Ferdinando Galiani

Rosario Patalano

Ferdinando Galiani

Economist, Diplomat and Philosopher in the Age of Enlightenment

palgrave
macmillan

Rosario Patalano
University of Naples Federico II
Naples, Italy

ISBN 978-3-032-02792-4 ISBN 978-3-032-02793-1 (eBook)
https://doi.org/10.1007/978-3-032-02793-1

This Palgrave Macmillan imprint is published by the registered company Springer Nature Switzerland AG.
The registered company address is: Gewerbestrasse 11, 6330 Cham, Switzerland

To my wife, Anna, and my son, Luca

Competing Interests The author has no competing interests to declare that are relevant to the content of this manuscript.

Contents

Abbreviations

BSNSP	Biblioteca della Società Napoletana di Storia Patria
MS	Manuscript
s.l.	*sine loco* (without place of publication)
s.n.	*sine nomine* (without name of publisher)

List of Figures

List of Tables

CHAPTER 1

Introduction

[The King] called together his architects and his priests and
bade them build him a labyrinth so confused and so subtle
that the most prudent men would not venture to enter it,
and those who did would lose their way.
Most unseemly was the edifice that resulted,
for it is the prerogative of God, not man,
to strike confusion and inspire wonder.
Borges 1949 [1998]: 263–264

The intellectual figure of Ferdinando Galiani (1728–1787) has the complex structure of a labyrinth. His many interests form an inextricable maze of blind paths, walls and hedges, traps and false doors. Whoever enters it with the certainty of immediately finding the way out, will soon find himself its prisoner and the interpretative path taken will soon prove to be misleading. The labyrinth of his complex thinking is the very image of eighteenth-century Naples built on a dense and intricate tangle of alleys, as it appears on the topographical map drawn by Giovanni Carafa, Duke of Noja (1775).

The Neapolitan abbot thus escapes any interpretation that would attempt to enclose his thought within the narrow limits of a simplified and hasty classification. The complexity of the "Galiani labyrinth" has obliged scholars to take limited routes or choose already beaten paths where it is

R. Patalano, *Ferdinando Galiani*,
https://doi.org/10.1007/978-3-032-02793-1_1

easier to find the exit. Partial paths have thus generated a myriad of specialised studies on Galiani the economist, Galiani the refined scholar of antiquities, Galiani the politician and diplomat, Galiani the man of letters and the Latinist, and even Galiani the libertine and worldly entertainer of brilliant salon conversations. This vast literature has certainly played an important role in deepening various aspects of his thought, but has offered a partial portrait of the Neapolitan abbot's complex, varied and unsystematic intellectual contribution. The dispersion of these Galiani studies among various sources makes it necessary to produce an overall synthesis that can serve as a starting point for further in-depth studies. The absence of a synthesis of Galiani's biographical story, based on the most important and significant specialist studies dedicated to him, is a historiographical gap that is no longer acceptable.

Filling this gap means reconstructing the "Galiani labyrinth", using the partial reconstructions as known paths to define its structure. The only way out of a labyrinth is to know the structure of the labyrinth itself, and the most appropriate key to understanding Galiani is the reconstruction of his complex human story in the context of his time.

The first reconstruction of the labyrinth was precocious: just a few months after the abbot's death, his nephew Luigi Diodati published the first biography (Diodati 1788). Despite its hagiographic character, Diodati's biography is based on a wealth of documentation defined by direct testimony and is a source of unpublished letters and writings now dispersed, becoming the basis for several nineteenth-century biographical reconstructions. Galiani was presented by Diodati as one of the main protagonists of Neapolitan intellectual and political life, an image that contrasted sharply with the isolation he experienced in the latter part of his life and with the "light" image of Galiani disseminated in the early nineteenth century based on the edition of his correspondence with French friends and certain memoirs. Thus arose the historiographical tradition of the "two Galians": the serious one, exalted by the patriotic rhetoric of national supremacy, typical of nineteenth-century Italy, was contrasted with the *petit Arlequin* celebrated by a certain kind of French literature. Two images that formed the blind paths of the labyrinth.

At the end of the nineteenth century, the figure of Galiani began to stimulate scholarly curiosity, opening up other paths in the labyrinth that led to another attempt at biographical synthesis by the Latinist Carlo Pascal (1885). In the same years, an obscure German philosopher, Friedrich Nietzsche, elevated Galiani to the genius of cynicism in the Age of Enlightenment by contrasting him with the hypocrite Voltaire (Nietzsche 1886 [2002]: 28). The archives were scoured in search of documents on the human life of the Neapolitan abbot and it was in this context that the figure of Fausto Nicolini emerged, who for half a century linked his entire scholarly activity to the "Galiani labyrinth".

It was Benedetto Croce who raised the question of Galiani's manuscripts, in the first issue of *La Critica*, in the possession of the Nicolini family, calling for a systematic inventory and urging the publication of the most interesting unpublished ones (Croce 1903: 239). Croce's appeal was immediately answered, in the same journal, by the young Fausto Nicolini who published an initial inventory of the manuscripts and initiated the publication of the first unpublished ones, taken from the correspondence (Nicolini 1903). Nicolini's indefatigable activity moved along two paths: philological research, with the aim of purging the vast correspondence of apocrypha and errors, and popularisation, publishing anthologies and reconstructions of Galiani's thought that were widely circulated. Nicolini was responsible for the first attempt to unravel the labyrinth by inserting Galiani into the autochthonous Neapolitan tradition of thought, highlighting, with daring and often forced comparisons, the links with Giambattista Vico. Unfortunately, his production was scattered in dozens of studies and was never concentrated in a general synthesis; he was not even able to publish a complete critical edition of Galiani's correspondence. The labyrinth absorbed him entirely and he never found his way out again.

At the same time, economic science was appropriating the economist Galiani, seen as a forerunner of the marginalist school or the labour theory of value, in the wake of the attention paid to him by Karl Marx. The great historian of economic thought, Joseph Alois Schumpeter drew an inspired portrait of him, calling him "a typical eighteenth-century abbé, sparkling with esprit" (Schumpeter 1954 [2006]: 278). The paths of the labyrinth became more and more intricate.

In the second half of the twentieth century, thanks to the research conducted by Franco Venturi, Galiani was included in the context of Italian Enlightenment culture, albeit in a slightly minor position, less involved in the general reform movement. His extraneousness to the reform movement was later strongly emphasised by Furio Diaz, to whom we owe the publication of an important anthological collection (Galiani 1975) and a more careful consideration of Galiani's activity as a government advisor (Diaz 1973).

In more recent years, other attempts have been made to unravel the path of the "Galiani labyrinth". Paolo Amodio's reconstruction, which provides a unitary interpretation of Galiani in the light of the libertine tradition of thought (Amodio 1997a, 1997b), Koen Stapelbroek's synthesis, which attempts to read Galiani's thought through the category of sociality (Stapelbroek 2008a, 2008b), and finally Azzurra Mauro's reconstruction, which places Galiani in the context of the circulation of ideas between Naples and Paris, focusing on the reciprocal influence of the two capitals (Mauro 2017a, 2017b, 2021). The approach adopted by Mauro is certainly a valid starting point for delving into the labyrinth, especially for its attention to unpublished production (with the valuable and careful publication of early unpublished works). However, both Mauro's work and Amodio and Stapelbroek's syntheses overlook Galiani's contribution to the nascent economic science, arbitrarily depriving his thought of an essential component.

Due to the absence of modern translations of his major works, Galiani remains an author still unknown to the larger international public. A French translation of *Della Moneta* (promised by the abbot André Morellet, a friend of Galiani, but of which there is no trace) was recently edited by André Tiran (Galiani 2005),[1] but in English, the only available translation of the same work is the one edited by Peter Toscano in 1977, which unfortunately is not considered very accurate from a philological point of view (Galiani 1977). The *Dialogues*, written in French, the other important works in Italian not dedicated to economic topics and the enormous correspondence, written in both Italian and French, remain largely unknown. The language barrier has prevented an appropriate assessment of the importance of Galiani's thought, reserving his knowledge to a small *élite* of scholars.

The present work offers a synthesis of Galiani's thought based on the most important specialist studies and the available critical editions of his correspondence and works, giving due space to the contribution that the Neapolitan abbot made to eighteenth century economic science as an essential element of his intellectual production.[2] It offers an English

[1] A previous partial French translation is edited by Georges-Henri Bousquet and Jean Crisafulli, see Galiani (1955).

[2] The texts of the correspondence are taken from the edition edited by Lucien Perey and Gaston Maugras, which is considered the most reliable collection (see Galiani 1881a) and from the more recent edition edited by Daniel Maggetti and George Dulac in 5 volumes (Galiani and d'Épinay 1992, 1993, 1994, 1996, 1997), but which is limited to the corre-

language summary that leaves much room for "Galiani's words" in order to help overcome the language barrier in the absence of an adequate English translation of his works. Galiani disliked translations, considered them a stretch, and wished Horace to be read in the original Latin so as not to lose any of his authentic freshness. A position that was certainly shareable, not least because of Galiani's brilliant prose, but which would have condemned him to being known only to the few interested parties capable of understanding eighteenth century Italian and French. The Neapolitan abbot certainly deserves a wider audience that today can only be reached through the English language.

The translation of the quotations from Galiani's works was carried out with the help of Joan McMullin, who took care of the linguistic revision of the whole text. Idiomatic terms and linguistic peculiarities, not only in French or Italian, but also in the Neapolitan dialect (which Galiani considered to be a veritable language), were translated, but the original expression was always quoted where necessary. In the translation, an attempt has been made to minimise the loss of philological rigour, whose strict (perhaps excessive) respect has been a limitation for the dissemination of Galiani's works.

An extensive apparatus of notes (a typical vice of the Italian academic tradition) complements the text with references to Galiani's published and unpublished writings and the rich secondary literature consulted. The historical reconstruction did not stop at the study of the published texts, but went as far as the analysis of the manuscripts (correspondence, unpublished texts and manuscript version of published treatises), which was of great help in the interpretation of Ferdinando Galiani's theory of value. In this case, in fact, the manuscript of the treatise *Della Moneta*, kept in the library of the *Società Napoletana di Storia Patria* (BSNSP), presents

spondence between Madame d'Épinay and Galiani, plus an Italian edition edited by Stefano Rapisarda, based partly on the French edition edited by Maggetti and Dulac and partly on the Perey-Maugras edition (always limited to the correspondence between Madame d'Épinay and Neapolitan abbot, see d'Épinay and Galiani 1996). Errors in the Perey-Maugras edition have been corrected and supplemented with editions by Fausto Nicolini and Daniel Maggetti and George Dulac. The correspondence with Bernardo Tanucci, kept in the State Archives in Naples and destroyed during the Nazi occupation in 1943, is taken from the edition edited by Augusto Bazzoni, amended by Fausto Nicolini's edition of Tanucci's letters to Galiani and the nineteenth-century copies donated to the Archive by the heirs of Augusto Pierantoni and the anthology edited by Furio Diaz and Luciano Guerci (see Bazzoni 1880a, 1880b; Nicolini 1914 and Galiani 1975).

interesting variants on the published text in the very chapter in which the theory of value is set out, and has been unjustly underestimated until now.

Bibliographical research has been greatly facilitated by modern computer technology that has made most of the original eighteenth-century digitised texts available online, and especially the enormous quantity of Galiani's manuscripts (of the three Galiani, one should say, as a large part of the manuscripts belong to his uncle Celestino and his brother Berardo), 74 volumes, most of which are still unpublished and kept at the Library of the *Società Napoletana di Storia Patria*, which are now easily accessible on the Web. Franco Venturi's dream of having a single national library, "in which one could reasonably expect to find every book and paper that has appeared in every corner of one's own country from the invention of printing to the present day" (Venturi 1998: xix), has been realised by the Internet, which has indeed gone far beyond the Italian historian's expectations, making available to scholars not only Italian texts, but the entire complex and varied intellectual production of the eighteenth century.

However, the language barrier remains a limitation and the hope is that this synthesis work will be followed by an English translation of Galiani's two main works, *Della Moneta* and the *Dialogues.*

With the perspective of delving into the roots of Galiani's thought, the book opens with Chap. 2 about the reconstruction of the intellectual, social and political context characterising the Kingdom of Naples in the first half of the eighteenth century. A political periphery, but intellectually lively, capable both of dialoguing with the most advanced part of European culture and of opposing innovations coming from abroad, in the name of defending an indigenous tradition.[3] Neapolitan intellectual life was thus profoundly divided by the opposing conceptions engaged in a clash considered decisive: all European intellectual currents were reproduced in Naples with a greater polemical intensity, exploding, as happens to a gas compressed in a confined space, in violent and bitter confrontations. Scholastics, Cartesians, Newtonians, sceptics, libertines, neo-Platonists and finally the supporters of the nascent "Enlightenment", found in the southern capital their own corner from which to do battle; an unprecedented ferment, a curious crossroads of themes and currents, destined to feed the thought of the most original philosopher of the eighteenth

[3] Several studies have shown that Naples, despite being a political periphery, was able to absorb and rework the different intellectual ferments that came from France and England above all, see Chiosi (1992); Imbruglia (2000).

century, Giambattista Vico. It was in this terrain of intellectual contention that Ferdinando's compact personality was formed, under the guidance of his uncle, Celestino Galiani, a Newtonian, who was entrusted with the responsibility of governing Neapolitan intellectual life.

Chapter 3 deals with the complex problem of monetary stabilisation in the Kingdom of Naples. In the course of the eighteenth century, all major European powers achieved the goal of a stable currency, or more precisely, permanently tied their monetary units to a fixed quantity of precious metal. This established the principle that money is no longer the exclusive domain of princes. Behind this choice there were economic and political reasons. Monarchies increasingly needed financial help to conduct their wars of supremacy and the productive and commercial wealth of a nation became the condition for being able to establish a policy of hegemony on the European continent and in the rest of the world. On the other hand, there could be no commercial expansion without a prior and opportune display of force and wars were always followed by trade agreements that were enormously advantageous for the victors. Political power was thus in turn a necessary condition for economic supremacy. The interests in play naturally converged towards a compromise and the ground on which this understanding was reached was precisely monetary policy. Money began to be regarded as an untouchable standard on which was based the establishment of fiduciary relations between the state and its subjects. This enabled economic activity to take place in the complete absence of inflationary disturbances, so dangerous not only for economic life but also for the very stability of social relations. Needless to underline how the subject of monetary stabilisation nurtured a theoretical debate on the very nature and role of money, which constitutes one of the most important chapters in the history of economic thought. It began with the contribution of John Locke, who became interested in economic issues at the urging of his political referents in Parliament. In the midst of the controversy stirred up by the proposals to set a minimum interest rate by law and to implement a devaluation of monetary units, the English philosopher founded the principles of monetary stabilisation on theoretical grounds. His systematisation of the theory of money would have great success and would remain an obligatory reference point throughout the eighteenth century. On the continent, John Law was to make another important theoretical contribution to support his proposal for a paper currency, the only form of standard that seemed possible to him in the face of the stresses caused to the monetary system by the fluctuating value of metals. Paradoxically, what was intended to be a proposal for stabilisation, in fact ended up being the most dramatic episode of monetary disorder of the eighteenth century. Law's legacy was taken up in a different way by Jean-François Melon and his opponent Charles Dutot, with the polemic over the role of monetary devaluations, which Melon judged not only legitimate but also positive if implemented to reduce excessively burdensome debts. Voltaire and Montesquieu also entered the controversy, which became a central topic in Enlightenment culture. Melon's work would be discussed throughout the eighteenth century, but would receive little acclaim, as the emerging trend was in favour of stabilisation. Thus between the 1730s and 1750s the theme of stable money was taken up by Richard Cantillon,[4] François Véron Duverger de Forbonnais[5] and Davis Hume,[6] and in these terms it passed into much of Enlightenment culture and was consolidated in economic thought. At the beginning of the nineteenth century, David Ricardo, with a certain serenity, could only state: "So much has already been written on currency, that of those who give their attention to such subjects, none but the prejudiced are ignorant of its true principles" (Ricardo 1821: 421).

Chapter 3 addresses the issue of monetary stabilisation in a context like the Kingdom of Naples, located on the periphery of the world-economy, with social structures still predominantly feudal, where the merchant class was weak, agriculture was in a state of subsistence, industrial activities were almost non-existent and Spanish fiscal policy had impoverished state finances. The monetary problems that plagued the Kingdom throughout the seventeenth century fostered copious literature on the government of money and other economic issues. Neapolitan culture therefore had a marked sensitivity to economic problems and this weighed heavily in its ability to receive and elaborate on the principles of monetary stabilisation. Rejecting en bloc the model of economic policy proposed by Melon was Carlo Antonio Broggia, who was linked to the anti-Cartesian philosophy

[4] "The nominal value of coins matters little or not at all provided it be permanent" (Cantillon 1755 [2010]: 223).

[5] "The truth is that it is important to leave it [money] as it is; that among France's prosperities, the current stability of currencies must count above all" (Forbonnais 1755: 970).

[6] "Money having merely a fictitious value, arising from the agreement and convention of men, the greater or less plenty of it is of no consequence, if we consider a nation within itself; and the quantity of specie, when once fixt, tho' never so large, has no other effect, than to oblige everyone to tell out a greater number of those shining bits of metal, for cloaths, furniture, or equipage, without increasing any one convenience of life" (Hume 1752: 63).

of Paolo Mattia Doria and Giambattista Vico. Broggia's work was later extensively used for the treatment of monetary policy by the Modenese historian Ludovico Antonio Muratori in his treatise *Della Pubblica Felicità*. Muratori, who combated the amorality of politics, also regarded the maintenance of the standard as part of the good Prince's duties. Needless to say, the great fortune that Muratori's work enjoyed in Italian reformist culture contributed in no small measure to the spread of the concept of stabilisation among Italian intellectuals. The defence of stable money was also supported by the aristocratic Trojano Spinelli, who had no direct affinity with the philosophical approach of Doria and Vico, and indeed was extremely familiar with the work of Locke.

What united these different orientations on the issue of stabilisation was precisely the rejection of the split between morality and politics, and the fact that this critique of the *Reason of State* was the defining element of those who defended monetary stability is proven to the contrary by the only author who assessed Melon's proposals on the government of the currency favourably, namely the young Ferdinando Galiani.

The justification of the *Reason of State* in the specific field of absolutist politics and admiration for Niccolò Machiavelli were a common theme for the group that gathered around Bartolemeo Intieri in the 1740s. The reference to the Italian philosophical and political tradition led them to consider politics a social mechanics, governed by the same empirical elements that guided physical research. In this perspective they had criticised Montesquieu's work for the absence of pragmatism, while they had warmly welcomed Melon's essay, which perfectly met their realistic demands for desirable reform from the point of view of the state's interest, despite the recognition of the social costs involved. Intieri and his circle had a very clear influence on the young Galiani, who through this mediation reevaluated the greatness of Italian Renaissance political thought, and not only Machiavelli, but also Guicciardini, acquiring the realistic approach that characterised his entire thought.

Chapters 4 and 5 tackle the work of Galiani's precocious genius, *Della Moneta*, with a detailed description of his contribution to monetary theory and monetary policy problems, in which he takes positions close to Melon that are not entirely compatible with the aims of stabilisation.

Chapter 6 deals with Galiani's multiple intellectual interests cultivated between 1751 and 1759, the years in which, after a journey to Italy to promote *Della Moneta*, he abandoned his monetary studies to concentrate on a variety of literary and scholarly interests. And these were also the years of the break with Intieri's group that marked the rise of Antonio Genovesi and the foundation of the first university chair specifically for the new economic science.

Chapter 7 reconstructs the ten-year stay in Paris. In his role as diplomatic representative of the Neapolitan court, Galiani came into contact with the core promoter of French (and thus European) Enlightenment culture, becoming an assiduous and admired frequenter of salons. His correspondence with the minister Bernardo Tanucci reveals the political and diplomatic issues that the abbot had to deal with during this period, using his particular skill to maintain the neutrality of the Neapolitan kingdom when faced with urging from the French to join the *Pacte de Famille*, designed to reunite the various branches of the Bourbon dynasty under French control. From Paris, Galiani observed the dramatic famine that hit the Neapolitan economy and became involved in the debate on the liberalisation of the grain trade, supported by the physiocratic school. However, after a careful analysis of the particular characteristics of the grain trade, the Neapolitan abbot, with his *Dialogues*, launched a polemic with physiocracy, destined to last many years and to intersect with the various agrarian crises that characterised the French economy in the 1770s. It was also a clash of a methodological nature, where Galiani's Newtonianism was opposed to the Cartesianism of the *économistes*. A diplomatic incident in which Galiani was involved interrupted his French sojourn.

Chapter 8 deals with the years of Galiani's maturity, spent in nostalgia for Paris and isolation in the Neapolitan intellectual context that now appeared alien to him. Galiani maintained a close correspondence with Madame d'Épinay and various exponents of Enlightenment culture, Denis Diderot, Friedrich Melchior von Grimm and Baron d'Holbach. Occupying important positions in the Neapolitan administration, the role of the Neapolitan abbot at this stage of his existence came very close to the characteristics of *cameralism*, especially due to his close relations with the court of Ferdinand IV and Maria Carolina. In this position as advisor, he drafted several reports on different subjects and in particular one of his essays on international law, supporting the reasons of neutral powers against belligerent parties. Although he achieved international fame by attracting the interest of some courts, such as that of St Petersburg, Galiani remained in Naples, where he cultivated various literary interests, attempting to re-edit his works (he only succeeded in updating *Della Moneta* with some notes) and leaving numerous works unfinished.

The epilogue (Chap. 9) attempts to address the Galiani labyrinth as a historiographical puzzle that is still unsolved and is open to new interpretations.

Naples, Federico II University
April 2025

References[7]

Primary Sources

Cantillon, R. (1755) [2010]. *Essai sur la nature du commerce en général. Traduit de l'anglois*, London: Fletcher Gyles. English Translation: *An Essay on Economic Theory*, Translated by C. Saucier, edited by M. Thornton. Auburn: Ludwig von Mises Institute.

Diodati, L. (1788). *Vita dell'abate Ferdinando Galiani*. Naples: Orsino.

Forbonnais, Véron de F. L. (1755). Espèces. In *Encyclopédie, ou dictionnaire raisonné des sciences, des arts et des métiers*, Tome V. Paris: Briasson, David l'aîné, Le Breton, Imprimeur ordinaire du Roy, Durand, pp. 957–970.

Galiani, F. (1881a). *Écrivains du XVIII siècle – Correspondance avec Madame d'Épinay, Madame Necker, Madame Geoffrin etc., Diderot, Grimm, d'Alembert, de Sartine, d'Holbach, etc. Nouvelle édition, entièrement rétablie d'après les textes originaux, augmentée de tous les passages supprimés et d'un grand nombre de lettres inédites, avec une étude sur sa vie et les oeuvres de Galiani*, edited by L. Perey, G. Maugras, 2 voll. Paris: Calmann Levy.

Galiani, F. (1955). *De La Monnaie. Traduit et analysé avec bibliographie, introduction et notes*, edited by G.-H. Bousquet, J. Crisafulli. Paris: Librairie Marcel Rivière.

Galiani, F. (1975). *Opere di Ferdinando Galiani*, edited by F. Diaz e L. Guerci, in *Letteratura italiana. Storia e testi. Illuministi italiani*, tomo VI. Milan- Naples: Ricciardi.

Galiani, F. (1977). *On Money*. A Translation of Della Moneta by Ferdinado Galiani by Peter R. Toscano. Ann Arbor: University Microfilm International.

Galiani, F. (2005). *De la Monnaie - Della Moneta*, édité et traduit sous la direction d'André Tiran, traduction coordonnée par Anne Machet. Paris: Economica

Galiani, F., d'Épinay, L. (1992). *Correspondance. Vol. I (1769–1770)*, présentation de G. Dulac, texte établi et annoté par D. Maggetti, en collaboration avec G. Dulac. Paris: Les Editions Desjonquères.

[7] The abbreviations "s.l." and "s.n." stand for the Latin terms *sine loco* (without place of publication) and *sine nomine* (without name of publisher).

Galiani, F., d'Épinay, L. (1993). *Correspondance. Vol. II (1771–Février 1772)*, présentation de G. Dulac, texte établi et annoté par D. Maggetti, en collaboration avec G. Dulac. Paris: Les Editions Desjonquères.

Galiani, F., d'Épinay, L. (1994). *Correspondance. Vol. III (Mars 1772–Mai 1773)*, présentation de G. Dulac, texte établi et annoté par D. Maggetti, en collaboration avec G. Dulac. Paris: Les Editions Desjonquères.

Galiani, F., d'Épinay, L. (1996). *Correspondance. Vol. IV (Juin 1773–Mai 1775)*, présentation de Georges Dulac, texte établi et annoté par Daniel Maggetti, en collaboration avec Georges Dulac, Paris: Les Editions Desjonquères.

Galiani, F., d'Épinay, L. (1997). *Correspondance. Vol. V (June 1775–Juillet 1782)*, présentation de G. Dulac, texte établi et annoté par D. Maggetti, en collaboration avec G. Dulac. Paris: Les Editions Desjonquères.

Hume, D. (1752). *Political discourses.* Edinburgh: Fleming.

Ricardo, D. (1821). *On the Principles of Political Economy, and Taxation.* London: John Murray.

Secondary Sources

Amodio, P. (1997a). *Il disincanto della ragione e l'assolutezza del bonheur: studio sull'abate Galiani*, Naples: Guida.

Amodio, P. (1997b). La diffusione del pensiero di John Locke a Napoli nell'età di Vico, contributo critico-bibliografico. *Atti dell'Accademia di Scienze Morali e Politiche*, CVII, pp. 183–194.

Bazzoni, A. (1880a). "Carteggio dell'abate Ferdinando Galiani col Marchese Tanucci (1759–1769)", *Archivio Storico Italiano,* Vol. 5, No. 117, pp. 367–375.

Bazzoni, A. (1880b). *Lettere di Ferdinando Galiani al Marchese Bernardo Tanucci.* Florence: Vieusseux.

Borges, J. L. (1949) [1998]. Los dos reyes y los dos laberintos. In *L'Aleph*, Buenos Aires: Editorial Losada. English translation: The Two Kings and the Two Labyrinths. In J. L. Borges. *Collected Fictions,* translated by Hurley, A. London: Penguin Books, 1998.

Chiosi, E. (1992). *Lo spirito del secolo. Politica e religione a Napoli nell'età dell'Illuminismo.* Naples: Giannini.

Croce, B. (1903). I manoscritti dell'abate Galiani. *La Critica. Rivista di Letteratura, Storia e Filosofia*, Vol. 1, pp. 236–240.

Diaz, F. (1973). L'abate Galiani consigliere di commercio estero del Regno di Napoli. In F. Diaz, *Per una storia illuministica.* Naples: Guida, pp. 289–364.

Imbruglia, G. (2000). *Naples in the Eighteenth Century: The Birth and Death of a Nation State.* Cambridge: Cambridge University Press.

Mauro, A. (2017a). *Un philosophe des Lumières entre Naples et Paris: Ferdinando Galiani (1728–1787)*. Thèse de Doctorate de l'Université Toulouse le Mirail - Toulouse II.

Mauro, A. (2017b). L'abbé Galiani alias le chevalier Zanobi: un philosophe qui "ne croit rien en rien sur rien de rien". *Littératures Classiques*, 93, pp. 155–167.

Mauro, A. (2021). *Un philosophe des Lumières entre Naples et Paris: Ferdinando Galiani (1728–1787)*. Oxford: Oxford University Press.

Nicolini, F. (1903). "*I manoscritti dell'abate Galiani*", La Critica. Rivista di Letteratura, Storia e Filosofia, Vol. 1, pp. 393–400.

Nicolini, F. (1914). Introduzione. In B. Tanucci, *Lettere a Ferdinando Galiani*, edited by F. Nicolini. Bari: Laterza, pp. vi–xix.

Nietzsche, F. (1886) [2002]. *Jenseits von Gut und Böse, Vorspiel einer Philosophie der Zukunft*, Leipzig: Druck und Verlag. English Translation, *Beyond Good and Evil Prelude to a Philosophy of the Future*, edited by Horstmann, R.-P., Norman, J., Cambridge: Cambridge University Press, 2002.

Pascal, C. (1885). *Sulla vita e sulle opera di Ferdinando Galiani*. Naples: Morano.

Schumpeter, J. A. (1954) [2006]. *History of Economic Analysis*. London: Routledge.

Stapelbroek, K. (2008a). *Love, Self-Deceit and Money. Commerce and Morality in the Early Neapolitan Enlightenment*. Toronto: University of Toronto Press.

Stapelbroek, K. (2008b). Universal Society, Commerce and the Rights of Neutral Trade: Martin Hübner, Emer de Vattel and Ferdinando Galiani. In P. Korkman, V. Mäkinen, (eds.) *Universalism in International Law and Political Philosophy*, COLLeGIUM: Studies Across Disciplines in the Arts and Humanities, vol. 4, Helsinki: Helsinki Collegium for Advanced Studies, pp. 63–89.

Venturi, F. (1998). *Settecento riformatore. Da Muratori a Beccaria*, Turin: Einaudi.

CHAPTER 2

The Intellectual Education of the Young Ferdinando Galiani (1728–1749)

Naples and its surroundings in the map of the Duke of Noja (1775). https://commons.wikimedia.org/wiki/File:Map_of_the_Duke_of_Noja_(Naples_section).png; https://maps.biblhertz.it/map?name=noia; High resolution (https://upload.wikimedia.org/wikipedia/commons/2/27/Map_of_the_Duke_of_Noja_%28Naples_section%29.png)

R. Patalano, *Ferdinando Galiani*,
https://doi.org/10.1007/978-3-032-02793-1_2

2.1 The Kingdom of Naples in the First Half of the Eighteenth Century: Projects of Reform and Dynastic Subjugation

When Ferdinando Galiani was born, on 2 December 1728,[1] the Kingdom of Naples had been a possession of the Austrian branch of the Habsburg crown for about twenty years. The imperial troops had wrested the Kingdom of Naples from the new Bourbon dynasty that had ascended to the Spanish throne, thus putting an end to the Spanish domination which had lasted almost two centuries. The change of regime was favored by the alternating fortunes on the battlefields which marked the long confrontation between the great European powers, known as the *War of the Spanish Succession* (1701–1714). The victories of Eugene of Savoy in Lombardy had allowed the Holy Roman Emperor, Joseph I, to achieve his dynastic objectives in Southern Italy, to the benefit of his brother Charles, pretender to the Spanish crown and rival to Philip of Bourbon. The city of Naples, the capital of the Kingdom, surrendered to the imperial troops of Count Wirich Philipp von Daun, in July 1707 without putting up any resistance, a clear sign of a country exhausted and in the throes of a serious social and political crisis. The outcome of the war sanctioned by the Treaties of Utrecht and Rastatt (1713–1714) assigned the Spanish throne to the Bourbons and the Duchy of Milan and the Kingdom of Naples to the Habsburgs, starting the period of Austrian dominance in Italy.

This change of regime would not have caused excessive trauma in a small provincial city like Chieti, where Galiani was born. His father, Matteo (1684–1748), held the role of Royal Auditor in that city, similar to that of a modern-day court judge, a role that was conferred for two years and which forced the family to move around the Kingdom several times.[2]

[1] Ferdinando Galiani's letter to Madame d'Épinay, Naples, 13 December 1770, published in Galiani (1881a, vol I: 315); Galiani and d'Épinay (1992, vol. I: 315). See also Diodati (1788: 2). His complete first name was Ferdinando Ernesto Francesco-Saverio Pier-Celestino, see his birth certificate in BSNSP, XXXI.A.08, folio 1.

[2] Matteo Galiani was born in San Giovanni Rotondo (Foggia), graduated in *utroque iure* (civil and canon law), and began a career as a provincial magistrate. in 1712 he married Anna Maria Ciaburri (1692–?), by whom he had seven sons, five females and two males (Berardo and Ferdinando). Promoted in 1727 to *proprietario fiscale* (*King's Attorney*) and in 1738, *caporuota* (*President of Tribunal Section*), he concluded his career with the title of marquis and member of the *Sacro Regio Consiglio* (*Sacred Royal Council*), the highest Neapolitan judicial body. See Nicolini (1918a: 154–155); see also Ademollo (1880); Pascal (1885: 2).

Matteo Galiani, despite coming from a poor family (Ferrone 1995: 124, see also Nicolini 1951, Galiani, MS-1), managed to raise his status to the level of the provincial middle class, still partly linked to the feudal world, but also projected towards the interests of royal absolutism and its mercantilist politics. In the final period of Spanish rule these classes had been called to take on government responsibilities, and Habsburg reformism drew them even further into its orbit by practicing a policy of breaking down ecclesiastical and noble privileges.

His older brother, Nicholas (1681–1753), had undertaken a brilliant ecclesiastical career by entering the monastic order of the Celestines, under the name of Celestino: a university professor in 1718, he became attorney general (1723) and abbot general of the order (1728), he was then archbishop of Taranto and Thessaloniki, finishing his *cursus honorum*, in 1732, with the prestigious position of *Cappellano Maggiore* of the Kingdom of Naples, a sort of minister of culture and education. Celestino was the main point of reference for the intellectual formation of the young Ferdinando (Nicolini 1918a: 152–153; Ferrone 1995: 124).[3]

It was precisely the imperial government's jurisdictional policy which, meeting with local anticurialism, had the effect of creating a kind of alliance between the *ceto civile* (*civil class*) employed in administration and law, the most enlightened part of the clergy (of which Celestino was a typical example) and the Habsburgs (Carpanetto and Ricuperati 1987: 147–148; Schipa 1904: 625–644).[4] The most prominent exponents of the Neapolitan *ceto civile*, from Serafino Biscardi (1643–1711) to Alessandro Riccardi (1678–1726), Gaetano Argento (1661–1730), Pietro Contegna (1670–1745?), Francesco Ventura (?–1759), Costantino Grimaldi (1667–1750) and the better-known Pietro Giannone (1676–1748), supported the Habsburg policy of strengthening state institutions and exploiting local wealth more rationally in an attempt to modernize the socio-economic structure of the Kingdom. On the other hand, together with the people, they had remained indifferent in the face of the failed anti-Spanish conspiracy hatched in 1701 by a part of the Neapolitan nobility, known as the *Conspiracy of the Prince of Macchia*. This plot aimed at

[3] Galiani's autobiography entitled *Ristretto della vita di Celestino Galiani*, BSNSP, XXXI. C. 7, is published in Natale, 2002a. See also Natale (2002b) and the biographical notes written by his nephew (*Vita di Celestino Galiani tratta dalle memorie da lui stesso lasciate e distesa da Ferd.o Galiano suo nipote*, BSNSP, XXXI.C.8, folios 65v–68v).

[4] On the specific features of this alliance, as it was conceived by Alessandro Riccardi, one of the main exponents of the Neapolitan *ceto civile*, see Ricuperati (1969).

the independence of the Kingdom under Archduke Charles of Habsburg, and viewed the Austrian Imperial House as one of the potential allies for their possible return to a ruling role in Neapolitan society, significantly reduced by the Spanish viceroys.[5]

The Austrians had found a country bled dry by excessive tax pressure (the main cause of the revolt of 1647–48), dreadful plague epidemics (1656, 1691), recurring famines and devastating earthquakes (1631, 1688) (Lepre 1986a: 298–312; Gentilcore 2013).[6] Agricultural production, especially grain, by the end of the seventeenth century was already barely sufficient to feed a growing population, effectively dispelling the celebrated myth of the fertility of the southern lands.[7]

[5] The conspirators did not accept the decision of Charles II of Habsburg who, without heirs, had designated Philip of Bourbon, nephew of Louis XIV, as his successor to the Spanish Throne, and they instead recognized Archduke Charles of Habsburg, second son of Leopold I, Holy Roman Emperor, as the legitimate heir. The conspiracy, which aimed to take over the city of Naples and eliminate the Spanish Viceroy, Duke of Medinaceli, was discovered and, after trying in vain to rouse the people, some of the conspirators were arrested and sentenced to death while others managed to escape, only to return to the Kingdom following the imperial armies. On the Conspiracy of the Prince of Macchia, see Vico (1703 [1992]); Doria (1710c [1981]: 72, 98); Granito (1861); Morandi (1939), Galasso (1982: 651–662); Musi (2007a); Gallo (2018). According to Benedetto Croce, the conspiracy "in spite or perhaps because of the fact that it flaunted the idea of an independent Kingdom, with a prince of its own, was essentially an attempt, reactionary in character, of the old barons to win back their power" (Croce 1925b [1970]: 128; see Lepre 1986b: 82). Croce's opinion has been revised by more recent historiography, in particular for Francesca Fausta Gallo: "The conspiracy represents an important moment in the history of the Kingdom in the decades of the crisis of European conscience, precisely because it reveals political ideas and principles, institutional proposals, economic conceptions, cultural models which, reworked and put on the agenda during the period of Austrian domination of the Kingdom, later found their most complete realization with the establishment of the independent Bourbon Kingdom of Naples" (Gallo 2018: 22).

[6] "The tax system created by the Spaniards in the South was a colossal structure of occupation and redistribution of resources from the top to the base of the system; different classes, groups and economic interests participated in the management of the apparatus. The Spanish-Neapolitan state thus created a model of integration between administration, economy and society destined to last well beyond the two centuries of domination" (Musi 1991: 21).

[7] "The nation was for centuries praised, envied, and coveted, as a paradise or a promised land, on account of the wealth of gifts with which nature has endowed it. More recently it has been disdained and pitied for its aridity, and indeed the fertility of Campania, and of certain parts of the Apulian coast, which caught the eye of earlier beholders, has the quality of a stage set, with behind it broad areas of unproductive land, characterized by expanses of bare rock, trickling streams, a low rainfall and rampant malaria" (Croce 1925b [1970]: 45).

Throughout Southern Italy, static wheat growing dominated, with low productivity, lacking technical development and managed by large feudal estates (Lepre 1986a: 109–112, 165–181; Astarita 1992). The increase in cereal production at the end of the seventeenth century was not the effect of an increase in productivity but was due to the extension of the area under cultivation which caused the contraction of breeding and wool production, previously important components of the southern economy (Marino 1988; Rossi 2010). The feudal structure that governed production relations in the southern countryside allowed a certain social equilibrium: the feudal lords (generally referred to as *baroni*, barons) were guaranteed a rent without significant investments, the amount of which essentially depended on the price of cereals, which rose in times of famine;[8] peasants were guaranteed civic use, i.e. community rights of gathering, hunting, collecting wood and grazing, which enabled them to integrate their income in periods of production crisis.[9] The management of administrative justice and rights, reserved to the barons, allowed the withdrawal of other resources in order to integrate losses in periods of low prices and keep the consistency of the rent constant.[10] This equilibrium, also favored by a long period of stationary cereal prices, stabilized social relations, offering the possibility of compensating for production variations, inte-

[8] "In the provinces the barons found themselves up against the corporations or communes, which struggled, with varying energy and fortune, but uninterruptedly, to defend the rights bequeathed to them by ancient custom and consecrated by written statutes, and to better their lot. Generally speaking, baronial power had come to be considered an evil, and there was an effort to shake it off, or, when this was impossible, to weaken it or to choose the lesser of two evils" (Croce 1925b [1970]: 121). See also Villari (1961).

[9] As Paolo Mattia Doria wrote, the condition of the peasants was dramatic: "This people is destined to carry all the weight that is necessary to feed and nourish not only the rapacity of the ruling nation, but all those orders that it has associated with it to be able to dominate in peace and without danger [...]. The poor peasant of the kingdom is the one upon whom all the weight of tyranny falls and is now reduced like the beasts, that is, never to enjoy those foods they carry on their backs, because the misery of these has reached such a level that only in the most serious and extreme illnesses they eat wheat bread, and at all other times, they eat nothing but corn bread and herbs seasoned with oil and salt, and of meat and other foods they have no idea" (Doria 1710c [1981]: 101).

[10] A series of "regal rights" guaranteed the feudal lords economic, political and social power over the fiefdom and included: civil and criminal jurisdiction of first and second instance; the appointment of judges in trials relating to their jurisdiction; the possibility of granting pardons to offenders after compensation of the injured party; the maintenance of public places and roads (known as "Portolania's jurisdiction"); the possibility of handling cases of minor matters; the minting of weights and measures. See Rovito (1987); Rao (1997).

grating losses and normalizing food consumption, but it also constituted a factor of staticity, because it prevented experimentation with farming innovations, condemning southern agriculture to chronic stagnation (Carpanetto and Ricuperati 1987: 25–28; Lepre 1981; Bevilacqua 1982).[11] In this context there were few areas of innovation, essentially concentrated in Puglia, marked by a particular production structure, the *masseria*, based on the use of salaried workers, on intensive production and aimed at the marketing of grain. Due to its character, the *masseria* attracted substantial investments, encouraged advanced production and management methods, even if it did not develop a capitalist type of work organization (Lepre 1963; Carpanetto and Ricuperati 1987: 27).

Mining production was almost completely absent and in any case limited to minerals of little or secondary importance, with the exception of the iron ore mined in Stilo, in Calabria, and almost all the products of the metallurgical industry came from England, Germany and Austria (Carpanetto and Ricuperati 1993: 70). The Neapolitan manufacturers that had in the past been well known, especially for silk, were no longer able to compete either internationally or on the domestic market due to the mediocre quality of their products. The limited manufacturing production was therefore entirely intended to satisfy internal demand, which was not particularly discerning, and for some products such as iron it was not even able to fully satisfy the needs of the Kingdom. The merchant navy was also insufficient, based on small coastal navigation and unable to fully cover the Kingdom's transport needs, consequently foreign trade and even part of local traffic were entrusted to foreign ships.[12] Internal trade was scarce due to the inadequate road network and navigation was constantly threatened by North African piracy, which also made the coasts unsafe.[13]

[11] Aurelio Lepre has reconstructed the ten-year series of wheat prices, in *Ducats* per *tomolo*, based on purchases from Neapolitan monasteries (see Table 2.1).

[12] On the economic situation of the Kingdom of Naples in the period of Austrian domination, a primary source is found in Paolo Mattia Doria's writings (see Doria 1710b [1973]; Schipa 1899; Di Vittorio 1969, 1973; Romano 1976; Russo and Guasti 2010; Cataldo 2020).

[13] "A twofold pressure had prevented the Mezzogiorno from escaping its underdeveloped condition: the continuous piratical plundering, especially from North Africa on the one hand, and the French, Dutch and English maritime trade on the other hand, which took advantage of those difficulties and favoured their persistence, since it transformed them into conditions to its own advantage. The two external forces, North African piracy and the trade of maritime powers, were linked by strong common interests" (Ajello 2001: 21).

Table 2.1 Ten-year series of wheat prices index (1650–1700)

	Ducats per tomolo	*Index*
1651–1660	1.47	100
1661–1670	1.06	72
1671–1680	1.06	72
1681–1690	1.19	80
1691–1700	1.17	79

Source: Lepre (1986b: 37)

On this fragile economic structure stood, like an enormous head, the capital, Naples, which constituted a distinctive reality in the complex social formation of the Kingdom. At the beginning of the eighteenth century, Naples, with its 220,000 inhabitants, shared the demographic record in Europe with Paris.[14] Over the course of the previous century, as a result of socio-political crises (the anti-Spanish insurrection of 1647), natural cataclysms (eruption of Vesuvius in 1631 and earthquake in 1688) and plague epidemics (in 1656 and 1691), Naples had lost a third of its population, which at the height of its demographic expansion amounted to 300,000 inhabitants at the beginning of the seventeenth century. 40% of the entire population of the Kingdom was concentrated in an area of 50/60 kilometers around Naples, and the overcrowding and chaotic urban development were evident to foreign visitors (Lepre 1986a: 252–257; Muto 2013; Valerio 2013).[15] The abnormal growth of Naples was due to the political, administrative and economic centrality that it had assumed within the institutional organization of the Spanish Viceroyalty (Musi 2007a). The control of the capital effectively ensured the Spaniards the control of the entire Kingdom and for this reason they favored immigration from the countryside, granting the numerous plebs fiscal privileges (inhabitants were exempt from direct taxes and taxed exclusively on consumption by means of duties and levies) as well as food ration assistance (called *Annona*).

[14] "The population rose from 186,000 inhabitants in 1688 to 220,000 in 1707, to 310,000 in 1742. In 1763, 337,000 inhabitants were attributed to the city; at the end of the century, contemporaries believed that its population was around 400,000 inhabitants, a figure which, although undoubtedly appearing too high, compared to that provided by the censuses which would be carried out in the nineteenth century, confirms the constant development of the city" (Lepre 1986b: 45). See also Doria (1710c [1981]); Carafa (1750); Goudar (1769); Venturi (1971a); Galasso (1982 and 2003); Rao (2005: 39–45).

[15] On the anti-Spanish insurrection, see Lepre (1986a: 269–298); Calabria (1991); Musi (2002, 2013); Rovito (2003); Villari (2012).

The presence of the viceregal court then attracted the barons who established their residence in the city, making Naples a center of rent spending and thus ensuring its economic supremacy. Various activities grew up around the needs of the nobility and the clergy, especially the textile industry, which in the mid-seventeenth century constituted 24% of the city's economic activities (Carpanetto and Ricuperati 1987: 17), though over the course of the century production had moved to the provinces and wool had largely replaced silk (Lepre 1986b: 47). The seaport also constituted an active component, as the main terminal point for the traffic of cereals and other agricultural products coming from the fertile region of Puglia and intended to feed the city, whose agricultural surroundings could not provide products in the necessary quantities.

The pacification of the city, and therefore of the entire Kingdom, was based on an efficient food ration system (*Annona*), which had become the fulcrum of great economic and political interests, and which effectively gave the capital the monopoly on the grain trade. The *Annona system*, inherited from ancient Rome, corresponded to the functions of a modern welfare and social protection system, guaranteeing food assistance to the growing masses of impoverished peasants coming from the countryside. The *Annona* had to ensure that the price of bread did not undergo drastic increases that could trigger social unrest, and it was therefore necessary to guarantee the overcrowded city a constant supply of grain according to its needs. Due to this essential function, the *Annona* had become an important institution, the center of a complex network of relationships that concentrated various interests, from city administration officials to great merchants, noble producers, speculators and usurers.

The persistence of feudal structures in southern society favored a polarization around two opposing social blocks: the peasants and the feudal lords. The condition of the peasants depended on contractual relationships, the characteristics of the soil cultivated and local political constraints.[16] The differences in the feudal class were due to the extension of

[16] A particular example of contractual relations in the Neapolitan countrysides was the *contratto alla voce (voice contract)*, a special advance purchase and sale contract practiced in the Mezzogiorno from the late Middle Ages until the nineteenth century, in relation to the oil and grain trade. In this contractual system, the merchant, buyer of agricultural products, advanced to the selling peasant, a certain sum of money or a certain quantity of goods (seeds and foodstuffs) valued in money. The parties did not establish the price of the future product (*voice price*) at the time of the agreement but referred to the *voce* that was established on a certain market place at harvest time. For some historians the *voce* contract was "a means of gaining control over overall production,

the property and the origins of the noble title: the larger fiefdoms, with jurisdiction over vast territories, belonged to the older nobility, while the more recently appointed feudal lords were not as powerful and rich, even if more numerous (Lepre 1986a: 113–117, 147–164; Carpanetto and Ricuperati 1987: 62).[17] The *comuni* (*demaniali* or *infeudati*), called *università*, bore almost the entire tax burden, and this was the reason for the high number of poor people in the provinces and the spread of banditry. Between these two opposite poles, in the province of the Kingdom, there was a varied middle class made up of merchants, tenants, state officials, magistrates, completely devoid of political power.[18] Matteo Galiani therefore belonged to this provincial middle class.

The social structure was much more complex in the capital (Venturi 1971a; Lepre 1986a: 103–109; Ajello 2001: 20). The noble class was composed of a more recent component of Spanish origin, created at the beginning of the sixteenth century, which occupied the top levels of government and administration, and of an indigenous component of ancient origin, which drew its wealth from feudal rents, from the income connected to administrative roles, from the proceeds of public debt and

while remaining outside real participation in agricultural management" (Macry 1972: 884) and through which a "parasitic hierarchy was organised on the productive agricultural base, which determined artificial and very wide margins of income for the unrestrained usurious speculation to which it gave rise and which culminated in the great merchant (usually a foreigner)" (Galasso 1992: 282). These contracts could have as their object, instead of an advance sale, a loan of grain. In essence, they consisted of a real loan to the peasants, who were then forced into debt to repay the higher sums received at the time of the advance, as it was seldom the buyer who remitted more money, since the item was lower than the agreed price. See also Bianchini (1839: 234); Villari (1961: 40–41); Chorley (1965) and Placanica (1982). Recently, the negative character of the *contratto alla voce* has been reconsidered in the light of a neo-institutionalist approach, according to which the *voce system* assumed the role of an instrument to contain transaction costs and risks associated with commercial exchange in the modern Mezzogiorno (Ciccolella and Guenzi 2008: 45). See also Marino (1982).

[17] The political power of the barons had been greatly reduced during the period of Spanish rule: "The kings of Spain did not only prevent the survival or renewal of the barons' political power; they also, through their viceroys, contrived to reduce the barons to the condition of subjects, on a level with the other social classes" (Croce 1925b [1970]: 99).

[18] "The dwindling wealth of the barons contributed in large part to the growing prosperity of the two main segments of the middle class, composed of speculators and lawyers. The former were tax contractors, grain exporters, bankers, and moneylenders, some of them native-born but many of them Genoese, who had taken over these functions from the Florentines and other foreign merchants who had carried on trade and finance in the old Kingdom. The Neapolitans called them Jews, borrowing this appellation from its rightful owners, who had been driven out by the viceroy Toledo" (Croce 1925b [1970]: 116–117).

mercantile activity.[19] Not all nobles had access to political power: at the end of the seventeenth century there was a contrast between the so-called "nobiltà di seggio" (*nobility of the seat*), around 130 families who controlled the city administration, owners of rich assets and with strong ties to the barons of the province, and the so-called "nobiltà fuori seggio" (*nobility outside the seat*), who were effectively excluded from political power (Carpanetto and Ricuperati 1993: 82; Schipa 1904: 645–666). The *Seggi* (also called *Sedili* or *Piazze*), six in number, were the institutional structures through which power was exercised, corresponding to various neighborhoods of the city. Five of them were reserved for the nobles and the sixth for the people.[20] The *Seggi* elected a *Giunta* (*Council*) made up of 5 nobles and the *Eletto del Popolo* (*Elected Representative of the People*) who had broad powers in the fields of urban planning, taxation, *Annona* and the management of public order.[21] The control of the *Annona*, which the nobles exercised in concert with the *Eletto del Popolo*, was particularly important, as the decisions of the Giunta regulated the price of bread, which was often subordinated to speculative interest (Schipa 1904: 35–36; see also Doria 1710c [1981]).[22] The political weight of the noble seats was

[19] "The barons, together with the clergy, made up the class of landowners or, more properly, large landowners. Beside the fruit of the land, they had many other sources of income, through monopolies and various forms of service and the exercise of certain jurisdictions which not only produced money but also afforded the means of imposing local domination, respect for their rights of ownership, and toleration of their abuses. The landowning barons did not work their land or even supervise its administration. This latter task was turned over to agents and lawyers, while the great majority of barons lived most of the year in the capital. They lived ostentatiously and luxuriously, without taking any public responsibility except for the enrollment of their younger sons in the militia and without exercising any productive activity" (Croce 1925b [1970]: 115). Formally, the barons were obliged to pay three taxes: *adoa* (a tax on exemption from military obligations), *relevio* (an inheritance tax), *quindemo* (another inheritance tax to be paid every 15 years). Because of the numerous exemptions enjoyed by the privileged classes and the lack of a land register that allowed for real taxation based on property owned, these taxes did not yield a great revenue (Bianchini 1839: 375).

[20] The Sedili of the nobility were: *Capuana, Montagna, Nilo, Forcella, Porto, Portanova*, to which was added *Sedile del Popolo* (see Croce 1925b [1970]: 84, and Schipa 1904: 34–37).

[21] "The Spanish Monarchy favored and exalted the development of the functions of the Capital, ceding a significant share of the power to centralize political-administrative decisions to the Neapolitan Ministry, and entrusting the metropolitan government to the Seggi" (Musi 1991: 20–21).

[22] "The fame that surrounded those city magistrates was unfavorable just as their main assignment was harmful to the general economy of the Kingdom. In the task of annually supplying the capital with what was needed for its subsistence, the *Eletto del Popolo* either formed the supplies by buying or had the royal power send commissioners to the provinces

obviously not homogeneous, but depended on the assets and prestige of the aristocrats who composed them. The Austrian occupation had, however, changed the balance by increasing the weight of the minor nobility, as many families of older nobility had opposed the change of regime (Carpanetto and Ricuperati 1987: 63).

Between the city nobility and the people there was a varied middle class, which was referred to as the *ceto civile*, made up of magistrates, lawyers, officials, university professors, but also elements of the nobility linked to administrative functions. Part of the *ceto civile* had political ties with the nobility, united by the fight against the excessive power of the ecclesiastical authorities and in defense of the role of the state. The most homogeneous nucleus of the *ceto civile* was made up of the so-called *Ministero Togato* (*Togate Ministry*, Rovito 1981; Lepre 1986b: 79; Musi 1986; Carpanetto and Ricuperati 1987: 63) composed of a component very similar to the French *Nobles of the Robe*, an *élite* that possessed a defined ideological identity and a common professional education as jurists and members of the judicial institutions, such as the *Camera della Sommaria* (*Chamber of the Sommaria*, which dealt with both administrative affairs and judicial cases concerning taxation), the *Consiglio Collaterale* (*Collateral Council*, which had cumulative chancery, legislative and administrative functions, suppressed in 1735 and replaced by the *Real Camera di Santa Chiara*, *Royal Chamber of Santa Chiara*), the *Sacro Real Consiglio* and the *Grande Corte della Vicaria* (*Sacred Royal Council* and the *Grand Court of the Vicaria*), which performed tasks of judicial institutions (Doria 1710c [1981]: 82–107; Lepre 1986a: 136–147; Intorcia 1987).[23] During the

to "bargain", that is to stock up on the necessary foodstuffs. Private individuals were therefore forced to sell at a low price, the rich to lend money, the landowners to reveal their harvests annually and not to keep or accumulate them beyond their own use. Purchases were then prohibited within a radius of twenty or thirty miles from Naples, exports from the capital and often from entire provinces and sometimes from the entire Kingdom were prohibited. The lack of probity of those elected was blamed for the disorder of the administration. It was alleged that, for illicit personal profits, they charged high prices, to the detriment of the treasury and the public" (Schipa 1904: 35). An emblematic episode was the lynching of the *Eletto del Popolo* Giovan Vincenzo Starace during the revolt of 1585 (see Marino 2007: 407–409).

[23] Raffaele Ajello has underlined the analogy between the French nobility and the Neapolitan *togati*: "Paris and Naples at the end of the seventeenth century expressed, despite the obvious differences, the conditions of social and cultural milieu that are in a phase of transition from feudalism to capitalism, characterized by a very strong presence of pre-bureaucratic ministerial apparatuses" (Ajello 1981: xvi). Moreover "legal scholars and theo-

Austrian period the *ceto civile* was quite numerous, estimated between 26,000 and 50,000 people (Carpanetto and Ricuperati 1987: 64). The forensic career was the only means of social mobility, and many young provincials undertook this career to seek a better position in a society that did not offer many opportunities.[24]

The existence of this particular social class, which cannot be defined either as a productive bourgeoisie or as a bureaucracy, is a typical product of a particular *Ancien Régime* society, the effect of a compromise between feudal power and the needs of an absolute state (Musi 1991: 15–21).[25] The *ceto civile*, in this context, was at the center of a complex network of economic and political interests, which involved the business and assets of the aristocracy, and which found form in the judicial disputes that fueled the frenetic Neapolitan judicial life (see Croce 1925b [1970]: 141–142).[26] Even in the context of these ties, the *ceto civile* attempted to counter both the traditional power of the barons and the domination of the Church.[27]

rists, doctors, lawyers and magistrates always looked at Paris and the political, social and cultural phenomena that occurred there (from technical-juridical production to historiographical production, from the development of Parliaments to the organization of the State) as their inspiration. In this way, a counterthrust was created with respect to the centripetal influences of both the Church of Rome and the Spanish court and administration, and the constitutional autonomy of the Neapolitan state was celebrated" (Ajello 1980: 8). On the structure of the various Neapolitan magistracies, see Schipa (1904: chap. III).

[24] At the end of the seventeenth century, an important exponent of the Togate Ministry, Francesco D'Andrea, exalted the legal profession which in Naples, as in no other city in the world, allowed men of "the lowest plebs, and of the most humble land of the Kingdom", with no other quality if not one's own merit, "to ascend to great positions and immense riches" (D'Andrea 1696a [1919]: 284–285; see also Lepre 1986b: 77). The venality of office and titles was also an important means of social mobility.

[25] "In the Mezzogiorno, government was entrusted, for centuries, to the jurists: that is, to a social group that was not uncultured, but incapable of stimulating real productivity, a governing class hostile to novelty, inclined to bookish education and idealistic formalisms" (Ajello 2001: 22).

[26] The Kingdom's judicial history was punctuated by interminable disputes between the tax authorities and barons, between barons and universities, and in Naples a rich jurisprudence on feudal succession had developed which theoretically recognised the figure of the sovereign at the origin of the feud, his prerogatives and his discretion in changing the conditions of its use, but in fact guaranteed baronial autonomy and the transmission of the feudal patrimony within the usurping family through majorascato and fidecommissum.

[27] According to Raffaele Ajello, the first Spanish viceroys, Don Pedro de Toledo and Pedro Pachedo, distrusting the Neapolitan aristocracy (the ancient *Nobles of the Sword*), considered not very faithful to the Spanish monarchy (just as they had opposed the Aragonese monarchy), implemented a series of reforms to remove the barons from the top positions of the

This contrast cannot be called a real class struggle, since the social prerequisites for it were still missing.[28] The new viceregal policy inaugurated by the Marquis of Carpio in 1683 provoked an intensification of the anti-Baronial struggle, led by the *ceto civile*, which under his rule assumed a leading role in the administration, initiating a process that led it to assume a greater political and social prominence in city life, which was further consolidated in the transition from the Spaniards to the Austrians.

The varied Neapolitan social structure was completed by the presence of a mercantile and professional class, especially doctors, apothecaries, architects, who, despite accumulating considerable assets, were excluded from the centers of power, which, as has been said, were concentrated in forensic activities. A particular role was then covered by the clergy to whom the monopoly of education and control of public morals was

institutions of the Kingdom, replacing them with pro-Spanish jurists. In this way, the nobility of the Kingdom was disarmed and greatly reduced in its political-military role, making the Kingdom dependent on the Spanish militias, while the *togati* (the new *Nobles of the Robe*) played the role of mediators between the viceregal authority and the people, adapting to a "compromising pragmatism" marked by a tendency towards compliance and uncritical servility which would explain the historical inability of the southern ruling classes to promote economic and social development (see Ajello 1994, 1996). Ajello's thesis is anticipated by Croce: "The kings of Spain did not only prevent the survival or renewal of the barons' political power; they also, through their viceroys, contrived to reduce the barons to the condition of subjects, on a level with the other social classes" (Croce 1925b [1970]: 99).

[28] "The class logic of Neapolitan society continued to be the logic of a disorganically complex society [...] in which the physiognomy of the classes and the processes of their formation, their turnover and their relationships were sclerotic and marginal and at the same time chaotically tumultuous" (Galasso 1976: 165), however "in the face of the royal bureaucracy, the nobility stood out more than ever as the only true and great antagonist, not simply as an organized social force (this was, for example, also the clergy) but as a class, that is, as a homogeneous and spontaneous social position, emerging from the slow sedimentation of the process of historical evolution of a society even above and beyond the material continuity of the elements that composed it" (Galasso 1976: 175–176). Aurelio Lepre formulates a similar opinion: "The *ceto civile* did not constitute a class. Even at the end of the seventeenth century and in the first decades of the following century, only the nobility could be considered such", though a pre-bourgeois spirit could be recognized in it (Lepre 1986b: 82). According to Raffaele Colapietra, "the legal profession, bound as it was to viceregal power, to juridical and economic immobility and administrative disorder, could not be considered a ruling class, a title that belonged to the aristocracy, the only class that had class consciousness and autonomy of government" (Colapietra 1961: 202). See also Quazza (1971: 63–85).

formally attributed, but who were certainly not alien to civil life and the economic and political interests that characterized it.[29]

Finally, at the base of the social pyramid there were the plebs, also varied, who made a living from small commercial and artisanal activities or as servants supported by the aristocratic income, or from occasional jobs in port activities. The poorest component, the underclassmen, referred to by the derogatory term *lazzari*, lived on public assistance, thanks to the *Annona* system, or the charity of the Church, which traditionally protected them (Schipa 1904: 666–683; Croce 1925b [1970]: 119–120).[30]

Only towards the end of the *War of the Spanish Succession* (1714) was the imperial government able to intervene more concretely in the economic life of the Kingdom, partly exploiting the positive economic cycle that began with the brief interlude of peace.[31]

The Neapolitan Kingdom, together with Flanders and the Adriatic provinces, constituted the only possessions of the vast Habsburg continental empire on which a mercantilist policy and serious competition with the great maritime powers could be founded. The Habsburg monarchy derived 30% of its revenue from the Italian dominions, where 37% of its population resided (Alatri 1989: 43).[32] For this reason, Anselm Franz Friedrich von Fleischmann, "one of the most prominent experts in political economy at the Austrian court" (Ajello 1969: 841) had moved to Naples as economic advisor to the Viceroy, cardinal Michael Friedrich

[29] The political influence of the Church was enormous: Paolo Mattia Doria underlined that power in the Kingdom was in fact divided in half between ecclesiastical authority and viceregal authority. Furthermore the clergy enjoyed "many privileges of the courts and a great deal of wealth", which allowed them to have "dominance over the conclave and the Court of Rome" and "to be able to command more despotically in the Kingdom of Naples and the rest of Europe" (Doria 1710b [1973]: 30).

[30] The presence of a vast and miserable urban underclass contrasted with the natural beauty of the landscape and the healthy climate, which is why since the sixteenth century in Europe the Kingdom of Naples was described as "a paradise, but one peopled by devils" (see Croce 1925b [1970]: 75, see also Croce 1923 [2006]: 11–21).

[31] An initial reformist attempt had been initiated by viceroy Cardinal Vincenzo Grimani (1708–1710), the "most active in creating the lines of a Habsburg policy in the south: a vigorous polemic on [ecclesiastical] benefices, creation of the *Giunta di Commercio*, alliance with the *ceto civile*, restoration of the royal patrimony, social stability by guaranteeing bread to the plebs" (Ricuperati 1970: 110). The imposition of new taxes provoked a reaction from the people and the attempt foundered with the death of the viceroy (Galasso 1989a: 202–208).

[32] In Europe, the Italian provinces were called "Les Indes de la Cour de Vienne" (see Doria 1984: 34).

Graf von Althann; but the implementation of every mercantilist project clashed with the problem of the weakness of the Neapolitan state structures, characterized by the almost total transfer of tax revenues to private individuals.

For this reason the Austrian authorities, supported by the Neapolitan *ceto civile*, developed the project for the establishment of the *Banco di San Carlo* in 1726 ("the most important episode of Austrian reformism", Ricuperati 1972: 405), which in the initial intentions was to: reduce ecclesiastical property, forcing ecclesiastical bodies to cede their real estate assets to the State and thus liquidating the institution of *manomorta* (*mortmain*); reconstruct the state's assets, buy back the ceded feudal rights, gifts and tax revenues sold off by the previous regime; suppress all *Banchi Pubblici* (public banks) operating in the Kingdom of Naples and replace them with a single entity, the *Banco di San Carlo* (Di Vittorio 2010). The *ceto civile,* incapable of fighting the privileges of the nobility largely aligned with the anti-curial party, supported the measures against the huge ecclesiastical wealth, and saw the clergy as "the weak link in the chain of the established order" (Lepre 1986b: 83). The implementation mechanism was entirely based on the abolition of Church privileges: with the suppression of the public banks, the ecclesiastics forced to sell their properties would not have found any other profitable use for the liquid capital made than to deposit it in the new bank, at 3% interest. The *Banco* would thus have had the financial means to buy back the fiscal rents (called *arrendamenti*). The owners of these assets, receiving money, could have easily and advantageously used it in the purchase of real estate sold by the ecclesiastics. The latter, by depositing money in the *Banco*, would have enabled it to buy back the fiscal rents and thus create a theoretically self-sufficient capital circulation. The possibility of doing good business at the expense of ecclesiastical assets would have served to attenuate the opposition of the owners of fiscal rents (Ajello 1969: 818–819). The only realistic element of this enormous round of money lay in the possibility of new investment opportunities for the rarefied Neapolitan capital market: for this reason it could have met the favor of classes interested in new earning opportunities, but it strangely ignored ecclesiastical opposition. To this was added the danger of an uprising of the plebs in favor of the public banks, traditionally engaged in assistance to the poor; a fact that weighed against granting the monopoly to the *Banco di San Carlo.*

The result of all this friction and resistance was the Pragmatics of 18 March 1728, which reduced the functions of the *Banco* by entrusting it only with the right to repurchase the revenues of the Royal Treasury that had been transferred. Soon its action was completely canceled by the financial needs of the Habsburgs, involved in the new *War of the Polish Succession* (1733–1738).[33]

Monetary policy was even less dynamic: the problems inherited from Spanish rule remained unchanged, i.e. the circulation of clipped coins, and the export and hoarding of good ones, while paper money circulation, which always acted as a substitute for metal money, was subjected to serious crises of confidence.[34] The repercussions of the failure of the *Systéme de Law* in France were also added to the disadvantage of paper circulation, which even pushed Charles VI to prohibit, with a specific policy, the use of bank notes in his domains.

Thus at the beginning of the 1730s a contradiction arose between the reformist intentions declared by the Viennese court and their actual implementation, linked to the contingent interests of imperial power policy, which was decided elsewhere and of which the Neapolitan area, merely a province in a vast empire, paid the costs in terms of human and material resources.[35] The lesson had now been learned: any attempt to modernize the Kingdom depended on the regaining of political independence. For this reason the *ceto civile* immediately sided in favor of Charles of Bourbon and offered its collaboration without too many reservations.[36]

The Austrian domination over Southern Italy fell apart as easily as the Spanish one had fallen apart twenty-seven years earlier. The dynastic ambitions of Elisabetta Farnese, Queen Consort of Philip V of Spain, heir of the Farnese and Medici families, and therefore interested in taking possession of the duchy of Parma and Piacenza and the Grand Duchy of Tuscany, her huge dowry, were linked to the Bourbon aims (largely defined by the political strategy of Cardinal Giulio Alberoni) of expelling the Habsburgs

[33] Tax revenues increased from 1,500,000 ducats in 1707 to more than 2,500,000; the increase was mostly due to new taxes.

[34] The Banco dell'Annunziata failed in early 1702 following the panic caused by the news of the death of Charles II and the disorder caused by the Macchia Conspiracy.

[35] According to Michelangelo Schipa, the Austrian government imposed a series of extraordinary taxes (donativi) on the Viceroyalty of Naples, the amount of which exceeded 3 million 200 thousand ducats (Schipa 1904: 9).

[36] "The emergence of a new awareness of the interests of the kingdom was not due to the affirmation of a new class, but rather to the increasingly frequent comparison that intellectuals made between the conditions of the South and those of other European countries" (Lepre 1986b: 87).

from Italy and restoring Spanish rule in the peninsula. A good means of realizing these different goals was found in Charles of Bourbon, eldest son of the second marriage of Philip V of Spain and Elisabetta Farnese (Ajello 1977). The Treaty of Vienna (1731) resolved the long-standing dispute over the fate of the Duchy of Parma and Piacenza and the Grand Duchy of Tuscany by assigning them to Charles (Alatri 1989: 19–20; Ajello 2001: 15–17). But this solution was destined to be temporary in the precarious European balance. The death, in 1733, of Augustus II of Poland triggered another succession crisis, starting a new conflict which on the Italian front saw France and Spain, allied in the first Bourbon family pact, opposed to Austria.

In February 1734, Charles of Bourbon joined the sixteen thousand Spanish soldiers of the Duke of Montemar in Siena, took command and headed South, while a Spanish naval squadron blocked the Gulf of Naples. On 25 March the Spanish army crossed the borders of the Neapolitan Kingdom and on 13 April, Montemar conquered the capital without encountering resistance (Schipa 1904: 99–131). The Habsburg troops, who retreated to Puglia, were defeated under the walls of Bitonto on 25 May. In September the "military march" ended with the conquest of Palermo (Alatri 1989: 62–63). With the Treaty of Vienna, signed in November 1738, Austria renounced its rights to Naples, Sicily and the State of the Presidi in favor of Charles of Bourbon who after more than two centuries returned independence, at least formally, to the Kingdom of Naples.

The foundation of an independent kingdom and the presence of a young monarch were two new elements, which contributed to fueling new hopes in all classes of Neapolitan society. In this climate it was not difficult to seek and find support to consolidate the new principality.[37] Despite the harsh purge of the "Austrian party",[38] the new sovereign offered the *ceto civile*, largely involved in the Austrian regime, the possibility of collaborating, while he promised the aristocracy and the clergy greater consideration for their role in society. To gain the favor of the

[37] "For the first time in southern history, political thought faced with full awareness and with strong hopes of success the problem that was already affecting the civil life of the most advanced countries in Europe, and which can be indicated with the dual concept: productivity-parasitism" (Ajello 1985: 115–116). See also Rao (1983); Chiosi (1986a); Spagnoletti (1997); Mafrici (1998); Caridi (2006, 2014); Galasso (2007).

[38] For this purpose, the *Giunta degli Inconfidenti* (*Council of the Untrustworthy*) was established, see Schipa (1904: 341–360); Venturi (1998: 30–33).

people, Charles solemnly affirmed, even before the Spanish army crossed the borders, that the new dynasty relieved "the Kingdom from every imposition, especially from those established by the insatiable greed of the Alemannic government".[39] Thus began under these auspices what Bernardo Tanucci called "the heroic time of the dynasty",[40] which essentially coincided with a serious effort to build and initiate the structures of an Absolute State. In an attempt to achieve this goal, the government moved along three lines: the delimitation of ecclesiastical power; the definition of the powers of the nobility and the role of the *ceto civile*; the reform and reorganization of the fiscal and administrative system.

Between 1734 and 1741, a series of mercantilist-inspired reforms were initiated, mostly borrowed from French models adapted to the Spanish situation. The close link with Spain was in fact an essential characteristic of this first phase of Bourbon rule. The protagonists of Neapolitan politics, Manuel de Benavides y Aragón Count (later Duke) of Santisteban (Italianized as Santo Stefano, 1734–1738) and José Joaquín de Montealegre, Marquis (later Duke) of Salas (1738–1746), were Spaniards in very close contact with the court of Madrid. Furthermore, the responsibility of *Sopraintendente Generale dell'Azienda* (*General Superintendent of the Agency*, a sort of modern Chancellor of the Exchequer)[41] was entrusted to the Sicilian Giovanni Brancaccio (De Caro 1971), coming from the Spanish financial administration and therefore linked to the same owner of the *Secretariat of State* of Madrid and leader of the *Afrancesado*

[39] See Ajello (1972: 486). This measure had been proclaimed in the Edict of Civita Castellana of 14 March 1734.

[40] "The foundation, and heroic time of this Court begins with the Treaty of Seville [1729], and ends at the departure of the Count of S. Stefano [Santisteban, 1738]" (Bernardo Tanucci letter to Luigi Viviani, Naples August 29, 1758, in Viviani della Robbia 1942, vo. II: 57). As Anna Maria Rao has pointed out, the expression coined by Tanucci refers to the years 1728–1736 and not - contrary to Raffaele Ajello (1972) - to the following decade (see Rao 2009: 317–320).

[41] An institution borrowed from France and transplanted to Spain by the French financier Giovanni Orry in 1713; in Naples it was then established in 1737 *Segreteria di Stato del Dispaccio di Azienda e Commercio (Secretariat of State for Commerce)*, which represented a decisive step towards the unification of the financial administration. The Superintendency, the Sommaria, the Chamber of Santa Chiara, the Delegates of the Arrendamenti, those of the Public Banks, the Annona Councils, the Customs of Foggia and Abruzzo, the Supreme Magistrate of Commerce and the Land and Sea Consulate depended on it. See Coniglio (1981: 39–41), Ajello (1972: 568) and Zilli (1990: 35–36). On the organisation of Charles' government, see Salvati (1962).

party (pro-French party), José Patiño Rosales, who had proposed him to that appointment.[42] But, alongside the nucleus of Spanish officials, a group of exponents of the Neapolitan *ceto civile* was immediately added in 1735, called to lead the *Giunta del Commercio* (*Trade Council*), the new body created to re-establish and promote the trade of the Kingdom; among these the prominent personality was Francesco Ventura.[43] "The appointment in the *Giunta del Commercio* of a group of jurists, who are homogeneous from an ideological and cultural point of view, was an important sign of the new political direction of the government; but this choice was further characterized by the fact that for the first time some merchants were placed alongside the lawyers, with equal rights and authority" (Ajello 1972: 586, see also Caridi 2011: 105–106).

Thus began in the summer of 1735 the attempt to lay the foundations of an absolute and mercantilist State.[44] For this purpose it was necessary to reorganize the entire fiscal administration, imitating the most developed European models, set a budget forecast for expenses, unify all cash operations in a single treasury, redeem and reorganize surrenders, eliminate the clergy's fiscal immunities and reduce the sale of public offices (*venalite des*

[42] Between 1734 and 1738, Santisteban occupied a prominent position in the *Council of State*, the government that Charles had established when he was still Duke of Parma and destined to define the lines of Neapolitan politics. The Council was composed not only of Santisteban, Mayor of the palace, but also of Montealegre, appointed secretary of state for foreign affairs, Giovanni Brancaccio (finance), Gaetano Brancone (ecclesiastical affairs) and Bernardo Tanucci (justice). Santisteban was removed in 1738 due to a court conspiracy of aristocrats close to Queen Maria Amalia, who disagreed with ecclesiastical policy, and control of the government passed to Montealegre (Schipa 1904: 333–339). Tanucci commented on the transfer of power as the end of the heroic period of the monarchy. On Santisteban and Montealegre and their role in Neapolitan politics see Schipa (1904: 339–340, 361–365); Ajello (1972: 498–502); Coniglio (1981); Chiosi (1986a: 384–396); Rao (1989: 218–230); Ajello (2001: 30–39). On the *Afranzesado* party, initiated by the French personnel sent by Luigi XIV to support the government of Philip V, see Ajello (1985).

[43] A certain role was played by Pietro Contegna and above all by Jean Baptiste Vaucoulleur: "a Frenchman who, having devoted himself for a long time to the study of commerce, manufacturing, customs and finances" (Schipa 1904: 561–566), had become a trusted consultant of the *Giunta*. See also Caridi (2011: 96–101).

[44] An example of the mercantilist policy is the introduction of a tax on the rents of foreigners and feudal lords not resident in the Kingdom, known as *valimento*, which was levied permanently in the early years of the new regime, the purpose of which was to discourage the purchase or possession of property in the kingdom by foreigners and to curb the flight of capital abroad, where rents were spent. On the financial situation of the Kingdom at the advent of the new regime, see Romano (1946).

offices).[45] The reforms of the following years were an attempt, often carried out under difficult circumstances, to achieve these objectives. But not all of the *ceto civile* supported Brancaccio's policy. A number of members of the Neapolitan judiciary, who had in fact been deprived of their authority, hindered him (judging him inadequate in experience and education) and had a great influence on the implementation of the reform policy (De Caro 1971; Caridi 2011: 107).

The most important result that Brancaccio achieved was the establishment of the *Catasto Onciario* (*Onciary Cadaster*)[46] in 1741, with the aim of obtaining "that the burdens are equally distributed, and that the poor are not burdened with more than their weak strength and the rich pay according to their possessions" (Prammatiche 1804: 360), and which, for the first time, established the tax on the property of the clergy.[47] Apart from the declared intentions, the reform was seriously affected by "the exemptions and privileges, the inequality between rich and poor (whereby the richer one was, the less, in proportion, one paid), the confirmation of the personal tax on land and labour of workers, the complex artificial mechanism for the distribution of taxes, the summary and approximate estimates of stable assets: these are all elements that indicate how the Neapolitan cadaster remains much inferior to the almost contemporary tax censuses in Lombardy and in Piedmont" (Villani 1977: 105–153, see also Zilli 1990; Bulgarelli Lukacs 2004).

[45] Possession of an office permitted the *right of substitution* (*diritto di sostituzione*: the officeholder could appoint a deputy to manage the office or rent out the entire office in exchange for a fixed income) and the *right of extension* (*diritto di ampliazione*: the officeholder could extend the original right to third parties designated by him, usually his family members, thus legitimising de facto inheritance of public offices). In September 1735, Montealegre forbade the Sommaria from further enforcing these rights in order to break up the network of patronage rooted locally, as it was known that the acquisition of offices constituted a way of investing one's capital and did not respond to any desire to fill roles generally considered suitable for individuals of modest status (Zilli 1990: 39; see also Comparato 1974; Mantelli 1986).

[46] On the relationship between the cadaster and the *Oncia*, the money of account of the Kingdom, from which its name derives see Giliberti (1921: 34–36).

[47] "This was the truly new part of the taxation and, even if there was the aim of increasing public revenues in this way, it opened the country to modern principles of understanding relations with the clergy, but not with the nobility, who continued to enjoy privileges for tax exemptions" (Coniglio 1981: 93). For further details on the functioning of the *Catasto Onciario*, see Villani (1977: 105–153).

The results in terms of commercial policy were even more limited. In this important area of trade policy it was a question of overcoming an age-old divide. It was enough to see the state of the Neapolitan fleet reduced to very few ships to despair of the concrete possibility of commercial development.

The *Giunta*'s activity was simply contradictory: on the one hand it attempted to encourage the liberalization of trade in raw materials (wheat, silk, oil, almonds, wine, foodstuffs, wool and livestock), essentially accepting the subordinate role assigned to Southern Italy within the world economy.[48] On the other hand it attempted to compete with the great maritime nations, concluding a commercial treaty with the Ottoman Empire (April 1740) and its regencies of Algiers, Tripoli and Tunis (June 1741); a fact which only aroused the hostility of France, since trade between the Levant and the Kingdom of Naples was actually very limited; the treaty with Constantinople was the only agreement completed (Romano 1948, 1951; Coniglio 1981: 107; Venturi 1998: 72–75). Other negotiations were started in this period with Sweden (June 1742), Denmark (April 1748) and Holland (August 1753). There were few who clearly saw the impossibility of adopting a mercantilist policy.

Despite these innovations, the fiscal policy proposed by Brancaccio followed the Spanish tradition of extraordinary finance, based on *donativi* (*donations*) and occasional withdrawals, justified by emergency measures, without a program that harmonized the government's action and without an effective correspondence between the available resources in the country and the needs imposed by political independence. For the first four years of the Kingdom, Santisteban did not act with the necessary determination against the conservative forces of the nobility, the church and the judicial apparatus, furthermore the influence of the Queen Mother Elisabetta Farnese was significant.[49] On the other hand, reformist positions had coalesced around Montealegre, ready to give their contribution both on the anti- Roman curia front and on that of resistance to the privileges of the nobility and the judiciary. A more incisive reformist policy therefore began to be introduced only after Santisteban's departure.

[48] Useful information on the position of the Kingdom of Naples in the context of Mediterranean trade can be found in Romano (1976: 67–160).

[49] According to Michelangelo Schipa, Santisteban "did not know how or did not want to train a Prince who emerged from his hands capable of governing with his head" (Schipa 1904: 71).

The *Giunta* was suppressed in 1739 and replaced by a new institution, the *Supremo Magistrato di Commercio* (*Supreme Magistrate of Commerce*), strongly desired by Montealegre and entrusted to Francesco Ventura, in a climate of very close collaboration between the government and the *ceto civile* (Ajello 1972: 650, see also Allocati 1955; Caridi 2011).[50] Thus a real judiciary was created, modeled once again on the French experience, with the task of removing the obstacles that hindered the development of commercial activities. The new institution immediately "entered objective competition with the existing magistracies, because it offered notable and substantial advantages compared to all the others: a rapid, simplified, informal rite, free from traditional constraints and complications; a body in which the commercial technicians worked alongside pure lawyers; use of the Italian language in documents which constituted a record in the Neapolitan courts; significant reduction of jurisdictional rights. The other magistracies of the city saw their jurisdictional affairs reduced and it was not just a question of prestige, either for the ministers (or judges) or for the magistrates (or chancellors) and much less for the nobles, courtiers, capitalists" (Ajello 1972: 652).

Another important measure taken to attract capital and business initiatives was the edict of 1740 which allowed the entry of Jews into the Kingdom (the rights granted were broader than those enjoyed by the Jews in the city of Livorno). Needless to say, this measure did not meet with great consensus among the population and further stiffened the positions of the Neapolitan clergy, already dissatisfied with the limitation of privileges suffered in the concordat of the following year.[51] The concordat, in fact, signed in June 1741, after long negotiations conducted with the Holy See by the Cappelano Maggiore, Celestino Galiani, established the principle of the subordination of ecclesiastical assets to taxation, albeit with some restrictions in immediate execution, and drastically reduced the right to asylum.[52] The Church, in exchange for this downsizing which ended years of conflict, retained the privilege of preventive censorship of

[50] Between the end of the imperial government and the beginning of the Bourbon one, proposals for the establishment of a specific institution dedicated to trade had been outlined by Serafino Biscardi ([1993]), Federico Valignani ([2001]) and Gregorio Grimaldi ([2001]). See also De Tiberiis (2001) and Pilati (2001).

[51] Other members of *ceto civile*, such as Pietro Contegna, and of ecclesiastical world, such as Celestino Galiani, were supporters of the edict on the Jews, see Lissa (2020).

[52] According to Franco Venturi, the ecclesiastical policy of the Bourbon government was a kind of "Giannonism without Giannone" (Venturi 1998: 24).

the press and obtained the right to participate with its own judges in lay tribunals for crimes committed by ecclesiastics (Nicolini 1931: 83–86).

But after 1741, despite the projects initiated and implemented, the impetus of the reformist action ended up being ultimately stifled: the balance that had accompanied the advent of the new dynasty was now broken in the face of the concrete choices that had been made and which affected many privileges.[53] A series of events contributed to creating the turning point in Neapolitan politics.

In August 1742, the presence of an English naval fleet in the Gulf of Naples and the mere threat of the capital being bombed were enough to extract the King's promise to withdraw from participation alongside Spain in the *War of the Austrian Succession*.[54] The following year a violent plague epidemic in Messina (1743–1744) revealed the weakness of the administrative structures, still undermined by corruption and privilege. Finally in 1744, on the field of Velletri, the King was saved only by "a good dose of luck" (Venturi 1998: 88; see also Schipa 1904: 438–444) and by the loyalty shown by the barons, confirmed even if the Austrian army had announced itself with a manifesto in which it promised the re-establishment of the ancient privileges of the nobility and the resumption of the fight against the Curia, thus earning the sympathies of many exponents of the ceto civile. Charles defeated the imperials at Velletri, but he was able to take advantage of the warning and changed his policy in a direction more favorable to the baronial class, now seen as the only sure support of the Kingdom. The law of 1738 on feudal jurisdiction was immediately eliminated; in 1746 the powers of the *Supreme Magistrate of Commerce* were

[53] According to Ilaria Zilli, the *War of the Austrian Succession* was the real cause of the royal failure on the front of reforms and the collapse of state finances. In fact, the analysis of the Kingdom's budgets reveals that the crisis of the 1740s was overcome only after the Treaty of Aix-la-Chapelle (1748). The agreement inaugurated a long period of peace for the Kingdom, allowing, in her opinion, a second economic recovery from the years 1753–54 until Charles's departure for Spain in 1759 (Zilli 1990: 70). An opinion that confirms Michelangelo Schipa's negative view of the early Bourbon period, subordinated to the Spanish court (Schipa 1904: 455). According to Raffaele Ajello, "from 1734 to 1746, Naples' stronger ties with Madrid benefited the Kingdom" (Ajello 2001: 29) and he evaluates Montealegre's government positively (Ajello 2001: 30–39).

[54] "A humiliation all the more bitter since the appearance of the English ships and their casual behavior were linked to a threatened revolt of the plebs of Naples, to a clear allusion to the discontent that was spreading in the kingdom and to the fragility of the entire government system of Charles of Bourbon" (Venturi 1998: 81–82). See also Schipa (1904: 408–417).

reduced and the edict on the Jews was revoked (Giura 1978; Caridi 2011: 122–124). In the same year Montealegre was dismissed and the government passed into the hands of the Marquis Giovanni Fogliani d'Aragona (Schipa 1904: 456–458). Alongside the latter, the Tuscan Bernardo Tanucci, who until then had remained in the background, acquired an increasingly prominent role (Schipa 1904: 452–454; Imbruglia 2019).[55]

In those years the Neapolitan politics was entirely dominated by the problem of succession to the Spanish throne, a fact which, according to what was established in Aix-la-Chapelle in 1748, would have determined the passage of Naples and Sicily to the cadet branch of the Bourbon-Parma.

In the new climate the plans for reform weakened, despite the influence of the reformist party led by Niccolò Fraggianni (1686–1763) (Di Rienzo 1977; Zambelli 1985; Di Donato 1989; Ajello 2001: 44–48; Ferrone 2012: 8–10); and the only initiative worthy of note developed by the finance administration, governed by Leopoldo de Gregorio (Schipa 1904: 472–473; Strazzullo 1997), was the institution of the *Giunta delle Ricompre* (*Repurchase Council*), which was supposed to redeem the public assets that had been largely sold off. In practice it was an attempt to achieve the creation of a consolidated public debt (Bianchini 1839: 427–429; Ricca-Salerno 1896: 395; Zilli 1990: 19). But at the end of Charles' reign only a little of the revenue transferred had been repurchased and the consolidation operation ended only in 1806 with the establishment of the *Great Book of Public Debt*.

[55] "The initiative of Montealegre and his passionate and intense way of interpreting his function in the Sicilies backfired on him: a few years before disgrace contributed to isolating him from his own protectors, his activism was already reproached as adventurous imprudence, his spirit of initiative led to a backlash, and an equal and opposite reaction, when his government fell. The ambiguous moral fabric dominant in the old culture swallowed up his reforms like quicksand, closing in on them, and what prevailed was indifference to the new and an excess of caution, which are the best alibi for inertia" (Ajello 2001: 35). Montealegre's dismissal was made possible by the death of Philip VI in the same year, 1746. Queen Maria Amalia was interested in freeing the king from dependence on the able minister and on maternal influences, which did not always coincide with the real interests of the Kingdom. Even important exponents of the government such as Tanucci could not stand the close link between Naples and Spain: "More and more the world is made to believe that we are a Spanish province - the minister wrote - and [...] that this king is a representation of the other" (Letter to Corsini, 23 December 1741, Tanucci 1980a: 522–523). On the antagonism between Tanucci and Montealegre, see Ajello (2001: 25). Tanucci was Secretary of Justice from 1734 to 1755; after Fogliani's departure in 1755, he was responsible for the navy, trade, justice and the royal house; from 1759 he assumed position of *First Secretary* (a sort of Prime Minister) until 1776 (see Salvati 1962: 80).

From June 1755, with the dismissal of Marquis Giovanni Fogliani, King Charles took direct control of the government, abolishing the post of first secretary and moving towards a policy of "immobilism", increasingly restricted by compromises with the conservative party. Thus Charles' reign ended in 1759, when he was called to the Spanish throne and the Neapolitan Kingdom was entrusted to a Council of Regency. The reforms, even if they had taken place, "had not found a precise center in the desire to create a state and military power for the new sovereign, nor had they centered on an attempt at *felicitas populi*. They had followed an uncertain trend between one thing and another in the absence of any desire to establish priorities and to glimpse a rhythm, a development program" (Venturi 1998: 81; see also Caridi 2011, 2012).

2.2 Neapolitan Intellectual Life Between Tradition and Innovation

In the last decades of the seventeenth century, Neapolitan intellectual life went through a lively phase, emerging from the torpor of Counter-Reformation conformism (De Giovanni 1970). Dominican Thomism, Franciscan Scotism and Jesuit neo-Thomism, hegemonic schools of thought after the Council of Trent, had completely overshadowed the great season of Neapolitan Humanism and Renaissance, which had produced the great personalities of Giovanni Pontano (1429–1503), Bernardino Telesio (1509–1588), Giovanni Battista Della Porta (1535–1615), Giordano Bruno (1548–1600) and Tommaso Campanella (1568–1639). The complex philosophical constructions of these thinkers had tackled with originality a heterogeneous variety of subjects ranging from occult philosophy, astrology, alchemy, mathematics, meteorology to natural philosophy (Garin 2008: 427–487, 561–596; Galasso 1982: 86). However, in the interstices left vacant by the strict ecclesiastical control, a substantial literature of a technical nature, but of good quality, had developed in the first half of the seventeenth century dedicated exclusively to the serious social emergencies that plagued the Kingdom of Naples, such as public health, monetary disorder, the functioning of the *Annona* and major judicial disputes.[56] These were themes that the official culture,

[56] On economic matters see De Santis (1605a, 1605b); Serra (1613); Turbolo (1616); Biblia (1621); Lunetti (1621, 1630); Tapia (1638); Enriquez de Fonseca (1681a). In the field of medical science, see Severino (1653).

focusing mainly on the great philosophical and theological systems, had neglected altogether, revealing, as an attentive protagonist of Neapolitan intellectual life, Vincenzo D'Onofrio (1618–1692), noted, a lack of interest in disciplines "whose usefulness was unknown" and which were instead "very necessary, both for life and for the perfect knowledge of the other sciences" (D'Onofrio 1653 [1932]: 246).

A new impetus to Neapolitan intellectual life came from Viceroy Iñigo Vélez de Guevara, Count of Oñate (1648–1653), who had the delicate task of restoring the authority of the Spanish government in Naples after the 1647–48 revolt, a task he fulfilled without excess, punishing only the leaders of the revolt and defeating the French attempts to take over the Kingdom. To foster reconciliation, he implemented a policy of promoting cultural activities by reopening the university and restarting the initiatives of the *Accademia degli Oziosi* (*Academy of the Idle*, active in Naples since 1611) (Giannone 1723, vol. IV: 391; De Miranda 2005), entrusting, however, the Jesuits with an enormous power to control Neapolitan intellectual life. The "paternalistic and moralizing" regime (Galasso 1982: 86), established by the Count of Oñate, left some space for stimuli of intellectual renewal in a context that was politically quiet, but marked by a growing and unstoppable intellectual vivacity (Galasso 1982: 92). The viceroy listened to the urging of an important member of the *ceto civile*, Francesco D'Andrea (1625–1698), and re-established the university chair of mathematics, entrusting it to Tommaso Cornelio (1614–1684), a leading figure in the dissemination of Descartes' and Gassendi's philosophy in the Kingdom (Giannone 1723, vol. IV: 391).[57] In the last decade of the seventeenth century in the Kingdom of Naples, as in other regions of Europe, mathematical science was considered an essential part of human knowledge, and its applications went beyond the narrow field of

[57] Besides Tommaso Cornelio, the leading figures of the tradition of Cartesian studies in Naples were Antonio de Monforte (1644–1717), Giacinto de Cristofaro (1667–1725) and Agostino Ariani (1672–1748) (see Barbieri 1778 and Amodeo 1924: chap. 1). In his *Autobiography*, Vico states that Descartes' philosophy in the last decade of the seventeenth century was "at the height of its renown among the established men of letters" (Vico 1728 [1975]: 132). Cornelius' presence in Naples was seen as a real intellectual breakthrough, as described by D'Andrea: "in the year of our Lord 1649 Naples saw the arrival of Tommaso Cornelio to whom our city owes all that is known today of the most truthful in philosophy and medicine, I was the first to embrace that way of philosophizing he proposed by bringing to Naples the work of Renato delle Carte [Descartes], whose name had been unknown to us until that time" (D'Andrea 1696a [1990]: 203).

mathematicians. This interest in mathematics became common among intellectual élites, favoring the general adoption of Descartes's algebraic geometry and the rapid algebraization of mathematical language (Garin 2008: vol. I, ch. 24). In the same years, legal culture was also renewed by taking Hugo Grotius' natural law theories as a point of reference.[58]

All these different signs of renewal converged in the experience of the *Accademia degli Investiganti* (*Academy of Investigators*, active since 1649, but formally established in 1663 on the initiative of the Benedictine Juan Caramuel y Lóbkowitz and Andrea Concublet) destined to play the role of a melting pot of heterogeneous theoretical directions: "the innovators endeavoured to follow Bacon, Hobbes, Galilei, Descartes, Gassendi, Malebranche, Spinoza, Grotius together [and] the situation was somewhat paradoxical. Experimentalism, probabilism, historical sensitivity, scientific-naturalistic interests gave way to metaphysical rationalism, mathematical deductivism, natural law, strong and persistent theological interests" (Galasso 1982: 111; see also Fish 1953; Mastellone 1963; De Giovanni 1970; Torrini 1981; Carpanetto and Ricuperati 1987: 80–81; Labellarte 2019: 23–30).[59] In this heterogeneous mixture, the amalgam was the legacy of the Renaissance tradition, in the sense of experimentalism and empiricism, combined with Cartesian reason with the intention of countering the old authority of Aristotle.[60] This characteristic would

[58] Particularly interesting for the technical expertise achieved by the Neapolitan legal school is the involvement of Neapolitan jurists in the issue of the so-called *Right of Devolution* (*Ius Devolutionis*), the alleged right over Flanders of Louis XIV of France. The Spanish government commissioned the jurist Francesco D'Andrea to write an opinion on the subject (D'Andrea 1667). On D'Andrea, see De Giovanni (1958); Mastellone (1969); Galasso (1982: 106–107); Ascione (1994); Robertson (2005: 152–153).

[59] An initial attempt to open up Neapolitan culture to philosophical innovations was made in 1645 by Camillo Colonna, with the foundation of the *Accademia Colonnese* or also of the *Mortelle*, which died out in 1657, whose main aim was to apply the empirical method, but was hindered by official science, still tied to Aristotelianism, by the threats of the Inquisition and by the plague epidemic of 1656, which rekindled superstitions and reinforced religious control over intellectual life (Galasso 1982: 89–90; Setaro 2021: 260).

[60] "The poles of renewal promoted by the Investigators lay somewhat outside the horizon of the new modern physical science, which would progress and triumph on the Galileo-Newton axis. Both Porzio's mechanistic naturalism and Di Capua's vitalistic naturalism, as well as their experimentalism, founded on empirical observation and relative induction, and alien to imaginary and mathematical experimentation, and as well as their probabilism and their rudimentary assertion of a historicity (and therefore perfectibility) of truth, refer, other than those of the modern physical and mathematical sciences, to Bacon, above all, and also to the Italian naturalism of the late Renaissance" (Galasso 1989a: 122).

facilitate the reception of Newtonian philosophy in the following years. The philosophical renewal led to a different commitment of the intellectual classes, no longer antagonistic or subservient, but prudent advocates of a transformation of the Kingdom, following more advanced social and cultural models (this is also evidenced by the development of large library collections, also open to the public, and relations with foreign scientific societies and academies, such as the *Royal Society*).[61] However, this season was short-lived, around 1670 the Academy's activity began to wane and three tendencies emerged: one line tended towards a moderate form of libertinism, taking a *libertas philosophandi* approach,[62] another component was directed towards anti-curialism, contesting ecclesiastical privileges and Jesuit interference in intellectual life, and a third trend attempted a metaphysical restoration, finding a point of reference in the new *Palatine Academy* (Rotta 1978: 843–848), founded in 1698 by viceroy Luis Francisco de la Cerda y Aragón, duke of Medinaceli (1695–1702). In many intellectuals, these different tendencies tended to overlap, marking phases of intellectual life that were not always coherent and linear.

The controversies that animated Neapolitan intellectual life in this period did not have an abstract character, but were linked to real needs, first of all the effort to understand the tumultuous social transformations that preluded the collapse of the *Ancien Régime*; to favor, emulate or, on the contrary, preclude the path taken by the most powerful States and Princes; to respond, in some way, to Italian decadence. Adherence to the philosophical principles of the *veteres*, as opponents of the modern philosophy supported by the *iuvenes*, did not always imply a conservative vision on social issues.

The most significant figure of these tendencies characterising Neapolitan intellectual life in the last decades of the seventeenth century was Giuseppe

[61] Particularly important was the rich library of Giuseppe Valletta, consisting of more than sixteen thousand printed volumes and manuscripts, which offered intellectuals of the time a broad panorama of contemporary European literature. After his death, part of the library's holdings formed the founding nucleus of the Girolamini Library, at the suggestion of the philosopher Giambattista Vico (see Comparato 1970; Galasso 1982: 90–94, 405–408; Trombetta 2002: 326–344). In 1690, on the initiative of Cardinal Francesco Maria Brancaccio, the first Neapolitan public library was established with an endowment of around 55,000 volumes.

[62] The term "libertine" or "freethinker" was generally equated with the term atheist, and it was used very generically to target anyone who strayed from the Aristotelian-scholastic tradition (see Mastellone 1963; Bianchi 1979, 1984; Bertelli 1980; Gregory 1981; Zoli 1989; Foucault 2010; Beniscelli 2012a, 2012b).

Valletta, a member of the *ceto civile* of humble origins, who later became rich with a successful career as a lawyer and who cultivated mercantile interests (De Giovanni 1968; Comparato 1970). He was an example of social ascent and intellectual emancipation despite the limitations imposed by a stagnant aristocratic society. Valletta, together with Francesco D'Andrea, renewed Neapolitan legal culture by opening it up to the influence of natural law, particularly in the approach of Grotius. In this perspective he defended essentially bourgeois values, such as the rejection of policies attempting to manipulate money (Valletta, MS, written between 1675–1676). By entering into correspondence with the Protestant world and assimilating, through his rich library collection, the most important philosophical and scientific innovations, Valletta asserted the autonomy of philosophical reflection, drawing accusations of libertinism and atheism. But Neapolitan libertinism had a moderate character, as heir to the humanist tradition, and was far from the radicalism of Bernard de Fontanelle, Charles de Saint-Évremond and Pierre Bayle.

Nonetheless, the Jesuits and the Roman Curia, in order to put a stop to these tendencies that severely limited the cultural hegemony of the Church and the credibility of the traditional faith, did not hesitate, in 1688, to open the process of Inquisition against some exponents of the Neapolitan intellectual world, accused of atheism. This resulted in the long judicial affair known as the "atheist trial" (1688–1697) (Osbat 1971; Rack 1973; Galasso 1982: 444–473; Setaro 2021), which represented another important moment in the emancipation of Neapolitan culture from ecclesiastical control and Aristotelian-scholastic hegemony.

As is known, the Spanish-style Inquisition (called "*a modo di Spagna*"), in which inquisitors were appointed directly by the sovereign, did not operate in Naples: two popular uprisings, in 1510 and 1547, had prevented its establishment, which is why a specific, complex system in inquisitorial matters was created in Naples based on local bishops who acted with the support of inquisitors appointed by the Holy Office in Rome, which in this way acted indirectly (Amabile 1892: 54–75; Romeo 1976: 5–109; Fiorelli 2009).[63] The lengthy trial obviously did not only concern

[63] "The only strength demonstrated by the legal apparatus was the tendency to resist Roman arrogance and to preserve a certain freedom of movement for European culture. The defence against the Spanish Holy Office, imposed on the viceroys by the lay magistrates and the nobles, was the greatest merit of the local ruling class: but even that intolerance arose largely from the defence of the *roba*; that is, of privilege" (Ajello 2001: 22).

the defendants, but all the intellectuals who supported the new culture; in fact, the inquisitors also asked for D'Andrea's arrest, a request that the viceroy, Francisco de Benavides, Count of Santisteban (1688–1696) rejected.[64] The trial provoked a clash between the ecclesiastical power, the civil judicial power, represented by the togate ministers, and the sovereign power represented by the viceroy, leading to a profound rupture in the Neapolitan intellectual world itself. The lengthy trial, although without proof of the defendants' guilt, ended with particularly severe punishments, but it also showed that the *ceto civile* was now able to resist ecclesiastical power and to drag part of the nobility and the people into this confrontation, while maintaining the neutrality of the viceregal authority.[65] The legitimacy of the trial and the role of the Inquisition were in fact debated by the most prominent members of the *ceto civile*: in 1693 Valletta published the *Procedimento Ordinario e Canonico nelle Cause che si trattano nel Tribunale del Sant'Uffizio nella Città e nel Regno di Napoli* (*Ordinary and Canonical Proceedings in the Causes Dealt with in the Court of the Holy Office in the City and Kingdom of Naples*), in which he retraced the history of the Church, emphasised its process of straying from the original spirit and judged the Inquisition Court an institution not only governed by backward and unjust rules, but contrary to the laws of nature, since the accusers could not present any evidence, nor could the accused defend themselves, and in his conclusions he called for the definitive separation of Church and State (Valletta, MS-1, 1693).[66] Valletta also intervened to defend modern philosophy, represented by the experimental approach and corpuscular physics, defined by Bacon, Gassendi and Descartes, against ancient and scholastic Aristotelianism (Labellarte 2019). This theme underlies the *Lettera in difesa della moderna filosofia e de' coltivatori di essa* (*Letter in Defence of Modern Philosophy and the Cultivators of it*, written in

[64] The four main defendants, were Basilio Giannelli (remembered for his poetic activity), Giacinto De Cristoforo (mathematician and author of a history of science and letters) well-known and respected in the literary milieu of Naples, Filippo Belli and Francesco Paolo Manuzzi, modest characters who had come to Naples to complete their law studies and who, at the end of the trial, abruptly returned to their homeland without a trace.

[65] The Seggi constituted a Deputation against the Holy Office and sent a delegation to Spain to beg for Naples' privilege of exemption from the Inquisition, showing the unity between the viceregal government, the nobility of the *seggi* and the jurists (Mastellone 1965: 71).

[66] This contribution was commissioned in 1691 by the Deputation to address the historical-legal issues raised by the trial.

1693–97, but published in 1732) and the *Istoria filosofica* (*Philosophical History*, probably written in 1697–1704, Valletta [1975]), in which he shows that modern theses take up a very ancient philosophical tradition dating back to Moses, from which it then passed on to the various oriental 'wisdoms', then to Pythagoras, Democritus, Plato and Epicurus, a homogeneous tradition against which Aristotelianism stands as a deviation (see Giansiracusa 1988; Labellarte 2019: 119–206).[67]

The substantial defeat of the ecclesiastical authorities, who had failed to restore either cultural hegemony or the role of the Inquisition, gave greater impetus to the fight against the privileges of the Church. The political-cultural elite who had led the clash against the Roman Curia and the Jesuits, and who constituted the most advanced part of the *ceto civile*, had been able to build a broad consensus on the anti-curialist programme, which involved both the autonomist aspirations of the nobility and popular and bourgeois intolerance towards ecclesiastical intrusiveness in daily life (Galasso 1982: 420).

Thus began the great season of Neapolitan anti-Curialism led by such notable personalities of the *ceto civile* as Gaetano Argento, Pietro Giannone, Costantino Grimaldi, and supported by the new Austrian regime (Lauro 1974). In *Dell'istoria civile del regno di Napoli*, published by Giannone in 1723, the jurisdictionalist program found its highest expression, but also its turning point. The emphasis on the word *"civil"* encapsulates the purpose of the work, aimed at "giving an exact and distinct cognisance of the political and temporal state of the Kingdom" over fifteen centuries, and to "see how and when the ecclesiastics were introduced into the empire, and what new input it brought to the Kingdom" and how "against all the laws of government, one empire was able to establish itself in another, and how often the priesthood, abusing the devotion of the people and its spiritual power, prevailed over the temporal government of the Kingdom" (Giannone 1723: 24–25).[68] The polemical intent was clear, but Giannone was overwhelmed by the ruthless campaign that the ecclesiastical authorities waged against him, accusing him of denying not only the principal dogmas of the Christian faith (the ordination of bishops, purgatory,

[67] Giovan Battista De Benedictis (1694), a Jesuit, had attacked Cartesian philosophy with a pamphlet in defense of Aristotelianism and scholasticism, soliciting polemical responses from Valletta and Costantino Grimaldi (1725). On the controversies that arose in Naples around the spread of Cartesianism, see Belgioioso (1992, 1999, 2005); Marcialis (1996); Lojacono (2003); Girard (2011, 2017).

[68] On Pietro Giannone see Ricuperati (1970, 2001); Ajello (1975, 1980).

miracles, the intercession of saints), but also devotions dear to the people such as the miracle of San Gennaro. Giannone, fearing the violence of the superstitious populace, cleverly stirred up against him, and not defended by the viceroy Cardinal von Althann, sought refuge in Vienna, where he was welcomed into the court circle linked to the *Hofbibliothek* and to Prince Eugene of Savoy.[69] As his fame began to spread all over Europe, he devoted himself to defending the *Istoria civile* and writing a new work, the *Triregno*, which remained unfinished. His human story coincided with the historical parabola of anti-Curialism and when this faded throughout Europe at the turn of the first half of the eighteenth century, Giannone was isolated, forced to wander between Venice and Geneva, and then ended his existence as a prisoner of the Savoy sovereign.[70]

At the advent of the new Kingdom, in which Giannone had hoped in vain to play a role, the political and cultural context had changed profoundly and Neapolitan intellectual life had lost its unity of purpose. The united reaction against the Inquisition was over and deep contrasts were emerging. New stimuli had come from post-Cartesian European literature, not only Spinoza, but Fontanelle and above all Locke and Mandeville questioned the foundations of traditional religious morality, to which was added the materialism and mechanism prevalent in the new physical science of Anglo-Dutch origin. Faced with these new trends, one part of Neapolitan culture reacted by attempting to elaborate alternative models based on the recovery of tradition, fearing not only the collapse of faith, but the crisis of all religiosity, "in a country already in itself more inclined to indulge in the forms of religion than to intimately cultivate its substance; there was fear of the unstoppable growth of selfishness, in a society, like the Neapolitan one, deeply divided, lacking in community spirit, incapable even of configuring its overall interests and dedicating even the slightest commitment to them" (Ajello 1978: 997). Another part, instead, assimilated the new models, albeit in a moderate and prudent manner, avoiding any excesses as far as possible, in an attempt to implement a modernisation of society, imitating the more evolved models.

[69] On the role of viceroy Althann in the anti-curial controversy see Ajello (1976a).

[70] The weapon of jurisdictionalism had been used by Vienna to press the Roman Curia for clearly defined and delimited concessions. Emperor Joseph I, the one who had instigated the fight, died in 1711 and his successor, Charles VI, strongly toned down the anti-Curial policy by acting in a new European political situation that required him to behave differently.

And it was in the midst of this fracture that the formation of the young Galiani took place.

2.3 The Traditionalists: Paolo Mattia Doria and Giambattista Vico

The Atheists trial had marked the high point of the spread of Cartesian thought in Neapolitan culture, revealing the weakness of scholastic Aristitotelism, which was no longer able to hegemonize intellectual life. It was, however, a spurious Cartesianism, which contained conflicting elements, in which currents derived from the Renaissance naturalistic and Platonising tradition were juxtaposed with rationalistic experimentalism, hardly reconcilable tendencies that would soon take opposite directions. Cartesianism had become "a garment too tight for the new rationalist and scientific demands that had matured thanks to it" (Galasso 1989b: 246) and a substantial part of the Neapolitan *intelligentsia* considered the philosophy of John Locke and Isaac Newton as adequate answers to the unresolved aporias of Cartesian philosophy. That solution that was rejected by another minority part of the Neapolitan cultural world that, instead, went beyond Descartes, re-evaluating Platonic metaphysics and condemning the materialism and sensualism that, in their opinion, was the foundation of modern doctrines.

From this camp of the traditionalists emerged the two figures of Paolo Mattia Doria (1667–1746) and Giambattista Vico (1668–1744), protagonists of a real *philosophical restoration*.[71]

Born into a very rich and illustrious Genoese family (that had given as many as five doges to the Republic between the sixteenth and seventeenth centuries), Doria moved to Naples in 1690 to collect some credits claimed by his family (Rotta 1978: 840; Scazzieri 2011; Belgioioso 2012). The cumbersome Neapolitan justice system forced him, in order to assert his interests, to study the *scientia iuris*, which he did with brilliant results, as he managed to prevail, in a succession case, over Gaetano Argento, then

[71] The intellectual link between Doria and Vico is described by the latter in his *Autobiography*: "Doria, as fine a philosopher as he was a gentleman, was the first with whom Vico could begin to discuss metaphysics. What Doria admired as sublime, great and new in Descartes, Vico remarked to be old and common knowledge among the Platonists. But in Doria's discourse he perceived a mind that often gave forth lightning-like flashes of Platonic divinity, so that thenceforth they remained linked in a noble and faithful friendship" (Vico 1728 [1975]: 129).

considered the prince of the Neapolitan forum.[72] Attracted by the lively Neapolitan culture, Doria became one of its active protagonists, finding in Cartesian rationalism an adequate answer to the problems of physics and mathematics, which were at the centre of his interests in an early phase of his intellectual career. Soon, however, Doria moved away from the prevailing Cartesian model, proposing an anti-Cartesian counter-revolution, based on the systematic refutation of the analytical approach (Doria 1726; Amodeo 1924, vol I: 29–35). By now firmly aligned with the "ancients", a proponent of a reappraisal of Platonic idealism with Christian elements, Doria contributed to the re-foundation of the *Accademia degli Oziosi* whose activities were opposed to the *Accademia delle Scienze* founded by Celestino Galiani and close to Newtonism and Lockism, which characterized the principlae content of the philosophy of the "moderns".[73]

For Doria, the use of Cartesian analytical calculus (*algebra*) deprives geometry of the need for demonstrations, limiting its pedagogical value and heuristic effectiveness (Doria 1721: 23–24; see Conti 1981).[74] Doria, following Neoplatonic tradition, assigns a central role to the rehabilitation of Euclidean geometry in his controversy with modern mathematical methodology, supporting the merits of the ancient authors versus the moderns (called *Algebrists*). More specifically, Doria rejected all developments accomplished in mathematics after Descartes' revolution, and in particular opposed differential calculus, considering it a deviation from the logical foundations of Greek geometry (Amodeo 1924, chap. I; Ferrone 1995: 525–540).[75]

[72] On Doria see Vidal (1953); Galasso (1973); Zambelli (1972: 294–320); Zambelli (1973); Conti (1975, 1978); Ajello (1976a: 391–419); Rotta (1978: 837–870); Ricuperati (1979); Belgioioso (1981); Nuzzo (1984); Papuli (1985); Ferrone (1995: 211–220); Israel (2001: 670–674); Stapelbroek (2008a: 90–106).

[73] Koen Stapelbroek points out the affinity between Doria's *anti-modernist querelle* and that conducted by Fénelon in France (Stapelbroek 2008a: 94, see also Riley 2001).

[74] "In Euclid's coherent method, it is the mind that reasons; by contrast, in the calculus of the *algebrists,* it is the pen that reasons, not the mind" (Doria 1738: 16). See also Doria (1721, 1724, 1728, 1732, 1739).

[75] "The *Algebrists* need to be banished from studies; by reducing geometry to abstract calculus, they take away its best quality, which is to produce logic" (Doria 1729: 479). Euclidean geometry is considered an important discipline in the education of the Prince. Doria's anti-cartesianism is part of a general opposition to the indiscriminate use of algebraic analysis and the claim that everything, especially geometry, can be reduced to mere calculus. It is well known that Isaac Newton claimed in the *Preface* to the *Principia* that "geometry is founded in mechanical practice" (Newton 1687 [1729]: [4]), and Gottfried Wilhelm von

According to Doria, the uncritical acceptance of Cartesian methodology had not only resulted in the decline of philosophical and scientific research but was the cause of a general decadence of civil life (Doria 1721: 36). Doria thus rejected all modern philosophy by proposing an original reading of the "contemporary world", which was entrusted to his major work *La vita civile* (*The Civil Life*, in various editions, Doria 1709, 1710a, 1710b, 1710c, 1729, 1740a, 1740b, 1753), compared by some reviewers to the works of Hugo Grotius and Samuel von Pufendorf (Le Clerc 1716).

The central theme is the definition of the characteristics of civil life, the essence of which lies - according to Doria - in the "mutual aid of the virtues and natural faculties that men give each other in order to achieve human happiness" (Doria 1729: 88).

Civil life is like a human body whose perfection consists of three things: "good constitution of the body, perfect vital virtue that animates it, and the right exercise of these virtues" (Doria 1729: 83). The good and happy constitution of the civil body and of the State is the order and form of government, vital virtue is the virtue of the men who make up civil life, and the exercise of vital virtue is the right use of virtues in the arts of peace and war (Doria 1729: 84).

Therefore, it is virtue, not vice, that is the foundation of civil society, "from which we can see how far from the truth Thomas Hobbes and Machiavelli have gone, who thought that man by his very nature always hated other men" (Doria 1729: 23).[76] Thus, rather than a *Leviathan* guarding men, the state, the "orders among citizens", appear to be founded on the need for mutual aid.

Once the orders are established, civil life - for Doria - can take three forms: "the *pure military life* (*vita pura militare*), when a people are united under a captain; the *civil economic* (sober) *life* (*vita civile economica*) when they unite under civil law, but with a frugal and moderate level; and the *pompous civil life* (*vita civile pomposa*) when they live in a more cultured and dignified manner" (Doria 1729: 110). The three forms of *civil life* are not only bound together by an evolutionary line from barbarous to pompous, but Doria leaves open the possibility that from a higher

Leibniz defended the model of linear analysis, based on Euclid's *Elements*. In the analytical field, Doria's contribution was weak, as was shown by his erroneous attempt to use elementary method to solve the problem of doubling the cube (*Delian Problem*), see Amodeo (1924, chap. 1).

[76] On the criticism of Hobbes in the context of Neapolitan intellectual life see Robertson, 2013).

life one can fall to a lower one. The moderate civil life passes into the pompous one if it is sustained by conquests or by lasting peace, so as to allow wealth and then luxury and idleness; but it can also fall into the barbarous life if the internal equilibium changes in favour of the military order, or civil wars are fought (Doria 1729: 121–122).[77]

In *civil economic life*, society is governed according to *orders* that correspond to real mutual needs, hence the main division between owners and servants. The owners are the possessors of land and goods, who act as fathers of families, the servants are the plebs destined to work the fields and cultivate the arts for the convenience and service of the men in the cities. But this idea of owner and servant must not give rise to the abuse of confusing servant with slave; in well-ordered civil life there is no real difference between the owners of the fields and the servant, nor any real inequality between one and the other, because "the former is a mere administrator and the latter an executor, the former is obliged to contribute with his labour and his mind, the latter with only the labour of his arms, the former is obliged by law to distribute to many what he takes from the fields and to have his livelihood as profit and for the servitude he maintains. And this is because the master works not only with labour, but with thought, and the servant only with the mechanical labour of his arms, deriving the benefit of being well governed and maintained by the master's thought, so it is only fair that so much benefit is compensated with mechanical servitude. So the whole difference between the servant and the master is that the latter maintains and directs the other by his prudence, and the former, not being in government but fit only for servile work, is governed and acts as a servant. In this law lies all the mutual aid of one to another which is the essence of civilised life" (Doria 1729: 104).

If the true essence of civil society is, for Doria, mutual aid between men, economic life takes on a central role in fostering and sustaining this solidarity or leading to its ruin. "Economy has no other object - Doria writes - than the preservation of one's possessions", which "depends on good distribution, fair and well-regulated increase" (Doria 1729: 316). Both misers and spendthrifts therefore sin: the right behavior towards wealth lies in the middle, in the mentality of the "father of the family" (Doria 1729: 316).

[77] The concept of balance of power is mentioned here; on the relations between Montesquieu and Doria, see Vidal (1953: 20). For Doria's position against despotism, see Comparato (2011).

To avoid straying from just moderation, it is necessary to distinguish "the natural economy from the abstract, i.e. the former has for its object the good order, good distribution and increase of real goods, and the latter has for its object the conservation and increase of money that is imaginary wealth" (Doria 1729: 318). The Prince, too, must be able to distinguish between natural and abstract economics; the first has for its object the good distribution of the tax burden, the other the increase of the state's commercial power. The abstract economy is - in Doria's thinking - subordinate to the natural one, because the Prince "must not neglect the preservation and increase of the number of the subjects and the cultivation of the lands that are their natural yields" (Doria 1729: 322).

Right economic governance must therefore be based primarily on a balanced distribution of taxes, because "those who possess more wealth must contribute more to the prince" and what remains for the richest must be spent so that the poor can earn a living (Doria 1729: 322). The Prince must also ensure an appropriate distribution of economic activities and avoid the formation of monopolistic positions and the concentration of wealth, but respect the autonomy of private individuals in the economic sphere.[78] The Prince must also distribute the population throughout the kingdom, avoiding the crowding of capital cities and the depopulation of the countryside; if a kingdom is overpopulated, the useful remedy is the foundation of colonies (Doria 1729: 326–327). But the Prince must above all else keep the faith: "A Prince or a republic that does not observe the faith cannot keep commerce alive and flourishing in his kingdom, because no one is willing to contract with him, since he does not consider his promises to be sure; and in this way his tributes cannot find tenants who will make them profitable; his fields have no one who will take the burden of cultivating them; nor can any of his revenues be administered with advantage; nor can the subject merchants find trust with foreigners, their goods being exposed to the violence of the Prince; and finally, in the urgent necessities of the dangers of the state, he will find no credit either with his subjects or with foreigners and will be forced to resort to violence

[78] "Wealth must not be equal, but distributed with right proportion, so that they become as equals, and this equality, which is not visible to the people, must be cared for and maintained by the magistrates who preside over the economy, who must ensure that the riches are possessed in fair proportion and used or spent by all in such a way that all the gold and silver of the city is continually moving; for it is the same in kingdoms as in human bodies, where, if the blood stagnates and stops in one part, it does not give life to the other parts and where it stops it corrupts" (Doria 1729: 325).

against his own subjects, and increasing the misery of the latter, he will soon find himself lord of a miserable state and will be forced to surrender to the force of his enemies" (Doria 1729: 329). To achieve these objectives, the Prince must employ "two kinds of ministers": those who are "purely practical", who "preside over the cultivation of the fields and see to it that the negligence of landowners does not render the fruitful countryside deserted, [and are] employed in the collection of taxes and other revenues of the public treasury"; and those who preside over "the entire economy of the kingdom" (Doria 1729: 332). They, of unblemished faith and probity, must be able to understand abstract economics, "they must be fully informed of the affairs of the world and be well instructed in arithmetic and geography and navigation, for it must be their care to maintain and increase commerce, which without the practice and knowledge of the affairs of all countries cannot be accomplished" (Doria 1729: 333). While recognising that trade increases the wealth of kingdoms and is also a very useful tool to provide "the people with a certain kind of erudition and culture in their customs" (Doria 1729: 334), Doria did not propose mercantilist policies, because he considered it harmful to subordinate politics to mercantile needs and interests.[79]

An example of the damage mercantilist policy causes the state is the exploitation of new lands in America and Asia. According to Doria, the West Indies have only increased the quantity of precious metals, but "it is certain that gold and silver have no intrinsic value in themselves, and that they are nothing but metals which, by the most ancient common consent of all learned nations, men have used as signs for the purpose of indicating the prices of commodities and regulating the exchanges of goods necessary for life or pleasure" (Doria 1729: 335). Doria thus follows the

[79] "Merchants are detrimental to the state when they want to mix in politics, which depends on other principles; for if those who hold the reins of government stumble over this pernicious defect of giving them all into the hands of merchants, true politics, justice and the whole economy of the state will be neglected, and those trades and commerce, which would be of great use to the republics, will in the long run cause damage and misery: because if good politics is neglected, the good and useful economy of the state is also damaged. This is what we see happening in our Europe today" (Doria 1729: 334–335). According to Maria Luisa Pesante, "Doria's merchant is not simply the one who trades, but the one who has credit, even better, the one who creates credit. He acts in a sphere that is indeterminate with respect to the fundamental command relationship between masters who are owners of the land and servants" (Pesante 2000: 683).

Platonic tradition that attributes a secondary role to money, as a sign of wealth, but not wealth in itself.[80]

The abundance of money has fuelled the consumption of luxury and favoured commercial speculation, "so that a great number of men tempted by the hope of great gains neglect the cultivation of the fields and those real trades that can be done in their own country" (Doria 1729: 335–336). Even more damaging for European countries is the trade with the East Indies, which is like "a chasm into which all the gold and silver that comes to Europe from the West Indies is submerged without ever coming out" (Doria 1729: 336). Doria very clearly identified the reasons for the disadvantageous trade with the East: Oriental princes bought few European goods by bartering them with their own products; goods bought in the East were only for luxury, they were paid high prices even though they had no high intrinsic value, and many Oriental commodities could be replaced by local products to satisfy the same needs; finally, Oriental princes indulged in competition between Europeans, making high profits from the duties and taxes they imposed on their commodities (Doria 1729: 336–338).

Trade with Asian countries may have benefited a few nations like Holland, France or England, because they resold Eastern commodities to other countries on the Old Continent, but the continuous flow of money to the East Indies was increasingly out of balance and sooner or later the impoverishment of Europe, according to Doria, would shrink the outlet markets, involving those nations in misery as well. The mercantilist policy of the European sovereigns was mainly directed towards the creation of merchant companies for the West and East India trade, neglecting domestic trade, the only profitable one, since true and useful trade consists of the

[80] Plato dates back to the idea of a dual monetary circulation, consisting of a money token (without a high intrinsic value,) reserved for domestic transactions, and a coin minted in precious metal, as can be seen from the fragment shown, and destined for international exchange (see Plato 2013, Book II: 79; Schumpeter 1954 [2006]: 53). While contesting Law's system, an example of mercantilist *cabala* (Doria 1740b [1981]: 207), Doria does not reject the concept of money creation from credit, as he writes in the *Vita Civile*: "[Merchants], with a more subtle and ingenious system, thought to give actual value to the word alone. And they made it so that the mere voice and the mere order of another man of known faith [...] should be received for actual money [...]. And this is the order of the merchants, to whose faith alone consists the whole essence, vigour and maintenance of commerce" (Doria 1729: 335).

good cultivation of the land (from which the abundance of goods is produced), and the virtue of the magistrates (Doria 1729: 346).

Solicited by a request from Gennaro D'Andrea (1637–1710), a high-ranking member of the *ceto civile* and regent of the Consiglio Collaterale, Doria wrote, between 1709 and 1710, a *Relazione dello stato politico, economico e civile del regno di Napoli nel tempo ch'è stato governato dai Spagnuoli, prima dell'entrata dell'armi tedesche in detto regno* (*Report on the political, economic and civil state of the Kingdom of Naples during the time it was ruled by the Spaniards, before the entry of German arms into the Kingdom*), which remained unpublished, in which he analysed the viceregal government experience in the light of the principles of good governance defined in the *Vita Civile* (Doria 1710c [1981], see also Doria 1710b [1973]). Rather than upholding those principles, according to Doria, the Spanish government had betrayed them all "in order to secure a long domination over the Kingdom of Naples and a broad authority over the rest of Italy" (Doria 1981: 49). The Spaniards, in fact, established certain principles of government which caused the Kingdom's backwardness.

The Spaniards had governed according to the principle of *divide et impera* to which they added that of *depauperandum esse regionem*: the ancient nobility was weakened by distributing new titles and debasing its political role, while in exchange tyranny was allowed in the lands of their dominion; "discord was sown between the nobility and the higher barons, between the people and the nobility, between the civil and the lower classes" (Doria 1710c [1981]: 54); the ecclesiastics were granted great privileges, "in order to obtain dominion over the conclave, and over the court of Rome, and to be able to command more despotically in the Kingdom of Naples" (Doria 1710c [1981]: 53); the intellectuals were humiliated and reduced to courtiers or directed to a forensic career;[81] all trade was prevented 'by spoiling the ports and forbidding the building of vessels (Doria 1710c [1981]: 53–54); finally, "they sacrificed justice to the *Reason of State*, because in order to impede all trade, they destroyed good faith, which is its support, they gave wide latitude to slander in all kinds of

[81] "In Naples, the doctorate was made common, because everyone could easily aspire to it, and then the hand was so extended to grant such a degree, making the examination for its acquisition very easy, and in a very short time Naples was filled with doctors (and thanks to the way the laws were handled) the courts were filled with slanderers" (Doria 1710c [1981]: 55).

contracts and went so far as to tolerate forgers, who are nowhere else tolerated and so lightly punished as in Naples" (Doria 1710c [1981]: 58).[82] This system allowed the viceroys to rule the kingdom without any limits and control, exploiting the country for their own political purposes. The system became even more corrupt after Masaniello's revolt: the Spaniards feared the people of the capital and therefore "let them enjoy a great abundance in living, burdening them with a few tax burdens, so as to keep these people content", but "they have greatly harmed the people of the Kingdom, who are forced to suffer every injury in the sale of agricultural production to maintain the abundance of the capital city" (Doria 1710c [1981]: 74).[83] Such a policy caused the outsized growth of Naples, "a serious defect of the Kingdom". The Spanish system of government was made possible by the temperament of the Neapolitan people: "inclined to malice", which "makes the state subject to two dangers, namely to sudden revolutions and popular uprisings, because of their impetus, with which the Neapolitans abound, and to conspiracies, because of their melancholic thinking" (Doria 1710c [1981]: 78).

Doria's *Relazione*, requested by a high-ranking member of the *togate* ministry, revealed the author's connection with the ruling class and the reformist instances that the latter manifested at the beginning of Austrian regime and that Doria skilfully emphasised through his severe criticism of Spanish rule. The Genoese nobleman was considered a point of reference (Vico himself dedicated *De antiquissima Italorum sapientia*, one of his most important works, to him), at a time of difficult transition between two regimes, based on the success of his *Vita Civile* and the idea of a perfect Platonic republic that he proposed. The intellectual isolation that Doria suffered in his later years did not, therefore, derive from his political views and criticism of the Spanish regime, but from his adherence to

[82] Doria's thesis on the absence of public faith as the main cause of underdevelopment was taken up by Antony Pagden (1988). The lack of public faith explains - according to Doria - the failure of the banks and also of the annona system, which is only an instrument of speculation and exploitation of the provinces (Doria 1710c [1981]: 91, 110–111).

[83] "This population, therefore, is the one destined to carry all the weight that is necessary to feed and nourish not only the rapacity of the ruling nation, but all those orders, which it has brought together to be able in peace and without danger to dominate. This population feeds the barons with its servitude: it feeds the ecclesiastical order and the civil [...]. Finally, the poor peasant of the kingdom is the one upon whom the whole weight of tyranny falls, so that he is now reduced like the beasts, that is, never to taste of those foods, which they carry on their shoulders" (Doria 1710c [1981]: 101).

metaphysical Platonism, his clear rejection of the Cartesian method and Lockian empiricism (which he called *sensism*), from his attempt to oppose modern thought by revaluing Euclidean geometry, by inisistently proposing his mathematical discoveries (duplication of the cube, trisection of the angle), which were fiercely criticized and attracted much irony in the scientific community (see Doria 1715, 1722; Conti 1981).[84]

However, Doria's reputation as an expert interpreter of the Neapolitan reality remained intact, so much so that in 1740, in the context of the new Bourbon regime, Ventura president of the *Supreme Magistrate of Commerce* (and nephew of D'Andrea) asked him to draw up another *Report* on the economy of the Kingdom (Doria 1740b [1981]), in which the Genoese philosopher proposed a development model for the Neapolitan Kingdom.

Doria rejected the economic experience of more developed countries, proposing as an alternative the ideal of a society founded on Christian values, consistent with the Neoplatonic philosophical approach defined in his *Vita Civile*.[85] His model of development is based on the assumption that the Neapolitan Kingdom is endowed with "an abundance of all goods necessary for living' and that its inhabitants "not only have no need for the goods of other countries, but can in great abundance supply them to other countries" (Doria 1740b [1981]: 145), a happy condition that has the

[84] This took him, as he himself writes in his autobiography, from "an author not only credited, but also envied in Europe", to an object of scornful derision (Doria 1981: 423; Galasso 1989b: 243). It was probably his 'unfortunate' (Rotta 1978: 870) *Nuovo metodo per trovare tra due linee rette date infinite medie continue proporzionali* (*New method for finding infinite continuous proportional averages between two given straight lines*, Doria 1715) that marked the break with the Neapolitan and European intellectual milieu, causing his isolation on a scientific level. However, for Rotta, Doria's isolation can be attributed to his "impotence as a Catholic possessed by a strong passion for justice in the face of an ecclesiastical structure too intimately interwoven with an unjust society" (Rotta 1978: 870).

[85] Doria was not entirely isolated in the European intellectual context, "when he drew from Platonic maxims tools for analysis, criticism and reform of the social and economic situation in the Kingdom of Naples. [..] A Platonic matrix provided vocabulary and categorizations for analysing trade and its effects on the orders of civil society, from Harrington to Neville, from Davenant to James Steuart, with the slow construction of a model of the commercial economy of the moderns in both normative and analytical terms. This is not to imply that a tradition of Platonizing discourse was uniquely and exclusively producing an analysis and normativity of economic life; it does, however, indicate that the language in which a powerful metaphysics had been formulated could still be used up to the mid-eighteenth century, with varying degrees of adherence to the metaphysics itself, but in a recognizable way, to categorize the problems of coeval societies" (Pesante 2000: 681).

added advantage its favourable geographical position "to trade with all parts of Europe, Africa and Asia Minor" (Doria 1740b [1981]: 145).

If this is its natural condition, "the one and only way in which trade can be expanded in the Kingdom of Naples is to strengthen the faith between citizens by means of strict justice in contracts, to reduce the length of litigation, to promote the cultivation of the land, to punish with severe punishment usury, monopolies and malicious bankruptcies, to introduce manufactures into the Kingdom, punish the frauds that are perpetrated in the *Annona* and the harassment of sailors on embarkation, raise the duties on goods that are not necessary for living, that come from outside and, on the other hand, set a low price to goods that are exported, never alter the taxes and other impositions, so that foreigners who want to trade in the Kingdom may find in this trade their profit and their security" (Doria 1740b [1981]: 184).

According to Doria the the trade policy recipe proposed by the "cabalists" appeared unrealistic. These supporters of enterprises and trading companies, raised to the status of statesmen and political advisors, (Pesante 2000: 687), wanted the Kingdom of Naples engaged in interoceanic trade. "The trade with Smyrna, with Constantinople and the other cities of the Levant, the trade with the East Indies, with the West Indies and with all the other parts of the world would in fact make the English, the Dutch and perhaps the French jealous, because the Kingdom of Naples and that of Sicily could supply the Turks with the same goods that the English, the Dutch and the French supply them and this with greater ease because of the greater proximity and perhaps even at a better price than that of the aforementioned nations. Since the trade of the Kingdom of Naples could therefore be very damaging to that of the maritime powers, this extensive trade could provoke a war with those powers with the forces of which the two Sicilies could never match" (Doria 1740b [1981]: 172).[86]

Doria had thus realised that in the "crystallisation" of trade relations at international level dominated by the great powers, the only lever for economic development remained the domestic market, to which he gave priority (Doria 1740b [1981]: 146). The fair demand for "certain rules", necessary for the market to function, could only come through a radical reform of the state and feudal economic relations, taking as a model the

[86] Doria proposed the establishment of an institution called the *Compagnia di San Gennaro* or *Banco di San Gennaro* to foster internal economic development on the model of the Genovese *Banco di San Giorgio*, see Doria (1740b [1981]: 209), and Venturi (1998:45).

English mixed government (of which he was an admirer, not criticizing Locke's political philosopher theses, see Vidal 1953: 135–136; Galasso 1989b: 254) or the Dutch constitutional system (Rotta 1978: 854).

Despite his adherence to a form of Christian Platonism, Doria was accused of Spinozism and the last of his works *Idea di una perfetta Repubblica* (*Idea of a Perfect Republic*) ended up being publicly burnt in 1753 in press drafts, along with the manuscript, because it was considered seditious against the prince and contrary to religion (Zambelli 1972: 300–301; Rotta 1978: 868; Ajello 2001: 43–44).

Another powerful blow to the modern philosophy of Descartes and Locke was dealt by Vico in *De nostris temporis studiorum ratione* (*On the study methods of our time*, Vico 1709 [1990], see Perkinson 1976 and Lilla 1993) and, more systematically, in *De antiquissima italorum sapientia ex linguae latinae originibus eruenda* (*On the ancient wisdom of the Italians taken from the origins of the Latin language*, Vico 1710 [1988]). In these works, Vico rejects Descartes' idea that the mathematical method alone is the legitimate source of knowledge in all domains of human inquiry. Against this Cartesian model of epistemology, Vico argues that rhetoric provides a superior instrument of knowledge for inquiring into the field of the *humanities*, such as anthropology, archaeology, history, law, arts and linguistics, and that the use of abstract calculus in the natural sciences represents an involution compared to the experimental methodology followed by the Galilean school.[87] Nevertheless, Vico does not reject all forms of mathematical knowledge, because, following the Platonic Renaissance tradition, he attributes a privileged position to geometry (Agrimi 1992; Lachterman 1980).

[87] "The sympathy with experimental methods which as we have seen estranged Vico from the French tendency of thought, that is from Cartesianism, and directed him towards the Italian and English schools of Galileo and Bacon, led him on the other hand to a hostile attitude towards Aristotelianism and scholasticism" (Croce 1913: 15). For Vico, the English school were right in not allowing physical science to be taught in the mathematical style. "Accordingly, we must reintroduce and maintain the experimental method in physical science, as opposed to this mathematical method; the English tendency as opposed to the French; the cautious use made of mathematics by Galileo and his school, as against the Cartesians' reckless and presumptuous employment of it" (Croce 1913: 13–14). The link between the Galilean school and Vico is also emphasised by Nicola Badaloni (1984: 3). Of all the moderns, Vico saved only Isaac Newton and Gottfried Wilhelm von Leibniz, "two foremost minds of our age" (Vico 1744 [1948]: 92), considering them exponents of the experimental method (see McMullin and Pompa 1976). Vico sent the first edition of *Scienza Nuova* to Newton (Vico's letter to Giuseppe Athias, 25 February 1726, published in Vico [1992]: 134). On Vico's thought about modern science, see Gualtieri (2019).

In this domain, man's knowledge is identical in character with God's, perfect and demonstrative, assuring the truth of the concepts. Vico, in fact, postulates that the "true is what is made" (*verum esse ipsum factum*) and God possesses universal knowledge because he made the universe (Vico 1710 [1988]: 45; Morrison 1978). Similarly, mankind only has knowledge of human history because man made it. This is also the case of geometry: it is true because man made it in his universal capacity for abstraction.[88] Thus, the validity of geometry does not derive from the Cartesian principle of evidence, but from identifying knowledge with creation, and that is why geometry can be called a constructive science.[89]

Vico disapproves of the generalization of Descartes' geometrical method, because it "applies only to measures and numbers. All other topics are quite incapable of it. Such a method cannot be applied if the terms are not first defined, the axioms established, and the questions to be asked agreed on. But in physics it is not names that we have to define, but things. There is no thesis here that is not subject to debate, and we cannot put any questions to stubborn nature" (Vico 1710 [1988]: 181).

The geometry stressed by Vico is *Euclidean*, or *synthetic* methodology, not the Cartesian *analytical* approach, which is deemed a danger, because, according to the Neapolitan philosopher, it results in a mere algebraic verbalism, in "empty affectations" (Vico 1710 [1988]: 18) without real contents.[90] Consistent with this criticism, Vico applies a Euclidian

[88] "We are able to demonstrate geometrical propositions because we create them; were it possible for us to supply demonstrations of propositions of physics, we would be capable of creating them *ex nihilo* as well" (Vico 1709 [1990]: 23).

[89] "You can see that the same fate has befallen both human knowledge and chemistry. For just as chemistry in its pursuit of a vain goal has unintentionally given birth to an art that is effective and most beneficial to mankind – pharmaceutics – so likewise the quest of human curiosity for a truth denied to man by nature has begotten two sciences that are most useful to society – arithmetic and geometry – and from these, in turn, it has begotten mechanics, the parent of all arts necessary to mankind" (Vico 1710 [1988]: 51–52).

[90] "Synthetic geometry is more certain than, and thus preferable to Cartesian geometry. The former proceeds from the indefinite power of known postulates to the unknown. Analytical geometry starts - Vico argues - from infinite and descends to minima. Cartesian method is bound to be foundationally uncertain in so far as it assumes a given and then proceeds to divide it into simpler figures until it reaches a minimum element. The product of analytic geometry is certain, but its starting point is not. Synthetic geometry, on other hand, begins with a starting point that, as made and construed are the image of divine creativity" (Vico 1710 [1988]: 27). According to Croce, Vico in any case attributes a secondary importance to geometry in the structure of knowledge. This opinion is contested by David Lachterman (1980). See also Goetsch (1995a).

geometrical nomenclature to his *Principi di Scienza Nuova* (*Principle of New Science*, 1725 [2002]; 1744 [1948]), using axioms, reasonable postulates and clarified definitions in order to present the basic principles (called, again in Euclidian terminology, *elements*) of new science.[91] This geometrical mode of presentation is probably adopted for rhetorical and pedagogical purposes.[92]

Despite the aridity of his prose, the baroque complexity of his language and the apparent abstractness of his arguments, Vico also grasped, with great insight, certain trends in eighteenth-century society. Social life, as defined in the *Scienza Nuova*, is the product of three factors: religion, marriage and burial (see Steinke 2022). No civilization, or organized assembly of men, can arise if these three factors are not present, even in different forms. Social bonds, according to Vico, have a religious origin and *Providence* operates in it (Mazzola 1998a, 1998b; Israel 2001: 664–670; Stapelbroek 2008a: 106–126).[93]

In axioms LXVI and LXVII of his *Scienza Nuova*, Vico outlined a staged theory of the development of societies: "Men first feel necessity, then look for utility, next attend to comfort, still later amuse themselves with pleasure, thence grow dissolute in luxury, and finally go mad and waste their substance" (Vico 1744 [1948]: 70, § 241); and "the nature of peoples is first crude, then severe, then benign, then delicate, finally dissolute" (Vico 1744 [1948]: 70, § 242). In these two concise concepts, Vico encapsulated the entire evolution of nations from the state of nature to the luxuries of the European courts;[94] this path was not conceived as a linear development from the first to the last stage, far from it: the highest

[91] About the philological problems present in Vico's terminology, see Goetsch (1995a: chap. 8). On recent interpretations of Vico's philosophy, see Marshall (2011).

[92] See also Vico (1709 [1990]: 14). "Linear Euclidean geometry - Vico asserts - is in a certain sense a graphic art which at once invigorates memory by the great number of its elements, refines imagination with its delicate figures as with so many drawings described in the subtlest lines, and quickens perception which must survey all these figures and among them all collect those which are needed to demonstrate the magnitude which is required: all this to bear fruit, at the time of mature judgment, in an eloquent, lively and penetrating wisdom" (Vico 1728 [1975]: 124). By contrast, the analytical approach "obscures their imagination, enfeebles their memory, renders their perception sluggish, and slackens their understanding" (Vico 1728 [1975]: 124).

[93] "Vico, in developing the concept of Providence, directly confronts seventeenth-century theological rationalism, but on the other hand, it is affected by the cultural climate favorable to Newtonian natural theology, which had a wide echo even among enlightened Italian Catholics" (Mazzola 1998a:113).

[94] On Vico's concept of the state of nature, see Costelloe (1999).

point reached by society could open a period of crisis and lead to the "recurrence", the return, of "barbarism". The evolutionary factor is defined in the relationship between man and nature and thus refers to a utilitarian concept of nature, along a path leading from necessity to luxury and waste.

If, as happens at a high level of civilisation, a nation "become naturally slaves of their unrestrained passions of luxury, effeminacy, avarice, envy, pride and vanity and, in pursuit of the pleasures of their dissolute life, were falling back into all the vices characteristic of the most abject slaves (having become liars, tricksters, calumniators, thieves, cowards and pretenders)" (Vico 1744 [1948]: 380–381, § 1105), then Providence will find a solution.[95] It first ordains "that there be found among these peoples a man like Augustus to arise and establish himself as a monarch and, by force of arms, take in hand all the orders and all the laws, which, though sprung from liberty, no longer avail to regulate and hold it within bounds" (Vico 1744 [1948]: 380, § 1104). But "if Providence does not find such a remedy within, it seeks it outside", it decrees these corrupt peoples "become slaves by the natural law of nations which springs from the nature of such nations, and that they become subject to better nations which, having conquered them by arms, preserve them as subject provinces" (Vico 1744 [1948]: 381, § 1105). But if peoples persist in their civil disease and cannot agree to find a peacemaking monarch among themselves, and not even from without they are conquered and preserved by better nations, then providence decrees that "through obstinate factions and desperate civil wars, they shall turn their cities into forests and the forests into dens and lairs of men. In this way, through long centuries of barbarism, rust will consume the misbegotten subtleties of malicious wits, that have turned them into beasts made more inhuman by the barbarism of reflection than the first

[95] "There is Divine Providence that is a Divine Legislative Mind, which out of the passions of men, each bent on his private advantage, for the sake of which they would live like wild beasts in the wilderness, has made the civil orders by which they may live in human society" (Vico 1744 [1948]: 56, § 133). According To Albert Hirschman: "This is clearly one of those statements to which Vico owes his fame as an extraordinarily seminal mind. Hegel's Cunning of Reason, the Freudian concept of sublimation and, once again, Adam Smith's Invisible Hand can all be read into these two pregnant sentences. But there is no elaboration and we are left in the dark about the conditions under which that marvelous metamorphosis of destructive passions into virtues actually takes place" (Hirschman 1977: 17). The problem of reconciling private vices and collective welfare, for Hirschman, is solved by Bernarde de Mandeville.

men had been made by the barbarism of sense" (Vico 1744 [1948]: 381, § 5). And the latter is to be preferred to the barbarity of reflection, which supports and defends unbridled passions, because the latter is "a generous savagery, against which one could defend oneself or take flight or be on one's guard", but the former is "a base savagery, under soft words and embraces, plots against the life and fortune" (Vico 1744 [1948]: 381, § 1105).

With these reflections Vico interpreted the crisis of *Ancien Régime* society, prophesying its imminent destruction. According to the Neapolitan philosopher, the development of trade and the monetary economy are among the causes that favour destruction.[96] This is a particularly interesting aspect in Vico's thought that has many points of contact with Doria's critical reflection. Commerce - Vico states - arises from the wealth of cities and "the term commerce is derived from that first merces or payment in the world, the fields which the heroes gave the *famuli* [servants] under the aforesaid law obliging the latter to serve them" (Vico 1744 [1948]: 14–15, §26, original italics). The monetary economy, arising after barter, "began late, after the civil empires were founded, so that we read of no coined money in either of the two poems of Homer" (Vico 1744 [1948]: 16, § 28). Coined money is a product of aristocratic society ("family coats-of-arms", Vico 1744 [1948]: 16, §28), whose military insignia "gave their imprint to coins" (Vico 1744 [1948]: 16, §28). Monetary circulation therefore has a purely political origin and is closely linked to the public treasury, i.e. the fiscal needs of the state to pay wages "to the plebs in war time" (and the word *aeraria*, according to Vico, has its root in *aes*, which was precisely the ancient name of the Roman bronze coin) (Vico 1744 [1948]: 15, § 26, original italics). Vico identified early coinage with medals of aristocratic origin: "when commerce by means of coined money was introduced, it was found that these medals were suitable for use as coins, which indeed were for that reason called *monetae* from *monendo* by the Latins [...]. In like fashion from the Greek *nomos* came *nomisma* as Aristotle tells us; and perhaps from it too came the Latin *numus* [...]. In French too law is called *loi*, and the metal for coins, *aloi*. These terms can

[96] In the allegorical painting that Vico puts before his *Scienza Nuova*, trade and the monetary economy are represented by a bag of money. It is not difficult to assume that the image of the purse is a reference to the concept of monetary economy as speculation. The emotional impact caused by the failure of John Law's *Système* could not fail to influence Vico's conservative view.

have had no other origin than the law or right signified by the hieroglyph, which is precisely the use of medals. All of which is strikingly confirmed by the following names of coins: *Ducat* from *ducendo*, which is said of captains; *Soldo*, whence soldier; and *Scudo*, a defensive arm, which originally meant the escutcheon or field of family arms, which in the beginning was the tilled land of each father in the time of the families, as will be shown later. This will shed light on the many ancient medals" (Vico 1744 [1948]: 146–147, § 487, original italics, see also 126–127, § 433).[97]

He also made a lucid analysis of the Neapolitan kingdom, in which "social life was characterised by a low plebeian class without any political consciousness, a middle class that was an enemy of disorder and indulged in idleness, a nobility that combined arrogance towards the plebeians with contempt for public activities, and was agitated internally by mutual discontent and hostility. All this, in a general malpractice, characterised by frivolity, ostentation and blazing pageantry" (Vico 1703 [1992]: 196).

In spite of the fact that in his autobiography, Vico wants to present himself as an isolated intellectual, as a "stranger" in his fatherland (Vico 1728 [1975]: 125), more recent historiography has shown that his apparently abstract reflections have a "substantial political character" (Giarrizzo 1981: 55; see also Costa 1976; Vaughan 1972; Ajello 1976a; Galasso 1989c).[98] As university professor of rhetoric (from 1698), one of his tasks was to inaugurate the academic year with an oration (seven, between 1699 and 1708) read to students, colleagues and the Neapolitan intelligentsia. He then had politically sensitive tasks such as the celebrations planned during Philip V's stay in Naples (Galasso 1989: 274) and was then appointed royal historiographer in 1735, which represented an institutional recognition for him, desired by the new Bourbon regime. He was also commissioned by the government to write a chronicle of the anti-Spanish Conspiracy of the Prince of Macchia (1701, Vico 1703 [1992]),

[97] The identification of ancient coins with medals was a legacy of the late Renaissance, when numismatics began to develop (see Vico 1555, a homonym of the Neapolitan philosopher). This identification is also reflected in the *Encyclopédie* (1765: 229–259, entry signed D.J, identified as Louis de Jaucourt). See also Muratori (1750a, 1750b) and Carli (1751); Venturi (1998: 457).

[98] "Vico's isolation within Naples in the 1730s and early 1740s should not be exaggerated. In 1732 Galiani himself intervened on Vico's behalf with cardinal Neri Corsini, nephew of Pope Clement XII (to whom Vico had presented a copy of the second *New Science* to follow his gift of the first in 1725), in a further effort to secure financial subvention" (Robertson 2005: 253).

which was not approved and thus remained unpublished, and in 1713, again by government commission, a biography of Marshal Antonio Carafa. His stature as a philosopher was also recognised by the *Novatores* and he had the support of Celestino Galiani (with whom he had been in contact since the 1720s and to whom he had sent a copy of the first edition of his *Scienza Nuova*). Despite the difficulties of his academic career (he never obtained a law tenure, which would have provided him with a better standard of living) and a certain suspicion on the part of the ecclesiastical authorities, Vico expressed political positions "common to the educated class that had found in the forum, in offices and, ultimately, in studies the road to success. The positions of this class suggested concord of orders, civil peace, and the flourishing of moral and economic life based on the advice of the wise: which concretely meant the disciplining of baronage, politicization of the middle class, pre-eminence of the forum and offices, intimate collaboration between intellectuals and the Palace" (Galasso 1989: 274).[99]

2.4 The Innovators: Celestino Galiani and Bartolomeo Intieri

The Neo-Platonism of Vico and Doria was a minority position in the conservative camp and was even regarded with suspicion by the dominant component, represented by ecclesiastical orthodoxy, according to which everything that moved outside of Aristotelian-Scholasticism was to be rejected as sensualism, Epicureanism, materialism and atheism. Both Vico and Doria were subjected to censure by the same Catholic traditionalist circles they sought to defend. Their condition was aggravated by the emergence of a new party that began to gain strength in the late 1720s, partly because it was supported by high members of the *ceto civile* and the Viennese court (represented by the Viceroy, Count Harrach), as well as young members of the Neapolitan intelligentsia, inclined to follow the most innovative trends in European culture. The group was further

[99] It is important to emphasise that Vico was educated as a jurist and his intellectual path was no different from that of a typical member of the *ceto civile*. He himself describes his jurist formation in his autobiography, speaking in the third person: "When he had studied both institutes in the texts of civil and canon law alike, without taking any heed of the so-called materials to be learned within the five-year period of legal training, he decided to apply for admission to the courts" (Vico 1728 [1975]: 110). On Vico and the Neapolitan political and social reality, see Stone (1997) and Naddeo (2011).

strengthened by the appointment in 1731 of Celestino Galiani as *Cappelllano Maggiore*, an extremely important position to initiate a reform of the education system and by this route attempt a modernisation of the decrepit educational structures in the Neapolitan kingdom, considering the school system as an essential requirement for the formation of a modern state. From 1732 despite the resistance, he undertook to carry out a reform of university studies which would open the Neapolitan university to the influence of the new European culture. At the end of the 1730s, Galiani was intent on this work, as an exponent of an Enlightened Catholicism, imbued with a secular morality, inclined to rationalism and a spirit of tolerance, very different from the inquisitorial climate that had dominated the Neapolitan capital in the last years of the seventeenth century.[100]

Celestino Galiani's education reflected all the stages of emancipation that Italian philosophical culture had experienced on its way to finally arriving at the Enlightenment: from Galilean experimentalism, to the enthusiastic adhesion to the Cartesian method to dispel the last elements of Aristotelianism, to the suggestions aroused by the works of Baruch Spinoza (certainly dangerous in terms of orthodoxy) and Pierre Gassendi, to the themes of natural law, to Locke's empiricism (even more hated by the ecclesiastical authorities), to the mathematical reason enunciated by Newton's *Principia*, of which he was a careful reader and commentator.[101] All these steps had been assimilated and placed the Neapolitan clergyman at the centre of a vast network of relations, making him an essential element of the intellectual renewal of early eighteenth-century Italy. Within this framework, however, he wanted to reserve a special role for himself, "avoiding the publication of his writings, exchanging thousands of letters in Italy and abroad, organizing academies, dedicating enormous time to the instruction of men destined for brilliant ecclesiastical careers and positions in the institutions of various Italian states, and soliciting philosophical-

[100] The spirit of tolerance that characterized Celestino Galiani was fully revealed when the Jews entered the Kingdom of Naples. In his *Parere teologico sopra alcuni punti appartenenti all'introduzione degli Ebrei ne' due Regni di Napoli e Sicilia* (Galiani, MSCG-2), requested by Montaleagre, Galiani claimed the extraneousness of the state in matters of religious controversy.

[101] See Galiani's manuscript, *Osservazioni sopra il libro di Newton, intitolato Principia Mathematica* (Galiani, MSCG-3). Celestino Galiani, together with Bartolomeo Intieri, had edited an edition of Gassendi's *Opera Omnia*, see Gassendi (1727) and Ferrone (1995: 57–62). On Celestino Galiani's Newtonism, see Feingold (2004: 86–87).

scientific debates" (Ferrone 1995: 124).[102] This prudent behavior shielded him from possible persecution by the Inquisition. An experience Celestino had known at the beginning of his career, when as a teacher of dogmatic theology, he based his teaching on new historical-philological criteria enriched by his personal knowledge of the Hebrew language (Ferrone 1995: 152–157; Costa 2009, 2011). And in 1711, for his interpretative theses, he was accused by the Inquisition of Jansenism and of serious errors in biblical exegesis, from which he was exonerated only in 1713, through the direct intervention of Pope Clement XI. This affair did not interrupt his work as a disseminator of modern European culture and his moderatism allowed him to carry out some important diplomatic missions to the Holy See on behalf of both the Austrian government and the new Bourbon Kingdom.[103]

Galiani's university reform project was elaborated under the influence of Newtonian natural philosophy and Lockean rationalism, definitely rejecting Cartesian epistemological approach.[104] In Naples, as in other parts of Italy, Newton's scientific program is associated to the great

[102] As has been amply demonstrated by Vincenzo Ferrone (1995). However, Fausto Nicolini the first to draw attention to this singular figure, see Nicolini (1931, 1951). Croce defines Celestino as a "man of encyclopedic learning" (Croce 1925b [1970]: 179). See also Di Rienzo (1998); Stapelbroek (2008a: 57–87); Iovine (2009).

[103] His position as Cappellano Maggiore was confirmed by the new Bourbon regime, but he was always viewed with distrust as a member of the "Austrian party". In particular, Tanucci emphasised that without his intervention, Galiani "would have been dethroned in our entrance by the bigot Santo Stefano to whom the cardinal archbishop [Giuseppe Spinelli] and Cardinal Belluga had presented the good chaplain as a heretic and unbeliever" (Bernardo Tanucci's letter to Francesco Nefetti, Naples, 30 May 1752, in Tanucci 1980a: 5–6).

[104] On the reform of university studies proposed by Galiani, see Origlia (1754: 246–260); Schipa (1904: 692–694); Zambelli (1977); Mazzola (1998a: 236–237); Iovine (2001: 390–399; 469–472). Galiani proposed the abolition of eight chairs that he considered unnecessary (three in law, two in medicine, one in logic and metaphysics, ethics and Scotus' theology), replacing them with new ones (law of nature and nations, law of the Kingdom, botany, experimental physics, theoretical physics, ecclesiastical history, hebrew language, a second chair in mathematics, anatomy and surgery). The reform, implemented in the 1740s, partially realized Galiani's proposals (also due to the distrust of the Curia which placed Galiani under investigation for his suspected adhesion to Lockean philosophy): only two law chairs were abolished, the two chairs of logic and metaphysics were merged, anatomy was separated from surgery, and the chairs of Law of the Kingdom, mathematics, botany and chemistry, and astronomy were established. The five chairs of theology were not suppressed and ecclesiastical control was confirmed.

heritage of Galileo Galilei's experimentalism and this explains its fast spread (Frisi 1775; Casini 1983a, 1983b; Ferrone 1995: 129; Mazzotti 2013).[105]

The reform of the mathematical teaching method was an essential element of this project of modernization. Galiani established two chairs of mathematics, assigned to Nicola Antonio De Martino (1701–1769) and his brother Pietro (1707–1746), both Newtonians and well-informed on the development of infinitesimal calculus.[106] Two more chairs of Theoretical and Experimental Physics were established in 1740 and assigned respectively to Newtonian physicians Mario Lama and Giuseppe Orlandi (1713–1776). Advanced mathematics was taught also in several religious and military colleges with practical applications and Celestino Galiani himself was a brilliant mathematician and one of the first Italians to use the new algorithms of infinitesimal calculus (Palladino 1988).[107] The establishment of the *Accademia delle Science* (1732), designed to spread rationalist philosophy, completed the modernization of the education system in the Kingdom of Naples (Ferrone 1995: 201–202; Iovine 2001: 378–385).[108] The nascent group of Neapolitan Newtonians therefore gave additional support to the fight against the Cartesian school, decreeing its decline once and for all. Newton's inductive approach contrasted with Descartes' deductivistic and aprioristic methodology and offered a new paradigm for scientific analysis (Cohen 1971: 227–251), providing a solution to the epistemological debate in Naples on the role of mathematical knowledge. Moreover, Neo-Platonic deism, followed by the Newtonians, introduced a clear distinction between religion and science.

Celestino Galiani accepted a particular interpretation of Newton's thought proposed by Dutch Newtonian scientists Willem Jacob's Gravesande (1688–1742) and Petrus van Musschenbroek (1692–1762)

[105] On the condition of the University and the various cultural institutions in Naples, see Rao (2005: 45–57, 63–69); Chiosi (2005).

[106] Respectively the Chair of Geometry and Mathematics and the Chair of Astronomy and Seamanship. A third chair of Arithmetic and Algebra was established in 1762. Previously, the mathematics chair was assigned to the Cartesian, Agostino Ariani (1672–1748).

[107] The wide diffusion of differential calculus in Naples is shown by several textbooks published in the last half of the Eighteenth Century, especially by Giuseppe Marzucco (1757) and Vito Caravelli and Vincenzo Porto (1786).

[108] The academy, modelled on its French homologue, was divided into six classes: Geometry, Astronomy, Mechanics, General Physics, Chemistry, Natural History and Anatomy. Various experimental activities were started in the academy following the Newtonian method.

('sGravesande 1723; Musschenbroek 1745). This Newtonian experimentalism was prevalent within *Accademia delle Scienze* and promoted the shifting of interests from natural to social disciplines (Ferrone 1995: 230).

The extension of Newtonian methodology favored the application of mathematical tools to social phenomenon, which were considered measurable and could therefore be represented with formal algorithms. Celestino Galiani, in his unpublished essay, *Ricerche intorno alle prime origini della scienza morale* (*Investigations around the first origins of moral science,* Galiani, MSCG), written probably between 1720 and 1730 (Ferrone 1995: 168–176), makes an initial attempt to define measurable arguments in the ethical doctrine.[109]

This project was mainly based on the philosophical doctrine of pleasure and pain, following the hedonistic doctrine of Locke's *Essay Concerning Human Understanding* (Ferrone 1995: 173), even if expressed in a moderate form (Galiani, MSCG: folios 61–62).[110] Pleasure and pain (taken from the second book of Locke's *Essay*) are considered two prime principles of human life and immediately interpreted in terms of mathematical calculus.[111] According to Galiani, pleasure and pain are relative concepts, subordinated to quantity and duration and for this reason can be calculated (Galiani, MSCG, folios 303r–304v), anticipating Pierre-Louis Moreau de Maupertius' *Essay de philosophie morale* (1749), which theorizes, for the first time explicitly, the possibility of mathematical calculation of pleasure and pain. Moreover, in his essay, Galiani not only attempts to apply differential calculus, but also some notions of probability calculus,

[109] The manuscript is written in two versions collected in the Library of the *Società Napoletana di Storia Patria* (XXI.B.1, folios 174–266 and XXXI.C.1, folios 1–68). Unless otherwise indicated, the quotations are from manuscript XXXI.C.1, indicated as MSCG. On the different version of Galiani'manuscript, see Ferrone (1995: 320, footnote 25) and Stapelbroek (2008a: 57, footnote 3).

[110] "Man is therefore by nature inclined to preserve himself as far as he can, and therefore by instinct of the same nature loves, pleases and fights pain" (Galiani, MSCG: folio 21r, see also folios 69r–72r). All the works of the English philosopher were put on the *Index librorum prohibitorum* in 1734. See Ferrone (1995: 201–204). On the diffusion of Locke's thought in Naples, see Amodio (1997a) and De Scisciolo (1997).

[111] Celestino clearly expresses a concept that comes very close to marginal utility: "Whoever burns with thirst, falling into a source of clear, limpid, sweet, fresh water, rejoices wholeheartedly, and drinking it feels great pleasure: as his thirst is quenched, the pleasure diminishes: so in all other things preceded by great desire, when they are obtained, they rejoice and delight us, but when they are not desired with a desire that disturbs us, acquiring and possessing them cause us little pleasure" (Galiani, MSCG: folios 61v–62r).

even if he does not achieve significant results (Ferrone 1995: 331, footnote 31).[112]

Following Bayle, Galiani, unlike Vico, did not consider religion as the aggregate and founding factor of human societies and therefore admitted the existence of atheistic societies (Galiani, MSCG: folio 65r).[113] Society for Galiani finds its foundation in the natural sociality of man.[114] This human sociality and interaction, which is also expressed through language, is referred to by the term commercio (commerce, Galiani, MSCG: folios 8v; 16r, 18r).[115] The state of nature is not a Hobbesian condition of conflict, but consists of peaceful and cooperative human aggregations, whose main purpose is to obtain from Nature the resources indispensable for survival (Galiani, MSCG: folio 8r). The foundation of society is the utility and advantage that aggregation gives to the individual, which explains why "in the Scienza Morale, utilitarianism is conceived as the true driving force of history" (Ferrone 1995: 174; Stapelbroek 2008a: 71).[116]

Vico's discourse is thus overturned: religion, for Galiani, is no longer an overriding factor as a sentimental and innate element but is a product of rationality that man can only develop when he has definitively solved the problem of his survival.[117] The religious phenomenon thus belongs to

[112] See Celestino Galiani, *Intorno ai calcoli differenziale e integrale* (Galiani, MSCG-4). See also Palladino (1988).

[113] "We understand from the ancient stories and report of the travels made by our contemporaries, above all to America, Africa and Asia, that there were once and still today are entire people - almost all those who call themselves savages [...] - who do not have in any form that concept of a most perfect being which we express with the name of God. Instead, some of them have no religion at all, and no concept of something superior of which one one could hope for or fear anything" (Galiani, MSCG: folios 40v–41r. English translation in Ferrone 1995: 170). On the reception of Bayle's thought in Italy, see Garin (1970); Pii (1972); Borghero (1996).

[114] There is a law of nature that "not only prescribes man's duties towards others, but also those he must perform towards himself and his Creator" (Galiani, MSCG: folio 19r).

[115] "Without any commerce of men with each other, let alone of the male with the female, the human species would very soon come to an end. Therefore it is necessary for at least the male with the female to unite in order to preserve the species" (Galiani, MSCG: folio 16v).

[116] Man "not only abhors pain but instinctively is of nature most inclined towards pleasure and the easy life, and consequently he is by nature inclined towards society, that is, towards living in common with other men where he encounters far greater comforts and joys than in solitude" (Galiani, MSCG: folio 17v. English translation in Ferrone 1995: 174).

[117] "The man we suppose fell from the clouds, who alone in the midst of incultivated and uninhabited jungles goes all day around searching for acorns or apples to eat, would find it difficult in his miserable state to elevate his mind to seek sublime truths. The sciences are the

an advanced state of social development and finds its basis in reason (Galiani, MSCG: folio 24r) and the idea of God is not innate and simple, but as a complex idea it is the product of complex reflection (Galiani, MSCG: folio 41v).

The utilitarian and rationalistic approach also distinguishes Galiani from another version of moderate Catholicism, that of Antonio Ludovico Muratori (1672–1750), who, in his *Filosofia Morale* (1735), reproposed the thesis of religious hymnatism and Catholic Stoicism. His social model reproposed the Catholic vision of a harmonious society, in which conflicts are absent, governed by good governance and charitable solidarity. It was an ideal model, therefore, that rejected all forms of individualism for a morality based more on common sense than on a detailed analysis of the motives for human action (Venturi 1998: 180). Galiani's approach was quite different, aimed at researching "the foundations of an ethics renewed only with the cognitive tool of reason, without any religious conditioning" (Ferrone 1995: 179).

At the end of the 1740s Newtonian experimentalism was definitely well established in Naples (Ferrone 1995: 248) and started to be applied to social sciences, particularly to economic analysis, called science of commerce and already considered an autonomous discipline. Neapolitan Newtonians were interested to establish a close connection between the physical order and the social and economic order, defining a Newtonian approach to social science, which can be regarded as a Newtonian version of social mathematics. This approach to social science was related to the idea of civic progress and to programs of political reforms.

An important support for Galiani's reforms was procured by the Tuscan priest Bartolomeo Intieri (1677–1757),[118] a self-educated mathematician

daughters of reflection, and reflection recognizes as its mother leisure, quiet and the easy life. When man, not distracted by necessities of body and life, can turn his thoughts where it pleases him most, then he usually dedicates himself to seeking the hidden causes of the effects evident to him. [...] Once the city were formed, the owenership of goods introduced, and the skills most necessary for comfortable living found, then many found themselves in the state of not having to think about needs of the body, and therefore they enjoyed tranquil leisure, and quite a few of them were able to apply themselves to reflecting on their own ideas and hence giving birth to science" (Galiani, MSCG: folio 24r. English translation in Ferrone 1995: 170–171).

[118] Galiani's appointment as Cappellano Maggiore was welcomed with great enthusiasm by Intieri: "The Emperor has done an Emperor-like action by entrusting the office of Cappellano Maggiore to Galiani. I felt a consolation that I have not had for many and many years, believing that this great man is such that he has no equal and can put human letters in good order,

and physician, interested in the economic development of the Kingdom (Fubini Leuzzi 2004; Ferrone 1995: 43–45; 223–238).[119] Ordained a priest shortly before 1703, he participated unsuccessfully in the competition for a mathematics professorship at the Neapolitan university. The mathematical sciences were therefore his first passion and his work *Apollonius ac Serenus Promotus* (Intieri 1704) was also reviewed in the *Acta Eruditorum* of Leipzig (1706: 274–276), but he was essentially a practical spirit.[120] As early as 1711, he was administrator of the Benevento fiefs of the Rinuccini family, to which were added the Corsini's properties in Santa Maria Capua Vetere and the allodial properties of the De' Medici, scattered throughout the Kingdom. In this capacity, he devoted himself to experimenting with new technologies to be applied to cereal production and trade.[121] His attention turned above all to methods of preserving grain, and he worked for many years on experimenting with a stove, the results of which he was to entrust to his best-known printed work, *Della perfetta conservazione del grano* (*The perfect storage of grain*, Intieri 1754).[122] This approach took him away from metaphysics[123] and brought him closer to scientific problems, to Galilei's experimental method, which had come back to life and spread with Newton's works. From this perspective, he actively participated in the work of the *Accademia delle Scienze*,

which if they take good root will hardly be uprooted any more, at least for centuries, despite all the effort that the barbarians will make, of whom we have many, but which are beginning to lose. Our university under the direction of this great man, who has all the confidence of the Court of Vienna, will wash away certain stains that now soil it" (Bartolomeo Intieri's letter to Giovanni Bottari, Naples, 16 December 1731, Biblioteca Corsiniana, Rome, published in Iovine 2001:375).

[119] A complete and documented biography of Bartolomeo Intieri has not yet been written; at the moment, apart from the classic work by Giuseppe Maria Galanti (1783) and the biography of Antonio Genovesi by Giacomo Racioppi (1871: 83–101), there are only partial reconstructions on this figure, in particular see Venturi (1959a, 1959b, 1998: 552–562); Ferrone (1995: chap. VI); Perna (1984: 1269–1279); Fubini Leuzzi (2004); Stapelbroek (2008a: 62–65); Iovine (2009).

[120] See also Intieri (1703, 1706, 1716).

[121] Galiani in *Della Moneta* describes one of the agronomic techniques experimented by Intieri (Galiani 1780: 405–407).

[122] Written in collaboration with Ferdinando Galiani. On these experiments and imitations of Intieri's stove, see Perna (1984: 1272–1276).

[123] "This Fusco, if I am not mistaken, physician to the King, [...] has published a little book on Aristotle. This is how time is wasted" (Intieri's letter to Celestino Galiani, Naples, 30 December 1738, BSNSP, XXXI.A.7: folio 24v.). His role model remained Bernard de Fontenelle, who had played an important role as a populariser of science in France.

urging above all the purchase of scientific machines to conduct experiments (Ferrone 1995: 205). Thus, his approach to economic problems did not come about through moral philosophy, rather it was his profession and his scientific mentality that drove him to take an interest in the social problems of Southern Italy and to participate in that anxiety for renewal that ran through almost the entire Neapolitan *intelligentsia* between the last period of Austrian rule and the early Bourbon period.[124]

Around the 1720s, a trade school, or something similar, was operating in Naples, founded by Intieri together with his friend Alessandro Rinuccini di Folco (1685–1758).[125] Intieri's interest in economic theory deepened in the late 1730s, after reading Jean-François Melon's *Essai politique sur le commerce* (Melon 1736), a work that was widely circulated, especially in Italy, and that played the same role in the first half of the eighteenth century as Adam Smith's *Inquiry* would play in the following century. Melon had been one of John Law's collaborators and after the collapse of the *Système* had become the regent's secretary (Bouzinac 1906: 25–27; Harsin 1928: 236–246; Gonnard 1935: chap. VII)); he had thus shared most of the economic policy decisions that aimed to undermine Britain's commercial hegemony. The *Essai* was therefore not the fruit of abstract thought, but the synthesis of concrete government experience; perhaps for this reason Melon's maxims enjoyed a great reputation, even after Nicolas Dutot's severe refutation of some of his opinions on financial matters (Dutot 1738; Velde 2012). It was precisely through the *Essai* that the free-thinking ideas of Bernard de Mandeville, expressed in his famous *The Fable of the Bees* (Mandeville 1714), penetrated continental Europe, and especially Italy; a work in which every ethical discourse was overturned,

[124]The connection between the innovators and the Court of Vienna was very strong in the last years of Austrian rule and this fuelled much mistrust in the new Bourbon regime. In particular, Intieri was very close to Count Harrach, viceroy of Naples between 1728 and 1733. In a letter, he praised the viceroy's policy: "Now we have here our viceroy Count Harrach, who as soon as he arrived gave proof of wise justice, which had fled from this kingdom frightened by the extravagant and unbearable genius of those who governed before. But now it seems that after a long storm the sun is showing itself. Everything the Viceroy has done since he entered the Kingdom is no other than prudence, justice, and a clear sign of good talent" (Bartolomeo Intieri's letter to Bartolomeo Corsini, Naples, 17 December 1728, Archivio Privato Corsini, Florence,published in Iovine 2001: 375).

[125]This is what Antonio Genovesi wrote in his autobiography: "He [Intieri] had set up a studio on behalf of the Rinuccini house and raised skilled young men there. This studio passed into the hands of Marquis Rinuccini, as Intieri, loving a quieter life, retired" (Genovesi [1997]: 71–72).

with the conception that private vices generated public prosperity. Melon's *Essai* offered Intieri and his circle the opportunity to come into contact with the economic problems of the more developed countries, France first of all, which in the first decades of the eighteenth century had experienced the convulsive transformations caused by the *Système*, and of which this work was a kind of direct testimony.[126]

Intieri's correspondence permits the reconstruction of the fundamental lines of his economic thought.

Melon's analysis, detached from any moral implications (even slavery was justified, see Melon 1736: chap.V), must have been particularly appealing to those in search of a correct scientific understanding of the complex problems of Neapolitan society. Economic culture, according to Intieri, was completely lacking in the Kingdom: "I agree," he wrote to Celestino Galiani, "that the *Science of Commerce* can be learnt with a few books by those with a straight and clear mind, but reading and re-reading helps a lot. The Prince and the Prime Minister must not waste time reading such books, but those who must advise them must have read a lot, and discussed a lot with experienced merchants. Without much reading and long meditation, he who advises can never persuade the Prince or the Prime Minister. One who does not understand something perfectly cannot even make another understand it. The lack of intelligence of the ministers who make up the *Giunta del Commercio* has produced the Government's unhelpful resolutions. […] Man cannot meditate if he has not first filled his head with various notions from books".[127]

But many barriers had to be overcome to foster the spread of economic culture. Referring to the controversy aroused in Paris by Melon's work, Intieri wrote to Galiani: "The Abbot Antonini […] writes to me

[126] In the group gathered around Intieri and Rinuccini were the young Ferdinando Galiani, the two Orlandi brothers, Celestino (1704–1775) the physicist Giuseppe (1712–1776), who later introduced Antonio Genovesi. Rinuccini followed Locke's approach and was well versed in the English language, unlike Intieri who instead showed sympathy for Melon (see Iovine 1999: 207–209).

[127] Bartolomeo Intieri's letter to Celestino Galiani, Naples, 13 January 1739 (BSNSP, XXXI.A.7, folio 25v.). Intieri was also critical of the policy of the *Magistrato di Commercio*: "Our *Magistrato di Commercio* has published a decree for the manufacture of silk. I feel that it will not be observed even now that it comes to light, and perhaps with good reason because it is considered contrary to the improvement of this most useful art" (Bartolomeo Intieri's letter to Celestino Galiani, Naples, 19 June 1741, BSNSP, XXXI.A.7, folio 41). The Intieri group was thus not aligned with the economic policy of the government of the newly born Bourbon kingdom, and dissent was quite strong.

something that may be surprising. The author of *Essai Politique sur le Commerce* did not even know Latin [...] His opponent Dutot does not even understand it. Your most illustrious Excellency knows better than I do how judiciously the aforementioned *Essai* was written, and here it is true that the Latin language necessary for those who wish to be literate is a great waste of time. A third would be enough to learn my mother tongue perfectly and all the more employed in the sciences would bear great fruit".[128] Intellectuals therefore had to abandon "useless vanities" and turn to the useful study of economics.[129]

In the meantime, he followed with keen interest the debate taking place in France on the "author of the never quite praised book entitled *Essai Politique sur le Commerce*"[130] and expressed the hope that "by printing and reprinting treatises, dissertations, reflections, essays, considerations, and the like on the elements of commerce, someone, deafened by such noises, will want to be informed about them, and by starting out of pretense and curiosity, will not finally put into practice those maxims that have hitherto been despised by past ministers of monarchs".[131] And he

[128] Bartolomeo Intieri's letter to Celestino Galiani, Naples, 4 October 1738 (BSNSP, XXXI.A.7, folio 3v.). And again in another letter to Celestino Galiani, he wrote: "Vast, noble and useful matter [commerce]. If the literate attach themselves to this they are freed from the bad reputation of being useless as they really are" (Naples, 7 February 1739, BSNSP, XXXI.A.7, folio 34v.)

[129] Bartolomeo Intieri's letter to Celestino Galiani, Naples, 11 November 1738, BSNSP, XXXI.A.7, folio 12.

[130] Bartolomeo Intieri's letter to Celestino Galiani, Naples, 18 November 173, BSNSP, XXXI.A.7, folio 17v. Intieri disputed Voltaire's criticism of Melon (Bartolomeo Intieri's letter to Celestino Galiani, 11 November 1738, BSNSP, XXXI.A.7, folio 12).

[131] He was aware of Voltaire's letter against Melon (Voltaire 1738a, 1738b), on which he wrote: "As for the criticism [by Voltaire to Melon] I believe it arose more from the innate genius we have of speaking evil than from Melon's merit" (Intieri's letter to Celestino Galiani, Naples 11 November 1738, BSNSP, XXXI.A.7, folio 12) and Dutot's essay, eagerly awaited ("it seems to me a thousand years to have Dutot's book, which should have arrived"; Intieri's letter to Celestino Galiani, Naples, 11 November 1738, BSNSP, XXXI.A.7, folio 12v.). The essay did not arrive until around 30 December 1738: "From Paris I got Dutot's book which deals with finances and trade against most of Melon's sentiments. It is two tomes. I have not had time to read it, I have seen a few things in passing. Great harm to the doctrine of commerce that the man who would have answered his opponent died" (Bartolomeo Intieri's letter to Celestino Galiani, Naples, 30 December 1738, BSNSP, XXXI.A.7, folio 24). From Amsterdam, he also waited for a work by the Abbot of Saint-Pierre. The contribution of Neapolitan writers did not escape him: he was familiar with the works of Serra and Turbolo: "I have found a certain booklet printed in Naples in 1629 by a certain Gian Donato Turbolo that deals with coins of the mint of this City and their weight

himself fulfilled this wish, entering into the heart of reflection on economic problems.

The Kingdom appeared to him to have great potential for development, both in material and human terms; and the government had to leverage this with a precise economic policy program:[132] "As for the perfection of the arts," Intieri wrote, "it cannot be denied that the Prince must use all diligence to promote it. To obtain it more easily, I think he should use more diligence for those arts to which his subjects are inclined. It cannot be denied that the subjects are more adept at agriculture not so much because of their experience as because of the wonderful fertility of the Kingdom. This in my opinion is the very noble art that must be promoted. Those who have written about commerce judge this to be the richest, and indeed if one were to calculate the fruit that the Kingdom of Naples could yield by sowing it all with wheat, it would be found to be greater than I think. I also consider that the subjects have an incredible ability to work the ordinary things that are of use to the poor, and according to the opinion of politicians, there is a very rich profit to be made from such work. Therefore, if one wished, I do not say to give total protection to commerce, but only to free it from the impediments of the past, [...] one could hope that what a wise Englishman said of this beautiful Kingdom in Utrecht would come true: that this Kingdom, despised by all, could become such as to make a good impression in Europe. And indeed, to consider that the great *Tavoliere di Puglia* serves only to support a few people is a very deplorable thing, whereas sowing it would bear immense fruit".[133]

and goodness" (Bartolomeo Intieri's letter to Celestino Galiani, Naples, 14 April 1739, BSNSP, XXXI.A.7, folio 38v.). Turbolo's preference for monetary devaluation also did not escape him, drawing an interesting parallel: "But what has caused me wonderment is that this good man has almost anticipated Melon, author of the golden booklet *Essai politique sur le commerce*" (Bartolomeo Intieri's letter to Celestino Galiani, Naples, 14 April 1739, BSNSP, XXXI.A.7, folio 38v.).

[132] He also wrote to Celestino Galiani: "For the rest, I am fully persuaded of the Kingdom's happy wealth that arises from any part of it [...] the brains of its subjects are skilled at everything and of excellent talent" (Bartolomeo Intieri's etter to Celestino Galiani, Naples, 11 October 1738, BSNSP, XXXI.A.7, folio 5v.). Ferdinando Galiani emphasised Intieri's optimistic spirit: "Bartolomeo Intieri alone, seeing clearly in the dark, delighted and rejoiced; he blessed the century, the Prince, the nation; he wished for that prosperity, which indeed came" (Galiani 1780: [15]).

[133] Bartolomeo Intieri's letter to Celestino Galiani, Naples, 13 January 1739 (BSNSP, XXXI.A.7, folios 26–26v.). In a later letter, he corrected this opinion: "If I had said that

The miserable condition of part of the population did not escape him: "The poor people lead a life similar in all aspects to that of the savages of Africa and America, that is, without the comfort of clothing, beds, furniture, without any pleasure, without any news or civilisation. It only differs from those savages, because the latter work little or nothing for others, but only for their own subsistence, while these [the Neapolitans] are condemned to endure hard labour like real donkeys. Yet this kind of miserable people living on the gates of Naples is known only to a few, whereas all travellers' papers are full of American savages."[134] And "to find in this country a person of the farmers' kind who has some quality of calculation and is able to write well is a very difficult if not impossible, and to employ certain people who have such a skill costs too much, not so much in terms of salary, but because they consider themselves to be of the *ceto civile* and of the literary kind, we do not know what treatment they want, besides that they are completely inexperienced in the countryside".[135] Even when the land promised abundance, it did not know how to make good use of it.[136]

He did not avoid expressing harsh judgements on the nobility: "If [it] will regain its former vigour, one can hope for every happy event, but in the meantime, it seems to me that at least few, or perhaps no one, studies the principles and nature of commerce in general".[137] It would therefore be useful for society if "the nobles would meditate on the nature of Trade and Finance, subjects worthy of their noble speculations due to their vastness and greatness and the wide field that remains to be worked on. The

Apulia, or the Tavoliere, should all be reduced to cultivation, I would have said the wrong thing, and in good spirits I say so. Neither is it all suitable for cultivation. My aim was that all that part suitable for cultivation should be cultivated [...]. I still agree that sheep are of great use to the Kingdom" (Bartolomeo Intieri's letter to Celestino Galiani, Naples, 31 January 1739, BSNSP, XXXI.A.7, folio 29v.).

[134] Bartolomeo Intieri's letter to Duke Filippo di Bartolomeo Corsini, Vico, 4 October 1741, in Florence Central Archives, Fondo Corsini, published in Iovine (1999: 202). The links with Tuscan correspondents revealed Intieri's contacts with Masonic circles (Venturi 1998: 54–55).

[135] Bartolomeo Intieri's Letter to Bartolomeo Corsini, Naples, 8 April 1727, Archivio Privato Corsini, Florence, published in Iovine (2001: 496).

[136] Bartolomeo Intieri's Letter to Duke Filippo di Bartolomeo Corsini, Naples 23 April 1752, Florence Central Archives, Fondo Corsini, published in Iovine (2001: 496).

[137] Bartolomeo Intieri's Letter to Senator Francesco Maria Buondelmonti, Naples, 18 November 1748, in Florence Central Archives, Fondo Buondelmonti, Room II, published in Iovine (1999: 219). On Buondelmonti see Venturi (1998: 55–56).

English have already started this work and the French are also getting busy",[138] but "to obtain this great advantage, it is necessary that the nobility think of other things than festivities and useless amusements which make them weak and hateful".[139] Intieri also accused the *ceto civile*: "Our courts are in a state of abatement and desolation due to the brazen petulance of magistrates and lawyers who have become unbearable",[140] and "our magistrates have been mortified by the Court and with universal approval. The jurist class still does not want to understand that magistrates are made and paid and honoured to do justice and give everyone what they are due and not to be tyrants, abusing laws and the authority of interpreters at their whim, so that the Republic is in turmoil, full of murders, discord and confusion".[141] He denounced their intrusiveness: "the subjection we have to jurists is such a great evil of this country and such a heavy burden, that I believe that much of the evil comes from them. It is certain that I would be content to do anything and not be around this arrogant, ignorant, wicked scoundrel. But since evil is incurable, one must be patient [...]. The greatest evil is that the jurists enter into all things".[142]

He also attacked traditional philosophy in the intellectual figure of Vico, defined as "Master Tisicuzzus [sufferer of consumption]", whose doctrine "has not yet been understood, except by brains made for the purpose, that is, who know madness. [...] To wish to print books that are understood only by a very few is the same as to wish to make a saint blaspheme".[143]

[138] Bartolomeo Intieri's Letter to Senator Francesco Maria Buondelmonti, Vico, 27 January 1749, in Florence Central Archives, Fondo Buondelmonti, Room II, published in Iovine (1999: 219–220).

[139] Bartolomeo Intieri's Letter to Senator Francesco Maria Buondelmonti, Naples, 16 December 1748, in Florence Central Archives, Fondo Buondelmonti, Room II, published in Iovine (1999: 219).

[140] Bartolomeo Intieri's Letter to Duke Filippo di Bartolomeo Corsini, Naples, 28 January 1753, in Florence Central Archives, Fondo Corsini, published in Iovine (1999: 218).

[141] Bartolomeo Intieri's letter to Senator Francesco Maria Buondelmonti, Naples, 19 July 1740, Florence Central Archives, Fondo Buondelmonti, Room II, published in Iovine (1999: 218).

[142] Bartolomeo Intieri's letter to Senator Francesco Maria Buondelmonti, Naples, Naples, 5 May 1730, Florence Central Archives, Fondo Buondelmonti, Room II, published in Iovine (2001: 378).

[143] Bartolomeo Intieri's letter to Duke Filippo di Bartolomeo Corsini, Vico, 26 July 1750, Florence Central Archives, Fondo Corsini, published in Iovine (1999: 216–217).

Finally, there was no lack of severe criticism for the clergy: '"Priests are enemies of trade and business and value money more today than a much larger sum after some time. They do not care about improvements, hopes and such things, but only care about the pure present. They do not want to hear of bad harvests, or misfortunes, or accidents, or low prices of foodstuffs, but only want money".[144]

For Intieri, therefore, the economy of the Kingdom had to specialise in cereal production and the manufacture of consumer goods; the latter was considered a sure means of enrichment more than luxury goods. Production had to be clearly aimed at export; and all those prohibitions and duties that opposed free trade had to be removed.

"Grain," he observed, "is a necessary commodity, so it is not to be feared that it will rot. It is enough that the King gives grain the same benefit as he gives wool. He does not make them pay any export duty [...]. The Poles, the English and others who have more infertile land than ours dispose of their grain and and why do we fear the export of our own? [...] Let the King mitigate this duty [...] and they will send away as much grain as has been produced, and I say that the Dutch and the Turks will come and take it, and this because of a certain and constant rule that men run where there is gain. England, which has a good nose, pays those who export, and we have put up endless obstacles. But what would it be like if we not only freed the export of this genre from the many impediments it has, but moreover used all diligence in cultivating this industry well, reducing it to greater perfection, which in my opinion could be done especially in Apulia. What if the Prince facilitated transport to the sea by building easy and comfortable roads. In short, it is certain that the Kingdom of Naples is the most fertile place in Italy and therefore the grain and all the rest of the provisions should come from here and not from Poland and England".[145]

This view thus presupposed the idea of a precise specialisation of the Kingdom within the international market; the existence of an international division of labour was thus clear to Intieri. Although he focused on agricultural development, he proposed a path that was diametrically opposed

[144] Bartolomeo Intieri's letter to Bartolomeo Corsini, Naples, 13 July 1728, Archivio Privato Corsini, Florence, cited in Iovine (2001: 377).

[145] Bartolomeo Intieri's letter to Celestino Galiani, Naples, 31 January 1739, BSNSP, XXXI.A.7, folios. 29v–30. Intieri feared above all crises of overproduction: "What Melon wisely writes is that abundant [harvests] are more to be feared than famines" (Bartolomeo Intieri's letter to Celestino Galiani, Naples, 23 January 1739, BSNSP, XXXI.A.7, folio 27v.)

to the one advocated by Doria: not internal trade, closing in on oneself, as the Genoese philosopher claimed, but being present on the foreign market with one's own production of better quality and at lower prices, because this allowed for the happy nature of the southern soil.

Activism in trade policy was to be an essential tool to achieve this goal, "but," Intieri pointed out, "I consider […] that we are very weak in dealing with trade, on the contrary we do not know true weakness and we believe others to be strong so we do nothing to err. But eventually we too will become more experienced".[146]

Monetary policy was also observed from the perspective of the foreign market. And on this point, the ideas expressed by Intieri were quite original: "It does not seem unnecessary to me,""he wrote to Celesino Galiani, "to note the people's error of disapproving the devaluation of money made by Count [of Santo Stefano], who instead did a singular benefit to the Kingdom, whereas Marquis Del Carpio, by increasing the weight of the money, caused grave harm […].To the peasant and to the majority of men who work only with their bodies as horses and donkeys do […], it is right to give no more than the very meagre pure food, a miserable outfit, considering also his miserable family […].In the Kingdom of Naples, the simple laborer (*bracciante*), i.e. the one who uses only his arms without using his beasts, as the beasts of burden do, is ordinarily given, between grain and money, the value of 30 [*Ducats*] per year. And so much is necessary for him to live miserably eating only bread. If there is anything left over, as indeed there is for him alone, he must spend it on his wife and more on paying taxes. This tariff is practised not only in the Kingdom but, I dare say, in the whole of Europe, and if there is any difference, it is due to the price of grain, of which the laborer must have a sufficient quantity, and the quality of the cold must also be taken into consideration, which forces the unfortunate man to provide himself with more suitable clothing. In the city, if he does the work of a servant of no skill […] he is owed 4 [*Ducats*] a month […]. And if we calculate the tax on bread, the payment of house rent and that expense of shoes and wigs, with a miserable rag of a shirt, we will find that for his necessary maintenance he barely has [*Ducats*] 30 or 38 a year left […].For the happiness of a state, these people deserve nothing more, because of the great abundance to be found there, not without Divine Providence. When the Marquis Del Carpio increased

[146] Bartolomeo Intieri's letter to Celestino Galiani, Naples, 30 December 1738, BSNSP, XXXI.A.7, folio 23r.

the weight of money, he also inadvertently increased the wages of these people and as a consequence grain, oil and everything else that was obtained from the Kingdom cost much more and as a consequence exports were less, at least for a few years, therefore little by little the wages would be lowered and finally little by little the Kingdom would be restored to the condition in which it is [...].In Rome, after the increase in the value of money, or even the decrease in weight, the opposite should have followed, that is, goods should be worth something more and the miserable people and even the rest of the wage-earners should be given more! But perhaps this did not happen because of the small and almost imperceptible alteration made. But money struck by the Carpio was so different in weight from that of the Count of Santo Stefano that it could not fail to cause a very strong alteration".[147]

Intieri justified Santo Stefano's monetary policy with special considerations. The increase in the weight of the currency led, according to the Tuscan priest, to an increase in wages in terms of the intrinsic value of money, at the same nominal value. In fact, employers, who previously paid wages in debased money, would after the reform be forced to pay wages to workers in good money.[148]

Intieri linked the rise in prices to the monetary policy of restoring the intrinsic value of money, identifying the social and economic damage from a policy of monetary stabilisation. The path followed was undoubtedly original, even if the entire argumentation remained confused. With it the Tuscan tried to apply a scientific method to the analysis of economic problems.[149]

[147] Bartolomeo Intieri's letter to Celestino Galiani, Naples, 13 January 1739 (BSNSP, XXXI.A.7, folios 16–17v). Ferdinando Galiani in 1750 considered 6 *Ducats* a month a poor salary. Michelangelo Schipa provides an interesting picture of the salaries of university professors in Naples around the 1740s, ranging from the very high salary of Biagio Troise (706 *Ducats* a year) to the very low salary of Antonio Genovesi (40 *Ducats* a year), which was even lower than what a janitor earned (60 *Ducats* a year) (Schipa 1904: 694), see also Romano (1968). Intieri refers to the monetary reform proposed by Viceroy Del Carpio in 1683, which established a restoration of the original value of the Neapolitan money (a policy similar to the reform implemented in England in the same years). In 1688, the Viceroy Count of Santo Stefano devalued the currency to prevent its export, as it was greatly overvalued in intrinsic value (see Dell'Erba 1935: 168–172; De Rosa 1987: 213–214).

[148] In the case of a revaluation of money, *Gresham's law* operated in reverse: it was the good money that drove out the bad, see Bloch (1954).

[149] Bartolomeo Intieri's analysis may fuel some erroneous conclusions about his contempt for the working classes. He was aware of the state of exploitation of the working population

The opinion that foreign trade was the main source of enrichment for the Kingdom was also confirmed by his analysis of the movements of the Neapolitan balance of payments: "Once the exportation of grains and oil ceased," he wrote in June 1741, "the exchange rates immediately increased for the foreign markets". He saw it was a sign that the situation of the Kingdom was very weak, if "the mere provision of money to be made in this city for the feast of St. Peter has the power to alter the exchange rate".[150]

The situation of monetary circulation in the Neapolitan Kingdom appeared serious to him: "I am astonished," he wrote, "how this city can be governed without cash, and if it is true that this is similar to blood, my astonishment grows. But just as blood, which makes its rounds with difficulty, generates evils in the body, so it also happens in this case". And he tried to give an explanation: "After all, I believe that money is held tight in the purses of the rich, for there could not be such a shortage of cash so soon, and besides, Spain must have sent a lot of money. Even the sordid gain that has been hoarded by scoundrels will be a good cause of such great distress, and without a strong and capable government this evil will not be remedied".[151]

In contrast to Intieri, who was optimistic about the Kingdom's potential, Rinuccini was more pessimistic considering the Neapolitan economy deprived of its own commercial autonomy and condemned to supplying raw materials to the trading powers, France and England in the first place.[152] He then attacked the nobility and the court that wasted money on luxury spending, neglecting the investments necessary for the economic development of the country. He pointed to mercantile republics such as Switzerland and Holland and constitutional monarchies such as England as examples of good governance: "Sovereigns think only of impoverishing their subjects, and that is promoting trade? I know that

in the Neapolitan Kingdom: "The population - he wrote in a letter to Celestino Galiani - cannot grow where there is no justice and where the poor are oppressed' (Bartolomeo Intieri's letter to Celestino Galiani, Naples, 31 January 1739, BSNSP, XXXI.A.7, folio 31).

[150] Bartolomeo Intieri's letter to Celestino Galiani, Naples, 19 June 1741 (BSNSP, XXXI.A.7, folio 41).

[151] Bartolomeo Intieri's letter to Celestino Galiani, Naples, 16 December 1738 (BSNSP, XXXI.A.7, folio 19v.).

[152] Alessandro Rinuccini's letters to Francesco Maria Buondelmonti, Archivio Privato Corsini, Florence, Fondo Buondelmonti: Naples, 15 August 1750; Naples, 20 December 1951; Naples, 25 July 1752; Naples, 21 August 1752, cited in Iovine (2001: 497). See also Iovine (2009).

wherever they increase duties, I mean in despotic dominions because it will not be so in the Swiss cantons, and where there is democracy in the government"[153] and the English people 'from their unfertile country with good government they know how to bring forth that fruit which others do not from more fertile countries; if this kingdom were in their hands they could pave it with gold and silver".[154]

In this intellectual climate, the young Ferdinando Galiani began his education under the guidance of his uncle Celestino.

2.5 The Education of a Precocious Talent

In July 1735, after having followed his father to Abruzzo, Apulia and Irpinia, Ferdinando, like his brother Berardo (1724–1774; Carrafiello 1998), was entrusted to the attentive tutelage of his uncle Celestino, who was responsible for establishing the educational path for the two youngsters (Diodati 1788: 3–4; Nicolini 1918a: 105–107). Celestino intended to give an erudite approach to teaching, not setting a precise orientation, ranging from the study of classical languages, and even Hebrew, to archaeology, from the natural sciences to the latest differential calculus, from law to philosophy, history and contemporary literature. In 1737, called to Rome to conduct the difficult negotiations for the Concordat between the Holy See and the Kingdom of Naples (concluded in 1741), Celestino entrusted the two young men to the Celestine Convent of San Pietro a Majella (De Majo 1998; Porta 2012) where they were tutored by important personalities of Neapolitan culture, primarily Celestino and Giuseppe Orlandi (the latter a tutor for scientific subjects and supervisor of education, Favino 2013) Antonio Morlando (teacher of Latin and classical literature) and Appiano Buonafede (1716–1793, teacher of philosophy, literature and theology, Salinari 1972).

Finally returning to Naples in 1741, Celestino was able to directly take care of his nephews' studies, completing their education. Berardo and

[153] Alessandro Rinuccini's letter to Francesco Maria Buondelmonti, Naples, 16 February 1753, Archivio Privato Corsini, Florence, Fondo Buondelmonti, published in Iovine (2001: 503).

[154] Alessandro Rinuccini's letter to Francesco Maria Buondelmonti, Naples, 4 September 1752, Archivio Privato Corsini, Florence, Fondo Buondelmonti, published in Iovine (2001: 498).

Ferdinando followed courses in civil and canon law with Marcello Cusano (later Archbishop of Palermo, Giannone's interlocutor in Vienna),[155] studied Greek and philosophy in depth under the guidance of Celestino himself and Hebrew with Savino Lattarulo (see Galiani, MS-23), and of course there was no shortage of scientific subjects, particularly mineralogy, geology and notions of geography, and mathematics with the new differential calculus. These subjects were complemented by learning modern languages, Spanish, French and English, with some knowledge of German. Ferdinando gave proof of his knowledge of these languages by translating some works and, at the tender age of 16, Locke's essay *Some Considerations on the Consequences of the Lowering of Interest and Raising the Value of Money* (remained unfinished and unpublished, see Galiani 1963: 380–389).[156] Finally, his education was enriched by studying music (he learned to play the harpsichord).[157]

If Ferdinando was essentially an eclectic in his interests, "not wanting to become rigid in a crude specialization"(Nicolini 1918a: 113), his brother Berardo, on the other hand, successfully dedicated himself to the study of archaeology, architecture and art history (he translated Vitruvius and was appointed *Academician of the Crusca*, see Carrafiello 1995).

It was a melting pot of disciplines, and in the midst of these what stood out, for young Ferdinando, was the "most difficult of all: politics" (Nicolini 1918a: 116), and through it, not yet clearly distinguished from the more general art of government, the brand new *science of commerce*, as Intieri

[155] Berardo was awarded the title of doctor in this subject in 1745, while Ferdinando only in 1766, in order to carry out his duties as Councillor of the *Tribunale di Commercio* (Nicolini 1918a: 113).

[156] According to Furio Diaz, the translation was interrupted because Galiani heard that a translation by Giovanni Francesco Pagnini and Angelo Tavanti was in progress, which was later published in Florence in 1751 (Diaz 1975a: xiii). But Galiani, in his *Note II* to the Second Edition of *Della Moneta*, states that he did not complete the translation for "the disgust that such disorder and breathless continuity, as the author had composed it, brought to his readers. Moreover, not adopting many of his principles and many of his sentiments, I saw that I would have been obliged to make long notes and refutations, instead it seemed to me better to spend the time to make this work [*Della Moneta*] containing only my thoughts" (Galiani 1780: 374). In a letter to Madame d'Épinay Galiani claimed to have completed the translation of Locke's treatise and added notes, see Ferdinando Galiani's letter to Madame d'Épinay, Naples, 13 Dicember 1770, published in Galiani, 1881a: vol. I, 317; Galiani and d'Épinay (1992, vol. I: 316).

[157] "All my studies have served me less than knowing how to play the harpsichord" (Ferdinando Galiani's letter to Domenico Sgueglia, Pisa, 27 March 1752, published in Galiani, 1975: 825).

called it, and of which the monetary problem was the most burning and complex topic.

The early works written between 1744 and 1748 show that Galiani was particularly fond of economic issues and found it a privileged terrain, even when the purpose of the work was purely an exercise in erudition: not only the barely drafted translation of Locke's essay (undertaken "for the study of the English language", Galiani 1780: 374), but also the essay, in Vico's style, *Dell'antichissima storia delle navigazioni nel Mediterraneo* (1746, *Of the ancient history of navigation in the Mediterranean*),[158] which also remained unfinished, and above all the dissertation *Sullo stato della moneta ai tempi della guerra troiana* (*On the state of money at the time of the Trojan War*), probably written between 1747 and 1748 (Diaz 1975a: xiii).[159] This dissertation was read in 1748 at the Neapolitan *Accademia degli Emuli*, as Galiani himself recalls in the notes to the second edition of *Della Moneta*, remarking, not without some satisfaction, that he had received an appreciation from the philologist, biblical scholar and archaeologist Alessio Simmaco Mazzocchi (Galiani 1780: 378).[160]

The analysis of the essay on money at the time of the Trojan War is of great interest, as it not only anticipates the theme of the origin of money later developed in *Della Moneta* (see Galiani [1751]: 9–13), but also represents an example of the method followed by Galiani and the original results he achieved.

Galiani rejected the thesis, then in vogue and also supported by Vico (1744 [1948]: 16, § 28), that there was no use of money in archaic Greece. He refuted the arguments put forward by the scholars one by one, with objections based on a historical and philological critique of Homer's texts

[158] The text was probably among Galiani's papers because it is mentioned by Diodati among unpublished works (Diodati 1788: 6, 93), but it has been lost, see Nicolini (1918: 149). In the Second Edition of *Della Moneta*, in *Notes IV* Galiani mentioned this early work and expressed his intention to finish it. In the essay, Galiani intended to unravel ancient mythologies by establishing analogies between the history of modern exploration and the ancient Greek history, being "persuaded that all history is nothing but a repetition of similar events, I believed to find many historical or physical truths rather than capricious and mendacious mythology" (Galiani 1780: Note IV, 375–376).

[159] The manuscript is kept in the BSNSP, XXXI A. 9.09, folios 155–182v. The text was published in Caracciolo and Merola (1963: 351–379) and *Note to the text*, xxxviii-xliii. See also Galiani, MS-51.

[160] See Nicolini (1918a: 113). According to Diodati, it was Mazzocchi"s praise that encouraged Galiani to study the subject of money in greater depth in order to write a treatise (Diodati 1788: 5). The *Accademia degli Emuli*, was a circle that met periodically in the home of the Neapolitan gentleman Girolamo Pandolfelli to discuss literary topics.

and other sources. In his criticism, Galiani clearly highlighted the inadequacy of traditional erudite culture: "most of those who aspire to be called erudite," he wrote, "do nothing more than copy one another, and, constantly quoting Homer, they never have the patience or curiosity, not to read him in full, but at least to compare and study those authorities which, on the faith of others, they have the audacity to quote" (Galiani 1748 [1963]: 351).

On this misreading of the texts, according to Galiani, scholars had assumed that there was no money in archaic Greece, based on the following arguments: 1. at that time there was an enormous scarcity of gold and silver and it was therefore impossible to use them as money; 2. The fact that there were practices such as "hospitality", which were intended to replace "commercial" relations made impossible by the absence of money; 3. in ancient texts, there was no explicit mention of money and "prices of things" were established on the basis of heads of cattle (Galiani 1748 [1963]: 352–356).

"All these arguments," the young Galiani remarked, "are negative: the force of which, though sufficient to prove when all other reasons are lacking, is nevertheless in itself very weak. Because all their force is founded on this tacit syllogism: that if there had been money, Homer would have named it; he did not name it, therefore there was no money [...]. All this apparatus of arguments will vanish when one can show a single sentence of Homer where money is mentioned" (Galiani 1748 [1963]: 361). These weak objections could be refuted by a more careful interpretation of the Homeric texts.

With regard to the first objection, the scarcity of precious metals did not allow the automatic conclusion that there was no use of money among the Greeks (Galiani 1748 [1963]: 362). The same situation of scarcity of gold and silver had occurred in the early days of Roman history and in the Middle Ages, and there was still monetary circulation, and at the time of the Trojan War, according to Galiani, there was no scarcity, as evidenced by the widespread use of precious metals for decorative purposes, but also by the exploitation of mines and the existence of large treasures held by other peoples known to the Greeks. Thus, the argument of scarcity was easily refutable (Galiani 1748 [1963]: 362). The argument of hospitality was also rejected, because this institution, which had a religious origin, also existed in the time of Caesar and Cicero, and it certainly cannot be inferred that there was no money at that time (Galiani 1748 [1963]: 364). The last argument, the absence of explicit references to money, was refuted by a detailed philological analysis of Homeric texts in which Galiani highlighted references to the existence of a piece of gold, "similar in every way to our money", called *Talent* (τάλαντον) (Galiani 1748 [1963]: 367).[161]

But Galiani was not satisfied to end his critique at this point, but he wanted to "forestall not only the opposing reasons, but all those that could still be opposed" to his thesis proving the existence of money at the time of the Trojan War (Galiani 1748 [1963]: 352).

To the objection that the *Talent* mentioned in the Homeric texts was not money but only a weight, Galiani replied that in the early days of its use money was identified with the weight of the metal of which it was made, and "the intrinsic nature of money" did not require the coinage to be sanctioned by the state authority (Galiani 1748 [1963]: 371). There were in fact peoples, such as the Chinese, Persians and Indians, who despite not having coinage, had monetary circulation because as "the learned John Locke" had shown, money originated by the "universal consent of men", as a public pledge "to receive from everyone the equivalent of what he has given", and not by intervention of the state authorities (Galiani 1748 [1963]: 372).

The essence of money (defined as the "metaphysics of commerce'", Galiani 1748 [1963]: 371) is that it "serves as a pledge to human society" and this function is not only reserved to precious metals, but "could still be performed, as it has sometimes been done, by stones, leather, bark, shells, fruit, all of which would be money, and finally by written notes" (Galiani 1748 [1963]: 372). However, the only ones that guarantee "comfort and full security" are metals, and among these mainly gold and silver. This is why men have chosen them as their common pledge. But precious metals also have another quality, that of being commodities, and "they serve men for vases, utensils, statues, tools and the like [...] and are considered not only for their weight, which is what constitutes their

[161] Galiani quotes several passages from the *Iliad* and *Odyssey* in which the *Talent* is mentioned: *Iliad* (Book IX, vv. 120–125; Book XIX, vv. 247–248; Book XXIII, vv. 269; Book XXIV, vv. 229–235; Book XXX, vv. 751); *Odyssey* (Book IV, v. 129; Book VIII, vv. 392–393; Book XIII, vv. 392–393). According to the most recent numismatic studies, the *Talent* (meaning "the weight a man can carry") was the highest measure of a weight system (*1 Talent = 30 heavy Minas = 60 light Mines*) of Babylonian origin, later adopted in Greece. Both the *Talent* and its sub-multliple, the *Mina*, were never minted because their weight values were too high; instead, the sub-multliple of the *Mina*, the *Shekel*, used in the East, and the *Drachma*, used in Greece, became minted coins. See Ridgeway (1887: 143–144). See also Brown (1998) who attributes a purely symbolic value to the talent.

intrinsic value, but also for their manufacture" (Galiani 1748 [1963]: 372). In their function as a pledge, they only pass from one hand to another without being consumed, and their value is therefore constituted by their weight alone, "i.e. the quantity, which constitutes the intrinsic value", linked to the total available mass of the same metal. The coinage is nothing more than a sign placed by public authority over a portion of metal to indicate its value, avoiding the inconvenience of having to weigh and divide the metal and the damage that would result from fraud. However, Galiani concluded, the state authority has abused this function by indicating values on minted money that are higher than the weight of the metal contained, but "this being a change in name only, it cannot change the very nature of the thing" (Galiani 1748 [1963]: 373).

The essential function of money is that of being, by consent, a means of payment. This particular function can be understood, Galiani remarked, if the distinction is made between barter (*permuta*) and sale (*vendita*): "Barter is to give one thing that is used in civil life for another that is useful. So to exchange a dress for a tomolo of flour is barter […] Here silver and gold (though they are the same metals that make up money) are considered according to their first quality, and are useful to society […]. Sale is giving one thing useful to civil life for another of no use, but which is only a sure pledge for the seller to receive the equivalent of what he has given. Thus to give a dress to get ten *Ducats* is sale, since those ten ducats serve neither to remove hunger nor thirst nor cold, but are only a sure pledge to get from others as much grain, wine, cloth, as is equivalent to the value of the dress given. Hence in India giving a piece of bread for ten almonds is sale, the almonds not for eating nor for any other use, but only as a pledge from the buyer. And so again, to give a dress for a note is a sale; and this is more clearly observed in the cities of merchants and in those where notes have a value almost equal to that of metallic money" (Galiani 1748 [1963]: 374).[162]

Galiani then formulated his thesis: the ancient Greeks used uncoined gold and copper (but not silver)[163] as a means of payment "to ransom

[162] This logical argument is very close to that of John Law: "Money is not the value for which goods are exchanged, but the value by which they are exchanged. The use of money is to buy goods, and silver while money is of no other use" (Law 1705: 82). Galiani also mentions Law's *Système* (Galiani 1748 [1963]: 374). On the relations between Law and Galiani, see Cesarano (1990).

[163] "There is no trace, to my knowledge, of silver money, nor silver is ever mentioned among the wealth and treasures, and this, as I have already said, is new evidence for me.

prisoners, to reward, to bet, to donate and finally to buy wine and other goods" (Galiani 1748 [1963]: 374), i.e. they used money.[164] The fact that they established prices in heads of cattle did not allow for the non-existence of money, because: (1) it is possible that this was only a usage derived from even earlier times:[165] (2) the Homeric texts were subsequent to the laws of Lycurgus, who "forbade his people the use of silver and gold money, which was then common in the rest of Greece, [and] only allowed them copper money";[166] (3) finally, more simply, an ox was a coin with this effigy, just as the horse was a Neapolitan copper coin (*Cavallo*).

Because, if it is certain that silver was in use at that time in furniture, vases or ornaments, one can never understand why it is not mentioned among the wealth, unless one assumes that other metals and not silver were used for money" (Galiani 1748 [1963]: 374). See also Ridgeway (1887: 133).

[164] Galiani's thesis is substantially accepted by modern historiography, supported by archaeological findings, in particular according to Mark Peacock: "To summarise the monetary aspects of Homer's epics, we may say that Homeric society was monetised to a low degree, if we compare it to societies in which one item, e.g. coin or currency, performs multiple functions of money, does so exclusively, and pervades most areas of social life. In Homer, only the measure of value function is performed exclusively by one unit (cattle). Other functions are performed by various goods; some of these goods perform only one function of money but not others, e.g. gold is used as a means of payment but neither as a medium of exchange nor as a measure of value" (Peacock 2011: 54). Other scholars emphasise the presence of "pre-monetary signs" and not actual money (Gernet 1968)

[165] "It is no less marvellous that in some countries, such as England and our Kingdom, everything is valued with a money that no longer exists, and this only because it once was there" (Galiani 1748 [1963]: 375).

[166] Vico in the *Chronological Table* of the *New Science* set the date of the Trojan War at 2820 of the world's years, while Lycurgus' political work ("Lycurgus gave his laws to the Spartans") is set at 3120, Homer's is instead dated at 3290 (see Vico 1744 [1948]: 41 § 84; 42 § 89). It is possible to note, only in passing, a logical difficulty in Galiani's argument. Assuming we have followed Vico's chronology, since Lycurgus' work is placed about three hundred years after the Trojan War, does the Homeric text testify to a society coeval with the poet or instead one more than four hundred years earlier (the time of Troy)? For Vico, Homer was not so much a real character as the symbol of Greek poetry in the heroic age. An interesting answer to this interpretative problem is formed by Paul Einzig: "The question is, was the system described by Homer in operation during the period of the Trojan war (about the thirteenth century B.C.) or during the much later period when the *Iliad* and the *Odyssey* was written (about the eighth century B.C.). We now know that the late Minoan and Mycenaean civilizations (sixteenth to twelfth century B.C.) had succeeded in developing an advanced form of metallic monetary system approaching the stage of coined money. […]. Homer, writing about a period corresponding to the most advanced phase of the Aegean civilization prior to the classical era of Hellas, describes a much more primitive system as having been in operation during the lifetime of Agamemnon of Mycenae. The apparent contra-

This early work by Galiani highlights some crucial influences characterizing this phase of his education. It is clear that Galiani is strongly influenced by the new philological method expounded by Vico in the *Scienza Nuova*, as demonstrated by the procedure with which he attempts to give an "authentic" reading of the Homeric poems, used as a historical source.[167] In the field of economic theory, Locke's influence is evident, however Galiani distances himself from absolute metallism, considering money above all a means of payment and recognising that it could have any material form: not only valuable commodities, but also common goods and even paper bills, because their function is only to be a pledge to facilitate transactions.[168]

Besides completing his education and producing his first works, Galiani laid the foundation for his professional future during these years. For those who wished to dedicate themselves to studies without substantial means at their disposal, the only path was to embrace an ecclesiastical career, in its various forms, which would provide them with a rent. This is what his uncle Celestino did, as did Antonio Genovesi a few years earlier, being ordained a priest in 1737. However, Ferdinando Galiani did not choose the path of the priesthood, but, in March 1745, took the vows of the so-called minor orders corresponding to the lowest ranks of the ecclesiastical hierarchy, which did not entail an actual sacramental ordination,

diction may presumably be accounted for by the fact that during the centuries that passed between the events and conditions described in the Iliad and the Odyssey and their recording by Homer there was an allround deterioration of civilization in the Aegean area as a result of the Doric invasion" (Einzig 1966: 222). The most recent historiography, however, denies that forms of monetary economy were developed in the Mycenaean age (see Nicolet-Pierre 2002: 90).

[167] "Fully adopting the historicist method, Galiani writes: "The term king (like almost all others), although used as if it meant the same, has very different meanings. For very differently it sounds in my mouth and in the mouth of one of our Neapolitans who lived at the time of Roger the Norman. The ideas of power, of wealth, of degree of authority, linked to the term king, are by far different and varied" (Galiani 1748 [1963]: 357). In a letter to Tanucci, Galiani described Vico: "The Frenchman [Nicolas-Antoine Boulanger] stole from Giambattista Vico, and did not quote him. But there are many who now know about the plagiarism here, and ask me for Vico's *Scienza nuova*, a book *made in the dark* by a man who had great enlightenment" (Ferdinando Galiani's letter to Bernardo Tanucci, Paris, 22 December 1766, published in Galiani, 1975: 928). On the relations between Ferdinando Galiani and Vico, see Nicolini (1918c).

[168] "Our right to class him [Locke] as a metallist can be fully established from the structure of his argument. Doubts might be raised, however, on the strength of Locke's statement that money exists by virtue of common consent" (Schumpeter 1954 [2006]: 277, footnote 6).

but nevertheless conferred the status of clergy on those who received them.[169] He was then appointed abbot of Santa Caterina dei Celani (a Neapolitan abbey whose assets included part of Lake Fusaro), ceded to him by his brother Berardo (Nicolini 1918a: 115), a position to which an ecclesiastical benefice was linked that would guarantee him the enjoyment of an ecclesiastical rent of six hundred *Ducats* per year. He later, in 1751, obtained by succession another abbot's benefice in Centola (in Province of Salerno), which gave him a rent of a further five hundred *Ducats* and the title of *Mitered Abbot* and *Monsignore* (Diodati 1788: 14–15).

To his undoubted talent, the young Galiani added a characteristic that accompanied him throughout his life: a playful and ironic spirit that characterised much of his literary production and his brilliant correspondence, and made him, in his maturity, a fascinating protagonist of literary salons and high-society circles.[170]

An early example of his abilities is the jocular work *Componimentii varj per la morte di Domenico Iannaccone Carnefice della Gran Corte della Vicaria* (*Miscellaneous compositions for the death of Domenico Iannaccone executioner of the Grand Court of Vicaria*, Galiani-Carcani, 1749), written in collaboration with Pasquale Carcani.[171] The work was written by Galiani to take revenge on Giannantonio Sergio, a Neapolitan lawyer and academician, who had prevented him from attending an academy meeting in place of his brother Berardo, but it was also an opportunity to criticise certain attitudes of the academics.[172] The same humour is found in a letter

[169] While wearing ecclesiastical robes and the typical tonsure, the abbot was dispensed from ecclesiastical obligations and given a benefice could devote himself to study.

[170] Galiani's writings are in the Library of the Società Napoletana di Storia Patria in a collection called *Archivio Galianeo* (consisting of 70 volumes, containing writings of various kinds). Entrusted, in 1787, by the abbot's testament to the Neapolitan lawyer Francesco Paolo Azzariti, the manuscripts were purchased by the Nicolini family and then donated to the Società Napoletana di Storia Patria, suffering no damage during the war. On Galiani's manuscripts and his dense correspondence, see Croce (1903); Nicolini (1908a, 1908b); Guerci (1972); Galasso (1989c). A detailed inventory of the manuscripts was compiled in 2023, see Inventario (2023).

[171] A manuscript copy is in BSNSP, XXIX.C.5.

[172] Giannantonio Sergio was a member of the Neapolitan forum, see Di Gennaro (1748). Other writings appeared in Naples under this name between 1747 and 1748 to celebrate religious or court events. Luigi Diodati describes the uproar caused by Galiani's writing as follows: "In conversations, nothing else was spoken of but this volume; everyone eagerly sought it out and, although many copies were distributed, they were not enough and countless other manuscripts were made. Many famous and respected men, who saw their style ridiculed, appealed to the king to discover the author" (Diodati 1788: 8, see Iovine 2001:

addressed, in December 1745, to an English Lord visiting or exiled in Naples, who had sent him his own translation or plagiarism of the *Dialogo de la bella creanza de le donne* better known as *Raffaella* by Alessandro Piccolomini (*Dialogue on the beautiful manners of women*, Piccolomini 1539; see Nicolini 1918a: 117).[173] The theme discussed is the relationship between men and women in social life, which then took the specific form of *cicisbeism*.[174] The seventeen-year-old Galiani already had clear enough ideas on the matter to assert that "from premeditated designs arises friendship or *cicisbeism*, and not love. And *cicisbeism* as it is devoid of the torments of an unhappy love, so it is devoid of the pleasures of a fortunate love" (Galiani, MS-2: folio 95). The role of the *cicisbeo* was thus purely social, not involving sentimental issues, and "love, that admirable *ressort* [impetus] that moves and gives life to human commerce" (Galiani, MS-2: folio 97r). Regarding this analogy between love and commerce, understood as human relations, Galiani followed the approach defined by his uncle Celestino. And, further on in the letter, Galiani, examining the subject with his method, i.e. "metaphysically", defined a curious classification of women: "the kinds of life that women live are six: p…[prostitutes], half-p…, honoured, half-honoured, devout and half-devout women. Now, of all these species, certainly the best must be the devout, as those who are always united with God and will go to Heaven. But, to speak of this world (for the other is not to be dealt with), I estimate that the best of all are the half-p… and the half-devout. Because the half-p… are those, *quae, si non caste, caute tamen vivunt* [*which, if not chaste, yet live cautiously*]; and the half-p… are those who, while inflamed with divine love are uplifted and intent on contemplating the shining stars of the empyrean, let the heavy and fragile body fall into the ditches. Other species of life are far worse. Because the p… being tinged with infamy, they are the abhorrence of their sex, as they are the love of the male sex, and then […] they remain abandoned even by men after paying the price. The honourable ones and those

444–445). The two authors, fearing they would be betrayed by the printer, turned themselves in to Justice Minister Tanucci who ordered them to do ten days of spiritual exercises.

[173] The text is preserved in the Società Napoletana di Storia Patria Library under the title *Lettera di Galiani a ignoto sulla natura dell'amore e sul cicibeismo* (Galiani, MS-2) and published by Nicolini (1918b: 117–121).

[174] *Cicibeismo* was a Genoese-origin custom, later spreading throughout Italy and Latin countries, to denote a habitual companion (also called *cavalier servente*) of a noble married woman. The term has an onomatopoeic origin, from whispering, "whispering in the ear", see Bizzocchi (2008).

who, while caring for the inner, do not care for the outer, are in a far worse condition, having neither servitude from men nor esteem from women. But of all these states, the one in which women are most inclined is that of the half devout, a life to be truly happy" (Galiani, MS-2: folio 98r–99r; Nicolini 1918a: 120). This view already reveals a cynical detachment from all forms of conformist hypocrisy, a characteristic of his character that did not always help him in human relations.

With the same spirit, the young Galiani tackled the complex theme of love in a lecture to the *Accademia degli Emuli* (Galiani, MS-3), in which various influences converged, from Locke's sensimism, which led to materialism, to Vico's philological research. Defining "love as that affection of the mind, whereby one often thinks of a person or a thing" (Galiani 1975: 690), Galiani argues that money, poetry, music, gambling, men, women, animals, flowers and even the most abstract and mental things can be objects of love. And love "is in itself neither pleasure nor pain, but can be both" (Galiani 1975: 690). Love is therefore a state of mind that depends on that part of the brain that excites the imagination, establishing associations between disparate and distinct ideas.[175] To heal from love, its opposite, hatred, which is also a state of mind and can be defined as "love of vengeance" (Galiani 1975: 693), is not enough; one must flee from thought and everything that can foster the lure of that thought. But if love is also suffering, and if it depends on the will to ignite the passions, "the question comes down to this: whether or not it is convenient to foment and maintain an amorous passion" (Galiani 1975: 694). The answer, according to Galiani, restricted to the case of love between a man and a woman, can only be given if one distinguishes the type of love, which can also take several forms simultaneously: "One can love a servant girl inasmuch as she has faithfully served us, inasmuch as she is beautiful in appearance, inasmuch as she is graceful: here are three of them together. To show that they are distinct, suppose this servant becomes a male, or becomes ugly; behold, one love ceases, and yet the other two remain, therefore they were different; she stole from her master, behold, another ceases, and yet

[175] In the manuscript on Platonic love, the definition becomes clearer: "love, a thing distinct in everything from lust, is a physical, purely mechanical affection of our body born involuntarily in us from that very cause that in our happy times has finally been discovered and under the name of the draw of attraction has been identified as the regulating cause of the universe" (Galiani, MS-4: folio 57v). The subject is also tackled in correspondence with Toccolino de' Lapi Toccoli, Count of Punghino, see BSNSP, XXXI. A. 10, folios 57r–59v. See also Stapelbroek (2008a: 129–133) and Mauro (2017a: 39–79).

the third still lasts, therefore it was different" (Galiani 1975: 695–696). These types of love are always lawful and convenient for all human and divine laws. Illicit are all the passions that derive from animal behaviour that cannot be defined as love. Even *cicisbeism* is not love, but only an external representation of it, because "the main essence of it, which consists in frequent thought, is absent" (Galiani 1975: 697). Such activity can only be useful if it is cultivated out of ambition and it appeared to Galiani as a vile and lowly practice, which in Naples, more than in other parts of Italy, had taken root, due to "'the gravity in men and reservedness in women", customs imposed by Spain, which for more than two hundred years had dominated (Galiani 1975: 699–700).

The theme of love must have particularly attracted the young Galiani, by then destined for an ecclesiastical career and celibacy. Another essay of his youthful reflections is in fact dedicated to *Platonic love* (Galiani, MS-4, see also Mauro 2017a: 59–75), considered by Galiani as a "continuation" of the previous lecture on the same theme of love. Platonic love for Galiani is a kind of "perturbation of reason, by which one pretends to justify a mechanical affection of the body, as a free operation of the mind" (Galiani, MS-4: folio 58v), and it is inappropriate to identify this affection with love, with which "it has no connection: consisting most of the time in mere talking, sometimes even in the intellectual part of the mind, but never in the senses"(Galiani, MS-4: folio 58v). Platonic love arises from a refusal, from a failure to satisfy feelings and senses, and serves to hide the loss of primitive affection. The unfortunate in love, the unhappy man who "receives nothing from his woman but repulses, scorn, cruelty, and rigours, what do you want him to do? His woman will not deceive him. Must he therefore always remain unhappy because he is not deceived? [...] Insensibly the man who does not find one who wants to deceive him and make him happy, let him deceive himself and make himself happy. [...] So as not to sadden himself with hateful truth" (Galiani, MS-4: folio 64r–64v). In this way he deceives himself and transforms his pain into an illusory but satisfying pleasure. "Happiness", Galiani asserted, following Jonathan Swift, "is the peaceful possession of the pleasure of being well and duly deceived" (Galiani, MS-4: folio 60r),[176] and when deception is difficult to reveal, it becomes the source of all our pleasure. "So if deception is stable, stable can be pleasure" (Galiani, MS-4: folio 62r). The conclusion to be

[176] "The possession of being well deceived" (Swift 1704: 175).

drawn is immediate for Galiani: if "man's ultimate end is happiness, this is found in pleasure, this in deception" (Galiani, MS-4: folio 63r).

Falsehood (*falsità*) and deception are for Galiani "homogenous to human nature", just as contrary to it are truth and disenchantment (Galiani, MS-4: folio 59r). All the ancient literature of fables and apologies demonstrates "how grateful is falsehood, how hateful and frowned upon the naked truth" (Galiani, MS-4: folio 59r). Even religion itself, according to the young abbot, repeating a theme developed in Vico's *Scienza Nuova*, has made use of fables, because "so great is the homogeneity of the lie to the human heart, that neither the deity of truth itself, nor the most effective remedies, nor the care of attentive ministers have ever been able to completely uproot it from its well-planted roots" (Galiani, MS-4: folio 59v). Locke showed that "outside our minds there is nothing but figure and motion, and yet everyone believes that outside us there are sounds, colours, tastes, and every other thing that we feel; hence we live in perpetual happy deception" (Galiani, MS-4: folio 61r–61v). The moral world not unlike the physical world is governed by a deceived and limited reason as are the senses. The "mutual" deception between men thus becomes a kind of providential remedy to achieve happiness (Galiani, MS-4: folio 66r).

And on religious themes, the young Galiani returned in a manuscript fortuitously found in 1956 at the British Museum in London by Fausto Nicolini and Franco Venturi, which appears as a chapter of a youthful work probably dealing with theological subjects (Galiani, MS-5, see Nicolini and Venturi 1956: 68).[177] Although it is only a fragment, the text is of great interest because it reveals a nonchalant approach in dealing, even with irony, with such a sensitive subject as the theses on the existence of God, a sign that his educational path had been broad and certainly not bound by strict adherence to religious orthodoxy.

According to Galiani, there are three theses on "God as creator and preserver of things"(Galiani, MS-5: 69): the Christian thesis, according to which God creates matter and form out of nothing, and "consequently he is an entity that is entirely distinct from matter and that necessarily exists" (Galiani, MS-5: 69); the thesis of the Pythagoreans, who hold that God gives form to pre-existing inert matter; the third thesis of the Stoics, Epicureans and Spinozists "does not admit God, when by God is meant an author of the world" (Galiani, MS-5: 70). To avoid falling into atheism,

[177] According to Marco Catucci, the fragment is supposed to have been written in his maturity, in the 1770s (see Catucci 1986: 122).

the latter identify God with the world itself. These theses elaborated by philosophers are not understood by the common people, "with regard to the creative cause, all these peoples who have no scientific culture, have never, or almost never, thought of it, therefore they have an obscure and indigestible idea of it and devote very little attention to it, all turned, as we see our Christians do, to placating and adoring these men who they believe, after death, have authority and power over them [...]. I could safely say that of a thousand Christians there is not one who believes that this world needs an efficient cause" (Galiani, MS-5: 71). The common people, both Christian and Jewish," Galiani observed, "are therefore idolatrous, they do not "intend anything by God other than what we mean either by the saint or by the evil spirit" (Galiani, MS-5: 71).

Despite the effort made by philosophers to define God and his attributes, Galiani believed that "the ideas which all philosophers (under this name I also mean Christian theologians) have of the creator entity are as ridiculous as those of the most foolish common people, although in appearance they seem to be very just. Both contain the great paralogism of applying to God the things and ideas that are convenient to man, but those of the common people have it more obvious, those of the scholars more abstruse and difficult. The Roman peasant makes Jupiter the eater of nectar, the Christian theologian makes him righteous: both say an absurdity" (Galiani, MS-5: 72). All explanations are equally ridiculous, unverifiable opinion and "the existence and main attributes of God" must be defined "by axiom" (Galiani, MS-5: 69). Even in these few interesting notations, the concept of the fantastic tale as the foundation of religious myth recurs, but Galiani goes much further than Vico by eliminating any difference between paganism, Judaism and Christianity in the common idolatry and superstition. This is an extremely dangerous thesis for a young man embarked on an ecclesiastical career.

To the subject of religiosity Galiani devoted particular attention in the same years. Among his writings there are fragments of essays dedicated to superstition (Galiani, MS-6),[178] to the *Antichrist* (Galiani, MS-7), to the *End of the World* (Galiani, MS-8), to the controversial subject of witchcraft

[178] "Superstition can rightly be defined as that religion which does not improve corrupt minds but by corrupt minds is entirely generated" (Galiani, MS-9: 819). See Mauro (2017a: 152–172).

(Galiani, MS-9)[179] and to Socrates as a victim of fanaticism (Galiani, MS-10).[180]

The analysis of these early writings by Galiani reveals two of his characteristics, which would accompany him throughout his activity as a writer: the heterogeneity and vastness of interests cultivated, the knowledge of an immense literature, from classical authors to Anglo-Saxon writers (and not only philosophers such as Locke, but also the nascent journalism of Joseph Addison and *The Spectator*), an effect of his very rich education; and the incompleteness and fragmentary nature in which his studies were scattered, an effect of a lazy character and a human nature more disposed to amusement than to systematic application. This is why his youthful writings have been called mere "exercises in rhetoric" (Diaz 1975a: xv). In more recent times, however, these writings have received special attention, and the theses on love as *self-deception* have been presented as the matrix of a new concept of sociality at the heart of Galiani's entire philosophy (Stapelbroek 2008a, 2020),[181] or as the first stage of libertine thinking and desecration of traditional morality (Amodio 1997a, 1997b).[182] To find a single guiding principle (love as self-deception) in a complex work such as Galiani's can construct a one-sided image of the Neapolitan abbot, imputing to him an extreme coherence of research, a virtue that can hardly be appropriate for a prolific and heterogeneous scholar, animated by multiple interests. And one can object to the thesis of the young Galiani's precocious libertinism by pointing out that his formative environment, although

[179] The eighteenth-century debate on the problem of witchcraft was particularly intense between the 1740s and the 17950s. Begun by Girolamo Tartarotti in 1744, it involved, among others, Gian Rinaldo Carli, Tommaso Maria Mamachi, Paolo Frisi and Scipione Maffei. See Venturi (1998: 355–383) and Parinetto (1974).

[180] "When I observe the superstition of the Athenians, I thank Heaven that I was not born among them, for what impiety can be greater than attributing the failings of mortals to the source of all perfection" (Galiani, MS-10: 702).

[181] "Once the principles of Galiani's political thought, which are most clearly present in his youthful readings, are better understood, the coherence in his writing career becomes clear and one can glean his vision of the future of Naples in the European states system" (Stapoelbroek 2008a: 7).

[182] "[Galiani] was endowed with an extraordinarily receptive nature, so much so that, rather than dispersing himself in erudition, he was able to develop, even at a very young age, a lively and highly personal intellectual position that was to be inextricably linked to an extremely unconventional lifestyle [...]. Whatever, in short, some critics may have wanted to see, for whom it was France that corrupted his morals, it is certain, however, that the characteristic duplicity of the libertine vocation was soon expressed in the erudite young abbot at the same time as the translation of Locke" (Amodio 1997a: 41–42).

intellectually open to all that was new, cannot be considered a circle of erudite freethinking, both because of the visible ecclesiastical responsibilities of his uncle Celestino (libertinism was identified with atheism by Catholic orthodoxy), and because libertinism no longer appeared as a novelty in intellectual life in the 1740s.[183]

Although these early works already reveal a great originality of thought (and cannot be considered mere exercises), they are still attempts and not systematic works from which generalising conclusions can be drawn about Galiani's entire intellectual career. This was admitted by Galiani himself when, in a note to the second edition of his *Della Moneta*, he wrote: "as young minds are inclined to enterprises much greater than their forces, which they do not know how to measure, I had truly imagined writing on the whole of political science, and many parts of it I had either drafted or prepared" (Galiani 1780: 393). A fragment of this planned treatise can be found in the manuscripts under the title *Dell'arte del governo, proemio* (*Of the Art of Government, Proem*, Galiani, MS-11), in which the young abbot addresses the issue of public happiness by identifying it with wealth: "Although moral philosophy teaches to despise the possession of wealth and its acquisition by a merchant, and not to regard it as a cause of happiness, politics takes it as an instrument of happiness, and it is therefore one of the things it kindly seeks to procure for its subjects" (Galiani, MS-11: 390). And without falling under the illusion, he repeated that: "the art of government is the art of giving happiness to many men united in society [...]. Politics concerns external causes. So the art of government is rather the art of preparing happiness than of giving it, and consists entirely in removing the external causes that produce unhappiness. Good government, therefore, is not that in which everyone is happy, since this government would never be there, but it is that in which everyone can be happy, when internal or particular causes do not prevent it. Tyranny is that government in which a few become happy at the expense and to the detriment of all the rest, who become unhappy" (Galiani, MS-11: 390).

This focus on wealth as the basis of public happiness shows that Galiani's main effort between 1747 (the year in which he probably began writing his dissertation on money at the time of the Trojan War) and 1750 was

[183] Paolo Amodio himself admits: "There is no doubt that the very structure of society, the modes of communication, publishing, the new spaces offered by government policy, the models of sociability, configure a context so different from that of the previous century, as to give different meaning to the word and, even more, to trends" (Amodio 1997a: 30).

therefore directed towards economic matters, and in particular monetary problems, which in those years were receiving great attention in Italy as a field of application for ambitious reform projects aimed at achieving good government.[184] Stimulated by this debate, the young Galiani tested his precocious talent on one of the most controversial and difficult subjects.

References[185]

Manuscript Sources

Galiani, C. MSCG. Ricerche intorno alle prime origini della scienza morale, manuscript kept in the Biblioteca Società Napoletana di Storia Patria, XXXI. C. 1, folios 1–68.

Galiani, C. MSCG-2. *Parere teologico sopra alcuni punti appartenenti all'introduzione degli Ebrei ne' due Regni di Napoli e Sicilia*, manuscript kept in the Biblioteca Società Napoletana di Storia Patria, XXXI.B.1, folios [244] 235–[267v] 258v.

Galiani, C. MSCG-4. *Intorno ai calcoli differenziale e integrale*, manuscript kept in the Biblioteca Società Napoletana di Storia Patria, XXXI.B.1, folios [302] 293–[307v] 298v.

Galiani, F. MS-1. *Notizie genealogiche dei Galiani*, Manuscript kept in the Biblioteca Società Napoletana di Storia Patria, XXXI. C. 8, folio 66.

Galiani, F. MS-2. *Lettera di Galiani a ignoto sulla natura dell'amore e sul cicisbeismo*, December 1745, Manuscript kept in the Biblioteca Società Napoletana di Storia Patria, XXXI. C. 19.05, folios 94r–99v, published in Nicolini, 1918b, pp. 117–121.

Galiani, F. MS-3. *Discorso sull'amore. Lezione accademica letta dall'abate Galiani nell'Accademia degli Emuli nel 1746*. Manuscript kept in the Biblioteca Società Napoletana di Storia Patria, XXXI. A. 09, folios 91r–100r, published in Galiani, 1975a, pp. 689–700.

[184] It is not certain whether the project to reprint seventeenth century texts published in Naples on monetary unrest and the economic and social problems of the Viceroyalty dates back to these early years, see Galiani MS-12. In a note in the second edition, Galiani returned to the project: "It would be a work worthy of a lover of these noble studies to collect and publish again, with clarifications and notes, the writings that then appeared on these subjects, the memory of which is now entirely lost" (Galiani 1780: Note XXIX, 408).

[185] The abbreviations "s.l." and "s.n." stand for the Latin terms *sine loco* (without place of publication) and *sine nomine* (without name of publisher).

Galiani, F. MS-4. *Lezione accademica sull'amor platonico.* Manuscript kept in the Biblioteca Società Napoletana di Storia Patria, XXX. C. 06, folios 57r–66r, published in Mauro 2017a, tome 2, pp. 454–464.

Galiani, F. MS-5. *Dell'idea di Dio*, Manuscript kept in the British Museum, Egerton Collection, 21, published in Nicolini-Venturi, 1956, pp. 67–73.

Galiani, F. MS-6. *Della superstizione, e delle cause di essa*, Manuscript kept in the Biblioteca Società Napoletana di Storia Patria, XXXI. A. 10, folios 124r–125v, published in Mauro 2017a, tome 2, pp. 469–471.

Galiani, F. MS-7. *Sull'Anticristo (al conte Punghino)*, Manuscript kept in the Biblioteca Società Napoletana di Storia Patria, XXXI. C. 12, folios 97r–102r, published in Mauro, 2017a, tome 2, pp. 472–477.

Galiani, F. MS-8. *Pensieri vari sulla durata e sulla fine del mondo*, Manuscript kept in the Biblioteca Società Napoletana di Storia Patria, XXXI. A. 10, folios 118r–120v, published in Mauro, 2017a, tome 2, pp. 478–480.

Galiani, F. MS-9. *Proemio di un'opera sulle streghe*, Manuscript kept in the Biblioteca Società Napoletana di Storia Patria, XXXI. C. 14, folios 146r–148r, published with this title in Galiani, 1975b, pp. 817–819.

Galiani, F. MS-10. *Sopra la morte di Socrate*, Manuscript kept in the Biblioteca Società Napoletana di Storia Patria, XXXI. A. 9, published in Galiani, 1975, pp. 701–703.

Galiani, F. MS-11. *Dell'arte del governo, proemio*, Manuscript kept in the Biblioteca Società Napoletana di Storia Patria, XXXI. C. 8, folios 1r–2v, published in Galiani, 1963, pp. 390–392.

Galiani, F. MS-12. *Proemio alla ristampa di libri che trattano dei disordini della moneta al tempo dei Viceré e cagioni delle misere condizioni del Regno*, Manuscript kept in the Biblioteca Società Napoletana di Storia Patria, XXXI. C. 8, folios Ir–IVv.

Galiani, F. MS-23. *Per il suo Maestro di Ebraico*, Manuscript kept in the Biblioteca Società Napoletana di Storia Patria, XXX. C. 12, folios: 99–101, partially published in Nicolini, 1975, p. 304.

Galiani, F. MS-51. *Sullo stato della moneta ai tempi della guerra troiana*, Manuscript kept in the Biblioteca Società Napoletana di Storia Patria, XXXI.A.09.09, folios 155–182v, published in Galiani, 1963, pp. 351–379.

Valletta, G. MS. *Risposta ad un Amico sopra le Ragioni della Città di Napoli per l'Assistenze domandate alla Fabrica della Nuova Moneta del Dottor Giuseppe Valletta*, manuscript kept in the Biblioteca Oratoriana dei Gerolamini in Naples (coll. MS. XXVIII.2.43, folios 225–261).

Valletta, G. MS-1. *Al nostro Santissimo Padre Innocentio duodecimo intorno al Procedimento ordinario e canonico nelle cause che si trattano nel tribunale del S. Officio nella Città e Regno di Napoli*, manuscript kept in the Biblioteca Nazionale di Napoli, MSS. XI. C. 10.

Primary Sources

Barbieri, M. (1778). *Notizie istoriche dei mattematici e filosofi del Regno di Napoli.* Naples: Vocola.

Biblia, F. (1621). *Discorso sopra l'Aggiustamento della Moneta e Cambii del Regno di Napoli. D'ordine dell'Ill.mo e R.mo Signor Cardinal Zapata Luogotenente e Capitan Generale per Sua Maestà in questo Regno di Napoli*, Naples: s.n.

Biscardi, S. [1993]. *Idea del governo politico ed economico del regno di Napoli*, in D. Luongo (ed.), *Mediazione ministeriale e ideologia economica.* Naples: Jovane.

Carafa, G. duca di Noja. (1750). *Lettera ad un amico contenente alcune considerazioni sull'utilità, e gloria, che si trarrebbe da una esatta carta topografica della città di Napoli, e del suo contado.* Naples: s.n.

Caravelli, V., Porto, V. (1786). *Trattati del calcolo differenziale di Vito Caravelli, e del calcolo integrale di Vincenzo Porto per uso del regale collegio militare.* Naples: Raimondi.

Carli, G. R. (1751). *Dell'origine e del commercio della moneta e dell'instituzione delle zecche d'Italia dalla decadenza dell'impero sino al secolo decimo settimo.* All'Haja [The Hague, but Venice]: s.n.

D'Andrea, F. (1667). *Risposta al trattato delle ragioni della Regina Cristianissima, sopra il Ducato di Brabante, et altri stati della Fiandra. Nella quale si dimostra l'ingiustizia della guerra mossa dal Re di Francia, per la conquista di quelle provincie; non ostante le ragioni, che si son pubblicate in suo nome, per la pretesa successione a favor della Regina Cristianissima.* Naples: s.n.

D'Andrea, F. (1696a) [1919]. Avvertimenti ai nipoti, *Archivio Storico per le Provincie Napoletane*, vol. 44, pp. 227–290, republished in N. Cortese (ed.) *I ricordi di un avvocato napoletano del Seicento: Francesco D'Andrea,* Naples: Lubrano, 1923.

De Benedictis, G. B (pseudonym Benedetto Aletino). (1694). *Lettere apologetiche in difesa della teologia scolastica e della filosofia peripatetica.* Naples: Raillard.

De Santis, M.A. (1605a). *Discorso di Marc'Antonio De Santis intorno alli effetti, che fa il cambio in Regno.* Naples: Costantino Vitali.

De Santis, M.A. (1605b). *Secondo Discorso di Marc'Antonio De Santis intorno alli effetti, che fa il cambio in Regno, sopra una risposta, che è stata fatta adverso del primo.* Naples: Felice Stigliola.

Di Gennaro, G. A. (1748). *Delle viziose maniere del difender le cause nel foro trattato di Giuseppe Aurelio Di Gennaro. Con una prefazione in cui si tratta dell'origine, e progressi dell'avvocazione, distesa da Giannantonio Sergio avvocato napoletano*, Venice: Bortoli.

Diodati, L. (1788). *Vita dell'abate Ferdinando Galiani.* Naples: Orsino.

D'Onofrio, V. (pseudonym Innocenzo Fuidoro). (1653?) [1932] *Successi del governo del Conte d'Oñatte 1648–1653.* Naples: Lubrano.

Doria, P. M. (1709). *La vita civile, e l'educazione del principe di P. M. Doria*. Francfort [but Naples]: s.n.

Doria, P. M. (1710a). *La vita civile di P. M. Doria, distinta in tre parti, aggiuntovi un trattato della educazione del principe. Seconda edizione dall'Autore ricorretta, ed accresciuta*. Augusta: Höpper.

Doria, P. M. (1710b) [1973], *Massime generali e particolare colle quali di tempo in tempo hanno gli Spagnoli governato il Regno di Napoli*, edited by V. Conti, with an introduction by G. Galasso. Naples: Guida (an earlier publication of excerpts from the Report is due to M. Schipa, with the title "Il Regno di Napoli descritto nel 1713 da P. M. Doria", *Archivio storico delle province napoletane*, 1899, fasc. I, pp. 25–84 e fasc. II pp. 329–350).

Doria, P. M. (1710c) [1981], "Relazione dello stato politico, economico e civile del regno di Napoli nel tempo ch'è stato governato dai Spagnuoli, prima dell'entrata dell'armi tedesche in detto regno", in *Manoscritti napoletani di Paolo Mattia Doria*. Galatina: Congedo, vol. 1, pp. 49–139.

Doria, P. M. (1715). *Nuovo metodo geometrico per trovare fra due linee rette date infinite medie continue proporzionali*. Antwerp: Cristoforo Plantini.

Doria, P. M. (1721). *Dissertazione di Paolo-Mattia Doria intorno alla nuova geometria di Cartesio: Con una Raccolta di tutte le dimostrazioni, e considerazionni dell' autore, pubblicate in varij tempi, ed in varie lettere, a fine di dimostrare geometricamente, che la parabola Apolloniana non hà le proprietà, che da geometri se l'assegnano*. Venice: s.n.

Doria, P. M. (1722). *Delle opere matematiche di Paolo Mattia Doria*. Venice: s.n.

Doria, P. M. (1724). *Discorsi Critici Filosofici intorno alla Filosofia degl'Antichi e de i Moderni; ed in particolare intorno alla Filosofia di Renato Des-Cartes. Con un progetto di una Metafisica*. Venice: s.n.

Doria, P. M. (1726). *Delle opere matematiche: Considerazione, dissertazioni, ed esercitazioni geometriche*, Naples: s.n.

Doria, P. M. (1728). *Filosofia di P, M Doria, con la quale si schiarisce quella di Platone; Dedicata all'Altezza Reale di Carlo Emanuele Principe di Piemonte. Volume primo continente le Nozioni di Logica, e le parti I. II. e III. della Metafisica [e] Volume secondo continente la Parte IV. della Morale, e le Parti V. e VI. della Morale Teorica e Pratica*. Amsterdam, [but Geneva: Stamperia del Tournes].

Doria, P. M. (1729). *La vita civile di P. M. Doria, con un trattato della educazione del principe. Terza impressione, dall'Autore ricorretta, e di molte aggiunzioni adornata*. Naples: Vocola.

Doria, P.M. (1732). *Difesa della metafisica degli antichi filosofi contro il Signor Giovanni Locke, ed alcuni altri moderni autori di P. M. Doria. Divisa in due parti*. Venice: s.n.

Doria, P. M. (1738) [1981]. Considerazioni Geometriche, Logiche e Metafisiche sopra li Elementi di Euclide, fatte a fine di prima disciplinare la mente umana nella sola vera ed unica Logica; secondo per unire nella mente umana la geometria e la logica alla metafisica, e per terzo ed ultimo per insegnare a dedurre dalle idee universali le proprietà particolari delle cose appartenenti alla fisica e alla Meccanica. In A. Spedicati (ed.), *Manoscritti napoletani di Paolo Mattia Doria.* Galatina: Congedo, 1981, vol. 3, pp. 1–20.

Doria, P. M. (1739). *Il Capitano filosofo*, Naples: Angelo Vocola

Doria, P. M. (1740a). *La vita civile di P. M. Doria, con un trattato della educazione del principe, quarta impressione.* Naples: Vocola.

Doria, P. M. (1740b) [1981]. Del commercio del regno di Napoli. Con l'aggiunta di un'Appendice, Nel quale s'indagano le cagioni generali e particolari, dalle quali il buono, e retto Commercio trae la sua origine; E si fà vedere il rapporto che il perfetto Commercio deve avere con gli altri Ordini, de' quali la Repubblica si compone. Lettera diretta al Signor D. Francesco Ventura, Degnissimo Presidente del Magistrato di Commercio. In G. Belgioioso (ed.), *Manoscritti napoletani di Paolo Mattia Doria.* Galatina: Congedo, 1981, vol 1, pp. 141–208.

Doria, P. M. (1753). *La vita civile di P. M. Doria, con un trattato della educazione del principe. Quinta impressione, dall'autore ricorretta, e di molte aggiunzioni adornata.* Naples: Vocola.

Doria, P. M. (1981). L'Arte di conoscere sé stesso, composto per l'amico Birago di Borgaro. In *Manoscritti napoletani di Paolo Mattia Doria*, P. De Fabrizio (ed.). Galatina: Congedo, vol. IV, pp. 411–431.

Dutot, N. (1738). *Réflexions politiques sur les finances et le commerce.* La Haye: Vaillant-Prevost.

Encyclopédie. (1765). *Encyclopédie, ou dictionnaire raisonné des sciences, des arts et des métiers,* Tome X. Neufchastel [but Paris]: Samuel Faulche.

Enríquez de Fonseca, L. (1681a) [1973]. *Discurso en orden a que à la moneda de vellon se disponga modo de uso por el qual sea mejor para los commercios que la moneda de plata.* Naples: Salvador Castaldo, Italian translation in R. Colapietra (ed.) *Problemi monetari negli scrittori napoletani del Seicento.* Rome: Accademia Nazionale dei Lincei, 1973, pp. 457–490.

Frisi, P. (1775). *Elogio del Galileo.* Milan: Agnelli.

Galanti, G. M. (1783). *Elogio storico del signor abate Antonio Genovesi pubblico professore di civil economia nell'Università di Napoli. Terza edizione notabilmente migliorata e corretta, ed accresciuta dell'elogio del signor Bartolomeo Intieri e di una lettera intorno al plagio letterario.* Florence: Pisoni.

Galiani, F. (1748) [1963]. *Sullo stato della moneta ai tempi della guerra troiana*, Manuscript kept in the Biblioteca Società Napoletana di Storia Patria, XXXI A. 9.09, folios 155–182v, published in Galiani, 1963, pp. 351–379.

Galiani, F. [1751] [published anonymous, with date of 1750]. *Della moneta. Libri cinque,* Naples: Giuseppe Raimondi.

Galiani, F. (1780). *Della moneta. Libri cinque. Edizione seconda.* Naples: Stamperia Simoniana.

Galiani, F. (1881a). *Écrivains du XVIII siècle – Correspondance avec Madame d'Épinay, Madame Necker, Madame Geoffrin etc., Diderot, Grimm, d'Alembert, de Sartine, d'Holbach, etc. Nouvelle édition, entièrement rétablie d'après les textes originaux, augmentée de tous les passages supprimés et d'un grand nombre de lettres inédites, avec une étude sur sa vie et les oeuvres de Galiani*, edited by L. Perey, G. Maugras, 2 voll. Paris: Calmann Levy.

Galiani, F. (1963). *Della Moneta*, edited by A. Merola, with introduction of A. Caracciolo, Milan: Feltrinelli.

Galiani, F. (1975). *Opere di Ferdinando Galiani*, edited by F. Diaz e L. Guerci, in *Letteratura italiana. Storia e testi. Illuministi italiani*, tomo VI. Milan-Naples: Ricciardi.

Galiani, F., d'Épinay, L. (1992). *Correspondance. Vol. I (1769–1770)*, présentation de G. Dulac, texte établi et annoté par D. Maggetti, en collaboration avec G. Dulac. Paris: Les Editions Desjonquères.

Gassendi, P. (1727). *Opera omnia in sex tomos divisa*. Florence: typis Regiae Celsitudinis.

Genovesi, A. [1997]. "Vita di Antonio Genovese". In F. Venturi (ed.) *Illuministi italiani. Riformatori* napoletani, vol. II, tomo I. Milan: Ricciardi - Mondadori, pp. 47–83.

Giannone, P. (1723). *Dell'istoria civile del Regno di Napoli libri 40 scritti da Pietro Giannone giureconsulto, ed avvocato napoletano. Tomo 4, in cui contiensi la politia del regno sotto Austriaci*. Naples: Nicolò Naso.

Goudar, A. (1769). *Naples. Ce qu'il faut faire pour rendre ce Royaume florissant, où l'on traite des avantages que le gouvernement peut retenir de la fertilité et de l'abondance de ses denrées, des facilités pour perfectionner les arts, de sa position favorable pour s'emparer des premières branches du commerce étranger*. Amsterdam: s.n.

Grimaldi, C. (1725). *Discussioni istoriche, teologiche, e filosofiche di Costantino Grimaldi fatte per occasione della risposta alle lettere apologetiche di Benedetto Aletino*. Lucca: s.n.

Grimaldi, G. [2001]. Considerazioni intorno al Commercio del Regno di Napoli. *Frontiera d'Europa*, VII, pp. 319–358.

Intieri, B. (1703). *Bartholomaei Intieri Florentini Aditus ad nova arcana geometrica detegenda editus ad Ill. et Ex. Dom. D. Hieronymum Onerum Cabanilium S. Marci marchionem*. Beneventi: Typ. Archiepiscopali.

Intieri, B. (1704). *Apollonius ac Serenus promotus, auctore Barrtholomaeo Intieri florentino ad illustrissimum et excellentissimum Dom. D. Hieronymum Onerum Cabanilium e comitibus Troiae et Montellae*. Naples: Sellitto.

Intieri, B. (1706). *Facilissimo metodo per la quadratura delle parabole di qualsivoglia grado, colla risposta alla questione proposta dal Sig. G. C. all'illustrissimo S. D. Serafino Biscardi patritio cosentino, reggente del Supremo Collateral Consiglio di Napoli*. Naples: s.n.

Intieri, B. (1716). *Nuova invenzione di fabbricar mulini a vento*. Naples: Mosca.

Intieri, B. (1754). *Della perfetta conservazione del grano. Discorso di Bartolomeo Intieri*. Naples: Giuseppe Raimondi.

Law, J. (1705). *Money and Trade Considered with a Proposal for Supplying the Nation with Money*. Edinburgh: Anderson.

Le Clerc, J. (1716). Article II. La Vita civile di Paolo Mattia Doria, distinta in tre Parti aggiuntovi un Trattato, della Educazione del Principe. Seconda Edizione, dall'Autore ricorretta ed accresciuta. *Bibliothèque ancienne et moderne pour servir de suite aux Bibliothèques universelle et choisie*, Tome V, Partie Prémiere, pp. 54–125.

Lunetti, V. (1621). *Espedienti a beneficio del Regno di Napoli, Real Patrimonio, d'intorno alle monete scarse, e cambio alto*. Naples: Tarquinio Prisco.

Lunetti, V. (1630). *Politica mercantile di Vettorio Lunetti. Dell'espedienti et arbitrij per publica utilità. Nelli quali con vere raggioni si mostrano le cause delli danni della città e regno di Napoli et il vero modo di rimediarli. Possono servire anche per dove fussi simili danni e si lascia per brevità li discorsi d'adornamenti e solo si accenna le materie delli grand'utili et incredibili avanzi per Sua Maestà e ben publico. E per trattarsi di servitio publico e di Sua Maestà non si deve disprezzare le proposte, se prima non s'intenda le raggioni*. Naples: Lazzaro Scorriggio.

Mandeville, B. de. (1714). *The Fable of the Bees: or, Private Vices, Publick Benefits*. London: Roberts.

Marzucco, G. (1757). *Riflessioni intorno alla quadratura del cerchio e delle curve*. Naples: Azzolino.

Melon, J-F. (1736). *Essai politique sur le commerce. Nouvelle édition. Cette édition est augmentée de sept chapitres et les lacunes des éditions précédentes y sont remplies*, s.l. s.n.

Muratori, L. A. [1750a]. "De moneta, sive jure condendi nummos. Dissertatio", in Argelati, F. (ed.) *De monetis Italiae variorum illustrium virorum Dissertationes, quarum nunc primum in lucem prodit*, IV Vol. Milan: Regia Curia, pp. 1–98.

Muratori, L. A. [1750b]. "De diversis pecuniae generibus, quae apud veteres in usu fuere. Dissertatio", in Argelati, F. (ed.) *De monetis Italiae variorum illustrium virorum Dissertationes, quarum nunc primum in lucem prodit,* IV Vol. Milan: Regia Curia, pp. 99–135.

Musschenbroek, P. van. [1745]. *Elementa physicae conscripta in usus accademicos*, edited by Giuseppe Orlandi and Antonio Genovesi, Naples: Benedetto Gessari.

Newton, I. (1687) [1729]. *Philosophiæ Naturalis Principia Mathematica*, London: Streater. English Translation: *The Mathematical Principles of Natural Philosophy*, translated by Andrew Motte, London: Benjamin Motte, 1729.

Origlia, G.G. (1754). *Istoria dello studio di Napoli*, vol. II. Naples: Simone.

Piccolomini, A. (1539). *Dialogo de la bella creanza de le donne*. Venice: Curtio Navò.

Plato. [2013]. *The Republic*. Translated by B. Jowett, Durham: Duke Classic.

Prammatiche. (1804). *Nuova collezione delle prammatiche del Regno di Napoli*, vol. VI. Naples: Stamperia Simoniana.

Serra, Antonio. (1613) [2011]. *Breve trattato delle cause che possono far abbondare li regni d'oro e d'argento dove non sono miniere, con applicazione al regno di Napoli diviso in tre parti.* Napoli: Lazzaro Scorriggio. English Translation: *A "Short Treatise" on the Wealth and Poverty of Nations*, Edited and with an Introduction by Sophus A. Reinert. Translated by Jonathan Hunt London – New York, Anthem Press, 2011.

Severino, M. A. (1653). *Therapeuta Neapolitanus.* Naples: Molli.

'sGravesande, W. J. (1723). *Philosophiae Newtonianae Institutiones, in usus academicos.* Leiden: Lugduni Batavorum.

Swift, J. (1704). *A Tale of a Tub: Written for the Universal Improvement of Mankind.* London: John Nutt.

Tanucci, B. (1980a). *Epistolario*, vol. I (1723–1746), R.P. Coppini, L. Del Bianco, Nieri, R. (eds). Rome: Edizioni di Storia e Letteratura.

Tapia, C. (1638). *Trattato dell'abbondanza, composto dal regente Carlo di Tapia, marchese di Belmonte, nel quale si mostrano le cause, dalle quali procede il mancamento delle vittovaglie et i rimedij che a ciascuna si possono dare; acciò non succeda, o succeduto non si senta, il danno di esso.* Naples: Roberto Mollo.

Turbolo, G.D. (1616). *Discorso della differenza et inegualità delle Monete del Regno di Napoli, con l'altre monete di Potentati convicini, e della causa della penuria di esse. Con l'espediente per lo aggiustamento e abbundanza sì delle monete di Regno come di forastiere. Per beneficio publico.* Naples: Tarquinio Longo.

Valignani, F. [2001]. Riflessioni sopra il Commercio del Regno di Napoli. *Frontiera d'Europa, società economia istituzioni diritto del Mezzogiorno d'Italia*, VII (2001), nn. 1–2, pp. 229–280.

Valletta, G. [1975]. Istoria filosofica. in G. Valletta, *Opere filosofiche*, edited by M. Rack, Florence: Olscki, pp. 221–386.

Vico, E. (1555). *Discorsi di Enea Vico Parmigiano sopra le medaglie degli antichi.* Venice: De Ferrari.

Vico, G.B. (1703) [1992] *Principum neapolitanorum coniurationis anni MDCCI historia*, published posthumously as *La congiura dei principi napoletani*, edited by C. Pandolfi, Naples: Morano, 1992.

Vico, G.B. (1709) [1990]. *De nostri temporis studiorumratione. Dissertatio a Joh. Baptista Vico.* Naples: Mosca. English Traslation *On the Study Methods of Our Time*, translated by Elio Gianturco, with a translation of *The Academies and the Relation between Philosophy and Eloquence (1737)* by Donald Phillip Verene, Ithaca: Cornell University Press, 1990.

Vico, G.B. (1710) [1988]. *De antiquissima Italorumsapientia ex linguae latinae origini bus eruenda. LibriTres*, Naples: Mosca. English translation *On the Most Ancient Wisdom of the Italians Unearthed from the Origins of the Latin*

Language, including *The Disputation with "The Giornale de' Letterati d'Italia"*, translated by L.M. Palmer, Ithaca: Cornell University Press, 1988.

Vico, G.B. (1725) [2002]. *The First New Science*, translated and edited by L. Pompa. Cambridge: Cambridge University Press.

Vico, G.B. (1728) [1975]. Vita di Giambattista Vico scritta da se medesimo. In *Raccolta di opuscoli scientifici e filologici*, edited by A. Calogerà, Venice: Cristoforo Zane, pp. 147–256. English translation *The Autobiography of Giambattista Vico, translated from the Italian by Max Harold Fisch and T. Goddard Bergin*. Ithaca: Cornell University Press, 1975.

Vico, G.B. (1744) [1948]. *Principi di Scienza Nuova d'intorno alla Comune Natura delle Nazioni, in questa terza impressione. Dal medesimo Autore in un gran numero di luoghi corretta, schiarita, e notabilmente accresciuta*. Naples: Stamperia Muziana. English translation *The New Science of Giambattista Vico*, by T. Goddard Bergin, Ithaca: Cornell University Press, 1948.

Vico, G.B. [1992]. *Epistole, con aggiunte le epistole dei suoi corrispondenti, a cura di Manuela Sanna, Prima Parte, 1693–1728*. Naples: Morano.

Voltaire [Arouet, F. M.]. 1738a. "Lettre a M. Thiriot sur l'ouvrage de M. Melon et sur celui de M. Dutot", in *Oeuvres Completes de Voltaire, v.1*, Paris, Dupont, 1824, pp. 157–175.

Voltaire [Arouet, F. M.]. (1738b). *Élémens de la philosophie de Newton*. London: s.n.

Secondary Sources

Ademollo, A. (1880). La famiglia e l'eredità dell'abate Galiani. *Nuova Antologia di Scienze, Lettere e Arti*, Volume LIII, Fascicolo XX, pp. 639–667.

Agrimi, M. (1992). Vico e la tradizione platonica. La filosofia dell'Umanità e la Storia Universale delle Nazioni. *Bollettino Del Centro di Studi Vichiani*, 22, pp. 65–102.

Ajello, R. (1969). Il Banco di San Carlo: organi di governo e opinione pubblica nel Regno di Napoli di fronte al problema della ricompera dei diritti fiscali. *Rivista Storica Italiana*, anno LXXXI (1969), fascicolo IV, pp. 812–881.

Ajello, R. (1972). La vita politica napoletana sotto Carlo di Borbone. In *Storia di Napoli*, vol. VII, Naples: Società editrice della Storia di Napoli, pp. 459–717.

Ajello, R. (1975). Pietro Giannone fra libertini e illuministi, *Rivista Storica Italiana*, LXXXVII, fasc. I, pp. 104–131.

Ajello, R. (1976a). La critica del regime in Doria, Intieri, Broggia. In R. Ajello (ed.) *Arcana juris. Diritto e politica nel. Settecento italiano*, Naples: Jovane, pp. 391–419.

Ajello, R. (1977). Carlo di Borbone. *Dizionario Biografico degli Italiani* - Volume 20, Rome: Treccani, *ad vocem*.

Ajello, R. (1978). Nota introduttiva alle opere di Carlo Antonio Broggia. In R. Ajello, (ed.) *La letteratura italiana. Storia e testi. Dal Muratori al Cesarotti*.

Politici ed economisti del primo Settecento, vol. 44, tomo V. Milan-Naples: Ricciardi, 1978, pp. 971–1032.

Ajello, R. (1980). Cartesianesimo e cultura oltremontana al tempo dell'*Istoria civile*. In R. Ajello (ed.), *Pietro Giannone e il suo tempo. Atti del Convegno di studi nel tricentenario della nascita*. Naples: Jovane, pp. 3–181.

Ajello, R. (1981). Introduzione. In P.L. Rovito, *Respublica dei togati. Giuristi e società nella Napoli del Seicento*. Naples: Jovane.

Ajello, R. (1985). Gli afrancesados a Napoli nella prima metà del Settecento. Idee e progetti di sviluppo. In M. Di Pinto (ed.), *I Borbone di Napoli e i Borbone di Spagna. Un bilancio storiografico*, vol. I. Naples: Guida, pp. 115–192.

Ajello, R. (1994). *Il problema storico del Mezzogiorno. L'anomalia socio-istituzionale dal Cinquecento al Settecento*. Naples: Jovene.

Ajello, R. (1996). *Una società anomala: il programma e la sconfitta della nobiltà napoletana in due memoriali cinquecenteschi*. Naples: ESI.

Ajello, R. (2001). Carlo di Borbone, Re delle Due Sicilie. In I. Ascione, (ed.), *Carlo di Borbone. Lettere Ai Sovrani di Spagna*, vol. I, 1720–1734. Rome: Ministero per i beni e le attività culturali, pp. 13–64.

Alatri, P. (1989). *L'Europa delle successioni (1731–1748)*. Palermo: Sellerio.

Allocati, A. (1955). Il Supremo Magistrato del Commercio del Regno di Napoli (1739–1806). *Studi economici*, anno X, 1955, n. 1–2, pp. 114–121.

Amabile, L. (1892). *Il Santo Officio della Inquisizione in Napoli*. Città di Castello: Lapi.

Amodeo, F. (1924). *Vita matematica napoletana*. Naples: Giannini.

Amodio, P. (1997a). *Il disincanto della ragione e l'assolutezza del bonheur: studio sull'abate Galiani*, Naples: Guida.

Amodio, P. (1997b). La diffusione del pensiero di John Locke a Napoli nell'età di Vico, contributo critico-bibliografico. *Atti dell'Accademia di Scienze Morali e Politiche*, CVII, pp. 183–194.

Ascione, I. (1994). *Il governo della prassi. L'esperienza ministeriale di Francesco D'Andrea*. Naples: Jovene.

Astarita, T. (1992). *The Continuity of Feudal Power: The Caracciolo Di Brienza in Spanish Naples*. Cambridge: Cambridge University Press.

Badaloni, N. (1984). *Introduzione a Vico*. Bari: Laterza.

Belgioioso, G. (1981). Introduzione. In G. Belgioioso (ed.), *Manoscritti napoletani di Paolo Mattia Doria*, vol. I. Galatina: Congedo, pp. 3–47.

Belgioioso, G. (1992). *Cultura a Napoli e cartesianesimo*. Galatina: Congedo.

Belgioioso, G. (1999). *La variata immagine di Descartes. Gli itinerari della metafisica tra Parigi e Napoli (1690–1733)*. Lecce: Milella.

Belgioioso, G. (2005). Images of Descartes in Italy. In T. M. Schmaltz (ed.), *Receptions of Descartes. Cartesianism and anti-Cartesianism in early modern Europe*. New York: Routledge, pp. 171–196.

Belgioioso, G. (2012). Paolo Mattia Doria. In *Il Contributo italiano alla storia del Pensiero: Filosofia,* Rome: Treccani, *ad vocem.*

Beniscelli, A. (2012a). *Libertini italiani.* Milan: Rizzoli.

Beniscelli, A. (2012b). Il funambolo e la dama. Dall'epistolario dell'abate Galiani e madame d'Épinay. In *Lumi inquieti: amicizie, passioni, viaggi di letterati nel Settecento.* Turin: Accademia University Press, pp. 85–100.

Bertelli, S. (1980). *Il libertinismo italiano.* Milan-Naples: Ricciardi.

Bevilacqua, P. (1982). Agricoltura e storia delle campagne nel Mezzogiorno d'Italia. *Studi Storici,* Jul.–Sep., 1982, Anno 23, No. 3, pp. 671–682.

Bianchi, L. (1979). Libertinismo e ateismo nel Seicento, *Studi Storici,* Anno 20, No. 4 (Oct.–Dec., 1979), pp. 881–886.

Bianchi, L. (1984). Il libertinismo in Italia nel XVII secolo: Aspetti e problemi. *Studi Storici,* Anno 25, No. 3 (Jul.–Sep., 1984), pp. 659–677.

Bianchini, L. (1839). *Storia delle finanze del Regno di Napoli.* Palermo: Lao.

Bizzocchi, R. (2008). *Cicisbei. Morale privata e identità nazionale in Italia.* Bari: Laterza.

Bloch, M. (1954). *Esquisse d'une histoire monétaire de l'Europe* (Cahiers des annales, N° 9). Paris: Colin.

Borghero, C. (1996). L'Italia in Bayle, Bayle in Italia: una ricerca mancata. In L. Bianchi (ed.) *Pierre Bayle e l'Italia.* Naples: Liguori, pp. 3–33.

Bouzinac, J. (1906). *Jean-François Melon, économiste.* Toulouse: Imprimerie Ouvrière.

Brown, A. (1998). Homeric Talents and the Ethics of Exchange. *The Journal of Hellenic Studies,* Vol. 118, pp. 165–172.

Bulgarelli Lukacs, A. (2004). *Alla ricerca del contribuente. Fisco, catasto, gruppi di potere, ceti emergenti nel Regno di Napoli nel XVIII secolo.* Naples: Edizioni Scientifiche Italiane.

Calabria, A. (1991). *The cost of empire: the finances of the Kingdom of Naples in the time of Spanish rule.* Cambridge: Cambridge University Press.

Caracciolo, A, Merola, A. (eds.). (1963). Introduzione. Galiani, F. *Della moneta e scritti inediti,* Milan: Feltrinelli.

Caridi, G. (2006). *Essere re e non essere re. Carlo di Borbone a Napoli e le attese deluse (1734–1738).* Soveria Mannelli: Rubbettino.

Caridi, G. (2011). Una riforma borbonica bloccata: il Supremo Magistrato di Commercio nel Regno di Napoli (1739–1746). *Mediterranea. Ricerche storiche,* 21, pp. 89–124.

Caridi, G. (2012). *La modernizzazione incompiuta nel Mezzogiorno borbonico (1738–1746).* Soveria Mannelli: Rubbettino.

Caridi, G. (2014). *Carlo III. Un grande re riformatore a Napoli e in Spagna,* Rome: Salerno Editrice.

Carpanetto, D., Ricuperati, G. (1987). *Italy in the Age of Reason: 1685–1789,* London - New York: Longman.

Carpanetto, D., Ricuperati, G. (1993). *L'Italia del Settecento. Crisi, trasformazioni, lumi*, Bari: Laterza.
Carrafiello, T. (1995). Berardo Galiani intendente di architettura (1724–1774). *Archivio Storico per le Province Napoletane*, Anno CXIII, pp. 245–379.
Carrafiello, T. (1998). Berardo Galiani. In *Dizionario Biografico degli Italiani* - Volume 51, Rome: Treccani, *ad vocem*.
Casini, P. (1983a). Newton in Italia, 1700–1740: note di ricerca. In P. Casini (ed.), *Newton e la coscienza europea*, Bologna 1983, pp. 173–227.
Casini, P. (1983b). Questioni sul newtonianesimo nel Settecento, in P. Rossi, (ed.), *Il Newtonianesimo nel Settecento*, Rome: Treccani, pp. 167–178.
Cataldo, V. (2020). *Napoli e le sue provincie durante il Viceregno austriaco (1707–1734)*. Soveria Mannelli: Rubbettino.
Catucci, M. (1986). *Galianea. Ferdinando Galiani tra letteratura ed economia*, Rome: Bulzoni.
Cesarano, F. (1990). Law and Galiani on money and monetary system. *History of Political Economy*, vol. 22, n. 2, pp. 321–340.
Chiosi, E. (1986a). Il Regno dal 1734 al 1799. In G. Galasso, R. Romeo (eds.), *Storia del Mezzogiorno*, Napoli: Edizioni del Sole, Vol. IV, pp. 384–396.
Chiosi, E. (2005). Istituzioni accademiche a Napoli nel Settecento: continuità e mutamenti. In J. Boutier, B. Marin, A. Romano, (eds.), *Naples, Rome, Florence. Une histoire comparée des milieux intellectuels italiens (XVII–XVIIIe siècles)*. Rome: Publications de l'École française de Rome, pp. 105–122.
Chorley, P. (1965). *Oil, Silk and Enlightenment. Economic Problems in XVIII Century Naples*. Naples: Istituto Italiano di Studi Storici.
Ciccolella, D., Guenzi, A. (2008). Scambi e gestione del rischio sui mercati locali e regionali. il contratto alla voce nel Mezzogiorno in Età Moderna. *Storia economica*, Anno XI, n. 1, pp. 41–79.
Cohen, B. I. (1971). *Introduction to Isaac Newton's Principia*. Harvard: Harvard University Press.
Colapietra, R. (1961). *Vita pubblica e classi politiche nel Viceregno napoletano (1656–1734)*. Rome: Storia e Letteratura.
Comparato, V. I. (1970). *Giuseppe Valletta. Un intellettuale napoletano della fine del Seicento*. Naples: Istituto Italiano Studi Storici.
Comparato, V. I.(1974). *Uffici e società a Napoli. Aspetti dell'ideologia del magistrato in età moderna*. Florence: Olschk.
Comparato, V. I. (2011). Platonismo e antidispotismo in Paolo Mattia Doria. In Canmpos Boralevi, L. (ed.), *Challenging Centralism. Decentramento e autonomie nel pensiero politico europeo,* Florece, Firenze University Press, pp. 99–110.
Coniglio, G. (1981). *I Borboni di Napoli*. Milan: dall'Oglio.
Conti, V. (1975). Paolo Mattia Doria e l'accademia di Medinacoeli. *Il Pensiero Politico*, 8 [2], pp. 203–218.

Conti, V. (1978). *Paolo Mattia Doria: Dalla Repubblica dei togati alla Repubblica dei notabili*. Florence: Olschki.

Conti, V. (1981). Le polemiche matematiche di P.M. Doria (con alcune lettere sconosciute). *Bollettino del Centro di Studi Vichiani*, 11, pp. 185–198.

Costa, G. (1976). Vico's Political Thought in His Time and Ours, *Social Research*, Vol. 43, No. 3, *Vico and Contemporary Thought*, pp. 612–624.

Costa, G. (2009). Celestini e inquisitori: Galiani, la Bibbia e la cultura napoletana. *Annali della Scuola Normale Superiore di Pisa. Classe di Lettere e Filosofia*, 2009, Serie 5, Vol. 1, No. 2, pp. 593–620.

Costa, G. (2011). *Celestino Galiani e la Sacra Scrittura: Alle radici del pensiero napoletano del Settecento*. Rome: Aracne.

Costelloe, T. M. (1999). The Concept of a State of Nature in Vico's New Science. *History of Philosophy Quarterly*, Vol. 16, No. 3, pp. 321–339.

Croce, B. (1903). I manoscritti dell'abate Galiani. *La Critica. Rivista di Letteratura, Storia e Filosofia*, Vol. 1, pp. 236–240.

Croce, B. (1913). *The philosophy of Giambattista Vico*, Translated by R. G. Collingwood. New York: Macmillan Company.

Croce, B. (1925b) [1970]. *Storia del Regno di Napoli*, Bari: Laterza. English translation *History of the Kingdom of Naples*. Chicago: Chicago University Press, 1970.

Croce, B. (1923) [2006]. Il paradiso abitato da diavoli. Conference read to the Neapolitan Society of Homeland History on 12 June 1923. In B. Croce (ed.), *Il paradiso abitato da diavoli*, Milan: Adelphi, 2006, pp. 11–21.

De Caro, G. (1971). Giovanni Brancaccio. In *Dizionario Biografico degli Italiani*, Vol. 13, *ad vocem*.

De Giovanni, B. (1958). *Filosofia e diritto in F. d'Andrea: contributo alla storia del previchismo*. Milan: Giuffrè.

De Giovanni, B. (1968). Cultura e vita civile in Giuseppe Valletta. In E. Sestan (ed.), *Saggi e ricerche sul Settecento*. Naples: Istituto Italiano per gli Studi Storici, pp. 1–47.

De Giovanni, B. (1970). La vita intellettuale a Napoli fra la metà del '600 e la restaurazione del Regno. In *Storia di Napoli*, vol. 6. *Tra Spagna e Austria*. Naples: Società Editrice Storia di Napoli, pp. 401–534.

Dell'Erba, L. (1932–1935) [1986]. *La riforma monetaria angioina e il suo sviluppo storico nel Reame di Napoli*, Sala Bolognese: Forni, 1986. First publication in *Archivio storico per le province napoletane*, Nuova Serie, anno XVIII–LVII, fascicolo I–IV, pp. 156–206; anno XIX–LVIII, fascicolo I–IV, pp. 5–66; anno XX–LIX, fascicolo I–IV, pp. 39–136; anno XXI–LX, fascicolo I–IV, pp. 46–158.

De Majo, S. (1998). Ferdinando Galiani. In *Dizionario Biografico degli Italiani*, volume 51, Rome: Treccani, *ad vocem*.

De Miranda, G. (2005). À de vagues desseins l'homme est toujours en proie. L'accademia degli Oziosi e i suoi antagonisti tra riti fondativi e costruzione

d'identità. In J. Boutier, B. Marin, A. Romano (eds.), Naples, Rome, Florence. Une histoire comparée des milieux intellectuels italiens (XVII–XVIII e siècles). Rome: Publications de l'École française de Rome, pp. 89–104.
De Rosa, L. (1987). *Il Mezzogiorno spagnolo tra crescita e decadenza*. Milan: Il Saggiatore.
De Scisciolo, N. (1997). Presenza lockiana a Napoli tra fine Seicento e inizio Settecento: dagli Investiganti alle eredità genovesiane. *Studi filosofici*, XX, pp. 73–111.
De Tiberiis G. F. (2001). Le riflessioni sopra il commercio di Federico Valignani. Alle origini del pensiero riformatore nel Regno di Napoli. *Frontiera d'Europa*, VII (2001), nn. 1–2, pp. 165–228.
Diaz, F. (1975a). Introduzione. In Galiani, F. *Opere*, edited by F. Diaz, L.Guerci, *Letteratura italiana. Storia e testi. Illuministi italiani*, tomo VI, Milan-Naples: Ricciardi, pp. ix–cvi.
Di Donato, F. (1989). La Segreteria del Regno e Niccolò Fragianni. *Archivio Storico per le Province Napoletane*, CVII, pp. 247–307.
Di Rienzo, E. (1977). Niccolò Fraggianni. In *Dizionario Biografico degli Italiani*, Vol. 49, *ad vocem*.
Di Rienzo, E. (1998). Celestino Galiani. In *Dizionario Biografico degli Italiani*, Vol. 51, *ad vocem*.
Di Vittorio, A. (1969). *Gli Austriaci e il Regno di Napoli. I. Le finanze pubbliche*. Naples: Giannini.
Di Vittorio, A. (1973). *Gli Austriaci e il Regno di Napoli. II. Ideologia e politica di sviluppo*. Naples: Giannini.
Di Vittorio, A. (2010). Economia e finanza pubblica nel Mezzogiorno austriaco (1707–1734). In S. Russo, N. Guasti, (eds.), *Il Viceregno austriaco (1707–1734)*, Rome, Carocci, pp. 53–63.
Doria, G. (1984). *Viaggiatori stranieri a Napoli*. Naples: Guida.
Einzig, P. (1966). *Primitive Money. In its Ethnological, Historical and Economic Aspects*. Second Edition, Revised and Enlarged, London: Pergamon Press.
Favino, F. (2013). Giuseppe Orlandi. In *Dizionario Biografico degli Italiani*, vol. 79, Rome: Treccani, *ad vocem*.
Feingold, M. (2004). *The Newtonian Moment: Isaac Newton and the Making of Modem Culture*, Oxford: Oxford University Press.
Ferrone, V. (1995). *The Intellectual Roots of the Italian Enlightenment: Newtonian Science, Religion, and Politics in the Early Eighteenth Century*. Atlantic Highlands: Humanities Press.
Ferrone, V. (2012). *The politics of Enlightenment: Republicanism, constitutionalism, and the rights of man in Gaetano Filangieri*. London: Anthem Press.
Fiorelli, V. (2009). *I sentieri dell'inquisitore. Sant'Uffizio, periferie ecclesiastiche e disciplinamento devozionale (1615–1678)*. Naples: Guida.

Fish, M.F. (1953). The Academy of Investigators. In E. Ashworth Underwood (ed.), *Science, Medicine and History: Essays on the Evolution of Scientific Thought and Medical Practice, Written in Honour of Charles Singer.* Oxford: Oxford University Press, pp. 521–563.

Foucault, D. (2010). *Histoire du libertinage: des goliards au marquis de Sade*, Paris: Perrin.

Fubini Leuzzi, M. (2004). Bartolomeo Intieri. In *Dizionario biografico degli italiani*, vol. 62, Rome: Istituto dell'Enciclopedia Italiana, *ad vocem.*

Galasso, G. (1973). Introduction. In Paolo Mattia Doria, *Massime del governo spagnolo a Napoli* (editeb by V. Conti), Naples: Guida.

Galasso, G. (1976). Napoli nel viceregno spagnolo dal 1648 al 1696. In *Storia di Napoli*, volume VI. Naples: Società Editrice Storia di Napoli.

Galasso, G. (1982). *Napoli spagnola dopo Masaniello*, Florence: Sansoni.

Galasso, G. (1989a). Mito e storia di Galileo nel Mezzogiorno. In G. Galasso (ed.), *La filosofia in soccorso de' governi. La cultura napoletana del Settecento.* Naples: Guida, pp. 119–135.

Galasso, G. (1989b). Doria: il governo spagnolo a Napoli e i problemi del Regno, In G. Galasso, (ed.) *La filosofia in soccorso de' governi. La cultura napoletana del Settecento*, Naples: Guida, pp. 193–232.

Galasso, G. (1989c). Doria: cultura e filosofia delle riforme. In G. Galasso, (ed.), *La filosofia in soccorso de' governi. La cultura napoletana del Settecento.* Naples: Guida, pp. 233–256.

Galasso, G. (1992). *Economia e società nella Calabria del Cinquecento.* Naples: Guida.

Galasso, G. (2003). *Napoli capitale. Identità politica e identità cittadina. Studi e ricerche 1266–1860.* Naples: Electa.

Galasso, G. (2007). *Storia del Regno di Napoli.* Vol. IV. *Il Mezzogiorno borbonico e napoleonico* (1734–1815). Turin: Utet.

Gallo, F. F. (2018). *La congiura di Macchia. Cultura e conflitto politico a Napoli nel primo Settecento.* Rome: Viella.

Garin, E. (1970). Per una storia dei rapporti fra Bayle e l'Italia. In E. Garin (ed.), *Dal Rinascimento all'Illuminismo. Studi e ricerche*, Pisa: Nistri-Lischi, pp. 157–172.

Garin, E. (2008). *History of Italian Philosophy*, vol. I, edited by G. Pinton, Amsterdam-New York: Rodopi.

Gentilcore, D. (2013). Tempi sì calamitosi: Epidemic Disease and Public Health. In T. Astarita, (ed.), *A Companion to Early Modern Naples.* Leiden-Boston: Brill, pp. 281–306.

Gernet, L. (1968). *Anthropologie de la Grèce Antique.* Paris: Masper.

Giansiracusa, L. (1988). La giustificazione storica del corpuscolarismo nella Istoria Filosofica di Giuseppe Valletta. *Rivista di Storia della Filosofia*, Vol. 43, No. 1, pp. 181–191.

Giarrizzo, G. (1981). *Vico, la politica e la storia*, Naples: Guida.

Giliberti, L. (1921). *Sul Catasto Onciario e l'Oncia di Carlini e di Grana*. Naples: Tipografia Cimmaruta.

Girard, P. (2011). Matérialisme et politique. Les enjeux de la réception du cartésianisme à Naples à l'âge classique. *Corpus, revue de philosophie*, 61, pp. 113–132.

Girard, P. (2017). L'émergence des Lumières à Naples entre matérialisme et radicalité. *Archives de Philosophie*, Vol. 80, No. 3, *L'invention de la modernité à Naples*, pp. 417–434.

Giura, V. (1978). *Gli ebrei e la ripresa economica del Regno di Napoli 1740–1747*. Genève: Droz.

Goetsch, J. R. (1995a). *Vico's Axioms. The Geometry of the Human World*. New Haven: Yale University Press.

Gonnard, R. (1935). *Histoire des doctrines monétaire dans ses rapports avec l'histoire des monnaies*. Paris: Librairie du Recueil Sirey.

Granito, A. (1861). *Storia della congiura del principe di Macchia e dell'occupazione fatta dalle armi austriache del Regno di Napoli nel 1707*. Naples: Stamperia dell'Iride.

Gregory, T. (1981). Il libertinismo della prima metà del Seicento: stato attuale degli studi e prospettive di ricerca. In T. Gregory, G. Paganini, G. Canziani, O. Pompeo Faracovi, D. Pastine (eds.), *Ricerche su letteratura libertina e letteratura clandestina nel Seicento*. Florence: La Nuova Italia, pp. 3–47.

Gualtieri, G. A. (2019). La concezione della scienza nella filosofia di Giambattista Vico. *I castelli di Yale. Quaderni di Filosofia*, VII, 2019, 1–2, pp. 125–170.

Guerci, L. (1972). Aspetti e problemi dell'epistolario di Ferdinando Galiani. *Rivista Storica Italiana*, 84, pp. 80–110.

Harsin, P. (1928). *Les doctrine monétaires et financières en France du XVIe au XVIIIe siécle*. Paris: Alcan.

Hirschman, A. O. (1977). *The Passions and the Interests: Political Arguments for Capitalism before its Triumph*, Princeton: Princeton University Press.

Imbruglia, G. (2019). Bernardo Tanucci. In *Dizionario Biografico degli Italiani* - Volume 93, Rome: Treccani, *ad vocem*.

Intorcia, G. (1987). *Magistrature del Regno di Napoli. Analisi prosopografica. Secoli XVI–XVII*. Naple: Jovene.

Inventario. (2023). *Inventario Manoscritti Galiani – Società Napoletana di Storia Patria*, available on line http://www.storiapatrianapoli.it/getFile.php?id=276.

Iovine, R. (1999). Il trattato Della moneta di Ferdinando Galiani. La dialettica politica a favore e contro la pubblicazione. *Frontiera d'Europa*, 1999, n. 1, pp. 173–236.

Iovine, R. (2001). Una cattedra per Genovesi nella crisi della cultyura moderna a Napoli. *Frontiera d'Europa*, 2001, n. 1–2, pp. 359–532.

Iovine, R. (2009). Celestino Galiani, Bartolomeo Intieri, Alessandro Rinuccini: difficoltà di sviluppo dell'ideologia economica nelle Sicilie (1700–1750) In

A. Alimento (ed.), *Modelli d'oltre confine: prospettive economiche e sociali negli antichi stati italiani*. Rome: Edizioni Storia e Letteratura, pp. 67–87.
Israel, J. I. (2001). *Radical Enlightenment: Philosophy and the Making of Modernity 1650–1750*. Oxford: Oxford University Press.
Labellarte, A. (2019). *Atomismo e corpuscolarismo nella Napoli di fine Seicento*, Rome: Armando Editore.
Lachterman, D. R. (1980). Vico, Doria e la geometria sintetica. *Bollettino del Centro di Studi Vichiani*, X, pp. 10–35.
Lauro, A. (1974). *Il giurisdizionalismo pregiannoniano nel Regno di Napoli. Problema e bibliografia (1563–1723)*. Rome: Edizioni di Storia e Letteratura.
Lepre, A. (1963). *Contadini, borghesi ed operai nel tramonto del feudalesimo napoletano*. Milan: Feltrinelli.
Lepre, A. (1981). La crisi del XVII secolo nel Mezzogiorno d'Italia. *Studi Storici*, Jan.–Mar., 1981, Anno 22, No. 1, pp. 51–77.
Lepre, A. (1986a). *Storia del Mezzogiorno d'Italia*, Vol. I. *La lunga durata e la crisi (1500–1656)*, Naples: Liguori.
Lepre, A. (1986b). *Storia del Mezzogiorno d'Italia*, Vol. II. *Dall'Antico Regime alla società borghese (1657–1860)*, Naples: Liguori.
Lilla, M. (1993). *G.B. Vico: The Making of an Anti-Modern*. Cambridge, Mass.: Harvard University Press.
Lissa, A. 2020. In difesa degli ebrei: Pietro Contegna (1679–1745) e Celestino Galiani (1681–1753). Due intellettuali non conformisti nel Regno di Napoli e delle due Sicilie. *Materia Giudaica*, 2020, XXV, pp. 469–480.
Lojacono, E. (2003). *Immagini di René Descartes nella cultura napoletana (1644–1755)*. Lecce: Conte.
Macry, P. (1972). Ceto mercantile e azienda agricola nel Regno di Napoli: il contratto alla voce. *Quaderni Storici*, Vol. 7, No. 21 (3), *Agricoltura - Proprietà – Mercati*, pp. 851–909.
Mafrici, M. (1998). *Il re delle speranze. Carlo di Borbone da Madrid a Napoli*, Naples: Edizioni Scientifiche Italiane Comparato 1970.
Mantelli, R. (1986). *Il pubblico impiego nell'economia del Regno di Napoli*. Naples: Istituto Italiano per gli Studi Filosofici.
Marcialis, M. T. (1996). Il Cogito e la coscienza. letture cartesiane nella Napoli settecentesca. *Rivista di Storia della Filosofia*, Vol. 51, No. 3 (1996), pp. 581–612.
Marino, J. A. (1982). Economic Idylls and Pastoral Realities: The Trickster Economy in the Kingdom of Naples. *Comparative Studies in Society and History*, Vol. 24, No. 2, pp. 211–234.
Marino, J. A. (1988). *Pastoral Economics in the Kingdom of Naples*. Baltimore: Johns Hopkins University Press.

Marino, J. A. (2007). The Rural World in Italy under Spanish Rule. In Dandelet, T. J., Marino, J. A. (eds.), *Spain in Italy. Politics, Society, and Religion 1500–1700*, Leiden: Brill, pp. 405–432.

Marshall, D. L. (2011). The Current State of Vico Scholarship. *Journal of the History of Ideas*, Vol. 72, No. 1, pp. 141–160.

Mastellone, S. (1963). Il libertinismo erudito a Napoli nella seconda metà del seicento. *Critica Storica*, Anno II, n. 6, pp. 451–463.

Mastellone, S. (1965). *Pensiero politico e vita culturale a Napoli nella seconda metà del Seicento*. Florence: D'Anna.

Mastellone, S. (1969). *Francesco d'Andrea politico e giurista (1648–1698): l'ascesa del ceto civile*. Florence: Olschki.

Mauro, A. (2017a). *Un philosophe des Lumières entre Naples et Paris: Ferdinando Galiani (1728–1787)*. Thèse de Doctorate de l'Université Toulouse le Mirail - Toulouse II.

Mazzola, R. (1998a). Religione e Provvidenza in Vico. *Bollettino del Centro di Studi Vichiani*, Anno XXVI–XXVII, pp. 101–126.

Mazzola, R. (1998b). Università e società a Napoli tra Sei e Settecento. *Bollettino del Centro di Studi Vichiani*, anno XXVIII, pp. 227–238.

Mazzotti, M. (2013). Il newtonianesimo e la scienza del Settecento. In *Il Contributo italiano alla storia del Pensiero – Scienze*. Roma: Istituto dell'Enciclopedia Treccani.

McMullin E., Pompa, L. (1976). Vico's Theory of Science. *Social Research*, Vol. 43, No. 3, *Vico and Contemporary Thought*, pp. 450–483.

Morandi, C. (1939). Partiti politici a Napoli durante la Guerra di Successione spagnola. *Rivista storica italiana*, serie V, vol. IV, pp. 557–571.

Morrison, J. C. (1978). Vico's Principle of Verum is Factum and the Problem of Historicism. *Journal of the History of Ideas*, Vol. 39, No. 4, pp. 579–595.

Musi, A. (1986). Tra burocrati e notabili. Potere e istituzioni nella Napoli del Seicento. *Bollettino del Centro di Studi Vichiani*, Anno XVI, pp. 157–176.

Musi, A. (1991). *Mezzogiorno spagnolo: la via napoletana allo stato moderno*. Naples: Guida Editori.

Musi, A. (2002). *La rivolta di Masaniello nella scena politica barocca*. Naples: Guida.

Musi, A. (2007a). Politica e cultura a Napoli tra il crepuscolo del sistema imperiale spagnolo e l'avvento degli Asburgo d'Austria (1698–1707). In A. Álvarez-Ossorio Alvariño, B.J. García García, V. León Sanz, (eds.). *La pérdida de Europa. La guerra de Sucesión por la Monarquía de España*. Madrid: EFCA pp. 785–797.

Musi, A. (2013). *L'impero dei viceré*, Bologna: Il Mulino.

Muto, G. (2013). "Urban Structures and Population", in T. Astarita, (ed.), *A Companion to Early Modern Naples*. Leiden-Boston: Brill, pp. 35–62.

Naddeo, B.A. (2011). *Vico and Naples: the urban origins of modern social theory*. Ithaca: Cornell University.

Natale, M. (2002a). Ecletticismo teoretico e pragmatismo, alle origini delle riforme illuministiche. L'autobiografia di Celestino Galiani. *Frontiera d'Europa* (2002/1), pp. 115–219.

Natale, M. (2002b). Notazioni integrative: continuità degli orientamenti empiristici da Francesco d'Andrea a Celestino Galiani. *Frontiera d'Europa* (2002/2), pp. 5–78.

Nicolet-Pierre, H. (2002). *Numismatique grecque*. Paris: Colin.

Nicolini, F. (1908a). I manoscritti di Ferdinando Galiani, *Archivio storico per le province napoletane*, 33 (1908), pp. 171–197.

Nicolini, F. (1908b). Intorno a Ferdinando Galiani a proposito di una pubblicazione recente. *Giornale Storico della letteratura italiana*, Volume LII, pp. 1–55.

Nicolini, F. (1918a). La famiglia dell'abate Galiani, *Archivio Storico Italiano*, Vol. 76, No. 3/4 (291/292), pp. 136–157.

Nicolini, F. (1918b). La puerizia e l'adolescenza dell'abate Galiani (1735–1745). Notize, lettere, versi, documenti, *Archivio Storico per le Province Napoletane*, Nuova serie Anno IV, XLIII. dell'intera collezione, Vol. IV, pp. 105–132.

Nicolini, F. (1931) *Monsignor Celestino Galiani. Saggio biografico*. Naples: Società Napoletana di Storia Patria.

Nicolini, F. (1951). *Un grande educatore italiano. Celestino Galiani*, Naples: Giannini.

Nicolini, F., Venturi, F. (1956). Inedito dell'abate Galiani. *Giornale Storico della letteratura italiana*, LXXIII, 1956, pp. 67–73.

Nuzzo, E. (1984). *Verso la "Vita civile": antropologia e politica nelle lezioni accademiche di Gregorio Caloprese e Paolo Mattia Doria*, Naples: Guida.

Osbat, L. (1971). *L'inquisizione a Napoli. Il processo agli ateisti*. Rome: Edizioni Storia e Letteratura.

Pagden, A. (1988). The Destruction of Trust and its Economic Consequences in the Case of Eighteenth-century Naples. In D. Gambetta, (ed.), *Trust: Making and Breaking Cooperative Relations*. Oxford: Basil Blackwell, pp. 127–141.

Palladino, F. (1988). La formazione scientifico-matematica di Celestino Galiani. *Bollettino del Centro di Studi Vichiani*, Anno XXVII–XXVII, pp. 253–262.

Papuli, G. (ed.) (1985). *P.M. Doria fra rinnovamento e tradizione*. Galatina: Congedo.

Parinetto, L. (1974). *Magia e ragione. Una polemica sulle streghe in Italia intorno al 1750*. Florence: La Nuova Italia.

Pascal, C. (1885). *Sulla vita e sulle opera di Ferdinando Galiani*. Naples: Morano.

Peacock, M. S. (2011). The Political Economy of Homeric Society and the Origins of Money. *Contributions to Political Economy*, 30, pp. 47–65.

Perkinson, H. J. (1976). Vico and the Methods of Study of Our Time. *Social Research*, Vol. 43, No. 4, *Vico and Contemporary Thought*, pp. 753–767.

Perna. M. L. (1984). Nota critica. In A. Genovesi, *Scritti economici*. Naples: Istituto Italiano per gli Studi Filosofici, pp. 1269–1279.

Pesante, M. L. (2000). Il commercio nella repubblica, *Quaderni storici*, Nuova Serie, Vol. 35, No. 105 (3), *Etiche economiche*, pp. 655–695.

Pii, E. (1972). Bayle e la cultura napoletana intorno al 1750. *Il Pensiero Politico*, 5[3], pp. 509–516.

Pilati, R. (2001). Del commercio: Gregorio Grimaldi e il riformismo napoletano nella prima età borbonica. *Frontiera d'Europa*, VII, nn. 1–2, pp. 281–318.

Placanica, A. (1982). *Moneta prestiti usure nel Mezzogiorno moderno*. Naples: Società Editrice Napoletana.

Porta, P. L. (2012). Ferdinando Galiani. *Il Contributo Italiano alla Storia del Pensiero. Economia*. Rome: Treccani, pp. 352–357.

Quazza, G. (1971). Rifeudalizzazione e ceto civile. In G. Quazza, *La decadenza italiana nella storia europea. Saggi sul Sei-Settecento*. Turin: Einaudi, pp. 63–85.

Racioppi, G. (1871). *Antonio Genovesi*. Naples: Morano.

Rack, M. (1973). Note napoletane. I processi del 1688–1697. *Giornale critico della filosofia italiana*, pp. 52–82.

Rao, A. M. (1983). *Il Regno di Napoli nel Settecento*. Naples: Guida.

Rao, A. M. (1989). Il riformismo borbonico a Napoli. In G. Cherubini, F. Della Peruta, E. Lepore, M. Mazza, G. Mori, G. Procacci, R. Villari (eds.), *Storia della società italiana*. Milan: Teti, pp. 218–230.

Rao, A. M. (1997). *L 'amaro delia feudalità. La devoluzione di Anione e la questione feudale a Napoli alla fine del '700*. Naples: Luciano.

Rao, A. M. (2005). Fra amministrazione e politica. Gli ambienti intellettuali napoletani. In J. Boutier, B. Marin, A. Romano (eds.), *Naples, Rome, Florence. Une histoire comparée des milieux intellectuels italiens (XVII–XVIII e siècles)*. Rome: Publications de l'École française de Rome, pp. 35–88.

Rao, A.M. (2009). L'apprendistato di un re: Carlo di Borbone a Napoli. In G. Fragnito (ed.), *Elisabetta Farnese principessa di Parma e regina di Spagna*. Rome: Viella, pp. 317–333.

Ricca-Salerno, G. (1896). *Storia delle dottrine finanziarie in Italia. Seconda edizione intieramente rifatta*. Palermo: Reber.

Ricuperati, G. (1969). Alessandro Riccardi e le richieste del ceto civile all'Austria nel 1707. *Rivista storica italiana,* anno LXXXI (1969), fascicolo IV, pp. 745–777.

Ricuperati, G. (1970). *L'esperienza civile e religiosa di Pietro Giannone*. Milan-Naples: Ricciardi

Ricuperati, G. (1972). Napoli e i viceré austriaci (1707–1734). In *Storia di Napoli*, volume VII, Naples: Società Editrice Storia di Napoli, pp. 349–457.

Ricuperati, G. (1979). A proposito di P.M. Doria. *Rivista Storica Italiana*, 91, pp. 261–285.

Ricuperati, G. (2001). *La città terrena di Pietro Giannone: un itinerario tra crisi della coscienza europea e illuminismo radicale*. Florence: Olschki.

Ridgeway, W. (1887). The Homeric Talent, Its Origin, Value, and Affinities. *The Journal of Hellenic Studies*, Vol. 8, pp. 133–158.

Riley P. (2001). Rousseau, Fénelon, and the Quarrel between the Ancients and the Moderns. In *The Cambridge Companion to Rousseau*. Cambridge: Cambridge University Press, pp. 2001: 78–93.

Robertson, J. (2005). *The Case for the Enlightenment. Scotland and Naples 1680–1760*. Cambridge: Cambridge University Press.

Robertson, J. (2013). Sacred history and political thought: Neapolitan responses to the problem of sociability after Hobbes. *The Historical Journal*, Vol. 56, No. 1, pp. 1–29.

Romano, R. (1946). La situazione finanziaria del Regno di Napoli attraverso il bilancio generate dell'anno 1734. *Archivio Storico per le Province Napoletane*, nuova serie, anno XXX, pp. 161–168.

Romano, R. (1948). Un tentativo di stipulazione di trattato commerciale tra Napoli e Venezia nel 1739. *Studi Economici ed Aziendali*, Anno III, pp. 1–16.

Romano, R. (1951). *Le commerce du Royaume de Naples avec la France et les pays de l'Adriatique an XVIII siécle*. Paris: Armand Colin.

Romano, R. (1968). *Prezzi, salari e servizi a Napoli nel secolo XVIII (1734–1806)*. Milan: Banca Commerciale Italiana.

Romano, R. (1976). *Dal Viceregno al Regno. Storia Economica*. Turin: Einaudi.

Romeo, G. (1976). Per la Storia del Sant'Ufficio a Napoli tra '500 e '600. Documenti e problem. *Campania Sacra*, VII, pp. 5–109.

Rossi, R. (2010). Il mercato laniero nel Regno di Napoli durante il Viceregno austriaco. Persistenze e mutamenti. In S. Russo, N. Guasti (eds.), *Il Viceregno austriaco (1707–1734)*. Rome, Carocci, pp. 137–153.

Rotta, S. (1978). Introduzione a Paolo Mattia Doria. In R. Ajello, M. Berengo (eds.) *Politici ed economisti del primo settecento, dal Muratori al Cesarotti, La letteratura Italiana, Storia e testi*, vol. 5, Naples-Milan: Ricciardi, pp. 837–870.

Rovito, P. L. (1981). *La Respublica dei togati. Giuristi e società nella Napoli del Seicento.*Naples: Jovene.

Rovito, P. L. (1987). Funzioni pubbliche e capitalismo signorile nel feudo napoletano del Seicento. *Bollettino del Centro di Studi Vichiani*, Anno XVI, pp. 95–156.

Rovito, P. L. (2003). *Il viceregno spagnolo di Napoli*. Naples: Arte Tipografica.

Russo, S., Guasti, N. (eds.). (2010). *Il Viceregno austriaco (1707–1734)*. Rome: Carocci.

Salinari, G. (1972). Appiano Buonafede. In *Dizionario Biografico degli Italiani*, Volume 15, Rome: Treccani, *ad vocem*.

Salvati, C. (1962). L'azienda e le altre Segreterie di Stato durante il primo periodo borbonico (1734–1806). *Quaderni della Rassegna degli Archivi di Stato*, 14, pp. 1–62.

Scazzieri, R. 2011. Paolo Mattia Doria. In *Il Contributo Italiano alla Storia del Pensiero. Economia*. Rome: Treccani, pp. 326–331.

Schipa, M. (1899). Il Regno di Napoli descritto nel 1713 da P. M. Doria. *Archivio Storico per le Province Napoletane*, 1899, Anno XXIV, fascicolo I, IV, pp. 25–84; 329–350.

Schipa, M. (1904). *Il Regno di Napoli al tempo di Carlo di Borbone*. Naples: Pierro.

Schumpeter, J. A. (1954) [2006]. *History of Economic Analysis*. London: Routledge.

Setaro, P. (2021). Una città in fermento. Gli intellettuali napoletani e il ruolo del viceré Francisco de Benavides, IX conte di Santisteban (1688–1696), *Pedralbes*, 41, pp. 255–298.

Spagnoletti, A. (1997). *Storia del Regno delle Due Sicilie*, Bologna: il Mulino.

Stapelbroek, K. (2008a). *Love, Self-Deceit and Money. Commerce and Morality in the Early Neapolitan Enlightenment*. Toronto: University of Toronto Press.

Stapelbroek, K. (2020). *Commercio, passioni e mercato. Napoli nell'Europa del Settecento*, Milan: Franco Angeli.

Steinke, H. (2022). Religion, Marriage, and Burial in Vico's Scienza nuova: A Reappraisal. *Laboratorio dell'ISPF* (Istituto per la storia del pensiero filosofico e scientifico moderno), XIX, n. 8, 2022.

Stone, H. S. (1997). *Vico's Cultural History. The Production and Transmission of Ideas in Naples 1685–1750*. New York: Brill.

Strazzullo, F. (1997). *Il marchese di Squillace. Leopoldo de Gregorio ministro di Carlo di Borbone*. Naples: Liguori.

Torrini, M. (1981). L'accademia degli Investiganti. Napoli 1663–1670. *Quaderni storici*, Vol. 16, No. 48 (3), *Accademie scientifiche del 600; Professioni borghesi*, pp. 845–883.

Trombetta, V. (2002). *Storia e cultura delle biblioteche napoletane*. Naples: Vivarium.

Valerio, V. (2013). Representation and Self-Perception: Plans and Views of Naples in the Early Modern Period. In T. Astarita (ed.), *A Companion to Early Modern Naples*. Leiden-Boston: Brill, pp. 63–88.

Vaughan, F. (1972). *The Political Philosophy of Giambattista Vico an Introduction to La Scienza Nuova*. The Hague: Martinus Nijhoff.

Velde, F. (2012). The Life and Times of Nicolas Dutot. *Journal of the History of Economic Thought*, Vol. 34, 1, pp. 67–107.

Venturi F. (1959a). Alle origini dell'Illuminismo napoletano. Dal carteggio di Bartolomeo Intieri. *Rivista Storica Italiana*, a. LXXI, fascicolo III, pp. 416–456.

Venturi, F. (1959b). Was ist Aufklärung? Sapere aude. *Rivista Storica Italiana*, a. LXXI, fascicolo II, pp. 119–128.

Venturi, F. (1971a). *Utopia and Reform in the Enlightenment*, Cambridge: Cambridge University Press.

Venturi, F. (1998). *Settecento riformatore. Da Muratori a Beccaria*, Turin: Einaudi.

Vidal, E. (1953). *Il pensiero civile di P.M. Doria negli scritti inediti: con il testo del manoscritto Del Commercio del Regno di Napoli*. Milan: Giuffrè.
Villani, P. (1977). *Mezzogiorno tra riforme e rivoluzione*. Bari: Laterza.
Villari, R. (1961). *Mezzogiorno e contadini nell'età moderna*, Bari: Laterza.
Villari, R. (2012). *Un sogno di libertà. Napoli nel declino di un impero. 1585–1648*. Milan: Mondadori.
Viviani Della Robbia, E. (1942). *Bernardo Tanucci e il suo più importante carteggio*. Florence: Sansoni.
Zambelli, P. (1972). *La formazione filosofica di Antonio Genovesi*, Naples: Morano.
Zambelli, P. (1973). Il rogo postumo di Paolo Mattia Doria. In *Ricerche sulla cultura dell'Italia moderna*, Bari: Laterza, pp. 149–198.
Zambelli, P. (1977). Prime iniziative di un Cappellano Maggiore. Una lettera inedita di Celestino Galiani. *Bollettino del Centro di Studi Vichiani,* Anno VII, pp. 113–121.
Zambelli, P. (1985). Letture vichiane e illuministiche del Segretario del Regno Niccolò Fraggianni. *Bollettino del Centro di Studi Vichiani*, Anno XIV–XV (1984–5), pp. 215–227.
Zilli, I. (1990). *Carlo di Borbone e la rinascita del Regno di Napoli. Le finanze pubbliche (1734–1742)*. Naples: ESI.
Zoli, S. (1989). *Europa libertina tra Controriforma e Illuminismo: l'Oriente dei libertini e le origini dell'illuminismo: studi e ricerche*. Bologna: Capelli.

CHAPTER 3

Towards *Della Moneta* (1743–1750)

3.1 Monetary Troubles in the Kingdom of Naples

It would not be possible to fully understand the treatise that the young Galiani published anonymously in Naples, in the autumn of 1751, without collocating it in the debate that took place in Italy from the early 1740s on the complex issues of monetary policy. The growing attention to the problems of money circulation was one of the elements by which the political and social backwardness of Italian States was measured in comparison to the choices made in more advanced countries, stimulating the formulation of economic reform projects. This renewed interest had its origins in the Italian tradition outlined by Gasparo Scaruffi (1519–1584) and Bernardo Davanzati (1529–1606) at the end of the sixteenth century, and which had continued throughout the seventeenth century, finding its most mature developments in Naples, given the situation of serious disorder in monetary circulation.

Despite the high level and intensity of the debate on monetary issues evident in the seventeenth-century Italian literature, the Italian States in the mid-eighteenth century had not yet completed, and in some cases, as in the Kingdom of Naples, had not even begun, reforms aimed at

R. Patalano, *Ferdinando Galiani*,
https://doi.org/10.1007/978-3-032-02793-1_3

monetary stabilization, imitating the path followed by Spain and England, and later by France.[1]

It was in fact Spain, in the last phase of the Habsburg monarchy, that initiated the process of monetary stabilization: in 1686, billon coins were withdrawn from circulation, *Silver Real* was devalued by 20%, but only for internal circulation, to prevent its export from the kingdom, without altering the silver coin in the colonial empire (*Real de a Ocho*, *Piece of Eight*, also known as the *Spanish Dollar*) and a double minting system was adopted, following the Dutch example (Vilar 1991).[2]

A decade later, a similar reform, known as the *Great Recoinage* of 1696, was implemented in England, demonetising the debased coinage and issuing the new full-weight currency (called *Guinea*). This choice, followed by deflationist effects, laid the foundations of the modern monetary system based on the gold standard (Vilar 1991: 211).[3] The stabilization process in France followed an extremely tortuous path, passing through the controversial experience of Law's *Système* (1716–1720), ending with the reforms of 1726. Again, a drastic deflationary policy was adopted, by increasing the value of the *Silver Mark* (Vilar 1991: ch. XXVI).

[1] The term *stabilization*, coined in the late nineteenth century by theorists advocating bimetallism (Schumpeter 1954 [2006]: 1042), entered the economic vocabulary after the monetary crises of the 1920s (among which the most serious was German hyperinflation). It was intended to denote the set of deflationary policies aimed at stabilizing the purchasing power of money (ensuring price stability) and encouraging a return to the monetary equilibrium of the gold standard system (albeit in the new form of the gold exchange standard). The term has passed into historiography to refer to the policies that were adopted from the last decade of the seventeenth century with the aim of remedying the disturbances in the circulation of money (Vilar 1991: chapters 25 and 27).

[2] Dutch monetary reform of early seventeenth-century introduced the distinction between a circulating currency, destined to internal exchanges, the level of which depended on the state, and a stable, international money used in international transactions and big business (Vilar 1991: chap. XXII). In Spain, Charles's reform introduced the distinction between *Plata Nueva* and *Plata Vieja*. On the structure of monetary systems in the eighteenth century, see Muldrew (2019).

[3] This reform was supported by John Locke and contrasted by William Lowndes, Secretary to the Treasury, who proposed a considerable money devaluation (Locke 1692, 1695, 1696a, 1696b; Lowndes 1695). Isaac Newton, as Master of the Mint, executed the reform, making a mistake in the valuation of bimetallic ratio that established a *de facto* gold standard in England (on debate on the *Great Recoinage* see Fay 1932; Horsefield 1960; Vilar 1991: chap. XXXIII; Kelly 1991; Chown 1996: chap. 6; Sargent and Velde 2002: 261–299; Kleer 2004; Davies 2002: 245–248). For a survey of the eighteenth century ethical, political and cultural debate on money, see Wennerlind (2019); Codr (2019); Carey (2019).

The common feature of all these reforms is the restoration of the intrinsic value of money, following the approach of the Scholastic tradition, according to which the intrinsic value of money is intangible because its alteration seriously invalidates its function as a medium of exchange, weakening the social consensus on monetary value.[4] This approach was adopted by natural law theorists, especially John Locke, and re-proposed as an epistemological framework for monetary policies.

This movement towards monetary stabilization, beyond its ideological and political justifications, was a consequence of increasing commercial competition between the great powers. The necessary condition for participation in the great commercial game is, in fact, that money, used in a certain space of sovereignty, must be valued as closely as possible to its intrinsic value or its "real parity". This presupposes that the purchasing power of coinage is as close as possible to market value of the specific amount of precious metal it contains (gold or silver). In this context, the main responsibility of government is to maintain the value of money as far as possible unchanged in terms of the intrinsic metal, avoiding direct and indirect manipulation.[5] This stability assures the use of national currency in international transactions, because it is exchanged as a commodity, according to its intrinsic value. Gold and silver play the role of international money, while national coinages are no more than local manifestations of the universal purchasing power of precious metals.

In the Italian States the problem of stabilization played a crucial role in the reform policies of the eighteenth century. The heritage of the previous century was particularly severe in the former Spanish domains, like the Kingdom of Naples and the Duchy of Milan.

In the Kingdom of Naples, during Spanish rule (1503–1707), monetary policy was totally subordinated to the fiscal needs of the *Monarchia Universalis*, which was engaged in continuous wars with the Ottoman

[4] The argument against inflation was put forward by St. Thomas Aquinas, Jean Buridan and other Scholastic authors (School of Paris), but only Nicholas Oresme clearly defined various aspects of the problem in a treatise, the first systematic essay on money (*De mutanione monetarum ac varioatione facta per reges* written in 1355, the first of the printed editions appearing in 1484, Oresme 1484 [1956]). See Brants (1895); Bridrey (1906); Souffrin and Segonds (1988); Gillard (1990); Langholm (1992); Nederman (2000); Hülsmann (2008). Later these arguments were taken up by the School of Salamanca (Luis Saravia de la Calle, Martín Azpilcueta, Tomás de Mercado).

[5] Stabilization is also made possible by introducing significant technical innovations in the minting process (see Caden 2019: 25–52).

Empire and the emerging national sovereignties (the Kingdom of France and the Dutch Republic, above all). In this context, the monetary history of the Kingdom of Naples under Spanish domination can be summarized as follows (Serra 1613; Turbolo 1616, 1629; Vergara 1715; Bianchini 1839: 254–266; Dell'Erba 1932–1935 [1986]; De Rosa 1955; Romano 1970):[6]

a. Gold coin (*Ducato* and *Scudo*)[7] was generally stable, but its role in domestic monetary circulation was marginal, while, in contrast, its high value was appreciated abroad.[8] The Spanish authorities preferred not to devalue gold money during the financial crisis, in order to maintain their uniformity in standard and to promote their use as an international currency (gold *Ducats* had not been minted since 1649). This policy defended the interests of *rentiers* at the expense of the merchant class, more inclined to devaluation measures. For its high intrinsic value and undervalued legal tender, Neapolitan gold coins "escaped" from the Kingdom as soon as they were minted. The outflow of gold was increased by tributes owed to Spain and to the Church and trade deficits.
b. The situation of silver coins (*Carlino*, see Fig. 3.1) was quite different, marked by significant fluctuations in value. Silver currency was devalued during crises (between 1503 and 1621 the *Carlino* was devalued by 31% in weight) and then drastically revalued (the *Carlino* was revalued in 1622 by 19% in weight), causing severe deflationist effects. Exchange rate movements reflected these fluctuations (De Rosa 1955: 372–378) and the Spanish government's attempt to maintain monetary stability was nullified by a very poor

[6] From the end of the fifteenth century, the Neapolitan monetary system was founded on the equivalence *1 Ducato (Ducat) = 5 Tarì = 10 Carlini (Carlins)= 100 Grana (Grains)= 1200 Cavalli*.

[7] The *Ducato* was the standard of the Neapolitan monetary system and was also used as the money of account.

[8] *Neapolitan Scudo*, particularly valued for its high intrinsic value, was included in the so-called *Scudo delle Cinque Stampe*, with other prized gold coins (namely the *Scudo of Venice, Milan, Genoa*, and *Castile*), these currencies (regarded *de facto* as international currencies) were convertible into the *Scudo di Marco*, unit of account used in the Genovese exchange fairs (Lyon and Bisenzone) between the sixteenth and seventeenth centuries; see Boyer-Xambeu et al. (1986: 73).

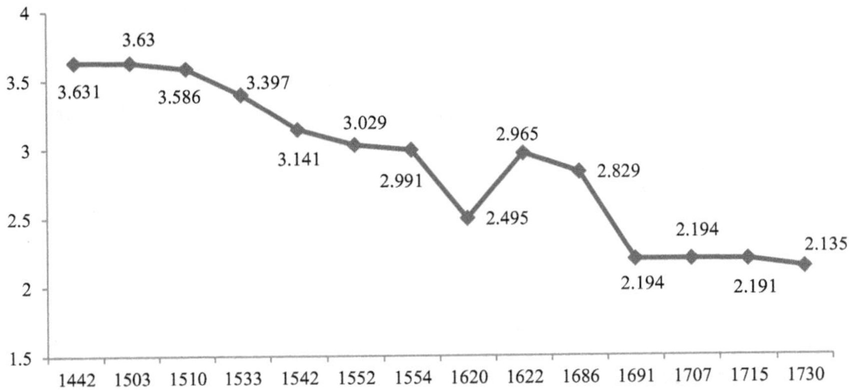

Fig. 3.1 Weight in grams of the silver coin (*Carlino*) (1442–1730). Source: Dell'Erba (1932–1935 [1986]); Muto (1986: 180)

intrinsic standard of the currency in circulation (the clipped coins called *mala moneta*).[9]

c. Copper money (*Cavallo, Tornese*, see Fig. 3.2) suffered severe pressures: it was devalued in weight and was undoubtedly the money most affected by falsifications (billon coins were never minted during the Spanish domination). The people suffered the consequences of these devaluations, responding with violent riots. The quality of copper currency was the main problem of the Neapolitan monetary system.[10]

[9] Several times during Spanish domination the Government ordered that money was to be valued by its weight and not by its legal value. The bad silver money was called *Zannetta*, the *Half Carlino* minted in 1583 by the Viceroy Juan de Zúñiga, with a weight (1.381 grams) that did not correspond to its multiple the *Carlino* (which was 2.991 grams and half should therefore have been about 1.495 grams), which led to some confusion in the already chaotic Neapolitan monetary circulation. These coins then suffered continuous clipping, so much so that their intrinsic value was so greatly devalued that they merited the title of *mala moneta*, reduced as they were to a quarter of their original value. In 1609, Viceroy Pimentel d'Errera wanted to impose the exchange of clipped coins, prohibiting their use in trade, a measure that greatly damaged Neapolitan public banks. The measure excluded *Zannette*, which could still be exchanged at nominal value. A few days later, the viceroy was forced by strong protests to admit all coins into circulation, using the emergency expedient of valuing them according to their intrinsic value (Dell'Erba 1932–1935 [1986]: 145).

[10] "The rise of copper production in central Europe from the end of the fifteenth century had already opened up prospects for a copper coinage. In the sixteenth century the issues of

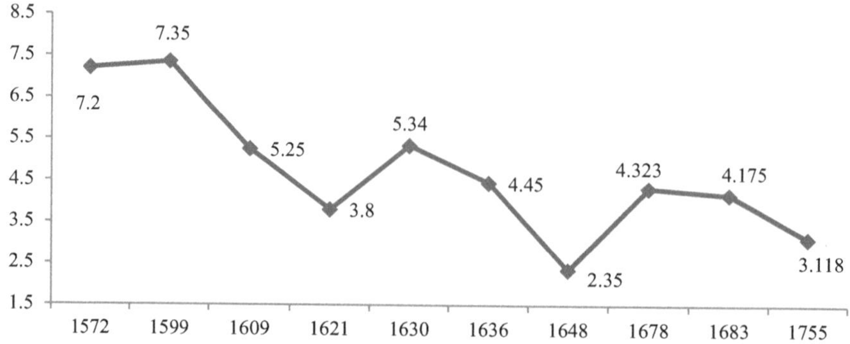

Fig. 3.2 Weight in grams of the copper coin (*Tornese*) (1572–1755). Source: Dell'Erba (1932–1935 [1986])

d. In order to combat debasement of coins and to increase the amount of currency in circulation, the Spanish Government authorized the circulation of deposit certificates (called *fedi di credito*) issued by the Neapolitan public banks and generally accepted as means of payment. The Neapolitan authorities supported the public banks and *de facto* transformed deposit certificates into legal tender, alleviating the scarcity of metallic money (De Rosa 2004; Costabile and Neal 2018).

The state of disorder in the monetary system of the Viceroyalty stimulated reflection on possible solutions.[11] Thus a copious literature emerged

copper money multiplied: in principle they still remained limited in extent and consisted only of small coin. The great need for money by the authorities during the wars of religion, and the vigorous expansion of copper production and copper supplies during the seventeenth century, removed all restraints. [...]. As a result of the gigantic increase in the issue of copper coins, the unit of account devalued so quickly and alarmingly that economic confidence was destroyed. This in turn psychologically prepared the population for demotion of the smaller coinage to a subsidiary currency and even to the status of token money" (Van Der Wee 1977: 298–299).

[11] The link between the development of monetary theory and crisis episodes was outlined by John Hicks: "Monetary theory is less abstract than most economic theory; it cannot avoid a relation to reality, which in other economic theory is sometimes missing. It belongs to monetary history, in a way that economic theory does not always belong to economic history. [...]. It is noticeable, on the one hand, that a large part of the best work on money is topical. It has been prompted by particular episodes, by particular experiences of the writer's own time.[...]. Sometimes what is sought is a general understanding; but with monetary

in Naples during the seventeenth century, which prepared the ground for the mature elaborations of the following century. The solutions proposed in an attempt to solve the serious problems of monetary circulation were diverse and often conflicting (Colapietra 1973; Muto 1986; De Rosa 1987, 1995; Rosselli 2000; Patalano and Reinert 2016; Velde 2020).

The seventeenth century opened on the need to impose political control of the exchange rate, a solution proposed by Marc'Antonio De Santis, a Neapolitan merchant advisor of the *Regia Camera della Sommaria*, then adopted between 1607 and 1609 by the Viceroy Count of Bonavente, without success (De Santis 1605a, 1605b; Serra 1613 [2011]). Against measures of administrative control and restrictive interventions on monetary outflows, Antonio Serra (imprisoned probably for debt motives and exponent of the economic interests of Genoese merchants and bankers, see Patalano and Reinert 2016: 2; Patalano 2016), whose work was destined by the depth of its analysis to influence the economic thinking of the Intierian circle and the young Galiani, proposed a policy of monetary stability, based on the preservation of the right proportion of value between different metals (Serra 1613 [2011]: 235).[12] In the same years, the philosopher Tommaso Campanella also intervened from prison to propose remedies against currency devaluation, a sign that monetary problems were taking on a central dimension as a factor in the economic and social crisis (Campanella 1608 [1973]: 84–110, see Costabile and Velde 2023). The debate between De Santis and Serra identified two positions that would confront each other in the following years, respectively that of the party of national merchants, in favour of regulatory measures and protectionism, and that of the Genovese party, representing the interests of foreign markets, which instead advocated substantially free-trade measures.

A few years later, urged on by the authorities, Fabrizio Biblia proposed a general reform of monetary circulation based on the withdrawal of debased currency to be replaced with revalued and intrinsically restored

theory it is more often a particular understanding, an understanding directed towards a particular problem, normally a problem of the time at which the work in question is written. So monetary theories arise out of monetary disturbances" (Hicks 1967: 156).

[12] "This man, whom I dare to compare to the French Melon and the English Locke, but who surpasses them both for having lived so long before and in a century of darkness and error in economic science; this man of discerning intellect, of sound judgment, was disrespected while he lived and remained after death forgotten, along with his book. No one ever quoted it, and perhaps the only copy that Bartolommeo Intieri possessed of it, and donated to me, was saved from oblivion" (Galiani 1780: 410).

coinage (Biblia 1621).[13] This reform proposal was accepted by Viceroy Cardinal Antonio Zapata, but caused a drastic deflation (De Rosa 1994: lvii–lviii). This measure was strongly contested by Giovanni Donato Turbolo, who argued, contrary to the policy adopted, that it was necessary to devalue the Neapolitan currency by adjusting it to the devaluation suffered by silver so as to favour exports from the Kingdom (Turbolo 1629).

The debate on monetary reforms waned in intensity in the following decades with the increasingly pressing needs imposed by the conflict in which the Spanish monarchy was engaged and as the reformist prospects came to an end following revolutionary events and devastating epidemics and natural disasters. The new political context is anticipated by the proposals expressed in *Politica Mercatile* by Vettorio Lunetti (1630), a government advisor on fiscal matters during the viceroyalty of the Duke of Medina (1637–1643), who partly took up the free-trade demands of the Genoese party and partly proposed drastic regulatory measures to mobilize local resources for the needs of war. Closer to the traditional vision of the Genoese party were the proposals formulated by Cornelio Spinola (1590–1652), consul in Naples of the Genoese nation almost continuously from 1617 to 1649 (Montacutelli 2018), who collected proposals from the most eminent personalities of the Kingdom, commenting on them with his own opinions (*Progetto di economie varie sopra tributi e imposizioni, imposte o da imporsi nel Regno di Napoli*, drafted probably between the spring of 1641 and the winter of 1642–43, see Galasso 1959: 39–44; Colapietra 1973: 64–79; Musi 2004; Montacutelli 2018).[14] Many of Spinola's opinions focus on the poor state of monetary circulation consisting of devalued copper and silver coins and the role of public banks in encouraging the circulation of bad money and promoting inflationary processes for the granting of easy credit (see Spinola, MS: folios 208, 260, 263). The deterioration of copper and silver coins continued in the years following the 1647 revolt, taking on dramatic characteristics. A possible solution was suggested by a Spanish physician Luis Enríquez de Fonseca (1620–1687), administrator and treasurer of the royal rents in Malaga and

[13] To avoid the practice of clipping coins to obtain precious metal, Biblia proposed minting coins composed of two concentric circles, one on the extreme side with the right face value and the inner one with half the face value but twice as much precious metal. The new coin was to circulate by weight (Biblia 1621: 6–7).

[14] *Plan of various economies on taxes and impositions, imposed or to be imposed in the Kingdom of Naples.* The bulky manuscript of 849 folios is kept in the National Library in Naples (XI.E.31).

later in Naples with administrative duties, who proposed reintroducing the billon coinage into the Kingdom, according to the Segovia method, no longer minted since the beginning of Spanish rule.[15] Being unfalsifiable, the billon valued by weight, according to Enríquez de Fonseca, had undoubted advantages over silver and copper and in order to facilitate its circulation, without incurring the high transport and transaction costs, he proposed the establishment of "authentic billon banks", with the task of issuing deposit certificates, following the example of the *fedi di credito* issued by public banks, whose function as guarantors of monetary circulation was praised by Enríquez de Fonseca (Enríquez de Fonseca 1681a [1973]; 1681b [1973]).

Despite all efforts, in the last decade of seventeenth century the monetary circulation in the Kingdom of Naples was in a poor state, as a result of Gresham's law: clipped and devalued silver and copper coins (the latter often counterfeited) circulated with fiduciary money, issued by Neapolitan public banks, and foreign coins of bad alloy.[16] In this period, Naples also lost the role of market of exchange, a sign of progressive marginalization in international trade.

During the reign of Charles II of Habsburg, an attempt to reform the Neapolitan monetary system, stimulated by Castilian reforms, was made by the Viceroy Marquis of Carpio (1683–1687) and his successor Count of Santisteban (1688–1696). For this purpose, in 1683, Viceroy Carpio established a Governmental Commission (called *Giunta per la fabbrica della moneta nuova, Council for the new coin fabrication*) designed to preside over the coining of new money (in the original weight and alloy) and

[15] Hammered coinage was used until the sixteenth century. In 1551, German technicians invented a process whereby metal was flattened in a hydraulic rolling mill with two parallel rollers, and then stamped by the same process. Hydraulic mills were introduced in Segovia in 1585.

[16] "The discomfort was increasing, and large quantities of completely counterfeit coins were also being introduced by local and foreign counterfeiters, and the people could no longer afford it, since they could not buy enough to eat with their coins in their hands, even if they paid inflated prices, and merchants refused to accept them, and even people became suspicious of accepting these coins, especially the tari, due to the large quantities of counterfeit or low silver circulating. Repeated laws of prohibitions and threats were to no effect, and in order to avoid conflict among citizens, experts had to be appointed to recognise good coins and have them accepted in the trade" (Dell'Erba 1932–1935 [1986]: 168). On the problem of small change, see Sargent and Velde (2002).

the withdrawing of clipped silver coins from circulation.[17] In November 1687, the money exchange operation was suspended due to the death of Carpio. His successor, Santisteban, blocked the issue of the new currency because the new coins were richer in silver than their nominal value, and if placed in circulation would immediately disappear either to be melted down or exported. It was therefore necessary to establish these coins on their correct market value, increasing the nominal value by 10% (Bianchini 1839: 264–265; Dell'Erba 1932–1935 [1986]: 172; De Rosa 1987: 212–246); three other devalued coins were then minted (with less metal content). In 1691, a further 20% raise in nominal value of all coins minted since 1683 had to be made in order to stop the outflow of money from the Kingdom, which had occurred as a result of another significant increase in the price of silver. To further stabilize the Neapolitan monetary system, the nominal value of the minted silver was adjusted to the commercial value of the raw metal, so as to avoid any speculation on Neapolitan money, and then other coins were minted, all with reduced weight (by 14.3%).This manoeuvre was intended to create the preconditions for the stabilization of the silver coinage, but another essential element for establishing total monetary stability was missing: in fact, no attention was paid to the copper coinage, which was further reduced in weight under the reigns of Charles II and Philip V, despite the fact that alteration had been curtailed with the introduction of new minting methods. The problem of copper coinage remained a heavy legacy for subsequent regimes.[18]

The monetary policy did not change under Austrian domination of Naples (1707–1735) and the Kingdom suffered from an intense shortage of metallic money. The possibility of a monetary reform was hindered by

[17] "The remedy against clipping, which could not be defeated even with the death penalty, was arduous, and the Viceroy called for consultation an assembly of persons suitable to give practical advice; there were many meetings and discussions [...] and finally the remedy against clipping was found, that is, to fix the contour of the coin with a design, instead of leaving it smooth, and by removing the design, not only was the clipping made evident, but the coin could be rejected. This simple step solved the problem completely and effectively, and had never before been conceived; perhaps the solution was made easy by the use of scales in minting" (Dell'Erba 1932–1935 [1986]: 169). The cost of the operation, around two million *Ducats*, was financed with the levying of new taxes and a loan underwritten by the public banks, well disposed to find employment opportunities in the rarefied Neapolitan economy.

[18] The *Grano*, a key copper coin, lost 15.1 % of its weight in the 1680 coinage compared to the 1630 coinage; in the 1701 coinage it lost a further 4 % of its weight compared to the 1680 coinage. The problem of the status and role of small change was common to all monetary systems, see Sargent and Velde (2002).

the limited availability of precious metals, as the price of silver had increased since the end of the sixteenth century. The Austrians therefore had great difficulty in minting coins, and if we exclude the minting of *Carlini* to be thrown to the people during the entry of the imperial troops into Naples, the first issue took place only in 1715, respecting the intrinsic value of the Spanish coins of 1691; however, the mint made no profit, given the high price of silver.

Fifteen years later the situation was still marked by a strong shortage of metallic currency and Viceroy Aloys von Harrach (1728–1733) started a new minting, this time reducing the weight of the silver coins (the *Carlino* was reduced by 2.5% compared to the last Spanish coinage), thus aligning them with the changed commercial value of silver. Nothing was done to improve the situation of the copper coin, because a new mintage would have entailed a further reduction in its weight, a measure difficult for the common people to accept. In the same way the minting of a new gold coin was avoided, because to be accepted in exchanges it had to at least be of equal value with the Spanish *Dobla* and would thus have been minted at a loss to the State. A new gold coinage would impose a strong revaluation in weight to guarantee its acceptability in international trade, a choice that would have caused a heavy loss in terms of seigniorage revenues.

At the end of Austrian domination, the monetary question in the Kingdom of Naples therefore still remained open, and while in other parts of Europe stabilization tendencies were already consolidated, in the Neapolitan area there were still only timid attempts.

Having regained its independence, under the rule of King Charles of Bourbon, the Kingdom of Naples required a monetary reform, not only to consolidate political power, but also to respond to the challenges imposed by increasing commercial competition and to avoid economic marginalization. The Neapolitan government began a monetary reform programme, appointing a specific committee, called *Deputazione delle Monete* (*Coinage Committee*),[19] to inquire into the monetary confusion created by the War of Austrian Succession and to introduce measures of monetary stabilization, already widely invoked.

At the beginning of his reign, coins, absolutely necessary to pay the troops, were made of Mexican silver brought from Spain. During the whole of 1734 five hundred thousand pieces of raw silver and one million

[19] This committee was an ancient institution, made up of 23 members, convened to test coins when the government ordered new coinage (see Galanti 1788: 364).

eight hundred thousand pieces of *Real de a Ocho*, to be melted down into new currency, flowed in from Madrid (Ajello 1972: 545–546). With these resources, in 1749 new gold (*Oncia, Doppia* and *Zecchino*) and silver coins (*Carlino*) were minted (Schipa 1904: 589–590; Giustiniani 1804: 364). The new gold coin was minted eighty years after the last gold minting to enhance the prestige of the new kingdom and, for the first time, the ancient unit of account, the *Gold Ounce*, established by the Normans, was actually minted.

One feature of the stabilization policy, namely the creation of strong currencies to be used mainly in international trade, was thus implemented in Naples. However, it was only one feature, which alone could certainly not complete a much more complex process.

The most serious mistakes were made in the area of silver coinage. While many Italian States, and most European ones, had reduced the weight of their coins, or worsened the alloy or made frequent increases, which were all manoeuvres carried out in relation to the changing price of silver, the Kingdom of Naples remained on the old value, heedless of the effects this would have on its monetary circulation. In fact, a gap was immediately created between foreign coins and Neapolitan currency, which took on the characteristic of a strong currency and was therefore particularly sought after. The outflow of coins from the Kingdom was also favoured by the fact that the gold/silver ratio was in those same years lower in Europe than that legally established in Naples.[20] Both of these trends worked against the stabilization of the Neapolitan currency.

A careful policy of balancing the value of the minted coin against the market value of the raw metal was the essential manoeuvre to keep the currency within its political space. Although one of the first acts in the area of currency government in the new Bourbon Kingdom was, in 1745, the alignment of Sicilian and Neapolitan currencies, which was the first step towards the constitution of a single monetary unit for the entire Kingdom, not much attention was paid to changes in the trading prices of precious metals, nor was an appropriate tariff policy adopted with regard to foreign currencies. The large quantity of silver coins minted at the beginning of Charles's reign, thanks to Spanish silver, did not immediately make the

[20] In Naples the bimetallic *gold/silver ratio* was 1:14.46 while on average in Hamburg in the years 1751–1760 the *gold/silver ratio* was 1:14.56. The *gold/silver ratio* was 1:14.67 for the northern Italian States (see Shaw 1896: 157–159; Messedaglia 1881: 75).

seriousness of the situation felt;[21] the problem would then explode at the end of the century with a new and more serious rarefaction of monetary circulation.

Coinage was very problematic as there was a disproportion of the intrinsic value compared to the nominal value between the *Zecchino* and the *Doppia*. Between 1749 and 1756, gold coins were minted with a face value of 2 (called *Neapolitan Uncia*), 4 and 6 *Ducats*, with the gold/silver ratio fixed 1 to 14½.[22] Neapolitan gold coins were subject to speculation, because their intrinsic value was too high compared to other foreign gold coins (Diodati 1790: 42; Dell'Erba 1932–1935 [1986]: 59). Consequently, at the end of eighteenth century, the Kingdom of Naples faced a gold shortage problem.[23]

Thus, a characteristic element of stabilization was missing in the Kingdom of Naples: the undervaluation of the currency intended for internal payments (generally silver), in order to avoid its exportation and to supply the circulation with sufficient means of payment.

Disastrous decisions were then made regarding copper coinage. At the advent of Charles, the circulation of *black coins* consisted of old eroded coins issued during the reigns of Charles II and Philip V and even those minted during the Masaniello uprising by the Duke of Guise, which were de facto *token money*, so reduced was their weight.[24] The copper coins had undergone continuous devaluation, to the detriment of the people who used them in small payments and to the advantage of the wealthy classes

[21] "The mass of silver coined in the first three years of the reign of King Charles of Bourbon, to which was added coins from as far back as Charles II of Spain and others from Sicily, was so great that the mint was left idle until the year 1747" (Dell'Erba 1932–1935 [1986]: 183). Also contributing to the situation was the influx of Brazilian gold, which for a time turned the ratio between the two metals to the advantage of silver.

[22] "A Spanish vessel arrived from Cadiz with 2 million Mexican ingots and also an English one" (Alessandro Rinuccini's letter to Francesco Maria Buondelmonti, Archivio Privato Corsini, Fondo Buondelmonti, Naples, 23 December 1753, publisched in Iovine 2001: 489). "Roman *Zecchini* flooded the city and the Kingdom. The government wisely deprived them of the quality of money and placed them among the goods be negotiated, like cloth and grain" (Alessandro Rinuccini's letter to Duke Filippo di Bartolomeo Corsini, Naples, 18 November 1748, Archivio Privato Corsini, Fondo Corsini, published in Iovine 2001: 489–490).

[23] By melting the Neapolitan silver and gold coins, a greater quantity of metal was obtained than that contained in the coins of other Italian States or France; there was therefore an incentive to seek them out, see Diodati (1790: 37–39).

[24] In average, the reduction compared to the legal weight was 2/3 (see L. Dell'Erba 1932–1935 [1986]: 303).

who could speculate on the premium the silver coin gained over the copper coin.

The problem of copper coinage was certainly discussed in the *Deputazione delle Monete*, which was established in 1749, but the destruction of the Neapolitan archives during the last war prevents us from reconstructing this exactly. However, the decision was taken in 1755 and a new copper coin was issued, with a further reduction in weight. Another essential element of stabilization was thus missing. The copper coin had to be accepted, enjoying the confidence of the people: this effect could only be achieved by a general exchange of the eroded currency and its replacement with coins that ensured stability and certainty, as was the case in other European States, but this choice was not made.

In the Kingdom of Naples, there was no interest in stabilizing the copper coinage, since the only consideration was the revenues of the mint, which could benefit greatly from the minting of devalued money. It is no surprise that the measure was not passed until 1755, when all reformist aspirations had been abandoned. The issue of these coins aroused great protest and in August 1757 the coinage, which had begun in May 1756, was suspended (see Galiani 1780: Note XIII, 391–392). Thus, the use of more advanced technical tools for minting and the indication of the face value on the effigy of the coins were seen as a *mere façade*. One only has to compare, without going too far, the monetary policy followed in Naples with the great reforms carried out in Piedmont and Austrian Lombardy to appreciate how far it was from the concrete experiences of stabilization (Vianello 1939: xix; Tucci 1986; Felloni 1998; Amato 1999: 97–139; Tiran 2014).

The Kingdom of Sardinia stabilized its currency, operating in the most drastic way possible, through an almost total recasting of the metallic circulating currency. The *General Coinage* of 1755 was implemented by minting one national coin for each monetary metal and two national coins, of different alloy, in billon. In this way, the Savoy's Kingdom had an internal reference system on which to base the valuation of circulating foreign noble coins, indeed, it was precisely through proper and efficient valuation that their importation into the Kingdom was stimulated.

The imperial government of Lombardy solved the serious problem of monetary disorder as part of the organic reform of the administration. By the stabilization measures adopted in the edict of 1778, the devalued copper coinage was withdrawn from circulation and replaced with new coins of greater weight, a renewed mint was opened in Milan to mint the new noble gold and silver coins, foreign coins were valued according to their intrinsic value. This reform was also drastic, unlike the compromising attitudes that marked the monetary policy implemented by the Neapolitan Bourbon regime. An unsuccessful attempt was also made to establish a monetary convention between Habsburg Lombardy and Savoy Piedmont (Venturi 1998: 469).

The Republic of Venice began the stabilization process in 1722 by reforming the silver coin, stabilizing its value in 1733, while the Republic of Genoa partially reordered the monetary system in 1759, completing the stabilization in 1792 (Cipolla 1975: 79–80; Amato 1999: 27–41).

This is therefore the background of the facts underlying the young Galiani's theoretical reflection.

3.2 The Neapolitan Precursors: Carlo Antonio Broggia and Trojano Spinelli

A work of genius is always a *garret* that rests on a solid edifice of experience, the bricks of which are laid by precursors that may or may not be recognised. In the *Avviso* (*Preface*) to the Second Edition of *Della Moneta*, Ferdinando Galiani acknowledged his debt to Carlo Antonio Broggia (1698–1767) and Trojano Spinelli (1712–1777), two writers of very different social origins, education and temperament, who had variously participated in the debate on monetary stabilization (Galiani 1780: *Avviso* [12–14]).

According to Galiani, Broggia was a "man of genius", "who was the first [in the Kingdom of Naples] to promote the study of a very useful and noble science [of money]", but "he wanted to be valued, to be then employed in government offices and to rise to better fortune. This ambition, encountering adverse circumstances, later led him to a tragic and pitiable end" (Galiani 1780: *Avviso* [12]).[25] Galiani recalled that while opposing Broggia in all his opinions, he chose "not to quote him, not to fight him, never to refute him; respecting in him a living author who had written with good intentions" (Galiani 1780: *Avviso* [13]).

Broggia belonged to a rich family of spice merchants of Venetian origin, working as an *aromatarius*, that is, a wholesale grocery trader. His rather

[25] "Only one person was able to observe the Neapolitan reality of those decisive years with freedom of judgement and independence of character, finding in himself enough courage to openly proclaim his ideas and publicly state his conclusions" (Venturi 1998: 89).

poor health and the daily difficulties of commercial practice did not prevent him from completing his intellectual formation which brought him into contact with Paolo Mattia Doria and Giambattista Vico, his two main intellectual reference points. A decisive influence also came from his frequent contacts with the intellectual circle gathered around Celestino Galiani and Bartolomeo Intieri, from which Broggia inherited the impulse to confront reality, avoiding closing himself off in sterile providentialism. It was through the mediation of Intieri that Broggia, most likely, knew Jean François Melon's treatise.[26]

These are, broadly speaking, the paths that led to Broggia's intellectual maturation and to the publication in 1743 of his main work: the *Trattato de' tributi, delle monete e del governo politico della sanità* (*Treatise on taxes, money, and the policy of public health*) (Broggia 1743), which is "the main economic treatise published in Italy before Galiani's *Della Moneta*" (Venturi 1998: 147).

Broggia's *Treatise* had the merit of awakening attention to monetary and fiscal policy among intellectuals and men of government: Ludovico Antonio Muratori took from Broggia most of his arguments on taxes and coins contained in *Della pubblica felicità*;[27] in Milan, the trade councillor

[26] Melon's *Essai*, also as a critical pole, was certainly an essential point of reference for Broggia, because through the French author, the Neapolitan merchant came into contact with Anglo-Saxon economic culture (William Petty first and then John Law) and especially with French economic culture (in particular Vauban's proposals for tax reform). See Ajello (1978: 1102). Broggia mainly contested Melon's pro-devaluation and pro-inflation views, and a specific unpublished treatise then dealt with contesting Melon's theses on luxury (Broggia [2004]). In a letter to Ludovico Antonio Muratori, Broggia described his relationship with Melon's *Essai*: "Many beautiful demonstrations you will have occasion to observe in this book. But consider the many erroneous and noxious things that are there, coloured and presented as good and necessary. The whole chapter on Luxury is especially filled with them. It seems to me that with all justice I attack this author in my treatise on money and I deem such a criticism worthy of reading" (Broggia's Letter to Muratori, Naples, 29 June 1745, published in Dal Pane 1958: 644).

[27] Particularly chapters XXII, XXIII and XXIV of *Della pubblica felicità* (Muratori 1749). Muratori observed: "Carl'Antonio Broggia, a Neapolitan merchant in one of his works printed in Naples in 1743, being a person of great intelligence and experience in public commerce, has wisely treated tributes better than those who handle digests and paragraphs, he makes known how to establish tributes, and how many disturbances can arise from personal tributes, and from others which impede trade and especially fall upon the farmers, artisans and other persons with their industry and toil, useful or necessary to the public" (Muratori 1749: 334) and he referred to "the useful treatise on money by the praised Carl'Antonio Broggia to which anyone who wishes to see this matter well discussed for the benefit of their

Giuseppe Forziati and Pompeo Neri had widely praised him, and even outside the Italian context, he was noticed and appreciated by the minister of the Palatine Elector, Giuseppe Fontanesi, with whom the Neapolitan merchant corresponded frequently.[28]

Broggia's aim is openly political, as evidenced by the dedication to the State Secretary Montealegre. Relations between Broggia and the powerful member of the Bourbon court must have been quite frequent, if the Neapolitan merchant even offered to act as a military adviser to the Bourbon minister, sending him, on the battlefield of Velletri, the treatise (which remained unpublished and preserved among the Broggia papers at the National Library of Naples) *Della Trinciera Mobbile* (*About the Mobile Trench*), accompanied by the wooden model of this war machine designed for the defense of the infantry (Broggia 1754: 11). Some time earlier, in 1742, Broggia presented to Montealegre one of his memoirs, today unfortunately lost, entitled *Il ristoro della Spagna, causato dalla Libertà, concessa alle Nazioni amiche, del Commercio d'America* (*The reinforcement of Spain, caused by the Freedom, granted to friendly nations, of American Commerce*, of which Broggia provides a summary in the *Memoria ad oggetto di varie politiche ed economiche ragioni* (*Memoire on various political and economic reasons*, see Broggia 1754) and the essay *Sulla Dogana* (*On Customs* unpublished kept in the National Library of Naples).

When Broggia published the *Treatise* he was convinced that his advice would be well received and would provide adequate guidance to illuminate the vast subject of taxes and money, "on which the legislator must decide with the utmost attention" (Broggia 1743: i). But despite all his efforts; Broggia remained on the margins of Neapolitan political life (Broggia 1754: xix; Patalano 2011, 2020a, 2020b).

country can turn" (Muratori 1749: 373). Broggia's correspondence with the Modenese historian is undoubtedly one of the most interesting events in his intellectual biography. The epistolary relationship probably began in February 1745, when Broggia sent Muratori a copy of his *Treatise*. The correspondence continued until July 1746 and the discussion focused on Melon's *Essai*, which the Neapolitan merchant had the merit of introducing to Muratori (he sent him a copy), and then on the problem of luxury and of ecclesiastical property, for which the Modenese historian recommended a certain moderation to the Neapolitan correspondent (Broggia 1978: 1100–1110, see Dal Pane 1958; Ajello 1978: 1102–1105: 1111–1124). On the relations between Muratori and Neapolitan intellectuals, see Schipa (1902).

[28] He had come into contact with Giuseppe Fontanesi in 1751 and the correspondence was then resumed after his exile between 1764 and 1765. See Ajello (1978: 1105–1106, 1125–1155).

In 1754, called upon to express his opinion on some issues such as the repurchase of public debt, the organization of the national cadastre and the minting of the new copper coin, Broggia openly contested the policy of the Neapolitan minister Leopoldo De Gregorio, Marquis of Squillace, thus arousing bitter controversy to which he replied the following year with a polemical pamphlet (Broggia 1755). By unmasking the private interests that were hidden behind the proposals of the Marquis of Squillace (Broggia 1755: xvi), Broggia invoked the intervention of the King, but his accusations were too explicit and they violated state secrets. The Court's reaction was violent: Broggia was exiled to Pantelleria and then to Palermo for six years.[29]

Despite his unfortunate political experience, Broggia has the merit of having initiated the debate on "history, nature, reform of money [...] the most important in the political and economic field" (Venturi 1998: 443), outlining an initial organic theoretical framework for a subject that in Naples had produced a great many specialised writings, incapable, however, of rising above a purely empirical treatment of monetary problems. Broggia, instead, was among the first to attempt to define policy solutions based on a theory of money.

On the nature of money, while adhering to the traditional view marked by the Aristotelian-Scholastic *metallist* doctrine, Broggia differed from it in some original insights. According to Broggia, money is "the price of all things that are bought and sold" (Broggia 1743: 175), that is, a general measure. The experience of mankind has overcome the inconveniences of barter, with the use of "pieces" of precious metal, used as a means of exchange and measure of value. Precious metals can take on this important role as they only have an *opinion price* and are not necessary for life (Broggia 1743: 175). Money, therefore, is not a commodity like any other: it derives its value from the recognised preciousness of the material from which it is made, which serves no other purpose than decoration and ornament;[30] when it fulfills this function it does not change its character,

[29] He would return to Naples only after the transfer of De Gregorio to Madrid in the entourage of Charles, crowned King of Spain.

[30] Gasparo Scaruffi also claimed that money had no other uses: "When [gold and silver] are reduced and made into money, they cannot rightly be called commodities by reason of their being; because they become and are then made the basis, the foundation and are a public measure common to all to make contracts for merchandise and many other things. [Crafted metal, gold, silver and copper] changes its name into that of the object made and is named necklace or other, and the same when they are reduced to money, because they change their

that is, it is not consumed for vital needs and can always be brought back to monetary use even in the form of a piece of jewellery, if exchanged for other goods. Implicitly Broggia points out that the use of common commodities as a unit of account and medium of exchange would entail problems since these also have other uses that can affect the monetary function they are invested with (like livestock or wheat, whose source of value is always connected to the necessary needs of life). The main function of money, as a measure and as an intermediary of exchanges, is to allow the circulation of wealth, but, since the metallic commodity-money is in itself a precious object, men have transformed their material wealth into coins (Broggia 1743: 177).

Thus the third traditional function of money is outlined, that of being a store of value, but this function generates the negative effect of hoarding, stopping the exchange circuit, because money, once "enclosed in the casket, the owner does not fear that it will either become worm-eaten or rot or die or deteriorate, as would happen if the value consisted of cloths, fruits, fodder, flocks, land and other things that require care and much inspection" (Broggia 1743: 179).

Inevitably, in the monetary economy, purchases and sales are not synchronous and the money must be temporarily set aside as a deposit in view of future payments. Banks have been set up for this function, collecting the savings set aside in cash and crediting the sums in accounts that can be transferred by negotiable deposit certificates (Broggia 1743: 389–390; see also Broggia [2004]). Broggia attributes to the bank the function of monetary creation, expressly speaking of duplication of value. In fact, individuals use only part of their reserves, which are also facilitated by the bank, and the idle sums can be used for credit operations, to the benefit of all industrial activity and the needs of a state. Thus the bank also creates the link between savings and investments: this is its most important function, because "the more money is naturally pushed to be deposited, the more a clear and industrious policy must push it back into circulation" (Broggia 1743: 403).

name and are named only with the name of the money" (Scaruffi 1582: 24, 26). The origin of money as an object of ornament is also accepted by contemporary scholars, such as William W. Carlile (1901: part 2, chap. 2). Marcel Mauss also argues that the function of precious objects in archaic societies corresponds to the modern function of money; moreover, the good used as money and as a store of value is modified in such a way that its original use as a consumer good is inhibited (Mauss 1923–24).

Hoarding is not the only danger that can threaten the stability of the monetary system. A more serious threat comes from the political authority, which can modify the value of money to its own advantage. The intervention of the state authority must only improve the use of the monetary instrument, guaranteeing its certainty as a measure and consequently its universal acceptability as a means of payment (Broggia 1743: 176).[31] But, according to Broggia, the major problems for monetary systems and for the stability of the measure-money derive from this continuous modification of the commercial relationship between metals.[32]

Copper money is a different matter. Broggia considers it to be of very low value and stable; in fact, copper is the metal which "is not pushed into both private and public deposits" (Broggia 1743: 235); in short, it is the "ultimate money" that "appreciates and is not appreciated". Owing to these characteristics its function is essential in the monetary system, as "not being able to appreciate from another money of lower value, because this money does not exist" (Broggia 1743: 269), it becomes a fundamental money, and resembles the "roots of a plant, which although they are the lowest and the least considered by most, they are important [...]. This money must be seriously considered by the legislator not so much for its value as for the wonderful role it plays" (Broggia 1743: 383). Copper, according to Broggia, for its stability in value is therefore the most suitable metal to assume the function of standard (Monroe 1923:110).[33]

[31] Regarding political interventions, Broggia proposes a change in terminology, specifying that the increase of money (*aumento*) concerns the increase in the number of coins in circulation at the same weight and intrinsic value, while there is a decrease (*diminuzione*) when the new coins have a lower weight and intrinsic value, even if they are multiplied in number. Instead *alzamento* (raising) or *sbassamento* (lowering) relate to the price of the currency in units of account (Broggia 1743: 184–186). In the Middle Ages, the focus was on the quantum of metal represented by a unit of account; thus an increase from 5 *Lira* to 6 *Lira* meant that the *Lira*, which represented, for example, 32 grams of gold, represented only 29 grams of gold, so it was said that money (of account) was weakened (or strengthened). At the end of the fourteenth century the term of comparison is reversed and the point of reference becomes the unit of account, the change from 5 to 6 *Lira* would be referred to as of "increase" (augmentation), and in the opposite case of "decrease" (diminution) (see Bloch 1954: 60–61).

[32] This is also James Steuart's primary concern, see Steuart (1767 vol I: 526, 532, 540).

[33] Also Giambattista Vasco, following Broggia, considers copper money the most suitable for the role of standard, see Vasco (1772: 80). Joseph Harris, on the other hand, has a different opinion and considers copper unstable, see Harris (1757: 45).

Broggia's concern is to continuously turn the *wheel of trade*, and the crisis and the stagnation of production activities can paradoxically be caused by the abundance of money, so that a state, even if it is rich in money and precious metals, will lack the necessary goods (Broggia 1743: 184). The case of Spain is repeatedly recalled by Broggia to underline the validity of his opinion with a concrete example.

The main task of the political authority must be to guarantee the movement of wealth, especially by stimulating industry. The other important task of the political authorities must therefore be to maintain monetary stability. Monetary values can be altered not only by arbitrary acts of the Prince to intentionally lower their metallic content (strongly condemned, in total contrast to Melon's theses), but also as a result of external circumstances due both to the events of international trade and to variations in the available stock of precious metals.

Greater instability of the monetary system, according to Broggia, is caused by the continuous modifications of the commercial relationship between gold and silver. To avoid leaving the internal monetary system at the mercy of the events of the world trade in precious metals and all other commodities, it is necessary to establish government interventions, which Broggia calls *reductions* (*riduzioni*), explicitly referring to medical terminology to underline that these monetary policies are destined to reset what has changed due to accidental circumstances, above all the fracture between the legal and market value of bullion, correcting their alignment. This operation does not entail any sort of quantitative decrease but only a restoration of equilibrium (*legitimate reductions*). Broggia distinguishes *legitimate reductions* from *illegitimate* ones, which are motivated solely by the needs of the state and not by changes in trade or in the quantity of metals and their market value. Such reductions can cause even more damage to the state than disinterest and laxity (Broggia 1743: 229). This is demonstrated by the state of the Neapolitan currency as a result of the reforms of the Viceroy Count of Santo Stefano, implemented at the end of the eighteenth century.[34]

According to Broggia, money must be unalterable in its intrinsic value, but variable in its nominal value in accordance with the variations of the market value of precious metals (Broggia 1743: 189). Therefore, there is

[34] His predecessor, Marquis del Carpio, had, according to Broggia, correctly implemented the reform by proposing a restoration of the intrinsic value of silver currency (Broggia 1743: 208).

no reduction in the intervention that restores the original weight of the coins, modified following shearing or wear; an operation that is described with the term *compensation* or *restoration* (*risarcimento* or *restaurazione*).

The instrument that the authority can manipulate is *imaginary money* (or *money of account*), which, not being *actual money*, coined in a particular metal, remains immune from the fluctuations deriving from metal trade, and whose value is *permanently fixed* in its price (*extrinsic value*).[35] It is money of account, created to escape the diminution of the intrinsic nature of effective coined money (Broggia 1743: 289): its creation is therefore always linked to the devaluation of a minted coin, initially used as a money of account, and "once actually real" (Broggia 1743: 292).

In short, *imaginary money* arises from a particular metamorphosis, which for Broggia is a real historical process: on the one hand the money of account actually minted dematerializes, transforming the original intrinsic metal *quantum* into an ideal, while retaining the name *ab antiquo*; on the other hand, it indirectly acquires another materialization, since its

[35] In medieval and early modern monetary systems there was a separation between unit of account and means of payment, and one unit of account could be equivalent to a certain number of real circulating coins: this unit of account was called *imaginary* because it was never coined (see Einaudi 1936 [2006]: 153). On the concept of *imaginary money* in the Italian writers of the eighteenth century, see Neri (1751: 49–50); Carli (1766: 13–14); Galiani ([1751]: 97–99); Einaudi (1936 [2006]); Loria (1936); Jannaccone (1946); Tucci (1996) and Amato (1999: 18, 24). According to Pasquale Jannaccone, *imaginary money* had to be logically distinguished from *money of account* and *ideal money*, because "the introduction of a *money of account*, i.e. a numerary with a constant denomination, is the remedy to resolve the confusion in counting generated by the co-existence of several currencies as means of payment" (Jannaccone 1946: 31); *imaginary money*, as a constant quantity of metal (gold, silver or copper) resolves "the uncertainty of the quantum of metal due in debit and credit relationships, caused by alterations in the title or weight of current currencies, or in the relationship between them, or between them and the money of account" (Jannaccone 1946: 31–32); the *ideal money*, with constant purchasing power, "remedies the frequent and often violent perturbation of prices" (Jannaccone 1946: 32). Instead, Einaudi, following Broggia, emphasises the role of the *imaginary money* as an instrument for balancing the monetary system: "The function of *imaginary money* in a country that had adopted the bimetallic standard was consequently that of keeping the monetary system in equilibrium. This objective was achieved by the simple process of crying the currency up or down, that is, by increasing or decreasing the current rates in money of account of the real coins. If this were done carefully, the legal rates would at all times be in accordance with the ratio between the prices of gold and silver, as determined by market conditions" (Einaudi 1936 [2006]: 153).

price is made up of copper (if it has the role of unit of account) or silver (if it is used for exchange) actually minted (Broggia 1743: 286).

Faced with changes in the market price of precious metals, the monetary authority must consequently change the value of the *imaginary money*, varying the so-called *tariff*, that is, the price in units of account per weight of metal. If, for example, the market price of gold increased compared to that of silver, it was necessary to immediately modify the legal bimetallic ratio, increasing the rate in favour of gold, thus preventing an outflow of the latter from the State.

Through the maneuver of *imaginary money*, the government of money could therefore be constructed - according to Broggia - in flexible terms in order to correct and neutralize the damage produced by fluctuations in the value of metals.[36]

Resorting to the maneuver on tariffs appears the extreme attempt to preserve a certain degree of monetary sovereignty without undermining the supremacy of the market as regulator of international commodity money. For Broggia, the tariff policy had to be applied actively and not only as a response to external fluctuations, in order to retain the national currency and attract foreign currency (Broggia 1743: 319), a maneuver to be implemented in the case of a trade deficit (on this point Broggia anticipates concerns and solutions that found full theoretical definition only in the nineteenth century).[37]

Broggia's main concern was with the status of the copper mintage, to which he attributed fundamental importance for the stability of the monetary system, but the copper money problem was not addressed and postponed. Only in 1754 was the question revived and Broggia was finally consulted by exponents of the Bourbon court on the project of withdrawing copper coins from circulation and minting new copper coins at a lower intrinsic value and in greater quantities than the old withdrawn coins, in

[36] Following lines of reflection similar to those of Broggia, James Steuart also considers the metallic monetary system unstable and proposes, in a more radical way, to adopt a conventional standard ("a unit which the invention of men, instructed in the arts of commerce") such as the *bank florin*, an abstract unit of account issued by the Amsterdam Wisselbank, which "stands invariable like a rock in the sea" (Steuart 1767 vol.I: 531). In less radical terms, Steuart proposes a monometallic system (Steuart 1767 vol.I: 543).

[37] A similar attempt to those defined by William Stanley Jevons (1884), Alfred Marshall (1926: 101–102) and Irving Fisher (1913) in the early nineteenth century, to sterilize monetary systems from fluctuations in the value of gold.

order to make a profit for the court and the contractor of the operation (Broggia 1754: xxii).

According to Broggia the new copper coin was to be minted with full intrinsic value (with a weight of 6.237 grams, without high seigniorage rights). Minting it with a smaller amount of copper - he observed - would be a very serious mistake and would cause serious damage due to the disproportion between copper and silver coins in terms of the ratio between intrinsic values (Broggia 1754: xli).This proposal was sent to the members of Charles's government, but without success. The plan to reconstitute a new copper coin with a lower intrinsic value was accepted and Broggia found it necessary to inform public opinion of the serious damage that would be caused to the state. He did so in the most radical way possible, by publishing a pamphlet addressed to the king himself (Broggia 1755).

Broggia warned the court against possible speculations on copper coins that would cause imbalances in the entire monetary system. First of all, the devaluation of copper affected the proportion between it and the gold and silver coins, requiring an overall realignment. On the other hand, the devaluation inflated the currency, as private individuals had an interest in bringing antique metals and coins to the mint, profiting from the difference between intrinsic and nominal value. Broggia also rejected the plan to mint the copper coin with an intrinsic value equal to that of the debased coins in circulation, and to remedy the disproportion with the other silver coins by simply increasing their price (nominal value) relative to copper. In this case, the silver coin of account would be changed by altering all the contractual relations already established (Broggia 1755: xi).

Once again Broggia peremptorily reiterated the need for a stabilizing monetary policy. The copper coin is - Broggia observes - "fundamental currency" and more than any other has to keep its intrinsic value intact, "because if the intrinsic value of silver coin decreases it abounds and drives gold out of circulation; if the intrinsic value of gold coin decreases, it abounds and silver is driven out. But if the intrinsic value of copper coin has decreased, it abounds and both gold and silver are expelled from the state, and State remains suffocated and flooded with a vile currency" (Broggia 1755: xi).

The direct appeal to the sovereign and to the general public with the quite explicit allusion to the popular revolt that would inevitably follow the devaluation of the copper coin, were arguments strong enough to be tolerated. From June 1755, with the dismissal of the Marquis Giovanni Fogliani, King Charles assumed direct control of the government by abolishing the office of first secretary. The Kingdom was moving towards a policy of "immobility", increasingly restricted by compromises and dominated by the financial problem, tendencies which would be accentuated in the age of the Regency.

The outcome of this affair was dramatic for Broggia, who paid for his political passion with prison and exile. The minting of the new copper coin, in accordance with de Gregorio's plan, was started in May 1756, but was then suspended in August 1757, a fact that once again testifies to the inaction into which the Neapolitan government had now fallen.[38]

The year 1755 therefore represents a turning point in the affairs of the government of money, marking the departure of two of the main protagonists of the debate of the previous years; stabilizing policies would be implemented in other parts of Italy, especially in Piedmont and Lombardy (see Amato 1999: 43–105).

Very different from Broggia's fate was the role of Trojano Spinelli, duke of Aquaro and Laurino, member of a distinguished family of the Neapolitan aristocracy and member of the *Deputazione delle Monete* (Patalano 2017). In is essay on money, *Riflessioni politiche sopra alcuni punti della Scienza della Moneta* (*Political Reflections on Some Points of Monetary Science*), published anonymously and undated, but probably around 1749, the Neapolitan aristocrat intended to provide a proposal for gold coinage and for the nominal value of circulating coins (Spinelli 1749: 3), two important measures to achieve monetary stabilization, discussed in the *Deputazione*.

Spinelli's proposals were presented as the results of an in-depth study on the difficult and little-known science of money (Spinelli 1749: 3). With the intent of providing a clear understanding of the basis of the science of money, in the first of three books of his *Riflessioni*, Spinelli chooses to present the arguments with "definitions, [and] some axioms", using the Euclidean geometrical method (Spinelli 1749: 2–3). The main propositions, geometrically demonstrated, are presented in the last part of book (Spinelli 1749: 63–73).

Spinelli uses the geometrical method, and the axiomatization of concepts, to deal with a difficult and controversial subject with the authority and neutrality of a "scientific point of view". This intent is revealed in the title of the essay, in which the term "political" – in the sense of art of

[38] *Prammatica LVII De Monetis*, On the copper coin, May 16, 1756.

government, according to the eighteenth-century lexicon – is based on scientific reasoning.

While the formal presentation follows the Euclidean method, the arguments originate from the tradition of Roman Law,[39] and the main concepts derive from medieval and modern monetary literature (above all Bernardo Davanzati and Jean François Melon), and from the school of Natural Law (above all Samuel Pufendorf and, albeit implicitly, John Locke).[40]

These complex influences are summarized in *Definition VIII*, in which Spinelli explains his conception of money: "Money in general", he argues, "is a portion of whatever material that is made by people as the price and measure of things, to contract equally, and that serves as a pledge, that is equivalent of all goods and of everything that is in commerce" (Spinelli 1749: 7–8).

This concept of money, consistent with the metallist tradition, is logically preceded by some definitions of value: "The intrinsic value of whatever material, is its price, that is, the estimate in the common opinion of mankind (*Definition I*) [and] the extrinsic value of material is the value imposed by order and will of the Prince and the Republic (*Definition II*)" (Spinelli 1749: 5).

Using a terminology common in Roman studies, Spinelli defines the two boundaries of money value: the market, represented by intrinsic value, and the political authority, represented by nominal value, called extrinsic value (which coincides with the Scholastic concept of *valor impositus*). The market and the political authority, as subjects of value, are evident definitions that do not need proof, just like the concepts of point and line in Euclidean geometry. The influence of the Italian tradition, above all Davanzati (1588: 20), is evident, but it is possible to recognize a link with Locke's theories. More specifically, definite traces of the English philosopher's ideas are contained in the following concepts: the uselessness of precious metals to the life of man (Locke 1714: 171); the origin of money as a *tacit agreement* (Locke 1714: 168); metallic money as a *pledge* (Locke 1692: 30), intrinsic value as a result of *common valuation* (Locke 1695:

[39] The main sources quoted by Spinelli are: the jurist Julius Paulus (*Corpus Juris Civilis, lex I, Origo, De Contrahenda emptione*); Biel (1583); Bruno (1584); Favre or Fabri (1598); Cujas (1618) and celebrated Bible exegetist Calmet (1734).

[40] Davanzati (1582 [1804] and 1588 [1804]); Abbé de Saint-Pierre (1733), Pufendorf (1672); Le Blanc (1690); Locke (1696a); Savary (1723), Melon (1736); Deschamps and Paris-Duverney (1740).

1). Although he did not quote it directly, Spinelli knew *Treatise of Government* and the monetary pamphlets (*Some Considerations* and *Further Considerations*), in spite of the fact that all Locke's works were inserted in 1731 in the Holy Office's List of Prohibited Books.

Following the logic structure of Euclide's *Elements*, Spinelli relies on axioms, used, in conformity with the geometrical method, as primitive propositions, self-evident and true, accepted as the basis of every other statement. Using geometry, the science of measurement and proportion, Spinelli intends to present the science of money as a *science of proportion*, in which the different elements that determine the value of money (nominal value, intrinsic value, alloy) are linked between them on the basis of certain ratios.

Locke's influence is even decisive in the field of monetary policy: in *Axiom VI*, in fact, Spinelli adopts the stabilization principle, asserting that: "A stronger currency is in general a greater good, than a weaker currency, all other things being equal" (Spinelli 1749: 11).To maintain a strong, stable currency, it is necessary to maintain a certain ratio between these different elements, as is the case of geometrical figures.

In *Definition X* and *Axiom VII*, Spinelli implicitly touches upon the problem of the devaluation of money. This is the subject of the Second Book of Spinelli's essay, dedicated to the demonstration that any alteration of money's extrinsic value determines political and social instability, because these measures are unfair and very damaging for the people and the Prince (Spinelli 1749: 13).

Following the terminology used in the sixteenth century and Locke's monetary pamphlets (Locke 1692: 134–135, 137–138), Spinelli uses the term *aumento* (from the French *augmentation*) for: (1) the operation that increases, pursuant to law, the extrinsic value of coins in circulation above their intrinsic value; (2) the melting of all coins to mint a new standard containing a low mass of precious metals (in the Scholastic tradition this manipulation is called *debasement*) (Spinelli 1749: 29).[41]

[41] John Locke called this operation "raising of coin" (Locke 1695: 11), but in Eighteenth century England, French terminology was adopted, under the influence of Savary's *Dictionaire universel du commerce*: Malachy Postlethwayt's translation of *Dictionnaire Universal*, uses the term "augmentation and diminution of the coin in denomination" (Postlethwayt 1749: 34), see also Postlethwayt (1774) under the entry "Coin"

In both cases, recalling Spinelli's terminology, the intrinsic value is manipulated, altering the ratio between the market value of bullion (gold, silver or copper) and the nominal value of coin.

A general raising of the nominal value of money, according to Spinelli, is unfair, because it cheats the people, stealing purchasing power from one side and giving it to another (Spinelli 1749: 13). This political choice invalidates the role of the public authority, called on to guarantee, with a public mark, the quality, weight, and fineness of metals contained in the coins (Spinelli 1749: 14). Moreover, manipulation creates injustice by damaging natural law, because the debtor has a contractual obligation with the creditor in virtue of an oath that is above civil law and the sovereign authority (Spinelli 1749: 18). Finally, the alteration of extrinsic value damages the economy as a whole, since it causes a generalized rise in prices, damaging foreign trade. In fact, if the domestic market is open to international trade, internal inflation benefits foreign merchants (Spinelli 1749: 20–21).

Inflation, shortage and stagnation are inevitable outcomes of money raising. In essence, according to Spinelli, to raise the money is equivalent to imposing a perpetual tax on all revenues, credits, and salaries, because, as a duty, a devalued coin deprives the subjects of a part of their wealth. Without exception creditor and debtor will be damaged by the alteration of money, because the debtor, too, once he is released, will suffer the negative effect of inflation on his wealth and income.[42]

If the alterations of money are frequent and are carried out without urgency, then a climate of mistrust will spread in the society, weakening the State authority and the mutual confidence among the subjects, making it difficult to contract loans (Spinelli 1749: 24).

The damages of raising the value of money are sustained not only by the people, but also by the Prince himself. First to all, the Prince will be paid with less weight of metal, inasmuch as the taxes are paid with local (and devalued) coins (Spinelli 1749: 26). Secondly, the massive poverty of the country, caused by inflation and economic stagnation, makes the collection of taxes and tariffs more difficult, impoverishing the treasury (Spinelli 1749: 27). The reduction of income from taxes corresponds to an increase in the amount of government spending abroad, and an

[42] Spinelli rejects Melon's argument on the generalized gains from sales in a state of increasing prices (Melon 1736: 222).

additional disadvantage concerns the need to increase the wages of troops and mercenaries, to avoid riots and mutinies (Spinelli 1749: 28–29).

However the Prince can gain from monetary manipulation: in the case of an increase in the extrinsic value of money, the burden of the public debt is reduced (creditors of the State are forced to receive less and to accept bad and overvalued money in payment for debts) and the Prince's treasury increases in nominal value; in the case of debasement, the Prince can gain from the exchange of the old currency with the new (devalued) one, acquiring the difference in precious metal between old and new coins (Spinelli 1749: 30). This device is useful when the public debt is too high and the government cannot raise new taxes, but it is a temporary solution, because it weakens the confidence in the state authority, giving rise to considerable problems.

The same disadvantages recur when the public authority modifies the extrinsic value of certain types of currency (gold, silver or copper money), leaving the rest unchanged. But in this case, additional problems are determined by the disproportion between the new devalued coins and the remaining unchanged money. Primarily, the partial alteration modifies the bimetallic ratio, encouraging arbitrage opportunities and speculation (Spinelli 1749: 35). According to Spinelli, all these arguments show that the augmentation of coins is very dangerous for the social stability of the Kingdom of Naples, and, in a case of emergency, a better alternative would be to raise taxes or public debt.

Coherently with his analysis, Spinelli considered any modification of monetary equilibrium extremely dangerous, proposing a defense of the "status quo".[43] The coinage of new gold money, to celebrate political independence under the new dynasty, could be a factor of instability, modifying the fragile ratios among kinds of money. More specifically, it was extremely difficult to determine the exact bimetallic ratio, to avoid dangerous speculation on the national currency (Spinelli 1749: 60).

Faced with the uncertain path of monetary reform, Spinelli considered it a better solution not to mint gold coins but to use foreign gold currencies valuated according to market value, and not by decree (Spinelli 1749: 62).[44] This political choice was praised by Galiani many years later (Galiani

[43] For this reason, he positively judged the reform of the Marquis of Carpio aimed at restoring the original value of silver currency (Spinelli 1749: 30–32).

[44] Broggia had a different opinion, proposing a new coinage of gold and silver coins at full weight and encouraging the importations of full-weight foreign currencies (Broggia 1743: 319, 337).

1780: *Avviso* [14]). The Kingdom of Naples – Spinelli argued – rich in agricultural products and raw materials, would always have a surplus in its trade balance, and consequently would not be devoid of good foreign currency, both silver and gold (Spinelli 1749: 62).

The lack of historical documents leaves many questions unanswered about the role played by Spinelli in the *Deputazione*: whether his opinion was broadly shared by other members or was merely a minority position. In his treatise on money published a few years earlier, Broggia proposed a different solution, based on variations of the extrinsic value, in order to adjust the legal value of money in unit of account (*imaginary money*) to the market fluctuation of bimetallic ratio (Broggia 1743: 190). Broggia proposed a flexible policy of stabilization and called this device correct setting, using medical terminology, because this procedure heals the fracture between the legal and market value of bullion and corrects their alignment. This operation does not entail any sort of quantitative decrease but only a restoration of equilibrium. According to Broggia, money must be unalterable in its intrinsic value, but variable in its nominal value in accordance with the variations of the market value of precious metals (Broggia 1743: 189).

In Spinelli's essay there is no mention of copper coinage, which was the weak point of the Neapolitan monetary system. His concept of monetary stability coincided with the stability of full-bodied gold and silver coins, known as *Grossi* in Italy, *Gros* in France, and *Groats* in England (Cipolla 1967: 14–15; 42–51). This type of money was used for the payment of rent and for importing luxury goods: its devaluation would have reduced the purchasing power of the aristocracy, threatening its social supremacy.

Spinelli's opinions represented the "fear of inflation" of the upper-class. The high rate of inflation that occurred during the period of price revolution, from the second half of the fifteenth century to the first halfu of the seventeenth century, caused a general impoverishment of the oldest class of European nobility (*Nobles of the Sword*). The inflationary process eroded the value of rent, the main source of wealth of the old aristocracy, favouring the rise of new classes and upsetting the social establishment. In his essay, Spinelli emphasized the social damage deriving from inflation, attributing the responsibility to government manipulations. The dramatic effects caused by the collapse of Law's System showed that political decisions could threaten social stability.

In the same years in which Broggia and Spinelli were closing their treaties and Galiani was taking his first steps, interest in monetary matters had grown throughout Italy, and discussing *good money* was no longer a matter reserved for politicians or the select few who were familiar with complex monetary matters. The Italian States were just then emerging from the War of the Austrian Succession and a long period of peace (which was to last until 1792) was beginning for the peninsula, a propitious opportunity to put their troubled finances in order and to imitate the monetary stabilization processes underway in much of Europe. Also changing was the attitude of the intellectuals who were increasingly interested in participating directly in major political decisions, at first only as advisors, but then increasingly in the first person, in that season of happy symbiosis that, for many of them, was to be enlightened absolutism.

Like a spreading wave, in the 1750s interest in monetary matters spread from Naples to Rome and then to Florence and Milan. At the beginning of 1750, Giovannantonio Fabrini's book, *Dell'indole e qualità naturali e civili della moneta e de' principi istorici e naturali de' contratti* (*On the nature and natural and civil qualities of money and the historical and natural principles of contracts*, Fabrini 1750) was published anonymously in Rome, and shortly afterwards the work *Del commercio* (*Of trade*), by the Roman banker Gerolamo Belloni (1750). In Florence, at the beginning of 1751, Gianfrancesco Pagnini and Angelo Tavanti, published, not without difficulty, Locke's monetary works (Locke 1751). Thus the theorist of the great English coinage, always present in the Italian debate, appeared in the light of day to support with his authority many opinions that had already manifested themselves and appeared consolidated.[45] Finally, in March 1751, Muratori's erudite pupil Filippo Argelati began his collection of monetary writings (Argelati 1750), among which the discovery of the outstanding hitherto unpublished treatise by Geminiano Montanari.[46]

In all these works, albeit in different ways, the principle of monetary stabilization was reaffirmed and the need to initiate a decisive monetary reform, seen as an indispensable condition for the economic recovery of the Italian States, was manifested (Venturi 1998: 445–468).

[45] The appendix included Giovanni Pagnini's essay, *Saggio sopra il giusto pregio delle cose, la giusta valuta della moneta e sopra il commercio dei romani*.

[46] In the third volume of Argelati's collection was the *Trattato del valore delle monete in tutti gli Stati*, written in 1680. Geminiano Montanari (1633–1687) was a professor of astronomy in Bologna and Padua.

3.3 The Genesis of *Della Moneta*

In this context, the young Galiani completed his treatise, the "masterpiece that came out of the discussion on money" (Venturi 1998: 490), between the last months of 1750 and the beginning of 1751 and, having taken the decision to publish it anonymously, awaited the necessary printing licence (*imprimatur*), which arrived only at the beginning of September 1751, after a path not without its pitfalls (Iovine 1999). The news that a treatise on the complex subject of money would be published had been circulating since July 1751, and not only in Italy, fuelling the curiosity of intellectuals and politicians who were increasingly interested in this topic.[47]

The genesis of the treatise, composed, as Galiani stated, as early as 1749, when he had not yet reached the age of twenty-one (Galiani 1780: *Avviso* [8]), is not entirely clear, first of all because of the decision to publish the work anonymously and without the knowledge of his uncle Celestine and the circle of friends and educators that surrounded him. Thirty years later, in the *Avviso* preceding the Second Edition, Galiani himself clarified the reasons for his choice: "it pleased [the author] to write and publish it with such secrecy that he hid it from everyone, even from his illustrious uncle Monsignor Galiani, only to pleasantly surprise him later, as happened. And it was even more difficult to keep this secret, because living under his strict care and discipline and in his own home, he was perpetually under observation. In addition, Monsignor Galiani, by virtue of the office of Cappellano Maggiore that he gloriously exercised, had so much authority and so much vigilance over the University, over all men of letters and over the books that were printed in Naples, that it seemed impossible to conceal anything from him in this area. And yet the secret, entrusted to just two young men of his age, was kept" (Galiani 1780: *Avviso* [8]). The two young men who knew the secret were Pasquale Carcani (1721–1783), and Pasquale di Tommasi (1712–1787),[48] who, in

[47] From Geneva, the Scottish philosopher David Fordyce wrote: "the title and author of a small but learned work just published in Naples on coinage" (David Fordyce's letter to Ferdinando Galiani, Geneva, 28 July 1751, BSNSP, XXXI.B.18: folio 23r. See Iovine 1999: 180).

[48] Pasquale Carcani, a man of letters and jurist, member of the *Accademia Ercolanese* (of which he became secretary) and the *Accademia degli Emuli*, later became one of Bernardo Tanucci's main collaborators, from 1759 to 1776, as an officer in the secretariat of foreign affairs. Pasquale di Tommasi, also a scholar, edited the Neapolitan reprint of the fourth edition of the *Vocabolario dell'Accademia della Crusca* in 1746.

Galiani's tale, were in charge of requesting the various permissions and overseeing the printing of the text.

This narration at a long distance from the events may have been emphasised by Galiani himself in order to increase the fame of his youthful talent, but also to dispel any possible suspicions about the role played by his uncle Celestino in the affair, who supposedly did not know the true authorship of the work until two months after the treatise's publication in early September 1751.

Fausto Nicolini has refuted this account on the basis of archive documents and proved that Celestino Galiani was aware of the author's identity at least as early as September 1751.[49] In more recent years, Raffaele Iovine has argued that the Chaplain Major was not only fully aware of the work's authorship from the beginning, but that he had also skilfully guided the complex approval process, which was partly under his control, by entrusting the drafting of reports to two "censors of convenience" linked to the *novatores* milieu (Iovine 1999: 177).[50]

According to Iovine, Bartolomeo Intieri also knew the author from the beginning and, together with Celestino, "contributed to the political-cultural operation that the team wanted to carry out, spreading the rumours of the imminent publication and emphasising, on the one hand, its novelty and critical approach, and on the other, its perfect alignment with the interests of the Kingdom and the Monarchy" (Iovine 1999: 179). The close link between the ideas of Intieri's circle and the theses expressed

[49] Nicolini cites the letter that Domenico Sgueglia, Celestino Galiani's secretary, sent to Ferdinando on 23 September 1751: "This morning, in Portici, our Monsignor had a long talk about the work with Marquis Fraggianni. I believe that the same [...] made him confess that you are the author of it. I have been called upon to confirm in what terrible circumstances of time and things you composed it" (Domenico Sgueglia's letter to Ferdinando Galiani, Naples, 23 September 1751, BSNSP, XXXI B 18.08, folio 37r, published in Nicolini 1908a: 8). This document would suggest that Celestine knew the authorship of the work from the beginning of its drafting. In a letter to Giovanni Gaetano Bottari, Celestino nevertheless stated that he was the last to know the paternity of *Della Moneta*: "About the book *Della Moneta*, without exaggeration, I was one of the last to know the author, although it was later discovered through someone who was a participant in the secret that it was not other than my nephew Ferdinando" (Celestino Galiani's letter to Giovanni Gaetano Bottari, Naples, 11 December, 1751, Biblioteca Corsiniana di Roma, MS. Cors. 1580. 32.E. 1, folios 228r–228v, published in Catucci 1986: 24).

[50] The two revisers were Giovanni Maria della Torre, an Episcopal censor and professor of physics linked to Abbot Antonio Genovesi, himself a *protégé* of Celestino Galiani, and the jurist Bernardo D'Ambrosio, a royal reviser, professor of Civil Institutions, chosen by Celestino himself (Iovine 1999: 177).

in *Della Moneta* was immediately evident,[51] and Carlo Antonio Broggia did not hesitate to attribute the work's authorship to Intieri himself, considering Ferdinando a mere figurehead (Broggia [1978]: 1136).[52] Instead, the available documents show that Intieri had no role other than that of an interested reader at the printing stage. As Galiani's first biographer, Luigi Diodati, points out, Intieri's letter to Ferdinando, dated 13 August 1751, would have made no sense (Diodati 1788: 13).[53] Intieri's letter to Celestino Galiani dated 25 September 1751 would show that it was only in mid-September, after publication therefore, that the Tuscan was aware that the real author was that young man, who had sent him his treatise "on witches and spells" just a month earlier:[54] "Until eight days ago, I would

[51] The influence of Intieri's circle was admitted by Galiani himself thirty years later in a report drafted for the government: "at that tender age when I made that book [*Della Moneta*] [I] did not know the kingdom well enough to be able to give authority to my opinions: but these were the thoughts of Bartolommeo Intieri, of Marquis Rinuccini, the greatest men in the study of public economy at that time, and Marquis Fraggianni, President Ventura and Monsig. Galiani my uncle" (Galiani, MS-14: 743).

[52] Broggia wrote: "to avoid putting himself in danger [...] [Intieri] wanted to publish anonymously and procured Galiani to pass himself off as its author. And so this sucker accepted the party without thinking of the rest and without even noticing a passage in the work [...] in which it is clearly argued and seen that the author speaks as a man of a very advanced age, which in 1750 was the septuagenarian Intieri" (Broggia's letter to Giovan Giuseppe Fontanesi, Naples, 26 March, 1765, in Biblioteca Nazionale Napoli, XXI. 16, no. 5, published in Ajello 1978: 1136–1137). Broggia refers to some phrases in *Della Moneta* that seemed to attest to the author's advanced age: "Because in old men the great ideas and the continual agitation born of internal anguish, and deterioration of the organs, are always a sign of approaching irreparable death" (Galiani [1751]: 370). In the second edition of 1780, in Note III, Galiani made it clear that in order to dissimulate, he had deceived the reader by pretending that "the author of the book was a serious man, of mature age, battered and wearied by adverse fortune, and come to the tedium of a world too well known" (Galiani 1780: 375).

[53] "I have read, and with inexplicable admiration and delight, the treatise on money, with the last pages you were pleased to send me; and not only have I read it, but I have written more about it to all my friends, touched by the strength made to me by the stupendous talent of a man, who, without a doubt, has earned the first place in this sort of subject [...]. We shall hear what applause he will receive from the public, who will admire his modesty" (Bartolomeo Intieri's letter to Ferdinando Galiani, Massa Equana, 13 August 1751, BSNSP, XXXI.B.18: folio 27v.; also published by Nicolini 1908a: 4). Luigi Diodati wrote that "[Ferdinando] was obliged to read it [to Celestino], as he used to read other new books in the hours of his rest" (Diodati 1788: 12). It is probable, therefore, that Ferdinando also sent the proofs to Intieri, who thanked him in the above-mentioned letter.

[54] Ferdinando Galiani's letter to Bartolomeo Intieri, Naples, 15 July 1751 (BSNSP, XXXI.C.14: folios 14,15). This is the only available letter from Ferdinando to Intieri (pub-

not have believed that a young man of 22 years of age was capable of composing a work such as that which forms the book of money; a subject difficult to scholars, crude and indigestible to merchants themselves, to whom it is nevertheless unknown, as is well known to all. But, having heard a few pieces of the most difficult things sketched by the admirable talent of Don Ferdinando and, not withdrawn into solitude, but in the midst of the happiest and most numerous conversations of this great city, I confess, most illustrious *Monsignore*, I confess, with astonishment, that I was surprised by the admirable and portentous talent of this most worthy nephew of yours, who I believe has surpassed all others, not to say young men of letters of his age, who have been so far, but many others of a more experienced age".[55]

A few days later, Intieri wrote directly to Ferdinando, now recognised as the author of the work: "Hearing from everywhere that you have been named as the author of the book *Della Moneta*, and being such that it deserves all the esteem of men of letters, and experts in this very important subject, as is known from the opinion that they are beginning to give it in Rome, I also, following the public voice and fame, will esteem you as such, and therefore as such I rejoice, and I congratulate you *Signore* author of the most beautiful, and noble, and useful work, and therefore worthy to be read by every man who loves society, the good, and the advancement of this art".[56]

Celestino and Intieri supported the work because it represented ideas broadly shared by the *novatores* and contributed to the renewal he desired.[57] And indeed, when the censorship process came to a halt, despite two favourable reports in March and June 1751, the Cappellano Maggiore

lished in Galiani 1975: 814–816; only the *Proemio* of the treatise *Sulla superstizione* is preserved, see MS-9). A few days later, writing to Antonio Cocchi, Intieri still did not know the author: "We have under our eyes a treatise on money. The author is unknown, but, whoever he is, he seems to me a talent of the first rank" (Bartolomeo Intieri's letter to Antonio Cocchi, Massa Equana, 16 August 1751; published in Venturi 1959a: 431).

[55] Bartolomeo Intieri's letter to Celestino Galiani, Massa Equana, 25 September 1751 (BSNSP, XXXI.B.18: folios 40–41; also published in Nicolini 1908a: 6).

[56] Bartolomeo Intieri's letter to Ferdinando Galiani, Massa Equana, 28 September 1751 (BSNSP, XXXI.B.18: folio 44, also published in Iovine 1999: 231).

[57] Celestino Galiani's role is evident in a letter from Intieri: "This book was printed by a person who claimed not to know the real author. The Cappellano Maggiore entrusted its revision to a public law professor. A rumour immediately spread in the literary circles of the goodness of this work and the Cappellano Maggiore himself said it was admirable and loudly shouted that it was worthy of dedication to the King" (Bartolomeo Intieri's letter to

intervened to overcome the obstacle. The procedure had been blocked because Galiani, wishing to remain anonymous, had asked the printer Giuseppe Raimondi to submit the dedication to the Sovereign in his own name (Galiani 1780: 371). This procedure, Galiani wrote, "seemed singular and daring" (Galiani 1780: 371) and the Court asked the auditors for a further report, which this time was not entirely favourable. In a letter to the Florentine senator and patrician Leonardo del Riccio, Intieri summed up the affair: "there is said to be an order from the Court that a *Compendium* of the doctrine of this book be delivered by the reviser, His Majesty wishing to be informed before publication. The author was unknown and still is. Nearly three months have passed in this state of uncertainty, and the more the glory and merit of the work has grown, the more the difficulties have grown, to such an extent that one has almost despaired of obtaining the licence".[58] For Intieri "the obstacle" came from the royal auditor, who was "little versed in such matters".[59]

According to Iovine, the delay in granting Galiani's request stemmed from an emerging political opposition to the publication of the treaty, which was seen as detrimental to the sovereign power to define the value of money.[60] An accusation, after all, that was absolutely unfounded, as Galiani's treaty did not deny this sovereignty.

The opposition involved elements of the court, primarily Bernardo Tanucci, who did not want to come into conflict with the conservative party close to the Sovereign, and exponents of the *ceto civile* wary of the innovative proposals supported by the Cappellano Maggiore's *entourage*. Specifically, Tanucci judged the treatise to be "full of advanced paralogisms, disorder and other people's stuff, and much of it used by Machiavelli

Leonardo del Riccio, Massa Equana, 10 October 1751, in Naldini - del Riccio Private Archive, Florence, published in Iovine 1999: 183).

[58] "The edition of the book was suspended, as it was accused of limiting the authority of the supreme authorities regarding the increase or decrease of the value of money" (Barolomeo Intieri's letter to Leonardo del Riccio, Massa Equana, 3 September 1751, in Archivio Privato Naldini - del Riccio, Florence, published in Iovine 1999: 183).

[59] Bartolomeo Intieri's letter to Duke Filippo di Bartolomeo Corsini, Massa Equana, 6 August 1751, Archivio Privato Corsini, Fondo Corsini, published in Iovine (1999: 180).

[60] See Bartolomeo Intieri's letter to Leonardo del Riccio, Massa Equana, 10 ottobre 1751, in Archivio Privato Naldini – del Riccio, Florence, published in Iovine (1999: 184).

in other guises and for other purposes".[61] The exponents of the conservatively oriented *ceto civile* were unable "to grasp the new theoretical stimuli offered by the new science, but rejected them by clinging to an ostentatious presumption of superiority and distrust of the new" (Iovine 1999: 215).

The novatores party had, however, won important positions of power in the previous years, and Celestino Galiani had no difficulty in resolving the impasse by finding appropriate support in one of the most enlightened exponents of the *ceto civile*: the Delegate of the Royal Jurisdiction Nicolò Fraggianni. Ferdinando himself, thirty years later, wanted to give Fraggianni credit for allowing the book to be published by overcoming the obstacles placed by the Court.[62]

With the dedication "Al Serenissimo e clementissimo Re Carlo" ("To the Most Serene and Most Clement King Charles"), accepted on 28 August 1751 with a dispatch to the Camera di Santa Chiara, the book could finally be published. On 10 September, the work received the Imprimatur and was printed a few days later.[63]

[61] Bernardo Tanucci's letter to Francesco Nefetti, Naples, 8 February 1752, published in Tanucci (1980a: 740). See also Bernardo Tanucci's letter to Francesco Nefetti, Naples, 26, October 1751, published in Tanucci (1980a: 718).

[62] "The King asked the opinion of Marquis Nicola Fraggianni, Delegate of the Royal Jurisdiction, whether such a dedication should be accepted, and in a statement he gave a favourable opinion of the request at a time when the author was entirely unknown to him, and he could not guess or imagine that the author was the same young man Galiani, whom he often saw in his home" (Galiani 1780: 371). Broggia described the episode in polemical terms in a letter to Fontanesi, pointing out that the reviewer had only read the first two chapters of the treatise, leaving out precisely those dealing with monetary policies (Carlo Antonio Broggia's letter to Giovan Giuseppe Fontanesi, Naples, 26 March, 1765, in Biblioteca Nazionale Napoli, XXI. 16, no. 5, published in Ajello (1978: 1139) Fraggianni's favourable opinion (*consulta*) is published in the second edition of *Della Moneta* (Galiani 1780: 371–372).

[63] The printer received exclusive rights (jus prohibendi) for 10 years (Iovine 1999: 230). On 17 September 1751, Intieri sent several copies to Bartolomeo Corsini (see Bartolomeo Intieri's letter to Bartolomeo Corsini, Massa Equana, 17 September 1751, Archivio Privato Corsini, Fondo Corsini, published in Iovine 1999: 230).

References[64]

Manuscript Sources

Galiani, F. MS-9. Proemio di un'opera sulle streghe, Manuscript kept in the Biblioteca Società Napoletana di Storia Patria, XXXI. C. 14, folios 146r–148r, published with this title in Galiani, 1975, pp. 817–819.

Galiani, F. MS-14. Sui contratti alla voce. Manuscript kept in the Biblioteca Società Napoletana di Storia Patria, XXXI. A. 10, published in Galiani, 1975, pp. 742–745 and in Galiani, 1999, pp. 77–80.

Spinola, C. MS. Progetto di economie varie sopra tributi e imposizioni, imposte o da imporsi nel Regno di Napoli, manuscript kept in the National Library Vittorio Emanuele III in Naples (coll. XI.E.31).

Primary Sources

Abbé de Saint-Pierre, C. I. Castel de. (1733). Discours contre l'augmentation des monnoyes et en faveur des annuitez. In *Ouvrage politique par M. l'Abbé de Saint Pierre*, Rotterdam: Jean Daniel Beman, Tome II: 199–230.

Argelati, F. (ed.). (1750). *De monetis Italiae variorum illustrium virorum dissertationes, quarum pars nunc primum in lucem prodit.* Milan: in regia Curia ex Aedibus Palatinis.

Belloni, G. (1750). *Del commercio dissertazione del sig. marchese Girolamo Belloni.* Rome: Pagliarini.

Biblia, F. (1621). *Discorso sopra l'Aggiustamento della Moneta e Cambii del Regno di Napoli. D'ordine dell'Ill.mo e R.mo Signor Cardinal Zapata Luogotenente e Capitan Generale per Sua Maestà in questo Regno di Napoli*, Naples: s.n.

Biel, G. (1583). *De monetarum potestate simul et utilitate libellus*, in *Tractatus varii atque utiles de monetis earumque mutatione ac falsitate in gratiam studiosorum ac practicorum collecti.* Coloniae Agrippinae: Apud Theodorum Baunium.

Broggia, C. A. (1743). *Trattato de' tributi, delle monete e del governo politico della sanità. Opera di stato, e di commercio, di polizia e di finanza: molto, alla felicità de' popoli, alla robustezza degli stati, ed alla gloria e possanza maggiore de' principi, conferente e necessaria.* Naples: Pietro Palombo.

Broggia, C. A. (1754). *Memoria ad oggetto di varie politiche ed economiche ragioni e temi di utili raccordi che in causa del monetaggio di Napoli s'espongono e propongono agli spettabili signori, convocati di real ordine dall'illustre marchese di*

[64]The abbreviations "s.l." and "s.n." stand for the Latin terms *sine loco* (without place of publication) and *sine nomine* (without name of publisher).

Vallesantoro Segretario di Stato della Reale Azienda. E incidentalmente con quest'occasione si risolve la sì difficile e strepitosa controversia sulla ricompra delle pubbliche entrate, o siano arrendamenti, alienati col patto di non ricomprare: così detto dazione in solutum. Si ragiona del censimento, o sia catasto, proponendosi il modo di farlo col desiato frutto e senza intoppi. E s'espone il saggio, o sia l'idea di sette utili trattati, da pubblicarsi. De' quali nella qui addietro pagina si contiene il titolo, 15 febbraio 1754. Naples: s.n.

Broggia, C. A. (1755). *Risposte alle obiezzioni state fatte da varj soggetti intorno al sistema del prezzo corrente, che assolutamente dee tenersi per la ricompera degli arrendamenti e similmente a quelle state anche fatte intorno alla rinovazione della moneta di rame che dee anch'essa avere tutto quel valore intrinseco che di giustizia gli spetta; e tanta farsene, che non ecceda il puro bisogno degli scambj minuti. Da umiliarsi a Sua Maestà che Dio sempre guardi, e feliciti di Carlo Antonio Broggia, a dì 14 novembre 1755.* Naples: s.n.

Broggia, C. A. (1978). Lettere a Muratori e Fontanesi. In R. Ajello, (ed.) *La letteratura italiana. Storia e testi. Dal Muratori al Cesarotti. Politici ed economisti del primo Settecento,* vol. 44, tomo V. Milan-Naples: Ricciardi, pp. 1100–1155.

Broggia, C. A. [2004]. *Il Banco ed il Monte de' pegni. Del lusso,* with the introducion by De Rosa, L. and Graziani, A., edited by R. Patalano. Naples: La Città del Sole.

Bruno, A. (1584). *Tractatus de augmento et diminutione monetarum,* in *Tractatus illustrium in utraque tum pontificii tum caesarei jurisfacultate juriscultorum.* Venetiis: s.n.

Calmet, A. A. (1734). *Disquisitiones de monetae signatae, vetustatae,* in *Prolegomena et dissertationes in omnes et singulos Sacrae Scripturae libros.* Venice: apud Christophorum Zane.

Campanella, T. (1608) [1973]. Arbitrii sopra l'aumento dell'entrate del Regno. In *Problemi monetari negli scrittori napoletani del Seicento,* edited by R. Colapietra, pp. 85–110. Rome: Accademia Nazionale dei Lincei.

Carli, G. R. (1766). *Osservazioni preventive al piano intorno alle monete di Milano.* Milan: Galeazzi.

Cujas, J. (1618). *Iacobi Cujacii Observationum libri XIX.* Lutetiae Parisiorum: s.n.

Davanzati, B. (1582) [1804]. *Notizia de' cambj,* in *Scrittori classici italiani di Economia Politica,* Parte antica, Tomo II, Milan: De Stefanis, 1804.

Davanzati, B. (1588) [1804]. *Lezione delle monete,* Firenze, in *Scrittori classici italiani di Economia Politica,* Parte antica, Tomo II. Milan: De Stefanis, 1804.

De Santis, M.A. (1605a). *Discorso di Marc'Antonio De Santis intorno alli effetti, che fa il cambio in Regno.* Naples: Costantino Vitali.

De Santis, M.A. (1605b). *Secondo Discorso di Marc'Antonio De Santis intorno alli effetti, che fa il cambio in Regno, sopra una risposta, che è stata fatta adverso del primo.* Naples: Felice Stigliola.

Deschamps, F.-M.-C., Paris-Duverney, J. (1740). *Examen du Livre intitulé: Réflexions politiques sur les finances et le commerce.* La Haie: Vaillant & Prevôt.

Diodati, L. (1788). *Vita dell'abate Ferdinando Galiani*. Naples: Orsino.

Diodati, L. (1790). *Dello stato presente della moneta nel regno di Napoli, e della necessità di un alzamento libri due*. Naples: Michele Migliaccio.

Enríquez de Fonseca, L. (1681a) [1973]. *Discurso en orden a que à la moneda de vellon se disponga modo de uso por el qual sea mejor para los commercios que la moneda de plata*. Naples: Salvador Castaldo, Italian translation in R. Colapietra (ed.) *Problemi monetari negli scrittori napoletani del Seicento*. Rome: Accademia Nazionale dei Lincei, 1973, pp. 457–490.

Enríquez de Fonseca, L. (1681b) [1973]. *Tratado y discurso sobre la moneda de el Reyno de Napoles. Su estado, el origen de sus daños, el remedio para su consummo*. Naples: Salvador Castaldo. Italian translation in R. Colapietra (ed.) *Problemi monetari negli scrittori napoletani del Seicento*. Rome: Accademia Nazionale dei Lincei, 1973, pp. 491–500.

Fabrini, G. (1750). *Dell'indole e qualità naturali e civili della moneta e de' principi istorici e naturali de' contratti. Dissertazioni*. Rome: Pagliarini.

Favre, A., Fabri, A. (1598). *Tractatus de variis nummariorum debitorum solutionibus* [...] *adversus Carolum Molinaeum: ejusdem disputatio de patrui hereditate inter solos fratrum filios, utrum in capita an in stirpes dividenda*, s.l: s.n.

Galanti G. M. (1788). *Nuova Descrizione Storica e geografica delle Sicilie dell'avvocato Giuseppe M.a Galanti tomo II*. Naples: Gabinetto Letterario.

Galiani, F. [1751] [published anonymous, with date of 1750]. *Della moneta. Libri cinque*, Naples: Giuseppe Raimondi.

Galiani, F. (1780). *Della moneta. Libri cinque. Edizione seconda*. Naples: Stamperia Simoniana.

Giustiniani L. (1804). *Nuova collezione delle Prammatiche del Regno di Napoli*, tomo VII. Naples: Stamperia Simoniana.

Harris J. (1757). *An Essay Upon Money and Coins*. London: Hawkins.

Le Blanc, F. (1690). Traité historique des monnayes de France depuis le commencement de la monarchie jusqu'à present. Paris: s.n.

Locke, J. (1692). *Some Considerations of the Consequences of the Lowering of Interest, and Raising the Value of Money. In a letter sent to a Member of Parliament*. London, Awnsham and John Churchill, at the Black-Swan in Pater-Noster-Row.

Locke, J. (1695). *Further Considerations Concerning Raising the Value of Money Wherein Mr. Lowndes's Arguments for it in his late Report concerning An Essay for the Amendment of Silver Coins, are particularly Examined by John Locke*. London: A. and J. Churchill at the Black Swan in Pater-Noster-Row.

Locke, J. (1696a). *Some considerations of the consequences of the lowering of interest, and raising the value of money. In a letter sent to a Member of Parliament. The second edition corrected*. London: printed for Awnsham and John Churchil.

Locke, J. (1696b). *Several papers relating to money, interest, and trade, & c*, London: Printed for A. and J. Churchill.

Locke, J. (1714). *Two Treatises of Government. In the Former, the false Principles and Foundation of Sir Robert Filmer, and his Followers, are detected and overthrown. The Latter is an Essay concerning the true Original, Extent, and End of Civil Government*, in *Works of John Locke*, vol. II. London: Churchill.

Locke, J. (1751). *Ragionamenti sopra la moneta, l'interesse del denaro, le finanze e il commercio, scritti e pubblicati in diverse occasioni dal signor Giovanni Locke. Tradotti la prima volta dall'inglese con varie annotazioni*, 2 tomi. Florence: Andrea Bonducci.

Lowndes, W. (1695). *A Report Containing an Essay for the Amendment of the Silver Coins*. London: s.n.

Lunetti, V. (1630). *Politica mercantile di Vettorio Lunetti. Dell'espedienti et arbitrij per publica utilità. Nelli quali con vere raggioni si mostrano le cause delli danni della città e regno di Napoli et il vero modo di rimediarli. Possono servire anche per dove fussi simili danni e si lascia per brevità li discorsi d'adornamenti e solo si accenna le materie delli grand'utili et incredibili avanzi per Sua Maestà e ben publico. E per trattarsi di servitio publico e di Sua Maestà non si deve disprezzare le proposte, se prima non s'intenda le raggioni*. Naples: Lazzaro Scorriggio.

Melon, J-F. (1736). *Essai politique sur le commerce. Nouvelle édition. Cette édition est augmentée de sept chapitres et les lacunes des éditions précédentes y sont remplies*, s.l. s.n.

Muratori L. A. (1749). *Della pubblica felicità oggetto de' buoni principi*, Lucca [but Venice]: s. n.

Neri P. [1751]. *Osservazioni sopra il prezzo legale delle monete e la difficoltà di prefinirlo e sostenerlo*. Milan: Malatesta.

Oresme, N. (1484) [1956]. *The De moneta of Nicole Oresme, and English Mint documents*, translated from the Latin with Introduction and Notes by C. Johnson. London: Thomas Nelson and Sons.

Postlethwayt, M. (1749). *A Dissertation on the Plan, Use, and Importance, of the Universal Dictionary of Trade and Commerce*. London: John and Paul Knapton.

Postlethwayt, M. (1774). *The Universal Dictionary of Trade and Commerce, with Large Additions and Improvements, Adapting the Same to the Present State of British Affairs in America Since the Last Treaty of Peace Made in the Year 1763*. London: Printed for W. Strahan, J and F. Rivington.

Pufendorf, S. (1672). *De jure naturae et gentium libri octo*. Londini Scanorum.

Savary, J. (1723). *Dictionnaire universel de commerce*. Paris: J. Estienne.

Scaruffi, G. (1582). *L'alitinonfo, per fare ragione, et concordanza d'oro, e d'argento; che servirà in universale; tanto per provvedere agli infiniti abusi del tosare, et guastare monete; quanto per regolare ogni sorte di pagamenti, et ridurre anco tutto il mondo ad una sola moneta*. Reggio Emilia: Hercoliano Bartoli.

Serra, Antonio. (1613) [2011]. *Breve trattato delle cause che possono far abbondare li regni d'oro e d'argento dove non sono miniere, con applicazione al regno di Napoli diviso in tre parti*. Napoli: Lazzaro Scorriggio. English Translation: *A "Short Treatise" on the Wealth and Poverty of Nations*, Edited and with an

Introduction by Sophus A. Reinert. Translated by Jonathan Hunt London – New York, Anthem Press, 2011.

Spinelli, T. [1749]. *Riflessioni politiche sopra alcuni punti della Scienza della Moneta. Al Sig. D. Domenico Caracciolo dei Marchesi di Capriglia*. Naples: s.n.

Steuart J. (1767). *An Inquiry into the Principles of Political Economy being an Essay on the Science of Domestic Policy in Free Nations. in which are particularly considered Population, Agriculture, Trade, Industry, Money, Coin, Interest, Circulation, Banks, Exchange, Public Credit, and Taxes by Sir James Steuart, Bart.* London: Millar and Cadell.

Tanucci, B. (1980a). *Epistolario*, vol. I (1723–1746), R.P. Coppini, L. Del Bianco, Nieri, R. (eds). Rome: Edizioni di Storia e Letteratura.

Turbolo, G.D. (1616). *Discorso della differenza et inegualità delle Monete del Regno di Napoli, con l'altre monete di Potentati convicini, e della causa della penuria di esse. Con l'espediente per lo aggiustamento e abbundanza sì delle monete di Regno come di forastiere. Per beneficio publico.* Naples: Tarquinio Longo.

Turbolo, G.D. (1629). *Discorso sopra le monete del Regno di Napoli per la renouatione della lega di esse monete, ordinata ed eseguita nell'anno 1622. E degli effetti da quella preceduti. E se il cambio alto per estra Regno sia d'utile ò danno a' Regnicoli. Con diverse Relationi e copie d'altri discorsi, dati fuora nell'anni 1618, 619 et 620 pertinenti alla medesima materia*. Naples: s.n.

Vasco G. (1772). *Della moneta saggio politico*. Milan: Galeazzi

Vergara, C. A. (1715). *Monete del Regno di Napoli di Ruggiero Primo Re sino all'Augustissimo Regnante Carlo VI Imperatore e III Re Cattolico raccolte e spiegate da Don Cesare Antonio Vergara dottore dell'una e dell'altra legge*. Rome: Gonzaga.

Secondary Sources

Ajello, R. (1972). La vita politica napoletana sotto Carlo di Borbone. In *Storia di Napoli*, vol. VII, Naples: Società editrice della Storia di Napoli, pp. 459–717.

Ajello, R. (1978). Nota introduttiva alle opere di Carlo Antonio Broggia. In R. Ajello, (ed.) *La letteratura italiana. Storia e testi. Dal Muratori al Cesarotti. Politici ed economisti del primo Settecento*, vol. 44, tomo V. Milan-Naples: Ricciardi, 1978, pp. 971–1032.

Amato, M. (1999). Il bivio della moneta. Problemi monetari e pensiero del denaro nel Settecento italiano. Milan: Egea.

Bianchini, L. (1839). *Storia delle finanze del Regno di Napoli*. Palermo: Lao.

Bloch, M. (1954). *Esquisse d'une histoire monétaire de l'Europe* (Cahiers des annales, N° 9). Paris: Colin.

Boyer-Xambeu, M.-T., Deleplace, G., Gillard, L. (1986). *Private Money & Public Currency. The 16th Century Challenge*. Armonk-London: Sharpe.

Brants, V. (1895) [1970]. *L'économie politique au Moyen-Age: esquisse des théories économiques professées par les écrivains des XIIIe et XIVe siècles*. New York: Franklin.

Bridrey, E. (1906). *La théorie de la monnaie au XIVe siècle, Nicolas Oresme*. Paris: Giard & Brière.

Caden, M. (2019). Money and its Technologies: Industrial Opposition and the Problem of Trust. In C. Desan (ed.) *A Cultural History of Money*, Vol. IV, *A Cultural History of Money in the Age of Enlightenment*. London: Bloomsbury Academic, pp. 25–52.

Carey, D. (2019). Money and the Issues of the Age: Thinking about Money in the Eighteenth Century. In C. Desan (ed.) *A Cultural History of Money*, Vol. IV, *A Cultural History of Money in the Age of Enlightenment*. London: Bloomsbury Academic, pp. 163–186.

Carlile W. W. (1901). *The Evolution of Modern Money*. London: Palgrave.

Catucci, M. (1986). *Galianea. Ferdinando Galiani tra letteratura ed economia*, Rome: Bulzoni.

Chown J. (1996). *A History of Money From Ad 800*. London, Routledge.

Cipolla, C. (1967). *Money, Prices and Civilization in the Mediterranean World: Fifth to Seventeenth Century*. New York, Gordian Press.

Cipolla, C. (1975). *Le avventure della lira*. Bologna: Il Mulino.

Codr, D. (2019). Money, Ritual, and Religion: A secularization story. In Desan. C. (ed.) *A Cultural History of Money*, Vol. IV, *A Cultural History of Money in the Age of Enlightenment*. London: Bloomsbury Academic, pp. 75–94.

Colapietra, R. (ed.) (1973). *Problemi monetari negli scrittori napoletani del Seicento*. Rome: Accademia Nazionale dei Lincei.

Costabile, L., Neal, L. (2018). *Financial Innovation and Resilience. A Comparative Perspective on the Public Banks of Naples (1462–1808)*. London: Palgrave Macmillan.

Costabile, L., Velde, F. (2023). Tax Erosion in Seventeenth-Century Naples: Tommaso Campanella on Causes and Remedies. *History of Political Economy*, 55: 5, pp. 929–962

Dal Pane, L. (1958). Di un' opera sconosciuta di Carlo Antonio Broggia e del suo carteggio con L. A. Muratori. *Giornale degli Economisti e Annali di Economia*, Nuova Serie, Anno 17, No. 11/12, pp. 638–661.

Davies, G. (2002). *A History of Money. From Ancient Times to the Present Day*. Cardiff: University of Wales Press.

Dell'Erba, L. (1932–1935) [1986]. *La riforma monetaria angioina e il suo sviluppo storico nel Reame di Napoli*, Sala Bolognese: Forni, 1986. First publication in *Archivio storico per le province napoletane*, Nuova Serie, anno XVIII–LVII, fascicolo I–IV, pp. 156–206; anno XIX–LVIII, fascicolo I–IV, pp. 5–66; anno XX–LIX, fascicolo I–IV, pp. 39–136; anno XXI–LX, fascicolo I–IV, pp. 46–158.

De Rosa, L. (1955). *I cambi esteri del Regno di Napoli dal 1591 al 1707*. Naples: Biblioteca del Bollettino dell'Archivio storico del Banco di Napoli.

De Rosa, L. (1987). *Il Mezzogiorno spagnolo tra crescita e decadenza*. Milan: Il Saggiatore.

De Rosa, L. (1994). Introduzione. In L. De Rosa (ed.) *Il Mezzogiorno agli inizi del '600*, Bari: Laterza.

De Rosa, L. (1995). Galiani e il commercio dei grani. In L. De Rosa, (ed.), *Economisti merdionali*. Naples: Istituto Italiano per gli Studi Filosofici, pp. 117–189.

De Rosa, L. (2004). L'archivio del Banco di Napoli e l'attività dei banchi pubblici napoletani. *De Computis. Spanish Journal of Accounting History*, N.1, pp. 54–66.

Einaudi, L. (1936) [2006]. The Theory of Imaginary Money from Charlemagne to the French Revolution. *Rivista di storia economica*, 1936, I, pp. 1–35. In L. Einaudi, R. Faucci, R. Marchionatti (eds.) *Luigi Einaudi Selected Economic Essays*. London: Palgrave Macmillan, Vol. II, pp. 153–181.

Fay, C. R. (1932). Locke Versus Lowndes. *The Cambridge Historical Journal* IV, no. 2, pp. 149–155.

Felloni, G. (1998). Finanze statali, emissioni monetarie ed alterazioni della moneta di conto in Italia nei secoli XVI–XVIII. In *Scritti di Storia Economica*, Genoa: Società Ligure di Storia Patria, pp. 471–496.

Fisher, I. (1913). A Compensated Dollar. *Quarterly Journal of Economics*, vol. 27, n. 2, pp. 213–235.

Galasso, G. (1959). Contributo alla storia delle finanze del regno di Napoli nella prima metà del Seicento. *Annuario dell'Istituto storico italiano per l'età moderna e contemporanea*, Vol. XI, pp. 5–106.

Gillard, L. (1990). Nicole Oresme, économiste. *Revue historique* 279, CCLXXIX, vol. 279 (1), (1990), pp. 3–39.

Hicks, J. (1967). *Critical essays in monetary theory*. Oxford: Claredon Press.

Horsefield, J. K. (1960). *British Monetary Experiments, 1650–1710*. Cambridge, MA: Harvard University Press.

Hülsmann, J. G. (2008). *The Ethics Of Money Production*. Auburn: Alabama Ludwig von Mises Institute.

Iovine, R. (1999). Il trattato Della moneta di Ferdinando Galiani. La dialettica politica a favore e contro la pubblicazione. *Frontiera d'Europa*, 1999, n. 1, pp. 173–236.

Iovine, R. (2001). Una cattedra per Genovesi nella crisi della cultyura moderna a Napoli. *Frontiera d'Europa*, 2001, n. 1–2, pp. 359–532.

Jannaccone, P. (1946). *Moneta e lavoro*. Torino: Utet.

Jevons, W. S. (1884). *Investigations in Currency and Finance*. London: Macmillan

Kelly, P. H. (1991). Introduction. In P. H. Kelly (ed.), *Locke on Money*, ed., Oxford: Clarendon Press.

Kleer, R. (2004). The Ruine of Their Diana: Lowndes, Locke, and the Bankers. *History of Political Economy* 36, no. 3, pp. 533–556.

Langholm, O. (1992). *Economics in the Medieval Schools: Wealth, Exchange, Value, Money and Usury According to the Paris Theological Tradition, 1200–1350*. Leiden: Brill.

Loria, A. (1936). Intorno alla funzione della moneta immaginaria (con osservazioni di Luigi Einaudi). *Rivista di Storia Economica*, Anno I, Numero 4, pp. 299–308.

Marshall A. (1926). *Official Papers.* London: Macmillan.

Mauss, M. (1923–24). Essai sur le don. Forme et raison de l'échange dans les sociétés archaïques. *Année sociologique*, Seconde Série, I Année, pp. 30–186.

Messedaglia, A. (1881). La teoria e la statistica dei metalli preziosi quale preliminare allo studio delle presenti questioni monetarie. *Archivio di statistica*, Anno VI, fasc. I, Estratto, Turin: Loesher.

Monroe, A. E. (1923). *Monetary Theory Before Adam Smith*, Cambridge (MS): Harvard University Press.

Montacutelli, M. (2018). Cornelio Spinola. In *Dizionario Biografico degli Italiani* - Volume 93, Rome: Treccani, *ad vocem*.

Muldrew, C. (2019). Money and the Everyday: New Practices in the Enlightenment. In C. Desan (ed.) *A Cultural History of Money*, Vol. IV, *A Cultural History of Money in the Age of Enlightenment*. London: Bloomsbury Academic, pp. 95–120.

Musi, A. (2004). Il console genovese a Napoli Cornelio Spinola (1621–1648) e i problemi di economia e di finanze nel Seicento mediterraneo *Archivio storico per le province napoletane*, CXXII, pp. 167–183.

Muto, G. (1986). Il problema monetario tra teoria e pratica di governo. *Bollettino del Centro di Studi Vichiani*, anno XVI, 1986, pp. 177–196.

Nederman, C. J. (2000). Community and the Rise of Commercial Society: Political Economy and Political Theory in Nicholas Oresme's *De Moneta*. *History of Political Thought*, 21, no. 1, pp. 2–15.

Nicolini, F. (1908a). I manoscritti di Ferdinando Galiani, *Archivio storico per le province napoletane*, 33 (1908), pp. 171–197.

Patalano, R. (2011). Carlo Antonio Broggia. In *Il Contributo Italiano alla Storia del Pensiero. Economia*. Rome: Treccani, pp. 287–291.

Patalano, R. (2016). Serra's Brief Treatise in a World-System Perspective: The Dutch Miracle and Italian Decadence in the Early 17th Century. In R. Patalano, S. A. Reinert, (eds.), *Antonio Serra and the Economics of Good Government, in Antonio Serra and the Economics of Good Government*, London: Palgrave Macmillan, pp. 63–88.

Patalano, R. (2017). Geometry of Money in the Neapolitan Eighteenth Century: Trojano Spinelli's Riflessioni Politiche. *History of Political Economy*, 49:4, pp. 631–666.

Patalano, R. (2020a). Carlo Antonio Broggia, a money doctor in adverse circumstances. *History of Economic Thought and Policy*, 2–2020, pp. 9–37.

Patalano, R. (2020b). Ferdinando Galiani's Newtonian Social Mathematics. *Journal of the History of Economic Thought*, Vol. 42, 3, pp. 357–383.

Patalano, R., Reinert, S. A. (eds.) (2016). *Antonio Serra and the economics of good government*, New York: Palgrave Macmillan.

Romano, R. (1970). Economia e finanza nella Napoli spagnola. In *Storia di Napoli*, volume VI, Naples: Società Editrice Storia di Napoli, pp. 537–606.

Rosselli, A. (2000). Early Views on Monetary Policy: The Neapolitan Debate on the Theory of Exchange. *History of Political Economy*, 32:1, pp. 61–82.

Sargent, T. J, Velde, F. R. (2002). *The Big Problem of Small Change*. Princeton: Princeton University Pres.

Schipa, M. (1902). *Il Muratori e la cultura napoletana del suo tempo*. Naples: Pierro.

Schipa, M. (1904). *Il Regno di Napoli al tempo di Carlo di Borbone*. Naples: Pierro.

Schumpeter, J. A. (1954) [2006]. *History of Economic Analysis*. London: Routledge.

Shaw, W. (1896). *The history of currency, 1252 to 1894,* Second Edition, New York: Burt Franklin.

Souffrin, P., Segonds, A. P. (eds.). (1988). *Nicolas Oresme, Tradition et innovation chez un intellectuel du XIVe siècle*. Paris: Les Belles Lettres.

Tiran, A. (2014). La monnaie ct les prix dans la pensée italienne au dix-huitième siècle. In J Blanc, L. Desmedt (eds.) *Les Pensées monétaires dans l'histoire. L'Europe, 1517–1776*. Paris: Classiques Garnier, pp. 645–700.

Tucci, U. (1986). Monete e riforme monetarie nell'Italia del Settecento. *Rivista Storica Italiana*, Anno XCVIII, I, pp. 78–119.

Tucci, U. (1996). Teoria e pratica delle idee monetarie di Gian Rinaldo Carli. *Acta Historiae*, V, pp. 11–24.

Van Der Wee, H. (1977). Monetary, Credit and Banking Systems. In *The Cambridge Economic History*, volume V, Cambridge; Cambridge University Press, pp. 290–392.

Velde, F. (2020). The Money Doctors of Seventeenth-Century Naples. *Capitalism: A Journal of History and Economics*, Volume 1, Number 2, Spring m2020, pp. 405–455.

Venturi F. (1959a). Alle origini dell'Illuminismo napoletano. Dal carteggio di Bartolomeo Intieri. *Rivista Storica Italiana*, a. LXXI, fascicolo III, pp. 416–456.

Venturi, F. (1998). *Settecento riformatore. Da Muratori a Beccaria*, Turin: Einaudi.

Vianello, A. (ed.) (1939). La riforma monetaria in Lombardia nella Seconda metà del '700. Milan: Bocconi.

Vilar, Pierre. (1991). *A History of Gold and Money, 1450 to 1920*. London: Verso.

Wennerlind, C. (2019). Money and its Ideas: Enlightenment debates about the Morality of Money. In C. Desan (ed.) *A Cultural History of Money*, Vol. IV, *A Cultural History of Money in the Age of Enlightenment*. London: Bloomsbury Academic, pp. 53–74.

CHAPTER 4

Della Moneta: The Pure Theory of Money

4.1 Nature, Functions and Origin of Money

"I have decided to write and, depending on my strength and talent, to illustrate the nature and qualities of money, that is, of those metals which the learned nations use to give and take as the equivalent of everything else: a subject as much for its great usefulness as for the obscurity that covers it, worthy to be studied and known much more than it is by the men appointed to command" (Galiani [1751]: 1).[1] Thus Galiani, pretending to be an old man,[2] wrote in the *Introduction* to his treatise, attacking those intellectuals who had "always neglected to examine the exact regulation of money" (Galiani [1751] *Proemio* [2]) useful to society, a lacuna from which the historians had not escaped, who although they considered themselves "masters of politics", had taught more "the art of acquiring

[1] The quotations from *Della Moneta* were translated into English by the author. The only English translation of *Della Moneta* currently available is by Peter Toscano (Galiani 1977), but it is not accurate and often fails to capture the true meaning of Galiani's thought.

[2] "In order to conceal myself better, it seemed to me convenient to pretend that the author of the book was a grave man, of mature age, fought and wearied by adverse fortune, and arrived at the tedium of a world too well known; and this pretence and innocent mischief were so useful to me, that nothing helped more to make people applaud the book and not let the author be guessed. Without this warning, one would not understand the reason for some of the phrases scattered throughout the book" (Galiani 1780: Note III, 375, see also Note XV, 393).

R. Patalano, *Ferdinando Galiani*,
https://doi.org/10.1007/978-3-032-02793-1_4

and preserving the dominion of Princes, than of making the obedience of subjects happy and sweet" (Galiani [1751]: *Proemio* [2]). Among them was "the immortal Muratori", who in his *Della Pubblica Felicità*, "with a naive confession of impotence" (Galiani [1751]: *Proemio* [2]) had commendably neglected to deal with the subject of money, avoiding a presumptuous dissertation on a subject he ignored.

In the midst of this desert, Galiani only saw the works of "Signor Melun", "a man of the greatest intellect, and of a truly honest and virtuous soul" (Galiani [1751]: *Proemio* [3]), of John Locke, "from whom it would have been desirable that in what he wrote more method and order could be discerned; and that not an informal letter, but an orderly work had been done by such a man" (Galiani [1751]: *Proemio* [3]) and also the Neapolitans, Broggia and Spinelli, deserved honourable mention, "of whom, one the entire science of money, the other of devaluation (called *alzamento*) had treated with praise"(Galiani [1751]: *Proemio* [3]).

Although he had "taken from them various concepts", he did not choose to quote them, "because", Galiani remarked, "the things I deal with, I desire that they have their force from reason, not from authority [...] knowing that the demonstration of truth is in itself a most powerful confutation of the false: and the pomp of quoting [...] I believe that it is always caused by littleness of mind" (Galiani [1751]:*Proemio* [3]).[3] Still contrasting traditional culture, he therefore chose a simple and direct method, seeking "greater clarity" and staying away from any "locution of sublime geometry" (Galiani [1751]: *Proemio* [4]).

And Galiani's choice of originality is evident in his method: the argumentation with which he studies the complex phenomenon of money is twofold: on the one hand a *deductive method*, on the other a continuous *historical specification* of what was established in the sphere of pure

[3] In the second edition, Galiani specified this choice in a note: "It is easy to see from reading this book that it was my intention to mention by name as little as possible those writers to whom I would be opposed, as it seems to me that sentiments, and not names of persons, are to be opposed by those who hold a contrary opinion. Moreover, I foresaw that, when it became known that I was the author, many would be scandalised to see a young man lacking in reverence for some venerated name" (Galiani 1780: Note I, 373). The venerable names under criticism were Bernardo Davanzati and Abbé de Saint-Pierre.

abstraction.[4] An alternation of *theoretical abstract* and *historical concrete* thus characterises the first two books of Galiani's work.

The way the young abbot defines the nature of money in the *First Chapter* of the *Second Book*, is essentially *deductive*.[5] Rejecting the opinions of philosophers who had considered the introduction of money "as the origin of all guilt and fomenting of bad inclinations" (Galiani [1751]: 88), Galiani reaffirmed the social usefulness of the monetary instrument, the fruit of the "perfection of civil society" (Galiani [1751]: 89). Men need to exchange goods with each other to satisfy each other's needs; trade is nothing but "a communication that men make among themselves of their efforts to meet common needs" (Galiani [1751]: 89). Exchange is therefore a human necessity, and everything that facilitates it is "also very useful" (Galiani [1751]: 89).

The first form of exchange is the simple barter "of things for things", but it is of great "inconvenience [...] because it is too difficult to know who lacks the thing that I have in abundance, or who has the thing that I am missing, nor can all things be transported, nor kept for a long time, nor equalized or divided according perhaps to the present and common need" (Galiani [1751]: 89–90).[6]

Galiani summarises in these few lines the traditional theses on the difficulties arising from a barter system, inherited from the Aristotelian tradition: the problem of the two wants not coinciding; difficulty in storing value; lack of division of goods and lack of a common measure of value

[4] Galiani emphasises the importance of history from the first pages of *Della Moneta*: "the art of government, more than any other without scholars, has been conducted up to the present day, and provided only with the materials from which it can be portrayed. These are contained in history. History is an unbroken narrative of the errors and punishments of mankind: from which it is easy, by meditating on it and on the errors of others, becoming wise, to amend the former or repair the latter. And not unlike the astronomical observations of many centuries, it was not difficult to define the system of the motion of the planets, so it is in the science of governing" (Galiani [1751]: [14–15]). On the distinction between the two levels of analysis, see Cesarano (1995: 102).

[5] The priority of the deductive method unites Galiani with modern thinking: "One of the chief things which monetary theory ought to explain is the evolution of money. If we can reduce the main lines of that evolution to a logical pattern, we shall not only have thrown light upon history, but we shall also have deepened our understanding of money, even modern money, itself" (Hicks 1967: 2)

[6] According to Filippo Cesarano, Galiani's analysis anticipates the theses of Carl Menger and Robert Jones on the origin of money (see Cesarano 1995: 99; Menger 1892; Jones 1976), but it is a very forced interpretation.

("nor equalized").[7] But in order to arrive at a definition of the historical necessity of commodity money, he follows an original path compared to the arguments of the Aristotelian tradition, deepening the analysis of the nature of the monetary instrument. The necessity of money has an anthropological cause, as it is a product of man's selfish nature. To demonstrate this concept, Galiani uses an argument to the contrary by hypothesising the existence of a communitarian society, such as that of "many religious orders, [which] happily and better than others live in communion", where the goods resulting from work are stored in "open and communal" warehouses from which each person withdraws according to his needs (Galiani [1751]: 90).[8] This type of society, in which there is a division of labour but goods are not traded on the market and distribution is centralised, has no need of money if its members maintain virtuous behaviour, but if even a small part of the population has opportunistic behaviour and lives "unjustly off the labours of others" in a social context in which "here would be no way to enrich or impoverish" (Galiani [1751]: 90), even the honest industrious person would no longer have any incentive to work and would also claim to live lavishly without effort. Such a society, undermined at its

[7] Aristotele ([1998], Book I, 9, 1257a: 15–16). Aristotelian tradition is, however, contradictory on the nature of money. In the *Politics*, Aristotle defines the characteristics of metallic money, in the *Nicomachean Ethics* he abandons the concept of commodity money to define money as ***nomisma***, "because it exists not by nature but by convention (***nomos***), and it is in our power to change its value and to render it worthless "(Aristotle [2004], Book V, 1133 a: 90, see Schumpeter 1954 [2006]: 57–62; Gordon 1961: 612). The scholastic tradition (*feudal theory of money*, Bridrey 1906: 101–177) proposed a particular interpretation of Aristotelian thought that was based more on the *Ethics* than on the *Politics*, which was later known and translated into Latin. This conception placed more emphasis on the conventional character of the monetary instrument than on its nature as a commodity. Money was thus reduced to a mere conventional instrument, a measure of values, and as such fell within the specific domain of State authority, becoming the highest expression of sovereignty. It was therefore fully justifiable that the prince could change the currency according to his needs. Galiani strongly contested the thesis held by the Aristotelian tradition (consisting of jurists and moralists) that considered money to be a creation of the law, believing that Davanzati, Locke, Broggia and Montesquieu were also still partly linked to that tradition (Galiani [1751]: 25–26).

[8] The concept of a society governed by communitarian principles is a typical theme of utopian literature: "Whatever each household produces is stored in warehouses, each kind of goods in its own place. Here the head of every household looks for what he or his family needs, and carries off what he wants without any sort of payment or compensation" (More 1516 [2002]: 55).

foundation by opportunistic behaviour stemming from man's egoistic nature, could therefore not survive for long.[9]

This communitarian society cannot therefore survive because it is completely incompatible with the nature of man, who always seeks his own gain with the minimum effort and sacrifice and "always careful not to be defrauded of their pleasures" (Galiani [1751]: 27). Galiani therefore accepted, without theological scruples, the principle of *self-interest* as prime mover of the economic order. His vision, however, is not optimistic: a sceptical conception of human behaviour is prevalent in his analysis, echoing the views of Niccolò Machiavelli and Thomas Hobbes.[10] According to Machiavelli, "all men are bad, and will always, when they have free field, give loose to their evil inclinations" (Machiavelli 1531 [1883]: 31), and "they are ungrateful, fickle, dissembling, hypocritical, cowardly, and greedy" (Machiavelli 1532 [1976]: 271). Community life can only remain if these inclinations of men are controlled and limited, as the Prince must do. A line of thought that goes all the way back to Hobbes, according to whom human action is expressed through acts of mutual diffidence.[11] These are conceptions that profoundly influenced the young Galiani, and which would remain fundamental constants in his thinking, sometimes described as excessively cynical.

To deal with opportunistic behaviour, it is necessary to introduce rules imposed by an authority that tries to repress it. The state of nature is, according to Galiani, a "most unhappy" condition. in which man is

[9] In the *Dialogues*, Galiani returned to the subject of monastic communities considering their limited number: "In a small administration, it would not be possible to introduce great abuses, it would be guarded too closely, it would not be possible to rehabilitate much" (Galiani 1770a: 37).

[10] In a youthful manuscript dedicated to superstition, Galiani wrote: "Man is born with a vile and infirm soul. Because he is vile, he is timid, envious, and enjoys the evil of others. Because he is timid, he is credulous, a liar, and in offences vindictive and cruel" (Galiani, MS-6: 469).

[11] "And from this diffidence of one another, there is no way for any man to secure himself, so reasonable as anticipation; that is, by force, or wiles, to master the persons of all men he can, so long, till he see no other power great enough to endanger him: and this is no more than his own conservation requireth, and is generally allowed" (Hobbes 1651 [1909]: 95). See Holt (2004) and on the influence of Hobbes in eighteenth century Italy, see Garin (1962). On Machiavelli's view of human nature, see Femia (2004: 63–85). Even Giuseppe Pecchio, who does not avoid criticism of Galiani, notes Machiavelli's influence on the Neapolitan abbot (Pecchio 1849: 84). On the "selfish hypothesis", the idea of self-interest as the motive of human action in pre-Smithian thought, see Force (2003).

"similar in everything to brutes" and it is "the orders of civilised society, which from the feral life and natural inclinations to maleficence, cruelty, hatred, envy and rapacity withdraw us" (Galiani [1751]:87–88). The role Galiani attributes to public authority follows the Hobbesian line and this approach is present as early as the *Dedication* to the Sovereign: "as men were drawn from the feral life and the unhappy state of nature and reduced to civil society, they unanimously resigned the defence of their rights to the Prince and to him all care for peace and tranquillity abandoned" (Galiani [1751]: *Dedica* [1]).

This Machiavellian-Hobbesian conception of the state of nature distances the young Galiani from the thesis of peaceful and cooperative human groupings advocated by his uncle Celestino, distances him from Intieri's optimism, and brings him closer to Vico for whom man is animated by bestial passions that are only corrected by religion, considered as the foundation of civil society.[12] Instead, for the young abbot, men guided by selfish interests ("insatiable animal [...] but rational and careful", Galiani [1751]:114) and dominated by opportunistic behaviour cannot build solid societies, which are only possible if there are institutions capable of imposing virtuous behaviour or repressing opportunistic ones.[13] But on the other hand, no social order can be founded on virtue alone: "nations and kingdoms will have ruinous and vacillating government if the virtue that sustains it is not joined to mundane interest, [the strength of which is always inexpugnable in even vicious human souls], since vast bodies cannot fully purge themselves of the bad germs that are born in them" (Galiani [1751]: 95).

Indeed, the warehouse system can exist if the rule is established that each person must receive the equivalent of what they have given to society

[12] The state of nature defined by Vico as "feral state" has marked elements of affinity with Hobbes' conception. "It was a nature all fierce and cruel; but, through that same error of their imagination, men had a terrible fear of the gods whom they themselves had created. From his period there remained two eternal properties: one, that religion is the only means powerful enough to restrain the fierceness of peoples; and the other, that religions prosper when those who preside over them are themselves inwardly reverent" (Vico 1744 [1948]: 317, § 916). On the controversial relationship between Vico and Hobbes, see Nicolini (1942, 1950); Nagy (2012). On the "state of nature" in Vico, see Costelloe (1999).

[13] The pessimistic view clearly separates Galiani from the erudite libertinism of Saint-Évremond, Mandeville and Bayle, for whom egoism and other vices are positive elements that should not be repressed but seconded, as they coincide with the interests of the state and society.

through their work and no more.[14] In this way each person who brings the product of his labour to the common warehouse obtains a *bullettino* (*note*), "conceived in these terms: *That he who has put into the public warehouses so much of such stuff, let us say for example 100 pairs of shoes, for the value of which he remains a creditor of the society*" (Galiani [1751]: 91, original italics).[15] To facilitate exchanges, rather than marking on the note the quantity of a specific good that the holder would have the right to take, a mechanism that would be as inefficient as barter, it would be necessary that "at the gates of all warehouses notes were freely received, so that everyone could obtain what he needed" (Galiani [1751]:91); and when the counter-value marked on the bulletin was covered, it was returned or destroyed.[16] In order to make the various goods commensurable, the Prince should establish a "value to all things [...] declaring, for example, that a bushel of wheat corresponds to as much wine, as much meat, as much oil, as much clothing, as much cheese, etc" (Galiani [1751]: 91). The public authority has the task of defining the relative prices between goods, so that "it would be known how much one belongs to each one to

[14]This type of society is governed by the law of labour-value. Galiani's *bollettini*, at this stage of his analysis, are similar to the *labour-notes* devised by Robert Owen and other utopian socialists..

[15]In a similar theoretical context, the possibility that each warehouse official does not issue notes but directly informs the other warehouse officials of the credit of each party with the community (and therefore of the right to withdraw goods from the warehouses) has been examined by Robert Lucas (1980). Carlo Benetti identifies the case in question with the "troc parfait" (Benetti 1994: 1180, see also Benetti 2018). According to Filippo Cesarano, this conception is an anticipation of modern theories that consider money as an instrument for "the production of information relevant to the respect of the budget constraint" (Cesarano 1995: 100–101). In particular, Cesarano identifies a certain affinity on the theoretical level with the *record-keeping system* defined by Joseph Ostroy (1973). See also Patalano and Realfonzo (2001).

[16]Warehouse officials act as certifiers who witness each agent's entitlement to make withdrawals. This is an approach compatibile with the *witness theory* on the origin of money put forward by Gunnar Heinsohn and Otto Steiger (1983: 19). There is also a clear similarity with the method adopted by Joseph Alois Schumpeter in *Das Wesen des Geldes*, and in particular with the theoretical case of the socialist economy: "we will have before us a system of book-keeping equivalences, illustrating numerically the whole economic life of the community and in which every element corresponds to an element in the economic circuit. We could assume that everything takes place in the records of the account books of the headquarters, acknowledging every member's entitlement to consume and debiting him with his withdrawals [...]. We could however imagine that the labour-slips are physically made out at the headquarters and given to the members, who later hand them in to the warehouses" (Schumpeter 1970: 108).

receive for what he has done, and when that his credit is equalized" (Galiani [1751]: 91–92).

A public authority implies the existence of a bureaucratic apparatus, even a simple one, made up of officials not directly involved in the production process, and to guarantee its function it is necessary to give the bureaucrats an amount of goods "proportionate to the importance and merit of their service" (Galiani [1751]: 92). The balance between the goods available in the general warehouse and the notes must always be maintained to avoid the disturbance of order and public confidence, and to this end, a certain number of bulletins must be given to the Prince and his bureaucratic apparatus, obliging "the citizens to bring, gratis, that is, without receiving a note, as many goods into the warehouses, as the sum of all that is given to the Prince to distribute to the ministers of society" (Galiani [1751]: 92). In the model of economy outlined by Galiani *notes* are the simple instruments of social accounting; they allow the contribution to production and the withdrawals from the communal warehouse to be measured, so that the latter do not exceed the former for each individual (budget constraint).[17]

However, even in this system - Galiani noted - opportunistic behaviour can occur either by directly falsifying the notes or through the frauds that warehousemen can commit in order to favour relatives and friends, by writing on the credit notes "a price higher than the goods brought, declaring, for example, he who brought only ten shoes to be the creditor of 1,000 pounds of bread, as if he had brought not ten but one hundred pounds: which would make the appearance of warehouses more stocked with goods than they actually are" (Galiani [1751]: 92–93). To avoid this problem the intervention of the public authority is again required, so that

[17] Galiani's argument is not very dissimilar to some of the definitions found in a general economic equilibrium model. A simple formalisation clarifies this statement: For each individual i-th of this community, the product of its labour constitutes its initial endowment w_i (which is not necessarily a single good, but can also be a vector of goods). Once the price system in the vector $[p]$ has been identified, the value of the endowment is also determined, thus:

$$[p]\ w_i = v_i$$

The variable v_i indicates precisely the *bullettini* (notes) in the possession of each individual, which can be exchanged for other goods in stock. Given that $[x]$ is the vector of goods, the subject can exchange while respecting its budget constraint (the purchasing power of its endowment), i.e:

$$[p]\ [x] \leq v_i$$

the Prince, having chosen a good as the unit of account (a pound of bread, for example), fixes the value of each *note*, distributing them to the keepers, who in turn are to give the notes to those who introduce goods into the warehouse and to receive them from those who take goods out: "then no longer would the whole price be expressed on one note, but he who brings in goods of more value than a pound of bread, would take as many bulletins as would equal the value of that" (Galiani [1751]: 93). This step marks the introduction of a common unit of account (the pound of bread), sanctioned by the public authority, with which an accurate accounting of the goods brought in and taken out of storage can be kept. The definition of a unit of account is therefore the founding act of money since being a unit of account constitutes its essence.[18]

This institutional expedient would remedy "the confusion of the various characters, the falsification, the continual formation of new notes; the keepers could keep their accounts exactly, and finally if it were certain that the notes would not be rejected by anyone for fear of fraud, it would seem that with these orders a society could be held and preserved"

[18] Galiani's analysis is very similar to the theory of money developed by John Maynard Keynes, who attributed the original function of unit of account to money: "Money itself, namely that by delivery of which debt contracts and price contracts are discharged, and in the shape of which a store of general purchasing power is held, derives its character from its relationship to the money of account, since the debts and prices must first have been expressed in terms of the latter. Something which is merely used as a convenient medium of exchange on the spot may approach to being money, inasmuch as it may represent a means of holding general purchasing power. But if this is all, we have scarcely emerged from the stage of barter. Money proper in the full sense of the term can only exist in relation to a money of account" (Keynes 1930, vol. I: 3). Very different is the *commodity-money theory*, which considers the function of exchange intermediary as primary: "Considering the market at any point in time, the logical precedence of the use of intermediation is demonstrated by the dependence of current nominal prices on the last actual prices. That is, from the prices that were determined by the exchange as it took place. Then, because if one considers the question from its dynamic aspect, one has to imagine - going backwards in the price series - an initial instant in which money appeared on the market. At that instant the only possible prices had to be, of necessity, the actual prices, as nominal prices could not be quoted for lack of experience. Sound logical reasons therefore recommend removing the value-measuring function from the group of independent monetary functions. Money measures value because it acts as an intermediary of exchange, and the proposition remains true even if the two tasks are performed by different things" (Federici 1941: 19; see also Cesarano 1995: 99).

(Galiani [1751]: 93). The notes took on the function of a means of payment.

At this point Galiani's deductive argumentation was interrupted, he tried to specify historically what he had logically affirmed. He looked for "whether historians or travellers told of any nation that by example confirmed my ideas", but "behold, a veil almost fell from my eyes and I realised that I had inadvertently arrived in the present world" (Galiani [1751]: 93–94).

Thus, it was clear to him that:

1. "commerce and money, its prime mover, have led us from the miserable state of nature in which each one thinks for himself to the happiest state of common life, in which each one thinks for all and works hard: and in this state, not from the principle of virtue and piety alone [...] but for the purpose of private interest and the comfort of each one, we are preserved" (Galiani [1751]: 94).
2. The *notes* were money "which is a representation of the claim that a person has on society, because of the labours incurred by him or by others for him" (Galiani [1751]: 94).
3. Common warehouses were to be replaced by private workshops, and keepers by their own interest, "the strength of which is always invincible even in vicious human souls", because in society virtue must be combined with worldly interest, "since the vast bodies cannot be fully purged of the evil germs that are born in them" (Galiani [1751]: 94–95).
4. The *notes* given gratis to the Prince and officials were simply duties and tributes, then distributed partly in wages to employees and partly in expenses of the Prince (Galiani [1751]: 95).
5. Precious metals (gold and silver in the first place) used as materials of the *notes* solved the inconveniences caused by the use of any alternative materials. The *moneta optima* is therefore metallic money, because it insures against the fraud of private individuals and the abuse that the Prince can make of it. In fact "if the matter did not contain all the value that money has, the Prince could print an excessive number of *notes*; and this mere doubt that he could do so is enough to decrease its price and stop its circulation. But metallic money cannot be multiplied except by God, and to want to dig it up or buy it involves as much expense as it is worth, and so there is no gain in increasing it: and therefore it is of the greatest importance

that money be made of such a material that all value has it natural and intrinsic, and not ideal" (Galiani [1751]: 95–96).

It is clear from all this argumentation that Galiani did not make the mistake, identified by Schumpeter, of confusing the purely *logical aspect* of the nature of money with its *historical characteristic*.[19] For Galiani, the logical nature of money is as a credit that allows the bearer to withdraw goods from the social warehouse: its materialization in a metallic form is the best solution to the inconveniences that arise from the use of other material means and which can call into question the maintenance of that trust on which the credit relationship represented by money is essentially based. The metallic form of money, its identification with a particular commodity such as gold, silver and copper, is only a historical product, a fact, but this does not exclude that among other peoples and in other periods of history, with the same meaning of money, other metallic materials have been used, such as bronze, brass, iron and even lead, and "in addition to this, there is no lack of nations that do not use metals, but use either fruit, as of bitter almonds in Cambaia [Cambodia], cocoa and mais in some places in America, or salt, as it is in Abyssinia, or sea shells. These things, whether they are money or not, when the words are disputed, much could be said in argument; but the dispute would be about names and not about things" (Galiani [1751]: 3).

The distinction between the *logical nature* and the *historical specification* of money appeared quite clear to Galiani, even in the functions that the monetary institution performs in reality: "money is of two kinds", he wrote "*ideal* and *real*, and it is used for two different purposes, to value things and to buy things" (Galiani [1751]: 67).

In its *ideal* use, "money is a common measure for knowing the price of everything [...] which means that a single voice, a single number is sufficient to evaluate everything, since the price consists of a proportion, which is best expressed and understood by numbers" (Galiani [1751]: 67).[20]

[19] "It is not true that, as a matter of pure logic, money essentially consists in, or must be backed by, a commodity or several commodities whose exchange value as commodities are the logical basis of their value as money" (Schumpeter 1954 [2006]: 276). According to Luigi Einaudi: "Galiani possessed the necessary investigative tool for the purpose, and while he did not know it by the name of the method of consecutive approximations, he knew how to handle it magnificently" (Einaudi 1949 [2014]: 234).

[20] This concept is well specified in the manuscript of *Della Moneta* kept in the library of *the Società Napoletana di Storia Patria*. Galiani defines money as "a common measure of the

In its *real* use, money buys goods that are valued by it.[21] For this function, it needs to be *materialised*, money must take real form and act as *tertium permutationis* (or *quid pro quo*), an intermediary of exchanges, a means of payment given in exchange for goods, and this has historically occurred mainly with precious metal coins. Considered in this *real dimension*, money is made up of "pieces of metal by public authority divided into parts either equal or proportionate to each other, which are given and taken with certainty by all as a pledge and perpetual security to have from others the equivalent of what was given to have these pieces of metal" (Galiani [1751]:68).[22]

Following Galiani's reasoning, it can be said that his *metallism* is *historically conditioned*: *perpetual security* could be provided by other pledges or simple accounting records, it is only the *state of confidence* at a given time and among given peoples that defines the materialisation of money, but this is contingent and remains distinct from its essence.[23]

And it is again the level of confidence that justifies particular institutions such as the Neapolitan public banks, which hoarded metallic money by forcing depositors to use deposit cerficates (called *fedi di credito*) to make payments; a particular rule that could be explained by the particular temperament of the Neapolitan people "inclined to quarrels and denial. The *fedi di credito* secure not only the payment, but its title with certain specific institutions. And so what is done elsewhere by the force of laws and the stimulus of gain, is done among us by corrupt customs and bad trust" (Galiani [1751]: 342, see Costabile 2016; Costabile - Neal 2018).

Galiani's analysis may seem deeply contradictory, oscillating between logical cartalism (*bollettini, notes*) and pratical metallism, if the deductive analysis, which defines the concept of money as valid *sub specie eaternitatis*,

relations of things in human commerce. That such is money to those who meditate on it requires no other evidence.[...]. It is not required to have any intrinsic value, but rather a number, and an abstract name suffice for this use, because they are sufficient to serve as a common measure. That this is true, it suffices to consider ideal [imaginary] money and the peoples who use them, and it will be seen that a single abstract name of something that does not exist is sufficient for this use" (Galiani, MS-13: folios 25r, 28r)

[21] Galiani defines the characteristics of a monetary economy in the sense that "money buys goods, but goods don't buy money" (Patinkin 1956: 1, see also Clower 1967).

[22] Locke's influence in defining metallic money as a *pledge* (Locke 1692: 30).

[23] In the manuscript of the treatise: "It is also seen by the case that during the space of some time coins have been sheared and counterfeited, or altered among an entire nation. Because men in taking money only seek the security of being able to give it for a thing of equal value to that which they have given for it" (Galiani, MS-13: folio 28).

is not distinguished from the historical specification, which instead defines money *sub specie temporis*, as it evolved in a given society and in a certain historical phase. Money is, essentially, the unit of account in social bookkeeping, the unit of measurement conventionally (and therefore arbitrarily) equated with the value of a given commodity or of a basket of commodities. This makes it possible to have a system of calculating the total value of production and the agents' claims to it.

According to the double method used by the young abbot, therefore, money is a *social institution* based on confidence and consensus, the metallic form it has taken is historically determined by the degree of confidence and is not a logical necessity. In this sense, Galiani's theory cannot be considered a metallist theory, according to which "it is logically essential for money to consist of, or to be covered by, some commodity" (Schumpeter 1954 [2006]: 274). The result achieved by Galiani's theory has many points of contact with some modern analyses of the monetary phenomenon, especially those referring to the *institutional theory of money*. According to these approaches money is neither a commodity, nor a contract, nor a creation of the state, but only a product of confidence (Aglietta and Orléan 2018: 103): "what matters [in a monetary economy] is the existence of social institutions condoned by either custom or law that enable individuals to trade efficiently if they follow certain rules" (Clower 1969: 13), and the aim of the "theory of money as an institutional mechanism is precisely to study the confidence-creating mechanism that evolved in order to support the accettability of money as *quid pro quo* in a world of imperfect information or, put another way, of potential fraudolent agents" (Giannini 2011: 9).[24]

Indeed, Galiani paid particular attention to the forms of *representation of money*, considering them as "manifestations of a debt" and relating their value specifically to confidence (Galiani [1751]:319).[25] "Their value", so he wrote, "is composed of the certainty of the debt, the punctuality of the debtor and the veracity of the sign. When all three of these requirements

[24]The institutional theory of money, which finds its forerunners in George Simmel (1907 [2004]) and François Simiand (1934), is distinguished into a neo-institutionalist approach (Richter 1988; Giannini 2011: chap.I) and a regulationist approach (Aglietta and Orléan 1982; Aglietta 2018). According to Paola Dongili, money in Galiani is a tool for lowering transaction costs in a context of information asymmetry, see Dongili, 1988: 18. See also Davis (2020).

[25]Representation (*représentation*) is a term used by Melon to refer to all forms of paper circulation and credit (Melon 1736: 7).

are in the highest degree certain, the representation equals the value of the thing represented [...].Therefore, such representations, easily finding those who accept them, become money, which can be said to be in all respects equal to the real one, were it not that they become bad and false as soon as they lose some of the aforesaid attributes, which, not being intrinsic to their nature, do not remain so firmly attached to them as the beauty and splendour of the metals that make up the real money" (Galiani [1751]:319–320).

Representations of money, such as paper money, can only exist, without being threatened by opportunistic behaviour, under certain circumstances: when their security "is founded on the terror of laws prohibiting their easy imitation" (as in the case of so-called *money of necessity*) and for "this reason they could only be used for a short time" (Galiani [1751]: 320); in the case of sieges, where promises of payment are drawn up for use at the end of the conflict; in the case of small, strongly united communities motivated by religious or political principles, such as the Quakers in Pennsylvania who used a paper currency without any particular problems (Galiani [1751]: 322–323).[26]

However, Galiani, while limiting its importance, did not reject metallism, believing that *moneta optima*, given the state of confidence, should only be based on gold, silver and copper.[27]

Real money, that is, "money that buys" must - according to the young abbot - meet two requisites in order to be used:

1. that it is universally accepted;
2. that it is not excessively voluminous and uncomfortable to transport and exchange (Galiani [1751]: 75).[28]

A good to be accepted by all as money must possess four qualities:

[26] On the diffusion of paper money in the English colonies of North America, see Weiss 1970.

[27] "Metallic money is seen as superior to paper on practical grounds, such as the fact that a piece of paper is far easier to duplicate than a piece of gold. In other words, money could be made of paper in principle, but it is wiser not to do so" (Rosselli 2001: 48). According to Lilia Costabile, Galiani developed a complex monetary model based on the coexistence of metallic and fiduciary circulation (Costabile 2016).

[28] Both of these requisites were known in Galiani's time, as they had already been clarified by scholastic philosophers.

1. it must have an intrinsic and real value unanimously estimated by all;
2. its value must be easily recognisable;
3. it must be difficult to falsify;
4. it must be storable for a long time (Galiani [1751]: 75–76).

The application of these criteria to the universe of goods known to man, leads to the selection of "those that nature has destined to serve as money by suitably endowing them" (Galiani [1751]: 76). First of all, all things that have no intrinsic value, but conventional value, are excluded: "because it is certainly less secure to have a good whose value depends on public convention and faith than to have those that have a value because they are necessary or useful to man" (Galiani [1751]:76). For this reason, the use of paper money or leather money cannot be accepted for long. Their acceptability is in fact limited to a particular community that has chosen to make use of them, but "the gap between public faith and common thinking is great. The latter is as universal as it is immutable, the former is extended no further than those persons and peoples who have agreed upon it, and is disturbed at every slightest accident, and therefore a people cannot use only represented money for long" (Galiani [1751]:76–77).

All goods that depend on the "tyranny of fashion" are also excluded, because if public faith is vacillating, the volubility of the "popular imagination" is even more so. Even more to be excluded are those goods that have value only for the particular religious faith or customs of a people. From this selection, only precious metals, and in particular gold and silver, can survive, as these satisfy the requirement of universal acceptability more than any other (Galiani [1751]: 77).

Regarding the second requirement (the immediate ascertainability of value), precious metals are the only goods that can be valued with respect to quantity (weight), quality (goodness) being unique or easily reducible to the same degree.[29] Their ductility allows them to be easily valued even if divided, because "of two pieces of gold I can make one [...] but of two diamonds there is no art of making one" (Galiani [1751]: 78). Their value is then clearly separated from the work that is applied to transform them into precious objects, as this art can simply be lost through casting; not so a cut gemstone (Galiani [1751]: 79). Falsifying metals is impossible, as

[29] "Metals are used for money because they have value, and they do not have value because they are used for money" (Galiani [1751]:55).

well as multiplying them. And even if this could be done, their value would decrease drastically until it would be nullified: "the Author of Nature will never allow the beautiful order of the universe, which all on money, as on its axis is maintained and turned, to be broken by Alchemy" (Galiani [1751]: 83). The mineralogical characteristics of precious metals then establish their immutability over time, justifying the fulfilment of the last requirement: long conservation.[30]

If precious metal in a society composed of selfish and opportunistic individuals is absolutely necessary for *real money*, it is also necessary for *ideal money*, even if this connection does not immediately appear, as it consists of the name alone (Galiani [1751]: 84). Instead, the link between metallic money and ideal money has a historical foundation, because: "an ideal money can only be introduced into a country by means of the real one, and wherever *imaginary money* is used for counting, it is certain that this money was once real, as is known from experience" (Galiani [1751]: 84). The link also exists from a logical point of view, because the essential function of ideal money is to be a measure, and "the measures must be stable and fixed as much as possible, but this stability cannot be found in any human thing" (Galiani [1751]: 84). However, it can be approached with a measure that has "a slow mutation and a steady progression either increasing or decreasing, which by no event is shaken and highly disturbed" (Galiani [1751]:84). Precious metals possess this property because they have an almost constant price, being subject neither to wide fluctuations in quantity, except for the discovery of new mines (which is a very rare event), nor to variations in consumption, which by universal estimation is the same everywhere (Galiani [1751]:84–85).[31]

[30] The analysis of these characteristics was meticulously conducted and revealed Galiani's interest in the geological sciences, which would later lead to the writing of a work on these topics (see Galiani 1772). In *Della Moneta,* Galiani mentions the burning lens of Ehrenfried Walther von Tschirnhausen, the metal experiments of Robert Boyle, Wilhelm Homberg and René-Antoine Ferchault de Réaumur (Galiani [1751]: 72–73; 81).

[31] In *Della Moneta* manuscript, the thesis appears more clearly defined: "Everything that is in human commerce can serve as a common measure of things, thus grain and wine etc.. But it is understood that to perform this function well, a kind is required whose value is fixed, that is, whose utility and scarcity is always the same [...]. This requirement, therefore, that money must be of a kind whose value, i.e. the relationship of which to other things, depending on utility and scfarcity, must be as fixed as possible, already excludes a very large number of kinds from being money, and makes us increasingly aware of the real reason why metals, by common consent, are destined for this use" (Galiani, MS-13: folios 26–27).

Metals are therefore suitable not only as a means of payment and medium of exchange, but also as a unit of account, and therefore they "must be considered as ***naturally money***" ("***naturalmente moneta***", Galiani [1751]: 85).

Having clarified the nature and functions of money, Galiani adopted a historicist approach to trace an admirable synthesis of the origin and evolution of the monetary instrument, from the beginnings of mankind to the society in which he lived.[32] His clear position for the historicist method led him to describe the theory that men at an indefinite time came together and decided to use metals for money as ridiculous: "Where are these congresses, these conventions of the whole of mankind? What is the century, what is the place, what are the deputies by means of which the Spaniards and the Chinese, the Goths and the Africans agreed so firmly, that for so many centuries afterwards, when even one people was unaware of the existence of the other, they never changed their ideas? And yet it must be said that when all men agree in the same sentiment, and in that sentiment they endure for many centuries, it is not these congresses held at the foot of the Tower of Babylon or at the exit of the Ark; it is the dispositions of our souls and the intrinsic constitutions of things: because these are really always the same, and have always been the same at all times" (Galiani [1751]: 66).[33]

Metallic money therefore follows its own historical evolution. The first metals known to mankind - Galiani remarked - must have been iron and copper. In fact, these metals are not found hidden in the depths of the earth, but are quite easily found on the surface. Their particular characteristics could be discovered through the curiosity of men "which is so much greater in proportion to the greater the needs and the more unknown are the properties of the materials [...].Even the case, to which the discovery of great things is normally due, could have done so; for men, having put them near the fire to shrink and support wood, must have seen them with

[32] "Galiani was permeated with a historicist spirit and, in his way of seeing things, the general is always found alongside the particular, just as the abstract, the ideal and the imagined are found alongside the concrete, the effectual, the real" (Einaudi 1949 [2014]: 237). The historicist approach also emerges in the severe critique of Montesquieu's *De l'esprit des lois*: "a book full of maxims that will seem true only to those born in Paris, and born there in the eighteenth century of human redemption" (Galiani [1751]:340). On the relationship between Galiani and Montesquieu, see Venturi (1998: 565–566).

[33] The term tacit agreement is used by Locke: "the Invention of Money, and the tacit Agreement of Men to put a value on it" (Locke 1714: 168).

wonder liquefy. Or finally, from the eruptions of volcanoes, which sometimes threw down torrents of liquefied metals, men must have learned the art of working iron" (Galiani [1751]: 4).

Gold and silver were discovered later, only after a certain development of the art of metallurgy when the properties of the metals were known. Gold was first found in the sands of rivers and then, deducing that water carried what was stored in the bowels of the earth, men began to dig in the mountains and along with the yellow metal they also found silver. Having discovered the most precious metals, men - struck by their singular beauty - initially used them as ornaments, as demonstrated by the custom of the most backward peoples (Galiani [1751]: 5).[34]

But the quantity of precious metals available would have been very little, if it had not been increased through trade, i.e. the peoples who had large quantities of it exchanged it for other goods; thus from the east coast of Africa (the legendary ancient *Ofir*) and from Spain came the large quantities of precious metals used for the great treasures of Asia and Egypt (Galiani [1751]: 6–7).[35] The Phoenicians and the Tyrians engaged in this trade and acquired a monopoly on it, and it was they who, by bringing large quantities of precious metals to Greece and Asia Minor, spread the use of metallic money.

In fact, by practising exchange between goods and precious metals, people realised that since the value of metal was always equal, it could only be regulated by quantity, so for greater convenience they established certain standard weights and measures, according to which the metal could be easily valued. Once metals were divided into standard quantities, it was easy for the public authority, which regulated markets and trade, to authenticate these weights with its own mark (Galiani [1751]: 8). Thus was born the minted coin.

The historical reconstruction confirms the results of the deductive analysis, which Galiani conducted on the nature of money; indeed:

[34] Vico's influence on these theses is evident: "Uniform ideas originating among entire peoples unknown to each other must have a common ground of truth (Vico 1744 [1948]: *Element XIII*, 57) and: "The nature of things is nothing but their coming into being (*nascimento*) at certain times and in certain fashions. Whenever the time and fashion is thus and so, such and not otherwise are the things that come into being" (Vico 1744 [1948]: *Element XIV*, 58). Even Broggia recognised that the first function of precious metals was to be objects of ornament (Broggia 1743:175).

[35] The similarity traced by Galiani between the Mediterranean basin in antiquity and the Oceans of the Modern Age is also highly effective and evocative.

1. relative prices of goods are defined as a priority;
2. precious metals are traded as surplus by peoples who hold them in large quantities, in exchange for other goods; surplus goods acquire the same function as *notes*;
3. metallic money for its characteristics is chosen as the standard, the first step towards its acceptance as *tertium permutationis* and thus as *currency*;
4. public authority comes only at the end to enshrine certainty and confidence in the new instrument with the coinage.[36] But for Galiani, as he had already made clear in his youthful dissertation, the weighed metal is already the currency, since "it is difficult to determine the origin of money if there is a difference between weighed metal and coin" (Galiani [1751]: 8).

Once the use of minted coinage was established, great riches flowed into the ancient world as its borders expanded with the conquests of Alexander and Rome, and - Galiani observed – "wealth was the companion of arms and obeyed the vicissitudes of these" (Galiani [1751]:13). And in fact, with the decline of the Roman Empire, the abundance of precious metals also vanished; first they were distributed to the Germanic peoples as tribute to keep the peace, then following the invasions, the stagnation of trade led to the rarity of gold "and the value of things seemed consequently very low" (Galiani [1751]:15). On this poverty was based the feudal regime and the natural economy, "because the sovereigns and masters could not collect duties other than in personal services, or in the fruits of the land" (Galiani [1751]:15).

The thirst for precious metals was so great in Europe that, after the discovery of the New World, "in a few years, all the metal that the Indians had collected over so many centuries was taken from America" (Galiani [1751]: 16). The river of gold and silver allowed Europe to fill itself with magnificence, but to the detriment of the hard exploitation of the peoples of America and Africa, "it being very true to those who reflect well, that one people cannot enrich itself without making another poor and unhappy" (Galiani [1751]: 17).

[36] "If money is the nerves of the civil body, of which the Prince is the head, with which it is kept united and vigorous, and if it makes use of its forces to preserve itself, then it has rightly been known at all times that Princes must be the supreme, just and wise regulators of money" (Galiani [1751]: *Dedica* [2]).

Europe's fate would have been quite different – Galiani observed – if the gateway to the East had not been opened at the same time and "India, arid of silver" had absorbed "the excessive quantity that was stagnating in Europe; so that the value of metals did not vary among us in proportion to the quantity that came from America, but much less [...].This state of affairs still continues. The new India sends us the metals, we spend a great amount on luxury, a little is used to increase the quantity of currency, and therefore it is always decreasing in value, although insensibly; we keep a lot of it in utensils, the rest is sent to ancient India, which in return gives us a great many of the comforts of life [...]. If this use were not made of gold and silver, these metals would no longer be riches; but when they were equally abundant as copper they would be equally valuable" (Galiani [1751]:17).[37]

4.2 The Theory of Value

Having identified the nature of money, characterised its functions and admirably outlined its origin, the young Galiani turned to the controversial question of the value of the monetary instrument, identified in its *optima* form with the precious metal.

If the complex subject of money aspires to be a science, he observed, it must be based on "certain principles [...] because there is no science where there is no demonstration and certainty" (Galiani [1751]:28). Opinions that attribute the value of money to "a purely chimerical and arbitrary value" must be rejected, as well as those who "believe that the consensus of men who have determined to use money gives to these metals, which they liked to use, that merit which they did not have in

[37] Galiani formulates a more complex reasoning than what Schumpeter calls simple metallism, i.e., "theoretical metallism without the specifically quantity-theorem element in it" (Schumpeter 1954 [2006]: 299). In fact, Galiani distinguishes in the production of gold a component for industrial uses (the exchange value of which, according to Schumpeter, depends on the form of the demand curve of gold as a commodity, and thus is not only related to supply) and a component for monetary uses: "It is the increase in this quantity which, the purchasing power of the total monetary stock remaining constant, is the immediate cause of the resulting fall in the exchange value of the monetary unit" (Schumpeter 1954 [2006]: 298). In Galiani's argument, it is interesting to emphasise that in his view the luxury consumption of gold would stop its use as currency and slow down the process of depreciation of its value. Also interesting is the relationship that Galiani establishes between the exploitation of mines and the value of metals: the more the latter decreases, the more mines are abandoned, because it is no longer useful to exploit them.

themselves" (Galiani [1751]: 25), a theory sustained above all by the Aristotelians, "from which moralists and jurists derive" (Galiani [1751]:26).[38] All these conceptions, once applied, have been "fatal and productive of tears" to the people who had suffered them. The opposition to them was weak, because "these opinions cannot be contradicted without destroying their basis: therefore I do not know, nor can I understand how it was possible that Locke, Davanzati, Broggia, the author of the work *Sul Commercio* [Girolamo Belloni], and the other of the *Spirito delle leggi*, with not a few others, not denying the first principle, had contrary sentiments and solidly built upon a false foundation without feeling either the weakness of this or the vacillation of that. Therefore I, before anyone else, with all my study, will try to demonstrate what I have been convinced of for a long time, that not only the metals that make up money, but everything else in the world, without exception, has its natural value, derived from certain, general and constant principles; that neither caprice, nor law, nor the prince, nor anything else can do violence to these principles and their effect [...]. On this foundation whatever edifice is erected will be durable and eternal" (Galiani [1751]: 26–27).[39] The scientific explanation of monetary phenomena thus had its cornerstone in the definition of a universal law, which Galiani found, almost like a new gravitational principle, in the concept of value.

In a first and more general definition, Galiani observes, "the value of things (since I generally speak of all things) is established by many as the estimate that men have of it" (Galiani [1751]:27), but this definition appears insufficient, obscure and ambiguous to him, and it must be further specified: "Estimate, or value, *is an idea of proportion between the possession of one thing, and that of another in a man's concept.* So when it is said that ten *staja* of wheat are worth as much as a *barrel* of wine, it is expressing a proportion of equality between possession of one thing and

[38] Galiani refers to the conventional theory of money indicated by Aristotle in the pages of the *Ethica Nicomachea* (Aristotle [2004]: V, 5, 11), reproposed by the Spanish scholastic Diego Covarrubias y Leuva (1512–1577), professor in Salamanca, and substantially accepted by the legal tradition (Covarrubias 1556).

[39] Galiani refers to what Montesquieu writes in Book XXII, Chap. II of *De l'esprit des loix* (Montesquieu 1748). Intieri's group was particularly adverse to Montesquieu's political work. Intieri and Galiani moved along a line of defence of absolutism, and the theorist of the division of powers appeared to them as a defender of the particularism of parliaments (see Venturi 1998: 566). *Sul Commercio* was published in December 1750 and certainly known to Galiani.

another. It follows that men, always careful not to be defrauded of their own pleasures, exchange one thing for another; for in equality there is neither loss nor deception (Galiani [1751]:27, italics added).[40]

The *Della Moneta* manuscript proves particularly useful for clarifying some of Galiani's concepts that in the edited text appear particularly obscure or are expressed too briefly.[41] To be precise, the criticism of the concept of estimate is much more complex in the manuscript. The Neapolitan *abbé* writes as follows: "*Definition*: The value of a thing might be defined as the estimate that men have of it, but in a clearer term it must be said to be the comparison or the relationship of one thing to all others that are in human commerce. *Explanation:* Since estimate has various degrees and does not properly express what value is, which also has various

[40] The *Stajo* was a unit of measurement of capacity for wheat and cereals, used in Italy before the adoption of the metric system, with different values from place to place, in the Kingdom of Naples, a stajo was equal to 10.081 *litres.*

[41] The existence of the *Della Moneta* manuscript has been known for some time, but inexplicably it has been neglected, even by the most thorough scholars. It already appears in the catalogue of manuscripts published by Nicolini, 1908b: 172. According to Alberto Caracciolo and Alberto Merola, editors of a critical edition, "Of the manuscript of the *Della Moneta*, only a few scattered folios remain in the numerous codes of the Galiani fund at the library" (Caracciolo and Merola 1963: xxxviii). That opinion is also shared by Furio Diaz, author of an important synthesis of Galiani's works: "The *Della Moneta* manuscript has been lost, except for a few scattered folios preserved among Galiani's manuscripts" (Diaz 1975a: 3). The *Della Moneta* manuscript is kept in the library of the Società Napoletana di Storia Patria in location XXIX. E.13. The manuscript (Galiani, MS-13), of about five hundred numbered folios, contains a large part of the treatise and some annotations which were placed as an appendix to the second edition of 1780. For this reason it is not possible to establish a precise dating of these unpublished pages, and the doubt remains as to whether it is a collection of preparatory works for the first edition of 1751, or text revisions made later and then brought together (Galiani did not make substantial changes to the second edition but updated the footnotes in that version). Compared to the edited text, the manuscript presents some interesting variations regarding the chapter on value, which appears as the Second Chapter in the First Book of the printed edition, with the title: *Declaration of principles from which the value of all things arises. Of utility and scarcity, stable principles of value. Many objections are answered* while in the unpublished text it appears with a different title: *Of the value of money, or of the metals of which money is composed, and of the method for determining it.* The chapter on value in the manuscript is divided into three parts: from folio 21 to folio 44 there is most of the *Second Chapter* of the *First Book* of the edited text, and precisely the observations relating to utility, to which are added the reflections on the common measure of things that in the printed text would be inserted in the *Second Chapter* of the *Second Book.* From folio 85 to 90 there are other reflections contained mainly in the *Second Chapter* of the *First Book* of the edited text, and finally from folio 472 to 489 there is the treatment of the problem of scarcity, the subject of the same *Second Chapter* of the *First Book* of the published text.

degrees, and of which estimate is more a synonym, equally obscure, it is better said to be a statement of the relationship between one thing and another [...] *Corollaries*: (1) It now appears that the relations by varying always vary in value, and that this always happens when one of the two terms varies, such being the nature of every relation [...]. (2) As these relationships depend in large part on the will and passion of men, and in part on the various times and states of things, it is clear that values are never fixed but vary according to these reasons. [...]. Having said this, who does not see how great a need there is for a common measure to which, once one thing is related, one knows at once the relationship of that thing to all the others that are also determined in this common measure" (Galiani, MS-13: folios 21–24; italics added).

And in the manuscript, he more fully specifies the necessary and sufficient conditions for the exchange: "When one thing is bought, exchanged, and converted for another, this one in that case is equivalent to that one [....] so if a tomolo of wheat is given in a country for a barrel of wine, it is a sign that the one is equivalent to the other, for if all men in a country make this contract, it is a sign that the experience and attention of all has verified the one to be of equal value to the other. If it is only one man who makes this exchange and this purchase, yet it is certain that in the particular need of this worth, and in his way of thinking the two things are equivalent, that is to say, that in the idea and needs of the buyer and seller it is that each believes he has by the exchange [...] gained, or at least not lost. This happens when the thing given, in the hand of him who had it, was superfluous and useless, and he who receives it did not have it, and it was necessary to him. Thus two different things can in the idea of two men be of equal value, because one has need of the one, the other needs the other" (Galiani, MS-13: folio 85).[42]

In the exchange, each one sells and buys goods according to his own evaluations; although free in determining the value of goods, meeting each other on the market they must exchange according to the *proportion of equality*, otherwise they would not meet a corresponding demand for their products. In establishing this equality, there is no attention to any moral norm based on ethical principles external to the exchange, rather the latter is regulated by the protection of one's own interest (*experience and attention*), by the conservation and satisfaction of one's pleasure ("always very careful not to be defrauded of their own pleasures, they

[42] The *tomolo*, an ancient unit of measurement, corresponded to 55.32 *litres* today.

exchange one thing for another; because in equality there is no loss, nor deception" (Galiani [1751]: 27) and by the guarantee that in the exchange there is no loss or deceit. Individual impulses to exchange (what is superfluous for one is necessary for the other and vice versa) must therefore deal with elements external to the single will: no man can impose his estimate on others, exchange is always a relationship between individuals and it is determined through a conciliation of wills. Although the process of exchange arises from individual needs, it ends with a result that is always social, that is, generally shared by the agents who operate within a given community. The possibility of reconciling the different needs is in fact offered by the guarantee that the exchange takes place according to criteria of equality.

Onto the body of the Aristotelian-Scholastic conception (the *exchange of equals*, that is according to *commutative justice*), Galiani grafts principles deduced from the philosophy of natural law and from the *new social morality*.[43] It is a composite approach that will accompany the entire construction of the law of value: if the exchange takes place according to *proportions of equality*, and exchange is actually determined only through the determination of these proportions, value is necessarily a *measure*, expressible according to relations of quantity.

This measure oscillates between subjective considerations and objective constraints, and "since the dispositions of human souls and their needs are varied, the value of things varies" (Galiani [1751]: 27). Some are "more generally enjoyed and demanded than others, they have a value that is called current, and others are evaluated only by the desire of those who wish to have them and those who can provide them" (Galiani [1751]: 27–28). But these oscillations move around a single law, because the

[43] Bernard de Mandeville represents the positions of this ethical approach well. One possible channel through which hedonism could enter the logical structure of scholastic theory was the concept of *complacipilitas*, which "is undoubtedly a subjective element, since it sees value as depending on the desire to acquire and possess one thing over another. This desire, it is worth underlining, is not only regulated by physical needs, as are hunger and thirst, but also by the imagination and taste of the individual and by the fashion and rules of conduct imposed by society." (de Roover 1971: 48). See Mandeville (1714). While denying these theories an analytical character, Pasinetti observes that in them "we can find allusions to subjective elements (which derive from the concept of estimate), allusions to objective elements (which refer to costs and labour), allusions to the functioning of a presumably efficient mechanism (competitive markets) and many other ideas" (Pasinetti 1989: 233).

measure of the value is "a ratio; and this is composed of two ratios, which I express with the names of *Utility* and *Scarcity*" (Galiani [1751]:28).[44]

The law of value therefore operates in a complex manner, being based not on "one principle alone, [but on] many which join together to form a compound reason" (Galiani [1751]:34), with which it is possible to explain the paradoxes that seem irresolvable, such as air and water, which are very useful elements for human life, but have no value, because they lack scarcity; and instead a sack of sand from Japan is a rare thing, but if it didn't have a particular use it would have no value (Galiani [1751]: 28).[45]

It is not possible to support interpretations that bring Galiani's theory of value under a single determinant (either *Utility* or *Scarcity*). The interpretation that considers Galiani a precursor of the theories of marginal utility is the most entrenched in the literature following the ***marginalist revolution*** in the 1880s–1890s,[46] which also marked the rediscovery of the economist Galiani, who had been almost forgotten in the first half of the nineteenth century. Less widespread is the thesis, but supported by authoritative economists, which links the theory of the Neapolitan *abbé* to labour value.[47] Equally rare, but essentially correct, is the opinion that considers Galiani's theory of value a synthesis between *scarcity* and *utility*

[44] Following Schumpeter, the word *rarità* is translated as *scarcity* (see Schumpeter 1954 [2006]: 287).

[45] Galiani criticizes Bernardo Davanzati for not resolving the paradox of value by not clearly understanding the composite law of value (cf. Galiani [1751]: 34). But the criticism is unjustified: the attentive Schumpeter notes it when he writes, "In developing Davanzati's argument, he [Galiani] writes in a vein of quite unwarranted superiority" (Schumpeter 1954 [2006]: 286). On the paradox of value see Stephenson (1972).

[46] Menger (1871: 108); Graziani (1889: 99–106); Pantaleoni (1889: 97, 111, 118, 124, 272); Cossa (1892: 267; 300–301); Dubois (1897: 849–864, 917–930); Einaudi (1953: 286); Tagliacozzo (1937: xliii) (who considered him a forerunner of the Austrian theory, see also Cubeddu 2024); Spooner (1956); Kauder (1965: 22–25); Hutchison (1988: 257–258); Pribram (1983: 115–117); Eusepi (1992: 103); Giocoli (1999: 69–93); Giocoli (2001); Screpanti and Zamagni (2005: 60). Against the interpretations of Galiani as a forerunner of marginalism, see Lebrun (1962: 329–358). An original interpretation of the theory of value as a description of the hierarchical order of society was proposed by Bensimon (2018).

[47] According to Jean Baptiste Say: "One of te most striking peculiarities of this work [*Della Moneta*], is that it contains some of the rudiments of the doctrine of Adam Smith, among others, that labour is the sole creator of value of things or wealth" (Say 1843: xxxi). Karl Marx, an attentive reader of Galiani, considers his theory of value in terms of labour-value (see Marx 1859 [1904]: 65. footnote 1). John Ramsay McCulloch also considers Galiani's theory an anticipation of theories of labour value, underlining the influence of Locke (McCulloch 1864: 12).

(Loria 1882: 31; Schumpeter 1954 [2006]: 287).[48] Indeed, Galiani's value theory is an effective synthesis of different traditions: the scholastic one of *utility-scarcity*, the one elaborated in the field of *natural law* (the idea that labour is an essential element of value, formulated in England, above all by William Petty and John Locke, certainly known to Galiani) and that of the *new social morality*[49] which legitimises the principle of *self-interest* as prime mover of the economic order.

It is a question of explaining this complexity of value law, specifying the concepts of utility and scarcity: if in fact - observes Galiani – it is not clear what the substance of value is, one cannot have proven principles on which to base the price of things, and "there is no science where there is no demonstration and certainty" (Galiani [1751]:28). First of all, it is necessary to clarify the concept "of the utility of things and how this is measured" (Galiani [1751]:28).

4.2.1 Utility

Utility - Galiani asserts - is "the aptitude that a thing has for giving us happiness", and he further specifies that if "man is composed of passions which move him with unequal strength. Satisfying them is pleasure. The acquisition of pleasure is happiness [...]. Utility is what a true pleasure produces for us, that is, it satisfies the stimulus of a passion" (Galiani [1751]: 28).

The concept of utility had first been defined in the economic thought of Scholasticism as *utilitas* (called *indigentia* by Thomas Aquinas)[50] but it

[48] Achille Loria considers Galiani an anticipator of Nassau Senior's theory, according to which value is determined by utility, limitation in supply and transferableness (see Senior 1836: 6–13). According to Schumpeter: "While Galiani thus foreshadowed much later developments (marginal utility), he also anticipated the value theory of the next hundred years (Ricardo and Marx). For, with surprising abruptness, he turns from *rarità*, by way of quantity of commodities, to labour (*fatica*) and forthwith enthrones it as the only factor of production and the only circumstance *che dá valore alla cosa*. In one sense this spoils his theory of value, but in another it is highly interesting" (Schumpeter 1954 [2006]: 287, original italics).

[49] The concept of a new morality was defined by Paul Hazard (1953: 289).

[50] Scholasticism had inherited the concept of utility from Saint Augustine who had defined two kinds of utility, one according to the order of nature, from inanimate things to living beings, up to man, who occupied the highest place; the other based on a subjective value criterion: "For instance, would not anyone prefer to have food in his house rather than fleas? There is nothing surprising in this, for we find the same criterion operating in the value we place on human beings, for all the undoubted worth of a human [...].Rational consideration

was a concept closely connected to man's needs, always theologically dominated and therefore not always able to explain all real human behaviour. The *new social morality* had placed the category of human passions at the centre of its vision, considering their satisfaction as a condition of man's happiness (Hazard 1953: 289). Galiani fully accepts the philosophical tradition of the eighteenth century conceiving man as a mixture of reason and altruistic and selfish passions. It is the eternal movement of passions which therefore characterises man's needs: "Once the passions we have in common with animals and which are determined by the conservation of the individual and of the species [eating, drinking, sleeping], are satisfied, other passions arise within man, none of which is as strong as the desire to stand out, and to be superior among others" (Galiani [1751]: 30).

And of these "the limit and the boundaries cannot be found; it being very true that as soon as one ceases to need one thing by obtaining it, one begins to have another by desiring it" (Galiani [1751]: 30; 1977: 23). Galiani pushed the hedonistic principle to its extreme consequences, making it a real tool for evaluating human actions: "All those pleasures, i.e., those satisfactions of one passion, which prick and torment the other passion, are not perfect pleasures, but if the pain they cause is less than the pleasure, they are pleasures but imperfect and senseless, if it is greater they are false pleasures, or true pains, and inconveniences" (Galiani, MS-13: folio 31).

The intellectual environment in which Galiani had grown up was not extraneous to certain philosophical approaches, the breeding ground of hedonism: his uncle Celestino and his educator, in his unpublished treatise *Ricerche intorno alle prime origini della scienza morale* (*Investigations around the first origins of moral science*), clearly followed hedonistic principles, even if expressed in a moderate form (Galiani, MSCG: folios 61–62). Galiani embraced this conception but, living in an environment that was still unwilling to accept the new morality, he had to temper his enthusiasm, distancing himself from vulgar Epicureanism and libertinism.[51]

decides on the position of each thing in the scale of importance, on its own merits, whereas need only thinks of its own interests" (Augustine 1972: book. XI, chap. XVI, 447. See also Thomas Aquinas 1920: [42257]; see also Schumpeter 1954 [2006]: 94; de Roover 1955, 1971: 46–75; Chafuen 2003: 106–107; Chaplygina and Lapidus 2016: 24).

[51] "Because I'm not an Epicurean, I don't even want to seem so, allow me to explain myself a little [...]. The pleasures of this life, which do not harm those of the other, are true and perfect, but those which in that life will produce pain (since the disparity between the plea-

Galiani explicitly refers to the concept of utility as the fulfillment of a wish; it is therefore immediately identified or measured through the quantity of the good actually consumed. The young *abbé* is therefore aware that a subjective magnitude can only be measured indirectly, "by the outward phenomena".[52] Schumpeter states that in Galiani's analysis he does not have any concept of marginal utility (Schumpeter 1954 [2006]: 287), however Galiani was not lacking in analytical instruments capable of facilitating the understanding of the phenomenon of diminishing marginal utility: his uncle Celestino was one of the first Italian scholars of the differential calculus elaborated by Gottfried Wilhelm von Leibniz and Isaac Newton, he established chairs of mathematics and of theoretical and experimental physics and advanced mathematics was taught also in several religious and military colleges with practical applications (Palladino 1988), and also Intieri followed a method, based on a Newtonian approach, as an essential element of modernization project of Neapolitan culture. Ferdinando certainly must have known differential calculus and possessed the analytical tools, even if this did not lead him to an explicit formulation of the principle of marginal utility.[53]

sures and pains of one life and the other is infinite), however great the enjoyment here and small the evil there, pleasures and liars will always be liars" (Galiani [1751]: 28). See also Galiani, MS-13, folio 31. Even Celestino tempered the hedonistic approach, observing in his manuscript on moral science, that in addition to physical good and evil, there is "another species of good and evil called moral, which is nothing other than the uniformity, and dissimilarity of human actions from the Law [of Nature]. Operations conforming to the Laws are called good, and the non-compliant ones bad, as they cause us some good, and physical harm. For example, he who transgresses the law of temperance gets drunk: and although he finds pleasure in the act of drinking, with this action, he incurs the infamy of men, a thing which in itself afflicts, and which usually deprives him of many real conveniences, and furthermore makes him deserving of the punishment God threatens to the intemperate" (Galiani, MSCG: folios 60–61).

[52] This expression is Alfred Marshall's, but it represents Galiani's thought well (Marshall 1920: 92).

[53] Celestino clearly expresses a concept that comes very close to marginal utility: "Whoever burns with thirst, falling into a source of clear, limpid, sweet, fresh water, rejoices wholeheartedly, and drinking it feels great pleasure: as his thirst is quenched, the pleasure diminishes: so in all other things preceded by great desire, when they are obtained, they rejoice and delight us, but when they are not desired with a desire that disturbs us, acquiring and possessing them cause us little pleasure" (Galiani, MSCG: folios 61–62). See Rossetti (1942).

4.2.2 *Scarcity*

Scarcity is the other component that Galiani places at the basis of value: "I call scarcity the proportion that exists between the quantity of a thing and the use that is made of it. I call use both the destruction and the occupation of a thing, which prevents the desire of another from being satisfied while one is using it" (Galiani [1751]: 38).

The concept of scarcity had come to the forefront of economic thought since the thirteenth century, thanks to Peter John Olivi, and was then taken up again by Antonino of Florence and Bernardino of Siena, who distinguished between *raritas* (scarcity/rarity), *difficultas* (cost) and *virtuositas* (use-value) as objective components of value, and *complacibilitas* (desirability), depending on the individual's subjective estimate.[54]

The first element to consider in calculating scarcity is therefore the total quantity of a good in a given period. The other element is what Galiani calls *use*, meaning the consumption (*distruggimento*) and appropriation (*occupazione*) of goods by each individual.[55] In practice Galiani recognises that every private good is characterized by excludability and rivalry in consumption. The Neapolitan *abbé* essentially refers to goods that satisfy a private use; water and air are not included, because they are not scarce.

There is a non-negligible difference between *use-consumption* and *use-appropriation*, as: "the destruction [*use-consumption*] of a thing raises its price more than its removal from trade [*use-appropriation*]. This is because its destruction completely eliminates all hope, while its removal preserves its value in accordance with the probability that the thing will be used and returned again to circulation and trade" (Galiani [1751]: 38).

This statement is particularly important for the value of money. Galiani believes that it has not been debased in an exact proportion to the mass of metal coming from the New World, only because a part of this has been removed from monetary use and turned to other uses, arising mainly from luxury. However, it is easy to understand what could have happened if this quantity had suddenly been coined.

[54] Antonino of Florence (1485: Pt. 2, Tit. 1, Chap. 8 and 16); Pribram (1983: 23–25). On Antonino of Florence and Bernardino of Siena, see de Roover (1967); Nuccio (1987: 2573–2684; 2733–2814).

[55] The case of the paintings reported by Galiani himself is quite emblematic: "For example, let there be one hundred paintings displayed for sale; if a gentleman buys fifty, the paintings become almost doubly rare, not because they are consumed, but because they are the fifty removed from sale (Galiani [1751]:38).

Total quantity and use do not directly define scarcity, which derives from the "proportion" that is formed between the two aspects. It can therefore be said that the more the quantity increases, the more the scarcity decreases and the more its use (*consumption-appropriation*) increases, the more the scarcity increases; but quantity and use simply define the available quantity of a good, therefore the scarcity decreases as the available quantity increases.[56]

The analysis of the manuscript is of great help in defining the concept of scarcity more precisely: "Value is composed of utility and *difficulty of purchasing* a thing. This truth is understood very well by those who consider that air and water, which are very useful elements for life, have no value because no effort or difficulty costs them to acquire them, and conversely to have a handful of sand from the sea of Japan is something that would be very difficult to obtain, but given that it had no particular merit or utility it would have no value" (Galiani, MS-13: folio 30).

The *paradox of value* is interpreted here in light of the relationship between *utility* and *difficulty of purchasing*.[57] Scarcity is therefore nothing more than difficulty in obtaining the availability of a good. This interpretation is also confirmed by the following passage, again taken from the manuscript: "The other principle on which the value of things depends is, as I said, *scarcity*. Under this heading I include both the quantity of production, the *labour* (*fatica*) it costs to reduce it to that state, and the decrease in consumption" (Galiani, MS-13: folio 482).[58]

[56] Nicola Giocoli has interpreted scarcity as a ratio that "depends upon a subjective component, consumption, and a seemingly objective one, the stock of the 'thing' in question" (Giocoli 2001: 102). If this were the case, Galiani would no longer have distinguished the subjective determinant, utility, from the objective determinant, scarcity, a distinction which seems to be the basis of his entire argument. It is obvious that scarcity depends on need, but Galiani's aim is to keep the two components of value conceptually separate, so need would therefore fall within the scope of utility.

[57] According to Schumpeter: "The famous paradox of value, which was gravely discussed again in the nineteenth century - the fact that obviously useful things fetch a low price and much less 'necessary' ones a high price - had been resolved several times before. But never before, or for more than a century to come, was this theory put forth so completely and with so full a sense of its importance" (Schumpeter 1954 [2006]: 287).

[58] Following Schumpeter the word *fatica* is translated as *labour* (Schumpeter 1954 [2006]: 287). Luigi Pasinetti identifies the concept of *fatica* with Smith's concept of "toil and trouble" (Pasinetti 1986: 413). Translating it as labour better captures the meaning of the word *fatica*, which in the Neapolitan dialect indicates work activity in a generic sense.

At this point we see a logical sequence between ***production - difficulty of purchasing - total quantity - available quantity - scarcity.*** On the basis of this logical sequence, goods are distinguished by Galiani into two classes:

a. goods obtained "from the different abundance with which *Nature* produces them"; and "they are the kinds that reproduce after a short time and are consumed with destruction: such as the fruits of the earth and animals" (Galiani [1751]: 38–39).
b. goods obtained "from the various efforts and work that are expended" (Galiani [1751]: 38).

For the first class of goods, the quantity depends not exclusively on human intervention, but also, and above all, on *Nature*: "In them with the same labour (*fatica*) it is possible, according to the variety of seasons, to harvest eight or ten times greater than what was achieved shortly before (Galiani [1751]: 38).[59] In this class of goods, human intervention can also be increased, but the result is not always a proportional increase in production, given that a drought can ruin the entire harvest even if farmers have expended more energy and resources than the previous year. However, human intervention is always required as the fruits do not move spontaneously to the mouth. "It is impossible", Galiani writes in the manuscript, "to find things of value in which some small amount of labour has not been expended, because for example wild fruits, the snails that are on the shore, require at least the labour of being collected, and of being displayed on sale" (Galiani, MS-13: folio 482). The quantity of the first class of goods is therefore linked to random phenomena due to *Nature* which influence the production result. Galiani is, however, essentially interested in the measurement of this uncertain component[60] based on the principles of probability calculation, which received great attention in the eighteenth

[59] More precisely in the manuscript: "The quantity of the harvest contributes to the value mainly in plants and animals and in their fruit, because the cultivation of a field always costs approximately the same labour (with the difference being negligible), although the production of a quantity of fruits depends on the order of the seasons, and can at times be eight or ten times greater than what has been produced at other times. Such a great difference that the scarcity depends so largely on it, and absorbs all the other component reasons, and makes them not very important" (Galiani, MS-13: folio 480).

[60] *Dialogues*, Galiani (1770a):

century, and it can be said that Galiani favours a type of objective probability attributable to what modern economists call *risk*.[61]

The quantity of the second class of goods is more directly related to labour; *Nature* acts only upstream of the production process, determining the overall amount of resources to be exploited. Relevant examples of this are: "Certain goods, such as minerals, stones, marble, which are not variously produced every year, but were all together scattered throughout the world, and of which the collection corresponds to our will; because if more people are employed there, more can be obtained from the maternal womb. So if you want to do calculations on this class of goods, you don't have to calculate anything other than labour, since the quantity of material corresponds only to this" (Galiani [1751]:39). In this case, he further observed in the manuscript, "the quantity of the product is nothing other than the *difficulty of purchasing*, that is, the command of many people, the layout of the site, the abundance of the mine, in short, the quantity of labour and time that its purchase costs" (Galiani, MS-13: folio 482). Even manufactured goods are under direct human control and therefore they too are determined only by the labour applied.

Galiani does not define a pure *labour-value* theory of value, but a *labour-cost* theory, and does not ignore utility, as a further essential determinant of value. The labour, without prejudice to utility, is exclusive, as a component of the cost, for some types of goods in which *Nature* no longer influences the quantity (manufactured goods and partly mineral resources), but for others, especially agricultural products, there remains cooperation on the production result due to natural agents.[62]

[61] See Galiani [1751]: 349-350). In his mature work *Dialogues*, written under the strong emotion of the devastanting crisis of 1764 (especially in the Neapolitan area), Galiani considerably toned down these certainties (see Galiani 1770a: 111-114). For the link between Galiani and the calculation of probability, see Giocoli (1997). The calculus of probability was part of Celestino's interests and he had dedicated an early contribution to the study of the *lotto* game, see Galiani MSCG-1.

[62] Galiani does not believe in the generosity of *Nature*, a concept he will state more clearly in the *Dialogues*: "Nature is something immense, indefinite, the worthy work of its creator. And who are we? Insects, atoms, nothing. Let's compare ourselves. There is no doubt nature always faithfully returns to the laws its author gave it to last an indefinite time. No doubt it brings everything back into equilibrium; but we don't need to wait for this return and this equilibrium. We are too small; time, space and movement are nothing before it; but we cannot wait. So let us not make an alliance with nature; it would be too disproportionate. Our task here on earth is to to fight it. Look around you. Look at the cultivated fields, the foreign plants introduced into our climes, the ships, tamed animals, the houses, the streets, the har-

The labour element now remains to be determined.

4.2.3 The Calculation of Labour

When calculating the contribution of labour to the value of a good, three variables must be taken into account: "the number of people, the time, and the different price of the people who work" (Galiani [1751]: 40).[63] Galiani is therefore once again interested in measurement in the attempt to construct objective and quantifiable concepts. He explicitly declares this when he refers to calculation and at this point carries out a crucial operation by representing in quantity the elements that mark the difficulty of production and the cost.

The number of people employed corresponds to the value of the wages paid for the time spent working, since "no one works except to live, nor can he work if he doesn't live" (Galiani [1751]:40). In his calculation Galiani refers first of all to the subsistence wage, which can be seen from the following passage: "If the work of fifty people is required to manufacture a bale of cloth [...], this cloth is worth a price equal to the expense of nourishment of these fifty men, for a time equal to that of the work: that if twenty are employed for a full day, ten for a half and twenty for three days, the value of the cloth will be equal to the nourishment of a man for eighty-five days; and of these days the first earn twenty, the second five, the third sixty. This is evident, assuming that these people all have equal wages" (Galiani [1751]: 40).

The time factor is also related to a measure expressed in wages. The time must be calculated not only by taking into account the duration of the work actually done, but also the necessary rest, "because he must eat even during that period" (Galiani [1751]: 40). This rest may be made longer than necessary by the customs and laws of a country. The observance of religious holy days of obligation is very dangerous for a country because it makes "goods more expensive than elsewhere" (Galiani [1751]:

bours harbours, dykes, causeways. These are the entrenchments in which we fight; all the pleasures of life and almost our very existence are the price of victory. With our little art and the spirit that God has given us, we fight nature and often succeed in overcoming and mastering it by using its forces against it. A singular battle, and one that makes man the image of his creator" (Galiani 1770a: 235).

[63] A similar calculation is proposed by James Steuart (1767: vol. I, 181–182).

41).[64] The calculation is carried out by Galiani again referring to the subsistence wage: "Assuming that a man working three hundred days in a year produces one hundred pairs of shoes, the value of these must correspond to his entire subsistance for an entire year. If another man, working three hundred and sixty days, produces one hundred and twenty pairs of shoes, he will sell his product one-fifth less, not having the need to make any other greater wage from one hundred and twenty pairs of shoes than what the first man draws from his one hundred (Galiani [1751]: 41).[65]

Finally, over time, the period of study and apprenticeship for the exercise of a profession and an art must also be calculated, the search for the client, as happens for artists, and finally the natural interruption for occupations that they cannot be carried out assiduously; in all these cases the salary must cover subsistence for the periods in which one cannot work (in these cases the socially necessary time is lengthened).

Apparently it is more difficult to calculate the varied nature of human talents, "from which the different price of labour arises", but the general principles of value are also valid for this, as "the value of men's talents is appreciated in the same way as that of inanimate things, and it is based on the same principles of scarcity and utility combined together" (Galiani [1751]: 42). Thus, out of a thousand men, six hundred, for example, are uniquely suited to agriculture, three hundred inclined to the manufacture of various arts, fifty to the richer trade, and fifty have a flair for studies and disciplines. Therefore, the merit of a man of letters compared to the peasant will be in reciprocal ratio of this number, that is, 600 to 50, or 12 times greater (see Galiani [1751]: 42). The scarcity of talents is therefore the joint result of Nature and labour. However, taking into account these complex determinations, the subsistence wage undoubtedly remains the most suitable measure of labour.

The calculation of the quantity of labour obviously depends on the type of good produced. Galiani distinguishes:

[64] On the reduction of religious holy days, see Galiani, MS-25. On the controversy over the reduction of religious holy days of obligation, see Venturi (1998: 136–138).

[65] Galiani's reasoning here is based on the identification of the subsistence wage as a factor determining the difficulty of purchasing. It seems that this concept is very close to that of "socially necessary labour time" defined by Karl Marx in Book I of *Das Kapital* (Marx 1867). A country that produces beyond the socially necessary time is destined to suffer competition from other countries that have a time that is more in line with the socially necessary one. In fact, the prices of the shoes produced are lower and this means that the "lazy" shoemaker can remain without his minimum subsistence level.

a. goods reproducible through the joint action of man and nature (agricultural products):
b. goods reproducible by human action (manufactured goods);
c. non-reproducible goods, given in terms of stocks, and made usable by human action (metals);
d. non-reproducible goods resulting from genius (artworks).

Non-reproducible goods (c) can be taken in large quantities from the "river banks", only by applying increasing quantities of labour, and for this reason gold is worth more than sand, because "if someone wants to fill a sack with sand in a quarter of an hour, he can easily do it, but if he wants it full of gold, he will need many whole years to collect the very scarce grains of gold" (Galiani [1751]:40). This means that these goods cost many hours of work, while the reproducible ones (a and b) cost on average a few hours of work, beyond the uncertainty about the production result. Obviously for artworks the calculation of the necessary work escapes any precise quantification.

The scarcity of a good can therefore be measured with the hours of labour required to obtain a unit of finished product. If we multiply these hours of labour by the subsistence wage, expressed in terms of the quantity of grain needed to feed a worker daily, we will obtain the real cost for each category of goods (Galiani 1780: note X). Therefore, the scarcity of a good can ultimately be represented by the cost in terms of the *quantity of labour necessary*, and traced back to a *labour cost* or *real cost*.

Galiani's concern is aimed at identifying a fundamental law of value. Everything must therefore be brought under the two determinants: utility and scarcity. This operation succeeds perfectly in the analysis of its only possible exception: *fashion*. A very significant phenomenon for the society of his times, which could lead to considering a cause of value external to those indicated, fashion, according to Galiani, "is an illness of the cerebrum common to the nations of Europe, because of which many things are rendered of little value simply because they are not new" (Galiani [1751]:46). It arises above all from the desire to imitate the customs "of the most dominant nations" and it "is entirely in the realm of the beautiful" (Galiani [1751]:46). However, fashion does not change the law of value, because the pleasure that a luxury good can cause can be related to the category of utility.

Galiani thus demonstrated that the principles from which value derives are "certain, constant, universal"; despite being varied, they are not "capricious" and their variation follows an exact and immutable order and rule, based on needs and pleasures and therefore "on the internal constitution of man" (Galiani [1751]: 45).

4.2.4 The Determination of Price

The analysis of the determinants of value is necessary to explain exchange. For Galiani, in fact, value is always "an idea of proportion between the possession of one thing and that of another in the concept of man", and defines the center of gravity around which the price or exchange value must revolve (and for this reason in the text, value and price are often synonymous).[66]

The actual exchange is therefore determined by the price and this must ensure, in coherence with the principle of value, an "equal proportion between having one thing or the other". This applies to all goods found on the market; therefore there are no inestimable values (i.e., not comparable like the Venus de' Medici). These goods do not have "infinite value", as has been erroneously said by many, but their price corresponds "always to the needs or desires of the buyer, and to the esteem of the seller, joined together, which form a composite reason" (Galiani [1751]: 47).

The acquisition of the utility of a good that we do not possess constitutes the subjective impulse that determines the exchange (if there were no exchange, to acquire utility we would have to work directly): "Wealth", he writes again in the manuscript, "consists in the possession of something that is not useful or necessary for me, but is necessary, or at least useful for others. The greater the number of these things that someone possesses, the less need he has of them, that is, the less useful or necessary they are for him, and the more useful and necessary they are for many other men, the greater the wealth" (Galiani, MS-13: folio 89).[67]

The entire exchange mechanism is, according to Galiani, based on the link between *utility - possession - satisfaction of needs - exchange of the superfluous with the necessary* or *with the desired*. Once again, a subjective

[66] Galiani, like the Scholastics, often uses value and price as synonyms, revealing their influence in this too. Regarding his doctrine of interest, he admitted using arguments typical of Scholastic doctrine (Galiani 1780, note xxxiv).

[67] In the published text Galiani writes more succinctly "wealth is the possession of something that is more desired by others than by the owner" (Galiani [1751]: 148). Money is always wealth only because it has the requirement of being able to be exchanged with all goods and therefore of always being useful.

quantity (utility) is revealed only through an objective measurement (quantity exchanged).[68] Reasoning on the example of Galiani, a miser will never find his accumulated wealth useless, the fact that he does not attempt to sell indicates that his subjective threshold of satisfaction has not been reached, but it is through the zero quantity, that is, a measure, that this subjective condition is revealed.

Establishing the price is the last stage of Galiani's analysis. The conceptual scheme that he developed is based on three steps: *value - exchange - price*. Two of these steps have the characteristics of abstract analysis conducted on a logical level, namely establishing the value and the principles that regulate the exchange. The last step, the definition of the mechanism that determines the actual prices, implies a change in perspective by moving to the concrete economic reality, and therefore onto the empirical level.

But, having reached this point in the analysis, Galiani realizes a problem that seems to bring him back to the starting point: "It is very difficult", he wrote, "and often impossible to make this calculation [i.e. calculate the price] from its principles; which would be, as logicians say, *a priori*: since it is certain that just as *scarcity* and value depend on consumption, so consumption conforms and varies according to value: and from this concatenation the problem becomes indeterminate, as it always is when two unknown quantities, which have some relation to each other, meet" (Galiani [1751]: 48).

Galiani has followed an *a priori* demonstration, proceeding from cause to effect, revealing on this point of his analysis, once again, the link with the method of scholastic doctrine, which considered this argumentation

[68] According to Schumpeter, "Having resolutely defined the term Value to mean a relation of subjective equivalence between a quantity of one commodity and a quantity of another - the objective equivalences on the market are treated as a special case of this, but he did not work out the transition from subjective to objective values" (Schumpeter 1954 [2006]: 286–287). This difficulty is attributable, according to the Austrian economist, above all to the absence of a concept of marginal utility (Schumpeter 1954 [2006]: 287).

procedure the perfect one.[69] But then he realizes that in reality there is no separation between the two causes of value, which are interdependent.[70]

The problem of the interdependence between prices and quantities and between supply and demand has been resolved at the level of economic analysis with the partial equilibrium approach and the distinction between short and long term: "There is no doubt that if in a country one hundred thousand barrels of wine are collected, and the inhabitants consume the same number, if due to a war with the arrival of a large army the consumption increases, increasing its scarcity, the price would increase, but if by chance, as the drinkers increase, the product increases due to very abundant harvest, the scarcity does not change, the price does not change. Now let it be clear that men, enticed by gain and profit, always procure things that are easy to consume, in such a way that the quantity of manufacturing corresponds to consumption, so that the price does not increase at all" (Galiani, MS-13: folio 472, see also Galiani [1751]: 49).

Obviously, he was also unable to explain the fluctuations around the equilibrium prices.[71] It is a deadlock on the analytical level that would be overcome by subsequent monocausal explanations of value, based either on utility (Turgot 1769 [2011]; Condillac 1776; Say 1843) or on labour (Smith 1776 partially, and Ricardo 1817; Marx 1859 [1904]), which, as it is known, would fall into other contradictions. A composite conception of the law of value, in terms very similar to how Galiani had set it out, would return only with Alfred Marshall's synthesis.[72]

[69] In Aristotelian logic the *a priori* is "what is prior and best known by nature", as opposed to the *a posteriori*, that is "what is prior and best known to us" (Aristotle, *Posterior Analytics*, I, 2; Aristotle, [1993]: 3) in the first case the Greek philosopher refers to what it is farthest from sensation (the universal) and with the second to what is closest to it (individuals). In scholastic terminology this notion is the basis of the so-called *a priori* demonstration (or *propter quid* or perfect demonstration) which proceeds from the cause to the effects, that is, from what is first according to nature, or absolutely, to what is first for us.

[70] "Galiani, very happy in posing the problem, was not so happy in solving it. His solution is nothing but a banality" (Loria 1882: 37).

[71] According to André Tiran, Galiani provides a qualitative assessment rather than a quantitative analysis of value (Tiran 2018: 88).

[72] "We might as reasonably dispute whether it is the upper or the under blade of a pair of scissors that cuts a piece of paper, as whether value is governed by utility or cost of production" (Marshall 1920: 362). And: "The cost of production principle and the final utility principle are undoubtedly component parts of the one all-ruling law of supply and demand; each may be compared to one blade of a pair of scissors. When one blade is held still, and the cutting is effected by moving the other, we may say with careless brevity that the cutting is

If consumption is regulated by utility and scarcity by labour, these two quantities can have a different influence on the price, depending on the type of good and the specific market situation: technical constraints and tastes come into conflict on the market.

At this point it is appropriate to better clarify the concepts that are starting to look like an intricate maze:

a. In many goods - Galiani writes - "scarcity and abundance suddenly change due to external causes without the work of man, but due to the order of the seasons. In these kinds of goods the price follows the scarcity" (Galiani [1751]: 49). These are agricultural products, or those in which Nature fixes the available quantity. The key factor for the price is therefore their scarcity.
b. There are goods which are less rare and which are widely consumed, because "whatever is worth less is consumed more willingly"; the only limit will be given by the difficulty of production, and by "the inconvenience and effort that it costs to purchase". The price can increase and therefore entirely follow the scarcity only if the supply remains fixed. Also in these circumstances "consumption is regulated by the price that arises from scarcity" (Galiani [1751]: 48).
c. While goods that "are not subject to the variety of collections have no other extrinsic reason to change their *scarcity* than fashion" (Galiani [1751]: 50), and from this that "being more esteemed or less, and more sought after or less, they become more expensive or less, and thus vary in their consumption" (Galiani, MS-13: folio 477). The normal behavior of these goods is to adapt supply to demand, so the price always fluctuates in relation to the "right value" (Galiani, MS-13: folio 473).

Finally, in other cases what is of utmost importance in fixing the price is the demand (use, consumption and therefore utility). This is the case of the precious metals that came from the New World in great abundance: if their consumption (demand) for luxury had not increased, their price would have fallen, and this is what prevented the complete collapse of all monetary systems based on metals. "Except in extraordinary cases" - Galiani pointed out - "when due to an unforeseen accident either

done by the second; but the statement is not one to be made formally, and defended deliberately" (Marshall 1920: 826). See also Schumpeter (1954 [2006]: 888–889).

consumption increases or the quantity of something is lacking, in any other case when abundance lowers prices, consumption keeps them high, and thus a proportionate balance is maintained" (Galiani, MS-13: folio 478).

Ascertaining the mechanism that determines actual prices involves an empirical perspective that strongly limits the prediction of hypotheses.[73] For this reason it is impossible to establish the price *a priori* ("from its principles"), because this achievement requires a perfect knowledge of thousands and thousands of variables that determine the final price. Moreover, "the calculations of political arithmetic are a risky matter. They are the source of serious errors, for they must all be made without any confirmation or endorsement by the principles; and only principles devoted to such studies could verify such facts and events" (Galiani [1751]:58).

The calculation of price *a priori* is impossible, but this limit of human reason is corrected by a providential *Supreme Hand* (or *Providence*) which creates an equilibrium.[74] This tendency to equilibrium derives "not from human prudence and virtue but from the lowest stimuli of all private gain", "transforming selfish instincts into social wealth" (Galiani [1751]:50).[75] This *Supreme Hand* works similarly to Newtonian gravitational theory, and the different individual interests, like different bodies in physics, become interdependent and reciprocally influenced, directed toward a harmonious systematic order by an invisible force of attraction (a sort of moral gravity).[76] The equilibrium is based upon two principles: first, the initial variations should not be taken into account but only the permanent and stationary states, since in the latter the equilibrium is always found, as happens in a vessel, when the water, after irregular move-

[73] However, some essential elements that contributed to the determination of the current price did not escape him: the different productivity between nations; the different level of income; different consumption habits; the distance from the markets; the level of taxation; the weight of commercial intermediation; the risks, including the damage caused to sellers by the existence of smuggling and fraud.

[74] According to Cesarano (1976, 1999), the concept of natural equilibrium can be taken as the methodological foundation of *Della Moneta*.

[75] The analogy with Smith' s concept of *Invisible Hand* is evident; see Paganelli (2018).

[76] "First, that we must not take into account the first movements in any thing, but the permanent and fixed states, and in this there is always order and equality; as, if in a vase of water there is any mutation, after a confused and irregular beating the regulated level follows. Secondly, that one cannot give in nature an accident, which leads things to infinite extremity; but a certain moral gravity, which is in everything, always draws them back from the infinite straight line, twisting them in a circle, perpetual yes, but finite" (Galiani, [1751]:52).

ment, returns to its original level; second, there is always a moral or physical gravity that prevents extreme movements (see Galiani [1751]: 51–52; see also Cesarano 1976: 382). Consistent with a Newtonian approach, according to Galiani: "The laws of commerce correspond to those of gravity and fluids [...].What gravity is in physics, is the desire to gain, or to live happily, in man; and, that being the case, all the physical laws of bodies can be perfectly verified in the morals of our life by those who know how to meditate on them" (Galiani [1751]: 52).

The equilibrium is not a simple product of natural laws but is historically determined. For this reason, Galiani is more interested in the forces that restore the equilibrium than in the static analysis of equilibrium, as is shown by the well-known example of the sudden conversion of a Muslim population that modifies the structure of demand and supply in a certain market (Galiani [1751]:51). This is an extremely modern approach as it is centered on the study of the mechanisms that lead to market equilibrium. Moreover, the adjustment process towards an equilibrium is not conceived as instantaneous or a-temporal but is slow and irregular, always able to cause real effects (Giocoli 2001: 120).

4.2.5 The Legacy

Despite its analytical richness (the highest point reached in the eighteenth century, Schumpeter 1954 [2006]: 286), the theory of value probably still had too many scholastic residues (which Galiani freed himself from later) to be accepted by the new Enlightenment mentality, and the theory of interest met with the same rejection, due to the moral concerns with which it was imbued.[77]

While the historian must understand the doctrines in their "entirety of place and time" (Michels 1932: 81), a theory is effective on an analytical level if it gives rise to a school of interpreters, popularizers and continuers. This does not happen for Galiani's theory of value. The reason for this failure is to be found in the theoretical impasse that opposes the deductive analysis of the determinants of value to the empirical analysis of the reality that leads to the formation of market prices, or rather in the impossibility of finding a bridge that allows one to pass to the explanation of real phenomena starting from theoretical principles.

[77] "It must not be forgotten that the theory he developed was really that of the scholastics" (Schumpeter 1954 [2006]: 286). See also de Roover (1955: 182).

Della Moneta was circulated widely in Italy and was certainly known in France, so much so that André Morellet wanted to translate it.[78] Galiani's attempt to establish a law of value by proposing a synthesis of utility and labor was rejected and attention shifted directly to market phenomena. In Galiani we still find principles that a few years later would appear antithetical, shoulder to shoulder, in fact during the eighteenth century the reflection on value was to continue, taking two different paths: on the one hand the path of utility and on the other that of labor value or labor-cost value.

This change of perspective appears clearly in Anne Robert Jacques Turgot's analysis. For Turgot, who knew *Della Moneta* (Turgot 1769 [2011]: 172): "It is impossible to express value in itself; and all that human language can express in this regard is that the value of one thing equals the value of another [...].Value, like size, has no other measure than itself, and if values are measured by comparison with other values, as length is measured by comparison with other lengths, then, in both means of comparison, there is no fundamental unit given by nature, there is only an arbitrary unit given by convention" (Turgot 1769 [2011]: 179).

It is therefore useless to define value, since in fact it is identified with price: "the two words value and price, although expressing fundamentally different ideas, can, without causing inconvenience, be substituted for each other in daily speech, when rigorous precision is not required" (Turgot 1769 [2011]: 179–180).

The results of Turgot's analysis have a certain importance: prices lead to values and there is no need to arrive at an exact measurement of value in itself which thus becomes an irrelevant abstract noun; value is traced back by Turgot to the sole component of utility, that is, to the subjective elements; scarcity is also conceived in subjective terms and simply becomes an opportunity cost. Condillac's analysis is less complex and rather vaguely bases value on utility, needs and use (Condillac 1776: 9).[79]

[78] "Morellet undertook a translation of *Della Moneta* in French, but the precise date of this translation and whether it was eventually published remain a mystery" (Legris 2001: 185).

[79] The relationship between Galiani and the two highest representatives of eighteenth-century utilitarianism, Turgot and Condillac, is described thus by Giorgio Tagliacozzo, "Turgot did not surpass Galiani as regards the subjective value, both because his expressions appear to us, in some points, less conscious, and for the lesser breadth given to the topic, and - finally - for having completely neglected - as Menger would later - value-cost relationships; instead he surpassed him - developing a point on which Galiani had not dwelt (despite having mentioned it in relation to the value of unique things and monopolies), that is, the objective consequences of the subjective analysis carried out - in his very interesting theory

The category of value is identified with the value of exchange-price, starting a tradition of thought that would be codified by the marginalist revolution of the late Nineteenth century.

Adam Smith also bases his analysis on a single factor, following the vigorous natural law tradition, with the aim of arriving at an explanation of the price phenomenon. Smith, distinguishing between *value in use* and *value in exchange* (Smith 1776, vol. I: 43), breaks the connection in the analysis of value between utility and labor, focusing attention on labor as a measure of exchange value to explain the formation of prices in a market economy.[80] In this approach, the element that underlies the value is identified as social effort: "The only true cost of production, from the point of view of society as a whole, was the expenditure of human labor. In the creation of wealth, certainly, labor co-operated with land, although even here labor was regarded as the "father" or "active principle" of wealth, whereas land was visualised as the passive "mother". But the creation of value was the prerogative of labor alone" (Meek 1973: 44).

This is a significant difference compared to Galiani's complex analysis of *Nature's* active role in the production process. Both Turgot's and Smith's approaches lead to a simplification of the theory of value, reducing or completely eliminating what is considered secondary and expanding what is instead considered essential, giving rise to two incompatible theoretical approaches, until Marshall's synthesis.[81]

A similar simplification process also characterizes the emerging economic science in Italy. Antonio Genovesi, holder of the first university chair of political economy in Europe (established at the Univerity of Naples in 1754 and called *Commercio e Meccanica*) and an expression of the same intellectual circle gathered around Celestino Galiani and Intieri, in which the young Ferdinando had acquired his first analytical notions,

of exchange value. With this he completed Galiani's system, to form an overall system comparable in structure to the Mengerian system (value-exchange-price)" (Tagliacozzo 1937: XLVII). To frame Turgot's analytical contribution, cf. Groenewegen (1970, 1977).

[80] The Smithian approach is anticipated by Francis Hutcheson, for whom: "Prices or values in commerce do not at all follow the real use or importance of goods for the support, or natural pleasure of life" (Hutcheson 1755, vol. II: 53).

[81] "Since the end of eighteenth century, economic theorists have concentrated on fewer and fewer basic elements. On the concept of value, they have narrowed themselves down to a choice between two quite different and alternative routes: the objective route of a cost-of-production and, more particularly, of a labor theory of value; and the subjective route of a marginal utility theory of value" (Pasinetti 1986: 415).

does not take up and develop the theory of the Neapolitan *abbé*.[82] While recognizing the need to anchor the value of money to a general law of value, Genovesi takes a completely different path, developing not a complete theory of value, but only an explanation of the way in which market prices are formed.[83] Genovesi essentially defines the law of demand (needs) and supply (quantity) and explicitly refers to market phenomena to confirm his statements on value. The path chosen by Cesare Beccaria and Pietro Verri is similar to that of Genovesi: the concepts of utility and scarcity are mentioned, but the reflection remains limited to the explanation of market phenomena, the analytical path is the reverse of that traced by Galiani: if for the Neapolitan *abbé*, in fact, the market phenomenon is only the last stage of the analysis, for his followers instead everything is explained starting from the observation of market phenomena. Verri will take this simplification to its extreme consequences, also removing the word value from his argument to replace it with that of price.[84]

4.3 Real and Imaginary Money: The Characteristics of Monetary Systems

By linking the value of the *moneta optima* to the value of the commodity from which it is made, Galiani succeeded in his aim of firmly anchoring monetary matters to a scientific principle, removing them from the realm

[82] According to Michele Troisi, critical attempts that belittle Genovesi by comparing him with Galiani do not hold up: "the two authors move on a substantially different level. If Galiani has greater refinement of intelligence and depth of analysis, Genovesi appears much more systematic and broader-minded. We are faced with two temperaments, which are reflected in their respective works: one is an acute, but cold and often skeptical observer of social facts and human passions; the other above all a teacher and ardent reformer" (Troisi 1941: 38). Other scholars, however, have underlined the continuity between Galiani's theory of value and that of Genovesi (Nuccio 1967: cxviii). Eluggero Pii recognizes that Galiani's formulation is clearer, however believes that the concepts of need and quantity, defined by Genovesi, are analogous to those of utility and scarcity developed by Galiani (Pii 1984: 182).

[83] "The value of things is in direct proportion to needs, and inverse to quantities, and the value of thing to thing is in reciprocal proportion to their quantities, i.e. masses" (Genovesi 1757: 44).

[84] "So what are the elements that form the price? It is certainly not only utility that constitutes it [...] Not even the mere scarcity of a commodity is enough to give it a price", Verri (1771: 19). Beccaria, however, will still formally distinguish value from price (Beccaria 1804: 344–356).

of arbitrariness.[85] Generally speaking, and Locke had already shown this, the value of precious metals was established relative to that of other commodities (in other words, simply as a relative price), but it had to be made clear that the mass of metals did not have only one use; a distinction had to be made between the component intended for industrial purposes and the other for monetary use, and it could be shown that metals "have much more value as metals than as money, and it can be concluded that they are used for money because they have value, and not worth because they are used as money" (Galiani [1751]:54–55).

Galiani demonstrated his thesis by calculating that the mass of uncoined silver in the Kingdom of Naples was four times greater than the amount coined, and that therefore the value of silver for non-monetary uses was four times greater than the amount of coined metal. If the metal were not used for alternative uses, the mines would no longer be exploited when the states were saturated by circulating money and the price of the metal would consequently be altered, but instead, Galiani observed, although the mass of silver increased by five hundred million in the Kingdom in half a century, its value did not decrease in the same proportion because luxury sustained the price of the metal (Galiani [1751]:59).

All this confirmed his theory that the formation of the relative price of metal as a common commodity (i.e. destined for consumer use) anticipated its use as a monetary instrument, and that therefore the use of metals as currency was not a "free and capricious choice" of men but was dictated by necessity and the very nature of metals (Galiani [1751]:61).

Once he had secured the theoretical foundation for his arguments, the young Galiani addressed the complex reality of monetary systems based on the coexistence of *imaginary money* and *real currency*, minted in gold, silver, copper and the various billon alloys, as well as its relatively widespread *representations* (notes).

Imaginary money, Galiani remarked, is such because it does not correspond to any actually minted piece of metal and its only function is to serve as a unit of account. *Imaginary money* is the oldest monetary unit in

[85] "[I have] shown that gold and silver have true intrinsic value, which derives neither from their use as currency, nor from our caprice, nor from the consensus of nations. To do this, it is agreed to develop the principles of the value of all things in general, and to adapt them to gold and silver. I then made it known that they not only had this intrinsic value before, but they have it now that they are used as money, because they are worth much more, and are used both as metals and as money" (Galiani [1751]: 63).

any monetary system, as its origin is linked to continuous processes of devaluation that debased it to the point of dematerialisation.[86]

The *imaginary money* account system had been introduced mainly by custom ("they have no law to compel them"), although states, such as France, had regulated the matter with "strict edicts", stipulating that "only with some currencies could one contract and contract, and not with others" (Galiani [1751]:97). The monetary system, almost everywhere, was characterised by several coins linked together by not a fractional number, as multiple or submultiple of twenty or twelve.[87]

Unlike other writers who had considered the money of account (on an imaginary or real basis) immutable or more wisely, like Broggia, had pegged it to the value of copper money, subject to less variation, Galiani rejected any idea of immutability for monetary values: "Nothing is less to be hoped for in this world", Galiani observed, "than perpetual stability and firmness; for this is repugnant to all orders and to the very genius of nature […] therefore a constant and unchangeable measure is not to be hoped for, nor is it to be sought", rather a slow mutation should be hoped for (Galiani [1751]:99).[88] The metal ensured with its slow mutation a tendentially stable measure, but it was nevertheless destined to change, due to its greater or lesser abundance, even without manipulation by Princes, modifying the prices of goods, since "the price is a ratio […] in order to change it requires that only one of the terms be changed; if the

[86] In the second edition, Galiani pointed out that: "Everything said in this chapter and the following ones about imaginary money, or money of account, is intended to refute the work of Carlo Broggia, in which he greatly exalted money of account and proposed introducing it among us" (Galiani 1780: Note VIII, 380). However, many of Galiani's arguments followed Broggia's theory (Broggia 1743: 286).

[87] Galiani referred to the proportions established by the Carolingian reform of the ninth century, when the relationship *1 Libra = 20 Solidi = 240 Denarii* was established. Galiani then recalled that in Naples people counted in ducats and *Tarì* (royal coins), in grana corresponding to the twentieth part of the *Tarì* (actual copper coin), in turn divided into twelve parts, called *Cavalli* (no longer coined due to their excessive exiguity of value). The Neapolitan system of account was based on the coexistence of real and imaginary money.

[88] In the first edition, there is no explicit reference to Broggia, while in the second edition, in *Note VIII*, Galiani wrote: "Everything that is said in this chapter and the following ones about imaginary money, or money of account, is intended to refute the work of Carlo Antonio Broggia, in which he greatly exalted money of account, and proposed introducing it among us, as if our *Ducato* were not also an *imaginary money* today, since none is minted of this value" (Galiani 1780: 380).

value of the currency does not change, it is enough that the price of what it measures changes" (Galiani [1751]: 102).

If the Prince were to insist on the invariability of prices, his measure would be ineffective, because "what the Prince does not do about the prices of goods, the multitude does, and with justice; the price being a measure of the people's labours, it is to the people's advantage to dispose of it" (Galiani [1751]:102) and the state authority is obliged, if it wishes to be obeyed, to conform to the measures adopted by the people. "Therefore", he concluded, "this invariable money is a dream, a frenzy: every new mine that becomes richer, quickly varies all the measures" (Galiani [1751]:103).

By persisting in the search for immutable measures, alternatives to metal could be sought in vain, employing as alternative standards wheat, or any other commodity used as a primary commodity (rice, maize, fish) and therefore widely available, but these commodities were subject to the fluctuations of the seasons and their price in the short term was very changeable. Galiani, however, recognised that commodities such as grain had a stable value over the long term, while money, on the other hand, fluctuated greatly, and proposed to use grain only as a long-term measure. Perhaps - the young abbot pointed out with subtle irony - the only fixed measure is man himself, because "there is nothing after the elements more necessary to man than man; and on the varying quantity of men depends the price of everything" (104).[89] And for this reason, the only one who used a valid measure were the peoples of the Guinean coast, who fixed

[89] Intieri had expressed a certain disappointment at this Galiani's statement: "Until now I have no other doubt than what you observe about the common, constant unchanging measure that you believe man can be. I do not understand and believe that among created things, to speak as a philosopher, none is stable, neither the sun, nor the stars, nor anything" (Bartolomeo Intieri's letter to Ferdinando Galiani, Massa Equana, 6 October 1751, BSNSP, XXXI.B.18: folio 51r). Thirty years later, in *Note X* of the second edition of his treatise, Galiani returned to the problem and wrote: "I have understood that using the price of slaves (as I then thought could be done) is not satisfactory [...] and it seems that it can be done thus. By reducing in value all that a man needs to live, seeking therefore that lowest and most wretched state, to which a poor man may be reduced by living. This amount reduced to this term will be the constant fixed value that will give the idea of the proportions of wealth and the state of money in every century and in every nation; because it expresses the proportion that a physical man, i.e., stripped of all moral value and considered almost a brute of the kind to whom beauty or intellect do not give value, but simply a beast of burden, has with the rest of society" (Galiani 1780: Note X, 382). The theme of the search for an invariable measure of values would also propel David Ricardo's investigation a century later.

prices on the basis of slaves, making the man their money, since he was "invariable and easy to compute, when in him we value, as they do, only the qualities of the body".[90]

Measures aimed at artificially changing the use of units of account in order to ensure price invariability were therefore ineffective. This was demonstrated, according to Galiani, by the case of Henry III's France, which in 1577 prohibited counting in *Libra, Solidus* and *Denarius*, as had been customary since the time of Charlemagne, and introduced the use of a new unit of account: the gold *Scudo*. Such a measure was dictated above all by the fear of a general increase in the price of goods, but it proved useless, indeed inflation ran even faster (it was at the beginning of the price revolution) and his successor Henry IV, in 1602, decided to return to the old system of account, in turn blaming the calculation in gold *Scudo* for the price increase. This example offered Galiani an opportunity to counter the idea that high prices were always an evil to be rejected: "A great enemy to the good actions of the Prince are the cries of his people; not because they are always unjust, but because they are not always to be heard" (Galiani [1751]: 113).

A general increase in prices was wrongly perceived by the people as a sign of a worsening of their condition, prompting the authorities to enact laws and statutes to lower prices, which then turned out to be ineffective and counterproductive (Galiani [1751]: 113). Four types of popular errors (*abbagli*), according to Galiani, were spreading as a result of a generalised price increase.

Complaints about the alleged existence of famine and misery were the first popular error, because famine and misery should produce depopulation, and when this does not occur, it simply means that the country enjoys abundance (Galiani [1751]:114). Secondly, when industry grows in a country, credits to foreign countries increase and money comes in from abroad, consequently everything appears more expensive, but the increase in the price of goods leads to a proportional increase in incomes

[90] The way in which African peoples bargained and traded had also attracted the attention of Montesquieu: "The blacks on the coast of Africa have a sign of values without money; it is a purely ideal sign, founded on the degree of esteem they have in mind for each commodity in proportion to their need for it. A certain product or commodity is worth three macutes; another, six macutes; another, ten macutes; it is as if they simply said three, six, and ten. The price is formed by the comparison they make of all the commodities with each other; so, there is nothing that is only money, but each kind of commodity is money for the other" (Montesquieu 1748 [1989]: Book XXII, chap. 8, 404).

and therefore the complaint is not justified. According to Galiani, the price increase due to famine is quite different from the beneficial inflation produced by prosperity: during a famine situation, the price increase is momentary and followed by deflation; in contrast, during a prosperous situation, the increase in prices is durable and increasing (as was the case in England and France) (Galiani [1751]: 115–116).[91] The third error derives from the assumption that the Prince is primarily responsible for inflation, because he has tyrannically increased taxes. In reality - Galiani objected - the increase in taxation is only a consequence of general inflation, as the levy is always proportionate to the state's expenses and these are almost entirely made up of the remuneration of its employees. A continuous increase in prices always causes an increase in taxes if the Prince does not want to fail (Galiani [1751]: 119). Finally, the last error, which attributed inflation to the Prince's luxury spending, was easily rejected: the presence of a court and the consequent sumptuousness of expenditure, generated "by opulence and the very fast circulation of money" must have led the people to look with "an eye of disdain for that unhappy time spent as a province of a kingdom, where assets were poorer because money was absorbed by the distant court" (Galiani [1751]: 119).

Having clarified the essential characteristics of *imaginary money* in its function as a unit of account, the young Galiani tackled the problems arising from the material and real form assumed by money. Gold, silver and copper were the most widely used metals with a decreasing degree of value to give material form to coins (Galiani [1751]:3). This diversity of monetary metals is explained - according to Galiani - by the needs of commerce: minute and therefore more frequent payments could not be made with gold coins, nor could major payments be made with small copper coins, from which it follows that "commerce has more need of copper than of any other currency, then of gold, and finally of silver" (Galiani [1751]:141).

[91] Galiani effectively remarked that famine did not always cause an increase in prices. When the crisis was generalised to many harvests, there was a general impoverishment of the population and producers had to lower prices to find an adequate outlet for their products. As a result, prices fell instead of rising as expected. On the other hand, when harvests were plentiful, prices were expected to fall, but the general prosperity and the resulting profits allowed producers to keep some of their product while waiting for prices to rise. In this case, prices could remain constant or even rise (Galiani [1751]: 117–119).

Copper, therefore, despite being the most contemptible of all metals, is undoubtedly the most useful for coinage.[92] To confirm this, Galiani observed, one need only take as evidence the monetary history of ancient peoples, who often used (this was the case with the Spartans and the Romans in the Republican era) only copper coins. This utility is essentially due to its low value, which makes it possible to buy the cheapest things and therefore the most useful, widespread and necessary for life. And because of this low value, copper coin escapes fraud and forgery and "with more confidence it is trafficked. Men dislike small and pitiful gains, when they are surrounded by great dangers" (Galiani [1751]:130). No one has any incentive to counterfeit it: neither the Prince, who only uses the most precious metals; nor the mint administrators, who would gain little from counterfeiting and thus risk harsh penalties for nothing; nor have the people ever paid attention to the intrinsic value, "because when fraud is not feared, the effects of consumption and time [on coins] are not estimated" (Galiani [1751]: 130).

According to Galiani, the circulation of copper coins therefore was on a fiduciary basis; no one cared about keeping the copper coins intact; no one cared about accepting good coins and rejecting bad ones, as was the case with gold and silver. The copper coin in fact circulated in the Kingdom of Naples, debased and halved in value, thus as a representation, a sort of "leather coin" (Galiani [1751]: 131).

It was precisely these qualities that led to the copper coin being proposed as a money of account (it was Broggia's proposal), a measure that was already implemented in Castile with the *Maravedì* (Velde and Weber 2000). This opinion was certainly more sensible than the one that wanted to base the system of account on silver coins, but it was certainly not right, as:

1. copper was always in an exchange relationship with other coins, being part of a monetary system. In particular, silver coin is the currency closest to it, and therefore "as long as copper is bound and tied by law to silver, it will be dragged along by it in all its mutations" (Galiani [1751]: 131). Counting in *Grana* (copper) or *Ducats* (silver) was only a difference of name, not of reality.

[92] Galiani specifies that under the name of copper, it includes all lower metals and the coin made of billon (Galiani [1751]:117–129).

2. Even if copper had not been included in a system, as was the case among the Chinese, who minted only copper coinage, leaving gold and silver to free private bargaining, its adoption as a money of account would have been completely ineffective. In fact, "since it is necessary that large payments be made in silver or gold, the account in copper would be useless, and by the force of the nature of things, would return to that in silver and gold" (Galiani [1751]:131). In short, the money of account will always coincide with the actual money with which one pays.
3. The supposed immutability of copper coinage was an unfounded thesis, as it always had a relative price that could change due to changes in the value of gold and silver (Galiani [1751]:134–135).

Another factor that influenced the material form of the coin was the alloy. Metals - Galiani argued - are never found in nature in their pure state and are always alloyed with some other, less valuable metal species. The alloy responds to two needs:

1. the high costs that would have to be incurred to mint a perfectly pure coin: the maximum purity can be as high as 23¾ carats of fine out of a total of 24 for gold coinage (purity that is realised by the *Venetian Zecchino*) and 11 ounces of fine out of a total of 12 for silver coinage (this is the case for French coins) (Galiani [1751]:166–167).
2. the high ductility that pure gold possesses would prevent it from performing its monetary use without inconvenience: the alloy simply serves to make it more tempered. Pure silver, on the other hand, would be too brittle and could not withstand even the operation of minting, so it is more resistant when alloyed (Galiani [1751]:167).

The alloy - he went on to explain - in itself does not harm the currency and is absolutely not a *criterium divisionis* to distinguish good money from bad. The currency coined with a great deal of alloy is not bad for this, but because the authority has imposed by "fraud or force of law" that it be accepted as having the value corresponding to the weight of pure metal (Galiani [1751]:172). This is demonstrated by the circulation in many countries of a coin "composed of half a precious metal, and half a base metal, called *billon* by the French, and *vellon* by the Spaniards", and no one refuses them (Galiani [1751]:173).

However, its utility should not be overemphasised, as Broggia had done (this time quoted). For this it was necessary to respond to all the arguments put forward by the Neapolitan merchant in support of the introduction of the *billon*:

1. it was not, in Galiani's opinion, entirely justified that the small silver coin was subject to rapid consumption, since this was very small and therefore almost imperceptible in relation to the circulating money supply (Galiani [1751]: 173).[93]
2. Also to be rejected was Broggia's thesis that with *billon* one could use all the poorer quality silver that was brought to the mint, coining it in alloy rather than incurring the high costs of refining it. In fact, Galiani calculated that even the minting of *billon* itself cost "almost twice as much as silver", so there was no advantage (Galiani [1751]:174).[94]
3. Finally, he rejected Broggia's last argument, that *billon* facilitated retail trade, replying that gold and silver were abundant and copper coins were beginning to be removed from circulation, so it would not have been useful to promote them (Galiani [1751]:175).

To complete the analysis of the monetary system, Galiani introduced the topic of coinage regulated by public authority, with different powers. In the case of paper circulation, the coinage was replaced by the signature on the banknotes, and this signature constituted its entire value. Therefore - Galiani concluded – "the notes have no value other than the extrinsic; nor can they be said to have more intrinsic value than the half *Baiocco* which the paper is worth" (Galiani [1751]:158). For metal coins, on the other hand, the coinage represented the value they already possessed as the intrinsic value of the metal, and if the Prince wanted to impose an extrinsic one "this did not [destroy] the intrinsic one, but [they] remained both together" (Galiani [1751]:159). The coinage of a metallic money was a "revelation of intrinsic value made by public authority" (Galiani [1751]:158). The extrinsic value given by the coinage to the metallic money would have been accepted only within the space of sovereignty; the

[93] This consumption was calculated by Galiani as five per cent of the entire circulating money.

[94] The expense of minting billon coins was onerous for both the alloy and the copper lost in it.

other value, the intrinsic one, would have been recognised everywhere. The Prince therefore had no choice but to align the extrinsic value as much as possible with the intrinsic value, the latter always being "independent of its use for currency" (Galiani [1751]:159).[95]

On the problem of seigniorage and the expenses related to coinage operations, Galiani rejected, with very harsh judgments, the proposal made two centuries earlier by Bernardo Davanzati, namely that coins should be minted without seigniorage and by minimising expenses, so as to impose a value equal to the intrinsic value (Galiani [1751]:160–162; see Davanzati 1588 [1804]: 45–46). If the public authority had renounced its minting rights - Galiani objected - coins would no longer have been minted as there was no profit to be made from the minting operation. The full intrinsic monetary circulation would have stimulated the fusion of coins for industrial use by goldsmiths (because it was easier to use coins than to buy raw metal), and the mint would have been forced to produce new coins to offset the low circulation, increasing costs for the community, as the English experience of the *Great Recoinage* proved (Galiani [1751]:163). To avoid such distortions, the nominal value of the minted coin had to be slightly higher than the intrinsic value of the metal it contained to cover costs and also the seigniorage right, "but since this [was] a fixed and invariable expense, the variation in the value of the coin depended entirely on the variance of the metal" (Galiani [1751]:178).

4.4 Fiduciary Money and Bank

In Galiani's conception, metallic money was the *moneta optima*, but this did not exclude the use of monetary instruments other than metal, which were essentially based on the fiduciary relationship between the issuer and the user. Indeed, the Neapolitan abbot acknowledged their importance, warning the reader that "it would be advisable to compose a work at least equal to the present one" (Galiani [1751]: 319) in order to deal with them adequately.

[95] In the manuscript of the treatise, Galiani wrote: "The extrinsic value [...] is nothing other than the certification of the sovereign, i.e. of the law, that in such a form of metal, for example in the *Scudo*, which has such an imprint, there is such a quantity of money. This by its nature must not be a new declaration of quantity, but a simple statement of the quantity, i.e. the weight of the coin, which must be added to the intrinsic value of the coin, and this value is the value of the metal" (Galiani,MS-13: folio 21r).

Confidence was therefore an essential element in guaranteeing the use of these *representations* of money, and the greatest effort of the issuing authority was directed precisely at preventing counterfeiting by the most effective means (signature, royal seal, particularity of the paper).

Regarding the origin, Galiani distinguishes between fiduciary money born of debt relations between private individuals and forms arising from the needs of the state (such as *obsidional* currencies).[96] And both types could be interest-bearing.

Only papers (*carte*) issued with the guarantee of public authority could have a wide circulation, unlike those issued by private individuals, which were rarely accepted and therefore had no monetary function. In most cases, the issuance of paper money was due to exceptional circumstances, such as in Pennsylvania, where the use of paper money was established to the point of completely replacing metal circulation. This phenomenon was, according to Galiani, quite exceptional and can be explained by the particular circumstances of American economic and social life:

- first of all, the almost absolute observance of laws, which is a direct consequence of the strict morality imposed on the population by the Quaker faith;
- the presence of savage peoples on the borders and therefore the impossibility of being subjected to counterfeiting of paper currency;
- the existence of a single trade channel to England, which made the mutual settlement of debts easy (Galiani [1751]:: 322–323).

The American experience of state-issued paper money was therefore inimitable, so Galiani limited his analysis to all the other more widespread paper currencies, which had "originated either from deposits, or from loans, or from the union of companies" (Galiani [1751]: 323).[97]

The most important of these was bank money, which was created, according to Galiani, for the needs of commerce, as precious metals had become insufficient to support the volume of trade and, a fact not to be

[96] "Issued by the commanders of the besieged cities, when money was lacking and all external communication was interrupted, it was agreed to dispense to the soldiers, instead of money, certain signs and promises of payment, payable immediately the anguish of the siege was lifted" (Galiani [1751]:320).

[97] Galiani distinguished between public loans that could bear temporary yields (bank deposits lent to the state; annuities, *arrendamenti*, tributes) or life-long yields (*tontine*) or loans made to private individuals for the needs of commerce and industry (company shares).

underestimated, after the discovery of the Indies, “the same gold that had lost value in comparison with the prices of many goods, gave great inconvenience and danger to be transported and trafficked” (Galiani [1751]:323–324). The origin of these monetary surrogates was directly linked to the state of public confidence and the credibility enjoyed by the Princes; where these requirements were lacking, other precious commodities were used, such as diamonds in China, and this proved that the monetary instrument was always linked to the level of confidence.

The first banks (*banchi*), established on the initiative of private capital (mainly Italian), were “very useful”, as “merchants found as much money as they wanted without paying great usury, and money did not rest idly in the hands of the inexpert to move and traffic it” (Galiani [1751]:325; see Costabile 2016; Costabile- Neal 2018). The faith and honesty of the bankers underpinned the credit function exercised by the banks and the consequent possibility of multiplying the monetary means in circulation. In this way the currency was “doubled with the creation of an equal amount of paper money, which is not obtained by sending goods to India, as in the case of precious metals” (Galiani [1751]:325–326). This function was, however, particularly delicate: “since markets in those times were subject to countless misfortunes no less due to the adversity of fate than to the malice of men less wealthy and more powerful than them, it often happened that by going bankrupt, credits were lost; and many remained very poor with useless credit cards in their hands” (Galiani [1751]: 326). Hence the need to establish public banks guaranteed by the state authority (*banchi pubblici*), such as those in Venice, Amsterdam, Hamburg, founded on the wealth of private merchants, or like the Bank of England, founded on the public treasury (*exchequer*).

Banks based on mercantile wealth mainly performed a payment function, by means of giro transfers defined on a bank account unit permanently linked to a quantum of precious metal, which could generate a premium of bank money over coins, or by issuing *certificates of deposit* (called *fedi di credito* in Neapolitan public banks) admitted into circulation, even by force of law, as a substitute for coins. Added to this was the traditional function of depositing, without paying any interest and with limits, often a real ban, on withdrawing the sums held on deposit.[98]

[98] However, Galiani advised that allowing the withdrawal of the deposited sums strengthened confidence.

Banks guaranteed by the state used private wealth for public needs, and since the Republic distinct from private individuals was "a chimerical entity", they became "creditors of themselves without realising it" and this allowed the multiplication of money and just as the "merchants did not leave their deposits buried, so the republics with bank money helped their grave needs [...] so that it has changed its nature, and from a deposit has become a loan made to the public, but a loan, unlike fiscal rents (*arrendamenti*), gratis and without interest" (Galiani [1751]: 327–328).

The case of the Bank of England was different: founded as well on the basis of a loan that private individuals had made to the Prince, the peculiarity of this institution was the issue of *notes* (*fedi*), which circulated with variable value, being linked to the uncertainty of their actual convertibility, and "of this probability a trade was made, and according to the greater or lesser probability varied the value of these credits" (Galiani [1751]: 328–329).

The subordination of these institutions to the needs of the state was not always, according to Galiani, a positive fact: the experience of John Law's *Banque Générale* demonstrated this. Galiani also attempted to make an objective judgement on this matter, consistent with his scientific purpose. In his opinion, the premises of the Law's *Système* were well-founded, but its implementation led to the abuse of paper money, which then led to its collapse. France emerging from Louis XIV's wars of supremacy was "devoid of currency" and filled with worthless *billets d'état*. The remedy could only be the bankruptcy of the state, since there was no metal to withdraw that mass of devalued paper money. Bankruptcy and the consequent destruction of paper money would have left the country without currency, and - he observed – "when a state loses its currency it is like a craftsman who in extreme indigence sells the instruments of his art. Then he is ruined forever, having no money to buy back the instruments of his work, nor instruments to buy money by working. Thus France could not restore herself with industry and peace, because without money there was no development of industry" (Galiani [1751]: 330–331; see Cesarano 1990). Law's proposal was a viable alternative to bankruptcy: state notes could be extinguished with new paper money, "in which there was confidence, to bring foreign silver and gold back to France. When France was then sufficiently rehabilitated, the new papers were also to have the same fate as the former" (Galiani [1751]: 330–331). But the issuance of notes soon overstepped its initial limits and turned into a colossal speculation; paper turned into shares in trading companies, circulating with increasing premiums.[99] The high issuance of notes soon led to an increase in prices, the only effect of which was the extinction of all debts, census and public rents. Law's system collapsed "because it was conducted to an extreme: France having found herself healthy after such great accidents, because the peasant did not feel the evil of the system, and the land and its fruits were favoured by the system, which increased its prices and consumption" (Galiani [1751]:334). According to Galiani, in spite of all its limitations, the system devised by Law, "a man of admirable and very rare talent, but without virtue and religion" (Galiani [1751]:330), had played the role of a *Jewish Jubilee* by extinguishing debts.

Finally, Galiani paid particular attention to the Neapolitan banks, which were considered to be a national institution, governed directly by private individuals and managed according to principles of honesty and public utility, and which had greatly benefited the population. Unlike the banks operating in republics, which are "designed to multiply the currency, to help the state and are supported by the public confidence", the banks established under a monarchy, "are only designed to keep currency and better circulate it" (Galiani [1751]:341). The main function of the Neapolitan banks was to safeguard money in a context in which the character of the people was inclined to litigiousness and fraud, "and so what elsewhere is done by the force of laws and the stimulus of gain, among us is done by corrupt customs and bad faith. But it cannot be denied that to

[99] In the second edition of *Della Moneta*, Galiani explained the reason for the failure of the *Système*: Law's aim was to recover the amount of money that had left France as a result of the wars and to this end: "[Law] had to calculate (and it was not difficult) how much the currency of France had been in 1698, the time of its greatest prosperity: let us suppose five hundred million *Lire*. Then it had to be estimated how much could have flowed out: let's assume three hundred million. So the bank, which with notes, i.e. paper money, undertakes to make the outgoing money appear as existing, it only needed to be three hundred million *Lire* [...].Fifteen years of peace was to be sufficient for full recovery. In this time, all ***notes*** were to be repaid and converted into actual currency, starting with twenty million a year and increasing thereafter. In this way, notes would not be discredited, because the prospect and certainty that a paper could soon be converted into money would always ensure its acceptance and circulation. After the fifteen years, the bank had to be abolished [...]. Law erred in this: that he believed he could pay off all the state's debts with notes, and therefore created them in proportion to the mass of the entire debt of the crown of France. A very serious and unforgivable mistake for such a great man; because one thing does not concern the other; because it is neither useful nor practicable to pay off all the debts of the state; because finally, when this is possible, justice requires that it be done with real money, and not with the imposture of a paper, which represents nothing actually existing and nothing probable in the future" (Galiani 1780: Note XXX, 411–412).

have made the Banks serve the extinction of litigation was a good and judicious thing" (Galiani [1751]: 342).

However, in the young abbot's opinion, some improvements should be made:

- first of all unify the seven banks into one, or more simply that the *fedi di credito* issued by one were also accepted by the others;
- establish that the closing of the account should all be done on the same day, so that no fraud could be committed on the clearing entries;
- reduce the number of notaries called upon for authentication operations, so as to speed up the recognition of the *fedi di credito* and ensure their wider circulation;
- establish banks in other provinces of the Kingdom (mainly in Gallipoli and Foggia) (Galiani [1751]: 342).

4.5 Nature of Interest and Exchange Rate

Galiani's scientific system could not be complete without mentioning the "serious, difficult and dangerous subject" of interest (Galiani [1751]: 346). A matter from which the young abbot would have "gladly abstained" if he had "been able to do so decently", since "contracts involving charging interest on money" were notoriously the subject of the most violent disputes, in which one entered with "the same spirit that a soldier would have regarding those who came to steal his money or his bread" (Galiani [1751]: 346–347). Many of these disputes were due to the passion for justice that led to the defence of the poor, and "for this reason," he observed, "all the centuries up to the fifteenth have been filled with voices agreeing to blame any charging of interest on money and detesting it" (Galiani [1751]: 348). But after the great inflation of the sixteenth century, the expulsion of the Jews, the institution of the *Monti di Pietà* (*Mounts of Piety*) and the public debt, all rents had been eroded and usury had been "almost extinguished", placating the common people, and "it was an admirable accident to see acute minds emerge to protect and support usury that was already dead and when alive had not been defended by anyone" (Galiani [1751]: 348). Thus, interest was justified in France by the erudite Claudio Salmasio[100] and thanks to the Jansenist Dutchman Nicholas Broedersen, the issue had been brought within the confines of Catholicism (see Broedersen 1743), provoking the controversy between Scipione Maffei and Daniele Concina in Italy, finally Pope Benedict XIV himself intervened to close the controversy with his Papal Bull *Vix Pervenit.*[101] Although he attributed valid reasons to the opponents of usury (such as Concina), the young Galiani concluded that those who defended interest-bearing loans also had "many both plausible and specious reasons in their favour" and he remained convinced that "when one sees the truth almost divided into two opposing judgements, and inclining no more to one than to the other, it is appropriate that there is some mistake or deception of words in the midst of it: since truth with its light immediately discovers its origin and its connection with all other truths, and blackens the false so decisively that it is impossible not to notice it" (Galiani [1751]: 349).

He therefore applied to the question of interest his method that skilfully alternated, by the force of lucid arguments, ***pars destruens*** and ***pars costruens***. What was ***not*** interest, in his view?

[100] Galiani Italianised the name of Claudius Salmasius, who took up the Calvinist view on the justification of usury (see Salmasius 1638, 1639). On Salmasius' theory of interest, see Böhm-Bawerk, E. (1884 [1890]: 35–40).

[101] At the beginning of 1744, the learned Venetian, Scipione Maffei, published a treatise on interest, *Dell'impiego del denaro* (*About the use of money*, Maffei 1744), in which he challenged the prevailing prejudice, treating the question of lending at interest as a "human matter", and distinguishing the execrable usury that "sucks the blood of the poor" (Maffei 1744: 218), from the normal and lawful use of money, which was defined as legitimate and beneficial because it was destined not for the poor, but for Princes, great merchants and landlords, and for which there could be no moral condemnation, since it was no longer "a question of those who ask for help to feed or clothe themselves and their families, as was the case among the Jews. In our days, thousands of *Scudi* and tens of thousands and hundreds of thousands and millions more are asked for" (Maffei 1744: 122). The ensuing debate was harsh (Venturi 1998: 117–136). And it was in Naples that a fervent Dominican preacher, Father Daniele Concina, was to print his violent pamphlet against Maffei, a work even written with the support and approval of the Neapolitan clergy (it was physically written in the Neapolitan Dominican convents of Santa Caterina a Formello and San Domenico Maggiore) and dedicated to Charles of Bourbon: "Daniele Concina had evidently sought and found in Naples a broad base for his opposition to Maffei" (Venturi 1998: 133). Only the presence of an enlightened pontiff, such as Benedict XIV, prevented the controversy from assuming the bleak features of the Inquisition. The Pope himself intervened with the encyclical *Vix Pervenit* (November 1745, see Benedict XIV 1746), formulating a Solomonic judgment of pacification, which however left everyone unsatisfied. See also Ballerini (1744), in defence of Catholic dogmas.

It was certainly not profit and gain derived from money, as Broedersen asserted, since "any profit, great or small, given by money, which is by its nature fruitless, is blameworthy: nor can it be called the fruit of labours, since labours are made by the borrower and not by the giver" (Galiani [1751]:352), but theologians were also wrong, who demanded from the loan contract the "*equivalent and nothing more*" (Galiani[1751]: 352). Reasoning about the meaning of "equivalent", one realised that the "nothing more principle" was unfair.

Under these assumptions, the basis of the loan surplus could only be justified by a difference in values. It is clear that the usefulness of two sums of money for the same person at different times may be different; the lender certainly finds the sum of money less useful (having less value) in the present and perhaps more useful in the future; this is just one implication that is entirely consistent with Galiani's theory of value, but he does not go down the subjectivist path.[102]

In Galiani's metallist conception, a sum of money is nothing more than a quantity of metal, and its value is therefore linked to the value of the coins in two different periods. Several times Galiani repeated that the value of metals is constant over the years, or suffers very slow fluctuations, abstracting from the malicious manipulation of Princes, so on this side there can be no change in value (following the Aristotelian tradition, money does not yield in itself). So where does the difference come from?

"The intrinsic value," he remarked, "was always changeable according to the degrees of probability of having and not having to enjoy something; and [...] one hundred *Ducats* away from the hand of any person, when they have a hundred degrees of probability of not being lost and ten of

[102] As Nicola Giocoli rightly notes, on this road he would encounter the Daniel Bernoulli's theories, which would provide him with valuable tools to resolve the question of interest from a subjectivist point of view (Giocoli 1997: 25). Convinced that Galiani's theory of interest is a 'fruit' of his subjective theory of value is Giorgio Tagliacozzo (1937: xlviii–xlix). Einaudi also moves in the same direction, considering Galiani's theory "a way of making values that are numerically different but distant in time subjectively identical" (Einaudi 1949 [2014] : 245). Nevertheless, he recognises that "Here Galiani did not apply his theory of decreasing degrees of utility, and did not add that, if there is equality at the margin, there could be intramarginal exchanges leading to a psychological benefit (of pleasure (as Galiani would put it) from the exchange between present and future. [...].Galiani deserves the merit, a remarkable merit indeed, of having anticipated the theories (of the Austrian school, etc.) that identify interest as the tool to be used to equalize present and future goods. He had already perceived that interest, while most often being positive, may also be negative" (Einaudi 1949 [2014] : 245).

being lost, become ninety *Ducats* present, and for ninety they have to be valued in any contract of gambling or barter" (Galiani [1751]:350). And he concluded, "among men, there is no price other than pleasure, nor is it bought except for comfort; and since one cannot feel pleasure without the discomfort and annoyance of others, one pays only the damage and deprivation of pleasure caused to others. To keep someone in *heartbeats* (*batticuore*) is pain: therefore it must be paid for. That which is called the fruit of money, when it is lawful, is nothing else than the price of *heartbeats*; and he that believeth it to be otherwise, is deceived" (Galiani [1751]: 353–354).

Interest is thus only traced back to subjective elements (*heartbeats*) through objective determinants (*uncertainty-risk*). There is no uncertainty and thus no justification for a premium on a sum that is held in the coffers as a pledge, or at least this is infinitely less than the money lent, even though subjectively the holder of that pledged sum, like Molière's miser, may manifest permanent apprehension. The interest depended on the uncertainty regarding the repayment of the sum loaned: the law of exchange value, which operated in terms of time, implied that the two quantities had to be equal, otherwise there could be no exchange, and "where the intrinsic price is increased and diminished by *risk* and *inconvenience* (*incomodo*), restoring the equality cannot be called profit" (Galiani [1751]: 351–352). Galiani identified the cause of interest in the borrower's discomfort.[103]

The surplus was not an intrinsic factor in the loan contract as such, but as he clarified, "it is as varied as the degree of probability of loss is almost infinitely various, which, just as it is sometimes very great (as in maritime

[103] According to Richard Cantillon, interest depended "on the lenders' apprehension and the borrowers' needs" (Cantillon 1755 [2010]: 95). Galiani "on the lenders' apprehension noted by Cantillon, but not on the need of borrowers identifies the cause of interest" (Catucci 1986: 45). Catucci emphasises the affinities between Galiani and Cantillon: "It is not impossible that [Galiani] had the English edition on which Postlethwayt relied in his *Dissertation on the plan, Use and Importance of the Universal Dictionary of Trade* (1749), which contains some six thousand words [of the *Essai*][...][Galiani] could have been in possession of the original [*Essai*] now disappeared, or of some pirated edition, obtained with other English books from his friend and correspondent in Livorno George Jackson ("[Jackson] he was a wealthy English merchant living in Livorno. A man of considerable culture and passionate bibliophile, he was in contact with lntieri, Rinuccini and Cocchi", Galiani, 1975: Guerci' s note, 836; see also Rotta 1973: 113–115). In any case, the affinities in the treatment of the subject, even more than in the theory itself, are remarkable, at least in terms of interest' (Catucci 1986: 46). On Cantillon and Galiani, see Lanzillo (1939).

usury), so it sometimes descends to zero (as it is in the Banks and Companies of the Republics), and sometimes even below zero, taking in negative quantities (as happened in France at the time of the Law system)" (Galiani [1751]: 354). Therefore, interest can be called an *apparent surplus* (*sovrappiù apparente*) (Galiani [1751]:351).

Galiani keeps the argument in an objective approach, pointing out that "false thinking is then [...] to find disparity between the poor and the rich, and to confuse justice with compassion. The just can be rightly demanded and claimed as much from the richest and happiest as from the most unfortunate: the unjust cannot be demanded from anyone" (Galiani [1751]: 352). He wanted to avoid a direct confrontation with the ecclesiastic authorities and had decided to stay on the same ground as them, using their same arguments and even their own sources.

The relationship between interest and *heartbeat* constitutes one of the first applications of probability calculus to the economic sphere (in terms of the expected value rule) and Galiani was among the first social scientists to realise that the structure of the natural sciences, based on a probabilistic model, is perfectly adaptable to social and economic analysis.[104] The calculation of probability, as is well known, had received a great deal of attention in the eighteenth century, even the widespread use of gambling among the aristocracy. Galiani privileges a type of objective probability that can be related to what modern economists call risk and reveals his optimism in the scientific progress achieved in this field: "Over many centuries of ignorance men have been so terrorized of chance events and by sheer luck that they have fled from them in fear, as from an untamed, kicking horse from whom they would flee with fright, seeking refuge out of reach. The light of true science has led them, finally, to the discovery that nothing is less fortuitous than chance events. Such events have a constant order and a controlled rule, such that it is possible to find a proportional relationship between the certainty of the present and the uncertainty of the future. Thus, as he quieted his fear, little by little, man began to familiarize himself with the idea of luck, to manage and manipulate it. For the first time, one hears discussions concerning justice in games of pure

[104] The probabilistic model was also proposed by Georges-Louis Leclerc de Buffon as opposed to the deterministic model of d'Alembert; see Buffon (1766). For the link between Galiani and the calculus of probability, cf. Giocoli (1997).

chance. Though previously scorned, in the hands of Bernoulli,[105] the art of forecasting becomes a branch of mathematics and of truth. From games, men proceeded to more serious matters such as navigation, human longevity, and the harvests of the fields, for so long all subject to chance. These were measured, valued, and insured, against the wiles of fortune, placing human prudence in reins and in chains. [...] Thus, [thanks] to mathematic[s], many conventions were put straight again, and the justice which the darkness of false science had expelled was recalled. In the face of chance, human daring was calculated and restricted between stable limits" (Galiani [1751]:349–350; see also Giocoli 2001: 127–128). The reference to mathematics, in a context that had experienced a vigorous debate on its foundations, could have provoked some risk of reaction, but it was used in neutral terms, only to ground the calculation of interest.[106]

Even on the issue of interest, Galiani irrupted with his scientific approach, using incontrovertible theses based on the force of facts. He then ably confirmed these findings by referring to passages from the Papal

[105] According to Emil Kauder (1965: 35) and Terence Hutchison (1988: 263), Galiani refers to Daniel Bernoulli, the author who wrote *Specimen Theoriae Novae de Mensura Sortis* in 1738 (also known as *Saint Petersburg Paradox*, see Bernoulli 1738 [1954]). Nicola Giocoli rejects this thesis, arguing that the reference to Bernoulli concerns Jacobus Bernoulli and his *Ars coniectandi. Tractatus de seriebus infinitis* (1713). It had already been argued by Furio Diaz and Luciano Guerci (see Galiani 1975: 251–252). A review of opinions for or against this attribution can be found in Giocoli (1997). Even if Galiani had known Daniel Bernouilli's arguments on the difference between ***mathematical expectation*** (or ***expected value***) and ***moral expectation***, he would have 'ignored' them, because they did not conform to his purpose. For Nicola Giocoli, Daniel Bernoulli's theses "are absolutely consistent with the framework of the theory of value in Book I" (Giocoli 1997: 25), although he also notes that Galiani is "not interested in the level of the lender's wealth because his goal is to demonstrate that there is no ethical argument against interest" (Giocoli 1997: 27). On Daniel Bernoulli's theory, see also Jordan (1924) and Stigler (1996).

[106] In the second edition of 1780, in *Note XXXIV*, he noted with self-congratulation: "When I published these thoughts of mine on the justice and injustice of the fruit of money, I expected to encounter great opposition and censure from moralists of some party, and on the contrary praise and approval from those who shared my opinion, but to my surprise, no praise and no blame was made to me: hence I learnt that to please the Scholastics it is not only necessary to unite with them in sentiments, but also to use the same kind of arguments: and for this reason any truth of the schools, which will be demonstrated by some with mathematical calculus, obfuscates them, nauseates them, and makes them displeased. However, I believe I have (whatever the scholastics say) given here the general equation of justice of all contracts, which is always reduced to this: that whatever varies the reason for our pleasure, must vary the sum of the equivalent thing which must be given in exchange (Galiani 1780: 414–415).

Bull *Vix Pervenit*, which had closed the Catholic controversy on the legitimacy of the interest rate. Always careful to distinguish usury, unmerited gain, from the interest that ensured the equity of the loan, Galiani addressed his possible opponents, observing that: "in any country where the repayment of the equivalent would always be measured by the equality of the weight of the metal without any other consideration, it is certain that borrowing would be difficult and very rare. Now if, in order to stimulate men to lend, a company of rich merchants decided to insure those who lend by a percentage paid by the borrower, would such insurance be legitimate or illegitimate? Having resolved this, the other question must be resolved. If the lender, not caring for extraneous security, were to collect the insurance price himself, would the nature of the contract change, and from just become sinful?" (Galiani [1751]:355).

Interest was thus the price of insurance against risk (the premium, in modern terminology),[107] and the fruit of the money "stands in that proportion to the capital, as the probability of loss stands to the probability of restitution" (Galiani [1751]: 357). This thesis can be basically traced back to the scholastic conception of *lucrum cessans-damnum emergens.*[108] The difference between the lender and the player who threw the money on the green table was precisely the need for the insurance required by the former

[107] Eugen von Böhm-Bawerk, who considered Galiani a forerunner of his theory of interest (since he explained interest as the *agio* of present goods over future ones), recognised it as incomplete because it was based solely on the difference in the certainty of enjoying them, or rather on the consideration of interest as an insurance premium (see Böhm-Bawerk 1884 [1890]: 50). "But unfortunately the inference which Galiani draws from this idea is very unsatisfactory. The reason that present sums of money are, as a rule, more valuable than future sums he finds exclusively in the different degree of their security. A claim to future payment of a sum of money is exposed to many dangers, and on that account is less valued than an equally large present sum. In so far as interest is paid to balance these dangers, it appears in the light of an insurance premium. [...].This was of course thoroughly to misunderstand the nature of loan interest" (Böhm-Bawerk 1884 [1890]: 50).

[108] On this Thomistic conception see Schumpeter (1954 [2006]: 98–102) and Pribram (1983: 16–20). Moreover, Galiani also confirmed that he remained on the terrain of the arguments used by the scholastics. According to Richard Cantillon: "The Casuists, who hardly appear to be suited to judge the nature of interest and matters of trade, conceived a term (*damnum emergens*), reluctant though they were to approve of these high rates of interest. [...]They are, or appear to be, a little more scrupulous concerning money loans, even though they are basically the same thing. Nevertheless, they still tolerate these loans through a distinction (*lucrum cessans*) of their own conception. [...]Nothing is more entertaining than the multiplicity of civil and church laws made in every century relating to the subject of the interest rate, always uselessly and always by philosophers ignorant of trade" (Cantillon 1755 [2010]: 95–96).

as opposed to the latter. This was the only subjective implication, since from an objective point of view uncertainty operated in both cases. Like all insurance, it was based on the modern calculation of probabilities, i.e. on objective quantities that could be dominated by the new mathematical science.

Galiani's theory of interest was closely linked to scholastic doctrine in that:

- it was considered a monetary phenomenon (and for this reason compared to the exchange rate);
- its explanation was approached with strong ethical concerns: one had to justify interest;
- time did not justify interest, but was only the place where the uncertainty extended; money deposited in banks, even if implicitly concerning a time difference and a loan, did not justify interest because there was no uncertainty about repayment (or at least at the time of deposit there were certain guarantees that the sum was not lost);
- there was no explicit reference to who used the sums, although the use of the money in economic enterprises was recognised (maritime trade was cited as an example). However, Galiani always assessed their degree of uncertainty and not the productive result that would follow.[109]

The relationship between interest and *heartbeats* was also confirmed by the economic policy measures identified to minimise the interest rate, namely:

- avoid the monopoly of money: "where there is a crowd of offerers, the conditions of the offer cannot be harsh. So shall the poor be treated without cruelty" (Galiani [1751]: 357);
- ensure the restitution of money, i.e. reduce uncertainty. "Therefore - he observed - it has not only been the abundance of precious metals that has lowered and almost extinguished usury for the last two cen-

[109] According to Marco Catucci: "Galiani provides several explanations of interest, not just one. The most important theory, the accomplished one, based on the alea of the loan, uses the papal bull as a starting point, pretending to be a simple commentary on it. But there is also mention of a more speculative and new theory, without theological underpinnings, concerning time; and finally a hedonistic theory" (Catucci 1986: 50).

turies; but principally the sweetness of government enjoyed in almost every kingdom. Let litigation be brief, justice certain, much industry in the people, and parsimony, and all the rich will be inclined to lend" (Galiani [1751]:356–357);
- reduce the public debt.

He extensively dwelled on the latter issue, considering it the "best way to diminish interest" (Galiani [1751]: 357). The debt to which Galiani referred was essentially the floating debt, created "by the necessities of wars [and] made fruitful by dismembering a portion of duties, and granting it to lenders, who share the profit among themselves" (Galiani [1751]: 358). The Prince's wealth was based on tributes and was always spent for the benefit of the citizens, "therefore if he has spent the money lent to him he has already returned it" (Galiani [1751]: 358).[110] Even when the Sovereign resorted to loans, the possibility of repaying them or paying interest was sustained on the imposition of new tributes, and it all became a big circle, and therefore - he observed – "the loan rendered with new money collected from those who lent, is no different from the unrendered" (Galiani [1751]: 359).

If this was the nature of public debt, its benefits were indicated thus:

- the weight of the large sum collected for necessities was distributed over several years;
- it was useful "for traffic and contracts", because of the lesser degree of uncertainty that fiscal rents possessed with respect to the land rent itself;
- it was the safest form of investment (income) for churches, hospitals, pious places (Galiani [1751]:359–360).

But in contrast there were the damages caused by the public debt, which if they did not outweigh the benefits, at least equalled them:

[110] Previously Galiani had stated that the Prince should not "regulate expenditure on rents, but these [rents] on that [expenditure], which, when he is just, he will endeavour to make as little as possible" (Galiani [1751]: 237). The abbot echoed a statement by Melon: "Private persons regulate their expences according to their income but the king regulateth his revenue, according to the expences that are necessary for the preservation of the state" (Melon 1739: 258). And it is a well-known statement by Melon that: "the debt of a state are debts due from the right hands to the left, whereby the Body will not find it self weakened, if it hath the necessary quantity of aliments, and they are proprely distribuited" (Melon 1739: 329).

- the secure rents of the public debt favoured the laziness of the rich and oppressed the poor for the tribute that had to be imposed to sustain its burden;
- investiments in public debt by ensuring secure incomes directly damaged agriculture by decreasing the value of land. The land thus remained "in the hands of miserable peasants, deprived of the support of the rich in cultivation. And it will always be worse cultivated that country, where the land is broken up into innumerable pieces of land owned by very poor people, compared to that where the settlers paid with the salaries of the rich owners of vast estates, do not run the risks of bad harvests" (Galiani [1751]: 359–360).
- covering extraordinary needs, especially after sustaining a war, most often required recourse to foreign credit, as the people found themselves immiserated and weakened by misfortune; this was equivalent to placing the country at the mercy of the foreigner, and was certainly the most serious damage (Galiani [1751]: 361).

The question of interest rate regulation therefore had to be tackled on the terrain of real economic facts and certainly not related to the impositions of the law, as Locke had already shown. Even more useless was the demand to ensure the equality of the loan with the legal obligation to return the same weight of metal received, because the changes in the intrinsic value of the currency, "almost as variable as the extrinsic, destroy all equality" (Galiani [1751]: 362). But everything was subject to change over time due to the instability of human affairs, and census, rents, mortgages and annuities of fiefs varied according to the movements of the population, the value of the currency, prices, customs and fashion, due to causes that no law, even the most respected and severe, could consider as immutable.

Even the exchange rate (*cambio*) had the same nature as interest and obeyed the same laws: "exchange and interest [are] brothers to each other. The one is the equalization between present money and money far from a place, made with an *apparent surplus* which is added sometimes to present money, sometimes to far money, in order to create equality between the intrinsic value of one or the other diminished by the lesser convenience or the greater danger. Interest is the same thing, but between present money and money which is distant in time, with the latter working in the same way as distance: and the foundation of the one contract and the other is the equality of the true intrinsic value. So true is this, that sometimes in the exchange the present money is worth less than the distant money and is called an exchange *below par* (*sotto del pari*); and the papers representing the money, which are nothing more than future money, are often worth more than the cash, and this more is called *agio*" (Galiani [1751]: 351).

True exchange[111] was, according to Galiani, bills of exchange. Essentialy, it was linked to commercial transactions and the state of the balance of trade: for this reason the abbot called it the "thermometer of states" and "the pulse of the civil body of society". The Prince had to pay particular attention to it precisely as a revelation of the sickness or well-being of a society, and not as an illusory source of enrichment, as some of the writers involved would have him believe".[112] A high exchange rate (excess demand for bills of exchange) favourable to bankers and speculators meant poverty and the decadence of a state; conversely, a low exchange rate meant a position of distinct commercial advantage. Exchange rate movements fluctuated around the so-called *par of exchange* (*cambio alla pari)*, represented by the ratio between the intrinsic values (weight of the metal contained) of the two currencies, "whatever more is taken from the equivalent weight of metal, it must not exceed the price of transport combined with the price of all degrees of risk, to which the metal transported is subjected"; this is the limit of the price of exchange rates, "beyond which they cannot remain permanently and for a long time".

Good exchange rate governance required, however, very careful evaluations of the overall commercial activity of a country. The high exchange rate with respect to all the mercantile centres was certainly a bad thing, but the exchange rate with respect to one or a few centres was not. On the other hand, if economic integration between two regions was very strong, as was the case between Naples and Sicily and the Papal State, the high exchange rate should not be too worrisome because it never led to the impoverishment of the country, since the money that went out came back in through other channels and often without using bills of exchange.[113]

[111] Distinct from what Galiani called *natural exchange*, coinciding with *manual exchange operations.*

[112] In *Note XXXV*, Galiani clarifies that the allusion was to Broggia and Gerolamo Belloni, whom he later attacks as being guilty of having treated the subject of foreign exchange from the point of view of interested parties, being merchants and bankers (Galiani 1780: 415). In the case of Broggia, this criticism is once again unfair, as the Neapolitan merchant had made a lengthy analysis of the dangers inherent in foreign exchange speculation.

[113] This was the case of the Abruzzese economy integrated into the Papal State, so much so that it could be said that "Rome was fed by the Abruzzi", since the Roman countryside was cultivated with the work of Abruzzese peasants; even if the exchange rate between the two countries was high, Abruzzese peasants always returned to the Kingdom "with a few *Zecchino* saved" and the shortage of money was not felt (Galiani [1751]: : 369).

References[114]

Manuscript Sources

Galiani, C. MSCG. Ricerche intorno alle prime origini della scienza morale, manuscript kept in the Biblioteca Società Napoletana di Storia Patria, XXXI. C. 1, folios 1–68.

Galiani, C. MSCG-1. Riflessioni sopra la natura dei lotti e loro giusti valori, manuscript kept in the Biblioteca Universitaria Bologna, Ms. 992, folios 26–94.

Galiani, F. MS-6. Della superstizione, e delle cause di essa, Manuscript kept in the Biblioteca Società Napoletana di Storia Patria, XXXI. A. 10, folios 124r–125v, published in Mauro 2017a, tome 2, pp. 469–471.

Galiani, F. MS-13. Della Moneta. Manuscript kept in the Biblioteca Società Napoletana di Storia Patria, XXIX. E. 13.

Galiani, F. MS-25. Per la riduzione delle feste, Manuscript kept in the Biblioteca Società Napoletana di Storia Patria, XXX. A. 10, folios 133r–144v, published in Galiani, 1999, pp. 51–55.

Primary Sources

Antonino of Florence. (1485). *Summa Theologiae Moralis*. Venice: Andreas de Paltasichis.

Aristotle. [1993]. *Posterior Analytics*, translated by J. Barnes, Oxford: Claredon Press.

Aristotle. [1998]. *Politics*. Translated, with introduction and notes, by CDC. Reeve, Indianapolis: Hackett Publishing Company.

Aristotle. [2004]. *Nicomachean Ethics*. Translated and edited by R. Crisp, Cambridge: Cambridge University Press.

Augustine of Hippo. [1972]. *City of God*, London: Penguin.

Ballerini, P. (1744). *La dottrina della Chiesa Cattolica circa l'usura dichiarata e dimostrata contro le pretese della novella opera intitolata Dell'impiego del denaro libri tre*. Bologna: Tommaso Colli.

Beccaria Bonesana, C. (1804). Elementi di economia pubblica. in *Scrittori classici italiani di economia politica*. Parte Moderna, Tomo XI, edited by P. Custodi. Milan: Destefanis.

Benedict XIV. (1746). *Bullarium*, vol. 1. Rome: Typ. de Propaganda Fide, pp. 578–581.

[114] The abbreviations "s.l." and "s.n." stand for the Latin terms *sine loco* (without place of publication) and *sine nomine* (without name of publisher).

Bernoulli, D. (1738) [1954]. Specimen Theoriae Novae de Mensura Sortis. *Commentarii Academiae Scientiarum Imperialis Petropolitanae*, Tomus V, pp. 175–192, published as Exposition of a New Theory on the Measurement of Risk, *Econometrica*, 1954, vol. 22, n. 1, pp. 23–36.

Broedersen, N. (1743). De usuris licitis et illicitis vulgo nunc compensatoriis et lucratoriis secundum jus naturale, divinum Veteris atque Novi Testamenti, ecclesiasticum et civile [...] Libri XII. Haag: Gosse.

Broggia, C. A. (1743). *Trattato de' tributi, delle monete e del governo politico della sanità. Opera di stato, e di commercio, di polizia e di finanza: molto, alla felicità de' popoli, alla robustezza degli stati, ed alla gloria e possanza maggiore de' principi, conferente e necessaria*. Naples: Pietro Palombo.

Buffon, G.-L. Leclerc de. (1766). *Histoire naturelle, générale et particulière avec la description du cabinet du roi*, tome XIV. Paris: Imprimerie royale.

Cantillon, R. (1755) [2010]. *Essai sur la nature du commerce en général. Traduit de l'anglois,* London: Fletcher Gyles. English Translation: *An Essay on Economic Theory*, Translated by C. Saucier, edited by M. Thornton. Auburn: Ludwig von Mises Institute.

Condillac, E. Bonnot de. (1776). *Le commerce et le gouvernement, considérés relativement l'un à l'autre: Ouvrage élémentaire*. Amsterdam: chez Jombert & Cellot.

Covarrubias y Leuva, D. (1556). *Veterum collatio numismatum, cum his quae modo exendutur.* Salamaca: apud Iunt. Granatae.

Davanzati, B. (1588) [1804]. *Lezione delle monete,* Firenze, in *Scrittori classici italiani di Economia Politica,* Parte antica, Tomo II. Milan: De Stefanis, 1804.

Galiani, F. [1751] [published anonymous, with date of 1750]. *Della moneta. Libri cinque,* Naples: Giuseppe Raimondi.

Galiani, F. (1770a). *Dialogues sur le commerce des bleds.* London [but Paris]: Merlin.

Galiani, F. (1772). *Catalogo delle materie appartenenti al Vesuvio contenute nel Museo, con alcune brevi osservazioni. Opera del celebre autore de' Dialoghi sul commercio de' grani.* London [but Florence]: s.n.

Galiani, F. (1780). *Della moneta. Libri cinque. Edizione seconda.* Naples: Stamperia Simoniana.

Galiani, F. (1975). *Opere di Ferdinando Galiani*, edited by F. Diaz e L. Guerci, in *Letteratura italiana. Storia e testi. Illuministi italiani*, tomo VI. Milan-Naples: Ricciardi.

Galiani, F. (1977). *On Money.* A Translation of Della Moneta by Ferdinado Galiani by Peter R. Toscano. Ann Arbor: University Microfilm International.

Galiani, F. (1999). *Scritti di politica economica*, edited by F. Cesarano. Lanciano: Rocco Carabba.

Genovesi, A. (1757). *Storia del commercio della Gran Brettagna scritta da John Cary mercatante di Bristol. Tradotta in nostra volgar lingua da Pietro Genovesi giureconsulto napoletano, con un Ragionamento sul commercio in universale, e alcune annotazioni riguardanti l'economia del nostro Regno di Antonio Genovesi R. Professore di Commercio e di Meccanica nella Cattedra Intieriana*, tomi 2. Naples: Benedetto Gessari.

Hobbes, T. (1651) [1909]. *Hobbes's Leviathan*. Reprinted from the Edition of 1651, with an Essay by G. Pogson Smith. Oxfrord: Claredon Press.

Hutcheson, F. (1755). *A System of Moral Philosophy: In Three Books*, vol. II. London: Millar.

Locke, J. (1692). *Some Considerations of the Consequences of the Lowering of Interest, and Raising the Value of Money. In a letter sent to a Member of Parliament*. London, Awnsham and John Churchill, at the Black-Swan in Pater-Noster-Row.

Locke, J. (1714). *Two Treatises of Government. In the Former, the false Principles and Foundation of Sir Robert Filmer, and his Followers, are detected and overthrown. The Latter is an Essay concerning the true Original, Extent, and End of Civil Government*, in *Works of John Locke*, vol. II. London: Churchill.

Machiavelli, N. (1531) [1883]. *Discorsi sopra la prima Deca di Tito Livio*. Florence: Bernardo Giunti. English translation by N H. Thomson, *Discourses on the First Decade of Titus Livius*. London: Kegan.

Machiavelli, N. (1532) [1976]. *Il principe di Nicchol̀o Machiavello al magnifico Lorenzo di Piero de Medici*. Rome: Antonio Blado d'Asola. English Translation, *The Prince*, translated, with introduction and notes by J. B. Atkinson. Indianapolis: Hackett Publishing Company.

Maffei, S. (1744). *Dell'impiego del danaro libri tre*. Verona: Giannalberto Tumermani.

Mandeville, B. de. (1714). *The Fable of the Bees: or, Private Vices, Publick Benefits*. London: Roberts.

Melon, J-F. (1736). *Essai politique sur le commerce. Nouvelle édition. Cette édition est augmentée de sept chapitres et les lacunes des éditions précédentes y sont remplies*, s.l. s.n.

Melon, J-F. (1739). *A Political Essay Upon Commerce: Written in French by Monsieur M* Translated, with Some Annotations and Remarks, by David Bindon, Esq*. Dublin: Printed for P. Crampton.

Montesquieu, C.-L. de Secondat. (1748) [1989]. *De l'esprit des loix. Ou Du rapport que les loix doivent avoir avec la constitution de chaque gouvernement, les moeurs, le climat, la religion, le commerce*, Genève: Barillot & Fils. English Translation, *The Spirit of the Laws*, edited by A. M. Cohler, B. C. Miller, H. S. Stone. Cambridge: Cambridge University Press.

More, T. (1516) [2002]. *Utopia*. G. M Logan, R. M. Adams (eds.) Cambridge: Cambridge University Press.

Ricardo, D. (1817). *On the Principles of Political Economy and Taxation*. London: John Murray.

Salmasius, C. (1638). *De Usuris Liber*, Leiden: Bonaventura and Abraham Elzevier.

Salmasius, C. (1639). *De modo usurarum liber*, Leiden: Bonaventura and Abraham Elzevier.

Say, J.-B. (1843). *A Treatise on Political Economy: Or the Production, Distribution, and Consumption of Wealth*, Philadelaphia: Grigg & Elliot.

Senior, N. W. (1836). *An Outline of the Science of Political Economy.* London: Clowes.

Smith, A. (1776). *An Inquiry Into the Nature and Causes of the Wealth of Nations. In Two Volumes.* London: Strahan.

Steuart J. (1767). *An Inquiry into the Principles of Political Economy being an Essay on the Science of Domestic Policy in Free Nations. in which are particularly considered Population, Agriculture, Trade, Industry, Money, Coin, Interest, Circulation, Banks, Exchange, Public Credit, and Taxes by Sir James Steuart, Bart.* London: Millar and Cadell.

Thomas Aquinas. [1920]. *The Summa Theologiæ of St. Thomas Aquinas.* London: Benziger Brothers.

Turgot, A.R.M. (1769) [2011]. Valeurs et Monnaies: Projet d'article. In *The Turgot Collection. Writings, Speeches, and Letters*, edited by D. Gordon, Auburn: Ludwig von Mises Institute, pp. 163–184.

Verri, P. (1771). *Meditazioni sulla economia politica con annotazioni.* Venice: Pasquali

Vico, G.B. (1744) [1948]. *Principi di Scienza Nuova d'intorno alla Comune Natura delle Nazioni, in questa terza impressione. Dal medesimo Autore in un gran numero di luoghi corretta, schiarita, e notabilmente accresciuta.* Naples: Stamperia Muziana. English translation *The New Science of Giambattista Vico*, by T. Goddard Bergin, Ithaca: Cornell University Press, 1948.

Secondary Sources

Aglietta, M. (2018). *Money. 5,000 Years of Debt and Power.* London: Verso.

Aglietta, M., Orléan, A. (1982). *La violence de la monnaie.* Paris: PUF.

Aglietta, M., Orléan, A. (2018). Réflexions sur la nature de la monnaie. In R. Boyer, (ed.), *La Théorie de la Régulation au fil du temps. Suivre l'évolution d'un paradigme au gré des transformations des capitalismes contemporains.* La Plaine Saint-Denis: Éditions des maisons des sciences de l'homme associées, pp. 103–109.

Benetti, C. (1994). Troc, bons d'achat et monnaie: La conception de Ferdinando Galiani. *Revue économique*, Vol. 45, No. 5, *Monnaie bancaire étalon-or et change: Les leçons des Classiques*, pp. 1177–1187.

Benetti, C. (2018). Échange, prix et monnaie dans le 1er chapitre du livre II de *Della moneta.* In A. Tiran, C. Carnino (eds.), *Ferdinando Galiani, économie et politique.* Paris: Classiques Garnier, pp. 193–210.

Bensimon, G. (2018). Une interprétation de la théorie de la valeur de Galiani. In A. Tiran, Carnino, C. (eds.), *Ferdinando Galiani, économie et politique*. Paris: Classiques Garnier, pp. 223–250.

Böhm-Bawerk, E. (1884) [1890]. *Geshischte und Kritik der Kapitalzins Theorien*, Innsbruck: Verlag; English Translation. *Capital and Interest. A Critical History of Economical Theory*, London: Macmillan.

Bridrey, E. (1906). *La théorie de la monnaie au XIVe siècle, Nicolas Oresme*. Paris: Giard & Brière.

Caracciolo, A, Merola, A. (eds.). (1963). Introduzione. Galiani, F. *Della moneta e scritti inediti*, Milan: Feltrinelli.

Catucci, M. (1986). *Galianea. Ferdinando Galiani tra letteratura ed economia*, Rome: Bulzoni.

Cesarano, F. (1976). Monetary Theory in Ferdinando Galiani's *Della Moneta*. *History of Political Economy*, 8 (3), pp. 380–399.

Cesarano, F. (1990). Law and Galiani on money and monetary system. *History of Political Economy*, vol. 22, n. 2, pp. 321–340.

Cesarano, F. (1995). Galiani e il ruolo della politica economica. In A. Roncaglia (ed.) *Alle origini del pensiero economico in Italia*. Bologna: Il Mulino, pp. 97–120.

Cesarano, F. (1999). Introduzione. In F. Galiani, *Scritti di Politica Economica*. Lanciano: Rocco Carabba, pp. vii–xix.

Chafuen, A. A. (2003). *Faith and Liberty. The Economic Thought of the Late Scholastics*. London: Lexington Books.

Chaplygina I., Lapidus, A. (2016). Economic Thought in Scholasticism. In *Handbook on the History of Economic Analysis*, Volume II, *Schools of Thought in Economics*, edited by G. Faccarello, H. D. Kurz. Cheltenham: Edward Elgar Publishing, pp. 20–42.

Clower, R. (1967). A Reconsideration of the Microfoundations of Monetary Theory. *Economic Inquiry*, vol. 6, 1, pp. 1–8.

Clower, R. (1969). Introduction. In R.Clower (ed.) *Monetary Theory: Selected Readings*, Hammondsworth: Penguin.

Cossa L. (1892). *Introduzione allo studio dell'economia politica*. Milan: Hoepli.

Costelloe, T. M. (1999). The Concept of a State of Nature in Vico's New Science. *History of Philosophy Quarterly*, Vol. 16, No. 3, pp. 321–339.

Costabile, L (2016). The value and security of money. Metallic and fiduciary media in Ferdinando Galiani's Della moneta. The European Journal of the History of Economic Thought, Vol. 23, Issue, 3, pp. 400–424.

Costabile, L., Neal, L. (2018). *Financial Innovation and Resilience. A Comparative Perspective on the Public Banks of Naples* (1462–1808). London: Palgrave Macmillan.

Cubeddu, R. (2024). Galiani, Menger and Other Austrians. *History of Economic Ideas*, XXXII, 3, pp. 63–83.

Davis, A. E. (2020). Money as Social Institution: Its Historical Emergence and Political Implicationsin. In S. Pressman (ed.) *How Social Forces Impact the Economy*. London: Routledge, pp. 81–96.

de Roover, R. (1955). Scholastic Economics: Survival and Lasting Influence from the Sixteenth Century to Adam Smith. *The Quarterly Journal of Economics*, Vol. 69, No. 2, pp. 161–190.

de Roover, R. (1967). *San Bernardino of Siena and Sant'Antonino of Florence: the Two Great Economic Thinkers of the Middle Ages*. Cambrige: Harvard University Printing Office.

de Roover, R. (1971). *La pensée économique des scolastiques doctrines et méthodes*, Paris: Vrin.

Diaz, F. (1975a). Introduzione. In Galiani, F. *Opere*, edited by F. Diaz, L.Guerci, *Letteratura italiana. Storia e testi. Illuministi italiani*, tomo VI, Milan-Naples: Ricciardi, pp. ix–cvi.

Dongili, P. (1988). Ferdinando Galiani: *Della moneta. Rivista Internazionale di Scienze Economiche e Commerciali*, Vol. 35, N. 1, pp. 11–28.

Dubois, A. (1897). Les théories psycologiques de la valeur au XVIIIe siècle. *Revue d'économie politique*, XI, pp. 849–864, pp. 917–930.

Einaudi, L. (1949) [2014]. Galiani, the economist. In *Rendiconti della Classe di Scienze morali, storiche e filologiche*, Series VIII, vol. IV, issue 3–4, March–April 1949, In L. Einaudi, R. Faucci, R. Marchionatti (eds.) *Luigi Einaudi Selected Economic Essays*. London: Palgrave Macmillan, vol II, pp. 227–264.

Einaudi, L. (1953). *Saggi bibliografici e storici intorno alle dottrine economiche*, Rome: Edizioni Storia e Letteratura.

Eusepi, G. (1992). Galiani teorico del valore soggettivo. In N. Acocella, G. M. Rey, M. Tiberi (eds.), *Saggi di politica economica in onore di Federico Caffé*, Milan: Angeli, pp. 93–118.

Federici, L. (1941). *La moneta e l'oro*. Milan: Casa Editrice Ambrosiana.

Femia, J.V. (2004). *Machiavelli Revisited*, Cardiff: University of Wales Press.

Force, P. (2003). *Self-Interest before Adam Smith. A Genealogy of Economic Science*, Cambridge: Cambridge University Press.

Garin, E. (1962). Appunti per una storia della fortuna di Hobbes nel Settecento italiano. *Rivista Critica di Storia della Filosofia*, Ottobre–Dicembre 1962, Vol. 17, No. 4, pp. 514–527.

Giannini, C. (2011). *The Age of Central Banks*. Cheltenham: Elgar.

Giocoli, N. (1997). La teoria dell'interesse di Ferdinando Galiani e l'ipotesi di Bernoulli: una grande occasione perduta?. *Il pensiero economico italiano*, 5 (1), pp. 7–37.

Giocoli, N. (1999). La teoria del valore di Ferdinando Galiani: un'interpretazione unitaria. *Storia del pensiero economico*, n. 38, pp. 69–93.

Giocoli, N. (2001). Value and Interest in Ferdinando Galiani's *Della Moneta*. *History of Economic Ideas*, Vol. 9, No. 3, Special Issue: *"Della Moneta" by Ferdinando Galiani: a Quarter Millennium Assessment* (2001), pp. 95–135.

Gordon, B. J. (1961). Aristotle, Schumpeter, and the Metalist Tradition. *The Quarterly Journal of Economics*, vol. 75, No. 4, pp. 608–614.

Graziani, A. (1889). *Storia critica della teoria del valore in Italia*. Milan: Hoepli.

Groenewegen, P. (1970). A Reappraisal of Turgot's Theory of Value, Exchange, and Price Determination. *History of Political Economy*, vol. II, pp. 177–196.

Groenewegen, P. D. (1977). *The Economics of A. R. J. Turgot*, The Hague: Martinus Nijhoff.

Hazard, P. (1953). *The European Mind. The Critical Years* (1680–1715). New Haven: Yale University Press.

Heinsohn, G., Steiger, O. (1983). Private Property, Debts and Interest or: the Origin of Money and the Rise and Fall of Monetary Economies. *Studi economici*, 21, pp. 3–56.

Hicks, J. (1967). *Critical essays in monetary theory*. Oxford: Claredon Press.

Holt, R. (2004). Fear Prudence: Hobbes and Williamson on the Morality of Contracting. *Journal of Economic Issues*, 38:4, pp. 1021–1036.

Hutchison, T. (1988). *Before Adam Smith. The Emergence of Political Economy 1662–1776*. Oxford: Basil Blackwell.

Jones, R.A. (1976). The Origin and Development of Media of Exchange. *Journal of Political Economy*, Vol. 84, No. 4, Part 1, pp. 757–776.

Jordan, C. (1924). On Daniel Bernoulli's Moral Expectation and on a New Conception of Expectation. *The American Mathematical Monthly*, Vol. 31, No. 4, pp. 183–190.

Kauder, E. (1965). *A History of Marginal Utility Theory*. Princeton: Princeton University Press.

Keynes, J. M. (1930). *A Treatise on Money*. Volume I. *The Pure Theory of Money*. London: Macmillan.

Lanzillo, A. (1939). Relazione tra il Cantillon e il Galiani. *Rivista di storia economica*, Anno IV, 2, pp. 201–218.

Lebrun, P. (1962). Réflexions méthodologiques sur l'histoire des théories et des doctrines économiques. La soidisant modernité de Ferdinando Galiani. In *Studi in onore di Amintore Fanfani*, VI, Milan: Giuffré, pp. 329–358.

Legris, A. (2001). Galiani, Della Moneta and the French Economists. *History of Economic Ideas*, 2001, Vol. 9, No. 3, *Special Issue: "Della Moneta" by Ferdinando Galiani: A Quarter Millennium Assessment* (2001), pp. 183–216.

Loria, A. (1882). La teoria del valore negli economisti italiani. *Archivio giuridico*, vol. XVIII, pp. 3–66.

Lucas, R. (1980). Equilibrium in a Pure Currency Economy. In J.H. Kareken, N. Wallace, (eds.), *Models of Monetary Economies*. Minneapolis: Federal Reserve Bank of Minneapolis, pp. 131–145.

Mauro, A. (2017a). *Un philosophe des Lumières entre Naples et Paris: Ferdinando Galiani (1728–1787)*. Thèse de Doctorate de l'Université Toulouse le Mirail - Toulouse II.

Marshall, A. (1920). *Principles of Economics*, (8th ed.). London: Macmillan & C.
Marx, K. (1859) [1904]. *Zur Kritik der politischen Ökonomie*. Berlin: Duncker. English Translation. *A Contribution to the Critique of Political Economy*, Chicago: Kerr & C.
Marx, K. (1867). *Das Kapital, Kritik der Politischen Ökonomie*, Erster Band: *Der Produktionsprozess des Kapitals*, Hamburg: Meissner.
McCulloch, J. R. (1864). *The Principles of Political Economy* (5th ed.). Edinburgh: Black.
Meek, R.L. (1973). *Studies in the labour theory of value*. New York: Monthly Review Pres.
Menger, C. (1871). *Grundsätze der Volkswirthschaftslehre*. Wien: Wilhelm Braumüller.
Menger, C. (1892). On the Origin of Money. *The Economic Journal*, Vol. 2, No. 6 (Jun., 1892), pp. 239–255.
Michels, R. (1932). *Introduzione alla storia delle dottrine economiche e politiche*, Bologna: Zanichelli.
Nagy, J. (2012). Vico Contra Hobbes. *Información Filosófica*, Vol. IX, N. 18, pp. 101–124.
Nicolini, F. (1908b). Intorno a Ferdinando Galiani a proposito di una pubblicazione recente. *Giornale Storico della letteratura italiana*, Volume LII, pp. 1–55.
Nicolini, F. (1942). Vico, Hobbes e una postilla inedita alla Scienza Nuova. *Atti dell'Accademia di scienze morali e politiche della Società Reale di Napoli*, vol. LXI.
Nicolini, F. (1950). *Di alcuni rapporti ideali tra il Vico e il Hobbes con qualche riferimento al Machiavelli*. Rome: Edizioni di Storia e Letteratura.
Nuccio, O. (1967). Introduzione. In *Scrittori classici italiani di economia politica*, parte moderna, tomo sesto, Rome: Bizzari, pp. i–lxxxiii.
Nuccio, O. (1987). *Il pensiero economico italiano. Le Fonti. 1050–1450. L'etica laica e la formazione dello spirito economico*, Vol. 1, Libro III. Sassari: Gallizzi.
Ostroy, J.M. (1973). The Informational Efficiency of Monetary Exchange. *American Economic Review*, 63 (4), pp. 597–609.
Paganelli, M.P. (2018). De la monnaie. Ferdinando Galiani et Adam Smith. In A. Tiran, Carnino, C. (eds.), *Ferdinando Galiani, économie et politique*. Paris: Classiques Garnier, pp. 211–222.
Palladino, F. (1988). La formazione scientifico-matematica di Celestino Galiani. *Bollettino del Centro di Studi Vichiani*, Anno XXVII–XXVII, pp. 253–262.
Pantaleoni, M. (1889). *Principii di economia pura*. Florence: Barbera.
Pasinetti, L. (1986). Theory of Value - A Source of Alternative Paradigms in Economic Analysis. In M. Baranzini, R. Scazzieri (eds.), *Foundations of Economics - Structures of Inquiry and Economic Theory*. Oxford: Basil Blackwell, pp. 409–431.

Pasinetti, L. (ed.) (1989). *Aspetti controversi della teoria del valore*. Bologna: Il Mulino.

Patalano, R., Realfonzo, R. 2001. On Money by Ferdinando Galiani: Notes, Social Accounting and Confidence. *History of Economic Ideas*, Vol. 9, No. 3, *Special Issue: "Della Moneta" by Ferdinando Galiani: A Quarter Millennium Assessment*, pp. 61–94.

Patinkin, D. (1956). *Money, Interest, and Prices; An Integration of Monetary and Value Theory*. Evanston, Illinois: Row, Peterson and Co.

Pecchio, G. (1849). *Storia dell'economia pubblica in Italia. Ossia epilogo critico degli economisti italiani preceduto da un'introduzione. Terza edizione*. Lugano: Tipografia della Svizzera Italiana.

Pii, E. (1984). *Antonio Genovesi. Dalla politica economica alla politica civile*. Florence: Olschki.

Pribram, K. (1983). *A history of economic reasoning*. New York: John Hopkins University Press.

Richter, R. (1988). The New Institutional Economics Applied to Monetary Economics. *Journal of Institutional and Theoretical Economics*, Vol. 144, No. 1, pp. 208–224.

Rosselli, A. (2001). The Role of The Precious Metals in *Della Moneta* by Ferdinando Galiani. *History of Economic Ideas*, Vol. 9, No. 3, pp. 43–60.

Rossetti, G. (1942). Galiani e la teoria dei gradi finali di utilità. *Rivista di Storia Economica*, Anno VII, pp. 111–116

Rotta, S. (ed.) (1973). *L'illuminismo a Genova. Lettere di P.P. Celesia e F. Galiani*, Florence: La Nuova Italia.

Schumpeter, J. A. (1954) [2006]. *History of Economic Analysis*. London: Routledge.

Schumpeter, J. A. (1970). *Das Wesen des Geldes*, Mann, F.K. (ed.), Gottingen: Ruprecht & Vandenhoeck.

Screpanti, E., Zamagni, S. (2005). *An Outline of the History of Economic Thought. Second Edition Revised and Expanded*. Oxford: Oxford University Press.

Simiand, F. (1934). La monnaie, réalité sociale. *Les Annales Sociologiques*, série D, fascicule 1, pp. 1–54.

Simmel, G. (1907) [2004]. *Philosophie des Geldes*, Leipzig, Duncker & Humblot. English Translation, *The Philosophy of Money*, London: Routledge.

Spooner, F. C. (1956). The Principle of Utility: The Contribution of Ferdinando Galiani. *Cambridge Historical Journal*, 12 (1), pp. 81–82.

Stephenson, M. A. (1972). The Paradox of Value: A Suggested Interpretation. *History of Political Economy*, 4 (1), pp. 127–139.

Stigler, S. (1996). The Bernoullis of Basel. *Journal of Econometrics*, vol. 75, n°1, pp. 7–13.

Tagliacozzo, G. (1937). *Economisti napoletani dei secoli XVII e XVIII*. Bologna: Cappelli.

Tiran, A. 2018. Galiani (1728–1787) et Della Moneta (1751). In A. Tiran, C. Carnino, (eds.), *Ferdinando Galiani, économie et politique.* Paris: Classiques Garnier, pp. 57–94.

Troisi, M. (1941). Aspetti teorici e normativi del sistema di economia civile di Antonio Genovesi. Il valore e la dottrina monetario-creditizia (con appendice di documenti inediti). *Rassegna Monetaria*, anno XXXVIII, n. 5, maggio 1941, pp. 729–761.

Velde, F. R., Weber, W. E. (2000). Fiat money in 17th century Castile. *Federal Reserve Bank of Minneapolis and University of Minnesota Minneapolis.*

Venturi, F. (1998). *Settecento riformatore. Da Muratori a Beccaria*, Turin: Einaudi.

Weiss, R. W. (1970). "The Issue of Paper Money in the American Colonies, 1720–1774", *The Journal of Economic History*, Vol. 30, No. 4, pp. 770–784.

CHAPTER 5

Della Moneta: The Monetary Policy

5.1 The Problem of Monetary Mutations

In the *Third Book* of his work, Galiani tackled the issue of money manipulation, and this was undoubtedly the main obstacle standing in the way of his scientific investigation. He was aware of this, and emphatically underlined that he was beginning to deal with "serious matters, and of such great importance, that most writers have disputed on these alone, as if the entire knowledge of money were included in them" (Galiani [1751]: 177). And indeed serious matters were those concerning the mutations that had caused "the most calamitous events and the most sensational operations". On this matter, too, it was necessary to clarify, to clear the field of confusion and errors, caused mostly by the fact that "when men reason about interest and gain, they always let themselves be carried away either by excessive fear or by disordered greed, and since the decisions of the authorities are almost always moved or suspended either by the advice of private individuals or by the cries of the multitude, it rarely happens that they are directed to the general utility" (Galiani [1751]: 178).

His first objective was therefore to appropriately classify the matter: the first step towards any treatment that claimed to be scientific. Mutations occurred for:

R. Patalano, *Ferdinando Galiani*,
https://doi.org/10.1007/978-3-032-02793-1_5

1. *natural causes*, such as discovery of new mines (which altered the exchange ratio between metals), or changes in habits and luxury (which directly affected the amount of gold available for monetary uses), or the natural wear and tear of circulating money;
2. *artificial causes*, due to the Princes, who changed the alloy, or the weight, or established by authority of law a new extrinsic value; or by the initiative of private individuals with the fraudulent operations of clipping (Galiani [1751]: 196).

The mutation, as we have seen, could concern:

1. only a part of the currency (a metal or a single kind of currency) and Galiani indicated it with the term of *sproporzione* (*disproportion*).
2. the entire monetary mass in circulation, and it was indicated with the term of *alzamento* (*raising*) (Galiani [1751]: 196–197).[1] Galiani rejected the terminological innovation introduced by Broggia, who aimed to distinguish variations in the extrinsic (nominal price of the coin, called *alzamento*) from those in the intrinsic value (variation of goodness and weight, called *mutazione*) (Broggia 1743: 184–186), and, instead, is much closer to the French tradition of the concept of *augmentation*, which was taken up by Spinelli as *aumento* (Spinelli [1749]: 29).[2]

[1] The terminology used to indicate mutation was very complex, before the sixteenth century the mutation of money "is called a weakening of the unit of account (in terms of metal represented) if a coin of écu actually in circulation is declared by royal edict to henceforth be worth, say, twenty sous in the unit of account instead of the previous ten, that is, if one sou is represented by half the quantity of metal, and if the footing of écu is raised in proportion. The term strengthening the unit of account is used for the reversal of the operation, which diminishes the value of a given weight of metal. This was perceived, incidentally, as a return of good money. Between two coins, the good one is consequently the one with a lower footing, the other being the bad one" (Boyer-Xambeu et al. 1986: 52). In the sixteenth century "the vocabulary was reversed, and this operation was from then on called raising or increasing metallic coins; in fact, there was an increase in the number of coins made from marc of metal, or in the number of sous for which this coin was to circulate. On the on hand, a decrease of coins implied that the same quantity of coined metal was worth a smaller amount of the unit of account" (Boyer-Xambeu et al. 1986: 65).

[2] According to Trojano Spinelli, the increase of the currency consisted either of the modification "by virtue of an edict or a new law", of the extrinsic value of the coins already minted; or in the melting of the entire mass of coins, to "make others of lesser alloy, i.e. less strong than the old ones" (Spinelli [1749]: 29). In the only English translation, which is not very reliable, edited by Peter Toscano, the term *alzamento* is translated as "raising the coins"

The first problem of a monetary system based on several metals was determined by fluctuations in their value. This problem had been the focus of Broggia's attention, but for Galiani it took on a different importance, as for him the movements in the value of metals had never been so significant as to seriously threaten monetary stability. And he proved this by appealing to history, which was once again called upon to confirm his thesis.

According to Galiani, in the time of King Darius of Persia, the ratio of gold to silver was established at around 1:13. By the time of Republican Rome, the ratio had changed to 1:15; then in the early imperial age it was at 1:12.5, closing at the fall of the empire at around 1:14.4. "In the barbarian centuries silver became very rare, and therefore the ratio changed, falling almost to 10 percent, but in this state very little remained" (Galiani [1751]: 194), because at the beginning of the fourteenth century it returned to the ratio of 1:12. "It remained in these terms until the discovery of the Indies with little fluctuation, and a century and more after that discovery had not changed much. Then, from a century onwards, it has been growing so much that it is now very close to that of 1 in 15, the greatest of all" (Galiani [1751]: 195).

Thus, there were no *exogenous causes* of instability for *monetary equilibrium*, as Broggia believed, but problems could only arise from *endogenous impulses*, as a result of wrong choices by the authority in charge of monetary policy. In fact, it was up to the political authority, in the context of the coinage function, to establish *ex lege* the proportion between coins of different metals and between monetary types of the same material. The constancy over long periods of time between the values of metals - Galiani argued - has made mistakes rare, and in ancient times committing them did not matter much, "because the neighbouring peoples were barbarian, uncouth, and lacking in all commerce, they could not absorb good money and return the bad, and therefore that authority that the Romans had over money, no Prince can use it today without damage" (Galiani [1751]: 195).

The reason for the increased attention required of Princes to establish legal ratios between monetary species was essentially due to the enormous fragmentation of political space, and not to be able to quickly change this legal ratio "has been at all times and is a source of grave evils" (Galiani [1751]: 180). In this context, even small movements in the ratio of metals

(Galiani 1977; Annalisa Rosselli translates as "augmentation of money", but then she leaves the word *alzamento* in the text (see Rosselli 2001: 45; 55–57).

could create monetary imbalances in countries that did not quickly adjust the legal proportion to the changing commercial course or that persisted in maintaining and setting proportions different from the natural ones. With great clarity, Galiani described the effects of an erroneous monetary policy as follows: "Let it be established that today the natural proportion between gold and silver is that whoever possesses one pound of gold is equally well endowed as one who has about 15 *pounds* of silver. The public authority now arrives and makes 13 *pounds* of silver equal to one of gold. It is immediately profitable to pay in silver because no longer 15 *pounds*, but only 13 *pounds* must be given to satisfy the debt of one *pound* of gold. It is advantageous to send gold where it is still valued at 15 *pounds* of silver. A man who had 30 *pounds* of silver in revenue and 15 *pounds* of debt, having made this change will have 17 *pounds* of revenue and 13 *pounds* of debt: therefore the gold disappears and the silver multiplies. If this legal ratio persists, all the gold will leave the country. If, once the loss of a much-needed money is known, the law is abolished, the damage done will be demonstrated because, supposing that while the disproportion was in force, 100,000 *ounces* of gold were exported and exchanged for silver, 1,300,000 *ounces* of silver would have flowed in. If the lost gold should be taken back, does this state obtain another 100,000 *ounces* of gold? No: for it must be taken back from the countries where the laws of those who have lost it do not arrive, and where the *ounce* of gold is worth 15 *ounces* of silver; so that only 86,666 ounces will be returned. All the remainder, which is not little, the state has lost forever and has gone into the hands of wiser people" (Galiani [1751]: 181–182).

And with an argument from the Aristotelian tradition, he condemned the speculative nature of this type of enrichment: "When the proportion between two commodities is in natural terms," he wrote, "only he who is really in need exchanges, the rest of men do not, but by changing this proportion, one of them acquires less value than is right and the other more. So it will be profitable, even for those who have no need, to give the one and take the other. Thus is born a way of earning money defined not by nature, but by law: hence is born a trade that anyone can and does ply without effort and without talent. Therefore the thing which is valued less than its natural value will be scarce, and the other which has replaced it will overabound; nor will it be able, if the force of law remains, to increase its value and so return to equilibrium" (Galiani [1751]: 181).

A legal ratio that did not respect the market ratio - according to Galiani - favoured above all foreign speculators, but the most serious damage was the unjust gains obtained by speculation to the advantage of a small fraction of citizens, an inequity that generated tyranny, a "bad order, in which those who are useless or harmful to others acquire wealth" (Galiani [1751]: 183).[3]

The law could therefore be a source of various evils, but Galiani rejected the principle advanced by Locke that public authority should never intervene in matters of price (Locke 1692: 31). If the law was right - the young abbot objected - it became a "confirmation of nature" and not a negation of it, and often a public measure could even strengthen actions of natural forces (Galiani [1751]: 183). Trade had to occur in full and natural freedom, as the state could not regulate men's pleasures and desires in minute detail, and the prices that arose from mutual consent had to be regarded as conforming to nature. If these were the natural circumstances, laws became necessary "only to make the consensus true, and to remove the frauds and deceptions, which by distorting ideas [made] the estimate and consensus false" (Galiani [1751]: 184). Measures on the criteria for defining the goodness of traded goods and those on the measurement system were very useful, but price interventions were not always beneficial.

The *Assisa*, i.e. the political price set for certain basic commodities, was certainly a more damaging system of price regulation, as this measure was taken to "satisfy the foolish minds of the lowest citizens" and was punctually disregarded by the control officers themselves, who allowed the price to be slightly higher than the political one (Galiani [1751]: 185).[4] The application of a fixed price (*Assisa*) to the currency, besides being an irrational measure,[5] would easily have caused the problem of the disproportion of the monetary system.[6]

[3] Schumpeter points out that Galiani implicitly believes that a bimetallic system in which the ratio between the two metals is legally fixed is indeterminate, a characteristic that was later identified by Léon Walras (see Schumpeter 1954 [2006]: 284, footnote 16). See Walras (1881).

[4] Galiani related the uselessness of the *Assisa* to the growth of working class income, believing that "when buyers are richer than sellers, the law has to favour the seller, and not the buyer, because the price is always more disadvantageous to those who have a greater desire to sell because they are more needy" (Galiani [1751]: 185–186).

[5] "Because to fix a ratio you have to hold both terms fixed; and so if you want to fix the price of money, it would be better to give it to wheat, wine, oil, and everything in the end. This is impossibile" (Galiani [1751]: 179).

[6] "This proportion established by the authority of the law, without being able to be changed according to natural movements, has been at all times, and is, the source of grave evils" (Galiani [1751]: 179).

Hence, there was to be no *Assisa*, or fixed price, which could lead to the peril of disproportion, but no free market either, because the latter would have damaged:

1. the rapidity of transactions, as currencies in circulation were not easily valued against each other;
2. citizens, especially the weaker ones, who were unable to establish the value of a newly minted coin without a precise indication from the mint;
3. all forms of contracts in which the parties did not establish values in a precise monetary unit (Galiani [1751]: 187).

The most suitable method for ensuring limited flexibility in the price of currency, the system known as *Voce* (*Voice* or *Voice-Price*) which corresponded to a "fixed, but not forced price," had to be carefully considered.[7] Such a system "serves as a rule for contracts in which two have spontaneously agreed to be at the price of the item: and so the freedom to contract is mixed with the necessity of a fixed rule, and the force is free agreement, not the law that establishes the *Voce*" (Galiani [1751]: 185). Trade regulated according to this system was the usual practice for buying and selling almost all essential goods in the Kingdom of Naples and "to this institution - Galiani observed - we owe all our trade" (Galiani [1751]: 186). This form of pricing seemed to the young abbot the most appropriate way to regulate monetary values: "This giving of a voice-price [...] to all coins avoids all dangers. The voice would be nothing more than the price at which the coin leaves the mint; after it leaves, no one should be forced to respect that same price, but the money should be treated as merchandise: and when common consent differs from the price of the mint, the mint should conform to that of the multitude, which when left at liberty always follows the truth" (Galiani [1751]: 188).[8] The value of money would thus

[7] The *voice-price* was set by the contractual parties in relation to changing market conditions. Galiani intended to apply to monetary matters the practice of fixing prices *by voice* as used since the Middle Ages in agricultural trade. However, this practice often concealed a usurious contract, which Galiani was not unaware of (see Galiani, MS-14: 745).

[8] Luigi Einaudi called this system of flexibility the *Galianean Clause*, considering it a "practical remedy" similar to that which governs the fixing of legal interest in today's societies (Einaudi 1936 [2006]: 172): "the system proposed by Galiani lay in supposing that mints should issue gold florins and silver scudos weighing 120 grains of fine metal, and that the proclamation should state that negotiations were to be compulsorily conducted in liras of

be regulated like interest, "which is set at 4 percent, but it is not forbidden to make it greater or lesser by convention" (Galiani [1751]: 187).

The *voice* system assigned the monetary authority the task of setting a reference price that could be changed by the agreement of the contracting parties in relation to market changes in the value of metals. When the variation from the original mint price became general, the monetary authority in turn had to adjust by changing the price. The system envisaged by Broggia was much more rigid, as it was based on changes in imaginary money and rapid interventions by the authorities, which Galiani considered difficult to implement

Another natural cause of mutation was the wear and tear of the coined metal, a not insignificant problem because "although it is true that it proceeds with slow steps, and does not produce fear in the people, when it grows a lot, it is necessary to correct it" (Galiani [1751]: 197).

The depletion (*struggimento*) of coins in his opinion depended on two factors (Galiani [1751]: 198):

1. the continuous use made, which clearly affected the smaller coins, used in very small and therefore more frequent exchanges;
2. the diameter of the coins, as consumption varied in inverse proportion to this size: in short, the larger the coin, the less quickly it was consumed.

The most common remedy lay in the use of billon coins, an alloy of copper and silver, but according to Galiani this measure was totally insufficient and harmful, because it involved high minting costs, did not prevent the practice of coin clipping, thus introducing an additional problem; and, in contexts where it was not traditionally used, it fuelled mistrust among the people for a coin that appeared to be counterfeit (as demonstrated by the experience of the Kingdom of Naples) (Galiani [1751]: 199, see also Galiani 1780: Note XIX, 399). If it was mainly small coins that were affected by wear and tear, the remedy could only be the minting of new coins with "greater thickness, imitating in this the wisdom of the

account, thus also stating a rate of 24 liras for the florin and of 2 liras for the scudo, applicable unless a contrary agreement existed [...] Thus, the *Galianean Clause* could give the money of account system the maximum elasticity. The right to 'illicit' negotiation would probably have paved the way to slower changes in 'proclaimed' rates; and in the meantime, there would have been no interest in exporting or in melting down any of the circulating denominations of gold or silver coins" (Einaudi 1949 [2014]: 261).

Greeks and Romans" (Galiani [1751]: 200). When coins were excessively worn, the only remedy was their withdrawal from circulation and the minting of new coins restored in their weight. The costs of the operation had to be borne by the community, through the imposition of a tax.[9] The timing of the new coinage had to be very fast and cover the entirety of the currency species concerned so as not to introduce disproportions (Galiani [1751]: 200).

Once the natural causes had been clarified, Galiani dealt with the mutations produced by private individuals and authorities. Above all, it was clipping that caused serious damage to the stability of the monetary system, because:

1. it caused disputes between buyers and sellers over the actual value of the monetary unit used as a means of payment;
2. it induced private individuals, especially foreigners, to even clip good money, as the reduced currency circulated at the same value (Galiani [1751]: 203–204).

Obviously the most immediate remedy was the harsh repression of the clippers, but if this decisive action was not possible, it was better to "do nothing at all [...] and wait patiently for better times" (Galiani [1751]: 205). Replacing metal currency with notes was difficult and could lead to even easier fraud.

A partial substitution of the clipped coin for good coin would have produced further inconveniences: "When in a country," Galiani noted, "there are two generations of currency, one good, and the other bad, the bad makes the good hide or drives it away, when there is a balance between them, if the good is much more numerous, the other loses its value, and is accepted with distrust or mostly rejected. If there is very little good currency, it either goes away or remains hoarded. These are all three great

[9] According to Galiani, there were two ways to finance this expenditure: either make the currency pay for it directly (by changing the weight or alloy, or by raising it), or impose new duties. In the case of a partial monetary reform (i.e. affecting only one species of currency), the first solution had to be ruled out because it caused disproportion; in the case of a general reform, both solutions could be practised, as the Count of Santo Stefano had done. The model of the massive English *Great Recoinage* of 1696 had been based on the imposition of new taxes.

evils that either disrupt trade or bleed the state" (Galiani [1751]: 205–206).[10]

A properly planned currency replacement had to take these drawbacks into account and be based on an exact calculation of expenditure, including the value of the worn metal to be restored, seigniorage and minting costs:

1. In the case where the state could fully bear the expense of a new coinage, it was necessary to issue an amount of new money equalling at least two-thirds of the old one. The old currency was then to be immediately put out of circulation, so that everyone would "compete for change, but even two-thirds of the total mass could not all be dried up in a few days" (Galiani [1751]: 206–207). With the metal of the old coins, new ones were minted until all the bad coinage was "netted". This was the method followed by the Viceroy Count of Santisteban, which Galiani considered to be the best monetary reform, "containing all possible savings and no pain" (Galiani [1751]: 207).[11]
2. In the case where the state was unable to pay the cost, the best remedy was to mint the new currency, as long as the state treasury allowed it, and to leave the old one still in circulation, stipulating that it be valued by weight. But such a measure, Galiani pointed out, could only be successfully adopted if the clippers were effectively combated and the state enjoyed great confidence (Galiani [1751]: 207).[12]

[10] Galiani noted the contrary workings of Gresham's law, which occurs following major inflationary pressures, when the state introduces good money that drives out the bad.

[11] Galiani also defended Count of Santisteban's policy, as did Intieri. On the contrary, the measure of the Count of Lemos in 1611 had caused serious damage, as the change of currency had been partial, only banning major coins and leaving *Zannette* in circulation.

[12] This was not the case during the reform of Cardinal Zapata (in 1622), who even promised the future abolition of *Zannette* without detriment to the holders. According to Galiani, this decision caused a further shearing of these coins. Other mistakes were made by the Count of Lemos, who "ordered that the large sheared coins should no longer be used, and moved by a false appearance of necessity, he allowed the continued use of *Zannette*, and *Cinquine*, low silver coins which were worse than the others. Therefore to those who brought in large sheared coins, the mint and the Banks began to give small coins that were much more sheared and corrupt. In four days the people were almost rioting" (Galiani [1751]: 207).

A more delicate and complex topic was the manipulation performed by Princes. This - Galiani emphasized - no longer involved the *tacit* manipulation of goodness and weight, a falsification operation entirely similar to that of the clippers and widely practised in the barbarian centuries. In his century, on the other hand, mutations occurred *overtly*, by edict, and were often the result of bad advice. In fact, he showed that most of them produced totally negligible effects:

1. the mutation of the proportion between copper and the richer metals, "if it is not very great, has no effect […]. The reason is that between copper and the higher metals there is no equality of strength. Copper is at least six or eight times lower in quantity, but equally in circulation […]. Bad copper always remains, and even when it is valued more than is right, it never attains the strength to compete with silver and gold" (Galiani [1751]: 213–214).
2. the disproportion introduced between gold and silver was more effective because the yellow metal was "more agile in going and coming" (Galiani [1751]: 214).
3. the disproportion introduced between coins of the same metal caused more damage than that introduced between different metals, making it easier for speculation by foreigners, who, as in the case of clipped coins, could introduce bad money and withdraw the good (Galiani [1751]: 214).

These measures brought no benefit to the state, since the disproportion:

1. produced a freeze on one part of the money supply, causing the other to vanish;
2. benefited foreigners and the more "mischievous" subjects;
3. did not bring about any automatic rebalancing mechanism, other than the total outflow of the disadvantaged currency (Galiani [1751]: 215).

To remedy the damage, it was necessary to intervene by completely eliminating the disproportion between coins of the same metal and in the case of the disproportion between different metals, leaving the rebalancing to the free market and then taking the equilibrium value as the new legal ratio (Galiani [1751]: 216–217).

5.2 The General *Alzamento* as an Exceptional Instrument of Fiscal Policy

Galiani distinguished between *disproportion* (mutation of a part of the currency) and *general alzamento* (*general augmentation*) that affected the entire circulating currency. On this policy, which had been both fiercely opposed and highly praised, Galiani wanted to clarify, once again taking a scientific point of view. To do so, he began his analysis with definitions: "*alzamento,*" he wrote, "is done either by a law or by melting the coins and decreasing their weight or carat quality" (Galiani [1751]: 221).

A few examples may clarify the concept expressed by Galiani:

1. If *general alzamento* is applied to the intrinsic value of coins, this directly alters the ratio of *commodity/monetised metal* for all commodities, which leads to an increase in nominal prices.[13]
2. If *general alzamento* concerns *imaginary money*, there is a devaluation of the latter in terms of the ideal quantum of metal contained.[14]

There were, for Galiani, three ways to carry out *alzamento* (Galiani [1751]: 250–251):

1. by *merco* (*marking*).[15] By affixing marks on the old coins that expressed the change in their value. A procedure widely used in

[13]Given a real coin of 1 *Carlino* which contains 10 grains of silver and which can buy 1 *Tomolo* of wheat, if the monetary authority reduces the intrinsic value of the *Carlino* to 0.9 grains of silver, without altering the relative price of wheat (i.e. without other intervening factors which alter the total quantity of wheat thus altering its relative price), 1 *Carlino* can only buy 0.9 *Tomolo* of wheat. In other words, the price of 1 *Tomolo* of wheat has increased to 1.11 *Carlini*.

[14]Let the *Scudo* be an actual coin, with a metal intrinsic value equal to 10 *Acini* of silver, and let the imaginary money be valued at 2 *Lire*. In essence, through the mediation of the actual coin, 1 *Lira*, the *imaginary money*, ideally contains 5 *Acini* of silver. The authority at some point raises the unit value of the *Scudo* from 2 to 3 *Lire*, so 3 *Lire* will contain 10 *Acini* of silver, and 1 *Lira* will contain only 3.3 *Acini* of silver. So there is a devaluation of the unit of account in terms of the ideal metal contained, and *voice-prices* will rise automatically. "This was the simplest and cheapest way of carrying out a devaluation in the old kind of monetary system where there was an accounting currency. Yet it was not so very different from the practices of today: in the French devaluation of 1958 it was decreed, from one day to the next, that the franc would be worth 20 percent less in terms of gold or foreign currencies" (Vilar 1991: 219). See Boyer-Xambeu et al. (1986: 52).

[15]See also Galiani, MS-26.

earlier times, but which, according to Galiani, left the possibility of fraud;
2. by *new coinage*. A procedure widely used in France, but one that entailed expense and could lead to inconvenience for the currency exchange operation;
3. by *simple edicts*. This procedure was regarded as the best, unless the state was in a situation of scarce monetary circulation.

This manoeuver was followed by a general increase in prices, because it "does not produce mutation of anything, but only of the *voce* (*voice*)" (Galiani [1751]: 223).

Like any effective scientific arrangement of a controversial subject, Galiani's argumentation proceeded by a *pars destruens* and a *pars costruens*.

The young abbot attacked the false ideas about the benefit and damage caused by such a policy:

1. First of all, *alzamento* could not be dismissed as damaging in all circumstances, because such a judgement could not be attributed to human affairs always "mixed with good and evil", and each had to be properly evaluated to establish the true utility of an action (Galiani [1751]: 227).
2. This policy did not cause the impoverishment of the Prince, who "for instant gain [would lose] a large part of his income", nor that of the people (Galiani [1751]: 227). Assuming that the Prince collected less public revenue after the *alzamento*, this deficit, consisting mainly of tributes, lowered the fiscal burden on citizens, and a sovereign's primary motive had to be the welfare of his subjects, since "the measure of the Prince's utility [is] the utility of his people" (Galiani [1751]: 230).
3. being a mutation of *voices* and not of *things*, *alzamento* could not even enrich the Prince, just as an increase in the unit of length could not transform an army of dwarfs into one of giants, and the Prince who claimed this would be accused of madness. "But," Galiani noted sarcastically, "men laugh if you promise to make them longer, they do not laugh if one refers to enrichment: they are so much more blinded by the greed of possessing things than by that of having a considerable stature" (Galiani [1751]: 226).

All these fallacious arguments were based on the thesis that *alzamento* caused a mechanical sequence between price rises, impoverishment of the population, fall in consumption and reduction of government revenues. But if the prices of commodities rise only by *voice*, the populace are equally impoverished only by *voice*: "the only real effect of *alzamento* is to discharge the debtor from having to repay the same sum he received for a debt contracted before the change in the price of money; but such a change, since it is between two individuals, cannot produce less revenue for the state. The Prince, who is the greatest debtor of all, is also disobligated; and if in this way he makes any one poor, it cannot be said that this causes him loss, but at most it does not cause him gain, diminishing the burden of tribute by as much as the debt is diminished" (Galiani [1751]: 233).[16]

All these false opinions derived - according to Galiani - from a substantial misunderstanding of the real effects of *alzamento* and the way it worked. Only Melon, a "man [who] was far superior to all in acuity of intellect and experience of human affairs", had come closest to the truth, not afraid to stand "against the tide" (Galiani [1751]: 233). This truth was that *alzamento* "is a profit that the Prince and the state derive from the slowness with which the multitude changes the connection of ideas about the prices of goods and money" (Galiani [1751]: 222).[17]

In the human mind - he observed – "things and voices [are] miserably joined together and united" (Galiani [1751]: 226) and this connection is the foundation of the "greatest work of our mind, which is the basis of all science [...] [and] on which the most singular and extraordinary recommendations are built" (Galiani [1751]: 222–223).[18]

[16] According to Franco Venturi: "Galiani had thus attempted to replace his generation's programme of monetary stability, reorganised taxation, and reforms with the "expedient of controlled inflation" (Venturi 1998: 497). See also Diaz (1975a: xxviii–xxix). Galiani considered deflation to be the worst evil, see also Galiani (1780: Note XI: 384–385).

[17] In the *Dialogues*, Galiani confirms this characteristic of human nature: "[Man] is a ductile matter on the leash of habit. He assumes all the folds, all the forms one wishes to give him without destroying himself; by means of habit he is able to give his strengths, his nature, his primitive being, an extension that would seem impossible at first and, what is even more singular, as soon as he has adapted himself, he realises that it is completely natural for him, that he has always existed and could not be otherwise, that this is his physical state" (Galiani 1770a: 229).

[18] Galiani bases his analysis on Locke's theory of language and knowledge, contained in *Book III* (*Of Words*) and *Book IV* (*Of Knowledge and Opinion*) of the *Essay Concerning*

The granting of an honour is based on the connection of ideas between the title and the nobility of the holder: "if a Prince declares all his subjects noble, he does not increase their honour, but strips it from the word *Nobility*, of which he changes the meaning" (Galiani [1751]: 223). If a Prince granted his staff a decoration, it would no longer be a decoration, but would assume the value of a livery in the judgement of the people: "because from the truth the multitude draws and conceives ideas, to these it couples the sounds of voices; by using the right power over the voices, the Prince gains the good of the state, which is the supreme law [...] if he abuses it, the connection is dissolved, the voices change meaning, things remain the same and the insuperable force of nature wins" (Galiani [1751]: 223).[19]

The effect of *alzamento* is based on the connection of ideas between goods and their prices, a connection that is not unlike the one that links noble titles to the idea of nobility. Once the monetary authority has decreed an *alzamento*, the connection between prices and goods slowly changes: "because men who are used to paying one ducat for food, when they have in their hands a thing called one *Ducato*, want to exchange it for food; and until they realise [the changed value], they complain of the avarice of those who deny the goods, or foolishly blame others for making everything more expensive" (Galiani [1751]: 224).

Alzamento can only have real effects if the price change occurs slowly, so that it is not immediately perceived by the people and the ideal connection between prices and commodities is not immediately broken. If, in fact, the increase in prices "occurs on the same day on which the *alzamento* is carried out [...] it would have no real consequence; nor would that law by which it was decreed that currencies, instead of being denominated with Italian names, should be denominated with Latin, Greek or

Human Understanding (see Locke 1748), published in 1690 and known in French and Latin versions. Locke's theory also had an influence on Vico's philosophy, see Costa (1970).

[19] On the inertia of the connection between words and ideas, Locke wrote: "But essences being taken for ideas established in the mind, with names annexed to them, they are supposed to remain steadily the same, whatever mutations the particular substances are liable to. For, whatever becomes of Alexander and Bucephalus, the ideas to which man and horse are annexed, are supposed nevertheless to remain the same; and so the essences of those species are preserved whole and undestroyed, whatever changes happen to any or all of the individuals of those species [...].The doctrine of the immutability of essences proves them to be only abstract ideas; and is founded on the relation established between them and certain sounds as signs of them; and will always be true, as long as the same name can have the same signification" (Locke 1748, vol II: 24).

Hebrew names" (Galiani [1751]: 224). The increase in prices works like the medicine of *alzamento*, "just as the morning fog is cleared by the sun", but it takes time for the sun to rise (Galiani [1751]: 224). If a Prince, having known this fact, were to practise *alzamento* every month, he would destroy any connection of ideas between prices and goods and make it completely useless.

Alzamento therefore only works in the interval in which the price rise progresses "bit by bit [...] according to the disposition of human minds" until it is annihilated: "the whole effect of *alzamento* is in this space that runs between the change made by the Prince and that of the people, after which the former vanishes and remains cancelled" (Galiani [1751]: 234). The larger this space, the greater the benefits. *Alzamento* is a dynamic process that can be distinguished in different phases:

a. *First phase*

"The Prince applies a mutation of *voices* to the currency: in appearance he does not seem to be less indebted than before, paying similar *voice-prices* if not with equal money: in reality, without increasing rents, he decreases the debt. Hence it is that all the harm of *alzamento* falls first on those who are paid by him" (Galiani [1751]: 234). The Prince can either reduce the intrinsic value of actual money (*devaluation of coins*) or increase the value of coins in terms of *imaginary money* (*alzamento* of actual money in unity of account, but devaluation of *imaginary money*). In both cases, as the debtor he will have to give back less metal to his creditors than he received.[20] If, for example, his debt amounted to 10,000 *pounds* of silver for the payment of wages to his employees (from the prime minister to the last soldier), this quantum of metal would materialise, according to the monetary system, in 148,000 *Piastres* of silver, which have a value in units of account of 177,600 *Ducats*, and it is in the latter value that his debt is

[20] "If *Peter* borroweth one hundred *Louis d'or* from *James*, he will become debtor to *James*, for two thousand four hundred *Livres*, nominal value. If on the next day, the King doth diminish the price of the *Mark* weight of gold by one sixth, and thereby reduce the *Louis d'or* to twenty *Livres*, Peter cannot pay his debt to *James*, but by giving him one hundred and twenty *Louis d'or* of the same weight and fineness he received. What *James* gaineth by this supposition, he would have lost, if there had been a proportionable increase of nominal value of the coin; for then *Peter* would have discharged his debt, with a smaller number of *Louis d'or*, of the same weight and fineness than he had received" (Melon 1739: 216–217, original italics).

expressed.[21] If the Prince proceeds to a general *alzamento*, he may establish that the silver *Piastre* (coin) contains less silver or he may increase its value in *Ducats*. If he chooses the latter solution and raises the *Piastre* from 1.2 to 1.5 *Ducats*, the *Ducat* will no longer contain the same quantum of metal.[22] His debt of 177,600 *Ducats* will be paid with 118,400 *Piastres* equal to a quantum of metal of 8000 *pounds*.[23] With a simple change of *voice*, the Sovereign's debt was reduced by 2000 *pounds*.[24]

b. *Second phase*

Those who obtained their credit satisfaction with fewer *Piastres*, but at the same nominal value, "do not perceive the change, buying as before" (Galiani [1751]: 234). The *Ducat*, unit of account, made it possible to buy the same quantity of goods as before (a *tomolo* of wheat is nominally still worth a *Ducat*), even though fewer *Piastres*, and therefore less metal, had to be paid for it. There has thus been an alteration in the relative price of the monetary metal with respect to other goods, but it has not yet been perceived by the agents, who look exclusively at nominal values (they are affected by *money illusion*, using terminology from modern economic theory, see Fisher 1928).

c. *Third phase*

The perception of the change in the relative price of the monetary metal with respect to goods occurs only because the country is open to foreign trade, indeed "if this mutation occurred in an island separated from all foreign trade, the change of ancient ideas would be very slow, and perhaps the natural idea of the value of metals would change. But in trade, the first to change is the exchange rate, the *thermometer of states*" (Galiani [1751]: 234).

[21] The example refers to money in force in the Kingdom of Naples at the time of Charles III, the silver *Piastra* contained about 23 grams of fine silver. Each *Piastra* was worth 1.2 *Ducats* of account.

[22] If 1.2 *Ducats* are equal to 23 grams of silver, then one *Ducat* is equivalent to 19.16 grams of silver; if 1.5 *Ducats* are worth 23 grams, one *Ducat* is equivalent to only 15.33 grams of silver.

[23] 148,000 *Piastre* are now worth 222,000 *Ducats*.

[24] The case of the direct devaluation of the *Piastre*'s intrinsic value is easily understood and therefore requires no special clarification.

d. *Fourth phase*

"When the exchange rate has been changed, the price of foreign goods immediately changes: if a merchant has bought a commodity in one country for one *ounce* of silver and takes it to another country where the *Ducat* used to weigh one *ounce*, but after *alzamento* weighs only 4/5 of an ounce, he certainly cannot sell the commodity for one *Ducat*, since the exchange rate, which has already aligned with the true value, makes him on his return the owner of 4/5 of an *ounce*, and not of a whole *ounce* of silver" (Galiani [1751]: 234–235). Thus, the change in the relative price between monetary metal and goods is first perceived by foreign merchants, who trade on the basis of metal standards, i.e. looking exclusively at weight and not at nominal value. The result is an increase in the price of foreign goods, until the original relative price between monetary metal and goods imported from the country that made the *alzamento* is restored. The first to perceive the inflationary pressure will therefore be those who import goods from abroad.

e. *Fifth Phase*

"Once foreign goods have become more expensive, those who can no longer buy them seek to make a profit from their own rents, which are the native productions of the place, and sell them more expensively to citizens and foreigners" (Galiani [1751]: 235). This increase in prices does not cause a net disadvantage for foreigners, because "he who comes from abroad to buy what used to be worth a hundred *Ducats*, and finds it worth a hundred and ten, doesn't mind any, as long as he receives his hundred *Scudi* in his homeland" (Galiani [1751]: 235).[25] For the citizens, on the other hand, the damage is considerable, "because paying credits and wages in money that is only in name the same as before, it is hard to have to buy with the old weight and with changing prices for those who receive with the same price and not with the same weight" (Galiani [1751]: 235–236).

[25] An ounce of silver always buys the same quantity of goods, whether it be ten *Ducats* or twelve. In contrast, if the increase in the price of goods is due to their scarcity, it will be necessary to surrender more than one ounce of silver to obtain the same quantity of goods.

f. *Sixth phase*

Thus the *money illusion* begins to fade and the reality of the change in the relative *commodity/monetary price* becomes clear: "to console himself each one increases the price of what he sells or rents, houses, lands, furniture; and while these people are compensated, the damage returns from where it first began, that is, to the Prince's employees, who, continuing to have the same wage, do not gain the same comfort from it. The protests of these people force the Prince in the end to increase wages, and everything falls ultimately on the Sovereign" (Galiani [1751]: 236). The final position will consist of a nominal debt of 220,000 *Ducats*, corresponding to 100,000 *pounds* of silver, but it is possible that the increase requested will be even higher and lead to a further increase in the debt, to the Prince's disadvantage.

The whole effect of *alzamento* lies in the *delay*, more or less extensive, with which the Prince suffers the damage.[26] Several conditions are required to ensure that this monetary manoeuvre is effective:

a. the mutation does not have to be implemented frequently and neither does it have to be announced before being implemented. The *alzamento* can only work if it is unexpected and rare, acting as an exogenous shock in a situation of unchanged expectations.[27]
b. the country must have a favourable position in foreign trade, so that it does not have to import large quantities of goods. A high volume of imports would immediately trigger the increase of domestic prices (Galiani [1751]: 237).

[26] According to Paola Dongili, the *alzamento*: "implies an understanding of an essential feature of a monetary economy, namely that while money expands the possibilities of recourse to the market, the generalised use of money constitutes a constraint on exchange techniques themselves and is a source of possible instability by separating the exchange of good against good into two separate transactions. In fact, contracts are concluded in (imaginary) money, and therefore those who receive their income on a contractual basis experience a real change in income, until they manage to change the terms of the contract, with a resulting change in their real demand for goods" (Dongili 1988: 25). It is therefore not: "an anticipation of the concept of monetary illusion or, in other words, of traders' expectations about prices with an elasticity of less than unity" (Dongili 1988: 25).

[27] The effectiveness of an economic policy is thus based on unexpected variations with unchanged expectations. An insight that undoubtedly anticipates the themes of *New Classical Macroeconomics*.

c. the rise in domestic prices must take place slowly, so as to foster the beneficial effects of the *alzamento*.
d. the bargaining power of those who serve the Prince must not be excessively high, so much so that they are forced to raise their wages more than proportionally to the price increase and thus the *alzamento*. In such cases the whole operation would result in a net disadvantage for the Prince (Galiani [1751]: 236).

These somewhat limiting circumstances obliged the Prince to take this measure only in case of extreme evils in order to postpone the damage (Galiani [1751]: 236).

The existence of a high government debt was the extreme case in which the use of *alzamento* is "a remedy to increase and pay debts at the same time [and] it is convenient," he concluded, "to worry about debts contracted for exorbitant expenses, not about their extinction, which must be done at any cost, and which is achieved by *alzamento*" (Galiani [1751]: 242).[28] Such manipulation therefore had the same "effect as a bankruptcy, but the damage [was] slower and spread out over everyone, so [it was] less stinging and clamorous", and in addition, it contained a saving of expenditure for a certain period of time.[29] In the truce of the public debt granted by *alzamento*, the Prince could remedy his financial situation and then cure the fever caused with the medicine of taxes, increasing them, "according to the mutation […] and then everything is as if it had never happened, and only ideas and names remain changed without harm" (Galiani [1751]: 236). And if the medicine were not sufficient, the state would be dead and destroyed "and it is not worth regretting having cured it with all extreme art" (Galiani [1751]: 236). In short, *alzamento* acted more as an instrument of fiscal policy than of monetary policy.[30]

[28] Broggia had formulated a similar proposal, according to which "a decrease in the weight or goodness of the currency might not be detrimental to the state, but only to commerce, when the public treasury is burdened with immense debts, for which large sums of interest must be paid annually, absorbing almost all the Prince's income" (Broggia 1743: 258).

[29] See the precise observations of Luigi Einaudi (1949 [2014]: 247–264) and Filippo Cesarano (1995: 108–114).

[30] A similar view is expressed by John Maynard Keynes in his *Tract on Monetary Reform*: "When the piled-up debt demands more than a tolerable proportion, relief has usually been sought in one or other of two out of the three possible methods. The first is Repudiation. But, except as the accompaniment of Revolution, this method is too crude, too deliberate, and too obvious in its incidence. The victims are immediately aware and cry out too loud; so that, in the absence of Revolution, this solution may be ruled out at present, as regards inter-

Having clarified what, in his opinion, was the authentic nature of *alzamento*, Galiani was able to reject false opinions about it (formulated mainly by Abbé de Saint-Pierre) and show its true usefulness and the damage that its imprudent use could cause.[31]

Alzamento was certainly a violence of the state, but it was certainly more serious than the violence of war, which Princes also used without hesitation, and it was not a tyrannical and unjust measure.[32] Nothing was to be feared from a just government that responded to "extreme necessity" with a manoeuvre on currency, without resorting to other more violent means such as the devastation of the countryside, the looting of churches and the requisitioning of all the precious metals in the banks (Galiani [1751]: 239). The choice of not honouring part of the contracted debt burdened only the wealthy financiers of the public treasury and much less the "unhappy peasant", thus achieving a more balanced distribution of the damage caused by excessive state indebtedness (Galiani [1751]: 240).[33] Nor was it a tribute, as it did not involve a permanent transfer of wealth, but only a temporary and particular one (burdening a specific class of citizens who were creditors of the Prince), and in the final position it could also lead to less income for the Sovereign (Galiani [1751]: 242). Not so the measures concerning the issue of *fiat money*, since "the royal notes are an effort made by the state above the sum of duties and are

nal debt, in Western Europe. The second method is Currency Depreciation, which becomes Devaluation when it is fixed and confirmed by law. In the countries of Europe lately belligerent, this expedient has been adopted, already on a scale which reduces the real burden of the debt by from 50 to 100 percent. In Germany the National Debt has been by these means practically obliterated, and the bond-holders have lost everything" (Keynes 1923: 64–65). See also Cesarano (1995: 113).

[31] See Abbé de Saint Pierre (1733, T. II: 199–230).

[32] "The luxury of monarchies are wars, from the effects of which one cannot escape in peace, without all being reduced to a frugal life" (Galiani [1751]: 261–262).

[33] "It is just that duty falls not on all equally, but on the strongest shoulders. Now the people who have tithes and fixed rents, are the ancient lords, the pious places rich and the opulent churches and monasteries: nor are tithes paid to peasants. Those who rent are not only the privileged, but the idle and niggardly, the more worthy to pay, as without increasing the wealth of the state they consume not only their own, but also foreign wealth. Nor must we be frightened by the tender voices of orphans, widows, virgins and pupils; for these are very few. The true orphan, the true poor is the industrious peasant, the artisan, the seaman and the merchant. Of these one must have compassion; and they are the ones who, being rent-takers, gain for *alzamento*" (Galiani [1751]: 252–253).

therefore a duty taken in advance" (Galiani [1751]: 242).[34] Through this additional issue of paper money, the state paid its expenses immediately, and at the same time withdrew some of the private wealth, which sooner or later had to be called in to pay off the debt incurred through new taxes. *Alzamento* did not impoverish the country, as it did not permanently affect the royal treasury, but only affected the circulation of money, decreasing "the amount of money circulating between the subjects and the Prince" (Galiani [1751]: 243), and this could even be useful to trade that used money in excess of its needs.[35] The effects on foreign trade were also not to be feared. The consequent increase in the price of domestic goods could be reduced by eliminating export duties (except for raw materials), while the increase in the price of imported goods could act as a stimulus to boost local production and improve the balance of trade.[36] *Alzamento* did not favour speculative behaviour by encouraging the withdrawal of goods from the market in expectation of a price increase, because the "merchant either sells at old prices and has coin of worse condition, or he increases the price, and has more coins, but equal weight of metal, and thus he does not improve his position. Therefore it is no use waiting" (Galiani [1751]: 245). Thus, the criticism traditionally raised against *alzamento* was fallacious and besides, public confidence was not threatened if the remedy of *alzamento* was only practised in a state of necessity.

While rejecting the false damages, Galiani showed what the real ones were:

1. in circumstances where it was "unnecessary and pernicious" to reduce the remuneration of the Prince's employees (this was the case with uprisings of poorly paid mercenaries) (Galiani [1751]: 245).

[34] According to Annalisa Rosselli: "The discussion on *alzamento* confirms Galiani's identification of money with its metal content" (Rosselli 2001: 57).

[35] Bernardo Davanzati in particular had argued that *alzamento* impoverished both the Prince, condemning him to less revenue, and the people, who saw their purchasing power reduced (see Davanzati 1588 [1804]: 41).

[36] Galiani remarked: "It is true that [after the raising] the foreigner will pay in new money [...], but the foreigner, having to submit to the prices he finds raised, will pay for the more expensive goods, even if with lighter coin, and so what he saves on weight by losing on number, he gains nothing" (Galiani [1751]: 263) and "it is then most false that foreign trade suffers, because the change in exchange rates makes foreigners insensitive to the rise" (Galiani [1751]: 263). "Hence, the fear that [...] has been expressed of the introduction of foreign minted coins is without foundation since, where there is no disproportion between metals, there can be no profit in minting." (Galiani [1751]: 263).

2. Melon's argument that *alzamento* benefited the debtor by favouring the poor, always in debt, must be rejected as a misleading "syllogism":[37] "The deception lies in this", Galiani argued, "that rich is *he who can benefit from the labours of others without paying an equivalent amount of labour, having his own labours, or the labours of his forefathers made before him and converted into money.* He is rich who has much money and is a creditor of labour; the poor man has no money but is a creditor of the rich man by his labour which he owes him. Therefore, since money and labours stand in opposite balances, the rich man is the debtor of money, the poor man the creditor. [...]. *Alzamento* does not benefit the debtor of labour, but the debtor of money so it benefits the rich, so that with greater labour one may acquire the same true value of metal [...]. Therefore it is unjust because it enriches the rich and aggravates the poor" (Galiani [1751]: 245–246).[38] Thus, *alzamento*, by benefiting the debtor, accrued to the benefit of the rich, forcing the poor [the creditor] to work harder to procure the same amount of metal he earned before the manoeuvre or to ask, at his own risk, for an increase in his wage. However, "when the state is troubled, the Prince, who for being the richest person is the greatest debtor of money, becomes poor of money; and therefore it profiteth him to be a creditor of the same labours by the ministers, notwithstanding that he doth not satisfy the same debt. To the utility of the Prince, who is the centre of society, having to yield that of every one, even if the poor man be aggravated, it is not fitting to regret it" (Galiani [1751]: 183).
3. Contrary to Melon's argument, *alzamento* was not to be used as an instrument to reduce taxes, which could be reduced directly without

[37] "Diminutions favour the creditor, and Augmentations, the Debtor: and supposing all other things are equal, in matters of the state, it is the debtor, who ought to be favoured" (Melon 1739: 217).

[38] The phrase in italics is in quotation marks in the original text (also in the 1780 edition, Galiani 1780: 245). For some scholars the passage is an apocryphal transcription of a concept expressed by Melon (see Diaz 1975a: 183), others, such as Fausto Nicolini and Alberto Merola, attribute it to Galiani (1915, 1963). Following this latter interpretation, the quotation mark can be considered a rhetorical emphasis. A probable analogy with Melon may be the following passage: "The rich man employs the mercenary for a modest wage [...]. The worker's wealth consists of secure work, which gives him the means to provide for his family" (Melon 1736: 291).

using such a sensible measure outside the circumstances that made it necessary (Galiani [1751]: 247).[39]

4. Finally, the view, also supported by Melon, that *alzamento* should be implemented when the tax burden was unbearable and expenditure could not be sustained for special emergencies (in the event of war for example), was not acceptable. In these circumstances, Galiani recommended the emission of *fiat money* or selling state revenue to private individuals (*arrendamenti*) to rake in resources.[40]

In the face of these real damages, there were three advantages for the Prince:

a. In the event of a serious emergency, *alzamento* acted as a "better remedy" than an expansion of public debt or an issuance of government bonds (Galiani [1751]: 250).
b. The temporary reduction in public spending was the most important effect, as the state could avoid raising taxes, simply by spending less (in terms of a smaller amount of precious metal sold for payments) (Galiani [1751]: 250).
c. *Alzamento*, being a "fiction of payment," was a means of debt settlement and as such it avoided the "damage" caused by the Prince's bankruptcy. At a disadvantage were all those who lived on fixed rents, "the lazy and the negligent, who are so much more entitled to pay, when without increasing the wealth of the state they consume not only their own, but also foreign wealth" (Galiani [1751]: 250). *Alzamento* also did justice to the countless disputes between private individuals for the execution of debts. These "disputes," Galiani concluded, "multiply ideal wealth and diminish real wealth: because a thousand *Ducats* demanded by one and not paid by another, appear to be two thousand for those who are expecting them shortly, boasting of having them as well as those who have them without security [...]. It is therefore the worthy care of a Prince to discourage

[39] "The augmentation of money to obtain the right of seigniorage in a recast is pernicious. The augmentation of money, to relieve the ploughman burdened with taxes, is necessary" (Melon 1736: 247). In the English translation (Melon 1739) there is no chapter XIX from which the quotation is taken.

[40] "Since the taxation required to pay the state's expenses is such that taxpayers, despite military executions, no longer have enough to pay them through the sale of their assets, what should the legislature do?" (Melon 1736: 240).

> those who hope for greater riches than those which really exist, so that, recognising themselves poor, they work: and therefore the extinction of debts and of all claims, whatever they may be, produces great benefits for a state" (Galiani [1751]: 250).

Following his method, Galiani completed the deductive analysis with a historical contextualisation that was intended to confirm his theses. France during the Regency of Louis Philippe d'Orléans provided an excellent *case study*. In 1718, Marc-René de Voyer, Marquis d'Argenson, President of the Council of Finance, proposed to the Regent a general *alzamento* of gold and silver coinage by one third of the old value. The public debt (around 200 million *Lire*), consisting of circulating titles subject to speculation, would thus have been reduced and the court would suffer a general failure "as all the wise men had foreseen, and it was necessity" (Galiani [1751]: 260).[41] But Parliament opposed this measure motivated more by "private indignation and the appetite for popular applause than by mature consideration" (Galiani [1751]: 260).[42] The manoeuvre was not to be revealed "to the multitude, to whom it was expedient not to make it clearly perceived" (Galiani [1751]: 261). Despite the opposition of Parliament, Galiani concluded, the *alzamento* was carried out, but was then overwhelmed by the collapse of Law's *Sistéme* and could not exert its effects.[43]

[41] "A particular person brings 125 silver *Marks* to the mint, which are worth 5000 *Lire* of what is 40 to the *Mark*, and brings 2000 *Lire* of *state notes*; he then takes back 7000 *Lire* of new money, which weighs no more than 116 *Marks*: so that he loses all his notes, and 9 *Marks* out of 125" (Galiani [1751]: 261).

[42] Opposing the traditional objections: "*alzamento* made trade impossible, exchange rates extremely high, foreign merchandise double in price, with French money among foreigners still at the same *coinfoot* [*Münzfuß*] as their own. The convenience of counterfeiting and the temptation of immense profit could fill France with adulterated coins. Internal trade was also damaged by *alzamento*, which diminished consumption". (Galiani [1751]: 265).

[43] The devaluation implemented by d'Argenson in May 1718 was one of the many episodes of changes in the value of metallic money adopted during Law's Système (there were about twenty between 1718 and 1720). The *Livre Tournois* with the devaluation of 1718 became the 900th part of the gold *Mark* and the 60th part of the silver *Mark*, in October 1720 it became the 1350th part of the first and the 90th part of the second (Jannaccone 1946: 198). The role of the Marquis d'Argenson in the affair of Law's Système was complex: "on his appointment, even though it was intended that he should work jointly with Law, he intrigued against Law, linking up with the financiers and searching out bankers and enemies opposed to [Law]" (Murphy 1997: 178). Galiani did not relate the raising manoeuvre to the primary need of the Système, which was to make paper money more stable than metallic money and

With his *alzamento* theory, Galiani questioned the two most important principles on which monetary stabilisation policy was founded: the immutability of monetary values[44] and the need for public debt to be placed under the control of creditors through institutions created *ad hoc* (such as the *Bank of England*). The young abbot proposed an expedient by which the Prince could obtain a truce from his creditors without being forced to suffer blackmail, guaranteeing him a margin of autonomy with respect to the financing needs of a modern state, avoiding extreme remedies, as had happened in France with Law's Système. His perspective was still that of floating debt and not the well-ordered requirements of raking in the resources required for consolidated debt. He then rejected that which would be - from England to France - the main means of covering public expenditure in emergency situations: the issue of *fiat money* (a measure that, once the emergency was over, was always traceable to the consolidated public debt system). On the problem of public debt, Galiani supported the arguments of absolutism (his disdain for parliaments and assemblies is clear and would be consistently maintained), defending the Prince's right to break free from all conditioning.

Galiani's *alzamento* theory describes the inflationary mechanism in terms very similar to the analyses of Richard Cantillon and David Hume. According to Cantillon: "[Locke] has clearly seen that the abundance of money makes everything more expensive but he has not considered how this happens. The great difficulty of this question lies in knowing in what way and in what proportion the increase of money raises the price of

to progressively reduce the debt burden. The conflict between d'Argenson and Parliament was an episode in French absolutist politics: "[d'Argenson's] appointment was an indication of the Regent's intent to take a strong stance against the Parliament. As the Lieutenant-Général de Police he had already been involved in a number of disputes with the Parliament, which disliked Argenson intensely, to the point of attempting to have him brought before the Chamber of Justice on the pretext of corrupt behaviour. By vesting the two positions - Keeper of the Seals and Minister of Finance - under Argenson's control the Regent was sending a strong message to the Parliament that he was no longer prepared to tolerate its interference in the executive decision-making process" (Murphy 1997: 178). On the dispute between d'Argenson and Parliament see also Hurt (2002: 149–172).

[44] In the following years, Galiani was more sensitive to the problem of inflation, as he wrote in the *Dialogues*: "The inner happiness of a man's heart, true happiness (which is quite different from foolishness) is the effect of rest and security he has on his state and future. If the monetary value of all things changes, confusion takes possession of all hearts, fate is unknown, and happiness disappears. This effect that the increase in currency infallibly produces is even more terrible if it results from the increase in the price of goods" (Galiani 1770a: 280).

things" (Cantillon 1755 [2010]: 148). Cantillon fills Locke's lacuna by demonstrating that when the quantity of money increases, not only does the absolute level of prices increase, but also the relative price structure undergoes various changes in relation to the initial nature of the money supply, the categories that receive the new money and their consequent demand for products. Hume also approaches the problem in similar terms: "We must consider, that, though the high price of commodities is a necessary consequence of the increase of gold and silver, yet it follows not immediately upon that increase; but some time is required before the money circulates through the whole state, and makes its effect be felt on all ranks of people. At first, no alteration is perceived; by degree the prices rise, first of one commodity, then of another; till the whole at last reaches a just proportion with the new quantity of specie which is in the Kingdom. In my opinion, it is only in the interval or intermediate situation, between the acquisition of money and rise of prices, that the increasing quantity of gold and silver is favourable to industry" (Hume 1752: 47). This differential mechanism caused by an increase in the money supply is known as the *Cantillon effect* (Blaug 1985: 20–21). Galiani's analysis is similar to Hume's position, emphasising the time lag in the price change process.

5.3 The Problems of Monetary Circulation

The analysis of the problems of monetary circulation occupies a significant part of Galiani's work. The aim is once again to provide a scientific basis for monetary policy proposals and to remove the subject of money from the realm of opinion. The most significant problem of money circulation was certainly that of the quantity of money needed to turn "the several wheels of trade" (Locke 1692: 17). How much money had to be created to satisfy the needs of commerce?

Galiani knew the answer given by Locke, who identified the proportion between money and trade as the way to follow, although the English philosopher warned that the calculation was rather difficult, since this proportion depended not only on the amount of money in circulation, but also on its "velocity of circulation".[45] However, according to Locke, it was possible to formulate "some probable guess [considering] how much

[45] "This shows the necessity of some proportion of money to trade: but what proportion that is, is hard to determine because it depends not merely on the quantity of money, but the quickness of its circulation" (Locke 1692: 32). The concept of the velocity of circulation of

money it is necessary to suppose must rest constantly in each Man's Hands, as requisite to the carrying on of trade" (Locke 1692: 32–33).

Locke's calculation is known to have anticipated the "transactions balances approach" (Pierce and Tysome 1985: 40–44) which directly links the quantity of money to the volume of payments to be made, an approach that is largely dependent on the conception of money as a *pledge*, emphasising its function as an intermediary of exchanges. "Every man", Locke wrote, "must have at least so much money, or so timely recruits, as may in hand, or in a short distance of time, satisfy his creditor who supplies him with the necessaries of life, or of his trade" (Locke 1692: 32).[46] In this approach, the quantity of money in circulation largely depends on institutional factors such as the payment system existing in a certain economic system.

According to Locke, money was exchanged between four classes of agents: "the landholder, whose land affords the materials; the labourer, who works them; the broker, i.e., the merchant and shopkeeper, who distributes them to those that want them; and the consumer, who spends them" (Locke 1692: 29–30). It was quite easy to establish the needs of the workers, as they lived *from hand to mouth* (Locke 1692: 33),[47] satisfied by the purchase of "victuals, clothes, and tools: all which may very well be provided, without any great sum of money lying still in their hands. The labourers, therefore, being usually paid once a week [...] we may suppose there is constantly amongst them, one with another, or those who are to pay them, always one week's wages in ready money" (Locke 1692: 33). The amount of money needed by landowners could also be determined on the basis of rent payments by their tenants, and thus "we cannot but suppose that between the landlord and tenant, there must necessarily be at least a quarter of the yearly revenue of the land constantly in their hands" (Locke 1692: 37). The quantity of money needed by the brokers amounted to "at least one-twentieth part of their yearly return" (Locke 1692: 39). The consumers, finally, were the landowners or workers or brokers themselves, and very few were those who consume without belonging to these

money was first formulated by William Petty in his *Verbum Sapienti* (Petty 1691) and then taken up by Locke (1692). See Monroe (1923: 166–169) and Ullmer (2011).

[46] "The necessity, therefore, of a proportion of money to trade, depends on money, not as counters, for the reckoning may be kept, or transferred by writing, but on money as a pledge, which writing cannot supply the place of: since the bill, bond, or other note of debt" (Locke 1692: 30–31).

[47] In English in Galiani's text (Galiani [1751]: 274).

categories (women, gamblers, educated people and their servants) (Locke 1692: 42). The calculation was determined as follows: "it cannot well be thought that less than one-fiftieth part of the labourer's wages, one-fourth part of the landholder's yearly revenue, and one-twentieth part of the broker's yearly returns in ready money, will be enough to drive the trade of any country. At least to put it beyond exception low enough, it cannot be imagined that less than one moiety of this, i.e. less than one-hundredth part of the labourer's yearly wages, one-eighth part of the landholder's yearly revenue, and one-fortieth part of the broker's yearly returns, in ready money, can be enough to move the several wheels of trade, and keep up commerce, in that life and thriving posture it should be" (Locke 1692: 40–41).

Galiani contested some of the criteria of this calculation: "since there are many who unite more than one class, being landlords, shopkeepers and consumers together. Of women, ecclesiastics, ministers, and countless other states, it is not possible to calculate from these traces, nor of public duties and the course of money" (Galiani [1751]: 275). However, he considered these observations by Locke to be "very useful and judicious" and proposed to apply them to the Neapolitan situation, merging them with the similar method followed by Petty (Galiani [1751]: 275).[48] Although convinced that this kind of calculation would not capture "the exact

[48] Melon dedicated the entire XXIV chapter of his *Essai* to *political arithmetic* (Melon 1736: 318–357), and it is likely that through this source Galiani knew Petty's work. Petty's calculation of the quantity of money needed for trade is contained in Chapter XI of his *Political Arithmetick* (Petty 1690: 111). Galiani also shows that he knows of a different method developed by "another writer of the same nation, a little while ago, [who] wishing to prove that the debts of the state were not so great as they appeared, has summed up the value of England very ingeniously, though with very long operation. His method I do not venture to follow, though I know the result to be true; while of this nation as the valour of operation overflows into temerity, so the acuteness of thought often departs from the truth, following on to the abstruse and strange" (Galiani [1751]: 275–276). According to Alberto Merola, the writer cited by Galiani might be Josiah Tucker (Galiani 1963: 232), author of *A Brief Essay on the Advantages and Disadvantages which Respectively Attend France and Great Britain, with Regard to Trade* (Tucker 1749), but there is no reference in this essay to calculations of the national debt. The essay Galiani refers to may be the anonymous author of a *Memoire* on the English public debt, quoted by Melon in chapter XXIII of his *Essai*, the excerpt of which (the Frenchman recalls) had appeared in the gazettes of the time (Melon 1736: 296). Melon may refer to some texts on the English public debt published in the 1720s, in particular the essays by Nathaniel Gould (1726, 1727) and William Pulteney Bath (1727) published anonymously. See Ahn (2023).

truth", taking "a shortcut [...] within certain boundaries of truth", would reach valid conclusions (Galiani [1751]: 276).

The first step was to establish the total amount of money in the Kingdom of Naples and in this regard Galiani observed that: "there was just under a million and a half *Ducats* in copper coin, almost six million in silver, and ten at most in gold, including also that money which is in the Pubblic Banks, and which does not exceed three million *Ducats.* Since this money must be used for the trade of all the goods consumed there, it is now convenient to try to know how many of them there are, to see if they can be moved by eighteen million *Ducats* alone" (Galiani [1751]: 275).

Taking, as stated above, the simplest way, Galiani established that the total consumption in the Kingdom was equal to "the full amount of its products", considering - under normal conditions - that the Kingdom's trade was always in equilibrium (Galiani [1751]: 276).[49] It was therefore sufficient to know the total annual consumption. This was the easiest way to calculate: consumer goods had to be necessarily purchased by an end-user; if there was not the amount of money needed to secure these transactions, it was effectively out of a monetary economy and back to barter.[50] Against possible objections he observed: "what I say does not seem little, because the great lords spend most of their income to feed those who serve them, and I already count this money in the expenditure of the latter, and I do not even mention public duties, because it is all included in the expenditure of those people who live on the money and mercies of the sovereign" (Galiani [1751]: 277). In his calculation, therefore, only expenditure that "produces consumption and not [...] that which enriches another, such as gambling, gifts or wages" (Galiani [1751]: 277).

In the provinces of the Kingdom, Galiani set the minimum subsistence amount (food, accommodation and clothing) at 2 *Ducats* a month, assuming that in the countryside most of the necessities were taken from

[49] "Because", he noted, "although a great many kinds come from outside for consumption, many of the locals go away. And without considering how much they amount to, it is certain from the effects that the two values are almost equal: since the Kingdom is neither exaggeratedly enriched nor impoverished, of which one or the other effect is inevitable when there is a great imbalance between the inflow and outflow" (Galiani [1751]: 276).

[50] Following Locke: "The farmer not having money to pay the labourer, supplies him with corn, which, in this great plenty, the labourer will have at his own rate, or else not take it off his hands for wages. And as for the workmen, who are employed in our manufactures, especially the woollen one, these the clothier, having ready money to pay, furnishes with the necessaries of life, and so trucks commodities for work" (Locke 1692: 34).

self-consumption; in the capital city, on the other hand, this minimum was increased to 6 *Ducats*, and - he observed - those who "live on less have their food, clothing or housing paid by others" (Galiani [1751]: 277). Taking into account the expenses of the rich for their own personal consumption, the calculation could rise to around 7 or 8 *Ducats* for each man a month; however, this amount was reduced if it was considered that women and children consumed "very little", and so Galiani fixed individual consumption at 4 *Ducats* a month for each man. This amount multiplied by the Kingdom's population of three million gave a monthly total of 12 million *Ducats*, and the value of the goods consumed in one year amounted to 144 million *Ducats* (Galiani [1751]: 277, see also Galiani 1780, Note XXVI: 404–405). This volume of transactions was - according to the young abbot - sufficiently supported by an effective money of 18 million *Ducats*: "so that it is enough for all the money to pass through eight different hands in a year in the form of payment, to satisfy so much trade" (Galiani [1751]: 277).[51]

Galiani therefore correctly defines the concept of the velocity of circulation of money (called *velocità di giro*), calculating it directly as the ratio between the value of the volume of transactions and the stock of circulating money. By considering only goods destined for final consumption and therefore actually sold, i.e. exchanged for money, the young Galiani avoided the difficulty of considering goods that are exchanged from one hand to another in the various production stages and that could generate duplication in the calculation; he then excluded services, as he considered them indirectly in the wages paid to domestic servants and civil servants and which were always ultimately expressed as the quantity of consumer goods exchanged. The total value of exchanged goods also represents the level of prosperity of a society, indeed, if the personal consumption of the peasants were to include the spices and powder of the aristocrats, the value of transactions would increase and it would be necessary to raise the velocity of circulation and/or increase the required money supply. The quantity of money is only related to the mass of personal consumer goods, and the

[51] According to Monroe: "Galiani's analysis also shows the influence of Locke, but his point of view is rather different. With him it is not so much a question of how much money a country needs, given a certain velocity of circulation, but how rapid the circulation must be to enable a given supply of money to suffice. In the case of Naples he computes that the existing monetary stock must circulate about eight times a year if it is to do the work required of it; and concludes that, since this seems a very moderate rate, there is every reason to believe that the country has money enough for its trade" (Monroe 1923: 167).

problem of hoarded money, which is in fact no longer used as a pledge, is avoided as it is withdrawn from circulation. The quantity of money necessary for the functioning of a monetary economy is thus identified, given the velocity of circulation, which is dependent on institutional factors.

The result that the young Galiani had arrived at allowed him to define the circulation of money: "I say *to run* money (*correre la moneta*) for the passage which it makes from one hand into another, as the price of labour or efforts (*fatiche*); so that it produces for the one who gives it, the purchase and consumption of some utility; because when it is transferred otherwise, it makes a useless circulation [...] and without presupposing many useful commodities that can be trafficked, money can only make a vain and fruitless circulation" (Galiani [1751]: 271).

The circulation (*giro*) of money was real wealth only if supported by production and consumption, otherwise the entire economy assumed the nature of a gambling table, on which money passed hundreds of times from one hand to another, but the total sum always remained the same. The same phenomenon happened with the nobility who, motivated by luxury, spent continuously, always borrowing. Their money revolved rapidly from one hand to the other but was based on unreal wealth and sooner or later both the poverty of the lords and that of their creditors would be discovered (Galiani [1751]: 272). However, a fast circulation of money could encourage "industries" and its stagnation could suffocate them. Therefore the Prince had to give special attention to the state of the money supply, but he should not be seduced by those superficial opinions that considered the increase in the quantity of money to be the panacea for the ills of the economy: "The quantity of money," Galiani observed, "must not be increased, except when it appears to be insufficient to move all commerce without hindering it and leaving it dry" (Galiani [1751]: 273). "It is [rather] the velocity of circulation of money, not the quantity of metals, that makes money appear much or little" (Galiani [1751]: 57) and therefore this variable needed to be controlled.

The stagnation of the currency produced, in fact, many "adverse effects":[52]

[52] Galiani took up the analogy, already established by Petty, between blood circulation and money circulation: "The political body is like man, in which the large veins serve for nothing more than to lead the blood into the ultimate and smallest veins: in these the new generation of meat and limbs is made, and the nourishment of the machine: when the blood is emptied, the capillary and most useful veins dry out and the remainder collects in the largest cavities, from which no nutriment comes" (Galiani [1751]: 279).

1. The scarcity of currency ruined agriculture and manufacturing above all. The damage was most severe for the farmers who were forced, especially in the Kingdom, to sell their produce on the market at low prices, resulting in their general impoverishment and the consequent reduction of the land they cultivated (Galiani [1751]: 279).
2. Those who used a salaried labour force no longer paid their employees in money, but used consumer goods, often of poor quality; a fact that caused further impoverishment of the working population (Galiani [1751]: 280).
3. The scarce currency favoured monopoly positions, because "where there are few sellers, or few buyers, there is hardly freedom in prices" (Galiani [1751]: 280).
4. Finally, the concentration of scarce currency in a few hands was the mother of usury "and of that spice of gains that we have dressed up and embellished with the name of interest" and which for Galiani took on the same nature as speculation on goods bought at a low price and resold at a high one (Galiani [1751]: 282). The remedy could not be to increase the quantity of money, as the net flow of money would always end up in the hands of the few who already had it; instead, it was necessary to increase the value of money, to make it pass through more hands and this was demonstrated - in his opinion - by the different level of the cost of money in the provinces (around 7–9 percent) and in the capital (around 3–5 percent). In the countryside "for the most part... there is only one who has money to give; in the capital there are almost infinite" (Galiani [1751]: 281).

In order to increase the money circulation, it was necessary to intervene on institutional factors:

1. by increasing the frequency of payments for smaller amounts so as to facilitate the circulation of money and avoid keeping it "idle and hoarded" (Galiani [1751]: 283);[53]
2. by encouraging the establishment of fairs and large markets, where transactions required limited currency, ensuring its quick circulation from one hand to another, to the great benefit of buyers who found lower prices. The Kingdom, due to its geographical position as a

[53] Locke had proposed the same remedy (Locke 1692: 36–38).

peninsula, "accessible from all sides with little expense" could rely on this system more than any other Italian region (Galiani [1751]: 283–284).

3. by reinforcing the system of *voice-contracts* (*contratti alla voce*) to facilitate the transfer of money to those who needed it, but *voice-prices* (*prezzi alla voce*) had be well calculated so as not to damage any party (Galiani [1751]: 284).[54]
4. by setting the payment of taxes in accordance with the natural timing of production activities, so that those who "must pay always have money in hand" (Galiani [1751]: 284). Moreover, Galiani pointed out, it would be better if the Prince did not always demand tributes in cash, but could request their collection by directly taking the goods he needed. This avoided the intermediation of the merchant class, which was detrimental to producers and the Sovereign himself.
5. by ensuring the brevity of legal disputes, which froze large sums of money for interminable periods (Galiani [1751]: 285).[55]
6. by guaranteeing the freedom to transfer money, without any particular legal constraints such as fideicommissum, legitimacy, legacy, dowry, etc. (Galiani [1751]: 285).
7. by not hindering the luxury consumption of the court and the nobility.

Luxury was a controversial topic, capable of arousing bitter opposition, comparable only to that which the word usury evoked. Galiani addressed the topic in his own way, claiming a scientific position on the matter. Whatever the moral opinion - the young abbot argued – it is certain that luxury "is the son of peace, of good government, and of the perfection of the arts useful to society; brother therefore of terrestrial happiness: since luxury cannot be anything other than the introduction of those professions, and the sale of those goods for pleasure, not of absolute necessity for life" Galiani [1751]: 285; see also Carnino 2018; Stapelbroek

[54] Galiani returned to the problem in the second edition, lamenting the negligence of magistrates in setting a correct voice-price (Galiani 1780, Note XXI: 400; see also Galiani, MS-14).

[55] "The disproportionate size of the capital, and the disproportionate size of the tribunal: these two things were once evils, but, as every disease in time either heals itself, or changes the complexion of the body in such a way that it becomes accustomed to the evil and converts it into its own nature, these today are no longer evils" (Galiani [1751]: 286).

2018). The development of luxury consumption followed the increase in population, which in turn was the product of peace and good government, and the perfecting of production, "which is nothing other than the discovery of new methods of making a manufacture with fewer people, or (which is the same) in less time than before" (Galiani [1751]: 289). Luxury consumption represented new labour demand for the growing population and also compensated for the loss of employment in the essential goods sectors. Luxury was a sign of decadence for society, but it was not unlike the ripening of grain: wanting to prevent luxury in prosperity was "like wanting the long-grown crops not to bear fruit in the summer, or to keep them green after the fruit has been harvested" (Galiani [1751]: 289). Luxury, contrary to Melon's view,[56] was the consequence and not the cause of good government and economic development. It could be a dangerous phase for society if it induced corruption in customs, and if it constituted, due to the strong propensity for imports, a means of reducing national wealth, but these disadvantages could be remedied by good organisation of government and greater local production. The greatest utility of luxury, however, was in the redistribution of wealth and the social mobility that followed it. "If by luxury the noble families become impoverished and extinct, the popular ones multiply and rise. There is only one difference: that the old families, having arisen in ferocious times, have no other origin than in arms, nor other riches than those that rapacity, wars and discord gave them. The new ones have grown with industry, in peace, in centuries of luxury. Of which ways of growing, which is better, it is easy to define" (Galiani [1751]: 290). Such intense redistribution could only come from the destruction and upheavals of war; luxury instead peacefully moved money that would otherwise have remained immobile to the prejudice of society.

Galiani thus attributed to changes in the circulation of money a much broader effect than simply an increase in monetary means, rejecting the traditional view that established an automatic link between an increase in the money supply and real wealth.[57] If, in fact, the quantity of money in

[56] "Luxury is an extraordinary sumptuousness, proceeding from the riches and security of a Government. It will be always found attendant upon every well-governed society. Whoever findeth himself possessed of great plenty, will be desiderous to enjoy it" (Melon 1739: 174).

[57] In particular, Galiani challenged the rather superficial statements of Antonio Ludovico Muratori, for whom "the whole economic government of a country is [reduced] to one very important maxim: that is, that as little money as possible should go out of the state and as much as possible should be introduced into it" (Muratori 1749: 204).

circulation was doubled without correcting its circulation and distribution, the only effect was an increase of prices of the *quantum* of metal, with the consequence of "having to exchange with six ounces of metal what one previously had with three" (Galiani [1751]: 294). Reference variable was always the quantity of money needed for transactions, and an increase in the money supply beyond this limit only produced inflationary effects. The country that retained quantities of metal not needed for its trade held "its superfluous unreasonably" (Galiani [1751]: 311), causing the collapse of its value: in short, as with any other commodity, the quantity of money was also subject to the law of value.

The excess money, in an agricultural country like the Kingdom of Naples, would have increased the amount of manufactured goods imported from abroad, especially luxury goods, and with the money obtained, foreigners would have been able to buy necessary goods such as grain, wine, oil, "and thus become nourished, populated, and made strong and formidable" (Galiani [1751]: 295). The high price (in terms of the *quantum* of metal) of domestic products discouraged those importers who came from countries "where due to the scarcity of the currency [...] a high price is disadvantageous" (Galiani [1751]: 296), consequently diminishing trade outlets.

Moreover, the population emigrated, affected by rising domestic prices and reduced employment opportunities, moving to countries where the cost of living was lower, and the outflow was never compensated, for the same reasons, by immigration from abroad. According to Galiani, the condition of England was an example of this evolution: it had attracted large sums of money with its commercial policy, losing many inhabitants and was only saved from decadence by "the excellence of its manufactures" (Galiani [1751]: 297).

Galiani, in his analysis of *alzamento*, had explained that for foreign merchants this manoeuvre did not entail any damage, because the quantity of coins in a country remained unchanged and therefore for a foreign buyer a *tomolo* of Neapolitan wheat was always exchanged for 1 *ounce* of silver, whether this was represented in 10 *Ducats* or 12 or 8. If, on the other hand, a country had an abundance of metal, because it had discovered a mine on its territory and began to mint coins without limit, the ratio between the quantity of goods and the metal minted was altered (1 *ounce* of silver was no longer sufficient to buy a *tomolo* of wheat, but 1.5 was needed). This analysis explained what had happened to Spain after the discovery of the West Indies, with the inflow of large quantities of metals that had caused an increase in domestic prices, a reduction in exports, an increase in imports and a general impoverishment of the country.[58]

The precious metal, for a country that had no mines, was not obtained gratis but had to be acquired by selling its production surplus. This expense could be justified if the state had to be provided with the quantity of money needed for transactions, but beyond this amount the exchange of surplus metal for useful goods was disadvantageous.[59] The exploitation of one's own mines was also unprofitable, an effort that impoverished the country and neither was it worth fighting so many wars and wasting so many resources to conquer them (Galiani [1751]: 297–298).

The idea that the minting of coins alone could secure wealth for the Prince and the people was also ridiculous. Seigniorage rights could only amount to a maximum of 2 percent, and therefore could never constitute a source of enrichment for the Sovereign, as could be the duty on agricultural or industrial activity. Regarding the benefits for the people, Galiani observed that the activity of the mint, not supported by economic prosperity, finished by being similar to the illusion of that very poor man who had gone to live near a mint hoping to "intercept" in his room the coins flowing from the mint press. The minting activity in these circumstances had the same effect as the increase in expenditure by an occupying army, which filled the country with money but did not enrich it, "and after a few years the money was collected in neighbouring provinces" (Galiani [1751]: 297–303).

The policy of filling the treasury was effective in republics such as Holland, Switzerland, Genoa and Venice, which were devoid of natural resources and which "have sought every way to multiply money, the acquisition of which was for them almost a conquest of new lands; but those people will be foolish who, living in the midst of fertile lands [as happens to the Neapolitans], and cultivating them badly, moved by puerile envy, will try to imitate unsuitably those who are in a very different situation. Parity with others is not always achieved by imitating and following them" (Galiani [1751]: 297–303).[60]

[58] Broggia had also linked the excessive increase in currency in circulation with the impoverishment of Spain (Broggia 1743: 184)

[59] On this issue, Galiani quoted Locke and his statement: "riches do not consist of having more gold and silver, but in having more in proportion than the rest of the world, or than our neighbours" (Locke 1696a: 15).

[60] This statement as an anticipation of the methodological relativism that Galiani would uphold in his mature work *Dialogues sur le commerce des bleds* (Galiani 1770a).

Also to be rejected were the measures prohibiting the "extraction of money". They, like all laws that violated individual interest, "reason and natural justice" (Galiani [1751]: 307), remained largely ignored, and were therefore completely useless. Their ineffectiveness was all the greater because even if the subjects had respected them, it would have been the Prince himself who violated them, and if both had respected them, great damage would still have resulted.

Private individuals could violate the ban on exporting coins and metals either by fraud (transporting them clandestinely) or by buying bills of exchange (*lettere di cambio*) to pay for their imports, as long as the volume of exports allowed it.[61] If the bills of exchange in circulation were entirely purchased by private trade, the Prince was obliged to break the law in order to be able to pay for representation expenses at foreign courts or missions or costs necessary to maintain distant possessions: "So when the sale that a Kingdom makes of its native goods is greater than the purchase of foreign goods, the prohibition is useless, as there is never a lack of bills of exchange to those who ask for them; if it is equal, the Prince is forced to commit what his people do not dare to do; when it is less, it would be harmful both to the people and to the prince not to break the law" (Galiani [1751]: 310). In fact, a country could be in a trade deficit for two opposing reasons: either because it had reached a high level of prosperity and could afford to buy luxury goods, with voluptuary consumption being the greatest effect of the wealth and prosperity achieved by a society, or it was in a state of calamity and money extraction was really the *only medicine*: "If we lack the grain of our land", Galiani concluded, "extracting money to buy the grain of others is a remedy for famine; and either the gold must be made edible or it must leave the country" (Galiani [1751]: 312).

With the same criterion, Galiani explained the necessity of exporting capital in excess, a phenomenon that arose from "excessive prosperity and opulence", generated "by industry and great parsimony" and which characterised the economic life of the great mercantile republics (Galiani [1751]: 314).

Investment opportunities thus moved capital, just as fluids flowed with different impetus through channels of different diameter. As long as the

[61] "Assuming, therefore, that our kingdom exports four million *Ducats* of goods, it is clear that without transgressing the law, its inhabitants can buy another four million *Ducats* of foreign goods with bills of exchange, and the kingdom's bills of exchange are thus extinguished" (Galiani [1751]: 310).

domestic trade ensured rich earnings, there was no reason to deploy one's wealth elsewhere, but when the profit margin was shrinking, money was withdrawn and stagnated in the coffers. It was therefore necessary to find other outlets for the money to move with the same impetus and these channels could also be found abroad, with the export of capital. A law that prevented this natural course of things would have been disregarded or would have caused great harm to the state, since the abundance of money would have lowered its relative value compared to other commodities, turning what was wealth into poverty.

From these experiences, Galiani drew his warning: "Therefore, I think that all the maxims of good government can be reduced to this one, that in a principality the law that forbids something must never duel with the profit that counsels it" (Galiani [1751]: 307). Galiani essentially adhered to free-market principles, of which France would become the champion a few years later.

5.4 Monetary Policy as Part of Economic Policy

The young Galiani had reconstructed monetary matters on a scientific basis with the aim of providing the Prince and his ministers with a treatise on which to base their concrete monetary policy choices. In this, his aim was not unlike that of Broggia and Spinelli, who had preceded him in the difficult role of advisors to the Prince (see Broggia 1743: 208; Spinelli 1749: 30–32). However, Galiani had seen things from a more unprejudiced point of view, stating several times in the course of the work (think of the question of the rise or the problem of luxury) that he sought only the truth of the facts, over and above the moral implications that might arise from his positions. After all, he had decided to publish his work anonymously also because he was aware of the dangerous character of many of his statements. Even after his authorship was known to all, the fact that he was a young clergyman with no concrete material interests if not the aspiration to still be able to serve his Prince, gave him the aura of an expert, brilliant and ingenious, which he skilfully exploited in the long journey he made in Italy between 1751 and 1752, preceded, we might say, at every stage by the fame that by then accompanied his treatise everywhere. In the dedication to the work, addressed to King Charles, he promised to explain "no less the true principles of the science of money than the history of our currency under your most prudent government" (Galiani [1751]: 12–13).

Regarding the monetary policy followed in Naples in the previous century, the deepest discontinuity between Galiani and his predecessors, Broggia and Spinelli, was the positive assessment of the viceroy Santo Stefano's monetary reforms, and this view was also shared by Intieri. The young abbot noted: "Very few understand what was done then, and why; but all confidently discuss and decide about it. Some say it was an *alzamento*, some that it was most damaging; and some give one opinion of it, and some another. The truth is that it was nothing of the sort, but only a correction of a mistake made by the Marquis of Carpio. In minting the silver coin, the Marquis had wished to make it equal to the Roman, so that there would be no need to study the exchange rate. A pointless desire, and perhaps even a dangerous one. He did not realise how inferior our copper coinage was to the Roman currency in the quantity of metal. By making the *Ducat* (*Ducatone*) of 100 *Grana*, he was giving the *Grana* an extrinsic value that was almost 50 percent higher than the true value. This made the silver go out and the copper stay in. It was therefore necessary to change this proportion and lower the price of copper: and this is what was done. If the money of account had not been changed at the same time, there would have been no increase [...] and the *Ducat* having nevertheless been raised to only 100 *Grana*, there followed an increase which, apart from changing the names of the price of goods and foreign exchange, did no other damage, as it could not by its very nature do so, and served to pay a large part of the expenses of coinage" (Galiani [1751]: 218–219).[62]

The principles that had inspired that reform were considered by Galiani to be still valid, as they would ensure the stability of the Neapolitan currency for many years. In particular, he defended the decision not to mint fully intrinsic copper coins; a policy followed under the reigns of Charles II and Philip V, with the aim of restoring the original intrinsic value.[63] This devaluation had been, according to Galiani, a necessity imposed by circumstances that had allowed the Kingdom not to be deprived of the amount of copper needed for small transactions.

The thesis advocated by Broggia (1743: 312), which wanted a complete restoration of copper currency, was rejected by the young abbot:

[62] Cesare Antonio Vergara had considered this manoeuvre to be at the origin of the alteration of exchange rates and prices in the Kingdom and of serious damage to the country's economy (Vergara 1715: 174–175). See also Galiani (1780: Note XVIII, 396–398).

[63] A thesis that Galiani confirmed thirty years later in the second edition of *Della Moneta* (see Galiani 1780: Note XIII, 391–392).

"the copper coin is preferable to being weak than strong, because when it is very good, it is driven out by silver, and this is a great evil, when it is very bad, it remains, but it does not have the strength to drive out silver against which it cannot compete, and when it does drive it out it is a lesser evil. Trade needs copper more than any other currency" (Galiani [1751]: 141). He therefore recommended:

- the re-minting of copper coins with an intrinsic value reduced by 11 percent compared to the nominal value (Galiani considered this devaluation insensitive to encourage possible speculation, as the coin was on average devalued compared to the extrinsic value by 25 percent, so the new coin was only 14 percent better than the old one). In essence, the overvaluation of the copper coin compared to the intrinsic value had to be maintained and its circulation as a *fiat money* guaranteed (Galiani [1751]: 140–141);
- minting was to take place a "little bit per year", without carrying out total currency exchange operations, which were very dangerous because they would certainly have led to easy speculation on the new currency compared to the old one in circulation (Galiani [1751]: 141).

Silver coinage was also, according to Galiani, in a "very good state and order" and he recognised that "the prudence of those who govern us today has known this to be true, and has minted the new coins imitating the old ones" in weight and alloy (Galiani [1751]: 141, see also Galiani 1780: Note XIV, 392–393). There was no need to carry out an *alzamento* of the silver coin to bring its value into line with the changed course of the raw metal, as this in his opinion had remained unchanged, but if it had been necessary, it would have been better "advice to change the value of copper and gold. The proportion is the same, but not the effect. If copper is changed, trade suffers less disturbance in the change of prices; if gold is changed, it being all foreign among us, the subjects will not fear it" (Galiani [1751]: 143–144).

For gold coinage, the principle had to be established that it should circulate by weight, and the minting authority only had to ensure its veracity. This was essentially what was done with the minting of Neapolitan *Ounces*, *Doppie* and *Zecchini* in November 1749. Regarding the billon coins, Galiani believed that they should be withdrawn from circulation and replaced with small silver coins. Finally, a large state like the Kingdom of Naples and Sicily had to exclude foreign silver coins from its internal circulation, while it could admit gold coins, but allowing them to be valued according to weight, in the same way as raw metal (Galiani [1751]: 305–306, see also Galaini 1780: Note XVI, 394–395).[64]

However, Galiani considered such monetary policy measures insufficient if they were not accompanied by an intensive stimulus to economic activity. There clearly emerged from his analysis the difference between the real economy and the monetary measures called upon to represent it and which he considered to be subordinate to it: "I propose - he wrote - to define the utility and necessity of money, and its proper limits, so that men, fleeing from that common error whereby they exchange images for things, tools for work, may know that the metal of coins is a luxury commodity and not a necessary one; money is not wealth, but its image and its means of circulation: from this circulation, although it may happen sometimes that true wealth is increased, countless times it only seems to happen, and this is not true. Not unlike one who swiftly moves a burning coal around, making the eye believe that a whole wheel of fire is in his hands, while the rapid mutation seems to men a duplicated presence" (Galiani [1751]: 147).

This efficacious metaphor was evoked in order to easily dismiss all the definitions that had been given to money: from the nerve of war to second blood, and which were only illusory attributes, as illusory as Midas' fortune had been. Metals were certainly useful to life, but if wealth came from the superfluous, gold and silver could only attract man at a certain stage of economic development, when "the first needs [were] easily satisfied" (Galiani [1751]: 149), and when luxury was the mirror of a prosperous state far from famine. The accumulation of treasures had to be kept within certain limits, and the prince's greatest care had to be for the only true wealth: man.

Population growth was the most obvious sign of the development and welfare of a state; such an objective could be achieved, according to Galiani, by appropriate means:

- the "right justice and freedom", i.e. good laws, which were to allow "the peaceful exercise of that which by right reason, and true religion (which is the same), is not forbidden, nor detrimental to the good of the whole state" (Galiani [1751]: 155–156);

[64] A small state, which could not help but admit them, had to underestimate its own in order to defend its monetary stability.

- the presence of military virtues and "wise providences" of health, to defend themselves against all enemies, especially the invisible ones (plagues) (Galiani [1751]: 156);
- the fair distribution of taxes, so that the tax burden necessary for the state does not cause loss of wealth by damaging trade and the arts (Galiani [1751]: 156);[65]
- the fair testamentary distribution of wealth, so that restrictions on succession (majoras and fedecommissum) do not induce younger sons to forced celibacy;
- political independence since without an autonomous Prince there could be no security of political stability, and this was a prerequisite for establishing good laws (Galiani [1751]: 156)
- but the most important requirement was the development of agriculture; it was to be favoured more than anything else, and more than trade, because "man is an animal that feeds on the land" (Galiani [1751]: 156). Opinions that exalted trade and disdained agriculture, thus overturning the natural order, were false. "It must be persuaded - he asserted - that trade without an increase of agriculture is a spectre and a vain shadow. And although commerce and agriculture are linked together in such a way that each is both the effect and cause of the other, a closer look will reveal that agriculture is always anterior to commerce: for prosperous commerce comes from the abundance of superfluous goods, and agriculture from agriculture, which is made by the people, the people by freedom, and freedom by fair government" (Galiani [1751]: 345). Even the great empires of the maritime powers were founded on the exploitation of "great lands", cultivated by "great numbers of slaves. But - Galiani concluded - because they are far away, we cry trade instead of saying arms and military virtue. On maps we can measure the lesser of their colonies, and find it almost as large as the whole Kingdom of Naples" (Galiani [1751]: 343).[66]

[65] "All their evil is in three points: either that they are not universal, or that they are badly placed, or badly used and distributed" (Galiani [1751]: 121).

[66] He remarked: "So that the trade which we lament the loss of, and blame ourselves for, we shall regain by discovering in the Mediterranean some place full of whales, some herring shore, or some shoal of cod; and when we have cut the Suez Strait we shall go before others to Arabia and the Indies, and the Moluccas, Ceilan [Ceylon], Batavia, and the Cape will be ours" (Galiani [1751]: 344–345).

This last point reveals Galiani's substantial adherence to the economic policy objectives pursued by much of the Neapolitan *intelligentsia*, from Doria to Broggia to Intieri. For him, too, it was necessary to remove all obstacles to increased agricultural production, first of all the disproportionate weight of taxation, its inequality, which weighed too heavily on the provinces and almost completely spared capital, i.e. it affected production and exempted rent.

Without pursuing easy illusions of enrichment, the Kingdom had to exploit its greatest advantage: the fertility provided by the climate. However, the young abbot did not accept the role of periphery that the Neapolitan region was assuming in world trade and warned, noting that, "Since our Kingdom abundantly produces all that is sought after, we can buy nothing but goods of luxury and pleasure. And this is nothing other than to promote the sale of the industries of others, to reward their sweat, to increase their wealth, and to give them the means of being able to come with that same money to buy our grain, wine and oil, and thus feed themselves, populate themselves and make themselves strong and formidable to us" (Galiani [1751]: 294). But how much he believed in the real possibility that Italy could emerge from this state of decadence and dependency is revealed in the last words of the work: "However, it grieves me and afflicts me that while the Kingdoms of Naples and Sicily are resurgent and rising with the presence of their own sovereign, the rest of Italy is noticeably lacking and declining from day to day. There are many signs of this decline, the greatest of which is the infinite discourse and the innumerable number of reforms, improvements, laws and institutions on government, commerce and all the orders of the civil state, made by every side and in competition" (Galiani [1751]: 370).

These words were written to describe, in his opinion, the critical situation of the other Italian states, but paradoxically they were more applicable to the situation of the southern Kingdom, taking on almost the character of an omen and a sad prophecy of the near end of so many hopes and plans.[67]

[67] According to Franco Venturi, this epilogue reveals the young Galiani's scepticism: "Galiani's splendid intelligence had burned itself out in these pages, finally leaving the ashes of his scepticism. He had penetrated the mechanisms of money, of inflation, had illustrated in a new way the relationships between law, economics and politics. Now he saw a sign of death in the debates of his contemporaries, in that desire for reform that barely surfaced in the discussions taking place in Venice, Milan, and Florence. [...].His passion for effectual reality, his Machiavellianism, his acceptance of authority, of war, his pity for the useless cries

References[68]

Manuscript Sources

Galiani, F. MS-14. Sui contratti alla voce. Manuscript kept in the Biblioteca Società Napoletana di Storia Patria, XXXI. A. 10, published in Galiani, 1975, pp. 742–745 and in Galiani, 1999, pp. 77–80.

Galiani, F. MS-26. Parere sul merco generale dell'oro e dell'argento, Manuscript kept in the Biblioteca Società Napoletana di Storia Patria XXX.C.1, folios 205r–207v, published in Galiani, 1963, pp. 398–400.

Primary Sources

Abbé de Saint-Pierre, C. I. Castel de. (1733). Discours contre l'augmentation des monnoyes et en faveur des annuitez. In *Ouvrage politique par M. l'Abbé de Saint Pierre*, Rotterdam: Jean Daniel Beman, Tome II: 199–230.

Broggia, C. A. (1743). *Trattato de' tributi, delle monete e del governo politico della sanità. Opera di stato, e di commercio, di polizia e di finanza: molto, alla felicità de' popoli, alla robustezza degli stati, ed alla gloria e possanza maggiore de' principi, conferente e necessaria*. Naples: Pietro Palombo.

Cantillon, R. (1755) [2010]. *Essai sur la nature du commerce en général. Traduit de l'anglois,* London: Fletcher Gyles. English Translation: *An Essay on Economic Theory*, Translated by C. Saucier, edited by M. Thornton. Auburn: Ludwig von Mises Institute.

Davanzati, B. (1588) [1804]. *Lezione delle monete,* Firenze, in *Scrittori classici italiani di Economia Politica,* Parte antica, Tomo II. Milan: De Stefanis, 1804.

Davanzati, B. (1696). *Discours Upon Coins, by Signor Bernardo Davanzati, A Gentleman of Florence*. London: Printed Awnsham and Churchill.

Galiani, F. [1751] [published anonymous, with date of 1750]. *Della moneta. Libri cinque,* Naples: Giuseppe Raimondi.

Galiani, F. (1780). *Della moneta. Libri cinque. Edizione seconda*. Naples: Stamperia Simoniana.

Galiani, F. (1915). *Della Moneta*, edited by F. Nicolini. Bari: Laterza.

Galiani, F. (1963). *Della Moneta*, edited by A. Merola, with introduction of A. Caracciolo, Milan: Feltrinelli.

of the common people led him to disbelieve and misunderstand a movement for reform that was certainly born of internal anguish, but was no indication of near irreparable death. His great book ended on a false note" (Venturi 1998: 502).

[68] The abbreviations "s.l." and "s.n." stand for the Latin terms *sine loco* (without place of publication) and *sine nomine* (without name of publisher).

Galiani, F. (1770a). *Dialogues sur le commerce des bleds.* London [but Paris]: Merlin.

Galiani, F. (1977). *On Money.* A Translation of Della Moneta by Ferdinado Galiani by Peter R. Toscano. Ann Arbor: University Microfilm International.

Gould, N. (1726). *An Essay on the Public Debts of this Kingdom.* London: Peele.

Gould, N. (1727). *A Defence of an Essay on the Public Debts, etc., in Answer to a State of the National Debt, etc.* London: Peele.

Hume, D. (1752). *Political discourses.* Edinburgh: Fleming.

Locke, J. (1692). *Some Considerations of the Consequences of the Lowering of Interest, and Raising the Value of Money. In a letter sent to a Member of Parliament.* London, Awnsham and John Churchill, at the Black-Swan in Pater-Noster-Row.

Locke, J. (1696a). *Some considerations of the consequences of the lowering of interest, and raising the value of money. In a letter sent to a Member of Parliament.* The second edition corrected. London: printed for Awnsham and John Churchil.

Locke, J. (1748). *An essay concerning human understanding. In four books. Written by John Locke, Gent. The thirteenth edition*, 2 vols. London: printed for S. Birt, D. Browne, C. Hitch, J. Hodges, J. Oswald.

Melon, J-F. (1736). *Essai politique sur le commerce. Nouvelle édition. Cette édition est augmentée de sept chapitres et les lacunes des éditions précédentes y sont remplies*, s.l. s.n.

Melon, J-F. (1739). *A Political Essay Upon Commerce: Written in French by Monsieur M* Translated, with Some Annotations and Remarks, by David Bindon, Esq.* Dublin: Printed for P. Crampton.

Muratori L. A. (1749). *Della pubblica felicità oggetto de' buoni principi*, Lucca [but Venice]: s. n.

Petty, W. (1690). *Political Arithmetick.* London: Clavel.

Petty, W. (1691). *Verbum Sapienti*, addendum to the *Political Anatomy of Ireland*, London: Brown and Rogers.

Pulteney Bath, W. (1727). *A state of the national debt, etc., With the payments made towards its discharge out of the sinking fund.* London: Francklin.

Spinelli, T. [1749]. *Riflessioni politiche sopra alcuni punti della Scienza della Moneta. Al Sig. D. Domenico Caracciolo dei Marchesi di Capriglia.* Naples: s.n.

Tucker, J. (1749). *A Brief Essay on the Advantages and Disadvantages which Respectively Attend France and Great Britain, with Regard to Trade.* London: Trye.

Vergara, C. A. (1715). *Monete del Regno di Napoli di Ruggiero Primo Re sino all'Augustissimo Regnante Carlo VI Imperatore e III Re Cattolico raccolte e spiegate da Don Cesare Antonio Vergara dottore dell'una e dell'altra legge.* Rome: Gonzaga.

Secondary Sources

Ahn, D. (2023). The War of Jenkins' Ear and the Spectre of French Universal Monarchy. *Global Intellectual History*, Volume, 10, Issue, 1, pp 1–22.

Blaug, M. (1985). *Economic Theory in Retrospect. Fourth Edition*. Cambridge: Cambridge University Press.

Boyer-Xambeu, M.-T., Deleplace, G., Gillard, L. (1986). *Private Money & Public Currency. The 16th Century Challenge*. Armonk-London: Sharpe.

Carnino, C. (2018). Le luxe "frère du bonheur terrestre". Ferdinando Galiani entre économie et politique. In A. Tiran, C. Carnino (eds.), *Ferdinando Galiani, économie et politique*. Paris: Classiques Garnier, pp. 437–456.

Cesarano, F. (1995). Galiani e il ruolo della politica economica. In A. Roncaglia (ed.) *Alle origini del pensiero economico in Italia*. Bologna: Il Mulino, pp. 97–120.

Costa, G. (1970). Vico e Locke. *Giornale critico della filosofia italiana*, vol. XLIX, pp. 344–361.

Diaz, F. (1975a). Introduzione. In Galiani, F. Opere, edited by F. Diaz, L.Guerci, *Letteratura italiana. Storia e testi*. Illuministi italiani,tomo VI, Milan-Naples: Ricciardi, pp. ix–cvi.

Dongili, P. (1988). Ferdinando Galiani: *Della moneta. Rivista Internazionale di Scienze Economiche e Commerciali*, Vol. 35, N. 1, pp. 11–28.

Einaudi, L. (1936) [2006]. The Theory of Imaginary Money from Charlemagne to the French Revolution. *Rivista di storia economica*, 1936, I, pp. 1–35. In L. Einaudi, R. Faucci, R. Marchionatti (eds.) *Luigi Einaudi Selected Economic Essays*. London: Palgrave Macmillan, Vol. II, pp. 153–181.

Einaudi, L. (1949) [2014]. Galiani, the economist. In *Rendiconti della Classe di Scienze morali, storiche e filologiche*, Series VIII, vol. IV, issue 3–4, March–April 1949, In L. Einaudi, R. Faucci, R. Marchionatti (eds.) *Luigi Einaudi Selected Economic Essays*. London: Palgrave Macmillan, vol II, pp. 227–264.

Fisher, I. (1928). *The Money Illusion*, New York: Adelphi Company.

Hurt, J. J. (2002). *Louis XIV and the Parlements. The assertion of royal authority*. Manchester: Manchester University Press.

Jannaccone, P. (1946). *Moneta e lavoro*. Torino: Utet.

Keynes, J.M. (1923). *A Tract on Monetary Reform*. London: Macmillan.

Monroe, A. E. (1923). *Monetary Theory Before Adam Smith*, Cambridge (MS): Harvard University Press.

Murphy, A. E. (1997). *John Law. Economic Theorist and Policy-Maker*. Oxford: Claredon Press.

Pierce, D. G., Tysome, P. J. (1985). *Monetary Economics. Theories, Evidence and Policy*, Second Edition, London: Butterworths

Rosselli, A. (2001). The Role of The Precious Metals in *Della Moneta* by Ferdinando Galiani. *History of Economic Ideas*, Vol. 9, No. 3, pp. 43–60.

Schumpeter, J. A. (1954) [2006]. *History of Economic Analysis.* London: Routledge.

Stapelbroek, K. (2018). Les fondements de l'économie politique de Galiani: L'art du gouvernement, le luxe et l'histoire de l'humanité. In A. Tiran, C. Carnino, (eds.), *Ferdinando Galiani, économie et politique.* Paris: Classiques Garnier, pp. 457–483.

Ullmer, J. H. (2011). The scientific method of Sir William Petty. *Erasmus Journal for Philosophy and Economics*, Volume 4, Issue 2, pp. 1–19.

Venturi, F. (1998). *Settecento riformatore. Da Muratori a Beccaria*, Turin: Einaudi.

Vilar, Pierre. (1991). *A History of Gold and Money, 1450 to 1920.* London: Verso.

Walras, L. (1881). *Théorie mathématique du bimétallisme*, Paris: Guillamin.

CHAPTER 6

Interlude (1751–1759)

6.1 Galiani the Money Doctor[1]

In the space of just two years, between 1750 and 1752, nine treatises dedicated to monetary problems (including *Della Moneta*) were published in the various Italian states (see Table 6.1), works dictated by the need for economic reforms at the beginning of a decade that marked the end of dynastic wars favouring a political stabilisation.[2] Interest in economic issues not only moved bankers, administrators or jurists, but above all scholars who came out of their *ivory towers* to confront real problems. Ludovico Antonio Muratori had led the way by examining, not without difficulty, the "great jumble" ("gran guazzabuglio", Muratori 1749: 193, see also Muratori 1750a, 1750b) of monetary policy. Another scholar, equally uninvolved in any commercial practice, Scipione Maffei, had attempted to modernise Catholic doctrine by pointing out the lawful boundaries of interest (Maffei 1744).

[1] The term *money doctor* was attributed in the 1920s to the US economist Edwin Walter Kemmerer who headed several missions sponsored by the *League for Nations* and the US government to support monetary stabilisation policies, see Kemmerer (1993); Flandreau (2003).

[2] The Florentine bibliographical journal, *Novelle della Repubblica Letteraria*, called this interest in money matters a "fashion", without however understanding its deeper nature. On the debate see Tucci (1986); Venturi (1998: chap. VII); Stapelbroek (2005).

R. Patalano, *Ferdinando Galiani*,
https://doi.org/10.1007/978-3-032-02793-1_6

Table 6.1 Treatises on monetary themes published in Italy between 1750 and 1752[a]

Fabrini, G. A. *Dell'indole e qualità naturali e civili della moneta e de' principii istorici e naturali de' contratti*	Rome	1750
Belloni, G. *Del Commercio*	Rome	1750
Galiani, F. *Della Moneta Libri Cinque*	Naples	1751
Carli, G. *Dell'origine e del commercio della moneta e dell'instituzione delle zecche d'Italia dalla decadenza dell'Impero sino al secolo decimo settimo*	[Venice]	1751
Neri, P. *Osservazioni sopra il prezzo legale delle monete, e le difficoltà di prefinirlo, e di sostenerlo*	Milan	1751
Pagnini, G. *Saggio sopra il giusto pregio delle cose, la giusta valuta della moneta e sopra il commercio dei Romani*	Florence	1751
Costantini, G. *Delle monete in senso pratico, e morale. Ragionamento diviso in sette capitoli*	Venice	1751
Argelati, F. *De monetis Italiae variorum illustrium virorum dissertationes, quarum pars nunc primum in lucem prodit*	Milan	1751–1752
Capello, P. G. *Nuovo trattato del modo di regolare la moneta*	Venice	1752

[a] Fabrini, *On the nature and natural and civil qualities of money and the historical and natural principles of contracts;* Belloni, *Of Commerce;* Carli, *On the origin and trade of money and the establishment of mints in Italy from the decadence of the Empire to the seventeenth century;* Neri, *Observations on the legal price of money, and the difficulties of predefining and sustaining it;* Pagnini, *Essay on the Proper Value of Things, the Correct Value of Money and on Roman Trade;* Costantini, *On money in a practical and moral sense. Argument divided into seven chapters;* Argelati, *Dissertations of various eminent men on the coins of Italy, parts of which are now published for the first time;* Capello, *New treatise on the regulation of money*

The Italian debate was entirely dominated by Nicolas Dutot's critique of the theoretical and political positions of Melon and Law, contained in his *Réflexions politiques sur les finances et le commerce* (Dutot 1738; Velde 2012), to which were added the theses of Locke (translated into Italian by Giovan Francesco Pagnini and Angelo Maria Tavanti just in 1751, see Locke 1751) and those of Abbé de Saint-Pierre (1733). Dutot set out the principle of monetary stabilisation (which soon became a *dogma*): "sound policy does not allow the numerical value of money to be touched once it has been established: it is the pledge or equivalent of our reciprocal exchanges, and the measure that regulates the value of the goods exchanged. Money must therefore not be altered, just as other measures must not be altered" (Dutot 1738: 3, 109). And following Locke: "gold and silver money is not only a common measure, it is also a pledge which has a real value like other commodities. The unenlightened people need such a pledge to secure themselves against authority, at least until they have no more to fear from that side" (Dutot 1738: 234–235). Weakened money could be considered counterfeit and its alteration in any form spoiled circulation and damaged trade (Dutot 1738: 167). Dutot's arguments were almost unanimously accepted among the protagonists of the debate, with the exception of Intieri[3] and the young Galiani both of whom instead praised Melon's pragmatism.[4]

The publication of *Della Moneta* thus took place in a political and intellectual climate that was not favourable to bold ideas such as those expressed by the young *abate*. Moreover, Galiani had strongly criticised the Italian scholarly tradition, a criticism made worse by the author's young age, and this did not encourage a benevolent reception of his work.[5]

In Naples, meanwhile, with the dismissal of Montealegre (1746), King Charles had taken over the government of the Kingdom directly (advised by Queen Maria Amalia who was subject to the various court intrigues). He showed a more prudent attitude and sacrificed some important reforms implemented in the previous years: the role of the *Supremo Magistrato del Commercio* was severely reduced,[6] the edict on the Jews was revoked and the reform of legal institutions was greatly slowed down. In this climate, the party of the reformers lost considerable political clout.

The contrasting responses that the young Galiani's work received in Naples is evidence of the difficulties facing the reformers. *Della Moneta*,

[3] "From Paris I got Du Tot's book which deals with finances and trade opposing most of Melon's sentiments. It is two tomes in octavo. I have not had time to read it, I have seen a few things in passing and I agree with the sentiments of Abate Antonini [Annibale], who is in Paris, who considered Melon a man of profound knowledge. It is a great loss to the doctrine of commerce that the man who would have replied to his opponent is dead and that this war over such a noble and useful science would have involved others" (Bartolomeo Intieri's letter to Celestino Galiani, Naples, 30 December 1738, BSNSP, XXXI.A.7, folio 24).

[4] "Among those who treat of money, I alone see that the author of the *Essai sur le commerce* stands out as a man of the greatest intellect and of a truly honest and virtuous spirit. But, since he did not combine in his work the demonstrations with the truths taught, just as his thought was better than anyone else, so it was less than any other who followed, and was read only to be refuted by those who were not endowed with the sharpness of mind to understand it" (Galiani [1751]: [15–16]).

[5] "The great and immortal Ludovico Antonio Muratori, in his last work *Della pubblica felicitá*, which was *morientis senis quasi cygnea vox*, has, with a naive confession of impotence, passed over this part concerning money: much more praiseworthy than if, as others may have done, he had presumptuously reasoned about what he did not understand" (Galiani [1751] [15], italics added).

[6] Initially invested with very broad jurisdiction, it was then limited to cases between foreigners or between Neapolitans and foreigners over foreign goods.

wrote Intieri to Duke Filippo di Bartolomeo Corsini, in September 1751, "has moved the public curiosity to read it, [for] the excessive praise with which it has been raised to the stars by those who have read it. They want him [Galiani] to have surpassed all the writers on this subject, even Locke, reputed so far to be the most remarkable. Our Davanzati is the most criticized of all the writers he has examined. These early praises have irritated many according to the habit of men, and it may happen that some unpleasant thrashings are heard".[7] The praise became harsh criticism when the identity of the author became known. Intieri reported this to his Tuscan correspondent: "This book, which has made known how weak the human mind is when judging a work, was elevated to the stars as the work of an enlightened head and mind while the author remained hidden [...] it is not credible how much they have lacerated, despised, blamed it, as a booklet most foolish, inept and deserving only of laughter and to be used for wrapping anchovies".[8] The intensity of the criticism was so strong that Celestino himself tried to distance himself from his nephew's work,[9] prompting a reaction from Intieri.[10] Criticism and perplexity were also voiced in court circles, manifested as early as the difficult phase of

[7] Bartolomeo Intieri's letter to Filippo di Bartolomeo Corsini, Massa Equana, 17 September 1751, Archivio Privato Corsini, Florence, Fondo Corsini, published in Iovine (1999: 230).

[8] Bartolomeo Intieri's letter to Filippo di Bartolomeo Corsini, Naples, 6 November 1751, Archivio Privato Corsini, Florence, Fondo Corsini, published in Iovine (1999: 231). See also Bartolomeo Intieri's letter to Leonardo Del Riccio, Massa Equana, 10 October 1751, in Archivi (1989: 80–81), published in Iovine (1999: 232).

[9] Celestino's perplexities were communicated to Giovanni Gaetano Bottari: "Considering his fresh age, his book, if nothing else deserves sympathy and it can be seen that he will continue to study, Lord God has given him talents not to be a useless burden on earth" (Celestino Galiani's letter to Giovanni Gaetano Bottari, Naples, 11 December, 1751, Biblioteca Corsiniana di Roma, MS. Cors. 1580. 32.E. 1, folio 228v, published in Catucci 1986: 24).

[10] "But why criticise the book whose merit you have celebrated? But let us leave them to croak and let us fully enjoy and admire the supreme power of our Lord and Creator, who has endowed the human mind with such great fullness of his goodness, that we may hope that our grandchildren, through the precious gift of cultivating the mind with greater happiness and comfort than their ancestors, may enjoy a kind of golden age" (Bartolomeo Intieri's letter to Celestino Galiani, Massa Equana, 30 September 1751, BSNSP, XXXI.B.18 folio 46; also published in Iovine 1999: 233). And writing to Ferdinand, "Neither is it true what you tell me about Monsignor your uncle [Celestino]. Believe me, the thing goes the other way from what you imagine. I have two letters from this worthy prelate that say the opposite [...]. Do not be troubled by these rumours" (Bartolomeo Intieri's letter to Celestino Galiani, Massa Equana, 6 October 1751, BSNSP, XXXI.B.18: folio 52; also published in Iovine 1999: 233).

publication; in particular, Bernardo Tanucci was decidedly sceptical, reporting the prevailing opinions among Neapolitan intellectuals who judged the book to be "full of advanced paralogisms, disorder and stuff taken from others, and much of it by Machiavelli used in other guises and for other purposes".[11] Even the reformist party itself was split: Alessandro Rinuccini criticised *Della Moneta* extensively, and certainly also for the praise of Melon,[12] while Antonio Genovesi held it in high consideration.[13]

A harsh critic was Broggia, who in a note in his own handwriting on Troiano Spinelli's book wrote, "After the year 1743, i.e. after Broggia published his *Trattato delle monete*, first the present [Spinelli's *Riflessioni*] came out, then the one entitled *Della moneta* by an anonymous author. In Venice three anonymous authors have published three books on the same subject [Carli, Costantini, Capello]. In Modena, the immortal Lodovico Antonio Muratori has discussed it, but with worthy reserve and according to laws as a truly learned and sincere author. In Milan, President Neri did the same. In Rome, under the name of Belloni, a monkey has come out

[11] Bernardo Tanucci's letter to Francesco Nefetti, Naples, 8 February 1752, in Tanucci (1980b: 740). "A distinguished [...] official of the Secretary of State of my department has spoken with reproach of the book *Della Moneta*. The author [Ferdinando] suspected me of that judgement; hence the silence of the questioned Galiani, who knows that he owes me a great deal and owes me more than he knows, since without me, Galiani uncle [Celestino] would have been dethroned on our entry [1734] by the bigoted Santo Stefano to whom the cardinal archbishop [Spinelli] and cardinal Belluga had preached the good chaplain as a heretic and unbeliever [...]. Those Florentines [Intieri and Rinuccini], disgusted, have cooled towards me the Galianis [Celestino e Ferdinando], friends of those two shopkeepers who, like the Galianis, do not like everything that is Court and House of Spain and France" (Bernardo Tanucci's letter to Francesco Nefetti, Naples, 30 May 1752, published in Tanucci 1980b: 5–6).

[12] "When his [Galiani's] book about money and trade came out, the author was not known, it happened in his presence that I criticised it badly, which I would not have done if he had said he was the author, and then it must be seen whether the criticism is unfair to complain rightly" (Alessandro Rinuccini's letter to Francesco Maria Buondelmonti, Naples, 12 April 1752 Archivio Privato Corsini Fondo Buendelmonti, published in Iovine 1999: 210).

[13] In one of his notes on the Italian version of John Cary's *History of the Trade of Great Britain*, Genovesi referred to the "calculations of the illustrious author of the excellent book *Della Moneta*", regarding the amount of gold and silver, both in coinage and in jewellery and ornaments, existing in the kingdom (Cary 1757, vol. I: 156). And "one of the best and most reasoned books on the present theory [of money] is that of Abbot Galiani" (Genovesi 1767: 7).

that can pass, but it is all rubbish".[14] But the work that had aroused his critical acrimony the most was Galiani's own, which had prompted him, as was his wont, to fill pages and pages with notes intended as a precise refutation of Galiani's text. Broggia again rejected every contribution that came from abroad, curiously equating Melon with Locke and strongly belittling their contribution to the science of money.[15] "I have clearly shown", he wrote, "in Chapter XI and XII of my *Trattato delle Monete*, how erroneous Melon is; and especially on the proposition that, according to him, money can be altered to assist the needs of state" (Broggia, MSCAB: folio 5); as for the Englishman Locke, he had written "a shapeless and insulting letter, to which neither profit nor pleasure can be given" (Broggia, MSCAB: folio 6). Both - he concluded - "are Epicurean sophists and sceptics" (Broggia, MSCAB: folio 7). Instead, Muratori's contribution was re-evaluated, against the opinion of the Neapolitan abbot who had considered Muratori's expertise in monetary matters to be totally inadequate, whereas for Broggia, the historian had touched "all the right strings" and had "spoken much more than the anonymous [Galiani] [wanted] to suggest", and above all adhered to sound principles (Broggia, MSCAB: folio 3).[16]

On the other hand, favourable comments had come from reformist circles outside the Neapolitan kingdom, in particular praise from Antonio

[14] Broggia's annotation on page 72 of the copy of Trojano Spinelli's *Political Reflections*, kept at the Kress Library. See also Venturi (1998: 517).

[15] He had also done so for Melon's work, in the unpublished manuscript *Del lusso più nocevole allo Stato ed al commercio e de' suoi rimedi* (*On the luxury most harmful for the State and trade and its remedies*), kept in the National Library in Naples (Broggia [2004]).

[16] He completely ignored Galiani's aim of constructing a single law of value; the concept of utility was morally criticised as the product of "certain fashionable false philosophies, which we should discuss at length, if this were our only purpose. It is sufficient to reflect that with these beautiful propositions [about utility] one does nothing but encourage the most unbridled passions, and the filthiest and most fraudulent vices" (Broggia, MSCAB: folio 49). To Galiani's well-known assertion that man continually tried to satisfy ever new passions, Broggia replied: "Therefore, according to this crude discourse, it is fitting that man should satisfy all the most extravagant passions that he can, and to which his depraved will leads him and I would better say his bestiality. Therefore man cannot make use of reason, which for its true utility and goodness moves him to temperance. Therefore [...] he will never be able to make use of reason itself, which remedies the infinite and disordered impulses of self-love, and puts the necessary boundaries and order to the passions. And if evil is inevitable, then man has no free will, to follow order and escape disorder, to flee vice and follow virtue" (Broggia, MSCAB: folios 49–50). And he reiterated that "useful things are those that are dictated by reason, and as such are animated by honesty" (Broggia, MSCAB: folio 50).

Maria Niccolini and Giovanni Gaetano Bottari (Pasta 2013; Petrucci and Pignatelli 1971).[17] These favourable opinions must have induced the young Galiani, with Celestino's approval (or even urged by him), to undertake a journey to the various Italian states, between November 1751 and November 1752, partial evidence of which was entrusted to a *Diary* (Galiani, MS-15).[18] Even the choice of the journey was not without criticism, some calling it a voluntary exile, but Tanucci wanted to defend the young abbot this time and defined it as a journey "for erudition",[19] denying any political implications.[20]

Leaving Naples on 28 November 1751, together with his friend Pasquale Carcani, Galiani arrived in Rome on 2 December, welcomed into the convent of the Celestines by the Provincial Father Celestino Orlandi (Galiani, MS-15: 56r; Diodati 1788: 15). In the following days, he met various exponents of Roman intellectual life, in particular Bottari (Galiani, MS-15: 57r)[21] and Daniele Concina, the protagonist of the controversy with Scipione Maffei on usury (Galiani, MS-15: 57v). He was then received by various ecclesiastical authorities, including cardinals Silvio Valenti Gonzaga, Secretary of State to Pope Benedict XIV, Tiberio Carafa,

[17] See Giovanni Gaetano Bottari's letter to Celestino Galiani, Rome, 15 October 1751, BSNSP, XXXI.B.18: folio 56r (see Catucci 1986: 20–22); See also Bartolomeo Intieri's letter to Ferdinando Galiani, Massa Equana, 28 September 1751, BSNSP, XXXI.B.18: folio 44r; Bartolomeo Intieri's letter to Ferdinando Galiani, Massa Equana, 6 October 1751, BSNSP, XXXI.B.18: folio 52r; Bartolomeo Intieri's letter to Ferdinando Galiani, Naples, 16 January 1752, BSNSP, XXXI.B.18: folio 74r; Bartolomeo Intieri's letter to Ferdinando Galiani, Naples, 6 February 1752, BSNSP, XXXI.B.18: folio 81; Gaspare Cerati's letter to Ferdinando Galiani, Pisa, 20 October, 1751 (published in Nicoletti 2008: 39). See also Venturi (1998: 504–517), Iovine (1999: 233).

[18] The Diary is a notebook in which Galiani mainly used to record his daily expenses, but also observations and small chronicles about people he met and more curious circumstances and situations he experienced or witnessed along his itinerary. Another source for Galiani's journey is the correspondence with the secretary of Celestino, Domenico Sgueglia, from 3 December 1751 to 27 October 1752 (BSNSP, XXXI.C.16). The letters to Sgueglia were published in part in Galiani (1975: 820–830).

[19] Bernardo Tanucci's letter to Francesco Nefetti, Naples, 2 May 1752, published in Tanucci (1980b: 758).

[20] According to Diodati, Celestino organised the journey "to cultivate the spirit of his nephew" (Diodati 1788: 15).

[21] His uncle Celestino recommended him to Bottai: "I entrust him to you in order to enlighten him on the rarest and most beautiful things that are in this admirable and divine city, and that deserve to be observed by a foreigner travelling for education" (Celestino Galiani's letter to Giovanni Gaetano Bottari, Naples, 11 December, 1751, Biblioteca Corsiniana di Roma, MS. Cors. 1580. 32.E. 1, folio 228v, published in Catucci 1986: 24).

Francesco Landi, and Giuseppe Spinelli, former archbishop of Naples.[22] On 15 December he was "graciously received" by the Pope (Galiani, MS-15: 60v; Diodati 1788: 15–16).[23]

Despite the hospitality granted by the high ecclesiastical hierarchies, Galiani's theoretical positions were certainly not supported in Rome.[24] The year before, two important treatises dedicated to monetary issues had been published in the pontifical capital by the Tuscan jurist Giovanni Antonio Fabrini (*Dell'indole e qualità naturali e civili della moneta e de' principii istorici e naturali de' contratti*, Fabrini 1750) and the Roman banker Girolamo Belloni (*Del Commercio*, published in Latin and Italian; Belloni 1750; Reinert 2011a; Caracciolo 1970).

Fabrini, believing inflation to be a consequence of monetary mutations, reaffirmed the metallist dogma by defining money as "a natural body of gold, silver and copper, of certain weight and goodness, invented by men

[22] In 1746, the arrest of three clergymen accused of heresy caused a conflict between Cardinal Spinelli and exponents of the Neapolitan *ceto civile*, led by Nicolò Fraggianni, who feared the *de facto* establishment of the Roman Inquisition in the Kingdom. The protests and the threat of raising the populace induced the cardinal to desist from an ecclesiastical trial (see Venturi 1998: 537–538).

[23] "I was received on Wednesday by the Pope, who, although it was a day for an audience of ministers, had the memory to call me before the secretaries of the Congregations entered. He kept me a short time, but with an inexpressible humanity and majesty [...]. First he spoke to me about the health of Your Illustriousness, then he asked me about my eye disease; finally he spoke to me about the book *Della Moneta*, and praised it. He then went on to ask me about the collection on the death of Boja, and praised it highly. The discourse was brief. I asked him nothing and so we remained friends" (Ferdinando Galiani's letter to Celestino Galiani, 17 December 1751, published in Diodati 1788: 16).

[24] "I will tell you that I have more enemies here than men. Envy, hatred and other ugly passions, products of human malignity, had preceded me and my presence has perhaps increased them. In such a violent state, imagine how I can be. The Pope to whom I went on Wednesday greatly praised Jannaccone's collection" (Ferdinando Galiani's letter to Domenico Sgueglia, Rome, 17 December 1751, BSNSP, XXXI.C.16: folios 7r–7v, see also Galiani 1975: 821). And again, "Here I have seen no one, nor have I had occasion to speak about the book, as I have spoken of nothing" (Ferdinando Galiani's letter to Domenico Sgueglia, Rome, 3 December 1751, BSNSP, XXXI.C.16: folio 1v). The stay became more and more difficult as the days passed. "I have been in a great melancholy in this infamous country. It is impossible to have sufficient words to describe its ugliness. I refrain from going out as much as I can, and if I had money I would leave here immediately after Epiphany" (Ferdinando Galiani's letter to Domenico Sgueglia, Rome, 10 December 1751, BSNSP, XXXI.C.16: folio 4r). In the meantime, he asked Sgueglia to send him as many copies of his *Della Moneta* (Ferdinando Galiani's letter to Domenico Sgueglia, Rome, 24 December 1751, BSNSP, XXXI.C.16: folio 9r).

to know the relation of other bodies to themselves and to facilitate the exchange of all useful or abstract things" (Fabrini 1750: 13). The value of money is only given by its intrinsic, "and it is no use saying then that the eleventh century was worth twenty *Soldi*, if we do not know how these twenty *Soldi* correspond to ours, and in matter and weight, otherwise the comparison will be merely verbal" (Fabrini 1750: 24). The government, he said, "as custodian and administrator of the goods of each and all, does something corresponding to the good of its subjects if it maintains in the coined bodies the natural relation of metals to each other and to the species, and unites itself as far as possible with the rest of men, or at least with the most important part, which are the closest in situation and in trade" (Fabrini 1750: 76–77). And so if the Sovereign, who must be "an illustrious guardian of the Right of the People" (Fabrini 1750: 77), declared a numerical value greater than the intrinsic (*alzamento*) would do great harm to his subjects, as "the currency is naturally its intrinsic, which cannot disregard foreign trade without surrounding the state with walls like the Chinese [...] taking away from the citizens nothing less than the comforts of life" (Fabrini 1750: 77). It was then necessary to maintain the right proportion between the quantity of money and the needs of commerce, avoiding both excessive issues and drastic deflations, because "diminished beyond measure the sum of the coined bodies, the prices of things make enormous variations, and to the extent that money becomes incapable of measuring itself" (Fabrini 1750: 76). The "sublime mind of the Abbé de Saint Pierre" (Fabrini 1750: 25), and Locke's "high genius" (Fabrini 1750: 93) were Fabrini's main points of reference.

Along the same lines was Belloni's short treatise, according to which, "the system which is ordered and constructed by laws, and which constantly proceeds in reason of commerce, must not be altered, unless a notable variation arises from commerce itself" (Belloni 1750: 18). The profit of the Prince had to coincide with the profit of the people (Belloni 1750: 42) and *alzamento* did not entail any advantage for either the treasury or the subjects (Belloni 1750: 45): a concept that sounded like a condemnation for Galiani's theses.

Fabrini's and Belloni's treatises were not at the same level as *Della Moneta*, either in terms of originality or theoretical depth. Fabrini's style was pedantic and Belloni's was didactic with a late mercantilistic flavour (Marconcini 1931; Einaudi 1953: chapp. IV, X), which nevertheless had a decidedly more positive editorial fortune than that obtained by the

Neapolitan abbot.[25] Various editions of Belloni's treatise were printed in Italy (Livorno, Bologna, Milan, Venice) and abroad (Avignon, Leipzig, London, The Hague, Paris, Santiago) (Venturi 1998: 453; Caracciolo 1970) and the work was reviewed in various journals (*Journal Oeconomique*, *Novelle della Repubblica Letteraria*, *Giornale dei Letterati*, *Storia Letteraria d'Italia*).[26] The reputation he enjoyed as a banker and his close political relations must have facilitated the dissemination of his treatise.

Having finally left Rome at the end of March 1752 (Galiani, MS-15: folio 68r), after obtaining sufficient money, Galiani reached the Grand Duchy, first in Livorno and Pisa, then in Siena, Lucca and Florence (in April) where he came into contact with important exponents of Tuscan culture, facilitated in this by the ties that Intieri and Rinuccini had maintained with their homeland.[27] From Naples, Tanucci, always hostile towards the Galianis, wrote that the young abbot had been trained as a man of letters and was not a man of the world, emphasising, in his opinion, the cold reception he received in Pisa (Diaz 1975a: xxiii).[28] Galiani was in contact with Antonio Maria Niccolini (Pasta 2013) and especially Gaspare Cerati (Caffiero 1979; Venturi 1998: 507), to whom he confided his intention (never realised) to write a treatise on taxes (*De Re Tributaria*).[29] But even in Tuscany, any ambiguous references to Melon's theses were banished. In 1751, Gianfrancesco Pagnini and Angelo Tavanti

[25] "In spite of the laudatory reviews of the competent and Pietro Metastasio's congratulatory epistles on his dissertation *Del Commercio*, printed in various editions, both luxury and ordinary, it may well be catalogued among the post-mercantilist writings or among those precursors of corporatism [...], but it is certainly a fatuous head, scientifically full of mush. [...]. As I read, I realised that Belloni was a poor devil who strove, with a great confusion of words, to explain to others what he himself did not understand" (Einaudi 1953: x–xi).

[26] Belloni's late mercantilist theories were criticised by Marquis D'Argenson in an anonymous review in *Journal Oeconomique*, see D'Argenson (1751); Einaudi (1953: chap. IV); Malbranque (2021).

[27] "I repeat my anxiety to have the *Della Moneta* books sold, because they are much desired here, and little seen, and this harms me" (Ferdinando Galiani's letter to Domenico Sgueglia, Pisa, 17 April 1752, BSNSP, XXXI.C.16: folio 37r). On the Relations between Galiani and Tuscan Intellectuals, see Nicoletti (2011).

[28] The relations between Galiani and Tuscan correspondents have been explored by Giuseppe Nicoletti in several studies, cf. in particular Nicoletti (1985, 1992, 2008).

[29] Gaspare Cerati's letter to Ferdinando Galiani, Pisa, 10 February 1754, BSNSP, XXXI.C.9; folio 216v.

edited, not without difficulty, the Italian translation of Locke's monetary writings (Locke 1751; Venturi 1998: 479–483).[30]

As an appendix to the translation, an essay by Pagnini (1751) reiterated the principles of monetary stabilisation by placing them in a historical context. "What other effect, therefore," he wrote, re-proposing the usual argument, "than the ruin of his people can the law of that Prince, who, not content with the office of sovereign administrator of that universal instrument and measure of commerce, wishes to go so far as to prescribe to the currency of his state a value greater or less than that which is universally imposed on it by the others who must receive it, and on whose esteem it must consequently depend" (Pagnini 1751: 40–41). The right of Princes to manipulate the currency derived - according to Pagnini - from Roman law,[31] but such a policy was possible for a military power that derived all its wealth from expansion, but at a time when there was no state that "thought to derive its revenue and its maintenance from war and conquest", it must "regulate the currency according to the maxims of Locke and not those of Roman jurisprudence" (Pagnini 1751: 54). Industry and agriculture were the sources of wealth in contemporary society, but the different distribution of resources in the world made trade obligatory: "men and peoples concurring in trade are to be considered as a kind of society formed among themselves for the purpose of being able more easily to provide for their

[30] Galiani, as is well known, had attempted to translate Locke, but had then abandoned the work, which he found very arduous. In the second edition of *Della Moneta*, Galiani wrote: "John Locke's treatises, in English, *On the Interest of Money* and *On Coinage*, precede Melun's *Essay on Commerce*; but they were mentioned by me in second place, because I esteem them less. In 1750, the year in which I published this work, they had not been published in translation into any other language, but were shortly afterwards printed in Italian in Florence in 1751 by Giovanni Francesco Pagnini and Angelo Tavanti, learned men and friends of mine [...]. The Florentine translators added notes, reflections, commentaries and clarifications. They also dislodged and dismantled the whole text, so that they could divide it into chapters and sections, and give some order to the subjects. Despite so much effort, the work remained horribly obscure. I, who for my own study of the English language had made this translation in the year 1744, was reluctant to rework and publish it, precisely because I was aware of the disgust that this disorder and continuity without refinement, as composed by the author, caused in the readers. Moreover, since I did not adopt many of his principles and sentiments, I saw that I would have been obliged to make long notes and refutations, instead of which it seemed to me better to spend my time doing this work [*Della Moneta*], which contained only my thoughts" (Galiani 1780: 374).

[31] "By quantity of money the ancient jurists have commonly understood the estimate and denomination which is assigned to it by the authority of the sovereign, and not the body, or metal which in itself it contains" (Pagnini 1751: 45).

needs, and governed by the law of using, for determining the price of things, the same measure that is commonly used by the majority of them" (Pagnini 1751: 7–8). This universal measure was money, "copper, gold, silver, and anything in which it pleased men to unite eminently and virtually the value and price, the qualities and goodness of all others in order to use it as a measure" (Pagnini 1751: 23). The value of money is established - Pagnini concluded - "by the judgement of commercial society", i.e. the market which is the only authority capable of establishing the value of monetary measure.

An example of the mistrust of the Tuscans, by now on the road to economic liberalism, for the role that Galiani recognised in the state authority on the governance of money was offered by the review that appeared in the *Novelle Letterarie* by Giovanni Lami, who judged "what is discussed about the *alzamento* is very verbose and ripetitive" (Lami 1752: 826).[32] In Florence as in Rome, his erudition was appreciated more than his economic ideas: he was, in fact, welcomed into the academies of *Colombaria* and *Crusca*, and into *Arcadia* under the name *Sterofante Pisindeo* (Diaz 1975a: XXXII).

[32] Galiani met Lami in Siena (Galiani, MS-15: folio 165r; Diaz 1975a: xxiv). *Novelle Letterarie* dedicated two reviews to *Della Moneta*, in June 1752 and December 1752, formulating two very different opinions: the first rather benevolent recension was followed by a very critical one on certain points such as the theory of *alzamento* and the question of interest. According to Furio Diaz, "The explanation, which relates precisely to the point of the dissemination and echoes of the Galiani book, is perhaps to be found in the fact [...] feared by Intieri and the Galiani, that at the time of the first mention, in June 1752, the reviewer, who was Larni himself, did not know the name of the author but, like many others in Italy, suspected it was Celestino Galiani ("Who the author is I do not know, because he did not put his name to it: but they say he is a learned prelate, no less a loyal subject to that King than a zealous citizen"). When the second excerpt was published in December 1752, the identity of the author - in the person of Celestino's young and unknown nephew - had already been widely leaked, and this knowledge also explains the tone of superiority with which Lami begins his article, saying that he had "almost forgotten" that he had begun to "give an account of the *Treatise on Money*" in a previous page, promising to continue it in a later issue. Finally, Lami's opinion may have been influenced by the reading he probably did between the first and second extracts of some of the other writings on money that came out at the time, all of which were directed against devaluations and *alzamento*, which Galiani had defended to a certain extent, and in favour of revaluations, perhaps with new coin mintings, which Galiani, in his inclination towards anything that could stimulate investment and the circulation of money, had not taken into consideration" (Galiani 1975: 8–9, Diaz's note).

Leaving Florence, Galiani passed through Bologna, Ferrara, Padua and Verona (May–June 1752)[33] and arrived in Venice (June–August 1752), finding a more favourable climate for discussing monetary matters,[34] but the stay was not pleasant.[35] He met Girolamo Costantini through Pier Giovanni Capello, who in turn introduced him to political authorities, such as Andrea Tron, and intellectual personalities, such as the erudite Marco Foscarini (Gullino 2020; Del Negro 1998). In particular with Tron, who was responsible for coinage, he discussed the Venetian *Zecchini*, a gold coin that was particularly popular at the time (Galiani, MS-15: 77r).[36]

The Republic of Venice was certainly the least willing to accept innovative ideas and among his Venetian interlocutors, Galiani found the same exaltation as Locke and Dutot. Conservative monetary policies were, however, an indication of decadence rather than strength.

The year before, Costantini had published his *Delle monete in senso pratico e morale*, in which he reiterated with various arguments the damage caused by alterations (Costantini 1751: 33–38), but recognised the state's right to *regulate* a very delicate matter for social and economic stability (Costantini 1751: 68). Costantini used the term currency regulation in the sense of stabilisation since political power could only confirm the "correct value of the intrinsic" (Costantini 1751: 72).[37] A few years later, Costantini published the first Italian translation of the essays by Melon, Dutot and the Abbé de Saint Pierre (Costantini 1754). The decision to publish the two opposing visions together was intended to refute

[33] See the correspondence with Domenico Squeglia (BSNSP, XXXI.C.16: folios 44r–46r). Celestino recommended his nephew to visit Scipione Maffei in Verona, see Celestino Galiani's letter to Ferdinando Galiani, Naples, 6 June 1752, BSNSP, XXXI.C.16; folio 163v.

[34] "Here, my books *Della Moneta* are much requested, so it is necessary to send them to me, it is not credible, and yet it is true, that in the last two years sixteen new authors have appeared in the light saying bestialities on money" (Ferdinando Galiani's letter to Domenico Sgueglia, Venice, 17 June 1752, BSNSP, XXXI.C.16: folio 47r).

[35] "I would have a thousand things to write, but I do not have time: I will say one: the excellent definition of Venice is Boccaccio's: *a city receptacle of every kind of trash*" (Ferdinando Galiani's letter to Domenico Sgueglia, Venice, 19 July 1752, BSNSP, XXXI.C.16: folio 60r, italics added. See also Boccaccio [2003]: 266).

[36] "Venice, the citadel of twenty-four-carat *Zecchini* and *Ducats* of excellent silver, guardian of a tradition of flawless and elegantly minted coins" (Venturi 1998: 510). See Tucci (1981: 275–316); Amato (1999: 187–238). For Galiani's assessment of the monetary institutions of the Venetian Republic, see Galiani ([1751]: Book IV, Chap. IV).

[37] "It is enough for each State to keep its currency valued as nearly as possible at the right intrinsic value of gold and silver, always preserving the strict proportion, and taking care that it is not altered by the arbitrariness of private individuals" (Costantini 1751: 83).

Melon's false arguments on *alzamento* with Dutot's "deeper meditations", so "that anyone who has hitherto been a follower of Melon's opinion, as was among others the very clear author of the work entitled *Della Moneta* [...] will change his mind and finally subscribe to the true and sound defence of Locke, Dutot, and many other worthy men, both from beyond the Alps and from Italy" (Costantini 1754).

Similar ideas had been expressed by Pier Giovanni Capello in his *Nuovo trattato del modo di regolare la moneta* (Capello 1752),[38] also providing data, collected in twelve tables, on the value of coins, the ratio between gold and silver and the relative traffic in Italian cities (Genoa, Florence, Rome, Milan, Naples, Venice) in the main foreign centres (London, Vienna, Cadiz, Lisbon, Alexandria, Constantinople) (Capello 1752: [10]).

Galiani had met, in Milan and not in Venice, the Venetian Gian Rinaldo Carli,[39] who had contributed to the debate on the governance of money with *Dell'origine e del commercio della moneta* (Carli 1751; Apih 1977; Tucci 1996; Trampus 2011a; Tusset 2020). Because of the authority that Carli enjoyed as a scholar and because he was one of the leading figures in imperial economic and financial policy in the Milanese state, the text was destined to have great influence, and not only in Italy.[40] Carli distinguished two types of alterations, those on intrinsic value (*alloy alteration*) and those on extrinsic value (*price alteration*), and considered them to be the main cause of Italian economic decadence. One of the historical examples he provided in support of his thesis was the Neapolitan monetary policy implemented by Marquess of Carpio and Count of Santisteban, echoing Broggia's thesis (Carli 1751: 60). In contrast, the Most Serene Republic of Venice was held up as an example "of probity and prudence to all other

[38] "The nominal value of coins in its true meaning is nothing other than the measure of money. Its function is the same as the function of the scales. What does the scale do? It indicates with its signs how much is the thing weighed. If the scales are scarce or overflowing, they speak falsely, and deceive, so the nominal value, which is the numerical reason for calculation, tells the quantity of metal in each coin [...]. It must not therefore be believed that placing a higher nominal value on one coin than on another will accredit the more highly valued coin; on the contrary, the less valued coins will be accepted as containing a greater quantity of metal by comparison. Thus it is not to the Prince's advantage to give more nominal value to one coin than to another, except to all his own over foreign ones" (Capello 1752: 46–47).

[39] Ferdinando Galiani's letter to Domenico Sgueglia, Venice, 12 August 1752, BSNSP, XXXI.C.16: folio 63r.

[40] Carli himself emphasised this: "Such was the faith lent to this work that it was received as a diplomatic work" (Carli 1784: tome II: 489–490).

nations" because it was able to keep its monetary system "always in perfect equilibrium" (Carli 1751: 62).

The particular geographical position of the Italian peninsula determined the vocation of its states to trade and "no *Trading Nation* can make arbitrary alterations to its currencies without ruining itself. I say *Trading Nation* that which, not living in isolation, has its interest tied to foreigners, I say *arbitrary alteration* that which is detached from the consent of others, and I say finally *on currencies*, because this alteration can fall as much on its own currencies as on the currencies of others" (Carli 1751: 34).[41] Therefore "any country in Italy that assigns a lower price to currencies than that which is due, if it has more active than passive trade within Italy itself, loses the trade itself: if it has more passive than active trade, immense losses are encountered and if it has nothing greater than the other, it will not lose in the trade of merchandise, but will lose in the trade of currencies, which will reduce it to such a state that it will be left without gold or silver at all" (Carli 1751: 67). Once the correct proportion has been altered, there is no mechanism capable of restoring the equilibrium: "some mathematicians have made us believe that money is like water, which after much running and twisting, finally finds its equilibrium again: the thing, however, is totally different, and particularly in Italy" (Carli 1751: 65). The proportion to be respected is the "common proportion of metals" (Carli 1751: 47), adjusting the nominal value as much as possible to the intrinsic value of the metal: "the greatest caution must therefore consist in the proportion of the metals, which depends on the consensus of the Nations; and this proportion should be changed in relation to the quantity or scarcity of the metals themselves, from which the coins are formed" (Carli 1751: 75).[42] A country cannot establish laws on

[41] Carli was aware of the global effects caused by different monetary policies: "From small alterations, prodigious effects arise, from which the magical chain of evils is formed. Nor is there any distance that saves, as trade approaches every remotest nation. Who would say that the scarcity of silver from the East Indies, in grace of which it is valued there a third more than in Europe, alters the proportions of metals and forms one of the main elements of Italy's confusion? What shall we say now about the mutations, which here and there frequently occur only for interest and profit? Will not these upset the whole system of currencies in a moment? Yes, of course, if it is true that Italy is an inch of earth compared to the whole world" (Carli 1751: 80).

[42] "Just as the price of any other commodity is regulated in Italy on the prices of those Nations in which they arrive at first hand, so too must the price of metals be absolutely established on that of the fortunate peoples, who are the first to have them and to adjust them in proportion to their scarcity or abundance" (Carli 1751: 86).

commodities as precious as metals and must uphold only two principles: "I. not to alter the price of money, because both trade and the money itself are lost; II. not to alter the alloy of money, because trade, money and credit are lost" (Carli 1751: 75–76). "This general maxim and the first of monetary theory", Carli concluded, has seldom been followed in Italy, damaging "our present commerce", since it is "general the disproportion of currency price, whereby the cities remain in the end with copper alone" (Carli 1751: 87).

In August, Galiani reached Milan,[43] and, still short of money, found hospitality with "gentlemen of the highest sphere" ("Count Federico Borromeo, the Count of Castelbarco [probably Cesare Ercole], Prince Trivulzio [probably Antonio Tolomeo]") and stayed "in small monetary councils [...] with President Neri and the Venetian Count Carli, both authors of books on money"[44] also meeting with Filippo Argelati.

Pompeo Neri, as is well known, had held important governmental responsibilities first in Florence and then in Milan, and in 1750 took part in the complex and fruitless negotiations between the Kingdom of Savoy and the imperial government for a monetary agreement aimed at fixing the ratio between gold and silver and their respective value for the two states (Venturi 1998: 469–473; Amato 1999: 39–40; Tiran 2011; Verga 2013). The negotiation offered Neri the opportunity to express in *Osservazioni sopra il prezzo legale delle monete* his proposals for monetary policy (Neri 1751). "Money", he observed, "is a mass of metal formed by the authority by some mark which serves as an attestation of the quantity it contains" (Neri 1751: 43). State authority in monetary matters only has the role of attesting intrinsic value and alteration would be as useless as "any attestation to authenticate an untrue calculation" (Neri 1751: 45).[45] Galiani's theses about *alzamento* must have appeared to him as a dangerous heresy and he did not hesitate to refute the positions of the Neapolitan

[43] Ferdinando Galiani's letter to Domenico Sgueglia, Milan, 9 August 1752, BSNSP, XXXI.C.16: folio 61r.

[44] Ferdinando Galiani's letter to Domenico Sgueglia, Milan, 12 August 1752, BSNSP, XXXI.C.16: folio 63r.

[45] "What seems an absurdity in the measures of length and gravity is done, by almost universal abuse of the mints, in the measures of value, from which is subtracted not only what is needed to reimburse the expenses of legalising the currency, but also what more must be subtracted to exact a duty and to satisfy the rapacity of the mint-makers. In all this manufacture everything is defined according to the will of the legislator, but the ultimate consequence is never submitted to his authority" (Neri 1751: 72).

abbot in a second memoir, written in January 1752 and drafted as an appendix to the *Osservazioni*, published in 1759 in the fifth volume of Argelati's collection (Neri 1759: 180). Notwithstanding that "the author deserves infinite praise for many truths, which he has well expressed in his book, I do not remain truly persuaded that the arbitrary *alzamento* of the currency is less harmful than bankruptcy, the evils of the *alzamento* seeming to me to be more extensive, more important, more casually thrown upon the people, and especially upon the poor, as they are all the creditors of their own labours" (Neri 1759: 179). And he briefly rejected Galiani's thesis, stating "in the first place because I have no memory that any state has ever been able to free itself from servitude, neither by force of bankruptcy, nor by force of *alzamento*. And in the second place, because the supposed benefits of the *alzamento* are already confessed to be limited to a period of time, which I believe to be of very short duration, or rather momentary, since the prices of the most important commodities for human life, and those that the state, which is supposed to be reduced to extreme necessities, may need, are immediately affected by the imbalance of the currency" (Neri 1759: 179).

And the young Neapolitan abbot's arguments could not even be accepted by Filippo Argelati, who devoted himself to collecting texts by Italian writers about monetary problems (*De Monetis Italiae*, Argelati 1750–1752), bringing to the forefront of the debate the *Trattato del valore delle monete in tutti gli Stati* (*Treatise on the Value of Money in All States*) written in 1683 by the Modenese astronomer and mathematician Geminiano Montanari and hitherto unpublished (Montanari 1683a [1750]).[46]

Montanari's treatise not only provided further support for stabilisation advocates, but introduced a new element into the debate by establishing a link between currency manipulation and speculative activities. He declared, "It is not at the Prince's command to value currencies at his own discretion, except for small copper coins, because any small imbalance between the prices, which he establishes out of common proportion, excites the merchants to profit, which they readily make from the errors of those in command to the detriment of their subjects and of true mercantile activity" (Montanari 1683a [1750]: 14). Thus, according to Montanari, the

[46] In 1759 Carlo Casanova, after Argelati's death, published another treatise by Montanari, *La Zecca in Consulta di Stato*, in volume VI of Argelati's collection, see Montanari (1683b [1759]).

decadence of Italian society derives from speculation on money, which occurred "mainly because, most of the richest Italian merchants being involved in the money trade, they neglected the gains that made their ancestors great, and allowed the supremacy to pass to France, England, Holland and elsewhere, to the infinite detriment and shame of Italy" (Montanari 1683b [1759]: 39).

On 19 September 1752, Galiani arrived in Turin[47] and met King Charles Emmanuel III, with whom he had a brief conversation, thus described in his diary, "The King of Sardinia spoke to me at length about money. He told me that Locke's system of not valuing gold in his states was not useful because the people of Geneva traffic in silver for export. He told me that in his states 10 million *Lire* of silk was made a year, that this brought in a great deal of money from France, that in some years as much as 4 million had come in. That he certainly knew that the commerce of his kingdom was more active than passive, that the production surplus of his people made the governance of money very difficult, because for every small gain new money was extracted and introduced from abroad. He told me that in the time of his government he had seen the entire currency of his state changed more than six times. He told me that lately he had had to ban certain coins of Genoa, with very unfair value. He spoke to me with praise of President Neri's book, confirmed that in his reign his ministers had made great mistakes by understanding nothing of the subject and complicated errors upon errors, but that he now forced them to study. He was familiar with the translation of Locke's book done in Florence. [...] Then the Duke of Savoy [Victor Amadeus] came in and the King told me he was his son and then introduced me saying, "Come, I am here talking to a Neapolitan abbot". The Duke of Savoy began to discuss the matter, showing that he understood it quite well. He was convinced that silver increases its price for luxury consumption. On this the King told me that he did not understand how silver could be so rare and at the same time seem to diminish in value compared to gold, and spoke to me of the trade that is made with India in gold. He then went on to talk about the importance of agriculture, and the duke gave me the example of the Egyptians and the ancient Romans, from which I knew he had read Rollin, and said some other good things.[48] Then the King told me that in order not to

[47] Francesco Garro's letter to Ferdinando Galiani, Turin, 19 September 1752, BSNSP, XXXI.B.18: folio 157r.

[48] Charles Rollin was the author of summaries of ancient history.

corrupt the troop and have the money spent equally everywhere, he kept his troop distributed throughout the state and no more than four battalions in Turin. Then he told President Garro to let me see everything, adding that it would not take long, and he dismissed me" (Galiani, MS-15: folios 87r–88r).[49]

Galiani had initially planned to continue his journey to Paris, via Genoa and Marseilles,[50] but gave up the plan and left Milan in October to return to Naples in early November 1752.

6.2 The Rupture with Intieri-Genovesi's Project and Scholarly Studies

The long journey across the peninsula provided Galiani with the opportunity to forge contacts with leading Italian intellectuals, with whom he corresponded extensively in the following years. However, the young abbot was appreciated as a refined intellectual and nephew of the *Cappellano Maggiore* of the Kingdom of Naples, but his views on monetary policy did not receive full support. Certainly *Della Moneta* had been appreciated, but the admiration, never hidden, for Melon and the nonchalance with which the author had treated the subject of *alzamento*, considered by his interlocutors to be a sort of heresy, weighed heavily on the judgement of his contemporaries. Nor was there an understanding of the complex exposition of the theory of value, which found no critical response, except for rare and superficial quotations.[51] The figure and work of Galiani portrayed by Costantini in his *Caso di monete imprestate* (*Case of Borrowed Money,* Costantini 1753), can be considered representative of an opinion widely shared by supporters of monetary stabilisation policies: "It is a great fatality of our times that when some witty and erudite writer, such as Abbot Galiani, makes an assertion that either does not please, or is not well understood, or is not entirely in keeping with his duty, he is, so to speak, stoned to death, as if his entire work deserved common disapproval. This must be said not out of partiality: I can in no way approve what he

[49] Diodati in his biography of Galiani reports the event in another form by drawing news from a letter Ferdinand sent to his uncle Celestino, see Diodati (1788: 17–18). See also Venturi (1998: 595–506).

[50] "From Genoa I embark for Marseille and from there go to Paris" (Ferdinando Galiani's letter to Domenico Sgueglia, Venice, 17 June 1752, BSNSP, XXXI.C.16: folio 48r).

[51] An example of this was the way Costantini quoted Galiani's law of value (Costantini 1753: 37–38).

writes in Chapter III of Book III of his work [...] where he treats of the *alzamento*, that is, of the mutation of the proportion of currency, from p. 221 to p. 259. I cannot, I say, absolutely adhere to his sentiments, since my opinion is very different, sharing the reasons that the Abbé de Saint Pierre, Dutot, and other good men from the other side of the Alps, and from Italy especially, asserted against Monsieur Melon, who was followed and defended by the Abbot of Naples; and it is superfluous to mention here: but he is also worthy of comprehension, because he had political considerations concerning the maxims of the Kingdom of Naples, on whose system he applied his propositions" (Costantini 1753: 37).

For more affinity with the emerging orthodoxy in monetary matters, Broggia certainly received more support (especially from Carli and Neri).[52] Even those who had had words of praise for *Della Moneta*, such as Bottari, did not fully grasp its value and preferred to fall back on Spinelli's more "practical" text.[53] Galiani himself realised the cold reception his work received, saying, "So far, I must confess to you that I have more obligation to the *Raccolta* [the verses for Iannaccone] than to the book [*Della moneta*]: and all my studies have served me less than knowing how to play the harpsichord".[54]

Nevertheless, *Della Moneta* for depth and style clearly surpasses all other contemporary writings about monetary matters, which often

[52] See Carli (1751: 59); Neri (1751: 54, 58–59).

[53] "Our most honourable Prince has sent the Duke a book *Della Moneta*, of which one had no previous knowledge, and yet it is sold, and the booksellers would take it in exchange for excellent books. I have seen Broggia mentioned in it, and if you could get it from your secretary I would gladly take it [...]. About this Broggia here, not even his name is known. I browsed through the anonymous book and it seemed to me to be full of beautiful thoughts, beautiful speculations, much useful information, and many practical teachings; it is true, that I wished the author, whoever he may be, had better stitched together all these things and drawn all these lines together, or more clearly determined points. The fact that he also wanted to write elegantly and in the style of French writers makes him sometimes obscure, because he uses phrases in a different sense from that, which we have had up to now, and he uses Tuscan phrases, but not in a Tuscan way. Besides, the book is good and there is much to be gleaned from it, but in practice Spinelli's is better. I do not even know why in the Introduction the anonymous person wanted to praise Melon and Locke's priority of writing on this subject rather than an Italian. I thought he had no news about Davanzati, and for that I excused him. But then I saw that he mentions him several times, but only to attack him soundly" (Giovanni Bottari's letter to Celestino Galiani, Rome, 15 October 1751, BSNSP, XXXI. B. 18: folios 55r–55v, published in Catucci 1986: 20–22).

[54] Ferdinando Galiani's letter to Domenico Sgueglia, Pisa, 27 March 1752, BSNSP, XXXI.C.16: folio 34r.

present confusing and repetitive arguments accompanied by crude technicalities. Only Argelati, who appreciated the work more than others, asked him to publish one of his dissertations in the collection *De Monetis Italiae*,[55] but Galiani's interest in economic matters was waning and he would soon turn his attention mainly to scholarly literary studies.

Intieri had bitterly rejected Galiani's criticism, demanding "from which school come this lot of beastly men who are more ignorant than night and more petulant, arrogant and contemptuous than ignorance itself!".[56] This is evidence that Galiani was still in close contact with the elderly Tuscan intellectual at that time. The product of this intense relationship was the work *Della perfetta conservazione del grano* (*About the perfect storage of grain*, Intieri 1754), to which Galiani contributed the actual drafting[57]

[55] See Filippo Argelati's letter to Ferdinando Galiani, 18 August 1753, BSNSP, XXXI. C. 9: foliod 106r–106v.

[56] Bartolomeo Intieri's letter to Ferdinando Galiani, Massa Equana, 4 March 1752, BSNSP, XXXI. B. 18: folios 88–89. Intieri's criticism was addressed to Costantini.

[57] Galiani claimed authorship of the work in the *Foreword* (*Avviso*) to the second edition of *Della Moneta*, in which he wrote that the book "under the name of Intieri (who invented the machine), was published by Galiani himself" (Galiani 1780: [15]). Even in correspondence, Galiani attributed the authorship of the work to himself (Ferdinando Galiani's letter to Francesco Bottari, Naples, 27 July 1754, published in Galiani 1975: 839). He was explicit in a letter to Lorenzo Mehus: "I have been busy writing a short work on the conservation of wheat and on a stove machine invented for this purpose by Bartolomeo Intieri your fellow citizen under whose name the work is published" (Ferdinando Galiani's letter to Lorenzo Mehus, Naples, 7 May 1753, published in Galiani 1975: 1055). Further evidence is offered by a letter to Galiani from George Jackon, an English bibliophile and merchant living in Livorno: "I thought I might read your name on the front of the aforesaid *Discorso*, having seen it in the aforementioned letter from your mind and from your pen, but I found it without knowing why it was published under the name of Bartolomeo Intieri well known to me" (George Jakson's letter to Ferdinando Galiani, Livorno, 5 May 1755, BSNSP, XXXI.B.19: folio 16r.). And in a letter to Madame d'Epinay: "In 1754, he was eighty-two years old and almost blind. I wanted the world to know about this useful machine. So I wrote a little book entitled: *Della perfetta conservazione del Grano*; and as I have never wanted to put my name on any of my works, I wanted it to bear the name of the inventor of the machine; but everyone knows that it is mine, and I believe that Grimm, Diderot, the Baron [d'Holbach], and perhaps others have it in Paris, and know this story as well as Abbé Morellet" (Ferdinando Galiani's letter to Madame d'Épinay, Naples, 13 December, 1770, in Galiani 1975: 1055; Galiani and d'Épinay 1992, vol I: 314). According to Diodati: "Galiani had no other part than that of writing the book; since the design and materials were all Intieri's [...]. This information is confirmed to me by my wise and honoured friend Giovanni Lembo, Elected of the People, who was a pupil of Intieri and Rinuccini. He added that Abbot Intieri, as a reward for the work, gave Galiani some *Doppioni* from Portugal. Intieri himself confessed this to Domenico Diodati, my brother [...]. In fact, following Galiani's example, he wanted

(his brother Berardo had drawn the plates), but the ideas and experiences narrated belonged entirely to Intieri.[58]

The *Proem*[59] was really Intieri's testament: "I depart from this life," he began, "happy to see that I leave mankind in a much better state than that in which I found it. The enlightenment of letters, the virtues of princes, the placidity of morals among the people, the arts useful to life, commerce, agriculture, have in the brief space of my life grown and spread so much, that an interior presage comforts me to believe, and to firmly hope, that in a very short time they will have to reach where not only *History* has never told us they have reached, but our thoughts themselves had perhaps never hoped to be able to see them one day. Little will our Europe enjoy a happy *Golden Age*, not rough and sylvan, as the poets dream of it, but cultured and citizenised, full of arts, comforts and comforts of life" (Intieri 1754: [10–11]). This *Golden Age* was indeed imminent, because as he wrote, "if we measure the progress of man made in the last three centuries, and compare it with everything else, we shall find it disproportionately greater" (Intieri 1754: [11]); and he attributed this strong acceleration of progress to the invention of the printing press and also observed, "perhaps in a little while it will make the sciences penetrate among the most uncouth peasants, and every peasant will then know as much as the mayor, and the notary of his village does today" (Intieri 1754: [14]).[60]

my brother to write two dissertations; one on the *palorcio*, i.e. the machine he invented to bring snow down from the mountain of Vico to the sea without the help of men or animal power, and the other on a machine to make a carriage go without horses" (Diodati 1788: 20–21). On the *palorcio* see Intieri (1754: 42–43).

[58] Galiani had already been working on this work since the spring of 1753 (Ferdinando Galiani's letter to Lorenzo Mehus, Naples, 5 May 1753, Biblioteca Riccardiana, Florence, Ms. 3494). The work was to be published in March 1754. See also Perna (1984: 1276–1277).

[59] Venturi attributes the *Proem* entirely to Galiani (Venturi 1998: 506), of the opposite opinion is Salvatore Rotta who attributes it to Intieri (Rotta 1973: 152), according to Maria Luisa Perna it is a product of Antonio Genovesi (Perna 1984: 1278).

[60] The publication of *Perfetta Conservazione* was not without obstacles, as can be deduced from a letter sent to Ferdinando, stating, "I was quite surprised by what you pointed out to me in your letter of 2 September regarding the bitter criticism, which was made by the reviewers, of the beautiful preface to the stove book" (Gaspare Cerati's letter to Ferdinando Galiani, 4 September 1754, BSNSP, XXXI.C.9: folio 222r.). See the observations of the ecclesiastical censorship and reply (BSNSP, XXX. C. 12: folios 123r–129r, published in Mauro 2017a: 465–468). The reply, most likely written by the young Galiani, is very resolute: "Please, Ecclesiastical Reviser, with your great and well known equity and learning, to reflect that the authority of the Revisers does not extend so far as to compel those who print to adopt the opinions and systems embraced by them, but only to compel them to abstain

One cannot fail to recognise in these concepts the Enlightenment approach, the certainty that the path of Reason was unstoppable and that the only problem actually concerned the most effective and widespread diffusion of the new ideas. It is basically, with all due distinctions, the same impulse that in those same years animated the group of *philosophes encyclopédistes* in France and that determined the rise and success of the first great enterprise of scientific divulgation in history.

Meanwhile, Celestino's death, on 26 July 1753, was to radically change Galiani's social position.[61] On the young abbot fell the mistrust that court circles had reserved, especially in his later years, for his uncle Celestino, who was forced to leave his post as Cappellano Maggiore in May 1753, forcibly retired due to his state of health, despite the fact that he had asked to be allowed to continue his duties.[62] The innovations he had introduced into university life and the protection he had always reserved for non-

from following those opinions which the Church has condemned and proscribed, and which are contrary to good morals, or the rights of sovereigns. Whether the press has been useful or harmful is still undecided; nor has the Church ever vituperated the praises of the press, but rather allowed the printing of the Breviary, the Rituals, the Communion Books, the Conception Books, and finally all sacred and liturgical books" (BSNSP, XXX. C. 12: folios 125r, published in Mauro 2017a: 466). The work was translated into French in 1770 (Intieri 1770), but according to Galiani the invention was plagiarised by the French agronomist Henri-Louis Duhamel du Monceau, to whom his brother Berardo had sent his drawings for revision, see Duhamel du Monceau (1753) and Ferdinando Galiani's letter to Madame d'Epinay, Naples, 13 December, 1770, in Galiani (1975: 1056); Galiani and d'Épinay (1992, vol. I: 314).

[61] A few months earlier, in February 1752, Celestino's health had deteriorated and Ferdinand revealed a certain coolness and indifference, a typical trait of his character: "I would like to go to Tuscany, but many write to me that it would be scandalous in the eyes of the world, and indeed they cry out why I have not returned to Naples. I have no heart to return to Naples, both because it would break the path I have embarked upon, which in that case will never be done again, and also because I would not want Monsignor [Celestino] to be displeased. To tell you my heart, I have no wish to be present at the misfortune, as it is something I cannot remedy by presence" (Ferdinando Galiani's letter to Domenico Squeglia, Rome, 25 February 1752, BSNSP, XXXI.C.16: 27r–27v). His indifference was also noted by Denis Diderot: "The Abbé Galiani greatly surprised me by confessing that he had never cried in his life, and that the loss of his father, brothers, sister and lovers had not cost him a single tear" (Denis Diderot's letter to Sophie Volland, 20 September 1760, published in Diderot 1955, vol. III: 76).

[62] The circumstances are described in detail in Iovine (2001: 473–477). The post of Cappellano Maggiore was entrusted to Nicola De Rosa, Bishop of Pozzuoli, who had conservative views on the organisation of studies, privileging legal and theological subjects over natural sciences.

conformist intellectuals were no longer tolerated either in Naples or Rome (he had even been accused of Jansenism).[63] Immediately after his death, his figure was the object of calumnies that tended to discredit his scientific and moral stature. In this climate, Ferdinando's requests to obtain certain benefits belonging to his uncle were rejected by the Roman Curia.[64] Tanucci cynically reported that the abbot, after the death of his uncle had returned "*ad plebem* and no word of him is heard in this large population".[65]

In the same months, the relationship with Intieri also tended to weaken. Galiani himself testified to one of his correspondents: "[Intieri] falls in love and gets bored with things in weeks. I also incurred his displeasure, for after having been the object of his love and thoughts for many months,

[63] "Certainly my uncle was not a Jansenist; he had too much Newton in his body" (Ferdinando Galiani's letter to Francesco Sanseverino, Naples, 12 April 1777, BSNSP, XXX.C.12: folio 268, see Galiani 1975: 1144).

[64] Ferdinando learned from Niccolini the negative outcome of the request: "This is the second time that I write to you with extreme regret and pain. The first was for the death of your uncle, the second will be in having to give you the inauspicious news that your request for Monsignor your uncle's benefits has been refused by the Pope [...]. Your uncle is dead, so as much as his memory makes a breach in Cardinal Valenti, so little does it make a breach in him, to say the least. In this agitation therefore, which is always increasing, the death of Monsignor Galiani occurred. At the news that reached the Pope, Monsignor Gorgoni, Bishop of Atri, a Celestine monk, was present. He was either not a friend of your uncle or aimed at his benefits and immediately attacked the memory of the deceased by saying that he was very scandalously rich [...]. Your memorial, your letter and the offices of Cardinal Valenti have remained ineffective. You therefore need other conjunctures for you to be able to be consoled, and I flatter myself that they have to happen, because Cardinal Valenti is angry and it takes time because you have been painted with His Holiness not in matters of doctrine, not in matters of lust, which would be fatal points, but for slander and that is to say, freedom of speech" (Antonio Niccolini's letter to Ferdinando Galiani, Rome, 10 September 1753, BSNSP, XXXI. B. 18: folio 253r). See Ferdinando Galiani's letter to Benedict XIV (BSNSP, XXX. C. 12: folios 1–2) in which he requests the allocation of the benefits that belonged to his uncle.

[65] Bernardo Tanucci's letter to Francesco Nefetti, Naples, 6 November 1753, in Tanucci (1980b: 113). In a letter to Benedict XIV Galiani described his economic condition: "The state in which we are now living after his death certainly deserves compassion [...]. I have inherited nothing from my parents other than ten Neapolitan ducats a month, nor can I hope for more from them. My brother, having five female sisters, and an aunt to feed, and a wife and two daughters, in addition to those who are likely to come, is so restricted in his measures, that if the pity of the King of Naples does not help him (which is not certain), he will not be able to maintain himself decently in Naples [...]. In such a state of circumstances I owe it to the singular munificence of Your Holiness not to medicate thanks to those two benefits, which I obtained some time ago" (Ferdinando Galiani's letter to Pope Benedict XIV, BSNSP, XXX. C. 12: folios 1).

he grew bored, forgot about me, and almost took an aversion to me. The same happened to Genovesi, for whom he showed so much love with his actions. And finally also from Rinuccini he parted. Moreover, a vase that breaks after 78 years does not deserve to be accused of fragility, and as he is, our Intieri is better than dead".[66]

After Celestino's death, Intieri's aim was to reproduce on a larger scale the work he had done with a small group of Neapolitan intellectuals and of which Abbot Antonio Genovesi provided an effective description: "Most of the discourses, in Intieri's small but brilliant conversation, were about the progress of human reason, the arts, commerce, state economy, mechanics, physics. Intieri was thus an enemy of useless abstractions and pedantic literary studies, from which men can derive no real fruit. As he had much practice in the things of the world and had in these sciences much study, he was regarded by all as an oracle. Certainly his opinion was excellent. Now, in short, the discourses all began to turn towards the economy of the state, and mechanics. He began to be persuaded that in all the Academies of Europe there should be a professor of economics and trade, and that it would be barbaric to want to follow, without any change, the literary culture of past centuries, that human reason, thanks to the press and the trade of nations, had made great progress, and that for this reason new ideas, new things, new ways of living, new ways of reasoning, or calculating ideas and things, and consequently new sciences infinitely more useful, should be pursued and spread among the lowest part of the people, and no longer attend only to speculation as in former times" (Genovesi [1997]: 73).

In order to disseminate this reform project, Intieri moved in two directions: to ensure a wide dissemination through the press of the most modern ideas that had already developed in more advanced Europe, with particular regard to progress in applied economics (and his treatise on the stove, represented the first conscious piece of this programme), and at the same time to insert the new economic science into academic studies, reproducing at an institutional level what had been the main objective of his cenacle: the formation of a new class of intellectuals dedicated to the study of economic and social problems and capable of providing the framework for a new corpus of state civil servants.

[66] Ferdinando Galiani's letter to Giovanni Bottari, Naples, 3 August 1754, Galiani (1975: 842–843). On the Galiani-Bottari correspondence, cf. Felici (1972).

Intieri believed it was possible, at the end of his life, to realise these projects for which he had worked silently for years, defying, in a conservative political climate distrustful of any form of innovation, the authority of the Church and the vanity and inertia of power. He had sought, in his intellectual circle, the figure to whom he could entrust the task of continuing and implementing his programme. At different times he had seen in the talent of the very young Ferdinando Galiani, in the monk Celestino Orlandi, "very studious" (Genovesi [1997]: 74)[67] in economic sciences, the possible successors in his work, but in the end only Antonio Genovesi seemed suitable to carry on his path.[68]

Galiani was too young and being notoriously undisciplined and unsystematic was not suited to teaching. Moreover, he had always had a sceptical attitude, which emerged in some places in his *Della Moneta*,[69] and a sign of how he judged Interi's project is contained in a letter of May 1754: "Intieri founded a chair of *Commercio e Meccanica* (*Commerce and Mechanics*) to be taught in Italian, and Genovesi will teach. Men take care of things when they are nearing their end, not when they are in bloom [...] and when your republic [Florence] was richer than Holland is today, no one thought of founding academies of agriculture, nor of translating Locke".[70]

Abbot Genovesi had been introduced to Intieri's cenacle by the physicist Giuseppe Orlandi around 1748–49 (Ferrone 1995: 253), but

[67] Genovesi himself affirms this: "Since he [Intieri] was at the time a close friend of Celestino Orlandi, a Celestine monk and former procurator general of the order, now bishop of Molfetta, a man of a great and fine mind, of lovable manners, and a scholar of these sciences, and who was my close friend, I believed that he wanted to involve him. I was convinced of the usefulness of this decision and did not cease to encourage him" (Genovesi [1997]: 74).

[68] Again Genovesi narrated the circumstances in which this choice occurred: "one day, [Intieri] more clearly explained to me that he had set his eyes on me. I thanked him for the love and esteem he had for me, but I told him he had to think better because, for the kind of studies I had done, I did not think I was in a position to satisfy his idea. From then on, I never spoke to him about it again, not wanting to abuse his friendship" (Genovesi [1997]: 74).

[69] In the Introduction to the Second Book of *Della Moneta* Galiani had mocked the Golden Age (Galiani [1751]: 87–88), provoking Intieri's reaction, see Bartolomeo Intieri's letter to Ferdinando Galiani, Massa Equana, 12 October 1751, BSNSP, XXXI.B.18: folios 53r–54v, see also Venturi (1998: 559). In this same letter, Intieri disputed Galiani's statement that man was a "constant measure", because in his opinion nothing was stable and constant in nature (folio 51r, see Galiani 1975: 5–6, Diaz's note).

[70] Ferdinando Galiani's letter to Lorenzo Mehus, Naples, 28 May 1753, in Galiani (1975: 837–838).

according to Genovesi himself in his autobiography, it was only in 1751 that "Intieri began to have a special friendship for me and to have the pleasure of having me to lunch often" (Genovesi [1997]: 72; Catucci 1984: 57–58). In those same years, Genovesi was barred from ascending to the chair of theology, the last step in a "rapid and fortunate" (Venturi 1998: 631) academic career, which began in 1741 as a professor of metaphysics. He had been promoted to that position by Celestino Galiani himself, who was engaged in radically reforming the Neapolitan university institute and therefore interested in young people who revealed a certain talent, and the abbot from the province of Salerno had attracted his attention.[71]

In 1745, Genovesi had become a professor of ethics (Venturi 1997: 12) and had by then, with his first book, the *Elementa Metaphysicae* (Genovesi 1743), a work inspired by the new philosophy of Newton and Locke, gained a reputation as an anti-Aristotelian philosopher. This put him in contact with that project of philosophical renewal with a European scope, which turned above all to English culture, Baconian empiricism, Lockian philosophy and finally Newtonian science as the foundations of the new thought, the new mentality and *libertas philosophandi* itself. Genovesi's path was thus in tune with what was emerging in France with the group gathered around Denis Diderot.[72] The *Elementa* was published without the imprimatur of archiepiscopal censorship (because the author refused to suppress certain passages), but with royal approval. This episode marked the beginning of a series of negative reactions to him from ecclesiastical circles.

However, Genovesi "did not become a pure Lockian, a Condillac *avant la lettre*, nor a man with an integral Newtonian scientific mentality. The metaphysical, systematic need was deep and rooted in him" (Venturi 1997: 8). An opinion that is confirmed by the *Disputatio psichico-historica de rerum corporearum origine et constitutione*, Genovesi's preface to the *Elementa physicae* by the Dutch Newtonian scientist Peter van Musschenbroek, published in collaboration with Giuseppe Orlandi and marking the definitive introduction of Newtonian science into Neapolitan

[71] Celestino Galiani is the protagonist of a dialogue written by Genovesi for the reform of university studies (see Genovesi 1763 [2008]).

[72] The similarity not only intellectually but also due to Genovesi's physical resemblance to Diderot was supported by Galiani (Ferdinando Galiani's letter to Bernardo Tanucci, Paris, 12 November 1764, in Galiani 1975: 914).

culture (Genovesi 1745). In this work, Genovesi provided an original interpretation of Newtonian science, placing it within a broad historical synthesis, which attempted to reconstruct the evolution of scientific doctrines since antiquity.[73] However, this moderate line did not save the Neapolitan abbot from suspicion of heresy. These were the years when the Neapolitan Church, led by Cardinal Giuseppe Spinelli, was attempting to regain control over cultural life, even fearing the possibility of the introduction of the Inquisition tribunal. Genovesi aspired to the prestigious chair of theology, whose tenure would have ensured a complete victory for those committed to the renewal of Neapolitan intellectual life, but his opponents accused him of heresy. The court initiated inquisitorial proceedings against the abbot, who was placed in the hands of a "Spanish Jesuit devoid of the spirit of modern philosophy" (Genovesi [1997]: 61). Divisions within the Neapolitan clergy saved Genovesi, who avoided persecution but had to give up his chair (Genovesi [1997]: 62–63, see Iovine 2001: 427–443).

Being isolated, Genovesi had found a solid point of reference in the aged Intieri; on the other hand, the Tuscan himself saw in him the great educator, the man capable of continuing his pedagogical work.[74] Moreover, he had the necessary philosophical depth, he had proven to have a good knowledge of the contemporary scientific movement, and had long been attentive to developments in economic science; in short, he had all the right requisites to be the holder of the new chair of *Commercio e Meccanica* (*Commerce and Mechanics*), which Intieri was preparing to found, at his own expense, in the Neapolitan university.

[73] According to Vincenzo Ferrone: "Genovesi's Newtonianism expounded in a rather dense section of the *Disputatio* ultimately appeared in a form quite different from the phenomenalist and Lockianism form propagated during the 1730s and 1740s in the Accademia delle Scienze by the followers of the Neapolitan *novatores* that was unusually tied to the pantheist hypothesis of the *anima mundi*" (Ferrone 1995: 249). In short, in Genovesi the Locke-Newton nexus was missing and Newtonian science was reread with the aim of smoothing out possible heterodox implications. Of an opposite opinion is Paola Zambelli who sustains the coherence of Genovesi's thought with respect to the genuine message of European rationalism from Wolff to Locke, see Zambelli (1972: 712).

[74] Genovesi's talents as a pedagogue had been demonstrated in the field. In 1738, Celestino Galiani had appreciated his talents on reading the manuscripts of the lectures he gave in his public school (Villari 1958: 7). When he obtained the chair in ethics, the number of his students rose to two hundred from the few dozen who attended his predecessor's lectures. In 1746, to avert his decision to abandon the teaching of Metaphysics that he performed free of charge, the students sent a petition to the King, see Iovine (2001: 427–429).

This chair for the teaching of the brand new science of economics was to be innovative in form as well, so much so that in the testamentary dispositions, in addition to the 300 *Ducats* of annual income to pay the holders and the appointment of Genovesi as the first professor, it established for the future the public competition, the exclusion of regular clergy from teaching, and the obligation to hold lectures in Italian.[75] But Intieri's project can lay claim to another important record: the chair was the first one specifically dedicated to teaching economics at university level.[76]

The term *mechanics*, which was then placed in the name of the chair, is not clearly interpreted: it may be thought that the intention was to immediately emphasise the reference to the laws of physics and mathematics, considered inseparable from economics, and basically to present the intellectual path of Intieri himself, who had moved, as we know, from the mathematical and physical sciences to economics, as an educational model; or, as Giacomo Racioppi has pointed out, "that chair was called *Commerce and Mechanics* by its founder, meaning, as I think, the teaching of agricultural and manufacturing industry in general. Remember how Genovesi himself, in his very first writings on economics, said mechanics was that teaching, which through the invention of tools and mechanisms, intended to promote the fertility of the earth and to do a lot in a short time and with little labour. [...] But that chair Genovesi himself and his contemporaries wanted to name it *Intieriana*" (Racioppi 1871: 105–106).[77]

In March 1754, King Charles approved the Intierian project[78] and the first lecture was held on 5 November 1754, to great public interest. This

[75] "This decision was unprecedented in the history of the Italian university" (Pennisi 1987: 150; see also the observations of Villari 1958: 36–37, who defines this choice by Genovesi as evidence of a "popular school" programme).

[76] Much controversy has arisen over the primacy attributed to the Genovesi chair in the academic teaching of economics (see Michels 1916: 600–605). But Intieri himself was aware of this distinction, writing, "Soon this public will enjoy the first opening of the chair of *Meccanica e Commercio*, to which Genovesi is prepared" (Intieri's letter to Antonio Cocchi, Naples, 18 June 1754, published in Venturi 1959a: 449).

[77] Of the same opinion is Eluggero Pii: "The chair had to deal with Commerce and Mechanics; if the term mechanics recalled the founder's practical inventions - the ropeway, the stove, etc. - the other term indicated exchange in the stage following subsistence production, encompassing all economic activities and all causes of productivity. By also assigning the metaphysician Genovesi to fill the new chair, the promise of global teaching was ensured" (Pii 1984: 47).

[78] "The new chair was not the expression of a decision by Charles of Bourbon to inaugurate a new course of reforming policy; instead, it was the promoters of the initiative who

was emphasised by Genovesi himself in his autobiography, when he observed the "great concourse of all classes of people" and the satisfaction of Intieri, who "seeing the happy outcome was delighted" (Genovesi [1997]: 78).[79]

Shortly before, in January 1754, Genovesi's first work implementing Intieri's programme had been published as an introduction to the text by Ubaldo Montelatici, founder of the Georgofili, with the title *Discorso sopra il vero fine delle lettere e delle scienze* (*Discourse on the True Purpose of Literature and Science*), and was dedicated precisely to the Tuscan patron (Genovesi 1753). The Intieri programme was thus welcomed by Genovesi and founded on solid institutional elements; however, the political climate was not calm. This is revealed in a letter by the abbot, in which, describing the extraordinary public success of his first lectures, he wrote, "I fear,

attempted by this means to insert themselves into active politics, hoping to characterise the policy of the Sovereign" (Pii 1984: 45). For Franco Venturi, the name of the Intieri chair communicates "what were the dominant passions of [Intieri's] life: commerce and technology" (Venturi 1960a: 511). The institution of the chair was not without difficulties, see Iovine (2001: 522–529).

[79] Thus Genovesi described the success of his first lectures: "On the fifth day of the current month [November 1754] I gave my preliminary presentation, i.e. the opening of the new chair, to an extraordinary audience, even though I had not made any invitations. I spoke for an hour, not only without having prepared anything, but without having written anything about what I said. With all this, the speech was greeted with applause, and immediately spread throughout the city... The following day, I began my lectures. I was amazed to hear Italian being taught [...] There were about 100 students. The young people do not yet understand the full utility of these subjects, and where one does not hear Justinian or Gallienus being quoted, they are not over-impressed. But one must go forward with courage: one must break this ice. A great movement has arisen from these lectures in the city, and all classes are asking for books on economics, commerce, the arts, agriculture, and this is a good principle. What pleases me is that at Court there are confidants of the sovereign, who diligently inform themselves" (Antonio Genovesi's letter to Giuseppe De Sanctis, Naples, 23 November 1754, published in Venturi 1997: 293–294). Genovesi thus achieved his aim of seeking "the great public" (Pii 1984: 17). Michelangelo Schipa described the institution of the chair as "the greatest event of the century" (Schipa 1924: 436). Contemporaries had the same perception, see Origlia (1754: 308–309). And Intieri: "Now more than ever I enjoy and am happy and thinking of the happiness of this kingdom all given over to the study of physics and especially of mechanics and useful and healthy mechanics, the promotion of trade, the foundations of some academies not of useless trifles, such as poetry and other trivialities, but of very useful studies, which promote trade and above all the most holy agriculture" (Intieri's letter to Antonio Cocchi, Naples, 18 June 1754, published in Venturi 1959a: 449).

however, those who do not understand the true usefulness of the sovereign and his vassals. God save me from some storm".[80]

In these difficult circumstances, while Genovesi was destined to occupy the scene completely, Galiani and Broggia stood in the background, the former was now caught up in other interests, while the merchant had definitively fallen into disgrace and even been expelled from the city for openly criticising the work of the government.

Ferdinando therefore remained alien to this reform movement that found its pivot in Genovesi and took refuge in studies (literary critique, numismatics, natural sciences, archaeology, witnessed by the dense correspondence).[81] Perhaps disappointed by the way his work had been received, perhaps because of a mentality alien to a pedagogical calling, perhaps because of his superficial, lazy and worldly nature, which "had evidently had the better of him in determining the direction of his activity. [And] it had certainly seemed easier and more comfortable for him to take refuge in an erudite-literary operosity, at times salacious and merely playful, at times more serious and fruitful" (Diaz 1975a: xli).[82]

The intense correspondence that Galiani kept with various intellectuals reveals his many interests cultivated between 1752 and 1759. It was perhaps the most important legacy that his uncle Celestino left to the young abbot, because the correspondents were all linked by long friendship to the Cappellano Maggiore (Guerci 1975a: 793). The names that recurred most frequently in the correspondence of these years were those of Gaspare Cerati (1690–1769, Caffiero 1979; Galiani and Cerati 2008), at that time provveditore generale of the University of Pisa; Antonio Cocchi

[80] Antonio Genovesi's letter to Giuseppe De Sanctis, Naples, 23 November 1754, published in Venturi (1997: 294).

[81] Genovesi however knew Galiani's work, describing it as an illustrious and excellent *Della Moneta* (see Genovesi 1757, vol 1: 184). An opinion confirmed in the *Lezioni*: "one of the best and most reasoned books on the theory of value is that of Abbot Galiani" (Genovesi 1767: 7). On the relations between Galiani and Genovesi, see Catucci (1984). Galiani did not have a favourable opinion of Genovesi's chair, a few years later he confided to one of his correspondents: "A chair of commerce has been vacant here since Genovesi's death; but it must be awarded by selection [...]. It seems that it will die suppressed and forgotten. Chairs of commerce are not studies for monarchical countries" (Ferdinando Galiani's letter to Lorenzo Mehus, Naples, 12 July 1774, published in Galiani 1975: 1108).

[82] Cardinal Luigi Valenti, with whom he was in contact in order to obtain certain benefits, reproached him for his "indolence" in which he was "engulfed" (Luigi Valenti's letter to Ferdinando Galiani, Rome, 7 February 1755, BSNSP, XXXI.C.9: folio 151r). See also BSNSP, XXXI.C 17.

(1695–1758, Baldini 1982), physician and naturalist; Antonio Niccolini (1701–1769), jurist; and Giovanni Gaetano Bottari (1689–1771, Petrucci and Pignatelli 1971; Galiani and Bottari 1972), scholar and theologian: "are some of the most representative names of that generation of men of culture open to innovative influences, but certainly not to be defined as Enlightenment, whose reflections were exercised on ecclesiastical history, theological questions, moral problems and the reform of the Church [...]; men who were united by a precise anti-Jansenistic attitude and a firm polemic against papal temporalism, which in Bottari, Niccolini and Cerati, despite the variety of nuances, are at one with an assiduous labour around the problem of Jansenism" (Guerci 1975a: 793).[83]

Apart from this group of Celestino's friends was the erudite Lorenzo Mehus (1717–1802, Flori 2009; Galiani and Mehus 2002), whom Galiani met on his journey in Tuscany, and with whom the Neapolitan abbot kept up an intense correspondence, dealing not only with erudition and archaeology (*antiquaria*), but also with political issues, a sign that his interest in the reality of his time had not abandoned him.

In 1755, Galiani undertook a collection of all the geological material from the eruptions of Vesuvius, and he "was the first to collect and gather all the different stones and materials of which he brought together one hundred and forty-one different kinds, and with them made a new and curious museum" (Diodati 1788: 21–22).[84] According to Diodati, the

[83] According to Luciano Guerci: "There was not in Galiani, nor will there ever be, a conscious pro-Jansenist attitude involving meditation and taking a stand on doctrinal issues. On the contrary, his intolerance and mockery for theological disputes and aversion to the fanaticism of the Jansenists can be constantly traced [...]. It was therefore anti-Curialism and anti-Jansenism that brought Galiani closer to the Bottari and the Niccolini: an attitude that can be traced back to a political dimension in which the moral tension, the vision of a purified Church and the anxiety for religious renewal typical of the young Ferdinando's Roman correspondents were significantly translated" (Guerci 1975a: 795). Galiani's rejection of Jansenism is clear: "Jansenists are as bad as all fanatics, and a fanatic is always anyone who makes a dogma of acting out of impulse, either you call it efficacious grace, or you call it cacodemonic, or you call it inspiration, or you call it destiny. The various names are made by the Jansenists, the Cybele Gauls, the Quakers, the Mohammedans, and Maratti. They are names. But renouncing one's calculating reason of yes and no is always the definition of fanaticism" (Ferdinando Galiani's letter to Francesco Sanseverino, Naples, 12 April 1777, BSNSP, XXX.C.12: folio 268, see Galiani 1975: 1144).

[84] See Ferdinando Galiani's letter to Madame d'Épinay, Naples, 13 December 1770, published in Galiani (1975: 1057); Galiani and d'Épinay (1992, vol. I: 315). The catalogue would be published in 1772, without Galiani's knowledge, under the title *Catalogo delle materie appartenenti al Vesuvio contenute nel Museo, con alcune brevi osservazioni* (*Catalogue*

collection, accompanied by a description, was sent to Rome to Pope Benedict XIV who, in return for the gift, conferred on him the benefices of the Amalfi rectory that gave 400 ducats of annual rent (Diodati 1788: 21–22).[85]

In December 1755, Galiani was appointed by the Sovereign as one of the 15 members of the *Accademia Ercolanese*, founded in the same year to study archaeological finds from the cities buried by the eruption of Vesuvius in 79 AD (Castaldi 1840; Pane 1975; Chiosi 1986a; Rao 1996).

of the materials belonging to Vesuvius contained in the Museum, with some brief remarks, Galiani 1772), and republished in 1779 (Galiani 1779a). See Duhem (1953). A manuscript entitled *Il Vesuvio* and addressed to Benedict XIV is in BSNSP, XXIX.C.5: folios 1–82; see also Ferdinando Galiani's letter to Benedict XIV, BSNSP, XXX. C. 12: folios 3–8. The publication was made without Galiani's knowledge: "You know that just twenty years ago I wrote a dissertation on Vesuvius, which I dedicated to Pope Lambertini, without printing it. Two years ago it was printed clandestinely in Florence with many errors and without my knowledge: this is the very booklet I sent to Grimm. This year I wanted to have this more corrected edition reprinted in Naples, but the consequences of my brother's death prevented me from doing so. I hope that a time will come when no one dying will embarrass me any more, and then I will do this second edition" (Ferdinando Galiani's letter to Madame d'Épinay, Naples, 25 February 1775, published in Galiani 1881a: Vol. II, 386; Galiani and d'Épinay 1996, vol IV: 228). See also Ferdinando Galiani's letter to Lorenzo Mehus, Naples, 15 December 1772, published in Galiani and Mehus (2002: 103), and Galiani (1975: 1057).

[85] See Ferdinando Galiani's letter to Pope Benedict XIV, BSNSP, XXX.C.12: folios 3–11. Diodati published the pontiff's letter of thanks dated 18 April 1755 (Diodati 1788: 21–22). He informed various correspondents of his new passsion. "I say, therefore, that ever since the last eruption last December I had the desire to present the Pope with a museum of Vesuvian stones to be sent to the Institute of Bologna [...] but in collecting and putting them together I found so many materials, so curious and forming such a united and linked system, that it was appropriate for me to make a small book on Vesuvius" (Ferdinando Galiani's letter to Antonio Cocchi, Naples, 15 April 1755, published in Venturi 1959a: 455). "I wanted to make a gift to His Holiness of Vesuvian stones, and I began to collect them. When they were put together, I discovered many curious things, which form almost a complete system, and I can pride myself on having seen more on Vesuvius than all the previous ones. It was therefore necessary to put these discoveries down on paper, and if they are printed, Your Excellency will be among the first to receive them from me" (Ferdinando Galiani's letter to Gaspare Cerati, Naples, 21 April 1755, published in Nicoletti 2008: 95). The correspondence confirms the benefit obtained from the Pope: "I am delighted with the happy outcome of your manoeuvres at the papal court, and that among other things, you have succeeded in fooling [coglionare] a Pope who was a curial in matters of interest. Bravo my Galiani. I do not doubt at all that if you send Etna to the Archbishop of Cologne, since you have dedicated Vesuvius to the Pope, he will make you his first court official. You have succeeded in the miracle of *Dic ut lapides isti panes fiant*" (Pietro Paolo Celesia's letter to Ferdinando Galiani, Genoa, 4 October 1755, published in Rotta 1973: 198).

It was Tanucci who proposed him[86] and Galiani devoted himself to the study of ancient paintings, collaborating on the compilation of a volume (Accademici Ercolanesi, 1757),[87] which, according to Diodati, earned him a pension of 150 *Ducats* per year, granted as a reward by the King (Diodati 1788: 23).[88] A trace of this activity by Galiani is the manuscript entitled *Pitture antiche che si conservano nella Real Villa di Portici, dissotterrate per ordine della Maestà del Re Carlo* (*Ancient paintings preserved in the Royal Villa of Portici, unearthed by order of the Majesty of King Charles*, Galiani, MS-16, dated 5 March 1756), which was ready for printing but never published and was recently rediscovered (D'Alconzo 2020a: 203; D'Alconzo 2020b; D'Alconzo 2020c), in which the abbot traced a history of the painting techniques used in antiquity, consulting ancient and contemporary sources and once again demonstrating not only his erudition, but an analytical method he had already pioneered in *Della Moneta*.

Galiani was by then a man of learning in the service of the monarchy, far from the civic involvement that both his uncle Celestino and Intieri had hoped for and promoted for his pupils, and his brother Berardo also followed the same path as an architect (Carrafiello 1995).

[86] See Bernardo Tanucci's letter to Ferdinando Galiani, Naples, 13 December 1755, BSNSP, XXXI. A. 8: folio 11. "The King has established an Academy of 15 subjects for the illustration of the monuments of Herculaneum, there is Mazzocchi, Partillo author of the beautiful book of the Via Appia, various learned young men of the country, and they have done me the honour of being part of it" (Ferdinando Galiani's letter to Gaspare Cerati, Naples, 23 November 1755, published in Nicoletti 2008: 105). Tanucci had moderately modified his opinion on *Della Moneta*: "Galiani's book is good, but I find in it some omissions and propositions that I do not find indubitable. Much Locke and much Machiavelli" (Bernardo Tanucci's letter to Domenico Caracciolo, Naples, 11 November 1756, published in Tanucci 1984: 169–170).

[87] This volume, on which Galiani had collaborated, was judged negatively by Johann Joachim Winckelmann, who also contested the conduct of the excavations and polemised several times with the theses of the Neapolitan scholars, in particular Berardo Galiani, Giacomo Martorelli and Alessio Simmaco Mazzocchi (see Guida 2010: 421; Strazzullo 1982; D'Alconzo 2019a). However, Winckelmann appreciated Ferdinando's erudition (letter of 9 May 1758, see Guida 2010: 418).

[88] In a letter to Madame d'Épinay, Galiani wrote: "I worked hard on the first volume of the plates" (Ferdinando Galiani's letter to Madame d'Épinay, Naples, 13 December 1770, published in Galiani 1975: 1057; Galiani and d'Épinay 1992, vol. I: 315). See also Bernardo Tanucci's letter to Ferdinando Galiani, Caserta, 20 January, 1758, BSNSP, XXXI. A.8: folio 15r. According to Furio Diaz this collaboration is doubtful (Galiani 1975: 1057), but is confirmed by the most recent studies, see D'Alconzo (2020a: 203); D'Alconzo (2020b); D'Alconzo 2020c. In the same period, according to Diodati, Galiani was commissioned by the academics to create a model for an equestrian statue of the Sovereign (Diodati 1788: 24).

An example of Galiani's research interests during this period is the incomplete essay *Degli uomini di statura straordinaria, e de' giganti* (*About Men of Extraordinary Stature and Giants*, Galiani, MS-17), written between 1757 and 1758, drafts of which are kept in the Library of the Neapolitan Society of National History.[89] The essay was inspired by the curiosity aroused by the presence in Naples at the end of 1757 of a young Irish traveller Cornelius Magrath, whose height was about 2 metres 30 centimetres.[90]

The event offered Galiani the opportunity to compile in a study "what is found in writers of all kinds about giants" (Galiani, MS-17: folios 164r–164v) in order to distinguish in this literature "which statures are clearly fabulous, which are less far-fetched, and which are certain and sure" (Galiani, MS-17: folio 166r). Galiani's interest ranged between anthropology and mythology, and provided a further opportunity to attack a certain kind of erudition lacking any analytical foundation,[91] and not without his usual irony.[92]

The myth of the giants was familiar in Neapolitan culture: it had been placed by Vico at the centre of his reflection on the early stages of human history, following the *Great Flood*, to describe the extreme conditions of violence and bestiality that, according to the Neapolitan philosopher,

[89] "The work, begun perhaps as early as 1757, was already being printed long before it was completed in 1758 [...]. Of it, therefore, only the introduction and the first three chapters have come down to us in two copies of drafts (columns and pages) with hand-written corrections, plus a long fragment of the fourth chapter, partly in drafts (only two columns), partly in manuscript (nine pages, some hand-written, some copied)" (Nicolini 1918b:196, BSNSP, XXXI. C. 12, folios 164r–203r.). Another part of the manuscript (a few pages) is contained in another volume (XXXI. C. 8, folios 16v–18v).

[90] Galiani himself reports its measurement as "eight Neapolitan palms and seven fingers, measured on 17 December 1757" (Galiani, MS-17: folio 164r).

[91] He attacked Abbot Jean-Marie de La Marque de Tilladet, "who, passionate about such beautiful things as giants seemed to him to be, is not content to meet some of them by misfortune, but finds them everywhere, welcomes them, even intrudes them into every foundation of monarchies and colonies, uses them for all his needs and offers them ready to serve any scholar in need" (Galiani, MS-17: folio 168r; see De Tilladet de La Marque 1718: 158–163, see also Céard 2007).

[92] "If our style is in some parts funny and playful, we ask the reader not to blame us. The subject matter itself does not require such seriousness, and this discourse is only meant to be read in idle hours for people with nothing to do. Finally, when all is lacking, *ridentum dicere verum: quid vetat?*" (Galiani, MS-17: folio 170r).

characterised primitive humanity.[93] According to Vico, after the Flood part of the surviving humanity renounced the true religion of their common father Noah and dissolved marriages and dispersed into the great forests. In this savage condition, mothers abandoned their children, who grew up without hearing a human voice and assuming gigantic stature because "to exert themselves to penetrate the great forest, grown extremely dense from the flood, would flex and contract their muscles in these exertions, and thus absorb nitrous salts into their bodies in greater abundance. They would be quite without that fear of gods, fathers and teachers which chills and benumbs even the most exuberant in childhood. They must therefore have grown robust, vigorous, excessively big in brawn and bone, to the point of becoming giants" (Vico 1744 [1948]: 101). For Vico, gigantism was therefore the effect of a primordial and savage state, from which the Jews, who continued to follow the ancient religion of Noah, had been immune.[94] By civilisation, the "cleanliness of body and fear of gods and of fathers [..] the giants diminished to our normal stature" (Vico 1744 [1948]: 102). The presence of these giants in human history was testified, according to Vico, by language and mythology (Mazzola 1994).

Unlike Vico, who is not mentioned in the manuscript but whose work was certainly known to him,[95] Galiani did not attribute any real and historical significance to the giants, considering only their presence in popular culture. "All less cultured peoples and all the rude and barbarous centuries," he wrote, "are equally filled and pervaded by the belief in giants.

[93] "By long residence and burial of their dead they came to found and divide the first dominions of the earth, whose lords were called giants, a Greek word meaning children of the earth, i.e. descendants of those who have been buried" (Vico 1744 [1948]: 8).

[94] "The entire first world of men must be divided into two kinds: the first, men of normal size, which includes the Hebrews only; the second, giants, who were the founders of the gentile nations. Of the giants there were in turn two kinds: the first, the sons of Earth, or nobles, from whom, as being giants in the full sense of the term, the age of giants took its name (and it is these whom sacred history defines as strong famous and powerful men of the age); the second, less properly so called, those other giants who were subjugated [by the former]" (Vico 1744 [1948]: 103).

[95] According to Fausto Nicolini, Galiani's essay on giants was strongly influenced by the *Scienza Nuova* (Nicolini 1918b: 196–202), while for Furio Diaz, Galiani's reflection has strong affinities with Hobbes' thought (Diaz 1975a: xxxiii–xxxiv). For Marco Catucci, "Galiani occupies no place in the history of Vichism: Vico was a metaphysician, Galiani an empiricist whose anti-Enlightenment polemic consisted mainly of criticising the metaphysical residues that invalidated the theories of his French friends and their Italian emulators. If one really considered it indispensable to find an antecedent, one could point to Galilei, with his scientific method, which had nothing to do with Vico" (Catucci 1986: 11).

Man, in his crude and natural state of corruption, is a credulous, cruel and superstitious animal; and these three vices are so deeply rooted in him, that they almost form his definition. All three of these faults are represented in the idea of giants, pleasing on the one hand the credulity of a bizarre and novel imagination, and on the other hand the natural cruelty of man, who takes pleasure in thinking how bloodthirsty and deadly giants are, as well as their strength. Finally, superstition, being but a cowardice and fear derived from no just principle, has naturally led to believing giants and fearing them" (Galiani, MS-17: folio 170r). Every nation had found in the myth of the giants, as in "all other wondrous things a necessary adornment" of its origins (Galiani, MS-17: folio 176r). And Jewish culture was no exception (contrary to what Vico argued), for "rabbis and Talmudists raised a forest of fables in the very field of truth, and were the most lying commentators on the truest of all books, well disposed to tell fables about giants, making this seem to be a particular passion of the Jews" (Galiani, MS-17: folio 171v).[96]

Through the myth of the giants, Galiani recognised the characteristics of human nature: "wicked, proud, cruel and full of every vice and offence: a clear indication of the inner feeling and knowledge [...] that man, in his corrupt nature, does as much evil as he cannot and does not have the strength, and that it is the same to increase their power or to increase their perversity" (Galiani, MS-17: folio 180r). And in the giants, Galiani read the founding act of society: "It is therefore certain that the first to emerge from the state of nature, i.e. from equality, had to be the strongest men, who, being equally more ferocious and more vicious, had to be the first to subjugate the weaker ones and to plunder them", but the subjugated men "realised that the strength of the many united is always greater than that of any individual, [and] formed the consensus of forces and the conspiracy of minds to sustain themselves, which is called society. Thus force generated reason. [...] Every society, having in itself a representative force, was able to subject to the duties of equality those who, feeling stronger and more powerful, wanted to wrong them. Hence reason is the force of the whole, directed to support the good of the whole, and to oppose the

[96] According to Vico: "the entire original human race was divided into two species: one of giants, the other of men of normal stature; the former gentiles, the latter Hebrews. Also that this difference can only have come about as the result of the savage education of the former and the human education of the latter. Hence that the Hebrews had a different origin from that of the gentiles" (Vico 1744 [1948]: 62).

specific forces that try to destroy or disturb it" (Galiani, MS-17: folio 18v). And again, reason was invoked to dispel lies because "men cannot be persuaded of uniformity in the laws of nature, and that ancient times were like the present, and distant countries like their neighbours. Therefore fable and falsehood always lurks, and makes its room in the times, or hidden places, and when the light of history or the attention of travellers illuminates and illustrates the times or hidden places, it quickly flees and goes further away. In Homer's time, the fables were set in Sicily and Campania, countries then believed to be very distant from Greece, in Augustus' time they were in the Indies beyond the Ganges, and now they are in the Magellanic lands. They will also flee from there and go either underground or to the Moon" (Galiani, MS-17: folio 177v).

The distance from Vico is remarkable and the points of contact with Enlightenment thought are evident, a sign that Galiani's thinking, despite his scholarly studies and occasional curiosities that characterised his intellectual engagement, was not extraneous to the themes that were at the heart of the movement and that found their point of reference in the *Encyclopédie*.

The death of Prospero Lambertini, Pope Benedict XIV, in May 1758, forced Galiani to leave his refuge of scholarship (which he himself calls "involuntary idleness") not only to pay homage to the figure of the deceased pontiff, but also to extol the political model he had embodied. In July 1758, the Neapolitan abbot published the oration *Delle lodi di papa Benedetto XIV* (*In praise of Pope Benedict XIV*, Galiani 1758), which can be regarded as a portrait of the virtues of the ideal ruler and an example of good government.[97] "Those who study," Galiani began, "the ancient histories of the popes, many will find that they were nephews or related to more ancient popes, and others will be of noble lineage or very rich family, and not a few will finally be seen to have been elevated by their sovereigns if not to the highest dignity, at least brought to the path, [but] very few and almost none will be found who alone, armed with their own virtue, reached [the papal throne]" (Galiani 1758: 9). This was the case of Prospero Lambertini, who had "no uncle, no close relation as pontiff, prince or cardinal, nor among his ancestors other than the old glory of arms and wars [...]. No support of powerful relatives in Rome, no recent

[97] Galiani defined *Delle lodi* as his best work (Ferdinando Galiani's letter to Madame d'Épinay, Naples, 13 December 1770, published in Galiani 1881a: vol. I, 316; Galiani and d'Épinay 1992, vol. I: 316).

merit of his relatives in that Court, lastly no riches at birth that paved or shortened his path" (Galiani 1758: 8). A man who had overcome every obstacle solely on the basis of his own virtues: "truth in words, greatness in thoughts, simplicity in manners, candour of mind, temperance in all actions, uprightness of will, honesty in acting, prudence in commanding, supreme doctrine, and incomparable wisdom" (Galiani 1758: 11). In contrast to those who laboured to seek power and hold on to it, Benedict XIV did not prepare his good fortune, but went along with it and "waited for it patiently, almost sleeping and unconcerned" (Galiani 1758: 11). Lambertini revealed these qualities, according to Galiani, in his delicate role as *Promoter of the Faith*, with the task of bringing arguments that called into question the virtues and miracles of candidates for canonisation during a canonical process. A task that required balancing skills because it had to reconcile "the common interest of the universal Church [...], the interest of the venerable man himself, to whom no greater prominence can be given than to make him pass under the most severe scrutiny; the interest of Christian morality leaning on the opposite side of the balance; the interest of all the saints, whose honours are sought to be communicated; the interest of God, whose first and full devotion is the first and only that those who resemble him can in some form share" (Galiani 1758: 13–14).

Because of these qualities, despite the division that opposed the different parties in the Roman Curia, Cardinal Lambertini was chosen as pontiff, and even in that office: "he was a great prince, but not in placid and tranquil times: he was in the midst of the tremors of those wars that shook Europe from its hinges and lacerated unhappy Italy, and cruelly afflicted and damaged its state, while epidemics of the most necessary animals, deadly plagues, violent tremors, and unusual floods ravaged every province of his country. He was an excellent pastor of the universal Church, but not at a fortunate age: he had to govern it when countless new sects and unprecedented errors swarmed from all sides, when Catholicism was burning with internecine discord, when respect for the supreme pontificate, the privileges of the ecclesiastics, and his authority were beginning to be regarded in many parts with hostility. He was a learned teacher, but not in ignorant and blind centuries: achieved the name in the brightest light of letters in the greatest fervour of the press, of writing, of controversies, of studies, of universities. He was a saint, but not in the earliest centuries of recent and flourishing Christian virtue: he knew how to be so in the midst of grievous corruption. He was a most vigilant bishop, but not among the first pastors of the Church, when the ferocity of persecutions, and the opposing vices of heathenism sufficiently inspired Christians with the fervour and example of holiness of morals. He was a most ardent patron of all the arts and sciences, but not in the happy age of Leo X. He had the pain of having to do so in ours, where, in spite of every human effort, the fatal order of worldly things wants Italy to be the beginning of their decadence" (Galiani 1758: 19–20).

But his greatest quality as a sovereign was the "virtue of refraining from doing [*di non fare*]. That of which I say is a most difficult science, a companion of sublime talents and sound advice, which even the greatest men have often lacked. Through it we know how much is to be expected from the natural medicine of time, and how much is to be forgiven from the indocility or heated imagination of men. And it is made a science all the more precious, the more obscure and less guided by the prize of popular acclaim. And indeed everyone can see that, while so many speak of the deeds Pope Benedict vigorously performed, almost no one remembers the many he prudently refrained from doing" (Galiani 1758: 33–34).[98]

The "do-nothing" thus became for Galiani a form of policy dictated by prudent waiting, a view that contrasted sharply with the activism of the reformers and placed him even further away from Intieri's vision.

The solemn commitment to the death of a Pope, who had played an important role in the young abbot's life, was followed by the occasional writings and works of disengagement, in a continuous alternation of the serious and the facetious. The occasion was offered by a social event celebrated every New Year's Eve during which the Ladies and Cicisbei were drawn by lot, a tradition that Galiani judged: "noble in its origin, useful in its constitution, pious in theory, meritorious in practice" (*Orazione recitata in una assemblea nel capo dell'anno 1759 in occasione di tirare a sorte i cicisbei e le cicisbee*, *Oration delivered in an assembly at the start of the year 1759 on the occasion of the drawing of lots for cicisbei and Ladies*, Galiani 1759 [1825]: 7).[99] In the short work, Galiani ironically returned to the theme of cicisbeism, considered a useful institution that alleviated the "torment that a young man suffers in having a squalid old woman beside

[98] Galiani refers above all to the tolerant position taken by Benedict XIV in relation to the Jansenist movement that had found great consensus among the clergy in France and threatened a schism. The Pope therefore avoided rigidly applying the bull *Unigenitus* with which, in 1713, Clement XI had condemned 101 propositions contained in the *Nouveau Testament en français avec des Réflexions morales sur chaque verset* (1677) by Pasquier Quesnel.

[99] The text circulated in manuscript and was printed between 1787–1788, followed by two other Neapolitan editions in 1825 and 1842.

him, or that a smart young woman suffers in having a shabby old lover or husband beside her", bonds that not even death could alleviate, since "the beneficial use of certain *aqua vitae* has been lacking" (Galiani 1759 [1825]: 11). Cicisbeism was thus a useful social institution that "balances and counterbalances the opposing ingredients of love" (Galiani 1759 [1825]: 10). The ceremony of the drawing of lots leads - according to Galiani - the social figure of the cicisbeo to its extreme consequences, in that it eliminates any choice dictated by sentiment, preference or opportunism: "ennoble yourselves by being initiated into our famous custom, make yourselves useful to society with unlimited and casual love; let pity be kindled in you by the meditation of resignation; mortify yourselves by living" (Galiani 1759 [1825]: 12).[100] Galiani's writing had a fine ironic tone, and it is difficult to separate the serious subject from the disguised criticism that the Neapolitan abbot was addressing to the customs of his time.

The period of disengagement and scholarship came to an abrupt end in the winter of 1759, when Minister Tanucci entrusted Galiani with the delicate position of Embassy Secretary in the Kingdom of France.

References[101]

Manuscript Sources

Broggia, C. A. MSCAB. Del pubblico interesse economico, politico, morale, di stato, e di commercio. Sostenuto e difeso contro gli errori, e le insidie de' falsi dotti. Dissertazioni varie, del tutto utili e necessarie per la civile scienza: Di C. A. Broggia. Prodotte in occasione di farsi gli esami, le risposte, e le note critiche su di un'opera intitolata: Della Moneta libri cinque, impressa in Napoli nel 1750, di autore anonimo. Manuscript kept in the Kress Library - Harvard University.

Galiani, F. MS-15. Diario 1751–1752. Manuscript kept in the Biblioteca Società Napoletana di Storia Patria, XXXI. C. 22.

Galiani, F. MS-16. Pitture antiche che si conservano nella Real Villa di Portici, dissotterrate per ordine della Maestà del Re Carlo, Manuscript kept in the Biblioteca Società Napoletana di Storia Patria, XXXI. C. 12.

[100] For other interpretations see Bizzocchi (2008: 210–211); Novi Chavarria (2008: 8–85); Mauro (2017a: 75–77).

[101] The abbreviations "s.l." and "s.n." stand for the Latin terms *sine loco* (without place of publication) and *sine nomine* (without name of publisher).

Galiani, F. MS-17. Degli uomini di grandezza straordinaria e de' giganti. Discorso. Manuscript kept in the Biblioteca Società Napoletana di Storia Patria, XXXI. C. 8, folios 16v–18v; XXXI C 12, folios 164r–203r.

Primary Sources

Abbé de Saint-Pierre, C. I. Castel de. (1733). Discours contre l'augmentation des monnoyes et en faveur des annuitez. In *Ouvrage politique par M. l'Abbé de Saint Pierre*, Rotterdam: Jean Daniel Beman, Tome II: 199–230.

Accademici Ercolanesi. (1757). Le pitture antiche di Ercolano e contorni incise con qualche spiegazione, tomo I. Naples: Regia Stamperia.

Argelati, F. (ed.). (1750). *De monetis Italiae variorum illustrium virorum dissertationes, quarum pars nunc primum in lucem prodit*. Milan: in regia Curia ex Aedibus Palatinis.

Belloni, G. (1750). *Del commercio dissertazione del sig. marchese Girolamo Belloni*. Rome: Pagliarini.

Boccaccio, G. [2003]. *The Decameron*, Translated with an Introduction and Notes by G. H. McWilliam. New York: Penguin.

Broggia, C. A. [2004]. *Il Banco ed il Monte de' pegni. Del lusso*, with the introducion by De Rosa, L. and Graziani, A., edited by R. Patalano. Naples: La Città del Sole.

Capello, P. G. (1752). *Nuovo trattato del modo di regolare la moneta*. Venice: Baseggio.

Carli, G. R. (1751). *Dell'origine e del commercio della moneta e dell'instituzione delle zecche d'Italia dalla decadenza dell'impero sino al secolo decimo settimo*. All'Haja [The Hague, but Venice]: s.n.

Carli, G.R. (1784). *Opere*, tomo II. Milan: Monastero di Sant'Ambrogio.

Cary, J. (1757). *Storia del commercio della Gran Brettagna scritta da John Cary con un ragionamento sul commercio in universale, e alcune annotazioni riguardanti l'economia del nostro regno*, edited by Genovesi A., vol. I. Naples: Benedetto Gessari.

Costantini, G. (1751). *Delle monete in senso pratico, e morale. Ragionamento diviso in sette capitoli, dedicato a quelli, che prender si vorranno la pena di leggerlo*. Venice: Occhi.

Costantini, G. (1753). *Caso di monete imprestate. Dialogo*. Venice: Bertoli.

Costantini, G. (1754) (ed.). *Delle monete, controversia agitata tra due celebri scrittori oltramontani, i signori Melon, e Du Tot*. Venice: Zatta.

D'Argenson, R. L. de Voyer de Paulmy. (1751). Lettre à l'auteur du Journal œconomique au sujet de la Dissertation sur le commerce de M. le Marquis Belloni, *Journal Œconomique*, April 1751, pp. 107–117.

De Tilladet de La Marque, J.-M. (1718). Sur les géants. *Histoire de l'Académie royale des inscriptions et belles-lettres: depuis son établissement jusqu'a present*, vol. 1. La Haye: chez la veuve d'Abr. Troyel, pp. 158–163.

Diderot, D. (1955). *Correspondence*, edited by G. Roth, 13 vols. Paris: Editions de minuit.

Diodati, L. (1788). *Vita dell'abate Ferdinando Galiani*. Naples: Orsino.

Duhamel du Monceau, H. L. (1753). *Traité de la Conservation des Grains et en particulier du Froment*. Paris: Guérin & Delatour.

Dutot, N. (1738). *Réflexions politiques sur les finances et le commerce*. La Haye: Vaillant-Prevost.

Fabrini, G. (1750). *Dell'indole e qualità naturali e civili della moneta e de' principi istorici e naturali de' contratti. Dissertazioni*. Rome: Pagliarini.

Galiani, F. [1751] [published anonymous, with date of 1750]. *Della moneta. Libri cinque*, Naples: Giuseppe Raimondi.

Galiani, F. (1758). *Delle lodi di papa Benedetto XIV. Orazione*. Naples: Giuseppe Raimondi.

Galiani, F. (1759) [1825]. *Orazione recitata in una assemblea nel capo dell'anno 1759 in occasione di tirare a sorte i cicisbei e le cicisbee*. Naples: Seguin.

Galiani, F. (1772). *Catalogo delle materie appartenenti al Vesuvio contenute nel Museo, con alcune brevi osservazioni. Opera del celebre autore de' Dialoghi sul commercio de' grani*. London [but Florence]: s.n.

Galiani, F. (1779a). Osservazioni sopra il Vesuvio dell'abate Ferdinando Galiani. In *Dei vulcani e monti ignivomi più noti, e distintamente del Vesuvio, Osservazioni fisiche e notizie istoriche di uomini insigni di vari tempi, raccolte con diligenza e divise in due tomi*. Livorno: Calderon e Faine, Tomo I, pp. lxi–lxx, 1–149.

Galiani, F. (1780). *Della moneta. Libri cinque. Edizione seconda*. Naples: Stamperia Simoniana.

Galiani, F. (1881a). *Écrivains du XVIII siècle – Correspondance avec Madame d'Épinay, Madame Necker, Madame Geoffrin etc., Diderot, Grimm, d'Alembert, de Sartine, d'Holbach, etc. Nouvelle édition, entièrement rétablie d'après les textes originaux, augmentée de tous les passages supprimés et d'un grand nombre de lettres inédites, avec une étude sur sa vie et les oeuvres de Galiani*, edited by L. Perey, G. Maugras, 2 voll. Paris: Calmann Levy.

Galiani, F. (1975). *Opere di Ferdinando Galiani*, edited by F. Diaz e L. Guerci, in *Letteratura italiana. Storia e testi. Illuministi italiani*, tomo VI. Milan-Naples: Ricciardi.

Galiani, F., Bottari, G.G. (1972). *Il carteggio Galiani-Bottari (1751–1759)*, edited by L. Felici. Rome: Fratelli Palombi.

Galiani, F., Cerati, G. (2008). *Carteggio (1749–1758)*, edited by G. Nicoletti, Naples: Bibliopolis.

Galiani, F., d'Épinay, L. (1992). *Correspondance. Vol. I (1769–1770)*, présentation de G. Dulac, texte établi et annoté par D. Maggetti, en collaboration avec G. Dulac. Paris: Les Editions Desjonquères.

Galiani, F., d'Épinay, L. (1996). *Correspondance. Vol. IV (Juin 1773–Mai 1775)*, présentation de Georges Dulac, texte établi et annoté par Daniel Maggetti, en collaboration avec Georges Dulac, Paris: Les Editions Desjonquères.

Galiani, F., Mehus, L. (2002). *Carteggio (1753–1786)*, edited by G. Nicoletti, Naples: Bibliopolis.

Genovesi, A. (1743). *Elementa Metaphysicae in usum privatorum adolescentium mathematicumin morem adornata. Pars prior. Ontosofia*. Naples: Gessari.

Genovesi, A. (1745). *Elementa physicae conscripta in usus academicos a Petro van Musschenbroeck, quibus nunc primum in gratiam studiosae iuventutis accedunt ab alienis manibus ubique auctaria et notae, disputatio physico-historica de rerum corporearum origine, ac demum de rebus coelestibus tractatus*. Naples: Palumbo.

Genovesi, A. (1753). Discorso sopra il vero fine delle lettere e delle scienze. In U. Montelatici, *Ragionamento sopra i mezzi più necessarj per far rifiorire l'agricoltura del p. abate d. Ubaldo Montelatici della congregazione laterarense colla Relazione dell'erba orobanche detta volgarmente succiamele e del modo di estirparla del celebre Pier-Antonio Micheli con un discorso di Antonio Genovesi Regio Professore d'Etica sopra il vero fine delle lettere e delle scienze. Il tutto dedicato al signor Bartolomeo Intieri*. Naples: Giovanni di Simone, pp. iii–cvi.

Genovesi, A. (1757). *Storia del commercio della Gran Brettagna scritta da John Cary mercatante di Bristol. Tradotta in nostra volgar lingua da Pietro Genovesi giureconsulto napoletano, con un Ragionamento sul commercio in universale, e alcune annotazioni riguardanti l'economia del nostro Regno di Antonio Genovesi R. Professore di Commercio e di Meccanica nella Cattedra Intieriana*, tomi 2. Naples: Benedetto Gessari.

Genovesi, A. [1763] [2008]. Dialogo fra il Galiani, il Bembo ed il Fraggianni sulla riforma degli studi in Napoli. In Genovesi, A, *Dialoghi e altri scritti intorno alle Lezioni di Commercio*, edited by E. Pii, Naples: Istituto Italiano per gli Studi Filosofici, pp. 398–405.

Genovesi, A. (1767). *Delle lezioni di commercio o sia d'economia civile da leggersi nella Cattedra Interiana dell'ab.Genovesi regio cattedratico. Parte seconda pel secondo semestre*. Naples: Fratelli Di Simone.

Genovesi, A. [1997]. "Vita di Antonio Genovese". In F. Venturi (ed.) *Illuministi italiani. Riformatori* napoletani, vol. II, tomo I. Milan: Ricciardi - Mondadori, pp. 47–83.

Intieri, B. (1754). *Della perfetta conservazione del grano. Discorso di Bartolomeo Intieri*. Naples: Giuseppe Raimondi.

Intieri, B. (1770). *L'Art de conserver les Grains, par Barthelemy Inthiery. Ouvrage traduit de l'Italien, par les soins de M. D.N.E.* [Louis Joseph Bellepierre de Neuve-Église]. Paris: Saugrain le jeune.

Lami, G. (1752). [Della Moneta Review]. In *Novelle Letterarie pubblicate in Firenze*, Anno MDCCLII, Tomo XIII, n. 52, pp. 825–830.

Locke, J. (1751). *Ragionamenti sopra la moneta, l'interesse del denaro, le finanze e il commercio, scritti e pubblicati in diverse occasioni dal signor Giovanni Locke. Tradotti la prima volta dall'inglese con varie annotazioni*, 2 tomi. Florence: Andrea Bonducci.

Maffei, S. (1744). *Dell'impiego del danaro libri tre*. Verona: Giannalberto Tumermani.

Montanari, G. (1683a) [1750], *Trattato del valore delle monete in tutti gli Stati*, in F. Argelati, *Tractatus de monetis Italiae appendix seu de monetis Italiae*, pars III, 1750, Milan: Regia Curia ex Aedibus Palatinis, pp. 1–16.

Montanari, G. (1683b) [1759]. *La Zecca in Consulta di Stato del dottor Geminano Montanari, pubblico professore di matematica nella Università di Padova. Trattato mercantile*, in F. Argelati, *Tractatus de monetis Italiae appendix seu de monetis Italiae*, pars VI, 1759, Milan: Regia Curia ex Aedibus Palatinis, pp. 5–70.

Muratori L. A. (1749). *Della pubblica felicità oggetto de' buoni principi*, Lucca [but Venice]: s. n.

Muratori, L. A. [1750a]. "De moneta, sive jure condendi nummos. Dissertatio", in Argelati, F. (ed.) *De monetis Italiae variorum illustrium virorum Dissertationes, quarum nunc primum in lucem prodit*, IV Vol. Milan: Regia Curia, pp. 1–98.

Muratori, L. A. [1750b]. "De diversis pecuniae generibus, quae apud veteres in usu fuere. Dissertatio", in Argelati, F. (ed.) *De monetis Italiae variorum illustrium virorum Dissertationes, quarum nunc primum in lucem prodit*, IV Vol. Milan: Regia Curia, pp. 99–135.

Neri P. [1751]. *Osservazioni sopra il prezzo legale delle monete e la difficoltà di prefinirlo e sostenerlo*. Milan: Malatesta.

Neri, P. [1759]. Appendice alle *Osservazioni*. In F. Argelati, (ed.), *De monetis Italiae variorum illustrium virorum dissertationes, quarum pars nunc primum in lucem prodit*. Milan: Regia Curia ex Aedibus Palatinis, Vol. V, pp. 147–180.

Origlia, G.G. (1754). *Istoria dello studio di Napoli*, vol. II. Naples: Simone.

Pagnini, G. (1751). *Saggio sopra il giusto pregio delle cose, la giusta valuta della moneta e sopra il commercio dei Romani*. In G. Pagnini, A. Tavanti, (eds), Locke, J. *Ragionamenti sopra la moneta l'interesse del danaro le finanze e il commercio scritti e pubblicati in diverse occasioni dal signor Giovanni Locke tradotti per la prima volta dall'inglese con varie annotazioni*. Florence: Bonducci, vol II, pp. [1]–116.

Tanucci, B. (1980b). *Epistolario*, vol. II (1746–1752), R.P. Coppini, Nieri, R. (eds.), Rome: Edizioni Storia e Letteratura.

Tanucci, B. (1984). *Epistolario*, vol. IV (1756–1757), L. Del Bianco (ed.), Rome: Edizioni Storia e Letteratura.

Vico, G.B. (1744) [1948]. *Principi di Scienza Nuova d'intorno alla Comune Natura delle Nazioni, in questa terza impressione. Dal medesimo Autore in un gran numero di luoghi corretta, schiarita, e notabilmente accresciuta*. Naples: Stamperia Muziana. English translation *The New Science of Giambattista Vico*, by T. Goddard Bergin, Ithaca: Cornell University Press, 1948.

Secondary Sources

Amato, M. (1999). Il bivio della moneta. Problemi monetari e pensiero del denaro nel Settecento italiano. Milan: Egea.

Apih, E. (1977). Gian Rinaldo Carli. In *Dizionario Biografico degli Italiani* - Volume 20, Rome: Treccani, *ad vocem*.

Archivi. (1989). *Archivi dell'aristocrazia fiorentina. Mostra di documenti privati restaurati a cura della Sovrintendenza Archivistica per la Toscana tra il 1977 e il 1989*. Florence: Biblioteca Medicea Laurenziana.

Baldini, U. (1982). Antonio Cocchi. In *Dizionario Biografico degli Italiani* - Volume 26, Rome: Treccani, *ad vocem*.

Bizzocchi, R. (2008). *Cicisbei. Morale privata e identità nazionale in Italia*. Bari: Laterza.

Caffiero, M. (1979). Gaspare Cerati. In *Dizionario Biografico degli Italiani* - Volume 23, Rome: Treccani, *ad vocem*.

Caracciolo, A. (1970). Girolamo Belloni. In *Dizionario Biografico degli Italiani* - Volume 7, Rome: Treccani, *ad vocem*.

Carrafiello, T. (1995). Berardo Galiani intendente di architettura (1724–1774). *Archivio Storico per le Province Napoletane*, Anno CXIII, pp. 245–379.

Castaldi, G. (1840). *Della Regale Accademia Ercolanese dalla sua fondazione sinora con un cenno biografico de' suoi soci ordinari*. Naples: Porcelli.

Catucci, M. (1984). Antonio Genovesi e Ferdinando Galiani. *Esperienze Letterarie*, anno IX, N. 4, pp. 57–62.

Catucci, M. (1986). *Galianea. Ferdinando Galiani tra letteratura ed economia*, Rome: Bulzoni.

Céard, J. (2007). Les géants selon Dom Calmet. In M. Closson, M. White-Le Goff (eds.) *Les Géants entre mythe et literature*. Arras: Artois Presses Université, pp. 37–46.

Chiosi, E. (1986a). Il Regno dal 1734 al 1799. In G. Galasso, R. Romeo (eds.), *Storia del Mezzogiorno*, Napoli: Edizioni del Sole, Vol. IV, pp. 384–396.

D'Alconzo, P. (2019a). Parole e immagini. La diffusione delle antichità vesuviane negli anni di Carlo di Borbone: iniziative istituzionali, carteggi, riproduzioni grafiche. In P.G. Guzzo, M.R. Esposito, N. Ossanna Cavadini, (eds.), *Ercolano e Pompei. Visioni di una scoperta*, Milan: Skira, pp. 54–73.

D'Alconzo, P. (2020a). Ferdinando Galiani e le antichità, tra istituzioni, collezionismo e mercato. In P. Giulierini, A. Coralini, E. Calandra, (eds.), *Miniere Della*

Memoria, Scavi in archivi, depositi e biblioteche, Naples: All'Insegna del Giglio, pp. 201–233.

D'Alconzo, P. (2020b). Rileggere la pittura antica attraverso una fonte manoscritta inedita: Ferdinando Galiani e i dipinti del Museo Ercolanese. In P. Giulierini, A. Coralini, Sampaolo, V. (eds.), *Picta fragmenta. Rileggendo la pittura vesuviana, Atti del Convegno Internazionale* (Napoli, 13–15 settembre 2018). Milan: Silvana Editorale.

D'Alconzo, P. (2020c). Egli è il primo de' Sovrani, ch'abbia fatto uno scavamento così vasto, durevole, e dovizioso: scavo e pubblicazione dei reperti vesuviani in un manoscritto galianeo del 1756, *Studi e ricerche del Parco archeologico di Pompei*, 43, 2020, pp. 103–123.

Del Negro, P. (1998). Marco Foscarini. In *Dizionario Biografico degli Italiani*, volume 49, Rome: Treccani, *ad vocem*.

Diaz, F. (1975a). Introduzione. In Galiani, F. *Opere,* edited by F. Diaz, L.Guerci, *Letteratura italiana. Storia e testi. Illuministi italiani*, tomo VI, Milan-Naples: Ricciardi, pp. ix–cvi.

Duhem, J. (1953). Bibliotheca Vesuvina d'après le manuscrit dressé par Galiani pour le pape Benoit XIV. *Bullettin du bibliophile et du bibliothécaire*, n. 2, pp. 59–73.

Einaudi, L. (1953). *Saggi bibliografici e storici intorno alle dottrine economiche*, Rome: Edizioni Storia e Letteratura.

Felici, L. (1972). *Il carteggio Galiani-Bottari (1751–1759)*. Rome: Fratelli Palombi.

Ferrone, V. (1995). *The Intellectual Roots of the Italian Enlightenment: Newtonian Science, Religion, and Politics in the Early Eighteenth Century*. Atlantic Highlands: Humanities Press.

Flandreau M. (ed.). (2003). *Money Doctors. The Experience of International Financial Advising 1850–2000*. London - New York: Routledge.

Flori, M. C. (2009). Lorenzo Mehus. In *Dizionario biografico degli italiani*, vol. 73, Rome: Istituto dell' Enciclopedia Italiana, *ad vocem*.

Guerci, L. (1975a). Epistolario. Preliminari. In F.Diaz, L. Guerci, (eds), Galiani, F. *Opere, Letteratura italiana. Storia e testi. Illuministi italiani*, tomo VI, Milan-Naples: Ricciardi, pp. 783–814.

Guida, A. (2010). Un omaggio in greco di Winckelmann a Galiani. *Eikasmos*, 21, pp. 417–422.

Gullino, G. (2020). Andrea Tron. In *Dizionario Biografico degli Italiani*, volume 97, Rome: Treccani, *ad vocem*.

Iovine, R. (1999). Il trattato Della moneta di Ferdinando Galiani. La dialettica politica a favore e contro la pubblicazione. *Frontiera d'Europa*, 1999, n. 1, pp. 173–236.

Iovine, R. (2001). Una cattedra per Genovesi nella crisi della cultyura moderna a Napoli. *Frontiera d'Europa*, 2001, n. 1–2, pp. 359–532.

Kemmerer, D. L. (1993). Princeton's Money Doctor: Professor E. W. Kemmerer and the Gold Standard. *The Princeton University Library Chronicle*, Vol. 55, No. 1, pp. 8–42.

Malbranque, B. (2021). Foreword to the General Directing of Trade Cannot Be a Science: D'Argenson's 1751 Commentary Essay and the Response to It. *Econ Journal Watch* 18(2), September 2021, pp. 257–277.

Marconcini, F. (1931). Momento mercantilista settecentesco: la dissertazione sopra il commercio di Girolamo Belloni, banchiere romano. *Rivista internazionale di scienze sociali*, s. 3, II, pp. 104–180. 393–416.

Mauro, A. (2017a). *Un philosophe des Lumières entre Naples et Paris: Ferdinando Galiani (1728–1787)*. Thèse de Doctorate de l'Université Toulouse le Mirail - Toulouse II.

Mazzola, R. (1994). I giganti in Vico. *Bollettino del Centro di Studi Vichiani*, Anno XXIV–XXV, pp. 49–78.

Michels, R. (1916). Controversie sulla prima cattedra di scienza economica. *Rivista Italiana di Sociologia*, anno XX, fasc. V–VI, settembre-dicembre 1916, pp. 600–605.

Nicoletti, G. (1985). Il primo soggiorno fiorentino di Ferdinando Galiani e il suo carteggio inedito con Anton Francesco Gori. In *Studi di filologia e critica offerti dagli allievi a Lanfranco Caretti*, Rome: Salerno editrice, vol. I, pp. 355–401.

Nicoletti, G. (1992). Un altro recupero galianeo: il carteggio inedito con Antonio Niccolini (1752–1755). *Studi Italiani*, IV (1992), 7, pp. 149–188.

Nicoletti, G. (ed.). (2008). Galiani F., Cerati, G. *Carteggio (1749–1758)*. Naples: Bibliopolis.

Nicoletti, G. (2011). Fra erudizione, antiquaria e amministrazione: Ferdinando Galiani e gli amici di Toscana. In C. Viola (ed.), *Le carte vive. Epistolari e carteggi nel Settecento*, Atti del I Convegno internazionale del Centro di Ricerca sugli Epistolari del Settecento, Rome: Edizioni di Storia e Letteratura, pp. 135–160.

Nicolini, F. (1918b). La puerizia e l'adolescenza dell'abate Galiani (1735–1745). Notize, lettere, versi, documenti, *Archivio Storico per le Province Napoletane*, Nuova serie Anno IV, XLIII. dell'intera collezione, Vol. IV, pp. 105–132.

Novi Chavarria, E. (2008). Forme e spazi della sociabilità aristocratica napoletana nel Settecento. In R. Bizzocchi, A. Pacini, *Sociabilità aristocratica in età moderna. Il caso genovese: paradigmi, interpretazioni e confronti*. Pisa: Edizioni Plus, pp. 73–86.

Pane, R. (1975). Ferdinando Galiani e l'antico. In *Convegno italo-francese sul tema Ferdinando Galiani* (Roma, 25–27 maggio 1972), Rome: Accademia Nazionale dei Lincei, pp. 201–211.

Pasta, R. (2013). Antonio Maria Niccolini. In *Dizionario Biografico degli Italiani*, Vol. 78, *ad vocem*.

Pennisi, A. (1987). *La linguistica dei mercatanti. Filosofia linguistica e filosofia civile da Vico a Cuoco*, Naples: Guida.

Perna. M. L. (1984). Nota critica. In A. Genovesi, *Scritti economici*. Naples: Istituto Italiano per gli Studi Filosofici, pp. 1269–1279.

Petrucci, A., Pignatelli, G. (1971). Giovanni Gaetano Bottari. In *Dizionario Biografico degli Italiani*, Vol. 13, *ad vocem*.

Pii, E. (1984). *Antonio Genovesi. Dalla politica economica alla politica civile*. Florence: Olschki.

Racioppi, G. (1871). *Antonio Genovesi*. Naples: Morano.

Rao, A. M. (1996). Tra erudizione e scienze: l'antiquaria a Napoli alla fine del Settecento. In C. Montepaone (ed.), *L'incidenza dell'antico. Studi in memoria di Ettore Lepore*, vol. III. Naples: Luciano, pp. 91–135.

Reinert, S. A. (2011a). Girolamo Belloni. In *Il Contributo Italiano alla Storia del Pensiero. Economia*. Rome: Treccani, pp. 271–274.

Rotta, S. (ed.) (1973). *L'illuminismo a Genova. Lettere di P.P. Celesia e F. Galiani*, Florence: La Nuova Italia.

Schipa, M. (1924). L'Università di Napoli nel secolo XVIII. In *Storia dell'Università di Napoli*. Naples: Ricciardi, pp. 436–466.

Stapelbroek, K. (2005). The Devaluation Controversy in Eighteenth-Century Italy. *History of Economic Ideas*, Vol. 13, No. 2, pp. 79–110.

Strazzullo, F. (1982). Il "Ragguaglio di Parnaso" dell'abate Galiani e la reazione dei napoletani a Winckelmann. In *Scritti in onore di Ottavio Morisani*, Catania: Università degli studi, pp. 415–425.

Tiran, A. (2011). Pompeo Neri. In *Il Contributo Italiano alla Storia del Pensiero. Economia*. Rome: Treccani, pp. 380–383.

Trampus, A. (2011a). Gian Rinaldo Carli. In *Il Contributo Italiano alla Storia del Pensiero. Economia*. Rome: Treccani, pp. 299–303.

Tucci, U. (1981). Le emissioni monetarie di Venezia e i movimenti internazionali dell'oro. In *Mercanti, navi, monete nel Cinquecento veneziano*, Bologna: Il Mulino, pp. 275–316.

Tucci, U. (1986). Monete e riforme monetarie nell'Italia del Settecento. *Rivista Storica Italiana*, Anno XCVIII, I, pp. 78–119.

Tucci, U. (1996). Teoria e pratica delle idee monetarie di Gian Rinaldo Carli. *Acta Historiae*, V, pp. 11–24.

Tusset, G. (2020). Gian Rinaldo Carli (1720–1795): Diagnosis and treatment of a monetary plague. *History of Economic Thought and Policy*, 2–2020, pp. 39–65.

Velde, F. (2012). The Life and Times of Nicolas Dutot. *Journal of the History of Economic Thought*, Vol. 34, 1, pp. 67–107.

Venturi F. (1959a). Alle origini dell'Illuminismo napoletano. Dal carteggio di Bartolomeo Intieri. *Rivista Storica Italiana*, a. LXXI, fascicolo III, pp. 416–456.

Venturi, F. (1960a). Le lezioni di commercio di Antonio Genovesi. Manoscritti, edizioni e traduzioni. *Rivista Storica italiana*, anno LXXII, fascicolo III, pp. 511–530.

Venturi, F. (1997). Nota introduttiva. In F. Venturi (ed.) *Illuministi italiani. Riformatori napoletani*, vol. II, tomo I. Milano: Mondadori, pp. 3–46.

Venturi, F. (1998). *Settecento riformatore. Da Muratori a Beccaria*, Turin: Einaudi.

Verga, M. (2013). Pompeo Neri. In *Dizionario Biografico degli Italiani*, Vol. 78, *ad vocem*.

Villari, L. (1958). *Il pensiero economico di Antonio Genovesi*. Florence: Le Monnier.

Zambelli, P. (1972). *La formazione filosofica di Antonio Genovesi*, Naples: Morano.

CHAPTER 7

Paris and the Anti-physiocratic Querelle (1759–1770)

Abbé Galiani by Jacob Gillberg. Source: Bildarchiv **Austria**

7.1 Diplomatic Agent in Paris

On 10 January 1759, Galiani was appointed Officer of the Secretariat of State and the Royal House and was sent to Paris as Embassy Secretary with a salary of 1200 *Ducats* per year (Diodati 1788: 26). According to Fausto

R. Patalano, *Ferdinando Galiani*,
https://doi.org/10.1007/978-3-032-02793-1_7

Nicolini, "Tanucci had sent Galiani from Naples to Paris for the apparently modest position of secretary to the Neapolitan embassy, but with the secret task, anything but modest, of secretly replacing in the handling of the most important and delicate affairs, that real nobody who was the titular ambassador, the Count of Cantillana" (Nicolini 1959a: xi).[1] José de Baeza Vicentelo y Manrique, Count of Cantillana (later Marquis of Castromonte) and Grandee of Spain (1695–1770, De Caro 1975) had been running the Parisian embassy since 1753, but his style was evidently not appreciated by Tanucci, who turned our abbot, immersed in his jokes and erudite curiosities, into a diplomatic agent, literally catapulting him from peripheral Naples to Paris, the centre of European civilisation and home of the Enlightenment.

Tanucci's diffidence for the exponents of the "Austrian party" had initially also affected Galiani,[2] but in 1755 the Neapolitan minister had included him among the members of the *Accademia Ercolanese*, of which Pasquale Carcani (1721–1783), a friend of the young abbot (he was co-author of the *Componimentii varj per la morte di Domenico Iannaccone*) in close contact with Tanucci himself, had been appointed secretary. In 1759, Carcani was appointed Officer of the Secretariat of Foreign Affairs and the Royal House, the same position as Galiani, beginning a close collaboration with Tanucci (De Rosa 1834: 64–68). In the absence of documents that can shed light on the relationship between Galiani and Tanucci, it is very likely that Carcani acted as a go-between, introducing the young abbot into the sphere of the minister's collaborators.[3] The relationship between Galiani and Tanucci was not without clashes and controversies, as Galiani recalled when the minister fell from office: "everyone knew that Tanucci did not love me".[4]

Galiani thus began his long career as a diplomatic agent and advisor to the Neapolitan government. The new prestigious position was not received

[1] It was Domenico Caracciolo, at that time ambassador in Turin, who advised Tanucci to support Cantillana with a young intelligence (Domenico Caracciolo's letter to Bernardo Tanucci, Turin, 17 January 1759, published in Schipa 1904: 541).

[2] See Tanucci's letter to Francesco Nefetti, Naples, 6 November 1753, published in Tanucci (1980b: 113).

[3] He was probably employed by Tanucci as an assistant secretary (*alunno di segreteria*) without salary, see Tanucci (1985: 605, footnote) and De Lucia (1984).

[4] Ferdinando Galiani' letter to Madame d'Épinay, Naples, 28 December 1776, published in Galiani (1881a, vol II: 489); Galiani and d'Épinay (1997, vol V: 125).

with great enthusiasm by Galiani, who gave a frank account of his state of mind in his correspondence with the Neapolitan minister.[5]

Leaving Naples at the end of April 1759, Galiani reached Nice from Genoa by sea, escaping the English naval blockade and avoiding the plague-stricken city of Marseilles,[6] then from Lyon he finally arrived in Paris on 7 June.[7] Southern France appeared to him depopulated: "one passes twenty or thirty miles without encountering a house, and from the top of the hills one can discover nothing but very few and very small villages. I counted how many people I found on the road from Antibes to Aix, and in a hundred and thirty miles of road I hardly found seventy or eighty people in all. Provence is also uncultivated. Of the Dauphiné I cannot judge, except that part which can be seen from the bank of the Rhone, it is truly the *butirro* [pulp] of France, and therefore it is well cultivated".[8]

[5] "In the correspondence between the Neapolitan Foreign Ministry and the Neapolitan embassy in Paris, it was usual to exchange (a) an official letter (or, as they used to say at the time, "d'offizio") written by a secretary of the minister Tanucci (mostly Pasquale Carcani) and signed by the minister, as well as two confidential letters signed by Tanucci himself, one to Cantillana, the other to Galiani; (b) an official letter written by Galiani and signed by Cantillana, as well as two confidential letters by Cantillana and Galiani respectively" (Galiani 1959, Fausto Nicolini's note: 330). Galiani's letters to Tanucci, written on behalf of the ambassador, and the autographs of the confidential letters, kept in the State Archives in Naples, were destroyed in the fire set by the retreating Nazi army in September 1943. Some nineteenth-century copies of the confidential letters are preserved, bound in two volumes (Museo 99 A 88 and Museo 99 A 89) containing correspondence from 1 May 1759 to 11 August 1769 (see Guerci 1975a: 848). Part of the correspondence between Galiani and Tanucci was published by Augusto Bazzoni between 1869 and 1880 (176 letters, see also Bazzoni 1880b; see Nicolini 1914: viii). Extensive excerpts of Galiani's letters were published by Nicolini in the edition of Tanucci's letters to Galiani (Tanucci 1914). Other unpublished letters by Tanucci were published by Gaspare De Caro (1962). Another collection of Galiani's letters from the Parisian period is published in Galiani (1975: 849–985). In this work, the analysis of the correspondence is based on the letters published in Bazzoni (1880b) (in some cases verified with copies in the State Archives), Nicolini (1914) and the collection edited by Diaz and Guerci (Galiani 1975).

[6] Ferdinando Galiani's letter to Bernardo Tanucci, Genoa, 17 May 1759, published in Bazzoni (1869a: 15).

[7] Ferdinando Galiani's letter to Bernardo Tanucci, Paris, 11 June 1759, published in Bazzoni (1869a: 17).

[8] Ferdinando Galiani's letter to Bernardo Tanucci, Lyon, 1 June 1759, published in Bazzoni (1869a: 16). Quesnay, in his articles for the *Encyclopédie*, *Fermier* and *Grain*, denounced the backward state of French agriculture and the consequent demographic crisis: "One hundred years ago the Kingdom numbered some twenty-four million people: after forty years of almost continuous wars and after the revocation of the *Edict of Nantes*, according to the census of 1700 they still numbered nineteen million five hundred thousand; but

The "immense" Paris then appeared to him to be a difficult city: "my health here does not overcome the defects of the site with as much strength as I would like. Truly the enterprise is hard. Bad and oppressive air, poisonous waters, unbelievable strangeness of climate, no snow, no fruit, no cheese, no maritime delights are all fair violence to a Neapolitan machine: but the hardest is the violence done here continually to nature, and the lacerations that my poor sense suffers".[9] And again a few weeks later: "I am already deceived, and I know, that I am not suited to Paris. My dress, my features, my character, my way of thinking, and all my other natural defects will always render me here unbearable to the French and boring to myself".[10] The situation was also aggravated by his health condition, as syphilis began to undermine his body (Nicolini 1914: xvii). Galiani's malaise became despair in the early 1760s: "Sir, it is impossible for me to stay in Paris: ten months of fever is the least of what I have suffered. An ambassadorship, a cardinalate, would not tempt me to stay here".[11]

the ruinous war of succession to the Spanish crown, the diminution of the Kingdom's revenue caused by obstacles to trade and arbitrary impositions, the misery of the countryside, desertion outside the Kingdom, the influx of serfs forced by poverty and militia to retire to the great cities where dissoluteness takes the place of marriage; the disorders of luxury, which unfortunately are compensated for by saving on reproduction; all these causes justify all too well the opinion of those who now reduce the number of men in the Kingdom to sixteen million; and a large number of them in the countryside are reduced to procuring their food by cultivating buckwheat or other cheap cereals; so they are not very useful to the State for their work and consumption" (Quesnay 1757: 830). As economic history studies show, the years in which Quesnay and Galiani observed the agrarian and demographic crisis marked the turning point, see Toutain (1961).

[9] Ferdinando Galiani's letter to Bernardo Tanucci, Paris, 27 June 1759, published in Bazzoni (1869a: 18).

[10] Ferdinando Galiani's letter to Bernardo Tanucci, Paris, 30 July 1759, published in Bazzoni (1869a: 19).

[11] Ferdinando Galiani's letter to Bernardo Tanucci, Paris, 10 March 1760, published in Bazzoni (1869a: 11). "The city is immense. [...]. It would be necessary to have a man in Versailles where the service of the King would require us to be. But the love of entertainment keep ambassadors in Paris, so now it is not permissible to go there. Lastly, it would be useful for there to be someone to watch the ambassadors themselves, and how I wish you had made me spy, I would certainly have more share in your compassion" (Ferdinando Galiani's letter to Bernardo Tanucci, Paris, 21 April 1750, published in Bazzoni 1869a: 25–26). In a letter to his brother Berardo, he wrote: "my health is getting worse by the day. The boredom and abomination of this country I can neither describe nor tell you about [...] I have no new interesting news for you here, except that this is the most messed-up country that dishonours the face of the earth" (Ferdinando Galiani's letter to Berardo Galiani, Paris, 1 October 1759,

His position also appeared difficult to him due to the distracted presence of Cantillana: "I have had the pain of finding him burdened with melancholy and disturbances for his interests in Spain, which are being ruined by the quarrels that have arisen against him in the present lamentable situation of that great kingdom".[12] And he was certainly not made any easier by the first impression made on him by the principal French minister, Étienne François de Choiseul: "I was introduced to the Duke of Choiseul, who for a second was pleased to look at me. I wouldn't even dream of him viewing business the way he looked at me; that would be too superficial".[13] Finally, few relationships made the beginning of his Parisian stay lonely.[14]

When Galiani assumed his diplomatic office, the Kingdom of France was engaged in the *Seven Years War* (1756–1763, see Riley 1986), as an ally of the Habsburg Monarchy (with the *Treaty of Versailles*, concluded in

BSNSP, XXXI.B. 17: folios 237r–237v, 238r.). Again in November 1759, Tanucci wrote to Charles III: "The Council of Regency is in doubt as to whether to allow Galiani to resign from the position of embassy secretary in Paris in order to become an officer of the secretariat with 40 *Ducats* a month, which they assigned to him as a fixed sum" (Bernardo Tanucci's letter to King Charles, Naples, 6 November 1759, published in Tanucci 1969: 24).

[12] Ferdinando Galiani's letter to Bernardo Tanucci, Paris, 11 June 1759, published in Bazzoni (1869a: 17). Galiani's opinion about Cantillana was not negative: "Far too from obstinacy and submissiveness, he showed constant calm, tranquillity and demeanour in the face of the impetuous outbursts, now of fury, now of feigned affection from that minister [Choiseul]: so that all the waves of that stormy sea broke against him, like a hard, motionless rock. Far from soliciting with haste and from complaining with bitterness, he performed calmly and gave a faithful account of all that his court instructed, without love, without hate, of which every cause was far from him" (Galiani, MS-20: 311).

[13] Ferdinando Galiani's letter to Bernardo Tanucci, Paris, 25 June 1759, published in Bazzoni (1869a: 18).

[14] "I tried to see the Marquis de Puisieux to execute the commission entrusted to me by Your Excellency; but the Swiss told me he was invisible. Perhaps he had found the *heliotrope* that Calandrino went searching for down the Mugnone. I will try again as many times as I can. From the moment I arrived, I would have liked to see this gentleman, who was very kind to my uncle; but having heard from many people, and from my compatriots who are here, that he does not remember Naples, that he never speaks of this period of his life, and that he does not show much benevolence to those who come from there, I did not want to run the risk of a cold reception. The Frenchman in Paris does not esteem, does not love, and remembers nothing. I noticed this in Judge [balio] de Fleury [avocat général of the Paris Parliament] who certainly loved Naples and left it with sorrow and now speaks of it as of a dream" (Ferdinando Galiani's letter to Bernardo Tanucci, Paris, 30 July 1759, published in Bazzoni 1869a: 19). Calandrino and the *heliotrope* is a novella narrated by Elissa in the eighth day of the *Decameron*, the one dedicated to tales of mockery and jokes between men and women. See Boccaccio ([2003]: 496–503).

1756, which had marked the so-called *Diplomatic Revolution*) and Russia, against Great Britain and Prussia. In November 1757, the Franco-Austrian coalition had been defeated at Rossbach by Frederick II's Prussians. This defeat, experienced traumatically, had contributed to the removal of Cardinal de Bernis, the protagonist of the Franco-Austrian entente, who intended to start peace negotiations. The Marquise de Pompadour and the pro-Austrian party of the Court, on the other hand, wanted to continue the war and favoured, in December 1758, the accession of Choiseul with the task of continuing the conflict. But the French were still defeated in August 1759 at Minden and at sea, in Lagos.

The colonial rivalry between France and Great Britain motivated the continuation of the war that took place with mixed fortunes in North America and India. In the first half of the eighteenth century, thanks to its geographical position on the Atlantic and the Mediterranean, France had gained control of important trading centres in Europe, Asia and America to the detriment of its British competitors. Although Law's system had had negative effects on credit institutions, its policy of cheap money stimulated activity and caused a redistribution of wealth: "Commerce and industry profited, and the great roads and canals planned by Law were not all abandoned. Lorient, the headquarters of the Company of the Indies, slowly grew in importance, as did Nouvelle-Orleans, founded in America. Overseas trade had received a considerable impetus and attention had been directed to the possibilities of the colonies. In France landowners who were lucky enough to profit in the early stages of the System and get out in time had been able to free their land from debt. While many families had been ruined, others had risen from poverty to riches. The redistribution of wealth and the consequent confusion of classes which resulted from the crash was its most marked result [...]. A generation of nouveaux riches emerged out of the crash of the System" (Cobban 1966: 223–224). France had become a European leader in the trade of luxury goods (mirrors, Sèvres porcelain, furniture, French lace) and controlled much of the trade in colonial goods, primarily sugar. The French controlled a few centres in India (Chandernagore in the hinterland of Bengal and Pondicherry on the south-eastern coast), contending with the English and Dutch for the Indian cinnamon and cotton trade. In North America, the French had primacy in the exploration of new territories, also facilitated by good relations with the indigenous peoples, and the resulting occupations were an obstacle to the inland expansion of the coastal British colonies. Monetary stability had favoured commercial development[15] and "French trade practically doubled between 1715 and 1740, and again doubled between then and 1763, and with its growth the merchant class of the ports began to rival the wealth of the financiers" (Cobban 1966: 237, see also Dockès 1969; Daudin and Crouzet 2004).

The French economy was based on agriculture, which was still heavily conditioned by periodic famines and institutional constraints, but thanks to a better utilisation of the factors of production, also highlighted by contemporary observers such as François Quesnay (1756a, 1757), it was able to ensure greater productivity.[16] French industry was scattered and fragmented, managed by merchant manufacturers and located in the countryside, where it was possible to utilise abundant cheap labour, raw materials (flax, hemp, wool), combustibles (mainly wood and then coal) and hydraulic energy (Dockès 1969: 195). Alongside this rural proto-industry, there was metallurgical production for military needs, subsidised by the state and consisting of substantial urban production concentrations (Daudin and Crouzet 2004: 35). A semi-craft production for luxury goods completed the picture.

In this evolving economic context, French politics was dominated by court intrigues: "the struggles of court factions emerged as the real structure of government in France. Favourites and mistresses competed for influence over the king. Transient alliances were perpetually being formed and dissolved among the coteries at Versailles. Women made and unmade the alliances of court faction" (Cobban 1966: 227).

Internal political stability was threatened by various forces that blocked all attempts at reform and weakened traditional power structures. The Catholic Church, the cornerstone of the Most Christian Monarchy, was delegitimised by the Jansenist movement[17] and the criticism of the *phi-*

[15] "The perpetual fluctuations in the value of the *Ecu* and the *Louis d'Or* were brought to an end by the stabilisation of the currency in 1726, at the rate of 24 *Livres* to the *Louis d'Or*" (Cobban 1966: 237).

[16] According to Jean-Claude Toutain, in the second half of the eighteenth century, France's agricultural production grew at an average annual rate of 0.50%, while the population grew by 0.35% per year. A decisive role in this increase in production was played by cereals especially wheat, the yield of which rose from 1 to 6–7 (see Toutain 1961).

[17] Galiani's judgement on the Jansenists was severe: "The Jansenists were a society of learned theologians who coupled much devotion and mysticism with new opinions on the Sacraments and Divine Grace. These together with the decadence of letters are ended here. They have been succeeded by a few unknown men who, with fanaticism and miracles, would like to support those opinions that they can no longer defend with erudition and knowl-

losphes, but still had the strength to block important tax reforms, such as the one proposed by *Contrôleur général des Finances*, Jean-Baptiste de Machault d'Arnouville, in 1750, which aimed to institute a general income tax, without class exceptions (called *vingtième*) and which was successfully opposed by the high clergy, the nobility and provincial parliaments.

The fiscal crisis of the state and the privileges granted to the clergy and nobility created strong social tensions with the bourgeois and working classes (both urban and rural). The political tension shifted the balance of power between local parliaments (led by the *noblesse de robe*) and the royal power, and clashes were frequent (Swann 1995).

The political decadence and economic and social difficulties contrasted strongly with the liveliness that characterised French intellectual life, in which Galiani was beginning to immerse himself.

The 1750s marked the spread of Enlightenment culture on a European scale, an event that was materialised in the success of the *Encyclopédie*, the publishing enterprise directed by Denis Diderot and Jean-Baptiste Le Rond d'Alembert that was definitively consolidated after the setback of 1752.[18] The new scientific system gave ample space to the study of society: in the framework called *Système figuré des connaissances humaines*, which appeared in the first volume of the *Encyclopédie*: the *Science de l'Homme* was dominated by *Raison* as was the *Science de la Nature*, while *Histoire* was placed in the field of *Memoire*. In this system, *Science Œconomique* appeared as a branch of *Science Morale Particulier* or *Science des Loix ou Jurisprudence*, alongside *Science Politique* and *Science du Droit Naturel*; the economic subject matter was distributed between *Jurisprudence Naturelle* (the duties of man in isolation), *Jurisprudence Politique* (man in

edge" (Ferdinando Galiani's letter to Bernardo Tanucci, Paris, 14 April 1760, published in Galiani 1975: 850–851).

[18] The attacks on the *Encyclopédie* were conducted mainly by the clergy, in particular the Jesuits, who used the accusation of plagiarism to block the publication of the various volumes. In reality, this accusation, even if used instrumentally, was not without some reason: Diderot and d'Alembert, who were entrusted with the editorship of the work, chose to make use of already existing material for most of the articles. The contributors had the task of revising and editing already existing articles (from various sources); often this revision led to an *ex novo* remaking of the entries; an operation that was necessary to overcome the gaps and inadequacies in the original material. In 1752, the Jesuits, contesting the orthodoxy of the theological entries drafted by Abbot de Prades, managed to obtain a royal decree to seize the first two volumes of the work (published in 1751), but the political protections enjoyed by the authors resolved the issue positively and this event marked the first victory of the *philosophes* against the clergy.

society) and *Jurisprudence Œconomique* ("the science of human duties in the family"). Although still defined in relation to morality and law, economics thus gained a place in the Enlightenment tree of knowledge; this was the first step towards the recognition of a scientific dignity for the subject of economics.[19]

In those same years, in fact, a group of young intellectuals interested in economic problems had gathered in Paris around the new *intendant du commerce*, Vincent de Gournay,[20] who had the great merit of making "France the centre of the most lively discussions of the subject in Europe at that time" (Venturi 1971a: 124). First of all, it included François Véron de Forbonnais, then Claudes-Jacques Herbert, George-Marie Butel-Dumont, Louis-Joseph Plumard de Dangeul and the young Anne Robert Jacques Turgot (Galiani's peer), all of whom were committed to understanding the reasons for British success in the commercial field and to preparing the means to overcome the gap, supporting the attempts at fiscal and economic reform initiated by the *Contrôleur général des finances*, Jean-Baptiste de Machault d'Arnouville. But their horizon of analysis is even more interesting because it was not restricted to the France-Great Britain confrontation: they looked beyond the Pyrenees, to Spain in decadence and the proposals for reform that were formulated by Spanish writers, and they also looked closely at Italy. All the best European economic literature passed through Paris: Forbonnais, in addition to writing articles on political economy for the *Encyclopédie* (*Change, Concurrance, Culture des terres and Espèce*), later collected by him under the name *Eléments du commerce* (Forbonnais 1754), translated Charles King's work, *The British merchant*, to which he added the *Discours préliminaire* and the essay *Idée générale du commerce de la Grande Bratagne* (King 1753) and the treatise by the Spaniard Geronimo de Uztàriz, *Theorica y practica de commercio y marina* (Uztàriz 1753); Plumard de Dangeul had translated the work of another Spanish reformer Bernardo de Ulloa, *Restablecimiento de las fabricas y comercio español* (Ulloa 1753) (thus not only English, but also Spanish production passed through French mediation) and, under the

[19]The article *Economie politique* was written by Jean Jacques Rousseau and later published separately as *Discours sur l'œconomie politique* in 1758. However, Jean-Claude Perrot notes, the meaning Rousseau attributed to the term was still linked to the "Greek domestic economy" and dealt with "from family economics to the constitutional aspects of society, neglecting all macro-economics" (Perrot 1992: 67).

[20]On Gournay see Schelle (1897); Diaz (1962; 29–41); Hutchison (1988: 224–225); Meyssonnier (1990); Charles (2011).

name of John Nickolls, had published the important comparison between the English and French economies (Nickolls 1754); Butel-Dumont had translated John Cary's work *An essay on the state of England* (Cary 1755) and together with de Gournay that of Josiah Child, *A discours about trade* (Child 1754) Montesquieu's son (Jean Baptiste de Secondat) translated Joshua Gee's book, *The trade and navigation* (Gee 1749) and finally Claude-Jacques Herbert published his *Essai sur la police générale des grains* (Herbert 1753). Victor Riqueti, Marquis de Mirabeau published the first volume of *L'ami du people* (Mirabeu 1756). Richard Cantillon's essays (1755) and the translation of David Hume's essays (1754–56) then circulated. In Naples, meanwhile, Genovesi avidly read this literature, where he found ideas for his university lectures.

A few months before Galiani arrived in Paris, in December 1758, Madame Pompadour's doctor and *Encyclopédie* contributor, François Quesnay, had drafted the first manuscript version of the *Tableau économique* (followed by a second printed edition in the spring of 1759 and a third in 1760), which would become the theoretical foundation of the *Physiocratic School* (or *Sect of Économistes*, as it was nicknamed by its many detractors), which would have great influence on the economic policy of the French monarchy in the following decade.[21] Despite his constant complaints and desire to return to Naples, Galiani was immersed in a social and intellectual context that could not fail to stimulate his lively intelligence and irresistible curiosity.

In March 1760, Cantillana left Paris temporarily (until August) to attend to matters of inheritance in Spain and Galiani was appointed *chargé d'affaires*, assuming greater visibility in the diplomatic context.[22] At that time, Charles Emanuel III of Savoy was mediating between England and France to assert Savoy's rights over Piacenza, wresting it from the Duchy

[21] Quesnay had published two entries in the *Encyclopédie*: *Fermiers* in volume VI (Quesnay 1756a) and *Grains* in volume VII (Quesnay 1757).

[22] "I enjoy here all the prerogatives, distinctions and acts that belong to *chargés*. Such they all believed me to be because the embassy secretary is considered to be a *chargé* in the absence of his ambassador. So there is no need for an introduction since I go and lunch with the minister [...] like everyone else. The presentation that Cantillana made of me on my arrival is like confirmation; here even after death it is good. And perhaps my rank is higher than that of *chargé*. So I lack only two things: money and health. I see that it is impossible to recover both, but I want at least one" (Ferdinando Galiani's letter to Bernardo Tanucci, Paris, 7 April 1760, published in Bazzoni 1869a: 21–22).

of Parma, ruled by a branch of the Bourbons, and this alarmed Tanucci.[23] Galiani cleverly tried to dissimulate the opposition between Naples and Turin: "From the ambassador of Turin I have learned that the news in the Dutch gazettes about the apparent opposition between our court and that of Sardinia is without foundation, I have thought of making more frequent appearances with him, and together deride this bad news in public. Certainly nothing would be more fatal to the tranquillity and security of Italy than an inopportune division between its members at a time when they need to be extremely united in spirit, as they are in interests".[24] In June 1760, the question was resolved, as Galiani announced to Tanucci: "This minister [Choiseul] has spoken to me at length to assure me that there is no treaty between France and the King of Sardinia, except for a very tedious and thorny border treaty that is already almost finished".[25]

In the months of Cantillana's absence, the diplomatic responsibility fell entirely on Galiani, and together with the burdens came the honours of inclusion in high society.[26] "Welcomed as they were with enthusiasm, courted and vied for, foreign diplomats threw themselves into Parisian life and, having displayed a preference, they allowed themselves to be adopted by this or that group - often by more than one" (Craveri 2005: 292). *Salons* dominated Parisian intellectual and social life as spaces of autonomy, far from the control of the Court and the Church. Organised around aristocratic women on the basis of a code of conduct, these places were dedicated to cultured and refined conversation (Guerci 1975b: 615–619;

[23] "I noted that the minister of Sardinia had a very long conversation [with the king of France]. To guess the subject is difficult. Some time ago it was said that the King of France was in negotiation with the King of Sardinia over a certain change of borders in Provence, which would have prevented reciprocal compensation" (Ferdinando Galiani's letter to Bernardo Tanucci, Paris, 14 April 1760, published in Bazzoni 1869a: 23).

[24] Ferdinando Galiani's letter to Bernardo Tanucci, Paris, 28 April 1760, published in Bazzoni (1869a: 27).

[25] Ferdinando Galiani's letter to Bernardo Tanucci, Paris, 23 June 1760, published in Bazzoni (1869a: 31).

[26] In a letter to Charles of Bourbon, Tanucci announced that Galiani would keep his assignment in Paris (Bernardo Tanucci's letter to King Charles, Naples, 29 April 1760, published in Tanucci 1969: 36–37). A few days earlier, on 1 April, he had announced Galiani's return to Naples. Thus, the decision to stay in Paris was made by Galiani in April (cf. Bernardo Tanucci's letter to King Charles, Naples, 1 April 1760, published in Tanucci 1969: 34), but again in August Tanucci returned to Galiani's permanence in Paris (Bernardo Tanucci's letter to King Charles, Naples, 19 August 1760, published in Tanucci 1969: 47).

Dédéyan 1975; Fabre 1975; Goodman 1989; Lilti 2005).[27] Formally excluded from the educational system of the time but literate, aristocratic women opened their salons not only to philosophers, writers, artists and musicians, but also to politicians and diplomats, fostering intellectual confrontation and political discussion. And "by the 1760s, the Parisian salons, already at the center of Parisian social and intellectual life, had become centers of Enlightenment" (Goodman 1989: 331).[28]

Galiani was immediately fascinated by the way he could show off his brilliant conversation, made more amiable by his marked Neapolitan accent, and display his irony and profound culture, becoming "a major figure in all the Parisian salons" (Goodman 1989: 341).[29]

[27] "Rather than social climbers, the salonnieres of the Enlightenment must be viewed as intelligent, self-educated, and educating women who reshaped the social forms of their day to their own social, intellectual, and educational needs. The initial and primary purpose behind salons was to satisfy the self-determined educational needs of the women who started them" (Goodman 1989: 333).

[28] "It was thus a newly redefined social and intellectual space that was exploited by the men of the Enlightenment who saw themselves as engaged in a collective endeavor on the model of their *Encyclopedia*: a collective endeavor that needed a regular, institutional, social base. To understand their project of Enlightenment requires an understanding of how eighteenth-century salon women transformed a noble, leisure form of social gathering into a serious working space, and in so doing created the ground on which such a collective project could be carried out" (Goodman 1989: 332). On the intellectual and educational condition of women, Madame d'Épinay offers an excellent portrait: "I am profoundly ignorant, that is the truth. My whole education has been directed towards learning pleasant feminine activities [...]. How many subjects women cannot approach! The doctrines that belong to the science of administration, politics, commerce are alien and forbidden to them; they cannot - must not - meddle with them. And so the only great things by which educated or learned men can truly benefit their fellow men, the state, their country, have already been eliminated at the outset. The female sex is then left with nothing but the fine arts, domestic activities, the duties of society, and their fragile constitution, prevent women from the continuous and in-depth study of ancient languages, such as Greek, Latin, etc. Thus the only little interest remaining for one to cultivate is French, English, Italian literature" (Madame d'Épinay's letter to Ferdinando Galiani, Paris, 4 January 1771, published in D'Épinay and Galiani 1996: 254–255).

[29] In 1763, just a few years after his arrival in Paris, his fame had reached the court of King Louis XV, as Galiani himself recounted: "This Most Christian King on the first day I was here at court on seeing me immediately approached Cantillana, who was near a window in the room, and asking him about me said *on m' a dit qu'il a beaucoup d'esprit*. To the King no one objected, so Cantillana and Grimaldi said *oui* and went on to say of me what it is not. This royal decision (surely born of what the Duc de Duras and the Duc de Brissac, who love me very much, may perhaps have said to him) immediately became news, since kings do not say a word that is in vain. I consequently found myself exposed to a salvo of compliments, praise

The Neapolitan abbot assiduously frequented (on Fridays) the salon of Madame Marie-Thérèse Rodet Geoffrin (Nicolini 1954: 27), made famous by a famous painting by Charles Gabriel Lemonnier representing the reading of Voltaire's tragedy *The Orphan of China* (a tragedy about Ghengis Khan and his sons, published in 1755) and describing well the atmosphere that characterised these meetings.[30] He was often among the guests in the salon of Madamoiselle Jeanne Julie Éléonore de Lespinasse (Nicolini 1954: 36), Madame Suzanne Curchod de la Nasse, wife of the Swiss banker and future minister Jacques Necker (Nicolini 1959a: 377), and every Tuesday guest of Anne-Catherine de Ligniville and Claude-Adrien Helvetius (Nicolini 1954: 38; Guillois 1894), while on Thursdays and Sundays he was in the salon of Charlotte-Suzanne d'Aine baronne d'Holbach (Nicolini 1954: 38, 43). But over all prevailed his frequentation of Madame Louise d'Épinay's salon with whom he formed a lasting friendship and became her regular correspondent when he left Paris (Valentino 1952; Steegmuller 1983; Weinreb 1992; Anglani 1999).

Fausto Nicolini has often given a rather caricatured image of Galiani, a frequenter of society salons, describing him as a character endowed with a particular *vis comica* and for this reason well accepted, but the abbot offered original elements to the conversations coming from an intellectual

and celebrity" (Ferdinando Galiani's letter to Bernardo Tanucci, Compiègne, 18 July 1763, published in Bazzoni 1877a: 197–198). On the relations between Galiani and Jean Paul Timoléon de Cossé, 7th Duke of Brissac, see Nicolini (1954:115–124).

[30] The painting was commissioned by Joséphine de Beauharnais to adorn the Château de la Malmaison. The painter depicts a reunion of all the famous people who might have been present in Madame Geoffrin's salon, such as the leading figures of the *Enlightenment*, Rousseau, Montesquieu, Diderot, d'Alembert, Quesnay, Helvetius, Buffon, politicians such as Choiseul, diplomats, poets and minor literary figures, gathered around the bust of the exiled Voltaire. According to Dena Goodman: "Geoffrin, who acted as a mentor and model for other salonnières, was responsible for two innovations that set Enlightenment salons apart from their predecessors and from other social and literacy gatherings of the day. She invented the Enlightenment salon. First, she made the one-o'clock dinner rather than the traditional late-night supper the sociable meal of the day, and thus she opened up the whole afternoon for talk. Second, she regulated these dinners, fixing a specific day of the week for them. After Geoffrin launched her weekly dinners, the Parisian salon took on the form that made it the social base of the Enlightenment Republic of Letters: a regular and regulated formal gathering hosted by a woman in her own home which served as a forum and locus of intellectual activity" (Goodman 1994: 90–91).

world, the Neapolitan one, which had absorbed and reworked the main European cultural currents, expressing its own identity.[31]

Jean-François Marmontel in his *Mémoires* drew an iconic portrait of Galiani: "Abbot Galiani was, in his own person, the smallest and most graceful Harlequin that Italy has ever produced, but on the shoulders of that Harlequin was the head of Machiavelli. He was Epicurean in philosophy and melancholic in spirit, and since he saw everything from the comic side, there was nothing either in politics or in morals about which he did not have some good tale to tell, and these tales always fell to the point and had all the salt of an ingenious and unexpected allusion. Imagine the manner of telling and gesticulating with the most instinctive grace, and you can imagine the pleasure that the contrast between the profound sense of the tale and the comic air of the narrator gave us. I am not exaggerating if I tell you that one would forget everything else and listen to him for hours on end. Then, having played the character, he had fulfilled his part in society, and sad and mute, in a corner, he seemed to wait impatiently for the words of the chief actor to return to the scene" (Marmontel 1804, vol II: 121–122).[32] Giacomo Casanova, who met him in Paris during those years, also drew an effective portrait of him: "The Abbé was very witty. He had an extraordinary knack for giving his most serious remarks a tinge of humor, and always with a straight face, speaking French very well with the incorrigible Neapolitan accent, which made him a favorite in all circles" (Casanova 2006: 585). Another Italian, Alessandro Verri, wrote to his brother Pietro: "This abbot [Galiani], who has a hundred spirits and not a quarter heart, is the fashionable man of Paris, he is sought after, he is known everywhere [...]. Beccaria and I had lunch with him at Madame Geoffrin's, and I assure you that the abbot always shone [...]. This is certain, that Galiani used to go to all our companies and that where he is everyone is silent and lets him shine".[33] And he described him rather

[31] Nicolini (1914: xvii–xviii); Nicolini (1954: 7–14). On the literature that reductively presents Galiani as a kind of *jester*, see Diaz (1975a: cxviii).

[32] For the cynical and realistic approach with which he pronounced his comments, sometimes veritable verdicts, and for his constant references to Niccolò Machiavelli, Galiani was known in Parisian salons by the nickname of *Machiavellino*. In a letter to Madame d'Épinay he refers to Abbot Morellet in connection with the nickname: "he reciprocates my affection although he thinks I am *Machiavellino*" (Ferdinando Galiani's letter to Madame d'Épinay, Naples, 27 January 1770, published in Galiani 1881a, vol I: 57).

[33] Alessandro Verri's letter to Pietro Verri, London, 15 January 1767, published in Verri (1980: 249–250).

scornfully: "a little *abatuccio* of a figure who has curious Neapolitan gesticulations, a buffoonish muzzle, and the French tongue in his mouth is a very expressive third species".[34]

And lastly, Denis Diderot, who was bound to him by close friendship, described him as follows: "Abbot Galiani entered [Madame d'Épinay's house], and with the kindly abbot, cheerfulness, imagination, wit, madness, joking and everything that makes one forget sorrows and life".[35] Diderot also gave a description of Galiani's conversation, often based on paradox: "I went to dinner at Baron [d'Holbach], where I found Naigeon, Suard, Abbé Morellet and Abbé Galiani. Galiani was very cheerful. He showed us that the place in the world where people do least what they want is the freest: Constantinople is an example of this, where there are almost no brakes on action and no freedom. [...] I madly love this abbot, who almost always grasps the oldest things from some secret corner that no one has looked at".[36]

Although he frequented the highest intellectual figures, in addition to Diderot he was linked to Paul Henri Thiry d'Holbach, Claude-Adrien Helvétius, Abbé André Morellet (whom he met in Naples in 1758 and who introduced him to the Paris salons), Jean-Baptiste d'Alembert, Jean-Baptiste Suard, Friedrich Melchior von Grimm, Galiani remained immune to the conformism that often characterised the cultured conversation of the Parisian salons, displaying an intellectual autonomy of his own (which he revealed in his frequent correspondence).[37] And this non-conformism

[34] Alessandro Verri's letter to Pietro Verri, 29 August 1769, published in Verri (1911, vol. III: 46).

[35] Denis Diderot's letter to Sophie Volland, Paris, 25 November 1760, published in Diderot (1955, vol. III: 268–269).

[36] Denis Diderot's letter to Sophie Volland, undated fragment, published in Diderot (1950, vol. II: 266). "I would like much more to tell you these things in person than to write them down, to see your wig leaning against the corner of the chimney and your head smoking, and to hear you start a subject, follow it, delve into it and, as you go along, throw rays of light into the darkest corners of literature, antiquity, politics, philosophy and morality" (Denis Diderot's letter to Ferdinando Galiani, Paris, 25 Mai 1773, in Galiani 1881a: vol. II, 222; see also Galiani, 1881b: vol. II, 57–58: Diderot 1875a, vol. VI: 302). On the relationship between Galiani and Diderot, see Dieckmann (1975); Davison (1985); Catucci (1986) and Cohen (1988). Among his Parisian friends, Galiani was particularly close to the Italian physician Angelo Gatti, an advocate of vaccination who was well established in French society: he was physician to the Helvétius couple, to Madame d'Épinay, to the Duchess of Choiseul, the minister's wife, and was advisor to Louis XV, see Nicolini (1929: 234).

[37] "Certainly Galiani arrived in Paris with a fully completed cultural and intellectual formation: he did not mature in the light of French theories, he always remained himself, ambassador, not only of the Kingdom but also of a different culture" (Catucci 1986: 12).

he expressed above all by opposing the theories of the Quesnay School, which in the 1760s were accepted as dogmas in the cultural and political circles of Paris and Versailles.[38]

Despite his worldly companionship, Galiani intelligently fulfilled his mission as a diplomatic agent, effectively assuming the role that formally fell to Cantillana (Diaz 1975a: xlv; Skornicki 2018).[39] The condition of the Neapolitan kingdom was very delicate: in October 1759, Charles had succeeded Ferdinand VI on the Spanish throne, leaving the responsibility of government, due to the minority of his successor Ferdinand, to a Council of Regency, of which Tanucci was the eminent personality. The kingdom, formally independent, was in fact under the guardianship of Charles III, as evidenced by the intense correspondence with Tanucci. The allied courts of Paris and Vienna tried to bring the kingdom into their sphere of influence.

The main issue between 1760 and 1761 was the complex diplomatic work that led to the stipulation, in August 1761, of the *Third Pacte de Famille* conceived by Choiseul as the basis of a new European order in an anti-British function and presented as a great diplomatic success.[40] Dynastic

[38] "Physiocracy was nonexistent in 1750. Tout Paris and still more Versailles talked about it from 1760 to 1770. Practically everybody (excluding professed economists) had forgotten it by 1780" (Schumpeter 1954 [2006]: 220). See Bauer (1890).

[39] This primary role attributed to Galiani was explicitly stated by Tanucci to the French ambassador in Naples: "Marquis of Tanucci has asked me to tell you expressly, Monseigneur, that although the Count of Cantillana has returned to Paris to resume his ministry to the King, he begs you to kindly continue to show the same kindness to Abbé Galiani, and to regard him as secrétaire to the King of the Two Sicilies" (Mathieu de Basquiat de La Houze's dispatch to duc de Choiseul, Naples, 27 Septembre 1760, quoted in Galiani 1881a: Vol. I, xxxviii–xxxix). On Galiani's diplomatic activity, see Diaz (1975b). On Mathieu de Basquiat, Baron de la Houzesee, chargé d'affaires in Naples between 1759 and 1762, see Galiani (1975: 853).

[40] "The *Pacte de Famille* is appreciated in this nation, I do not refer to the common people, who seeing a powerful relief in an unhappy war must naturally rejoice, but I refer also to the learned and the prudent. Every quarrel with the Spaniards is over here, and every animosity of nation will soon be over. All hope of the French having a place in Italy is likewise ended. It is therefore infinitely pleasing to see the tranquillity of this part and the seats of the princes of Italy, originally French, assured. I would add to this that the Infante Philip is singularly loved here, and Parma is considered a French colony for the many who have moved here [...]. Choiseul is and always will be as I believed it to be. All Bourbon and nothing else. I don't believe that the French will become good at joining us. The French are only good at home. Let the cabinets be united. Let the nations remain as God made them" (Ferdinando Galiani's letter to Bernardo Tanucci, Paris, 4 January 1762, published in Bazzoni 1875b:

connections between the Bourbons justified a political and military alliance, but their economic interests were divergent: Choiseul wanted to impose free trade on Spain so as to find new markets for French goods in the vast Spanish empire, while Charles III had the opposite need to protect his market to support the recovery of the Spanish economy after decades of decline.[41] Philip I of Bourbon, Duke of Parma adhered to the pact, but the Regency of Naples maintained a detached attitude, stalling (Diaz 1975a: xlv, see Orain and Reinert 2022).[42] Tanucci, aware of the different balance of power, wanted to defend the Kingdom's neutrality, avoiding involving it in a conflict, especially with the British (as had happened in 1742, when the Kingdom's weakness was revealed), and at the same time he wanted to guarantee margins of autonomy for commercial policy.[43] A strategy that was supported by Charles III (Skornicki 2018: 326).[44]

Galiani obviously supported this line of neutrality and disengagement, sharing above all his fear of British power. Writing to Tanucci in October 1762, the Neapolitan diplomat excellently summarised the political framework and his diplomatic strategy: "Victory smiles on them [the British] from all sides. They believe they have a powerful and defenceless America in front of them, and can plunder it at their leisure in a few months. The English custom, copied from the ancient Romans, of dividing everything among the soldiers is the secret to conquering half the world. Already the

45). On the *Pacte de Famille* see Soulange-Bodin (1894); Bourguet (1907); Blart (1915); Ozanam (1961); Lopez-Cordon Cortezo (2003); Skornicki (2018); Van Kley (2018: 196–242).

[41] The pact for commercial purposes was also supported by de Gournay: "The two Crowns therefore have an equal interest in helping each other, not only by the aid of their arms, but also by promoting the respective Trade of their Subjects. [...] We can therefore see how important it is for the Courts to consult each other and to join together to protect and increase the Trade of their subjects" (de Gournay, MS: folios 1–2, published in Skornicki 2018: 324).

[42] "The Bourbons are kinsmen and friends, and of excellent blood, so that only the perpetuity of concord should be suspected. The ministers and the people are not of the same temperament nor of the same education and discipline" (Bernardo Tanucci's letter to Ferdinando Galiani, Naples, 8 January 1763, published in Tanucci 1914, vol. I: 3).

[43] "Weak as we are, we will have to observe the treaties to the overbearing nations, who will make as many conventions towards us as they wish, certain of which we will be able to make no complaints other than words" (Bernardo Tanucci's letter to Domenico Caracciolo, Naples, 2 June 1766, published in Migliorini 1979: 187).

[44] On Neapolitan diplomacy in the eighteenth century, see Maiorini (2000). On the political role of trade treaties, see Alimento and Stapelbroek (2017).

adresse of the city of London to the King says manifestly, that there will be no peace without the dissolution of the *Pacte de Famille*. If it were my turn, I, would break it with a stroke of my pen. The heart of sovereigns has no need for written treaties. We will always be sons of Spain, and there is no greater treaty than this bond. [...] On this we must count. We can also count on France as much as the heart and genius of the sovereign can influence his cabinet, which is often more powerful than he is. [...] Without treaties, Spain will gain, we will gain, and perhaps France will also gain. Every treaty is a debt [*taccolo*]. Every privilege creates more envy than good, and reciprocity always destroys profit. Treaties with the Turk and the Pope, weak and disordered powers. With others no treaties".[45] Behind the alleged dynastic solidarity Galiani identified the French threat to the economic interests of the Neapolitan kingdom.[46] The good formal relationship with Choiseul[47] then cleverly allowed him to conceal the Neapolitan opposition to the Pact.[48] But it was an asymmetrical relationship,

[45] Ferdinando Galiani's letter to Bernardo Tanucci, Fontainebleau, 18 October 1762, published in Galiani (1975: 869–870).

[46] "The *Pacte de Famille* required to be enlightened and retouched by particular treaties of commerce, which each of the Bourbon nations had to extend separately, and in relation to its own particular advantages and situation. The Hispanic treaty was undoubtedly one thing, the Sicilian treaty was another, the Parma treaty was another in relation to the French" (Ferdinando Galiani's letter to Bernardo Tanucci, Paris, 6 Dicember 1762, published in Galiani 1975: 872).

[47] "It is so rare and difficult to be able to speak to Choiseul, that although our conversation did not last long, it did not fail to excite the wonder of many, and I received compliments of felicitation from some foreign ministers, that the Duke had done me the honour of speaking to me principally on a day when almost no one had been able to speak" (Ferdinando Galiani's letter to Bernardo Tanucci, Paris, 31 August 1761, published in Bazzoni 1875a: 527). "I had the honour to dine again at the Duke of Choiseul's, who always welcomes me with equal love and kindness. It is very difficult to approach one who always has more than forty people at table" (Ferdinando Galiani's letter to Bernardo Tanucci, Paris, 15 August 1763, published in Galiani 1975: 878). Tanucci also confirmed the excellent relationship between Galiani and the French minister: "He entered Choiseul's good graces with some singularity" (Bernardo Tanucci's letter to King Charles, Portici, 1 April 1760, published in Tanucci 1969: 51).

[48] "[Choiseul] told me (but did not show anger in his face) that new complaints and reported speeches had arrived, from which it appeared that Your Excellency blamed and had an aversion to the *Pacte de Famille*. I immediately and boldly replied that I could not believe these reports. That I knew that Your Excellency had contributed more than any other to the *Pacte de Famille* by recommending this bond and always instilling it in the mind of the most wise Catholic King, and that this had been the only instruction given me when I came here. As the Duke of Choiseul listened to me patiently, I did not want to leave off telling him (and I told him so a little warmly) that the sentiments and heart of a man who for thirty years has

Galiani, at least from what appeared from his correspondence, admired Choiseul,[49] but the latter did not reciprocate with the same feeling.[50] Choiseul had, however, realised that the Neapolitan Regency had no interest in the Pact and accused Tanucci's policy of Machiavellianism.[51] The doubts and perplexities of the Neapolitan government were expressed in a document prepared by Galiani, *Notes au Pacte de Famille*, probably

enjoyed the honour of a distinguished esteem from the great Catholic King, and whom three French ambassadors all living have treated with great esteem, although he did not have the ministry of Foreign Affairs, must not depend on the judgement of a *nouveau venu* [the French ambassador in Naples, Aimeric-Joseph-Jacques, marquis de Durfort]" (Ferdinando Galiani's letter to Bernardo Tanucci, Paris, 15 August 1763, published in Galiani 1975: 878–879).

[49] "His [Choiseul's] maxims seem to me true, wise, and that can lead this Kingdom to salvation, and Europe to the desired peace" (Ferdinando Galiani's letter to Bernardo Tanucci, Paris, 15 August 1760, published in Bazzoni 1869b: 41). "I never cease to admire Choiseul" (Ferdinando Galiani's letter to Bernardo Tanucci, Paris, 31 August 1760, published in Galiani 1975: 857). "Certainly the parsimony (*spirito di economia*) that Choiseul has is the great, indeed the only antidote to cure all the ills of political bodies as is the diet for natural bodies. He made a campaign in Germany this year with two armies (nor is it his fault that it was not more brilliant) and he did it not only with the same amount of money spent in other years, but they say he saved twenty million. It is certain that the rents were sufficient, and to continue the war this new year, no new impositions will be placed" (Ferdinando Galiani's letter to Bernardo Tanucci, Paris, 16 November 1761, published in Bazzoni 1875b: 41).

[50] "The abbé Galiani is nothing but a flat buffoon and a little wit, whom I have treated much better here than he deserves, and who in the hope of making a fortune gave himself up slavishly to Tanucci's passion against France" (Duc de Choiseul's letter to Martial Dumas de Boisgramont, Versailles, 29 July 1766, Archives du Ministère des Affaires Étrangères, Correspondance Politique, Naples 86, folio 288, published in Skornicki 2018: 327). And: "The Abbé Galiani is nothing but a Fanfaron who plays all sorts of notes in succession, sometimes with a form of wit, and more often with great malice; his praises or his criticisms deserve only much contempt, and I am very much inclined to believe that Tanucci appreciates the services that this flat buffoon [has not ceased] to render, and employs him only for things for which the instruments used need neither great light nor even the most common virtues" (Duc de Choiseul's letter to Bérenger, Versailles, 29 January 1766, Archives du Ministère des Affaires Étrangères, Correspondance Politique, Naples 92, folio 18, published in Skornicki 2018: 327).

[51] "It seems to me that it is from Machiavelli's *The Prince* that this minister [Tanucci] has drawn his morality, and it is certainly destructive of good faith and of all confidence, you have been very careful not to point out the absurdity and indecency of the remarks he has made to you on this subject, and the unjust suspicions he has shown you about our fidelity to our commitments. It is indeed too fastidious to deal with men in whom one finds nothing but artifice and dissimulation" (Duc de Choiseul's letter to Louis César Renaud Viscount de Choiseul, ambassador in Naples, Versailles, 14 Février 1769, Archives du Ministère des Affaires Étrangères, Correspondance Politique, Naples 89, folio 56).

written in 1761 before the Pact was formally signed between France and Spain. According to Galiani: "Treaties must foresee the most remote times and all future contingents as far as is humanly possible. The *Pacte de Famille* is even more than any other treaty built for eternity; thus it must be as valid and well constructed as is possible to the powers of the human mind" (Galiani, MS-18: 704). First of all, he proposed restricting mutual aid to only the case of aggression in Europe by England and Holland, declaring the Neapolitan Kingdom extraneous to the disputes that arose in other theatres in which it had no direct interests and to avoid unnecessary retaliation against its commercial activity (Galiani, MS-18: 704–705). The treaty was also to ensure that the member states of the alliance could maintain their neutrality in the event of war. A clause that was established for the benefit of the weaker states, Parma and Naples: "It may be in the interest and even the usefulness of France or Spain that these sovereigns maintain neutrality in several circumstances. Thus it is right that, without breaking the bonds of love, friendship and attachment, they should maintain a peace which they could not sometimes break without exposing themselves to the risk of losing their states, or of making immense efforts on the part of France and Spain to support them" (Galiani, MS-18: 705). In the case of neutrality, the same clauses as for the cities of the Hanseatic League would apply to the commercial fleet, so as to avoid seizures and attacks by privateers (Galiani, MS-18: 705). Furthermore, the alliance should not harm the commercial activities of the member states, because "the *Pacte de Famille* are based on a guarantee and a mutual alliance between the sovereigns of the August Family, the strongest and closest that has ever been conceived between sovereigns; it is to this fundamental basis that everything must relate. Now it is clear that, as a consequence of the same principles, the interests of the finances of each sovereign, the profit of his customs, must above all be owed to the others: for the richer and more powerful their ally, the better his finances, the more he will be a good and useful ally. Thus the increase in the customs of one's ally must be preferred to the illegitimate gains of a few merchants, whom one must not excessively seek to protect" (Galiani, MS-18: 705).[52]

[52] The question of customs tariffs was of particular interest to the Neapolitan government, and Galiani attempted to study the complex French tax system: "To send Your Excellency distinct news of what our goods pay in France, I set out to study the book entitled *Le Tarif*. But, seeing that I understood it little, I consulted experts. They all agreed with me that the tariff is a chaos in which no one understands anything" (Ferdinando Galiani's letter to Bernardo Tanucci, Paris, 21 March 1763, published in Tanucci 1914, vol. I: 23). Galiani was

In a memoir written in 1784 for Queen of Naples, Maria Carolina, Galiani reconstructed the political events of the *Pacte de Famille* in detail: "When this [the *Pacte*] was stipulated the Duke of Choiseul showed that he was persuaded that the Court of Naples would be pleased with the participation (albeit unknowingly) and would immediately adhere. He had the dexterity to make even the Catholic King [Charles III] believe it, full of tenderness for this son of his [Ferdinand IV], and persuaded that the Kingdoms of Sicily were of such intrinsic weakness that they could live on nothing but support and protection. [...]. France was not surprised at our silence as long as that [Seven-Year] war lasted, and did not insist on adherence to the *Pacte*. On the contrary, it was agreed with the Catholic King that we would wait for the time of peace so that an underage King assisted by a mediocre regency would not find himself in the embarrassments of a war. But after the preliminaries of Fontainebleau on 3 November 1762 [which anticipated the *Peace of Paris* that would mark the end of the *Seven Years' War*], the Duke of Choiseul's irritation and resentment at seeing the Regency of Naples stalling and shying away from adhering to the *Pacte de Famille* was great. Tanucci added another reason to this irritation by denying France the right to cut timber in Calabria for the re-establishment of its navy, and did other things almost in spite of himself: but the famine in Naples in 1764 served as an excuse to interrupt the discussion of other affairs and saved Tanucci [...]. Finally, towards the end of that year, the King of the Two Sicilies [Ferdinand IV] came to the last straits with respect to the adhesion of the King and the Regency begged and obtained from the Catholic King a dispensation, not without reproaches of lack of wisdom and gratitude" (Galiani, MS-19: 356–357).[53]

aware of the asymmetrical conditions in which the Neapolitan trade was taking place: "As for textiles, I see very large Italian velvets and damasks coming here [to France] to sell; as they come from Genoa, they could come from Naples if we knew how to manufacture them and if there were not that absurdity among us of a large duty on the output of our manufactures" (Ferdinando Galiani's letter to Bernardo Tanucci, Paris, 14 November 1763, published in Galiani 1975: 887).

[53] Galiani told Tanucci of the Duke of Choiseul's disappointment, which he had ably mitigated: "Turning, therefore, to the matter of the building timbers, I told him that I was astonished to hear that they had been denied, while (as far as I knew) I had understood that they had been granted, and in the same way that the King now gloriously reigning in Spain recently granted them [...]. I therefore begged His Excellency to be persuaded that it was not from coldness of heart, nor from a lack of goodwill, but from the authority and weight of what was done by the Catholic King that the decision taken today by the Regency was born. It seemed to me with my speech that I had partly quelled the commotion in which he

During his entire activity as a diplomat and advisor, Galiani defended two principles: the right to neutrality and the supremacy of national commercial interests over dynastic claims. These two principles were systematically violated by the great powers that protected their interests against weaker states, such as the Kingdom of Naples, by force.

This asymmetry in trade relations was revealed by the issue of the "right of inspection" of ships entering foreign ports. The privilege of exemption from customs inspections had been granted to the English in the *Treaty of Madrid* (1667), later extended to the Dutch and French through the most-favoured-nation clause in the *Treaty of Utrecht* (1713). The right of inspection was closely connected to the control of smuggling, which the French in particular practised in their trade relations with the Neapolitan kingdom, causing great damage (Clemente 2003). For the Neapolitan government, the *Pacte de Famille* had introduced *de facto* equal treatment for the member states and consequently Neapolitan ships were also to be exempt from inspection, but the *fermiers* of Languedoc and Provence continued to subject Neapolitan vessels to inspection.[54] Galiani put the question in terms of principle: "From the news I have, I see that the privileges of exemption from visitation are no longer applied on our small Neapolitan boats in Provence. If a pound of tobacco can be found even on the high seas on a Neapolitan vessel, it is enough for the *fermiers généraux* to eat the whole crew alive. Or why should we who are a race of *Lestrigon* and *Cyclopes* not do the same? Why do so many smugglers from Provence come to bring tobacco to the wharf?".[55] And to make the right effective, he advocated the construction of an adequate naval force: "I would very

showed me to be, and he told me that he would speak to me more comfortably about it" (Ferdinando Galiani's letter to Bernardo Tanucci, Compiègne, 18 July 1763, publisched in Bazzoni 1877a: 197). Tanucci had great faith in Galiani's persuasive abilities: "having the abbot with his prudence and good manners sweetened the bitterness with which the duke of Choiseul spoke to him about the two problems [timber and visits], perhaps the duke will have spoken in the Council with cold blood" (Bernardo Tanucci's letter to Cantillana, Naples, 6 August 1763, published in Tanucci 1997: 379). See Diaz (1975b: 84).

[54] According to Furio Diaz, the *fermiers'* behaviour was suggested by the French government as retaliation for the Neapolitan resistance to adhering to the *Pacte de Famille* (Diaz 1975b: 84). Tanucci himself related the inspections to the announcement of the Franco-Spanish Pact, see Bernardo Tanucci's letter to Ferdinando Galiani, Naples, 6 August 1763, published in Tanucci (1914, vol. I: 56); Bernardo Tanucci's letters to King Charles, Naples, 7 December 1762 and 5 April 1763, published in Tanucci (1969: 141, 153).

[55] Ferdinando Galiani's letter to Bernardo Tanucci, Paris, 4 January 1762, publisched in Bazzoni (1875b: 45).

much enjoy if Naples had the love of the navy and the art of building vessels [...]. But even if we did not need it, we could make warships and sell them to Spain and France with great profit as the Genoese do. We have wood, pitch and iron all in Calabria and we do not lack hemp. Here, the vessels are estimated at ten thousand lire per cannon [...]. Your Excellency will be able to know how much our vessels cost and will surely find almost a third less in what the *San Filippo* and *San Carlo* [Neapolitan theatres] cost, with all that the King was lavishly robbed".[56] The Neapolitan government had tried in retaliation to subject the French ships to inspection as well, but they refused all control and preferred to unload "elsewhere the goods destined here [to the Neapolitan kingdom]".[57]

The question of inspections also offered Galiani an opportunity to clarify the weakness of Neapolitan maritime trade and the necessity of smuggling.[58] In December 1762, the Neapolitan government had banned the smuggling of Neapolitan goods to the coasts of foreign countries, for Galiani the edict was a mistake that risked destroying the Neapolitan navy: "The trade of the two Sicilies," he observed, "is all done with feluccas and small ships, which do not have a capacity of sixty tons. Each felucca has between seven and ten men and sometimes more crew. With the same number of men the Dutch etc. run a vessel of two or three hundred tons, and with sixteen or seventeen men a vessel of five hundred. The size of this cargo can therefore well provide for the expenses and nourishment of the people. But what can a small felucca carry (unless it be laden with diamonds) that is sufficient to cover the expenses of the crew and the profit to the merchant? That profit which commerce does not bring, therefore, comes from smuggling. If this is eliminated, feluccas will no longer go round the world, because in general it cannot be profitable to put ten men to carry forty or fifty tons of goods, while the foreigner with the same number brings us three or four hundred. We must therefore privilege our trade. We must imitate the wise nations, the English, the Dutch, the

[56] Ferdinando Galiani's letter to Bernardo Tanucci, Paris, 25 January 1762, publisched in Bazzoni (1875b: 47).

[57] Bernardo Tanucci's letter to Ferdinando Galiani, Naples 17 July 1763, published in Tanucci (1914, vol. I: 49).

[58] "The ease with which smuggling can be paid for must now play an important role in considerations of the finances and trade of nations, because all nations now agree that their own manufactures must be encouraged and foreign ones discouraged, and they have all done so in more or less the same way, by imposing high taxes or imposing absolute bans on everything foreign" (Galiani 1770a: 221–222).

French, etc., who either prohibit or impose a tax of at least five per cent. on all merchandise of any kind that is brought into our ports by non-national vessels. In general, it is necessary to ensure that a duty discourages foreigners from bringing into our ports not only their own goods, but sometimes those of our own kingdom, or of Sicily to Naples. When the Neapolitans sail with large ships, no longer with oars, but with sails, then it will be possible to say that we will have commerce: up to now we have nothing but contraband to let us survive".[59] The characteristics of the Neapolitan maritime trade were imposed - according to Galiani - by the insecure conditions in which navigation in the central Mediterranean was carried out due to the presence of Turkish and Barbary pirates. Rowing feluccas could evade pirate ships by always sailing close to the coast, but this obliged a reduced volume of trade; the use of tartanes would have allowed a larger volume of trade, but would also have exposed it more to piracy: "I conclude that we must clean our seas, favour tartanes more than feluccas, and our own more than foreigners with an imposition, which foreigners cannot complain about, because they have the same in their countries".[60]

7.2 The Great Famine of 1763–1764 and the Liberalisation of the Grain Trade in France

Galiani's role as a diplomatic agent became even more delicate in 1764, when a terrible famine devastated the Kingdom of Naples, an event that halted the process of development of the Neapolitan economy, which had hitherto been growing "not overwhelmingly, but regularly" (Villani 1977:

[59] Ferdinando Galiani's letter to Bernardo Tanucci, Paris, 7 February 1763, published in Galiani (1975: 882). "Small vessels and smuggling are synonymous. Large ships and non-smuggling are also synonymous. This is the one and only reason why the English do not do it, the French do. The sailor of any nation smuggles when he can. English small ships do not come to us. There is too much sea between us. On the Channel coast it is incredible how much smuggling the English do. The reason is in the very nature of the thing. A big vessel does not enter the bays, where a gust of wind might smash it against the shore. It has no time to waste doing the small trade of smuggling. What its large crew eats in the meantime would be worth more than the profit of smuggling. Quite the contrary is the case with small vessels for reasons that are easy to understand, and above all because the master of it is some poor devil who has nothing to lose and everything to risk" (Ferdinando Galiani's letter to Bernardo Tanucci, Paris, 12 September 1763, published in Galiani 1975: 882–883).

[60] Ferdinando Galiani's letter to Bernardo Tanucci, Paris, 7 February 1763, published in Galiani (1975: 882).

1, see also Clemente and Russo 2019). The famine was a typical *Ancien Régime* crisis and affected the whole of Europe, with particularly severe effects. The downturn had started in 1758–1759, when the Capitanata harvest was completely lost, causing a famine that was resolved with a special supply of grain from Sicily and continued with a series of bad years (in 1761 and 1763), albeit with varying intensity, until 1766. It "highlighted profound imbalances, provoked sharp price increases,[61] triggered speculative and inflationary phenomena, favoured the owners of land rent and mercantile capital, and worsened the living conditions of the growing peasant population, which found no opportunity in other sectors of production" (Villani 1977: 2). The crisis reached its peak in 1764 when, in the overpopulated Neapolitan capital, as many as 40,000 people died and in the whole kingdom deaths numbered about 200,000:[62] "The tragedy was of such magnitude that the entire eighteenth-century generation remembered this memorable moment with indignation and grief" (Venturi 1973: 394). It was quite clear that the crisis had been exacerbated by the dysfunction of the *Annona* system, the poor state of the road infrastructure, speculative behaviour and the deficit in state finances, factors that had impeded supply possibilities.[63] The famine was seen as the result, almost taken for granted, of the failure of the reformist policy, putting the entire Neapolitan ruling class under accusation.

The Neapolitan government did not deal with the situation in a timely manner and, in a system of administered prices, this initial passivity facilitated *agiotage* by the large commercial intermediaries, with the inevitable decrease in the quantity of circulating goods and the consequent bread riots. The famine was particularly severe in the provinces, while in the

[61] In just one year, the price of wheat went from thirteen *Carlins* to seven *Ducats* per tomolo (Villari 1958: 38).

[62] Carpanetto and Ricuperati (1993: 262). There is, however, no unanimity on the extent of famine-induced mortality, see Lepre (1986a: 59).

[63] "At the first news of the famine, the vicious circle of crises in the modern age came to an end: the poor harvest fuelled the fear of hunger and drove people to hoard and hide grain. Speculative manoeuvres increased the difficulties of supply and drove up prices [...]. Hoarding undoubtedly had a strong negative influence, but this was not so much due to hoarding per se as to the commercial system of the kingdom. [...] The largest quantities of the grain available for trade were in the hands of the great barons who received it from the peasants in the form of rents. It was they who profited most from the high prices and made good money even in times of famine. [...] Against the powerful barons, requisition measures could not be effective [...]. It was this system of power that speculated on famine and which the government was unable to undermine, even when it endangered public order" (Lepre 1986b: 61–62).

capital the impact was less violent: there was no complete lack of bread, but it was "scarce, difficult and laborious to buy, but not impossible, nor desperate" (Sarcone 1765: 255).[64] The famine was followed by an epidemic: "Horrible miseries were experienced in places far from the city capital, in some of which the famine made its most terrible effects felt, the poor and miserable people, abandoned to the stimuli of a raging hunger, were forced to feed themselves with the vilest food, to live on pure herbaceous substances cooked and seasoned with salt and oil, and the most miserable were reduced to eating uncooked grass" (Sarcone 1765: 256), and Antonio Genovesi gave a dramatic testimony: "In the month of April, those who had eaten nothing but herbs began to die, either of weakness or of small fevers: because the famine was so great. In May the capital was infected. The disease grew in June and early July. The dead rose to 300 a day [...]. There is no doubt that the evil did not start from bad and evil food".[65]

In March 1764, Galiani observed the devastating effects of the famine from Paris, writing "the news of the famine in Naples afflicts me infinitely" and proposed a solution to Tanucci: "We must inoculate against smallpox, and abandon all the cures to protect against contagion, which man makes, and which are ineffective. Grain famine must be counteracted by growing a plant that, at least qualitatively, takes the place of grain when it is lacking corn is one of these. In fact, since there has been maize in Europe there have been fewer famines.[66] But this alone is not enough. I see half the world, that is, all the new world, using for bread a root, which has a thousand different names in America. It is called *Manioc* etc. It is basically

[64] "Here we have had a dreadful famine, which is now almost entirely vanished in the capital city, which we owe to the provident care of Marquis Tanucci, but in most provinces it is still raging with much mortality" (Antonio Genovesi's letter to Michele Torcia, Naples, 29 April 1764, in Genovesi 1774, vol. II: 4).

[65] Antonio Genovesi's letter to Michele Torcia, Naples, 30 July 1764, published in Genovesi (1774, vol. II: 17). The physician Michele Sarcone gave an accurate description of the conditions of the city of Naples invaded by poor peasants from the provinces, victims of the famine: "It was pitiful to see from everywhere wandering through the streets not men, but living, pale, scattered, ragged corps" (Sarcone 1765: 258). In the *Dialogues* Galiani wrote "Naples, a city of three hundred and fifty thousand inhabitants, had five hundred thousand inhabitants in the winter of 1764, and all the inhabitants of the countriside, another six hundred thousand, came to the city every day to buy bread" (Galiani 1770a: 55). See also Fasano (1765); Mazzola (2020).

[66] Maize had been introduced into the Kingdom of Naples and was widespread, supplementing the diet of the working classes, see Lepre (1986b: 56–59).

equivalent to the *potatoes* of Spain and Ireland. This island lives on them, and where before it was deserted for lack of grain it is now populated. I see all the people here surviving the winter on these potatoes, which have various names: they are called *pommes de terre*, *topinambours* etc. […]. […]. Now then, if our Abruzzi, Basilicata, Calabria Citra etc., mountainous and partly cold countries, had this plant, how much less wheat would they need! This plant is born without cultivatione and in the most ungrateful soils, and has the advantage that it comes in winter, and one is in time to sow it when one has seen the outcome of the wheat harvest".[67] And, with his usual cynical irony, pointed out "the substance is that in just forty years this crop brought over from America has already covered the countryside of Ireland, England, Germany, Switzerland, and almost all of France. If one counts that in all this time more than a thousand dissertations on the administration of grain have come out, which have come to nothing, one has to say that a potato is better than a pamphlet".[68]

Galiani blamed the famine on a mentality that was closed to innovations, and especially on the *Annona* system: "Oh! old Intieri and the good Rinuccini said so well, that this *Annona* magistrate of the Most Excellent City was the ruin of the Kingdom and the capital. The only science of these lords is to starve the Kingdom to maintain the abundance of the *Masaniello*. Here all their knowledge, all their providence is reduced. Providence that is easy and lucrative because it is armed by force. As soon as the harvest fails, they begin to say that there is infinite grain hidden in the Kingdom, that there are usurers, impostors, who do not want to sell it, that they are in Benevento (like witches). The one is as false as the other. In the meantime, they devastate the Kingdom, they set low prices forcibly, and take away a hoped-for fortune from the farmers. Distrust is established, bad faith, trade is disrupted, and one is either up to his neck or drowns […]. Damn all the *Annona*, all the magistrates and all the rules".[69]

[67] Ferdinando Galiani's letter to Bernardo Tanucci, Paris, 19 March 1764, published in Galiani (1959: 298–299).

[68] Ferdinando Galiani's letter to Bernardo Tanucci, Paris, 30 April 1764, published in Galiani (1975: 902).

[69] Ferdinando Galiani's letter to Bernardo Tanucci, Paris, 26 March 1764, published in Bazzoni (1877b: 41–42). The Neapolitan *Annona* system operated according to the principle of hoarding, which involved sending commissioners or contractors to the provinces to buy the quantity of grain needed to fill the city deposits, the so-called *grain pits*, at a fixed price. This system obviously provoked local rebellions as peasants and smallholders refused

As a diplomatic agent, Galiani had helped find sources of grain supplies for the Kingdom,[70] the Neapolitan government by using local merchants had advanced large sums to import wheat from other Italian regions and even from England, but had not made any requests to France, despite having had an "extra-huge harvest" in 1764, because, since the export of grain was forbidden, it could be acquired by smuggling and furthermore, even though they had obtained a permit from the government, the French would use intermediaries in Genoa and Livorno in order to make more profit (Galiani, MS-20: 308).[71] The situation was also worsened by the hostile political climate with Choiseul showing "rancour and hostility on every occasion" for Naples' uncertain adherence to the *Pacte de Famille* (Galiani, MS-20: 308). Galiani, in a memoir, *Istoria vera della controversia de' grani di Marsiglia scritta da persona ben informata, col parere sulla giustizia delle pretensioni delle parti litiganti* (*True story of the Marseilles grain dispute written by a well-informed person, with an opinion on the justice of the claims of the disputing parties*), written in 1772 (Galiani, MS-20), meticulously described the fraudulent supply of grain by the Neapolitan consul in Marseilles, Francesco Hombrados, which gave rise to a long legal dispute.[72]

to deliver the grain at lower prices than the free market would set. The *Annona* system also favoured overpopulation in Naples because the poorest peasants, unable to find food in the province, moved to the capital where they would find bread, even of very poor quality, and avoid starvation. "In 1764, the beggars from the provinces who flocked to Naples rose to fifty thousand" (Galiani 1959: 300, Nicolini's note). A severe critic of the *Annona* system was also Paolo Mattia Doria, who denounced its defects, see Doria (1710a [1981]: 114–116).

[70] "For my part, I did what I could. I also tried to send grain to Your Excellency and although I did not have the commission I would have had the courage, but I was dismayed that it was not possible to getit to Naples before May and perhaps June" (Ferdinando Galiani's letter to Bernardo Tanucci, Paris, 26 March 1764, published in Bazzoni 1877b: 42).

[71] "The grain from the generous hand of the Catholic King [of Spain] given to us will have served to bring even more on their own account and to the profit of those French merchants who were in charge of sending them. Grain has also been brought by other daring men trusting in the justice of Your Excellency, but the terror of the exorbitant fees of the *Annona* discourages most of them. [...] That very grain, which the Genoese have seized from us, will then be taken by the merchants to Naples, and sold for twice as much" (Ferdinando Galiani's letter to Bernardo Tanucci, Paris, 7 May 1764, published in Bazzoni 1878a: 18–19).

[72] The intricate issue is described in detail by Fausto Nicolini (see the note by Fausto Nicolini, in Tanucci 1914, vol. I: 130–133). The Neapolitan government ordered the purchase of French wheat in Marseilles through commercial intermediaries, but France kept its export prohibition and the transaction was not completed. So the Neapolitan government directly ordered Consul Hombrados to buy as much grain as possible to send to Naples, in

The episode revealed the confused way in which the Neapolitan ruling class had managed the famine and also the inadequacy of institutional mechanisms, such as the *Annona*, no longer able to cope efficiently with crises.[73] The importing of grain at high prices was bleeding the meagre Neapolitan finances dry, and Galiani proposed a solution to deal with the emergency situation: "Why don't we have the silver from the churches (obliged by their essence to be mothers, and nourishers of the poor) taken to the mint?".[74] On a voluntary basis, a part, of the ecclesiastical treasures could be monetised and the churches would be paid interest of 4% per annum on the value of the objects ceded, until the capital was returned. The cost of the transaction could be covered by a tribute. "This most appropriate opportunity would serve to put back into circulation and commerce immense masses of metal that we keep idle and that are one of our great evils. It is not necessary to touch the banks, but to make a debt to the churches, which possess so much idle metal, to pay them the interest, and also to repay the capital, what harm is there? Who can cry out? The most sacred vessels and reliquaries would have to be left behind, but

the hope that dynastic ties would induce the French government to lift the export ban. But this was not the case and the Neapolitan government revoked the order. Hombrados made an agreement with some speculators and, on behalf of the Neapolitan government, bought some 80,000 *tomoli* of wheat to send to Naples, at very high prices. The grain arrived in Naples in June 1764, but in very poor condition, and the following July France lifted the export prohibition. Galiani wrote to Tanucci, "It is certain that the famine in Naples was made and willed by those who closed the port of Marseilles, and by those who, despite our prayers, prolonged and then refused to buy grain here from our court in order to boast of their gains and excessive profit of the merchants" (Ferdinando Galiani's letter to Bernardo Tanucci, Paris, 23 April 1764, published in Galiani 1975: 900). The episode is also taken up in the *Dialogues*: "Will you then turn to your neighbours? But since they have robbed some of your grain, that is proof that they had not enough of it; so either they will not give you any, or it will be yours that they will sell to you, but rotten during the transport, and overcharged with double the freight, and with all that their greed could have calculated of profit. So you can only turn to the farthest countries. This help will be weak, will arrive late and will cost enormously" (Galiani 1770a: 54–55). On trade flows in the world grain market in the eighteenth century, see Dobado-González - Garzía-Hiernaux - Guerrero (2012). On Francisco Hombrados Malo, see Carrino (2021).

[73] "If Your Excellency can abolish the annona [...] for one year only [and] grant a right on all that grain or flour that any baker or private individual will freely bring into Naples [...] do so, and you will have saved the Kingdom. If you cannot, weep like Jeremiah and abandon a city which God has abandoned" (Ferdinando Galiani's letter to Bernardo Tanucci, Paris, 2 November 1767, published in Galiani 1959: 327–328). See also Macry (1974).

[74] Ferdinando Galiani's letter to Bernardo Tanucci, Paris, 7 May 1764, published in Bazzoni (1878a: 19).

candlesticks, frets, antependium, statues, everything would be minted and the friars would find themselves enriched with a considerable annual income. Perhaps some would shout, not that they do not know the utility, but only about the future omen of infidelity, and ill-payment from the royal treasury. But it is necessary above all things to introduce into Naples the credit of the *Royal Exchequer* and the mutual trust between it and the people: that the people should willingly bring their money to the King, and the King should always find it in the pockets of his subjects. [...]. It can begin with the friars and not with the banks for if the friars lack faith, less evil: if the banks, most grave and supreme evil, and which would be our total ruin".[75]

He therefore admonished Tanucci to quickly adopt such a measure to prevent the famine from having even more negative effects on the already fragile economy of the Kingdom: "Reflect, Your Excellency, on the great amount of money that has gone out, or that remains, owing to the Kingdom for so much foreign grain bought, and you will see with your wise mind that the decrease in the volume of metal, which was among us, must necessarily produce very high exchange rates, very high prices of many kinds of things, and above all the low price of our own goods, that is, oil, silk, wine etc. All the effects of the mass of metal diminished and restricted in the hands of a few merchants, who have made great profit in the public calamity. So if new metal is not recast in the mass of the little that circulates now, the convalescence of our Kingdom will last many years. It will remain without strength, without commerce, always languishing. It is therefore necessary to mint and coin money to meet the debt that the royal treasury will have contracted, to compensate for the collections of this calamitous year, which will be very large. Woe if the royal treasury were to fall behind in its payments. It would halt the circle of money, which is the only thing that can cure us. Languor and inertia, natural effects of the little circle of money, would continue".[76]

[75] Ferdinando Galiani's letter to Bernardo Tanucci, Paris, 7 May 1764, published in Bazzoni (1878a: 20).

[76] Ferdinando Galiani's letter to Bernardo Tanucci, Paris, 7 May 1764, published in Bazzoni (1878a: 19–20). But a week later, the abbot was more pessimistic: "There remains the dear price, which is not an evil that can be medicated by commerce and industry that is introduced into a people. But, when the juice and substance of a nation is drunk up all by the friars, barons and *paglietti* [epithet for Neapolitan lawyers], idle and bad people, it is a difficult business to put the money into circulation" (Ferdinando Galiani's letter to Bernardo Tanucci, Paris, 14 May 1764, published in Galiani 1959: 305).

The Neapolitan tragedy had been consummated when the *Contrôleur Général des Finances*, Clément Charles François de L'Averdy, passed the measures to liberalise the grain trade, with the edicts of May 1763 and July 1764, which marked the greatest success of the physiocratic school.[77] The policy of liberalisation had long been advocated by a large part of the *intelligentsia* as a prerequisite for restoring in France the productive centrality of the agricultural sector, which had been severely downgraded by mercantilist policies (Perrot 1988: 509, 520).[78]

As early as the end of the seventeenth century, Pierre Le Pesant, Sieur de Boisguilbert (1696 [1843], 1707a [1843], 1707b [1843]; Faccarello 1999) had made this point in explicit opposition to Colbert's system. For Boisguillebert, France possessed a competitive advantage in the production of wheat, wine, and salt, the foundation and cause of all the wealth of Europe (Boisguilbert 1696 [1843]: 172–173). According to Boisguilbert, the mercantilist policy proposed by Colbert ignored this competitive advantage by subordinating agriculture to the development of manufacturing. In the Colbert system, the agricultural sector, according to Boisguilbert, had the sole function of providing cheap means of subsistence to keep wages down. Added to this was the unfair system of taxation based on the *Taille*, which as a direct tax, applied arbitrarily, hit the French peasantry and the productive classes, reducing disposable income and thus consumption (Boisguilbert 1696 [1843]: 181). To maintain low prices and avoid famine, Colbert's system completely banned the export of grain and instead favoured its import (edicts of 1664 and 1667), applying a customs policy diametrically opposed to that applied to manufactures. A

[77] With the declaration of May 1763 and the edict of July 1764, the government liberalised the circulation of grain between the provinces of the Kingdom of France, abolishing passports and special authorisations, and allowed the export of grain and flour through certain ports on condition that the price did not exceed a certain level. However, a special regime for the capital and certain market and duty rights remained in force. Implementing the two measures were the *Contrôleur Général des Finances* Henri Léonard J. B. Bertin and C. C. F. de L'Averdy, supported by Choiseul, under the influence of physiocratic theories. See Dockés (1969: 186–187) and Charbit (2002: 857). For a detailed analysis on grain policy in eighteenth-century France, see Kaplan (1976). On the problems associated with liberalisation see Harcourt (2011).

[78] Galiani also positively assessed the French government's political choices: "This free internal trade in grain and the external trade that will soon be instituted, this establishment of an amortisement fund, these colleges of agriculture, this war on the *tuile* arbitraire are all great things done" (Ferdinando Galiani's letter to Bernardo Tanucci, Paris, 5 March 1764, published in Galiani 1959: 297).

system of internal customs made trade between province and province difficult, increasing transport costs. Thus, provinces in overproduction could not dispose of their products either abroad or in other provinces of the Kingdom in famine (Boisguilbert 1696 [1843]: 233–234). The lack of outlets caused overproduction in the most fertile regions, which was followed by a fall in prices, incomes and rents received on land. Farmers sold at a loss, reducing investments and improvements, thus decreasing the cultivated area. If this was compounded by a bad year, a deflationary crisis quickly spread to other regions (Boisguilbert 1696 [1843]: 201; Boisguilbert 1707a [1843]: 400).

The supposed advantage that France enjoyed in the context of protectionism thus turned into its opposite by generating the crises of overproduction in which, according to Boisguilbert, the agricultural sector had been for years. Faced with the severity of deflation all remedies were justified, even that of destroying the abundant harvest, as the Dutch often did (Boisguilbert 1696 [1843]: 202). Agricultural overproduction in France could be solved, according to Boisguillebert, by allowing complete freedom for foreigners to buy grain at any time and in any quantity (Boisguilbert 1707b [1843]: 377). By allowing free domestic trade and freedom of export, prices would never be too low nor too high (Boisguilbert 1705 [1843]: 275). Exports were also to be supported with premiums, following the English example (Boisguilbert 1705 [1843]: 344), but the domestic market was to be protected, maintaining protective duties on grain, removing them only in times of famine. Boisguillebert therefore proposed a "conditional free trade", taking the defence of the domestic market as a priority. With Boisguilbert, the idea was thus affirmed that exports benefit domestic agricultural production by sustaining incomes and prices for the benefit of society as a whole. This policy prescription was based on the assumption that the French agricultural sector, and cereal production in particular, had an advantage over other countries and that without external trade outlets France was condemned to overproduction and deflation of prices and incomes in the agricultural sector.

Ideas in favour of liberalising the grain trade began to penetrate the political sphere only in the 1750s, under the influence of the group of reformers gathered around the new intendant of commerce Vincent de Gournay.[79] The political proposals for the liberalisation of the grain trade

[79] Other writers during the eighteenth century shared Boisguilbert's opinion, see Melon (1736); Dupin (1748); Machault D'Arnouville (1749); Glineur (2005: 296); Herbert

were largely presented in Claude-Jacques Herbert's *Essai sur la police general des grains* (1753), a pamphlet that was particularly successful, even outside France (it was translated by Genovesi, see Herbert 1765), in which he proposed, overcoming Boisguillebert's protectionist concerns, the total liberalisation of the grain trade, which was seen as the only solution to the problem of famine.

With the advent of the *Physiocratie*, the question of the liberalisation of the grain trade became an essential part of a theoretical system and was presented in a scientific form that gave it the status of an absolute truth.

In his articles *Fermiers* and *Grains*, written for the *Encyclopédie*, Quesnay outlined the essentials of the physiocratic conception of grain production and trade. If the only productive sector is agriculture, Quesnay observed, i.e. the only one capable of creating the *net product*, it follows that the increase in national wealth can only be generated by its strengthening. This strengthening could be achieved by extending the *grande culture*, based on the intensive use of capital (with the use of horses) and the management entrusted to tenant farmers (*fermiers*), and by reducing the amount of land cultivated with the traditional labour-intensive *petit culture* (with the use of oxen) and directed mainly to the subsistence of the peasant (Quesnay 1756a: 529). In the provinces where *petit culture* was practised, land was cultivated with barley, oats, buckwheat, maize and very low-value products that barely ensured survival (Quesnay 1756a: 538). The peasant did not have sufficient capital to cultivate wheat in large quantities, which was the only way of making a profit (Quesnay 1756a: 529). In the provinces where *grande culture* prevailed, the land was prepared for the production of grain, and the peasants, obtaining more surplus, diversified their production and also devoted themselves to handicrafts (Quesnay 1756a: 537).

The enormous backwardness of French agriculture was due to the shortage of tenant farmers (Quesnay 1756a: 532) and the excessive regulation of the market, culminating in the prohibition of free trade, which had the effect of lowering the price of grain (Quesnay 1756a: 532). The sufficiently high price (*bon prix,* good price) served to cover expenses and to give an adequate profit margin to those who were able to provide the nation with an annual increase in real wealth. The policy of low grain prices, underpinning the strict regulation of trade, tended to favour city

(1753: 134–135, 162); Vivens, Chevalier de (1756, part I, chap. IX); Forbonnais (1758, t. I: 295–297); Abeille (1760, 1763, 1764, 1768).

dwellers, labourers and artisans in the manufactures above all, who obtained bread at low prices (Quesnay 1757: 813).

In order to encourage good prices, it was necessary, according to Quesnay, to immediately remove the ban on *free trade* (Quesnay 1756a: 536). The liberalisation of exports had to be accompanied by the removal of internal barriers and natural obstacles in order to favour national trade. By abolishing internal customs and improving the communication infrastructure (roads and canals) it would be possible to quickly transfer grain from the surplus provinces to those affected by the famine.[80]

For Quesnay and his school, it was therefore a matter of reversing the entire trade policy set by Colbert, wrongly directed towards the export of luxury manufactures in the production of which the kingdom had no advantage, as it did not possess the raw materials and skills to manufacture "belles étoffes et les draps fins" (Quesnay 1757: 812). Competition with other manufacturing countries had resulted in a trade war that had prompted the adoption of retaliatory protectionist measures with the effect of minimising mutual trade and leaving the agricultural sector in uncertainty (Quesnay 1757: 812). The development of manufacturing had therefore not given France any advantage (Quesnay 1757: 821). A nation with little production and trade in agricultural commodities remained uncertain in its wealth, and even if it engaged in manufacturing trade to survive (Quesnay 1757: 827). In the physiocratic view, foreign trade and the liberalisation of domestic trade were necessary conditions to ensure a stable and adequate price level in the agricultural sector. Quesnay stated this explicitly in the article *Hommes*, intended for the *Encyclopédie*

[80] According to some scholars, free trade was not regarded by the physiocrats as a dogma, but rather as a secondary choice: "Quesnay taught laissez-faire and free trade as absolute norms of political wisdom. But these imperatives must be viewed in the light of the physiocrats' hostility to all kinds of privileges and to a great many things that seemed to them to be abuses, monopoly positions among others. Since these could not have been abolished without a good deal of governmental interference, Quesnay urged upon government what really was an activist policy, and not at all one of doing nothing. Moreover, in spite of his wholesale condemnation of government regulation or control, it is important to observe that what he actually faced were regulations that were inherited from the past and no longer fitted current conditions: the absolute norm of laissez-faire acquires in such a case a relative significance that differs greatly from what its absolutism suggests. Finally, we must not forget that French agriculture in 1760 was not interested in protection: there was no danger of large wheat imports as a normal phenomenon; and free trade in agricultural products would have, if anything, increased their prices" (Schumpeter 1954 [2006]: 222).

and never published due to the censorship problems the latter ran into (Quesnay 1757–1758 [2005]: 277).

The same idea was present in other exponents of the school, and is clearly expressed by the agronomist Henry Pattullo who wrote: "The true object of the free exportation of grain, must only be to avoid non-values and expenses, to maintain them at a price more or less equal and sufficient to support the revenues of the goods of the nations, to compensate the farmer for his expenses, and to procure him a profit proportionate to his advances, and to the risks to which he is exposed" (Pattullo 1758: 218).

Quesnay tended to emphasise that the *bon prix* was not a high price, but only a price sufficient to prevent the loss of value of grain (Quesnay 1757: 830). The export of grain, generalised and not limited to certain provinces (Quesnay 1757: 829), was thus - according to Quesnay - the essential condition for the recovery of French agriculture (Quesnay 1757: 825). France was facilitated in this by its favourable geographical position, between the Atlantic and the Mediterranean (Quesnay 1757: 825). The commercialisation of the products of the soil also allowed France to develop the trade in manufactured goods, as it could always pay, in proportion to the income from its landed property, labourers and artisans (Quesnay 1757: 827). Neither regulations nor *Annona* policies were needed (Quesnay 1757: 825), free trade, which had been considered the main cause of famines, on the contrary, constituted their major antidote, as England's experience showed (Quesnay 1757: 825). Nor was competition from other nations, particularly the fertile American colonies, to be feared, as the quality of French grains was clearly superior (Quesnay 1757:825).

In synthetic terms, the economic geography of wheat proposed by Quesnay was essentially deterministic: wheat had to be cultivated on the land best suited to receive it and thus most productive, the surpluses obtained in this way were sent to the regions in deficit and exported. In the event of generalised famine, the free import of grain from abroad made it possible to solve crises. In the same deterministic terms, manufacturing was also rejected as it was not only a sterile activity, but also because it was not justified by French geography due to the absence of raw materials (Quesnay and Du Pont de Nemours 1768, Note sur la Maxime IX: 112–113).

An agricultural nation therefore had to favour active foreign trade in its commodities and practise passive foreign trade in manufactured goods. This type of trade allowed an agricultural country supremacy, both because it would never fear that its trade, as was the case for manufactured goods (and even more so for luxury goods), could be taken away from it by rival competitors, and because it would never be tributary to any other country possessing the raw materials necessary for industry (Quesnay 1757: 827).

These were the theories that influenced political choices in France.[81]

7.3 *Naples, Paris, London: The Genesis of the* Dialogues

Galiani had closely followed the liberalisation process and the political debate, giving an extensive report to Tanucci in a memoir, *Storia dell'avvenuto sugli editti del libero commercio de' grani in Francia promulgati nel 1763 e 1764* (*History of the edicts of free trade in grain in France promulgated in 1763 and 1764*), probably written in 1765 (Galiani, MS-21).

The Neapolitan abbot described in detail the interests of the provincial intendants (*intendants provinciaux*) who were entrusted with the control of the grain trade: "as soon as they realised that the province entrusted to them was insufficiently provided for, they began to close their eyes and let those merchants, who enjoyed and had deserved their confidence and good grace, export the consignments of grain that they had stockpiled. Sometimes they even granted these permits in writing, but never for free. The stewards also had another strange authority, which was that of forbidding grain to go out of their province into another province of France, or brought from it into this one; and, as not all the provinces of that monarchy are fertile in grain, and some lack it completely, so it was in their power to bring about abundance or famine whenever and wherever they pleased. The one and the other was equally profitable to them and to their

[81] Schumpeter tends to downplay the political influence of physiocracy: "Expressed in terms of that particular environment, Quesnay's success was primarily a *succès de salon*. Polite society talked physiocracy for a time but very few people outside took much notice of it except by way of sneering at it. There was thus a physiocrat fashion but there was no physiocrat movement in the sense in which there was (and is) a Marxist movement, especially not one rooted in agrarian class interests. But what about the political influence of the physiocrats of which we read so much? What about their historic role in combating privilege, abuses, and all the horrors of protection?" (Schumpeter 1954 [2006]: 222). On the evolution of the Physiocratic movement, see: Higgs (1897); Schelle (1907); Weulersse (1910); Beer (1939); Villari (1965); Fox-Genovese (1976); Vaggi (1987); Sonenscher (2002); Charles and Théré (2007); Vardi (2012); Charles and Théré (2019). On the relationship between Physiocratic theories and Italian economic thought, see Villari (1968).

merchants" (Galiani, MS-21: 315–316). Such arbitrary behaviour had ruined French agriculture and no reforms had been implemented since the *Contrôleur Général* was chosen from among the intendants, who in turn were chosen from eighty families and thus "all of them relatives or close friends of each other [...]. This shows how damaging it is to restrict the offices of administration to a particular class of families, who can by kinship or friendship connect and hold themselves together" (Galiani, MS-21: 316). The appointment of Clément Charles François de L'Averdy, a member of a parliament and a stranger to the intendants, to the position of *Contrôleur Général*, broke, according to Galiani, the network of interests and initiated the reforms, inspired above all by Abbot André Morellet and Louis Paul Abeille, *Inspector General of Manufactures*, both of whom Galiani described as "very special friends in Paris" (Galiani, MS-21: 317). The measures convinced the King and the parliaments, but not the intendants who opposed them, impeding transport and rousing the rabble. The famine in Naples was indicated as the effect of trade liberalisation, but Abbot Morellet proved that there had never been free trade in the Neapolitan Kingdom, confuting all opposition.[82]

Galiani concluded his memoir by emphasising the benefits of free trade: "From this history we know that to refuse the free trade in grain or the fixed, perpetual, irrevocable tariff in the form of customs duty - which is the same as liberty - is not the effect of ignorance or prejudice or panic or old habit, but is malice, self-interest, the aim of profit. Everyone knows the good of liberty, but to those who can be privileged, while others are held back, common liberty is no good. [...]. I wanted to write down all this history that I have seen so that in countries where the good of a fixed and regulated administration is to be established, it will be known what and how much war is to be endured. Let there be no fear of events elsewhere, and let it be known that in the end this war will be won with constancy and firmness, since it was won in France, a country that at present enjoys neither the advantage of a vigorous administration in the prince, nor that of a perfect subordination in the inferiors" (Galiani, MS-21: 321–322).[83]

[82] According to Fausto Nicolini, the inspiration for Morellet's pamphlet was Galiani himself (Morellet 1764; Galiani 1959: 306, footnote 1 and 318–319).

[83] Galiani's advocacy of free trade is, according to Furio Diaz, "distracted and badly informed" and his remarks "appear rather general and a tad superficial" (Diaz 1975a: lii) and "in Galiani, busy with his diplomatic relations and in the flattering events of his salon conversation, in contact with the most famous *gens de lettre* of Paris, the specific study of the ele-

The decision to liberalise the grain trade in a country as extensive as the French Kingdom, according to the abbot, obliged the neighbouring states to adopt the same measures: "the free exportation of the grains of France will be a great detriment to our commerce if we do not endeavour to imitate it. Here they have known this great truth, that the only preservative from famine, is free trade and exporting, because this increases the cultivation, and when much grain is sown, always either much or little is harvested, but those who sow little, sometimes reap nothing".[84]

The memoir had been written in Naples where Galiani had returned due to his poor health. In December 1764, in fact, he wrote to Tanucci that French doctors had recommended a period of treatment at the

ments and materials that could have been relevant in that attempt, does not appear - and [there is] a certain improvisation, haste, and therefore sometimes superficiality" (Diaz 1975a: liii). A free trade stance for the grain trade was also taken by Intieri: "Grain is a very necessary commodity, so there is no need to fear it rotting. It is enough that the King gives to grain the same as he gives to the wool that the sheep makes. He does not charge duty on them and the Sicilians come and take it. The Poles, the English and others who have more infertile land than ours dispose of their grain and we have to fear the outcome of ours? [...]. Let the King mitigate this duty [...] and we will send away as much grain as ever is made, and I say that the Dutch and the Turk will come and take it, and this because of a certain and constant rule that men run where there is profit. England that has a good nose pays those who export it, and we besides the tax have put infinite hindrances. But what would happen if we not only freed the exportation of this kind from the many impediments it has, but moreover used all diligence to cultivate this industry well, to reduce it to greater perfection, which in my opinion could be done especially in Apulia, which would be if the Prince facilitated transport to the sea by making roads easy and comfortable. In short, it is certain that the Kingdom of Naples is the most fertile place in Italy and therefore the grain and all the rest of the provisions should come from here and not from Poland and England" (Bartolomeo Intieri's letter to Celestino Galiani, Naples, 31 January 1739, BSNSP, XXXI.A.7: folios 29v–30r). Intieri feared crises of overproduction: "What Melon wisely writes is that, on reflection, those [harvests] of abundance are more to be feared than famines" (Bartolomeo Intieri's letter to Celestino Galiani, Naples, 23 Jamuary 1739, BSNSP, XXXI.A.7: folio 27v). "You must be convinced - wrote Galiani in *Della Moneta* - that trade without the increase of agriculture (because we have none) is a spectre and a vain shadow. And although commerce and agriculture are linked together in such a way that each is the effect and cause of the other; yet if we look more closely, we will find that agriculture always precedes commerce: because flourishing commerce comes from the abundance of superfluous goods, and these derive from agriculture, which is made by the population; the population by freedom; freedom by just government" (Galiani [1751]: 345).

[84] Ferdinando Galiani's letter to Bernardo Tanucci, Paris, 25 July 1764, published in Bazzoni (1878a: 21).

thermal waters of Barège, in the Pyrenees.[85] But Galiani considered this stay to be out of his financial reach and asked Tanucci permission to return to Naples for six months, to take care of himself in Ischia and also to pursue certain family affairs.[86] The abbot left Paris at the end of April 1765 and did not return to the French capital until November 1766 (Diodati 1788: 47).[87]

Important assignments had kept Galiani in Naples for twice the requested period of leave. Tanucci had appreciated his work at the embassy and proposed to the King to assign him, at the end of his diplomatic mission, to the Secretariat of State,[88] but probably this role in the Neapolitan bureaucracy was not particularly appreciated by the abbot, who, as Tanucci wrote to Charles III, aspired to "a supernumerary position in the Magistrate of Commerce, i.e. advisor. But the Regency cannot make supernumeraries, and I am not sure that he persists in this desire".[89] In the face of the King's refusal to give this supernumerary position, Tanucci did not know how to please Galiani.[90] In December 1765, he proposed Galiani

[85] Galiani also had problems with his eyes, as he wrote to Tanucci: "the ophthalmologists I consulted for my eye problems have all unanimously urged me to make use of a special mineral water (*acqua ferrata*), which flows in Passi (which is the Posillipo of Paris). They say that this mineral water will thin my humours, do a hundred good things to my blood, and in sustance I will not go blind. I believe nothing of it, but in sustance fear makes me determine to follow their advice" (Ferdinando Galiani's letter to Bernardo Tanucci, Paris, 27 June 1763, published in Bazzoni 1876b: 252).

[86] Ferdinando Galiani's letter to Bernardo Tanucci, Paris, 24 December 1764, quoted in Tanucci (1914: 221) (Nicolini's footnote). See also il documento in BSNSP, XXXI.A. 8: folio 29r.

[87] The return to Naples was not a particularly happy experience for the Abbé, as we learn from a letter by Domenico Caracciolo: "I well believe that after many years of being away, the indecent shouts must be a wonder to each of us. Or unruly gestures and the swearing of our compatriots" (Domenico Caracciolo's letter to Ferdinando Galiani, London, 2 July 1765, published in Nicolini 1954: 28).

[88] Bernardo Tanucci's letter to King Charles, Naples, 13 August 1765, published in Tanucci (1969: 278).

[89] Bernardo Tanucci's letter to King Charles, Naples, 24 September 1765, published in Tanucci (1969: 283–284). Even when he returned to Paris, Galiani asked Tanucci for a secure position for himself and his brother Berardo: "I am very ready to return to keep you whatever company you wish, but you know the conditions. Either my brother or I must be accommodated. So it depends on when Your Excellency wills it, or rather, when (as I hope) he can freely and effectively will it" (Ferdinando Galiani's letter to Bernardo Tanucci, Paris, 1 December 1766, publisched in Bazzoni 1878b: 453).

[90] Bernardo Tanucci's letter to King Charles, Portici, 5 November 1765, published in Tanucci (1969: 290).

as ambassador to Denmark and emphasised that his ecclesiastical status should not be an obstacle for such a function in a Protestant state, because "before Luther and Calvin corrupted our holy religion, and the Christian nations were divided, ambassadors and other ecclesiastical representatives were frequent. Afterwards there is no lack of examples".[91]

In April 1766, Galiani was preparing to return to France, but Tanucci still wanted to keep him in Naples to appoint him as a member of a commission created to draft the commercial treaty that King Charles had ordered to be concluded with France. Genovesi was also a member of the commission, headed by Juan Asensio de Goyzueta, *Segretario di Azienda e Commercio*. This proposal was opposed by the Prince of San Nicandro, Tanucci's opponent in the Regency Council, arguing that "as Galiani was a friend of Choiseul, it would be better if he were in France, and present there he could persuade him on the matters of the treaty", but Tanucci objected that Cantillana's jealousy should be avoided and proposed strengthening the abbot's role by appointing him advisor to the *Magistrate of Commerce*, a position that when he returned to France "would give him a certain credit and perhaps greater access".[92] A proof that Galiani's role had become essential at Louis XV's court. From what Tanucci reported to King Charles, Galiani was rather sceptical about the French willingness to conclude a treaty with Naples, believing that negotiations had been initiated "on the sole pretext of suspending the inspections [carried out by the Neapolitans on French ships] and continuing the smuggling here, since it is certain that for one Sicilian vessel, which happens to be in the ports of France, one hundred Frenchmen come to the ports and harbours and beaches of Sicily, and make a great profit for the French, who unfortunately resented not being able to trade here, obstinate as they were not to receive inspections".[93]

[91] Bernardo Tanucci's letter to King Charles, Naples, 17 December 1765, published in Tanucci (1969: 296–297).

[92] Bernardo Tanucci's letter to King Charles, Portici, 29 April 1766, published in Tanucci (1969: 316).

[93] Bernardo Tanucci's letter to King Charles, Portici, 13 May 1766, published in Tanucci (1969: 318–319). A few days later, Tanucci confirmed Galiani's suspicions to the King: "The proposal of the treaty of commerce was a way out so as not to be able to sustain the violence and injustice and false complaints, and a cunning compensation for not being able to resist the cries of the Provençals, who wanted at any cost, even to be inspected, to recover the trade that was so advantageous to them in the Sicilies, and to put to sleep the affair of the inspections, returning them to the not to be done, which is so advantageous to the French. You see, Your Majesty, that the suspension of the visits will not be for that short time that Choiseul

Galiani's scepticism also concerned the actual will of the Neapolitan government to conclude the treaty. Many years later, the abbot, reconstructing the complex negotiations with France for Queen Maria Carolina, wrote: "On 7 May 1766, by a dispatch, a council was established under the direction of Marquis Goyzueta, composed of the President of the *Magistrate of Commerce*, Giambattista Iannucci, the Secretary of this tribunal, Vincenzo Boraggine, Abbot Galiani, freshly elected advisor of the same tribunal, and who was then in Naples by licence, the merchant Giovanni Lembo, *Eletto del Popolo*, and the professor Antonio Genovesi. And this council was to discuss the subjects and articles of the future treaty. The mere reading of the members of a council so strangely coupled and composed of people inexperienced in the art of negotiating with sovereigns, was enough for the wise men to realise that nothing was to be concluded, and so it was, in fact, not even once did it meet" (Galiani, MS-19: 357–358).

On 11 June 1766, Galiani, who in the meantime had graduated in *utroque iure*, i.e. in civil and canon law (Tanucci 1914: vol. 2: 2, Nicolini's footnote), was appointed as advisor (consigliere) to the *Supreme Magistrate of Commerce* (a degree was a prerequisite for assuming this office) and in the Council "everyone willingly gave his vote".[94] Tanucci had intended, together with some members of the Council, to keep Galiani in Naples again, but the majority authorised his departure for France in August 1766. Tanucci feared that Galiani's departure would be considered by the French government "a sign of little intention to make the treaty".[95]

The return journey to France was "very happy".[96] Galiani had stopped in Milan, welcomed by Count Karl Joseph von Firmian, Maria Theresa's minister plenipotentiary in the Duchy of Milan (and former ambassador to Naples).[97] Milan appeared to Galiani a rich city: "This country has flour-

said, but will probably be at the Greek Kalends, so that Galiani's suspicions are verified, who about Choiseul's way of thinking has guessed and ascertained more than one thing" (Bernardo Tanucci's letter to King Charles, Naples, 17 June 1766, published in Tanucci 1969: 325).

[94] Bernardo Tanucci's letter to King Charles, Naples, 10 June 1766, published in Tanucci (1969: 323).

[95] Bernardo Tanucci's letter to King Charles, Naples, 26 August 1766, published in Tanucci (1969: 337).

[96] Ferdinando Galiani's letter to Bernardo Tanucci, Paris, 17 November 1766, published in Bazzoni (1878b: 449).

[97] "From him I have received the most distinguished refinements he could ever imagine and desire. He does the same with any Neapolitan who comes here, and is truly a good friend

ished again under his [Firmian] beneficent and philosophical hand. One does not see a single poor person in the streets. The farmer is rich, and happy, and the town has a beautiful air of prosperity. [...] The book *Dei Delitti e delle Pene* (*Of Crimes and Punishments*) has been seen, and there is already a huddle of many young nobles, who study and think, and whom the people therefore believe to be unbelievers, as centuries ago they would have believed them to be sorcerers".[98]

His return to Paris was not equally happy, Galiani was received coldly by Choiseul and reported to Tanucci as follows: "I have been assured that from Naples very bad things have been written about me to the Duke of Choiseul, claiming that I have spoken badly of him. No one knows the contrary better than Your Excellency. But a calumny and a lie without proof is the easiest thing and the least ingenious, I am not worried, because since I know how frank, sincere and truth-loving the Duke of Choiseul is, and that he willingly converses and lets people speak, with no man in the world will I have an easier time justifying myself than with him and return to his good grace. On the contrary, I will say that in a certain way I rejoice that this foolish imposture has been made to me, because [...] he will love me more than before after he has satisfied himself. With open-hearted people reconciliations succeed very well".[99] In the report written for Maria Carolina many years later, Galiani accused Tanucci of having "made him obnoxious to that ministry, since [the Neapolitan minister] had deliberately caused the French to know all the secret enlightenments he had received from him [Galiani] concerning the warnings to be had in order not to harm the Neapolitans, should they wish to embrace the articles of the *Pacte de Famille* relating to trade" (Galiani, MS-19: 358).

both of the King and of the Neapolitans. Much has been said with him about Your Excellency and everything I have told him he has understood with that pleasure that transpires in a beautiful, grateful and reminiscent soul" (Ferdinando Galiani's letter to Bernardo Tanucci, Milan, 25 October 1766, published in Bazzoni 1878b: 448).

[98] Ferdinando Galiani's letter to Bernardo Tanucci, Milan, 25 October 1766, published in Bazzoni (1878b: 448).

[99] Ferdinando Galiani's letter to Bernardo Tanucci, Paris, 17 November 1766, published in Bazzoni (1878b: 449).

A few days later, Galiani reported that the climate had changed for the better,[100] even recovering the relationship with Choiseul.[101]

Galiani was now perfectly integrated into French *haute société* and considered Paris his homeland of choice, and felt valued and appreciated for his merits and not for friendship or family, as he was valued in Naples.[102] From his privileged observatory, he closely followed every intellectual, political and economic phenomenon, responding in detail to the various questions posed by Tanucci.

He gave the Neapolitan minister detailed information on the enterprise of the century, the *Encyclopédie*, which he followed closely thanks to his

[100] The Parisians "have welcomed me with such love, that I am much more loved in Paris than in Naples. Such love can be forgiven for the much fog in this climate, the lack of appetite, the convulsions of the nerves, the headache I have here" (Ferdinando Galiani's letter to Bernardo Tanucci, Paris, 24 November 1766, published in Bazzoni 1878b: 450).

[101] "I was not deceived in what I foresaw when I wrote to Your Excellency that I entirely trusted in the frankness and love of truth, which resides in the soul of the Duke of Choiseul. In fact, last Tuesday, when I went to Versailles, as soon as he saw me, he told me everything that had been written against me from Naples and (but always keeping a laughing and placid face) he told me that they had written that I had rendered all the baddest services I could to France, that I had exacerbated the ministers' tempers, put thorns in their affairs and, finally, that I was to blame for everything. I did not flinch at such an incredible narration, but defended and justified myself with all the vigour and strength that innocence gave me, the notorious falsehood of the facts, and the all too well-known mendacity of the writer [...]. He heard everything with infinite benevolence and kindness, he did not dispute, he did not oppose. He conceded many things" (Ferdinando Galiani's letter to Bernardo Tanucci, Paris, 1 December 1766, published in Bazzoni 1878b: 451).

[102] "Your Excellency asks me for an explanation of my Parisian love, and never ceases to be surprised by my predilection for Paris. Here I will explain myself. I have no other sure love in Naples, nor can I assertively say that I am loved by anyone other than Your Excellency [...]. The others who loved me and said they loved me, did they love Galiani, or did they love Tanucci's friend? Was it ray or reverberation? Did those relatives, friends, etc. love me, or the Councillor of Commerce? Did the same honest people love me, or the nephew of that Monsignor Galiani who made one a bishop, gave the other a cathedra, the other what do I know? Was it gratitude or inclination? [...] In Paris, I am all me." (Ferdinando Galiani's letter to Bernardo Tanucci, Paris, 5 December 1766, published in Bazzoni 1878b: 454). And again he repeated the same thought: "a little body like mine, not made for conflict, weak in health and also lazy by habit, not armed with seat relatives of major scoundrels who have swindled fiefs, forged writs, [...] finally, who has almost no homeland, and has no one else in his homeland but a foreigner, Tanucci, among the infinite pagan peoples, is not made to skirmish, resist, whirl in the vortex, and spin, he is striated matter, he is of the intermundium, he is crust, excrement, deposition. And because every body tends to its own place, therefore I fell in Paris, where I will most likely remain for ever" (Ferdinando Galiani's letter to Bernardo Tanucci, Paris, 23 February 1767, published in Bazzoni 1878c: 24).

friendship with Diderot and d'Alembert: "This dictionary is an enterprise made by seven or eight men of letters. Diderot was at the head of it all, and charged with the mixing and amalgamation. Diderot is a man of more d literary interests than any other Frenchman I know. He knows enough Latin and Italian, and loves it. The dominant passion in him was metaphysics; I could therefore compare him to our Genovesi to whom he also resembles very much in features, voice etc. He gave excellent precepts on drama and made two mediocre comedies. [...] D'Alembert was in charge of geometrical and mathematical articles. D'Alembert [...] is jovial, gay, sometimes a jester, a good friend of the Italians and a great admirer of them. If he has not quoted them, it is because it is not the custom of the French nation to quote, much less the custom of geometers. [...]. Seven volumes had appeared when the work ran aground. The booksellers cried out; the venture was for three million *Lire*, there being (unbelievably) four thousand three hundred subscribers or shall we say associates. Since the art of typography has been in the world, there is no example of a book enterprise so costly, and so lucrative".[103]

In February 1767, the *Caisse d'Escompte* was created under the direction of Jean-Joseph de Laborde, the King's banker at the time. Tanucci, intrigued, asked Galiani about this new institution, who replied with a detailed analysis of the French kingdom's financial system: "The King has three hundred and twenty million rents a year, of which 124 million are paid by the *fermiers généraux* who have five *grosses fermes* and a few small ones under contract, i.e. salt, tobacco, wine, internal and external customs, state lands, etc. The remaining 200 million are obtained from capitation, twentieths, free gifts, clergy, cutting, post, *parties casuelles*, saleable charges etc. The sum paid by the *fermiers*, must all be given to the royal treasury, but as the state has 97 million in annual debt [...] therefore the product of the *fermiers* is intended to make these payments. So from the *fermes* only about 27 million goes into the royal treasury (if these are allocated to the *Caisse d'Amortissement*), all the rest is transferred from the King's *fermiers* to the rent or lifetime annuity payers, or to the Hôtel de Ville or other state debt payers. So those *fermiers*, so harshly attacked in the past, today give nothing to the King. They flay the people to pay the people, and by a very long, nefarious process, they give back to the same

[103] Ferdinando Galiani's letter to Bernardo Tanucci, Paris, 12 November 1764, published in Galiani (1975: 914–915). On the relationship between Galiani and Genovesi, see Stapelbroek (2006).

people. But for all the remaining 200 million, which in essence is all the King's net income, to a very great extent there is no obligation to pay it in Paris. For example, the provinces are not obliged to give free donations other than in their own capitals. It is up to the royal treasury to think about what it wants to use them for or to take them to Paris. Your Excellency will see, therefore, that the royal treasury, in order to collect these two hundred million a year, needs either a huge transport of cash or an immense circulation of bills of exchange within the Kingdom, i.e. from Lyons, Marseilles, Rouen, etc. to Paris. To pay for the King's spending on war, navy, etc. requires the same amount of money, either in transport or in bills of exchange. [...]. So, to make this infinite movement of money, it took a merchant, or rather a financier, to manage the entire royal treasury. He keeps the budget clear, so that it appears that everything has come in and gone out of the royal treasury, although indeed much is spent there, much passes from place to place without coming to Paris, and circulates in a thousand ways. It is necessary to plug holes and gaps with bills of exchange so that there is never a shortage of what is called *le service* here, i.e. this prompt distribution of money and payments to those who are owed. This is what is called the *banquier de la cour*. He, by means of his bills of exchange, must ensure that the money is found wherever the King needs it, and bring it in and out at the same time. But since sometimes in one month more is spent than is collected, and on the contrary in another month more is collected than is spent, the *court banker* makes up for these shortcomings with long-dated bills of exchange, payable, say, in three, four, six months, but never more than a year, because he makes adjustments, and calculates that in that given time and city the royal treasury will have enough to pay the bill. This long internal bill of exchange issued by the royal treasury is called a *rescription*, and has here the value of cash. One immediately finds someone who will take it and give cash like the *polizze di banco* [*fedi di credito*] in Naples [...]. This was one of the main operations carried out by the *court banker*. In addition to the management of the royal treasury, he had his own liquid assets of a few million. When there was no money in the royal treasury he would pay in bills of exchange at three months, for example, then with the liquid assets he would discount those who wanted the cash, and keep three months' interest. Here fraud could come in, for he could pretend that there was no money in the royal treasury, and make the cash he gave appear to be his own money, and thus draw interest on a capital which was not his own but that of the King. [...] Between this and many other arbitrages, profits etc. the *court banker* here earns in time of peace four or five million a year, and much more in time of war. Enormous, monstrous, scandalous wealth, which has no example in any other country, nor is there any other office here that resembles it. Now, de Laborde, who has become very rich, having more than 25 million, and wants to retire, has proposed that the banker should no longer be one person, but a company. There are countless reasons for companies that exist in Europe. This one had the difference that the company was very numerous, being composed of sixty thousand shares. The people soon realised, that so much money was not needed for the internal exchange, which could be done very well with eight or ten million, and they understood that under this guise it was a new loan, which the King wanted to make. Without the necessary attention, the bank will fail. But de Laborde will continue *il service*, and if he leaves, there will be no shortage of takers, for the thing is too good, there is no risk, and there is endless and stomach-churning profit".[104]

In the summer of 1767, the Neapolitan ambassador in London, Domenico Caracciolo (Scibilia 1976), passed through Paris and met Galiani, with whom he was on friendly terms (Nicolini 1954: 15–54).[105] The meeting aroused the Abbé's curiosity for English society and he wrote to Tanucci: "Caracciolo's arrival here has given me the desire to accompany him when he returns to England, stay there for a month, see London and return immediately. The cause of this desire is easy to guess. I want to

[104] Ferdinando Galiani's letter to Bernardo Tanucci, Paris, 2 March 1767, published in Bazzoni (1878c: 26–28) (italics added). On Laborde and the Caisse d'Escompte, see Durand (1969: 75–111). As Galiani predicted, the Caisse was suppressed three years later. Another project presented by the Anglo-Swiss merchant Isaac Panchaud in March 1769 proposed the liquidation of the Company of the Indies and its transformation into a public bank intended to support trade by opening credits. Supported by Abbot Morellet, the project failed. Galiani told Tanucci: "Regarding the new bank that is to be made here, the painful memory of Law, and of the Mississippi, is too fresh; but something will have to be done. This year cannot go like the others. [...] This financial trouble here began in 1756 [...]. The gigantic body had strength and lived. But having gained nothing in the six years of perfect peace, now that the Corsican war has come, which is bound to be costly, and that others are expected, the evil has been discovered and it is great. A resounding failure seems inevitable. Perhaps all the perpetual rents will be reduced to half, all the pensions to two thirds, and so we will be able to go on for some more time" (Ferdinando Galiani's letter to Bernardo Tanucci, Paris, 3 April 1769, published in Galiani 1975: 982).

[105] The correspondence between Galiani and Caracciolo is kept in the Library of the Società Napoletana di Storia Patria, XXX.B.17: folios 50–59; XXXI.C.14: folios 4–43.

educate myself. *I am commerce, I am politics*: one must see the metropolis of these two things".[106]

Galiani finally obtained permission to visit England between November and December 1767 and in a letter to Tanucci described his impressions on English society, writing,"I thank you very much for allowing me to see this very worthy country, which I found very different from the idea I had based on the descriptions of others. To tell you what I think of it would be a long story. In short, I will tell you that I find it very similar to Italy, and infinitely distant from France. [...] It is evident that [the English] have taken the good line of the true and the real, therefore they will go further than the French, and will be what the Italians were when they were one nation, and what they would be again if they were again to be one monarchy. But they will never be what the Italians were or could be. This is hindered by the climate, the infertile land, the population, which is not and cannot be more than nine million, i.e. at least one third less than the current Italian population. Finally, their position as an island impedes all trade by land with neighbouring powers, which, when it is short-haul, is much less costly than navigation. Their present power seems to me similar to that of the Jesuits. The result of great industry, of infinite suffering, of great parsimony, of enthusiastic love for public affairs, for the holy institute, in a word, effort, violence towards the lazy and profligate nature made by enthusiasm and producing more credit than strength, [...] more fear than harm, more lightning than thunder, more appearance than duration".[107] The negative opinion was confirmed in the *Dialogues*, where

[106] Ferdinando Galiani's letter to Bernardo Tanucci, Paris, 24 August 1767, published in Tanucci (1914, vol II: 117) (italics added). Caracciolo had already invited him a few years earlier, but without success: "I speak seriously. It is an absolute disgrace that you do not want to take a tour of this country. Come! You don't have to spend a *Cavallo* [Neapolitan copper coin of little value]. Come to my house. You will lack nothing [...]. Comedies, operas, balls, the Parliament and the countryside. Write and come! I will make you laugh and amuse you. We will take a tour together of the most beautiful things in the provinces: the universities, the casinos, the men of letters, the politicians, the p... We will mix the sacred with the profane" (Domenico Caracciolo's letter to Ferdinando Galiani, London, 6 December 1764, published in Nicolini 1954: 23).

[107] Ferdinando Galiani's letter to Bernardo Tanucci, London, 7 December 1767, published in Bazzoni (1879a: 173–174). A few weeks later he specified: "When I said England resembled Italy it was not metaphysical, studied, calculated speculation, it was physical sense because in London I believed I was in Italy. The climate was much softer than in Paris, the houses with Italian architecture, a lot of brick, low roofs, facades on the street, portly men, badly combed, without powder, without hats, [...] women without red, all covered up, little

Galiani observed: "the English nation, although hard-working, industrious and patient, has not yet been able to develop its manufactures to the extent it would like. For they will always lose in competition not only with the French, but also with the Germans. No matter how many laws the English make, their morals resist them, and morals are always stronger than laws" (Galiani 1770a: 29).

Moreover, Galiani did not admire the English political system based on the role of parliament. "Today England," he wrote in the *Dialogues,* "is the most complicated political machine in Europe and perhaps in the world. This country is at once agricultural, manufacturing, warlike, and commercial; it is, in spite of its size, by nature entirely situated in seaports [...]. Its government is the most mixed, the most artificially composed that has ever existed. Finally, its morals, character, soil, climate, production, political relations, strength, weakness, resistance, everything is particular to this country, which is different from the rest of the world and often unique in its kind" (Galiani 1770a: 65).

David Hume, who had been in Paris between 1763 and 1766 as secretary of the British embassy, was well acquainted with Galiani's views and most probably he knew him personally, both because of the institutional relationships linked to their work as diplomatic agents and because they both belonged to the same circle of friends as Diderot (cf. Pupo 2020: 22) and frequented Parisian salons, including that of Madame de Geoffrin. To their mutual friend Morellet, Hume wrote: "The Abbé Galiani goes to Naples: he does well to leave Paris before I come thither; for I should certainly put him to death for all the ill he has spoken of England. But it has happened, as was fortold by his friend, Caracciolo, who said that the Abbé would remain two months in this country, would speak all himself, would not allow an Englishman to utter a syllable; and after returning would give the character of the nation during the rest of his life, as if he

hats on their heads, richly ill-dressed ladies, everything finally reminded me of Italy, that is, not all Italy, but that which has republics, either living or extinct, Tuscany and Lombardy. This outward and corporeal form of England I found similar to Italy. The costume is certainly dissimilar, except for the seriousness, which seems to me equal in the two nations, that is in London and in Venice, or Genoa" (Ferdinando Galiani's letter to Bernardo Tanucci, Paris, 8 February 1768, published in Bazzoni 1879a: 175). Diodati reports in his biography of a trip to Holland in the same period "to observe the state and cultivation of the United Provinces", but there is no trace of it in the documents (Diodati 1788: 48–49).

were perfectly well acquainted with them".[108] In *Della Moneta*, Galiani drew an unhappy picture of the English nation, attributing it to its wealth: "The orders of the English government are most able to bring into England immense sums of money; not caring for the high price of food and grain itself, so long as it is always exported, and sold to neighbouring peoples. The effects of these orders have been, that the population has not grown in England as much as it could, given the coming of very few foreigners. [...] Many arts, such as printing, have declined, as the English cannot sell books cheaply, and foreigners do not want to buy them at such a high price: and if it were not for the excellence of the manufactures, nothing that comes from England would be bought. [...] Finally, English themselves take greater pleasure in travelling as rich men than in living as poor men at home, and by their travels they have irreparably opened a door to the drain of so much of their wealth" (Galiani [1751]: 296–297).[109] In a letter to Tanucci, Abbot Galiani was even more explicit: "What says Your Excellency of this brazenness with which the English have told all Europe that they have no law of nations [*ius gentium*], nor know them, that they know nothing but the acts of Parliament. I could not refrain from saying to the British Embassy Secretary,[110] who was saying this nonsense: so you are not people, what animal is an Englishman then? They must be beavers, or the like, who have a peculiar justice among themselves but none in common with man".[111]

[108] David Hume's letter to Abbé Morellet, London, 10 July 1769, published in Hume (2011: 205–206). Spartaco Pupo emphasises the relationship between Hume and Galiani, calling Hume "an occult mentor of Galiani", see Pupo (2020: 21). Unlike Hume, Edward Gibbon was a great admirer of the Neapolitan abbot and did not hesitate to quote him in his monumental work *The History of the Decline and Fall of the Roman Empire*: "laughing philosopher, the Abbé Galliani, (*Dialogues sur le Commerce des Bleds*,) may truly affirm, that it was the residence of the rois très Chrétiens en très chevelus" (Gibbon 1788: 17; see Galiani 1770a: 120).

[109] In the *Dialogues*, *Le Chevalier* prophesied the American Revolution, stating that "the enormous cost of food [has] caused such a large number of English men and manufactures to return to America, from where they are already looking menacingly at their imprudent metropolis" (Galiani 1770a: 153).

[110] It is very likely that the embassy secretary Galiani refers to is Hume himself who held that position at that time. According to Marco Catucci, who cites this letter as evidence, the meeting (or clash) certainly took place (see Catucci 1986: 80). On Hume's role in eighteenth-century Italy, see Baldi (1983); Pupo (2020).

[111] Ferdinando Galiani's letter to Bernardo Tanucci, Paris, 30 April 1764, published in Galiani (1975: 903). A concept again reiterated: "A powerful and glorious nation, which claims to be supremely cultured, declared to all the nations of Europe, only two years ago,

And likewise Galiani condemned the French assemblies: "Parliaments in France obey no one"[112] and "Parliament is no longer, as it once was, the idol of the nation. Full of presumptuous and ignorant youths, it is in the greatest urgencies of the state all occupied in its private affairs, it protects the Jansenists, whom fanaticism has made ridiculous, and fights against the court more to defend the interests of their financiers than to succour the needs of the nation".[113] The presence of parliaments in the state apparatus was for Galiani a medieval residue and characterised a form of government that he called "despotic aristocratic". In *Della Moneta* he explained its genesis and characteristics in depth: "[Aristocratic despotism] necessarily arose from the fusion of the two nations, the conqueror and the defeated. The old inhabitants became slaves of the barbarians, but as they lived among themselves aristocratically before, so they wished to continue. And so, forming among them that Senate, which they called Parliament, they chose one to whom they gave nothing regal but their name and insignia and their spontaneous submission. Thus the kings had neither soldiers, nor revenues, nor ministers of their own, besides their hereditary ones, but the electors, who, being all despotic in their own lands, had soldiers, duties and riches, they [kings] had to make use of. Such government still lasts in part in Germany and Poland, elsewhere not so much as in past centuries" (Galiani [1751]: 257). The king's power was severely limited: "the offices of the magistrates cannot be suppressed, which is why the King takes an indirect way of intimidating the Parliaments [...] by putting [its member] in a fortress: all these ways are weak and inef-

that it does not know the law of nations [*jus gentium*], nor that it exists in its own country; and it has adduced this reason, which is only suitable for barbarians, and this law of nations is not confirmed by any act of its Parliament. That is to say, this nation knows no obligation of justice other than towards its own population, or towards those who are united to it by treaty in the bond of social humanity" (Galiani, MS-24: 718–719).

112 Ferdinando Galiani's letter to Bernardo Tanucci, Paris, 16 June 1760, published in Bazzoni (1869a: 30).

113 Ferdinando Galiani's letter to Bernardo Tanucci, Paris, 14 July 1760, published in Bazzoni (1869a: 33). "Because of their medieval origins and their constant resistance to the unifying and centralising work of the monarchy, parliaments appeared to Galiani to be highly criticisable, symbolising perhaps the most notable obstacle to the development of royal absolutism" (Ghisalberti 1975: 60). In a letter to Tanucci, Galiani specified his opinion: "Perhaps in the long term it is better for a state to have a parliament than not to have one, but in the principles of a kingdom a little despotism is not bad, otherwise the creation is tardier" (Ferdinando Galiani's letter to Bernardo Tanucci, Paris, 30 April 1764, published in Galiani 1959: 301–302).

fective, because in essence he cannot deprive them of their power nor decapitate any of them. Another way would remain for the King, and that would be to fill the Parliaments with people loyal to him. This has been neglected too much in the past; it can be done in the future. Hitherto the Parliaments themselves have substituted for their vacant members, and the King was content with a simple assent and approval, almost always accepting the appointment. Furthermore, Parliaments have taken it upon themselves to say we do not want it when some person disliked by them wants to enter their body. Finally, once the King has received the office, he can no longer do great harm to the member of Parliament [...]. This is the origin of the great power of Parliaments".[114] And in almost prophetic terms he highlighted the conflict between royal government and Parliament, a conflict that would later explode with the Revolution: "Parliaments have always fought of jurisdiction with the *Conseil*. The King has supported the *Conseil*, the people have loved Parliaments. In sustance, true majesty is not offended by these disputes. The nation profits is a corrupt tribunal such as the *Conseil*, and full of people born of and attached to finance, is crushed, as it will soon be".[115]

His defence of the absolute monarchy led him to reject both the egalitarian theses of Jean-Jacques Rousseau and Montesquieu's advocacy of mixed governments (Ghisalberti 1975: 65).[116]

In particular, he rejected egalitarianism, for as he wrote in the *Dialogues*: "Property and freedom are sacred rights for man, they are the first of all

[114] Ferdinando Galiani's letter to Bernardo Tanucci, Paris, 9 January 1764, published in Galiani (1975: 893).

[115] Ferdinando Galiani's letter to Bernardo Tanucci, Paris, 19 March 1764, published in Galiani (1975: 896).

[116] In the second edition of *Della Moneta* Galiani's opinion on Montesquieu's work was decidedly negative: "President Montesquieu's hate for any absolute government shines through in all his writings, although he tried to disguise it by changing the meaning of the most widespread voices, and calling "monarchy" a mixed and quasi-republican government, such as he wanted it to be, but not such as France was, and giving the names 'despotism' and 'tyranny' to the existing monarchies. He multiplies the accusations against monarchies as much as he can, and glosses over their merits. He confuses the faults of rulers with the intrinsic vice of monarchical forms, and always wants to draw a general maxim from a particular case. Invaded by his spirit, other parliamentarians led that ancient and necessary body to total ruin in just a few years; and so the book *On the Spirit of the Laws* caused as much damage as it could to France, for whose good it seemed written and intended" (Galiani 1780: Note XXXI, 413). Pier Luigi Porta, on the other hand, considers the models of agricultural and industrial society developed by Galiani as clearly influenced by Montesquieu's thought, see Porta (1995: 130).

rights, they are inherent in us, they constitute our political essence just as the body and soul constitute our physique; beyond the ties that bind us to society, nothing must disturb them. Interest and damage caused by a third person belong to justice; general interest and damage belong to politics. But when these two great, powerful and exacting divinities are appeased, nothing hurts them any more, nothing affects them; man then assumes his rights, becomes once more proprietary and free, and I do not know any other legitimate power on earth that can deprive him. Neither the caprice of a despot on the one hand, nor the speculations of a metaphysician on the other, nor the senseless cries of the multitude, nor the unfounded alarms of a government unjust through weakness and arbitrary through timidity, have any legitimate rights or valid excuses for meddling in our affairs" (Galiani 1770a: 210–211).

Instead, he admired Chinese despotism: "Long live the Chinese! It is an ancient nation, which regards itself as a nation of naughty infants, while we swell in importance because we run across seas and continents. [...] Everywhere we [Europeans] bring war, discord, our bars of gold, our guns, our Gospel, our syphilis".[117]

In March 1768, Galiani, replying to Tanucci, noted the first elements of dissent in French society, but still showed confidence in the measures to liberalise the grain trade: "Your Excellency having written to me several times about grain, it is necessary for me to send you a little book published here recently that has met with universal approval, and while, in the current scarcity, minds began to waver and some law or ordinance was wanted, it confirmed the only mother of abundance is absolute freedom. The book is written with great simplicity and clarity. I believe that Genovesi, who has already translated a book on the *Police du grains* [by Herbert], should also translate this one. Good government must march together with the light and education of the people, otherwise it will be blamed. By persisting in the maxims of liberty, grain prices have fallen and there is no longer any fear of shortage this year".[118]

[117] Ferdinando Galiani's letter to Madame d'Épinay, Naples, 12 May 1770, published in Galiani (1881a: vol. I, 144).

[118] Ferdinando Galiani's letter to Bernardo Tanucci, Paris, 7 March 1768, published in Tanucci (1914, vol. II: 184). See Venturi (1960a: 47); Minerbi (1973: 151, footnote). The book to which Galiani refers may be "one of the pamphlets written by Abbot Nicolas Baudeau in 1768 to address the criticism that was beginning to be levelled in France against the rules of liberty: either the *Avis au peuple sur son premier besoin* or the *Lettres sur les*

His brief period in London had allowed him to directly observe the economic and social conditions of the British kingdom, which in 1768 had been shaken by popular uprisings, known as 'Wilkes and liberty', in support of the populist politician John Wilkes, who had lived in exile in France, between 1763 and 1764, frequenting Madame d'Holbach's salon, and then moved to Italy, where he frequented Galiani in Naples, between 1765 and 1766 (Nicolini 1954: 177–180; Barnes 1930: 23–48).[119] The English revolt was seen by Galiani as an effect of the liberalisation of the grain trade, the cost of which was borne by the working classes. With an unusual feeling of solidarity with the people, the Neapolitan abbot clarified his thoughts on these events in a letter to Madame d'Épinay a few years later: "All the current political systems of all the nations of the world are based on ancient violence, committed and perpetrated against the possessors of the only true goods. All have ridden roughshod over the peasants. Kings, Popes, Parliaments, Sorbonne, Faculties, Chapters of the Order of the Holy Spirit, and even the Chapter of Saint Michel, all have ridden on top of them and debased the price of grain. The English dared to touch the price of grain, and instantly Wilkes and the Middlesex *franc-tenancier* [*free tenant*] challenged the King and the Lords and the Commons, and in London you might see a carter carrying grain, fighting with a Viscount of Great Britain. The English had to stop the export of grain abruptly, in order to put a stop to the progressive enrichment of the tenant farmers, who were almost about to overthrow the whole political machine of the state".[120]

He was probably struck by the trade restrictions established by the *Navigation Act*, which imposed, as is well known, that most maritime trade should be conducted using British ships and crews, generating revenue and strengthening British maritime and economic power. In the autumn of 1768, Galiani focused his attention on the possibility of

émeutes populaires que cause la cherté des grains, et sur les precautions du moment" (Baudeau 1768; Turgot 1768; see Galiani 1975: 603, editor's footnote).

[119] For the debate on grain exports in Britain, see Young (1770).

[120] Ferdinando Galiani's letter to Madame d'Épinay, Naples, 22 December 1770, published in Galiani (1881a: vol. I, 329–330); Galiani and d'Épinay (1992, vol. I: 322). "For the last ten years, the English themselves have placed obstacles in the way of their freedom and commerce, despite their form of government being essentially free and commercial" (Ferdinando Galiani's letter to Madame d'Épinay, Naples, 3 June 1775, published in Galiani 1975: 1117; Galiani and d'Épinay 1992, vol. V: 32). In England, the *free tenant* depended exclusively on the king's power and owned lands in full ownership, called *Allods.*

applying the same kind of restrictions to Neapolitan trade, establishing a monopoly on the transport of some goods: "It is enough for foreigners to take away from us, silks, wines, canapes, manna, liquorices, wools, cotton [...] and all. By grace, the grain remains to us. It will be said to the contrary, that our merchants will cry out having difficulty in finding ships of our own. There can be no such difficulty, since there are eight hundred Neapolitan ships, and perhaps when there is difficulty, I will reply: so much the better. Less grain will go out, it will go out *guttatim* [drop by drop], and not in a landslide; our ships will make more voyages to and from, and will earn more freights: our navy will grow, and then there will no longer be a shortage of national ships [...]. Certainly France will not cry out. London never takes grain from foreign countries. If it opened its doors last year, it will soon close them again [...]. So if the routes to Sicily were only granted to our ships, it would be a great good. If this is not to be done, then at least the fee should be four *Carlini* for foreigners and three for nationals".[121]

In November 1768, Galiani began to publicly criticise physiocratic theories and the policy of liberalisation in the parisian salons of Madame d'Épinay and Baron d'Holbach.[122] Denis Diderot gave a direct account of Abbé's opinion: "[Galiani] preached extensively against the exportation of grain, for a reason which is not common: it is that bad laws must persist wherever there are not men of sufficient intellect in the ministry to enforce good ones, and to foresee the inconveniences of the most advantageous innovations. He preached against the favour given to agriculture for a very strange reason: he said that agriculture was the most important of all conditions, and that it had taken more than four thousand years of effort to debase it, and that to try to bring it out of this debasement was to work to reduce the dukes and peers to nothing, and to bring the king into

[121] Ferdinando Galiani's letter to Bernardo Tanucci, Paris, 7 November 1768, published in Bazzoni (1879b: 370–371). See also Ferdinando Galiani's letter to Bernardo Tanucci, Paris, 19 December 1768, published in Galiani (1959: 332–333).

[122] According to Nicolini: "Certain indications would suggest that the visit in England and Caracciolo's speeches were not extraneous to that economic conversion determined in Galiani at the beginning of 1768 and for which from being a partisan of the unlimited freedom of grain exportation and friend and supporter of the physiocrats that he was still in 1765, he became, first with words and then with writing, a combative opponent of that and of these" (Nicolini 1954: 33). Pier Luigi Porta also shares this opinion, see Porta (1995: 125–126).

parliament accompanied by twelve bakers".[123] And again a few days later: "Finally Abbé Galiani explained himself clearly. Either there is nothing proved in politics or it is proved that exporting is madness. [...]. I prostrated myself before him to publish his ideas. Here is just one of his principles: what does it mean to sell grain? It means exchanging grain for money. You don't know what you are talking about: it is exchanging grain for grain. Can you ever exchange the grain you have with advantage for the grain that will be sold to you? He has shown us all the branches of this law, and they are immense. He explained to us the cause of the present high price, and we saw that no one had suspected it".[124]

Galiani's criticism was part of a broad movement of opposition to the edicts of 1763 and 1764. While the *conomistes* tried to use their influence at Court to enact further liberalist reforms, aiming at the abolition of the guilds, many provincial parliaments opposed the implementation of the liberalisation measures and uprisings occurred in 1768 in Maine, Normandy and Touraine, triggered by the increase in the price of bread.[125] The liberalisation policy had caused a serious supply crisis threatening the subsistence regime of the poorest part of the French population. The free market favouring the entry of foreign merchants into the trade caused effects very similar to those of a famine on the supply chain, to which was added a series of bad harvests and "both in terms of causes and effects, it became impossible to disentangle liberalization from the shortage or, to put it in the language of the time, to distinguish the real dearth from the artificial one" (Kaplan 1982: 52; Kaplan 1976: chap. 3; Hufton 1983). The whole of France was panic-stricken by the famine, which the continu-

[123] Denis Diderot's letter to Sofia Volland, Paris, 12 November 1768, published in Galiani (1959: 335). On the relation between Diderot and Physiocracy, see Strenski (1967) and Minerbi (1973).

[124] Denis Diderot's letter to Sofia Volland, Paris, 22 November 1768, published in Galiani (1959: 335–336).

[125] "The high price of wheat, which had begun to be perceived in 1766, only intensified during 1767. On 2 December 1767, [...] bread, which had been rising since the previous month of August, when it had been paid at 2 *Soldos* and 6 *Deniers* per *pound*, was being sold at the market on the basis of 3 *Soldos* and 3 *Deniers*, despite the fact that the harvest had not been bad that year; this increase was attributed to the excessive exportation of wheat outside the Kingdom. The population of the towns began to clamour, to make what Le Trosne himself called small riots; they were supported by the bourgeoisie who lived off their rents, who earned nothing at the time from the increase in goods, and who regretted the price of the bread they ate as stolen from their little fantasies of luxury and decorum" (Weulersse 1910, vol. I: 155).

ous rise in prices fuelled: "consumer uprisings occurred throughout the kingdom and were frequently tolerated or even supported by the local police who, in this fashion, rioted against the liberal laws that tied their hands. From above: the coalition of the people and the police was reinforced by several parliaments, a number of intendants, and a group of philosophes" (Kaplan 1982: 52–53). In order to avoid unrest in the capital, L'Averdy entrusted the management of the Parisian supplies to a company led by a former baker named Pierre-Simon Malisset ("an audacious and highly skilled baker-businessman", Kaplan 1996: 443), supported by three wealthy officials experienced in financial affairs and international trade. The contract allowed the company, within certain limits, to profit from the grain and flour trade and Malisset used the link with the Court for his own business. This fuelled rumours among the population that the King had entrusted Malisset's company with the monopoly of the grain trade and the contract began to be referred to as the *Pacte de Famine* (Cahen 1926).[126] By the autumn of 1768, the price of bread had reached double the price considered normal and L'Averdy was forced to resign, replaced first by Étienne Maynon d'Invault and after only a year by Abbot Joseph Marie Terray, who repealed the liberalisation edicts in 1770.

In this context, Galiani's criticism, formulated precisely at the most acute moment of the crisis, was not isolated, but was part of a framework of opposition to the theoretical foundations and political proposals of the Quesnay school.

This opposition was manifested in a number of contributions that appeared between 1767 and 1768, notably the essays by Jean Joseph Louis Graslin (1767, see Orain 2019), François Véron Duverger de Forbonnais (1767, see Charles and Orain 2019) and Gabriel Bonnot, known as Abbé de Mably (1768) (Weulersse 1910: 151–180; Pribram 1983: 113–114; Ferrand and Orain 2019). Forbonnais strongly criticised the theoretical principles underlying the *Tableau* and the economic policy proposals set out in the articles *Fermiers* and *Grains*. Graslin, while adhering to liberalist principles, contested the physiocratic principle of the exclusive productivity of the agricultural sector, contrasting it with the productivity of labour, anticipating Adam Smith's critique. Finally, the

[126] Jean-Charles-Guillaume Le Prévôt de Beaumont denounced the supposed *Pacte de Famine* conspiracy to the Parliament of Rouen, accusing de L'Averdy of having created a monopoly on the grain trade and personally enriching himself. Owing to these denunciations, he was arrested in November 1768 and imprisoned for 21 years.

most radical critique was that of Mably, who rejected the reduction of the moral order to the natural order and virtue to self-interest, contested the private ownership of land and considered the extreme inequality of fortunes as a radical vice of society: the entire political, moral and social philosophy of the *conomistes* was totally condemned. Other criticisms were made by leading protagonists of French intellectual life: Jean Jacques Rousseau contested enlightened despotism (Rousseau 1767 [1997]; Pénigaud 2015), Voltaire wrote a satire of the physiocratic system in *L'Homme au quarante écu* (Voltaire 1768; Ousselin 1999), Grimm criticised the fanaticism and esotericism that characterised the Quesnay school (Grimm 1878: 170–171; 1878: 31–32; 1879: 429–432).

It is probable that Galiani, who was always interested in French granary policy,[127] was familiar with this critical literature, the subject of discussion in the salons he frequented most assiduously, those of Madame d'Épinay and Madame d'Holbach, and from these conversations, and the increasingly critical social situation (Weulersse 1910, vol. I: 180–185), came the idea of giving his thoughts the form of *Dialogues*, as if he wanted to reproduce the atmosphere of the typically animated and brilliant discussions of the Parisian salons.[128] Accepting insistent invitations, such as Diderot's, the Abbé began writing the *Dialogues* between the end of 1768 and the beginning of 1769, while continuing his activities as a diplomatic agent.[129] Nothing could have foreseen what was to happen in the spring of

[127] "[About the increase in the price of grain] I have spoken with many magistrates here in the past few days and mainly with Sartine [Gabriel de], lieutenant of police, a man of high merit" (Ferdinando Galiani's letter to Bernardo Tanucci, Paris, November 2, 1767, published in Tanucci 1914, vol. 2: 140).

[128] "The discussion was not limited to the circle of theorists and specialists. The grain trade was more than ever a topic of social conversation. The Edict of 1764 was being criticized along with the latest tragedy and novel, and the pamphlets in question were displayed on salon shelves, along with fashionable books. They were not always read: the extreme boredom they caused served as an excuse; but they were still obliged to have an opinion about them" (Gaudemet 1899: 129).

[129] The physiocratic journal *Éphémérides du citoyen ou Bibliothèque raisonnée des sciences morales et politiques* informed its readers in May 1769 of the imminent publication of a book against Quesnay's doctrines: "The Citizen Philosophers, whose pupils we have the honour to be and whose organs we sometimes are, are threatened by a large book that, according to the Friends of its Authors, will pulverise the doctrine we are trying to spread. This doctrine, however, is based solely on the evidence of natural laws, which must affect thinking men, and the force of this evidence, which shows how the interests of Sovereigns and Nations mingle and reconcile, must inevitably lead to universal agreement, when it is clearly demonstrated. We therefore find it difficult to believe that such a doctrine will be pulverised. We find it

1769 that would lead to Galiani's departure from Paris and his forced return to Naples.

Despite himself, Galiani was at the center of a delicate diplomatic incident between Naples and Paris. The reason for diplomatic tension between England and France was still the *Pacte de Famille* and the extension of the Bourbon alliance to Austria through marriage arrangements. To restore the threatened European equilibrium, London had formed alliances with Russia and Denmark, but the political crisis in Sweden between the two opposing factions of the *Hattpartiet* (the *Hats Party*), which had returned to power in 1769 and favoured an alliance with France, and *Mösspartiet* (the *Caps Party*), which was linked to Russia, again threatened European stability (Roberts 2003: 155–175). The British government then pushed Denmark to arm a fleet in support of the *Caps Party*, prompting a reaction from Paris, which threatened war against the Danes if they pursued their intent. France would involve all its allies in the war, first and foremost Spain and then Naples itself, not yet formally bound to the *Pacte de Famille* but certainly subordinate to the choices of the Spanish government. As the tension between London and Paris grew, Choiseul was informed of an alleged statement by Galiani to his friend Karl Heinrich von Gleichen, Danish ambassador in France, about the role of the Neapolitan Kingdom in the ongoing diplomatic affair.[130]

News of this allegedly imprudent statement by Galiani, made perhaps in March 1769, was reported to Tanucci by Girolamo Grimaldi, minister of Charles III: "It pains me to have to tell Your Excellency about a disgusting affair, and about which the King has exclusively ordered me to make Your Excellency a separate report".[131] And he detailed the incident in a report attached to the letter: "Gleichen warned his court that an insinuation had been made to him by the court of Naples, that Abbot Galiani [...], Tanucci's intimate confidant, had told him that the [Neapolitan] ministry had never adhered, and probably never would adhere, to the *Pacte de Famille*, and that the poor entente between the two ministries of

almost as difficult to believe that respectable people who profess to be philosophers had any part, as is alleged, in the work in which it is attacked." (Éphémérides 1769a: 132–133).

[130] Gleichen was ambassador in Naples between 1770 and 1771, where he assiduously frequented Galiani, forming a close friendship with him, see Ferdinando Galiani's letter to Madame d'Épinay, Naples, 22 December 1770, published in Galiani (1881a, vol I: 328); Galiani and d'Épinay (1992, vol. I: 321).

[131] Girolamo Grimaldi's letter to Bernardo Tanucci, Aranguez. 18 April 1769, published in Ferraioli (1880: 693). See also Nicolini (1929: 236–246).

France and Naples came from this. That his court wishing to disenchant Europe about the idea of its union with France and Spain, would take the first opportunity, that was not contrary to its own interests, to act differently from the courts of Versailles and Madrid. That consequently combining these notions with the assurance that the abbot could give Gleichen of the appreciation in Naples of His Danish Majesty's friendship, the result was that Gleichen could assure Bernstorff [Johann Hartwig Ernst von Bernstorff, Danish prime minister], not in the terms of a ministerial declaration, but as a confidential notice for which the abbot could answer, that the court of Naples, far from taking the slightest part in the declarations of France and Spain, would redouble its attention to increasing its union with Denmark. From this report Gleichen and Bernstorff, the ministers of the enemy courts of the Bourbons and Austria alliance derive the following inference: that since it had to be believed that an embassy secretary did not speak with so much confidence, if not certain of the way of thinking of his court, and this to be nevertheless governed by a young monarch, not being able to have any other sentiments, than those conveyed to him by the King of Spain, it therefore followed that Spain wavered in the alliance, so that this should not be believed to be inseparable, nor so fearful, as had hitherto been judged".[132] The consequence was drastic: "the remedy that the king proposes is to repeat to Copenhagen that declaration that [count of] Fuentes [Joaquin Atanasio Pignatelli d'Aragona, Spanish ambassador in Paris] already did [...] in order to disprove with this step the idea that there was coldness in the alliance. [...]. The King orders that the aforesaid abbot Galiani be immediately withdrawn from Paris, so as not to be exposed to new inconveniences as a result of his conversations, and His Majesty hopes that for his own interest, and just compliance, all the ministers of the Two Sicilies will be instructed not to show feelings different from those of the two crowns of the family, because whatever the events may be, always the bond of blood will concur in them [...]. I pity Your Excellency that because of the distorted way of thinking of one of his subordinates, and because of his recklessness in communicating it, he has to hear this complaint from the King, which, however, can only fall upon the author of the conversation. [...] The King thinks that by recalling Abbot Galiani at once the reason must not be communicated to him, and

[132] Girolamo Grimaldi's letter to Bernardo Tanucci, Aranguez. 18 April 1769, published in Ferraioli (1880: 691–692).

only on his arrival [in Naples] can it be thought, if it is convenient, to inform him".[133]

Because of his friendly relations with Gleichen, it is possible that Galiani might have confided his opinion on the diplomatic situation, which the Danish agent used to his advantage. And it is certain that Galiani's political positions were largely shared by Tanucci.[134] Many years later, in 1784, in an official report for Queen Maria Carolina, Galiani returned to this affair, attributing responsibility to Tanucci, who was removed from power in 1776 and had passed away in 1783. According to Galiani, Tanucci had artfully made known to the French all the secret advice received regarding precautions not to harm the Neapolitans, should they adhere to the *Pacte de Famille*, and this had provoked Choiseul's mistrust (Galiani, MS-19: 358). The crisis between France and Denmark was the opportunity that Choiseul sought to force the Neapolitan kingdom to join the Bourbon alliance, but 'Tanucci by means of Galiani [had] made known that the King of Sicily would not [enter] into this dispute, the Catholic King deplored Tanucci and authorised Galiani's recall from Paris' (Galiani, MS-19: 359). The Neapolitan abbot thus claimed after years his mere role as an instrument of the Neapolitan minister's policy.

Tanucci on May 6, 1769, sent a cold communication to Galiani in which he decreed his dismissal from the role of diplomatic agent: "It is the will of the King that Your Exellency in four days from this dispatch leave

[133] Girolamo Grimaldi's letter to Bernardo Tanucci, Aranguez. 18 April 1769, published in Ferraioli (1880: 693–694).

[134] Another element of tension between Naples and the French court was the question of Corsica; the correspondence between Tanucci and Galiani shows that both opposed the French conquest of Corsica. Moreover, Tanucci, in his youth, had been a schoolmate of the leader of the Corsican independence movement, Pasquale Paoli, whose father was then an exile in Naples. Galiani's opposition was well known, as evidenced by a number of testimonies, and in the absence of information, many believed that the Corsican question had been the reason for his expulsion from Paris. Doctor Gatti was convinced of this and referred Galiani to a conversation with the duchess Choiseul (Angelo Gatti's letter to Ferdinando Galiani, [Chanteloup], 31 [May 1769], published in Nicolini 1929: 238). A rumour that was quite widespread was also reported by Alessandro Verri: 'That famous abbot Galiani. [...] secretary of the embassy in Naples and a man of singular spirit, sought after by all, is now disgraced for having spoken freely about the Corsican war and the king's maitresse [Madame du Barry]' (Alessandro Verri's letter to Pietro Verri, Rome, 29 August 1769, published in Nicolini 1929: 256). See Nicolini (1929: 238).

Paris to return to Naples to his office as Advisor to the Magistrate of Commerce".[135]

A few days later, Tanucci wrote to King Charles to dispel any suspicions about his complicity in the affair, declaring that he had not given Galiani "any order that could have induced him to inconsiderate, imprudent and reckless conversation, which is supposedly made by him to the Danish minister [...]. Marquis Grimaldi will tell Your Majesty the prompt and easy obedience in recalling Galiani from Paris. He is being replaced by Perez, an officer of the secretariat, a tardy and heavy man, and capable only of writing a letter of general news, and at the antipodes of that vivacity which made Galiani err".[136]

While his removal from Paris was being decided, Galiani informed the Neapolitan minister about the diplomatic situation, giving his personal opinion: "I have seen a letter from the King of Prussia to d'Alembert, in which he discusses much about his transience and the short space of life he has left, and seems to be talking about death. He expresses himself angrily about the mutations that will happen in Sweden by, as he says, the French, but he declares himself very precisely, that he will not go to war on this account. I now unite with your Excellency's opinion that the warriors of the North will die of sleep, if London does not wake them up. Perhaps it is simulation all that they do and all was to get money from the British".[137]

Once he had learned of his sudden removal from office, Galiani wrote a dramatic letter to Tanucci: "A choleric discourse against me, in the most general terms, made by the Duke of Choiseul to Castromonte [Cantillana] about two months ago, has already made, combining the timing of the round of letters, my Ambassador and myself fear some news this week. Neither he nor I, however, were expecting the news that came. It seemed to me that since I have here two ambassadors, persons greater than any exception, who watch over my conduct who can bear witness to it, who being on the spot are as it were my natural judges, and who love me very

[135] Bernardo Tanucci's dispatch to Ferdinando Galiani, Portici, 6 May 1769, published in Ferraioli (1880: 695).

[136] Bernardo Tanucci's letter to King Charles, Portici, 9 May 1769, published in Tanucci (1969: 524–525). At this time Tanucci was "more in need of the support of the Spanish cabinet than ever, now that Queen Maria Carolina was beginning to show signs of wanting to get rid of him, had swallowed the bitter pill and disowned and sacrificed Galiani" (Nicolini 1929: 240–241).

[137] Ferdinando Galiani's letter to Bernardo Tanucci, Paris, 15 May 1769, published in Bazzoni (1880a: 372).

much, and are fully and in every respect satisfied with me, nothing could come to me that would be wrong. It did not go like that, and what happened to me is, after death, what I experience as the greatest of evils that could befall me. If I deserved it, I will conform; if I didn't deserve it, God forgive the injustice to those who did it to me [...]. Nothing else I can tell you except that the day I had the King's order I remained without being able to have lunch or dinner. At night I had a fever with strong convulsions. The next day I endeavored to go out to finish a commission already given me by the Lord Prince of Belmonte, who I believe is in the Queen's service. I seemed somewhat more relieved, but neither appetite nor strength nor sleep returned, and this is the fourth day of in appetence. I had a fever yesterday with new convulsions at night. What frightens me most is a kind of torpor in my side and right leg [...]. Meanwhile I settled my affairs as best I could. Sold the horses, the carriage, packed up my belongings".[138]

On May 30, 1769, the Neapolitan abbot took leave of the court: "Although very ill, I went to Versailles. The speech of the Duke [Choiseul] was of much consolation to me. He spoke with all frankness and candor in the presence of my Ambassador and then that of Spain. He attested that he had nothing personal against me, attested several times his personal friendship toward me. Nothing in my case of which I could repent, or should blush. He promised (and will undoubtedly do so) to bear witness to Your Excellency and the Marquis Grimaldi. He esteemed it convenient that I should take leave of the King, and this was done in the manner most distinguished, and most honourable to me according to style. Great were the welcomes, the kindnesses, the signs of regret at my departure [...]. I have had occasion to know love toward my person: so many distinctions, so many kindnesses have been better medicine to my health [...]; but the soul is dejected still and the body is not healthy in everything. Perhaps my fairytale is over. Thank God it ends without shame and without

[138] Ferdinando Galiani's letter to Bernardo Tanucci, Paris, 29 May 1769, published in Bazzoni (1880a: 373–374). Galiani did not know the cause of his departure and suspected the physician Angelo Gatti, see Nicolini (1929: 236). See Angelo Gatti's letter to Ferdinando Galiani, Chanteloup, 30 May 1769; Angelo Gatti's letter to Ferdinando Galiani, Chanteloup, 1 June, 1769, published in Nicolini (1929: 236–240).

embarrassment".[139] Ably Choiseul had given him hope of his return to Paris (Nicolini 1929: 241).[140]

He then asked Tanucci permission not to return to Naples but to stay in some city in Italy or Provence. Meanwhile, the Neapolitan minister attempted to lessen his discouragement by writing to him that he thought it more appropriate for him to be employed at the *Magistrate of Commerce* (with the salary of 1000 *Ducats* per year), because of the skills he had acquired "in the long practice of the embassy secretariat".[141] From Madrid, Grimaldi wrote to Tanucci to spare Galiani further punishment: "the Count of Fuentes, having been informed of the carelessness of Abbot Galiani, and the Duke of Choiseul as well, esteeming and loving him, and recognizing him no less capable of being employed with utility in the service of this monarch, on any committee, in which he may not injure by his imprudence; have recommended the aforesaid abbot to the King, and His Majesty has ordered me to write so that he may represent to this Sovereign, that after correcting the recklessness, and no longer able to commit it, he may deign to retain his grace".[142]

Galiani left Paris in mid-June 1769,[143] "having borrowed the thousand *Scudi* from the Count of Cantillana, to whose heirs he returned them punctually the following year, and having written to [his friend, the physician] Angelo Gatti a final letter, in which he recommended one of his Parisian lovers by whom he also had a son (Madame de La Daubinière),[144]

[139] Ferdinando Galiani's letter to Bernardo Tanucci, Paris, 3 June 1769, published in Bazzoni (1880a: 374–375).

[140] Writing to Gleichen many years later, Galiani reconsidered the incident: "The only fault I committed, is the one I did not commit, of being born Neapolitan; just as the best thing he did was to be born French and called Choiseul. Whatever spirit I had I could only have stayed another year in Paris, until Castromonte's death" (Ferdinando Galiani's letter to Karl Heinrich von Gleichen, Naples, 3 April 1773, published in Galiani 1881a, vol II: 195).

[141] Bernardo Tanucci's letter to Ferdinando Galiani, Portici, 27 June 1769, published in Ferraioli (1880: 697).

[142] Girolamo Grimaldi's letter to Bernardo Tanucci, Aranguez, 13 June 1769, published in Ferraioli (1880: 697).

[143] According to Nicolini, Galiani left on June 25 (Galiani 1959: xiv), but in a letter to d'Épinay, Galiani states that he left on June 14 (Galiani 1975: 985, footnote).

[144] See Angelo Gatti's letter to Ferdinando Galiani, Paris, 18 September 1769, published in Nicolini (1929: 254). See also Nicolini (1908b: 18–20). Some time later, the abbot wrote to Madame d'Épinay: "I must tell you that a feeling of humanity prompted me to give twelve *Livres* a month to a woman, so that she could bring up a child that an unnatural father abandoned after having begotten him clumsily. This lady's name is Madame de La Daubinière, in rue Saint-Honoré, opposite the little Hôtel de Noailles. Gatti was the payer of this annuity.

he left Paris with a broken heart, but not without taking with him in the post chair a girl destined to alleviate the boredom of the journey. His faith in the chimerical promises of Choiseul was still so great that, instead of continuing directly to Naples, he stopped over three months in Genoa, at the home, it seems, of his old friend and banker Pietro Paolo Celesia" (Nicolini 1929: 246).

Having just completed the long work on a map of the Kingdom of Naples[145] he entrusted the *Dialogues* into the hands of his closest Parisian friends, Madame d'Épinay and Diderot.

7.4 *Geoeconomics of Grain and Methodological Relativism: Galiani's* Dialogues

The circumstances under which Galiani completed the drafting of his *Dialogues* were clarified in a letter to Madame d'Épinay in early 1770: "Since the identity of the author is now known, I want to hope that friends have not been silent about the unfortunate circumstances under which the unlucky infant [the book] was conceived and aborted. Even I do not know

Do me the courtesy of paying Gatti, and entrusting the continuation of the help to this person, who will come to see you, and whom I recommend to you as warmly as possible. After you, she is the dearest thing I have left in Paris. She does not deserve her unfortunate fate and deserves your protection. I beg you not to give her twelve *Livres* more than once, as she may be tempted to spend it" (Ferdinando Galiani's letter to Madame d'Épinay, Naples, 8 September 1770, in Galiani 1881a, vol. I: 253–254; Galiani and d'Épinay 1992, vol. I: 251). On the relations between Gatti and Madame de La Daubinière, see Nicolini (1929: 246, 254, 264). Both the son attributed to Galiani and Madame de La Daubinière died shortly afterwards.

[145] Galiani had collaborated with the geographer Giovanni Antonio Rizzi-Zannoni on a map of the Kingdom of Naples, an enterprise that the abbot considered of primary importance: "at my own expense I am making out of it what may serve me for a good map of the Kingdom of Naples. If Your Excellency would protect this work, I could do something good and useful mainly for the navigation of our ill-known shores" (Ferdinando Galiani's letter to Bernardo Tanucci, Paris, September 27, 1762, published in Bazzoni 1876a: 245). The map was drawn up on the basis of a group of parchments, found by the abbot himself in the *Dépôt de la Guerre* in Versailles and copied in secret, concerning the Kingdom of Naples and Sicily, drawn up by order of King Alfonso V of Aragon around the middle of the fifteenth century and likely derived from census surveys. Since 1781, Rizzi-Zannoni worked on a new map of the kingdom commissioned by the Neapolitan government, which was completed in 1812. See Diodati (1788: 49–50); Blessich (1896); Principe (1993). On the Aragonese cartography and Galiani's eighteenth-century copies, see Valerio (2007).

what it is anymore, since I could not read it once with a cool mind. Having left the original manuscript in your hands, therefore I know nothing".[146]

The drafting of the *Dialogues* probably began in November 1768, when Galiani accepted the pressing invitation of his Parisian friends to give systematic form to his thoughts, and ended in the agitated days of June 1769, when he had been ordered to leave the French capital.[147] The *Dialogues* were written in great secrecy, even Tanucci, according to available correspondence, was not informed of the abbot's new commitment.[148]

The manuscript of the *Dialogues*, published by Philip Koch in 1968, provides a better insight into the stages of elaboration of the text. That manuscript was in the possession of Madame d'Épinay, later passed to Grimm and then came into the hands of Gaston Maugras, curator of Galiani's correspondence, and finally was acquired in 1953 by Harvard University's Houghton Library. According to Koch the manuscript held by the Houghton Library is to be regarded as the only manuscript on which corrections were made in the rather extensive interventions by Diderot and Madame d'Épinay to purify Galiani's not always perfect French and introduce other stylistic variants (Koch 1968: 26–9, 292–316; Koch 1961, 1975). This interpretation was opposed by Nicolini for whom the greatest similarities between the published text and the manuscript concerned the last dialogue, while for the other seven dialogues the differences were much greater and therefore the printed edition must have been based not on the "redaction or, rather, sketch represented by the Koch

[146] Ferdinando Galiani's letter to Madame d'Épinay, Naples, 27 January 1770, in Galiani (1881a, vol. I: 58–59); Galiani and d'Épinay (1992, vol. I: 111–112). Writing to one of his Italian correspondents, Galiani recalled again the circumstances in which he had completed the edition of his book: "It is very true that les *Dialogues sur les bleds* is a thing of mine, but roughened, and not polished, interrupted by my unexpected departure from Paris. I left the manuscript in the hands of a lady who, eight months after my departure, had it printed in Paris without my having had time to touch it up" (Ferdinando Galiani's letter to Lorenzo Mehus, Naples 7 May 1771, published in Galiani 1975: 993).

[147] "I wrote the last dialogue in haste, the day before I left, and I am surprised that it is no worse than it is" (Ferdinando Galiani's letter to Armand-Henri Baudouin, Naples, April 26, 1770, in Galiani 1881a, vol. I: 104).

[148] "You may be sure that if I could have confided to anyone the work of the *Dialogues*, which I was enjoying writing in Paris, it would have been to you in preference to anyone else and in every respect. But as I had no intention of leaving Paris so soon, I wanted to maintain the most perfect anonymity" (Ferdinando Galiani's letter to Joseph Pellerin, Naples, March 24, 1770, in Galiani 1881a, vol. I: 85).

edition, but on a second redaction drafted by Galiani himself" (Nicolini 1959a: xv–xxi). There is no trace of this second redaction in the available documents. In support of Nicolini's interpretation there are several arguments: (1) the existence of numerous major variants in the manuscript, even in the names of the characters; (2) the rapid revision of the manuscript that was accomplished in only 12 hours;[149] (3) the manuscript has many corrections, attributed to d'Épinay, that were not reflected in the printed edition; (4) the names of the protagonists could not be changed without Galiani's consent (see Galiani 1975, Diaz's note: 351–356). However, Furio Diaz observes, "the numerous corrections and variations made by Galiani himself interlinearly or in the margins of the manuscript, and the same formal and linguistic corrections added by d'Épinay suggest that this was the only integral version of the *Dialogues*, completed within the limits allowed to the author by his hasty return home. Nor do we see how in the few months in which, as per repeated assertions expressed in correspondence with his friends, he devoted himself to the composition of the *Dialogues* (November 1768–June 1769), the lazy Galiani could have added, to a redaction on which he had worked so hard including corrections and additions, a second and more complete draft. Finally, both dialogues VII and VIII in the manuscript appear to have been written in great haste and without thoughtful revision" (Galiani 1975, Diaz's notes: 354).

It is therefore possible to conclude, following Diaz, that "for all its ingenious finesse, Nicolini's hypothesis does not appear to be convincing, and that as things stand we must accept the text published by Koch as the only complete original manuscript of the *Dialogues*. With the consequence, of course, that the work done on it by Diderot and d'Épinay turns out to be of considerable consistency, to the point of having gone to press with a text that is almost new in formal terms, and also with few but significant substantial additions. A fact, this, that cannot come as a surprise to those who know Diderot's particular disposition to participate with entire passages of his own hand in the elaboration of his friends' works" (Galiani 1975, Diaz's note: 355, see also Guerci 1971).[150]

[149] "We locked ourselves away, the philosopher [Diderot] and I, and read and corrected with the greatest care, from eleven in the morning until midnight, without a moment's respite" (Madame d'Épinay's letter to Ferdinando Galiani, Aux Ternes, 26 July 1769, in Galiani 1959: 337–338; Galiani and d'Épinay 1992, vol. I: 60).

[150] According to Marco Catucci, Diderot's interventions were substantial and the *Dialogues* inspired two of his works, *Le Rêve de d'Alembert* (written in 1782) and *Paradoxe sur le comédien* (written between 1773 and 1777): "The revision of the *Dialogues* no longer seems

The reading of the manuscript is particularly interesting for the variation in the names of the protagonists, who up to the seventh dialogue are *Marquis Frangipane* and *Chevalier Painmollet*,[151] an ironic reference to the bread issue, characters that disappear in the eighth dialogue, the last, in which Galiani reverses the noble titles and changes the names, introducing on the scene *Chevalier Zenobi* and *Marquis de Roquemaure*, who appear in the printed text. In the fifth dialogue of the manuscript as well as in the published text, a third interlocutor appears, *Monsieur de Painbis C. du P. de...*, who in the last dialogue becomes the *President de... du P. de B.*, a secondary interlocutor whose function is to better clarify *Zenobi's* arguments.[152] Other characters are present in the manuscript: *Abbé Panartico* appears in the title of the third dialogue, but never enters the scene; a woman also appears in the second dialogue of the manuscript, probably to represent the famous guests of the Paris salons, such as Madame d'Épinay and Madame d'Holbach (Koch 1968: 37).

Behind the characters of the *Dialogues* it is possible to recognise real identities: *Frangipane-Zenobi* is Galiani's alter ego, *Painmollet - de Roquemaure* is identifiable in the figure of the Marquis Marc-Antoine-Nicolas de Croismare (Nicolini 1954: 125–150)[153] and, finally, *de Painbis C. du P. de... - Presidente de... du P. de B.* would be Armand-Henri-Baudouin de Guémadeuc, President of the *Chambre des requètes* of the Paris Parliament (Nicolini 1959a: 563–576).[154]

determined by a partial misunderstanding, but represents the tribute that had to be paid to make the work publishable, acceptable. A tribute that Diderot himself did not want to pay for the *Rêve* and the *Paradoxe*, which remained unpublished for a long time after his death. It is only due to a fortunate case of having such a genial censor, if even the printed edition, with all its limitations, with respect to the manuscript, can be considered a masterpiece, but by Diderot not by Galiani, by Diderot in a *Galianian phase*" (Catucci 1986: 103).

[151] Koch believes this name was taken from a contemporary work *Mémoire pour servir à l'histoire des révolutions du pain mollet*, by Charles Marie de La Condamine, published in 1768.

[152] According to Marco Catucci, the name Zanobi may have been taken from the novel by Alain-René Lesage, *Le Diable boiteux* (*The Devil upon Two Sticks*, Lesage 1707), in which a certain "Zanubio, cavalier napolitain" appears in chapter nine. See Catucci (1986: 80).

[153] Diderot traced the characteristics of the *Marquis de Roquemaure*: "he is a fiery interlocutor, slight, indiscreet, petulant, excessive in everything, good-hearted, honest, sensitive, superficial, short of education. The abbot [Galiani] makes him speak properly" (Diderot 1955: 16).

[154] "In my *Dialogues* he is the President" (Ferdinando Galiani's letter to Madame d'Épinay, Naples, 21 July 1770, published in Galiani 1881a, vol I: 204; Galiani and d'Épinay 1992, vol. I: 212). Diderot had a harsher opinion of the *President*, described as ignorant and well

On his journey to Naples, Galiani was not only nostalgic for the French capital, which he had left so abruptly, but also worried about the publication of his *Dialogues.* From Genoa, where he stayed for a long time, he wrote: "[I am] eager to learn that at last the scribblings have rounded the cape, overcoming the terrible parade of revision [...]. If we exclude this matter for everything else I feel calm".[155] A few days later, Madame d'Épinay informed Galiani on the progress made: "On my return from Bourgneuf, on the 10th of this month, I found the work in the hands of our friend, the magistrate [Antoine Raymonde de Sartine, lieutenant-general of police]. He had it for eight days. [...]. I wanted to know his opinion: he seemed well satisfied with the setting and the progress of the first five [dialogues] he had read, but unpleasantly struck by some jokes that in his opinion would spoil the work. I invited him to give it back to me [...] I read it, expressed the same opinion, and gave it to two persons of good taste to read it, without mentioning, as you can well imagine, the name that should be kept anonymous. The two were enthusiastic about it, absolutely exalted. [...] From the following day we locked ourselves away, the philosopher [Diderot] and I, and read and corrected it with the greatest care, from eleven in the morning until midnight, without a moment's respite. I returned it to de Sartine, who gave it back to me yesterday, giving me licence to print it".[156] Galiani, with his usual irony, responded to the objections and possible censure: "Regarding the buffoonery, far from agreeing with you, I found that there was not enough of it. You will say, "But they were not in good taste". So much the better, Madame! Do you think all readers have good taste? One has to please everyone. What bad jokes didn't the patriarch Voltaire publish? Finally I would have left them in, they could have made the book's fortune with fools, of which there are many. But let us think no more about it. When it is known in what a terrible state of pain and discomfort of mind this unfortunate work was conceived, realised and finished, and what kind of little runt it is, there will be nothing to say to the author, and the publishers will always have more

disposed towards Galiani's arguments (Diderot 1955: 12). "Entering the scene late [the President] has the task of placing himself above the parties; of helping both sides to clarify their thinking, so that he can - as a judge, and as such he is presented - draw conclusions, in the same way as in a judicial hearing, assigning the awards to those who have deserved them" (De Rosa 1995: 150).

[155] Ferdinando Galiani's letter to Madame d'Épinay, Genoa, 17 July 1769, in Galiani (1881a, vol. I: 15–16); Galiani and d'Épinay (1992, vol. I: 58).

[156] Madame d'Épinay's letter to Ferdinando Galiani, Aux Ternes, 26 July 1769, in Galiani (1959: 337–338); Galiani and d'Épinay (1992, vol. I: 60).

merit in having left it as it is than if they had redone it. I now eagerly await news about [...] the success of the project".[157]

The publication of the *Dialogues* was assigned to the publisher Merlin, who was supposed to pay 100 *Louis d'Or* to the author, and by September the printing was almost complete,[158] but in the following weeks the process slowed down due to the censorship officers[159] and their alleged sympathy for the physiocrats.[160] Sartine had an ambiguous attitude,[161] worried

[157] Ferdinando Galiani's letter to Madame d'Épinay, Genoa, 14 August 1769, published in Galiani (1975: 339–340); Galiani and d'Épinay (1992, vol. I: 61).

[158] Madame d'Épinay's letter to Ferdinando Galiani, Aux Ternes, 1 September 1769, published in Galiani (1959: 341); (Galiani and d'Épinay 1992, vol. I: 65–67); Madame d'Épinay's letter to Ferdinando Galiani, Aux Ternes, 18 September 1769, published in Galiani (1959: 342) (Galiani and d'Épinay 1992, vol. I: 71–72); Denis Diderot's letter to Ferdinando Galiani, s.l. 20 September 1769, published in Galiani (1959: 344–345); Madame d'Épinay's letter to Ferdinando Galiani, Paris, 29 September 1769, published in Galiani (1959: 345–346) (Galiani and d'Épinay 1992, vol. I: 76–78).

[159] "Since the last letter, I have not been able to wrest anything from censorship. It's a discouraging thing. Now the work has been stopped for four days, and these dogs of censors take twelve days to check each page" (Madame d'Épinay's letter to Ferdinando Galiani, Paris, 14 October 1769, published in Galiani 1959: 347; Galiani and d'Épinay 1992, vol. I: 90). "I really suffer and get impatient with the slowness of the press and the censors. For fifteen days I have not received a single page to correct. I continue without ceasing to harass the censors, but one is ill, the other is at Fontainebleau" (Madame d'Épinay's letter to Ferdinando Galiani, Paris, 23 October 1769, published in Galiani 1959: 348; Galiani and d'Épinay 1992, vol. I: 90).

[160] "The official [...] claims that the censor has more sympathy for the physiocrats than he does for parliament. He also insinuates that the censor disapproves of the book, and that (he suspects) he is keeping it blocked to prevent its release" (Madame d'Épinay's letter to Ferdinando Galiani, La Briche, 4 November 1769, published in Galiani 1959: 349; Galiani and d'Épinay 1992, vol. I: 93). And Galiani's reply: "Is it possible that the best of men, the most worthy magistrate, the man in the world who loves me the most, and whom I love and esteem the most, in short M. de Sartine, wants to ruin me along with an honest bookseller? Would you have believed it, Madame? Would you have believed that the only respectful book that has been published so far on matters of administration would encounter so many difficulties, while satires that would be the most gory, if they were not boring, can appear with permission? [...]. Will it prevent me from printing the work in Holland, or even here? A certain M. Godard [Ange Goudar], a famous writer on economics, has just printed here a terrible and violent work against our administration, entitled *Naples*, and they have allowed him to do so. Will M. de Sartine allow himself to be surpassed by us in the love of freedom of the press?" (Ferdinando Galiani's letter to madame d'Épinay, Naples, 18 December 1769, in Galiani 1959: 352; Galiani and d'Épinay 1992, vol. I: 102–103). See Goudar (1769). On Goudar, see Hauc (2004).

[161] However Galiani had a very good friendship with him, see Galiani (1959: 325–326). Nicolini's footnote.

about displeasing the new *Contrôleur Général des Finances*, Étienne Maynon d'Invault (who had succeeded de L'Averdy in September 1768) and Choiseul, both supporters of the *conomistes*,[162] and entrusted the censorship to a particularly harsh censor (Diderot 1955, vol IX: 138–139). Diderot responded to Galiani's impatience, abruptly, "Have you the devil in your body to cover me with insults in all languages dead and alive? The manuscript was copied, the copy read and reread with all the scruples of friendship, the work presented to the bookseller [...] then taken to the censor who held it for a long time; then it was strenuously defended against this censor who was a damned Capuchin, who had cut out half of the first dialogue; then given in full to the press, under whose screws we have been suffering for a month and will still have to suffer a fortnight".[163] The situation was only resolved at the end of December, when Maynon d'Invault was replaced by Abbot Joseph Marie Terray, a critic of the Quesnay school, and so Madame d'Épinay could announce to Galiani: "The work is finally printed. We shall meet next Thursday, myself, the philosopher [Diderot] and the prophet [Grimm] to reread it from beginning to end and check that no glaring error has escaped".[164] Finally, on 24 December 1769, the *Dialogues* could be published, although de Sartine still wanted to withhold the book for further scrupulous checks, arousing Madame d'Épinay's disapproval.[165]

The book, published anonymously with London as the fictitious place of printing, and without an indication of the publisher, began to circulate in early 1770 and the author's name was immediately known. With his usual irony, Galiani wrote: "I note, however, that it was necessary to fire a controller, cause huge bankruptcies and turn the state upside down to get my little book to appear. The night that gave birth to Hercules was not as

[162] See Diderot (1955, vol IX: 138–139); Diderot (1955, vol IX: 144, footnote 2). See also Madame d'Épinay's letter to Ferdinando Galiani, Paris, 24 December 1769, published in Galiani 1959: 353, see Nicolini's footnote (Galiani and d'Épinay 1992, vol. I: 105).

[163] Denis Diderot's letter to Ferdinando Galiani, Paris, 20 September 1769, published in Diderot (1955, vol. IX: 144–145). In actual fact, the censor was not a Capuchin, but an advisor to the Parliament of Paris (see Diderot 1955, vol. IX: 144, footnote 2).

[164] Madame d'Épinay's letter to Ferdinando Galiani, Paris, 11 December 1769, published in Galiani (1959: 351); Galiani and d'Épinay (1992, vol. I: 99–100).

[165] Madame d'Épinay's letter to Ferdinando Galiani, Paris, 24 December 1769, published in Galiani (1959: 353), see Nicolini's footnote. Another obstacle was the *Intendant General des Finances*, Jean-Charles-Philibert Trudaine de Montigny, also a supporter of the free grain trade, who had to give the final authorisation after printing.

long or stormy".[166] As soon as he was able to see it, he wrote to Madame d'Épinay: "I finally got a copy of the book that caused such a great noise in Paris, and I read it in one go, so much so that I can hardly remember anything of its contents now. Word of a connoisseur, it is a good book [...]. The changes I have found are few, but these few produce a very great effect. [...] I thank the benefactors. I cannot say the same for those who corrected the proofs!".[167] But, a few months later, writing to Lorenzo Mehus, he strongly downgraded his *Dialogues*: "It is very true that *les Dialogues sur les bleds* is a thing of mine, but roughened, and not polished, interrupted by my unexpected departure from Paris. I left the manuscript in the hands of a lady who, eight months after my departure, had it printed in Paris without my having had time to touch it up".[168]

Galiani would have liked to write a final dialogue, the ninth, in which he would "deal in depth with the policy necessary to define, in the system of general and constant permission to export and import, the storage and loading granaries that should be established in France and the measures to be taken to prevent cowardice".[169]

[166] Ferdinando Galiani's letter to Madame d'Épinay, Naples, 20 January 1770, published in Galiani (1959: 354); Galiani and d'Épinay (1992, vol. I: 108).

[167] Ferdinando Galiani's letter to Madame d'Épinay, Naples, 3 February 1770, published in Galiani (1881a, vol I: 64–65); Galiani and d'Épinay (1992, vol. I: 113).

[168] Ferdinando Galiani's letter to Lorenzo Mehus, Naples, 7 May 1771, published in Galiani (1975: 993).

[169] Ferdinando Galiani's letter to Madame d'Épinay, Naples, 21 July 1770, published in Galiani (1959: 403); Galiani and d'Épinay (1992, vol. I: 115). Galiani responded in this way to an objection by Diderot reported by d'Épinay: "Abbot Galiani, said he [Diderot], neglected to point out an observation about the difficulty of calculating the superfluous, which is common to all nations and to all men. There is always a certain quantity of bread (I mention bread, but I could also say of wheat) that does not participate in the normal circulation: and it is the quantity that is taken away through fear and greed. [...]. And to this quantity of wheat that is subtracted from the normal circulation by the rich and the well-to-do miser or coward, you must add another quantity: that which is subtracted by the poor who are alarmed. The poor who fear famine stock up four times as much foodstuffs as they really need. The opposite extremes come together and produce the same effect. Abbot Galiani has studied grain as an economist and as a politician: but he has yet to study it as a moralist, as the object of the greatest of needs, and as the occasion of the most atrocious cowardice and sometimes of the most revolting cupidity" (Madame d'Épinay's letter to Ferdinando Galiani, Paris, 28 June–1 July 1770, published in Galiani 1959: 401–402; Galiani and d'Épinay 1992, vol. I: 199–200). The need to complete the work with a ninth dialogue was in Galiani's plans: "I would like to add a dialogue to the second edition that will serve to illustrate the system of storage warehouses, the only one in France that can make the grain trade viable" (Ferdinando Galiani's letter to Madame d'Épinay, Naples, 27 January 1770, in Galiani

The choice made by Galiani to entrust his arguments to the light form of the dialogue to address such a delicate topic, at a time of serious political and social crisis, and in opposition to the power of a school, the physiocratic one, that was still hegemonic and enjoyed wide political consensus, may seem inappropriate.[170] But the dialogue was also the literary form chosen by Galileo Galilei to defend his theses against the Jesuits and to refute the Ptolemaic-Aristotelian system in support of the Copernican system (Galilei 1632).[171] And with the same objective of scientific criticism, Galiani intended to tackle the controversial issue of the liberalisation of the grain trade.[172]

Despite the fact that the *Dialogues* opens with a description of the famine that struck Italy in 1764 and 1765 (and the Italian *Chevalier Zenobi* witnessed it), the scenes take place in a convivial atmosphere characterised by lunches and dinners in which the shortages suffered by the French

1881a, vol I: 59; Galiani and d'Épinay 1992, vol. I: 112). See also Galiani's ironic response to Diderot's criticism (Ferdinando Galiani's letter to Madame d'Épinay, Naples, 21 July 1770, in Galiani 1881a, vol I: 206–207; Galiani and d'Épinay 1992, vol. I: 213–214).

[170] The choice of the dialogical form may also have been determined by the revival of this literary genre in France, with Fénelon and Fontanelle; an entry in the *Encyclopédie*, compiled by Jean-François Marmontel, see Catucci (1986: 79). According to Azzurra Mauro, the short essay *De l'opinion* written by Galiani in the early 1760s anticipates many arguments on rationality used in the *Dialogues* (Mauro 2017a: 176, see also Galiani, MS-22). On the *Dialogues*, see also Mauro (2017b).

[171] Luigi De Rosa, on the other hand, emphasises the influence of the Platonic *Dialogues* and the theory of contraries, referred to in the text: "your way of reasoning, which is somewhat like that of Socrates, and which always seems to be based on the opposite of what you intend to conclude next" (Galiani 1770a: 147). "As in Plato, in Galiani too, by his own admission, the method of small steps is followed [...]. As in Plato's dialogues, so in these of Galiani, the author is in the main character, in the one who analyses, or suggests the analysis and determines the conclusion, or causes it to be determined, by the maieutic method employed" (De Rosa 1995:149). According to Marco Catucci: "The *Dialogues* cannot be conveniently compared to the *Dialogo dei massimi sistemi* (*Dialogue Concerning the Two Chief World Systems*, see Galilei 1632), which is still too closely linked in its structure to the Platonic tradition" (Catucci 1986: 14). Instead, Galiani's work represents "one of the later examples of the literary genre that had as models the *Principe*, the *Cortegiano*, the *Galateo* [...]. The recovery of the sixteenth-century rhetorical tradition allows the author to satisfy his dramatic narrative vocation, preserving intact, or rather exalting the informative value of his work" (Catucci 1986: 29). See Machiavelli (1531 [1883]); Castiglione (1528); Della Casa (1558). On *Dialogue* as an apologue, see Deloche (1988). See also Finoli (1947).

[172] About Galiani's *Dialogues* see Gaudemet (1899); Gignoux (1922); Porta (1995); Faccarello (1998); Klotz (2000); Patalano (2018).

people are absent:[173] it is an apparently cynical choice, but one that intends to mark the detachment of scientific reflection from the constraints of the social and political context.[174] The discussion took place in less than a month, between 16 November and 14 December 1768, with several meetings on the same day (14 November and 24 November). *Chevalier Zenobi's* tight and witty arguments are based on his common sense ("common sense is the only sovereign court that never goes on holiday", Galiani 1770a: 22), and not on a knowledge of economic literature ("I read but little or not at all", Galiani 1770a: 95), the *Marquis de Roquemaure*, on the other hand, bases his assertions on a vast knowledge of physiocratic theories.[175]

The central thesis put forward by *Chevalier Zenobi*, Galiani's alter ego, in the various conversations that animated his dialogues with the *Marquis de Roquemaure* is based on the statement that grain cannot be considered just any commodity, it is, in fact: "can be regarded as a production of the

[173] "How is it possible that the good food we have just eaten has not banished from our minds a sad talk of famine? Let us enjoy the present, let us banish lugubrious ideas" (Galiani 1770a: 20).

[174] An opposing, rather original, thesis was put forward by Gianluigi Goggi, according to whom the *Dialogues* were a defence of the ruling class in the face of popular uprisings, and represented a clearly conservative political position: "Some documents show that the work was a reaction to a French situation, and more specifically to a very specific situation in Paris in October–November 1768. This was a subsistence crisis caused by the scarcity of harvests, which threatened to unleash social unrest or disturb public order. Faced with this situation, Galiani's point of view was the same as that of the police and its Lieutenant General Sartine. One could call it the point of view of the constituted authorities, which naturally led to a defensive reflex in the face of any threat of disorder. In November 1768, the fear of popular sedition, but also, more generally, of a revolution, linked to the bon prix and the free grain trade advocated by the Physiocrats, caused the authorities to take a series of measures to avert the imminent danger of disorder. At the ideological level, the clearest expression of this defensive reflex is the work of Galiani" (Goggi 1994: 296). Galiani's conservative inspiration would have been caused by his sojourn in England and direct observation of the Wilkes and liberty uprisings, which constituted proof that free trade measures "necessarily led to political democracy, shifting the balance of power in favour of the social stratum of free landowners. [...]. In Galiani's thought, England acted as a negative model of a political and social evolution that had to be controlled and even hindered" (Goggi 1994:297). A similar view is expressed by Marco Catucci: "Galiani is a man of the court, and the salon has partly taken the place of the court in the France of Louis XV. The courtier's job is to train and correct the Prince: a similar task falls to Chevalier Zanobi, who has to dispel the physiocratic enthusiasms of the Marquis de Roquemaure" (Catucci 1986: 74).

[175] In the *Dialogues*, Chevalier Zenobi states that he knows Riquetti's works, *Theorie de l'Impot* (Galiani 1770a: 95) and, *L'ami du l'homme* (Galiani 1770a: 149).

soil, and from this point of view it belongs to commerce and economic legislation. Then it can and must at the same time be regarded as the first necessity and the first care in the civil order of societies, and from this point of view it belongs to politics and the *Raison d'État*. Tell me, when you supply a frontier fortress, when you command an army, when you equip a ship, do you not think as much or even more about wheat, bread and biscuits than you do about gunpowder and cannon?" (Galiani 1770a: 30–31).[176]

The regulation of such an important commodity therefore belongs entirely to the *Reason of State*, to politics, and other considerations become absolutely secondary:[177] "After the elements, wheat is the greatest, the most pressing and the most continuous of man's needs. And as the elements, by their abundance, are not an object of commerce, wheat consequently becomes man's first need (Galiani 1770a: 131) [...]. To eat bread or not to eat bread is not a matter of taste, caprice or luxury; it is a necessity of every century and every age" (Galiani 1770a: 90).

This element of a "political" nature, which characterises not only wheat, but all other grains and more generally that which serves as common nourishment,[178] is, according to Galiani, completely ignored by the *conomistes*, who unlike the ancients who considered wheat in the light of politics and *Raison d'État*, treat it as a mere object of commerce (Galiani 1770a: 33). Thus their conclusions on the liberalisation of the grain trade are to be considered the product of an abstract determinism in which the political implications and historical-institutional premises of such a choice were not even considered (Galiani 1770a: 31).

[176] He reiterated this concept later: "What is truly superfluous to one people, is superfluous to all. Such are gems, porcelain, lace, embroidery, chevrons, etc.; and of such ornaments of luxury there may well be the ardent greed to possess them, but never the need. But that which is necessary to one people, such as grain, wine, oil, wood, metals, etc., can never be said to be superfluous to others, for all men have similar needs. It may, it is true, happen that at one time the need of one nation is urgent because it lacks a harvest, and another has a plentiful supply. But nature, in varying the vicissitudes of the seasons, has disposed, almost as a compensation for such a risk, that the necessary provisions for mankind can all be preserved for a not short space of time in the face of every adverse event" (Galiani 1782: 206–207).

[177] Still emphasising its strategic importance, he did not hesitate to assert that wheat is "a true munition of war" (Galiani 1770a: 50).

[178] "Under the name of *bled* [*blé* - *wheat*], I also mean rice, corn, méteil [a mixture of cereals], etc., and everything that serves as common food for rich and poor alike. To make it easier, I will only use the word *bled*" (Galiani 1770a: 131).

Abstract and misleading is also the fundamental principle that agriculture is the basis of every country's wealth (Galiani 1770a: 23). A principle that, according to Galiani, resolves itself into an axiom unverified by experience and easily refuted by its opposite. It is enough to cite the case, Galiani observes, of small states, such as Geneva, Lucca, Frankfurt, without territory, or with a limited territory, such as Holland and Genoa, which are rich and which certainly do not base their fortune on agriculture, which is completely non-existent or limited. Instead, the *deductive determinism* of Physiocrats should lead to opposite results in these cases. Even in large countries such as France, one cannot consider all wealth as the exclusive gift of agriculture, since the provinces comprising it are very diverse and in some agriculture may prevail in others industry, without primacy in the formation of national wealth being attributed to one or the other (Galiani 1770a: 26).

It follows that: "their principle, stated in general terms, is false and that to apply it to France, in particular, it would be necessary first to demonstrate that it is suitable for that country, which they have not done" (Galiani 1770a: 26). A similar error is made by Montesquieu, who: "has made nothing but mistakes of this kind, happy to discover the finest ideas, the most delicate relationships" (Galiani 1770a: 99). This is the method of the metaphysicians: "Their work is a true masterpiece of marquetry, or if you like, a mosaic. It consists of putting together an infinity of small detached pieces that they must not have made or altered, but which are existing, real, as nature gives them. From these parts, artistically glued, arranged and nuanced, there emerges a great picture and a new spectacle, although it is made entirely of parts that were scattered" (Galiani 1770a: 99–100). Generalisations constructed in this way therefore lead to error.

Equally erroneous is the uncritical application of instruments conceived in the past, in completely different circumstances, as is often the case in the regulation of grain policy, which in some states is even inspired by the legislation in force in the Roman Empire at the time of Augustus (Galiani 1770a: 6–7).

The preeminence attributed to agriculture is therefore the result of a generalisation and can easily be disputed.[179] First of all, manufacturing is

[179] "This principle, which they believe to be general, applies specifically only to purely agricultural countries. This false principle led them astray. Seeing grain in a country, they said that was wealth, that was income and that was spending. They thought they were in France. They saw complete and absolute freedom; they said: there is nothing like complete and abso-

not sterile, but it is "a species of production in that it adds to the raw material" (Galiani 1770a: 40).[180] Agricultural production is subject, then, to the uncertainty of the production result, subordinate as it is to the weather, while manufacturing, on the other hand, is immune to it (Galiani 1770a: 41). It can therefore be concluded that: "a purely agricultural people is the most unfortunate of peoples; left to servitude, superstition and indigence, it farms all the more poorly, as cultivation is its only occupation, and it suffers all the more the disgrace of famine, as it has only the produce of the land for its only good" (Galiani 1770a: 115). The farmer in his essence is comparable to a gambler: "I see him taking rolls of *Louis*, the price of sowing, ploughing and labour, and throwing them on a field against the elements and the seasons that hold sway" (Galiani 1770a: 110). On the contrary: "The manufacturer does not let himself be trampled underfoot; he leaves and takes with him his hands, which are his land and his treasure" Galiani 1770a: 114).[181]

Having eliminated the question of the primacy of the agricultural sector, Galiani challenges the dogma that a free trade policy is the best regulation of the grain trade. Such a policy cannot, in fact, be applied to small states without territory, which must necessarily have recourse both to public granaries to supply the population and to political control of the price

lute freedom to make agriculture flourish. As if the freedom to buy foreign goods was the same thing as selling one's own. Finally, they saw good and bad years in France and believed that there are good and bad years in everything, and did not take into account that the inversion of seasons, which produces barren years, is still better for a trading country than ordinary years. In barren years there is more movement, more transportation, more buildings occupied, more liveliness, more profit in the exchange from one place to another; so if in any year any country in Europe complains of famine, count on the Dutch banker rejoicing" (Galiani 1770a: 71–72).

[180] "The grain trade is not a manufacture, it adds nothing to the matter" (Galiani 1770a: 40), but maritime trade is: "transport from one country to another far away is a kind of manufacture, it adds something to the raw material, it adds freights and these freights employ and make a living for a number of people" (Galiani 1770a: 51).

[181] "It is from manufactures alone that you can hope for a prompt and equal circulation of wealth, the extinction of usury and contracts that are onerous for the borrower, the equality of the total product of the state in the midst of all vicissitudes, the equality consequently of the product of the taxes from which the strength of the state derives; any force that is not regulated and lasting, that comes in fits and starts, is useless. It is not a wind, it is a hurricane that shatters the mill and does not turn it. We must expect manufacturing industry to cure the two great evils of humanity, superstition and slavery. And these same factories, which are so important to preserve, are nevertheless very delicate to manage, because the manufacturer can leave while the farmer must stay" (Galiani 1770a: 121).

of grain, which must be kept as constant as possible (Galiani 1770a: 43).[182] In these countries, the strict rules of the *Annona*, which can easily be applied in limited territories, will still be useful. In these particular circumstances, the grain trade can be totally under state control. If, in fact, the management were assigned to a caste of merchants, injustice and inefficiency would ensue. Gains and losses of this trade must therefore be attributed to the state that can most easily bear the burden or utilise the advantages (Galiani 1770a: 40). Manufacturing will also be encouraged in these states, which becomes the only resource to be exchanged for agricultural commodities.

In states of medium size, not endowed with fertile land and located on favourable communication routes, with direct access to the sea or navigable rivers, the population will sustain itself by manufacturing and maritime trade, as is the case for Holland and Genoa (Galiani 1770a: 51).[183] Under these circumstances, the best policy will be to establish free trade in grain and eliminate any regulation of the *Annona*.[184] Generally, these countries regard the purchase of grain as their largest expense and to ensure a constant price they diversify their sources of supply.[185] Manufactures and ships

[182] "If a city should find itself enclosed by contagion, or inundated by flooding rivers, or ruined by tremors, or by fires, or finally struck down by some other misfortune, it is convenient for the Sovereign authority not to leave the prices of provisions, of materials to be manufactured, and of everything that has become urgently necessary at the mercy of avarice and the greed of vendors, but to set the price that I call *civil equity*" (Galiani 1782: 222).

[183] "Transport from one country to another very far away is a kind of manufacture; it adds to the raw material, it adds rental fee, and this rental fee employs and sustains many people" (Galiani 1770a: 51).

[184] "The *Annona* of a city or country whose doors cannot be closed at will with ease and security is detestable. It is an inconvenience and a tax in times of plenty, which only serves to starve people in times of shortage. Since the government relies on the supply of its warehouses, if these run out, all is lost. You cannot resort to your private merchants, because they have never traded in grain, since it was forbidden and smuggled. They do not know how to proceed or where to start, especially in difficult times. They have no correspondents, no shops of their own, no means of transport either by sea or land" (Galiani 1770a: 55).

[185] According to Marco Minerbi: "Galiani moves from a point of view that is undoubtedly backward (on the level of theory, method and ideology) even compared to other opponents of physiocracy, a point of view that can be defined as annonary: the grain problem never ceases to be treated essentially as a problem of supplying the city with the primary and fundamental means of subsistence; agriculture appears only as a subordinate and instrumental activity; the author of the *Dialogues* never departs from a vision of the city-countryside (or manufactures-agriculture) relationship close to that which, for centuries, reflected one of the fundamental aspects of Italy's economy, and against which only in a slightly earlier period had discordant voices been raised, voices to which Galiani remained distant and estranged, or at

provide the means to purchase it where it is most profitable. They do not suffer from the uncertainties of their incomes, since their wealth is based on industry, they only fear war that interrupts trade flows (Galiani 1770a: 63–64).

In contrast, for medium-sized but very fertile states, such as Sicily, or for those with a large extension, such as France, the harvest will depend on weather conditions and a year of abundance may be followed by a year of famine. The export of grain can only be allowed if the country has an abundance of commodities; in the opposite case "to carry abroad for free any grain you may need (I'm not saying in an exceptional case) but in one of those barren seasons that come back very often, three or four times in ten years, it's a very unfavourable trade" (Galiani 1770a: 146–147).

The increase in agricultural production is subject to the natural limit of arable land and even if the labour force is increased, it cannot increase beyond a certain limit (Galiani 1770a: 149–150). This production limit cannot apply to manufacturing states. The expansion of cultivation is possible for states that can exploit large territories and are not limited by natural barriers (Russia, colonies of America), not for countries like France or Great Britain, countries closed by natural and political borders. Generally, surplus grain, if it exists in countries like France, is the effect of a population deficit (Galiani 1770a: 169). However, even if there were a sufficient surplus, the grain trade would not be profitable. Wheat is a heavy commodity, voluminous and prone to perish; it can be traded between autumn and spring, in weather conditions that are the worst for shipping (Galiani 1770a: 170–171). Grain then grows everywhere while trade is sustained by need, hence profits are extremely variable and dependent on famines occurring in certain areas. To feed this trade requires a network of correspondents who signal local need, which is why it is easily carried out by large monopolistic companies (Galiani 1770a: 172–177). Moreover, if free trade is allowed, powerful companies cannot be prevented from hoarding it on the market, arousing the opposition of the population, even in times of plenty (Galiani 1770a: 179–181). On the other hand, the very location of the most fertile provinces in relation to national borders

least disinterested. To the physiocrats, who advocated the *bon prix* of grains, and who had identified the exchange between the sterile class and the productive class as one of the essential moments in the entire process of the economy, he countered the traditional concern for the cheap supply of cities, inherited from the practice of government traditionally followed by the various Italian states, and which had found, for example in Muratori, a spokesman who had justified and defended that practice" (Minerbi 1973: 160).

can have different effects: if the fertile provinces are close to the national borders, free trade will cause most of the grain to be exported abroad (this is the case in France), starving the internal provinces; if, on the other hand, the most fertile provinces are located in the centre of the country, free trade measures will facilitate internal trade (the case of Castile) (Galiani 1770a: 15–16).[186] Finally, internal trade is difficult, having to go through many intermediaries and the fact that the final product, bread, passes through too many hands increases its price without giving any advantage to the producers (Galiani 1770a: 197).

The only advantage of the grain trade is the impulse it can give to the development of the national navy, if navigation acts are imposed, as the case of England shows: "[it is] the only country which, up to the time of the Edict of 1764, allowed the wheat trade, with the restriction that only national ships were allowed, for I regard it as a restriction that the benefit was granted only to English ships. The effect was not the direct and immediate encouragement of cultivation, as the ignorant believe, but the encouragement of the navy. This flourishing navy gave impetus and movement to everything. Manufactures prospered, from which agriculture spread and improved" (Galiani 1770a: 217–218).[187]

Fertile countries of medium and large size, such as Turkey, Poland, and Sicily, although they had an active grain trade, they allowed foreigners to exercise it, and because of this they became impoverished, even discouraging agriculture itself, which had become unprofitable (Galiani 1770a: 217). All countries whose economy is mainly based on agriculture behave like gamblers. They gain riches at the beginning as easily as a gambler gains at the beginning of winning rounds. Prosperity leads to population growth and the need to defend themselves against other peoples, stimulating the warrior spirit. Soon, war becomes habitual both to the outside world and as a solution to internal struggles. Domestic wealth is thus reduced or destroyed and it will be necessary to trade with neighbours to obtain necessities. Trade is done in debt, since there is no manufacturing in the country, and this puts it at the mercy of foreign merchants. Soon the

[186] However, Galiani notes in the eighth and final dialogue, foreign trade always has several advantages over domestic trade (Galiani 1770a: 262–263).

[187] "To transport fifteen hundred thousand francs in gems, textiles, and Indian porcelain, one ship is enough; but to transport the same value in grain, forty good ships are not enough. Therefore, if you want to have a good navy, numerous and flourishing, that will go a long way, earn money and keep busy, wheat is infinitely better than any other commodity" (Galiani 1770a: 214–215).

money will disappear entirely for the benefit of foreigners and what remains will be concentrated in the hands of a few. Interest on money will be very high and it will be difficult without capital to improve productive activity. The concentration of wealth will favour luxury consumption at the expense of useful and essential consumption: "This is the origin of fiefs, domanial rights, ecclesiastical and seigneurial tithes; this is the birth either of anarchy, which you might otherwise call feudal government, or despotism. The latter can only accommodate the farmer, for the farmer is stuck to his land, he cannot take it with him, and if he leaves, having no knowledge of any trade, he has no means left to live, so he must stay and suffer" (Galiani 1770a: 114). This is the destiny of decadence of an agricultural people, which will be reflected in its institutional and social structures (Galiani 1770a: 74). The production and trade of manufactured goods provide advantages that agricultural activity cannot.[188] First of all, manufacturing production grows by the number of hands (Galiani 1770a: 150), while that of agricultural commodities, as mentioned above, is limited by the available land.[189] Industry therefore has increasing returns to scale and agriculture is dominated by decreasing returns to scale, the opposite of what the *conomistes* claimed (Galiani 1770a: 150–151).

The order of priorities identified by the physiocratic school must therefore be reversed: it is manufacturing that provides wealth while agriculture can provide subsistence. Trade in grain and other agricultural commodities may even cease altogether in a manufacturing country that has achieved food subsistence. And it can even go beyond this limit, since the wealth created by manufacturing can ensure the acquisition of commodities to make up the domestic deficit and support the surplus population (Galiani 1770a: 150–151). At this point, Galiani observes: "the art of government will have accomplished its masterpiece", forcing nature to perform "a miracle such as having more men on limited land than its forces and means can sustain" (Galiani 1770a: 151).

[188] "Any production, whether of land or art, which by its nature or by law must pass through several hands before reaching the consumer, must leave the first producer destitute [...]. Find a way for the same farmer to become a miller and a baker and sell bread at his barn door instead of grain, and you will see him get rich. This is so true that people, great calculators by instinct, try as much as possible to avoid some of the hands in between" (Galiani 1770a: 198–199).

[189] "The product of manufactures is unlimited, since it increases in proportion to the number of men. The product of commodities is limited and circumscribed by the extent of the soil" (Galiani 1770a: 153).

To ensure an increase in wealth, it is therefore the agricultural sector that must be placed in support of the manufacturing sector and economic policy must be in line with this. Measures in favour of grain exports can harm the population and thus the development of manufacturing, just as the high price of foodstuffs everywhere produces emigration and a reduction in industrial activities (Galiani 1770a: 153).[190]

The development of agriculture is always a consequence of the growth of manufacturing and trade: "Agriculture, being the basis of everything, receives all the stimulus, so there is no need to worry about it. Increase, enrich, make all other things prosper, and rest assured. When the farmer finds many consumers and rich consumers, it is impossible for him not to sell his produce well. If you want to see the truth of this even more clearly, look at Holland, the Republic of Genoa and other trading cities; they have no grain of their own production, but because they transport it from one nation to another, they have a beautiful navy, a happy and wealthy people, and also all the crops of which their soil is capable, pushed to the limits of art and industry. It is true that the Morean or Sicilian wheat trade allows olive, orange and cherry trees to bloom in the mountains around the Genoa coast. The Polish wheat trade makes tulips bloom in Holland, while the same wheat makes nothing bloom either on the banks of the Vistula or on the plains of Sparta and Agrigento" (Galiani 1770a: 217–218).

Galiani proposes a *possibilist approach* to economic geography in which production choices are not rigidly subordinated to the constraints of physical geography, but become active elements in the transformation of the territory.[191] It is enough to see the squalor of the countryside surrounding cities such as Rome and Madrid to demonstrate that without manufacturing there is no development of agriculture: "The same hand governs Rome and Bologna. The court never resides in Bologna [...]; but in compensation there are many factories in the city, and its territory is the best

[190] "Those who believed that the increase in the price of bread should be cheerfully supported with a view to the progress of agriculture were quite mistaken, and that to encourage cultivation, it is necessary to go about it in a completely different way and take a very different path from the one they have taken. With their expensive bread, they will starve the people, harm factories and make non-producing classes of men rich, and the price of wheat will remain almost at its former level and the farmer in his former poverty" (Galiani 1770a: 200). The concept of the bon prix is according to Galiani false and harmful (Galiani 1770a: 27–29).

[191] An approach that Galiani's analysis anticipates and that would be fully developed in the late nineteenth century by geographer Paul Vidal de la Blache.

cultivated in Italy. In Valencia and Catalonia, for some years now, factories and plants have sprung up, and these two provinces already have surprising cultivation. Walking through them, one would think one was in front of the gardens of Armide" (Galiani 1770a: 217–218).

On this point, Galiani follows Vico's view that the only determining factor is the historical and not the natural element. The thesis that industry is free from natural constraints is, however, taken from Antonio Serra's reading (Serra 1613).[192]

The virtuous circuit of wealth, as the story of the small and wealthy merchant republics also demonstrates, proceeds from industry to agriculture and not *vice versa*, as the physiocratic school states. It is the increase in manufacturing incomes that stimulates the demand for agricultural products and encourages their production and sale. If, on the other hand, agricultural incomes are increased, the result is not the same, as the life of the peasants is frugal and that of the nobles directed towards luxury consumption, which enriches foreign merchants. That is why around the great capitals of fertile countries one finds - Galiani observes - only squalor and misery generated by the spending on rents.[193]

Industry not only provides demand to the agricultural sector, but is also able to provide the necessary means to increase agricultural production, as

[192] In the second edition of *Della Moneta* Galiani gave an extremely positive assessment of Serra's work: "Anyone reading this treatise will surely be surprised and full of admiration to see how, in a century of total ignorance of economic science, its author had clear and correct ideas of the subject he wrote about and how soundly he judged the causes of our troubles and the only effective remedies [...]. I do not doubt to place him in the rank of the first and oldest writer of political and economic science and to grant Calabria also this hitherto unknown vaunt of having produced him [...]. This man, whom I dare to compare to Melon of the French and, in this part, to Locke of the English, but who surpasses them both for having lived so long before and in a century of darkness and error in economic science" (Galiani 1780: Note XXIX, 410–411). See Stapelbroek (2016)

[193] "If money is only in the hands of a rich consumer, it is still too far away from the peasant who cannot borrow it or circulate it in any way. What does it matter to rich lords where they get the luxuries of life, as long as they enjoy them? What does it matter to a cardinal or a Great of Spain where he gets the good fruit with which he wants to fill his table? One will get it from Tuscany, Malta or Naples; the other from Valencia. Greater or lesser expenditure will not stop them. So the money that runs out and falls out of the hands of the consumer takes a leap and goes to encourage a farmer, but God knows where. Thus you can have great consumer lords, very rich in the midst of a poor people and an uncultivated country; and if these examples do not convince you, here are others closer by, Compiègne and Fontainebleau. Every year the court has ten million spent there by the richest consumers in Europe" (Galiani 1770a: 119–120).

well as supplementary income necessary to limit fluctuations due to the ups and downs of the agricultural cycle (Galiani 1770a: 124–125).[194]

Policy proposals are consistent with this analysis: grain should be considered a raw material and its export discouraged (Galiani 1770a: 292–293). The edict of 1764 does the opposite, incentivising foreign trade to the detriment of domestic trade, for a number of reasons both economic (cheapness of transport costs by river; low storage costs on ships; cheapness of export trade as wholesale trade as opposed to domestic trade which is retail trade; profits caused by exchange rate fluctuations; international sales are made in gold money and not as in domestic retail trade with bad silver money; finally, trade over long distances takes place without any interference from the authorities) (Galiani 1770a: 262–264), and geographical (the proximity to the borders of the most fertile provinces) (Galiani 1770a: 264–265), thus condemning France to famine.

If, therefore, there is a centrifugal force that takes the grain out of the country, exposing it dangerously to famine, then internal trade must be encouraged and external trade discouraged. This can be achieved by using the tax system, which will operate like the sluices that direct the flow of water to the desired point, keeping it inside the country and not dispersing it outside. It will first be necessary to abolish the last legal restrictions on free internal trade, then to develop the roads and canals, infrastructures needed to facilitate trade between the provinces, forcing the nature of the physical spaces, and finally to impose customs barriers to increase the price of grain for export, which will be set in relation to the average term of the difference between export and internal circulation (Galiani 1770a: 273, 274–275, 278–279). The revenue from this tax should then be invested in infrastructure for domestic trade (Galiani 1770a: 311). A customs barrier should also be imposed on imports to defend domestic production in case of abundance when prices fall (Galiani 1770a: 308). In the event of famine, the opening of borders is useless as surplus countries not yet open to liberalisation such as France would close their borders or speculate on the price for political and enrichment purposes.

Criticising physiocratic theory, Galiani proposed an alternative methodological approach for the emerging economic science. First of all, Galiani

[194] "A manufacture can be run by a farmer's wife, daughters, brothers or cousins; in this way the money it brings in stays in the family and supports the cultivation of the land; it is used to make advances, to avoid hasty sales at a loss; without borrowing the farmer gets by" (Galiani 1770a: 119).

reaffirms the probabilistic model of science, adapted to social and economic analysis:[195] most economic actions, both by individual agents and governments, take place in a situation of uncertainty, and in this perspective the analysis of circumstances becomes the basic element of decision-making: "reason must be deduced from the intrinsic investigation of the nature of things and never use any other way" (Galiani 1770a: 166). And "this science of administration, this science called *économie politique*, by combining two words which in their natural meaning and according to Aristotle's definitions are contrary; this science [...] is much more complicated and much more difficult than we think. More difficult than one might think" (Galiani 1770a: 228).

According to this complex methodology, the indicators of a suitable policy are not those deduced from abstract axioms but those that are more useful and coherent to the prudence and wisdom of a particular society. Therefore, economic policy is reduced to being part of political science, as the art of government, in which the focus is not individual interest but the more complex context of *Raison d'État*. This view of economic policy as art is confirmed by Galiani through the analogy with the art of navigation (Galiani 1770a: 233–234). The general principle that must regulate the art of government is expressed in the Latin motto *"Nil repente!"* (*nothing suddenly*) (Galiani 1770a: 257).[196] Economic problems, Galiani argues, are complex because "when in a problem there are a lot of variables, the equation becomes indeterminate, or it belongs to the class of problems we call *maximis et minimis*, and such are in fact all political problems. It is a matter of obtaining the most possible good with the least possible evil. It is an approximation. Nothing in politics can be pushed to extreme limits. There is a point up to which the good is greater than the bad; if you overstep it, the bad prevails over the good" (Galiani 1770a: 229; see also Faccarello 1998: 128).[197] And "only the wise man can calculate it. The

[195] According to Giocoli, in the *Dialogues* Galiani abandons his youthful faith in probability calculus, expressed in *Della Moneta*, for a more complex concept of uncertainty (Giocoli 2001: 14, footnote).

[196] "Politics is nothing more than the science of preventing or stopping instantaneous movements that occur due to extraordinary causes and goes no further, since great revolutions are entirely the work of nature, man's strength can do nothing, and he, rather than being the author of them, is their main instrument and utensil" (Galiani 1770a: 237).

[197] "Virtue, the desire to do good, is a passion in us like all the others. It is rare to encounter; but when it does, it is too violent. It is even more violent than any other; for while the spur of goodness animates us, no bridle of remorse stops us. This violence and ardour gener-

people feel it by instinct. The ruling man realises it by time. The modern economist never suspects it" (Galiani 1770a: 230).

Galiani's *Dialogues* offers one of the first applications of calculus (or differential calculus) to economic problems in defining a situation of social equilibrium. The notion of *maximis et minimis*, referring to Gottfried Wilhelm Leibniz's *Nova Methodus pro Maximis et Minimis* (Leibniz 1684), can be applied to every political and economic problem in terms of *maximization/minimization* under constraints. However, mathematical formalization of economic and political problems, even though useful, has a limited domain of application and produces partial results, in the end leaving a degree of indeterminateness. This is a general principle that would be better defined later, in the writings of Galiani's maturity.

7.4.1 Appendix

The economic policy proposal of the Physiocratic school can be summarised using the *Heckscher-Ohlin model* (Heckscher 1919 [1950], Ohlin 1933) with two production factors land (T) and capital (C) and two products Wheat (g) and Cloth (m). Wheat is land-intensive, cloth is capital-intensive. Given the assumption of the exclusive productivity of the agricultural sector, the transformation curve assumes a concave upward trend. In this case, the returns of grain production (g) are increasing (the sector has a higher land factor intensity than manufacturing) and those of the manufacturing sector (m) are constant (AF curve in Fig. 7.1),[198] growing returns that are maximised with the spread of large-scale cultivation.

Point C corresponds to a situation of *Colbertian policy* in which resources are used for manufacturing production (m), sacrificing the agricultural sector. The spread of large-scale cultivation and the liberalisation of internal trade shift production from C to F at the point of physiocratic

ate enthusiasm. We convince ourselves what we wish without arguing and persuade others with the eagerness of argument, because we are virtuous. You do not give good reasons, but you have the frankness of truth, the courage of virtue, the fire of your own persuasion, and you lead others astray who see no reason to distrust you. Believe me: do not be afraid of rogues or villains, sooner or later they unmask themselves. Fear the honest man in error; he is in good faith with himself, he wants good and everyone trusts him; but unfortunately he is mistaken about the means of procuring it for men" (Galiani 1770a: 230–231).

[198] The two factors used are labour and capital. Large-scale culture is able to use large shares of capital, while manufacturing labour uses, in the physiocratic view, a larger share of labour.

autarky. The country thus specialises in grain production. External trade liberalisation makes it possible to exchange grain with manufactured goods on the foreign market, according to the prevailing international term of trade (straight line *tt'*), reaching the *S* point that ensures gains from trade. In this particular situation, the benefits of international trade are assured even if the international term of trade (*tt'*) coincides with the domestic reason for trade and could even worsen, within certain limits, without reducing the advantage assured to the country by international trade. The Physiocratic hypothesis predicts that the terms of trade are advantageous for grains on the international market with respect to the domestic terms of trade, so as to ensure the formation of a *bon prix*, as constant as possible, necessary to stimulate domestic production and to guarantee the formation of the rent.

The *Physiocratic policy* proposal thus aims at full specialisation consistent with the assumption that attributes increasing returns to scale to the grain sector. However, full specialisation becomes dangerous in the event of famine (this would correspond to an inward shift of the transformation

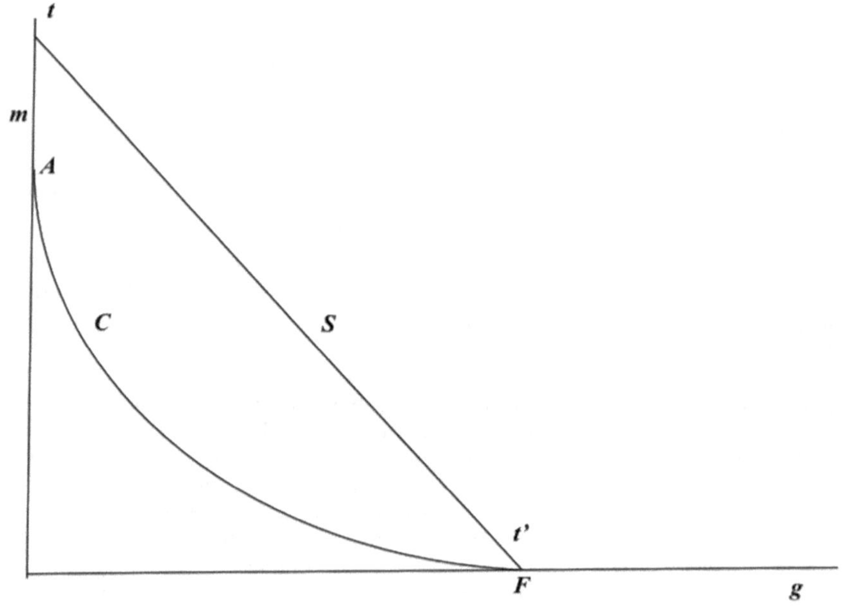

Fig. 7.1 Production possibilities frontier according to Physiocratic hypothesis

curve with a change in the internal terms of trade and lower total output). Vulnerability can only be tempered if the country has not become fully specialised, which goes against the basic assumptions on the exclusive productivity of the agricultural sector.

The contradictory elements in Physiocratic theory and policy proposals were the focus of Galiani's severe criticism. For the Neapolitan abbot, it is the manufacturing sector that has increasing returns to scale, while the agricultural sector is characterised by decreasing returns to scale. The two factors used in the production process are labour and land. In contrast to the Physiocratic hypothesis, Galiani considers manufacturing production to be characterised by increasing returns to scale, since it grows by reason of unlimited labour, while agricultural production is subject to decreasing returns to scale since it is limited by the exploitable land and is subject to the uncertainty of the final productive outcome. It should be noted that an explicit reference to the concept of capital as one of the determinants of production is absent in Galiani, whereas in Physiocracy it appears explicitly defined as an indispensable factor of agricultural production and implicitly of manufacturing production.

Galiani still describes a pre-capitalist society in which what prevails in craft production is essentially the quantity and quality of labour applied. Given the underlying assumptions, the production possibilities frontier (see Fig. 7.2, curve *AF*) will have to describe a product obtained at increasing returns, cloth (*m*), and a product obtained at decreasing returns, wheat (*g*), assuming a particular inverted *S-shape*, with an inflection point (*h*).[199] In this case, it will be convenient to specialise in the production of cloth (*m*) (point *F*) and to exchange on the market for wheat (*g*) (point *S*), according to the reason for exchange *tt'*.

As contemporary economic theory shows, in the case of variable returns to scale between two production sectors in the same country, specialisation and the relative gains from trade depend on the size of the country and the intensity with which returns to scale increase or decrease as production increases (Melvin 1969; Helpman 1981; Panagariya 1981; Das Satya 1982; Lawrence and Spiller 1983). Under these conditions, the pattern of trade cannot be unambiguously determined. Another element that complicates the analysis is the presence of transport costs, which are explicitly considered by Galiani and completely ignored in the physiocratic

[199] "The transformation curve has at least one point of inflection if there are increasing returns in one sector and decreasing returns in the other." (Gandolfo 2014: 54).

approach. Finally, Galiani also attributes to the manufacturing sector, thanks to the technical progress and income generated, a driving function in relation to the agricultural sector. In analytical terms, the progress of the manufacturing sector determines the forward shift of the production possibilities frontier.

Historical experience has shown that the application of free trade to the agricultural sector has not produced the results in terms of benefits predicted by theory (Boussard et al. 1995: 27). These effects are due to the particular characteristics of supply and demand for agricultural products, and for grain in particular. A policy of complete liberalisation leads to instability, because demand is inelastic and supply is subject to the vagaries of nature. Instability leads to uncertainty, determines price volatility, affecting them as market signals (Boussard et al. 1995: 49) and prevents the formation of efficient results, making decision-making by producers and consumers difficult. Further political assessments make total deregulation of the agricultural sector inadvisable, firstly because of the importance of food supplies (a problem known since antiquity) and because of the lobbying power wielded by producers, the basis of protectionist laws (such as the British *Corn Laws*) and the policy of subsidies (Atkin 1995: 46).

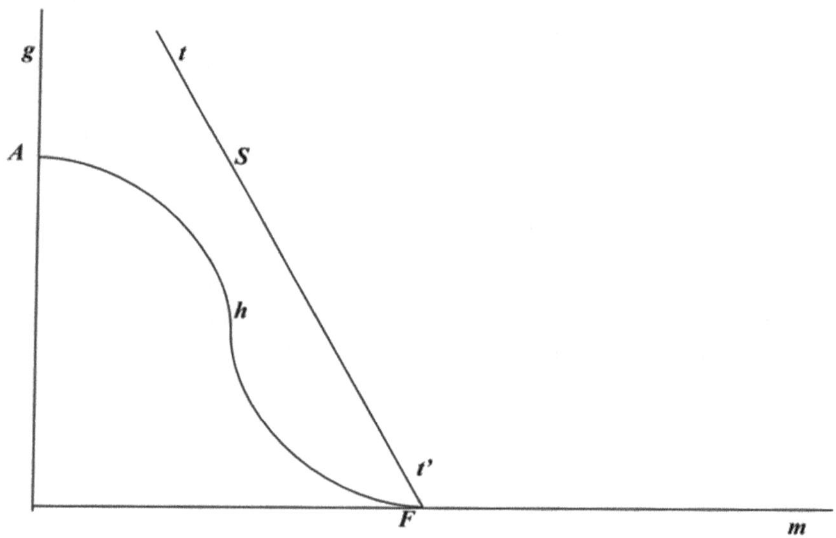

Fig. 7.2 Production possibilities frontier according to Galiani's hypothesis

Grain, as Galiani guessed, remains a political affair even today (Atkin 1995: 4) and only a very limited portion of production passes through world trade (Atkin 1995: 69) still using, as in the eighteenth century, a complicated marketing and intermediation structure (Atkin 1995: 101). Moreover, the tendency for agricultural prices to continually fall relative to industrial prices (known as the *Prebisch-Singer Hypothesis*) shows that Galiani's concerns about development possibilities based on agricultural specialisation were well-founded (Atkin 1995: 86).

References[200]

Manuscript Sources

De Gournay, J. MS. *Mémoire (sans titre).* Manuscript kept in the Archives Municipales de Saint-Brieuc, Fonds Gournay, Ms. 82.

Galiani, F. MS-18. *Notes au Pacte de Famille.* Manuscript kept in the Biblioteca Società Napoletana di Storia Patria, XXX. A. 10, folios 252r–261v. Folios 252r–257r, published in Galiani, 1975d, pp. 704–709.

Galiani, F. MS-19. *Breve racconto di quel che è a mia notizia rispetto al Trattato di navigazione e commercio colla Francia* (1784a). Manuscript kept in the Biblioteca Società Napoletana di Storia Patria, XXX. D. 3, folios 74r–81v, published in Diaz, 1973, pp. 354–364 and in Galiani, 1999a, pp. 125–131.

Galiani, F. MS-20. *Istoria vera della controversia de'grani di Marsiglia scritta da persona ben informata, col parere sulla giustizia delle pretensioni delle parti litiganti. Amsterdam 1772.* Manuscript kept in the Biblioteca Società Napoletana di Storia Patria, XXIX. C. 6, folios 1–111, partially published in Galiani, 1959a, pp. 307–313.

Galiani, F. MS-21. *Storia dell'avvenuto sugli editti del libero commercio de'grani in Francia promulgati nel 1763 e 1764.* Manuscript kept in the Biblioteca Società Napoletana di Storia Patria, XXX. C. 12, folios 23–39, published in Galiani, 1959b, pp. 315–322.

Galiani, F. MS-22. *De l'opinion*, Manuscript kept in the Turin State Archives, published in Nicolini, 1959b, pp. 139–156 ("the indication of the place where the fragment De l'opinion is kept is wrong, as Venturi pointed out: it is the Turin State Archives and not the British Museum", see Galiani, 1975e: Guerci's note: cxvii).

Galiani, F. MS-24. *Considerazioni sul Trattato di Commercio tra il Re e il Re Cristianissimo*, Manuscript kept in the Biblioteca Società Napoletana di Storia Patria, XXX.-A. 10, folios 183r–251v, partially published in Galiani, 1975f, pp. 717–734.

[200] The abbreviations "s.l." and "s.n." stand for the Latin terms *sine loco* (without place of publication) and *sine nomine* (without name of publisher).

Primary Sources

Abeille, L.-P. (1760). *Corps d'observations de la societe d'agriculture, de commerce et des arts établie par les États de Bretagne*, Rennes: Jacques Vatar.

Abeille, L.-P. (1763). *Lettre d'un négociant sur la nature du commerce des grains*, s.l: sn.

Abeille, L.-P. (1764). *Réflexions sur la police des grains en France et en Angleterre*, s.l: sn.

Abeille, L.-P. (1768). *Principes sur la liberté du commerce des grains*. Amsterdam [but Paris]: Desaint.

Baudeau, N. (1768). *Avis au peuple sur son premier besoin, ou Petits traités économiques*. Amsterdam: Hochereau.

Boccaccio, G. [2003]. *The Decameron*, Translated with an Introduction and Notes by G. H. McWilliam. New York: Penguin.

Boisguilbert, P. Le Pesant De. (1696) [1843]. *Le Détail de la France, la cause de la diminution de ses biens et la facilité du remède en fournissant en un mois tout l'argent dont le Roi a besoin et enrichissant tout le monde*, in E. Daire (ed.). *Économistes financiers du XVIII siècle*, tome I. Paris: Guillamine, 1843, pp. 171–266.

Boisguilbert, P. Le Pesant De. (1705) [1843]. *Le Factum de la France ou moyen très facile de faire recevoir au roi quatre-vingt millions par-dessus la capitation, praticables par deux heures de travail de Messieurs les Ministres et un mois d'exécution de la part des peoples*. In E. Daire (ed.). *Économistes financiers du XVIII siècle*, tome I, Paris: Guillamine, 1843, pp. 260–351.

Boisguilbert, P. Le Pesant De. (1707a) [1843]. *Dissertation sur la nature des richesses, de l'argent et des tributs: ou l'on decouvre la fausse idée qui règne dans le monde à l'égard de ces trois articles*, [S.l.]. In E. Daire (ed,) *Économistes financiers du XVIII siècle*, tome I, Paris: Guillamine, 1843, pp. 394–424.

Boisguilbert, P. Le Pesant De. (1707b) [1843]. *Traité de la nature, culture, commerce et intérêt des grains: tant par rapport au public, qu'a toutes les conditions d'un état*, [S.l.]. In E. Daire, (ed,) *Économistes financiers du XVIII siècle*, tome I, Paris, Guillamine, 1843, pp. 359–389.

Cantillon, R. (1755) [2010]. *Essai sur la nature du commerce en général. Traduit de l'anglois*, London: Fletcher Gyles. English Translation: *An Essay on Economic Theory*, Translated by C. Saucier, edited by M. Thornton. Auburn: Ludwig von Mises Institute.

Cary, J. (1755). *Essai sur l'état du commerce d'Angleterre, tomes 2*, Londres-Paris. Nyon-Vailant.

Casanova, G. (2006). *History of My Life*, first translated into english in accordance with the original french manuscript by W. R. Trask. New York: Everyman's Library.

Castiglione, B. (1528). *Il libro del Cortegiano*. Venice: Aldo Romano & d'Andrea d'Asola

Child, J. (1754). *Traités sur le commerce et les avantages qui résultent de l'intérêt de l'argent. Avec un petit Traité contre l'usure par Thomas Culpeper*. Amsterdam-Berlin: Jean Neaulme.

Della Casa, G. (1558). *Il Galateo overo de' costumi. Trattato di messer Giovanni della Casa, nel quale sotto la persona d'un vecchio idiota ammaestrante un suo giovanetto, si ragiona de modi, che si debbono o tenere, o schifare nella comune conversatione, cognominato Galatheo overo de costumi*. Venice: Bevilacqua.

D'Epinay, L., Galiani, F. (1996). *Epistolario 1769–1782*, edited by S.Rapisarda. Palermo: Sellerio.

Diderot, D. (1875a). Lettre à M. l'abbé Galiani sur le sixième ode du troisième livre d'Horace. In J. Assézat (ed.), *Œuvres Complètes de Diderot revues sur les éditions originals comprenant ce qui a été publié a diverses époques et les manuscrits inédits conserves à la bibliothèque de l'ermitage. notices, notes., table analytique étude sur Diderot et le mouvement philosophique au XVIII siècle*, Tome VI. Paris: Garnier, pp. 289–302.

Diderot, D. (1950). *Lettres à Sophie Volland*, edited by A. Babelon, 14th édition, 2 vols. Paris: Gallimard.

Diderot, D. (1955). *Correspondence*, edited by G. Roth, 13 vols. Paris: Editions de minuit.

Diodati, L. (1788). *Vita dell'abate Ferdinando Galiani*. Naples: Orsino.

Doria, P. M. (1710a). *La vita civile di P. M. Doria, distinta in tre parti, aggiuntovi un trattato della educazione del principe. Seconda edizione dall'Autore ricorretta, ed accresciuta*. Augusta: Höpper.

Dupin, C. (1748). *Mémoire sur les blés, avec un projet d'édit pour maintenir en tout temps la valeur des grains à un prix convenable au vendeur et à l'acheteur*. Paris: s.n.

Éphémérides. (1769a). Discussions qui surviennent et qui assurent les succèss de la verité. *Éphémérides du citoyen ou Bibliothèque raisonnée des sciences morales et politiques*, Tome V. Paris: Lacombre, pp. 132–133.

Fasano, T. (1765). *Della febbre epidemica sofferta in Napoli l'anno 1764. Libri 3*. Naples: Raimondi.

Forbonnais, Véron de F. L. (1754). *Eléments du commerce*, Leyde [but Paris]: Briasson-David l'aîné-Le Breton-Durand.

Forbonnais, Véron de F. L. (1758). *Recherches et considerations sur les finances de France*. Basel: s.n.

Forbonnais, Véron de, F. L. (1767). *Principes et observations oeconomiques*. Amsterdam: Rey.

Galiani, F. (1770a). *Dialogues sur le commerce des bleds*. London [but Paris]: Merlin.

Galiani, F. (1780). *Della moneta. Libri cinque. Edizione seconda*. Naples: Stamperia Simoniana.

Galiani, F. (1782). *De' doveri de' principi neutrali verso i principi guerreggianti: e di questi verso i neutrali. Libre due*. Naples: s.n.

Galiani, F. (1881a). *Écrivains du XVIII siècle – Correspondance avec Madame d'Épinay, Madame Necker, Madame Geoffrin etc., Diderot, Grimm, d'Alembert, de Sartine, d'Holbach, etc. Nouvelle édition, entièrement rétablie d'après les textes originaux, augmentée de tous les passages supprimés et d'un grand nombre de lettres inédites, avec une étude sur sa vie et les oeuvres de Galiani*, edited by L. Perey, G. Maugras, 2 voll. Paris: Calmann Levy.

Galiani, F. (1881b). *Lettres du XVII et XVIII siècle – Lettres de l'Abbé Galiani à Madame d'Épinay, Voltaire, Diderot, Grimm, le Baron d'Holbach, Morellet, Suart (sic), d'Alembert, Marmontel, la Vicomtesse de Belsunce, etc. Publiées d'après les éditions originales augmentées des variantes, de nombreuses notes et d'un Index avec notice biographique*, edited by E. Asse, 2 voll., Paris, G. Charpentier.

Galiani, F. (1959). *Dialogues sur le commerce des bleds. Giusta l'editio princeps del 1770 con appendici illustrative*, edited by F. Nicolini, Naples: Ricciardi

Galiani, F. (1975). *Opere di Ferdinando Galiani*, edited by F. Diaz e L. Guerci, in *Letteratura italiana. Storia e testi. Illuministi italiani*, tomo VI. Milan-Naples: Ricciardi.

Galiani, F., d'Épinay, L. (1992). *Correspondance. Vol. I (1769–1770)*, présentation de G. Dulac, texte établi et annoté par D. Maggetti, en collaboration avec G. Dulac. Paris: Les Editions Desjonquères.

Galiani, F., d'Épinay, L. (1997). *Correspondance. Vol. V (June 1775–Juillet 1782)*, présentation de G. Dulac, texte établi et annoté par D. Maggetti, en collaboration avec G. Dulac. Paris: Les Editions Desjonquères.

Galilei, G. (1632). *Dialogo di Galileo Galilei Linceo Matematico Sopraordinario dello Studio di Pisa e Filosofo e Matematico Primario del Serenissimo Gr. Duca di Toscana, dove nei congressi di quattro giornate si discorre sopra i due Massimi Sistemi del Mondo, Tolemaico e Copernicano, proponendo indeterminatamente le ragioni filosofiche e naturali tanto per l'una, quanto per l'altra parte.* Florence: Landini.

Gee, J. (1749). *Considérations sur le commerce et la navigation de la Grande-Bretagne. Ouvrage traduit de l Anglais, sur la quatrième edition.* London: Bettesworth & C.

Genovesi, A. (1774). *Lettere familiari dell'abate Antonio Genovesi, pubblicate da Domenico Forges Davanzati*, 2 voll. Naples: Stamperia Raimondiana.

Gibbon, E. (1788). *The History of the Decline and Fall of the Roman Empire*, Volume The Tenth. Dublin: Luke White.

Goudar, A. (1769). *Naples. Ce qu'il faut faire pour rendre ce Royaume florissant, où l'on traite des avantages que le gouvernement peut retenir de la fertilité et de l'abondance de ses denrées, des facilités pour perfectionner les arts, de sa position favorable pour s'emparer des premières branches du commerce étranger.* Amsterdam: s.n.

Graslin, J.J.L. (1767). *Essai analytique sur la richesse et sur l'impôt: où l'on réfute la nouvelle doctrine économique*, London: s.n.

Grimm, F. M. F. von. (1878). *Correspondance litteraire, philosophique et critique par Grimm*, vol. VI. Paris: Garnier.

Grimm, F. M. F. von. (1879). *Correspondance litteraire, philosophique et critique par Grimm*, vol. IX. Paris: Garnier.

Herbert, C. J. (1753). *Essai sur la police générale des grains.* London: s.n.

Herbert, C. J. (1765). *Riflessioni sull'economia generale de' grani tradotte dal francese, con un discorso preliminare del Signor Abbate Genovesi catedratico di commercio.* Naples: Gravier.

Hume, D. (2011). *The Letters of David Hume*, edited by J.Y.T. Greig. Oxford: Clarendon Press.

King, C. (1753). *Le négociants anglois ou traduction libre du livre intitulé The British merchant contenant diverses mémoires sur le commerce de l'Angleterre avec la France, le Portugal, l'Espagne, publié pour la première fois en 1713.* Dresde [but Paris]: Frères Estienne.

Leibniz, G. W. (1684). Nova Methodus pro Maximis et Minimis. *Acta Eruditorum*, 3, pp. 467–473.

Lesage, A.-R. (1707). *Le Diable boiteux.* Paris: Veuve Barbin.

Mably, Bonnot de G. (1768). *Doutes proposées aux Philosophes Économistes sur l'Ordre naturel et essentiel des sociétés politiques.* La Haye: Nyon.

Machault d'Arnouville, J-B. (1749). Mémoire sur le commerce des grains, partially published in ripubblicate in Dupont De Nemours, P.-S. 1789. *Analyse historique de la législation des grainsdepuis 1692, à laquelle on a donné la forme d'un rapport à l'Assemblée nationale.* Paris, chez Petit, pp. 13–44.

Machiavelli, N. (1531) [1883]. *Discorsi sopra la prima Deca di Tito Livio.* Florence: Bernardo Giunti. English translation by N H. Thomson, *Discourses on the First Decade of Titus Livius.* London: Kegan.

Marmontel, J.F. (1804). *Mémoires d'un père pour servir à l'instruction de ses enfants.* Paris: Xhrouet.

Melon, J-F. (1736). *Essai politique sur le commerce. Nouvelle édition. Cette édition est augmentée de sept chapitres et les lacunes des éditions précédentes y sont remplies*, s.l. s.n.

Mirabeu, V. Riqueti de. (1756). *L'ami des hommes ou Traité de la population*, Avignon: s.n.

Morellet, A. (1764). *Fragment d'une lettre sur le commerce des grains.* Paris: s. n.

Nickolls, J. [Plumard de Dangeul L.-J.]. (1754). *Rémarques sur les avantages et les désavantages de la France et de la Grande-Bretagne par rapport au commerce et aux autre sources de la puissance des états. Traduction de l'anglois du chevalire John Nickolls, troisième édition, augmentée d'un Essai sur la police et le commerce des grains.* Leyde [but Paris]: Estienne.

Pattullo, H. (1758). *Essai sur l'amélioration des terres.* Paris: Durand.

Quesnay, F. (1756a). Fermier. In D. Diderot, J. D'Alembert Le Ronde (eds.), *Encyclopédie, ou, Dictionnaire raisonné des sciences, des arts et des métiers*, tome VI. Paris: Briasson-David-Le Breton-Durand, pp. 528–540.

Quesnay, F. (1757). Grain. In D. Diderot, J. D'Alembert Le Ronde (eds.), *Encyclopédie, ou, Dictionnaire raisonné des sciences, des arts et des métiers*, tome VII, Paris: Briasson-David-Le Breton-Durand, pp. 812–833.

Quesnay, F. (1757–1758) [2005]. Homme. In C.Théré, L.Charles, J.-C. Perrot, (eds.) *Oeuvres économiques complètes et autres textes: Textes polémiques, Documents associés,* Tome Prémier. Paris: Institut national d'études démographiques, pp. 257–324.

Quesnay, F., Du Pont de Nemours, P. S. (1768). *Physiocratie, ou Constitution naturelle du gouvernement le plus avantageux au genre humain.* Leyde [but Paris]: Merlin.

Rousseau, J. J. (1767) = [1997]. Letter to Mirabeau. In *The social contract and other later political writings*, Cambridge: Cambridge University Press, pp. 268–271.

Sarcone, M. (1765). *Istoria ragionata de' mali osservati in Napoli nell'intero corso dell'anno 1764.* Naples: Stamperia Simoniana,

Serra, Antonio. (1613) [2011]. *Breve trattato delle cause che possono far abbondare li regni d'oro e d'argento dove non sono miniere, con applicazione al regno di Napoli diviso in tre parti.* Napoli: Lazzaro Scorriggio. English Translation: *A "Short Treatise" on the Wealth and Poverty of Nations*, Edited and with an Introduction by Sophus A. Reinert. Translated by Jonathan Hunt London – New York, Anthem Press, 2011.

Tanucci, B. (1914). *Lettere a Ferdinando Galiani*, edited by F. Nicolini, Bari: Laterza.

Tanucci, B. (1969). *Lettere di Bernardo Tanucci a Carlo III di Borbone (1759–1776)*, edited by R. Mincuzzi. Rome: Istituto per la Storia del Risorgimento Italiano.

Tanucci, B. (1980b). *Epistolario*, vol. II (1746–1752), R.P. Coppini, Nieri, R. (eds.), Rome: Edizioni Storia e Letteratura.

Tanucci, B. (1985). *Epistolario*, vol. V (1757–1758), G. de Lucia (ed.), Rome: Edizioni Storia e Letteratura.

Tanucci, B. (1997). *Epistolario*, vol. XII (1763–1764), M. C. Ferrari, (ed.), Naples: Società Napoletana di Storia Patria.

Turgot, A.R.M. (1768). *Lettres sur les émeutes populaires que cause la cherté des bleds et sur les précautions du moment.* s.l: s.n.

Ulloa, B. de. (1753). *Rétlabissement des manufactures et du commerce d'Espagne.* Paris: Frères Estienne.

Uztàriz, G. de. (1753). *Théorie et pratique du commerce et de la marine, traduction libre sur l'espagnol de Don Geronymo de Uztàriz, sur la seconde èdition de ce livre à Madrid en 1742.* Paris: Veuve Estienne

Verri, A., Verri, P. (1911). *Carteggio di Pietro e Alessandro Verri*, vol. III, edited by F. Novati, E. Greppi, Milan: Cogliati.

Verri, A., Verri, P. (1980). *In viaggio a Parigi e Londra (1766–1767). Carteggio di Pietro e Alessandro Verri*, edited by G. Gasperi, Milan: Adelphi.

Vivens, F. de Labat de. (1756). *Observation sur divers moyens de soutenir et d'encourager l'agricolture, principalment dans la Guyenne*, s.l, s.n.

Voltaire [Arouet, F. M.]. (1768). *L'Homme au quarante écu* London: s.n.

Young, A. (1770). *The Expediency of a Free Exportation of Corn at This Time*. London: Nicoll.

Secondary Sources

Alimento, A., Stapelbroek, K. (2017). *The Politics of Commercial Treaties. Balance of Power, Balance of Trade*. London: Palgrave Macmillan.

Anglani, B. (1999). I dialoghi dell'assenza. Il carteggio tra l'abate Galiani e Madame d'Èpinay. *Annali della Facoltà di Lingue e Letterature Straniere*. Terza Serie, XIII, pp. 269–293.

Atkin, M. (1995). *The international grain trade. Second Edition*. Cambridge: Woodhead.

Baldi, M. (1983). *David Hume nel Settecento Italiano*. Florence: La Nuova Italia Editrice.

Barnes, D. G. (1930). *A History of English Corn Laws: From 1660–1846*. London: Routledge.

Bauer, S. (1890). Studies on the Origin of the French Economists. *The Quarterly Journal of Economics*, Vol. 5, No. 1, pp. 100–107.

Bazzoni, A. (1869a). Carteggio dell'abate Ferdinando Galiani col Marchese Tanucci (1759–1769). *Archivio Storico Italiano*, Vol. 9, No. 2, pp. 10–36.

Bazzoni, A. (1869b). Carteggio dell'abate Ferdinando Galiani col Marchese Tanucci (1759–1769). *Archivio Storico Italiano*, Vol. 10, No. 1, pp. 40–57.

Bazzoni, A. (1875a). Carteggio dell'abate Ferdinando Galiani col Marchese Tanucci (1759–1769). *Archivio Storico Italiano*, Vol. 21, No. 87, pp. 516–527

Bazzoni, A. (1875b). Carteggio dell'abate Ferdinando Galiani col Marchese Tanucci (1759–1769). *Archivio Storico Italiano*, Vol. 22, No. 88, pp. 37–51.

Bazzoni, A. (1876a). "Carteggio dell'abate Ferdinando Galiani col Marchese Tanucci (1759–1769)", *Archivio Storico Italiano*, Vol. 23, No. 92, pp. 242–252.

Bazzoni, A. (1876b). Carteggio dell'abate Ferdinando Galiani col Marchese Tanucci (1759–1769). *Archivio Storico Italiano*, Vol. 24, No. 95, pp. 243–254.

Bazzoni, A. (1877a). Carteggio dell'abate Ferdinando Galiani col Marchese Tanucci (1759–1769). *Archivio Storico Italiano*, Vol. 25, No. 98, pp. 195–207.

Bazzoni, A. (1877b). Carteggio dell'abate Ferdinando Galiani col Marchese Tanucci (1759–1769). *Archivio Storico Italiano*, Vol. 26, No. 100, pp. 26–42.

Bazzoni, A. (1878a). Carteggio dell'abate Ferdinando Galiani col Marchese Tanucci (1759–1769), *Archivio Storico Italiano,* Vol. 1, No. 103, pp. 14–31.

Bazzoni, A. (1878b). Carteggio dell'abate Ferdinando Galiani col Marchese Tanucci (1759–1769). *Archivio Storico Italiano,* Vol. 1, No. 105, pp. Vol. 1, 445–459.

Bazzoni, A. (1878c). Carteggio dell'abate Ferdinando Galiani col Marchese Tanucci (1759–1769). *Archivio Storico Italiano,* Vol. 2, No. 106, pp. 23–31.

Bazzoni, A. (1879a). Carteggio dell'abate Ferdinando Galiani col Marchese Tanucci (1759–1769). *Archivio Storico Italiano,* Vol. 3, No. 110, pp. 171–183.

Bazzoni, A. (1879b). Carteggio dell'abate Ferdinando Galiani col Marchese Tanucci (1759–1769). *Archivio Storico Italiano,* Vol. 4, No. 114, pp. 361–375.

Bazzoni, A. (1880a). "Carteggio dell'abate Ferdinando Galiani col Marchese Tanucci (1759–1769)", *Archivio Storico Italiano,* Vol. 5, No. 117, pp. 367–375.

Bazzoni, A. (1880b). *Lettere di Ferdinando Galiani al Marchese Bernardo Tanucci.* Florence: Vieusseux.

Beer, M. (1939). *An Inquiry into Physiocracy.* London: Allen and Unwin.

Blart, L. (1915). *Les rapports de la France et de l'Espagne après le Pacte de Famille jusqu'à la fin du ministère du duc de Choiseul.* Paris: Librairie Félix Alcan.

Blessich A. (1896). L'Abate Galiani geografo. Contributo alla storia della geografia moderna. *Napoli Nobilissima,* Anno V, fasc. X, pp. 145–150.

Bourguet, A. (1907). *Étude sur la politique étrangère du duc de Choiseul.* Paris: Plon.

Boussard, J.-M., Gérard, F., Piketty, M.-G. (1995). *Libéraliser l'agriculture mondiale? Théories, modèles et réalités.* Montpellier: Cirad Centre de coopération en recherche agronomique pour le développement.

Cahen, L. (1926). Le Pacte de Famine et les spéculations sur les blés. *Revue Historique,* Tome 152, Fasc. 1, pp. 32–43.

Carpanetto, D., Ricuperati, G. (1993). *L'Italia del Settecento. Crisi, trasformazioni, lumi,* Bari: Laterza.

Carrino, A. (2021). *Francisco Hombrados Malo (secolo XVIII). Un uomo per tutte le stagioni.* Viterbo: Sette Città.

Catucci, M. (1986). *Galianea. Ferdinando Galiani tra letteratura ed economia,* Rome: Bulzoni.

Charbit, Y. (2002). The Political Failure of an Economic Theory: Physiocracy. *Population,* Vol. 57, No. 6, pp. 855–883.

Charles, L. (2011). Le cercle de Gournay: usages culturels et pratiques savants. In L Charles, F. Lefèbvre, C. Théré, (eds.), *Le cercle de Vincent de Gournay Savoirs économiques et pratiques administratives en France au milieu du XVIIIè siècle.* Paris: Ined, pp. 63–88.

Charles, L., Orain, A. (2019). François Véron de Forbonnais and the Invention of Antiphysiocracy. In S. L. Kaplan, S. A. Reinert (eds.), *The Economic Turn: Recasting Political Economy in Eighteenth-Century Europe.* London: Anthem Press, pp. 139–168.

Charles, L., Théré, C. (2007). François Quesnay: A Rural Socrates in Versailles?, *History of Political Economy*, 38, pp. 195–214.

Charles, L., Théré, C. (2019). The Physiocratic Movement: A Revision, in S. L. Kaplan, S. A. Reinert (eds.), *The Economic Turn: Recasting Political Economy in Eighteenth-Century Europe*. London: Anthem Press, pp. 35–70.

Clemente, A. (2003). Quando il reato non è peccato. Il contrabbando nel Regno di Napoli tra conflitti giurisdizionali, pluralismo istituzionale e quotidianità degli scambi (XVIII secolo). *Quaderni Storici*, 143, 2, pp. 359–394.

Clemente, A., Russo, S. (eds). (2019). *La polizia de' grani: mercati, regole e crisi di sussistenza nelle economie di antico regime*. Soveria Mannelli: Rubbettino.

Cobban, A. (1966). The Decline of Divine-Right Monarchy in France. In *The New Cambridge Modern History*. Volume VII The Old Regime (1713–63). Cambridge: Cambridge University Press, pp. 214–240.

Cohen, H. (1988). Diderot's machiavellian Harlequin: Ferdinando Galiani. *Studies on Voltaire and the eighteenth century*, n° 256, pp. 129–148.

Craveri, B. (2005). *The Age of Conversation*. New York: New York Review Books.

Das Satya, P. (1982). Economies of Scale, Imperfect Competition, and the Pattern of Trade. *The Economic Journal*, Vol. 92, No. 367, pp. 684–693.

Daudin, G., Crouzet, F. (2004). *Commerce et prospérité: la France au XVIIIe siècle*. Paris: Presses de l'université Paris-Sorbonne.

Davison, R. (1985). *Diderot et Galiani: étude d'une amitié philosophique*. Oxford: Voltaire Foundation.

De Caro, G. (1962). *Le carte Tanucci nell'Archivo General de Simancas*, Milan: Giuffré.

De Caro, G. (1975). José de Baeza Vicentelo y Manrique conte di Cantillana. In *Dizionario Biografico degli Italiani*, Vol. 18, *ad vocem*.

Dédéyan, C. (1975). L'Europe française à l'heure de Galiani. In *Convegno italo-francese sul tema Ferdinando Galiani* (Roma, 25–27 maggio 1972), Rome: Accademia Nazionale dei Lincei, pp. 380–389.

Deloche, R. (1988). En marge d'un bicentenaire: Galiani et l'apologue. *Revue économique*, Vol. 39, No. 6, pp. 1143–1157.

De Lucia, G. (1984). I collaboratori di Bernardo Tanucci nelle Segreterie di Stato durante il quinquennio 1755–1759. *Storia e Politica*, Anno XXIII, fasc. 1, pp. 73–94.

De Rosa C. A. (1834). *Ritratti poetici di alcuni uomini di lettere antichi e moderni del regno di Napoli*, Volume 1, Naples: Fibreno.

De Rosa, L. (1995). Galiani e il commercio dei grani. In L. De Rosa, (ed.), *Economisti merdionali*. Naples: Istituto Italiano per gli Studi Filosofici, pp. 117–189.

Diaz, F. (1962). *Filosofia e politica nel Settecento francese*. Turin: Einaudi.

Diaz, F. (1975a). Introduzione. In Galiani, F. *Opere*, edited by F. Diaz, L.Guerci, *Letteratura italiana. Storia e testi. Illuministi italiani*, tomo VI, Milan-Naples: Ricciardi, pp. ix–cvi.

Diaz, F. (1975b). La politica estera e i problemi economici del Regno di Napoli nell'opera di Ferdinando Galiani. In *Convegno italo-francese sul tema Ferdinando Galiani* (Roma, 25–27 maggio 1972), Rome: Accademia Nazionale dei Lincei, pp. 79–107.

Dieckmann, H. (1975). Diderot et Galiani. In *Convegno italo-francese sul tema Ferdinando Galiani* (Roma, 25–27 maggio 1972). Rome: Accademia Nazionale dei Lincei, pp. 309–331.

Dobado-González, R., García-Hiernaux, A., Guerrero, D.E. (2012). The Integration of Grain Markets in the Eighteenth Century: Early Rise of Globalization in the West. *The Journal of Economic History*, Vol. 72, No. 3, pp. 671–707.

Dockès, P. (1969). *L'espace dans la pensée économique du XVIe au XVIIIe* siècle. Paris: Flammarion.

Durand, Y-R. (1969). Introduction. In *Mémoires de Jean-Joseph de Laborde fermier général et banquier de la cour, Annuaire-Bulletin de la Société de l'histoire de France*, pp. 75–111.

Fabre, J. (1975). Galiani et la société française à l'époque de Louis XV. In *Convegno italo-francese sul tema Ferdinando Galiani* (Roma, 25–27 maggio 1972), Rome: Accademia Nazionale dei Lincei, pp. 159–176.

Faccarello, G. (1998). Galiani, Necker and Turgot. A debate on economic reform and policy in 18th Century France. In G. Faccarello (ed.), *Studies in the History of French Political Economy. From Bodin to Walras.* London: Routledge, pp. 120–195.

Faccarello, G. (1999). *The Foundations of «Laissez-Faire»: The Economics of Pierre de Boisguilbert.* London: Routledge.

Ferrand, J., Orain, A. (2019). Sensationism, Modern Natural Law and the Science of Commerce at the Heart of the Controversy between Mably and the Physiocrats. In S. L. Kaplan, S. A. Reinert (eds.), *The Economic Turn: Recasting Political Economy in Eighteenth-Century Europe.* London: Anthem Press, pp. 439–468.

Ferraioli, G. (1880). Un fallo diplomatico dell'abate Galiani. *Archivio storico per le province napoletane*, Anno V, Fascicolo IV, pp. 690–698.

Finoli, A.M. (1947). Osservazioni sulla lingua degli economisti italiani del Settecento. *Lingua nostra*, 8, pp. 108–112.

Fox-Genovese, E. A. (1976). *The Origins of Physiocracy: Economic Revolution and Social Order in Eighteenth-Century France*, Ithaca: Cornell University Press.

Gandolfo, G. (2014). *International Trade Theory and Policy.* Berlin: Springer.

Gaudemet, E. (1899). *L'abbé Galiani et la question du commerce des blés à la fin du règne de Louis XV.* Paris: Rousseau.

Ghisalberti, C. (1975). Ferdinando Galiani e il problema istituzionale. In *Convegno italo-francese sul tema Ferdinando Galiani* (Roma, 25–27 maggio 1972), Rome: Accademia Nazionale dei Lincei, pp. 49–65.

Gignoux C.-J. (1922). L'abbé Galiani et la querelle des grains au XVIIIe siècle. *Revue d'histoire économique et sociale*, Vol. 10, No. 1, pp. 17–37.

Giocoli, N. (2001). Value and Interest in Ferdinando Galiani's *Della Moneta*. *History of Economic Ideas*, Vol. 9, No. 3, Special Issue: *"Della Moneta" by Ferdinando Galiani: a Quarter Millennium Assessment* (2001), pp. 95–135.

Glineur, C. (2005). Entre libéralisme et protectionnisme: la politique pré-libérale du contrôleur général Moreau de Séchelles. *La Revue administrative*, 58e Année, No. 345, pp. 290–302.

Goggi, G. (1994). Galiani et l'Angleterre sur la genèse des dialogues sur les blés. *Dix-Huitieme Siecle*, n. 26, *Economie et politique*, pp. 295–316.

Goodman, D. (1989). Enlightenment Salons: The Convergence of Female and Philosophic Ambitions. *Eighteenth-Century Studies*, Vol. 22, No. 3, *Special Issue: The French Revolution in Culture*, pp. 329–350.

Goodman, D. (1994). *The Republic of Letters: A Cultural History of the French Enlightenment.* Ithaca: Cornell University Press.

Guerci, L. (1971). F. Galiani, Dialogues entre M. Marquis de Roquemaure, et Ms. le Chevalier Zanobi (a cura di P. Koch). *Rivista Storica Italiana*, Anno LXXXIII, fasc. I, pp. 178–189.

Guerci, L. (1975a). Epistolario. Preliminari. In F.Diaz, L. Guerci, (eds), Galiani, F. *Opere*, *Letteratura italiana. Storia e testi. Illuministi italiani*, tomo VI, Milan-Naples: Ricciardi, pp. 783–814.

Guerci, L (1975b). Croquis d'un dialogue sur les femmes. Preliminari. In F.Diaz, L. Guerci, (eds), Galiani, F. *Opere*, *Letteratura italiana. Storia e testi. Illuministi italiani*, tomo VI, Milan-Naples: Ricciardi, pp. 615–634.

Guillois, A. (1894). *Le salon de Madame Helvétius. Cabanis et les idéologues*, Paris: Calmann Lévy.

Harcourt, B. E. (2011). *The illusion of free markets: punishment and the myth of natural order.* Cambridge, Massachusetts: Harvard University Press.

Hauc, J.-C. (2004). *Ange Goudar: Un aventurier des Lumières.* Paris: Honoré Champion.

Heckscher, E. F. (1919) [1950] "The effects of foreign trade of the distribution of income". in H. S. Ellis, L. A. Metzler (eds.). *Readings in the theory of international trade.* London: Allen & Unwin, pp. 270–300.

Helpman, E. (1981). International Trade in the Presence of Product Differentiation, Economies of Scale and Monopolistic Competition: A Chamberlin-Heckscher-Ohlin Approach. *Journal of International Economics*, 11, 1981, pp. 305–340

Higgs, H. (1897). *The Physiocrats: Six Lectures on the French Economists of the 18th Century.* London: Macmillan.

Hufton, O. (1983). Social Conflict and the Grain Supply in Eighteenth-Century France. *The Journal of Interdisciplinary History*, Vol. 14, No. 2, pp. 303–331.

Hutchison, T. (1988). *Before Adam Smith. The Emergence of Political Economy 1662–1776*. Oxford: Basil Blackwell.

Kaplan, S. L. (1976). *Bread, politics and political economy in the reign of Louis XV*. The Hague: Martinus Nijhoff.

Kaplan, S. L. (1982). The Famine Plot Persuasion in Eighteenth-Century France. *Transactions of the American Philosophical Society*, Vol. 72, No. 3, pp. 1–79.

Kaplan, S. L. (1996). *The Bakers of Paris and the Bread Question. 1700–1775*, Durham: Duke University Press.

Klotz, G. (2000). La question des blés en France au dix-huitième siècle: Galiani, critique des physiocrates. *Il Pensiero Economico Italiano*, vol VIII, n. 2, pp. 147–183.

Koch, P. (1961). The Genesis of Galiani's Dialogues sur le Commerce Des Blés. *French Studies*, Volume XV issue 4, pp. 314–323.

Koch, P. (1968). Introduction. In F.Galiani, *Dialogues entre M. Marquis de Roquemaure et M. le chevalier Zanobi. Analecta Romanica*, Heft 21, Frankfurt am Main: Klostermann, pp. 1–51.

Koch, P. (1975). Les veritable Dialogues de Galiani. In *Convegno italo-francese sul tema Ferdinando Galiani* (Roma, 25–27 maggio 1972), Rome: Accademia Nazionale dei Lincei, pp. 185–197.

Lawrence C., Spiller P. T. (1983). Product Diversity, Economies of Scale, and International Trade. *The Quarterly Journal of Economics*, Vol. 98, No. 1, pp. 63–83.

Lepre, A. (1986a). *Storia del Mezzogiorno d'Italia*, Vol. I. *La lunga durata e la crisi (1500–1656)*, Naples: Liguori.

Lepre, A. (1986b). *Storia del Mezzogiorno d'Italia*, Vol. II. *Dall'Antico Regime alla società borghese (1657–1860)*, Naples: Liguori.

Lilti, A. (2005). *Le Monde des salons. Sociabilité et mondanité à Paris au XVIIIe siècle*. Paris: Fayard.

Lopez-Cordon Cortezo, M. V. (2003). Pacte de Famille ou intérêts d'État? La Monarchie française et la diplomatie espagnole du XVIIIe siècle. In L. Bély, (ed.), *La présence des Bourbons en Europe, XVIe–XXIe siècle*. Paris: PUF, pp. 185–220.

Macry, P. (1974). *Mercato e società nel Regno di Napoli. Commercio del grano e politica economica nel '700*. Naples: Guida.

Maiorini, M.G. (2000). Neapolitan Diplomacy in the Eighteenth Century: Policy and the Diplomatic Apparatus. In D. Frigo, (ed.) *Politics and Diplomacy in Early Modern Italy. The Structure of Diplomatic Practice, 1450–1800*. Cambridge: Cambridge University Press, pp. 176–209.

Mauro, A. (2017a). *Un philosophe des Lumières entre Naples et Paris: Ferdinando Galiani (1728–1787*). Thèse de Doctorate de l'Université Toulouse le Mirail - Toulouse II.

Mauro, A. (2017b). L'abbé Galiani alias le chevalier Zanobi: un philosophe qui "ne croit rien en rien sur rien de rien". *Littératures Classiques*, 93, pp. 155–167.

Mazzola, R. (2020). Napoli 1764. *Laboratorio dell'ISPF*, vol. XVII, 4, pp. 2–8.

Melvin, J.-R. (1969). Increasing Returns to Scale as a Determinant of Trade. *The Canadian Journal of Economics*, Vol. 2, pp. 389–402.

Meyssonnier, S. (1990). Vincent de Gournay (1712–1759) et la "Balance des homes". *Population* (French Edition), Vol. 45, No. 1, pp. 87–112.

Migliorini, A.V. (1979). I problemi del trattato franco-napoletano di navigazione e di commercio (1740–1766). *Rivista storica italiana*, XCI, 1, pp. 180–207.

Minerbi, M. (1973). Diderot, Galiani e la polemica sulla fisiocrazia (1767–1771). *Studi Storici*, Anno 14, No. 1, pp. 147–184

Nicolini, F. (1908b). Intorno a Ferdinando Galiani a proposito di una pubblicazione recente. *Giornale Storico della letteratura italiana*, Volume LII, pp. 1–55.

Nicolini, F. (1914). Introduzione. In B. Tanucci, *Lettere a Ferdinando Galiani*, edited by F. Nicolini. Bari: Laterza, pp. vi–xix.

Nicolini, F. (1929). Amici e corrispondenti dell'abate Ferdinando Galiani: I. Angelo Gatti (con nuove notize e documenti inediti sul richiamo del Galiani da Parigi). *Archivio Storico Italiano*, Vol. 87 (Serie 7, Vol. 12), No. 4 (332), pp. 233–272.

Nicolini, F. (1954). *Amici e corrispondenti francesi dell'abate Galiani. Notizie lettere documenti*. Naples: Banco di Napoli.

Nicolini, F. (1959a). Avvertenza. In F. Nicolini (ed.), F. Galiani, *Dialogues sur le commerce des bleds. Giusta l'editio princeps del 1770 con appendici illustrative*, Naples: Ricciardi, pp. ix–xxviii.

Ohlin, B. (1933). *Interregional and International trade*, Cambridge (Mass.): Harvard University Press.

Orain, A. (2019). Physiocrat Arithmetic versus Ratios: The Analytical Economics of Jean- Joseph- Louis Graslin. In S. L. Kaplan, S. A. Reinert (eds.), *The Economic Turn: Recasting Political Economy in Eighteenth-Century Europe*. London: Anthem Press, pp. 193–220.

Orain, A., Reinert, S. A. (2022). Small States in an Age of Empires: The Duchy of Parma's Colonial Moment, 1750–1770. *Capitalism: A Journal of History and Economics*, 3, no. 1 (Winter 2022), pp. 57–105.

Ousselin, E. (1999). L'Homme aux quarante écus: Voltaire économiste. *The French Review*, Vol. 72, No. 3, pp. 493–502.

Ozanam, D. (1961). Les origines du troisième Pacte de Famille (1761). *Revue d'histoire diplomatique*, octobre–décembre 1961, n. 4, pp. 307–340.

Panagariya, A. (1981). Variable Returns to Scale in Production and Patterns of Specialization. *The American Economic Review*, Vol. 71, pp. 221–230.

Patalano, R. (2018). Les *Dialogues* de Ferdinando Galiani et la Géoéconomie du commerce des grains à la fin du XVIIIe siècle. In A. Tiran, C. Carnino, (eds.), *Ferdinando Galiani, économie et politique*. Paris: Classiques Garnier, pp. 341–369.

Pénigaud, T. (2015). The political opposition of Rousseau to Physiocracy: government, interest, citizenship. *European Journal of the History of Economic Thought*, Vol. 22 Issue 3, pp. 473–499.

Perrot, J. C. (1988). "Les économistes, les philosophes et la population" in Jacques Dupâquier (ed.), *Histoire de la population française*, tome II: *De la Renaissance à 1789*, Paris: PUF, pp. 499–551.

Perrot, J.-C. (1992). *Une histoire intellectuelle de l'économie politique. XVIIe–XVIIIe siècle*. Paris: Éditions de l'École des Hautes Études en Sciences Sociales.

Porta, P. L. (1995). La concezione dello sviluppo economico nei Dialoghi sul commercio dei grani di Ferdinando Galiani. In A. Roncaglia, (ed.), *Le origini del pensiero eonomico in Italia*. Bologna: Il Mulino, pp. 121–140.

Pribram, K. (1983). *A history of economic reasoning*. New York: John Hopkins University Press.

Principe, I. (1993). La cartografia nel Regno di Napoli e l'Atlante di Giovanni Antonio Rizzi Zannoni. In G. A. Rizzi Zannoni, *Atlante del Regno di Napoli*, Soveria Mannelli: Rubbettino, pp. 13–45.

Pupo, S. (2020). Hume politico a Napoli. Per una rilettura della fortuna del "celebre scozzese" negli scritti degli illuministi meridionali. *(Il) Pensiero Politico. Rivista di Storia delle Idee Politiche e Sociali*, Anno LIII, n. 1, pp. 3–35.

Riley, J. C. (1986). *The Seven Years War and the Old Regime in France. The Economic and Financial Toll*. Princeton: Princeton University Press.

Roberts, M. (2003). *The Age of Liberty: Sweden 1719–1772*. Cambridge: Cambridge University Press.

Schelle, G. (1897). *Vincent de Gournay*, Paris: Guillaumin.

Schelle, G. (1907). *Le Docteur Quesnay. Chirurgien, Médecin de M.me de Pompadour et de Louis XV, Physiocrate*. Paris: Félix Alcan.

Schipa, M. (1904). *Il Regno di Napoli al tempo di Carlo di Borbone*. Naples: Pierro.

Schumpeter, J. A. (1954) [2006]. *History of Economic Analysis*. London: Routledge.

Scibilia, A. (1976). Domenico Caracciolo. In *Dizionario Biografico degli Italiani*, Volume 19, Rome: Treccani, *ad vocem*.

Skornicki, A. (2018). Le pour et le contre Galiani, la diplomatie et le commerce des blés. In A. Tiran, C. Carnino (eds.), *Economie et politique chez Ferdinando Galiani*. Paris: Classiques Garnier, pp. 319–340.

Soulange-Bodin, A. (1894). *La diplomatie de Louis XV et le Pacte de Famille*. Paris: Didier, Perrin & Cie.

Sonenscher, M. (2002). Physiocracy as a theodicy. *History of Political Thought*, 23, pp. 326–339.

Stapelbroek, K. (2006). Preserving the Neapolitan State: Antonio Genovesi and Ferdinando Galiani on commercial society and planning economic growth. *History of European Ideas*, Volume 32, Issue 4, pp. 406–429.

Stapelbroek, K. (2016), "To Console and Alleviate the Human Mind": Ferdinando Galiani's Attempted Republication of Serra in the 1750s, in Patalano, R., Reinert, S. A. (eds.), *Antonio Serra and the Economics of Good Government.* New York: Palgrave Macmillan, pp. 234–262.

Steegmuller, F. (1983). *A Woman, a Man, and Two Kingdoms: The Story of Madame d'Épinay and Abbé Galiani.* Princeton: Princeton University Press.

Strenski, E.M. (1967). Diderot, for and against the physiocrats. *Studies on Voltaire and the 18th Century*, vol. LVII, pp. 1435–1455.

Swann, J. (1995). *Politics and Parlamento of Paris under Louis XV (1754–1774).* Cambridge: Cambridge University Press.

Toutain, J. C. (1961). *Le produit de l'agriculture francaise de 1700 à 1958. La Croissance. Histoire Quantitative De L'Économie Francaise. Cahiers De L'Institut De Science Économique Appliquée*, Paris: Isea.

Vaggi, G. (1987). *The Economics of François Quesnay.* London: Macmillan.

Valentino, H. (1952). *Madame d'Èpinay, une femme d'esprit sous Louis XV*, Paris: Librairie Académique Perrin.

Valerio, V. (2007). Cartography in the Kingdom of Naples during the Early Modern Period. In D. Woodward, (ed.), *The History of Cartography, Volume 3. Cartography in the European Renaissance*, Chicago: The University Chicago Press, pp. 940–974.

Van Kley, D. K. (2018). *Reform Catholicism and the International Suppression of the Jesuits in Enlightenment Europe.* New Haven: Yale University Press.

Vardi, L. (2012). *The Physiocrats and the World of the Enlightenment.* Cambridge: Cambridge University Press.

Venturi, F. (1960a). Le lezioni di commercio di Antonio Genovesi. Manoscritti, edizioni e traduzioni. *Rivista Storica italiana*, anno LXXII, fascicolo III, pp. 511–530.

Venturi, F. (1971a). *Utopia and Reform in the Enlightenment*, Cambridge: Cambridge University Press.

Venturi, F. (1973). 1764: Napoli nell'anno della fame. *Rivista storica italiana*, Anno LXXXV fasc. 2, pp. 394–472.

Villani, P. (1977). *Mezzogiorno tra riforme e rivoluzione.* Bari: Laterza.

Villari, L. (1958). *Il pensiero economico di Antonio Genovesi.* Florence: Le Monnier.

Villari, L. (1965). La fisiocrazia nel dibattito illuministico. *Studi Storici*, Anno 6, No. 1, pp. 25–39.

Villari, L. (1968). Note sulla fisiocrazia e sugli economisti napoletani del '700. In E. Sestan (ed.), *Saggi e ricerche sul Settecento*, Naples: Istituto Italiano per gli Studi Filosofici, pp. 224–251.

Weinreb, R. (1992). *Eagle in a Gauze Cage: Louise d'Epinay, femme de lettres*, New York: AMS Press.

Weulersse, G. (1910). *Le mouvement physiocratique en France (de 1750 à 1770).* Paris: Alcan.

CHAPTER 8

The Last Years (1770–1787)

Portrait of Abbot Ferdinando Galiani, by Giuseppe Sanmartino, 1787, Museo Filangieri, Naples. https://it.wikipedia.org/wiki/Ferdinando_Galiani#/media/File:Ritratto_dell'abate_Ferdinando_Galiani.jpg

R. Patalano, *Ferdinando Galiani*,
https://doi.org/10.1007/978-3-032-02793-1_8

8.1 Galiani Under Attack: Cartesianism Versus Newtonianism

The polemical force of the *Dialogues* provoked equally strong reactions of dissent and consensus, and Galiani himself regarded his attack on the physiocratic school as a "bombshell".[1] A direct testimony to the climate generated by Galiani's work is offered by a letter that his friend Angelo Gatti sent him from Paris, in January 1770, a few days after the publication of the *Dialogues*: "It is necessary that I tell you more about the success of your book, however much you have received or are about to receive more precise and more detailed news from Madame d'Épinay. Since it was published, every day I have heard of it, and have sought opportunities to hear about it. An excellent, most useful book, according to some, full of new and profound views, *très agréable à lire, dialogué à merveille, etc.*: *detestable*, according to others, *full of errors, d'un mauvais ton, très prolixe, sans ordre*, etc., and, with all that, capable of making a very great impression on the public and of delaying the freedom of exportation for fifty years. The former are the indifferent, and one can say the public; the latter, the *Économistes* and those who had claimed to be for unlimited freedom or had promoted it. All of these, as a result, are shouting against you and your book and preparing to respond to you. Abbot Baudeau, who has been back from Poland for four months, has already made an excerpt, which is already printed in the *Ephémérides du citoyen*. La Rivière, auteur du *Despotisme légal*, is writing a book against you. But the most formidable of your opponents is Abbé Morellet, who works day and night to do a more voluminous work than yours against you, who are the enemy of all freedom, the friend of authority and despotism, and the scorner of *Économistes* and literate people in general. Your friends and his, in general, are enchanted with your book and disapprove of his anger against you and the publisher. But he does not want to listen to reason, and, under the pretext of avenging truth and liberty, wants to revenge his first opinion and his offended vanity. When the duke [Choiseul], the first promoter and protector of free exportation, heard that your work was against this freedom, he became extremely irate and deplored you in strong terms. I, being informed of this, told him that such was not the object of your book and that it deserved to be read by him as well. He told me that he would

[1] Ferdinando Galiani's letter to Madame d'Épinay, Naples, 18 November 1769, published in Galiani (1959: 350); Galiani and d'Épinay (1992, vol. I: 95).

read it, but I fear that he will not have had the time, and that the first impression against you will remain such as he received it from the two abbots Barthélemy and Beliardi".[2]

The intensity of the controversy was so great that still three years after the *Dialogues* were published, Marquis Caracciolo, the new ambassador to Paris after Cantillana's death, wrote to Galiani: "Those blessed *Dialogues* on the freedom of export have done you incredible harm in this country, because the *Économistes* have made horrible war on you and are constantly making war on you. I see first hand that opinions of whatever kind they are, religious or political or scientific, economic, speculative, practical [...], exalt the head, produce party spirit and form a sect. And every sect, having taken some kind of consistency, defends itself against its opponents and attacks them [...]. In short, the sectarians all employ the same means to triumph over their enemies; they all become friars, all priests, all fanatics [...]. Indeed now is the time that your divisive *Dialogues* is remembered in Paris, and the *Économistes* are shouting and exclaiming against you because of the present famine; the government having forbidden exportation for a long time, the maxim of the *Contrôleur General* [Abbot Terray] and commonly of all the ministers being contrary to free grain trade, [...] and, as you know, Abbot Morellet was forbidden to reply to your book. At present, despite all the provisions and all the orders, with bread being sold in many places at five *Soldi* a pound and numerous riots in several provinces, the old question is brought up again for the benefit of the *Économistes*".[3] And again: "Turgot and Abbot Morellet claim that no book has done as much damage to France as your *Dialogues* [...]. You say that your system about grains has either not been understood here or they have not wanted to understand it. I say to you what they say to me on that point. For the rest, I do not have to decide whether you are right or wrong, because one

[2] Angelo Gatti's letter to Ferdinando Galiani, Paris, 22 January 1770, published in Nicolini (1929: 260–263), see also Galiani (1959: 396–397). Giovanni Angelo Gatti (1724–1798), an Italian physician and professor at the University of Pisa, became famous for being the first inoculator in Tuscany and for contributing his studies to the spread of this practice. Gatti was appointed, "médicin consultant du roi" by the King of France Louis XV in 1763 and Particular Physician to the King of Naples Ferdinand IV in 1778. He was linked to Galiani by close friendship. On Gatti see Nicolini (1929) and Farinella (1999). Jean-Jacques Barthélemy and Alessandro Beliardi were agents who served the Duke of Choiseul.

[3] Domenico Caracciolo's letter to Ferdinando Galiani, Paris, 12 June 1773, published in Nicolini (1954: 45–46, see also Galiani, 1959: 595–597).

would have to examine your book thoroughly, which I regret to do now, and then my opinion is of no use".[4]

In a climate made difficult by popular uprisings caused by famine (still dominated by the alleged *Pacte de Famine*) and the parliaments' opposition to liberalisation,[5] the *Dialogues* took on the character of a political pamphlet opposing free trade policy choices and going beyond the limits of a purely intellectual polemic. The years 1769 and 1770 saw a severe subsistence crisis: supplies contracted, prices rose, and grain and bread riots swept large parts of the country. This crisis caused controversy on the implementation of economic liberalization policies, which were judged too abstract and inadequate for the French socio-economic situation.

In December 1769, Étienne Maynon d'Invault resigned and was replaced in the office of *Contrôleur Général des Finances* by Abbot Joseph Marie Terray: a political shift that heralded a change in grain policy.[6] In

[4] Domenico Caracciolo's letter to Ferdinando Galiani, sent at the same time but lost, cited in Diodati (1788: 54). A few years later, Caracciolo himself, as Viceroy of Sicily, faced a severe famine on the island (see Caracciolo 1785).

[5] "Another crisis was in the making as soon as the preceding one had been quelled. That it erupted, however, in 1770 and proved to be so violent seems to be directly related to the general economic crisis. Business distress and uncertainty made money, like grain, scarce. The financiers suffered setbacks and the government found it difficult to obtain large doses of fresh credit. Measured against the claims on the treasury one should say, more precisely, treasuries the increased revenue which Laverdy said liberalization produced was a mere trifle. Maynon D'Invault had a 55,000,000 *Livres* deficit, eighty millions in arrears, and was meeting the needs of 1769 with the anticipated receipts of 1770. "The finances of Your Majesty" the Controller-General confessed to the king, "are in the most horrible state of ruin". Facing imminent bankruptcy, Maynon resigned in December 1769. With him passed the last hope of liberalization" (Kaplan 1976: 490).

[6] "The departure of Maynon, a friend of the physiocrats and a stout defender of the liberal reforms, did not signify a determination within the royal council to change the grain policy. It was motivated by the financial *imbroglio*, not the subsistence crisis, two problems whose relationship at this point in time the king's advisers did not clearly perceive. [...] Terray [...] had not taken an active role in the parliamentary campaign against liberalization. Throughout his career as rapporteur of royal legislation he had shown singular talent for mediating between the desires of the sovereign court and those of the king. At the end of 1769 it was expected that he would devote all of his energies to the herculean task of restoring a semblance of order -to the crown's finances, leaving the subsistence question in the hands of the liberals Trudaine de Montigny and Albert [Intendants du commerce] who remained in charge of the grain department. Choiseul, whose influence in the council had not yet been undercut by Maupeou, detested the *Économistes* but remained a partisan of liberalization. At the moment Terray came to power, prices in Paris were still declining and the Parlement had lapsed into silence" (Kaplan 1976: 492).

July 1770, faced with revolts in the provinces,[7] Terray temporarily suspended the grain export decree and re-established a grain policy with the creation of granaries to counter the famine. This decision fuelled rumours about the *Pacte de Famine* and the alleged conspiracy uniting the court, aristocrats and speculators against the poor.

The events of the autumn of 1770 thus seemed to confirm Galiani's theses, but the polemic with Physiocracy initiated by the Neapolitan abbot was not only political for it involved the very methodological roots of the Quesnay School. Galiani, in fact, rejected a mechanistic application of deductive methodology to the social and economic system, drawing an appropriate epistemic distinction between natural science and the social and political sciences.

The enthusiasm for the ideal model of Newton's science, common in eighteenth-century culture, took on a special meaning in France, acquiring an original feature in its synthesis with the previous Cartesian tradition (Brunet 1931; Shank 2008). Although Voltaire, in his *Philosophie de Newton* (Voltaire 1738b), stressed the Newtonian empirical approach in contrast with Descartes, there remained a considerable legacy of Cartesian deductive methodology in authors like Montesquieu (1748 [1989]: 3–4) and d'Alembert (1743: ii–iii) (see Ingrao and Israel 1990: ch. 1; Oliveira 2017). According to d'Alembert, the true model of science, distinct from metaphysics, is based on mathematical and geometrical deductive methodology and every scientific discipline is composed of logical chains, originating in fundamental principles (Cane 1976).[8]

This particular approach, deeply influenced by the Cartesian legacy, which establishes a methodological monism in scientific research, finds a systematic application in the field of economic analysis with the Physiocratic School.[9] Although François Quesnay, the recognized founder of the

[7] "During the course of the summer and early fall disturbances marred the peace in Upper and Lower Normandy, the Hainaut, Picardy, Anjou, the Touraine, Auvergne, the Nivernais, Alsace, and Lorraine. Some of the most serious rioting occurred in Champagne" (Kaplan 1976: 499).

[8] In his *Discours préliminaire de l'Encyclopédie* (1751), d'Alembert recognizes that Cartesian mathematization paved the way for the Newtonian climax of the scientific revolution (d'Alembert 1751 [1995]: 78–79; Shank 2008: 16). d'Alembert can be regarded, like Christian Huygens, Gottfried Leibniz, and Johann Bernoulli, as a "Cartesian" opponent to the emerging Newtonian methodology. See also Brunet (1931).

[9] On the Cartesian influence on the Physiocratic movement, see also Bourthoumieux (1935); Schuhl (1938); Neill (1948, 1949); Hecht (1958); Kubota (1958); Foley (1973, 1976); Pribram (1983: ch. VII); Mirowski (1991: 154–158); Larrère (1994); Perru (1997:

school, followed an eclectic methodological approach and was often called the "Newton of new economic science" (Neill 1948: 169), Newtonian methodology and experimental approach remain extraneous to the Physiocrats.[10]

For the *Économistes*, economic laws, like natural laws, are immutable, based on simple, constant principles, deducible from the *ordre naturel*. They are the manifestation of the mechanical natural order, based upon the force of human self-interest and readable through the epistemological concept of *evidence* (Quesnay 1756b; see also Luftalla 1963; Fischman 1998).[11] As typical rationalists, the Physiocrats (who called themselves *Philosophes Économistes*) subscribed to the idea that economic concepts are written in the code of nature and can be read with the aid of *Reason* (Le Mercier de La Rivière 1767, vol. II: 120–121, 434; Dupont de Nemours 1768b) as intuitive and evident geometrical concepts. Consequently, economic analysis is an exact science, based on simple, constant principles, subject to invariable rules of natural laws, as indicated by the word *Physiocratie* (Dupont de Nemours 1768a), and subject to rational demonstration like the most certain physical sciences (Le Trosne 1766: 9; Le Trosne 1777: 320). Economic science constitutes a system, an "ensemble so united by a series of necessary and coherent deductions, that when the chain is broken one can present nothing more than scattered parts, isolated and disordered truths, parts of principles that are as obscure as the language is inexact" (Le Trosne 1777, vol. I: 492–493; see Neill 1949:

620–622); Roncaglia (2005: 96); Diemer and Guillemin (2013: 30–38). On Descartes's influence on the French Enlightenment, see Brockdorff (1937).

[10] According to Thomas Neill: "Except for him, the Physiocrats all subscribed to the deductive method of elucidating detailed laws of economic behaviour from innate principles" (Neill 1949: 541; see also Neill 1948: 170).

[11] "In seeking the specific laws of divinely inspired *ordre naturel* Quesnay employed one criterion, the precept of evidence which became the watchword of all physiocratic writings Evidence is basically the Cartesian intuition of eternal truth" (Koch 1968: 8). Georges Weulersse points out that [...] "Physiocratic evidence refers to Cartesian evidence. However, the latter did not apply to moral issues, and it is precisely to these that *Économistes* want to extend it" (Weulersse 1910, vol. II: 121). The concept of *evidence* becomes a polemical target of Galiani, with irony in the *Dialogues*: "It seemed evident to economists that the evidence of their evidence would make the advantage of free exportation evident to all nations, and that they would all adopt it" (Galiani 1770a: 301). And again: "Evidence is a rascal who owes everyone; he has promised and given tickets to all sciences and has only ever paid those land surveyors who have remained no less beggarly for it" (Galiani 1770a: 232).

541).[12] Operating on measurable objects, economic science "is apt to be subject to calculus" (Le Trosne 1777, vol. I: 320),[13] and the laws of this science are clearly discerned "by reflection, by judgment, by physical and moral arithmetic, by certain calculation" (Dupont de Nemours 1768a, vols. I, III; see Neill 1949: 543). Mathematical evidence is described by simple arithmetical and mechanical formulae (as in the *Tableau*) used to make intelligible political decisions.[14] Finally, civil and political laws must be dictated by the natural laws and must not interfere with them (*laissez-passer* and *free trade*).

Moreover, the Physiocratic movement was part of the rationalist stream of the French Enlightenment, strongly influenced by the mediation of Nicolas Malebranche, especially in the ethical vision and deistic optimism of the natural order.[15] The physiocratic school was by these characteristics structured as "a true sect *d'Illuminés*. They have prophecies, fables, visions and, above all, narcotic boredom".[16]

[12] Although Quesnay did not accept a rationalist treatment of social problems, his disciples considered deductive methodology more appropriate than the inductive approach for economic analysis because its fundamental principles are by nature quite evident and rapidly comprehensible by a series of incontestable logical deductions (Le Mercier de La Rivière 1767: 194–195; Le Trosne 1777, vol. I: 492–493; Morellet 1774: 28–29; see also Perrot 1992: 369).

[13] As "Descartes had applied mathematics to philosophy to create modern rationalism [...] in the same way the Physiocrats had applied mathematics to social matters to come out with the exact science of Physiocracy" (Neill 1949, p. 543).

[14] See Hoselitz (1968); Perrot (1992, p. 369); Cremaschi (2000: 713–718); Charles (2000, 2003, 2004). According to Diemer and Guillemin (2013, p. 37), the *Tableau* is similar to a machine or a mechanical system in which economic phenomena are reduced to physical phenomena, through a mechanical causality. The *Tableau* "can be seen as a transposition of the principles of Cartesian physics in the field of economic analysis" (Diemer and Guillemin 2013, p. 36).

[15] According to Edgard Allix: "It is Quesnay who transported Cartesianism into social science and he did so through Malebranche" (Allix 1911: 564). For Jean-Claude Perrot: "The imprint of Malebranche on Quesnay's thought is clearly identified" (Perrot 1992: 42).

[16] Ferdinando Galiani's letter to Madame d'Épinay, Naples, 28 April 1770, published in Galiani (1881a, vol I: 129); Galiani and d'Épinay (1992, vol. I: 155). And so judged Quesnay: "I believe Quesnay to be the *Antichrist*, and his rural physiognomy is the *Apocalypse*. This is more serious than you think. One day I'll have fun comparing Voltaire and Quesnay, and I intend to prove to you that this doctor is something else. He is something supernatural. He is sad and absurd, and he does not reject any fool among his disciples, as long as he is enthusiastic" (Ferdinando Galiani's letter to Madame d'Épinay, Naples, 28 April 1770, published in Galiani 1881a, vol I: 129; Galiani and d'Épinay 1992, vol. I: 155). See also Papi 1975.

Physiocratic economic analysis based on aprioristic assumptions (such as the *natural order* or the exclusive productivity of agriculture) can be called *Cartesian social mathematics*, inasmuch as "the Cartesian method was consciously and purposely cultivated by the Physiocrats" (Neill 1948: 168).[17] The mechanical logic of Descartes was adapted to the political project of the Physiocracy, characterizing economic science as a machine of wealth, of which the driving force is constituted by landowners and land rent (Diemer and Guillemin 2013, p. 38).[18]

This dominant Rationalist influence is evident in Physiocratic policy proposals, particularly on the issue of liberalization and deregulation of the grain trade, while Newtonian methodology, based on the experimental approach, remains extraneous to the Physiocratic movement. In contrast

[17] Karl Pribram uses the term "Cartesian economy" to define much of the French economic science of the eighteenth century, not limiting this definition only to the Physiocratic School (Pribram 1983: ch. VII). Some recent literature has greatly reduced, if not entirely eliminated, the rationalist Cartesian legacy on Quesnay's School, emphasizing other intellectual influences. This new view considers the sensualist approach predominant in the form of *sensualism normatif* (Steiner 1993, vol. I: 227–230); or *sentimental empiricism* (Riskin 2003), or *sensory evidence*, which elevates "Physiocracy to the rank of a science akin to geometry and physics" (Charles 2004: 465), considering the *Tableau* "a rational recreation" and "a sort of visual calculating machine for wealth" (Charles 2004: 469). The complex nature of the Physiocratic movement has been confirmed by Liana Vardi, who considers Quesnay's theory of knowledge a "sentimentalisme de la nature" vacillating "between Cartesian innateness and Lockean sensationalism" (Vardi 2012: 3). Similarly, for Gianni Vaggi: "Quesnay's methodology is an original mixture of rationalism and empiricism, and he was certainly influenced by authors like Locke and Descartes" (Vaggi 1987: 20). Vernard Foley also places Newton among the authors who influenced Quesnay's scientific method (Foley 1973: 145). The Newtonian influence on the Physiocratic movement was initially asserted by Mourant (1943). According to Thomas Neill: "in the Physiocrats [there are] mixed, but not integrated, elements of Cartesian rationalism, Lockean empiricism, Newtonian science and deistic optimism" (Neill, 1948: 153). Other commentators on Physiocracy have shown the close similarity between medieval economic thought and Quesnay's school, cf. Beer (1939), or the legacy of natural law, cf. Hasbach (1893).

[18] According to Karl Pribram, the Rationalist legacy revealed, on the political level, the conservative character of the Physiocratic School: "Cartesian philosophy provided a rallying point for more conservative minds and suggested a well-organized and clearly defined approach to the analysis of physical and social phenomena in terms of universally applicable principles. The Physiocratic doctrine was an outstanding achievement as an attempt to establish a generally valid system of social relationships in accordance with Cartesian philosophy" (Pribram 1983, p. 103; see also Laval-Reviglio 1987). "Rejecting Montesquieu's conception, after Quesnay, the Physiocrats defended legal despotism, a position that opened them to criticism in a world that was beginning to tire of full-blooded despotism" (Argemíd' Abadal 2012: 147).

to Physiocratic economic doctrine, based on the primacy of deductive methodology, in his *Dialogues* Galiani asserted, the realism of circumstance in economic science, as opposed to aprioristic axiomatic hypotheses and rationalist generalizations.[19]

Galiani's opposition to all kinds of hypostatization of concepts and apriorism, already clear in *Della Moneta*,[20] becomes the central nucleus of *Dialogues*. For this reason this work by Galiani represents an original methodological perspective, not a belated proposal of seventeenth-century mercantilist policies (as in Forbonnais's criticism; see Forbonnais 1767) and not even an anticipation of nineteenth-century protectionist theories.

According to Giorgio Tagliacozzo, a striking parallelism exists between Vico's attack on Cartesianism and Galiani's polemic against the Physiocrats, the representatives, in the field of economics, of the basic viewpoint of rationalism. As Vico was one of the first and most authoritative critics of Cartesianism, so Galiani was the first and the most forceful critic of abstract economic principles and metaphysical preconceptions (Tagliacozzo 1968: 109–110, see also Soliani and Clément 2018). This *Methodenstreit* is clearly expressed by Galiani in his well-known declaration of intents: "I'm for nothing. I'm for people not to reason falsely. The export of common sense is the only one which exasperates me" (Galiani 1770a: 12; Tagliacozzo 1968: 108). This statement echoes the Newtonian methodological maxim: *Hypotheses non fingo* (*I frame no hypotheses*, Newton 1713: 484; 1729, vol. II: 392). Galiani, in his criticism of Physiocracy, contrasts Newton to Descartes, claiming the realism of circumstance and aims for economic science as opposed to axiomatic hypotheses and metaphysical generalizations.

In line with Newtonian mathematical empiricism, Galiani proposes a limited formalization of economic laws, asserting the supremacy of historical and institutional contextualization over abstract theory (Einaudi 1949 [2014]: 237–238). In the field of economic analysis, Galiani, as a conscious follower of the Newtonian methodological lesson, proposes arguments based on real contents inserted in the historical context and rejects

[19] About Galiani's anti-Physiocrat dispute, see Gaudemet (1899); Koch (1961); Tagliacozzo (1968); Kaplan (1979, 2019a); Steegmuller (1988); Klotz (2000). Important exponents of French culture intervened against the Physiocrats; see Faccarello (1994).

[20] "Of the many errors by which our mind is beset and among which it perpetually wanders, very few would be left if it were possible to make people avoid those which stem from relative words taken in an absolute sense" (Galiani [1751]: 179; quoted in Tagliacozzo 1968: 103).

the apodictic truths of deductive methodology. According to this complex method, the appropriate measures of policy are not those resulting from abstract axioms but those that are more useful and more consistent with prudence and common sense. Galiani proposes a gradualist approach to policy making, rejecting the "shock therapy" proposed by the Physiocratic School and defining a conception of economic policy as a general art of government and as a component of political science.[21]

Under the influence of the Newtonian approach to scientific analysis, Galiani proposed a new paradigm for economic methodology, which can be called *Newtonian social mathematics* (Patalano 2020b). Despite the absence of systematic reasoning, Galiani's approach is an original contribution to the emerging connection between the evolution of economic knowledge and the rise of the scientific method.

Galiani's radical methodological opposition to Physiocratic theories could not go unnoticed and just a few days after publication, on 17 January 1770, before Galiani even received the book from Paris (in February 1770), the movement's journal, *Éphémérides du citoyen ou Bibliothèque raisonnée des sciences morales et politiques*,[22] directed by Pierre-Samuel Dupont de Nemours, launched a campaign against the *Dialogues*, revealing the identity of the author [called *L'Abbé G.*, a name that was also used by other critics of Galiani], whom the Neapolitan abbot had tried in vain to conceal under the name *Chevalier Zenobi*. A book that was described as "terrible, of which the *Philosophes*, friends of liberty, were strongly threatened for more than eight months, and of which we gave notice in May 1769" (Éphémérides 1769b: 197).[23]

The review (probably by Dupont de Nemours himself, Diaz 1975c: 348), captured all the antiphysiocratic arguments of the *Dialogues*, pointing out that: "This work is of no small importance, since it attempts nothing more than to establish that it is not the principles of natural law, nor the rules of justice that should decide on the administration of commerce; that regulations are preferable to freedom; that agriculture is not the source of wealth; that the science of government, instead of having large, simple and uniform principles, depends on a myriad of small notions as varied and multiplied as the smallest topographical details, and in the

[21] According to Filippo Cesarano (1999, p. xxxiii), Galiani's approach to economic policy anticipates the theory of Avinash Dixit (1996), who introduces a political dimension to the analysis. See also Cesarano (1986, 1995).

[22] On this journal, see Goutte (1994).

[23] See also Madame d'Épinay's letter to Ferdinando Galiani, Paris, 9 April 1770, published in d'Epinay and Galiani (1996: 76–77).

midst of which it would become impossible to distinguish an arbitrary operation from one founded on reason. So that the study of political economy would be no more than a means of varying in frivolous circles the conversations with which one seeks to escape boredom. If the Author is right, all the principles which we have hitherto expounded to our readers, which are the result of the meditations of the most enlightened citizens and philosophers, which have influenced legislation, which have gained the votes of the most illustrious societies and the most respectable magistrates, are nevertheless false and pernicious. The matter undoubtedly deserves to be clarified, and it will be" (Éphémérides 1769b: 194–196). And threatening further interventions: "We do not wish to deprive various writers whom we esteem of the honour and pleasure of convincing the author and bringing him back to the truth; but if others would not take the trouble, we would dare to offer him a complete, yet fairly brief refutation of his paradoxes, which are very long and very numerous" (Éphémérides 1769b: 196). After a brief review of the topics dealt with in the text, accompanied by less than flattering judgements,[24] the anonymous reviewer concluded with a personal attack, pitting Galiani against Cesare Beccaria: "*L'Abbé G.* therefore also neglected to educate himself, and in the law and the facts, and in the principles and consequences, and in the rules of mutual equity, and on the motives of well-understood interest. He thought he could remedy all this with indecent jokes. [...] Oh, that this is not the way in which his compatriot, Marquis de Beccaria, treats matters that can influence the happiness of mankind. On every page of the illustrious author of *Dei delitti e delle Pene* [*Crimes and Punishments*], we see that he seeks the truth in good faith; his soul speaks to all sensible lovers, and he speaks their language; we recognise that he is a man, and a good man at that. But it is impossible to guess what is hidden behind the mask with which *l'Abbé G.* likes to cover himself, and if it were possible to guess something by seeing the spectacle he tries to put on" (Éphémérides 1769b: 245–246).[25]

[24] "It is a delightful work, containing the world's most beautiful laughter, one or two very pleasant short stories, a few bedtime stories, a large number of jokes and quips, a great deal of affected and perhaps even more real incorrectness; some very noble pieces of poetry, some very big and very beautiful ideas; and then the perpetual pretence of treating serious topics frivolously and discussing the most interesting topics without caring about them" (Éphémérides 1769b: 246).

[25] The opinion of a significant exponent of the *Milanese School*, Alessandro Verri, was not very positive: "This man is a singular spirit, a composite of excellent *bons mots*, much grace, much comedy, infinite wit, but, in the end, without logic. And such a bizarre intellect, that I

The line taken by the physiocratic organ aimed to diminish the scientific value of the *Dialogues* by ridiculing the author's theses. A few weeks later, in February 1770, a new article in the *Éphémérides*, again signed anonymously by *Monsieur T.*, proposed another radical criticism: "[the fundamental principles], which are the only ones on the subject in question and which have been set out and developed these 14 years since in the sixth and seventh volumes of the *Encyclopédie*, under the entries *Farmers* and *Grains*, were undoubtedly sufficient to prevent educated men from considering *L'Abbé G.*'s book as a good work on the subject" (Éphémérides 1769c: 101–102).

The attack became more intense with the direct intervention, in the same volume of the *Éphémérides*, by one of the most prominent physiocratic exponents, Abbé Nicolas Baudeau, who, with his *Lettres sur les Dialogues anti-Économistes* (but only one was published, and later reprinted in Baudeau 1770), promised a pointed refutation of Galiani's theses (Baudeau 1769: 108–128), which still ended in personal attacks: "Where would be the fault, if by chance the wise and humane public did not take your Chevalier, half jester and half politician, for a philosopher who babbles, or for a statesman who confides, or for a good man who pleads the

could not define him. Now he has printed these dialogues, equally indefinable, except perhaps to say something excellent that Voltaire said, namely that they seemed to him to have been composed by Plato and Molière together. If you will read them, you will find that Voltaire says, in his usual way, that they are written in Plato's amiable and elegant manner of dialogue, and in the buffoonery of a comedian. I am not persuaded by what he says on the subject, but it is a reading that amuses me because of the gracefulness with which it is written: and what pleases me most, is to see the current tone of Paris painted in real life. The book has made a sensation; Morellet writes against it; indeed, there have been spicy letters between him and the author. Diderot is a bitter partisan of Galiani, and esteems his book highly. The French, whom I know here, cannot suffer him; not so much, I believe, for the cause of truth, as for the ridicule he gives to their tone, on which they have incredible claims. [...]. Most of the book is digression; it is, in short, a farce by a man of wit about the *Annona*" (Alessandro Verri's letter to Pietro Verri, Rome, 4 July 1770, published in Verri and Verri 1911: 373–374). And a few days later: "Having progressed further in Abbot Galiani's dialogues, I was disgusted. In the first few I was pleased by the oddity of it, but, then, he seems to me to be a complete fool and a perfect sophist: Zeno would have written so. To praise, or rather to admire himself, as he continually does, is a most disgusting thing; and if you take away the witty and some of the cheeky traits, there remains on the grains nothing but a skeleton of paralogisms. I make this protest to you, lest, if you ever read it, you lose my credit. The same abbot is also the author of a book on money that he printed some time ago" (Alessandro Verri's letter to Pietro Verri, Rome: 7 July 1770, published in Verri and Verri 1911: 378–379). See also Galiani (1959: 380–381).

cause of the poor people; but for an Abbé, who puts all his pleasure and glory in making them laugh and in mocking them? This glory is little, Monsieur l'Abbé" (Baudeau 1769: 119). And still along the same lines, the two letters by Abbé Pierre-Joseph-André Roubaud (1769: 179–216),[26] which were followed by six more letters, each devoted to a dialogue, collected in another volume (Roubaud 1770). The critical review of the *Éphémérides* was closed by Dupont de Nemours' contribution, which again extolled the *commedia dell'arte* character of the *Dialogues*[27] and announced, in a polemical escalation, Pierre-Paul-Henri Le Mercier de La Rivière's descent into the quarrel with his *L'intéret général de l'État* (Le Mercier de La Rivière 1770).

From Naples, Galiani, informed by Madame d'Épinay, followed the "stir"[28] (*bruit*) caused by his *Dialogues* and the evolution of the controversy with his usual irony, declaring himself ready to respond to criticism.[29] In particular, he was anxiously looking forward to the opinion of Voltaire and Turgot (of whom he had great esteem).[30] Voltaire judged the *Dialogues* very flatteringly: "As for the author, I can't recognise him, because as far as I know no one has written on this subject in France. This book is going to make me lose my sight. It seems to me that Plato and Molière got together to write this book".[31]

[26] "If, for example, you were to examine page by page the works of *Économistes* you oppose and do not know, would you not find at least a small apparent contradiction?" (Roubaud 1769:189–190).

[27] "In general, it is good to laugh, no doubt: but to laugh at the expense of people whose bread and freedom have been taken away would be a very cruel act" (Dupont de Nemours 1770a: 28). See also Dupont de Nemours (1770a).

[28] Ferdinando Galiani's letter to Madame d'Épinay, Naples, 3 February 1770, published in Galiani (1881a, vol I: 64); Galiani and d'Épinay (1992, vol. I: 113).

[29] "I have accepted criticism and even insults, so send me any that should be published. Should the insults be too violent, I will reply to the gentlemen farmers with a pamphlet depicting the God of gardens (by Horace), once a fig tree, now the God of *Économistes*, with the caption, *quantum vesica pepedi* [with as great an explosion as a burst bladder]" (Ferdinando Galiani's letter to Madame d'Épinay, Naples, 3 March 1770, published in Galiani 1881a, vol I: 81; Galiani and d'Épinay 1992, vol. I: 123).

[30] Ferdinando Galiani's letter to Madame d'Épinay, Naples, 27 January 1770, published in Galiani (1881a, vol I: 58); Galiani and d'Épinay (1992, vol. I: 111) (on Voltaire, see Pomeau 1975); Ferdinando Galiani's letter to Madame d'Épinay, Naples, 7 April 1770, published in Galiani (1881a, vol I: 100); Galiani and d'Épinay (1992, vol. I: 136) (on Turgot).

[31] Voltaire's letter to Denis Diderot, 10 January 1770, published in Galiani (1959: 373). See also Madame d'Épinay's letter to Ferdinando Galiani, Paris, 27 May 1770, published in Galiani (1959: 374) (Galiani and d'Épinay 1992, vol. I: 176) and Madame d'Épinay's letter

Not of the same tenor was Turgot's judgement, who wrote to Morellet as follows: "You are very severe, this is not a book that can be called bad, even if it supports a very bad cause; but it cannot be supported with more wit, more grace, more skill, more good jokes, more finesse even, and more discussion of details. Such a book, written with this elegance, this lightness of tone, this correctness and originality of expression, and by a foreigner, is perhaps a unique phenomenon. The work is very entertaining; and unfortunately it will be very difficult to respond in such a way as to dispel the seduction of what is specious in reasoning and piquant in form. I wish I had time, but I don't, and neither do you. Dupont is absorbed in his travels; Abbé Beaudeau will answer too much as an *économiste*, etc.".[32] And again in a letter to Madame de Lespinasse he gave an even harsher judgement: "The Abbé Galiani, beginning in Geneva to treat the question of free trade in grain, resembles one who, writing a book on the means employed by men to procure their livelihood, would make his first chapter on legless donkeys; or like a geometer who, treating the properties of triangles, would begin with white triangles as the simplest, and then treat blue triangles, then red triangles, and so on. I will also say, in general, that he who does not forget that there are political states separate from one another and constituted in different ways, will never deal well with any question of political economy. Nor do I like to see him always so cautious, so hostile to enthusiasms, so in agreement with all the *ne quid nimis*, and with all those people who enjoy the present and are quite happy to let the world go on as it is, because it is very good for them [...]. Oh, all these people must not like enthusiasm, and must call enthusiasm everything that attacks the infallibility of those in power, the admirable dogma of the Abbé, the policy of Pangloss, which he extends to all places and all times; I think I can give him a very good answer, but it requires a lot of art. *Économistes* are too self-confident to fight against a skilful *ferrailleur*".[33]

to Ferdinando Galiani, Paris, 29 October 1770, published in Galiani (1959: 375) (Galiani and d'Épinay 1992, vol. I: 283). See also in Voltaire's *Philosophical Dictionary* the item "Blé ou Bled" (Galiani 1959: 375–376).

[32] Anne Robert Jacques Turgot's letter to André Morellet, Paris, 19 January 1770, published in Morellet (1822: 193), see also Galiani (1959: 378–379).

[33] Anne Robert Jacques Turgot's letter to André Morellet, Paris, 19 January 1770, published in Morellet (1822: 194–195), see also Galiani (1959: 379–380). Madame d'Épinay reported a more positive opinion to Galiani: "I forgot to tell you Turgot's opinion: *Here is a terrible book*, he wrote to me, *who tries to refute it will break his nose and it will be refutations that no one will read. The book will have the fortune of the Spirit of the Laws*" (Madame

Positive judgements were obviously expressed by his friends who shared his criticism of Physiocracy, in particular Grimm (1829: 278–280).[34] And the *Dialogues* attracted the attention of the Empress of Russia, Catherine II (Galiani 1959: 383–387), the King of Prussia, Frederick II, and a few other crowned heads (Charles William Ferdinand of Brunswick-Wolfenbüttel, see Galiani 1959: 386) and courts of Europe, that of Madrid, in particular, to which is owed the Spanish translation of 1775 (Galiani 1775),[35] which was followed by several German translations (Galiani 1777, 1778 see Nicolini 1909a: 408; Braeuer 1975; Bernardini 2000; Reinert 2011a)[36] and a Russian translation made by Pierre Cuvilles at the initiative of the Imperial Academy of Sciences in Saint Petersburg (Galiani 1776; Gambacorta 1988: 336).

But his attention and expectations were mainly focused on the announced reply by Abbot André Morellet and so he wrote about it: "I should have guessed he would digress economically in the dictionary he is about to make, for the reason that d'Invaux paid him. I am wrong; but whatever he does, I will always love him, in spite of his answers, his retorts and his new rural physiognomy"[37] and "I am not surprised by Panurge's

d'Épinay's letter to Ferdinando Galiani, Aux Ternes, 18 March 1770, published in D'Epinay and Galiani 1996: 69; Galiani and d'Épinay 1992, vol. I: 128–129. Italic added). Galiani's reply was enthusiastic: "I am delighted with Turgot's judgment; my heart had sensed it. I had the highest regard for his excellent judgement, and I would always have bet that he would have enjoyed the *Dialogues*" (Ferdinando Galiani's letter to Madame d'Épinay, Naples, 7 April 1770, published in Galiani 1881a, vol. I: 100; Galiani and d'Épinay 1992, vol. I: 136).

[34] A positive review appeared in *Année Littéraire*, edited by Elia Fréron, see Madame d'Épinay's letter to Ferdinando Galiani's, Paris, 24 June 1770, published in Galiani (1959: 381) (Galiani and d'Épinay 1992, vol. I: 192); Ferdinando Galiani's letter to Madame d'Épinay, Naples, 14 July 1770, published in Galiani (1881a, vol I: 195–196) (Galiani and d'Épinay 1992, vol. I: 207); Ferdinando Galiani's letter to Madame d'Épinay, Naples, 27 July 1770, published in Galiani (1881a, vol I: 209–210) (Galiani and d'Épinay 1992, vol. I: 221).

[35] See Galiani (1959: 390–395); Astigarraga (2018).

[36] "The first German translation of the *Dialogues*, published in Paris in 1770 under the false indication of London, was by Barckhausen, one of the greatest connoisseurs and disseminators of Galiani's work in Germany at the time. It was published in Lemgo by Meyer, one of the publishers, however provincial, most closely associated with the *Aufklärung*, in 1777. Others followed: one the following year, without the translator's name, under the title *Handlung-Gespräch*; another in 1784, and a fourth in 1802" (Bernardini 2000: 4).

[37] Ferdinando Galiani's letter to Madame d'Épinay, Naples, 24 February 1770, published in Galiani (1881a, vol I: 73); Galiani and d'Épinay (1992, vol. I: 119–120).

[Morellet][38] contradictions.[39] He is a man with his heart in his head and his head in his heart. He reasons from passion and acts from principle. That is why I love him with all my heart, even if I reason differently, and he also loves me madly, even if he thinks I am *Machiavellino*. Moreover, I think that his heart, which is the most virtuous and the most beautiful in the world, will guide his head, and that he will end up not responding and loving me more. He will realise on the second or third reading of the work that Chevalier Zanobi does not believe or think a word of what he says; that he is the world's greatest sceptic and the world's greatest academic; that he believes nothing, in nothing, about nothing. [...] We are waiting to see how long Paris will continue not to listen to me and to warm up to an interminable question. Only Grimm had listened to me first, and had guessed that the book would remain without a conclusion: a conclusion had to be added, thanks to the Parisian viewers, who love to conclude. After all, the book is really a philosopher's book, and it alone is capable of forming a philosopher and a statesman; that is to say, a man who has the key to the mystery, and who knows that everything can be reduced to *zero*. Abbé Raynal is quite right to say that the work is deep. It is devilishly deep because it is hollow, and there is nothing underneath. Those who have said that the principles are too scattered have given the highest praise to the dialogue; but the style of dialogues is almost unknown in Paris. Those who take the trouble to link my ideas will perhaps guess the aim of the work".[40]

Morellet was a close friend of Galiani. He met him in Naples in 1758, when the French abbot was tutor to the son of the Marquis of Chaumont de la Galaizière, Chancellor of Lorraine, then a possession of the King of Poland, Stanislas Leszczyński. Morellet introduced Galiani in Parisian salons, particularly that of d'Holbach (Galiani 1959: 463, Nicolini's notes).[41] Morellet translated Beccaria's *Dei delitti e delle Pene* into French

[38] On the various names attributed to Morellet by Galiani and d'Épinay, see Galiani (1959: 465), Nicolini's note.

[39] "I repeat, Morellet was against free trade, I can prove it. I do not know if he knew it in the secret of his heart. It may have happened to him, like the prophet Balaam, who wanted to curse and bless; but it is a fact. This time the abbot was *Machiavellino*" (Ferdinando Galiani's letter to Madame d'Épinay, Naples, 5 May 1770, published in Galiani 1881a, vol I: 138–139; Galiani and d'Épinay 1992, vol. I: 161).

[40] Ferdinando Galiani's letter to Madame d'Épinay, Naples, 27 January 1770, published in Galiani (1881a, vol I: 56–58); Galiani and d'Épinay (1992, vol. I: 11–112).

[41] On Morellet's biography see Di Rienzo (1994).

(Morellet and Beccaria 1766) and may have attempted to translate *Della Moneta*.[42] A few months earlier, Morellet had polemicized with Jacques Necker over the policy towards the *Compagnie des Indes*, whose dissolution he proposed, opposing those who, like the Geneva banker, defended the legitimacy of the privileges attributed to the *Compagnie* (see Morellet 1769a; Necker 1769).[43] Madame d'Épinay had solicited Galiani's interest in the subject,[44] but the Neapolitan climate was not conducive to this new engagement.[45]

Morellet's intervention had been urged (and paid for) by the *Intendant des finances* Jean Charles Philibert Trudaine de Montigny, who was related to the *Contrôleur Général des Finances*, Étienne Maynon d'Invault, who had attempted to impede the publication of the *Dialogues*.[46] Galiani was aware of this "political interest": "They wrote to me that Abbé Morellet had received orders from the government to confute my *Dialogues*. So

[42] There is no trace of this translation, Galiani however mentions it in a letter to Morellet, which has been lost, and which the French abbot himself transcribes in a reply (André Morellet's letter to Ferdinando Galiani, Paris, 1 May 1770, published in Galiani 1959: 478).

[43] Madame d'Épinay reported the controversy to Galiani: "The poor man [Morellet] got himself into trouble with his *Mémoire* on the *Compagnie des Indes*. Necker's *Mémoire* is a masterpiece" (Madame d'Épinay's letter to Ferdinando Galiani, Paris, 18 September 1769, published in Galiani and d'Épinay 1992, vol. I: 73). See also the correspondence between Galiani and d'Holbach in the letters to the Neapolitan abbot of August and September 1769, see Nicolini (1929: 189, 193).

[44] Madame d'Épinay's letter to Ferdinando Galiani, Paris, 29 September 1769, published in Galiani and d'Épinay (1992, vol. I: 79). Galiani replied "I realise that I have an obligation to return to Paris, to write a booklet that will put an end to this affair, since to tell the truth, these are people who do not know how to make a count" (Ferdinando Galiani' letter to Madame d'Épinay, Genoa, 2 October 1769, published in Galiani 1881a, vol I: 32; Galiani and d'Épinay 1992, vol. I: 87).

[45] "If you do not restore my good humour, I will write to no one [...] and you want me to write about the East India Company! *I nunc et versus tecum meditare canoros* [*Go now, and meditate thy tuneful lays*]" (Ferdinando Galiani' letter to Madame d'Épinay, Naples, 18 December 1769, published in Galiani 1881a, vol I: 50–51; Galiani and d'Épinay 1992, vol. I: 104–105).

[46] In his *Mémoires*, Morellet admitted the contractual relationship that linked him to Trudaine: "The Minister of Finance, who paid me, naturally had to dispose of my time when he needed it. Trudaine de Montigny had the same right in his position as *Intendent des Finances et du Commerce*, and above all as my benefactor" (Morellet 1822, vol. I: 191). And "[The] *Réfutation des Dialogues de l'abbé Galliani sur le commerce des blés*, [was] made at the invitation of Trudaine de Montigny, to support the reasonable opinions of the ministry, and in particular of Duc de Choiseul, in favour of free trade" (Morellet 1822, vol. I: 192). On Morellet's defense of Physiocratie, see Kaplan (2019b).

they have declared him the guardian and gendarme of the *Économistes*? Is he under orders to hunt down us unfortunate little smugglers of rural philosophy? Patience! We will recommend our legs to save us. As for me, I galloped all the way to Naples and I think I am safe here".[47]

Galiani had also written to Morellet in a kind of open letter, using Baron d'Holbach as an intermediary,[48] but the text has been lost (Morellet did not divulge it) and its content must not have been particularly benevolent if the Neapolitan abbot made it clear to Madame d'Épinay: "I would prefer that no copies of the letter I wrote to Abbé Panurge be circulated. It is not devout enough for a letter written on Passion Saturday. Apart from that, I do not repudiate it".[49]

Morellet (classed as a "bad moralist" and "very bad economist" by Galiani[50]) replied with a long letter in which he responded to the irony of Galiani who had called his interest in the *Dialogues* an amusement: "I only want to defend a cause that I believe to be that of truth and public utility"[51] and associated Galiani with Necker because they both fought free trade.[52]

[47] Ferdinando Galiani's letter to Madame d'Épinay, Naples, 31 March 1770, published in Galiani (1881a, vol I: 90–91); Galiani and d'Épinay (1992, vol. I: 130–131).

[48] "I am sending you Abbé Morellet's open letter, and you will see that it is not meant to be read by everyone. The *Pusillus grex electorum* [*A small cohort of the elect*] must read it. No one must make a copy. Remember the place I occupy and the country I live in. Moreover, I don't think Abbé Morellet can change his mind about me. So I can rest assured" (Ferdinando Galiani's letter to Baron d'Holbach, Naples, 7 April 1770, published in Galiani 1881a, vol I: 92–93).

[49] Ferdinando Galiani's letter to Madame d'Épinay, Naples, 7 April 1770, published in Galiani (1881a, vol I: 97); Galiani and d'Épinay (1992, vol. I: 134). "Panurge had read your letter to d'Alembert and Lespinasse. Both said that nothing has ever come close to your letter in terms of finesse, grace and beauty from the pen of Voltaire or Montesquieu. He also wanted to read his reply, which to them, however, seemed deadly dull" (Madame d'Épinay's letter to Ferdinando Galiani, Paris, 7 May 1770, published in Galiani and d'Épinay 1992, vol. I: 163; d'Epinay and Galiani 1996: 100). Some passages from Galiani's letter are quoted in the reply that Morellet sent him (André Morellet's letter to Ferdinando Galiani, Paris, 1 May 1770, published in Galiani 1959: 473–486). The entire correspondence on the quarrel between Morellet and Galiani is published in Appendix Nine to the *Dialogues* of Nicolini's edition (see Galiani 1959: 463–717).

[50] Ferdinando Galiani's letter to Madame d'Épinay, Naples, 9 February 1771, published in Galiani (1881a, vol I: 355); Galiani and d'Épinay (1993, vol. II: 50).

[51] André Morellet's letter to Ferdinando Galiani, Paris, 1 May 1770, published in Galiani (1959: 474).

[52] Galiani admired Necker: "I am waiting for Necker's book, which I will read because it is easy to read and, above all, it is easy to understand. For political economy, Necker is like Bernoulli who surpassed even Newton in the elegance, clarity and brevity of his demonstra-

The French abbot then pointed out the contradiction between *Della Moneta*, in which he had supported the primacy of agriculture, and the *Dialogues* in which he had denied it.[53]

Morellet's response was deemed disappointing by Galiani,[54] who again attacked the Physiocrats in his reply: "I am for, not against, like the *Chevalier Zanobi*. Yes, I am in favour, and my whole book is in favour. But I am in favour without fanaticism, because fanaticism, or enthusiasm, has never seemed to me to be useful for anything except stirring up a revolt. That is the only difference between me and the *Économistes*, between their principles and mine. [...]. Finally, my dear Abbé, I await your book with the greatest impatience, to see myself vindicated in the eyes of France and cleansed of the infamy and nonsense that economists have spewed against me. These *Économistes* are furious, not because I have not adopted their principles, but because I have not adopted their style".[55]

Meanwhile, the group of *Encyclopédistes* hostile to the Physiocrats had organised themselves to block Morellet's criticism; a sign that the *Dialogues* had become an element in the political struggle between factions at court. It was once again Louise d'Épinay who informed Galiani: "Your friend [de Sartine] did not want Panurge's refutation to be published without a couple of censors being appointed. To fill one of these posts he chose the

tions. That is what I admire most about him" (Ferdinando Galiani's letter to Madame d'Épinay, Naples, 10 June 1775, published in Galiani 1881a, vol II: 412–413; Galiani and d'Épinay 1997, vol. V: 36). See also Ferdinando Galiani's letter to Madame d'Épinay, Naples, 22 July 1780, published in Galiani (1881a, vol II: 590–591); Galiani and d'Épinay (1997, vol. V: 224).

[53] "I do not know if you know of a way to reconcile such opposing principles; but until you give me an explanation, you will agree that I may have believed that the two works in which I make these statements are not based on the same principles, and that I may have fought the one with the other in mind" (André Morellet's letter to Ferdinando Galiani, Paris, 1 May 1770, published in Galiani 1959: 480). The concept was reiterated in the *Réfutation* (see Morellet 1774: 64–65).

[54] "I was expecting your reply this week. In the dispatch from the Minister of France I received a large parcel, the envelope of which, in an unknown handwriting, sealed with I don't know which stamp, contains a kind of letter, eight fat pages without a signature, in an unknown hand, and in which I see that they want me to believe that it is you who are writing to me; but neither the tone, nor the style, nor the thoughts, nor anything else resembles you" (Ferdinando Galiani's letter to André Morellet, Naples, 26 May 1770, published in Galiani 1881a: 152–153). The letter is also published in Galiani (1975: 1028–1034).

[55] Ferdinando Galiani's letter to André Morellet, Naples, 26 May 1770, published in Galiani (1881a: 158).

philosopher [Diderot], which seems to me extremely good"[56] and attached to the letter Diderot's report, which, although in favour of publication, gave a very negative opinion of it.[57]

At the beginning of April, as Madame d'Épinay announced to Galiani, Morellet's *Réfutation de l'ouvrage qui a pour titre Dialogues sur le Commerce des Bleds* (*Refutation of the work entitled Dialogues on the Grain Trade*) was ready for printing,[58] but Abbot Terray blocked its publication (Morellet, 1774: 7): the antiphysiocratic party was prevailing in French politics.[59] The *Réfutation* was published in November 1774,[60] when the balance of political power was again tilting in favour of the liberalists and Turgot had taken over the post of *Contrôleur Général,* instead of Terray, and by decree of the *Conseil du Roi* in September 1774 had restored free grain trade.[61]

[56] Madame d'Épinay's letter to Ferdinando Galiani, Paris, 18 March 1770, published in Galiani (1959: 467–468); Galiani and d'Épinay (1992, vol. I: 127).

[57] Diderot's report is published in Galiani (1959: 468–470). See Denis Diderot's letter to Antoine de Sartine, Paris, 10 March 1770, published in Diderot (1955, vol. X: 32–35).

[58] Madame d'Épinay's letter to Ferdinando Galiani, Paris, 9 April 1770, published in Galiani and d'Épinay (1992, vol. I: 137); D'Epinay and Galiani (1996: 77).

[59] "I have just found out that Panurge, after the letter you wrote to him, is convinced that you have received news of his book, and believes that this can only have happened because de Sartine gave it to me to read and I sent it to you" (Madame d'Épinay's letter to Ferdinando Galiani, Paris, 7 May 1770, published in Galiani and d'Épinay 1992, vol. I: 163; D'Epinay and Galiani 1996: 100).

[60] Galiani judged Morellet's book with cutting irony: "I opened Morellet's book, yawned and it fell out of my hands. As much as I want to read it, I feel that it is beyond my strength. I also feel that it would be impossible for me to refute it. It is so long! And it seems to me that it is a prestigious work, because every piece, every line, every syllogism in the book is well written, clear and right, and yet the whole thing is flat, obscure and false" (Ferdinando Galiani's letter to Madame d'Épinay, Naples, 3 June 1775, published in Galiani 1881a, vol II: 408–409; Galiani and d'Épinay 1997, vol. V: 31–32).

[61] Galiani's comments on Turgot were sarcastic, see Ferdinando Galiani's letter to Madame d'Épinay, Naples, 17 September 1774, published in Galiani (1881a, vol II: 345–346); Galiani and d'Épinay (1996, vol. IV: 183). And: "I knew of Turgot's hatred for my *Dialogues*; they will become even more hateful to him once this damned export has brought him down; wait" (Ferdinando Galiani's letter to Madame d'Épinay, Naples, 24 September 1774, published in Galiani 1881a, vol II: 347–348; Galiani and d'Épinay 1996, vol. IV: 186). And with malice: "I receive compliments from all sides, from Italy, Germany, etc., on the fact that it is believed that Turgot drew all the principles of his edict from my book, and that he adopted the whole system from it, in order to favour internal circulation, and to concern himself only with that? Please tell Morellet what I tell you, which is very true, and watch him die of pain" (Ferdinando Galiani's letter to Madame d'Épinay, Naples, 24 December 1774, published in Galiani 1881a, vol II: 373; Galiani and d'Épinay 1996, vol. IV: 210).

The *Réfutation* represented the most systematic attack on the *Dialogues*. Morellet's first objection was methodological and was summed up in the all-out defence of the primacy of deductivism over the empirical approach of the *Dialogues* (Morellet, 1774: 28–29). For Morellet, the empirical datum was misleading if one neglected to trace it back to the theoretical principle of individual interest: the effectiveness of a regulatory system was thus not based, as Galiani claimed, on particular circumstances, but on respect for the fundamental principle of individual interest as the cause of economic action.[62]

Morellet confirmed his doctrinaire approach: "Despite customs, character, and political relations, the causes that influence the production of grain and the reasons that determine the trade of this product are the same everywhere and require the same administration everywhere. The same applies to differences in soil, climate and production. If the soil is fertile for grain, if the climate is favourable for its cultivation, if the harvests are abundant, trade must be free; and if these circumstances are not favourable, trade must still be free, and man's industry will triumph over the demands of nature. In a word, whether there be little or much grain, this difference can never authorise the enactment of laws contrary to the right which every Proprietor must have, to use his land and the crops it produces as he pleases" (Morellet 1774: 49–50).

Morellet thus rejected the subtle distinctions that Galiani proposed between large and small sovereignties and between fertile and sterile countries, to reaffirm that the principle of free trade was valid *sub specie aeternitatis*, under all circumstances, since the foundation of any economic policy was only in the protection of private property rights (Morellet 1774: ch. 2, 3, 4). Differences in prices, the effect of different needs, moved goods between states and between the provinces of the same country (Morellet 1774: 255). If grain as a result of free trade escaped from the state, it was only because there was a relative advantage of price, not of geographical distance, which had to be bridged by the quantity exported.

[62] "The seller's interest, the price, thus becomes the true and only principle of the movement of grain. The construction of a road, of a canal, of structures, gives the grain the opportunity to move; but if we want to speak accurately, we must say that these are not the causes of the movement. The grain only starts when the foreigner makes a better price than the citizen and pays all the costs, risks and wages of the trader. These conditions, taken together, will be the cause of the grain leaving, and not the construction of the canal, which is only the means" (Morellet 1774: 35).

Morellet's arguments are based on the hypostatisation of abstract categories, such as property and individual interest: "The mere use of property can never be contrary to the general interest. On the contrary, the general interest is that every citizen should make the most varied, the most extensive, the most unlimited use of property, as long as it is limited to one thing and one person; it is from this activity and this freedom of each individual that the general good derives" (Morellet 1774: 109). When entering the economic field, Morellet attempted to refute the distinction between exclusively manufacturing countries and exclusively agricultural countries, considering it without a solid theoretical foundation and being only the result of legal prohibitions or popular mentality (Morellet 1774: 115). In his critique, Morellet completely ignored the assumption of Galiani's analysis that grain was a *sui generis* commodity, the central argument around which his policy proposal was built, focusing instead on refuting the thesis of the supremacy of the industrial sector over the agricultural sector.[63] On the argument of the opposing productivity of the agricultural and industrial sectors, Morellet counters with the concept of capitalist intensity of production processes. This is the only analytical argument of any substance that Morellet uses in objecting to Galiani: "The commodities trade and the manufacturing trade do not increase or decrease as a result of manpower, but as a result of the capital employed in exploiting the soil and in manufacturing; it is the large amount of capital applied that makes manpower work, and manpower can do nothing without capital" (Morellet 1774: 212). Given the non-existence of diminishing returns, there was no incompatibility between one and the other, but an agricultural country could accommodate any kind of industry and the circulation of wealth was only based on agricultural development (Morellet 1774: 214–216).

In the heart of Enlightenment Paris, an epistemological clash among the *Encyclopédistes* themselves was occurring around Galiani's *Dialogues* and the physiocratic doctrine: Diderot, who had been the censor of the *Réfutation*, wrote, in the last months of 1770, a reply against Morellet

[63] "All the wealth that exists in the Universe owes its existence to the cultivation of the soil. Without cultivation, they would not exist. If cultivation ceased, or if the earth were suddenly struck with sterility, the wealth that exists in the world today would be destroyed in a short time by use and consumption, and man, no longer able to bring it back from the soil through cultivation, would fall into a misery that would soon destroy the species" (Morellet 1774: 184).

that was not printed and was only published in 1963 under the title *Apologie de l'abbé Galiani* (Diderot 1770 [1963], see Kaplan 2019c).

"All that is found in the Économistes", wrote Diderot, "is well used against Abbot Galiani. [*La Réfutation*] is the work of a man of common sense, whereas the work of Abbot Galiani is that of a man of genius. Everything he says, good or bad, false or true, belongs to him. There is not a word in the other work that is the author's own. Only Abbot Galiani could have produced his book; anyone could have done Morellet's *Réfutation*" (Diderot 1770 [1963]: 73).

While Morellet's book was blocked, Galiani's anti-physiocratic polemic found new vigour in the massacre that took place in Paris on 30 May 1770, the day of the wedding between the *Dauphin* and Marie Antoinette, when many people were crushed in the throngs of the crowd attracted by the fireworks display set up for the occasion (Kaplan 1979: 6–10).[64] Madame d'Épinay informed Galiani a few days after the tragedy[65] and the abbot responded by attacking the *Économistes*: "The disaster of Paris, and the horrible massacre of the rue St. Honore made me shudder [...] Madame, I accuse the *Économistes.* They have preached property and liberty with such insistence, they have worked so hard at undermining the police, [public] order, the regulations; they have said so often that nature left to itself was so beautiful, functioned so well, put itself in equilibrium, etc., that finally, sure of their ownership of the street and of their liberty to walk, everyone wanted to profit from this. There is the beautiful fruit of their long sermon. The truth is, if [I] were [today] in Paris, and if [I] had my usual verve, this event alone would be enough for me to reply to the

[64] "The official list of the dead counted 132 names, though it is not clear if this included persons who subsequently died of wounds incurred on 30 May" (Kaplan 1979: 9). But "news of the disaster travelled with stunning rapidity, along with extravagant estimates of the number of victims. The *Correspondance litteraire* spread the word that "nearly a thousand" died. Simeon-Prosper Hardy, a Parisian bookdealer and diarist, heard several tabulations ranging from 367 to 1200. In one place Mercier gauged the casualties at 1800 and in another at 1200. A memoir attributed to the chiefs of the Guet claimed 600 fatalities, the same number fixed upon by the comte de Segur who had been on the scene. Another spectator wrote to a friend that 300 persons perished in the tumult. Baron d'Holbach, an eyewitness who had had to fight vigorously to escape with his life, reckoned the death toll at 200. His friend and fellow salonkeeper, Madame d'Épinay, informed her correspondents that 680 people died in the crushing on the street and another 200 drowned in the Seine where the furious momentum of the crowd had propelled them" (Kaplan 1979: 8).

[65] Madame d'Épinay's letter to Ferdinando Galiani, Paris, 1–3 June 1770, published in Galiani and d'Épinay (1992, vol. I: 180–181); d'Épinay and Galiani (1996: 113–114).

Économistes. I would make them understand that it is sufficient to spread the rumor that there will be total liberty in one place, and consequently a huge crowd, for the pickpockets, great monopolists in watches and snuff-boxes, to awaken instantaneously and conceive a scheme to capitalize upon the brawl [*bagarre*]. What I tell you is not a joke. Think about it, and you will discover the exactitude of the comparison".[66]

The fresh controversy was encouraged by the news from France announcing a new famine. Madame d'Épinay informed him in detail about grain price increases in the various French cities and the abbot wrote: "Due to a sort of foreboding, I have had it in mind for some time that, this very year, my *Dialogues* will produce the effect of having the Edict revoked, because there will be in France the famine that I predicted and foretold. This week, by chance, I came across an article in the Paris *Gazette* which seems to me to have been inserted specifically to calm the fears of certain provinces, because it announces with a kind of euphoria the arrival of a convoy of grain at Nantes. I ask you to inform me in detail about this, and about the price of the wheat that will go to Paris. Because, as men always judge by events, if wheat is expensive in Paris, I will be right, I will be a great man, a great politician, and Panurge and Pangloss will be fools. The price markets (halles) will be the thermometer of my praise".[67] As the famine intensified, Galiani raised the polemical tone even further: "What you tell me about the Ministry's orders to continue to speak well of my book and to attack *Économistes* does not surprise me. I have always been convinced that, sooner or later, the Ministry would realise the service I have rendered it by devoting myself, against a band of impudent and dishonest fanatics, to unmasking them and uncovering their foolish ambition and seditious opinions [...] I believe that the *Économistes* should already be content with having made the French miss out on bread without also

[66] Ferdinando Galiani's letter to Madame d'Épinay, Naples, 23 June 1770, published in Galiani (1881a, vol I: 175–176); Galiani and d'Épinay (1992, vol. I: 191–192) (English translation by Steven Laurence Kaplan, see Kaplan 1979: 23). However, Galiani was not interested in price movements: "I just want to know from one month to the next, in general, the state of shortage or abundance of food in Paris and the provinces; and I also want to know, in general, whether we are exporting, importing or transporting, and whether we are bearing, and to whom we are reporting the cause of the disgrace - that's all. Your economic tables make me queasy and take away a precious half-page" (Ferdinando Galiani's letter to Madame d'Épinay, Naples, 21 July 1770, published in Galiani 1881a, vol I: 205: Galiani and d'Épinay 1992, vol. I: 212).

[67] Ferdinando Galiani's letter to Madame d'Épinay, Naples, 9 June 1770, published in Galiani (1881a, vol I: 172–173); Galiani and d'Épinay (1992, vol. I: 186).

aiming to make a nation that is polite and lovable more than any other lose its morals and decency".[68] He was also irritated by yet another pamphlet written against him, this time in the form of a satire, by another exponent of physiocracy, Abbot Pierre-Joseph-André Roubaud: "I received the books […] I have already devoured them and read everything that was thrown up at me. This reading consoled me about losing a tooth while I was in the middle of a letter from Abbé *Ribaud* [Roubaud].[69] In all conscience, my beautiful Dame, they are too stupid; it is absolutely impossible to answer them a single line. The effrontery with which they make me say all the nonsense imaginable, even quoting pages from my book, would deserve to be taken to the police; and if I had been in Paris, I would have enjoyed suing them in Parliament for damages […]. I have nothing to answer and I am right. If there is a shortage in France, they will talk about wheat again and do me justice".[70] But a few days later, Galiani called for political intervention over the calumnies uttered by Abbot Roubaud: "Have you read the *Récréations économiques*? Read the sixth or seventh letter; see what it says about Abbé Galiani's monkey.[71] Notice that the author gives all authenticity to his book, and signs it, promising to answer to me and the public. […] I would like you to speak seriously to de Sartine about this. I believe that *Économistes* should be satisfied with making the French miss out on bread and give up making a nation that is courteous and amiable more than any other lose its morals and decency. Please inform de Sartine that, from the way these *Récréations* were printed, it seems indisputable that the police will admit this atrocious calumny launched not against the *Chevalier Zanobi*, but against the person of Abbé Galiani. If the police admit the most absurd calumnies, I have nothing to say. If de Sartine is angry and furious about this, as I think he is, please ask him, on my behalf, if he would have refused me in Paris, in the position I

[68] Ferdinando Galiani's letter to Madame d'Épinay, Naples, 27 July 1770, published in Galiani (1881a, vol I: 210–211); Galiani and d'Épinay (1992, vol. I: 221–222). Galiani refers to an intervention favourable to him that appeared in the *Année Littéraire* in June 1770 (see Madame d'Épinay's letter to Ferdinando Galiani, Paris, 24 June 1770, published in Galiani and d'Épinay 1992, vol. I: 192–193: d'Epinay and Galiani 1996: 128).

[69] Galiani plays with words by transforming *Roubaud* in *Ribaud*, ribald in French.

[70] Ferdinando Galiani's letter to Madame d'Épinay, Naples, 23 June 1770, published in Galiani (1881a, vol I: 176–177); Galiani and d'Épinay (1992, vol. I: 190).

[71] Galiani refers to an anecdote circulating in Paris about the monkey that Galiani was forced to kill because it allegedly tried to participate in an erotic encounter of his master. The infamous anecdote was also taken up by other detractors of Galiani (see Galiani 1975: 1046, footnote).

held, to send Abbé Roubaud to the Fort l'Évêque for a few weeks. I believe that, whether from afar or close up, I am still the same Abbé Galiani. Finally, I must confess that what burns me in this affair is to see that I have attracted the bite of the Roubaud monkey, precisely for wanting to defend de Sartine from the slanderous imputations that *Économistes*, led by Abbé Baudeau, spread against him in Paris in December 1768, accusing him and de Choiseul of being the cause of the high price of wheat".[72]

The crisis in France stimulated Galiani to further clarify his position on trade liberalisation. In a long letter to Jean-Baptiste-Antoine Suard in September 1770, the abbot established an interesting relationship between grain policy and forms of government: "In every government, grain legislation takes on the character of the spirit of the government itself. Under a despot, free exportation is impossible. The tyrant is too afraid of the cries of his starving slaves. In a democracy, free exportation is natural and infallible. Since the rulers and the ruled are the same people, trust is infinite. In a mixed and shared government, freedom can only be mixed and tempered. Corollary. If you interfere too much with the administration of laws in France, you alter the form and constitution of government, whether this change is the cause or the effect of complete freedom of exportation. Now, changing the form of government is a beautiful thing when done, but a very ugly thing to do. [...]. So keep your government and keep your grain. [...]. Since France, in its present state, is a kingdom of traders, navigators and manufacturers, all its wealth is concentrated on its borders. All the great and opulent cities are on its coasts. The interior is appallingly poor. The peripheral areas are where the money is. There is therefore a centrifugal force in France; it must be corrected, otherwise the grain will all go to the borders in barren years. It will then come out for another physical reason, which I will explain to you. Put a heavy weight on a *pâte*, on a fluid or soft matter; you will certainly flatten it, crush it, and create a centrifugal force in the matter, because it wants to escape under the weight. Now put a king, a parliament, a council, and the intendancies right in the middle of a country; these are heavy masses, and furiously so: you will immediately see as many people and as much food as possible escaping from the edges, if you do not correct the movement. The *Économistes* will tell you that they will prevent, with their frequent

[72] Ferdinando Galiani's letter to Madame d'Épinay, Naples, 27 July 1770, published in Galiani (1881a, vol I: 211–212); Galiani and d'Épinay (1992, vol. I: 222).

ephemeral (*éphémères*) pamphlets,[73] parliaments, stewards, etc., from weighing in on the *pâte*. Poor fanatical fools. They think that as soon as they have worked out a very common idea and scribbled it down in flat, bad French, it will immediately be implemented: not so; and parliaments will always stop, and councils will always declare, and *intendants* will always regulate, and always too much, and always within. [...] If I had said that by leaving exports free it was necessary to encourage, in the style of England, domestic traders, given the greater difficulty of roads and transit in the miserable inland provinces, all the *Économistes* would have kissed me on the forehead, and perhaps elsewhere.[74] I said the same thing, with the difference that instead of saying something absurd and impractical, I said something reasonable and easy. This is what I have done for domestic trade, but I have done much more. I have encouraged, guaranteed and made exports sacred and invulnerable. You have not done that and you blame me again. You have done the opposite; you have placed restrictions and modifications on freedom, as my dear Abbé Morellet, whom I still love and whom I would like to enlighten on these issues, told me. [...] From here I can see that my gentlemen *Économistes*, if they heard what I have to say, would stand up on their big boots and shout at me that I am an Italian, a Neapolitan, and perhaps a Ragusan, a Samaritan, a clergyman; and I would quietly reply that they are *Économistes*. They will call me *Machiavelli, Mazarin*, financier, skinner of the people, leech of the poor, etc. etc. I will call them poor fools, leeches of the haemorrhoidal veins, who want to correct nature and change men. After all, the French are like Italians".[75]

[73] Another play on words between *Éphémérides* and *éphémères*. By using the term éphémère Galiani was alluding to the *Éphémérides du citoyen*, organ of the *Économistes*.

[74] "The English had to quickly stop exports to halt the increase in peasant wealth, which would have brought down the entire political machine of the state" (Ferdinando Galiani's letter to Madame d'Épinay, Naples, 22 December 1770, published in Galiani 1881a, vol I: 330; Galiani and d'Épinay 1992, vol. I: 322). "The one nation that had been their work-horse abandoned them and reformed its incentive premium, as I had foreseen and predicted. They decided to rank the different wheat prices. It is a bad idea, not as good as mine, but not so bad in England, where wheat prices are more or less the same in all provinces because of the great ease of circulation. However, the system adopted in England is almost identical to mine" (Ferdinando Galiani's letter to Madame d'Épinay, Naples, 22 June 1771, published in Galiani 1881a, vol I: 410; Galiani and d'Épinay 1993, vol. II: 133).

[75] Ferdinando Galiani's letter to Jean-Baptiste-Antoine Suard, Naples, 8 September 1770, published in Galiani (1975: 1047–1053), see also Galiani (1881a, vol. I: 244–252). See also

The events now proved him right, and the Neapolitan abbot still took advantage of this to claim the validity of his theories: "I have been very happy, and not at all surprised, by the Council's decree. It is the first step towards the adoption of the complete theory that I advocate in my *Dialogues*, and do not doubt that my system will be applied in full [...].[76] I am absolutely right. In the meantime, the spirit of justice of the *Contrôlleur Général* should induce him to grant me some sort of reparation of honour, in exchange for the atrocious idiocies I have had to endure for having wished to render a service to the nation that had had the goodness to give me such a benevolent welcome. It cannot be denied that I was vilified in the sight of Europe by a bunch of physiocratic rogues. These were methods worthy of them, and I am not surprised. Rusticity is well suited to peasants, and peasants are villains *par excellence*".[77] And he was preparing for a new confrontation with the Quesnay school: "If I had been playing the game against *Économistes*, I would have written a dissertation to show that they are responsible for the *bagarre*, and I would have found the clearest passages in their works, in which they incite brawling, casting out all kinds of order, in favour of the only natural and essential order of freedom".[78]

The work that Galiani identified as the most suitable target for his polemical satire was de La Rivière's *L'interet Général de l'État* and he thus informed his Parisian correspondent: "I was idle when I decided to have

Ferdinando Galiani's letter to Jean-Baptiste-Antoine Suard, Naples, 15 December 1770, published in Galiani (1975: 1059–1064), see also Galiani (1881a, vol. I: 320–324).

[76] Galiani's friendship with de Sartine and Terray's anti-physiocratic policy led the *Économistes* to spread the rumour that the *Dialogues* had been written on commission from the party hostile to the Physiocrats (see Galiani 1968, Appendix B: 336 Koch's footnote). Galiani sent de Sartine two *Mémoires* (on the establishment of the Monte di Pietà in Paris and on the grain trade; see Ferdinando Galiani's letter to Madame d'Épinay, Naples, 28 April 1770, published in Galiani 1881a: 125; Galiani and d'Épinay 1992, vol. I: 153). The memoir on the Monte di Pietà is published in Galiani (1881a: 115–124); the memoir on the grain trade is published in Galiani (1959: 577–594).

[77] Ferdinando Galiani's letter to Madame d'Épinay, Naples, 11 August 1770, published in Galiani and d'Épinay (1992, vol. I: 230–231); d'Épinay and Galiani (1996:163–164). Grimm also supported him by giving him news: "While the *messieurs les ruraux* [physiocrats] still have the right to bake bread *chez la béurriere*, most of the inland provinces are starving, and this scourge has even spread to Alsace, a frontier province, one of the richest in the kingdom, which alone exported a prodigious amount of grain" (Friedrich Melchior von Grimm's letter to Ferdinando Galiani, Paris, 24 June 1770, published in Galiani 1959: 497).

[78] Ferdinando Galiani's letter to Madame d'Épinay, Naples, 11 August 1770, Galiani and d'Épinay (1992, vol. I: 232); published in d'Épinay and Galiani (1996: 165).

some fun, and I myself laughed at the madness that started in my brain. I promised you a dissertation on the *bagarre* and this is the beginning. [...]. You will understand nothing if you do not pick up de La Rivière's work and read it with that book open before your eyes. You will marvel at such a tight parody. If you read it twice, you will realise that it is not just a perfidious divertissement, but a real refutation, because even if I change the names of things, I leave all of de La Rivière's reasoning unchanged, and you will instantly discover how absurd and outlandish it is. Nevertheless, I doubt whether my *plaisanterie* (*joke*) is fit to be printed. It will not make anyone laugh, because no one will read de La Rivière's book. So it is enough for me to amuse Grimm, the philosopher [Diderot], the good Baron [d'Holbach] etc.".[79]

La Bagarre, whose original title is *L'intéret Général de l'État, ou la liberté des Bagarres [...] Avec la réfutation d' un nouveau Système de bagarre publié en forme de Feu d'Artifice. Par M. L. A. R. Économiste indigne*,[80] was written between August and October 1770, but the lost manuscript was found and published in 1979 by Steven Kaplan (1979).[81]

The Neapolitan abbot's aim was to demonstrate the abstractness of the *Économistes* arguments by revealing their deductive logic, and he therefore recommended that Madame d'Épinay read de La Rivière's text and then "make the comparison" with his parody.[82]

The text is constructed in two columns: on the left column are parts of de La Rivière's text, on the right column Galiani's parody (in the text published by Kaplan, the columns are reversed). *La Bagarre* is divided into chapters that correspond to those of *L'intéret Général*, in the third chapter appears an *Extrait des Ephémerides Économiques de Cracovic - Avertissement du Journaliste*, which was perhaps meant to serve as a preface to the text.

[79] Ferdinando Galiani's letter to Madame d'Épinay, Naples, 25 August 1770, published in Galiani (1881a, vol I: 237–238); Galiani and d'Épinay (1992, vol. I: 243–244). See also Ferdinando Galiani's letter to Madame d'Épinay, Naples, 13 October 1770, published in Galiani (1881a, vol I: 280) (Galiani and d'Épinay 1992, vol. I: 271); Ferdinando Galiani's letter to Madame d'Épinay, Naples, 27 October 1770, published in Galiani (1881a, vol I: 294) (Galiani and d'Épinay 1992, vol. I: 280); see also Galiani (1959: appendix eighth, 440–461) and Kaplan (1979).

[80] *The general interest of the State, or the freedom of brawl [...] With a refutation of a new system of brawl published in the form of fireworks. By Mr L. A. R. Unworthy economist.* M. L. A. R. are precisely the initials of de La Rivière.

[81] The manuscript is in the Bibliothèque Nationale de Paris, MSN.Naf. 22253.

[82] Ferdinando Galiani's letter to Madame d'Épinay, Naples, 13 October 1770, published in Galiani (1881a, vol I: 280); Galiani and d'Épinay (1992, vol. I: 274).

Confirming Galiani's habit of hiding behind fictional characters, the self-named *Polish Journaliste* clarified the meaning of the parody: "We hope that the public will be enchanted to see the progress that the new *Economic Science* and *Rural Philosophy* are making day by day among us. The immortal works published in France on these subjects, previously ignored, have excited and awakened, as it were, the spirits that languished in torpor and idleness at home. *Monsieur the Abbot of Radznomowintzokiso Kiski* has just devoted himself in a special way to the study of brawls (*bagarre*), an essential and fundamental part and a necessary and natural consequence of complete freedom, on which the glory and prosperity of the nation depends"[83] (Kaplan 1979: 87).

Some examples in Table 8.1 may clarify the meaning of Galiani's parody.

The decision to arrange de La Rivière's text and the parody synoptically was not Galiani's, but that of his Parisian friends: "Needless to tell you", wrote Madame d'Épinay, "how much Grimm and Diderot laughed at reading the last pare of the *Bagarre*. It is a true masterpiece. We always kept the fundamental work open before our eyes, and I think the parody should be printed in duplicate, the basic text on one side and your commentary opposite".[84] But Galiani did not approve this choice: "The only thing I recommend is that, should the work ever go to press, you should not think of placing the text and the parody in front of each other, half a page apart. Many translators have made this mistake and they have all regretted it. There is nothing that kills a translation or a parody more than this system".[85] Galiani, therefore, desired *La Bagarre* to circulate as an original text, an imitation that was meant to confuse and amuse.[86]

With his usual irony, Galiani diluted his anger with a satirical *operetta*, intended for a limited circulation for the circle of his Parisian friends, and which was not worth publishing at a time when Physiocracy was losing all

[83] The reference to Poland is justified by de La Rivière's designation as Prévot (provost) of Widzynisky in Poland, a governmental position of varying importance.

[84] Madame d'Épinay's letter to Ferdinando Galiani, Paris, 18 November 1770, published in Galiani and d'Épinay (1992, vol. I: 299); d'Épinay and Galiani (1996: 227).

[85] Ferdinando Galiani's letter to Madame d'Épinay, Naples, 2 February 1771, published in Galiani (1881a, vol I: 351); Galiani and d'Épinay (1993, vol. II: 44).

[86] "This fake de La Rivière that Galiani enjoys constructing, paradoxically, is supposed to show what the real de La Rivière is like: stupid and fervent, ambitious and naive; in short, an *économiste*, i.e., for Galiani, an epiphany of absurdity and nonsense. The fake is constructed using as much as possible the materials, the structures, of the original. The comic effect, irresistible, is mainly achieved by substituting a few common nouns for the technicalities of physiocratic jargon (slippers, carriages, digestion, walk)" (Catucci 1986: 111).

Table 8.1 The text of *La Bagarre*

L'intéret général de l' État	*La Bagarre*
Pour bien juger de ces précautions, il faut les considérer dans la nécessité dont elles paraissaient être pour assurer la subsistance des Vislles; il faut faire attention que le manque d'une liberté suffisante, et la faiblesse naturelle d'un commerce qui n'est point encore monté, les exposaient a une cherté trop considérable, pour ne pas se hâter de la prévenir par les opérations les plus promptes ou du moins de la diminuer	Pour bien juger de ces précautions, il faut les considérer dans la nécessite dont elles paraissent être pour assurer la sureté publique; il faut faire attention que le manque d'une habitude sufis ante aux bagarres et la faiblesse naturelle des coudes et des reins d'une quantité de gens dont la force des épaules n'est pas encore montée, les exposeraient a une presse trop considérable pour ne pas se hâter de la prévenir par des détachements de gardes a pied ou a cheval, ou du moins de la diminuer (Galiani 1770b [1979]: 69)
Qui dit Société, dit association. Qui dit un Corps politique, dit des hommes lies entre eux par un intérêt commun publiquement et généralement reconnu, pour la conservation duquel ils se sont unis. Au moyen de cet intérêt commun, il existe alors nécessairement une volonté commune, celle d'adopter tout ce qui convient a ce même intérêt, de rejeter tout ce qui lui est contraire; et cette volonté commune est la loi commune & fondamentale de la Société	Qui dit Société, dit association. Qui dit association, dit Société, et qui ne dit ni l'un ni l'autre, c'est une marque qu'il parlera d'autre chose. Qui dit une société *économistique*, dit des hommes lies ou a lier. Ils ont un intérêt commun, et au moyen de cet intérêt commun, il existe un jargon commun, et ce jargon commun, est la loi commune de la Secte, et la contre force de tout langage qui ne serait pas commun et qui lui serait opposée (Galiani 1770b [1979]: 71; italics added)
Aussi est-ce un grand malheur quand les différentes branches du Corps de la Magistrature ne sont pas d'accord entre elles sur ce qui concerne une nouvelle loi	Aussi est-ce un grand malheur quand les différentes branches du Corps de la Magistrature ne permettent pas aux Économistes de soutenir avec enthousiasme la liberté des bagarres (Galiani 1770b[1979]: 74)

(*continued*)

Table 8.1 (continued)

L'intéret général de l' État	*La Bagarre*
II n'est donc qu'un moyen pour les concilier; c'est deremonter jusqu'aux premiers principes de l'intérêt commun parmi nous et d'examiner rigoureusement les rapports de ces principes avec cette liberté	II n'est donc qu'un moyen pour les concilier; c'est de s'obstiner dans son avis malgré les raisonnements les plus clairs et les événements les plus fâcheux; c'est de remonter toujours a des idées vagues et générales sans vouloir jamais examiner rigoureusement ni l'application des théories, ni l'exception des règles, ni les Circonstances particulières (Galiani 1770b [1979]: 75)
Par rapport à ce qui dépend de nous, les causes immédiates de la reproduction annuelle des biens propres a nos consommations sont les travaux de la culture, et les avances que nous confions a la terre; pour augmenter la masse des reproductions, il faut donc augmenter la somme de ces avances et de ces travaux	Par rapport à ce qui dépend de nous, les causes immédiates de la promenade sont le plaisir de prendre l'air et le besoin d'aider à la digestion. Pour augmenter la masse des digestions, il faut donc augmenter les diners et les soupers (Galiani 1770b [1979]: 82)

the support it had enjoyed.[87] Madame d'Épinay wrote to him from Paris, "I can assure you that since your book came out they have lost all credence, especially since people are starving here. People everywhere mock their writings [...]. Except within their own tiny little clique, the *Physiocrats* are the object of universal ridicule, indeed I have even seen some supporters of certain points of their theories even laugh at those writings and especially at the authors [...]. They must be drowned in ridicule, which in Paris is more effective than reasoning. They are heavy and unreasonable, you are light and rational. You are the triumphant one and the public does you justice. Hear this: for the past month, business has taken me to

[87] "To be honest, I don't know whether to keep the joke going any longer. Nothing would be so easy for me, but I fear it would become monotonous. Besides, I am still distraught over the insults that have been thrown at my *Dialogues*, and I would rather have an honest reparation from de Sartine or the Abbé Terray, than a resounding revenge, directed against a bunch of *Économistes* who can be drowned in spittle, and yet will manage to form a powerful sect, and perhaps a religion, because they are sad and irrational, and have great sympathy for those riots, which should, according to them, restore equality of conditions" (Ferdinando Galiani's letter to Madame d'Épinay, Naples, 13 October 1770, published in Galiani 1881a, vol I: 280; Galiani and d'Épinay 1992, vol. I: 271).

frequent circles far removed from our own among people of the most diverse backgrounds. Well, there is only one voice and it is all in your favour".[88]

Meanwhile he claimed his primacy over the Physiocrats: "I am older than all the *Économistes*, since in 1749 I wrote my book on money and in 1754 that on grain. At that time the *secte économique* had not yet been born. Since these beasts regarded me as an intruder and a newcomer to their fold, I am quite happy for them to know that it is up to me to drive them out and remain where I have been for twenty years".[89]

In December 1770, Abbot Terray promulgated the decree on the grain trade that established free internal circulation and confirmed the restrictions on foreign trade (Kaplan 1976: 532–539; Girard 1924), measures that if not exactly inspired, were broadly akin to the positions expressed by Galiani. During this period, Galiani hoped to return to Paris, perhaps called by Abbot Terray and his friends, and had some further hopes when Caracciolo took on the role of ambassador, but the attempts were unsuccessful.

The polemic with the physiocratic school was never entirely over: in 1773 in a report on the *Annona of Genoa*, sent to Giovan Battista Grimaldi, Galiani outlined a scornful judgement of the Quesnay school: "This science that modern Frenchmen out of highest ignorance have called *economic*, when they should have called it *political*, is much more difficult than it appears. It is reduced to applying very simple general theories to very complicated specific cases. He who believes he knows it through only having understood is a fool, because its theoretical truths are so simple and clear that every child guesses them. It is as if he believes himself a sublime geometer, because he knows that the whole is greater than the parts [...]. But an immense, deep, complex science is required to apply them to a particular country. This science includes ethics, traditions, laws, commerce, agriculture and finance. Every variation makes different cases, and different applications of theories" (Galiani, MS-29: 735, italic added).[90]

[88] Madame d'Épinay's letter to Ferdinando Galiani, Paris, 7 November 1770, published in Galiani and d'Épinay (1992, vol. I: 294–295). On the decline of physiocracy see Charles (2015a); Charles (2015b).

[89] Ferdinando Galiani's letter to Madame d'Épinay, Naples, 13 December 1770, published in Galiani (1881a, vol I: 315); Galiani and d'Épinay (1992, vol. I: 315).

[90] The manuscript is undated, but the essay was transmitted by Giovan Battista Grimaldi in April 1773 (see Ferdinado Galiani's letter to Giovan Battista Grimaldi, Naples, 27 Aprile 1773, BSNSP, XXX.C.12: folios 83r–85r).

In the short paper, Galiani further specified certain concepts expressed in the *Dialogues* using "geometric" terminology, consisting of theorems and corollaries. Due to the smallness of its territory, the Republic of Genoa could only import grain without any constraints. The presence of a large port, seafaring skills and grain-rich neighbouring countries facilitated its supply and rendered an *Annona* system superfluous (Galiani, MS-29: 735–737). The particular situation in Genoa then allowed Galiani to take up the subject of granary warehouses, the subject of the planned ninth dialogue that he had not had time to write in Paris and that he would have liked to include in a second edition of the *Dialogues*.[91] He thus identified the structure of the *Annona* with the *provender's storehouse* (*magazino di provvisione*), consisting of grain collected by the Prince who had the exclusive right to buy and sell it (or to cede this right to others) with the obligation to give a fixed price to the bread, gaining in good years and losing in bad ones. Such an *Annona* system was "a monopoly armed by the power of the prince" (Galiani, MS-29: 738), was detrimental to trade and insufficient to cover needs in case of famine.

Moreover, this mechanism was an unnecessary waste of money (also needed to guard the storehouse and prevent the grain from rotting) as famines were becoming rarer due to the decrease in wars, advances in navigation, the end of piracy, the increasing productivity and extension of cultivated land and, "for the last and greatest reason", the presence of

[91] Ferdinando Galiani's letter to Madame d'Épinay, Naples, 27 January 1770, in Galiani (1881a, vol I: 59); Galiani and d'Épinay (1992, vol. I: 111). A few years later, Galiani took up the project for a second edition: "Are my *Dialogues* for sale? Have they been condemned? You encourage me to finish them. There is nothing so true that a tenth dialogue is missing: but the means to complete it! I lack verve, wit, strength, free time, everything. I can think of only one way to add something to a second edition: to include all the articles from the letters I wrote on the same subject to Suard, Morellet, to you, to de Sartine and to many others I no longer remember. I could also send you a consultation I did for the Republic of Genoa last year on the same issue of freedom of export. Finally, if there is anything I can do to make working with old productions of my mind more interesting, welcome! Otherwise, I do not see the possibility of adding anything" (Ferdinando Galiani's letter to Madame d'Épinay, Naples, 19 November 1774, in Galiani 1881a, vol II: 367; Galiani and d'Épinay 1996, vol. IV: 111). And: "if you think that a second edition of my *Dialogues* should be published, consider adding to it all the parts of my letters relating to the question. Also add to it the parody of de La Rivière's *L'intéret de l'État*, if you find it amusing; and in a word, compile, compile, compile everything you can find about me in Paris, but do not expect anything more from here. Since I have not succeeded in persuading exalted heads, I am losing courage" (Ferdinando Galiani's letter to Madame d'Épinay, Naples, 24 June 1775, in Galiani 1881a, vol II: 415–416; Galiani and d'Épinay 1997, vol. V: 38). See also Braeuer (1988).

alternative crops such as maize. The case of a *precautionary storehouse* (*magazzino di precauzione*) was different, consisting of vast quantities of grain that the Prince collected "without any idea of profit, without exclusive right, and only prepared to cope with unforeseen cases", and constituted a necessary expense like war provisions (Galiani, MS-29: 736–737). In case of need, such a warehouse would prevent the speculative activities of the merchants, "it will break the secret concerts and aims of the merchants. It will sell when and how much the band of merchants would not want to sell, and will put fear into them" (Galiani, MS-29: 738). Obviously Galiani applied his free-trade arguments to the Genoese Republic, and did not propose them as a general policy; rather, he took a further opportunity to distinguish his position from that of the physiocrats: "A hot-headed and unconsidered economist will now come along and say that neither warehouse is to be had. That indefinite liberty suffices for everything and is sufficient alone: that fears of plague and siege are dreams: that monopoly is a *chimera*: that the cries of useless clerks are seditious voices, that we must immolate ourselves to the goddess of Liberty: that those who govern had better not govern: and that the last of all would be to take the economists to govern the world in all its parts. Perhaps they will speak the truth; but they will not be heard or followed. Not even the liveliest and most resolute of nations [France] could follow them for a moment without much regret. Whoever wants to say impracticable things, say them as they do. Whoever wants feasible things, let him moderate this fervour for liberty" (Galiani, MS-29: 741, italics added).

And he reminded Madane d'Épinay that: "General theories and nothing are almost the same thing. The *Économistes* believed that with four rough, vague words and a dozen general arguments they knew everything, and I proved to them that they knew nothing".[92] He then gave a formal definition of political science: "Politics is the science that promotes the greatest possible good for men with the least possible pain, according to circumstances. This is a solution of the *De Maximis et Minimis problem*. Politics is a curve (a parabola) to be drawn. The abscissas will be the good, the ordinates will be the bad. The point will be found where the least possible pain meets the greatest good. This point solves the problem, and these are all human problems, because everything is a mixture of good and bad. You can see that in the beginning all political problems are repre-

[92] Ferdinando Galiani's letter to Madame d'Épinay, Naples, 6 November 1773, published in Galiani (1881a, vol. II: 274); Galiani and d'Épinay (1996, vol. IV: 88).

sented by an indeterminate equation which will be fixed when you apply it to particular cases. Do you ask yourself whether it is a good idea to grant full freedom to grain exports? This general problem can only be solved by an indefinite equation. Then you ask whether it is a good idea to grant export freedom to France in 1773. Then the problem is fixed, because you fix the country and the time; and the same equation, applied to the fixed case, can give either the positive statement or the negative. Politics is therefore the geometry of curves, the sublime geometry of governments, like the administration (police), it is plain and simple geometry: Euclid's six books [...]. Politics is thus not only a science of education, but in general a science of improvement [...]. Throw away from yourselves and from politics these great empty words about the strength of empires, their fall, their rise, etc. Do not love monsters of the imagination and moral beings. It should only be about the happiness of real people, of existing or planned individuals. Us and our children, that is all. The rest is fantasy".[93]

And returning once again to the most suitable policies to combat famine, Galiani observed: "All the countries of Europe that have experienced famine for nine years (i.e. since the beginning of the Polish turmoil, which is the sole cause) have issued edicts, and these edicts are just as they would have been issued three centuries ago, proving that the works of *Économistes* have neither enlightened nor persuaded any government. I feel sorry for them and for governments, because progress could have been made in grain policy over the last three centuries. But *Économistes* have not been able to teach it, nor have governments been able to learn it. That is what should have been taught and preached: 1. That the exact knowledge of the grain production of a kingdom in any given year, even if we could have it, is useless, leads nowhere and advances nothing. 2. That an absolute ban on exports is impractical and less advantageous than a heavy tax on exports. 3. That the price of grain should never be fixed. You want to know the harvest: nonsense. Fix the price: madness. Prohibit export: misery. The remedy to prevent famine was enunciated in my *Dialogues* to those who read them to the end. Two taxes. One on exports, the other on imports. There is only one remedy for the present famine. The government must convince itself that it is a calamity as great as war; a calamity worthy of its care, and just as millions and billions are spent on war, millions and billions must be spent on famine. Indebtedness. Buy anywhere at any price.

[93] Ferdinando Galiani's letter to Madame d'Épinay, Naples, 6 November 1773, published in Galiani (1881a, vol. II: 275–276); Galiani and d'Épinay (1996, vol. IV: 89); translated partially in Faccarello (1998: 160).

Sell at a loss. Strike monopolies, destroy merchants. Exporting must always be left to the merchants and must always be profitable for them, but importing must absolutely not be tolerated. Only the state can import grain from abroad".[94]

But Galiani's triumph was short-lived; 1774 marked the year of the *Économistes'* revival. Famine and hunger once again tormented France, marking the rise of Turgot to the position of *Contrôleur Général des Finances*,[95] who, being a convinced liberalist, restored the decrees liberalising the grain trade, despite strong opposition from the crown council and local parliaments, provoking a new heated debate with the anti-free trade interventions of Simon-Nicholas Henri Linguet (member of the Paris Parliament) and Jaques Necker (Linguet 1774; Necker 1775), to which was added, in defence of the physiocrats, the publication of Morellet's *Rèfutation* that finally saw the light of day (thanks to Turgot's intervention that had established freedom of the press),[96] Nicolas Baudeau's polemical response (1775) and the contributions of Nicolas de Condorcet, clearly in favour of the physiocracy (Condorcet 1774, 1776).

[94] Ferdinando Galiani's letter to Madame d'Épinay, Naples, 13 November 1773, published in Galiani (1881a, vol. II: 280–281); Galiani and d'Épinay (1996, vol. IV: 91–92).

[95] On the role of *Contrôleur*, Galiani was rather sceptical: 'What is a *Contrôleur Général*? A great player of *dice cups* (*gobeletes*). He has a magic wand in his hand, which we call letters patent and declarations, and he performs great sleights of hand, sometimes real, sometimes apparent' (Ferdinando Galiani's letter to Jean-Baptiste-Antoine Suard, Naples, 8 September 1770, published in Galiani 1975: 1049, see also Galiani 1881a, vol. I: 246).

[96] Galiani was also sceptical about freedom of the press: "God preserve you from the freedom of the press, established by edict. Nothing contributes more to making a nation vulgar, to destroying taste, to bastardising eloquence and every kind of spirit [...]. The constraint of modesty and the constraint of the press were the causes of the perfection of the spirit, taste and way of thinking of the French. Keep them both, otherwise you are lost. Freedom as such is good: we already enjoy it. It must exist de facto, and must be based solely on the personal virtues of the tolerant and magnanimous minister. In this way, the nation will care more for the minister who forgives, when he could punish. If freedom is granted by edict, the minister will no longer be appreciated and will be insulted, as is the case in London. The nation will become as coarse as the English and the point of honour (honour, the pivot of your monarchy) will suffer. You will be as coarse as the English, without being as robust; you will be as mad, but much less profound in your madness" (Ferdinando Galiani's letter to Madame d'Épinay, Naples, 24 September 1774, published in Galiani 1881a vol II: 348–349; Galiani and d'Épinay 1996, vol. IV: 186).

Madame d'Épinay regularly informed Galiani about the change in French politics implemented by the new sovereign Louis XVI[97] and the hostile feelings of the new *Contrôleur Général des Finances*, Turgot, towards him.[98] The Neapolitan abbot replied with his usual cold irony ("I knew of Turgot's hatred for my *Dialogues*; they will become even more hateful to him once this damned export has brought him down; just wait")[99] and with a prophecy: "Turgot was appointed *Contrôleur Général.* He will stay too short a time in place to carry out his systems. His administration of finances will resemble his brother's Cayenne. He will punish scoundrels; he will protest, he will get angry, he will want to do good, but he will encounter thorns, difficulties and scoundrels everywhere. His credit will diminish; he will be hated; it will be said that he is not good at his job; his enthusiasm will cool; he will retire, or be dismissed; and we will return once and for all from the error of having wanted to give a position like his, in a monarchy like yours, to a very virtuous and very philosophical man. It will be the free exportation of grain that will break his neck".[100] Madame d'Épinay exhorted him to publish a second edition of his *Dialogues* to contribute to the heated debate, also supported by freedom of the press.[101] But Galiani rejected the invitation, too busy with family problems, discouraged by his friend Caracciolo, and too lazy and bored to

[97] Louis XV had died in May 1774 and Galiani eulogised him: "The reign of Louis XV will be the most memorable for posterity. The latter will mention the century of Louis XIV only to say that Voltaire spoke of Louis XIV's century during the reign of Louis XV. Moreover, it was the latter century that produced Montesquieu, Voltaire, Diderot, d'Alembert, Boulanger, La Chalotais and the eclipse of the Jesuits. If we compare the cruelty of the persecution of Port-Royal with the gentleness of the persecution of the *Encyclopédistes*, we see the difference in the reigns, morals and hearts of the two kings. The first was a celebrity-seeker, who exchanged sensation for glory; the second was an honest man who did the most vulgar of jobs (that of king) with the greatest possible reluctance. For a long time we shall not find such a kingdom" (Ferdinando Galiani's letter to Madame d'Épinay, Naples, 28 May 1774, published in Galiani 1881a, vol II: 316; Galiani and d'Épinay 1996, vol. IV: 143–144).

[98] "I don't doubt that Turgot is devoted to you, because I don't know how anyone can dislike you, but I tell you that he and his people consider your book dangerous. They have already said so in his house and he himself has repeated it since he became Minister of Finance" (Madame d'Épinay's letter to Ferdinando Galiani, Paris, 5 September 1774, published in Galiani and d'Épinay 1996, vol. IV: 182; d'Épinay and Galiani 1996: 798).

[99] Ferdinando Galiani's letter to Madame d'Épinay, Naples, 24 September 1774, published in Galiani (1881a, vol II: 347–348); Galiani and d'Épinay (1996, vol. IV: 186).

[100] Ferdinando Galiani's letter to Madame d'Épinay, Naples, 17 September 1774, published in Galiani (1881a, vol II: 345–346); Galiani and d'Épinay (1996, vol. IV: 183–184).

[101] An article in favour of Galiani and against Morellet's arguments appeared in December 1774 in *Correspondance littéraire philosophique et critique* edited by Jacques-Henri Meister

take up the subject again, he observed sceptically: "Don't worry about the flood of pamphlets: people get tired of them. The first step forward that the *Contrôleur Général* wants to take, his ears will be scratched with shouts and a horrible din; and perhaps he will be so frightened that he will back down".[102]

In May 1775, a series of popular uprisings caused by the poor harvest and rising grain prices, known as the *Guerre des Farines*, forced the king to impose a price restraint and threatened the policy of liberalisation that Turgot defended for another year until his resignation. As usual, Madame d'Épinay informed him of the unrest in good time and Galiani analysed the situation with coldness and sarcasm: "My first reaction on reading your letter was to thank God I wasn't in Paris. I might have been put in prison there as the author of the revolt. It would have been right to find in my *Dialogues* that I had predicted and announced it, when I said that a statesman must foresee unforeseen events. This unworthy and occult *cabala*, which is undoubtedly the primary motive of popular imbecility, should have been foreseen [...]. The first problem a minister has to solve is to keep his position; and the more honest he thinks he is, the harder he has to work to stay there, so that he can do good for people for longer. If any good he would like to do exposes him to losing it, he must sacrifice it to his very existence. I hope that this event will have taught Turgot and the Abbé Morellet to know men and the world, which is not that of the works of *Économistes*. He will have seen that revolts caused by high prices are not impossible, as he believed. He calculated everything and only forgot the wickedness of men, and the envy that persecutes those in charge. You never know exactly how many enemies there are [...]. If his pain and that of the abbot served to make them do a little more justice to my *Dialogues*, or at least to my intentions, which result from my maxims as a whole, I would have gained much from this struggle, for there are no men whose esteem and friendship I hold more dear. They have great virtues and great genius. Perhaps they have stayed too long in government, and were not, like me, thrown into the midst of a court in their early years, to be the toy of fortune".[103]

(see Correspondance littéraire 1879: 514–518), encouraging Galiani's friends to propose a second edition of the *Dialogues*. See Galiani (1881a, vol. II: 350–415).

[102] Ferdinando Galiani's letter to Madame d'Épinay, Naples, 10 December 1774, published in Galiani (1881a, vol II: 371); Galiani and d'Épinay (1996, vol. IV: 207).

[103] Ferdinando Galiani's letter to Madame d'Épinay, Naples, 27 May 1775, published in Galiani (1881a, vol II: 405–407); Galiani and d'Épinay (1996, vol. IV: 249–250).

And still a few years later, when the controversy was over and the Physiocratic School had disappeared altogether, Galiani reiterated his criticism in the preface to the second edition of *Della Moneta*, stressing that, thanks to the Physiocrats, economic science: "before reaching maturity has come to the corruption of an obscure metaphysical jargon in the mouths of those who France wanted to call *Économistes*" (Galiani 1780: 3). And in *Note XXV*, the Neapolitan abbot responded in detail to an accusation by Morellet that he had evidently not accepted: "The illustrious friend of mine, the Abbot Morellet, was therefore dazzled when, in one of the refutations he had written, he thought he saw a contradiction between this book of mine on money [*Della Moneta*] and that one [*Dialogues*], and thus convinced me by applying to the export trade what I have generally and always said in favour of liberty. It has never been my opinion that the export trade in grain should be absolutely forbidden or stopped. I have only said, and continue to say, that it is to be hoped and wished for that moment when, owing to the increase of the population, and not to the prohibition of inappropriate laws, a nation is no longer in a condition to do so, and I would add that the Prince should rather sacrifice this trade to the increase of the population, than the latter to that" (Galiani 1780: 404). But by now those controversies were extinguished, the sect of *Économistes* almost forgotten, and Galiani could even judge with irony his *Dialogues* "which had so much praise, and so many confutations, and perhaps both unmerited" (Galiani 1780: 404).

8.2 The Return to Naples: Galiani Cameralist

Galiani experienced his abrupt departure from Paris as an existential drama: "Madame", he wrote to d'Épinay, "I cannot console myself with having left Paris [...]. I will succeed in overcoming the elements, nature, the joined gods and return to Paris. Yes, Paris is my homeland. Should I be exiled a hundred times, I will do everything I can to return again".[104] And again a few days later: "I've dropped anchor in Genoa, where the seabed is good and I'm safe from storms, so as not to be crashed by the currents onto the rocks in Naples. I have doubled anchors and winches, and hope to save myself from shipwreck. It is not about my happiness, it is

[104] Ferdinando Galiani's letter to Madame d'Épinay, Genoa, 17 July 1769, published in Galiani (1881a, vol I: 12–13); Galiani and d'Épinay (1992, vol. I: 52).

about life. Every day I feel inside me that it is physically impossible for me to live far from Paris".[105]

Having finally returned to Naples, Galiani did not expect to find anything but "envious, stupid and malicious people", while his true friends were in Paris.[106] Naples appeared boring to him: "Here I have nothing to torment me, except the absence of leisure, of pleasures, of friends, of pupils, of dinners, of lunches, of money, of health, of cheerfulness, of pleasant business, of love; but, in return, I have the minister's friendship, the envious man's anger, the risk of slander, of nuisances as far as the eye can see, of trials, of the palace, of the court, of bagpipes in the streets".[107] And desperate, he wrote to Baron d'Holbach: "As for me, I am bored to death here. I see no one but two or three Frenchmen. I am Gulliver returning from the land of the *Houyhnhnms*, now only keeping company with his two horses. I go on a few official visits to the wives of the two ministers of state and finance. And then I sleep or dream. What a life! There is nothing amusing here. No edicts, no reductions, no deductions, no suspension of payments. Life here is deathly uniform. Nothing is discussed, not even religion. Ah, my dear Paris! How I miss it!".[108]

Nor did the creation of a small *salon* in Naples console him: "Here I organised a miniature Paris. Gleichen, General Koch [Jean Baptiste de Koch], a Venetian resident, the secretary of the French embassy [Laurent Bérenger] and myself all dine together. We get together and we play at reciting Paris, like Nicolet plays Molière at the fair. During dinner, I delighted them with Voltaire's epistle and the prose ode you so kindly sent me. I thank you from the bottom of my heart and I beg you, and on behalf of myself and the whole brigade, to send me anything interesting and amusing that will be printed in Paris".[109]

[105] Ferdinando Galiani's letter to Madame d'Épinay, Genoa, 14 August 1769, published in Galiani (1881a, vol I: 18–19); Galiani and d'Épinay (1992, vol. I: 62).

[106] Ferdinando Galiani's letter to Madame d'Épinay, Genoa, 18 September 1769, published in Galiani (1881a, vol I: 29–30); Galiani and d'Épinay ("1992, vol. I: 72).

[107] Ferdinando Galiani's letter to Madame d'Épinay, Naples, 18 December 1769, published in Galiani (1881a, vol I: 50–51); Galiani and d'Épinay (1992, vol. I: 104).

[108] Ferdinando Galiani's letter to Baron d'Holbach, Naples, 7 April 1770, published in Galiani (1881a, vol I: 93–94).

[109] Ferdinando Galiani's letter to Madame d'Épinay, Naples, 22 December 1770, published in Galiani (1881a, vol I: 3280); Galiani and d'Épinay (1992, vol. I: 321).

Between the fleas (which infested Naples) and his illnesses (including problems with his eyesight),[110] Galiani would never see Paris again, although at first he had hopes of returning there, a hope fuelled by Choiseul's political misfortune.[111] Despite his nostalgia for Paris, Galiani had obtained a good position: "From my Court I received the most pompous of praises, in a dispatch that was even circulated through the city of Naples, regarding my qualities, my zeal and my probity in the services I rendered to the Crown. The salary for my office of Councillor of Commerce has been fixed at almost double what is usually paid to others. You may therefore tell your friends that the honour of their dear Galiani is safe".[112] In November 1770 he was appointed *Secretary* of the *Supreme Magistrate of Commerce.*[113] To return to Paris, without a well-paid official role, he would have had to give up all assignments and corresponding income, a decision he could never take: "You must know that if I left Naples, I would be begging in Paris. First I would have to give up my entire salary, which is half my income. But you will tell me that I still have at least six thousand *Francs* from my abbeys. That's not true. I would lose those too. Actually, the abbeys would not be taken away from me, but none of my peasants would ever think of paying me. Such is the state of anarchy in which we live, that no one fears the laws of justice, but in return fears injustice; and since I am a magistrate, I can do it. I am feared, I am paid. I was paid even when I was in Paris, because there I served the King; and it was clear that I had to go back to work; but if I had retired from service, I would not have been paid by anyone, because my income was in the abbeys, that is, in the estates of distant lands in the provinces. A Frenchman, much less an Englishman, does not know these risks. Wherever

[110] Ferdinando Galiani's letter to Madame d'Épinay, Naples, 23 June 1770, published in Galiani (1881a, vol I: 173); Galiani and d'Épinay (1992, vol. I: 191).

[111] Ferdinando Galiani's letter to Madame d'Épinay, Naples, 12 May 1770, published in Galiani (1881a, vol I: 141); Galiani and d'Épinay (1992, vol. I: 165).

[112] Ferdinando Galiani's letter to Madame d'Épinay, Genoa, 14 August 1769, published in Galiani (1881a, vol I: 19); Galiani and d'Épinay (1992, vol. I: 62).

[113] "I managed to get another position that earns me two thousand *Lire* a year and that does not involve any work: I am *Secretary of Commerce.* In the courts we call *secretaries* what you call *gens de roi.* I had been fighting for that position for a month and in the end I happily succeeded in obtaining it" (Ferdinando Galiani' letter to Madame d'Épinay, Naples, 24 November 1770, published in Galiani 1881a, vol I: 308; Galiani and d'Épinay 1992, vol. I: 301). See note on the appointment of Ferdinando Galiani as councillor of the *Supremo Tribunale del Commercio* signed by Juan Asensio de Goyzueta, Secretary of State, in BSNSP, XXX.C. 7: folios 131r–v [156r–v].

he is, the justice of his country protects his land ownership. Here one is only secure by dint of consideration. One has to be feared, and very much so, to be something in society. So you can understand that I cannot move from here unless I can find six thousand *Francs* in Paris".[114]

His responsibilities were spelled out in a letter to an Italian friend: "You ask me what office I have; I have a very low burden, but I am paid as if I were highly burdened. I am a councillor of trade, which means that I have to judge trade disputes between foreigners and our own. But the foreigners have such a bad opinion of us that they no longer trade with us, and if a dispute arises, they are more content to lose than to sue. Therefore my Court has no cases. So on this side I have a beautiful life. But the painful side comes from another office, which I also have, as *Secretary of Commerce*. This consists of giving opinions. There is nothing, no matter how small, on which the King does not ask for advice: there is no example of the advice given ever being followed; and yet neither he is unwilling to ask for it, nor we to give it. This is truly *improbus labor*, because the fact that we never see a harvest of the fruit sown is a most tedious thing".[115]

This "painful" assignment, as an expert (more or less listened to) on economic policy, projected Galiani into his new dimension as advisor to the Prince, initiating the *cameralist phase* of his intense intellectual activity.[116] However, he did not abandon his many literary interests, the learned studies he cultivated with a certain assiduity, his satirical vocation and his intense correspondence, especially with Madame d'Épinay and his French friends.

His new role as advisor was also the effect of the radical changes that affected the Kingdom's power structures between 1770 and 1780. In particular, Bernardo Tanucci's pre-eminent position began to be reduced with the coming of age of Ferdinand IV, reached in 1767, and above all due to the growing influence of Queen Maria Carolina, who assumed an increasingly important role in the Neapolitan court (Schipa 1938). A

[114] Ferdinando Galiani' letter to Madame d'Épinay, Naples, 6 June 1772, published in Galiani (1881a, vol II: 82); Galiani and d'Épinay (1994, vol. III: 64–65).

[115] Ferdinando Galiani's letter to [Paolo Antonio Menafoglio], Naples, 28 aprile 1772, published in Galiani (1975: 1081–1082).

[116] Federico D'Onofrio has pointed out a certain affinity between the concept of public happiness defined by Muratori and Genovesi and the German cameralist tradition, see D'Onofrio (2015). Certainly, Galiani is also part of this tradition and his affinities with Cameralism are even more marked because, unlike Muratori and Genovesi, he had direct governmental responsibilities.

member of the Council of State since 1771 and protector of Freemasonry that Tanucci had repressed, Maria Carolina wanted to remove the Kingdom from Spanish influence and bring it into the sphere of Austrian interests (Recca 2017; Mafrici 2020). Tanucci was now alienated from the policy followed by the Court and was finally dismissed in October 1776, replaced by Giuseppe Beccadelli Bologna, Marquis of Sambuca, "one of the most corrupt figures in the Kingdom" (Imbruglia 2019).[117]

Galiani very pragmatically adapted to the political change without any particular problems, following the behaviour of a court intellectual, always attentive to the fickle moods and without forging exclusive relationships, following the oldest Italian tradition of courtiers, with the feeling of a foreigner, more interested in what was happening in his adopted French homeland than in his native Naples.[118]

An example of his style is the negative judgement on Tanucci contained in an official report for Queen Maria Carolina in August 1784. Galiani downplayed the former minister's abilities, attributing his alleged diplomatic successes "solely to the vicissitudes of fate", for which he "scrounged the reputation of great minister in an event into which he had put nothing of his own", while some of his "rusticities [...] with a less favourable court would have spoilt everything" (Galiani, MS-19: 356). He also considered him to be "the manipulator of the fictitious famine" of 1764 that he had used to eliminate certain ministries with the "dexterity of passing them off as the culprits of the famine" (Galiani, MS-19: 357). Tanucci, Galiani continued, "never worked for the good of the state, he only vented his passions, his grudges, his personal resentments" (Galiani, MS-19: 357). Finally, he considered the minister to be completely unprepared for diplomatic activity: "It was a constant practice of Marquis Tanucci, as a result

[117] "Marquis Tanucci was relieved of his dicasteries, which were entrusted to the Marquis of Sambuca, a Sicilian; and he remained Minister of State without a dicastery. He would resemble de Maurepas, if the successor were his creature, but he was chosen by the king without his consent, and this makes all the difference. Such an event in the country of lethargy and sleep (like ours) is no small matter. In Paris, it would have caused no stir. However, for us it is a big deal, And I, who infinitely love noise and change, am delighted by this spectacle" (Ferdinando Galiani' letter to Madame d'Épinay, Naples, 2 November 1776, published in Galiani 1881a, vol II: 478; Galiani and d'Épinay 1997, vol. V: 113–114).

[118] "A minister only binds himself to people who have a devotion to him, and I cannot give myself, I could not even give myself to the devil. I am an autonomous man. I will have neither great fortune nor great persecution" (Ferdinando Galiani' letter to Madame d'Épinay, Naples, 28 December 1776, published in Galiani 1881a, vol II: 489–490; Galiani and d'Épinay 1997, vol. V: 125).

of mean and miscalculated frugality, never to use couriers in his negotiations. He sent everything by post, and always without a cipher, so that the other sovereigns always knew his thoughts and those of our ambassadors and emissaries who wrote to him. And so it is no wonder that he never succeeded in twenty-one years of ministry to conclude any alliance, treaty or convention of any kind. He did not even moderate his expressions in his confidences, rather he charged them with hateful personalities, so that whoever had to answer him was very embarrassed between having to displease him, or displease the minister of the court at which he resided" (Galiani, MS-19: 360).

The fall of Tanucci, therefore, did not involve him: "I cannot be involved in the misfortune of his [Tanucci's] creatures. Sambuca is an old and true friend of mine, as is his whole family; but he will not know what to do with me, for the same reason as Tanucci".[119]

However, his *cameralist phase* is of considerable interest, [and] "perhaps from a historical point of view, the most important category of Galiani's manuscripts" is that which includes "opinions, consultations, representations, etc." (Nicolini 1908a: 179). A second vocation, "the one that in his mature years juxtaposed the great charmeur of the Parisian salons, the witty author of literary operettas and linguistic and critical studies, and the very fine writer on economic matters, against the attentive and rather diligent official who became his government's advisor in the practice of commercial policy towards the countries with which the kingdom had the greatest relations or with which there was the opportunity to establish relations" (Diaz 1973: 291).[120] In the following years, Galiani obtained other important offices: in 1777, he was appointed president of the *Giunta dei reali allodiali* (*Royal Allodial Council*), which took care of the King's personal property, and tax lawyer (avvocato fiscale) in the same organism; in 1782, he was appointed *Consigliere del Consiglio supremo delle finanze* (*Councillor of the Supreme Council of Finances*) and in 1784

[119] Ferdinando Galiani' letter to Madame d'Épinay, Naples, 28 December 1776, published in Galiani (1881a, vol II: 489); Galiani and d'Épinay (1997, vol. V: 124–125).

[120] Galiani's qualities as an expert advisor are unanimously recognised: "Whether moralist or diplomat, *Machiavellino* brings to all the issues he deals with his lucid sense of expediency, his realistic assessment of the conditions within which political and economic action must take place. And from this point of view, the official duties he held after his return home seem to have strengthened his capacity for analysis and judgement" (Diaz 1975a: xxcv–xcvi). Similar opinions were expressed by Raffaele Guariglia (1914: 21) and Giuseppe Galasso (1989c: 360–361).

he became a member of the *Sopraintendenza del Fondo della Separazione* (*Superintendence of the Separation Fund*), which took care of military property.

A first opinion as a government advisor was drafted while he was still in Paris (dated 4 January 1768), as embassy secretary, and concerned proposals for the use of goods confiscated from the Society of Jesus, expelled from the Kingdom of Naples in November 1767 (Galiani, MS-27).[121] Galiani informed Tanucci on the policy followed in France, considered as model. He therefore proposed that all real estate belonging to the Jesuits be allocated to a single purpose: "Education is the first of the government's cares, the first impulse that moves every great monarchy, the first of all needs. The youth are the hope and the renewal of a nation. They are the posterity; they are those for whom everything is done by us. They are the love, and the sole care of nature" (Galiani, MS-27: 711). This single destination as colleges in the different provinces of the Kingdom would have prevented claims for other religious, hospital or military uses, and would have indicated, as had been done in France, the government's desire not to revoke the expulsion decision. He therefore proposed entrusting the government of the colleges following "the method we have used with such experimental success in all the pious works of banks, monasteries, conservatories, hospitals, which are the admiration of Europe" (Galiani, MS-27: 713). A successfully trialled public governance because "it is always good to introduce the least possible novelty in anything new that a country wants to do. The rules, methods, laws and customs to which a people is already accustomed prevent confusion, embarrassment and uncertainty, which is the evil of novelty. Now that the authority, jurisdiction etc. of governors, delegates etc. is well known in Naples, it will be

[121] "Each Jesuit, taken individually, was good, lovable, morose, whereas the Society, which was made up of the sum of individuals, was hateful, morally corrupt, pernicious" (Ferdinando Galiani's letter to Madame d'Épinay, Naples, 3 June 1775, published in Galiani 1881a, vol II: 409; Galiani and d'Épinay 1997, vol. V: 32). On the abolition of the Society of Jesus, see Robertazzi Delle Donne (1970); Renda (1970). The expulsion of the Society of Jesus (in 1767) caused significant effects on the economic level: in Sicily alone, the Jesuit patrimony amounted to about 40,000 hectares of land cultivated in various ways. The confiscated lands were not acquired by the State, but parcelled out and granted for use to peasants, in an attempt to put into practice Antonio Genovesi's programme, aimed at the creation of a class of independent farmers and the multiplication of small land ownership. The expulsion also freed up resources for the reform of the education system, for the numerous colleges seized were reopened following the reform plan outlined by Genovesi (see Genovesi 1781).

easy to adapt, and the new college will soon be in force and fully operational" (Galiani, MS-27: 713). He also advocated entrusting teaching in colleges to teachers chosen by the university, admitting "nobles and civilians (*ceto civile*) indiscriminately, and taking care not to make distinctions of class, since the *civilian class* is the one that in the kingdom lacks more than any other the means to give a regulated education to its children" (Galiani, MS-27: 715). These secular colleges would reduce the power of the clergy in the Kingdom's educational system based on seminaries that took in poor young men who were then forced to embark on an ecclesiastical career without a vocation.[122] Minister Tanucci's political choices, as is known, went in the direction desired by Galiani and Antonio Genovesi drew up a plan to reform teaching that introduced the Italian language into lessons and subjects of a technical-scientific nature (Galanti 1783: 144–160; Zazo 1929; Zambelli 1972: 775–777, 784–785).

Back in Naples, Galiani's advisory work focused mainly on the most important issues of foreign trade: from the resumption of negotiations for a trade treaty with France, to the shipping and trade treaty with the Russian Empire and the Ottoman Empire, and also with the newly founded republic of the United States. In all these he applied his analytical method. An example is the first chapters of the *Considerazioni sul Trattato di Commercio tra il Re e il Re Cristianissimo* (*Considerations on the Treaty of Commerce between the King and the Most Christian King*) (Galiani, MS-24).[123]

"Trade", wrote Galiani, "requires nothing but freedom and protection. Natural freedom, protection, which the law of nature and of people grants. That having been had, nothing is lacking. And if there were more, it would not be a treaty of commerce founded on equality and advantageous to the two peoples, but it would be a harsh condition of servitude, and inferiority imposed either as a result of previous victories, or allowed to slide due to the inaccuracy and stupidity of a weak and barbaric people, who contract

[122] "Almost all bishop have introduced the scandalous and cruel abuse that if seminarians who have reached the proper age do not enter the Church, their families must pay the seminary all the board for their studies. I do not cease to marvel how this violence, so contrary to natural liberty, so contrary to the choice of the state, so contrary to canonical and civil laws, and so used among us, has not yet excited the zeal of the King's ministers" (Galiani, MS-27: 715).

[123] The document was drafted during the French sojourn, in 1766, but resumed and updated probably between 1776 and 1777, when Galiani was appointed member of a commission that was to conclude the treaty with France, see Diaz (1973: 293).

with another more powerful, more industrious and more cunning" (Galiani, MS-24: 718).

Trade is the consequence of the peaceful existence of peoples, of their mutual knowledge and acceptance, which is why treaties between neighbouring peoples are very rare, treaties between distant peoples are much more frequent, and treaties between very distant countries with recent relations are necessary (Galiani, MS-24: 720). In the latter case, the treaty stipulated with "peoples first discovered and visited" essentially concerns three matters: "at sea, in port, or land" (Galiani, MS-24: 720). At sea, the treaty must ensure freedom of navigation and respect for the flag; in port, it must regulate the introduction or removal of goods, the payment of dues, inspections and customs tariffs; on land, it must allow freedom, security, and patronage of foreign merchants (Galiani, MS-24: 720). Trade treaties, if they arise from mutual convenience and equality of interests, contain nothing more than "an extension and declaration of what the law of nations and universal reason teaches, wants, prescribes: nothing else is envisaged in them, and nothing else is concerned, than to free foreigners from injustice, to combat partiality, excessive affection for the national" (Galiani, MS-24: 719). Instead, trade treaties that grant an advantage to one nation are "the effect of bullying (*prepotenza*) at sea, and of wars and victories" (Galiani, MS-24: 719). And also treaties that grant exclusive privileges, such as in France the exemption from the *droit d'aubaine*, which avoids the right of the French state to inherit the property of foreigners, or, like England, guarantee the rights of nations only to its own people and those of nations linked to it (Galiani, MS-24: 718–719).

Trade relations with France, Galiani noted, were regulated by the *Peace of the Pyrenees* (1659), signed by the Spanish monarchy for all its domains and thus also applied to the Neapolitan viceroyalty. This treaty that resulted from the Spanish defeat granted advantages to France, also due to the weakness of the vice royal government and the absence of a Neapolitan fleet, was to be considered abrogated by the subsequent peace treaties between the two kingdoms and as a result of the independence acquired by the Kingdom of Naples. The new relations, therefore, between the Two Sicilies and France had to be regulated according to principles of equal reciprocity, because "in the treaty to be stipulated, it must always be borne in mind that it is not from superiority of forces, and for the fate of wars and victories, but in the bosom of the deepest peace, from the sole desire of common advantage, and far from any need that the august sovereigns are moved to contract. Neither of the two nations should accept iniquitous conditions, and oppression, and servitude, but love and equality should dictate them" (Galiani, MS-24: 724). The whole story of the long negotiations for the treaty was summarised in a memorandum addressed to the Queen, Maria Carolina, in 1784 (Galiani, MS-19).

Galiani's view on foreign trade moved away from the English and French mercantilist models for an approach that was essentially free-trade in that he considered "happy and glorious that age in which without long treaties and copious articles of commerce, the act of peace alone and declared friendship will suffice to make navigation and traffic free and flourishing" (Galiani, MS-24: 719). These principles contrasted with some of the *Dialogues*' conclusions regarding grain protectionism. However, the typical political realism of the abbot emerged from the argument when he observed that when faced with disputes over treaty provisions, "better it will always be to live in indecision and uncertainty, which keeps us at liberty, than to come to a ruinous and fatal definition" (Galiani, MS-24: 734).[124]

France, according to Galiani, had always pursued a policy of hegemony towards the kingdoms ruled by the Bourbon dynasty (using the *Pacte de Famille*) and French interests did not coincide with those of the Neapolitan kingdom. This was why it was necessary to abandon any intention of a treaty with Versailles if France maintained its hegemonic pretensions and to propose "fair, useful, decent" conditions (Galiani, MS-19: 363) as laid down in the treaties with Holland, Denmark and Sweden, and on this same model to sign treaties with England and the Russian Empire.

For Galiani, the commercial policy of the Kingdom had to be directed towards the Levant, especially towards the Russian power that, following the conquest of the Crimea (which entered the Russian sphere with the *Peace of Küçük Kaynarca* in 1774), overlooked the Mediterranean. To the analysis of trade relations between Russia and the Kingdom of Naples, Galiani dedicated a specific report in October 1783, in which he detailed the conditions to make it viable (Galiani, MS-28, see Gambacorta 1988; Di Filippo 2005).[125] It was a trade that had to be conducted by sea and therefore needed guarantees on freedom of navigation: "Sicilian trade with Russia will not be a dream if the Dardanelles route is opened. On the

[124] On a free-trade line of thought is also the essay on the *Annona* of Genoa (Galiani, MS-29).

[125] See also Galiani, MS-52; Galiani, MS-53. The negotiations were conducted by two diplomats, Muzio da Gaeta, Duke of San Nicola and Antonino Maresca, Duke of Serracapriola.

contrary, it will be flourishing if attention is paid to it. One could open with Saint. Petersburg as long as the Ottoman affairs in the Black Sea do not have a fixed and decided state" (Galiani, MS-28: 335; see Mafrici 2011; Sirago 2018). The importance of the commercial relationship with the eastern Mediterranean had already been pointed out by Galiani in *Della Moneta*, even making a prophecy: "that trade of which we lament the loss, and blame ourselves for it, we will regain by discovering in the Mediterranean some place full of whales, some shore of herring, or some shoal of cod; and when we have cut the Suez Strait, we will go before others to Arabia and the Indies, and the Moluccas, Ceylon, Batavia and the Cape will be ours" (Galiani [1751]: 344–345).

To the relationship with the *Ottoman Sublime Porte*, Galiani devoted a report in 1784, written at the behest of Queen Maria Carolina, in which he drew an effective geopolitical portrait of the Mediterranean Sea and the opposing interests of the various powers. The excellent relations with the Ottoman power would facilitate the Kingdom's commercial activities and the intensification of the Neapolitan maritime traffic in the Black Sea would reduce the Russian maritime influence, more feared by the Turks (Galiani, MS-41: 121, see Galiani, MS-45; Barbagallo 1971; Diaz 1973: 320–326). Russia, too, could benefit from the Neapolitan maritime traffic with the Crimea, "because it would be years before it would have a merchant navy there to do all its own traffic and all the charters convenient to that trade" (Galiani, MS-41: 121). The increased presence of the Neapolitan merchant marine in trade with Russia would not provoke negative reactions from Austria, England, Holland and the Hanseatic League, because the Austrians used the Danube and the Nordic countries traded via the Baltic (Galiani, MS-41: 121). A negative reaction could come from Ragusa and Venice, which would reduce the freights granted by the Ottomans due to Neapolitan competition, and above all from the French, which "for many years now have been aiming to have the entire trade with the Ottoman Levant fall into their hands and make it a monopoly for their nation" (Galiani, MS-41: 122). The alliance and protection granted to the Barbary Princes of North Africa, the interest in Malta, the occupation of Corsica, the threats to Ragusa and the flattery to the Venetians and Genoese, and finally the aversion to the trade of Livorno, were, according to Galiani, clear indications of a strategic plan to dominate the trade in the Mediterranean.

Of course, in order to realistically achieve the goal of a commercial role in the eastern Mediterranean, it was necessary to provide the kingdom with an efficient navy and Galiani was pessimistic about this. Despite the efforts made by King Charles and Tanucci to strengthen the Neapolitan merchant and military fleet (see Sirago 2019), the state of the Neapolitan navy still appeared critical to Galiani due to three causes: "the bad faith of the masters and crews; their cowardice at the sight of the Barbary pirates; the inexperience of the pilots in sailing" (Galiani, MS-42: 134).[126] All these shortcomings were attributable, according to the Neapolitan abbot, to the absence of adequate economic incentives, both for ship owners and crews. He therefore proposed to set up a system of rewards for crews that captured Barbary ships, to award noble titles to captains who had demonstrated leadership skills, imitating the system in force in countries with a great seafaring tradition, such as England and Holland.

The attempt to reach an agreement with the Ottomans, entrusted to the diplomat William Maurice Ludolf (Galiani, MS-44; see Mafrici 2004), was unsuccessful due to the growing tension with Russia, which resulted in the Russian-Turkish war of 1787–1792, making trade across the Dardanelles difficult.

The offer of the newly-established Republic of the United States to establish trade relations with the Two Sicilies was substantially rejected by Galiani, for whom "admitting, indeed inviting North American merchants to our ports is a useful thing for our commerce, and to be defined also with solicitude. On the other hand, having our ships going to the ports of the United States of America is so far neither useful nor urgent to procure" (Galiani, MS-43: folio 1v). The Neapolitan abbot considered the initiative of the former British colonies not motivated by real economic interests, but a way to receive political recognition in Europe and "to rank among the other powers" (Galiani, MS-43: folio 2v) and proposed to wait prudently for Spain and France to make choices on formal agreements.[127]

[126] In order to strengthen the navy, Queen Maria Carolina called John Acton to Naples in 1778, who was destined to play an increasingly central role in the Neapolitan government.

[127] Galiani perceived the growing role of the rebel American colonies: "The time has come for the total collapse of Europe and the migration to America. Everything is falling apart here: religion, laws, arts, sciences: and everything will be rebuilt from scratch in America. This is not a joke, nor an idea drawn from English controversies: I said it, announced it, predicted it more than twenty years ago: and I have always seen my prophecies come true. So don't buy your house in Chaussée-d'Antin, you will buy it in Philadelphia. The misfortune is mine, because there are no abbeys in America" (Ferdinando Galiani's letter to Madame d'Épinay, Naples, 18 May 1776, published in Galiani 1881a, vol. II, 442–443; Galiani and d'Épinay 1997, vol. V: 75).

Galiani was therefore immune to the infatuation with rebel colonies that characterised many exponents of the Neapolitan Enlightenment, first and foremost Gaetano Filangieri, and adduced realistic reasons to his opinion, such as the scarcity of products that, according to him, the United States could offer, limited to tobacco, wood and wheat, which the Kingdom did not need, and above all the high risk of long-distance trade, as demonstrated by the difficulties experienced in trade with the West Indies (Galiani, MS-43: folio 2r).

The rebellion of the British colonies had led to tensions with England in previous years that Galiani probably wanted to avoid. In fact, during the American War of Independence, the free navigation in the Mediterranean of the Neapolitan fleet had been seriously threatened by the Royal Navy, which practised a systematic interdiction of the trade of states outside the conflict with its rebellious colonies, seizing and diverting neutral ships to English ports, under the pretext of considering them to be used to supply the rebellious colonies.

In response to this threat, on the initiative of the Empress of Russia, Catherine II, in 1780, the *League of Armed Neutrality* was established to defend free navigation (Kaplan 1995: 111–131). The League was joined by the kingdoms of Sweden and Denmark, joined by Prussia, Austria and Portugal in 1781, the Ottoman Empire in 1782 and the Kingdom of the Two Sicilies in 1783.[128] Adhesions induced by the fate of the United Provinces, which was involved in the conflict with England in December 1780.

In September 1778, Ferdinand IV had proclaimed his kingdom's neutrality in the Anglo-French conflict (which had begun in July 1778 and was later joined by Spain in June 1779). Galiani had taken part in the consultations for this choice[129] and following Catherine's declaration on neutrality, the Neapolitan abbot's study of the issue became the subject of a treatise on international law, *De' doveri de' principi neutrali verso i principi guerreggianti, e di questi verso i neutrali* (*Of the Duties of Neutral Princes towards the Fighting Princes, and of the latter towards the Neutrals,*

[128] See *Atto col quale Sua Maestà il Re delle Due Sicilie accede al sistema di neutralità marittima in favore del commercio e della navigazione*, in Archivio di Stato di Napoli, ME, 7396, see Monti (1942: 21–27) (which published the text of the *Treaty of Accession to the League*). See Trampus (2020: 103–105).

[129] The text of the edict of September 1778 proclaiming the neutrality of the Kingdom of Naples and the opinion of the Supreme Magistrate (of which Galiani was a member) are published in Monti (1942: 11–16).

Galiani 1782), begun in 1780[130] and laboriously completed two years later.[131]

The treatise was presented in a rather resigned manner, as an imperfect work, imposed by an "irresistible command", written "almost without the help of books [...] and by one who was among many tedious occupations distracted" (Galiani 1782: iii). It is unclear whether this statement was the usual dissimulation behind which Galiani liked to hide in order to confuse the reader and possible critics.[132] This too, like all his major works, was published anonymously. In reality, diplomatic matters could not have been foreign to him with the experience he gained during the decade in Paris.[133]

The treaty was intended to justify the policy of neutrality adopted by the Kingdom of Naples and defend the right of minor states not to be involved in wars between the great powers. This political line had been set by Tanucci, and Galiani had helped to define it in his diplomatic role in

[130] But the project of writing a treaty on international law had been in his interests since 1772: "I intend to study the law of nature in the works of de Buffon and on the basis of animals. In Abbé Prévost's collection of the *Travels*, I will look for the law of nations. The similarity between man and the dog forms the basis of my *Traité du Droit de la Paix et de la Guerre*; the similarity of man to the bull constitutes my principles of family law. After the two treatises on the law of nature and the law of nations comes my Public Law, which will be entitled: De l'Influence des Préjugés du Droit romain, sur le Système politique actuel de l'Europe" (Ferdinando Galiani's letter to Madame d'Épinay, Naples, 12 December 1772, published in Galiani 1881a, vol. II, 149–150; Galiani and d'Épinay 1994, vol. III: 172). See *Histoire générale des voyages*, in 15 volumes (1746–1759), by Antoine François Prévost d'Exiles.

[131] In a letter to Grimm in December 1780, Galiani mentioned the new work he had begun: "I have started a work on public law that I will publish in Italian, the only language I know at the moment. [...]. This book will be so heavy that people will swear it was written by Volfius or Puffendorfius. I fear I will not be able to finish this work, I am so discouraged [...] I only do this work for money. If it succeeds in Naples, I can earn four hundred francs by selling the whole edition. That's very little" (Ferdinando Galiani's letter to Friedrich Melchior von Grimm, Naples, 9 December 1780, published in Galiani 1881a, vol II: 602–603; see also Ferdinando Galiani's letter to Lorenzo Mehus, Naples, 25 June 1782, published in Galiani 1975: 1157–1158). See Diodati (1788: 76–78); Monti (1942); Demaria (1972); Galiani (1975: Guerci's Note, 645–650); Ghisalberti (1975); Catucci (1986: 143–157); Stapelbroek (2008b, 2011).

[132] According to Marco Catucci: "The obligation, as we learn from the correspondence, is a pure invention, a screen, as is the claim to have written without the help of books, and above all the speed of composition" (Catucci 1986: 147).

[133] A manuscript version of Galiani's treatise is kept in the Library of the Società Napoletana di Storia Patria (XXXI C 05). See Galiani (1975, Guerci's Note: 645–650).

France, as shown by the affair of the non-adhesion to the *Pacte de Famille*.[134]

In pursuit of this objective, Galiani divided the treatise into two parts: the first, broader, in which the subject of the duties of neutral princes was defined according to the principles of "pure morality and justice" (Galiani 1782: ix), while the second, just 21 pages long, was dedicated to the "maxims of that worldly policy, which under the name of *Reason of State* has been attempted to make tolerable to the peoples, and pleasing to the Sovereigns" (Galiani 1782: ix). Such a strict distinction was for Galiani necessary to avoid overlapping between the two distinct approaches, which was widely practised in *natural law* literature, and which caused "uncertainty in opinions, and mingling and contradiction in doctrines" (Galiani 1782: ix), mixing "the dictates of justice with the counsels of political prudence" (Galiani 1782: 5). The first part considered the issue of neutrality "as it should be", the second part, on the other hand, framed neutrality "as it was" in political reality. This distinction echoed Cicero's *De Officiis* (Cicero [1991]) based on the contrast between the honest-ethics of the first book and the useful-politics of the second book, whose maxims were often contrasted with those of modern writers.[135]

Galiani explicitly criticised the approach followed by Hugo Grotius in *De iure belli ac pacis* (*On the Law of War and Peace*, Grotius 1625 [2005])[136] and much of the Northern European natural law tradition (Galiani 1782: 274–275), which had completely ignored the subject of neutrality, with the exception of Emmeric de Vattel (1758, see Trampus 2020: 15–37) and the more profound Martin Hübner (1759).[137]

[134] The subject of neutrality had been addressed by Galiani in his report on the treaty of commerce with France in 1776 (see Galiani, MS-24; Monti 1942: 4–7; Guariglia 1914).

[135] On the relationship between Galiani and Cicero, see Catucci (1986: 147).

[136] "Hugh Grotius, who by the favour of his immense reading and prodigious memory, having embellished the old fabric of Public Law with a richly embroidered erudition, acquired fame as the founder of a science, which to the vagueness and lustre of that unusual ornament seemed entirely new, hardly devoted one or two chapters of his book *De Jure Belli, & Pacis* to speak of the rights and duties of neutrality" (Galiani 1782: 4). On the dissemination of Grotius' thought in Naples, see Conti (2002); Russo (2007). A translation of *De iure belli ac pacis* was published in Naples in 1777 (Grozio 1777).

[137] "This writer, however, did not deal generally with the duties of neutrality, except insofar as it was appropriate to illustrate the particular question of the seizure of ships, which he alone undertook to treat. I will not deny, however, that the work of this judicious jurist has been of great use to me, although in not a few opinions I have believed I must depart from him" (Galiani 1782: 5). See also Stapelbroek (2008b). Galiani planned a treatise against

The principles of pure morality that justified a prince's choice of neutrality had, according to Galiani, their foundation in natural law (*jus naturale*), but this doctrine had no solid theoretical basis, appealing from when needed to reason, conscience, the consensus of the people, the authority of philosophers, history, treaties, codes, and even the *Holy Scriptures*. This caused great uncertainty about principles. Instead, it became clear to Galiani that natural law, and the science of law in general, was nothing more than "a geometrical meditation on the truths that are deduced from certain principles, or axioms" (Galiani 1782: xi). As in geometry, in law too, a copious number of truths and solutions to problems could be deduced from a limited number of principles, just as innumerable demonstrations and truths descend from the single definition of the triangle. Galiani also followed a Newtonian methodology in this matter.

Following this intention, Galiani dedicated the first chapter of his treatise to *definitions* and *axioms*. The *first definition* concerned *sovereignty*, i.e. "any civilised society of men, under whatever species of government, be it monarchical, republican, or mixed, provided it has either absolute independence from any other, or as much independence as is sufficient to have the right of war and peace, and to be able freely and spontaneously to determine to remain neutral" (Galiani 1782: 6). Sovereignties could be in a *state of quiescence* (*second definition*) when the subjects of two nations, without any previous ties, met without conflict (as in the case of a contact between Neapolitans, Chinese or Hottentots). And it was the case of relations between distant peoples who peacefully entered into relations (Galiani 1782: 6). The *state of friendship* (*third definition*), on the other hand, is the knowledge and acquaintance between two peoples and between two sovereigns defined or not defined by treaties (the case of Neapolitans with respect to Hanseatic cities, Poland, Denmark or Sweden) (Galiani 1782: 6–7). And, finally, the *state of alliance* (*fourth definition*), established by two princes who have established a treaty providing for collaboration in the event of war. Consistent with these definitions, *neutrality* (*fifth definition*) is the condition of that "Prince, who, finding himself in a state of peace, friendship, or alliance with other Princes, who were at peace with each other, continues to remain in the same state towards them, even

Grotius: "the idea of composing this work came to me after being forced to read a few pages of Grotius (ah how delirious that man is)" (Ferdinando Galiani's letter to Madame d'Épinay, Naples, 24 May 1777, published in Galiani 1881a, vol. II, 509–510; Galiani and d'Épinay 1997, vol. V: 155–156).

though there has arisen either a rupture, or a fire of war between them" (Galiani 1782: 7). The term *neutrality* could contain an ambiguity, since neutral was the Prince who was completely extraneous to the conflict without having contact with the belligerents, and neutral could also be considered the Prince who equidistantly had commercial or other contacts with the belligerent parties. This is why he proposed specifying two forms of neutrality: *impartial refusal* (*imparziale rifiuto*, in the case of complete extraneousness to the conflict) and *impartial concession or tolerance* (*imparziale concessione* o *tolleranza*, in the case of contact with the belligerent parties) (Galiani 1782: 11).

To the *definitions*, Galiani added *axioms*: the principle that "all men are bound by duty of nature and humanity to provide other men with what benefits the needs and comforts of life, as far as they can, either to their profit, or without their harm" (*first axiom* called the *axiom of beneficence*) and that 'all men are obliged by the duty of nature and humanity not only not to harm other men, but to remove the causes, and to discourage the means by which men can harm each other, provided they can do so without danger of harm to themselves' (*second axiom*, called the *axiom of justice*) (Galiani 1782: 12). The limits within which human action (of *charity* and *justice*) occurs are defined by the benefit or absence of harm and thus always governed by shrewd selfishness.[138] Full altruism, unconditioned by advantage or absence of harm, does not belong to human nature nor to the essence of societies. And he further specified: "Justice is not to subtract or deny to others what belongs to them [...] but to give one's own to others, to lend one's own work never previously promised, belongs to charity, and one never has the right to demand it for justice. This is the substantial difference between the allied prince and the friend. From the

[138] "The beneficence of one who would free from the gallows, or from prison another man almost unknown to him, who has been deservedly condemned there, would be absurd. Such an action deserves no other title than foolishness or crime" (Galiani 1782: 36). Koen Stapelbroek advocates a different thesis according to which Galiani "defended the significance of the principles of beneficence and universal society and argued that people were naturally sociable. Yet, he was eager to distinguish his views from any kind of cosmopolitanism that stipulated that it was natural for people to have an equal amount of fellow-feeling, compassion and friendship for the whole of humankind" (Stapelbroek 2008b: 85). And "The driving principle of progress in the history of humankind and the rise of civilisation was beneficence, a natural love or friendship that people naturally felt and that held societies together. Beneficence was always related to commerce and the level of people's mutual understanding of their ideas" (Stapelbroek 2011: 169). But it is an interpretation that greatly forces Galiani's thinking, which is in a completely different direction.

ally, by justice, the aid stipulated and agreed upon is demanded; from the friend, it is implored by that feeling of humanity which one hopes to find in him. So it can never be said that he is unjust who refuses to lend his help and his work, but only that he can sometimes be called ruthless and inhuman" (Galiani 1782: 31). "One cannot confuse", Galiani concluded, "the constant and precise duties of *justice* with the impulses of *beneficence*" (Galiani 1782: 31).[139] That mistake is made by natural law theorists.

Having established the fundamental principles by applying the geometric method, Galiani drew certain consequences from them. Isolated sovereignties can be considered - Galiani observed - as men in the state of nature, "not yet bound, nor willing to spontaneously submit to any bond of civil society" (Galiani 1782: 14).[140] In the state of nature, men, like the sovereignties assimilated to them, have two duties: towards themselves and towards the species. And these are not two motives that run like parallel lines, but intersect, converge or diverge, and in the combination of these two different duties lies virtue: "Every moral question therefore is not a simple search for how in a given case one can do the greatest good to oneself, or even how one can do the greatest good to others; but it is a

[139] To clarify this point, Galiani gave an example: "Suppose one man owes another one hundred *Scudi* for the price of something sold to him, or for any other legal contract. Everyone understands that this man's debt is certainly fixed at one hundred *Scudi* neither more nor less. Now suppose on the other hand that an unfortunate man reduced to begging begs for charity from a rich man. It is a debt of charity to succour him. But how much must this rich man give to the poor? The sum is never fixed. There may be circumstances, that I do not say a hundred, but a thousand *Scudi* is such a small amount, that it deserves to be reproached as cruelty not to have given more. There may be other circumstances such that a single *Soldo* is sufficient charity. There may be no obligation to give anything, and there may be cases in which the use of charity would be a vice and a fault (which the algebraists would express by saying that charity then becomes one of the negative quantities). This is what I meant by saying that the duties of *justice* are to be considered as constant quantities; whereas those of *beneficence* are variable quantities, which may rise and fall according to the ordinates of certain curves, and reach zero, and even recede to the contrary. Nor can it be objected to me that even debts of justice may vary and diminish or increase, as if interest and usury had to be paid on a sum due: for on reflection everyone will understand that the amounts vary in debts of justice due to extrinsic causes (such as the delay of time, the distance of places from which the change arises, and other cases) whereas debts of charity are in themselves and intrinsically variant and indeterminate if they are not applied to the circumstances of each particular case" (Galiani 1782: 32).

[140] "Sovereignties are in a state of nature among themselves; they have no prince, no superior, no other guardian of their reasons, except their own forces, brought together by the bonds of friendship, or alliance" (Galiani 1782: 28).

compound problem, which always boils down to determining how in a given case one can do the greatest good to oneself with the least harm to others, or on the contrary how one can obtain the greatest good of other men with the least inconvenience to oneself" (Galiani 1782: 16–17). Galiani proposed a utilitarian type of morality, consistent with what he had defined in *Della Moneta*: human actions were to be judged according to the utility they generated for those who performed them and those who underwent them (Galiani 1782: 66, note).

The solution of ethical problems could follow the method that the *geometers* (mathematicians) called *De Maximis et Minimis*, "the theories of which are so admirably adapted to the study of morals, that it is strange that so little or nothing has been seen of their correlation so far" (Galiani 1782: 18). And of this method he gave an example applied to moral questions: "one might consider and express one class of human duties as the *abscissae*, another class as the *ordinates* of some *curve*. Then the boundary of human actions would be expressed by that curve, which would thus designate in its various points the quantity and the greater or lesser magnitude of virtues and vices. That is, one might sometimes consider the progression of human actions under the semblance of a circular curve, having for its tangent the perfection of the virtues. At one point the curve touches it, and wanting to push it further, it turns away from it and moves away from it as much as it had approached it. Thus with geometric clarity one can understand what men have said in a certain coarse way, that virtue lies in the middle; which is not always true" (Galiani 1782: 18, note). The human will assumed the form of a *hyperbola* between two *asymptotes*: "freedom and coercion, with which it does not entirely coincide, since there is no human act, however spontaneous, that does not have a little necessity mixed with it, nor, on the contrary, any violence or coercion that does not leave a little freedom to escape it: so that there is in nature neither perfect freedom nor perfect coercion of the will" (Galiani 1782: 412, note).[141] In a footnote to the text, Galiani drafts an example of geometrical formalization, using a coordinate system, in which the two contrasting human forces give rise to a circular curve, whose tangent represents the perfection of virtues (Galiani 1782: 18, footnote 1).[142] In this attempt at

[141] See Galiani (1782: 412, note). On ethical problems in Galiani, see Leonzio (2014). See also Catucci (1986: 149–150).

[142] Another example of Galiani's way of reasoning is offered by his correspondence. He writes: "If we create a calculated geometry, we find the *good* = *x*, the *evil* = *y*, and the equation

formalization, Galiani follows Leibniz's argument on the relation between geometrical quantities and the shape of a curve, and the Newtonian terminology (explicitly using the term *fluent*; Galiani 1782: 267), but he ignores the concept of functional relation, as the expression of the relationship between variables by means of ***equations***, outlined in Eulero's classic *Introductio in Analysin Infinitorum* of 1748 (Euler 1748). Galiani's method is completely influenced by the concept of calculus developed by Newton and Leibniz. In fact the principal object of study was the analysis of geometric curves, formulated in different methods for solving problems regarding curves, tangents to curves, areas under curves, lengths of curves, and velocities of points moving along curves (Kleiner 1989).

Galiani proposed a moral science that had to have geometric rigour in the clarity of its expressions and demonstrations, because its object, like geometry, consisted of comparable relations of magnitudes, which could be expressed by means of calculation (Galiani 1782: 16, 20 notes). The attempt to construct a moral discourse on axiomatic principles first outlined by Baruch Spinoza was taken up by Baron d'Holbach, Galiani's friend and correspondent, in his *Système de la Nature* (d'Holbach 1770 [1889]).[143]

Consistent with this approach of method, the same geometric and utilitarian proportions must be applied to war, which arises from the state of nature in which only force prevails and not law, guaranteeing the

will be: $+x - x = 0$; $+y - y = 0$" (Ferdinando Galiani's letter to Madame d'Epinay, Naples, 26 April 1777, published in Galiani 1881a, vol. II: 504; Galiani and d'Épinay 1997, vol. V: 150).

[143] "Morals is the science of the relations that subsist between the minds, the wills, and the actions of men, in the same manner that geometry is the science of the relations that are found between bodies. Morals would be a chimera and would have no certain principles, if it was not founded upon the knowledge of the motives which must necessarily have an influence upon the human will, and which must necessarily determine the actions of human beings" (D'Holbach 1770 [1889]: 98). Galiani knew d'Holbach's work and his opinion was not positive: "I leafed through *Système de la Nature*. It seems to me to be by the same hand that produced *Christianisme dévoilé* (D'Holbach 1766) and *Militaire philosophe* (Naigeon and D'Holbach 1768). It is too long. It does not seem to be written with composure, and this is a great flaw, because one might think that the author does not so much need to persuade others as to persuade himself. In essence, we do not know enough about nature to form a system" (Ferdinando Galiani's letter to Madame d'Épinay, Naples, 30 June 1770, published in Galiani 1881a, vol. I: 180–181; Galiani and d'Épinay 1992, vol. I: 196; see also Ferdinando Galiani's letter to baron d'Holbach, Naples, 24 July 1770, published in Galiani 1881a, vol. I: 203). "A copy with a dedication of the *Doveri* (kept in the Paris Bibliothèque Nationale) was sent to d'Holbach" (Galiani, 1975: 648, Guerci's note).

minimum violation of the axiom of beneficence compatible with the achievement of the object of war: "therefore the entire science of the law of war is also the study of the solution of a problem *de maximis et minimis*, and therefore, if, for example, to achieve a victory it is sufficient to kill one hundred men, one cannot kill one thousand. To do so is a violence, even if one acts against one's enemies, because these, although enemies, are men with whom there is an eternal bond of duty" (Galiani 1782: 22).[144]

The choice of neutrality must also be compatible - Galiani stated - with the axioms of beneficence and justice. Excluding in fact the case of distant states at war, disproportion of force with the belligerent parties and the absence of friendly relations, the question of the choice of neutrality arises for a "Prince not distant by situation of dominion, equally friendly with two others, not bound to any of them by a treaty of alliance,[145] and whose forces are such as to carry weight in the war, may, in the event of war between them, determine to remain neutral without failing in the duties of justice and friendship that he has with them" (Galiani 1782: 26–27). The rule that is applied to subjects not to intervene in the quarrels of others cannot be applied in the condition of the state of nature in which there is no higher authority legitimised to use force. Therefore, if a friendly state is attacked, intervention is required, except if the forces of the party attacked are sufficient to repel the aggressor and if there are doubts about the legitimacy of the aggression (Galiani 1782: 29–30). Intervention is not a matter of justice as Grotius claimed in the concept of just war, but of beneficence. Law, and therefore justice, can be claimed in treaties, but - Galiani concluded - if intervention is the effect of friendly succour, it pertains to the feeling of beneficence, which is the product of considerations

[144] "War is the greatest expense, the greatest damage, and the greatest danger to a sovereignty; so great are the consequences of the massacres, the devastation of fields and buildings, the debts, the tributes, the extraction of money, and the total depletion that war causes, to which ruin is often added the much greater consequence of alterations in the laws, customs, and even the constitution of the State. An earthquake, an epidemic, a fire, a famine, destroying one or more cities, though horrible calamities scourges of celestial wrath, are not comparable to this scourge, which man gives to himself: for neither the effect of them stretches so far, nor lasts so long, and because experience shows us, that from those aforementioned evils, those who remain, soon rise up, and rise again, whereas an unhappy war may go so far as to make a nation lose its independence and liberty forever: and in the opinion of wise men, slavery is worse than death" (Galiani 1782: 45–46).

[145] "An alliance contains the promise of the union either of all, or of one stipulated to quantity of forces in all the manifestly just wars of the ally, and also in the doubtful ones, in which there are reasons to be weighed for one side and for the other" (Galiani 1782: 131).

on the damage suffered by the aggrieved, on his forces, on the causes of the war and on the degree of friendship (Galiani 1782: 32–33). Only "when all these three reasons are united and come to be in that degree that geometers would say a maximum, the duty of beneficence can become as forcible and stringent as that of the most exact justice" (Galiani 1782: 34). And therefore "only in very few cases is it a forced duty not to remain neutral, but in very many one can or even must" (Galiani 1782: 38).

The choice of neutrality was thus a prerogative of sovereign states, "a natural right, inherent, innate, as much as that of equality, freedom, and independence between man and man in the so-called state of nature" (Galiani 1782: 141),[146] and "no sovereign has the right to compel another sovereignty that is absolute and independent of him, nor obliged by any pact, to join it and take part in the war that it wages or that is waged against it by a third power" (Galiani 1782: 140) and this principle must also be applied to states that are bound together by dynastic kinship (an explicit reference to the *Pacte de Famille* affair) (Galiani 1782: 88–100).

Having defined the nature of the choice of neutrality, Galiani discussed its consequences. Using the terminology of Newton's *Principia*, the Neapolitan abbot specified that the state of neutrality could not be considered a new condition in which the Prince found himself, but corresponded to a "permanence, a continuation of the previous state, coming precisely from the fact that no new cause had arisen with respect to him that obliged him to change it: and this is not only a general law of every Sovereignty, and of every man, but it is the same universal law of the whole of nature, called by the philosophers *force* of *inertia*, which reduces to this, that without a new cause there is no mutation of state or motion in any body" (Galiani 1782: 142; italics added). Unlike Grotius and other natural law scholars, Galiani did not interpret neutrality in terms of equal conduct towards belligerent parties, but more simply as the continuation of existing relations, especially trade relations.

[146] "This is the highest and most perfect right that can be comprehended in man. Natural freedom, or independence, is in morality what solidity, or impenetrability, is in physics. When the idea of solidity disappears, all matter vanishes, because if the bodies interpenetrate, the whole world becomes one atom. Behind the light of this idea, one understands well what is meant when it is said that by nature all men are equal. It means what a physicist means when he establishes that the solidity of a grain of sand is equal to that of a mountain. He does not measure size: he only says, that that grain is incompenetrable by the mountain, and therefore always remains an entity and cannot become a nothing in nature" (Galiani 1782: 141–142).

However - he observed - the state of neutrality imposes certain restrictions consistent with the principle of friendship and humanity and every sovereign is obliged "to remove not only all causes, but to divert the means, so that the warriors may prolong the duration of the war" (Galiani 1782: 149). Consequently, in the name of the right to property, the transit of belligerent armies through neutral territory must be prevented (Galiani 1782: 158–160), the right of asylum must also be allowed for deserters, for the right of responsibility (Galiani 1782: 182), the use of fortresses or infrastructures must not be allowed (Galiani 1782: 237).

The trade of neutral parties with the belligerent state can therefore legitimately continue if it concerns "all those things, which benefit the life and the harmless pleasure of men" (Galiani 1782: 150)[147] and does not become an activity of speculation (Galiani 1782: 221).[148] The belligerent parties have a duty not to hinder this kind of trade produced by the *impartial concession*, because the disadvantage suffered by a neutral people in being banned from trading during the entire duration of the war is so much greater than the advantage that the enemy of the war can expect from this embargo policy. And it is "a duty not of strict justice, but of equity, and of regard for the innocent, and impartial friend to whom there is no valid reason to cause so much harm" (Galiani 1782: 304).[149] Galiani

[147] Galiani defined a list of illegitimate goods: mules, horses, weapons, vessels, worked iron, sulphur, saltpetre, wood. Legitimate goods were unworked iron and hemp, tar, pitch, small timber, money and mercenary troops (Galiani 1782: 325–362).

[148] Exchanges between neutral and belligerent parties in a state of necessity must be regulated - Galiani specified - according to the price of natural equity dependent "on the general duties of humanity" (Galiani 1782: 218), which "may legitimately extend and embrace the fortunate profit made by the seller on the buyer's urgency, provided that the immoderate excess is contained" (Galiani 1782: 221).

[149] Galiani condemned smuggling not according to the right of belligerent parties (Galiani 1782: 320) but according to morality, "since to refrain from regularly supplying contraband of war to combatants is an honest duty of neutral parties, therefore any artifice, any fraud, any masquerade becomes indecent and undeserving of excuse" (Galiani 1782: 322). Galiani contested the opinion of the Tuscan jurist Giovanni Maria Lampredi, according to whom the transport of goods by the subjects of a neutral state on the territory of the belligerent state could be defined as smuggling, whereas if the transport was carried out by foreigners, it could not be defined as smuggling (Lampredi 1778: Pars III. Chap. 12. § 9. n. 4). And Galiani objected: "It is my constant habit, when I have to examine some question of law or morality, to see it under the most trivial and vulgar aspect: to strip it of all ornaments of maxims and general judgments, and to propose it as if I had to give it to the stupidest of the plebs to resolve. Doing so in this matter immediately reveals the fallacy of the distinction imagined by Lampredi. I propose to let one of the common people decide whether it can be

then condemned the activities of privateers and the violations of neutral ships permitted by maritime customs as defined by the *Libre de Consolat de Mar*, "which the coarseness and unhappiness of the [fourteenth] century immediately converted into a *Code of Laws* without it ever having any other intrinsic force of authority, except for a certain natural good sense of equity" (Galiani 1782: 468).

The right of neutral parties to maintain lawful trade was also to be defended with arms, "in the reasonableness of this natural defence of one's own well-being and comfort, no less than the preservation of any perfect right, stands the justice of the determination to form that alliance which today has assumed the name of *armed neutrality*" (Galiani 1782: 304). An apparently contradictory term that unites "the contrary ideas of peace, and of arms, of friendship towards both warriors, of distrust, and of apparatus against both", but which established a principle of rational conduct in confusion and arbitrariness (Galiani 1782: 284).

From neutrality conceived according to the abstract and ideal principles of justice and equity, Galiani went on to define neutrality according to the political reality of *Reason of State*, understood as "that science and that concatenation of counsels, which direct a Sovereignty solely to its enlargement by whatever means, making no other choice among the ways but to always prefer the most useful, the safest, the most effective" (Galiani 1782: 490). In this context where sovereignties are all at odds with each other, neutrality is viewed with distrust by the belligerent parties, because neutral countries get rich in wars.[150] It is therefore convenient for belligerent parties to negotiate with the more powerful neutral states to obtain their support or to ensure that they do not give it to the adversary, and it is convenient to invade small neighbouring neutral states to draw them into the war (Galiani 1782: 493–497). States at war must prevent neutral

said that the innkeepers do not supply the city of Naples with wine because they wait for those who go to their cellars to buy wine, and that only the oil sellers supply it because with a wineskin on their person they transport and sell house to house. The man of the people laughs in my face, telling me that both supply, both sell: only the oil vendor relieves the buyer of a penalty that he takes on himself by making him pay for it. This ordinary decision is enough to refute Lampredi's opinion" (Galiani 1782: 339). On the dispute between Galiani and Lampredi concerning the trade of neutral parties, see Vidari (1868); Miglio (1942).

[150] "Because the countries close to the war provide the armies with food and provisions of all kinds, and so they earn money from it; their maritime trade flourishes under the friendly flag of all; they collect the families expatriated and impoverished by the war, and so they acquire cultivators, artisans, manufacturers, so that their population grows more than what is lacking in those where the fire of the war has been more furious" (Galiani 1782: 493).

nations from profiting from trade and smuggling. For states that choose neutrality, the objective is simply to protect their own interests and take advantage of others' state of war (Galiani 1782: 503–510).

Despite the fact that Galiani had devoted only a few pages to the second book, this part was the real heart of the treatise, disproving everything that had been stated in the long first part.[151] Tacitus, Niccolò Machiavelli, Giovanni Botero, Traiano Boccalini, and even Francesco Guicciardini, i.e. the Italian tradition of political thought, burst onto the scene in the few final pages of the treatise, and the arrogance and harshness of treaties imposed by force emerged. Galiani so skillfully contrasted the abstractness of the principles of the first part with the concreteness of the political reality of the second part: the "as it is" prevailed over the "as it should be".[152] His role as advisor to the Prince certainly could not be based on the sterile academic arguments discussed in the first book; all his activity as diplomatic agent had been guided by the criteria of *Reason of State* and certainly not guided by abstract moral principles, in which the abbot had never believed.[153] Galiani himself claimed his realist vision in a letter to d'Épinay: "in politics, I only accept *Machiavellianism* (*Machiavélisme*) pure and simple, raw, green, in all its strength, in all its bitterness"[154].

Galiani loved the subtle art of dissimulation: he hid behind an old sage in *Della Moneta*, under the guise of the brilliant and sceptical Chevalier Zanobi in the *Dialogues*, and with the curious structure given to the *Doveri*, feigning an incomplete draft, he ridiculed the entire natural law tradition. As the anonymous reviewer of the *Novelle Letterarie* observed:

[151] A similar opinion on Galiani's work is in Demaria (1972: 648–650); Amodio (1997a: 308–324). Croce on the other hand held that "the political and Machiavellian Galiani wrote a refutation of the *Ragion di Stato*" (Croce 1932: 100, note).

[152] A very different position from Gaetano Filangieri for whom: "The great damage which the Shipowners have caused to be suffered in this last war, particularly to the nations of both hemispheres; the little advantage which the nations themselves have derived from it, from the ports of which they have been shipped; the progress which the system of armed neutrality is making: these are many causes, which give us reason to hope, that a new law will soon be added to the common law of nations, by which it will be forbidden to the belligerent nations, to have recourse in the future to this infamous means of harming their enemies at the expense of universal tranquillity" (Filangieri 1784: 385).

[153] In the second edition of *Della Moneta*, Galiani criticising Montesquieu reiterated: "He who writes about the arts of government has to say of things as they are, not as he would like them to be" (Galiani 1780: Notes XXXI, 413).

[154] Ferdinando Galiani's letter to Madame d'Épinay, Naples, 5 September 1772, published in Galiani (1881a, vol. II: 114); Galiani and d'Épinay (1994, vol. III: 104).

"The combination is curious, to have *Socrates* and *Machiavello* on the same scene" (Novelle Letterarie 1783: 206).

The criticism of natural law was not extraneous to the Neapolitan intellectual context. Vico had strongly criticised the doctrines of Hugo Grotius, Samuel Pufendorf and John Selden, accusing them of abstractionism because they ignored historical reality and "[they] failed to distinguish the natural law of the nations, which was coeval with their customs, from the natural law of the philosophers, which the latter grasped by force of reasoning" (Vico 1728 [1975], see Ruggiero 2018).[155] A critical position that Galiani took up in his *Doveri*.

The book did not have the success of the *Dialogues* although its approach to such a controversial topic did not go entirely unnoticed by the anonymous reviewer of the *Novelle Letterarie:* "The first two chapters especially show the man of great genius, both for the clarity and precision of his ideas, and for the subtle opinions he has on social duties and the rectitude of heart and mind in assigning the principles of justice, not confusing them, as even the early schoolmasters frequently did, with those of beneficence, equity, expediency, etc., and showing almost geometrically the difference [...]. In the other chapters he shows himself to be no less ingenious in the application of established principles than he is in the frankness of matters of state, and adorned with the finest erudition, not as Grotius and his followers accumulated ad nauseam. Everything is written with a certain liberty, which in great minds is not only tolerated, but admired and revered [...]. It is perhaps the first time that one speaks to kings, among themselves, as one speaks to other men in society" (Novelle letterarie 1783: 201, 206).[156] Galiani reacted "against the rampant anti-

[155] "The findings of English, Dutch, and German scholars in the seventeenth and eighteenth centuries with regards to the maxims of a just government, conducted on the basis of only rational evidence without considering the history of nations, seemed to him [Vico] wrongheaded and insufficient as a result of a lack of critical method [arte critica]". They had confused "the natural law of nations, coming out of their customs, with the natural law of philosophers, which they had understood as the force of reason" (Ferrone 2012: 73–74).

[156] On the limited fortune of the *Doveri*, see Galiani (1975: 648–649), Guerci's note. Galiani's essay had a more favourable reception in Germany, where it was also translated (see Galiani 1790; Bernardini 1995, 2000). See Karl Johann Friedrich Count von Medem's letter to Ferdinando Galiani, Berlin, 30 April 1785, who referred to the judgement of the King of Prussia expressed in a letter sent to him: "I am very grateful for the attention of the Abbé de Galiani in Naples. His work on the reciprocal duties of neutral powers, a copy of which he gave you to present to me, has been well received. I received it as a sign of his feelings for me, of which it will be a perpetual monument in my great Library in Berlin" (BSNSP, XXXI.A.13,

Romanist polemic", confirming "a constant and repeated adherence to the type of culture in which he had been formed and to which he did not want, despite his vast contacts with the Enlightenment, Italian and French intellectual world, to renounce in any way" (Ghisalberti 1975: 52).[157] And yet he did not avoid criticism of the jurists' interpretations of Roman law: "In the *Code* and in the following *Constitutions* of the Byzantine Empire, in matters concerning the general economy, the police, finances and trade, among the very few good laws, one finds a heap of very foolish ones, the work of the whim or inexperience of the worst princes who have dishonoured the throne. The moderns, however, have blindly worshipped them, leading them into error by believing they were created by the great Romans [...]. But those who meditate on them will spare themselves the trouble of reading the applauded modern works on the causes of the decadence of the Roman Empire, because in that filthy and false legislation they will immediately recognise the true causes that destroyed it" (Galiani 1782: 306–307).

His substantial adherence to a traditional view of legal relations, his critique of natural law in the version of Grotius' school (which brought him closer to Vico and the *veteres*) and his rejection of any reform of the existing institutional set-up distanced him from the innovative ferment that characterised Neapolitan culture in the 1780s.

While Galiani was slowly and laboriously writing his *Doveri,* the young Gaetano Filangeri published the first two volumes of his *Scienza della Legislazione* (*The Science of Legislation*), which immediately gained great acclaim. New intellectual figures emerged, "born of university reforms, of modern Masonic social patterns, and of the renewal of the academies and the publishing system after the tremendous 1764 famine had bared the worst injustice and structural backwardness of the Old Regime, the party of enlightened philosophers definitely appeared on the scene as a loud and effective force in the Kingdom's political struggle. [...] Cosmopolitans, lovers of civil liberty, they no longer limited themselves to addressing the

folio 253r, published in Flora 1927: 233). In order to learn about the reactions to the *Doveri* in the various Italian states, Galiani kept up correspondence with various local exponents, in particular Lorenzo Mehus in Florence, Benedetto Stay in Rome, and Giovan Battista Grimaldi in Genoa.

[157] Carlo Ghisalberti's opinion is strongly contested by Marco Catucci, according to whom Ghisalberti "reads *Corpus iuris civilis* instead of Roman laws. It is in fact only the *Digest*, the collection of *Responsa Prudentum*, that is the object of Galiani's admiration, not the entire *Corpus* of which he has not spared criticism" (Catucci 1986: 156).

sovereign to auspicate his assistance, but independently identified their principal interlocutor in public opinion. Unveiling the truth regarding the mechanisms of power to the citizenry, unmasking the enemies of justice and of equality, educating the people, and delineating the salient traits of a future just society through books and pamphlets had by then come to constitute their inalienable objectives" (Ferrone 2012: 11).

Galiani was extraneous to this new mentality and this new intellectual circle, even though he shared their criticism of the excessive power of the *togati*. He observed with disappointment the ferment that animated Neapolitan intellectual life: "Freedom is general here. Naturally it bears good fruit and bad, but the harvest of the good exceeds that of the bad; and in everything we must bless the government of the statue of liberty we enjoy, little enjoyed elsewhere. Surely that same impunity that makes a Sarcone vomit libels, encourages a Filangieri, a Galanti lawyer, to produce good books, and in this exchange we gain, because the good books remain, the bad ones rot on the dunghill that generated them".[158]

Nor was his opinion of reformist and enlightened intellectuals positive: "The inclination of all mediocre minds is to shine by the tone and flavour of the century. It requires much character in the soul to ignore endless fame and applause, as soon as one adopts the fashionable tone, and becomes Beccaria, Genovesi, Badaud [Nicolas Baudeau], Roubaud, etc".[159]

Galiani's substantial isolation in this new intellectual climate[160] was confirmed by his exclusion from the *Reale Accademia di Scienze e Belle Lettere* founded in Naples in June 1778.[161] Galiani expressed his irritation to Madame d'Épinay: "There is another thing that will seem even more surprising to you, because my own country was astonished. An *Academy of*

[158] Ferdinando Galiani's letter to Lorenzo Mehus, Naples, 25 June 1782, published in Galiani (1975: 1159).

[159] Ferdinando Galiani's letter to Baron Grimm, Naples, 20 March 1775, published in Galiani (1881a, vol. II, 392–393). Ironically, Galiani wrote Badaud instead of Baudeau: the term describes idle curiosity, gullibility, simpleminded foolishness and gaping ignorance.

[160] "I have been ignorant of what a conversation is for two years. In the absence of other reasonable animals, my only companion is a cat" (Ferdinando Galiani's letter to Madame Necker, Naples, 6 July 1771, published in Galiani 1881a, vol. I: 414). And: "My poor Neapolitans are completely unaware that I have published works, and if they knew, they would not care" (Ferdinando Galiani's letter to Madame d'Épinay, Naples, 10 May 1777, published in Galiani 1881a, vol. II: 506; Galiani and d'Épinay 1997, vol. V: 153).

[161] The new academy was directed by the physician Michele Sarcone, who excluded some Neapolitan cultural figures he disliked, such as Galiani, Gaetano Filangieri, Mario Pagano and Domenico Caracciolo.

Sciences and letters has been founded, and I am not one of them. Remember that man of letters, unknown to Diderot, who quietly said to him: *Sir, I work for the colonies!* I say the same thing: I am in Naples and work for Saint Petersburg!".[162] His hostility towards the new Academy grew over the years: "All they do is publish bloody satires against me. Fortunately, public opinion is on my side, and the authors of these satires are the object of absolute contempt. All this anger comes from a certain academy of sciences, which claims to have been founded here, of which I refused to be a member, as did some other men who also disdained it. This academy began by wanting to make an excellent and superior theriac than that of Venice, and by wanting to force the apothecaries to buy it. One can judge from this the character of this academy, which was founded more for financial purposes than for the advancement of human knowledge. I know that last year, when they wanted to found this academy here, they wrote to d'Alembert and others in France to tell them that they had been made honorary members. Please tell me if d'Alembert and the others accepted this honour and what was their response. There has been the deepest silence about their reply, so please let me know what is going on".[163]

Galiani's claim about his relationship with Saint Petersburg was not without reason: beyond his diplomatic role, Galiani was known in the Russian imperial court for his scholarly qualities. His *Dialogues* had been read with great interest in Saint Petersburg and also translated into Russian (Galiani 1776; Gambacorta 1988: 336). The esteem was reciprocal, as Galiani admired the form of enlightened despotism represented by Empress Catherine II[164] and prophesied: "The great ruler of Europe will be the prince of our Tartars, that is, the one who will own Poland, Russia and Prussia, and command the Baltic and the Black Sea. For the peoples

[162] Ferdinando Galiani's letter to Madame d'Épinay, Naples, 1 August 1778, published in Galiani (1881a, vol. II: 556, italic added); Galiani and d'Épinay (1997, vol. V: 192). See also Nicolini (1923: xxi–xxviii).

[163] Ferdinando Galiani's letter to Madame d'Épinay, Naples, 18 March 1780, published in Galiani (1881a, vol. II: 585–586); Galiani and d'Épinay (1997, vol. V: 221).

[164] "Catherine is a great woman because she is intolerant and conquering; and all great men have been intolerant, and we must be. If one encounters a foolish prince on one's path, one must preach tolerance to him, so that he falls into the trap and the crushed party has time to get back on its feet thanks to the tolerance granted to it and to crush the opponent in turn. The sermon on tolerance is therefore a sermon given to fools and tricksters, or people who have no interest in the matter" (Ferdinando Galiani's letter to Madame d'Épinay, Naples 22 June 1771, published in Galiani 1881a, vol. I: 407–408; Galiani and d'Épinay 1993, vol. II: 131). An attack also against Voltaire's principle of tolerance.

of the North will always be less vile than those of the South. The rest of the princes will be controlled by the policy of this predominant government".[165] The contacts were certainly favoured by the presence in Saint Petersburg of Diderot and especially Grimm, who became a trusted man of the czarina and her ambassador to the European courts, but due to his diplomatic experience, Galiani also had direct acquaintances with Russian political figures.[166] The *petit abbé* looked at these assignments with a certain scepticism[167] and, with his usual detached irony, doubted the diffusion of his thought at the Petersburg court: "I had suspected that the Empress of Russia knew me; in fact, since she sends presents to an infinity of writers she does not know, seeing that I did not receive any, I immediately said to myself: she must know me"[168]. Invited by Grimm to Saint Petersburg, Galiani declined, preferring "an epistolary exchange, more intense than hitherto [that] could delight the Empress at least as much as a face-to-face conversation and would cost her about a quarter of the cost of my trip and stay in Russia".[169] Certainly the abbot would have had more prestige in Saint Petersburg, as the empress was astonished at the secondary role attributed to him in Naples: "the head of that man [Galiani] is useless in Naples, his works are ignored and decrees are made in the old-fashioned way without making use of him and his wise ideas".[170] And indeed Catherine used Galiani for a number of commissions, such as the

[165] Ferdinando Galiani's letter to Madame d'Épinay, Naples, 27 April 1771, published in Galiani (1881a, vol. I: 387–388); Galiani and d'Épinay (1993, vol. II: 100). Catherine was repeatedly praised in her *Doveri*, see Galiani (1782: libro I, capo IX, par. I, capo x, par. II).

[166] In particular with Andrej Petrovič Šuvalov, who was his guest in Naples, see Ferdinando Galiani's letter to Madame d'Épinay, Naples, 13 April 1771, published in Galiani (1881a, vol. I: 381); Galiani and d'Épinay (1993, vol. II: 91). On the relationship between Catherine and the *philosophes*, see Zaretsky (2019).

[167] "In Paris philosophers stay in the open air, in Stockholm and Saint Petersburg they keep them in the warmth of greenhouses. In Naples we breed them in manure, because the climate is not favourable to them" (Ferdinando Galiani's letter to Madame d'Épinay, Naples, 18 June 1774, published in Galiani 1881a, vol. II: 322; Galiani and d'Épinay 1993, vol. IV, 1996: 151).

[168] Ferdinando Galiani's letter to Baron Grimm, Naples, 20 March 1775, published in Galiani (1881a, vol. II: 392). In reality, the empress had read the *Dialogues* and was fascinated by it, see Catherine's letter to Baron Grimm, 25 November 1777, published in Catherine II and Grimm (2016: 118).

[169] Ferdinando Galiani's letter to Madame d'Épinay, Naples, 31 May 1777, published in Galiani (1881a, vol. II: 512); Galiani and d'Épinay (1997, vol. V: 158–159).

[170] Catherine's letter to Baron Grimm, 30 November 1778, published in Catherine II and Grimm (2016: 191).

Latin inscription for the monument to Peter the Great,[171] the drafting of a celebratory work on the model of Plutarch's *Paralele Lives,* in which Catherine was to be compared to Louis XV,[172] and which was never completed,[173] and a programme for the celebrations of the twentieth anniversary of her coronation (Gambacorta 1988: 343). In return the empress had bought Berardo Galiani's library at a good price and rewarded Ferdinando with several medals (Gambacorta 1988: 343; Carrafiello 2019).[174]

Apart from formal tributes abroad or at home, such as that paid to him by Gaetano Filangieri,[175] the new generation saw Galiani as rather distant

[171] See Ferdinando Galiani's letter to Baron Grimm, Naples, 17 October 1772, published in Galiani (1881a, vol. II: 122–123).

[172] See Baron Grimm's letter to Ferdinando Galiani, Saint Petersburg, 3 December 1776, published in Galiani (1903–1904: 506).

[173] See Ferdinando Galiani's letter to Baron Grimm, Naples, 17 January 1777, published in Galiani (1903–1904: 509–511).

[174] "[Grimm] had the Empress of Russia buy my brother's books and prints at the price I asked for. The service consists in the fact that I took revenge on my kind compatriots, who wanted to buy it for nothing" (Ferdinando Galiani's letter to Madame d'Épinay, Naples, 20 July 1776, published in Galiani 1881a, vol. II: 457; Galiani and d'Épinay 1997, vol. V: 88–89).

[175] This is also demonstrated by the formal homage that Gaetano Filangieri dedicates to him in his *Scienza della legislazione*, but which is not followed by an effective understanding of Galiani's theses that are substantially misunderstood or removed altogether. In the second book of his *Scienza*, Filangieri wrote: "I do not undertake here to demonstrate the inconsistency of Melon's proposed system of regulating extraction by price. This erroneous system has been refuted to the point of evidence by a compatriot of mine in a work that does honour to the country where he was born. This is written in French and is entitled *Dialogues sur le commerce des Grains.* In this chapter, I would have been able to profit from the enlightenment of this great man, if I had not sworn, before beginning it, to close all the books that have appeared on this subject, and to think absolutely for myself. However, I do not wish to deny this writer the tribute of admiration. I must confess, that his dialogues surprised me. It is not possible to write on such a sterile subject with such elegance, with such brio with such amenity. It was reserved for the celebrated Galiani to bring to the grain warehouses those graces that Fontanelle had, with greater ease, brought to the graves of the dead" (Filangieri 1780: 129). And "the Abbot Galiani, this sublime genius, to whom as a good citizen I owe all gratitude for the honour, which with his talents, and with his writings, he has brought to my fatherland" (Filangieri 1780: 284). However the *Dialogues* were completely ignored in Naples, as Galiani himself pointed out: "All my *Dialogues* will remain stuck in my craw, seeing that in Naples they are not greatly appreciated" (Ferdinando Galiani's letter to Madame d'Épinay, Naples, 21 September 1771, published in Galiani 1881a, vol. I: 446; Galiani and d'Épinay 1993, vol. II: 199–200). See also for the relationship between Filangieri and Galiani, Catucci (1986: 143–145).

from their reformist goals. Evidence of this feeling of estrangement is given by Giuseppe Maria Galanti who, in his *Memorie*, drew a less than benevolent portrait of the *petit abbé* as a reviewer of his *Nuova descrizione storica e geografica delle Sicilie* (*New Historical and Geographical Description of the Sicilies,* Galanti 1786): "Galiani was a man of spirit, talent and certain knowledge, but animated by a malignant genius. He considered himself to be the only one in Naples who understood economic matters and with a frank and decisive air, he let the ministers of state know how true his imaginations were. He therefore did not think that a work was being done that could succeed because of the accuracy and abundance of the information that the king provided. [...]. The abbot kept a conduct that deluded me: he had me print almost the entire first volume, with those changes, modifications and corrections that he liked to prescribe [...]. [...]. The report finally had to be made to the King and Galiani described the work to him in the most odious colours. I, who, full of confidence, hope and gratitude towards the abbot, had urged the sovereign resolution, was struck down by the most intense pain" (Galanti 1997: 1002–1003).

In the meantime, Galiani continued his work as a consultant dealing with various economic policy issues. In particular, his attention, almost always prompted by contingent events, was focused on development issues and the reform of institutions.

Demographic issues had always been central to the Neapolitan abbot's thinking, ever since *Della Moneta* (Galiani [1751]: 155–156), and in the second edition of 1780, he reiterated that "a kingdom, if it were deserted of inhabitants, would be worth nothing, [and] is therefore worth in reason of the inhabitants" (Galiani 1780: *Notes XXVI*, 404), establishing the population of the Two Sicilies at 4 and a half million million and calculating an increase of approximately 1 million 300 thousand in thirty years (Galiani 1780*: Notes VI*, 378).

A specific memoir on the causes of the depopulation of the Sienese Maremma was dedicated to demographic problems (Galiani, MS-30).[176] Galiani identified two types of causes of depopulation: a *physical cause* and a *moral cause*, to which corresponded two types of remedies. He was clear about the condition of balance between population and local resource endowment (*carrying capacity*), a concept that Genovesi had also reflected

[176] According to Guerci, this memoir can be dated between 1775 and 1776, as is evident from the correspondence with Lorenzo Mehus (See Galiani 1975: Guerci's notes, 1123).

on in his *Lectures*, defining the "*right population*" (Genovesi 1765: 88). In the *Dialogues*, Galiani had reduced the constraint of the endowment of natural resources by also considering manufacturing production: "Agriculture will provide the population with its livelihood, but manufacturing alone will bring money and wealth to the state. You can even go beyond these limits and create a forced population, so large that you will be forced to travel to depopulated countries to buy, with the proceeds of the factories, the necessary foodstuffs for the surplus of people you will have to feed. Then the art of government will have accomplished its masterpiece, for the masterpiece of art is to force nature and compel her to perform such a miracle as that of having more people in a limited area of land than her forces and resources can support" (Galiani 1770a: 484). The condition of the *Maremma* offered Galiani the opportunity for a case study to reflect on the causes of population reduction. First of all, the Tuscan region had suffered the calamities that had struck Italy since the sixteenth century: "see the calamities in Siena, Pisa, Florence, Rome. Add to this the almost continuous plague that has covered Italy since 1492 [...]. Add to this the loss of its coastal ports, which had become Spanish garrisons, and the phenomenon will be explained" (Galiani, MS-30: 10). The major cause of the depopulation of the Maremma was not, in his opinion, the unhealthiness of the places, but emigration, which "arises from a general principle that the rich, industrious, affluent population attracts the poor and disadvantaged. Because everyone goes where they are better off, where they find more employment, more bread, more money. So that Florence and Livorno attract the Maremma and are the true swamps that depopulate it. Capitals and cities, which are centres of motion and wealth, attract because of their emptiness. If a plague removed twenty thousand souls from Livorno, the following year the same population would be seen there, but hardly a soul would remain in Massa and Grosseto. This explains why one does not see depopulation in countries where there has been a long destructive war. Wars are always waged on the plains and in the most fertile places for the convenience of the armies. These empty countries attract, and have something to attract, for the money left there by the armies. Depopulation follows in the neighbouring mountains" (Galiani, MS-30: 10). To counteract the trend of population decline, Galiani proposed first of all removing the physical causes with an adequate endowment of infrastructure and increasing the cultivable surface area, either by land reclamation or by reducing the land used for grazing. Emigration could only be stopped by establishing a centre of commerce to make the territory economically attractive, but he advised against encouraging colonies of foreigners that could only prosper "in a perfectly empty or new country like America", since the guest is "indolent and lazy", nostalgic for everything he leaves behind (Galiani, MS-30: 13). Nor was it useful to establish tax exemptions and privileges "because the worst would take advantage of them" (Galiani, MS-30: 13).

The reference to the reduction of land for pasture revealed Galiani's strong aversion to the pastoral economy practised in the Apulian plain and the tax system that regulated it for the benefit of the royal treasury. As is well known, the so-called *Dogana delle pecore di Foggia* (*Sheep Customhouse of Foggia*), established at the beginning of the fifteenth century, was a special jurisdiction to protect transhumant sheep-farming, which ensured tax revenues, meat and wool mainly destined for export, as there were no local manufacturing activities able to utilise the available raw material.[177] In a note to the second edition of *Della Moneta*, Galiani demolished the entire system: "I count among the greatest causes of damage the system of the *Dogana delle pecore di Foggia*: a system that to the vulgar seems sacred and precious, because it yields four hundred thousand ducats to the king: to the wise it seems absurd precisely because it sees only four hundred thousand ducats collected from an extension of land that could give two million; a province inhabited by one hundred thousand people that could feed and make three hundred thousand rich and happy; uncultivated land preferred to cultivated land; the food of beasts rather than that of man; the wandering life rather than the fixed life; haystacks rather than houses; the ravages of the seasons rather than the cover of stables, and finally to maintain a kind of rural industry that has no other similar example in cultured Europe, and only in desert Africa and barbarous Tartary" (Galiani 1780: *Notes XXXIII*, 414).

The earthquake that struck Calabria and eastern Sicily in February 1783 prompted Galiani to deal in a series of writings (partly spontaneous reflections in view of consultations, partly reports for the government)

[177] "The *Dogana* of Foggia maintained a vast network of sheepwalks between the mountains of the Abruzzi and the plains of Puglia. It rented winter pasture to sheepowners engaged in long-distance migration down from the mountains, as it regulated the land-use policy of indigenous landowners of the plains. Its tribunal moderated conflict between doganal participants in both civil and criminal cases. And finally, the customhouse served as economic consul between producers and merchants at the annual Foggian fair" (Marino 1988: 2).

with the backwardness of those regions and to promote reform projects.[178] Catastrophic events of this type, such as the Lisbon earthquake of 1755, had stimulated the Enlightenment intellectuals' reflection on the role of nature, dampening their initial optimistic approach,[179] but for Galiani, who in his writings, and especially in his *anti-Physiocratic* polemic, had repeatedly described nature as a malignant power averse to man, this event was not particularly traumatic, confirming his thesis. On the contrary, the destruction caused by the earthquake provided, in his view, the opportunity "to form a general plan for the rehabilitation" of the region (Galiani, MS-32: 752).

The calamity had been particularly destructive in that region because it had fallen on a weak social structure, characterised by three major problems: "the overbearance of the barons; the excessive wealth of the mortmain; the filth, misery, savagery and ferocity of those cities and peoples" (Galiani, MS-32: 752). And the small number of largely intermarried landholding barons, and the great distance from the centres of government, were at the root of the overbearing feudal power in the Calabrian provinces.[180] Galiani proposed as an initial remedy to administratively divide the province so as to reduce distances to facilitate royal and popular control over the barons. To avoid the excessive concentration of property, Galiani proposed the abolition of all *fideicommissum* established before 1783, "so that each baron could freely sell that fief that he considered convenient without the buyer being harassed in the future by those called to the *fideicommissum*. The apparent object of this law would be to put the barons in a position to restore the other fiefs by selling some of them. This law would put the circulation of money in that country into an extraordinary movement and activity" (Galiani, MS-32: 754). Another remedy was to favour the renewal of the baron class by welcoming nobles of mercantile origin. To limit the properties subject to ecclesiastical privilege, Galiani proposed not to rebuild some of the churches and monasteries that had been destroyed, also in order to make resources available for the

[178] See Galiani, MS-31; Galiani, MS-32; Galiani, MS-33; Galiani, MS-34; Galiani, MS-35.

[179] A typical example of the impact of these events on the *philosphes'* thinking is Voltaire's *Candide, ou l'Optimisme* (see Voltaire 1756; see also Voltaire 1759).

[180] "Catanzaro is not in the middle of this long province, but in one end of it, so that a subordinate of that province sometimes needs to walk four or five days to carry out an order from it. The common people, not having the strength to suffer the expense of invoking the sovereign's arm, fall under the yoke of the baron" (Galiani, MS-32: 753).

reconstruction of houses.[181] He also proposed not to rebuild villages that were far from communication routes (Galiani, MS-32: 755–756). Finally, the Neapolitan abbot proposed placing the reconstruction in the hands of a few magistrates, supported by technicians (Galiani, MS-31: 748–749).

Galiani devoted particular attention to the reconstruction of the city of Messina to which he attributed a vocation as a commercial emporium due to its favourable geographical position. Livorno and Marseilles were the model to follow and therefore local power had to be attributed to the merchant class, either by reducing the presence of the barons or by incentivising their participation in commercial activities like the Genoese nobles (Galiani, MS-34: 759). The Sicilian city was to be a free port facilitating the immigration of foreign merchants and ensuring the free exercise of different religions (Galiani, MS-34: 760). The construction of adequate infrastructure, such as the road to Palermo, cultural institutions such as the theatre (for the enjoyment of merchants), efficient courts to quickly settle disputes (prohibiting the excessive presence of the forensic class),[182] and a military garrison (to facilitate the circulation of money) would complete the picture of reconstruction (Galiani, MS-34: 760–761).

These reform ideas brought Galiani closer to the new Genovesian generation that was actively collaborating with the government in the 1780s.[183] In the same years, his friend Caracciolo, appointed Viceroy in Sicily, also proposed reform objectives (from the constitution of a land register to the abolition of feudal jurisdiction, see Schipa 1897), while

[181] "Calabria Ultra, not less than the entire Kingdom, has its cities built at random and without judgement, not in those places where the ancient Greeks and Romans planted them, but where chance has brought together inhabitants saved either from ancient earthquakes or from the desolations of long wars. They are therefore all most unhappy" (Galiani, MS-31: 749).

[182] "It will be good to prohibit Messina from keeping agents and lawyers here. It is incredible the voracity of Sicilian agents and Neapolitan *paglietti* (lawyers) to devour Sicily, and not content with plundering it, they slander ministers here giving their clients to understand that they have always spent money underhand, so that one hears endless filth" (Galiani, MS-31: 760–761).

[183] Furio Diaz is rather sceptical about the Neapolitan abbot's commitment to reform.: "A reforming sensibility thus emerges in *Machiavellino* on the tragic echo of the great natural disaster: even if the optimistic premise according to which, in 1783, "from the arrogance of the barons (which was once the general complaint of the whole Kingdom) the other provinces are largely freed, less so than this Calabria Ultra", makes the limits of such Galiani's reformism immediately evident [...] Not even a hint of the subversion of feudalism, but, as usual, a set of small administrative or legislative acts, here intended to mitigate the ills of a province, now exasperated by the ruins of the earthquake" (Diaz 1975a: civ).

many other exponents of the Genovesian school rose to important roles in the administration of the Kingdom, such as Giuseppe Palmieri (Director of Customs in Terra d'Otranto and later member of the Supreme Council of Finance), Giacinto Dragonetti (secretary of the Royal Chamber of Santa Chiara, then member of the Sacred Royal Council and finally president of the Grand Court of the Vicaria), Giovanni Filippo Delfico, Melchiorre Delfico (member of the Supreme Council of Finance), Domenico Grimaldi (councillor of the Supreme Council of Finance), the diplomat Michele Torcia,[184] Trojano Odazi (called in 1781 to fill the chair of *Commerce and Mechanics*, vacant since Genovesi's death) and Domenico Forges Davanzati. Most of them animated the pro-Jacobin movement in Naples, later collaborating with the Napoleonic regime.

However, Galiani lacked the political passion that characterised the new generation and his contribution was more directed towards efficiency objectives rather than a need for a general renewal of society and institutions.[185] Galiani therefore remained a conservative, steeped in political realism, sceptical, severely critical of vague reform projects, and certainly made even more pessimistic and cynical by his mature age.

His conservative stance emerged in connection with the controversy over the abolition of *voice* contracts (*contratti alla voce*). In a report for the King in December 1782, Galiani intervened in support of this ancient consuetude, claiming its "salutary, beneficial, necessary" use (Galiani, MS-14: 742, see Diaz 1975a: xcviii–c) against those who wanted to abolish it, because "either they do not understand the thing, or do not know the state of the kingdom, or are an enemy of the public good" (Galiani, MS-14: 742). According to Galiani, without this type of contract, money could neither be advanced to support agricultural production, nor provide security for the commercial intermediation of agricultural products. As long as the rules established by custom were observed, the price-regulating mechanism worked well, but as soon as "the people assigned to set the

[184] In correspondence with Galiani, but critical of the *Dialogues*, considered a text that is "facetious, witty, would never fall out of your hand, but without a grain of common sense [...] my creed is quite the opposite of yours" (Michele Torcia's letter to Ferdinando Galiani, Naples, 23 March 1776, BSNSP, XXX. B.17: folios 62r–63v).

[185] The reports on the way of organising the Kingdom's postal service (Galiani, MS-36, possibly written in 1777); on the use of the pensions awarded to Tanucci (Galiani, MS-37), which Galiani proposed to allocate to the Vicariate Court to recruit new magistrates; on the revenues of the municipality of Castellammare (Galiani, MS-38), written in March 1785 for John Acton.

prices, either through connivance or by prevarication altered the rules, one of the greatest evils that has ever been done to this kingdom was produced" (Galiani, MS-14: 742). Galiani therefore proposed to re-establish it in its original form, observing the ancient rules and imposing "in case of transgression very serious penalties" (Galiani, MS-14: 743). The original form stipulated that goods such as oil, grain, wool and cheese were regulated by this type of price, which "cannot, nor must ever serve in anything other than those contracts of money advance and stocking-up, in which it is spontaneously agreed to receive goods in exchange for money, at the *voice-price*. In any other contract or valuation whatsoever, it must be forbidden to make use of the *voice-price*" (Galiani, MS-14: 745; italics added). And he explained the reason for this limitation: "The *voice-price* is not the true and actual price, but it must be about eight or ten per cent less: and if it were not so, it would be disadvantageous for the person who advanced money. Because in this lower price the merchant must find compensation for money held, for the risk of his peasant debtor's insolvency to which he is exposed, and also for the expense, inconvenience, worry, and condition of the goods given to him in return for his money, which are always subject to decay, theft, deterioration, depreciation of price, etc., and which he cannot sell immediately, but must retain for some time to sell in a better condition" (Galiani, MS-14: 745; italics added). The *voice-price* could not be legitimately applied in conditions where no money was to be advanced, as in the case of requisitions for the passage of troops or for the *Annona*, because it would be an injustice to the farmer, "since the true price of the commodity should be valued about ten per cent higher than that of the voice", therefore "it is equally fatal errors to set *voices* too high, and to put them too low, because if the former ruin farmers, the latter ruin merchants, destroy trade, and in the end also damage farmers" (Galiani, MS-14: 745; italics added). Galiani ascribed the responsibility for the abuses to the interference of provincial magistrates, confirming what he had stated in a note in the second edition of *Della Moneta*, in which the intervention of the courts in revising the valuation of *voices*, had given rise to trials, disputes, uncertainties, controversies "between the voice made and the *voice* reformed" (Galiani 1780: *Notes XXI*, 406; italics added). In this confusion many had proposed the abolition of the *voice*. Galiani justified the *voice-price* as a tool to contain risks and transaction costs in the absence of efficient market mechanisms. The time for its abolition would come when "the opulence of the provinces and the wealth of the farmers will have come to the point of freeing them from the necessity of a contract, which in essence is nothing more than a sale of unripe fruit with an advance of money, on which a profit of uncertain interest is granted" (Galiani 1780: Notes XXI, 406). The Neapolitan abbot was silent on the responsibility of the major merchants who, in their position as monopolists, arbitrarily imposed the prices of foodstuffs, setting very high usury percentages for the loan of money that exceeded thirty per cent.[186]

Protests had been raised in various parts of the Kingdom and had urged the intervention of the newly established *Supreme Council of Finances*, of which Domenico Grimaldi and the president and tax lawyer of the *Sommaria*, Nicola d'Ajello, were members, along with Galiani (appointed councillor in November 1782) (Ciccolella 2016: 509).[187] Galiani's position was also substantially shared by Domenico Grimaldi, while d'Ajello referred to "fictitious buying and selling" made by farmers or markets to orientate the *voice* (Ciccolella 2016: 511). Trojano Odazi (see Odazi

[186] A large part of the historiography has emphasised the negative characteristics of the *voice-price* system, which was considered a usurious contract (Chorley 1965: 123; Placanica 1982: 30, 36) and "the *voice* system [...] tended to perpetuate the precariousness of the producer's economic position, while profiting commensurately from the merchant" (Chorley 1965: 123; see also Macry 1972: 864: Macry 1974). A review of this negative opinion has been proposed by Daniela Ciccolella and Alberto Guenzi, according to whom the *voice system* was "a multiform institution, characterised by a great capacity to adapt to different economic and social contexts that change over time. Therefore, the current representation of the contract, the automatisms on which it rests and the effects it asserts should be documented and periodised while, more generally, the interpretative schematism into which historiography has forced the *voice* contract has precluded a better understanding of its function and the non-pathological motives that must have contributed to the birth and survival of an institution spanning over five centuries of Southern history. A legal institution that, moreover, as such, should be framed not only in the social and economic context in which it originated and established itself, but also in the history of law and economic thought" (Ciccolella and Guenzi 2008: 44–45, see also Ciccolella 2016). Ciccolella and Guenzi's analysis confirms Galiani's theses on the institutional role of the *voice* system.

[187] Archivio di Stato di Napoli, Ministero delle Finanze, *Consulta relativa alle voci che si fanno delle derrate del Regno, fascicolo* 2885bis, reports: Ferdinando Galiani to the King, 25 December 1782; Domenico Grimaldi to the King, 13 January 1783; Nicola d'Ajello to the President of the Supreme Council of Finance, 21 January 1783. See also Archivio di Stato di Napoli, RCS, Consultationum, vol. 406, folio 184, *Consulta relativa ai contratti si fanno alla voce*, 2 March 1784 (see Ciccolella 2016: 507, 509, 524).

1782, 1783),[188] who was not particularly esteemed by Galiani, had intervened on the wisdom of abolishing the *voice* system.[189]

More innovative in their approach are the opinions on silk production (Galiani, MS-39) and soap production (Galiani, MS-40) in which Galiani proposed a free trade policy. For silk production, the Neapolitan abbot made use of Domenico Grimaldi's analysis (1780) and recommended retaining the duty because it was not too burdensome, but abolishing patents and restrictions on the internal circulation of the product and semi-finished products (Galiani, MS-39: 20–21). With regard to the production of soaps, once a flourishing industry that had declined due to both the imposition of duties on exports and the mercantilist policies of France, Holland and England, which had started their own productions by importing raw materials such as oils and soda from the Two Sicilies without constraints (Galiani, MS-39: 24), Galiani advocated the elimination of the duty and advised against granting exclusive rights to a few producers, declaring his preference for a competitive and emulative regime that would improve the product (Galiani, MS-39: 24–26).

The tedious application to the particular case did not prevent Galiani from raising his eyes to the general principles of good governance, and in the middle of a report it was possible to find a maxim of economic policy that revealed his great qualities: "the art of good governance", he observed

[188] Liberist positions had been expressed a few years earlier by Giacinto Bellitti (1771). Other interventions in the debate that continued after Galiani's death were offered by an anonymous author (1783) and Giuseppe Palmieri (1788). On the debate see Montaudo (2005: 415–443).

[189] "Troiano Odazi has been well placed here; he has a future assignment with current earnings. He will teach I don't know what sciences in a College of Nobles to be erected on Jesuit property, which is a long time from being implemented. In the meantime he has 300 *Ducats* a year. He owes this fortune to the Count of Kaunitz, who recommended him to the Sovereign" (Ferdinando Galiani's letter to Paolo Antonio Menafoglio, Naples, 28 April 1772, published in Galiani 1975: 1080). And he drew an unflattering portrait of him: "Troiano Odazi was born in Abruzzo. He did some studies there, obtained support from the Queen and a school for future disciples. He was supposed to teach the boarders of a noble college that was to replace the Novitiate of the Nefandi [the Nunziatella college ruled by wicked Jesuits]. Money was coming, and the pupils were not rushing in. He stayed there for two years, and yet (who would believe it?) he was unhappy, and went back to seeking Fortune as *Fiordiligi* sought *Brandimarte*. He is a very good man; he has nothing against himself, except a restlessness, and a painful internal feeling of non respondere *favorem speratum meritis*. He will ruin his fortune by seeking it" (Ferdinando Galiani's letter to Lorenzo Mehus, Naples, 12 July 1774, published in Galiani 1975: 1107–1108, see also editor's note: 1108). See also MS-54.

in one of his reports, “is similar to that of making great roads. One must not set out with great fury to do things [and] after they are done, believing them to be eternal, forget about them and think no more about them. On the contrary, one must always think about maintaining and touching up what has already been done, and it is always more difficult to maintain than to do” (Galiani, MS-39: 19).

In his later years, he would have liked to be involved in grain policy, but he was not consulted on such matters and his *Dialogues* were completely ignored:: “War in the West, plague in the East, famine in the interior. The prophet Nathan has enough to choose from. We had a bad harvest. We made regulations in the old way (because we are several centuries back), and immediately the price rose. You can well imagine that I am neither consulted, nor employed here, nor esteemed to hear anything on the subject. The reason is that everyone is completely unaware that I have written a book on the subject. It is known that I have written a work in French, but some people think it is a beautiful fairy tale novel, others that it is a poem”.[190]

8.3 The Delights of Exile

Living the last years of his life as an exile in his homeland, kept alive by the subtle thread that bound him to his French friends, through correspondence entrusted to the slow and uncertain mail service,[191] Galiani once again took refuge in various distractions (such as avid reading of travellers' and explorers' books) and learned studies, distancing himself, when possible, from the duties that his government advisory role imposed on him. This activity of his was not systematic, and satisfied his lively curiosity, limited only by his laziness: “his books could not be written except in spurts: as long as the road ran flat and straight, the nimble pen spun on the paper with the eagerness of an unbridled horse; but as soon as one obstacle arose (even if it was that of not finding a volume he needed), his innate laziness put the *démon écrivailleur* (as he called him) in hasty flight, and the book was no longer spoken of” (Nicolini 1909b: v).

[190] Ferdinando Galiani's letter to Madame d'Épinay, Naples, 1 August 1778, published in Galiani 1881a, vol. II, 555); Galiani and d'Épinay (1997, vol. V: 193–194).

[191] To avoid scattering the letters, Madame d'Épinay numbered them, see Madame d'Épinay's letter to Ferdinando Galiani, Aux Ternes, 18 March 1770, published in Galiani and d'Épinay (1992, vol. I: 128); D'Épinay and Galiani (1996: 69).

Due to his character, between 1770 and his death, the *petit abbé* (as Madame d'Épinay liked to call him) only completed three works, in addition to the *Doveri*: *Socrate immaginario* (*Imaginary Socrates*, Galiani and Lorenzi 1775), *Spaventosissima descrizione dell'eruzione del Vesuvio* (*Frightening description of the eruption of Vesuvius*, Galiani 1779b), *Del dialetto napoletano* (*Of the Neapolitan dialect*, Galiani 1779c), to which are added the notes to the second edition of *Della Moneta*,[192] the reprint of *Delle lodi di papa Benedetto XIV* (Galiani 1781) and the short *Croquis d'un dialogue sur les femmes*, sent in manuscript to Madame d'Épinay in a letter of April 1772 (*Sketch of a dialogue on women*, Galiani, MS-46).[193] The *Studi sopra Orazio* (*Studies on Horace* Galiani 1909),[194] begun in Paris, remained incomplete and the *Vocabolario delle parole del dialetto napoletano* (*Vocabulary of words in the Neapolitan dialect*, Galiani 1789) was published posthumously. Finally, the intense correspondence with Madame d'Épinay and other French interlocutors played an important

[192] Galiani in 1773 had started work on this second edition published in 1780: "I am busy reprinting my old work *Della Moneta*, written in Italian, which is completely out of print. I wanted to add something to it, but the older I get, the more I realise that in books there is always something to cut, never something to add. This does not coincide with the hopes of the publishers. They always want books to be big and fools (because only fools buy so many books) have the same desire. So I am working on expanding my work. They ask for notes; I will make some. But what do I put in them? Could you help me or let me help you find what I should add, please, to a work that you may know, because I have scattered several copies around Paris. You will answer me that you do not understand Italian, and even less the money of my country; but what does that matter? Do you not take notes without knowing the text? Haven't Horace, Aristotle, etc. had an infinite number of commentators? Help me, then, because I get tired of commenting myself, and I always find that I have said in the text what I would like to say in my notes" (Ferdinando Galiani's letter to Madame d'Épinay, Naples, 18 December 1773, published in Galiani 1881a, vol. II, 282–283; Galiani and d'Épinay 1993, vol. II: 98).

[193] Ferdinando Galiani's letter to Madame d'Épinay, Naples, 11 April 1772, published in Galiani (1881a: vol. I, 50–62). The text was included by Grimm in his *Correspondance littéraire*, 15 May 1772 (Grimm 1879, pp. 498–505), known to be written in manuscript form and intended for private circulation. The text was first published in 1784, in the *Journal des gens du monde*, II, pp. 65–83. See Nicolini (1909a: 411), Galiani (1975: Guerci's note, 615–633).

[194] Edited by Fausto Nicolini, see Nicolini (1909b), Nicolini (1975) and Nicolini (1978). To which must be added the *Catalogo delle materie appartenenti al Vesuvio contenute nel Museo, con alcune brevi osservazioni* (*Catalogue of the materials belonging to Vesuvius contained in the Museum, with some brief remarks*) published in 1772 without Galiani's knowledge (Galiani 1772).

role in the abbot's intellectual biography and can be considered a primary source for reconstructing his thinking, especially in his later years.[195]

Galiani himself was aware of this when he wrote to Madame d'Épinay: "You know well, my beautiful Madame, that our correspondence after our common death will be printed. What a pleasure for us! How it will amuse us! I am working hard to make my letters prevail over yours, and I am beginning to flatter myself that I will succeed. You will notice in yours a little too much monotony of friendship. Always tender, always caressing, always applauding, On the contrary, mine will have a fascinating variety: sometimes I play at offending you, sometimes I behave sarcastically, sometimes I start the letter with one tone and end it with another, and I always enjoy good health. Herein lies, above all, my great superiority".[196]

From the correspondence Galiani received those intellectual stimuli that were lacking in his increasingly despised Naples, where he felt crushed

[195] On the correspondence see Nicolini (1964); Diaz (1972, 1975); Dulac (1992); Rapisarda (1996); Amodio (1997a: 66–79); Anglani (1999); Beniscelli (2012a).

[196] Ferdinando Galiani's letter to Madame d'Épinay, Naples, 5 June 1773, published in Galiani (1881a, vol. II, 210); Galiani and d'Épinay (1996, vol. IV: 21). The vicissitudes of Galiani's correspondence are very complex and a systematic edition of his entire epistolary would be necessary. The subject was correctly addressed by Nicolini (see Nicolini 1964: 7–42). *French correspondence* (with French people or people living in France after his return to Naples in 1769, see Bedarida 1975) became a literary sensation in the early nineteenth century. Several letters had already been included in Grimm's *Correspondance*, which had a limited circulation, but a systematic collection, albeit marred by apocrypha and various philological errors, was published in 1818 in two different editions that appeared simultaneously (Galiani 1818a, 1818b), followed by another double edition in 1881 (Galiani 1881a, 1881b). The edition edited by Lucien Perey and Gaston Maugras is considered the most reliable collection, despite the presence of errors and censorship (se Amodio 1997a: 78). A more accurate edition of the French correspondence, limited to the letters between Madame d'Épinay and Galiani, was published by Daniel Maggetti and George Dulac in 5 volumes (Galiani and d'Épinay 1992, 1993, 1994, 1996, 1997). An Italian translation of the correspondence between d'Épinay and Galiani, based partly on the French edition edited by Maggetti and Dulac and partly on the Perey-Maugras edition, has been edited by Stefano Rapisarda (see d'Épinay and Galiani 1996). Before publication, many of the letters in the correspondence were already known in Europe, as evidenced by the letters that arrived in Warsaw in the summer of 1773 (Ferdinando Galiani's letter to Madame d'Épinay, Naples, 3 July 1773, published in Galiani 1881a, vol. II, 224–225; Galiani and d'Épinay 1996, vol. IV: 30).

by the "weight of an artificial idleness and forced lethargy",[197] and encircled by a "society of cannibals, anthropophagists, cyclops".[198]

In this rarefied climate in which he was forced to live, his interest in reflecting on the nature of women, education and religion arose from a suggestion that Madame d'Épinay offered him in one of her many letters, expressing her opinion on the *Essai sur le caractere, les moeurs et l'esprit des femmes dans les différens siècles* by Antoine-Léonard Thomas, a member of the *Académie française* (Thomas 1772).[199] Madame d'Épinay had read Thomas's recently published essay and argued for the equality of the sexes against the thesis of an ineradicable natural difference between male and female: "What is certain is that men and women have the same nature and physical constitution. Proof of this is that savage females are as robust and agile as savage males, and so it follows that the frailty of the constitution and organs of us women certainly depends on our upbringing, and is the effect of the role we have been assigned in society. Men and women, having the same nature and equal constitution, are capable of the same errors, the same virtues and the same vices. The virtues that have been ascribed to women, in general, are almost all virtues against nature, producing only small fictitious virtues and very concrete vices. It would take many generations to return to the way nature created us. We would not necessarily gain, but those who would certainly lose out are men. They are so happy that we are worse than we really are, after all they have done to distort us with their fine institutions. It is such an obvious thing in itself, that it does not even deserve to be stated, any more than all of Thomas' statements did".[200]

[197] Ferdinando Galiani's letter to Lorenzo Mehus, Naples, 28 November 1775, published in Galiani (1975: 610).

[198] Ferdinando Galiani's letter to Lorenzo Mehus, Napoli, 7 Dicember 1773, published in Galiani (1975: 1122). And again writing to Mehus: "The distance between me and the majority of my compatriots is immense. [...]. I wish their love far away, and enjoy their ineffectual hatred, which I pay for with equal disdain, very quietly" (Ferdinando Galiani's letter to Lorenzo Mehus, Naples, 28 November 1775, published in Galiani 1975: 610).

[199] Thomas' essay was criticised by Diderot (1875b) and Grimm (1879: 471–472). Madame d'Épinay tackled the issue of female education in *Les Conversations d'Émilie*, where she challenged Rousseau's theories (d'Épinay 1774, see Cherrad 2007).

[200] Madame d'Épinay's letter to Ferdinando Galiani, Paris, 14 March 1772, published in Galiani and d'Épinay (1994, vol. III 30–31); d'Epinay and Galiani (1996: 484–485). The text published in the *Correspondence* edited by Perey and Maugras (Galiani 1881a) has many changes compared to the manuscript preserved in BSNSP, see Galiani (1975; Guerci's notes, 631–632).

In response to d'Épinay, Galiani brought back the *Chevalier* and the *Marquis*, the protagonists of a brief but intense dialogue that revealed his unvarnished thoughts on topics widely debated in Enlightenment culture. First of all, the abbot confirmed the opinion on the natural weakness of women, defined as "an animal that is by nature weak and sickly" (Galiani, MS-46: 635, see Croce 1935; Albertone 2018; Montanile 2018), she is "weak in the apparatus of her muscles. Hence her withdrawn life, her attachment to the male of the species who provides her with sustenance, her occupations, trades, light clothing, etc." (Galiani, MS-46: 636), and she is naturally sick: "at first like all animals until she is fully grown. Then comes that well-known symptom which belongs to the whole class of *Bimanes* (two handed animals).[201] She falls ill for at least six days a month, that is, for a fifth of her life; then come the pregnancies and the feeding of the children, which are two very long and very serious illnesses. So they only have glimpses of health through continuous illness. Their character is affected by this almost habitual state. They are caressing and engaging like all sick people, but sometimes abrupt and capricious like all sick people. Easy to upset, easy to fix, like patients. They seek distraction and amusement, and nothing is enough to amuse them. Their imagination is in constant agitation, fear, hope, joy, despair, desire and disgust are imprinted

[201] Responding to Madame d'Épinay and Grimm, Galiani clarified the term "*bimanes*": "What? Are your minds ignorant of what the class of *bimanes* is? Theirs. That of apes and men. Buffon specified that bipeds are strictly speaking just birds; quadrupeds are all animals. Men and apes have two hands and two feet; that's why he calls them *bimanes*" (Ferdinando Galiani's letter to Madame d'Épinay, Naples, 13 June 1772, published in Galiani 1881a, vol. II: 85–86; Galiani and d'Épinay 1994, vol. III: 68–69). Galiani's reference is not precise as the term *Bimanes* was used by anthropologists at the end of the Eighteenth century to distinguish man from the ape called *Quadrumanes*. The *Bimanes/Quadrumanes* distinction introduced in 1766 by Georges-Louis Leclerc de Buffon (modelled on the term "quadrumane" coined by the English anatomist Edward Tyson in 1699 to refer to the chimpanzee) mitigated man's animality by justifying his particular nature as a product of Creation (see Buffon 1766: Tome XIV, 18; Tyson 1699; Senut 2012). It is not clear whether Galiani, aware of the distinction, wanted to ironically emphasise the link between man and ape or whether he incorrectly referred to the concept. Genovesi also took up the man/ape comparison in his *Lectures*: "Line up ten great orang-outangs (monkeys of human height and build, and that march straight), ten of the savages of the Australian lands described by Dampier, ten of our hairy-footed peasants of Basilicata, ten provincial semi-gentlemen of certain small lands, ten Neapolitan gentlemen of this age, ten Florentine gentlemen, and you will have a series of men ascending from unity to the highest" (Genovesi 1783: 206–207; see also Dampier 1697). Unlike Galiani, Genovesi followed Rousseau in positing education as the discriminating factor between man and animal.

more strongly in their minds and are more easily erased" (Galiani, MS-46: 637). And to Marquis' objection that woman's minority condition was the product of education, *Chevalier-Galiani* replied: "Three quarters of education is instinct, and consequently it is nature itself, a necessity, an organic law of our species" (Galiani, MS-46: 639). The connection between instinct and education is clarified in a letter to Madame d'Épinay: "My *Treatise on Education* is ready. I show that education is the same for man and beast. It can be reduced to these two points: Learning to endure injustice; learning to suffer boredom. What do you make a horse do in a riding school? The horse naturally does the stride, trot, gallop and walk. But he does this when he wants and according to his pleasure. We teach him to do these gaits against his reason (this is injustice), and to continue them for two hours (this is boredom). So whether we teach a child Latin, Greek or French, it is not the usefulness of the thing that matters, but the fact that he has to get used to doing someone else's will (and being bored), and being beaten by someone born his equal (and suffering). When he is used to it, he is ready, he is a social being, he goes out into the world, he respects magistrates, ministers, kings (and he does not complain about it). He performs the duties of his office, he is at his desk, or in court, or in the guardhouse [...]. If his behaviour is different, he is of no use in the social order. Education, therefore, is nothing but the domestication of natural instincts in favour of social duties. Education must amputate and mutilate instincts. If it does not do so, you have the poet, the improviser, the brave man, the painter, the prankster, the original, who revels and starves, unable to fit into one of the existing niches in the social order. England, the least educated nation in the universe, is consequently the greatest, the most embarrassing and soon the most wretched of all [...]. All methods of teaching science to children are false and absurd, because it is not a matter of learning geography or geometry, but of getting used to work, i.e. to boredom, to fix one's ideas on an object, etc. A child who knows all the capitals of the universe will not be accustomed to focusing on the balance of his income and expenditure, and little Geographer will be despoiled by the butler who administers his lands and go bankrupt in the midst of his capitals. Start from these theories, develop them, and you get a book that is the exact opposite of *Émile*'s, and for that reason better".[202]

[202] Ferdinando Galiani's letter to Madame d'Épinay, Naples, 4 August 1770, published in Galiani (1881a, vol. I: 216–218); Galiani and d'Épinay (1992, vol. I: 223–224) (italics added). And again against Rousseau: "It is madness to believe in the influence of air or milk

Galiani's theories on education are radically opposed to those of Rousseau, according to whom the educational process must indulge man's natural goodness, without using coercive means, and avoid as much as possible that society may corrupt it.[203] Finally, commenting on Madame d'Épinay's *Les Conversations d'Émilie*, he further specified his thoughts: "You argue that what we call the effect of chance does not exist in education; in part I agree and say that life is chance, but education isn't. It is true that education has a decisive influence on us, but do you know who is the preceptor who educates us? The century and the nation in which we come into the world. Thus, a man born today in Constantinople will be brought up as a *Turk*; in Rome, as a *Roman Apostolic Christian*; in Paris, as a refined mind, an *économiste-anglomaniac-ruralist*; in London, as a *damned colonialist*, and so on. Everything around us educates us, and the preceptor is an infinitely small entity. So you are right: good opportunities must be multiplied. You are also right when you say that it is easier to educate a female than a male because the female is much less subject to the influences of her environment".[204]

Morality itself is instinct, "just as dancing, music, singing, pleasures, and all these are not the effect of an education that alters nature, as fools believe; on the contrary, they are all effects of nature itself, which impels us to give this education, which is only its development" (Galiani, MS-46:

on children. But it is our fault to believe that children know nothing or almost nothing before the age at which they begin to speak. But since we cannot know what another being knows unless he speaks to us with his voice or with signs, we believe that children know nothing. This is a gross mistake. A man who had spent a year in London without learning a single word of the language would know an infinity of things about that country: the streets, the houses, the customs, the laws, the men, the offices, the political system, and so on. I see that my reflection destroys the whole system of *Émile* and the other pedagogues; but I conclude that at two years the thing is done; the folds of vices and virtues are given" (Ferdinando Galiani's letter to Madame d'Épinay, Naples, 19 January 1771, published in Galiani 1881a, vol. I: 342; Galiani and d'Épinay 1992, vol. I: 36).

[203] "Have you ever had the delusion to believe Rousseau and his *Émile*, and to believe that education, maxims and speeches have nothing to do with the organisation of heads? If you believe that, take a wolf and turn it into a dog, if you can" (Ferdinando Galiani's letter to Madame d'Épinay, Naples, 3 April 1773, published in Galiani 1881a, vol. II: 191–192; Galiani and d'Épinay 1994, vol. III: 223–224).

[204] Ferdinando Galiani's letter to Madame de Belsunce (daughter of Madame d'Épinay), Naples, 18 March 1775, published in (Galiani 1881a, vol. II: 388); Galiani and d'Épinay (1996, vol. IV: 231–232). Galiani's thought in relation to colonialism and the problem of slavery has been analyzed by Alessandro Tuccillo (2013: 202–214, 2018).

639–640). And Galiani also based the law of nations on instinct[205] and forms of government are linked to education which disciplines instincts: "In a republic there is less need for education than in a monarchy, and in despotism children must be kept in a menagerie, worse than slaves and women. Despotism among monks is the result of the unjust and tedious rigours of the novitiate; and this is the characteristic of the artificial and modern theocracy. The ancient and primitive theocracy began with the fear of thunder and earthquakes, created gods and saw them everywhere. Modern theocracy begins by wanting to purify men through austerities and macerations; once these men are accustomed to maximum suffering and problems, the pope, the abbot, the confessor, the novice master is a tyrant, a god; he is everything. He can do anything he wants with such a domesticated being. Public education leads to democracy, private education to despotism. There were no boarding schools in Constantinople, Spain or Portugal. The few that existed in these countries were run by Jesuits, with a cruelty that distorted them".[206]

Religion alone is the only part of education that is extraneous to instinct: "Nature gives us no instinct towards religion. It does not belong to any class of animal, we owe it entirely to education; and it is education alone that distinguishes man from beast. Religion is our characteristic trait. Instead of saying that man is a reasonable animal, we should say that man is a religious animal. All animals are reasonable; only man is religious. Morality, justice, virtue, feeling are instincts; faith in an invisible being is not" (Galiani, MS-46: 640–641). Animals are afraid of natural events, man believes in the existence of an invisible being who is the cause of events: "This is the general definition of religion, which includes both true and false religions. I would argue against all authority that everything that distinguishes man from beast is an effect of religion: society, politics, government, luxury, unequal conditions, the fine arts, and so on. We owe everything to this characteristic of our species" (Galiani, MS-46: 640–641).

Galiani's theological reflection is scattered and never organically defined, although the subject was constantly present, as his early manuscripts show (Galiani, MS-5, Galiani, MS-6; Galiani, MS-7). His interest

[205] An index to a treatise on law, planned and never written, was sent to Madame d'Épinay, see Ferdinando Galiani's letter to Madame d'Épinay, Naples, 24 May 1777, published in Galiani (1881a, vol. II, 509–510); Galiani and d'Épinay (1997, vol. V:155–156).

[206] Ferdinando Galiani's letter to Madame d'Épinay, Naples, 18 March 1775, published in Galiani (1881a, vol. I: 217–218); Galiani and d'Épinay (1996, vol. IV: 231–232).

is not surprising since he had received, under the guidance of his uncle Celestine, a thorough and solid preparation in the theological field, in particular in the scholastic tradition, which, as *Della Moneta* shows, he took up on delicate topics such as the theory of value and the question of the legitimacy of interest.

In a barely sketched essay, *De l'opinion* (Galiani, MS-22),[207] written during the second part of his Parisian sojourn, between 1766 and 1768 (Nicolini 1959b), Galiani made a distinction between abstract ideas "susceptible of evidence and demonstration" such as "time, space, motion and the reciprocal relations between quantities and qualities", which "make up what we call science properly so called" (Galiani, MS-22: 7) and all other ideas definable as opinions and governed by probability (Galiani, MS-22: 7). Pushed to the highest degree, probability takes on - according to Galiani - the force of demonstration and conjecture, but there are important differences between the two processes of knowledge: (1) probability has the need for external arguments, which are not necessary in demonstration; (2) it is necessary to accumulate arguments for probability, whereas demonstration has only one reason that is evident and true; (3) probabilities are quantifiable with more or less (*magis et minus*), "demonstrations have the force of an equal conviction" (Galiani, MS-22: 7); (4) "the proof of probability is always relative to each man and different between one man and another. The demonstration is absolute and always the same in the head of all men, except in the case of madness" (Galiani, MS-22: 7). And concluding Galiani gave his definition of opinion: "a belief founded on probabilities great and small, good or bad, but which belong neither to the class of demonstrations nor to that of proven facts, and which influences the habits, customs, laws, and happiness of men" (Galiani, MS-22: 8). In the planned essay, Galiani wanted to focus his attention "on the false opinions or errors of opinion that have caused harm to men" (Galiani, MS-22: 8), looking for the causes of their birth, establishment and downfall, excluding from the analysis the Christian faith and vulgar beliefs or errors based on weak probabilities that proved false over time, such as "the opinion that the ancients had of the existence of pygmies or the existence of the giants of the Australian lands" (Galiani, MS-22: 7). The cause of human opinions and errors originates, according

[207]With his usual dissimulating technique, Galiani attributed the essay, "translated from the Portuguese" to "M***. ancient reformed philosopher following the *Encyclopédie*" (Galiani, MS-22: 6).

to Galiani, from the "disproportion between our senses and the agents of nature. It acts through infinitely smaller bodies, or through infinitely greater forces, or through infinitely more complicated laws that our senses cannot grasp, nor can our imagination (which is but an inner sense organised by the fibres and nerves, where the ideas acquired through the senses are recorded, as in a table) be applied" (Galiani, MS-22: 8–9). For the physical difficulty, the only way nature has left for man to understand the causes of phenomena is the syllogism *post hoc, ergo propter hoc* (after this, therefore because of this) which is likewise, "the father of philosophical and historical truths (which are very different from geometrical truths) and of error" (Galiani, MS-22: 9).[208] In mathematical research, the error derives only from obscure ideas, in philosophical, physical and historical research, the error therefore derives from a defect in experience, since science is nothing but a multiplication of experiences and evidence is a mass of probabilities, i.e. of observations *post hoc, ergo propter hoc*. Once the erroneous opinion is introduced, it has an effect on habit and language,[209] it is passed on through laziness and the negligence of seeking other evidence, fuelling credulity, which is trust in the evidence provided by others (Galiani, MS-22: 9). The rule of analogy, also applied in scientific argumentation, being also a probability, is another source of erroneous opinions, yet without such a rule, "we will always be in a cruel uncertainty and in a laboured scepticism" (Galiani, MS-22: 11). The essence of the system is nothing other than the "fury to find in everything relations of analogy" (Galiani, MS-22: 11).

Opinion has a fundamental importance, "it is the king of the world", and is linked to strength and reason. Like an animal, man has an opinion of his strength based on experience, and similarly "reason is nothing but a force within the spirit" (Galiani, MS-22: 14). Opinions are consolidated through experience, memory and habit, they conform to reason at the outset, but are then imperceptibly falsified as circumstances change. In order to avoid the formulation of false opinions, it was necessary, according to Galiani: (1) to check probability with new experiences; (2) to mistrust anologies; (3) to avoid the systematic spirit, to "believe that nature is

[208] Commonplaces, trite statements, beliefs, superstitions and magical thinking are the result of this error.

[209] One cause of opinion according to Galiani comes from poetic language itself, such as puns, rhymes, comparisons (Galiani, MS-22: 13).

immense, infinite, varied, and that it is not bound to numbers, to petty relations" (Galiani, MS-22: 12).

On the stratification of opinions are built not only intellectual systems but sovereignties themselves: "What then is an old empire, an old belief? It is a residue of an ancient age preserved by memory and habit, despite changed circumstances (the empire of Germany, the court of Rome). But was this infantilism reasonable when it spread? Yes. When men believed that the sun revolved around the earth, that the earth was flat, etc., were they right? Yes, because the means of science and knowledge available to them at the time did not indicate anything else. This opinion, therefore, rightly dominated their childish reason" (Galiani, MS-22: 16). The process of consolidating a primitive opinion was the basis of pagan religions: "The war that man, in order to procure well-being, must wage against nature is the principle of society. By a puerile rule of analogy, man animated the elements and other bodies of nature. Hence the first vulgar ideas of religion. Air, water, the sun, mountains, the first deities. Proceeding on the same principle of analogy, man gave his gods his way of thinking, his tastes, wills, needs, whims, affections" (Galiani, MS-22: 18). For Galiani, there was no such thing as a natural, pure, simple religion, unmediated by the human mind, but even the religions of savage peoples were complex intellectual constructions. Voltaire was therefore wrong in assuming the existence of a natural religion: "he took the cream, the core, the substance of Christianity to fight Christianity with its cortex, which the misfortunes of the times, the barbarian peoples, gave it and which the Christians tolerated by considering it a cortex. Natural religion in Voltaire's sense is therefore true, but it is Christianity and not that which arose in the heads of the first men. *Primus in orbe Deos fecit timor* (*Fear first created gods in the world*).[210] The thunder, the storm troubled men; they wanted to dominate the thunder, the storm, they believed they were making an alliance with the beings who sent the thunder, the storm. This is the first religion. All ancient history, all travels attest to it" (Galiani, MS-22: 19). Primitive religion then became more complex in a second epoch of religious opinions that generated the theocracy, i.e. the link between political and religious power; the belief in gods returned to Earth then opened the third phase, characterised by theogonies and mythologies, based on the allegorical interpretations of historical facts (Galiani, MS-22: 19–20).

[210] See Vico (1744 [1948]: 64). See also Statius, *Thebaid*, 3, 661. These words also appear in a fragmentary poem attributed to Petronius (*Fragments*, 22. 1).

Galiani thus expressed an epistemological theory of opinion in which continuous experimental verification became the main tool for approaching truth. The absence of experimentation leads to fatalism.[211] His view was not very different from the concept of opinion defined in the *Encyclopédie*[212] and still follows a Newtonian approach.

He mistrusted every extreme religious position and opposed all forms of fanaticism, had an impatience with the theological disputes that pitted the Jansenists against the Jesuits, and admired the principle of tolerance embodied by Pope Benedict XIV. Galiani also rejected atheism and agnosticism because he considered religion to be the product of the imagination and therefore the concept of God was ineliminable from the human mind: "unbelief is the greatest effort the human spirit can make against its own instinct and pleasure. It means to deprive oneself perpetually of all the joys of imagination and the taste for the marvellous. It means renouncing the exploration of the entire field of knowledge, while man has an enormous lust for knowledge. It means always denying and doubting everything,

[211] "There is an error of reasoning in these large systems, which has lasted as long as they have existed. The error is that everyone agrees without anyone noticing. Yes, without a doubt, this world is a great machine, which moves and goes necessarily; but how many wheels does this machine have? That is what no one seeks, no one defines, no one asks. Is there any other main wheel besides the physical laws of the movement of gross matter and the physical laws of the movements of this subtle matter we call spirit? Are all these matters and laws known to us? In short, are there other spirits besides the human one that we know? Do rigged dice necessarily fall as much as unrigged dice, but do they fall differently, and are all these laws known to us? In short, are their minds other than the human one we know? The same applies to all other events. It would be necessary to know all the mechanisms" (Ferdinando Galiani's letter to Madame d'Épinay, Naples, 19 August 1770, published in Galiani 1881a: vol. I, 236; Galiani and d'Épinay 1992, vol. I: 238). And "Fatalism is the only system suited to savages, and if we understood the language of animals well, we would see that it is the only system of all beasts. Fatalism is the father and son of barbarism; it is its offspring, and then it feeds it; and do you know why? Because it is the laziest system, and therefore the most suitable for man" (Ferdinando Galiani's letter to Madame d'Épinay, Naples, 28 March 1772, published in Galiani 1881a, vol. II, 46; Galiani and d'Épinay 1994, vol. III: 41).

[212] "According to the Logicians, demonstration produces science or certain knowledge, and probable arguments produce opinion. Whenever the mind's consent to a truth proposed to it is accompanied by doubt, it is called opinion [...]. Moreover, since science is certain and self-evident, by its very presence it banishes all oscillation, and consequently the very opinion whose place it takes, and captures the entire mind with the brilliance of light [...]. Opinion and science are found in the same subject, there must be certainty and uncertainty at the same time, since without certainty there would be no science, and without uncertainty no opinion" (Boucher d'Argis 1765: 796–707).

and living in a perpetual squalor of ideas, knowledge, sublime doctrines, etc. What a desolating emptiness! What nothingness! What an effort! It is thus demonstrated that the vast majority of men (and especially women, whose imagination is twofold, since they have the imagination of the head and the imagination of the womb), cannot be incredulous, and those who can be, can only sustain the effort at the height of their soul's vigour and youth. If the soul grows old, faith immediately reappears".[213] For this reason, the craziest fanatic who "runs through the crowd" will always find a following, while the unbeliever "is an acrobat who does the most incredible tricks in the air, fluttering around on his rope. He fills all spectators with fear and amazement and no one is tempted to follow or imitate him".[214] Writing an avowedly atheistic work like the *Système de la Nature*, Baron d'Holbach "is a veritable *Abbé Terray of metaphysics*. He makes reductions, suspensions and failures of knowledge, pleasure and the human spirit".[215]

Atheists deny imagination when they assert that "if a God had made the world, it would undoubtedly be the best of worlds, but it is not; therefore there is no God [...]. This is the reasoning of the philosophers [...]. Do you not know that God created this world out of nothing? So we have God as father and nothingness as mother. Sure, our father is worth a lot, but our mother is worth nothing. We take from our father, but we also take from our mother. What is good in the world comes from the father, and what is bad comes from *Madame le néant*, our mother, who is not worth much. [...] The major term of their syllogism is false; so false that if it were true that this world is the best possible, it is evident that it would not have been created and God would not exist. Its imperfection is the most convincing proof of its creation and its subordination to a more perfect being".[216]

[213] Ferdinando Galiani's letter to Madame d'Épinay, Naples, 21 September 1776, published in Galiani (1881a, vol. II, 469); Galiani and d'Épinay (1997, vol. V: 102–103).

[214] Ferdinando Galiani's letter to Madame d'Épinay, Naples, 21 September 1776, published in Galiani (1881a, vol. II, 469); Galiani and d'Épinay (1997, vol. V: 103).

[215] Ferdinando Galiani's letter to Baron d'Holbach, Naples, 24 July 1770, published in Galiani (1881a: vol. I, 203).

[216] Ferdinando Galiani's letter to Abbé Mathieu Mayeul, Naples, 14 December 1771, published in Galiani (1881a: vol. I, 494–495). Similar ideas were already expressed in his youth by Galiani, as demonstrated by the fragment on the existence of God analysed in previous *Chapter 1* (see Galiani, MS-5). According to Galiani, d'Holbach's atheism is denial of imagination: "what is an atheist? He is a man, who destroys chimeras prejudicial to the human species, in order to reconduct men back to nature, to experience, and to reason. He is a

Nor did he accept Voltaire's deism as expressed in *Tout en Dieu*[217]: "He who says Everything in God, says clearly and bluntly that God is Everything; for he who says that two and three enter into five, says that five is nothing but the sum of three and two, and there is nothing more to add. How can one fill a pamphlet with something on which I could not even write twenty lines, and even resort to a comparison? This time Voltaire had the unlucky game. He wanted to look like a deist and ended up being an atheist without realising it. [...]. One should never get too excited about these arguments: they are slippery".[218] And Galiani gave a harsh opinion of him: "it is clear that he is a deist for political reasons. Thus atheists do not count him among their enemies, even though he writes against them. It is very pleasing that we have reached a point where Voltaire seems moderate in his views, and that he flatters himself that he is counted among the protectors of religion, and that we, instead of persecuting him, should protect and encourage him".[219]

To the two opposing visions Galiani had dedicated a dialogue, *Cela revient toujours au même* (*It always comes down to the same thing*, Galiani, MS-48), written in September 1770, inspired by Voltaire's *Dieu. Réponse au Système de la nature* (Voltaire 1770; Sasso 1978). The interlocutors in the short dialogue were Voltaire, Mirabaud (the name under which d'Holbach had published his book) and the "curé de Venise" as arbiter.[220] Galiani used the metaphor of *shoes* (*souliers*) to talk about religions and *cobblers* (*cordonniers*) to mean institutional clergy. As he reported to Madame d'Épinay: "I had begun to write an important dialogue on the

thinker, who, having meditated upon matter, its energy, its properties, and its modes of acting, has no occasion, in order to explain the phenomena of the universe, and the operations of nature, to invent ideal powers, imaginary intelligences, beings of the imagination, who, far from making him understand this nature better, do no more than render it capricious, inexplicable, unintelligible, and useless to the happiness of mankind" (D'Holbach 1770 [1889]: 300).

[217] *Tout en Dieu. Commentarie sur Malebranche*, published by Voltaire under the pseudonym of l'abbé de Tilladet (Voltaire 1769). This pamphlet that Voltaire, in 1769, addressed to d'Alembert was appreciated by Grimm, see Galiani (1881a, vol. I, 25–26).

[218] Ferdinando Galiani's letter to Madame d'Épinay, Naples, 20 January 1770, published in Galiani (1881a, vol. I, 54); Galiani and d'Épinay (1992, vol. I: 109).

[219] Ferdinando Galiani's letter to Madame d'Épinay, Naples, 8 August 1772, published in Galiani (1881a, vol. II, 103–104); Galiani and d'Épinay (1994, vol. III: 89).

[220] The manuscript was discovered by Nicolini among Galiani's manuscripts and later published in Nicolini (1909a, 1954). The "curé de Venise" is the abbot Jean-François Martin, a frequent visitor to Madame d'Épinay's circle.

subject: are shoes an invention of man or do they exist in nature independently of men? Should they be abolished or preserved? Are they good for you or bad for your feet? In my small treatise these questions, which are fundamental for shoemakers, would be thoroughly investigated".[221] In the dialogue, to Mirabaud-d'Holbach's thesis that shoe-religions are the work of humans, Voltaire retorts that "something so necessary, so widespread, so known at all times and in all places", cannot be attributable to human opinion "which is always wavering and uncertain, but to nature itself and its laws" (Galiani, MS-48: 208). The atheist Mirabaud-d'Holbach objects that shoes are the work of shoemakers because nobody is born with shoes and they are all different, expensive, cheap, narrow, wide, subject to fashion. Only common sense should guide the choice of shoes, Voltaire replies. In the end, the solution to the dispute is attributed to the curate who, with Solomonic judgement, sentences that the two interlocutors, being people of spirit, are always in agreement. This is how Galiani dismissed theological disputes, considering them useless.

This sceptical vision did not prevent Galiani from defining his own concept of God. Galiani's God is not a beneficent being, rather he is "a spoilt child who touches everything and often breaks everything he touches. Now, it would not be bad to take some caution against the wickedness of this undisciplined child, who is at home in this world and is called fate".[222] He loves to make fun of mankind and "laughs with all his heart at seeing men busy arranging the world for their own needs, while it is he, and he alone, without emulators, who arranges it at his whim and for his amusement".[223]

The apparatus of rules and rituals of religious confessions and the presence of the clergy mortified the instinctive and intimate nature of the religious spirit. With irony, using his passion for cats, the Neapolitan abbot

[221] Ferdinando Galiani's letter to Madame d'Épinay, Naples, 15 September 1770, published in Galiani (1881a: vol. I, 258); Galiani and d'Épinay (1992, vol. I: 254–255).

[222] Ferdinando Galiani's letter to Madame d'Épinay, Naples, 27 February 1773, published in Galiani (1881a, vol. II, 177); Galiani and d'Épinay (1994, vol. III: 206).

[223] Ferdinando Galiani's letter to Madame d'Épinay, Naples, 9 September 1780, published in Galiani (1881a, vol. II, 597); Galiani and d'Épinay (1997, vol. V: 229). On the concept of God in Galiani, see also Ferdinando Galiani's letter to Madame d'Épinay, Naples, 5 March 1774, published in Galiani (1881a, vol. II, 300) (Galiani and d'Épinay 1996, vol. IV: 124–125); Ferdinando Galiani's letter to Madame d'Épinay, Naples, 23 July 1774, published in Galiani (1881a, vol. II, 330) (Galiani and d'Épinay 1996, vol. IV: 165); Ferdinando Galiani's letter to Madame d'Épinay, Naples, 29 July 1775, published in Galiani (1881a, vol. II, 419) (Galiani and d'Épinay 1997, vol. V: 46).

described how positive religions came into being: "The cat first teaches her young to fear the human gods. Then she explains to them the theology and the two principles, the good man God and the bad dog Demon: then she dictates to them morals, war on mice and sparrows, etc.; finally she tells them about the future life and the heavenly *Ratapolis*, which is a city whose walls are made of parmesan cheese, floors of breadcrumbs, columns of eels, etc., and which is full of mice for their amusement. It teaches them respect for their fellow man. He inculcates in them respect for sterilised cats, who are predestined cats, called to this state by God man, to be happy in this world and the next, as a testimony to how fat they are; and for this reason they are exempt from taking mice. Finally, he recommends the most perfect resignation in case God-man calls them to this state of perfection, etc. etc".[224]

With an essentially malevolent God, such as Nature itself,[225] constituted religion could not play a positive role and in the *Doveri*, Galiani distinguished between true religion, linked to nature, and false positive religions: "That natural light of reason, which almost by instinct has led all men in every age to realise the existence of a Creator of ourselves and of the Universe, adds to these duties a third, namely that of man's obligations towards his Author. But the founders of false religions, passing themselves off as believers in and interpreters of the Numens, abused the universal belief in order to demand from the deluded mortals in their name many duties that are as burdensome to the multitude as they are useful and beneficial to them alone, and they thus placed the duties

[224] Ferdinando Galiani's letter to Madame d'Épinay, Naples, 22 December 1770, published in Galiani (1881a, vol. I, 331); Galiani and d'Épinay (1992, vol. I: 322–323).

[225] The concept is well expressed in a Galiani monologue reported in Abbot Morellet's *Memoires*, known as *le conte des dés pipes* (*the tale of the rigged dice*): "I suppose, gentlemen, that the one of you who is most convinced that the world is the work of chance, playing three dice, I won't say in a gambling den, but in the best house in Paris, his antagonist rolls once, twice, three times, four times, and finally constantly, a six. As long as the game goes on, my friend Diderot, who loses his money this way, will say without a moment's hesitation or doubt: The dice are rigged, I am in a game of hazard! Ah, philosopher! because ten or twelve throws of the dice have come out of the cylinder in such a way as to make you lose six francs, you firmly believe that it is a clever artificial manoeuvre, a very well-conceived cunning, and seeing in this universe such a prodigious number of combinations a thousand and a thousand times more difficult, and more complicated, and more sustained, and more useful, you do not suspect that the dice of nature are rigged and that there is a great cheat up there who is playing the game of cheating you" (Morellet 1822: 136–137). See also Brunetière (1881: 932–933); Van Bever (1976: 260); Marchal (1999: 1012).

towards the Numens in contrast to the other two natural duties. Hence the sacrifices of Ifigenies and a hundred other monstrosities. True religion, while it has secured our belief in and given us knowledge of the true God, has shown us that He does not demand of us anything other than our inner feelings of love, gratitude, and resignation. To demand also, and for our greater good, the exact fulfillment of those same duties towards ourselves, and towards our kind, which nature has pointed out to us. This is how, by the light of the true Faith, morality was for the first time reunited with religion" (Galiani 1782: 15, footnote 1). And in private correspondence he further specified his thoughts on the link between religion and nature as the foundation of true religion: "With your sad consubstantiality and transubstantiation, what do you expect us to do? There are two kinds of religion: that of the new peoples is cheerful and is nothing but agriculture, medicine, athletics and population. Those of the old peoples are sad and are only metaphysics, rhetoric, contemplation, elevation of the soul; they will cause the abandonment of cultivation, population, good health and pleasures. We are old".[226]

According to Galiani, the early Christians were nothing more than "an order of Freemasons who wanted to expand and proselytise" (Grimm 1878: 105). The nature of the Church according to the abbot "had always been that of a government and not a religion" (Grimm 1878: 116) and the same characteristic of Christian times was dictated by the demands of administrative efficiency: "as the number of religious increased, the *choir* had to be enlarged without taking away space from the *nave*. The multiplicity of instances with the [Christian] sect increased day by day, and requiring a redoubled solicitude, two tribunals were built similar to the one in the hemicycle, on the right and left. Abbot Galiani maintains that this is the true origin of the true cross, Greek or Latin, which is said to have been used in the first Christian temples to commemorate the sign of redemption; according to him, this form, the work of chance and

[226] Ferdinando Galiani's letter to Madame d'Épinay, Naples, 20 January 1770, published in Galiani (1881a: vol. I, 53–54); Galiani and d'Épinay (1992, vol. I: 108). "A druid was at the same time astrologer, magician, physician, surgeon, interpreter of oracles, legislator and, as if all this were little, also tragic and lyrical poet, author of dramas and hymns that he himself set to music, staged and sang. Blissful times! Today, however, all these charlatanships have been apportioned among different classes, and those who make a living from the one leave others to profit from the others in order to make money on the backs of their neighbours" (Galiani 1978: 296).

necessity, was never symbolic" (Grimm 1878: 108, see also Galiani 1909: 268–287).

Miracles also encouraged discipline and credulity, as in the case of the miracle of St. Gennaro's blood, about which Galiani showed his scepticism to Karl Heinrich von Gleichen, observing: "It seems that the early Christian priests found this chemical secret and, believing that this brownish gum was similar to curdled blood, said to themselves: Here is an excellent thing that can be as useful to us as to the pagan priests, and they used it as a pious fraud, very useful for the great success it had".[227]

In his study on Horace, Galiani puts forward a particular thesis on the establishment of Christianity in the Latin world: "In paganism there was no feast under which slaves were periodically entitled to a day of rest [...]. This is one of the main reasons why Christianity progressed so rapidly in the Roman world: slaves, whose numbers were four times greater than those of the free, were immediately enthusiastic about a religion that granted them a day of rest every week. No one can deny that Christianity set out to abolish (de facto, if not de jure) slavery and re-establish equality among men" (Galiani, MS-47; 241–242).[228]

Having reduced God to an instinctive imagination and positive religion to an institution, Galiani proposed a form of scepticism, rejecting the atheist and materialist positions of his Parisian friends,[229] Diderot and d'Holbach, while the influence of Vico was very clear, albeit suitably

[227] Gleichen (1868: 211–211), see also Galiani (1881a, vol. II, 652). Galiani's irony about miracles is well illustrated in a letter to Grimm, see Ferdinando Galiani's letter to Baron Grimm, Naples, 18 July 1772, published in Galiani (1881a, vol. II, 101–102). On superstitions and prophecies in his early writings, see Galiani, MS-6; Galiani, MS-7. On the difference between religion and superstition see Mauro (2017a: 137–141).

[228] For Greek religion, "mythology was nothing but national history altered and corrupted by tradition", of Etruscan origin, "the primitive Roman religion was nothing but a kind of rural philosophy, whose elements (astronomical principles and the like) had been divinised. As contacts between Rome and Magna Grecia became more frequent, Greek myths penetrated more and more into Rome, until, modified and adapted to the original local beliefs, they became the official state religion" (Galiani 1978: 274).

[229] According to Cesare Cases: "Galiani's attitude towards religion differs from that of the other Enlightenment thinkers. If he shares with them an aversion to all practised religions, he nevertheless arrives neither at the atheism of Diderot and d'Holbach, nor at the deism of Voltaire, but rather at a kind of religious agnosticism, for which the demonstration of the non-existence of God is just as uncertain as that of his existence" (Galiani 1957: 103). Paolo Amodio instead considers Galiani's thought to be an expression of atheistic libertinism, see Amodio (1997a: 245–252).

reinterpreted.[230] Instead, he underestimated Nicholas Boulanger's thought, who in his *L'Antiquité dévoilée par ses usages* (Boulanger 1766), proposed a critical analysis of the religious beliefs, customs and political institutions of ancient civilizations, questioning mythological narratives and religious explanations by interpreting them in light of more concrete considerations, such as the social, economic and political aspects of life in ancient societies.[231]

But in a city born for idleness, it was easier to devote oneself to quiet learned studies and literary amusements than to compromise oneself with dangerous and demanding arguments about religion: "This city condemned to idleness since the time of Horace and Virgil, *et in otio natam Parthenopem* [*Parthenope, born for the idle life*], will give me many more joys than I would like, and even more than I could wish for".[232]

And it was precisely the work of Quintus Horatius Flaccus that attracted his attention from his adolescence, justified by a kind of Epicurean affinity and supported by a thorough knowledge of the Latin language.[233] He had begun writing on Horace in Paris in 1764, in French, devoting himself to commentaries on the *Carmina* (*Odes*) and the *Epistula ad Pisones* (*Epistle to the Pisons*), but as he wrote to Madame d'Épinay "in France I have produced nothing but children and books that have never seen the light of

[230] "Fear first created gods in the world (*Primos in orbe deos fecit timor*): false religions were born not of imposture but of credulity" (Vico 1744 [1948]: 64, § 91). And "[post-diluvian men] pictured the sky to themselves as a great animated body, which in that aspect they called Jove, the first god of the so-called *gentes maiores*, who by the whistling of his bolts and the noise of his thunder was attempting to tell them something. And thus they began to exercise that natural curiosity which is the daughter of ignorance and the mother of knowledge, and which, opening the mind of man, gives birth to wonder" (Vico 1744 [1948]: 105–106, § 377).

[231] In a letter to Tanucci, Galiani wrote: "[In the] *L'antiquité dévoilé par ses usages* not much rigor is used, [...] it is all research on the origins of pagan ceremonies. The Frenchman stole from Giambattista Vico, and did not quote him. However, there are many who now know here the plagiarism, and ask me about Vico's *Scienza nuova*, a book done in the dark by a man who had great enlightenment" (Ferdinando Galiani's letter to Bernardo Tanucci, Paris, 22 December 1766, published in Galiani 1975: 928, see Tanucci's response in Tanucci 1914, vol. II: 21–22).

[232] Ferdinando Galiani's letter to Madame d'Épinay, Naples, 18 November 1769, published in Galiani and d'Épinay (1992, vol. I: 96); d'Epinay and Galiani (1996: 40).

[233] It is known that Galiani was also interested in epigraphy, see Nicolini (1904–1905); Nicolini (1908b); Pane (1975); Soldovieri (2019).

day".[234] In 1775, Galiani resumed his studies on Horace, writing in Italian, an introduction to the work, which should have been entitled *Pensieri liberi sopra Orazio* (*Free thoughts on Horace*), a *Vita di Orazio* (*Life of Horace*), which remained incomplete, a transcription of almost all of Horace's *Odes, Satires* and *Epistles* in chronological order, comments and notes only on the *Odes* and *Epodi* (*Epodes*), and an outline of a critical essay on Horace's Italian translations.[235]

In the preface, written in 1779, to his unfinished *Disegno di un'edizione di Orazio ordinate cronologicamente e commentate* (*Outline of a chronologically ordered and annotated edition of Horace*), the Neapolitan abbot recalled his tormented path: "I am no longer in the age or position to make books. I, too, suffered the evil of *typomania* in my youth, and I have, without serious fatigue or ugly scars, miraculously emerged from it safe and cured. The years, experience, the events of life, the spectacle of the others' fortunes and my own have produced disenchantment, nausea, idleness, apathy", but in order to satisfy his friends' insistent requests, he decided to compile "a great many thoughts on the life and works of Horace, which had been accumulated for a long time and which I could well say had already been published, because for several years, without ambition or interested aims, I have revealed them to everyone, either while sitting at the table, or while reasoning, or while walking" (Galiani 1978: 128).[236] Galiani's aim was "to write a life of Horace taken mainly from his own poems, enrich it with notes and quotations [...], and then publish all his poems again, arranged according to the order of times and

[234] Ferdinando Galiani's letter to Madame d'Épinay, Naples, 13 Dicember 1770, published in Galiani (1881a: vol. I, 316); Galiani and d'Épinay (1992, vol. I: 316). These works by Galiani were published under the title *Commentaires sur les Oeuvres d'Horace*, in 1765, in vols. V, VI and VII of the *Gazette littéraire de l'Europe*, and retouched in form by the editors. Another edition was published in 1821, by Vincent Campenon and Jean-Baptiste-Denis Després, see Galiani (1821). See Nicolini (1978: 114–116); Bracchi (1997: 85).

[235] The manuscripts are kept in the BSNSP (XXXI A 10; XXXI A 12; XXXII C 5; XXXII C 6; XXXII C 14) reordered and published by Fausto Nicolini, see Nicolini (1978). See also Paratore (1975).

[236] The work was also laborious due to the lack of books: "My Horace would progress if I had libraries here; but the lack of books, the problems I have to face to get them, hinder me, delay and delay my work to the point of making me disgusted" (Ferdinando Galiani's letter to Madame d'Épinay, Naples, 23 January 1779, published in Galiani 1881a, vol. II, 570; Galiani and d'Épinay 1997, vol. V: 205–206).

circumstances" (Galiani 1978: 131).[237] Not, therefore, a translation of which he saw the limits, observing that Horace "was possible to understand perfectly, [but] impossible to translate", and "whoever undertakes a translation in such a work, discovers in it so many beauties, that to want to try to translate them into another language, one immediately lacks the courage, the pen drops out of the hand and a certain eagerness and resentment arises within oneself at not being able to find equivalent phrases, always seeming to spoil and degrade a beautiful, inimitable, perfect expression" (Galiani 1978: 130). Galiani once again challenged the academic tradition and the countless "silly and insipid commentaries" by proposing an authentic historical-philological recovery of Horace's work (Galiani 1978: 225).[238]

His passion for the Latin poet was also motivated by a human sympathy (and affinity): "I am studying Horace. I now have a very clear idea of his life: he was unhappy, poor, mistreated by Maecenas who exploited him a great deal and did him no real benefit. Ancient Maecenas were the same as modern Maecenas. The world never changes".[239]

Galiani's detailed analysis of Horace's thought and society in the early imperial age of Augustus offered a number of opportunities to discuss contemporary culture and society. The injustice of the Roman tax system, for example, was compared to the disorder of the French tax system: "Inequality between privileged and non-privileged goods and a completely arbitrary tax on the latter: these are the main causes of the decline of agriculture among the Romans, and consequently of the fall of the Empire [...]. The inequality in the present French financial system seems to have had the same origin. The Frankish conquerors introduced in

[237] See Ferdinando Galiani's letter to Madame d'Épinay, Naples, 13 June 1778, published in Galiani (1881a, vol. II, 550); Galiani and d'Épinay (1997, vol. V: 190).

[238] "Search, first of all, and establish the time when the poem you want to understand was written; see the state of successes, thoughts and customs of that time, which the historians will give us; and Horace will be understood at once. It will become ten times more beautiful, more energetic, more sensible; the flights of fancy, the extravagant jumps, the incoherence, the obscurity will disappear; everything will be found clear, allusive, concatenated" (Galiani 1978: 225). "Galiani considers the errors of interpretation of the commentators who preceded him to be unforgivable, because they were caused by a lack of knowledge of Latin and an overly approximate translation criterion" (Bracchi 1997: 86).

[239] Ferdinando Galiani's letter to Madame d'Épinay, Naples, 19 August 1775, published in Galiani (1881a, vol. II, 421); Galiani and d'Épinay (1997, vol. V: 49–50). Fausto Nicolini emphasises the character and biographical affinities: "in Horace he loved the man, the man made so much in his image and likeness" (Galiani 1978: 122).

France the same distinction between their own property and families and that of the conquered Romans, and, naturally, the same inconveniences ensued. Can this be remedied? Certainly, but only when the French no longer give the phrase *je suis un gentilhomme* the importance that the ancient Romans attributed to the analogous phrase *civis romanus sum*" (Galiani 1978: 157). And in discussing the oligarchy that dominated Rome, Galiani turned his attention to the growing influence of the merchant class: "Not the least cause of the tendency towards oligarchy is trade, with its immense imbalance in the distribution of wealth, which ends up flowing almost all into a few hands. Proof of this are Holland, republican Florence, Genoa, Venice" (Galiani 1978: 192). In some other comments he identified himself with Horace: "Our poet was not simply a poet-friend of Maecenas; neither then, nor, for that matter, nowadays, were there people who had no other trade than that of writing verse. Besides being a poet, Horace was employed in the ministry of his patron; he was, indeed, his trusted man, his cabinet secretary, to put it in the current phrase. As such, he had the duty to occupy himself all day long with foreign policy and to know the minutest details; but, as a good philosopher and a better poet, he also had the duty to be cordially bored with the job that gave him bread, and, having left office, so to speak, not to worry about it at all" (Galiani 1978: 197). Which was precisely what Galiani did, devoting himself to his passions.

And from the need to forget the burdensome institutional duties was born the *Socrate Immaginario* (*Imaginary Socrates*) (Galiani and Lorenzi 1775; Lorenzi 1780), an *opera buffa*, partly in Neapolitan dialect, written in 1775 together with Giovanni Battista Lorenzi and set to music by Giovanni Paisiello.[240] In a letter of September 1775, the abbot described the plot of the work to Madame d'Épinay: "I will tell you about my comic opera: it is an imitation of Don Quixote. It is about a good provincial bourgeois [Don Tammaro Promontorio, an Apulian landlord] who has given himself the task of restoring the old philosophy, music, gymnastics and so on. He thinks he is Socrates: he has hired his barber [Mastro Antonio], whom he has turned into Plato (he is Sancho Panza); his wife [Donna Rosa] is grumpy and beats him all the time: so she is a Xantippe. He goes to his garden to consult his demon; finally he is made to drink a sleeping pill, believing it to be hemlock: and thanks to opium, when he

[240] Nicolini cites a 1775 edition (see Nicolini 1909a: 409); another edition of 1780 has only Lorenzi as author.

wakes up, he finds himself cured of his madness. This subject would be worthy of a merry romance, and is, in my opinion, the only one that could be as original as Don Quixote, and in line with the taste of our century. When the play is printed, I will send it to Caracciolo, and if he takes the trouble to explain the Neapolitan phrases and jokes to you, you will laugh".[241] The *opera* was performed in October 1775 and was also staged in the court theatre in the presence of the sovereigns, but it caused scandal and controversy, and the minister Tanucci suspended the performances on the orders of the King, who deemed it "indiscreet". Galiani, as usual, punctually reported the affair to his French correspondent: "I told you that I was busy working on a comic opera entitled *Socrate*s and that it had amused me greatly [...] You must therefore know that this opera was the most sublime of successes. It was banned by express order of His Majesty, after having been performed six times for the public and also once at court. This had not yet happened in Italy. In France, only *Tartufe* deserved this honour. So put *Socrates* on the same level as *Tartufe* for the noise it made, for the cabals, intrigues and wickedness it generated. This is my situation here, the fear my spirit inspires in the heads of fools; envy me and do not pity me, for this affair has done me no harm. You cannot imagine all the explanations that have been given to this work, all the allusions that have been found in it. Since the *Apocalypse*, nothing has ever been explained in such an amusing way".[242]

Writing to Lorenzo Mehus in November 1775, Galiani reconstructed the genesis of the work and denied its authorship: "*Socrate Immaginario* belongs to me as much as to you, or anyone else, who has not had the slightest part. It is the work of Giambattista Lorenzi, a man well known here for this kind of composition which he has been producing for fifteen

[241] Ferdinando Galiani's letter to Madame d'Épinay, Naples, 16 September 1775, published in Galiani (1881a, vol. II, 424); Galiani and d'Épinay (1997, vol. V: 53–54). See sulla trama del *Socrate Immaginario* see Nicolini (1909a: 398–400) e Catucci (1986: 127–139).

[242] Ferdinando Galiani's letter to Madame d'Épinay, Naples, 9 Dicember 1775, published in Galiani (1881a, vol. II, 430–431); Galiani and d'Épinay (1997, vol. V: 58). For the storyline see Nicolini (1909a: 398–399) and Del Donna (2012: 19). The opera was part of the dispute between supporters of Italian music, represented by Nicolò Piccinni and Giovanni Paisiello, and supporters of Christoph Willibald Gluck. Galiani obviously sided with the Italians: "Piccinni has just given our grand theatre an opera that surpasses all the good music that had been heard in Naples until now. Gluck's *Orpheus*, which was performed at Court at the same time, has been fearfully eclipsed by Piccinni's opera" (Ferdinando Galiani's letter to Madame d'Épinay, Naples, 15 February 1774, published in Galiani 1881a, vol. II, 296; Galiani and d'Épinay 1996, vol. IV: 120).

years, and he is the only one among us who succeeds. Therefore hated, and persecuted by the ignorant. [...] He is truly a man of spirit and knowledge: he is my friend and sometimes gives me the pleasure of dining with me. These lunches are all I have in common with *Socrate*. This *burletta* was performed here with due licence, and was perhaps enjoyed too much. The party of the *San Giovanni de' Fiorentini Theatre*, which is powerful, emulating the *Teatro Nuovo*, turned heaven and earth to ensure that this *burletta* would not harm the income of that other impresario. These were all the reasons for the war, and no others. *Socrate* was liked by the King for music. A plot was hatched and after seven performances, the *burletta* was ordered to be suspended, but without making any accusations against the author. Now it is said that it will be resumed, which seems difficult. However, the librettos have continued to be sold as long as there have been any, having never been banned. The King sings many arias from *Socrate*. The theatre has not closed".[243] And writing to Madame d'Épinay's daughter, "they staged [the *pièce*] and it aroused so much, but so much of a clamour that it ended up being banned by express order of His Majesty. You cannot imagine what joy I felt in the present circumstance, to see that the beautiful Neapolitan spirits arouse me at least as cordially as the Économistes. So, from now on, I have taken the solemn decision to do nothing more, to write nothing more, to publish nothing more".[244] And with a certain victimization he reported to D'Alembert: "My *Socrate Immaginario* had been authorised to be represented several times, because

[243] Ferdinando Galiani's letter to Lorenzo Mehus, Naples, 28 November 1775, published in Galiani (1975: 1119–1122). On the authorship of the work and Galiani's collaboration, there is no certainty. In this letter, Galiani claimed to have played no role. In others he claims his contribution: "I am besieged by a thousand annoyances, and I have nothing pleasant to do except my Horace and a comic *pièce* that I am busy having completed under my direction. It is called *The Imaginary Socrates*. There is nothing funnier in the world" (Ferdinando Galiani's letter to Madame d'Épinay, Naples, 9 September 1775, published in Galiani 1881a, vol. II, 422–423; Galiani and d'Épinay 1997, vol. V: 52). According to Luigi Diodati, Galiani had the idea for the work and integrated Lorenzi's draft with his own interventions (Diodati 1788: 52–63). Michele Scherillo considered Galiani as co-author of the work, a thesis accepted by Nicolini (see Scherillo 1886: 5–20; Nicolini 1908b: 12–15). Pietro Napoli-Signorelli denied any intervention by Galiani; Gaetano Amalfi admitted to an initial idea of his (see Napoli-Signorelli 1798: 193; Amalfi 1888a: 1–23), while for Vanda Monaco, *Socrates Imaginary* is by Galiani (Monaco 1968: 87–129). See Galiani (1975; Guerci's note, 1120); Scognamiglio (2010).

[244] Ferdinando Galiani's letter to Madame de Belsunce, Naples, 11 November 1775, published in Galiani (1881a, vol. II, 428); Galiani and d'Épinay (1997, vol. V: 56).

it was attributed to someone else, and as soon as it became known that I had drawn up the Plan, its representation was forbidden"[245]. The *pièce* was then performed again in the 1780 Carnival, obtaining royal permission (Pascal 1885: 82).

Beyond the entertainment offered to the public, *Socrate Immaginario* was above all a pungent satire by which Galiani returned in the last years of his life to attack, as he had done in his youth, academic and erudite culture; this time his satire was aimed at Saverio Mattei, professor of ancient Greek and Hebrew at the Neapolitan university, as well as a lawyer and exponent of the ceto civile (Rao 2008), but it was also an attack on Neo-Platonism.

Socrate Immaginario had been written partly in Neapolitan dialect, and in the same years Galiani was working on an essay on linguistics, *Del Dialetto Napoletano* (*Of Neapolitan Dialect*), published in 1779, further proof of his multiple interests (Galiani 1779b). In a letter to Madame d'Épinay, the *petit abbé* specified the genesis of the new book: "Not knowing what to do in order not to bore myself, and not being able to continue my work on Horace for lack of books and help, I undertook a work that had been suggested to me by Diderot. I worked on it for a month and it is not far from being printed. I am obliged to maintain the utmost secrecy, otherwise it would be forbidden, as happened with the work on Socrates. I am writing a dictionary of the Neapolitan dialect, with etymological and historical research on words peculiar to our idiom. This book will be curious, and useful to my country, moreover, very entertaining for those who know our dialect".[246]

With the usual dissimulation, the book on Neapolitan dialect was published with the false attribution to four anonymous *Accademici Amici della Patria* o *Filopatridi* (*Academic Friends of the Fatherland*).[247] The

[245] Ferdinando Galiani's letter to Jean Baptiste Le Rond d'Alembert, Naples, 28 November 1777, published in Galiani (1881a, vol. II, 538).

[246] Ferdinando Galiani's letter to Madame d'Épinay, Naples, 17 April 1779, published in Galiani (1881a, vol. II, 576–577); Galiani and d'Épinay (1997, vol. V: 212–213).

[247] "We were no more than five, but death, which always gets the best of us, having, not long ago, kidnapped one of us, reduced us to four [...]. Not by public authority, but of our own free will, being united in a friendly knot, we have assumed the name of 'academicians friends of the fatherland', for that ancient right, which reigns among Italians, to be able to call themselves academicians of any kind of study or liberal art, all those who have this in mind" (Galiani 1779c: 12–13). For Diodati the authorship of the work is entirely by Galiani (Diodati 1788: 71), Nicolini attributes a collaborative role to the erudite Gian Vincenzo Meola (Nicolini 1923: x). According to Luigi Serio, besides Galiani and Meola, the book was

choice of such attribution was linked to the "nationalistic" intent that characterised Galiani's essay. While at the instigation of Intieri and Genovesi, Italian took on an academic character by replacing Latin in university lecture halls (Nicolini 1923; Pennisi 1987; Amodio 1997a: 193–213), Galiani instead proposed elevating Neapolitan to the official language of the Kingdom. The 'negligent' Spanish domination, the inquisitorial weight of the Church and natural disasters had, according to the abbot, stifled the Neapolitan intellectual vivacity and withered the language born at the court of Frederick II of Swabia, and which would have been 'the general language of Italy, if that happy Campania and that Apulia which produced and nurtured it, had sustained itself as the first, and not as the lowest and most derelict of the Italian provinces' (Galiani 1779c: 8). The Neapolitan language had thus decayed into a dialect, full of "scurrilous obscenities", so much so that "speaking Neapolitan and buffoonery" was the same thing (Galiani 1779c: 8). He therefore proposed a work aimed at recovering the authentic language that had been corrupted over the centuries, providing "an essay on our grammar, a brief account of the origin and varied fortunes of our dialect and of the best writers who have handled it mainly in poetry, and a brief vocabulary of those of our voices that deviate the most from common Italian and of which the intelligence is obscure not only to foreigners but sometimes to our fellow citizens themselves" (Galiani 1779c: 9).

For Galiani, Neapolitan had its origin in the Greek Doric dialect, which compared to the other dialects of ancient Greece was characterised by open vowels and more pronounced consonants, features that the Neapolitan idiom had also preserved compared to Italian and could therefore be called "the Doric of the Italian favella" (Galiani 1779c: 16). The Neapolitan dialect originated from a *lingua franca*, a mixture of several languages, among which Greek and Latin stood out, born during the Longobard domination. It was a language without grammar, with altered pronunciation, without writing and handed down orally (Galiani 1779c: 54). This brought us to the thirteenth century, when Dante Alighieri perfected the nascent Italian language, which - Galiani observed - was little different from the Neapolitan dialect (Galiani 1779c: 59), but later the *Accademia della Crusca* eliminated all words from the Italian language that were not present in the Tuscan dialect. This tendency was also

composed by Pietro Napoli-Signorelli and Carlo Vespasiano (Serio 1780: 12), an opinion shared by Amalfi (1888b: 39–81). See on the attribution, Nicolini (1923: ix–xx).

reinforced by the greater zeal of Tuscan writers to write in Italian (Galiani 1779c: 59). Old Neapolitan preserved more than any other Italian dialect both the "greater conformity with Latin pronunciation" and the "greater quantity of Latin words preserved among us" (Galiani 1779c: 63). During the Aragonese domination, Neapolitan became an official and court language (Galiani 1779c: 101), but had no literature, as Neapolitan writers followed "the pen of Petrarch and Boccacio" (Galiani 1779c: 106).

A language that, at least in its original structure, was suitable for poetry and music (Galiani 1779c: 24) was corrupted by many writers, especially in the seventeenth century, and among these especially Giovan Battista Basile and Giulio Cesare Cortese (Galiani 1779c: 123), who had transcribed it "with a barbarous orthography", impeding correct pronunciation and reading, and thus "it seemed to everyone not to recognise under these distorted appearances a sweet dialect and a not unworthy offspring of the Italian favella, but some barbarous and unusual language" (Galiani 1779c: 41).[248] Basile "unfortunately for us, had the caprice to imitate Giovanni Boccaccio's incomparable *Decameron*, and composed a pentameron in Neapolitan dialect entitled *Lo cunto de li cunte* [*The Tale of Tales*] [...]. Such an undertaking completely lacked the talent to execute it. Lacking in every way either high genius or philosophy, happiness of invention or richness of knowledge to be able to imagine or decorate pretty or interesting or tragic or amusing or moral tales, he could think of nothing else but to write tales of fairies and ogres so insipid, monstrous and filthy that the Arabs themselves, the founders of this depraved taste, would have been ashamed to have imagined them. To the stupidity of invention corresponds the monstrosity of style" (Galiani 1779c: 123–124, see Basile 1674). Basile's book, according to Galiani, was fatal, not only disfiguring the dialect, but also contributing to a total corruption of the customs of the people, finding support from the Spanish government, which authorised several reprints, to influence the education of young people attracted by the vulgar entertainment the work contained (Galiani 1779c: 126).[249]

The intellectual renaissance that began with the independence of the Kingdom repudiated the Neapolitan dialect to embrace the Tuscan dialect

[248] An early example of corruption Galiani attributes to Boccaccio (Galiani 1779c: 78–80).

[249] Galiani's negative judgement contrasts sharply with the revaluation of Basile's work, initiated especially by Benedetto Croce, who called *Lo cunto de li cunti*, "the oldest, richest and most artistic of all popular storybooks" (Croce 1925a: 3), a classic of the Neapolitan literary tradition.

made sacred "by the indeclinable verdict of the Crusca" (Galiani 1779c: 140). Galiani's political objective was clearly at odds with this trend in Neapolitan culture. In order to restore the literary value of Neapolitan, the abbot proposed an official bilingualism that was to stimulate a renewed literature by remedying the errors made in the seventeenth century.[250] However, his intention to establish the illustrious Neapolitan language and codify a national language was implemented with arbitrary choices, excessive simplifications of grammar and 'ahistorical exclusions' (Catucci 1986: 167). The essay was supposed to be an introduction to the *Vocabolario del dialetto napoletano* (*Dictionary of Neapolitan Dialect*), later published posthumously (Galiani 1789); he also planned a second edition, but it was never published, absorbed as he was by his duties as advisor.

The interest shown by Galiani in minority languages was widespread in Enlightenment culture. The entry "Langue" in the *Encyclopédie*, compiled by Nicolas Beauzée, recognized that: "if a language is spoken by a nation made up of several peoples who are equal and independent in respect to each other and who generally use the same words and syntax, such as the Greeks in ancient times and the Italians and Germans today, each people can have its particular usages with respect to pronunciation or the endings of the same words, and these equally valid variations form the dialects of their national language" (Beauzée 1765: 249). And Turgot, who was assigned the *Étymologie* entry in the *Encyclopédie*, adopted a method of comparison as a tool of historical-etymological analysis: "When several of these primitive languages have been formed at the same time in different countries, the study of these different languages, of their dialects, of the variations they have undergone; the comparison of the different ways in which they have altered the same inflections, or the same sounds of the mother tongue, by making them their own; that of the opposite directions [...] in which they have diverted the meaning of the same expressions; the continuation of this comparison, throughout the course of their progress, and in their different periods, will serve a great deal to give insight into the

[250] A choice that seems at odds with what he argued in a letter to Madame d'Épinay against multilingualism: "If Europe had only one language, there would be no more intolerance. When people are similar, they love each other, and nothing makes us more dissimilar than not being able to understand each other when speaking. It is the difference in language that makes the species truly different. We are of the same family when we can understand each other well" (Ferdinando Galiani's letter to Madame d'Épinay, Naples, 27 March 1773, published in Galiani 1881a, vol. II, 189; Galiani and d'Épinay 1994, vol. III: 220).

origins of each of them: Thus Italian and Gascon, which come from Latin, like French, often have an intermediate word between a French word and a Latin word, whose transition would have seemed too abrupt and too improbable if we had wanted to derive one immediately from the other, Either the word actually became French only because it was borrowed from Italian or Gascon, which is very common, or these three languages were less different in the past than they are today" (Turgot 1756: 100).

Galiani's work, not "a simple grammatical-historical-bibliographical handbook of the Neapolitan dialect", but an essay "with two faces, serious-scientific and satirical-burlesque" (Nicolini 1923: xxxviii), was directed against official culture, especially against the new *Academy of Sciences* from which the abbot had been excluded, and for this antagonistic character it was the object of violent controversy.[251]

Satisfying his taste for lampoonery, in the same year, Galiani, under the pseudonym of Onofrio Galeota, published another burlesque satire on the eruption of Vesuvius in the summer of 1779, desecrating in his own way a tragic event, but also taking the opportunity to ironise on the new physics of electricity.[252]

Thus, Galiani's last years were spent between his commitments as a consultant, the many works that were planned, started and never completed,[253] and the correspondence that became increasingly rare as Madame d'Épinay's illness progressed, finally stopping in July 1782 (she died in April 1783).[254] He rarely left Naples and only for short trips, mainly taking care of his family after the death of his brother Berardo in 1774[255].

[251] Luigi Serio (1780) and the secretary of the Academy, Michele Sarcone (1780) intervened in the controversy with Galiani; on the controversy see Nicolini (1923: xxxiv–xlviii).

[252] On the pseudonym chosen by Galiani, see Croce (1954); Placanica (1982). Galiani published another work under the name Onofrio Galeota, see Galiani (1785) and Nicolini (1909a: 410–411). "This Galeota was a poor priest who lived by printing foolishness, easily purchased, because they were light reading" (Pascal 1885: 84).

[253] He also intended to reprint his early works, but only succeeded in publishing the second edition of *Della Moneta* and the *eulogy* of Benedict XIV (see Ferdinando Galiani's letter to Madame d'Épinay, Naples, 13 December 1770, published in Galiani 1881a: vol. I, 316; Galiani and d'Épinay 1992, vol. I: 316).

[254] "Madame d'Épinay is no more, I too have ceased to be! In your last letter you proposed to me to continue with you the correspondence that I had the honour of maintaining with her for so long; I feel all the price of the sacrifice that you deigned to impose on yourself; but how could I answer? My heart is no longer among the living, it is entirely in a tomb" (Ferdinando Galiani's letter to Madame du Boccage, Naples, 10 June 1783, published in Galiani1881a, vol. II, 634).

[255] "He has a wife, his wife's mother, and three daughters, none of them married; look what a frightful spectacle presents itself to my imagination! In all three cases, I am con-

In May 1785, debilitated by syphilis, he suffered an apoplectic stroke while attending a meeting of the *Giunta del Fondo di Separazione* of which he was a member. Due to his serious condition, it was not possible to transport him and he had to stay in the president's house for many days (Diodati 1788: 82). His recovery from the stroke was long and not complete, and fearing in May of the following year that he would suffer another attack, he took a trip to Apulia to enjoy the healthier air. Returning to Naples in June 1786, he resumed his activities, leading a more moderate life and staying in the countryside. Despite the precautions taken, his health did not improve and he was advised to travel through Italy, which he undertook between April and May 1787, visiting Venice, Padua and Modena.

Luigi Diodati's biography is a source of direct testimony of the last months of the abbot's life: having returned to Naples in June 1787, Galiani fell into "a tearful state and from day to day he lacked strength. Without losing his vivacity, he already felt that he had little more time left to live: so he said goodbye to all his friends, telling them that the dead were calling him, and that they had already sent him the invitation card for their conversation. Meanwhile, towards the months of July and August 1787, he had a swelling in his legs, a clear sign of dropsy, accompanied also by breathlessness. On the evening of 7 October, he wanted to go to Portici to pay his respects to the Sovereigns [...] Then both the King and the Queen, seeing him too ill [...] told him to call a doctor. [...] He retired the next morning to Naples, then called the celebrated doctor Domenico Cotugno, got into bed and it was clear that the illness was to take his life" (Diodati 1788: 84–85).[256]

Regretting not being able to finish his work on the port of Baia (Galiani, MS-49) and to complete the second map of the Kingdom of Naples, he died on 30 October 1787, receiving religious comforts. Shortly before his

demned to rule a terrible menagerie of five women, to be bored to death for the rest of my life, or at least for more than a year, chained in Naples, overseeing cotillons, and responsible for the food and care of a family" (Ferdinando Galiani's letter to Madame d'Épinay, Naples, 11 September 1773, published in Galiani 1881a, vol. II, 258; Galiani and d'Épinay 1996, vol. IV: 65).

[256] A few days before his death, Queen Marie Caroline wrote him a farewell letter, thanking him for his services to the crown, see Queen Marie Caroline's letter to Ferdinando Galiani, Naples 17 October 1787, published in Galiani (1881a, vol. II, 635–638); see also Ferdinando Galiani's letter to Queen Marie Caroline, Naples, 18 October 1787, published in Galiani (1881a, vol. II, 639–641).

death, he had dictated his will in which he indicated as his burial place the Church of the Ascension of the Celestines, next to the tomb of his uncle Celestine (Galiani, MS-50: 655). He left his manuscripts to his nephew Francesco Paolo Azzariti (Galiani, MS-50: 657): "eight very big tomes, which [contained] only the letters of Italian friends, in addition to fourteen other volumes which [included] the letters of several illustrious foreign men, of many Sovereigns and famous State ministries" (Diodati 1788: 19).[257]

References[258]

Manuscript Sources

Galiani, F. MS-5. *Dell'idea di Dio*, Manuscript kept in the British Museum, Egerton Collection, 21, published in Nicolini-Venturi, 1956, pp. 67–73.

Galiani, F. MS-6. *Della superstizione, e delle cause di essa*, Manuscript kept in the Biblioteca Società Napoletana di Storia Patria, XXXI. A. 10, folios 124r–125v, published in Mauro 2017a, tome 2, pp. 469–471.

Galiani, F. MS-7. *Sull'Anticristo (al conte Punghino)*, Manuscript kept in the Biblioteca Società Napoletana di Storia Patria, XXXI. C. 12, folios 97r–102r, published in Mauro, 2017a, tome 2, pp. 472–477.

[257] In a letter to Madame d'Épinay, Galiani mentioned several manuscripts completed and ready for publication: "My completed Italian manuscripts are a translation of Locke's work on currency, with notes; a translation in verse of the first book of Anti-Lucretius; some poems; a dissertation on giants and men of extraordinary stature; a dissertation on Carthaginian kings; several dissertations on learned subjects and two or three orations; a dissertation on the paintings of Herculaneum; one on Vesuvius; my French Horace, etc." (Ferdinando Galiani's letter to Madame d'Épinay, Naples, 13 December 1770, published in Galiani 1881a: vol. I, 317; Galiani and d'Épinay 1992, vol. I: 316). Among the assets constituting his inheritance was the sword of Cesare Borgia: "I have a very curious piece, the sword of Cesare Borgia, Duke of Valentinois, son of Pope Alexander VI, which he had made on purpose with emblems alluding to his future greatness and ambition. It is superfluous to tell you how, by what detours, this sword fell into my hands. I wanted to make a lucrative present of it to the Pope, and, according to my custom, to accompany it with an erudite dissertation to illustrate its emblems" (Ferdinando Galiani's letter to Madame d'Épinay, Naples, 2 October 1773, published in Galiani 1881a, vol. II, 269; Galiani and d'Épinay 1996, vol. IV: 75). According to Galiani's last wishes, the sword was to be sold, but if the transaction failed, the heirloom was to be donated to Empress Catherine (Galiani, MS-50: 657). On the Borgia sword, see Ademollo (1880: 660–667).

[258] The abbreviations "s.l." and "s.n." stand for the Latin terms *sine loco* (without place of publication) and *sine nomine* (without name of publisher).

Galiani, F. MS-14. *Sui contratti alla voce*. Manuscript kept in the Biblioteca Società Napoletana di Storia Patria, XXXI. A. 10, published in Galiani, 1975, pp. 742–745 and in Galiani, 1999, pp. 77–80.

Galiani, F. MS-19. *Breve racconto di quel che è a mia notizia rispetto al Trattato di navigazione e commercio colla Francia* (1784). Manuscript kept in the Biblioteca Società Napoletana di Storia Patria, XXX. D. 3, folios 74r–81v, published in Diaz, 1973, pp. 354–364 and in Galiani, 1999, pp. 125–131.

Galiani, F. MS-22. *De l'opinion*, Manuscript kept in the Turin State Archives, published in Nicolini, 1959c, pp. 139–156 ("the indication of the place where the fragment De l'opinion is kept is wrong, as Venturi pointed out: it is the Turin State Archives and not the British Museum", see Galiani, 1975: Guerci's note: cxvii).

Galiani, F. MS-24. *Considerazioni sul Trattato di Commercio tra il Re e il Re Cristianissimo*, Manuscript kept in the Biblioteca Società Napoletana di Storia Patria, XXX. A. 10, folios 183r–251v, partially published in Galiani, 1975, pp. 717–734.

Galiani, F. MS-27. *Piano di riforma proposto da Galiani dopo la cacciata dei gesuiti da Napoli*, Manuscript kept in the Biblioteca Società Napoletana di Storia Patria XXX. C. 12, folios 12v–19r, published in Galiani, 1975h, pp. 710–716.

Galiani, F. MS-28. *Relazione circa un progetto di trattato tra la Russia e il Regno di Sardegna e le prospettive di un trattato fra Russia e Regno di Napoli*, Manuscript kept in the Biblioteca Società Napoletana di Storia Patria XXX. A. 15, folios 59r–62r, published in Diaz, 1973, pp. 335–340.

Galiani, F. MS-29. *Sull'annona di Genova*, Manuscript kept in the Biblioteca Società Napoletana di Storia Patria XXX. C. 6, folios 50r–56v, published in Galiani, 1975, pp. 735–741; in Cesarano, 1999, pp. 69–74.

Galiani, F. MS-30. *Pensieri miei sulle cause della spopolazione della Maremma sanese e su' rimedi*, Manuscript kept in the Biblioteca Società Napoletana di Storia Patria XXX. C. 12.29, folios 164–170, published in Galiani, 1999: 9–13, see also Galiani, 1963: 393–397.

Galiani, F. MS-31. *Pensieri vari di Ferdinando Galiani sul tremuoto della Calabria Ultra e di Messina*, Manuscript kept in the Biblioteca Società Napoletana di Storia Patria XXX. D. 03, Folios 42r–45r, published in Galiani, 1975, pp. 748–751.

Galiani, F. MS-32. *Continuazione de' pensieri di Ferdinando Galiani sul tremuoto della Calabria*, Manuscript kept in the Biblioteca Società Napoletana di Storia Patria XXX. D. 03, folios 45r–48v, published in Galiani, 1975, pp. 752–756.

Galiani, F. MS-33. *Quarto foglio de' pensieri di Ferdinando Galiani sul tremuoto di Calabria, e sue conseguenze*, Manuscript kept in the Biblioteca Società Napoletana di Storia Patria XXX. D. 03, folios 49r–50v, published in Galiani, 1975, pp. 757–758.

Galiani, F. MS-34. *Pensieri generali sul ristabilimento di Messina*, Manuscript kept in the Biblioteca Società Napoletana di Storia Patria, XXX. D. 03, folios 39r–41v., published in Galiani, 1975, pp. 759–762.

Galiani, F. MS-35. *Parere sul disgombro e il riedificamento di Messina*, Manuscript kept in the Biblioteca Società Napoletana di Storia Patria, XXX. D. 03, folios 62r–65v, published in Galiani, 1975, pp. 763–766.

Galiani, F. MS-36. *Sul regolamento delle Poste del Regno*, Manuscript kept in the Biblioteca Società Napoletana di Storia Patria, XXXI. A. 10, folios 88r–103v, published in Galiani, 1999b, pp. 41–49.

Galiani, F. MS-37. *Dell'uso che potrebbe farsi delle pensioni di Tanucci*, Manuscript kept in the Biblioteca Società Napoletana di Storia Patria, XXX. C. 06, folios 8r–9v, published in Galiani, 1999c, pp. 33–34.

Galiani, F. MS-38. *Rapporto all'Acton sul Comune di Castellamare*, Manuscript kept in the Biblioteca Società Napoletana di Storia Patria, XXX. D. 03, folios 85v–89r, published in Galiani, 1975, pp. 774–779 e in Galiani, 1999, pp. 35–39.

Galiani, F. MS-39. *Parere riguardante i dazi della seta*, Manuscript kept in the Biblioteca Società Napoletana di Storia Patria, XXX. D. 03, folios 53–55; 83–85, published in Galiani, 1999, pp. 19–21.

Galiani, F. MS-40. *Per la privativa di una fabbrica di saponi*, Manuscript kept in the Biblioteca Società Napoletana di Storia Patria, XXXI. A. 10, folios 80r–87v, published in Galiani, 1999, pp. 23–26.

Galiani, F. MS-41. *Piano per conseguire dalla Porta Ottomana la libera navigazione del Mar Nero ai bastimenti mercantili delle Due Sicilie*, Manuscript kept in the Biblioteca Società Napoletana di Storia Patria, XXX. D. 03, folios 66r–68r, published in Galiani, 1999, pp. 121–123.

Galiani, F. MS-42. *Sulla decadenza della marineria*, Manuscript kept in the Biblioteca Società Napoletana di Storia Patria, XXX. C. 12., folios 40–43, published in Galiani, 1999, pp. 133–135.

Galiani, F. MS-43. *Parere sullo stabilimento di rapporti commerciali e d'amicizia con gli Stati Uniti* (1784), Manuscript kept in the Biblioteca Società Napoletana di Storia Patria, XXX. D. 03, folios 1–6.

Galiani, F. MS-44. *Istruzioni al conte Ludolf sulla libera navigazione del Mar Nero*, Manuscript kept in the Biblioteca Società Napoletana di Storia Patria, XXX. D. 03, folios 68v–70v.

Galiani, F. MS-45. *Considerazioni sul vantaggio che deriverebbe ai sudditi di S.M. Imperiale dalla libertà che avessero i bastimenti delle Due Sicilie di navigare fino all'imboccatura del Danubio*, Manuscript kept in the Biblioteca Società Napoletana di Storia Patria, XXX. D. 03, folios 71r–73r.

Galiani, F. MS-46. *Croquis d'un dialogue sur les femmes*, Manuscript kept in the Biblioteca Società Napoletana di Storia Patria, XXX. C. 12, Folios 212–218, published in Galiani, 1975, pp. 635–642; Galiani, 1881a, vol. II, pp. 50–62.

Galiani, F. MS-47. *Commento alle odi di Orazio*, Manuscript kept in the Biblioteca Società Napoletana di Storia Patria, XXXII C 6, published in Nicolini, 1978.

Galiani, F. MS-48. *Cela revient toujours au même*, Manuscript kept in the Biblioteca Società Napoletana di Storia Patria, XXX C 12, folios: 227–230, published in Nicolini, 1909a, pp. 253–258, and Galiani, 1954: 208–211.

Galiani, F. MS-49. *Piano per l'ancoraggio del porto di Baja*, Manuscript kept in the Biblioteca Società Napoletana di Storia Patria, XXXI. A. 10, folios: 60r–60v.

Galiani, F. MS-50. *Testamento*, Manuscript kept in the Biblioteca Società Napoletana di Storia Patria, XXXI. A. 08, folios: 85r–88r, published in Ademollo, 1880a, pp. 654–658.

Galiani, F. MS-52. *Projet d'un traité de commerce et de navigation entre Sa Majesté le Roi des Deux Sicilies, et Sa Majesté l'Imperatrice de toutes les Russies* (1785a), Manuscript kept in the Biblioteca Società Napoletana di Storia Patria, XXX. A. 15: folios 27r–34r [29–43].

Galiani, F. MS-53. *Riflessioni sul controprogetto del Duca di Serracapriola*, Manuscript kept in the Biblioteca Società Napoletana di Storia Patria, XXX. A. 15: folios 35–69bis [45–116].

Galiani, F. MS-54. *Sui contratti a voce. Confutazione della teoria di Odazi.* Manuscript kept in the Biblioteca Società Napoletana di Storia Patria, XXXI.A.10.10, folios 64r–65v.

Nicolini, B. (1975). Gli scritti galianei di Fausto Nicolini. In *Convegno italo-francese sul tema Ferdinando Galiani* (Roma, 25–27 maggio 1972), Rome: Accademia Nazionale dei Lincei, pp. 259–307.

Primary Sources

Basile, G.B. (1674). *Il pentamerone del cavalier Giovan Battista Basile, overo Lo cunto de li cunte trattenemiento de li peccerille di Gian Alesio Abbattutis.* Naples: Bulifon.

Baudeau, N. (1769). Lettres de M. l'abbé Baudeau, prevot mitré de Widzyniski, à M. l'abbé G.•••, sur ses Dialogues anti-Économistes, *Éphémérides du citoyen ou Bibliothèque raisonnée des sciences morales et politiques,*Tome XII. Paris: Lacombre, pp. 108–128.

Baudeau, N. (1770). *Lettres d'un Amateur à M. l'abbé G***, sur ses Dialogues anti-Économistes.* Paris: Lacombe.

Baudeau, N. (1775). *Eclaircissements demandés à M. N** [Necker], Sur ses Principes Economiques, & sur ses projets de législation; Au nom des Propriétaires fonciers & des Cultivateurs François. Extrait des Nouvelles Éphémérides Économiques.* Paris: Didot.

Beauzée, N. (1765). Langue. In *Encyclopédie, ou dictionnaire raisonné des sciences, des arts et des métiers,* Tome IX, Neufchastel [but Paris]: Samuel Faulche, pp. 149–266. English Translation *The Encyclopedia of Diderot & d'Alembert Collaborative Translation Project.* Translated by Julia Wallhager. Ann Arbor: Michigan Publishing, University of Michigan Library, 2015 (reference on line).

Bellitti, G. (1771). *Sul contratto detto alla voce.* Naples: s.n.

Boulanger, N. (1766). *L'Antiquité dévoilée par ses usages, ou Examen critique des principales opinions, cérémonies, institutions religieuses & politiques des différens peuples de la terre.* Amsterdam: chez Marc Michel.

Boucher d'Argis, A.-G. (1765). Opinion. In *Encyclopédie, ou dictionnaire raisonné des sciences, des arts et des métiers,* Tome XI. Neufchastel [but Paris]: Samuel Faulche, pp. 706–707.

Buffon, G.-L. Leclerc de. (1766). *Histoire naturelle, générale et particulière avec la description du cabinet du roi,* tome XIV. Paris: Imprimerie royale.

Caracciolo, D. (1785). *Riflessioni su l'economia e l'estrazione dei frumenti della Sicilia fatte in occasione delle carestia dell'indizione terza 1784 e 1785.* Palermo: Stamperia Reale.

Catherine II, and Grimm, F. M. (2016). *Une correspondance privée, artistique et politique au siècle des Lumières,* tome I, 1764–1778, edited by S. Karp. Moscow: Monuments de la pensée historique.

Cicero, M. T. [1991], *On Duties* [*De Officis*]. English Transation edited by Atkins, E. M.; Griffin, M. T. Cambridge: Cambridge University Press

Condorcet, M. J. A. N. de Caritat. (1774). *Lettres sur le commerce des grains.* Paris: Couturier Père.

Condorcet, M. J. A. N. de Caritat. (1776). *Réflexions sur le commerce des bleds,* Londres [Genève]: s.n.

Correspondance littéraire. (1879). *Correspondance, littéraire, philosophique et critique par Grimm, Diderot, Raynal, Meister, etc: revue sur les textes originaux.* Paris: Garnier.

d'Alembert, J-B. Le Rond. (1743). *Traité de dynamique.* Paris: David.

d'Alembert, J-B. Le Rond. (1751) [1995]. Discours préliminaire des Éditeurs. In *Encyclopédie, ou dictionnaire raisonné des sciences, des arts et des métiers,* tome I. Paris: Briasson, David l'aîné, Le Breton, Imprimeur ordinaire du Roy, Durand, pp. i–xlv. English Translation: *Preliminary Discourse to the Encyclopaedia of Diderot,* translated by R. N. Schwab with the collaboration of W. E. Rex. Chicago: University of Chicago Press.

Dampier, W. (1697). *A New Voyage Round the World.* London: James Knapton.

D'Epinay, L. (1774). *Les Conversations d'Émilie.* Paris: chez Pissot.

D'Epinay, L., Galiani, F. (1996). *Epistolario 1769–1782,* edited by S.Rapisarda. Palermo: Sellerio.

De Vattel, E. (1758). *Le droit des gens ou Principes de la loi naturelle appliqués à la conduite et aux affaires des nations et des souverains.* London: s.n.

D'Holbach, Thiry P. (1766). *Le Christianisme dévoilé ou Examen des principes et des effets de la religion chrétienne.* Londres: s.n.

D'Holbach, Thiry P. (1770) [1889]. *Système de la nature, ou Des loix du monde physique et du monde moral,* London: s.n. English translation, *The System of Nature.* Boston: Mendun, 1889.

Diderot, D. (1770) [1963]. Apologie de l'abbé Galiani. In D. Diderot, *Œuvres politiques*, edited by P. Vernière, Paris: Garnier, pp. 59–124.

Diderot, D. (1875b). Sur les femmes. In *Œuvres Complètes de Diderot revues sur les éditions originals comprenant ce qui a été publié a diverses époques et les manuscrits inédits conserves à la bibliothèque de l'ermitage. notices, notes., table analytique étude sur Diderot et le mouvement philosophique au XVIII siècle*, Tome II. Paris: Garnier, pp. 251–262.

Diderot, D. (1955). *Correspondence*, edited by G. Roth, 13 vols. Paris: Editions de minuit.

Diodati, L. (1788). *Vita dell'abate Ferdinando Galiani*. Naples: Orsino.

Dupont de Nemours, P. S. (1768a). *Physiocratie, ou Constitution naturelle du gouvernement le plus avantageux au genre humain*. Paris: Merlin.

Dupont de Nemours, P. S. (1768b). *De l'origine et des progrès d'une science nouvelle*. Paris: Chez Desaint.

Dupont de Nemours, P. S. (1770a). Avvertissement contenant le Table raisonnée des matières traitées dans les volumes de l'année précédente, *Éphémérides du citoyen ou Bibliothèque raisonnée des sciences morales et politiques*, Tome XI. Paris: Lacombre, pp. 5–111.

Éphémérides. (1769b). Supplement a l'article des critiques raisonnées, *Éphémérides du citoyen ou Bibliothèque raisonnée des sciences morales et politiques*, Tome XI. Paris: Lacombre, pp. 193–247.

Éphémérides. (1769c). Le bal de l'Opèra. Fable, par M. T. *Éphémérides du citoyen ou Bibliothèque raisonnée des sciences morales et politiques*, Tome XII. Paris: Lacombre, pp. 99–106.

Euler, L. (1748). *Introductio in Analys in Infinitorum*. Lausannae: apud Marcum Michaelem Bousquet et socios.

Filangieri, G. (1780). *La Scienza della Legislazione*, Tomo II. Naples: Stamperia Raimondiana.

Filangieri, G. (1784). *La Scienza della Legislazione*, edizione prima veneta, Tomo IV. Venice: Giovanni Vitto.

Flora, G. (1927). *Le più belle pagine di Ferdinando Galiani*, Milan: Treves.

Forbonnais, Véron de, F. L. (1767). *Principes et observations oeconomiques*. Amsterdam: Rey.

Galanti, G. M. (1783). *Elogio storico del signor abate Antonio Genovesi pubblico professore di civil economia nell'Università di Napoli. Terza edizione notabilmente migliorata e corretta, ed accresciuta dell'elogio del signor Bartolomeo Intieri e di una lettera intorno al plagio letterario*. Florence: Pisoni.

Galanti G. M. (1786). *Nuova Descrizione Storica e geografica delle Sicilie dell'avvocato Giuseppe M.a Galanti tomo I*. Naples: Gabinetto Letterario.

Galanti G. M. (1997). Memorie storiche del mio tempo. In F. Venturi, (ed.), *Illuministi italiani*, vol. II, Tomo II. Milan: Ricciardi-Mondadori, pp. 988–1020.

Galiani, F. (1751) [published anonymous, with date of 1750]. *Della moneta. Libri cinque.* Naples: Giuseppe Raimond.

Galiani, F. (1770a). *Dialogues sur le commerce des bleds.* London [but Paris]: Merlin.

Galiani, F. (1770b) [1979]. *L'intérêt géneral de l'État ou La liberté du commerce des bleds démontrée conforme au droit naturel; au droit public de la France; aux lois fondamentales du Royaume; à l'intérêt commun du souverain et de ses sujets dans tous les temps; avec la réfutation d'un nouveau système de bagarre publié en forme de feu d'artifice*, par M.L.A.R. economiste indigne, in La Bagarre: Galiani's Lost Parody, edited by S. L. Kaplan. The Hague: Martinus Nijhoff, pp. 65–116.

Galiani, F. (1772). *Catalogo delle materie appartenenti al Vesuvio contenute nel Museo, con alcune brevi osservazioni. Opera del celebre autore de' Dialoghi sul commercio de' grani.* London [but Florence]: s.n.

Galiani, F. (1775). *Diàlogos sobre el comercio de trigo, atribuidos al Abate Galiani.* Madrid: Joachin Ibarra.

Galiani, F. (1776). *Razgovory o chlebnom torge s francyskago perevedeny Petrom Kjuvil'e.* Saint Peterburg: Imperatorskaya Akademiya Nauk.

Galiani, F. (1777). *Dialogen über die Regierungskunst vornemlich in Rucksicht auf den Getreydehandel.* Lemgo: Meyerschen Buchhandlung.

Galiani, F. (1778). *Handlungs-Dialogen von Herrn Abbé* [Ferdinando] *Galenti* [Galiani], translated by W Berisch. Lipsia: Wirthgen.

Galiani, F. (1779b). *Spaventosissima descrizione dello spaventoso spavento, che ci spaventò tutti, coll'eruzione del Vesuvio, la sera dell'otto agosto del corrente anno, ma (per grazia di Dio) durò poco, di d. Onofrio Galeota, poeta e filosofo all'impronto - Fratiè, non m'ammalì - Il Teatro de' Fiorentini nel corrente dramma.* Naples: Stampato a spese dell'autore, e si vende grana sei a chi lo va a comprare.

Galiani, F. (1779c). *Del Dialetto napoletano, Deus nobis haec otia fecit.* Naples: Mazzola Vocola.

Galiani, F. (1780). *Della moneta. Libri cinque. Edizione seconda.* Naples: Stamperia Simoniana.

Galiani, F. (1781). *Delle lodi di papa Benedetto XIV, Orazione dedicata a Sua Eccellenza reverendissima mons. Lazaro Opizio Pallavicino, arcivescovo di Lepanto e nunzio apostolico.* Naples: Stamperia Simoniana.

Galiani, F. (1782). *De' doveri de' principi neutrali verso i principi guerreggianti: e di questi verso i neutrali. Libre due.* Naples: s.n.

Galiani, F. [Galeota, Onofrio]. (1785). *Guazzabuglio filosarmonico o sia miscellaneo versoprosaico sulle probole*, antiprobole ed aneddoto forense, di d. Onofrio Galeota, poeta e filosofo all'impronto . Fantasianapoli [Naples]: s.n.

Galiani, F. (1789). *Vocabolario delle parole del dialetto napoletano che più si scostano dal dialetto toscano, con alcune ricerche etimologiche sulle medesime, degli*

Accademici [oscuri] Filopatridi. Opera postuma supplita ed accresciuta notabilmente. Naples: Porcelli.

Galiani, F. (1790). *Recht der Neutralitaet. Oder: Von den gegenseitigen Pflichten neutraler und kriegfuehrender Maechte*. Leipzig: Georg Conrad Walthers Wittwe.

Galiani, F. (1818a). *Correspondance inédite de l'abbé Ferdinand Galiani, conseiller du Roi, pendant les années 1765 à 1783, avec Madame d'Épinay, le Baron d'Holbach, le Baron de Grimm, Diderot et autres personnages célèbres de ce temps; augmentée de plusiers lettres à Monseigneur Sanseverino, archevêque de Palerme, à M. le Marquis de Caraccioli, ambassadeur de Naples près la cour de France, à Voltaire, d'Alembert, Raynal, Marmontel, Thomas, Le Batteux, Madame du Bocage; précédée d'une notice historique sur l'abbé Galiani, par l'abbé Bart. Mercier de Saint Léger, bibliotethécaire de Sainte-Geneviève. A laquelle il a été ajoute diverses particularités inédites concernant la vie privée, les bons mots, le caractère original de l'auteur. Par M. C*** de S[t] M***. membre de plusieurs académies*, 2 voll., Paris: J. B. Dentu, imprimeur-libraire.

Galiani, F. (1818b). Correspondance inédite de M. l'abbé Ferdinand Galiani, conseiller du Roi de Naples, avec Mme d'Épinay, le Baron d'Holbach, le Baron Grimm et autres personnages célèbres du XVIIIe siècle. Édition imprimée sur le manuscrit autographe de l'auteur, revue et accompagnée de notes, par M*** [A.-A. Barbier], membre de plusiers académies. Précédée d'une notice historique sur la vie et les ouvrages de l'Auteur, par feu Ginguené, avec des notes par M. Salfi, et du Dialogue de l'abbé Galiani sur les femmes. Tome premier [-Tome second], 2 voll., Paris-Strasbourg-Londres: Treuttel et Würtz.

Galiani, F. (1821). *Oeuvres d'Horace, traduites par MM. Campenon et Després, accompagnées du Commentaire de l'abbé Galiani, précédées d'un essai sur la vie et les écrits d'Horace*. Paris: De Bure.

Galiani, F. (1881a). *Écrivains du XVIII siècle – Correspondance avec Madame d'Épinay, Madame Necker, Madame Geoffrin etc., Diderot, Grimm, d'Alembert, de Sartine, d'Holbach, etc. Nouvelle édition, entièrement rétablie d'après les textes originaux, augmentée de tous les passages supprimés et d'un grand nombre de lettres inédites, avec une étude sur sa vie et les oeuvres de Galiani*, edited by L. Perey, G. Maugras, 2 voll. Paris: Calmann Levy.

Galiani, F. (1881b). *Lettres du XVII et XVIII siècle – Lettres de l'Abbé Galiani à Madame d'Épinay, Voltaire, Diderot, Grimm, le Baron d'Holbach, Morellet, Suart (sic), d'Alembert, Marmontel, la Vicomtesse de Belsunce, etc. Publiées d'après les éditions originales augmentées des variantes, de nombreuses notes et d'un Index avec notice biographique*, edited by E. Asse, 2 voll., Paris, G. Charpentier.

Galiani, F. (1903–1904). Dal carteggio dell'abate Galiani. Lettere inedite del d'Holbach, Diderot, Signora d'Épinay, *La Critica: rivista di letteratura, storia e filosofia*, vol. I, pp. 477–491; vol. II, pp. 73–84; 155–168; 503–517.

Galiani, F. (1909). Gli studi sopra Orazio. In Nicolini, 1909a, pp. 1–160.

Galiani, F. (1957). *Dialogo sulle donne e altri scritti di Ferdinando Galiani*, edited by C. Cases, Milan: Feltrinelli.

Galiani, F. (1959). *Dialogues sur le commerce des bleds. Giusta l'editio princeps del 1770 con appendici illustrative*, edited by F. Nicolini, Naples: Ricciardi

Galiani, F. (1968). *Dialogues entre M. Marquis de Roquemaure et M. le chevalier Zanobi. The autograph manuscript of the Dialogues sur le commerce des bleds diplomatically edited with introduction, notes and appendices by Philip Koch*, Analecta Romanica, Heft 21, Frankfurt am Main: Klostermann.

Galiani, F. (1975). *Opere di Ferdinando Galiani*, edited by F. Diaz e L. Guerci, in *Letteratura italiana. Storia e testi. Illuministi italiani*, tomo VI. Milan-Naples: Ricciardi.

Galiani, F., d'Épinay, L. (1992). *Correspondance. Vol. I (1769–1770)*, présentation de G. Dulac, texte établi et annoté par D. Maggetti, en collaboration avec G. Dulac. Paris: Les Editions Desjonquères.

Galiani, F., d'Épinay, L. (1993). *Correspondance. Vol. II (1771–Février 1772)*, présentation de G. Dulac, texte établi et annoté par D. Maggetti, en collaboration avec G. Dulac. Paris: Les Editions Desjonquères.

Galiani, F., d'Épinay, L. (1994). *Correspondance. Vol. III (Mars 1772–Mai 1773)*, présentation de G. Dulac, texte établi et annoté par D. Maggetti, en collaboration avec G. Dulac. Paris: Les Editions Desjonquères.

Galiani, F., d'Épinay, L. (1996). *Correspondance. Vol. IV (Juin 1773–Mai 1775)*, présentation de Georges Dulac, texte établi et annoté par Daniel Maggetti, en collaboration avec Georges Dulac, Paris: Les Editions Desjonquères.

Galiani, F., d'Épinay, L. (1997). *Correspondance. Vol. V (June 1775–Juillet 1782)*, présentation de G. Dulac, texte établi et annoté par D. Maggetti, en collaboration avec G. Dulac. Paris: Les Editions Desjonquères.

Galiani, F., Lorenzi, G.B. (1775). *Socrate immaginario. Commedia per musica rappresentata nel Teatro Nuovo sopra Toledo, nell'autunno dell'anno 1775, con musica del Signor Giovanni Paisiello*, Naples: s.n.

Genovesi, A. (1765). *Delle lezioni di commercio o sia d'economia civile da leggersi nella Cattedra Interiana dell'ab.Genovesi regio cattedratico.* Parte prima pel primo semestre. Naples: Fratelli Simone..

Genovesi, A. (1781). "Piano delle scuole formato dall'Abate Genovesi in occasione di essere stati espulsi i gesuiti da Napoli", in Galanti, G. M. *Elogio storico del signor abate Antonio Genovesi.* Florence: Francesco Pisoni, pp. 108–120.

Genovesi, A. (1783). *Delle lezioni di commercio o sia d'economia civile da leggersi nella cattedra Interiana dell'ab. Genovesi regio cattedratico. Parte Prima, Terza edizione napoletana.* Naples: Stamperia Simoniana.

Gleichen, K. H. von. (1868). *Souvenirs de Charles-Henri Baron de Gleichen*, Paris: Techener.

Grimaldi, D. (1780). *Osservazioni economiche sopra la manifattura e commercio delle sete nel Regno di Napoli alle sue finanze* etc. Naples: Giuseppe Maria Porcelli.

Grimm, F. M. F. von. (1829). Sermon Philosophique. In *Correspondance littéraire, philosophique et critique de Grimm et de Diderot, depuis 1753 jusqu'en 1790*, Volume 16. Paris: Furne, pp. 265–288.

Grimm, F. M. F. von. (1878). *Correspondance litteraire, philosophique et critique par Grimm*, vol. VI. Paris: Garnier.

Grimm, F. M. F. von. (1879). *Correspondance litteraire, philosophique et critique par Grimm*, vol. IX. Paris: Garnier.

Grotius, H. (1625) [2005]. *De Jure belli ac pacis libri tres, in quibus jus naturae et gentium, item juris publici praecipua explicantur.* Paris: Nicolaum Byon, English translation, *The rights of war and peace*, edited and with an introduction by Richard Tuck, Indianapolis: Liberty Fund.

Grozio, U. (1777) Il dritto della guerra e della pace di Ugone Grozio colle note dello stesso autore, e di Giovanni Barbeyrac. Tradotto nell'idioma italiano dall'avvocato napoletano D. Antonio Porpora, Naples: Giuseppe De Dominicis.

Hübner, M. (1759). *De la saisie des bâtiments neutres ou du droit qu'ont les nations belligérantes d'arrêter les navires des peuples amis.* La Haye: s.n.

Lampredi, G.M. (1778). *Juris Publicis Universalis, sive Juris Naturae et Gentium Theoremata*, volume III. Livorno: Falurnus.

Le Mercier de La Rivière, P. P. F. J. H. (1767). *L'ordre naturel et essentiel des sociétés politiques.* Paris: Geuthner.

Le Mercier de La Rivière, P. P. F. J. H. (1770). *L'intéret général de l' État, ou la liberté du. commerce des blés démontrée conforme au droit naturel, au droit public de la France, aux loix fondamentales du Royaume, à l'intéret commun du souverain et de ses sujets dans tous les temps: avec la réfutation d'un nouveau systeme, publié en forme de dialogues sur le commerce des blés.* Amsterdam-Paris: Desaint.

Le Trosne, G.-F. (1766). De l'utilité des discussions économiques. *Journal de l'agriculture, du commerce et des finances,* VI, Premier Partie (July), pp. 8–85.

Le Trosne, G.-F. (1777). *De l'ordre social, ouvrage suivi d'un traité élémentaire sur la valeur, l'argent, la circulation, l'industrie et le commerce intérieur et extérieur.* Paris: chez les Frères Debure.

Linguet, S. N. H. (1774). *Du pain e du Bled*, London: s.n.

Lorenzi, G. B. (1780). *Socrate immaginario commedia per musica di Giambatista Lorenzi P. A. da rappresentarsi nel Teatro Nuovo sopra Toledo nella primavera di questo anno 1780.* Naples: s.n.

Montesquieu, C.-L. de Secondat. (1748) [1989]. *De l'esprit des loix. Ou Du rapport que les loix doivent avoir avec la constitution de chaque gouvernement, les moeurs, le climat, la religion, le commerce,* Genève: Barillot & Fils. English Translation, *The Spirit of the Laws*, edited by A. M. Cohler, B. C. Miller, H. S. Stone. Cambridge: Cambridge University Press.

Morellet, A. (1769a). *Mémoire sur la situation actuelle de la Compagnie des Indes, juin 1769*. Paris: Desaint.

Morellet, A. (1774). *Réfutation de l'ouvrage qui a pour Titre Dialogues sur le Commerce des Bleds*. London: s. n.

Morellet, A. (1822). *Mémoires inédits de l'abbé Morellet,... sur le dix-huitième siècle et sur la Révolution; précédés de l'éloge de l'abbé Morellet, par M. Lémontey*, Paris: Librarie Française de l'Advocat.

Morellet, A., Beccaria, C. (1766). *Traité des delits et des peines, traduit de l'Italien. D'après la troisieme edition, revue, corrigée & augmentée par l'auteur. Avec des additions de l'auteur, qui n'ont pas encore paru en Italien*, Philadelphia: s. n.

Naigeon, J. A., D'Holbach, Thiry P. H. [1768]. *Le militaire philosophe, ou, Difficultés sur la religion proposées au r. p. Malebranche, prétre de l'Oratoire*, London: s.n.

Napoli-Signorelli, P. (1798). *Il regno di Ferdinando IV adombrato in tre volumi in continuazione delle Vicende della coltura delle Sicilie*. Naples: Migliaccio.

Necker, J. [1769]. *Réponse au mémoire de M. l'abbé Morellet sur la Compagnie des Indes, imprimée en exécution de la délibération de Mrs les actionnaires, prise dans l'assemblée générale du 8 août 1769*. Paris: de l'Imprimerie Royale.

Necker, J. [1775]. *Sur la législation et le commerce des grains*, Paris: Pissot.

Newton, I. (1713). Scholium Generale. In *Philosophiae naturalis principia mathematica. Editio secunda*, Cambridge: Cornelius Crownfield, pp. 481–484.

Newton, I. (1729). *The Mathematical Principles of Natural Philosophy*, translated by Andrew Motte, London: Benjamin Motte.

Novelle letterarie. (1783). Review of *De' Doveri*. In *Novelle letterarie pubblicate in Firenze*, numero 13, 28 March 1783, column 201–206.

Odazi, T. (1782). *Riflessioni sui contratti alla voce*. Naples: s.n.

Odazi, T. (1783). *Della libertà de' prezzi, ossia della necessità di abolire i contratti alla voce per tutte le derrate di questo Regno*. Naples: Porsile.

Palmieri, G. (1788). *Riflessioni sulla pubblica felicità relativamente al Regno di Napoli. Seconda edizione dall'autore accresciuta*. Naples: Stamperia Flauto

Quesnay, F. (1756b). Évidence. In D. Diderot, J. d'Alembert Le Ronde (eds.), *Encyclopédie, ou, Dictionnaire raisonné des sciences, des arts et des métiers*, tome VI. Paris: Briasson-David-Le Breton-Durand, pp. 146–157.

Roubaud, P.-J.-A. (1769). Lettres de l' auteur des Représentations aux magistrats, à M. le chevalier Zanobi principal interlocuteur des Dialogues sur le commerce des blés. *Éphémérides du citoyen ou Bibliothèque raisonnée des sciences morales et politiques*, Tome XII. Paris: Lacombre, pp. 179–216.

Roubaud, P.-J.-A. (1770). *Récréations économiques, ou Lettres de l'auteur des Représentations aux magistrats à M. le chevalier Zanobi principal interlocuteur des Dialogues sur le commerce des blés* Amsterdam - Paris: Delalain.

Sarcone, M. (1780). *Lettera Terza. Ammonizione caritativa all'autore del libro intitolato Del dialetto napoletano*. [Naples]: Presso Ezechiele.

Serio, L. (1780). *Lo vernacchio. Risposta al Dialetto napoletano.* Naples: s.n.

Tanucci, B. (1914). *Lettere a Ferdinando Galiani*, edited by F. Nicolini, Bari: Laterza.

Thomas, A.-L. (1772). *Essai sur le caractere, les moeurs et l'esprit des femmes dans les différens siecles.* Paris: Moutard.

Turgot, A.R.M. (1756). Etymologie. In *Encyclopédie, ou dictionnaire raisonné des sciences, des arts et des métiers*, Tome VI, Neufchastel [but Paris]: Samuel Faulche, pp. 98–111.

Tyson, E. (1699). *Orang-outang, sive Homo sylvestris*, London: Printed for T. Bennett and D. Brown.

Verri, A., Verri, P. (1911). *Carteggio di Pietro e Alessandro Verri*, vol. III, edited by F. Novati, E. Greppi, Milan: Cogliati.

Vico, G.B. (1728) [1975]. Vita di Giambattista Vico scritta da se medesimo. In *Raccolta di opuscoli scientifici e filologici*, edited by A. Calogerà, Venice: Cristoforo Zane, pp. 147–256. English translation *The Autobiography of Giambattista Vico, translated from the Italian by Max Harold Fisch and T. Goddard Bergin.* Ithaca: Cornell University Press, 1975.

Vico, G.B. (1744) [1948]. *Principi di Scienza Nuova d'intorno alla Comune Natura delle Nazioni, in questa terza impressione. Dal medesimo Autore in un gran numero di luoghi corretta, schiarita, e notabilmente accresciuta.* Naples: Stamperia Muziana. English translation *The New Science of Giambattista Vico*, by T. Goddard Bergin, Ithaca: Cornell University Press, 1948.

Voltaire [Arouet, F. M.]. (1738b). *Élémens de la philosophie de Newton.* London: s.n.

Voltaire [Arouet, F. M.]. (1756). *Poemes sur la loi naturelle en IV chants et sur le désastre de Lisbonne.* Amsterdam: Ledet.

Voltaire [Arouet, F. M.]. (1759). *Candide, ou l'Optimisme. Traduit de l'allemande de Mr. le docyeur Ralph.* s.l: s.n.

Voltaire [Arouet, F. M.]. (1769). Tout en Dieu. Commentarie sur Malebranche. *Nouveaux melanges philosophiques, historiques, critiques*, Volume 8, pp. 289–306.

Voltaire [Arouet, F. M.]. (1770). *Dieu. Réponse de Mr. de Voltaire au Systême de la Nature.* Au Château de Ferney: s.n.

Secondary Sources

Ademollo, A. (1880). La famiglia e l'eredità dell'abate Galiani. *Nuova Antologia di Scienze, Lettere e Arti*, Volume LIII, Fascicolo XX, pp. 639–667.

Albertone, M. (2018). Au cœur des Lumières. Ferdinando Galiani et le *Croquis d'un Dialogue sur les femmes.* In A. Tiran, C. Carnino (eds.), *Ferdinando Galiani, économie et politique.* Paris: Classiques Garnier, pp. 155–170.

Allix, E. (1911). Le physicisme des physiocrates. *Revue d'économie politique*, Vol. XXV, n. 5, pp. 563–586.

Amalfi, G. (1888a). Chi ha scritto *Il Socrate immaginario*?. In *Dubbi sul Galiani*, Naples: Priore, pp. 1–23.

Amalfi, G. (1888b). Chi compose il libro Del dialetto napoletano?. In *Dubbi sul Galiani*, Naples: Priore, pp. 39–81.

Amodio, P. (1997a). *Il disincanto della ragione e l'assolutezza del bonheur: studio sull'abate Galiani*, Naples: Guida.

Anglani, B. (1999). I dialoghi dell'assenza. Il carteggio tra l'abate Galiani e Madame d'Èpinay. *Annali della Facoltà di Lingue e Letterature Straniere*. Terza Serie, XIII, pp. 269–293.

Argemíd' Abadal, L. (2012). The Physiocrats. In J. G. Backhaus, (ed.), *Handbook of the History of Economic Thought: Insights on the Founders of Modern Economics*. New York: Springer, pp. 137–160.

Astigarraga, J. (2018). Entre la Naples de Galiani, le Paris de Turgot et le Madrid de Campomanes. La traduction espagnole des *Dialogues sur le commerce des blés*. In A. Tiran, Carnino, C. (eds.), *Ferdinando Galiani, économie et politique*. Paris: Classiques Garnier, pp. 401–426.

Barbagallo, F. (1971). Discussioni e progetti sul commercio tra Napoli e Costantinopoli nel '700. *Rivista Storica Italiana*, Anno LXXXIII, II, pp. 264–296.

Bedarida, P. (1975). La correspondance française de l'Abbé Galiani. In *Convegno italo-francese sul tema Ferdinando Galiani* (Roma, 25–27 maggio 1972). Rome: Accademia Nazionale dei Lincei, pp. 13–23.

Beer, M. (1939). *An Inquiry into Physiocracy*. London: Allen and Unwin.

Beniscelli, A. (2012a). *Libertini italiani*. Milan: Rizzoli.

Bernardini, P. (1995). Il Diritto di Neutralità nel tardo giusnaturalismo tedesco e la traduzione del Galiani politico in Germania. *Materiali per una storia della cultura politica*, 25, pp. 291–312.

Bernardini, P. (2000). Arte di governo e diritto di neutralità nel tardo illuminismo tedesco. A proposito della traduzione del Galiani Politico in Germania. In La Manna, F. (ed.) *Commercium: scambi culturali italo-tedeschi nel XVIII secolo*. Florence: Olschki, pp. 3–25.

Bourthoumieux, C. (1935). *Le mythe de l'ordre naturel en économie politique depuis Quesnay*. Paris: M. Rivière.

Bracchi, C. (1997). Ferdinando Galiani lettore e critico di Orazio. *Italianistica: Rivista di letteratura italiana*, Vol. 26, No. 1, pp. 85–109.

Braeuer, W. (1975). Ferdinando Galiani et la culture allemande. In *Convegno italo-francese sul tema Ferdinando Galiani* (Roma, 25–27 maggio 1972). Rome: Accademia Nazionale dei Lincei, pp. 175–183.

Braeuer, W. (1988). Das fehlende letzte kapitel bei Galiani, *Rivista Internazionale di Scienze Economiche e Commerciali*. Vol. 35, N. 1, pp. 7–10.

Brockdorff, C. von. (1937). Descartes et les Lumières Françaises. *Revue de Métaphysique et de Morale*, 44, 1, pp. 305–324.

Brunet, P. (1931). *L'introduction des théories de Newton en France au dix-huitième siècle*. Volume 1. Paris: Blanchard.

Brunetière, F. (1881). Études sur le xviii siècle: III. l'abbé Galiani. *Revue des Deux Mondes*, Troisième Période, Vol. 45, No. 4, pp. 924–945.

Cane, E. (1976). Jean d'Alembert between Descartes and Newton: A Critique of Thomas L. Hankins' Position, *Isis*, 67, 2, pp. 274–278.

Carrafiello, T. (2019). *La biblioteca di Berardo Galiani. Vicende storiche e catalogo commentato, con un approfondimento sugli inediti galianei*. Florence: Altralinea.

Catucci, M. (1986). *Galianea. Ferdinando Galiani tra letteratura ed economia*, Rome: Bulzoni.

Cesarano, F. (1986). La teoria della politica economica nei *Dialogues* di Ferdinando Galiani. *Rivista di politica economica*, 12, pp. 1691–1706.

Cesarano, F. (1995). Galiani e il ruolo della politica economica. In A. Roncaglia (ed.) *Alle origini del pensiero economico in Italia*. Bologna: Il Mulino, pp. 97–120.

Cesarano, F. (1999). Introduzione. In F. Galiani, *Scritti di Politica Economica*. Lanciano: Rocco Carabba, pp. vii–xix.

Charles, L. (2000). From the *Encyclopédie* to the *Tableau économique*: Quesnay on Freedom of Grain Trade and Economic Growth. *The European Journal of History of Economic Thought*, 7 (1), pp. 1–21.

Charles, L. (2003). The Visual History of the Tableau Économique. *The European Journal of the History of Economic Thought*, 10 (4), pp. 527–550.

Charles, L. (2004). The Tableau Économique as Rational Recreation. *History of Political Economy*, 36 (3), pp. 445–474.

Charles, L. (2015a). Figures of Mockery. The Cultural Disqualification of Physiocracy (1760–1790). *The European Journal of the History of Economic Thought*, 22 (3), pp. 383–419.

Charles, L. (2015b). Jeux de mots, narrative and economic writing: The Rhetoric of Anti-physiocracy in French Economic Periodicals (1764–1769). *The European Journal of the History of Economic Thought*, 22, (3), pp. 359–382.

Cherrad, S. (2007). De l'éducation des mères à une possible éducation publique: mesdames d'Épinay et de Miremont. In I. Brouard-Arends, M.-E. Plagnol-Diéval (eds.), *Femmes éducatrices au siècle des Lumières*, Rennes: Presses Universitaires de Rennes, pp. 93–102.

Chorley, P. (1965). *Oil, Silk and Enlightenment. Economic Problems in XVIII Century Naples*. Naples: Istituto Italiano di Studi Storici.

Ciccolella, D. (2016). Il prezzo della patria. Stato, negozianti e regolazione dei prezzi alla voce nel Mezzogiorno nel secondo '700. *Storia economica*, Anno XIX, n. 2, pp. 491–530.

Ciccolella, D., Guenzi, A. (2008). Scambi e gestione del rischio sui mercati locali e regionali. il contratto alla voce nel Mezzogiorno in Età Moderna. *Storia economica*, Anno XI, n. 1, pp. 41–79.

Conti, V. (ed.) (2002) *La ricezione di Grozio a Napoli nel Settecento*. Florence: Centro Editoriale Toscano.

Cremaschi, S. (2000). Legge di Natura e Scienza Economica. *Quaderni storici, Nuova Serie, Etiche economiche*, 35, 105 (3), pp. 697–730.

Croce, B. (1925a). Giambattista Basile e l'elaborazione artistica delle fiabe popolari. Discorso. In G.B. Basile, *Il Pentamerone, ossia, La fiaba delle fiabe*, edited by B.Croce, Bari: Laterza, pp. 3–21.

Croce, B. (1932). *Conversazioni critiche*. IV serie. Bari: Laterza.

Croce, B. (1935). *Una lettera inedita della signora d' Épinay e il Dialogue sur les femmes dell'abate Galiani*, In Croce, B. Varietà di storia letteraria e civile , serie prima, Bari, Laterza, pp. 119–134.

Croce, B. 1949. Opuscoli e disegni giocosi dell'abate Galiani, in Croce, B. La letteratura italiana del Settecento, Bari: Laterza, pp. 287–289.

Croce, B. (1954). Don Onofrio Galeota poeta e filosofo napoletano. In *Aneddoti di varia letteratura*, vol III, Bari: Laterza, pp. 150–162.

D'Onofrio, F. (2015). On the Concept of "Felicitas Publica" in Eighteenth-Century Political Economy. *Journal of the History of Economic Thought*, Volume 37, Number 3, pp. 449–471.

Del Donna, A.R. (2012). *Opera, Theatrical Culture and Society in Late Eighteenth-Century Naples*. London: Routledge.

Demaria, G. (1972). La scienza politica di Ferdinando Galiani. *Giornale degli Economisti e Annali di Economia*, Nuova Serie, Anno 31, No. 9/10, pp. 624–677.

Di Filippo, M. (2005). Per una storia dei rapporti tra il Regno di Napoli e l'Impero russo. In D. Rizzi, A. Shishkin (eds.), *Archivio russo-italiano IV*, Avellino: Europa Orientalis - Istituto di Linguistica (Università di Salerno), pp. 243–295.

Diaz, F. (1972). Aspetti e problemi dell'epistolario di Ferdinando Galiani. *Rivista storica italiana*, Anno LXXXIV, fasc. I, pp. 80–110.

Diaz, F. (1973). L'abate Galiani consigliere di commercio estero del Regno di Napoli. In F. Diaz, *Per una storia illuministica*. Naples: Guida, pp. 289–364.

Diaz, F. (1975a). Introduzione. In Galiani, F. *Opere*, edited by F. Diaz, L.Guerci, *Letteratura italiana. Storia e testi. Illuministi italiani*, tomo VI, Milan-Naples: Ricciardi, pp. ix–cvi.

Diaz, F. (1975c). "Preliminari" ai *Dialogues*. In F. Diaz, L.Guerci (eds), F. Galiani, *Opere, Letteratura italiana. Storia e testi. Illuministi italiani*, tomo VI, Milan-Naples: Ricciardi, pp. 347–356.

Diemer, A., Guillemin H. (2013). La naissance de l'économie politique ou la fascination des penseurs de la société pour la physique, *Triangle, ISH Lyon, Séminaire Economie Politique*, 15 avril 2013.

Di Rienzo, E. (1994). *Alle origini della Francia contemporanea. Economia, politica e società nel pensiero di André Morellet: 1756–1819*, Naples: Edizioni Scientifiche Italiane.

Dixit, A. K. (1996). *The Making of Economic Policy: A Transaction-Cost Politics Perspective. Munich Lectures in Economics*. Cambridge (MS): MIT Press.

Dulac, G. (1992). Preface. In Galiani, F., d'Épinay, L. 1992. *Correspondance. Vol. I (1769–1770)*, présentation de G. Dulac, texte établi et annoté par D. Maggetti, en collaboration avec G. Dulac, Paris: Les Editions Desjonquères, pp. 7–34.

Einaudi, L. (1949) [2014]. Galiani, the economist. In *Rendiconti della Classe di Scienze morali, storiche e filologiche*, Series VIII, vol. IV, issue 3–4, March–April 1949, In L. Einaudi, R. Faucci, R. Marchionatti (eds.) *Luigi Einaudi Selected Economic Essays.* London: Palgrave Macmillan, vol II, pp. 227–264.

Faccarello, G. (1994). Nil repente!: Galiani and Necker on Economic Reforms. *European Journal of the History of Economic Thought,* 1 (3), pp. 519–550.

Faccarello, G. (1998). Galiani, Necker and Turgot. A debate on economic reform and policy in 18th Century France. In G. Faccarello (ed.), *Studies in the History of French Political Economy. From Bodin to Walras.* London: Routledge, pp. 120–195.

Farinella, C. (1999). Angelo Gatti. In *Dizionario Biografico degli Italiani*, Vol. 52, *ad vocem.*

Ferrone, V. (2012). *The politics of Enlightenment: Republicanism, constitutionalism, and the rights of man in Gaetano Filangieri.* London: Anthem Press.

Fischman, M. (1998). Le concept quesnayen d'ordre naturel. *Cahiers d'économie politique* 32, pp. 67–97.

Flora, G. (1927). Le più belle pagine di Ferdinando Galiani, Milan: Treves

Foley, V. (1973). An Origin to the Tableau Oeconomique. *History of Political Economy*, 5, pp. 121–150.

Foley, V. (1976). *The Social Physics of Adam Smith.* West Lafayette: Purdue University Press.

Galasso, G. (1989c). Doria: cultura e filosofia delle riforme. In G. Galasso, (ed.), *La filosofia in soccorso de' governi. La cultura napoletana del Settecento.* Naples: Guida, pp. 233–256.

Gambacorta, L. (1988). Ferdinando Galiani e la Russia. *Archivio Storico per le Province Napoletane*, Vol. CVI, pp. 335–346.

Gaudemet, E. (1899). *L'abbé Galiani et la question du commerce des blés à la fin du règne de Louis XV.* Paris: Rousseau.

Ghisalberti, C. (1975). Ferdinando Galiani e il problema istituzionale. In *Convegno italo-francese sul tema Ferdinando Galiani* (Roma, 25–27 maggio 1972), Rome: Accademia Nazionale dei Lincei, pp. 49–65.

Girard, R. (1924). *L'abbé Terray et la liberté du commerce des grains, 1769–1774.* Paris: Les Presses Universitaires de France.

Goutte, P.-H. (1994). Les Éphémérides du citoyen, instrument périodique au service de l'ordre naturel (1765–1772). *Dixhuitième Siècle*, n°26, 1994. *Economie et politique.* pp. 139–161.

Guariglia, R. (1914). Un mancato trattato di commercio tra le Due Sicilie e la Francia e un parere inedito dell'abate Galiani. *Rivista di diritto internazionale*, VIII, 1, pp. 1–21.

Hasbach, G. (1893). Les fondements philosophiques de l'économie politique de Quesnay et de Smith, *Revue d' économie politique*, 3 (Sept.), pp. 745–795.

Hecht, J. (1958). Le bicentenaire du *Tableau économique*: François Quesnay et la physiocratie. Présentation d'une publication de l' INED. *Population*, 13 (2), pp. 287–292.

Hoselitz, B. F. (1968). Agrarian Capitalism, the Natural Order of Things: François Quesnay. *Kyklos*, 21, pp. 637–664.

Imbruglia, G. (2019). Bernardo Tanucci. In *Dizionario Biografico degli Italiani* - Volume 93, Rome: Treccani, *ad vocem*.

Ingrao, B., Israel, G. (1990). *The Invisible Hand: Economic Equilibrium in the History of Science*, Cambridge: MIT Press.

Kaplan, H.H. (1995). *Russian Overseas Commerce with Great Britain During the Reign of Catherine II*. Philadelphia: American Philosophical Society.

Kaplan, S. L. (1976). *Bread, politics and political economy in the reign of Louis XV*. The Hague: Martinus Nijhoff.

Kaplan, S. L. (1979). *La bagarre: Galiani's "Lost" Parody*. The Hague: Martinus Nijhoff Publishers.

Kaplan, S. L. (2019a). Galiani: Grain and Governance. In S. L. Kaplan, S. A. Reinert (eds.), *The Economic Turn: Recasting Political Economy in Eighteenth-Century Europe*. London: Anthem Press, pp. 221–304.

Kaplan, S. L. (2019b). *Live and Die Proprietors and Free*: Morellet Dismantles the *Dialogues* and Defends the Radical Liberal Break. In S. L. Kaplan, S. A. Reinert (eds.), *The Economic Turn: Recasting Political Economy in Eighteenth-Century Europe*. London: Anthem Press, pp. 305–350.

Kaplan, S. L. (2019c). Is the Feeling of Humanity not more Sacred than The Right of Property?: Diderot's Antiphysiocracy in His Apology of Abbé Galiani. In S. L. Kaplan, S. A. Reinert (eds.), *The Economic Turn: Recasting Political Economy in Eighteenth-Century Europe*. London: Anthem Press, pp. 351–394.

Kleiner, I. (1989). Evolution of the Function Concept: A Brief Survey. *The College Mathematics Journal*, September 1989, Volume 20, Number 4, pp. 282–300.

Klotz, G. (2000). La question des blés en France au dix-huitième siècle: Galiani, critique des physiocrates. *Il Pensiero Economico Italiano*, vol VIII, n. 2, pp. 147–183.

Koch, P. (1961). The Genesis of Galiani's Dialogues sur le Commerce Des Blés. *French Studies*, Volume XV issue 4, pp. 314–323.

Koch, P. (1968). Introduction. In F.Galiani, *Dialogues entre M. Marquis de Roquemaure et M. le chevalier Zanobi. Analecta Romanica*, Heft 21, Frankfurt am Main: Klostermann, pp. 1–51.

Kubota, A. (1958). Quesnay, disciple de Malebranche. In *François Quesnay et la physiocratie*. Volume 1. Paris: INED, pp. 169–196.

Larrère, C. (1994). Malebranche revisité: l'économie naturelle des physiocrates. *Dix-huitième Siècle*, 26, pp. 117–138.

Laval-Reviglio, M.-C. (1987). Les conceptions politiques des physiocrates. *Revue française de science politique*, 37 (2), pp. 181–213.

Leonzio, E. (2014). L'abbé Galiani e il problema dell'etica tra politica e pedagogia. *Studi francesi*, 172 (LVIII, I), pp. 46–63.

Luftalla, M. (1963). L'évidence, fondement nécessaire et suffisant de l'ordre naturel chez Quesnay et Morelly. *Revue d'histoire économique et sociale*, 41 (2), pp. 213–249.

Macry, P. (1972). Ceto mercantile e azienda agricola nel Regno di Napoli: il contratto alla voce. *Quaderni Storici*, Vol. 7, No. 21 (3), *Agricoltura - Proprietà – Mercati*, pp. 851–909.

Macry, P. (1974). *Mercato e società nel Regno di Napoli. Commercio del grano e politica economica nel '700.* Naples: Guida.

Mafrici, M. V. (2004). Diplomazia e commercio tra il Regno di Napoli e la Sublime Porta: Guglielmo Maurizio Ludolf (1747–1789). In M. Mirella (ed.), *Rapporti diplomatici e scambi commerciali nel Mediterraneo moderno*, Soveria Mannelli: Rubbettino, pp. 151–172.

Mafrici, M. V. (2011). Le relazioni diplomatiche e commerciali tra il Regno di Napoli e l'Impero russo nel secolo dei Lumi. In P. Volpini, R. Sabbatini, (eds.). *Sulla diplomazia in età moderna. Politica, economia, religione. Annali di storia militare europea*, 3, Milan: Franco Angeli, pp. 219–240.

Mafrici, M. V. (2020). Maria Carolina d'Asburgo-Lorena e la politica internazionale napoletana (1770–1799). In G. Sodano, G. Brevetti, (eds.), *Io, la Regina. Maria Carolina d'Asburgo-Lorena e il suo tempo*, *Quaderni - Mediterranea - Ricerche storiche*, n. 37, pp. 25–50.

Marchal, F. (1999). Galiani, un modèle du Neveu de Rameau. Le prestige des mimes. *Revue d'Histoire littéraire de la France*, 99e Année, No. 5, pp. 1007–1020.

Marino, J. A. (1988). *Pastoral Economics in the Kingdom of Naples.* Baltimore: Johns Hopkins University Press.

Mauro, A. (2017a). *Un philosophe des Lumières entre Naples et Paris: Ferdinando Galiani (1728–1787*). Thèse de Doctorate de l'Université Toulouse le Mirail - Toulouse II.

Miglio, G.F. (1942). *La controversia sui limiti del commercio neutrale fra Giovanni Maria Lampredi e Ferdinando Galiani.* Rome: Ispi.

Mirowski, P. (1991). *More Heat than Light.* Cambridge: Cambridge University Press.

Monaco, V. (1968). *Giambattista Lorenzi e la commedia per musica*, Naples: Berisio.

Montanile, M. (2018). Il *Dialogue sur les femmes* di Ferdinando Galiani. In C. Passetti, L. Tufano (eds.), *Femminile e maschile nel Settecento.* Florence: Firenze University Press, pp. 81–93.

Montaudo, A. (2005). *L'olio nel Regno di Napoli nel XVIII secolo. Commercio, Annona e Arrendamenti.* Naples: Edizioni Scientifiche Italiane.

Monti, G.M. (1942). *La dottrina dell'abate Ferdinando Galiani sulla neutralità e l'adesione di Ferdinando IV alla Lega dei Neutri.* Milan: Ispi.

Mourant, J. A. (1943). *The Physiocratic Conception of Natural Law.* Chicago: University of Chicago Press.

Neill, T. P. (1948). Quesnay and Physiocracy. *Journal of the History of Ideas,* 9, 2 (April), pp. 153–173.

Neill, T. P. (1949). The Physiocrats' Concept of Economics. *The Quarterly Journal of Economics,* 63, 4, pp. 532–553.

Nicolini, F. (1904–1905). L'abate Galiani epigrafista. *Napoli Nobilissima,* s. 1, pp. 13, 27–30, 42–44; 14, 12–14, 73–77, 108–10.

Nicolini, F. (1908a). I manoscritti di Ferdinando Galiani, *Archivio storico per le province napoletane,* 33 (1908), pp. 171–197.

Nicolini, F. (1908b). Intorno a Ferdinando Galiani a proposito di una pubblicazione recente. *Giornale Storico della letteratura italiana,* Volume LII, pp. 1–55.

Nicolini, F. (ed.). (1909a). *Il pensiero dell'abate Galiani. Antologia di tutti i suoi scritti.* Bari: Laterza.

Nicolini, F. (1909b). Gli studi sopra Orazio dell'abate Ferdinando Galiani. In *Atti dell'Accademia Pontaniana,* anno XXXIX, Memoria VIII, pp. i–xvi; 1–160.

Nicolini, F. (1923). Introduzione. In Galiani, F., *Del dialetto napoletano,* edited by F. Nicolini. Naples: Ricciardi, pp. ix–lv.

Nicolini, F. (1929). Amici e corrispondenti dell'abate Ferdinando Galiani: I. Angelo Gatti (con nuove notize e documenti inediti sul richiamo del Galiani da Parigi). *Archivio Storico Italiano,* Vol. 87 (Serie 7, Vol. 12), No. 4 (332), pp. 233–272.

Nicolini, F. (1954). *Amici e corrispondenti francesi dell'abate Galiani. Notizie lettere documenti.* Naples: Banco di Napoli.

Nicolini, F. (1959b). Un inedito dell'abate Galiani. *Biblion,* I, pp. 139–156.

Nicolini, F. (1964). *Per una nuova edizione della corrispondenza francese dell'abate Galiani.* Naples: s.n.

Nicolini, B. (1975). *Gli scritti galianei di Fausto Nicolini.* In Convegno italo-francese sul tema Ferdinando Galiani (Roma, 25–27 maggio 1972), Rome: Accademia Nazionale dei Lincei, pp. 259–307.

Nicolini, F. (1978). L'Orazio dell'abate Galiani. *Accademia Nazionale dei Lincei, Memorie,* Serie VIII, vol.XXII, fascicolo 2, pp. 111–314.

Oliveira, A. R. E. (2017). d'Alembert: Between Newtonian Science and the Cartesian Inheritance. *Advances in Historical Studies,* 6, pp. 128–144.

Pane, R. (1975). Ferdinando Galiani e l'antico. In *Convegno italo-francese sul tema Ferdinando Galiani* (Roma, 25–27 maggio 1972), Rome: Accademia Nazionale dei Lincei, pp. 201–211.

Papi, G. U. (1975). "Ferdinando Galiani e l'economia". In *Convegno italo-francese sul tema Ferdinando Galiani* (Roma, 25–27 maggio 1972), Rome: Accademia Nazionale dei Lincei, pp. 25–46.

Paratore, E. (1975). Il commento a Orazio di Ferdinando Galiani. In *Convegno italo-francese sul tema Ferdinando Galiani* (Roma, 25–27 maggio 1972). Rome: Accademia Nazionale dei Lincei, pp. 365–379.

Pascal, C. (1885). *Sulla vita e sulle opera di Ferdinando Galiani*. Naples: Morano.

Patalano, R. (2020b). Ferdinando Galiani's Newtonian Social Mathematics. *Journal of the History of Economic Thought*, Vol. 42, 3, pp. 357–383.

Pennisi, A. (1987). *La linguistica dei mercatanti. Filosofia linguistica e filosofia civile da Vico a Cuoco*, Naples: Guida.

Perrot, J.-C. (1992). *Une histoire intellectuelle de l'économie politique. XVIIe–XVIIIe siècle*. Paris: Éditions de l'École des Hautes Études en Sciences Sociales.

Perru, O. (1997). Les physiocrates: La communauté est-elle de droit naturel?. *Revue Philosophique de Louvain*, quatrième série, 95 (4), pp. 617–638.

Placanica, A. (1982). *Moneta prestiti usure nel Mezzogiorno moderno*. Naples: Società Editrice Napoletana.

Pomeau, R. (1975). Galiani et Voltaire. In *Convegno italo-francese sul tema Ferdinando Galiani* (Roma, 25–27 maggio 1972). Rome: Accademia Nazionale dei Lincei, pp. 333–345.

Pribram, K. (1983). *A history of economic reasoning*. New York: John Hopkins University Press.

Rao, A. M. (2008). Saverio Mattei. In *Dizionario Biografico degli Italiani*, Vol. 72, *ad vocem*.

Rapisarda, S. (1996). Introduzione. In d'Épinay-Galiani, *Epistolario 1769–1782*, edited by S.Rapisarda. Palermo: Sellerio, pp. xviii–li.

Recca, C. (2017). *The Diary of Queen Maria Carolina of Naples, 1781–1785. New Evidence of Queenship at Court*. London: Palgrave Macmillan.

Reinert, S. A. (2011a). Girolamo Belloni. In *Il Contributo Italiano alla Storia del Pensiero. Economia*. Rome: Treccani, pp. 271–274.

Renda, F. (1970). *Bernardo Tanucci e i beni dei Gesuiti*. Catania: Università di Catania.

Riskin, J. (2003). The Spirit of System and the Fortunes of Physiocracy. *History of Political Economy*, 35, Suppl. 1, *Oeconomies in the Age of Newton*, edited by M. Schabas and N. de Marchi pp 42–73.

Robertazzi Delle Donne, E. (1970). *L'espulsione dei Gesuiti dal Regno di Napoli*. Naples: Libreria scientifica editrice.

Roncaglia, A. (2005). *The Wealth of Ideas*. Cambridge: Cambridge University Press.

Ruggiero, R. (2018). La nozione storica di diritto naturale nel pensiero di Vico tra *De ratione* e *De uno*. *Bollettino del Centro di Studi Vichiani*, Anno XLVIII, pp. 89–103.

Russo, F. (2007). Il desiderio della società. Sulla fortuna di Grozio tra Westfalia e Napoli. *Annali dell'Università Suor Orsola Benincasa*, anno 2006–2007.
Sasso, R. (1978). Voltaire et le système de la nature de d'Holbach. *Revue Internationale de Philosophie* Vol. 32, No. 124/125 (2/3), *Rousseau et Voltaire 1778–1978*, pp. 279–296.
Scherillo,M.(1886).IlSocrateimmaginario.Saggiocritico.InF.Galiani,G.B.Lorenzi, *Socrate Immaginario. Commedia per musica, preceduta da un saggio critico e con note del dottor M. Scherillo.* Milan: Sonzogno, pp. 5–20.
Schipa, M. (1897). *Un ministro napoletano nel secolo XVIII. Domenico Caracciolo.* Naples: Pierro.
Schipa, M. (1938). *Nel Regno di Ferdinando IV di Borbone.* Florence: Vallecchi.
Schuhl, P.-M. (1938). Malebranche et Quesnay. *Revue Philosophique de la France et de l'Étranger*, 125, 3/4, pp. 313–315.
Scognamiglio, A. (2010). Introduzione. In F. Galiani, *Socrate immaginario. Commedia per musica.* Naples: Denaro libri.
Senut, B. (2012). Fifty years of the Debate on the Origin of Human Bipedalism. *Journal of Biological Research - Bollettino della Società Italiana di Biologia Sperimentale*, 85 (1), pp. 37–46.
Shank, J. B. (2008). *The Newton Wars and the Beginning of the French Enlightenment.* Chicago: University of Chicago Press.
Sirago, M. (2018). Le rôle de Ferdinando Galiani à la signature du Traité de commerce entre la Russie et le Royaume des Deux-Siciles (1787). In A. Tiran, C. Carnino, (eds.), *Ferdinando Galiani, économie et politique.* Paris: Classiques Garnier, pp. 295–317.
Sirago, M. (2019). La politica marittima di Bernardo Tanucci nell'epistolario con Carlo III Re di Spagna. *Cuadernos de Ilustración y Romanticismo. Revista Digital del Grupo de Estudios del Siglo XVIII,* n° 25, pp. 507–538.
Soldovieri, U. (2019). L'Abate Galiani epigrafista. In L. Calvelli, G. Cresci Marrone, A. Buonopane, (eds.) *Altera pars laboris Studi sulla tradizione manoscritta delle iscrizioni antiche*, Venezia Edizioni Ca' Foscari pp. 304–322.
Soliani, R., Clément, A. (2018). Les fondaments philosophiques de l'approche èconomique de Ferdinando Galiani. In A. Tiran, C. Carnino, (eds.), *Ferdinando Galiani, économie et politique.* Paris: Classiques Garnier, pp. 121–154.
Stapelbroek, K. (2008b). Universal Society, Commerce and the Rights of Neutral Trade: Martin Hübner, Emer de Vattel and Ferdinando Galiani. In P. Korkman, V. Mäkinen, (eds.) *Universalism in International Law and Political Philosophy*, COLLeGIUM: Studies Across Disciplines in the Arts and Humanities, vol. 4, Helsinki: Helsinki Collegium for Advanced Studies, pp. 63–89.
Stapelbroek, K. (2011). The progress of humankind in Galiani's *Dei Doveri dei Principi Neutrali*: Natural law, Neapolitan trade and Catherine the Great. In Stapelbroek, K. (ed.) *Trade and War: The Neutrality of Commerce in the Inter-State System.* COLLeGIUM: Studies Across Disciplines in the Arts and

Humanities, vol. 10, Helsinki: Helsinki Collegium for Advanced Studies, pp. 161–183.

Steegmuller, F. (1988). The Abbé Galiani: The Laughing Philosopher. *The American Scholar*, 57, 4 (Autumn), pp. 589–597.

Steiner, P. (1993). L'économie politique du royaume agricole: François Quesnay, In A. Béraud, G. Faccarello, (eds.), *Nouvelle histoire de la pensée économique. Volume I, Des Scolastiques au classiques.* Paris: La Découverte, pp. 225–253.

Tagliacozzo, G. (1968). Economic Vichism (Vico, Galiani, Croce - Economics, Economic Liberalism). *BNL Quarterly Review*, 21 (85), pp. 96–119.

Trampus, A. (2020). *Emer de Vattel and the Politics of Good Government, Constitutionalism, Small States and the International System.* London: Palgrave Macmillan.

Tuccillo, A. (2013). *Il commercio infame. Antischiavismo e diritti dell'uomo nel Settecento italiano,* Naples: ClioPress.

Tuccillo, A. (2018). L'esprit de commerce à l'épreuve de la colonisation dans le traité *Della moneta*. In A. Tiran, C. Carnino, (eds.), *Ferdinando Galiani, économie et politique.* Paris: Classiques Garnier, pp. 485–505.

Vaggi, G. (1987). *The Economics of François Quesnay.* London: Macmillan.

Van Bever, P. (1976). L'abbé Galiani et les signes sociaux. *Etudes sur le XVIIIe siècle*, 3, pp. 255–263.

Vardi, L. (2012). *The Physiocrats and the World of the Enlightenment.* Cambridge: Cambridge University Press.

Vidari, E. (1868). Ferdinando Galiani, Giovanni Maria Lampredi e Alberto Domenico Azuni. *Archivio Giuridico,* vol. I, pp. 210–241.

Weulersse, G. (1910). *Le mouvement physiocratique en France (de 1750 à 1770).* Paris: Alcan.

Zambelli, P. (1972). *La formazione filosofica di Antonio Genovesi*, Naples: Morano.

Zaretsky, R. (2019). *Catherine & Diderot: The Empress, the Philosopher, and the Fate of the Enlightenment.* Cambridge (MS): Harvard University Press.

Zazo, A. (1929). Antonio Genovese e il suo contributo alle riforme scolastiche nel napoletano (1767–1769). *Samnium*, II, pp. 55–65

CHAPTER 9

Epilogue

The "Galiani labyrinth" remains an open historiographical problem. The question posed by Benedetto Croce at the beginning of the last century, when reviewing an anthological collection by Fausto Nicolini dedicated to the works of the Neapolitan *abbé*, is the clearest example of someone who remains locked in the labyrinth.

"Who was Abbot Galiani?", the Neapolitan philosopher asked himself, "Galiani, a man of varied and sound doctrine, versed in the natural sciences and mathematics, extremely well-versed in economic science, jurisprudence, history, languages, an exquisite Latinist, was not, perhaps, cut out to be what was expected of him: a great scientist, a great historian or a great philologist. The works that he outlined in these disciplines remained, almost all of them, in the form of sketches or fragments, or even mere titles. In all of his writings, he casts flashes of light; in none does this light focus to enduringly illuminate a wide expanse of facts. Only in pure economy did he truly advance the science (theory of economic value) in a youthful effort, which, however, he did not pursue and which did not produce a substantial body of doctrine. This has been explained (and the explanation was given by the author himself) by the laziness that dominated him; but that laziness remains to be explained. In truth, he did not possess that austere consciousness, as of a mission, that is necessary to consecrate oneself to science; he lacked enthusiasm, persistence and the spirit of sacrifice" (Croce 1909: 399–400). And he concluded: "Galiani

R. Patalano, *Ferdinando Galiani*,
https://doi.org/10.1007/978-3-032-02793-1_9

does not go beyond the eighteenth century (of which he shared the irreligious spirit, materialism and hedonism), or rather, perhaps, in some points, he does not even reach it; but he is nevertheless faced with it like an old man, who, unable to understand the new aspirations of the young, has sufficient experience and wisdom to perceive its childishness, smile at its illusions and foresee where he will break his neck" (Croce 1909: 404).

Croce dragged Abbé Galiani out of the eighteenth century, just as Friedrich Nietzsche had done a few years earlier, extolling precisely the flaws highlighted by the Neapolitan philosopher: "the Abbé Galiani, the most profound, discerning, and perhaps also the filthiest man of his century. He was much more profound than Voltaire, and consequently a lot quieter. But, as I have already suggested, what happens more often is that the scientific head is placed on an ape's body, a more subtle and exceptional understanding is put in a base soul" (Nietzsche 1886 [2002]: 28).

Galiani was thus destined for the same fate as Vico, both set outside their time. The literature on Galiani has largely followed this path: the Neapolitan *abbé* has been considered "by character and mental disposition rather alien to the spirit of the Enlightenment" (Diaz 1975a: xliii), or little inclined to the Enlightenment appeals of Celestino's and Intieri's circle (Ferrone 1995: 236), stressing his ambiguous, cynical, and Machiavellian nature (Venturi 1960b; Robertson 2000: 34) and his aptitude for the logic of paradox (typical of the Baroque period) (Ravix 2018), or highlighting his connection with the philosophy of Vico (Nicolini 1918b; Tagliacozzo 1968; Badaloni 1973; Davison 1988; Tiran 2018; Soliani and Clément 2018), or emphasizing his eclectic attitude poised between Epicurean libertinism and the Enlightenment (Amodio 1997a). An attempt to frame Galiani's thought in the context of the Enlightenment has recently been made by Koen Stapelbroek, but the outcome is ambiguous, since "in attempting to step outside of the ideological categories of eighteenth century political thought, Galiani also turned himself into an outsider to the Enlightenment" (Stapelbroek 2008a: 224). Azzurra Mauro recently placed Galiani's intellectual contribution in the context of

Enlightenment culture,[1] emphasising the non-systematic nature of his thought and calling him a "philosopher without philosophy".[2]

Galiani, on the other hand, follows a coherent scientific programme that is deeply embedded in the intellectual context of the eighteenth century, even if it is set in a particular and still "unenlightened" corner. The goal pursued in his main works, from the precocious *Della Moneta* to the mature and thoughtful *Dialogues* and *De' Doveri*, is to construct a form of *social mathematics*, applying Newtonian methodology to represent theories and analyse political, social, and economic problems. This original approach can be called *Newtonian social mathematics.* Like his uncle Celestino, Abbot Galiani "had too much Newton in his body"[3] and assimilated the latter's analytical method from his youth.[4]

This feature of Galiani's thought, fully integrated into the Enlightenment intellectual movement, has not been highlighted in the considerable critical literature, and his attempt to ground political and economic arguments on an analytical basis remains largely unexplored. The non-systematic nature of Galiani's insights, due to his laziness, largely justifies this underestimation of his scientific programme. Instead, despite the

[1] "His emancipatory method consists of two principles. The first is the construction of correct and valid reasoning, according to a concern, steeped in scientific spirit, of eighteenth-century philosophy. The second is the transmission of knowledge that does not become tradition, that refuses to become authority, contrary to the scholastic dream of totalisation. In this way, and to use Ernst Cassirer's expression, Galiani's philosophy, like that of the Enlightenment, does not reside in a doxology, but in the art and manner of conducting debates on ideas. Philosophy thus becomes a technique that challenges absolute assumptions and assertions: it is in the way in which discussion is guided [...] that Galiani also attempts to liberate man from intellectual slavery by removing him from idleness" (Mauro 2017b: 162).

[2] "Galiani also had a singular relationship with the status of philosopher, which he sought or rejected depending on place and circumstances. This ambivalence is the focus of a study that aims to reconsider the Neapolitan and Parisian contexts, where the terms 'philosopher' and 'philosopher' took on different meanings, practices and usages" (Mauro2017a: 18). According to Azzurra Mauro, "Galiani presents himself as the promoter of the new critical and philological method of searching for truth, based on a courageous analysis of texts and reality, as defined by Spinoza's exegetical experience. This approach totally invalidates the principle of authority. *Abbé* Galiani exasperates this challenge to the *ipse dixit* (in this case to the ideas of the Physiocrats)" (Mauro 2017b: 160).

[3] Ferdinando Galiani's letter to Francesco Sanseverino, Naples 12 April 1777, BSNSP, XXX.C.12: folio 268, see Galiani (1975: 1144).

[4] Newton's laws, according to the young Ferdinand, also governed the movement of angels and God himself, according to solidity and attraction (see Count Punghino's letter to Ferdinando Galiani, Barcellonette, 13 October 1748: BSNSP, XXXI C. 12, folio 19r.).

fragmentariness and the dispersion of his thought, Galiani has a coherent and unitary methodological project largely influenced by Newtonianism, which is known to have been an essential component of the Enlightenment debate.[5] The abbé Galiani follows an intellectual itinerary shared by other Newtonians in the same years, asserting the necessity of a general science of society in an intellectual context, the Neapolitan one, in which the application of a rigorous analytical methodology is considered an indispensable tool to understand and describe the complex structure of society, while at the same time highlighting the limits and dangers deriving from the extreme abstraction of social phenomena (Patalano 2020a).

In this perspective, Galiani's exclusion from the Enlightenment intellectual movement must be reviewed in light of this overlooked methodological approach. In fact, Galiani shares the Enlightenment call for a social science based on a rigorous method, but his approach is strongly realistic and remains immune from abstraction, connecting with the empirical versions of the Enlightenment movement. Galiani's approach manages to combine analytical rigor with the need for empirical evidence, represented, in the field of social science, by historical and institutional contextualization.

Galiani consistently adheres to Newtonianism as a methodological model to construct a conception of social science as a complex discourse that has both descriptive and normative value. Galiani's methodological maturation was completed with the *anti-Physiocratic*: in contrast with Physiocratic economic doctrine, based on the primacy of deductive methodology, the Neapolitan abbé claims for economic science the realism of circumstance against aprioristic axiomatic hypotheses and rationalist generalizations. Galiani's Newtonian social mathematics was opposed to the social mathematics of the Cartesian approach that characterised the Physiocratic School and other rationalist components of the Enlightenment.

Galiani's attempt is not isolated in the complex context of the European Enlightenment,[6] and it is useful to make a brief comparison with other contemporary Newtonian approaches.

[5] Newton's method was at the focus of d'Alembert's *Discours Préliminaire* to the *Encyclopédie* marking the shift from Descartes' rationalism toward empiricism, in which facts and concrete evidence were contrasted with *a priori* speculation, considered sources of error (see d'Alembert 1751 [1995]: xvii–xxviii. 82–84). On the spread of Newtonianism in the eighteenth century, see Llobera (1979); Casini (1983a, 1983b, 1988, 2006).

[6] On the complexity of the Enlightenment movement, see Ferrone (2019) and Outram (2019).

The reaction against an imprudent use of mathematical notation in economic analysis is the nucleus of Condorcet's *Tableau général de la science qui a pour objet l'application du calcul aux sciences politiques et morales* (Condorcet 1793 [1994]), which can be considered the social mathematics *Manifesto* (Ingrao and Israel 1990; Feldman 2005). Condorcet distinguishes this science from Petty's "Political Arithmetic" and Buffon's "Moral Arithmetic" (Condorcet 1793 [1994]: 93–94), limiting the application of *calcul* to moral and political sciences.[7] Using the French word *calcul*, Condorcet refers, above all, to calculus of probabilities as the main instrument for the development of the social sciences (Williams 2004: 104). The application of mathematical logic to social science requires a methodological elaboration to avoid abstract and naïve algebraic formalization. In the *Tableau*, Condorcet outlines a complex structure of new social mathematics, based on five preliminary theories: probability theory; theory of quantity (which includes the theory of money interest); theory of combination (algebraic basis for the calculus of probabilities); deductive theory (the method for deducing from observed facts either general facts or even more general laws); and the theory of mean values (Condorcet 1793 [1994]: 97). Among these preliminary theories, Condorcet does not mention differential and integral calculus, because he does not believe that they could be systematically applied to the political and moral sciences (Crépel and Rieucau 2005: 255).

Condorcet, like Galiani, is interested in the distinction between mathematics and economic analysis, underlining that "these two sciences must not be confused" (Condorcet 1793 [1994]: 109–110). Political economy provides theory and observation of facts, without calculus, while social mathematics offers solutions based on calculus, allowing policy makers to calculate the effects of measures adopted. Social mathematics is only a tool and involves the facts and ideas only as a foundation for the calculus of the solid basis (Laboulle 1939: 53; Crépel and Rieucau 2005: 266). Condorcet's approach preserves the Newtonian methodological paradigm, based on the observation of facts and on a limited application of mathematical tools.

[7] What Condorcet meant by "Mathématique Sociale" has been studied by several authors: see, in particular, Laboulle (1939); Granger (1956); Baker (1975); Williams (2004); Crépel and Gilain (1989); Perrot (1992: 357–376), Crépel and Rieucau (2005), Rothschild (2001, 2005).

In spite of different degrees of orderliness and political opinions, Galiani and Condorcet attempt to delineate a Newtonian solution to the epistemological debate on the role of mathematical knowledge in the social sciences.[8] But this approach did not develop further. In Scottish moral philosophy, Francis Hutcheson re-proposes the analogy between egoistic motives and the functioning of gravity in the physical laws, applying mathematical concepts to his analysis, arriving at a rigorous formulation of the utilitarian principle (Hutcheson 1725; Brooks and Aalto 1981; Pribram 1983: 121). However, Hutcheson's position remained isolated because neither David Hume nor Adam Smith made attempts to apply mathematical concepts to social science, proposing a sceptical Newtonianism.[9] For Hume, mathematics is not a useful tool in the field of moral philosophy and all attempts to extend this instrument beyond the bounds of abstract science "are mere sophistry and illusion" (Hume 1748: 252, see also Demeter 2014: 171–180). Even Smith, while proposing abstract concepts and generalizations, does not use mathematical formalizations showing a diffidence towards symbols and long chains of reasoning (Redman 1997: 215–218).

In Italy, Antonio Genovesi, at the end of the 1740s, started his collaboration with Intieri and Celestino Galiani, showing growing interest in social science, and particularly for the new economic discipline. But the role of Genovesi was ambiguous: his conception of *economia civile* (*civil economy*, Genovesi 1765, 1766, 1767) privileges an ethical and political perspective, completely neglecting the methodological connection between economic analysis and mathematical tools, drawing criticism from Pietro Verri for the lack of scientific rigour.[10] Nevertheless, Genovesi

[8] Condorcet, unlike the Neapolitan abbé, defended liberalisation measures (see Condorcet 1774). On the relation between Condorcet and the Physiocratic School, see Perrot (1992, pp. 358–376).

[9] For the concept of sceptical Newtonianism applied to Smith, see Cremaschi (1989). Foley (1976, chs. 2, 7, 9) considers Smith's methodology largely influenced by Cartesian philosophy rather than by Newton. See also Cremaschi (1981; 129). For common intellectual frameworks between Scottish and Neapolitan Enlightenment, see Robertson (1997, 2005).

[10] Pietro Verri's letter to his brother Alessandro, Milan 3 November 1766, published in Verri and Verri (1923: 32). See also Ferrone (1995: 260) and Carmagnani (2014). Lombard authors showed a greater attraction for the Cartesian model of social mathematics, falling into a naive application of mathematical formalization to economic reasoning. This is particularly evident in the sixth edition of Pietro Verri's *Reflections on Political Economy*, published in 1772, including some footnotes, attributed to the Milanese mathematician Paolo

is still interested to the Newtonian approach in the field of moral philosophy: in the *Diceosina* (Genovesi 1766. See D'Onofrio, 2015; Bruni 2017 he proposes an ethical system based on Newton's *Principia*, establishing a connection between the law of gravitation and human behaviour. Genovesi's underestimation of social mathematics in favour of the primacy of the political and ethical dimension in economic analysis, brings to a close the programme of research started by Celestino Galiani's circle.[11]

Since his youth, Galiani had understood that the new economic science was the scientific foundation supporting the *Ragion di Stato*. Within the framework of the natural laws that underpinned economic life, there was space for the art of government, still seen as being in the prince's best interest. The new Machiavelli, the new advisor to the Prince, was undoubtedly identified in the economist. He was consistently faithful to this principle throughout his intellectual life. At the peak of the Physiocratic controversy, writing to Madame d'Épinay, he described himself as a poor, failed economist ("je ne suis qu'un *pauvre économiste manqué*"[12]), showing his regret that he had not continuously developed his interest in economic analysis , distracted by his intellectual curiosity. But in this choice not to devote himself completely to economic science, in a systematic way as Antonio Genovesi did, was also the effect of the disappointment that followed the publication of *Della Moneta* and the tour in Italy between 1751 and 1752 in which his bold positions on devaluation were criticised and judged with distrust. His theory of *alzamento* placed him outside the movement in support of monetary stabilisation and revealed his Renaissance conception of politics, in which it was legitimate for the Prince to act according to the *Ragion di Stato* even against public morality: it was the apologia of enlightened absolutism, coloured by "Machiavellian complacency and cynical acceptance of even the coldest and harshest aspects of power and the State" (Venturi 1998: 498). This tendency justified the *cameralist phase* in the last period of his life, in which although he put forward proposals for reform and identified critical areas of the Kingdom's society and economy, he never fell into utopian projects, maintaining a

Frisi (1728–1784), in which an effort is made to translate economic arguments into mathematical equations (Bianchini 2002; Tubaro 2002). This attempt at formalization increased the opposition to applying mathematical tools to economic reasoning, and Verri eliminated Frisi's notes in the following edition of his *Reflections*.

[11] See Ferrone (1995); Casini (2006); Marcialis (2018).

[12] Ferdinando Galiani's letter to Madame d'Épinay, Naples, 13 Dicember 1770, published in Galiani (1881a, vol. I: 313); Galiani and d'Épinay (1992, vol. I: 313) (italics added).

very close bond with the court and in particular with Queen Maria Carolina, who dictated the programme of government of the Neapolitan kingdom. He was not fascinated by Freemasonry and remained outside of it, following Tanucci's diffidence; moreover, he always showed scepticism towards deism (and this choice weighed on his isolation).[13] He was certainly a conservative (although aware of the exploitation of the peasantry) and declared this without difficulty: "Monarchy is essentially based on inequality of conditions, inequality of conditions is based on low commodity prices, low commodity prices are based on coercion. Complete freedom causes the prices to rise and the peasants to become rich. The rich peasant does not care about military service, will no longer tolerate arbitrary taxes, abusive levies, etc.; he will be strong enough to no longer allow himself to be trampled on, either by revolt or legal action, and will have enough money to win court cases. Thus the republican form is realised, and finally the equality of conditions, after six thousand years of efforts to destroy it . [...]. I prefer monarchy because I feel much closer to the government than to the plough. I possess an income of fifteen thousand *Lire* which I would lose if the peasants became rich. If everyone behaved as I do and spoke according to his own interests, there would be an end to disputes in this world".[14] He supported Minister de Maupeou's policy against the power of parliaments[15] and opposed Turgot's abolition of the guilds.[16] He repeatedly showed his admiration for China as a model

[13] In 1738, Charles, following Spanish policy and papal guidelines, banned the establishment of Masonic lodges in the Kingdom of Naples, but the ban was not observed and many Masonic affiliations sprang up in the kingdom. The ban was renewed in 1746 and 1751 by Charles, and confirmed by Tanucci in September 1775, but these measures were never enforced. Moreover, Maria Carolina protected the lodges and did not hesitate to dismiss Tanucci to protect Masonic activities (see Francovich 1974: 200). For the relationship between Freemasonry and the Enlightenment, see Giarrizzo (1994); Beaurepaire (2003); Trampus (2011b).

[14] Ferdinando Galiani's letter to Madame d'Épinay, Naples, 2 January 1773, published in Galiani (1881a, vol. II: 154–155); Galiani and d'Épinay (1994, vol. III: 181–182).

[15] "Solve the unfortunate affair of parliaments and you will have had a brilliant start. If you want to believe me, keep the new system of parliaments [the one defined by the Maupeou reforms] and bring back the old ones. The new system is better; the old ones were better" (Ferdinando Galiani's letter to Madane d'Épinay, Naples, 18 June 1774, published in Galiani 1881a, vol. II: 321–322; Galiani and d'Épinay 1996, vol IV: 151).

[16] "As for the abolition of corporations, I say this in defiance of all fashionable thinkers and economists: it is madness, an error, an absurdity. [...] The more difficult, tiring and expensive something is, the more people love it, become attached to it, crave it. The most austere religious orders are those that have produced the greatest men. If you make the rules of the

of government destined to excel in the future,[17] attributing anthropological primacy to Asian ethnicity (another occasion to dispute Montesquieu's deterministic theories).[18]

In terms of economic analysis, Galiani's theory of value was certainly the highest point reached in the theoretical elaboration of eighteenth century Italian writers. The analysis of *Della moneta*'s manuscript has made it possible to define Galiani's theory of value as a synthesis of subjective elements (utility) and objective elements (scarcity, and thus labour and nature), or more precisely, it presents itself as the result of the development of two traditions, the scholastic (utility-scarcity) and the nascent hedonistic utilitarianism (of which uncle Celestino himself was a

fathers of Saint-Maur or the Jesuits easy and convenient, their order is destroyed; thus I am convinced that Turgot dealt a mortal blow to French manufacturing. Some skilled craftsmen will leave; others will become shallow in their work; and instead of establishing the spirit of emulation, he will have broken all the true energies of the human heart. This is my opinion" (Ferdinando Galiani's letter to Madame d'Épinay, Naples, 13 April 1776, published in Galiani 1881a, vol. II: 438–439; Galiani and d'Épinay 1996, vol V: 70–71).

[17] "At the two extremities of the great continent, there will be the Chinese on one side and the Europeans on the other, two more or less equal nations. They will have the same characteristics; they will have absolute government, tempered by forms, length of procedure, gentleness of customs; they will have many soldiers and little courage; much industry and little genius; many people and few happy people. The republics will disappear in Europe: they do not march in line with the monarchies, they lose ground and are sunk. Poland is proof of this: its disgrace preceeds that of the Italian republics, despised for their smallness, by a century at most. We will therefore be Chinese in a hundred years at most. I'm already having fun flattening my nose and stretching my ears from below, and I'm not doing too badly" (Ferdinando Galiani's letter to Madame d'Épinay, Naples, 24 July 1773, published in Galiani 1881a, vol. II: 236–237; Galiani and d'Épinay 1996, vol IV: 40–41).

[18] "Human beings have taken an immense amount of time to perfect themselves: the peoples of California and New Holland [Australia], who are three or four thousand years old, are still mere brutes. Perfectibility began to make great strides in Asia more than twelve thousand years ago, and God only knows how long before that only futile efforts had been made. If an Asiatic race had not passed into Europe and Africa, and if from Europe it had not passed into America, whence it went round the world, man would still be only the most mischievous, the most cunning, and the most skilful of apes: therefore perfectibility is not a gift of man as a whole, but of the white and bearded race alone. Through cross-breeding, the brown and bearded race, the brown and unbearded race and the black race have gained something. Everything that is said about climates is nonsense, a *non causa pro causa*, the most common fallacy of logic. Everything depends on race. The first, the noblest of races, comes by nature from northern Asia. The Russians are closer to it, which is why they have made more progress in fifty years than the Portuguese will in five hundred" (Ferdinando Galiani's letter to Madame d'Épinay, Naples, 12 October 1776, published in Galiani 1881a, vol. II: 473–474; Galiani and d'Épinay 1997, vol V: 108–109).

forerunner in Italy). The same compromise between different traditions of thought emerges with the theory of interest, in which advanced developments in the calculus of probability are embedded in an approach that still contains ethical concerns. But the ground on which Galiani emerges from his century is certainly the pure theory of money: the Neapolitan abbot rejects vulgar metallism, distinguishing between the *logical nature* and the *historical specification* of money and attributing to the latter the character of a *social institution*, based on *confidence* and *consensus*. The metallic form that money takes has only a *contingent cause*, historically determined by the degree of confidence, and is not a logical necessity.

Due to these characteristics, Galiani's work did not find immediate successors, but criticism (even if this was often full of admiration for the precocious talent demonstrated) and a certain substantial lack of understanding among his contemporaries, and this penalised the development of some of his important theoretical positions, which seemed to fall on deaf ears. In particular, the theory of value, practically ignored by his contemporaries, was later rediscovered by the marginalist economists of the nineteenth century, who however distorted its meaning, making Galiani a forerunner of the subjective theory of utility.

With the *Dialogues*, Galiani reached the peak of his prestige as an economist. With his analytical capacity and the solid strength of his arguments, he succeeded in influencing much of the French intellectual and political world. He succeeded in finding a place in the fracture between two currents of the French Enlightenment, the Cartesian school of Quesnay, and the empiricist school, largely influenced by Newtonism, supported by some of the *Encyclopédie*'s eminent contributors, in particular Diderot.

Galiani was therefore a man *of the eighteenth century* and *in the eighteenth century* sharing all its contradictions. Moreover, his constant dialogue with the highest personalities of the French Enlightenment (in particular his friend, Diderot), his assiduous frequentation of Parisian salons, his involvement in intellectual and political life from his privileged position as a diplomat, and the intense correspondence that followed his return home, make him a protagonist of that season.

The themes, the philosophical nodes, that were at the centre of the Enlightenment debate were also present in his critical reflection,[19] but in

[19] His view is not dissimilar to that outlined by Diderot in the *Encyclopédie* entry of his *Dictionnaire universel*: "We must thus take care to give the reasons of things, when there are some; assign the causes, when we know them; indicate the effects, when they are certain;

an original way, in the light of his intellectual training completed in contact with an original tradition of thought that had provided him with critical tools.[20] He therefore did not absorb Enlightenment ideas like a *tabula rasa*, but sifted them critically, with a sceptical streak, staying away from the easy enthusiasms of rationalism. He fused in his thought the Italian tradition of political science, Machiavelli in the first place (but also Giovanni Botero) and of natural science, and in Galileo he found the source of inspiration for the *Dialogues*, with the economic literature, especially Melon discussed and shared by Intieri, and the new Newtonian methodology, assimilated in his solid youthful education, directed by his Newtonian uncle Celestine. Vico's teaching was the basis of his radical aversion to Cartesianism and all forms of abstract rationalism, and certainly contributed to his interest in historical contextualisation and philological rigour, but his thought can in no way be considered a development of Vico's philosophy, as Nicolini has forcibly claimed.

His participation in the complex Enlightenment movement was unique: Galiani would never have interpreted Horace's *Sapere Aude!* as a motto[21] of emancipation characteristic of the *Aufklärung*, as Immanuel Kant was to do in the same years by forcing the concept ("*Dare to know; begin!*"),[22] but would more authentically leave it in its actual meaning ("*Dare to be wise: begin!*") of an exhortation not to hesitate because "the man who postpones the hour for right living is like the countryman waiting for the river to stop flowing: but on it glides and shall glide, rolling its waters for all time".[23]

resolve the conundrums through direct application of the principles; set forth truths; unmask errors; artfully discredit prejudices; teach men to doubt and wait; dispel ignorance; weigh the value of human knowledge; distinguish between true and false, true and plausible, plausible and miraculous or incredible, common phenomena from extraordinary phenomena, certain facts from doubtful facts, and those from facts absurd and counter to the natural order; become acquainted with the general course of events, and take each thing for what it is, and consequently inspire a desire for knowledge, a horror for lies and vice, and a love for virtue; for whatever has not happiness and virtue as its ultimate end is nought" (Diderot 1755 [2002]: 642).

[20] Galiani's contribution is a typical case of an intellectual being interpreted outside the national context, a historiographical approach defined by John Robertson (see Robertson 1997, 2005).

[21] "Dimidium facti, qui coepit, habet: sapere aude".

[22] Kant (1784), see also Venturi (1959a).

[23] Horace, *Epistle*, II, Lib. I, *Ad Lollium*, v. 40, English Translation, Horace ([2011]: 205).

References[24]

Primary Sources

Condorcet, M. J. A. N. de Caritat. (1774). *Lettres sur le commerce des grains*. Paris: Couturier Père.

Condorcet, M. J. A. N. de Caritat. (1793) [1994]. *Tableau général de la science qui a pour objet l'application du calcul aux sciences politiques et morales*. English translation: *Foundations of Social Choice and Political Theory*. Translated and edited by I. McLean and F. Ewitt. Cheltenham: Edward Elgar Publishing.

d'Alembert, J-B. Le Rond. (1751) [1995]. Discours préliminaire des Éditeurs. In *Encyclopédie, ou dictionnaire raisonné des sciences, des arts et des métiers*, tome I. Paris: Briasson, David l'aîné, Le Breton, Imprimeur ordinaire du Roy, Durand, pp. i–xlv. English Translation: *Preliminary Discourse to the Encyclopaedia of Diderot*, translated by R. N. Schwab with the collaboration of W. E. Rex. Chicago: University of Chicago Press.

Diderot, D. (1755) [2002]. Encyclopédie. In *Encyclopédie, ou dictionnaire raisonné des sciences, des arts et des métiers*, tome V. Paris: Briasson, David l'aîné, Le Breton, Imprimeur ordinaire du Roy, Durand, pp. 635–648. English Translation in *The Encyclopedia of Diderot & d'Alembert Collaborative Translation Project*. Translated by P. Stewart. Ann Arbor: Michigan Publishing, University of Michigan Library, 2002. On Line: http://hdl.handle.net/2027/spo.did2222.0000.004.

Galiani, F. (1881a). *Écrivains du XVIII siècle – Correspondance avec Madame d'Épinay, Madame Necker, Madame Geoffrin etc., Diderot, Grimm, d'Alembert, de Sartine, d'Holbach, etc. Nouvelle édition, entièrement rétablie d'après les textes originaux, augmentée de tous les passages supprimés et d'un grand nombre de lettres inédites, avec une étude sur sa vie et les oeuvres de Galiani*, edited by L. Perey, G. Maugras, 2 voll. Paris: Calmann Levy.

Galiani, F. (1975). *Opere di Ferdinando Galiani*, edited by F. Diaz e L. Guerci, in *Letteratura italiana. Storia e testi. Illuministi italiani*, tomo VI. Milan-Naples: Ricciardi.

Galiani, F., d'Épinay, L. (1992). *Correspondance. Vol. I (1769–1770)*, présentation de G. Dulac, texte établi et annoté par D. Maggetti, en collaboration avec G. Dulac. Paris: Les Editions Desjonquères.

Galiani, F., d'Épinay, L. (1994). *Correspondance. Vol. III (Mars 1772–Mai 1773)*, présentation de G. Dulac, texte établi et annoté par D. Maggetti, en collaboration avec G. Dulac. Paris: Les Editions Desjonquères.

[24]The abbreviations "s.l." and "s.n." stand for the Latin terms *sine loco* (without place of publication) and *sine nomine* (without name of publisher).

Galiani, F., d'Épinay, L. (1996). *Correspondance. Vol. IV (Juin 1773–Mai 1775)*, présentation de Georges Dulac, texte établi et annoté par Daniel Maggetti, en collaboration avec Georges Dulac, Paris: Les Editions Desjonquères.

Galiani, F., d'Épinay, L. (1997). *Correspondance. Vol. V (June 1775–Juillet 1782)*, présentation de G. Dulac, texte établi et annoté par D. Maggetti, en collaboration avec G. Dulac. Paris: Les Editions Desjonquères.

Genovesi, A. (1765). *Delle lezioni di commercio o sia d'economia civile da leggersi nella Cattedra Interiana dell'ab.Genovesi regio cattedratico.* Parte prima pel primo semestre. Naples: Fratelli Simone.

Genovesi, A. (1766). *Della Diceosina o sia filosofia del giusto e dell'onesto*, Naples: Stamperia Simoniana.

Genovesi, A. (1767). *Delle lezioni di commercio o sia d'economia civile da leggersi nella Cattedra Interiana dell'ab.Genovesi regio cattedratico. Parte seconda pel secondo semestre.* Naples: Fratelli Di Simone.

Horace. [2011]. *Satires and Epistles,* Translated by J. Davie, with an Introduction and Notes by R. Cowan. Oxford, Oxford University Press.

Hume, D. (1748). *Philosophical Essays Concerning Human Understanding.* London: Millar.

Hutcheson, F. (1725). *An Inquiry into the Original of Our Ideas of Beauty and Virtue.* London: J. Darby.

Kant, I. (1784). Beantwortung der Frage: Was ist Aufklärung?, *Berlinische Monatsschrift*, Band 12, pp. 481–494.

Verri, A., Verri, P. (1923). *Carteggio di Pietro e Alessandro Verri*, vol. I, edited by E. Greppi, A. Giulini, Milan: Cogliati.

Secondary Sources

Amodio, P. (1997a). *Il disincanto della ragione e l'assolutezza del bonheur: studio sull'abate Galiani*, Naples: Guida.

Badaloni, N. (1973). La cultura. In R. Romano e C. Vivanti (eds.), *Storia d'Italia*, vol. 3. *Dal primo Settecento all'Unità*. Turin: Einaudi, pp. 697–984.

Baker, K. M. (1975). *Condorcet from Natural Philosophy to Social Mathematics.* Chicago: The University of Chicago Press.

Beaurepaire, P.-Y. (2003). *L'espace des francs-maçons. Une sociabilité européenne au XVIIIe siècle.* Rennes: PUR.

Bianchini, M. (2002). *Bonheur public et méthode géométrique: enquête sur les économistes italiens (1711–1803).* Paris: Ined.

Brooks, G. P., Aalto, S. K. (1981). The Rise and Fall of Moral Algebra: Francis Hutcheson and the Mathematization of Psychology, *Journal of the History of the Behavioral Sciences*, 17, 3, pp. 343–356.

Bruni, L. (2017). On the Concept of Economia Civile and "Felicitas Publica": A Comment on Federico D'onofrio. *Journal of the History of Economic Thought*, Volume 39, Number 2, pp. 273–279.

Carmagnani, M. (2014). *Economia politica e morale pubblica. Pietro Verri e la cultura economica europea*. Bologna: Il Mulino.

Casini, P. (1983a). Newton in Italia, 1700–1740: note di ricerca. In P. Casini (ed.), *Newton e la coscienza europea*, Bologna 1983, pp. 173–227.

Casini, P. (1983b). Questioni sul newtonianesimo nel Settecento, in P. Rossi, (ed.), *Il Newtonianesimo nel Settecento*, Rome: Treccani, pp. 167–178.

Casini, P. (1988). Newton's *Principia* and the Philosophers of the Enlightenment. *Notes and Records of the Royal Society of London*, Vol. 42, No. 1, *Newton's Principia and Its Legacy*, pp. 35–52.

Casini, P. (2006). Il momento newtoniano in Italia: un post-scriptum. *Rivista di Storia della Filosofia*, Vol. 61, No. 2, pp. 299–316.

Cremaschi, S. (1981). Adam Smith, Newtonianism and Political Economy. *Manuscrito*, V (1), pp. 117–134.

Cremaschi, S. (1989). Adam Smith: Skeptical Newtonianism, Disenchanted Republicanism, and the Birth of Social Science. In Dascal, M., Gruengard, O. (eds.), *Knowledge and Politics: Case Studies in the Relationship Between Epistemology and Political Philosophy*. Boulder: Westview Press, pp. 83–110.

Crépel, P., Gilain, C. (eds). (1989). *Condorcet: mathématicien, économiste, philosophe, homme politique*. Paris: Minerve.

Crépel, P., Rieucau, J.-N. (2005). Condorcet's Social Mathematics: A Few Tables. *Social Choice and Welfare*, 25 (2/3), pp. 243–285.

Croce, B. (1909). Il pensiero dell'abate Galiani. *La Critica. Rivista di Letteratura, Storia e Filosofia*, Vol. 7, pp. 399–404.

Davison, R. (1988). Diderot, Galiani et Vico: un itinéraire Philosophique. *Diderot Studies*, Vol. 23, pp. 39–53.

Demeter, T. (2014). Enlarging the Bounds of Moral Philosophy: Newton's Method and Hume's Science of Man, in Z.Biener, E. Schliesser, (eds.), *Newton and Empiricism*. Cambridge: Cambridge University Press, pp. 171–180.

Diaz, F. (1975a). Introduzione. In Galiani, F. *Opere*, edited by F. Diaz, L.Guerci, *Letteratura italiana. Storia e testi. Illuministi italiani*, tomo VI, Milan-Naples: Ricciardi, pp. ix–cvi.

D'Onofrio, F. (2015). On the Concept of "Felicitas Publica" in Eighteenth-Century Political Economy. *Journal of the History of Economic Thought*, Volume 37, Number 3, pp. 449–471.

Feldman, J. (2005). Condorcet et la Mathematique Sociale: Enthousiasmes et Bemols. *Mathematics and Social Sciences*, 43, 172 (4): pp. 7–41.

Ferrone, V. (1995). *The Intellectual Roots of the Italian Enlightenment: Newtonian Science, Religion, and Politics in the Early Eighteenth Century*. Atlantic Highlands: Humanities Press.

Ferrone, V. (2019). *Il mondo dell'Illuminismo. Storia di una rivoluzione culturale.* Turin: Einaudi.

Foley, V. (1976). *The Social Physics of Adam Smith.* West Lafayette: Purdue University Press.

Francovich, C. (1974). *Storia della massoneria in Italia: Dalle origini alla Rivoluzione francese.* Florence: La Nuova Italia.

Giarrizzo, G. (1994). *Massoneria e Illuminismo nell'Europa del Settecento.* Venice: Marsilio.

Granger, G.-G. (1956). *La mathématique sociale du marquis de Condorcet.* Paris: PUF.

Ingrao, B., Israel, G. (1990). *The Invisible Hand: Economic Equilibrium in the History of Science*, Cambridge: MIT Press.

Laboulle, M. J. (1939). La Mathématique sociale: Condorcet et ses prédécesseurs. *Revue d'Histoire littéraire de la France*, 46 (1/2), pp. 33–55.

Llobera, J. R. 1979. "Newton, The Scientific Model, And Social Thought In The Enlightenment", *Dialectical Anthropology*, Vol. 4, No. 2, pp. 147–153

Marcialis, M. T. (2018). Percezioni e Idee. Il confronto tra Antonio Conti e Antonio Genovesi. *Rivista di Storia della Filosofia*, Vol. 73, No. 4, pp. 629–664.

Mauro, A. (2017a). *Un philosophe des Lumières entre Naples et Paris: Ferdinando Galiani (1728–1787).* Thèse de Doctorate de l'Université Toulouse le Mirail - Toulouse II.

Mauro, A. (2017b). L'abbé Galiani alias le chevalier Zanobi: un philosophe qui "ne croit rien en rien sur rien de rien". *Littératures Classiques*, 93, pp. 155–167.

Nicolini, F. (1918b). La puerizia e l'adolescenza dell'abate Galiani (1735–1745). Notize, lettere, versi, documenti, *Archivio Storico per le Province Napoletane,* Nuova serie Anno IV, XLIII. dell'intera collezione, Vol. IV, pp. 105–132.

Nietzsche, F. (1886) [2002]. *Jenseits von Gut und Böse, Vorspiel einer Philosophie der Zukunft,* Leipzig: Druck und Verlag. English Translation, *Beyond Good and Evil Prelude to a Philosophy of the Future,* edited by Horstmann, R.-P., Norman, J., Cambridge: Cambridge University Press, 2002.

Outram, D. (2019). *The Enlightenment.* Fourth Edition. Cambridghe: Cambridge Univesity Press.

Patalano, R. (2020a). Carlo Antonio Broggia, a money doctor in adverse circumstances. *History of Economic Thought and Policy*, 2–2020, pp. 9–37.

Perrot, J.-C. (1992). *Une histoire intellectuelle de l'économie politique. XVII*[e]*–XVIII*[e] *siècle.* Paris: Éditions de l'École des Hautes Études en Sciences Sociales.

Pribram, K. (1983). *A history of economic reasoning.* New York: John Hopkins University Press.

Ravix, J. (2018). Entre Arlequin et Machiavelli: Galiani économiste baroque. In A. Tiran, C. Carnino (eds.), *Ferdinando Galiani, économie et politique.* Paris: Classiques Garnier, pp. 95–120.

Redman, D. A. (1997). *The Rise of Political Economy as a Science: Methodology and the Classical Economists.* Cambridge, MA: MIT Press.

Robertson, J. (1997). The Enlightenment above National Context: Political Economy in Eighteenth-Century Scotland and Naples. *The Historical Journal*, Vol. 40, No. 3, pp. 667–697.

Robertson, J. (2000). Enlightenment and Revolution: Naples 1799. *Transactions of the Royal Historical Society. Sixth Series*, 10, pp. 17–44.

Robertson, J. (2005). *The Case for the Enlightenment. Scotland and Naples 1680–1760.* Cambridge: Cambridge University Press.

Rothschild, E. (2001). *Economic Sentiments: Adam Smith, Condorcet, and the Enlightenment.* Cambridge (MS): Harvard University Press.

Rothschild, E. (2005). Axiom, Theorem, Corollary, Etc.: Condorcet and Mathematical Economics. *Social Choice and Welfare*, 25, pp. 287–302.

Soliani, R., Clément, A. (2018). Les fondaments philosophiques de l'approche èconomique de Ferdinando Galiani. In A. Tiran, C. Carnino, (eds.), *Ferdinando Galiani, économie et politique.* Paris: Classiques Garnier, pp. 121–154.

Stapelbroek, K. (2008a). *Love, Self-Deceit and Money. Commerce and Morality in the Early Neapolitan Enlightenment.* Toronto: University of Toronto Press.

Tagliacozzo, G. (1968). Economic Vichism (Vico, Galiani, Croce - Economics, Economic Liberalism). *BNL Quarterly Review*, 21 (85), pp. 96–119.

Tiran, A. 2018. Galiani (1728–1787) et Della Moneta (1751). In A. Tiran, C. Carnino, (eds.), *Ferdinando Galiani, économie et politique.* Paris: Classiques Garnier, pp. 57–94.

Trampus, A. (2011b). *La massoneria nell'età moderna*: Bari: Laterza.

Tubaro, P. (2002). A Case Study in Early Mathematical Economics: Pietro Verri and Paolo Frisi, 1772. *Journal of the History of Economic Thought*, 24 (2), pp. 193–214.

Venturi F. (1959a). Alle origini dell'Illuminismo napoletano. Dal carteggio di Bartolomeo Intieri. *Rivista Storica Italiana*, a. LXXI, fascicolo III, pp. 416–456.

Venturi, F. (1960b). Galiani tra enciclopedisti e fisiocrati. *Rivista Storica Italiana*, anno LXXII, fascicolo I, pp. 45–64.

Venturi, F. (1998). *Settecento riformatore. Da Muratori a Beccaria*, Turin: Einaudi.

Williams, D. (2004). *Condorcet and Modernity.* Cambridge: Cambridge University Press.

References[1]

Manuscript Sources

Broggia, C. A. MSCAB. *Del pubblico interesse economico, politico, morale, di stato, e di commercio. Sostenuto e difeso contro gli errori, e le insidie de' falsi dotti. Dissertazioni varie, del tutto utili e necessarie per la civile scienza: Di C. A. Broggia. Prodotte in occasione di farsi gli esami, le risposte, e le note critiche su di un'opera intitolata: Della Moneta libri cinque, impressa in Napoli nel 1750, di autore anonimo*. Manuscript kept in the Kress Library - Harvard University.

De Gournay, J. MS. *Mémoire* (sans titre). Manuscript kept in the Archives Municipales de Saint-Brieuc, Fonds Gournay, Ms. 82.

Galiani, C. MSCG. *Ricerche intorno alle prime origini della scienza morale*, manuscript kept in the Biblioteca Società Napoletana di Storia Patria, XXXI. C. 1, folios 1–68.

Galiani, C. MSCG-1. *Riflessioni sopra la natura dei lotti e loro giusti valori*, manuscript kept in the Biblioteca Universitaria Bologna, Ms. 992, folios 26–94.

Galiani, C. MSCG-2. *Parere teologico sopra alcuni punti appartenenti all'introduzione degli Ebrei ne' due Regni di Napoli e Sicilia*, manuscript kept in the Biblioteca Società Napoletana di Storia Patria, XXXI.B.1, folios [244] 235–[267v] 258v.

Galiani, C. MSCG-3. *Osservazioni sopra il libro di Newton, intitolato Principia Mathematica*, manuscript kept in the Biblioteca Società Napoletana di Storia Patria, XXX. D. 2, folios 96–109v.

[1] The abbreviations "s.l." and "s.n." stand for the Latin terms *sine loco* (without place of publication) and *sine nomine* (without name of publisher).

R. Patalano, *Ferdinando Galiani*,
https://doi.org/10.1007/978-3-032-02793-1

Galiani, C. MSCG-4. *Intorno ai calcoli differenziale e integrale*, manuscript kept in the Biblioteca Società Napoletana di Storia Patria, XXXI.B.1, folios [302] 293–[307v] 298v.

Galiani, F. MS-1. *Notizie genealogiche dei Galiani*, Manuscript kept in the Biblioteca Società Napoletana di Storia Patria, XXXI C 8, folio 66.

Galiani, F. MS-2. *Lettera di Galiani a ignoto sulla natura dell'amore e sul cicisbeismo*, December 1745, Manuscript kept in the Biblioteca Società Napoletana di Storia Patria, XXXI. C.19.05, folios 94r–99v, published in Nicolini, 1918b, pp. 117–121.

Galiani, F. MS-3. *Discorso sull'amore. Lezione accademica letta dall'abate Galiani nell'Accademia degli Emuli nel 1746*. Manuscript kept in the Biblioteca Società Napoletana di Storia Patria, XXXI. A. 09, folios 91r–100r, published in Galiani, 1975, pp. 689–700.

Galiani, F. MS-4. *Lezione accademica sull'amor platonico*. Manuscript kept in the Biblioteca Società Napoletana di Storia Patria, XXX. C. 06, folios 57r–66r, published in Mauro 2017a, tome 2, pp. 454–464.

Galiani, F. MS-5. *Dell'idea di Dio*, Manuscript kept in the British Museum, Egerton Collection, 21, published in Nicolini-Venturi, 1956, pp. 67–73.

Galiani, F. MS-6. *Della superstizione, e delle cause di essa*, Manuscript kept in the Biblioteca Società Napoletana di Storia Patria, XXXI A 10, folios 124r–125v, published in Mauro 2017a, tome 2, pp. 469–471.

Galiani, F. MS-7. *Sull'Anticristo (al conte Punghino)*, Manuscript kept in the Biblioteca Società Napoletana di Storia Patria, XXXI. C. 12, folios 97r–102r, published in Mauro, 2017a, tome 2, pp. 472–477.

Galiani, F. MS-8. *Pensieri vari sulla durata e sulla fine del mondo*, Manuscript kept in the Biblioteca Società Napoletana di Storia Patria, XXXI. A. 10, folios 118r–120v, published in Mauro, 2017a, tome 2, pp. 478–480.

Galiani, F. MS-9. *Proemio di un'opera sulle streghe*, Manuscript kept in the Biblioteca Società Napoletana di Storia Patria, XXXI. C. 14, folios 146r–148r, published with this title in Galiani, 1975, pp. 817–819.

Galiani, F. MS-10. *Sopra la morte di Socrate*, Manuscript kept in the Biblioteca Società Napoletana di Storia Patria, XXXI. A. 9, published in Galiani, 1975, pp. 701–703.

Galiani, F. MS-11. *Dell'arte del governo, proemio*, Manuscript kept in the Biblioteca Società Napoletana di Storia Patria, XXXI. C. 8, folios 1r–2v, published in Galiani, 1963, pp. 390–392.

Galiani, F. MS-12. *Proemio alla ristampa di libri che trattano dei disordini della moneta al tempo dei Viceré e cagioni delle misere condizioni del Regno*, Manuscript kept in the Biblioteca Società Napoletana di Storia Patria, XXXI. C. 8, folios Ir–IVv.

Galiani, F. MS-13. *Della Moneta*. Manuscript kept in the Biblioteca Società Napoletana di Storia Patria, XXIX. E. 13.

Galiani, F. MS-14. *Sui contratti alla voce.* Manuscript kept in the Biblioteca Società Napoletana di Storia Patria, XXXI. A. 10, published in Galiani, 1975, pp. 742–745 and in Galiani, 1999, pp. 77–80.
Galiani, F. MS-15. *Diario 1751–1752.* Manuscript kept in the Biblioteca Società Napoletana di Storia Patria, XXXI. C. 22.
Galiani, F. MS-16. *Pitture antiche che si conservano nella Real Villa di Portici, dissotterrate per ordine della Maestà del Re Carlo,* Manuscript kept in the Biblioteca Società Napoletana di Storia Patria, XXXI. C. 12.
Galiani, F. MS-17. *Degli uomini di grandezza straordinaria e de' giganti. Discorso.* Manuscript kept in the Biblioteca Società Napoletana di Storia Patria, XXXI. C. 8, folios 16v–18v; XXXI C 12, folios 164r–203r.
Galiani, F. MS-18. *Notes au Pacte de Famille.* Manuscript kept in the Biblioteca Società Napoletana di Storia Patria, XXX. A. 10, folios 252r–261v. Folios 252r–257r, published in Galiani, 1975, pp. 704–709.
Galiani, F. MS-19. *Breve racconto di quel che è a mia notizia rispetto al Trattato di navigazione e commercio colla Francia* (1784a). Manuscript kept in the Biblioteca Società Napoletana di Storia Patria, XXX. D. 3, folios 74r–81v, published in Diaz, 1973, pp. 354–364 and in Galiani, 1999, pp. 125–131.
Galiani, F. MS-20. *Istoria vera della controversia de' grani di Marsiglia scritta da persona ben informata, col parere sulla giustizia delle pretensioni delle parti litiganti. Amsterdam 1772.* Manuscript kept in the Biblioteca Società Napoletana di Storia Patria, XXIX. C. 6, folios 1–111, partially published in Galiani, 1959, pp. 307–313.
Galiani, F. MS-21. *Storia dell'avvenuto sugli editti del libero commercio de' grani in Francia promulgati nel 1763 e 1764.* Manuscript kept in the Biblioteca Società Napoletana di Storia Patria, XXX. C.12, folios 23–39, published in Galiani, 1959, pp. 315–322.
Galiani, F. MS-22. *De l'opinion,* Manuscript kept in the Turin State Archives, published in Nicolini, 1959b, pp. 139–156 ("the indication of the place where the fragment *De l' opinion* is kept is wrong, as Venturi pointed out: it is the Turin State Archives and not the British Museum", see Galiani, 1975: Guerci's note: cxvii).
Galiani, F. MS-23. *Per il suo Maestro di Ebraico,* Manuscript kept in the Biblioteca Società Napoletana di Storia Patria, XXX. C. 12, folios: 99–101, partially published in Nicolini, 1975, p. 304.
Galiani, F. MS-24. *Considerazioni sul Trattato di Commercio tra il Re e il Re Cristianissimo,* Manuscript kept in the Biblioteca Società Napoletana di Storia Patria, XXX. A. 10, folios 183r–251v, partially published in Galiani, 1975, pp. 717–734.
Galiani, F. MS-25. *Per la riduzione delle feste,* Manuscript kept in the Biblioteca Società Napoletana di Storia Patria, XXX. A. 10, folios 133r–144v, published in Galiani, 1999, pp. 51–55.

Galiani, F. MS-26. *Parere sul merco generale dell'oro e dell'argento*, Manuscript kept in the Biblioteca Società Napoletana di Storia Patria XXX.C.1, folios 205r–207v, published in Galiani, 1963, pp. 398–400.
Galiani, F. MS-27. *Piano di riforma proposto da Galiani dopo la cacciata dei gesuiti da Napoli*, Manuscript kept in the Biblioteca Società Napoletana di Storia Patria XXX. C. 12, folios 12v–19r, published in Galiani, 1975, pp. 710–716.
Galiani, F. MS-28. *Relazione circa un progetto di trattato tra la Russia e il Regno di Sardegna e le prospettive di un trattato fra Russia e Regno di Napoli*, Manuscript kept in the Biblioteca Società Napoletana di Storia Patria XXX. A. 15, folios 59r–62r, published in Diaz, 1973, pp. 335–340.
Galiani, F. MS-29. *Sull'annona di Genova*, Manuscript kept in the Biblioteca Società Napoletana di Storia Patria XXX. C. 6, folios 50r–56v, published in Galiani, 1975, pp. 735–741; in Cesarano, 1999, pp. 69–74.
Galiani, F. MS-30. *Pensieri miei sulle cause della spopolazione della Maremma sanese e su' rimedi*, Manuscript kept in the Biblioteca Società Napoletana di Storia Patria XXX. C. 12.29, folios 164–170, published in Galiani, 1999: 9–13, see also Galiani, 1963: 393–397.
Galiani, F. MS-31. *Pensieri vari di Ferdinando Galiani sul tremuoto della Calabria Ultra e di Messina*, Manuscript kept in the Biblioteca Società Napoletana di Storia Patria XXX. D. 03, Folios 42r–45r, published in Galiani, 1975, pp. 748–751.
Galiani, F. MS-32. *Continuazione de' pensieri di Ferdinando Galiani sul tremuoto della Calabria*, Manuscript kept in the Biblioteca Società Napoletana di Storia Patria XXX. D. 03, folios 45r–48v, published in Galiani, 1975, pp. 752–756.
Galiani, F. MS-33. *Quarto foglio de' pensieri di Ferdinando Galiani sul tremuoto di Calabria, e sue conseguenze*, Manuscript kept in the Biblioteca Società Napoletana di Storia Patria XXX. D. 03, folios 49r–50v, published in Galiani, 1975, pp. 757–758.
Galiani, F. MS-34. *Pensieri generali sul ristabilimento di Messina*, Manuscript kept in the Biblioteca Società Napoletana di Storia Patria, XXX. D. 03, folios 39r–41v., published in Galiani, 1975, pp. 759–762.
Galiani, F. MS-35. *Parere sul disgombro e il riedificamento di Messina*, Manuscript kept in the Biblioteca Società Napoletana di Storia Patria, XXX. D. 03, folios 62r–65v, published in Galiani, 1975, pp. 763–766.
Galiani, F. MS-36. *Sul regolamento delle Poste del Regno*, Manuscript kept in the Biblioteca Società Napoletana di Storia Patria, XXXI. A. 10, folios 88r–103v, published in Galiani, 1999, pp. 41–49.
Galiani, F. MS-37. *Dell'uso che potrebbe farsi delle pensioni di Tanucci*, Manuscript kept in the Biblioteca Società Napoletana di Storia Patria, XXX. C. 06, folios 8r–9v, published in Galiani, 1999, pp. 33–34.
Galiani, F. MS-38. *Rapporto all'Acton sul Comune di Castellamare*, Manuscript kept in the Biblioteca Società Napoletana di Storia Patria, XXX. D. 03, folios

85v–89r, published in Galiani, 1975, pp. 774–779 e in Galiani, 1999, pp. 35–39.

Galiani, F. MS-39. *Parere riguardante i dazi della seta,* Manuscript kept in the Biblioteca Società Napoletana di Storia Patria, XXX. D. 03, folios 53–55; 83–85, published in Galiani, 1999, pp. 19–21.

Galiani, F. MS-40. *Per la privativa di una fabbrica di saponi,* Manuscript kept in the Biblioteca Società Napoletana di Storia Patria, XXXI. A. 10, folios 80r–87v, published in Galiani, 1999, pp. 23–26.

Galiani, F. MS-41. *Piano per conseguire dalla Porta Ottomana la libera navigazione del Mar Nero ai bastimenti mercantili delle Due Sicilie,* Manuscript kept in the Biblioteca Società Napoletana di Storia Patria, XXX. D. 03, folios 66r–68r, published in Galiani, 1999, pp. 121–123.

Galiani, F. MS-42. *Sulla decadenza della marineria,* Manuscript kept in the Biblioteca Società Napoletana di Storia Patria, XXX. C. 12., folios 40–43, published in Galiani, 1999, pp. 133–135.

Galiani, F. MS-43. *Parere sullo stabilimento di rapporti commerciali e d'amicizia con gli Stati Uniti* (1784), Manuscript kept in the Biblioteca Società Napoletana di Storia Patria, XXX. D. 03, folios 1–6.

Galiani, F. MS-44. *Istruzioni al conte Ludolf sulla libera navigazione del Mar Nero,* Manuscript kept in the Biblioteca Società Napoletana di Storia Patria, XXX. D. 03, folios 68v–70v.

Galiani, F. MS-45. *Considerazioni sul vantaggio che deriverebbe ai sudditi di S.M. Imperiale dalla libertà che avessero i bastimenti delle Due Sicilie di navigare fino all'imboccatura del Danubio,* Manuscript kept in the Biblioteca Società Napoletana di Storia Patria, XXX. D. 03, folios 71r–73r.

Galiani, F. MS-46. *Croquis d'un dialogue sur les femmes,* Manuscript kept in the Biblioteca Società Napoletana di Storia Patria, XXX. C. 12, Folios 212–218, published in Galiani, 1975, pp. 635–642; Galiani, 1881a, vol. II, pp. 50–62.

Galiani, F. MS-47. *Commento alle odi di Orazio,* Manuscript kept in the Biblioteca Società Napoletana di Storia Patria, XXXII. C. 6, published in Nicolini, 1978, pp. 154-255.

Galiani, F. MS-48. *Cela revient toujours au même,* Manuscript kept in the Biblioteca Società Napoletana di Storia Patria, XXX C 12, folios: 227–230, published in Nicolini, 1909a, pp. 253–258, and Galiani, 1957: 208–211.

Galiani, F. MS-49. *Piano per l'ancoraggio del porto di Baja,* Manuscript kept in the Biblioteca Società Napoletana di Storia Patria, XXXI. A. 10, folios: 60r–60v.

Galiani, F. MS-50. *Testamento,* Manuscript kept in the Biblioteca Società Napoletana di Storia Patria, XXXI. A. 08, folios: 85r–88r, published in Ademollo, 1880, pp. 654–658.

Galiani, F. MS-51. *Sullo stato della moneta ai tempi della guerra troiana,* Manuscript kept in the Biblioteca Società Napoletana di Storia Patria, XXXI.A.09.09, folios 155–182v, published in Galiani, 1963, pp. 351–379.

Galiani, F. MS-52. *Projet d'un traité de commerce et de navigation entre Sa Majesté le Roi des Deux Sicilies, et Sa Majesté l'Imperatrice de toutes les Russies* (1785), Manuscript kept in the Biblioteca Società Napoletana di Storia Patria, XXX. A. 15: folios 27r–34r [29–43].

Galiani, F. MS-53. *Riflessioni sul controprogetto del Duca di Serracapriola*, Manuscript kept in the Biblioteca Società Napoletana di Storia Patria, XXX. A. 15: folios 35–69bis [45–116].

Galiani, F. MS-54. *Sui contratti a voce.* Confutazione della teoria di Odazi. Manuscript kept in the Biblioteca Società Napoletana di Storia Patria, XXXI.A.10.10, folios 64r–65v.

Spinola, C. MS. *Progetto di economie varie sopra tributi e imposizioni, imposte o da imporsi nel Regno di Napoli,* manuscript kept in the National Library Vittorio Emanuele III in Naples (coll. XI.E.31).

Valletta, G. MS. *Risposta ad un Amico sopra le Ragioni della Città di Napoli per l'Assistenze domandate alla Fabrica della Nuova Moneta del Dottor Giuseppe Valletta*, manuscript kept in the Biblioteca Oratoriana dei Gerolamini in Naples (coll. MS. XXVIII.2.43, folios 225–261).

Valletta, G. MS-1. *Al nostro Santissimo Padre Innocentio duodecimo intorno al Procedimento ordinario e canonico nelle cause che si trattano nel tribunale del S. Officio nella Città e Regno di Napoli*, manuscript kept in the Biblioteca Nazionale di Napoli, MSS. XI. C. 10.

Primary Sources

Abbé de Saint-Pierre, C. I. Castel de. (1733). Discours contre l'augmentation des monnoyes et en faveur des annuitez. In *Ouvrage politique par M. l'Abbé de Saint Pierre*, Rotterdam: Jean Daniel Beman, Tome II: 199–230.

Abeille, L.-P. (1760). *Corps d'observations de la societe d'agriculture, de commerce et des arts établie par les États de Bretagne*, Rennes: Jacques Vatar.

Abeille, L.-P. (1763). *Lettre d'un négociant sur la nature du commerce des grains*, s.l: sn.

Abeille, L.-P. (1764). *Réflexions sur la police des grains en France et en Angleterre*, s.l: sn.

Abeille, L.-P. (1768). *Principes sur la liberté du commerce des grains.* Amsterdam [but Paris]: Desaint.

Accademici Ercolanesi. (1757). *Le pitture antiche di Ercolano e contorni incise con qualche spiegazione*, tomo I. Naples: Regia Stamperia.

Anonimo. (1783). *Lettera scritta ad un amico sul contratto detto alla Voce.* Naples: s.n.

Antonino of Florence. (1485). *Summa Theologiae Moralis.* Venice: Andreas de Paltasichis.

Argelati, F. (ed.). (1750). *De monetis Italiae variorum illustrium virorum dissertationes, quarum pars nunc primum in lucem prodit.* Milan: in regia Curia ex Aedibus Palatinis.

Aristotle. [1993]. *Posterior Analytics,* translated by J. Barnes, Oxford: Claredon Press.

Aristotle. [1998]. *Politics.* Translated, with introduction and notes, by CDC. Reeve, Indianapolis: Hackett Publishing Company.

Aristotle. [2004]. *Nicomachean Ethics.* Translated and edited by R. Crisp, Cambridge: Cambridge University Press.

Augustine of Hippo. [1972]. *City of God,* London: Penguin.

Ballerini, P. (1744). *La dottrina della Chiesa Cattolica circa l'usura dichiarata e dimostrata contro le pretese della novella opera intitolata Dell'impiego del denaro libri tre.* Bologna: Tommaso Colli.

Barbieri, M. (1778). *Notizie istoriche dei mattematici e filosofi del Regno di Napoli.* Naples: Vocola.

Basile, G.B. (1674). *Il pentamerone del cavalier Giovan Battista Basile, overo Lo cunto de li cunte trattenemiento de li peccerille di Gian Alesio Abbattutis.* Naples: Bulifon.

Baudeau, N. (1768). *Avis au peuple sur son premier besoin, ou Petits traités économiques.* Amsterdam: Hochereau.

Baudeau, N. (1769). Lettres de M. l'abbé Baudeau, prevot mitré de Widzyniski, à M. l'abbé G.•••, sur ses Dialogues anti-économistes, *Éphémérides du citoyen ou Bibliothèque raisonnée des sciences morales et politiques,*Tome XII. Paris: Lacombre, pp. 108–128.

Baudeau, N. (1770). *Lettres d'un Amateur à M. l'abbé G***, sur ses Dialogues anti-économistes.* Paris: Lacombe.

Baudeau, N. (1775). *Eclaircissements demandés à M. N** [Necker], Sur ses Principes Economiques, & sur ses projets de législation; Au nom des Propriétaires fonciers & des Cultivateurs François. Extrait des Nouvelles Éphémérides Économiques.* Paris: Didot.

Beauzée, N. (1765). Langue. In *Encyclopédie, ou dictionnaire raisonné des sciences, des arts et des métiers,* Tome IX, Neufchastel [but Paris]: Samuel Faulche, pp. 149–266. English Translation *The Encyclopedia of Diderot & d'Alembert Collaborative Translation Project.* Translated by Julia Wallhager. Ann Arbor: Michigan Publishing, University of Michigan Library, 2015 (reference on line).

Beccaria Bonesana, C. (1804). Elementi di economia pubblica. in *Scrittori classici italiani di economia politica.* Parte Moderna, Tomo XI, edited by P. Custodi. Milan: Destefanis.

Bellitti, G. (1771). *Sul contratto detto alla voce.* Naples: s.n.

Belloni, G. (1750). *Del commercio dissertazione del sig. marchese Girolamo Belloni.* Rome: Pagliarini.

Benedict XIV. (1746). *Bullarium*, vol. 1. Rome: Typ. de Propaganda Fide, pp. 578–581.

Bernoulli, D. (1738) [1954]. Specimen Theoriae Novae de Mensura Sortis. *Commentarii Academiae Scientiarum Imperialis Petropolitanae*, Tomus V, pp. 175–192, published as Exposition of a New Theory on the Measurement of Risk, *Econometrica*, 1954, vol. 22, n. 1, pp. 23–36.

Bernoulli, J. (1713). *Ars conjectandi, opus posthumum. Accedit Tractatus de seriebus infinitis, et epistola gallicé scripta de ludo pilae reticularis,* Basel: Impensis Thurnisiorum, fratrum.

Biblia, F. (1621). *Discorso sopra l'Aggiustamento della Moneta e Cambii del Regno di Napoli. D'ordine dell'Ill.mo e R.mo Signor Cardinal Zapata Luogotenente e Capitan Generale per Sua Maestà in questo Regno di Napoli*, Naples: s.n.

Biel, G. (1583). *De monetarum potestate simul et utilitate libellus*, in *Tractatus varii atque utiles de monetis earumque mutatione ac falsitate in gratiam studiosorum ac practicorum collecti.* Coloniae Agrippinae: Apud Theodorum Baunium.

Biscardi, S. [1993]. *Idea del governo politico ed economico del regno di Napoli*, in D. Luongo (ed.), *Mediazione ministeriale e ideologia economica*. Naples: Jovane.

Boccaccio, G. [2003]. *The Decameron*, Translated with an Introduction and Notes by G. H. McWilliam. New York: Penguin.

Boisguilbert, P. Le Pesant De. (1696) [1843]. *Le Détail de la France, la cause de la diminution de ses biens et la facilité du remède en fournissant en un mois tout l'argent dont le Roi a besoin et enrichissant tout le monde*, in E. Daire (ed.). Économistes financiers du XVIII siècle, tome I. Paris: Guillamine, 1843, pp. 171–266.

Boisguilbert, P. Le Pesant De. (1705) [1843]. *Le Factum de la France ou moyen très facile de faire recevoir au roi quatre-vingt millions par-dessus la capitation, praticables par deux heures de travail de Messieurs les Ministres et un mois d'exécution de la part des peoples.* In E. Daire (ed.). *Économistes financiers du XVIII siècle*, tome I, Paris: Guillamine, 1843, pp. 260–351.

Boisguilbert, P. Le Pesant De. (1707a) [1843]. *Dissertation sur la nature des richesses, de l'argent et des tributs: ou l'on decouvre la fausse idée qui règne dans le monde à l'égard de ces trois articles*, [S.l.]. In E. Daire (ed,) Économistes financiers du XVIII siècle, tome I, Paris: Guillamine, 1843, pp. 394–424.

Boisguilbert, P. Le Pesant De. (1707b) [1843]. *Traité de la nature, culture, commerce et intérêt des grains: tant par rapport au public, qu'a toutes les conditions d'un état*, [S.l.]. In E. Daire, (ed,) Économistes financiers du XVIII siècle, tome I, Paris, Guillamine, 1843, pp. 359–389.

Boulanger, N. (1766). *L'Antiquité dévoilée par ses usages, ou Examen critique des principales opinions, cérémonies, institutions religieuses & politiques des différens peuples de la terre.* Amsterdam: chez Marc Michel.

Boucher d'Argis, A.-G. (1765). Opinion. In *Encyclopédie, ou dictionnaire raisonné des sciences, des arts et des métiers*, Tome XI. Neufchastel [but Paris]: Samuel Faulche, pp. 706–707.

Broedersen, N. (1743). De usuris licitis et illicitis vulgo nunc compensatoriis et lucratoriis secundum jus naturale, divinum Veteris atque Novi Testamenti, ecclesiasticum et civile [...] Libri XII. Haag: Gosse.

Broggia, C. A. (1743). *Trattato de' tributi, delle monete e del governo politico della sanità. Opera di stato, e di commercio, di polizia e di finanza: molto, alla felicità de' popoli, alla robustezza degli stati, ed alla gloria e possanza maggiore de' principi, conferente e necessaria*. Naples: Pietro Palombo.

Broggia, C. A. (1754). *Memoria ad oggetto di varie politiche ed economiche ragioni e temi di utili raccordi che in causa del monetaggio di Napoli s'espongono e propongono agli spettabili signori, convocati di real ordine dall'illustre marchese di Vallesantoro Segretario di Stato della Reale Azienda. E incidentalmente con quest'occasione si risolve la sì difficile e strepitosa controversia sulla ricompra delle pubbliche entrate, o siano arrendamenti, alienati col patto di non ricomprare: così detto dazione in solutum. Si ragiona del censimento, o sia catasto, proponendosi il modo di farlo col desiato frutto e senza intoppi. E s'espone il saggio, o sia l'idea di sette utili trattati, da pubblicarsi. De' quali nella qui addietro pagina si contiene il titolo, 15 febbraio 1754*. Naples: s.n.

Broggia, C. A. (1755). *Risposte alle obiezzioni state fatte da varj soggetti intorno al sistema del prezzo corrente, che assolutamente dee tenersi per la ricompera degli arrendamenti e similmente a quelle state anche fatte intorno alla rinovazione della moneta di rame che dee anch'essa avere tutto quel valore intrinseco che di giustizia gli spetta; e tanta farsene, che non ecceda il puro bisogno degli scambj minuti. Da umiliarsi a Sua Maestà che Dio sempre guardi, e feliciti di Carlo Antonio Broggia, a dì 14 novembre 1755*. Naples: s.n.

Broggia, C. A. (1978). Lettere a Muratori e Fontanesi. In R. Ajello, (ed.) *La letteratura italiana. Storia e testi. Dal Muratori al Cesarotti. Politici ed economisti del primo Settecento*, vol. 44, tomo V. Milan-Naples: Ricciardi, pp. 1100–1155.

Broggia, C. A. [2004]. *Il Banco ed il Monte de' pegni. Del lusso*, with the introducion by De Rosa, L. and Graziani, A., edited by R. Patalano. Naples: La Città del Sole.

Bruno, A. (1584). *Tractatus de augmento et diminutione monetarum*, in *Tractatus illustrium in utraque tum pontificii tum caesarei jurisfacultate juriscultorum*. Venetiis: s.n.

Buffon, G.-L. Leclerc de. (1766). *Histoire naturelle, générale et particulière avec la description du cabinet du roi*, tome XIV. Paris: Imprimerie royale.

Calmet, A. A. (1734). *Disquisitiones de monetae signatae, vetustatae*, in *Prolegomena et dissertationes in omnes et singulos Sacrae Scripturae libros*. Venice: apud Christophorum Zane.

Campanella, T. (1608) [1973]. Arbitrii sopra l'aumento dell'entrate del Regno. In *Problemi monetari negli scrittori napoletani del Seicento*, edited by R. Colapietra, pp. 85–110. Rome: Accademia Nazionale dei Lincei.

Cantillon, R. (1755) [2010]. *Essai sur la nature du commerce en général. Traduit de l'anglois*, London: Fletcher Gyles. English Translation: *An Essay on Economic Theory*, Translated by C. Saucier, edited by M. Thornton. Auburn: Ludwig von Mises Institute.

Capello, P. G. (1752). *Nuovo trattato del modo di regolare la moneta*. Venice: Baseggio.

Caracciolo, D. (1785). *Riflessioni su l'economia e l'estrazione dei frumenti della Sicilia fatte in occasione delle carestia dell'indizione terza 1784 e 1785*. Palermo: Stamperia Reale.

Carafa, G. duca di Noja. (1750). *Lettera ad un amico contenente alcune considerazioni sull'utilità, e gloria, che si trarrebbe da una esatta carta topografica della città di Napoli, e del suo contado*. Naples: s.n.

Caravelli, V., Porto, V. (1786). *Trattati del calcolo differenziale di Vito Caravelli, e del calcolo integrale di Vincenzo Porto per uso del regale collegio militare*. Naples: Raimondi.

Carli, G. R. (1751). *Dell'origine e del commercio della moneta e dell'instituzione delle zecche d'Italia dalla decadenza dell'impero sino al secolo decimo settimo*. All'Haja [The Hague, but Venice]: s.n.

Carli, G.R. (1784). *Opere*, tomo II. Milan: Monastero di Sant'Ambrogio.

Cary, J. (1755). *Essai sur l'état du commerce d'Angleterre, tomes 2*, Londres-Paris. Nyon-Vailant.

Cary, J. (1757). *Storia del commercio della Gran Brettagna scritta da John Cary con un ragionamento sul commercio in universale, e alcune annotazioni riguardanti l'economia del nostro regno*, edited by Genovesi A., vol. I. Naples: Benedetto Gessari.

Casanova, G. (2006). *History of My Life*, first translated into english in accordance with the original french manuscript by W. R. Trask. New York: Everyman's Library.

Castiglione, B. (1528). *Il libro del Cortegiano*. Venice: Aldo Romano & d'Andrea d'Asola

Catherine II, and Grimm, F. M. (2016). *Une correspondance privée, artistique et politique au siècle des Lumières*, tome I, 1764–1778, edited by S. Karp. Moscow: Monuments de la pensée historique.

Child, J. (1754). *Traités sur le commerce et les avantages qui résultent de l'intérêt de l'argent. Avec un petit Traité contre l'usure par Thomas Culpeper*. Amsterdam-Berlin: Jean Neaulme.

Cicero, M. T. [1991], *On Duties* [*De Officis*]. English Transation edited by Atkins, E. M.; Griffin, M. T. Cambridge: Cambridge University Press

Concina, D. (1746). *Esposizione del dogma che la chiesa romana propone a credersi intorno l'usura colla confutazione del libro intitolato Dell'impiego del danaro.* Naples: Pietro Palumbo.

Condillac, E. Bonnot de. (1776). *Le commerce et le gouvernement, considérés relativement l'un à l'autre: Ouvrage élémentaire.* Amsterdam: chez Jombert & Cellot.

Condorcet, M. J. A. N. de Caritat. (1774). *Lettres sur le commerce des grains.* Paris: Couturier Père.

Condorcet, M. J. A. N. de Caritat. (1776). *Réflexions sur le commerce des bleds,* Londres [Genève]: s.n.

Condorcet, M. J. A. N. de Caritat. (1793) [1994]. *Tableau général de la science qui a pour objet l'application du calcul aux sciences politiques et morales.* English translation: *Foundations of Social Choice and Political Theory.* Translated and edited by I. McLean and F. Ewitt. Cheltenham: Edward Elgar Publishing.

Correspondance littéraire. (1879). *Correspondance, littéraire, philosophique et critique par Grimm, Diderot, Raynal, Meister, etc: revue sur les textes originaux.* Paris: Garnier.

Costantini, G. (1751). *Delle monete in senso pratico, e morale. Ragionamento diviso in sette capitoli, dedicato a quelli, che prender si vorranno la pena di leggerlo.* Venice: Occhi.

Costantini, G. (1753). *Caso di monete imprestate. Dialogo.* Venice: Bertoli.

Costantini, G. (1754) (ed.). *Delle monete, controversia agitata tra due celebri scrittori oltramontani, i signori Melon, e Du Tot.* Venice: Zatta.

Covarrubias y Leuva, D. (1556). *Veterum collatio numismatum, cum his quae modo exendutur.* Salamaca: apud Iunt. Granatae.

Cujas, J. (1618). *Iacobi Cujacii Observationum libri XIX.* Lutetiae Parisiorum: s.n.

d'Alembert, J-B. Le Rond. (1743). *Traité de dynamique.* Paris: David.

d'Alembert, J-B. Le Rond. (1751) [1995]. Discours préliminaire des Éditeurs. In *Encyclopédie, ou dictionnaire raisonné des sciences, des arts et des métiers,* tome I. Paris: Briasson, David l'aîné, Le Breton, Imprimeur ordinaire du Roy, Durand, pp. i–xlv. English Translation: *Preliminary Discourse to the Encyclopaedia of Diderot,* translated by R. N. Schwab with the collaboration of W. E. Rex. Chicago: University of Chicago Press.

D'Andrea, F. (1667). *Risposta al trattato delle ragioni della Regina Cristianissima, sopra il Ducato di Brabante, et altri stati della Fiandra. Nella quale si dimostra l'ingiustizia della guerra mossa dal Re di Francia, per la conquista di quelle provincie; non ostante le ragioni, che si son pubblicate in suo nome, per la pretesa successione a favor della Regina Cristianissima.* Naples: s.n.

D'Andrea, F. (1696a) [1919]. Avvertimenti ai nipoti, *Archivio Storico per le Provincie Napoletane,* vol. 44, pp. 227–290, republished in N. Cortese (ed.) *I ricordi di un avvocato napoletano del Seicento: Francesco D'Andrea,* Naples: Lubrano, 1923.

D'Andrea, F. (1696b) [1990]. *Avvertimenti ai nipoti*, Ascione, I. (ed.). Naples: Jovene, 1990.

D'Argenson, R. L. de Voyer de Paulmy. (1751). Lettre à l'auteur du Journal œconomique au sujet de la Dissertation sur le commerce de M. le Marquis Belloni, *Journal Œconomique*, April 1751, pp. 107–117.

Dampier, W. (1697). *A New Voyage Round the World*. London: James Knapton.

Davanzati, B. (1582) [1804]. *Notizia de' cambj*, in *Scrittori classici italiani di Economia Politica*, Parte antica, Tomo II, Milan: De Stefanis, 1804.

Davanzati, B. (1588) [1804]. *Lezione delle monete*, Firenze, in *Scrittori classici italiani di Economia Politica*, Parte antica, Tomo II. Milan: De Stefanis, 1804.

Davanzati, B. (1696). *Discours Upon Coins, by Signor Bernardo Davanzati, A Gentleman of Florence*. London: Printed Awnsham and Churchill.

De Benedictis, G. B (pseudonym Benedetto Aletino). (1694). *Lettere apologetiche in difesa della teologia scolastica e della filosofia peripatetica*. Naples: Raillard.

Della Casa, G. (1558). *Il Galateo overo de' costumi. Trattato di messer Giovanni della Casa, nel quale sotto la persona d'un vecchio idiota ammaestrante un suo giovanetto, si ragiona de modi, che si debbono o tenere, o schifare nella comune conversatione, cognominato Galatheo overo de costumi*. Venice: Bevilacqua.

d'Épinay, L. (1774). *Les Conversations d'Émilie*. Paris: chez Pissot.

d'Épinay, L., Galiani, F. (1996). *Epistolario 1769–1782*, edited by S.Rapisarda. Palermo: Sellerio.

De Santis, M.A. (1605a). *Discorso di Marc'Antonio De Santis intorno alli effetti, che fa il cambio in Regno*. Naples: Costantino Vitali.

De Santis, M.A. (1605b). *Secondo Discorso di Marc'Antonio De Santis intorno alli effetti, che fa il cambio in Regno, sopra una risposta, che è stata fatta adverso del primo*. Naples: Felice Stigliola.

Deschamps, F.-M.-C., Paris-Duverney, J. (1740). *Examen du Livre intitulé: Réflexions politiques sur les finances et le commerce*. La Haie: Vaillant & Prevôt.

De Tilladet de La Marque, J.-M. (1718). Sur les géants. *Histoire de l'Académie royale des inscriptions et belles-lettres: depuis son établissement jusqu'a present*, vol. 1. La Haye: chez la veuve d'Abr. Troyel, pp. 158–163.

De Vattel, E. (1758). *Le droit des gens ou Principes de la loi naturelle appliqués à la conduite et aux affaires des nations et des souverains*. London: s.n.

D'Holbach, Thiry P. (1766). *Le Christianisme dévoilé ou Examen des principes et des effets de la religion chrétienne*. Londres: s.n.

D'Holbach, Thiry P. (1770) [1889]. *Système de la nature, ou Des loix du monde physique et du monde moral*, London: s.n. English translation, *The System of Nature*. Boston: Mendun, 1889.

Diderot, D. (1755) [2002]. Encyclopédie. In *Encyclopédie, ou dictionnaire raisonné des sciences, des arts et des métiers*, tome V. Paris: Briasson, David l'aîné, Le Breton, Imprimeur ordinaire du Roy, Durand, pp. 635–648. English Translation in *The Encyclopedia of Diderot & d'Alembert Collaborative Translation Project*.

Translated by P. Stewart. Ann Arbor: Michigan Publishing, University of Michigan Library, 2002. On Line: http://hdl.handle.net/2027/spo.did2222.0000.004.

Diderot, D. (1770) [1963]. Apologie de l'abbé Galiani. In D. Diderot, *Œuvres politiques*, edited by P. Vernière, Paris: Garnier, pp. 59–124.

Diderot, D. (1875a). Lettre à M. l'abbé Galiani sur le sixième ode du troisième livre d'Horace. In J. Assézat (ed.), *Œuvres Complètes de Diderot revues sur les éditions originals comprenant ce qui a été publié a diverses époques et les manuscrits inédits conserves à la bibliothèque de l'ermitage. notices, notes., table analytique étude sur Diderot et le mouvement philosophique au XVIII siècle*, Tome VI. Paris: Garnier, pp. 289–302.

Diderot, D. (1875b). Sur les femmes. In *Œuvres Complètes de Diderot revues sur les éditions originals comprenant ce qui a été publié a diverses époques et les manuscrits inédits conserves à la bibliothèque de l'ermitage. notices, notes., table analytique étude sur Diderot et le mouvement philosophique au XVIII siècle*, Tome II. Paris: Garnier, pp. 251–262.

Diderot, D. (1950). *Lettres à Sophie Volland*, edited by A. Babelon, 14th édition, 2 vols. Paris: Gallimard.

Diderot, D. (1955). *Correspondence*, edited by G. Roth, 13 vols. Paris: Editions de minuit.

Di Gennaro, G. A. (1748). *Delle viziose maniere del difender le cause nel foro trattato di Giuseppe Aurelio Di Gennaro. Con una prefazione in cui si tratta dell'origine, e progressi dell'avvocazione, distesa da Giannantonio Sergio avvocato napoletano*, Venice: Bortoli.

Diodati, L. (1788). *Vita dell'abate Ferdinando Galiani.* Naples: Orsino.

Diodati, L. (1790). *Dello stato presente della moneta nel regno di Napoli, e della necessità di un alzamento libri due.* Naples: Michele Migliaccio.

D'Onofrio, V. (pseudonym Innocenzo Fuidoro). (1653?) [1932] *Successi del governo del Conte d'Oñatte 1648–1653.* Naples: Lubrano.

Doria, P. M. (1709). *La vita civile, e l'educazione del principe di P. M. Doria.* Francfort [but Naples]: s.n.

Doria, P. M. (1710a). *La vita civile di P. M. Doria, distinta in tre parti, aggiuntovi un trattato della educazione del principe. Seconda edizione dall'Autore ricorretta, ed accresciuta.* Augusta: Höpper.

Doria, P. M. (1710b) [1973], *Massime generali e particolare colle quali di tempo in tempo hanno gli Spagnoli governato il Regno di Napoli*, edited by V. Conti, with an introduction by G. Galasso. Naples: Guida (an earlier publication of excerpts from the Report is due to M. Schipa, with the title "Il Regno di Napoli descritto nel 1713 da P. M. Doria", *Archivio storico delle province napoletane*, 1899, fasc. I, pp. 25–84 e fasc. II pp. 329–350).

Doria, P. M. (1710c) [1981], "Relazione dello stato politico, economico e civile del regno di Napoli nel tempo ch'è stato governato dai Spagnuoli, prima dell'entrata dell'armi tedesche in detto regno", in *Manoscritti napoletani di Paolo Mattia Doria*. Galatina: Congedo, vol. 1, pp. 49–139.

Doria, P. M. (1715). *Nuovo metodo geometrico per trovare fra due linee rette date infinite medie continue proporzionali*. Antwerp: Cristoforo Plantini.

Doria, P. M. (1721). *Dissertazione di Paolo-Mattia Doria intorno alla nuova geometria di Cartesio: Con una Raccolta di tutte le dimostrazioni, e considerazionni dell' autore, pubblicate in varij tempi, ed in varie lettere, a fine di dimostrare geometricamente, che la parabola Apolloniana non hà le proprietà, che da geometri se l'assegnano*. Venice: s.n.

Doria, P. M. (1722). *Delle opere matematiche di Paolo Mattia Doria*. Venice: s.n.

Doria, P. M. (1724). *Discorsi Critici Filosofici intorno alla Filosofia degl'Antichi e de i Moderni; ed in particolare intorno alla Filosofia di Renato Des-Cartes. Con un progetto di una Metafisica*. Venice: s.n.

Doria, P. M. (1726). Delle opere matematiche: Considerazione, dissertazioni, ed esercitazioni geometriche, Naples: s.n.

Doria, P. M. (1728). *Filosofia di P, M Doria, con la quale si schiarisce quella di Platone; Dedicata all'Altezza Reale di Carlo Emanuele Principe di Piemonte. Volume primo continente le Nozioni di Logica, e le parti I. II. e III. della Metafisica [e] Volume secondo continente la Parte IV. della Morale, e le Parti V. e VI. della Morale Teorica e Pratica*. Amsterdam, [but Geneva: Stamperia del Tournes].

Doria, P. M. (1729). *La vita civile di P. M. Doria, con un trattato della educazione del principe. Terza impressione, dall'Autore ricorretta, e di molte aggiunzioni adornata*. Naples: Vocola.

Doria, P.M. (1732). *Difesa della metafisica degli antichi filosofi contro il Signor Giovanni Locke, ed alcuni altri moderni autori di P. M. Doria. Divisa in due parti*. Venice: s.n.

Doria, P. M. (1738) [1981]. Considerazioni Geometriche, Logiche e Metafisiche sopra li Elementi di Euclide, fatte a fine di prima disciplinare la mente umana nella sola vera ed unica Logica; secondo per unire nella mente umana la geometria e la logica alla metafisica, e per terzo ed ultimo per insegnare a dedurre dalle idee universali le proprietà particolari delle cose appartenenti alla fisica e alla Meccanica. In A. Spedicati (ed.), *Manoscritti napoletani di Paolo Mattia Doria*. Galatina: Congedo, 1981, vol. 3, pp. 1–20.

Doria, P. M. (1739). *Il Capitano filosofo*, Naples: Angelo Vocola

Doria, P. M. (1740a). *La vita civile di P. M. Doria, con un trattato della educazione del principe, quarta impressione*. Naples: Vocola.

Doria, P. M. (1740b) [1981]. Del commercio del regno di Napoli. Con l'aggiunta di un'Appendice, Nel quale s'indagano le cagioni generali e particolari, dalle quali il buono, e retto Commercio trae la sua origine; E si fà vedere il rapporto che il perfetto Commercio deve avere con gli altri Ordini, de' quali la Repubblica si compone. Lettera diretta al Signor D. Francesco Ventura, Degnissimo

Presidente del Magistrato di Commercio. In G. Belgioioso (ed.), *Manoscritti napoletani di Paolo Mattia Doria*. Galatina: Congedo, 1981, vol 1, pp. 141–208.

Doria, P. M. (1753). *La vita civile di P. M. Doria, con un trattato della educazione del principe. Quinta impressione, dall'autore ricorretta, e di molte aggiunzioni adornata*. Naples: Vocola.

Doria, P. M. (1981). L'Arte di conoscere sé stesso, composto per l'amico Birago di Borgaro. In *Manoscritti napoletani di Paolo Mattia Doria*, P. De Fabrizio (ed.). Galatina: Congedo, vol. IV, pp. 411–431.

Duhamel du Monceau, H. L. (1753). *Traité de la Conservation des Grains et en particulier du Froment*. Paris: Guérin & Delatour.

Dupin, C. (1748). *Mémoire sur les blés, avec un projet d'édit pour maintenir en tout temps la valeur des grains à un prix convenable au vendeur et à l'acheteur*. Paris: s.n.

Dupont de Nemours, P. S. (1768a). *Physiocratie, ou Constitution naturelle du gouvernement le plus avantageux au genre humain*. Paris: Merlin.

Dupont de Nemours, P. S. (1768b). *De l'origine et des progrès d'une science nouvelle*. Paris: Chez Desaint.

Dupont de Nemours, P. S. (1770a). Avvertissement contenant le Table raisonnée des matières traitées dans les volumes de l'année précédente, *Éphémérides du citoyen ou Bibliothèque raisonnée des sciences morales et politiques*, Tome XI. Paris: Lacombre, pp. 5–111.

Dupont de Nemours, P. S. (1770b). *Observations sur les eff ets de la liberti du commerce des grains et sur ceux des prohibitions*. Baste-Paris: s.n.

Dutot, N. (1738). *Réflexions politiques sur les finances et le commerce*. La Haye: Vaillant-Prevost.

Encyclopédie. (1765). *Encyclopédie, ou dictionnaire raisonné des sciences, des arts et des métiers*, Tome X. Neufchastel [but Paris]: Samuel Faulche.

Enríquez de Fonseca, L. (1681a) [1973]. *Discurso en orden a que à la moneda de vellon se disponga modo de uso por el qual sea mejor para los commercios que la moneda de plata*. Naples: Salvador Castaldo, Italian translation in R. Colapietra (ed.) *Problemi monetari negli scrittori napoletani del Seicento*. Rome: Accademia Nazionale dei Lincei, 1973, pp. 457–490.

Enríquez de Fonseca, L. (1681b) [1973]. *Tratado y discurso sobre la moneda de el Reyno de Napoles. Su estado, el origen de sus daños, el remedio para su consummo*. Naples: Salvador Castaldo. Italian translation in R. Colapietra (ed.) *Problemi monetari negli scrittori napoletani del Seicento*. Rome: Accademia Nazionale dei Lincei, 1973, pp. 491–500.

Éphémérides. (1769a). Discussions qui surviennent et qui assurent les succèss de la verité. *Éphémérides du citoyen ou Bibliothèque raisonnée des sciences morales et politiques*, Tome V. Paris: Lacombre, pp. 132–133.

Éphémérides. (1769b). Supplement a l'article des critiques raisonnées, *Éphémérides du citoyen ou Bibliothèque raisonnée des sciences morales et politiques*, Tome XI. Paris: Lacombre, pp. 193–247.

Éphémérides. (1769c). Le bal de l'Opèra. Fable, par M. T. *Éphémérides du citoyen ou Bibliothèque raisonnée des sciences morales et politiques*, Tome XII. Paris: Lacombre, pp. 99–106.

Euler, L. (1748). *Introductio in Analys in Infinitorum*. Lausannae: apud Marcum Michaelem Bousquet et socios.

Fabrini, G. (1750). *Dell'indole e qualità naturali e civili della moneta e de' principi istorici e naturali de' contratti. Dissertazioni*. Rome: Pagliarini.

Fasano, T. (1765). *Della febbre epidemica sofferta in Napoli l'anno 1764. Libri 3*. Naples: Raimondi.

Favre, A., Fabri, A. (1598). *Tractatus de variis nummariorum debitorum solutionibus* [...] *adversus Carolum Molinaeum: ejusdem disputatio de patrui hereditate inter solos fratrum filios, utrum in capita an in stirpes dividenda*, s.l: s.n.

Filangieri, G. (1780). *La Scienza della Legislazione*, Tomo II. Naples: Stamperia Raimondiana.

Filangieri, G. (1784). *La Scienza della Legislazione*, edizione prima veneta, Tomo IV. Venice: Giovanni Vitto.

Forbonnais, Véron de F. L. (1754). *Eléments du commerce*, Leyde [but Paris]: Briasson-David l'aîné-Le Breton-Durand.

Forbonnais, Véron de F. L. (1755). Espèces. In *Encyclopédie, ou dictionnaire raisonné des sciences, des arts et des métiers*, Tome V. Paris: Briasson, David l'aîné, Le Breton, Imprimeur ordinaire du Roy, Durand, pp. 957–970.

Forbonnais, Véron de F. L. (1758). *Recherches et considerations sur les finances de France*. Basel: s.n.

Forbonnais, Véron de, F. L. (1767). *Principes et observations oeconomiques*. Amsterdam: Rey.

Frisi, P. (1775). *Elogio del Galileo*. Milan: Agnelli.

Galanti, G. M. (1783). *Elogio storico del signor abate Antonio Genovesi pubblico professore di civil economia nell'Università di Napoli. Terza edizione notabilmente migliorata e corretta, ed accresciuta dell'elogio del signor Bartolomeo Intieri e di una lettera intorno al plagio letterario*. Florence: Pisoni.

Galanti G. M. (1786). *Nuova Descrizione Storica e geografica delle Sicilie dell'avvocato Giuseppe M.a Galanti tomo I*. Naples: Gabinetto Letterario.

Galanti G. M. (1788). *Nuova Descrizione Storica e geografica delle Sicilie dell'avvocato Giuseppe M.a Galanti tomo II*. Naples: Gabinetto Letterario.

Galanti G. M. (1997). Memorie storiche del mio tempo. In F. Venturi, (ed.), *Illuministi italiani*, vol. II, Tomo II. Milan: Ricciardi-Mondadori, pp. 988–1020.

Galiani, F. (1748) [1963]. *Sullo stato della moneta ai tempi della guerra troiana*, Manuscript kept in the Biblioteca Società Napoletana di Storia Patria, XXXI A. 9.09, folios 155–182v, published in Galiani, 1963, pp. 351–379.

Galiani, F. [1751] [published anonymous, with date of 1750]. *Della moneta. Libri cinque*. Naples: Giuseppe Raimond.

Galiani, F. (1758). *Delle lodi di papa Benedetto XIV. Orazione.* Naples: Giuseppe Raimondi.

Galiani, F. (1759) [1825]. *Orazione recitata in una assemblea nel capo dell'anno 1759 in occasione di tirare a sorte i cicisbei e le cicisbee.* Naples: Seguin.

Galiani, F. (1770a). *Dialogues sur le commerce des bleds.* London [but Paris]: Merlin.

Galiani, F. (1770b) [1979]. *L'intérêt géneral de l'État ou La liberté du commerce des bleds démontrée conforme au droit naturel; au droit public de la France; aux lois fondamentales du Royaume; à l'intérêt commun du souverain et de ses sujets dans tous les temps; avec la réfutation d'un nouveau système de bagarre publié en forme de feu d'artifice, par M.L.A.R. economiste indigne*, in *La Bagarre: Galiani's Lost Parody*, edited by S. L. Kaplan. The Hague: Martinus Nijhoff, pp. 65–116.

Galiani, F. (1772). *Catalogo delle materie appartenenti al Vesuvio contenute nel Museo, con alcune brevi osservazioni. Opera del celebre autore de' Dialoghi sul commercio de' grani.* London [but Florence]: s.n.

Galiani, F. (1775). *Diàlogos sobre el comercio de trigo, atribuidos al Abate Galiani.* Madrid: Joachin Ibarra.

Galiani, F. (1776). *Razgovory o chlebnom torge s francyskago perevedeny Petrom Kjuvil'e.* Saint Peterburg: Imperatorskaya Akademiya Nauk.

Galiani, F. (1777). *Dialogen über die Regierungskunst vornemlich in Rucksicht auf den Getreydehandel.* Lemgo: Meyerschen Buchhandlung.

Galiani, F. (1778). *Handlungs-Dialogen von Herrn Abbé* [Ferdinando] *Galenti* [Galiani], translated by W Berisch. Lipsia: Wirthgen.

Galiani, F. (1779a). Osservazioni sopra il Vesuvio dell'abate Ferdinando Galiani. In *Dei vulcani e monti ignivomi più noti, e distintamente del Vesuvio, Osservazioni fisiche e notizie istoriche di uomini insigni di vari tempi, raccolte con diligenza e divise in due tomi.* Livorno: Calderon e Faine, Tomo I, pp. lxi–lxx, 1–149.

Galiani, F. (1779b). *Spaventosissima descrizione dello spaventoso spavento, che ci spaventò tutti, coll'eruzione del Vesuvio, la sera dell'otto agosto del corrente anno, ma (per grazia di Dio) durò poco, di d. Onofrio Galeota, poeta e filosofo all'impronto - Fratiè, non m'ammalì - Il Teatro de' Fiorentini nel corrente dramma.* Naples: Stampato a spese dell'autore, e si vende grana sei a chi lo va a comprare.

Galiani, F. (1779c). *Del Dialetto napoletano, Deus nobis haec otia fecit.* Naples: Mazzola Vocola.

Galiani, F. (1780). *Della moneta. Libri cinque. Edizione seconda.* Naples: Stamperia Simoniana.

Galiani, F. (1781). *Delle lodi di papa Benedetto XIV, Orazione dedicata a Sua Eccellenza reverendissima mons. Lazaro Opizio Pallavicino, arcivescovo di Lepanto e nunzio apostolico.* Naples: Stamperia Simoniana.

Galiani, F. (1782). *De' doveri de' principi neutrali verso i principi guerreggianti:e di questi verso i neutrali. Libre due.* Naples: s.n.

Galiani, F. [Galeota, Onofrio]. (1785). *Guazzabuglio filosarmonico o sia miscellaneo versoprosaico sulle probole, antiprobole ed aneddoto forense, di d. Onofrio Galeota, poeta e filosofo all'impronto.* Fantasianapoli [Naples]: s.n.

Galiani, F. (1789). *Vocabolario delle parole del dialetto napoletano che più si scostano dal dialetto toscano, con alcune ricerche etimologiche sulle medesime, degli Accademici [oscuri] Filopatridi. Opera postuma supplita ed accresciuta notabilmente.* Naples: Porcelli.

Galiani, F. (1790). *Recht der Neutralitaet. Oder: Von den gegenseitigen Pflichten neutraler und kriegfuehrender Maechte.* Leipzig: Georg Conrad Walthers Wittwe.

Galiani, F. (1818a). *Correspondance inédite de l'abbé Ferdinand Galiani, conseiller du Roi, pendant les années 1765 à 1783, avec Madame d'Épinay, le Baron d'Holbach, le Baron de Grimm, Diderot et autres personnages célèbres de ce temps; augmentée de plusiers lettres à Monseigneur Sanseverino, archevêque de Palerme, à M. le Marquis de Caraccioli, ambassadeur de Naples près la cour de France, à Voltaire, d'Alembert, Raynal, Marmontel, Thomas, Le Batteux, Madame du Bocage; précédée d'une notice historique sur l'abbé Galiani, par l'abbé Bart. Mercier de Saint Léger, bibliotethécaire de Sainte-Geneviève. A laquelle il a été ajoute diverses particularités inédites concernant la vie privée, les bons mots, le caractère original de l'auteur. Par M. C*** de S[t]M***. membre de plusieurs académies,* 2 voll., Paris: J. B. Dentu, imprimeur-libraire.

Galiani, F. (1818b). *Correspondance inédite de M. l'abbé Ferdinand Galiani, conseiller du Roi de Naples, avec Mme d'Épinay, le Baron d'Holbach, le Baron Grimm et autres personnages célèbres du XVIIIe siècle. Édition imprimée sur le manuscrit autographe de l'auteur, revue et accompagnée de notes, par M*** [A.-A. Barbier], membre de plusiers académies. Précédée d'une notice historique sur la vie et les ouvrages de l'Auteur, par feu Ginguené, avec des notes par M. Salfi, et du Dialogue de l'abbé Galiani sur les femmes.* Tome premier [-Tome second], 2 voll., Paris-Strasbourg-Londres: Treuttel et Würtz.

Galiani, F. (1821). *Oeuvres d'Horace, traduites par MM. Campenon et Després, accompagnées du Commentaire de l'abbé Galiani, précédées d'un essai sur la vie et les écrits d'Horace.* Paris: De Bure.

Galiani, F. (1881a). *Écrivains du XVIII siècle – Correspondance avec Madame d'Épinay, Madame Necker, Madame Geoffrin etc., Diderot, Grimm, d'Alembert, de Sartine, d'Holbach, etc. Nouvelle édition, entièrement rétablie d'après les textes originaux, augmentée de tous les passages supprimés et d'un grand nombre de lettres inédites, avec une étude sur sa vie et les oeuvres de Galiani,* edited by L. Perey, G. Maugras, 2 voll. Paris: Calmann Levy.

Galiani, F. (1881b). *Lettres du XVII et XVIII siècle – Lettres de l'Abbé Galiani à Madame d'Épinay, Voltaire, Diderot, Grimm, le Baron d'Holbach, Morellet, Suart (sic), d'Alembert, Marmontel, la Vicomtesse de Belsunce, etc. Publiées d'après les éditions originales augmentées des variantes, de nombreuses notes et*

d'un Index avec notice biographique, edited by E. Asse, 2 voll., Paris, G. Charpentier.
Galiani, F. (1903–1904). Dal carteggio dell'abate Galiani. Lettere inedite del d'Holbach, Diderot, Signora d'Épinay, *La Critica: rivista di letteratura, storia e filosofia*, vol. I, pp. 477–491; vol. II, pp. 73–84; 155–168; 503–517.
Galiani, F. (1909). Gli studi sopra Orazio. In Nicolini, 1909a, pp. 1–160.
Galiani, F. (1915). *Della Moneta*, edited by F. Nicolini. Bari: Laterza.
Galiani, F. (1955). *De La Monnaie. Traduit et analysé avec bibliographie, introduction et notes*, edited by G.-H. Bousquet, J. Crisafulli. Paris: Librairie Marcel Rivière.
Galiani, F. (1957). *Dialogo sulle donne e altri scritti di Ferdinando Galiani*, edited by C. Cases, Milan: Feltrinelli.
Galiani, F. (1959). *Dialogues sur le commerce des bleds. Giusta l'editio princeps del 1770 con appendici illustrative*, edited by F. Nicolini, Naples: Ricciardi
Galiani, F. (1963). *Della Moneta*, edited by A. Merola, with introduction of A. Caracciolo, Milan: Feltrinelli.
Galiani, F. (1968). *Dialogues entre M. Marquis de Roquemaure et M. le chevalier Zanobi. The autograph manuscript of the Dialogues sur le commerce des bleds diplomatically edited with introduction, notes and appendices by Philip Koch*, Analecta Romanica, Heft 21, Frankfurt am Main: Klostermann.
Galiani, F. (1975). *Opere di Ferdinando Galiani*, edited by F. Diaz e L. Guerci, in *Letteratura italiana. Storia e testi. Illuministi italiani*, tomo VI. Milan-Naples: Ricciardi.
Galiani, F. (1977). *On Money*. A Translation of Della Moneta by Ferdinado Galiani by Peter R. Toscano. Ann Arbor: University Microfilm International.
Galiani, F. (1978). L'Orazio dell'abate Galiani, in Nicolini, 1978, pp. 111–314.
Galiani, F. (1999). *Scritti di politica economica*, edited by F. Cesarano. Lanciano: Rocco Carabba.
Galiani, F. (2005). *De la Monnaie - Della Moneta*, édité et traduit sous la direction d'André Tiran, traduction coordonnée par Anne Machet. Paris: Economica
Galiani, F., Bottari, G.G. (1972). *Il carteggio Galiani-Bottari (1751–1759)*, edited by L. Felici. Rome: Fratelli Palombi.
Galiani, F., Carcani, P. (1749). *Componimentii varj per la morte di Domenico Iannaccone Carnefice della Gran Corte della Vicaria, raccolti e dati alla luce da Giannantonio Sergio Avvocato Napoletano*. Naples: s.n.
Galiani, F., Cerati, G. (2008). *Carteggio (1749–1758)*, edited by G. Nicoletti, Naples: Bibliopolis.
Galiani, F., d'Épinay, L. (1992). *Correspondance. Vol. I (1769–1770)*, présentation de G. Dulac, texte établi et annoté par D. Maggetti, en collaboration avec G. Dulac. Paris: Les Editions Desjonquères.
Galiani, F., d'Épinay, L. (1993). *Correspondance. Vol. II (1771–Février 1772)*, présentation de G. Dulac, texte établi et annoté par D. Maggetti, en collaboration avec G. Dulac. Paris: Les Editions Desjonquères.

Galiani, F., d'Épinay, L. (1994). *Correspondance. Vol. III (Mars 1772–Mai 1773)*, présentation de G. Dulac, texte établi et annoté par D. Maggetti, en collaboration avec G. Dulac. Paris: Les Editions Desjonquères.

Galiani, F., d'Épinay, L. (1996). *Correspondance. Vol. IV (Juin 1773–Mai 1775)*, présentation de Georges Dulac, texte établi et annoté par Daniel Maggetti, en collaboration avec Georges Dulac, Paris: Les Editions Desjonquères.

Galiani, F., d'Épinay, L. (1997). *Correspondance. Vol. V (June 1775–Juillet 1782)*, présentation de G. Dulac, texte établi et annoté par D. Maggetti, en collaboration avec G. Dulac. Paris: Les Editions Desjonquères.

Galiani, F., Lorenzi, G.B. (1775). *Socrate immaginario. Commedia per musica rappresentata nel Teatro Nuovo sopra Toledo, nell'autunno dell'anno 1775, con musica del Signor Giovanni Paisiello*, Naples: s.n.

Galiani, F., Mehus, L. (2002). *Carteggio (1753–1786)*, edited by G. Nicoletti, Naples: Bibliopolis.

Galiani, F, Tanucci, B. (1880). *Lettere di Ferdinando Galiani al Marchese Bernardo Tanucci, pubblicate per cura di Augusto Bazzoni (1759–1769)*, Estratto dall' *Archivio storico italiano*, Serie III et IV (1869–1880). Florence: Vieusseux.

Galilei, G. (1632). *Dialogo di Galileo Galilei Linceo Matematico Sopraordinario dello Studio di Pisa e Filosofo e Matematico Primario del Serenissimo Gr. Duca di Toscana, dove nei congressi di quattro giornate si discorre sopra i due Massimi Sistemi del Mondo, Tolemaico e Copernicano, proponendo indeterminatamente le ragioni filosofiche e naturali tanto per l'una, quanto per l'altra parte*. Florence: Landini.

Gassendi, P. (1727). *Opera omnia in sex tomos divisa*. Florence: typis Regiae Celsitudinis.

Gee, J. (1749). *Considérations sur le commerce et la navigation de la Grande-Bretagne. Ouvrage traduit de l Anglais, sur la quatrième edition*. London: Bettesworth & C.

Genovesi, A. (1743). *Elementa Metaphysicae in usum privatorum adolescentium mathematicumin morem adornata. Pars prior. Ontosofia*. Naples: Gessari.

Genovesi, A. (1745). *Elementa physicae conscripta in usus academicos a Petro van Musschenbroeck, quibus nunc primum in gratiam studiosae iuventutis accedunt ab alienis manibus ubique auctaria et notae, disputatio physico-historica de rerum corporearum origine, ac demum de rebus coelestibus tractatus*. Naples: Palumbo.

Genovesi, A. (1753). Discorso sopra il vero fine delle lettere e delle scienze. In U. Montelatici, *Ragionamento sopra i mezzi più necessarj per far rifiorire l'agricoltura del p. abate d. Ubaldo Montelatici della congregazione laterarense colla Relazione dell'erba orobanche detta volgarmente succiamele e del modo di estirparla del celebre Pier-Antonio Micheli con un discorso di Antonio Genovesi Regio Professore d'Etica sopra il vero fine delle lettere e delle scienze. Il tutto dedicato al signor Bartolomeo Intieri*. Naples: Giovanni di Simone, pp. iii–cvi.

Genovesi, A. (1757). *Storia del commercio della Gran Brettagna scritta da John Cary mercatante di Bristol. Tradotta in nostra volgar lingua da Pietro Genovesi giureconsulto napoletano, con un Ragionamento sul commercio in universale, e alcune annotazioni riguardanti l'economia del nostro Regno di Antonio Genovesi R. Professore di Commercio e di Meccanica nella Cattedra Intieriana*, tomi 2. Naples: Benedetto Gessari.

Genovesi, A. [1763] [2008]. Dialogo fra il Galiani, il Bembo ed il Fraggianni sulla riforma degli studi in Napoli. In Genovesi, A, *Dialoghi e altri scritti intorno alle Lezioni di Commercio*, edited by E. Pii, Naples: Istituto Italiano per gli Studi Filosofici, pp. 398–405.

Genovesi, A. (1765). *Delle lezioni di commercio o sia d'economia civile da leggersi nella Cattedra Interiana dell'ab.Genovesi regio cattedratico.* Parte prima pel primo semestre. Naples: Fratelli Simone.

Genovesi, A. (1766). *Della Diceosina o sia filosofia del giusto e dell'onesto*, Naples: Stamperia Simoniana.

Genovesi, A. (1767). *Delle lezioni di commercio o sia d'economia civile da leggersi nella Cattedra Interiana dell'ab.Genovesi regio cattedratico. Parte seconda pel secondo semestre.* Naples: Fratelli Di Simone.

Genovesi, A. (1774). *Lettere familiari dell'abate Antonio Genovesi, pubblicate da Domenico Forges Davanzati*, 2 voll. Naples: Stamperia Raimondiana.

Genovesi, A. (1781). "Piano delle scuole formato dall'Abate Genovesi in occasione di essere stati espulsi i gesuiti da Napoli", in Galanti, G. M. *Elogio storico del signor abate Antonio Genovesi.* Florence: Francesco Pisoni, pp. 108–120.

Genovesi, A. (1783). *Delle lezioni di commercio o sia d'economia civile da leggersi nella cattedra Interiana dell'ab. Genovesi regio cattedratico. Parte Prima, Terza edizione napoletana.* Naples: Stamperia Simoniana.

Genovesi, A. [1997]. "Vita di Antonio Genovese". In F. Venturi (ed.) *Illuministi italiani. Riformatori* napoletani, vol. II, tomo I. Milan: Ricciardi - Mondadori, pp. 47–83.

Giannone, P. (1723). *Dell'istoria civile del Regno di Napoli libri 40 scritti da Pietro Giannone giureconsulto, ed avvocato napoletano. Tomo 4, in cui contiensi la politia del regno sotto Austriaci.* Naples: Nicolò Naso.

Gibbon, E. (1788). *The History of the Decline and Fall of the Roman Empire*, Volume The Tenth. Dublin: Luke White.

Giustiniani L. (1804). *Nuova collezione delle Prammatiche del Regno di Napoli*, tomo VII. Naples: Stamperia Simoniana.

Gleichen, K. H. von. (1868). *Souvenirs de Charles-Henri Baron de Gleichen*, Paris: Techener.

Goudar, A. (1769). *Naples. Ce qu'il faut faire pour rendre ce Royaume florissant, où l'on traite des avantages que le gouvernement peut retenir de la fertilité et de l'abondance de ses denrées, des facilités pour perfectionner les arts, de sa position favorable pour s'emparer des premières branches du commerce étranger.* Amsterdam: s.n.

Gould, N. (1726). *An Essay on the Public Debts of this Kingdom*. London: Peele.

Gould, N. (1727). *A Defence of an Essay on the Public Debts, etc., in Answer to a State of the National Debt, etc.* London: Peele.

Graslin, J.J.L. (1767). *Essai analytique sur la richesse et sur l'impôt: où l'on réfute la nouvelle doctrine économique,* London: s.n.

Grimaldi, C. (1725). *Discussioni istoriche, teologiche, e filosofiche di Costantino Grimaldi fatte per occasione della risposta alle lettere apologetiche di Benedetto Aletino*. Lucca: s.n.

Grimaldi, D. (1780). *Osservazioni economiche sopra la manifattura e commercio delle sete nel Regno di Napoli alle sue finanze* etc. Naples: Giuseppe Maria Porcelli.

Grimaldi, G. [2001]. Considerazioni intorno al Commercio del Regno di Napoli. *Frontiera d'Europa*, VII, pp. 319–358.

Grimm, F. M. F. von. (1829). Sermon Philosophique. In *Correspondance littéraire, philosophique et critique de Grimm et de Diderot, depuis 1753 jusqu'en 1790*, Volume 16. Paris: Furne, pp. 265–288.

Grimm, F. M. F. von. (1878). *Correspondance litteraire, philosophique et critique par Grimm*, vol. VI. Paris: Garnier.

Grimm, F. M. F. von. (1879). *Correspondance litteraire, philosophique et critique par Grimm*, vol. IX. Paris: Garnier.

Grotius, H. (1625) [2005]. *De Jure belli ac pacis libri tres, in quibus jus naturae et gentium, item juris publici praecipua explicantur*. Paris: Nicolaum Byon, English translation, *The rights of war and peace*, edited and with an introduction by Richard Tuck, Indianapolis: Liberty Fund.

Grotius, H. (1777). *Il diritto della guerra e della pace di Ugone Grozio, colle note dello stesso autore, e di Giovanni Barbeyrac. Tradotto nell'idioma italiano dall'avvocato napoletano Antonio Porpora*. Naples: De Dominicis.

Grozio, U. (1777). *Il dritto della guerra e della pace di Ugone Grozio colle note dello stesso autore, e di Giovanni Barbeyrac. Tradotto nell'idioma italiano dall'avvocato napoletano D. Antonio Porpora*, Naples: Giuseppe De Dominicis.

Harris J. (1757). *An Essay Upon Money and Coins*. London: Hawkins.

Herbert, C. J. (1753). *Essai sur la police générale des grains*. London: s.n.

Herbert, C. J. (1765). *Riflessioni sull'economia generale de' grani tradotte dal francese, con un discorso preliminare del Signor Abbate Genovesi catedratico di commercio*. Naples: Gravier.

Hobbes, T. (1651) [1909]. *Hobbes's Leviathan*. Reprinted from the Edition of 1651, with an Essay by G. Pogson Smith. Oxfrord: Claredon Press.

Horace. [2011]. *Satires and Epistles,* Translated by J. Davie, with an Introduction and Notes by R. Cowan. Oxford, Oxford University Press.

Hübner, M. (1759). *De la saisie des bâtiments neutres ou du droit qu'ont les nations belligérantes d'arrêter les navires des peuples amis*. La Haye: s.n.

Hume, D. (1748). *Philosophical Essays Concerning Human Understanding*. London: Millar.

Hume, D. (1752). *Political discourses*. Edinburgh: Fleming.

Hume, D. (1754). *Discours Politiques de Mr. David Hume, traduits de l'anglois par Mr de M***** [Éléazar de Mauvillon], Amsterdam: T. Schreuder et Pierre Mortier le jeune.

Hume, D. (2011). *The Letters of David Hume*, edited by J.Y.T. Greig. Oxford: Clarendon Press.

Hutcheson, F. (1725). *An Inquiry into the Original of Our Ideas of Beauty and Virtue*. London: J. Darby.

Hutcheson, F. (1755). *A System of Moral Philosophy: In Three Books*, vol. II. London: Millar.

Intieri, B. (1703). *Bartholomaei Intieri Florentini Aditus ad nova arcana geometrica detegenda editus ad Ill. et Ex. Dom. D. Hieronymum Onerum Cabanilium S. Marci marchionem*. Beneventi: Typ. Archiepiscopali.

Intieri, B. (1704). *Apollonius ac Serenus promotus, auctore Barrtholomaeo Intieri florentino ad illustrissimum et excellentissimum Dom. D. Hieronymum Onerum Cabanilium e comitibus Troiae et Montellae*. Naples: Sellitto.

Intieri, B. (1706). *Facilissimo metodo per la quadratura delle parabole di qualsivoglia grado, colla risposta alla questione proposta dal Sig. G. C. all'illustrissimo S. D. Serafino Biscardi patritio cosentino, reggente del Supremo Collateral Consiglio di Napoli*. Naples: s.n.

Intieri, B. (1716). *Nuova invenzione di fabbricar mulini a vento*. Naples: Mosca.

Intieri, B. (1754). *Della perfetta conservazione del grano. Discorso di Bartolomeo Intieri*. Naples: Giuseppe Raimondi.

Intieri, B. (1770). *L'Art de conserver les Grains, par Barthelemy Inthiery. Ouvrage traduit de l'Italien, par les soins de M. D.N.E.* [Louis Joseph Bellepierre de Neuve-Église]. Paris: Saugrain le jeune.

Kant, I. (1784). Beantwortung der Frage: Was ist Aufklärung?, *Berlinische Monatsschrift*, Band 12, pp. 481–494.

King, C. (1753). *Le négociants anglois ou traduction libre du livre intitulé The British merchant contenant diverses mémoires sur le commerce de l'Angleterre avec la France, le Portugal, l'Espagne, publié pour la première fois en 1713*. Dresde [but Paris]: Frères Estienne.

La Condamine, C. M. de. (1768). *Le pain mollet. Poëme*. s.l: s.n.

Lami, G. (1752). [Della Moneta Review]. In *Novelle Letterarie pubblicate in Firenze*, Anno MDCCLII, Tomo XIII, n. 52, pp. 825–830.

Lampredi, G.M. (1778). *Juris Publicis Universalis, sive Juris Naturae et Gentium Theoremata*, volume III. Livorno: Falurnus.

Law, J. (1705). *Money and Trade Considered with a Proposal for Supplying the Nation with Money*. Edinburgh: Anderson.

Le Blanc, F. (1690). Traité historique des monnayes de France depuis le commencement de la monarchie jusqu'à present. Paris: s.n.

Le Clerc, J. (1716). Article II. La Vita civile di Paolo Mattia Doria, distinta in tre Parti aggiuntovi un Trattato, della Educazione del Principe. Seconda Edizione, dall'Autore ricorretta ed accresciuta. *Bibliothèque ancienne et moderne pour servir de suite aux Bibliothèques universelle et choisie*, Tome V, Partie Prémiere, pp. 54–125.

Leibniz, G. W. (1684). Nova Methodus pro Maximis et Minimis. *Acta Eruditorum*, 3, pp. 467–473.

Le Mercier de La Rivière, P. P. F. J. H. (1767). *L'ordre naturel et essentiel des sociétés politiques.* Paris: Geuthner.

Le Mercier de La Rivière, P. P. F. J. H. (1770). *L'intéret général de l' État, ou la liberté du. commerce des blés démontrée conforme au droit naturel, au droit public de la France, aux loix fondamentales du Royaume, à l'intéret commun du souverain et de ses sujets dans tous les temps: avec la réfutation d'un nouveau systeme, publié en forme de dialogues sur le commerce des blés.* Amsterdam-Paris: Desaint.

Lesage, A.-R. (1707). *Le Diable boiteux.* Paris: Veuve Barbin.

Le Trosne, G.-F. (1766). De l'utilité des discussions économiques. *Journal de l'agriculture, du commerce et des finances,* VI, Premier Partie (July), pp. 8–85.

Le Trosne, G.-F. (1777). *De l'ordre social, ouvrage suivi d'un traité élémentaire sur la valeur, l'argent, la circulation, l'industrie et le commerce intérieur et extérieur.* Paris: chez les Frères Debure.

Linguet, S. N. H. (1774). *Du pain e du Bled*, London: s.n.

Locke, J. (1692). *Some Considerations of the Consequences of the Lowering of Interest, and Raising the Value of Money. In a letter sent to a Member of Parliament.* London, Awnsham and John Churchill, at the Black-Swan in Pater-Noster-Row.

Locke, J. (1695). *Further Considerations Concerning Raising the Value of Money Wherein Mr. Lowndes's Arguments for it in his late Report concerning An Essay for the Amendment of Silver Coins, are particularly Examined by John Locke.* London: A. and J. Churchill at the Black Swan in Pater-Noster-Row.

Locke, J. (1696a). *Some considerations of the consequences of the lowering of interest, and raising the value of money. In a letter sent to a Member of Parliament.The second edition corrected.* London: printed for Awnsham and John Churchil.

Locke, J. (1696b). *Several papers relating to money, interest, and trade, & c*, London: Printed for A. and J. Churchill.

Locke, J. (1714). *Two Treatises of Government. In the Former, the false Principles and Foundation of Sir Robert Filmer, and his Followers, are detected and overthrown. The Latter is an Essay concerning the true Original, Extent, and End of Civil Government*, in *Works of John Locke*, vol. II. London: Churchill.

Locke, J. (1748). *An essay concerning human understanding. In four books. Written by John Locke, Gent. The thirteenth edition*, 2 vols. London: printed for S. Birt, D. Browne, C. Hitch, J. Hodges, J. Oswald.

Locke, J. (1751). *Ragionamenti sopra la moneta, l'interesse del denaro, le finanze e il commercio, scritti e pubblicati in diverse occasioni dal signor Giovanni Locke. Tradotti la prima volta dall'inglese con varie annotazioni*, 2 tomi. Florence: Andrea Bonducci.

Lorenzi, G. B. (1780). *Socrate immaginario commedia per musica di Giambatista Lorenzi P. A. da rappresentarsi nel Teatro Nuovo sopra Toledo nella primavera di questo anno 1780*. Naples: s.n.

Lowndes, W. (1695). *A Report Containing an Essay for the Amendment of the Silver Coins*. London: s.n.

Lunetti, V. (1621). *Espedienti a beneficio del Regno di Napoli, Real Patrimonio, d'intorno alle monete scarse, e cambio alto*. Naples: Tarquinio Prisco.

Lunetti, V. (1630). *Politica mercantile di Vettorio Lunetti. Dell'espedienti et arbitrij per publica utilità. Nelli quali con vere raggioni si mostrano le cause delli danni della città e regno di Napoli et il vero modo di rimediarli. Possono servire anche per dove fussi simili danni e si lascia per brevità li discorsi d'adornamenti e solo si accenna le materie delli grand'utili et incredibili avanzi per Sua Maestà e ben publico. E per trattarsi di servitio publico e di Sua Maestà non si deve disprezzare le proposte, se prima non s'intenda le raggioni*. Naples: Lazzaro Scorriggio.

Mably, Bonnot de G. (1768). *Doutes proposées aux philosophes économistes sur l'Ordre naturel et essentiel des sociétés politiques*. La Haye: Nyon.

Machault d'Arnouville, J-B. (1749). Mémoire sur le commerce des grains, partially published in ripubblicate in Dupont De Nemours, P.-S. 1789. *Analyse historique de la législation des grainsdepuis 1692, à laquelle on a donné la forme d'un rapport à l'Assemblée nationale*. Paris, chez Petit, pp. 13–44.

Machiavelli, N. (1531) [1883]. *Discorsi sopra la prima Deca di Tito Livio*. Florence: Bernardo Giunti. English translation by N H. Thomson, *Discourses on the First Decade of Titus Livius*. London: Kegan.

Machiavelli, N. (1532) [1976]. *Il principe di Nicchold Machiavello al magnifico Lorenzo di Piero de Medici*. Rome: Antonio Blado d'Asola. English Translation, *The Prince*, translated, with introduction and notes by J. B. Atkinson. Indianapolis: Hackett Publishing Company.

Maffei, S. (1744). *Dell'impiego del danaro libri tre*. Verona: Giannalberto Tumermani.

Mandeville, B. de. (1714). *The Fable of the Bees: or, Private Vices, Publick Benefits*. London: Roberts.

Marmontel, J.F. (1804). *Mémoires d'un père pour servir à l'instruction de ses enfants*. Paris: Xhrouet.

Marzucco, G. (1757). *Riflessioni intorno alla quadratura del cerchio e delle curve*. Naples: Azzolino.

Maupertuis, P.-L. Moreau d. (1749). *Essai de philosophie morale*, Berlin: s.n.

Melon, J-F. (1736). *Essai politique sur le commerce. Nouvelle édition. Cette édition est augmentée de sept chapitres et les lacunes des éditions précédentes y sont remplies*, s.l. s.n.

Melon, J-F. (1739). *A Political Essay Upon Commerce: Written in French by Monsieur M* Translated, with Some Annotations and Remarks, by David Bindon, Esq.* Dublin: Printed for P. Crampton.

Mirabeu, V. Riqueti de. (1756). *L'ami des hommes ou Traité de la population*, Avignon: s.n.

Mirabeu, V. Riqueti de. (1760). *Théorie de l'impot*, s.l.: s. n.

Montanari, G. (1683a) [1750], *Trattato del valore delle monete in tutti gli Stati*, in F. Argelati, *Tractatus de monetis Italiae appendix seu de monetis Italiae*, pars III, 1750, Milan: Regia Curia ex Aedibus Palatinis, pp. 1–16.

Montanari, G. (1683b) [1759]. *La Zecca in Consulta di Stato del dottor Geminano Montanari, pubblico professore di matematica nella Università di Padova. Trattato mercantile*, in F. Argelati, *Tractatus de monetis Italiae appendix seu de monetis Italiae*, pars VI, 1759, Milan: Regia Curia ex Aedibus Palatinis, pp. 5–70.

Montesquieu, C.-L. de Secondat. (1748) [1989]. *De l'esprit des loix. Ou Du rapport que les loix doivent avoir avec la constitution de chaque gouvernement, les moeurs, le climat, la religion, le commerce*, Genève: Barillot & Fils. English Translation, *The Spirit of the Laws*, edited by A. M. Cohler, B. C. Miller, H. S. Stone. Cambridge: Cambridge University Press.

More, T. (1516) [2002]. *Utopia*. G. M Logan, R. M. Adams (eds.) Cambridge: Cambridge University Press.

Morellet, A. (1764). *Fragment d'une lettre sur le commerce des grains*. Paris: s. n.

Morellet, A. (1769a). *Mémoire sur la situation actuelle de la Compagnie des Indes, juin 1769*. Paris: Desaint.

Morellet, A. (1769b). *Examen de la Réponse de M. N** [Necker] Au Mémoire de M. l'Abbé Morellet Sur La Compagnie Des Indes*. Paris: Desaint.

Morellet, A. (1774). *Réfutation de l'ouvrage qui a pour Titre Dialogues sur le Commerce des Bleds*. London: s. n.

Morellet, A. (1822). *Mémoires inédits de l'abbé Morellet,... sur le dix-huitième siècle et sur la Révolution; précédés de l'éloge de l'abbé Morellet, par M. Lémontey*, Paris: Librarie Française de l'Advocat.

Morellet, A., Beccaria, C. (1766). *Traité des delits et des peines, traduit de l'Italien. D'après la troisieme edition, revue, corrigée & augmentée par l'auteur. Avec des additions de l'auteur, qui n'ont pas encore paru en Italien*, Philadelphia: s. n.

Muratori, L. A. (1735). *La filosofia morale esposta e proposta ai giovani*, Verona: Angelo Targa.

Muratori L. A. (1749). *Della pubblica felicità oggetto de' buoni principi*, Lucca [but Venice]: s. n.

Muratori, L. A. [1750a]. "De moneta, sive jure condendi nummos. Dissertatio", in Argelati, F. (ed.) *De monetis Italiae variorum illustrium virorum Dissertationes, quarum nunc primum in lucem prodit*, IV Vol. Milan: Regia Curia, pp. 1–98.

Muratori, L. A. [1750b]. "De diversis pecuniae generibus, quae apud veteres in usu fuere. Dissertatio", in Argelati, F. (ed.) *De monetis Italiae variorum illustrium virorum Dissertationes, quarum nunc primum in lucem prodit*, IV Vol. Milan: Regia Curia, pp. 99–135.

Musschenbroek, P. van. [1745]. *Elementa physicae conscripta in usus accademicos*, edited by Giuseppe Orlandi and Antonio Genovesi, Naples: Benedetto Gessari.

Naigeon, J. A., D'Holbach, Thiry P. H. [1768]. *Le militaire philosophe, ou, Difficultés sur la religion proposées au r. p. Malebranche, prétre de l'Oratoire*, London: s.n.

Napoli-Signorelli, P. (1798). *Il regno di Ferdinando IV adombrato in tre volumi in continuazione delle Vicende della coltura delle Sicilie*. Naples: Migliaccio.

Necker, J. [1769]. *Réponse au mémoire de M. l'abbé Morellet sur la Compagnie des Indes, imprimée en exécution de la délibération de Mrs les actionnaires, prise dans l'assemblée générale du 8 août 1769*. Paris: de l'Imprimerie Royale.

Necker, J. [1775]. *Sur la législation et le commerce des grains*, Paris: Pissot.

Neri P. [1751]. *Osservazioni sopra il prezzo legale delle monete e la difficoltà di prefinirlo e sostenerlo*. Milan: Malatesta.

Neri, P. [1759]. Appendice alle *Osservazioni*. In F. Argelati, (ed.), *De monetis Italiae variorum illustrium virorum dissertationes, quarum pars nunc primum in lucem prodit*. Milan: Regia Curia ex Aedibus Palatinis, Vol. V, pp. 147–180.

Newton, I. (1687) [1729]. *Philosophiæ Naturalis Principia Mathematica*, London: Streater. English Translation: *The Mathematical Principles of Natural Philosophy*, translated by Andrew Motte, London: Benjamin Motte, 1729.

Newton, I. (1713). Scholium Generale. In *Philosophiae naturalis principia mathematica. Editio secunda*, Cambridge: Cornelius Crownfield, pp. 481–484.

Newton, I. (1729). *The Mathematical Principles of Natural Philosophy*, translated by Andrew Motte, London: Benjamin Motte.

Nickolls, J. [Plumard de Dangeul L.-J.]. (1754). *Rémarques sur les avantages et les désavantages de la France et de la Grande-Bretagne par rapport au commerce et aux autre sources de la puissance des états. Traduction de l'anglois du chevalire John Nickolls, troisième édition, augmentée d'un Essai sur la police et le commerce des grains*. Leyde [but Paris]: Estienne.

Novelle letterarie. (1783). Review of *De' Doveri*. In *Novelle letterarie pubblicate in Firenze*, numero 13, 28 March 1783, column 201–206.

Odazi, T. (1782). *Riflessioni sui contratti alla voce*. Naples: s.n.

Odazi, T. (1783). *Della libertà de' prezzi, ossia della necessità di abolire i contratti alla voce per tutte le derrate di questo Regno*. Naples: Porsile.

Oresme, N. (1484) [1956]. *The De moneta of Nicole Oresme, and English Mint documents*, translated from the Latin with Introduction and Notes by C. Johnson. London: Thomas Nelson and Sons.

Origlia, G.G. (1754). *Istoria dello studio di Napoli*, vol. II. Naples: Simone.

Pagnini, G. (1751). *Saggio sopra il giusto pregio delle cose, la giusta valuta della moneta e sopra il commercio dei Romani*. In G. Pagnini, A. Tavanti, (eds), Locke, J. *Ragionamenti sopra la moneta l'interesse del danaro le finanze e il commercio scritti e pubblicati in diverse occasioni dal signor Giovanni Locke tradotti per la prima volta dall'inglese con varie annotazioni*. Florence: Bonducci, vol II, pp. [1]–116.

Palmieri, G. (1788). *Riflessioni sulla pubblica felicità relativamente al Regno di Napoli. Seconda edizione dall'autore accresciuta*. Naples: Stamperia Flauto

Pattullo, H. (1758). *Essai sur l'amélioration des terres*. Paris: Durand.

Petty, W. (1690). *Political Arithmetick*. London: Clavel.

Petty, W. (1691). *Verbum Sapienti*, addendum to the *Political Anatomy of Ireland*, London: Brown and Rogers.

Piccolomini, A. (1539). *Dialogo de la bella creanza de le donne*. Venice: Curtio Navò.

Plato. [2013]. *The Republic*. Translated by B. Jowett, Durham: Duke Classic.

Postlethwayt, M. (1749). *A Dissertation on the Plan, Use, and Importance, of the Universal Dictionary of Trade and Commerce*. London: John and Paul Knapton.

Postlethwayt, M. (1774). *The Universal Dictionary of Trade and Commerce, with Large Additions and Improvements, Adapting the Same to the Present State of British Affairs in America Since the Last Treaty of Peace Made in the Year 1763*. London: Printed for W. Strahan, J and F. Rivington.

Prammatiche. (1804). *Nuova collezione delle prammatiche del Regno di Napoli*, vol. VI. Naples: Stamperia Simoniana.

Prévost d'Exile, A-F. (1747). *Histoire générale des voyages, ou, Nouvelle collection de toutes les relations de voyage par mer et par terre: l'état actuel de toutes les nations, enrichie de cartes géographiques*, Volume 1. La Haye: chez Pierre de Hondt.

Pufendorf, S. (1672). *De jure naturae et gentium libri octo*. Londini Scanorum.

Pulteney Bath, W. (1727). *A state of the national debt, etc., With the payments made towards its discharge out of the sinking fund*. London: Francklin.

Quesnay, F. (1756a). Fermier. In D. Diderot, J. d'Alembert Le Ronde (eds.), *Encyclopédie, ou, Dictionnaire raisonné des sciences, des arts et des métiers*, tome VI. Paris: Briasson-David-Le Breton-Durand, pp. 528–540.

Quesnay, F. (1756b). Évidence. In D. Diderot, J. d'Alembert Le Ronde (eds.), *Encyclopédie, ou, Dictionnaire raisonné des sciences, des arts et des métiers*, tome VI. Paris: Briasson-David-Le Breton-Durand, pp. 146–157.

Quesnay, F. (1757). Grain. In D. Diderot, J. d'Alembert Le Ronde (eds.), *Encyclopédie, ou, Dictionnaire raisonné des sciences, des arts et des métiers*, tome VII, Paris: Briasson-David-Le Breton-Durand, pp. 812–833.

Quesnay, F. (1757–1758) [2005]. Homme. In C.Théré, L.Charles, J.-C. Perrot, (eds.) *Oeuvres économiques complètes et autres textes: Textes polémiques, Documents associés*, Tome Prémier. Paris: Institut national d'études démographiques, pp. 257–324.

Quesnay, F. (1758) [1888]. Maximes générales du Gouvernement économique d'un royaume agricole avec les Notes sur ces maxims. In *Oeuvres économiques et philosophiques de F. Quesnay accompagnées des éloges et d'autres travaux biographiques sur Quesnay par différents auteurs, publiées avec une introduction et des notes par Auguste Oncken*. Paris: Jules Peelman, pp. 330–358.

Quesnay, F., Du Pont de Nemours, P. S. (1768). *Physiocratie, ou Constitution naturelle du gouvernement le plus avantageux au genre humain*. Leyde [but Paris]: Merlin.

Ricardo, D. (1817). *On the Principles of Political Economy and Taxation*. London: John Murray.

Ricardo, D. (1821). *On the Principles of Political Economy, and Taxation*. London: John Murray.

Roubaud, P.-J.-A. (1769). Lettres de l' auteur des Représentations aux magistrats, à M. le chevalier Zanobi principal interlocuteur des Dialogues sur le commerce des blés. *Éphémérides du citoyen ou Bibliothèque raisonnée des sciences morales et politiques*, Tome XII. Paris: Lacombre, pp. 179–216.

Roubaud, P.-J.-A. (1770). *Récréations économiques, ou Lettres de l'auteur des Représentations aux magistrats à M. le chevalier Zanobi principal interlocuteur des Dialogues sur le commerce des blés* Amsterdam - Paris: Delalain.

Rousseau, J. J. (1758). *Discours sur l'oeconomie politique*. Geneva: chez Emanuel Du Villard.

Rousseau, J. J. (1762). *Émile ou De l'éducation*, La Haye [but Paris]: Jean Néaulme [but chez Nicolas Bonaventure Duchesne].

Rousseau, J. J. (1767) = [1997]. Letter to Mirabeau. In *The social contract and other later political writings*, Cambridge: Cambridge University Press, pp. 268–271.

Salmasius, C. (1638). *De Usuris Liber*, Leiden: Bonaventura and Abraham Elzevier.

Salmasius, C. (1639). *De modo usurarum liber*, Leiden: Bonaventura and Abraham Elzevier.

Sarcone, M. (1765). *Istoria ragionata de' mali osservati in Napoli nell'intero corso dell'anno 1764*. Naples: Stamperia Simoniana,

Sarcone, M. (1780). *Lettera Terza. Ammonizione caritativa all'autore del libro intitolato Del dialetto napoletano*. [Naples]: Presso Ezechiele.

Savary, J. (1723). *Dictionnaire universel de commerce*. Paris: J. Estienne.

Say, J.-B. (1843). *A Treatise on Political Economy: Or the Production, Distribution, and Consumption of Wealth*, Philadelaphia: Grigg & Elliot.

Scaruffi, G. (1582). *L'alitinonfo, per fare ragione, et concordanza d'oro, e d'argento; che servirà in universale; tanto per provvedere agli infiniti abusi del tosare, et guastare monete; quanto per regolare ogni sorte di pagamenti, et ridurre anco tutto il mondo ad una sola moneta*. Reggio Emilia: Hercoliano Bartoli.

Serio, L. (1780). *Lo vernacchio. Risposta al Dialetto napoletano*. Naples: s.n.

Serra, Antonio. (1613) [2011]. *Breve trattato delle cause che possono far abbondare li regni d'oro e d'argento dove non sono miniere, con applicazione al regno di Napoli diviso in tre parti.* Napoli: Lazzaro Scorriggio. English Translation: *A "Short Treatise" on the Wealth and Poverty of Nations*, Edited and with an Introduction by Sophus A. Reinert. Translated by Jonathan Hunt London – New York, Anthem Press, 2011.

Senior, N. W. (1836). *An Outline of the Science of Political Economy.* London: Clowes.

Severino, M. A. (1653). *Therapeuta Neapolitanus.* Naples: Molli.

'Sgravesande, W. J. (1723). *Philosophiae Newtonianae Institutiones, in usus academicos.* Leiden: Lugduni Batavorum.

Smith, A. (1776). *An Inquiry Into the Nature and Causes of the Wealth of Nations. In Two Volumes.* London: Strahan.

Spinelli, T. [1749]. *Riflessioni politiche sopra alcuni punti della Scienza della Moneta. Al Sig. D. Domenico Caracciolo dei Marchesi di Capriglia.* Naples: s.n.

Steuart J. (1767). *An Inquiry into the Principles of Political Economy being an Essay on the Science of Domestic Policy in Free Nations. in which are particularly considered Population, Agriculture, Trade, Industry, Money, Coin, Interest, Circulation, Banks, Exchange, Public Credit, and Taxes by Sir James Steuart, Bart.* London: Millar and Cadell.

Swift, J. (1704). *A Tale of a Tub: Written for the Universal Improvement of Mankind.* London: John Nutt.

Tanucci, B. (1914). *Lettere a Ferdinando Galiani*, edited by F. Nicolini, Bari: Laterza.

Tanucci, B. (1969). *Lettere di Bernardo Tanucci a Carlo III di Borbone (1759–1776)*, edited by R. Mincuzzi. Rome: Istituto per la Storia del Risorgimento Italiano.

Tanucci, B. (1980a). *Epistolario*, vol. I (1723–1746), R.P. Coppini, L. Del Bianco, Nieri, R. (eds). Rome: Edizioni di Storia e Letteratura.

Tanucci, B. (1980b). *Epistolario*, vol. II (1746–1752), R.P. Coppini, Nieri, R. (eds.), Rome: Edizioni Storia e Letteratura.

Tanucci, B. (1984). *Epistolario*, vol. IV (1756–1757), L. Del Bianco (ed.), Rome: Edizioni Storia e Letteratura.

Tanucci, B. (1985). *Epistolario*, vol. V (1757–1758), G. de Lucia (ed.), Rome: Edizioni Storia e Letteratura.

Tanucci, B. (1997). *Epistolario*, vol. XII (1763–1764), M. C. Ferrari, (ed.), Naples: Società Napoletana di Storia Patria.

Tapia, C. (1638). *Trattato dell'abbondanza, composto dal regente Carlo di Tapia, marchese di Belmonte, nel quale si mostrano le cause, dalle quali procede il mancamento delle vittovaglie et i rimedij che a ciascuna si possono dare; acciò non succeda, o succeduto non si senta, il danno di esso.* Naples: Roberto Mollo.

Thomas, A.-L. (1772). *Essai sur le caractere, les moeurs et l'esprit des femmes dans les différens siecles.* Paris: Moutard.

Thomas Aquinas. [1920]. *The Summa Theologiæ of St. Thomas Aquinas*. London: Benziger Brothers.

Tucker, J. (1749). *A Brief Essay on the Advantages and Disadvantages which Respectively Attend France and Great Britain, with Regard to Trade*. London: Trye.

Turbolo, G.D. (1616). *Discorso della differenza et inegualità delle Monete del Regno di Napoli, con l'altre monete di Potentati convicini, e della causa della penuria di esse. Con l'espediente per lo aggiustamento e abbundanza sì delle monete di Regno come di forastiere. Per beneficio publico.* Naples: Tarquinio Longo.

Turbolo, G.D. (1629). *Discorso sopra le monete del Regno di Napoli per la renouatione della lega di esse monete, ordinata ed eseguita nell'anno 1622. E degli effetti da quella preceduti. E se il cambio alto per estra Regno sia d'utile ò danno a' Regnicoli. Con diverse Relationi e copie d'altri discorsi, dati fuora nell'anni 1618, 619 et 620 pertinenti alla medesima materia*. Naples: s.n.

Turgot, A.R.M. (1756). Etymologie. In *Encyclopédie, ou dictionnaire raisonné des sciences, des arts et des métiers*, Tome VI, Neufchastel [but Paris]: Samuel Faulche, pp. 98–111.

Turgot, A.R.M. (1768). *Lettres sur les émeutes populaires que cause la cherté des bleds et sur les précautions du moment*. s.l: s.n.

Turgot, A.R.M. (1769) [2011]. Valeurs et Monnaies: Projet d'article. In *The Turgot Collection. Writings, Speeches, and Letters*, edited by D. Gordon, Auburn: Ludwig von Mises Institute, pp. 163–184.

Tyson, E. (1699). *Orang-outang, sive Homo sylvestris*, London: Printed for T. Bennett and D. Brown.

Ulloa, B. de. (1753). *Rétlabissement des manufactures et du commerce d'Espagne*. Paris: Frères Estienne.

Uztàriz, G. de. (1753). *Théorie et pratique du commerce et de la marine, traduction libre sur l'espagnol de Don Geronymo de Uztàriz, sur la seconde èdition de ce livre à Madrid en 1742*. Paris: Veuve Estienne

Valignani, F. [2001]. Riflessioni sopra il Commercio del Regno di Napoli. *Frontiera d'Europa, società economia istituzioni diritto del Mezzogiorno d'Italia*, VII (2001), nn. 1–2, pp. 229–280.

Valletta, G. (1732) [1975]. *Lettera del Signor Giuseppe Valletta in difesa della moderna filosofia e de' coltivatori di essa, indirizzata alla santità di Clemente XI. Aggiuntavi in fine un'osservazione sopra la medesima*. Rovereto: Berno. In G. Valletta, *Opere filosofiche*, edited by M. Rack, Florence: Olscki, pp. 76–215.

Valletta, G. [1975]. Istoria filosofica. in G. Valletta, *Opere filosofiche*, edited by M. Rack, Florence: Olscki, pp. 221–386.

Vasco G. (1772). *Della moneta saggio politico*. Milan: Galeazzi

Vergara, C. A. (1715). *Monete del Regno di Napoli di Ruggiero Primo Re sino all'Augustissimo Regnante Carlo VI Imperatore e III Re Cattolico raccolte e spiegate da Don Cesare Antonio Vergara dottore dell'una e dell'altra legge*. Rome: Gonzaga.

Verri, A., Verri, P. (1911). *Carteggio di Pietro e Alessandro Verri,* vol. III, edited by F. Novati, E. Greppi, Milan: Cogliati.

Verri, A., Verri, P. (1923). *Carteggio di Pietro e Alessandro Verri,* vol. I, edited by E. Greppi, A. Giulini, Milan: Cogliati.

Verri, A., Verri, P. (1980). *In viaggio a Parigi e Londra (1766–1767). Carteggio di Pietro e Alessandro Verri,* edited by G. Gasperi, Milan: Adelphi.

Verri, P. (1771). *Meditazioni sulla economia politica con annotazioni.* Venice: Pasquali

Vico, E. (1555). *Discorsi di Enea Vico Parmigiano sopra le medaglie degli antichi.* Venice: De Ferrari.

Vico, G.B. (1703) [1992] *Principum neapolitanorum coniurationis anni MDCCI historia,* published posthumously as *La congiura dei principi napoletani,* edited by C. Pandolfi, Naples: Morano, 1992.

Vico, G.B. (1709) [1990]. *De nostri temporis studiorumratione. Dissertatio a Joh. Baptista Vico.* Naples: Mosca. English Traslation *On the Study Methods of Our Time,* translated by Elio Gianturco, with a translation of *The Academies and the Relation between Philosophy and Eloquence (1737)* by Donald Phillip Verene, Ithaca: Cornell University Press, 1990.

Vico, G.B. (1710) [1988]. *De antiquissima Italorumsapientia ex linguae latinae origini bus eruenda. LibriTres,* Naples: Mosca. English translation *On the Most Ancient Wisdom of the Italians Unearthed from the Origins of the Latin Language,* including *The Disputation with "The Giornale de' Letterati d'Italia",* translated by L.M. Palmer, Ithaca: Cornell University Press, 1988.

Vico, G.B. (1725) [2002]. *The First New Science,* translated and edited by L. Pompa. Cambridge: Cambridge University Press.

Vico, G.B. (1728) [1975]. Vita di Giambattista Vico scritta da se medesimo. In *Raccolta di opuscoli scientifici e filologici,* edited by A. Calogerà, Venice: Cristoforo Zane, pp. 147–256. English translation *The Autobiography of Giambattista Vico, translated from the Italian by Max Harold Fisch and T. Goddard Bergin.* Ithaca: Cornell University Press, 1975.

Vico, G.B. (1744) [1948]. *Principi di Scienza Nuova d'intorno alla Comune Natura delle Nazioni, in questa terza impressione. Dal medesimo Autore in un gran numero di luoghi corretta, schiarita, e notabilmente accresciuta.* Naples: Stamperia Muziana. English translation *The New Science of Giambattista Vico,* by T. Goddard Bergin, Ithaca: Cornell University Press, 1948.

Vico, G.B. [1992]. *Epistole, con aggiunte le epistole dei suoi corrispondenti, a cura di Manuela Sanna, Prima Parte, 1693–1728.* Naples: Morano.

Vivens, F. de Labat de. (1756). *Observation sur divers moyens de soutenir et d'encourager l'agricolture, principalment dans la Guyenne,* s.l, s.n.

Voltaire [Arouet, F. M.]. 1738a. "Lettre a M. Thiriot sur l'ouvrage de M. Melon et sur celui de M. Dutot", in *Oeuvres Completes de Voltaire, v.1,* Paris, Dupont, 1824, pp. 157–175.

Voltaire [Arouet, F. M.]. (1738b). *Élémens de la philosophie de Newton*. London: s.n.
Voltaire [Arouet, F. M.]. (1756). *Poemes sur la loi naturelle en IV chants et sur le désastre de Lisbonne*. Amsterdam: Ledet.
Voltaire [Arouet, F. M.]. (1759). *Candide, ou l'Optimisme. Traduit de l'allemande de Mr. le docyeur Ralph*. s.l: s.n.
Voltaire [Arouet, F. M.]. (1767). *Dictionnaire philosophique, portatif. Sixieme Edition revue, corrigée & augmentée de XXXIV. Articles par l'Auteur*. London: s.n.
Voltaire [Arouet, F. M.]. (1768). *L'Homme au quarante écu* London: s.n.
Voltaire [Arouet, F. M.]. (1769). Tout en Dieu. Commentarie sur Malebranche. *Nouveaux melanges philosophiques, historiques, critiques*, Volume 8, pp. 289–306.
Voltaire [Arouet, F. M.]. (1770). *Dieu. Réponse de Mr. de Voltaire au Systême de la Nature*. Au Château de Ferney: s.n.
Young, A. (1770). *The Expediency of a Free Exportation of Corn at This Time*. London: Nicoll.

Secondary Sources

Ademollo, A. (1880). La famiglia e l'eredità dell'abate Galiani. *Nuova Antologia di Scienze, Lettere e Arti*, Volume LIII, Fascicolo XX, pp. 639–667.
Aglietta, M. (2018). *Money. 5,000 Years of Debt and Power*. London: Verso.
Aglietta, M., Orléan, A. (1982). *La violence de la monnaie*. Paris: PUF.
Aglietta, M., Orléan, A. (2018). Réflexions sur la nature de la monnaie. In R. Boyer, (ed.), *La Théorie de la Régulation au fil du temps. Suivre l'évolution d'un paradigme au gré des transformations des capitalismes contemporains*. La Plaine Saint-Denis: Éditions des maisons des sciences de l'homme associées, pp. 103–109.
Agrimi, M. (1992). Vico e la tradizione platonica. La filosofia dell'Umanità e la Storia Universale delle Nazioni. *Bollettino Del Centro di Studi Vichiani*, 22, pp. 65–102.
Ahn, D. (2023). The War of Jenkins' Ear and the Spectre of French Universal Monarchy. *Global Intellectual History*, Volume, 10, Issue, 1, pp 1–22.
Ajello, R. (1969). Il Banco di San Carlo: organi di governo e opinione pubblica nel Regno di Napoli di fronte al problema della ricompera dei diritti fiscali. *Rivista Storica Italiana*, anno LXXXI (1969), fascicolo IV, pp. 812–881.
Ajello, R. (1972). La vita politica napoletana sotto Carlo di Borbone. In *Storia di Napoli*, vol. VII, Naples: Società editrice della Storia di Napoli, pp. 459–717.
Ajello, R. (1975). Pietro Giannone fra libertini e illuministi, *Rivista Storica Italiana*, LXXXVII, fasc. I, pp. 104–131.
Ajello, R. (1976a). La critica del regime in Doria, Intieri, Broggia. In R. Ajello (ed.) *Arcana juris. Diritto e politica nel. Settecento italiano*, Naples: Jovane, pp. 391–419.

Ajello, R. (1976b). Vico e Riccardi nella crisi politica del 1726. In R. Ajello (ed.) *Arcana juris. Diritto e politica nel. Settecento italiano*, Naples: Jovane, pp. 149–228.

Ajello, R. (1977). Carlo di Borbone. *Dizionario Biografico degli Italiani* - Volume 20, Rome: Treccani, *ad vocem*.

Ajello, R. (1978). Nota introduttiva alle opere di Carlo Antonio Broggia. In R. Ajello, (ed.) *La letteratura italiana. Storia e testi. Dal Muratori al Cesarotti. Politici ed economisti del primo Settecento*, vol. 44, tomo V. Milan-Naples: Ricciardi, 1978, pp. 971–1032.

Ajello, R. (1980). Cartesianesimo e cultura oltremontana al tempo dell'*Istoria civile*. In R. Ajello (ed.), *Pietro Giannone e il suo tempo. Atti del Convegno di studi nel tricentenario della nascita*. Naples: Jovane, pp. 3–181.

Ajello, R. (1981). Introduzione. In P.L. Rovito, *Respublica dei togati. Giuristi e società nella Napoli del Seicento*. Naples: Jovane.

Ajello, R. (1985). Gli afrancesados a Napoli nella prima metà del Settecento. Idee e progetti di sviluppo. In M. Di Pinto (ed.), *I Borbone di Napoli e i Borbone di Spagna. Un bilancio storiografico*, vol. I. Naples: Guida, pp. 115–192.

Ajello, R. (1994). *Il problema storico del Mezzogiorno. L'anomalia socio-istituzionale dal Cinquecento al Settecento*. Naples: Jovene.

Ajello, R. (1996). *Una società anomala: il programma e la sconfitta della nobiltà napoletana in due memoriali cinquecenteschi*. Naples: ESI.

Ajello, R. (2001). Carlo di Borbone, Re delle Due Sicilie. In I. Ascione, (ed.), *Carlo di Borbone. Lettere Ai Sovrani di Spagna*, vol. I, 1720–1734. Rome: Ministero per i beni e le attività culturali, pp. 13–64.

Alatri, P. (1989). *L'Europa delle successioni (1731–1748)*. Palermo: Sellerio.

Albertone, M. (2018). Au cœur des Lumières. Ferdinando Galiani et le *Croquis d'un Dialogue sur les femmes*. In A. Tiran, C. Carnino (eds.), *Ferdinando Galiani, économie et politique*. Paris: Classiques Garnier, pp. 155–170.

Alimento, A., Stapelbroek, K. (2017). *The Politics of Commercial Treaties. Balance of Power, Balance of Trade*. London: Palgrave Macmillan.

Allix, E. (1911). Le physicisme des physiocrates. *Revue d'économie politique*, Vol. XXV, n. 5, pp. 563–586.

Allocati, A. (1955). Il Supremo Magistrato del Commercio del Regno di Napoli (1739–1806). *Studi economici*, anno X, 1955, n. 1–2, pp. 114–121.

Amabile, L. (1892). *Il Santo Officio della Inquisizione in Napoli*. Città di Castello: Lapi.

Amalfi, G. (1888a). Chi ha scritto *Il Socrate immaginario*?. In *Dubbi sul Galiani*, Naples: Priore, pp. 1–23.

Amalfi, G. (1888b). Chi compose il libro Del dialetto napoletano?. In *Dubbi sul Galiani*, Naples: Priore, pp. 39–81.

Amato, M. (1999). Il bivio della moneta. Problemi monetari e pensiero del denaro nel Settecento italiano. Milan: Egea.

Amodeo, F. (1924). *Vita matematica napoletana*. Naples: Giannini.
Amodio, P. (1997a). *Il disincanto della ragione e l'assolutezza del bonheur: studio sull'abate Galiani*, Naples: Guida.
Amodio, P. (1997b). La diffusione del pensiero di John Locke a Napoli nell'età di Vico, contributo critico-bibliografico. *Atti dell'Accademia di Scienze Morali e Politiche*, CVII, pp. 183–194.
Anglani, B. (1999). I dialoghi dell'assenza. Il carteggio tra l'abate Galiani e Madame d'Èpinay. *Annali della Facoltà di Lingue e Letterature Straniere*. Terza Serie, XIII, pp. 269–293.
Apih, E. (1977). Gian Rinaldo Carli. In *Dizionario Biografico degli Italiani* - Volume 20, Rome: Treccani, *ad vocem*.
Archivi. (1989). *Archivi dell'aristocrazia fiorentina. Mostra di documenti privati restaurati a cura della Sovrintendenza Archivistica per la Toscana tra il 1977 e il 1989*. Florence: Biblioteca Medicea Laurenziana.
Argemíd' Abadal, L. (2012). The Physiocrats. In J. G. Backhaus, (ed.), *Handbook of the History of Economic Thought: Insights on the Founders of Modern Economics*. New York: Springer, pp. 137–160.
Ascione, I. (1994). *Il governo della prassi. L'esperienza ministeriale di Francesco D'Andrea*. Naples: Jovene.
Astarita, T. (1992). *The Continuity of Feudal Power: The Caracciolo Di Brienza in Spanish Naples*. Cambridge: Cambridge University Press.
Astigarraga, J. (2018). Entre la Naples de Galiani, le Paris de Turgot et le Madrid de Campomanes. La traduction espagnole des *Dialogues sur le commerce des blés*. In A. Tiran, Carnino, C. (eds.), *Ferdinando Galiani, économie et politique*. Paris: Classiques Garnier, pp. 401–426.
Atkin, M. (1995). *The international grain trade. Second Edition*. Cambridge: Woodhead.
Badaloni, N. (1973). La cultura. In R. Romano e C. Vivanti (eds.), *Storia d'Italia*, vol. 3. *Dal primo Settecento all'Unità*. Turin: Einaudi, pp. 697–984.
Badaloni, N. (1984). *Introduzione a Vico*. Bari: Laterza.
Baldi, M. (1983). *David Hume nel Settecento Italiano*. Florence: La Nuova Italia Editrice.
Baker, K. M. (1975). *Condorcet from Natural Philosophy to Social Mathematics*. Chicago: The University of Chicago Press.
Baldini, U. (1982). Antonio Cocchi. In *Dizionario Biografico degli Italiani* - Volume 26, Rome: Treccani, *ad vocem*.
Barbagallo, F. (1971). Discussioni e progetti sul commercio tra Napoli e Costantinopoli nel '700. *Rivista Storica Italiana*, Anno LXXXIII, II, pp. 264–296.
Barnes, D. G. (1930). *A History of English Corn Laws: From 1660–1846*. London: Routledge.

Bauer, S. (1890). Studies on the Origin of the French Economists. *The Quarterly Journal of Economics*, Vol. 5, No. 1, pp. 100–107.

Bazzoni, A. (1869a). Carteggio dell'abate Ferdinando Galiani col Marchese Tanucci (1759–1769). *Archivio Storico Italiano*, Vol. 9, No. 2, pp. 10–36.

Bazzoni, A. (1869b). Carteggio dell'abate Ferdinando Galiani col Marchese Tanucci (1759–1769). *Archivio Storico Italiano*, Vol. 10, No. 1, pp. 40–57.

Bazzoni, A. (1875a). Carteggio dell'abate Ferdinando Galiani col Marchese Tanucci (1759–1769). *Archivio Storico Italiano*, Vol. 21, No. 87, pp. 516–527

Bazzoni, A. (1875b). Carteggio dell'abate Ferdinando Galiani col Marchese Tanucci (1759–1769). *Archivio Storico Italiano*, Vol. 22, No. 88, pp. 37–51.

Bazzoni, A. (1876a). "Carteggio dell'abate Ferdinando Galiani col Marchese Tanucci (1759–1769)", *Archivio Storico Italiano*, Vol. 23, No. 92, pp. 242–252.

Bazzoni, A. (1876b). Carteggio dell'abate Ferdinando Galiani col Marchese Tanucci (1759–1769). *Archivio Storico Italiano*, Vol. 24, No. 95, pp. 243–254.

Bazzoni, A. (1877a). Carteggio dell'abate Ferdinando Galiani col Marchese Tanucci (1759–1769). *Archivio Storico Italiano*, Vol. 25, No. 98, pp. 195–207.

Bazzoni, A. (1877b). Carteggio dell'abate Ferdinando Galiani col Marchese Tanucci (1759–1769). *Archivio Storico Italiano*, Vol. 26, No. 100, pp. 26–42.

Bazzoni, A. (1878a). Carteggio dell'abate Ferdinando Galiani col Marchese Tanucci (1759–1769), *Archivio Storico Italiano*, Vol. 1, No. 103, pp. 14–31.

Bazzoni, A. (1878b). Carteggio dell'abate Ferdinando Galiani col Marchese Tanucci (1759–1769). *Archivio Storico Italiano*, Vol. 1, No. 105, pp. Vol. 1, 445–459.

Bazzoni, A. (1878c). Carteggio dell'abate Ferdinando Galiani col Marchese Tanucci (1759–1769). *Archivio Storico Italiano*, Vol. 2, No. 106, pp. 23–31.

Bazzoni, A. (1879a). Carteggio dell'abate Ferdinando Galiani col Marchese Tanucci (1759–1769). *Archivio Storico Italiano*, Vol. 3, No. 110, pp. 171–183.

Bazzoni, A. (1879b). Carteggio dell'abate Ferdinando Galiani col Marchese Tanucci (1759–1769). *Archivio Storico Italiano*, Vol. 4, No. 114, pp. 361–375.

Bazzoni, A. (1880a). "Carteggio dell'abate Ferdinando Galiani col Marchese Tanucci (1759–1769)", *Archivio Storico Italiano*, Vol. 5, No. 117, pp. 367–375.

Bazzoni, A. (1880b). *Lettere di Ferdinando Galiani al Marchese Bernardo Tanucci*. Florence: Vieusseux.

Beaurepaire, P.-Y. (2003). *L'espace des francs-maçons. Une sociabilité européenne au XVIIIe siècle*. Rennes: PUR.

Bedarida, P. (1975). La correspondance française de l'Abbé Galiani. In *Convegno italo-francese sul tema Ferdinando Galiani* (Roma, 25–27 maggio 1972). Rome: Accademia Nazionale dei Lincei, pp. 13–23.

Beer, M. (1939). *An Inquiry into Physiocracy*. London: Allen and Unwin.

Belgioioso, G. (1981). Introduzione. In G. Belgioioso (ed.), *Manoscritti napoletani di Paolo Mattia Doria*, vol. I. Galatina: Congedo, pp. 3–47.

Belgioioso, G. (1992). *Cultura a Napoli e cartesianesimo*. Galatina: Congedo.

Belgioioso, G. (1999). *La variata immagine di Descartes. Gli itinerari della metafisica tra Parigi e Napoli (1690–1733)*. Lecce: Milella.
Belgioioso, G. (2005). Images of Descartes in Italy. In T. M. Schmaltz (ed.), *Receptions of Descartes. Cartesianism and anti-Cartesianism in early modern Europe*. New York: Routledge, pp. 171–196.
Belgioioso, G. (2012). Paolo Mattia Doria. In *Il Contributo italiano alla storia del Pensiero: Filosofia*, Rome: Treccani, *ad vocem*.
Benetti, C. (1994). Troc, bons d'achat et monnaie: La conception de Ferdinando Galiani. *Revue économique*, Vol. 45, No. 5, *Monnaie bancaire étalon-or et change: Les leçons des Classiques*, pp. 1177–1187.
Benetti, C. (2018). Échange, prix et monnaie dans le 1er chapitre du livre II de *Della moneta*. In A. Tiran, C. Carnino (eds.), *Ferdinando Galiani, économie et politique*. Paris: Classiques Garnier, pp. 193–210.
Beniscelli, A. (2012a). *Libertini italiani*. Milan: Rizzoli.
Beniscelli, A. (2012b). Il funambolo e la dama. Dall'epistolario dell'abate Galiani e madame d'Épinay. In *Lumi inquieti: amicizie, passioni, viaggi di letterati nel Settecento*. Turin: Accademia University Press, pp. 85–100.
Bensimon, G. (2018). Une interprétation de la théorie de la valeur de Galiani. In A. Tiran, Carnino, C. (eds.), *Ferdinando Galiani, économie et politique*. Paris: Classiques Garnier, pp. 223–250.
Bernardini, P. (1995). Il Diritto di Neutralità nel tardo giusnaturalismo tedesco e la traduzione del Galiani politico in Germania. *Materiali per una storia della cultura politica*, 25, pp. 291–312.
Bernardini, P. (2000). Arte di governo e diritto di neutralità nel tardo illuminismo tedesco. A proposito della traduzione del Galiani Politico in Germania. In La Manna, F. (ed.) *Commercium: scambi culturali italo-tedeschi nel XVIII secolo*. Florence: Olschki, pp. 3–25.
Bertelli, S. (1980). *Il libertinismo italiano*. Milan-Naples: Ricciardi.
Bevilacqua, P. (1982). Agricoltura e storia delle campagne nel Mezzogiorno d'Italia. *Studi Storici*, Jul.–Sep., 1982, Anno 23, No. 3, pp. 671–682.
Bianchi, L. (1979). Libertinismo e ateismo nel Seicento, *Studi Storici*, Anno 20, No. 4 (Oct.–Dec., 1979), pp. 881–886.
Bianchi, L. (1984). Il libertinismo in Italia nel XVII secolo: Aspetti e problemi. *Studi Storici*, Anno 25, No. 3 (Jul.–Sep., 1984), pp. 659–677.
Bianchini, L. (1839). *Storia delle finanze del Regno di Napoli*. Palermo: Lao.
Bianchini, M. (2002). *Bonheur public et méthode géométrique: enquête sur les économistes italiens (1711–1803)*. Paris: Ined.
Bizzocchi, R. (2008). *Cicisbei. Morale privata e identità nazionale in Italia*. Bari: Laterza.
Blart, L. (1915). *Les rapports de la France et de l'Espagne après le Pacte de Famille jusqu'à la fin du ministère du duc de Choiseul*. Paris: Librairie Félix Alcan.

Blaug, M. (1985). *Economic Theory in Retrospect. Fourth Edition*. Cambridge: Cambridge University Press.

Blessich A. (1896). L'Abate Galiani geografo. Contributo alla storia della geografia moderna. *Napoli Nobilissima*, Anno V, fasc. X, pp. 145–150.

Bloch, M. (1954). *Esquisse d'une histoire monétaire de l'Europe* (Cahiers des annales, N° 9). Paris: Colin.

Böhm-Bawerk, E. (1884) [1890]. *Geshischte und Kritik der Kapitalzins Theorien*, Innsbruck: Verlag; English Translation. *Capital and Interest. A Critical History of Economical Theory*, London: Macmillan.

Borges, J. L. (1949) [1998]. Los dos reyes y los dos laberintos. In *L'Aleph*, Buenos Aires: Editorial Losada. English translation: The Two Kings and the Two Labyrinths. In J. L. Borges. *Collected Fictions,* translated by Hurley, A. London: Penguin Books, 1998.

Borghero, C. (1996). L'Italia in Bayle, Bayle in Italia: una ricerca mancata. In L. Bianchi (ed.) *Pierre Bayle e l'Italia*. Naples: Liguori, pp. 3–33.

Bourguet, A. (1907). *Étude sur la politique étrangère du duc de Choiseul.* Paris: Plon.

Bourthoumieux, C. (1935). *Le mythe de l'ordre naturel en économie politique depuis Quesnay*. Paris: M. Rivière.

Boussard, J.-M., Gérard, F., Piketty, M.-G. (1995). *Libéraliser l'agriculture mondiale? Théories, modèles et réalités.* Montpellier: Cirad Centre de coopération en recherche agronomique pour le développement.

Bouzinac, J. (1906). *Jean-François Melon, économiste*. Toulouse: Imprimerie Ouvrière.

Boyer-Xambeu, M.-T., Deleplace, G., Gillard, L. (1986). *Private Money & Public Currency. The 16th Century Challenge*. Armonk-London: Sharpe.

Bracchi, C. (1997). Ferdinando Galiani lettore e critico di Orazio. *Italianistica: Rivista di letteratura italiana*, Vol. 26, No. 1, pp. 85–109.

Braeuer, W. (1975). Ferdinando Galiani et la culture allemande. In *Convegno italo-francese sul tema Ferdinando Galiani* (Roma, 25–27 maggio 1972). Rome: Accademia Nazionale dei Lincei, pp. 175–183.

Braeuer, W. (1988). Das fehlende letzte kapitel bei Galiani, *Rivista Internazionale di Scienze Economiche e Commerciali*. Vol. 35, N. 1, pp. 7–10.

Brants, V. (1895) [1970]. *L'économie politique au Moyen-Age: esquisse des théories économiques professées par les écrivains des XIIIe et XIVe siècles.* New York: Franklin.

Bridrey, E. (1906). *La théorie de la monnaie au XIVe siècle, Nicolas Oresme*. Paris: Giard & Brière.

Brockdorff, C. von. (1937). Descartes et les Lumières Françaises. *Revue de Métaphysique et de Morale*, 44, 1, pp. 305–324.

Brooks, G. P., Aalto, S. K. (1981). The Rise and Fall of Moral Algebra: Francis Hutcheson and the Mathematization of Psychology, *Journal of the History of the Behavioral Sciences,* 17, 3, pp. 343–356.

Brown, A. (1998). Homeric Talents and the Ethics of Exchange. *The Journal of Hellenic Studies,* Vol. 118, pp. 165–172.

Brunet, P. (1931). *L'introduction des théories de Newton en France au dix-huitième siècle.* Volume 1. Paris: Blanchard.

Brunetière, F. (1881). Études sur le xviii siècle: III. l'abbé Galiani. *Revue des Deux Mondes,* Troisième Période, Vol. 45, No. 4, pp. 924–945.

Bruni, L. (2017) On the Concept of Economia Civile and "Felicitas Publica": a Comment on Federico D'onofrio. Journal of the History of Economic Thought, Volume 39, Number 2, pp. 273–279.

Bulgarelli Lukacs, A. (2004). *Alla ricerca del contribuente. Fisco, catasto, gruppi di potere, ceti emergenti nel Regno di Napoli nel XVIII secolo.* Naples: Edizioni Scientifiche Italiane.

Caden, M. (2019). Money and its Technologies: Industrial Opposition and the Problem of Trust. In C. Desan (ed.) *A Cultural History of Money,* Vol. IV, *A Cultural History of Money in the Age of Enlightenment.* London: Bloomsbury Academic, pp. 25–52.

Caffiero, M. (1979). Gaspare Cerati. In *Dizionario Biografico degli Italiani* - Volume 23, Rome: Treccani, *ad vocem.*

Cahen, L. (1926). Le Pacte de Famine et les spéculations sur les blés. *Revue Historique,* Tome 152, Fasc. 1, pp. 32–43.

Calabria, A. (1991). *The cost of empire: the finances of the Kingdom of Naples in the time of Spanish rule.* Cambridge: Cambridge University Press.

Cane, E. (1976). Jean d'Alembert between Descartes and Newton: A Critique of Thomas L. Hankins' Position, *Isis,* 67, 2, pp. 274–278.

Caracciolo, A. (1970). Girolamo Belloni. In *Dizionario Biografico degli Italiani* - Volume 7, Rome: Treccani, *ad vocem.*

Caracciolo, A, Merola, A. (eds.). (1963). Introduzione. Galiani, F. *Della moneta e scritti inediti,* Milan: Feltrinelli.

Carey, D. (2019). Money and the Issues of the Age: Thinking about Money in the Eighteenth Century. In C. Desan (ed.) *A Cultural History of Money,* Vol. IV, *A Cultural History of Money in the Age of Enlightenment.* London: Bloomsbury Academic, pp. 163–186.

Caridi, G. (2006). *Essere re e non essere re. Carlo di Borbone a Napoli e le attese deluse (1734–1738).* Soveria Mannelli: Rubbettino.

Caridi, G. (2011). Una riforma borbonica bloccata: il Supremo Magistrato di Commercio nel Regno di Napoli (1739–1746). *Mediterranea. Ricerche storiche,* 21, pp. 89–124.

Caridi, G. (2012). *La modernizzazione incompiuta nel Mezzogiorno borbonico (1738–1746).* Soveria Mannelli: Rubbettino.

Caridi, G. (2014). Carlo III. Un grande re riformatore a Napoli e in Spagna, Rome: Salerno Editrice.

Carlile W. W. (1901). *The Evolution of Modern Money.* London: Palgrave.

Carmagnani, M. (2014). *Economia politica e morale pubblica. Pietro Verri e la cultura economica europea*. Bologna: Il Mulino.

Carnino, C. (2018). Le luxe "frère du bonheur terrestre". Ferdinando Galiani entre économie et politique. In A. Tiran, C. Carnino (eds.), *Ferdinando Galiani, économie et politique*. Paris: Classiques Garnier, pp. 437–456.

Carpanetto, D., Ricuperati, G. (1987). *Italy in the Age of Reason: 1685–1789*, London - New York: Longman.

Carpanetto, D., Ricuperati, G. (1993). *L'Italia del Settecento. Crisi, trasformazioni, lumi*, Bari: Laterza.

Carrafiello, T. (1995). Berardo Galiani intendente di architettura (1724–1774). *Archivio Storico per le Province Napoletane*, Anno CXIII, pp. 245–379.

Carrafiello, T. (1998). Berardo Galiani. In *Dizionario Biografico degli Italiani* - Volume 51, Rome: Treccani, *ad vocem*.

Carrafiello, T. (2019). *La biblioteca di Berardo Galiani. Vicende storiche e catalogo commentato, con un approfondimento sugli inediti galianei*. Florence: Altralinea.

Carrino, A. (2021). *Francisco Hombrados Malo (secolo XVIII). Un uomo per tutte le stagioni*. Viterbo: Sette Città.

Casini, P. (1983a). Newton in Italia, 1700–1740: note di ricerca. In P. Casini (ed.), *Newton e la coscienza europea*, Bologna 1983, pp. 173–227.

Casini, P. (1983b). Questioni sul newtonianesimo nel Settecento, in P. Rossi, (ed.), *Il Newtonianesimo nel Settecento*, Rome: Treccani, pp. 167–178.

Casini, P. (1988). Newton's *Principia* and the Philosophers of the Enlightenment. *Notes and Records of the Royal Society of London*, Vol. 42, No. 1, *Newton's Principia and Its Legacy*, pp. 35–52.

Casini, P. (2006). Il momento newtoniano in Italia: un post-scriptum. *Rivista di Storia della Filosofia*, Vol. 61, No. 2, pp. 299–316.

Cassirer, E. (1932). *Die Philosophie der Aufklärung*. Tübingen: Verlag von J.C.B. Mohr.

Castaldi, G. (1840). *Della Regale Accademia Ercolanese dalla sua fondazione sinora con un cenno biografico de' suoi soci ordinari*. Naples: Porcelli.

Cataldo, V. (2020). *Napoli e le sue provincie durante il Viceregno austriaco (1707–1734)*. Soveria Mannelli: Rubbettino.

Catucci, M. (1984). Antonio Genovesi e Ferdinando Galiani. *Esperienze Letterarie*, anno IX, N. 4, pp. 57–62.

Catucci, M. (1986). *Galianea. Ferdinando Galiani tra letteratura ed economia*, Rome: Bulzoni.

Céard, J. (2007). Les géants selon Dom Calmet. In M. Closson, M. White-Le Goff (eds.) *Les Géants entre mythe et literature*. Arras: Artois Presses Université, pp. 37–46.

Cesarano, F. (1976). Monetary Theory in Ferdinando Galiani's *Della Moneta*. *History of Political Economy*, 8 (3), pp. 380–399.

Cesarano, F. (1986). La teoria della politica economica nei *Dialogues* di Ferdinando Galiani. *Rivista di politica economica*, 12, pp. 1691–1706.
Cesarano, F. (1990). Law and Galiani on money and monetary system. *History of Political Economy*, vol. 22, n. 2, pp. 321–340.
Cesarano, F. (1995). Galiani e il ruolo della politica economica. In A. Roncaglia (ed.) *Alle origini del pensiero economico in Italia*. Bologna: Il Mulino, pp. 97–120.
Cesarano, F. (1999). Introduzione. In F. Galiani, *Scritti di Politica Economica*. Lanciano: Rocco Carabba, pp. vii–xix.
Chafuen, A. A. (2003). *Faith and Liberty. The Economic Thought of the Late Scholastics*. London: Lexington Books.
Chaplygina I., Lapidus, A. (2016). Economic Thought in Scholasticism. In *Handbook on the History of Economic Analysis*, Volume II, *Schools of Thought in Economics*, edited by G. Faccarello, H. D. Kurz. Cheltenham: Edward Elgar Publishing, pp. 20–42.
Charbit, Y. (2002). The Political Failure of an Economic Theory: Physiocracy. *Population*, Vol. 57, No. 6, pp. 855–883.
Charles, L. (2000). From the *Encyclopédie* to the *Tableau économique*: Quesnay on Freedom of Grain Trade and Economic Growth. *The European Journal of History of Economic Thought*, 7 (1), pp. 1–21.
Charles, L. (2003). The Visual History of the Tableau Économique. *The European Journal of the History of Economic Thought*, 10 (4), pp. 527–550.
Charles, L. (2004). The Tableau Économique as Rational Recreation. *History of Political Economy*, 36 (3), pp. 445–474.
Charles, L. (2011). Le cercle de Gournay: usages culturels et pratiques savants. In L Charles, F. Lefèbvre, C. Théré, (eds.), *Le cercle de Vincent de Gournay Savoirs économiques et pratiques administratives en France au milieu du XVIIIè siècle*. Paris: Ined, pp. 63–88.
Charles, L. (2015a). Figures of Mockery. The Cultural Disqualification of Physiocracy (1760–1790). *The European Journal of the History of Economic Thought*, 22 (3), pp. 383–419.
Charles, L. (2015b). Jeux de mots, narrative and economic writing: The Rhetoric of Anti-physiocracy in French Economic Periodicals (1764–1769). *The European Journal of the History of Economic Thought*, 22, (3), pp. 359–382.
Charles, L., Orain, A. (2019). François Véron de Forbonnais and the Invention of Antiphysiocracy. In S. L. Kaplan, S. A. Reinert (eds.), *The Economic Turn: Recasting Political Economy in Eighteenth-Century Europe*. London: Anthem Press, pp. 139–168.
Charles, L., Théré, C. (2007). François Quesnay: A Rural Socrates in Versailles?, *History of Political Economy*, 38, pp. 195–214.
Charles, L., Théré, C. (2019). The Physiocratic Movement: A Revision, in S. L. Kaplan, S. A. Reinert (eds.), *The Economic Turn: Recasting Political Economy in Eighteenth-Century Europe*. London: Anthem Press, pp. 35–70.

Cherrad, S. (2007). De l'éducation des mères à une possible éducation publique: mesdames d'Épinay et de Miremont. In I. Brouard-Arends, M.-E. Plagnol-Diéval (eds.), *Femmes éducatrices au siècle des Lumières*, Rennes: Presses Universitaires de Rennes, pp. 93–102.

Chiosi, E. (1992). *Lo spirito del secolo. Politica e religione a Napoli nell'età dell'Illuminismo*. Naples: Giannini.

Chiosi, E. (1986a). Il Regno dal 1734 al 1799. In G. Galasso, R. Romeo (eds.), *Storia del Mezzogiorno*, Napoli: Edizioni del Sole, Vol. IV, pp. 384–396.

Chiosi, E. (1986b). La Reale Accademia ercolanese. Bernardo Tanucci fra politica antiquaria. In R. Ajello, M. D'Addio (eds.), *Bernardo Tanucci statista letterato giurista, Atti del convegno internazionale di studi per il secondo centenario 1783–1983*, vol. II, Naples: Jovene, pp. 493–517.

Chiosi, E. (2005). Istituzioni accademiche a Napoli nel Settecento: continuità e mutamenti. In J. Boutier, B. Marin, A. Romano, (eds.), *Naples, Rome, Florence. Une histoire comparée des milieux intellectuels italiens (XVII–XVIIIe siècles)*. Rome: Publications de l'École française de Rome, pp. 105–122.

Chorley, P. (1965). *Oil, Silk and Enlightenment. Economic Problems in XVIII Century Naples*. Naples: Istituto Italiano di Studi Storici.

Chown J. (1996). *A History of Money From Ad 800*. London, Routledge.

Ciccolella, D. (2016). Il prezzo della patria. Stato, negozianti e regolazione dei prezzi alla voce nel Mezzogiorno nel secondo '700. *Storia economica*, Anno XIX, n. 2, pp. 491–530.

Ciccolella, D., Guenzi, A. (2008). Scambi e gestione del rischio sui mercati locali e regionali. il contratto alla voce nel Mezzogiorno in Età Moderna. *Storia economica*, Anno XI, n. 1, pp. 41–79.

Cipolla, C. (1967). *Money, Prices and Civilization in the Mediterranean World: Fifth to Seventeenth Century*. New York, Gordian Press.

Cipolla, C. (1975). *Le avventure della lira*. Bologna: Il Mulino.

Clemente, A. (2003). Quando il reato non è peccato. Il contrabbando nel Regno di Napoli tra conflitti giurisdizionali, pluralismo istituzionale e quotidianità degli scambi (XVIII secolo). *Quaderni Storici*, 143, 2, pp. 359–394.

Clemente, A., Russo, S. (eds). (2019). *La polizia de' grani: mercati, regole e crisi di sussistenza nelle economie di antico regime*. Soveria Mannelli: Rubbettino.

Clower, R. (1967). A Reconsideration of the Microfoundations of Monetary Theory. *Economic Inquiry*, vol. 6, 1, pp. 1–8.

Clower, R. (1969). Introduction. In R.Clower (ed.) *Monetary Theory: Selected Readings*, Hammondsworth: Penguin.

Cobban, A. (1966). The Decline of Divine-Right Monarchy in France. In *The New Cambridge Modern History*. Volume VII The Old Regime (1713–63). Cambridge: Cambridge University Press, pp. 214–240.

Codr, D. (2019). Money, Ritual, and Religion: A secularization story. In Desan. C. (ed.) *A Cultural History of Money*, Vol. IV, *A Cultural History of Money in the Age of Enlightenment*. London: Bloomsbury Academic, pp. 75–94.

Cohen, B. I. (1971). *Introduction to Isaac Newton's Principia*. Harvard: Harvard University Press.
Cohen, H. (1988). Diderot's machiavellian Harlequin: Ferdinando Galiani. *Studies on Voltaire and the eighteenth century*, n° 256, pp. 129–148.
Colapietra, R. (1961). *Vita pubblica e classi politiche nel Viceregno napoletano (1656–1734)*. Rome: Storia e Letteratura.
Colapietra, R. (ed.) (1973). *Problemi monetari negli scrittori napoletani del Seicento*. Rome: Accademia Nazionale dei Lincei.
Comparato, V. I. (1970). *Giuseppe Valletta. Un intellettuale napoletano della fine del Seicento*. Naples: Istituto Italiano Studi Storici.
Comparato, V. I.(1974). *Uffici e società a Napoli. Aspetti dell'ideologia del magistrato in età moderna*. Florence: Olschk.
Comparato, V. I. (2011). Platonismo e antidispotismo in Paolo Mattia Doria. In Canmpos Boralevi, L. (ed.), *Challenging Centralism. Decentramento e autonomie nel pensiero politico europeo,* Florece, Firenze University Press, pp. 99–110.
Coniglio, G. (1981). *I Borboni di Napoli*. Milan: dall'Oglio.
Conti, V. (1975). Paolo Mattia Doria e l'accademia di Medinacoeli. *Il Pensiero Politico*, 8 [2], pp. 203–218.
Conti, V. (1978). *Paolo Mattia Doria: Dalla Repubblica dei togati alla Repubblica dei notabili*. Florence: Olschki.
Conti, V. (1981). Le polemiche matematiche di P.M. Doria (con alcune lettere sconosciute). *Bollettino del Centro di Studi Vichiani*, 11, pp. 185–198.
Conti, V. (ed.) (2002) *La ricezione di Grozio a Napoli nel Settecento*. Florence: Centro Editoriale Toscano.
Cossa L. (1892). *Introduzione allo studio dell'economia politica*. Milan: Hoepli.
Costa, G. (1970). Vico e Locke. *Giornale critico della filosofia italiana*, vol. XLIX, pp. 344–361.
Costa, G. (1976). Vico's Political Thought in His Time and Ours, *Social Research*, Vol. 43, No. 3, *Vico and Contemporary Thought*, pp. 612–624.
Costa, G. (2009). Celestini e inquisitori: Galiani, la Bibbia e la cultura napoletana. *Annali della Scuola Normale Superiore di Pisa. Classe di Lettere e Filosofia*, 2009, Serie 5, Vol. 1, No. 2, pp. 593–620.
Costa, G. (2011). *Celestino Galiani e la Sacra Scrittura: Alle radici del pensiero napoletano del Settecento*. Rome: Aracne.
Costabile, L (2016). The value and security of money. Metallic and fiduciary media in Ferdinando Galiani's Della moneta. The European Journal of the History of Economic Thought, Vol. 23, Issue, 3, pp. 400–424.
Costabile, L., Neal, L. (2018). *Financial Innovation and Resilience. A Comparative Perspective on the Public Banks of Naples (1462–1808)*. London: Palgrave Macmillan.
Costabile, L., Velde, F. (2023). Tax Erosion in Seventeenth-Century Naples: Tommaso Campanella on Causes and Remedies. *History of Political Economy*, 55: 5, pp. 929–962

Costelloe, T. M. (1999). The Concept of a State of Nature in Vico's New Science. *History of Philosophy Quarterly*, Vol. 16, No. 3, pp. 321–339.

Craveri, B. (2005). *The Age of Conversation*. New York: New York Review Books.

Cremaschi, S. (1981). Adam Smith, Newtonianism and Political Economy. *Manuscrito*, V (1), pp. 117–134.

Cremaschi, S. (1989). Adam Smith: Skeptical Newtonianism, Disenchanted Republicanism, and the Birth of Social Science. In Dascal, M., Gruengard, O. (eds.), *Knowledge and Politics: Case Studies in the Relationship Between Epistemology and Political Philosophy*. Boulder: Westview Press, pp. 83–110.

Cremaschi, S. (2000). Legge di Natura e Scienza Economica. *Quaderni storici, Nuova Serie, Etiche economiche*, 35, 105 (3), pp. 697–730.

Crépel, P., Gilain, C. (eds). (1989). *Condorcet: mathématicien, économiste, philosophe, homme politique*. Paris: Minerve.

Crépel, P., Rieucau, J.-N. (2005). Condorcet's Social Mathematics: A Few Tables. *Social Choice and Welfare*, 25 (2/3), pp. 243–285.

Croce, B. (1903). I manoscritti dell'abate Galiani. *La Critica. Rivista di Letteratura, Storia e Filosofia*, Vol. 1, pp. 236–240.

Croce, B. (1909). Il pensiero dell'abate Galiani. *La Critica. Rivista di Letteratura, Storia e Filosofia*, Vol. 7, pp. 399–404.

Croce, B. (1913). *The philosophy of Giambattista Vico*, Translated by R. G. Collingwood. New York: Macmillan Company.

Croce, B. (1925a). Giambattista Basile e l'elaborazione artistica delle fiabe popolari. Discorso. In G.B. Basile, *Il Pentamerone, ossia, La fiaba delle fiabe*, edited by B.Croce, Bari: Laterza, pp. 3–21.

Croce, B. (1925b) [1970]. *Storia del Regno di Napoli*, Bari: Laterza. English translation *History of the Kingdom of Naples*. Chicago: Chicago University Press, 1970.

Croce, B. (1923) [2006]. Il paradiso abitato da diavoli. Conference read to the Neapolitan Society of Homeland History on 12 June 1923. In B. Croce (ed.), *Il paradiso abitato da diavoli*, Milan: Adelphi, 2006, pp. 11–21.

Croce, B. (1932). *Conversazioni critiche*. IV serie. Bari: Laterza.

Croce B. (1935). Una lettera inedita della signora d' Épinay e il Dialogue sur les femmes dell'abate Galiani, in Croce, B. Varietà di storia letteraria e civile, serie prima, Bari, Laterza, pp. 119–134.

Croce, B. (1949). Opuscoli e disegni giocosi dell'abate Galiani, in Croce, B. La letteratura italiana del Settecento, Bari: Laterza, pp. 287–289

Croce, B. (1954). Don Onofrio Galeota poeta e filosofo napoletano. In *Aneddoti di varia letteratura*, vol III, Bari: Laterza, pp. 150–162.

Cubeddu, R. (2024). Galiani, Menger and Other Austrians. *History of Economic Ideas*, XXXII, 3, pp. 63–83.

D'Alconzo, P. (2019a). Parole e immagini. La diffusione delle antichità vesuviane negli anni di Carlo di Borbone: iniziative istituzionali, carteggi, riproduzioni grafiche. In P.G. Guzzo, M.R. Esposito, N. Ossanna Cavadini, (eds.), *Ercolano e Pompei. Visioni di una scoperta,* Milan: Skira, pp. 54–73.

D'Alconzo, P. (2019b). La luna e i gamberi: Bernardo Tanucci, Ferdinando Galiani e l'affaire Winckelmann. In I. Bragantini, E. Morlicchio, (eds.), *Winckelmann e l'archeologia a Napoli. Atti dell'incontro di studi - Università degli Studi di Napoli L'Orientale,* Naples: Università degli Studi di Napoli "L'Orientale", pp. 101–132.

D'Alconzo, P. (2020). Egli è il primo de' Sovrani, ch'abbia fatto uno scavamento così vasto, durevole, e dovizioso: scavo e pubblicazione dei reperti vesuviani in un manoscritto galianeo del 1756, Studi e ricerche del Parco archeologico di Pompei, 43, 2020, pp. 103–123

D'Alconzo, P. (2020a). Ferdinando Galiani e le antichità, tra istituzioni, collezionismo e mercato. In P. Giulierini, A. Coralini, E. Calandra, (eds.), *Miniere Della Memoria, Scavi in archivi, depositi e biblioteche,* Naples: All'Insegna del Giglio, pp. 201–233.

D'Alconzo, P. (2020b). Rileggere la pittura antica attraverso una fonte manoscritta inedita: Ferdinando Galiani e i dipinti del Museo Ercolanese. In P. Giulierini, A. Coralini, Sampaolo, V. (eds.), *Picta fragmenta. Rileggendo la pittura vesuviana, Atti del Convegno Internazionale* (Napoli, 13–15 settembre 2018). Milan: Silvana Editorale.

D'Onofrio, F. (2015). On the Concept of "Felicitas Publica" in Eighteenth-Century Political Economy. *Journal of the History of Economic Thought,* Volume 37, Number 3, pp. 449–471.

Dal Pane, L. (1958). Di un' opera sconosciuta di Carlo Antonio Broggia e del suo carteggio con L. A. Muratori. *Giornale degli Economisti e Annali di Economia,* Nuova Serie, Anno 17, No. 11/12, pp. 638–661.

Das Satya, P. (1982). Economies of Scale, Imperfect Competition, and the Pattern of Trade. *The Economic Journal,* Vol. 92, No. 367, pp. 684–693.

Daudin, G., Crouzet, F. (2004). *Commerce et prospérité: la France au XVIIIe siècle.* Paris: Presses de l'université Paris-Sorbonne.

Davies, G. (2002). *A History of Money. From Ancient Times to the Present Day.* Cardiff: University of Wales Press.

Davis, A. E. (2020). Money as Social Institution: Its Historical Emergence and Political Implicationsin. In S. Pressman (ed.) *How Social Forces Impact the Economy.* London: Routledge, pp. 81–96.

Davison, R. (1985). *Diderot et Galiani: étude d'une amitié philosophique.* Oxford: Voltaire Foundation.

Davison, R. (1988). Diderot, Galiani et Vico: un itinéraire Philosophique. *Diderot Studies,* Vol. 23, pp. 39–53.

De Caro, G. (1962). *Le carte Tanucci nell'Archivo General de Simancas,* Milan: Giuffré.

De Caro, G. (1971). Giovanni Brancaccio. In *Dizionario Biografico degli Italiani*, Vol. 13, *ad vocem*.

De Caro, G. (1975). José de Baeza Vicentelo y Manrique conte di Cantillana. In *Dizionario Biografico degli Italiani*, Vol. 18, *ad vocem*.

De Giovanni, B. (1958). *Filosofia e diritto in F. d'Andrea: contributo alla storia del previchismo*. Milan: Giuffrè.

De Giovanni, B. (1968). Cultura e vita civile in Giuseppe Valletta. In E. Sestan (ed.), *Saggi e ricerche sul Settecento*. Naples: Istituto Italiano per gli Studi Storici, pp. 1–47.

De Giovanni, B. (1970). La vita intellettuale a Napoli fra la metà del '600 e la restaurazione del Regno. In *Storia di Napoli*, vol. 6. *Tra Spagna e Austria*. Naples: Società Editrice Storia di Napoli, pp. 401–534.

Del Donna, A.R. (2012). *Opera, Theatrical Culture and Society in Late Eighteenth-Century Naples*. London: Routledge.

Dell'Erba, L. (1932–1935) [1986]. *La riforma monetaria angioina e il suo sviluppo storico nel Reame di Napoli*, Sala Bolognese: Forni, 1986. First publication in *Archivio storico per le province napoletane*, Nuova Serie, anno XVIII–LVII, fascicolo I–IV, pp. 156–206; anno XIX–LVIII, fascicolo I–IV, pp. 5–66; anno XX–LIX, fascicolo I–IV, pp. 39–136; anno XXI–LX, fascicolo I–IV, pp. 46–158.

Del Negro, P. (1998). Marco Foscarini. In *Dizionario Biografico degli Italiani*, volume 49, Rome: Treccani, *ad vocem*.

Dédéyan, C. (1975). L'Europe française à l'heure de Galiani. In *Convegno italo-francese sul tema Ferdinando Galiani* (Roma, 25–27 maggio 1972), Rome: Accademia Nazionale dei Lincei, pp. 380–389.

Deloche, R. (1988). En marge d'un bicentenaire: Galiani et l'apologue. *Revue économique*, Vol. 39, No. 6, pp. 1143–1157.

De Lucia, G. (1984). I collaboratori di Bernardo Tanucci nelle Segreterie di Stato durante il quinquennio 1755–1759. *Storia e Politica*, Anno XXIII, fasc. 1, pp. 73–94.

De Majo, S. (1998). Ferdinando Galiani. In *Dizionario Biografico degli Italiani*, volume 51, Rome: Treccani, *ad vocem*.

Demaria, G. (1972). La scienza politica di Ferdinando Galiani. *Giornale degli Economisti e Annali di Economia*, Nuova Serie, Anno 31, No. 9/10, pp. 624–677.

Demeter, T. (2014). Enlarging the Bounds of Moral Philosophy: Newton's Method and Hume's Science of Man, in Z.Biener, E. Schliesser, (eds.), *Newton and Empiricism*. Cambridge: Cambridge University Press, pp. 171–180.

De Miranda, G. (2005). À de vagues desseins l'homme est toujours en proie. L'accademia degli Oziosi e i suoi antagonisti tra riti fondativi e costruzione d'identità. In J. Boutier, B. Marin, A. Romano (eds.), Naples, Rome, Florence. Une histoire comparée des milieux intellectuels italiens (XVII–XVIII e siècles). Rome: Publications de l'École française de Rome, pp. 89–104.

de Roover, R. (1955). Scholastic Economics: Survival and Lasting Influence from the Sixteenth Century to Adam Smith. *The Quarterly Journal of Economics*, Vol. 69, No. 2, pp. 161–190.

de Roover, R. (1967). *San Bernardino of Siena and Sant'Antonino of Florence: the Two Great Economic Thinkers of the Middle Ages*. Cambrige: Harvard University Printing Office.

de Roover, R. (1971). *La pensée économique des scolastiques doctrines et méthodes*, Paris: Vrin.

De Rosa C. A. (1834). *Ritratti poetici di alcuni uomini di lettere antichi e moderni del regno di Napoli*, Volume 1, Naples: Fibreno.

De Rosa, L. (1955). *I cambi esteri del Regno di Napoli dal 1591 al 1707*. Naples: Biblioteca del Bollettino dell'Archivio storico del Banco di Napoli.

De Rosa, L. (1987). *Il Mezzogiorno spagnolo tra crescita e decadenza*. Milan: Il Saggiatore.

De Rosa, L. (1994). Introduzione. In L. De Rosa (ed.) *Il Mezzogiorno agli inizi del '600*, Bari: Laterza.

De Rosa, L. (1995). Galiani e il commercio dei grani. In L. De Rosa, (ed.), *Economisti merdionali*. Naples: Istituto Italiano per gli Studi Filosofici, pp. 117–189.

De Rosa, L. (2004). L'archivio del Banco di Napoli e l'attività dei banchi pubblici napoletani, De Computis. Spanish Journal of Accounting History, N.1, pp. 54–66.

De Scisciolo, N. (1997). Presenza lockiana a Napoli tra fine Seicento e inizio Settecento: dagli Investiganti alle eredità genovesiane. *Studi filosofici*, XX, pp. 73–111.

De Tiberiis G. F. (2001). Le riflessioni sopra il commercio di Federico Valignani. Alle origini del pensiero riformatore nel Regno di Napoli. *Frontiera d'Europa*, VII (2001), nn. 1–2, pp. 165–228.

Di Filippo, M. (2005). Per una storia dei rapporti tra il Regno di Napoli e l'Impero russo. In D. Rizzi, A. Shishkin (eds.), *Archivio russo-italiano IV*, Avellino: Europa Orientalis - Istituto di Linguistica (Università di Salerno), pp. 243–295.

Diaz, F. (1962). *Filosofia e politica nel Settecento francese*. Turin: Einaudi.

Diaz, F. (1972). Aspetti e problemi dell'epistolario di Ferdinando Galiani. *Rivista storica italiana*, Anno LXXXIV, fasc. I, pp. 80–110.

Diaz, F. (1973). L'abate Galiani consigliere di commercio estero del Regno di Napoli. In F. Diaz, *Per una storia illuministica*. Naples: Guida, pp. 289–364.

Diaz, F. (1975a). Introduzione. In Galiani, F. *Opere*, edited by F. Diaz, L.Guerci, *Letteratura italiana. Storia e testi. Illuministi italiani*, tomo VI, Milan-Naples: Ricciardi, pp. ix–cvi.

Diaz, F. (1975b). La politica estera e i problemi economici del Regno di Napoli nell'opera di Ferdinando Galiani. In *Convegno italo-francese sul tema Ferdinando*

Galiani (Roma, 25–27 maggio 1972), Rome: Accademia Nazionale dei Lincei, pp. 79–107.

Diaz, F. (1975c). "Preliminari" ai *Dialogues*. In F. Diaz, L.Guerci (eds), F. Galiani, *Opere, Letteratura italiana. Storia e testi. Illuministi italiani*, tomo VI, Milan-Naples: Ricciardi, pp. 347–356.

Di Donato, F. (1989). La Segreteria del Regno e Niccolò Fragianni. *Archivio Storico per le Province Napoletane,* CVII, pp. 247–307.

Dieckmann, H. (1975). Diderot et Galiani. In *Convegno italo-francese sul tema Ferdinando Galiani* (Roma, 25–27 maggio 1972). Rome: Accademia Nazionale dei Lincei, pp. 309–331.

Diemer, A., Guillemin H. (2013). La naissance de l'économie politique ou la fascination des penseurs de la société pour la physique, *Triangle, ISH Lyon, Séminaire Economie Politique*, 15 avril 2013.

Di Rienzo, E. (1977). Niccolò Fraggianni. In *Dizionario Biografico degli Italiani*, Vol. 49, *ad vocem*.

Di Rienzo, E. (1994). *Alle origini della Francia contemporanea. Economia, politica e società nel pensiero di André Morellet: 1756–1819*, Naples: Edizioni Scientifiche Italiane.

Di Rienzo, E. (1998). Celestino Galiani. In *Dizionario Biografico degli Italiani*, Vol. 51, *ad vocem*.

Di Vittorio, A. (1969). *Gli Austriaci e il Regno di Napoli. I. Le finanze pubbliche*. Naples: Giannini.

Di Vittorio, A. (1973). *Gli Austriaci e il Regno di Napoli. II. Ideologia e politica di sviluppo*. Naples: Giannini.

Di Vittorio, A. (2010). Economia e finanza pubblica nel Mezzogiorno austriaco (1707–1734). In S. Russo, N. Guasti, (eds.), *Il Viceregno austriaco (1707–1734)*, Rome, Carocci, pp. 53–63.

Dixit, A. K. (1996). *The Making of Economic Policy: A Transaction-Cost Politics Perspective. Munich Lectures in Economics*. Cambridge (MS): MIT Press.

Dobado-González, R., García-Hiernaux, A., Guerrero, D.E. (2012). The Integration of Grain Markets in the Eighteenth Century: Early Rise of Globalization in the West. *The Journal of Economic History*, Vol. 72, No. 3, pp. 671–707.

Dockès, P. (1969). *L'espace dans la pensée économique du XVIe au XVIIIe* siècle. Paris: Flammarion.

Dongili, P. (1988). Ferdinando Galiani: *Della moneta. Rivista Internazionale di Scienze Economiche e Commerciali*, Vol. 35, N. 1, pp. 11–28.

Doria, G. (1984). *Viaggiatori stranieri a Napoli*. Naples: Guida.

Dubois, A. (1897). Les théories psycologiques de la valeur au XVIIIe siècle. *Revue d'économie politique*, XI, pp. 849–864, pp. 917–930.

Duhem, J. (1953). Bibliotheca Vesuvina d'après le manuscrit dressé par Galiani pour le pape Benoit XIV. *Bullettin du bibliophile et du bibliothécaire*, n. 2, pp. 59–73.

Dulac, G. (1992). Preface. In Galiani, F., d'Épinay, L. 1992. *Correspondance. Vol. I (1769–1770)*, présentation de G. Dulac, texte établi et annoté par D. Maggetti, en collaboration avec G. Dulac, Paris: Les Editions Desjonquères, pp. 7–34.

Durand, Y-R. (1969). Introduction. In *Mémoires de Jean-Joseph de Laborde fermier général et banquier de la cour, Annuaire-Bulletin de la Société de l'histoire de France*, pp. 75–111.

Einaudi, L. (1936) [2006]. The Theory of Imaginary Money from Charlemagne to the French Revolution. *Rivista di storia economica,* 1936, I, pp. 1–35. In L. Einaudi, R. Faucci, R. Marchionatti (eds.) *Luigi Einaudi Selected Economic Essays*. London: Palgrave Macmillan, Vol. II, pp. 153–181.

Einaudi, L. (1949) [2014]. Galiani, the economist. In *Rendiconti della Classe di Scienze morali, storiche e filologiche*, Series VIII, vol. IV, issue 3–4, March–April 1949, In L. Einaudi, R. Faucci, R. Marchionatti (eds.) *Luigi Einaudi Selected Economic Essays*. London: Palgrave Macmillan, vol II, pp. 227–264.

Einaudi, L. (1953). *Saggi bibliografici e storici intorno alle dottrine economiche*, Rome: Edizioni Storia e Letteratura.

Einzig, P. (1966). *Primitive Money. In its Ethnological, Historical and Economic Aspects*. Second Edition, Revised and Enlarged, London: Pergamon Press.

Eusepi, G. (1992). Galiani teorico del valore soggettivo. In N. Acocella, G. M. Rey, M. Tiberi (eds.), *Saggi di politica economica in onore di Federico Caffè*, Milan: Angeli, pp. 93–118.

Fabre, J. (1975). Galiani et la société française à l'époque de Louis XV. In *Convegno italo-francese sul tema Ferdinando Galiani* (Roma, 25–27 maggio 1972), Rome: Accademia Nazionale dei Lincei, pp. 159–176.

Faccarello, G. (1994). Nil repente!: Galiani and Necker on Economic Reforms. *European Journal of the History of Economic Thought,* 1 (3), pp. 519–550.

Faccarello, G. (1998). Galiani, Necker and Turgot. A debate on economic reform and policy in 18th Century France. In G. Faccarello (ed.), *Studies in the History of French Political Economy. From Bodin to Walras*. London: Routledge, pp. 120–195.

Faccarello, G. (1999). *The Foundations of "Laissez-Faire": The Economics of Pierre de Boisguilbert*. London: Routledge.

Farinella, C. (1999). Angelo Gatti. In *Dizionario Biografico degli Italiani*, Vol. 52, *ad vocem.*

Favino, F. (2013). Giuseppe Orlandi. In *Dizionario Biografico degli Italiani*, vol. 79, Rome: Treccani, *ad vocem.*

Fay, C. R. (1932). Locke Versus Lowndes. *The Cambridge Historical Journal* IV, no. 2, pp. 149–155.

Federici, L. (1941). *La moneta e l'oro.* Milan: Casa Editrice Ambrosiana.

Feingold, M. (2004). *The Newtonian Moment: Isaac Newton and the Making of Modem Culture*, Oxford: Oxford University Press.

Feldman, J. (2005). Condorcet et la Mathematique Sociale: Enthousiasmes et Bemols. *Mathematics and Social Sciences*, 43, 172 (4): pp. 7–41.

Felici, L. (1972). *Il carteggio Galiani-Bottari (1751–1759)*. Rome: Fratelli Palombi.

Felloni, G. (1998). Finanze statali, emissioni monetarie ed alterazioni della moneta di conto in Italia nei secoli XVI–XVIII. In *Scritti di Storia Economica*, Genoa: Società Ligure di Storia Patria, pp. 471–496.

Femia, J.V. (2004). *Machiavelli Revisited*, Cardiff: University of Wales Press.

Ferrand, J., Orain, A. (2019). Sensationism, Modern Natural Law and the Science of Commerce at the Heart of the Controversy between Mably and the Physiocrats. In S. L. Kaplan, S. A. Reinert (eds.), *The Economic Turn: Recasting Political Economy in Eighteenth-Century Europe*. London: Anthem Press, pp. 439–468.

Ferraioli, G. (1880). Un fallo diplomatico dell'abate Galiani. *Archivio storico per le province napoletane*, Anno V, Fascicolo IV, pp. 690–698.

Ferrone, V. (1995). *The Intellectual Roots of the Italian Enlightenment: Newtonian Science, Religion, and Politics in the Early Eighteenth Century*. Atlantic Highlands: Humanities Press.

Ferrone, V. (2012). *The politics of Enlightenment: Republicanism, constitutionalism, and the rights of man in Gaetano Filangieri*. London: Anthem Press.

Ferrone, V. (2019). *Il mondo dell'Illuminismo. Storia di una rivoluzione culturale*. Turin: Einaudi.

Finoli, A.M. (1947). Osservazioni sulla lingua degli economisti italiani del Settecento. *Lingua nostra*, 8, pp. 108–112.

Fiorelli, V. (2009). *I sentieri dell'inquisitore. Sant'Uffizio, periferie ecclesiastiche e disciplinamento devozionale (1615–1678)*. Naples: Guida.

Fish, M.F. (1953). The Academy of Investigators. In E. Ashworth Underwood (ed.), *Science, Medicine and History: Essays on the Evolution of Scientific Thought and Medical Practice, Written in Honour of Charles Singer.* Oxford: Oxford University Press, pp. 521–563.

Fisher, I. (1913). A Compensated Dollar. *Quarterly Journal of Economics*, vol. 27, n. 2, pp. 213–235.

Fisher, I. (1928). *The Money Illusion*, New York: Adelphi Company.

Fischman, M. (1998). Le concept quesnayen d'ordre naturel. *Cahiers d'économie politique* 32, pp. 67–97.

Flandreau M. (ed.). (2003). *Money Doctors. The Experience of International Financial Advising 1850–2000*. London - New York: Routledge.

Flora, G. (1927). Le più belle pagine di Ferdinando Galiani, Milan: Treves

Flori, M. C. (2009). Lorenzo Mehus. In *Dizionario biografico degli italiani*, vol. 73, Rome: Istituto dell' Enciclopedia Italiana, *ad vocem*.

Foley, V. (1973). An Origin to the Tableau Oeconomique. *History of Political Economy*, 5, pp. 121–150.

Foley, V. (1976). *The Social Physics of Adam Smith.* West Lafayette: Purdue University Press.

Force, P. (2003). *Self-Interest before Adam Smith. A Genealogy of Economic Science*, Cambridge: Cambridge University Press.

Foucault, D. (2010). *Histoire du libertinage: des goliards au marquis de Sade*, Paris: Perrin.

Fox-Genovese, E. A. (1976). *The Origins of Physiocracy: Economic Revolution and Social Order in Eighteenth-Century France,* Ithaca: Cornell University Press.

Francovich, C. (1974). *Storia della massoneria in Italia: Dalle origini alla Rivoluzione francese.* Florence: La Nuova Italia.

Fubini Leuzzi, M. (2004). Bartolomeo Intieri. In *Dizionario biografico degli italiani*, vol. 62, Rome: Istituto dell'Enciclopedia Italiana, *ad vocem.*

Galasso, G. (1959). Contributo alla storia delle finanze del regno di Napoli nella prima metà del Seicento. *Annuario dell'Istituto storico italiano per l'età moderna e contemporanea*, Vol. XI, pp. 5–106.

Galasso, G. (1973). Introduction. In Paolo Mattia Doria, *Massime del governo spagnolo a Napoli* (editeb by V. Conti), Naples: Guida.

Galasso, G. (1976). Napoli nel viceregno spagnolo dal 1648 al 1696. In *Storia di Napoli*, volume VI. Naples: Società Editrice Storia di Napoli.

Galasso, G. (1982). *Napoli spagnola dopo Masaniello*, Florence: Sansoni.

Galasso, G. (1989a). Mito e storia di Galileo nel Mezzogiorno. In G. Galasso (ed.), *La filosofia in soccorso de' governi. La cultura napoletana del Settecento.* Naples: Guida, pp. 119–135.

Galasso, G. (1989b). Doria: il governo spagnolo a Napoli e i problemi del Regno, In G. Galasso, (ed.) *La filosofia in soccorso de' governi. La cultura napoletana del Settecento*, Naples: Guida, pp. 193–232.

Galasso, G. (1989c). Doria: cultura e filosofia delle riforme. In G. Galasso, (ed.), *La filosofia in soccorso de' governi. La cultura napoletana del Settecento.* Naples: Guida, pp. 233–256.

Galasso, G. (1989d). I manoscritti napoletani dell'abate Galiani. In G. Galasso, (ed.) *La filosofia in soccorso de' governi. La cultura napoletana del Settecento.* Naples: Guida, pp. 353–368.

Galasso, G. (1992). *Economia e società nella Calabria del Cinquecento.* Naples: Guida.

Galasso, G. (2003). *Napoli capitale. Identità politica e identità cittadina. Studi e ricerche 1266–1860.* Naples: Electa.

Galasso, G. (2007). *Storia del Regno di Napoli.* Vol. IV. *Il Mezzogiorno borbonico e napoleonico* (1734–1815). Turin: Utet.

Gallo, F. F. (2018). *La congiura di Macchia. Cultura e conflitto politico a Napoli nel primo Settecento.* Rome: Viella.

Gambacorta, L. (1988). Ferdinando Galiani e la Russia. *Archivio Storico per le Province Napoletane*, Vol. CVI, pp. 335–346.

Gandolfo, G. (2014). *International Trade Theory and Policy.* Berlin: Springer.

Garin, E. (1962). Appunti per una storia della fortuna di Hobbes nel Settecento italiano. *Rivista Critica di Storia della Filosofia*, Ottobre–Dicembre 1962, Vol. 17, No. 4, pp. 514–527.

Garin, E. (1970). Per una storia dei rapporti fra Bayle e l'Italia. In E. Garin (ed.), *Dal Rinascimento all'Illuminismo. Studi e ricerche*, Pisa: Nistri-Lischi, pp. 157–172.

Garin, E. (2008). *History of Italian Philosophy*, vol. I, edited by G. Pinton, Amsterdam-New York: Rodopi.

Gaudemet, E. (1899). *L'abbé Galiani et la question du commerce des blés à la fin du règne de Louis XV.* Paris: Rousseau.

Gentilcore, D. (2013). Tempi sì calamitosi: Epidemic Disease and Public Health. In T. Astarita, (ed.), *A Companion to Early Modern Naples.* Leiden-Boston: Brill, pp. 281–306.

Gernet, L. (1968). *Anthropologie de la Grèce Antique.* Paris: Masper.

Giansiracusa, L. (1988). La giustificazione storica del corpuscolarismo nella Istoria Filosofica di Giuseppe Valletta. *Rivista di Storia della Filosofia*, Vol. 43, No. 1, pp. 181–191.

Ghisalberti, C. (1975). Ferdinando Galiani e il problema istituzionale. In *Convegno italo-francese sul tema Ferdinando Galiani* (Roma, 25–27 maggio 1972), Rome: Accademia Nazionale dei Lincei, pp. 49–65.

Giannini, C. (2011). *The Age of Central Banks.* Cheltenham: Elgar.

Giarrizzo, G. (1981). *Vico, la politica e la storia*, Naples: Guida.

Giarrizzo, G. (1994). *Massoneria e Illuminismo nell'Europa del Settecento.* Venice: Marsilio.

Gignoux C.-J. (1922). L'abbé Galiani et la querelle des grains au XVIIIe siècle. *Revue d'histoire économique et sociale*, Vol. 10, No. 1, pp. 17–37.

Giliberti, L. (1921). *Sul Catasto Onciario e l'Oncia di Carlini e di Grana.* Naples: Tipografia Cimmaruta.

Gillard, L. (1990). Nicole Oresme, économiste. *Revue historique* 279, CCLXXIX, vol. 279 (1), (1990), pp. 3–39.

Giocoli, N. (1997). La teoria dell'interesse di Ferdinando Galiani e l'ipotesi di Bernoulli: una grande occasione perduta?. *Il pensiero economico italiano*, 5 (1), pp. 7–37.

Giocoli, N. (1999). La teoria del valore di Ferdinando Galiani: un'interpretazione unitaria. *Storia del pensiero economico*, n. 38, pp. 69–93.

Giocoli, N. (2001). Value and Interest in Ferdinando Galiani's *Della Moneta. History of Economic Ideas*, Vol. 9, No. 3, Special Issue: *"Della Moneta" by Ferdinando Galiani: a Quarter Millennium Assessment* (2001), pp. 95–135.

Girard, P. (2011). Matérialisme et politique. Les enjeux de la réception du cartésianisme à Naples à l'âge classique. *Corpus, revue de philosophie*, 61, pp. 113–132.

Girard, P. (2017). L'émergence des Lumières à Naples entre matérialisme et radicalité. *Archives de Philosophie*, Vol. 80, No. 3, *L'invention de la modernité à Naples*, pp. 417–434.

Girard, R. (1924). *L'abbé Terray et la liberté du commerce des grains, 1769–1774*. Paris: Les Presses Universitaires de France.

Giura, V. (1978). *Gli ebrei e la ripresa economica del Regno di Napoli 1740–1747*. Genève: Droz.

Glineur, C. (2005). Entre libéralisme et protectionnisme: la politique pré-libérale du contrôleur général Moreau de Séchelles. *La Revue administrative*, 58e Année, No. 345, pp. 290–302.

Goetsch, J. R. (1995a). *Vico's Axioms. The Geometry of the Human World*. New Haven: Yale University Press.

Goetsch, J. R. (1995b). Vico's Speculative Geometry of the Civil World. *The Journal of Speculative Philosophy*, New Series, Vol. 9, No. 4, pp. 279–295.

Goggi, G. (1994). Galiani et l'Angleterre sur la genèse des dialogues sur les blés. *Dix-Huitieme Siecle*, n. 26, *Economie et politique*, pp. 295–316.

Gonnard, R. (1935). *Histoire des doctrines monétaire dans ses rapports avec l'histoire des monnaies*. Paris: Librairie du Recueil Sirey.

Goodman, D. (1989). Enlightenment Salons: The Convergence of Female and Philosophic Ambitions. *Eighteenth-Century Studies*, Vol. 22, No. 3, *Special Issue: The French Revolution in Culture*, pp. 329–350.

Goodman, D. (1994). *The Republic of Letters: A Cultural History of the French Enlightenment*. Ithaca: Cornell University Press.

Gordon, B. J. (1961). Aristotle, Schumpeter, and the Metalist Tradition. *The Quarterly Journal of Economics*, vol. 75, No. 4, pp. 608–614.

Goutte, P.-H. (1994). Les Éphémérides du citoyen, instrument périodique au service de l'ordre naturel (1765–1772). *Dixhuitième Siècle*, n°26, 1994. *Economie et politique*. pp. 139–161.

Granger, G.-G. (1956). *La mathématique sociale du marquis de Condorcet*. Paris: PUF.

Granito, A. (1861). *Storia della congiura del principe di Macchia e dell'occupazione fatta dalle armi austriache del Regno di Napoli nel 1707*. Naples: Stamperia dell'Iride.

Graziani, A. (1889). *Storia critica della teoria del valore in Italia*. Milan: Hoepli.

Gregory, T. (1981). Il libertinismo della prima metà del Seicento: stato attuale degli studi e prospettive di ricerca. In T. Gregory, G. Paganini, G. Canziani, O. Pompeo Faracovi, D. Pastine (eds.), *Ricerche su letteratura libertina e letteratura clandestina nel Seicento*. Florence: La Nuova Italia, pp. 3–47.

Groenewegen, P. (1970). A Reappraisal of Turgot's Theory of Value, Exchange, and Price Determination. *History of Political Economy*, vol. II, pp. 177–196.

Gualtieri, G. A. (2019). La concezione della scienza nella filosofia di Giambattista Vico. *I castelli di Yale. Quaderni di Filosofia*, VII, 2019, 1–2, pp. 125–170.

Guariglia, R. (1914). Un mancato trattato di commercio tra le Due Sicilie e la Francia e un parere inedito dell'abate Galiani. *Rivista di diritto internazionale*, VIII, 1, pp. 1–21.

Guerci, L. (1971). F. Galiani, Dialogues entre M. Marquis de Roquemaure, et Ms. le Chevalier Zanobi (a cura di P. Koch). *Rivista Storica Italiana*, Anno LXXXIII, fasc. I, pp. 178–189.

Guerci, L. (1972). Aspetti e problemi dell'epistolario di Ferdinando Galiani. *Rivista Storica Italiana*, 84, pp. 80–110.

Guerci, L. (1975a). Epistolario. Preliminari. In F.Diaz, L. Guerci, (eds), Galiani, F. *Opere*, *Letteratura italiana. Storia e testi. Illuministi italiani*, tomo VI, Milan-Naples: Ricciardi, pp. 783–814.

Guerci, L (1975b). Croquis d'un dialogue sur les femmes. Preliminari. In F.Diaz, L. Guerci, (eds), Galiani, F. *Opere*, *Letteratura italiana. Storia e testi. Illuministi italiani*, tomo VI, Milan-Naples: Ricciardi, pp. 615–634.

Guida, A. (2010). Un omaggio in greco di Winckelmann a Galiani. *Eikasmos*, 21, pp. 417–422.

Gullino, G. (2020). Andrea Tron. In *Dizionario Biografico degli Italiani*, volume 97, Rome: Treccani, *ad vocem*.

Guillois, A. (1894). *Le salon de Madame Helvétius. Cabanis et les idéologues*, Paris: Calmann Lévy.

Harcourt, B. E. (2011). *The illusion of free markets: punishment and the myth of natural order.* Cambridge, Massachusetts: Harvard University Press.

Harsin, P. (1928). *Les doctrine monétaires et financières en France du XVI*[e]*au XVIII*[e]*siécle*. Paris: Alcan.

Hasbach, G. (1893). Les fondements philosophiques de l'économie politique de Quesnay et de Smith, *Revue d' économie politique*, 3 (Sept.), pp. 745–795.

Hauc, J.-C. (2004). *Ange Goudar: Un aventurier des Lumières.* Paris: Honoré Champion.

Hazard, P. (1953). *The European Mind. The Critical Years* (1680–1715). New Haven: Yale University Press.

Hecht, J. (1958). Le bicentenaire du *Tableau économique*: François Quesnay et la physiocratie. Présentation d'une publication de l' INED. *Population*, 13 (2), pp. 287–292.

Heckscher, E. F. (1919) [1950] "The effects of foreign trade of the distribution of income". in H. S. Ellis, L. A. Metzler (eds.). *Readings in the theory of international trade.* London: Allen & Unwin, pp. 270–300.

Heinsohn, G., Steiger, O. (1983). Private Property, Debts and Interest or: the Origin of Money and the Rise and Fall of Monetary Economies. *Studi economici*, 21, pp. 3–56.

Helpman, E. (1981). International Trade in the Presence of Product Differentiation, Economies of Scale and Monopolistic Competition: A Chamberlin-Heckscher-Ohlin Approach. *Journal of International Economics*, 11, 1981, pp. 305–340

Hicks, J. (1967). *Critical essays in monetary theory.* Oxford: Claredon Press.
Higgs, H. (1897). *The Physiocrats: Six Lectures on the French Economists of the 18th Century.* London: Macmillan.
Hirschman, A. O. (1977). *The Passions and the Interests: Political Arguments for Capitalism before its Triumph*, Princeton: Princeton University Press.
Holt, R. (2004). Fear Prudence: Hobbes and Williamson on the Morality of Contracting. *Journal of Economic Issues*, 38:4, pp. 1021–1036.
Horsefield, J. K. (1960). *British Monetary Experiments, 1650–1710.* Cambridge, MA: Harvard University Press.
Hoselitz, B. F. (1968). Agrarian Capitalism, the Natural Order of Things: François Quesnay. *Kyklos*, 21, pp. 637–664.
Hufton, O. (1983). Social Conflict and the Grain Supply in Eighteenth-Century France. *The Journal of Interdisciplinary History*, Vol. 14, No. 2, pp. 303–331.
Hülsmann, J. G. (2008). *The Ethics Of Money Production.* Auburn: Alabama Ludwig von Mises Institute.
Hurt, J. J. (2002). *Louis XIV and the Parlements. The assertion of royal authority.* Manchester: Manchester University Press.
Hutchison, T. (1988). *Before Adam Smith. The Emergence of Political Economy 1662–1776.* Oxford: Basil Blackwell.
Imbruglia, G. (2000). *Naples in the Eighteenth Century: The Birth and Death of a Nation State.* Cambridge: Cambridge University Press.
Imbruglia, G. (2019). Bernardo Tanucci. In *Dizionario Biografico degli Italiani* - Volume 93, Rome: Treccani, *ad vocem.*
Ingrao, B., Israel, G. (1990). *The Invisible Hand: Economic Equilibrium in the History of Science*, Cambridge: MIT Press.
Intorcia, G. (1987). *Magistrature del Regno di Napoli. Analisi prosopografica. Secoli XVI–XVII.* Naple: Jovene.
Inventario. (2023). *Inventario Manoscritti Galiani – Società Napoletana di Storia Patria*, available on line http://www.storiapatrianapoli.it/getFile.php?id=276.
Iovine, R. (1999). Il trattato Della moneta di Ferdinando Galiani. La dialettica politica a favore e contro la pubblicazione. *Frontiera d'Europa*, 1999, n. 1, pp. 173–236.
Iovine, R. (2001). Una cattedra per Genovesi nella crisi della cultyura moderna a Napoli. *Frontiera d'Europa*, 2001, n. 1–2, pp. 359–532.
Iovine, R. (2009). Celestino Galiani, Bartolomeo Intieri, Alessandro Rinuccini: difficoltà di sviluppo dell'ideologia economica nelle Sicilie (1700–1750) In A. Alimento (ed.), *Modelli d'oltre confine: prospettive economiche e sociali negli antichi stati italiani.* Rome: Edizioni Storia e Letteratura, pp. 67–87.
Israel, J. I. (2001). *Radical Enlightenment: Philosophy and the Making of Modernity 1650–1750.* Oxford: Oxford University Press.
Jannaccone, P. (1946). *Moneta e lavoro.* Torino: Utet.
Jevons, W. S. (1884). *Investigations in Currency and Finance.* London: Macmillan

Jones, R.A. (1976). The Origin and Development of Media of Exchange. *Journal of Political Economy*, Vol. 84, No. 4, Part 1, pp. 757–776.

Jordan, C. (1924). On Daniel Bernoulli's Moral Expectation and on a New Conception of Expectation. *The American Mathematical Monthly*, Vol. 31, No. 4, pp. 183–190.

Kaplan, H.H. (1995). *Russian Overseas Commerce with Great Britain During the Reign of Catherine II*. Philadelphia: American Philosophical Society.

Kaplan, S. L. (1976). *Bread, politics and political economy in the reign of Louis XV*. The Hague: Martinus Nijhoff.

Kaplan, S. L. (1979). *La bagarre: Galiani's "Lost" Parody*. The Hague: Martinus Nijhoff Publishers.

Kaplan, S. L. (1982). The Famine Plot Persuasion in Eighteenth-Century France. *Transactions of the American Philosophical Society*, Vol. 72, No. 3, pp. 1–79.

Kaplan, S. L. (1996). *The Bakers of Paris and the Bread Question. 1700–1775*, Durham: Duke University Press.

Kaplan, S. L. (2019a). Galiani: Grain and Governance. In S. L. Kaplan, S. A. Reinert (eds.), *The Economic Turn: Recasting Political Economy in Eighteenth-Century Europe*. London: Anthem Press, pp. 221–304.

Kaplan, S. L. (2019b). *Live and Die Proprietors and Free*: Morellet Dismantles the *Dialogues* and Defends the Radical Liberal Break. In S. L. Kaplan, S. A. Reinert (eds.), *The Economic Turn: Recasting Political Economy in Eighteenth-Century Europe*. London: Anthem Press, pp. 305–350.

Kaplan, S. L. (2019c). Is the Feeling of Humanity not more Sacred than The Right of Property?: Diderot's Antiphysiocracy in His Apology of Abbé Galiani. In S. L. Kaplan, S. A. Reinert (eds.), *The Economic Turn: Recasting Political Economy in Eighteenth-Century Europe*. London: Anthem Press, pp. 351–394.

Kauder, E. (1965). *A History of Marginal Utility Theory*. Princeton: Princeton University Press.

Kelly, P. H. (1991). Introduction. In P. H. Kelly (ed.), *Locke on Money*, ed., Oxford: Clarendon Press.

Kemmerer, D. L. (1993). Princeton's Money Doctor: Professor E. W. Kemmerer and the Gold Standard. *The Princeton University Library Chronicle*, Vol. 55, No. 1, pp. 8–42.

Keynes, J.M. (1923). *A Tract on Monetary Reform*. London: Macmillan.

Keynes, J. M. (1930). *A Treatise on Money*. Volume I. *The Pure Theory of Money*. London: Macmillan.

Kleer, R. (2004). The Ruine of Their Diana: Lowndes, Locke, and the Bankers. *History of Political Economy* 36, no. 3, pp. 533–556.

Kleiner, I. (1989). Evolution of the Function Concept: A Brief Survey. *The College Mathematics Journal*, September 1989, Volume 20, Number 4, pp. 282–300.

Klotz, G. (2000). La question des blés en France au dix-huitième siècle: Galiani, critique des physiocrates. *Il Pensiero Economico Italiano*, vol VIII, n. 2, pp. 147–183.

Koch, P. (1961). The Genesis of Galiani's Dialogues sur le Commerce Des Blés. *French Studies*, Volume XV issue 4, pp. 314–323.

Koch, P. (1968). Introduction. In F.Galiani, *Dialogues entre M. Marquis de Roquemaure et M. le chevalier Zanobi. Analecta Romanica*, Heft 21, Frankfurt am Main: Klostermann, pp. 1–51.

Koch, P. (1975). Les veritable Dialogues de Galiani. In *Convegno italo-francese sul tema Ferdinando Galiani* (Roma, 25–27 maggio 1972), Rome: Accademia Nazionale dei Lincei, pp. 185–197.

Kubota, A. (1958). Quesnay, disciple de Malebranche. In *François Quesnay et la physiocratie*. Volume 1. Paris: INED, pp. 169–196.

Labellarte, A. (2019). *Atomismo e corpuscolarismo nella Napoli di fine Seicento*, Rome: Armando Editore.

Laboulle, M. J. (1939). La Mathématique sociale: Condorcet et ses prédécesseurs. *Revue d'Histoire littéraire de la France*, 46 (1/2), pp. 33–55.

Lachterman, D. R. (1980). Vico, Doria e la geometria sintetica. *Bollettino del Centro di Studi Vichiani*, X, pp. 10–35.

Langholm, O. (1992). *Economics in the Medieval Schools: Wealth, Exchange, Value, Money and Usury According to the Paris Theological Tradition, 1200–1350*. Leiden: Brill.

Lanzillo, A. (1939). Relazione tra il Cantillon e il Galiani. *Rivista di storia eco*nomica, Anno IV, 2, pp. 201–218.

Larrère, C. (1994). Malebranche revisité: l'économie naturelle des physiocrates. *Dix-huitième Siècle*, 26, pp. 117–138.

Lawrence C., Spiller P. T. (1983). Product Diversity, Economies of Scale, and International Trade. *The Quarterly Journal of Economics*, Vol. 98, No. 1, pp. 63–83.

Lauro, A. (1974). *Il giurisdizionalismo pregiannoniano nel Regno di Napoli. Problema e bibliografia (1563–1723)*. Rome: Edizioni di Storia e Letteratura.

Laval-Reviglio, M.-C. (1987). Les conceptions politiques des physiocrates. *Revue française de science politique*, 37 (2), pp. 181–213.

Lebrun, P. (1962). Réflexions méthodologiques sur l'histoire des théories et des doctrines économiques. La soidisant modernité de Ferdinando Galiani. In *Studi in onore di Amintore Fanfani*, VI, Milan: Giuffré, pp. 329–358.

Legris, A. (2001). Galiani, Della Moneta and the French Economists. *History of Economic Ideas*, 2001, Vol. 9, No. 3, *Special Issue: "Della Moneta" by Ferdinando Galiani: A Quarter Millennium Assessment* (2001), pp. 183–216.

Leonzio, E. (2014). L'abbé Galiani e il problema dell'etica tra politica e pedagogia. *Studi francesi*, 172 (LVIII, I), pp. 46–63.

Lepre, A. (1963). *Contadini, borghesi ed operai nel tramonto del feudalesimo napoletano*. Milan: Feltrinelli.

Lepre, A. (1981). La crisi del XVII secolo nel Mezzogiorno d'Italia. *Studi Storici*, Jan.–Mar., 1981, Anno 22, No. 1, pp. 51–77.

Lepre, A. (1986a). *Storia del Mezzogiorno d'Italia*, Vol. I. *La lunga durata e la crisi (1500–1656)*, Naples: Liguori.

Lepre, A. (1986b). *Storia del Mezzogiorno d'Italia*, Vol. II. *Dall'Antico Regime alla società borghese (1657–1860)*, Naples: Liguori.

Lilla, M. (1993). *G.B. Vico: The Making of an Anti-Modern*. Cambridge, Mass.: Harvard University Press.

Lilti, A. (2005). *Le Monde des salons. Sociabilité et mondanité à Paris au XVIIIe siècle*. Paris: Fayard.

Lissa, A. 2020. In difesa degli ebrei: Pietro Contegna (1679–1745) e Celestino Galiani (1681–1753). Due intellettuali non conformisti nel Regno di Napoli e delle due Sicilie. *Materia Giudaica*, 2020, XXV, pp. 469–480.

Llobera, J. R. 1979. "Newton, The Scientific Model, And Social Thought In The Enlightenment", *Dialectical Anthropology*, Vol. 4, No. 2, pp. 147–153

Lojacono, E. (2003). *Immagini di René Descartes nella cultura napoletana (1644–1755)*. Lecce: Conte.

Lopez-Cordon Cortezo, M. V. (2003). Pacte de Famille ou intérêts d'État? La Monarchie française et la diplomatie espagnole du XVIIIe siècle. In L. Bély, (ed.), *La présence des Bourbons en Europe, XVIe–XXIe siècle*. Paris: PUF, pp. 185–220.

Loria, A. (1882). La teoria del valore negli economisti italiani. *Archivio giuridico,* vol. XVIII, pp. 3–66.

Loria, A. (1936). Intorno alla funzione della moneta immaginaria (con osservazioni di Luigi Einaudi). *Rivista di Storia Economica*, Anno I, Numero 4, pp. 299–308.

Lucas, R. (1980). Equilibrium in a Pure Currency Economy. In J.H. Kareken, N. Wallace, (eds.), *Models of Monetary Economies*. Minneapolis: Federal Reserve Bank of Minneapolis, pp. 131–145.

Luftalla, M. (1963). L'évidence, fondement nécessaire et suffisant de l'ordre naturel chez Quesnay et Morelly. *Revue d'histoire économique et sociale*, 41 (2), pp. 213–249.

Macry, P. (1972). Ceto mercantile e azienda agricola nel Regno di Napoli: il contratto alla voce. *Quaderni Storici*, Vol. 7, No. 21 (3), *Agricoltura - Proprietà – Mercati*, pp. 851–909.

Macry, P. (1974). *Mercato e società nel Regno di Napoli. Commercio del grano e politica economica nel '700*. Naples: Guida.

Mafrici, M. (1998). Il re delle speranze. Carlo di Borbone da Madrid a Napoli, Naples. Edizioni Scientifiche Italiane

Mafrici, M. V. (2004). Diplomazia e commercio tra il Regno di Napoli e la Sublime Porta: Guglielmo Maurizio Ludolf (1747–1789). In M. Mirella (ed.), *Rapporti diplomatici e scambi commerciali nel Mediterraneo moderno*, Soveria Mannelli: Rubbettino, pp. 151–172.

Mafrici, M. V. (2011). Le relazioni diplomatiche e commerciali tra il Regno di Napoli e l'Impero russo nel secolo dei Lumi. In P. Volpini, R. Sabbatini, (eds.). *Sulla diplomazia in età moderna. Politica, economia, religione. Annali di storia militare europea*, 3, Milan: Franco Angeli, pp. 219–240.

Mafrici, M. V. (2020). Maria Carolina d'Asburgo-Lorena e la politica internazionale napoletana (1770–1799). In G. Sodano, G. Brevetti, (eds.), *Io, la Regina. Maria Carolina d'Asburgo-Lorena e il suo tempo, Quaderni - Mediterranea - Ricerche storiche*, n. 37, pp. 25–50.

Maiorini, M.G. (2000). Neapolitan Diplomacy in the Eighteenth Century: Policy and the Diplomatic Apparatus. In D. Frigo, (ed.) *Politics and Diplomacy in Early Modern Italy. The Structure of Diplomatic Practice, 1450–1800*. Cambridge: Cambridge University Press, pp. 176–209.

Malbranque, B. (2021). Foreword to the General Directing of Trade Cannot Be a Science: D'Argenson's 1751 Commentary Essay and the Response to It. *Econ Journal Watch* 18(2), September 2021, pp. 257–277.

Mantelli, R. (1986). *Il pubblico impiego nell'economia del Regno di Napoli*. Naples: Istituto Italiano per gli Studi Filosofici.

Marchal, F. (1999). Galiani, un modèle du Neveu de Rameau. Le prestige des mimes. *Revue d'Histoire littéraire de la France*, 99e Année, No. 5, pp. 1007–1020.

Marcialis, M. T. (1996). Il Cogito e la coscienza. letture cartesiane nella Napoli settecentesca. *Rivista di Storia della Filosofia*, Vol. 51, No. 3 (1996), pp. 581–612.

Marcialis, M. T. (2018). Percezioni e Idee. Il confronto tra Antonio Conti e Antonio Genovesi. *Rivista di Storia della Filosofia*, Vol. 73, No. 4, pp. 629–664.

Marconcini, F. (1931). Momento mercantilista settecentesco: la dissertazione sopra il commercio di Girolamo Belloni, banchiere romano. *Rivista internazionale di scienze sociali*, s. 3, II, pp. 104–180. 393–416.

Marino, J. A. (1982). Economic Idylls and Pastoral Realities: The Trickster Economy in the Kingdom of Naples. Comparative Studies in Society and History, Vol. 24, No. 2, pp. 211–234.

Marino, J. A. (1988). *Pastoral Economics in the Kingdom of Naples*. Baltimore: Johns Hopkins University Press.

Marino, J. A. (2007). The Rural World in Italy under Spanish Rule. In Dandelet, T. J., Marino, J. A. (eds.), *Spain in Italy. Politics, Society, and Religion 1500–1700*, Leiden: Brill, pp. 405–432.

Marshall, A. (1920). *Principles of Economics,* (8th ed.). London: Macmillan & C.

Marshall A. (1926). *Official Papers*. London: Macmillan.

Marshall, D. L. (2011). The Current State of Vico Scholarship. *Journal of the History of Ideas*, Vol. 72, No. 1, pp. 141–160.

Marx, K. (1859) [1904]. *Zur Kritik der politischen Ökonomie*. Berlin: Duncker. English Translation. *A Contribution to the Critique of Political Economy*, Chicago: Kerr & C.

Marx, K. (1867). *Das Kapital, Kritik der Politischen Ökonomie*, Erster Band: *Der Produktionsprozess des Kapitals*, Hamburg: Meissner.

Mastellone, S. (1963). Il libertinismo erudito a Napoli nella seconda metà del seicento. *Critica Storica*, Anno II, n. 6, pp. 451–463.

Mastellone, S. (1965). *Pensiero politico e vita culturale a Napoli nella seconda metà del Seicento*. Florence: D'Anna.

Mastellone, S. (1969). *Francesco d'Andrea politico e giurista (1648–1698): l'ascesa del ceto civile*. Florence: Olschki.

Mauro, A. (2017a). *Un philosophe des Lumières entre Naples et Paris: Ferdinando Galiani (1728–1787)*. Thèse de Doctorate de l'Université Toulouse le Mirail - Toulouse II.

Mauro, A. (2017b). L'abbé Galiani alias le chevalier Zanobi: un philosophe qui "ne croit rien en rien sur rien de rien". *Littératures Classiques*, 93, pp. 155–167.

Mauro, A. (2021). *Un philosophe des Lumières entre Naples et Paris: Ferdinando Galiani (1728–1787)*, Oxford: Oxford University Press.

Mauss, M. (1923–24). Essai sur le don. Forme et raison de l'échange dans les sociétés archaïques. *Année sociologique*, Seconde Série, I Année, pp. 30–186.

Mazzola, R. (1994). I giganti in Vico. *Bollettino del Centro di Studi Vichiani*, Anno XXIV–XXV, pp. 49–78.

Mazzola, R. (1998a). Religione e Provvidenza in Vico. *Bollettino del Centro di Studi Vichiani*, Anno XXVI–XXVII, pp. 101–126.

Mazzola, R. (1998b). Università e società a Napoli tra Sei e Settecento. *Bollettino del Centro di Studi Vichiani*, anno XXVIII, pp. 227–238.

Mazzola, R. (2020). Napoli 1764. *Laboratorio dell'ISPF*, vol. XVII, 4, pp. 2–8.

Mazzotti, M. (2013). Il newtonianesimo e la scienza del Settecento. In *Il Contributo italiano alla storia del Pensiero – Scienze*. Roma: Istituto dell'Enciclopedia Treccani.

McCulloch, J. R. (1864). *The Principles of Political Economy* (5th ed.). Edinburgh: Black.

McMullin E., Pompa, L. (1976). Vico's Theory of Science. *Social Research*, Vol. 43, No. 3, *Vico and Contemporary Thought*, pp. 450–483.

Meek, R.L. (1973). *Studies in the labour theory of value*. New York: Monthly Review Pres.

Melvin, J.-R. (1969). Increasing Returns to Scale as a Determinant of Trade. *The Canadian Journal of Economics*, Vol. 2, pp. 389–402.

Menger, C. (1871). *Grundsätze der Volkswirthschaftslehre*. Wien: Wilhelm Braumüller.

Menger, C. (1892). On the Origin of Money. *The Economic Journal*, Vol. 2, No. 6 (Jun., 1892), pp. 239–255.

Messedaglia, A. (1881). La teoria e la statistica dei metalli preziosi quale preliminare allo studio delle presenti questioni monetarie. *Archivio di statistica*, Anno VI, fasc. I, Estratto, Turin: Loesher.

Meyssonnier, S. (1990). Vincent de Gournay (1712–1759) et la "Balance des homes". *Population* (French Edition), Vol. 45, No. 1, pp. 87–112.
Michels, R. (1916). Controversie sulla prima cattedra di scienza economica. *Rivista Italiana di Sociologia*, anno XX, fasc. V–VI, settembre-dicembre 1916, pp. 600–605.
Michels, R. (1932). *Introduzione alla storia delle dottrine economiche e politiche*, Bologna: Zanichelli.
Miglio, G.F. (1942). *La controversia sui limiti del commercio neutrale fra Giovanni Maria Lampredi e Ferdinando Galiani*. Rome: Ispi.
Migliorini, A.V. (1979). I problemi del trattato franco-napoletano di navigazione e di commercio (1740–1766). *Rivista storica italiana*, XCI, 1, pp. 180–207.
Minerbi, M. (1973). Diderot, Galiani e la polemica sulla fisiocrazia (1767–1771). *Studi Storici,* Anno 14, No. 1, pp. 147–184
Mirowski, P. (1991). *More Heat than Light*. Cambridge: Cambridge University Press.
Monaco, V. (1968). *Giambattista Lorenzi e la commedia per musica*, Naples: Berisio.
Monroe, A. E. (1923). *Monetary Theory Before Adam Smith*, Cambridge (MS): Harvard University Press.
Montacutelli, M. (2018). Cornelio Spinola. In *Dizionario Biografico degli Italiani* - Volume 93, Rome: Treccani, *ad vocem*.
Montanile, M. (2018). Il *Dialogue sur les femmes* di Ferdinando Galiani. In C. Passetti, L. Tufano (eds.), *Femminile e maschile nel Settecento*. Florence: Firenze University Press, pp. 81–93.
Montaudo, A. (2005). *L'olio nel Regno di Napoli nel XVIII secolo. Commercio, Annona e Arrendamenti*. Naples: Edizioni Scientifiche Italiane.
Monti, G.M. (1942). *La dottrina dell'abate Ferdinando Galiani sulla neutralità e l'adesione di Ferdinando IV alla Lega dei Neutri*. Milan: Ispi.
Morandi, C. (1939). Partiti politici a Napoli durante la Guerra di Successione spagnola. *Rivista storica italiana*, serie V, vol. IV, pp. 557–571.
Morrison, J. C. (1978). Vico's Principle of Verum is Factum and the Problem of Historicism. *Journal of the History of Ideas*, Vol. 39, No. 4, pp. 579–595.
Mourant, J. A. (1943). *The Physiocratic Conception of Natural Law*. Chicago: University of Chicago Press.
Muldrew, C. (2019). Money and the Everyday: New Practices in the Enlightenment. In C. Desan (ed.) *A Cultural History of Money*, Vol. IV, *A Cultural History of Money in the Age of Enlightenment*. London: Bloomsbury Academic, pp. 95–120.
Murphy, A. E. (1997). *John Law. Economic Theorist and Policy-Maker*. Oxford: Claredon Press.
Musi, A. (1986). Tra burocrati e notabili. Potere e istituzioni nella Napoli del Seicento. *Bollettino del Centro di Studi Vichiani*, Anno XVI, pp. 157–176.

Musi, A. (1991). Mezzogiorno spagnolo: la via napoletana allo stato moderno. Naples. Guida Editori.

Musi, A. (2002). *La rivolta di Masaniello nella scena politica barocca*. Naples: Guida.

Musi, A. (2004). Il console genovese a Napoli Cornelio Spinola (1621–1648) e i problemi di economia e di finanze nel Seicento mediterraneo *Archivio storico per le province napoletane*, CXXII, pp. 167–183.

Musi, A. (2007a). Politica e cultura a Napoli tra il crepuscolo del sistema imperiale spagnolo e l'avvento degli Asburgo d'Austria (1698–1707). In A. Álvarez-Ossorio Alvariño, B.J. García García, V. León Sanz, (eds.). *La pérdida de Europa. La guerra de Sucesión por la Monarquía de España*. Madrid: EFCA pp. 785–797.

Musi, A. (2007b). The Kingdom of Naples in the Spanish Imperial System. In T. J. Dandelet, J. A. Marino, (eds.), *Spain in Italy. Politics, Society, and Religion 1500–1700*, Leiden: Brill, pp. 73–98.

Musi, A. (2013). *L'impero dei viceré*, Bologna: Il Mulino.

Muto, G. (2013). "Urban Structures and Population", in T. Astarita, (ed.), *A Companion to Early Modern Naples*. Leiden-Boston: Brill, pp. 35–62.

Muto, G. (1986). Il problema monetario tra teoria e pratica di governo. *Bollettino del Centro di Studi Vichiani*, anno XVI, 1986, pp. 177–196.

Naddeo, B.A. (2011). *Vico and Naples: the urban origins of modern social theory*. Ithaca: Cornell University.

Nagy, J. (2012). Vico Contra Hobbes. *Información Filosófica*, Vol. IX, N. 18, pp. 101–124.

Natale, M. (2002a). Eclettícismo teoretico e pragmatismo, alle origini delle riforme illuministiche. L'autobiografia di Celestino Galiani. *Frontiera d'Europa* (2002/1), pp. 115–219.

Natale, M. (2002b). Notazioni integrative: continuità degli orientamenti empiristici da Francesco d'Andrea a Celestino Galiani. *Frontiera d'Europa* (2002/2), pp. 5–78.

Nederman, C. J. (2000). Community and the Rise of Commercial Society: Political Economy and Political Theory in Nicholas Oresme's *De Moneta*. *History of Political Thought*, 21, no. 1, pp. 2–15.

Neill, T. P. (1948). Quesnay and Physiocracy. *Journal of the History of Ideas*, 9, 2 (April), pp. 153–173.

Neill, T. P. (1949). The Physiocrats' Concept of Economics. *The Quarterly Journal of Economics*, 63, 4, pp. 532–553.

Nicolet-Pierre, H. (2002). *Numismatique grecque*. Paris: Colin.

Nicoletti, G. (1985). Il primo soggiorno fiorentino di Ferdinando Galiani e il suo carteggio inedito con Anton Francesco Gori. In *Studi di filologia e critica offerti dagli allievi a Lanfranco Caretti*, Rome: Salerno editrice, vol. I, pp. 355–401.

Nicoletti, G. (1992). Un altro recupero galianeo: il carteggio inedito con Antonio Niccolini (1752–1755). *Studi Italiani*, IV (1992), 7, pp. 149–188.

Nicoletti, G. (ed.). (2008). Galiani F., Cerati, G. *Carteggio (1749–1758)*. Naples: Bibliopolis.

Nicoletti, G. (2011). Fra erudizione, antiquaria e amministrazione: Ferdinando Galiani e gli amici di Toscana. In C. Viola (ed.), *Le carte vive. Epistolari e carteggi nel Settecento*, Atti del I Convegno internazionale del Centro di Ricerca sugli Epistolari del Settecento, Rome: Edizioni di Storia e Letteratura, pp. 135–160.

Nicolini, B. (1975). Gli scritti galianei di Fausto Nicolini. In *Convegno italo-francese sul tema Ferdinando Galiani* (Roma, 25–27 maggio 1972), Rome: Accademia Nazionale dei Lincei, pp. 259–307.

Nicolini, F. (1903). "I manoscritti dell'abate Galiani", La Critica. Rivista di Letteratura, Storia e Filosofia, Vol. 1, pp. 393–400.

Nicolini, F. (1904–1905). L'abate Galiani epigrafista. *Napoli Nobilissima*, s. 1, pp. 13, 27–30, 42–44; 14, 12–14, 73–77, 108–10.

Nicolini, F. (1908a). I manoscritti di Ferdinando Galiani, *Archivio storico per le province napoletane*, 33 (1908), pp. 171–197.

Nicolini, F. (1908b). Intorno a Ferdinando Galiani a proposito di una pubblicazione recente. *Giornale Storico della letteratura italiana*, Volume LII, pp. 1–55.

Nicolini, F. (ed.). (1909a). *Il pensiero dell'abate Galiani. Antologia di tutti i suoi scritti*. Bari: Laterza.

Nicolini, F. (1909b). Gli studi sopra Orazio dell'abate Ferdinando Galiani. In *Atti dell'Accademia Pontaniana*, anno XXXIX, Memoria VIII, pp. i–xvi; 1–160.

Nicolini, F. (1914). Introduzione. In B. Tanucci, *Lettere a Ferdinando Galiani*, edited by F. Nicolini. Bari: Laterza, pp. vi–xix.

Nicolini, F. (1918a). La famiglia dell'abate Galiani, *Archivio Storico Italiano*, Vol. 76, No. 3/4 (291/292), pp. 136–157.

Nicolini, F. (1918b). La puerizia e l'adolescenza dell'abate Galiani (1735–1745). Notize, lettere, versi, documenti, *Archivio Storico per le Province Napoletane*, Nuova serie Anno IV, XLIII. dell'intera collezione, Vol. IV, pp. 105–132.

Nicolini, F. (1918c). Giambattista Vico e Ferdinando Galiani. Ricerca storica. *Giornale Storico della Letteratura Italiana*, Volume LXXI, pp. 137–207.

Nicolini, F. (1923). Introduzione. In Galiani, F., *Del dialetto napoletano*, edited by F. Nicolini. Naples: Ricciardi, pp. ix–lv.

Nicolini, F. (1929). Amici e corrispondenti dell'abate Ferdinando Galiani: I. Angelo Gatti (con nuove notize e documenti inediti sul richiamo del Galiani da Parigi). *Archivio Storico Italiano*, Vol. 87 (Serie 7, Vol. 12), No. 4 (332), pp. 233–272.

Nicolini, F. (1931) *Monsignor Celestino Galiani. Saggio biografico*. Naples: Società Napoletana di Storia Patria.

Nicolini, F. (1942). Vico, Hobbes e una postilla inedita alla Scienza Nuova. *Atti dell'Accademia di scienze morali e politiche della Società Reale di Napoli*, vol. LXI.

Nicolini, F. (1950). *Di alcuni rapporti ideali tra il Vico e il Hobbes con qualche riferimento al Machiavelli.* Rome: Edizioni di Storia e Letteratura.

Nicolini, F. (1951). *Un grande educatore italiano. Celestino Galiani*, Naples: Giannini.

Nicolini, F. (1954). *Amici e corrispondenti francesi dell'abate Galiani. Notizie lettere documenti.* Naples: Banco di Napoli.

Nicolini, F. (1959a). Avvertenza. In F. Nicolini (ed.), F. Galiani, *Dialogues sur le commerce des bleds. Giusta l'editio princeps del 1770 con appendici illustrative*, Naples: Ricciardi, pp. ix–xxviii.

Nicolini, F. (1959b). Un inedito dell'abate Galiani. *Biblion*, I, pp. 139–156.

Nicolini, F. (1964). *Per una nuova edizione della corrispondenza francese dell'abate Galiani.* Naples: s.n.

Nicolini, F. (1978). L'Orazio dell'abate Galiani. *Accademia Nazionale dei Lincei, Memorie*, Serie VIII, vol.XXII, fascicolo 2, pp. 111–314.

Nicolini, F., Venturi, F. (1956). Inedito dell'abate Galiani. *Giornale Storico della letteratura italiana*, LXXIII, 1956, pp. 67–73.

Nietzsche, F. (1886) [2002]. *Jenseits von Gut und Böse, Vorspiel einer Philosophie der Zukunft,* Leipzig: Druck und Verlag. English Translation, *Beyond Good and Evil Prelude to a Philosophy of the Future,* edited by Horstmann, R.-P., Norman, J., Cambridge: Cambridge University Press, 2002.

Novi Chavarria, E. (2008). Forme e spazi della sociabilità aristocratica napoletana nel Settecento. In R. Bizzocchi, A. Pacini, *Sociabilità aristocratica in età moderna. Il caso genovese: paradigmi, interpretazioni e confronti.* Pisa: Edizioni Plus, pp. 73–86.

Nuccio, O. (1967). Introduzione. In *Scrittori classici italiani di economia politica,* parte moderna, tomo sesto, Rome: Bizzari, pp. i–lxxxiii.

Nuccio, O. (1987). *Il pensiero economico italiano. Le Fonti. 1050–1450. L'etica laica e la formazione dello spirito economico*, Vol. 1, Libro III. Sassari: Gallizzi.

Nuzzo, E. (1984). *Verso la "Vita civile": antropologia e politica nelle lezioni accademiche di Gregorio Caloprese e Paolo Mattia Doria*, Naples: Guida.

Ohlin, B. (1933). *Interregional and International trade*, Cambridge (Mass.): Harvard University Press.

Oliveira, A. R. E. (2017). d'Alembert: Between Newtonian Science and the Cartesian Inheritance. *Advances in Historical Studies,* 6, pp. 128–144.

Orain, A. (2019). Physiocrat Arithmetic versus Ratios: The Analytical Economics of Jean- Joseph- Louis Graslin. In S. L. Kaplan, S. A. Reinert (eds.), *The Economic Turn: Recasting Political Economy in Eighteenth-Century Europe.* London: Anthem Press, pp. 193–220.

Orain, A., Reinert, S. A. (2022). Small States in an Age of Empires: The Duchy of Parma's Colonial Moment, 1750–1770. *Capitalism: A Journal of History and Economics,* 3, no. 1 (Winter 2022), pp. 57–105.

Osbat, L. (1971). *L'inquisizione a Napoli. Il processo agli ateisti*. Rome: Edizioni Storia e Letteratura.

Ostroy, J.M. (1973). The Informational Efficiency of Monetary Exchange. *American Economic Review*, 63 (4), pp. 597–609.

Ousselin, E. (1999). L'Homme aux quarante écus: Voltaire économiste. *The French Review*, Vol. 72, No. 3, pp. 493–502.

Outram, D. (2019). *The Enlightenment*. Fourth Edition. Cambridghe: Cambridge Univesity Press.

Ozanam, D. (1961). Les origines du troisième Pacte de Famille (1761). *Revue d'histoire diplomatique*, octobre–décembre 1961, n. 4, pp. 307–340.

Paganelli, M.P. (2018). De la monnaie. Ferdinando Galiani et Adam Smith. In A. Tiran, Carnino, C. (eds.), *Ferdinando Galiani, économie et politique*. Paris: Classiques Garnier, pp. 211–222.

Pagden, A. (1988). The Destruction of Trust and its Economic Consequences in the Case of Eighteenth-century Naples. In D. Gambetta, (ed.), *Trust: Making and Breaking Cooperative Relations*. Oxford: Basil Blackwell, pp. 127–141.

Palladino, F. (1984). Origine e diffusione del calcolo differenziale in Italia: con un'appendice di lettere inedite. *Giornale critico della filosofia italiana*, a. 63. (65.), fasc. 3., settembre-dicembre 1984, pp. 327–405.

Palladino, F. (1988). La formazione scientifico-matematica di Celestino Galiani. *Bollettino del Centro di Studi Vichiani*, Anno XXVII–XXVII, pp. 253–262.

Panagariya, A. (1981). Variable Returns to Scale in Production and Patterns of Specialization. *The American Economic Review*, Vol. 71, pp. 221–230.

Pane, R. (1975). Ferdinando Galiani e l'antico. In *Convegno italo-francese sul tema Ferdinando Galiani* (Roma, 25–27 maggio 1972), Rome: Accademia Nazionale dei Lincei, pp. 201–211.

Pantaleoni, M. (1889). *Principii di economia pura*. Florence: Barbera.

Papi, G. U. (1975). "Ferdinando Galiani e l'economia". In *Convegno italo-francese sul tema Ferdinando Galiani* (Roma, 25–27 maggio 1972), Rome: Accademia Nazionale dei Lincei, pp. 25–46.

Papuli, G. (ed.) (1985). *P.M. Doria fra rinnovamento e tradizione*. Galatina: Congedo.

Paratore, E. (1975). Il commento a Orazio di Ferdinando Galiani. In *Convegno italo-francese sul tema Ferdinando Galiani* (Roma, 25–27 maggio 1972). Rome: Accademia Nazionale dei Lincei, pp. 365–379.

Parinetto, L. (1974). *Magia e ragione. Una polemica sulle streghe in Italia intorno al 1750*. Florence: La Nuova Italia.

Pascal, C. (1885). *Sulla vita e sulle opera di Ferdinando Galiani*. Naples: Morano.

Pasinetti, L. (1986). Theory of Value - A Source of Alternative Paradigms in Economic Analysis. In M. Baranzini, R. Scazzieri (eds.), *Foundations of Economics - Structures of Inquiry and Economic Theory*. Oxford: Basil Blackwell, pp. 409–431.

Pasinetti, L. (ed.) (1989). *Aspetti controversi della teoria del valore*. Bologna: Il Mulino.

Pasta, R. (2013). Antonio Maria Niccolini. In *Dizionario Biografico degli Italiani*, Vol. 78, *ad vocem*.

Patalano, R. (2011). Carlo Antonio Broggia. In *Il Contributo Italiano alla Storia del Pensiero. Economia*. Rome: Treccani, pp. 287–291.

Patalano, R. (2016). Serra's Brief Treatise in a World-System Perspective: The Dutch Miracle and Italian Decadence in the Early 17th Century. In R. Patalano, S. A. Reinert, (eds.), *Antonio Serra and the Economics of Good Government, in Antonio Serra and the Economics of Good Government*, London: Palgrave Macmillan, pp. 63–88.

Patalano, R. (2017). Geometry of Money in the Neapolitan Eighteenth Century: Trojano Spinelli's Riflessioni Politiche. *History of Political Economy*, 49:4, pp. 631–666.

Patalano, R. (2018). Les *Dialogues* de Ferdinando Galiani et la Géoéconomie du commerce des grains à la fin du XVIIIe siècle. In A. Tiran, C. Carnino, (eds.), *Ferdinando Galiani, économie et politique*. Paris: Classiques Garnier, pp. 341–369.

Patalano, R. (2020a). Carlo Antonio Broggia, a money doctor in adverse circumstances. *History of Economic Thought and Policy*, 2–2020, pp. 9–37.

Patalano, R. (2020b). Ferdinando Galiani's Newtonian Social Mathematics. *Journal of the History of Economic Thought*, Vol. 42, 3, pp. 357–383.

Patalano, R., Realfonzo, R. 2001. On Money by Ferdinando Galiani: Notes, Social Accounting and Confidence. *History of Economic Ideas*, Vol. 9, No. 3, *Special Issue: "Della Moneta" by Ferdinando Galiani: A Quarter Millennium Assessment*, pp. 61–94.

Patalano, R., Reinert, S. A. (eds.) (2016). *Antonio Serra and the economics of good government*, New York: Palgrave Macmillan.

Patinkin, D. (1956). *Money, Interest, and Prices; An Integration of Monetary and Value Theory*. Evanston, Illinois: Row, Peterson and Co.

Peacock, M. S. (2011). The Political Economy of Homeric Society and the Origins of Money. *Contributions to Political Economy*, 30, pp. 47–65.

Pecchio, G. (1849). *Storia dell'economia pubblica in Italia. Ossia epilogo critico degli economisti italiani preceduto da un'introduzione. Terza edizione*. Lugano: Tipografia della Svizzera Italiana.

Pénigaud, T. (2015). The political opposition of Rousseau to Physiocracy: government, interest, citizenship. *European Journal of the History of Economic Thought*, Vol. 22 Issue 3, pp. 473–499.

Pennisi, A. (1987). *La linguistica dei mercatanti. Filosofia linguistica e filosofia civile da Vico a Cuoco*, Naples: Guida.

Perkinson, H. J. (1976). Vico and the Methods of Study of Our Time. *Social Research*, Vol. 43, No. 4, *Vico and Contemporary Thought*, pp. 753–767.

Perna. M. L. (1984). Nota critica. In A. Genovesi, *Scritti economici.* Naples: Istituto Italiano per gli Studi Filosofici, pp. 1269–1279.

Perrot, J. C. (1988). Les économistes, les philosophes et la population in Jacques Dupâquier (ed.), Histoire de la population française, tome II: De la Renaissance à 1789, Paris: PUF, pp. 499–551.

Perrot, J.-C. (1992). *Une histoire intellectuelle de l'économie politique. XVIIe–XVIII^{e}siècle.* Paris: Éditions de l'École des Hautes Études en Sciences Sociales.

Perru, O. (1997). Les physiocrates: La communauté est-elle de droit naturel?. *Revue Philosophique de Louvain*, quatrième série, 95 (4), pp. 617–638.

Pesante, M. L. (2000). Il commercio nella repubblica, *Quaderni storici*, Nuova Serie, Vol. 35, No. 105 (3), *Etiche economiche*, pp. 655–695.

Petrucci, A., Pignatelli, G. (1971). Giovanni Gaetano Bottari. In *Dizionario Biografico degli Italiani*, Vol. 13, *ad vocem.*

Pierce, D. G., Tysome, P. J. (1985). *Monetary Economics. Theories, Evidence and Policy*, Second Edition, London: Butterworths

Pii, E. (1972). Bayle e la cultura napoletana intorno al 1750. *Il Pensiero Politico*, 5[3], pp. 509–516.

Pii, E. (1984). *Antonio Genovesi. Dalla politica economica alla politica civile.* Florence: Olschki.

Pilati, R. (2001). Del commercio: Gregorio Grimaldi e il riformismo napoletano nella prima età borbonica. *Frontiera d'Europa,* VII, nn. 1–2, pp. 281–318.

Placanica, A. (1982). *Moneta prestiti usure nel Mezzogiorno moderno.* Naples: Società Editrice Napoletana.

Placanica, A. (2004). Ferdinando Galiani e il vero e falso Onofrio Galeota tra bizzarrie vesuviane e catastrofi calabresi. In A. Placanica, *Scritti*, tomo II, Soveria Manneli: Rubbettino, pp. 163–190.

Pomeau, R. (1975). Galiani et Voltaire. In *Convegno italo-francese sul tema Ferdinando Galiani* (Roma, 25–27 maggio 1972). Rome: Accademia Nazionale dei Lincei, pp. 333–345.

Porta, P. L. (1995). La concezione dello sviluppo economico nei Dialoghi sul commercio dei grani di Ferdinando Galiani. In A. Roncaglia, (ed.), *Le origini del pensiero eonomico in Italia.* Bologna: Il Mulino, pp. 121–140.

Porta, P. L. (2012). Ferdinando Galiani. *Il Contributo Italiano alla Storia del Pensiero. Economia.* Rome: Treccani, pp. 352–357.

Pribram, K. (1983). *A history of economic reasoning.* New York: John Hopkins University Press.

Principe, I. (1993). La cartografia nel Regno di Napoli e l'Atlante di Giovanni Antonio Rizzi Zannoni. In G. A. Rizzi Zannoni, *Atlante del Regno di Napoli*, Soveria Mannelli: Rubbettino, pp. 13–45.

Pupo, S. (2020). Hume politico a Napoli. Per una rilettura della fortuna del "celebre scozzese" negli scritti degli illuministi meridionali. *(Il) Pensiero Politico. Rivista di Storia delle Idee Politiche e Sociali*, Anno LIII, n. 1, pp. 3–35.

Quazza, G. (1971). Rifeudalizzazione e ceto civile. In G. Quazza, *La decadenza italiana nella storia europea. Saggi sul Sei-Settecento.* Turin: Einaudi, pp. 63–85.

Racioppi, G. (1871). *Antonio Genovesi.* Naples: Morano.

Rack, M. (1973). Note napoletane. I processi del 1688–1697. *Giornale critico della filosofia italiana*, pp. 52–82.

Rao, A. M. (1983). *Il Regno di Napoli nel Settecento.* Naples: Guida.

Rao, A. M. (1989). Il riformismo borbonico a Napoli. In G. Cherubini, F. Della Peruta, E. Lepore, M. Mazza, G. Mori, G. Procacci, R. Villari (eds.), *Storia della società italiana.* Milan: Teti, pp. 218–230.

Rao, A. M. (1996). Tra erudizione e scienze: l'antiquaria a Napoli alla fine del Settecento. In C. Montepaone (ed.), *L'incidenza dell'antico. Studi in memoria di Ettore Lepore*, vol. III. Naples: Luciano, pp. 91–135.

Rao, A. M. (1997). *L 'amaro delia feudalità. La devoluzione di Anione e la questione feudale a Napoli alla fine del '700.* Naples: Luciano.

Rao, A. M. (2005). Fra amministrazione e politica. Gli ambienti intellettuali napoletani. In J. Boutier, B. Marin, A. Romano (eds.), *Naples, Rome, Florence. Une histoire comparée des milieux intellectuels italiens (XVII–XVIII e siècles)*. Rome: Publications de l'École française de Rome, pp. 35–88.

Rao, A. M. (2008). Saverio Mattei. In *Dizionario Biografico degli Italiani*, Vol. 72, *ad vocem.*

Rao, A.M. (2009). L'apprendistato di un re: Carlo di Borbone a Napoli. In G. Fragnito (ed.), *Elisabetta Farnese principessa di Parma e regina di Spagna.* Rome: Viella, pp. 317–333.

Rapisarda, S. (1996). Introduzione. In d'Épinay-Galiani, *Epistolario 1769–1782*, edited by S.Rapisarda. Palermo: Sellerio, pp. xviii–li.

Ravix, J. (2018). Entre Arlequin et Machiavelli: Galiani économiste baroque. In A. Tiran, C. Carnino (eds.), *Ferdinando Galiani, économie et politique.* Paris: Classiques Garnier, pp. 95–120.

Recca, C. (2017). *The Diary of Queen Maria Carolina of Naples, 1781–1785. New Evidence of Queenship at Court.* London: Palgrave Macmillan.

Redman, D. A. (1997). *The Rise of Political Economy as a Science: Methodology and the Classical Economists.* Cambridge, MA: MIT Press.

Reinert, S. A. (2011a). Girolamo Belloni. In *Il Contributo Italiano alla Storia del Pensiero. Economia.* Rome: Treccani, pp. 271–274.

Reinert, S. A. (2011b). Another Grand Tour: Cameralism and Antiphysiocracy in Baden, Tuscany, and Denmark–Norway. In J. G. Backhaus (ed.), *Physiocracy, Antiphysiocracy and Pfeiffer.* New York: Springer, pp. 39–70.

Renda, F. (1970). *Bernardo Tanucci e i beni dei Gesuiti.* Catania: Università di Catania.

Ricca-Salerno, G. (1896). *Storia delle dottrine finanziarie in Italia. Seconda edizione intieramente rifatta.* Palermo: Reber.

Richter, R. (1988). The New Institutional Economics Applied to Monetary Economics. *Journal of Institutional and Theoretical Economics*, Vol. 144, No. 1, pp. 208–224.

Ricuperati, G. (1969). Alessandro Riccardi e le richieste del ceto civile all'Austria nel 1707. *Rivista storica italiana,* anno LXXXI (1969), fascicolo IV, pp. 745–777.

Ricuperati, G. (1970). *L'esperienza civile e religiosa di Pietro Giannone.* Milan-Naples: Ricciardi

Ricuperati, G. (1972). Napoli e i viceré austriaci (1707–1734). In *Storia di Napoli*, volume VII, Naples: Società Editrice Storia di Napoli, pp. 349–457.

Ricuperati, G. (1979). A proposito di P.M. Doria. *Rivista Storica Italiana*, 91, pp. 261–285.

Ricuperati, G. (2001). *La città terrena di Pietro Giannone: un itinerario tra crisi della coscienza europea e illuminismo radicale.* Florence: Olschki.

Ridgeway, W. (1887). The Homeric Talent, Its Origin, Value, and Affinities. *The Journal of Hellenic Studies*, Vol. 8, pp. 133–158.

Riley, J. C. (1986). *The Seven Years War and the Old Regime in France. The Economic and Financial Toll.* Princeton: Princeton University Press.

Riley P. (2001). Rousseau, Fénelon, and the Quarrel between the Ancients and the Moderns. In *The Cambridge Companion to Rousseau.* Cambridge: Cambridge University Press, pp. 2001: 78–93.

Riskin, J. (2003). The Spirit of System and the Fortunes of Physiocracy. *History of Political Economy,* 35, Suppl. 1, *Oeconomies in the Age of Newton,* edited by M. Schabas and N. de Marchi pp 42–73.

Robertazzi Delle Donne, E. (1970). *L'espulsione dei Gesuiti dal Regno di Napoli.* Naples: Libreria scientifica editrice.

Roberts, M. (2003). *The Age of Liberty: Sweden 1719–1772.* Cambridge: Cambridge University Press.

Robertson, J. (1997). The Enlightenment above National Context: Political Economy in Eighteenth-Century Scotland and Naples. *The Historical Journal*, Vol. 40, No. 3, pp. 667–697.

Robertson, J. (2000). Enlightenment and Revolution: Naples 1799. *Transactions of the Royal Historical Society. Sixth Series*, 10, pp. 17–44.

Robertson, J. (2005). *The Case for the Enlightenment. Scotland and Naples 1680–1760.* Cambridge: Cambridge University Press.

Robertson, J. (2013). Sacred history and political thought: Neapolitan responses to the problem of sociability after Hobbes. *The Historical Journal*, Vol. 56, No. 1, pp. 1–29.

Romano, R. (1946). La situazione finanziaria del Regno di Napoli attraverso il bilancio generate dell'anno 1734. *Archivio Storico per le Province Napoletane*, nuova serie, anno XXX, pp. 161–168.

Romano, R. (1948). Un tentativo di stipulazione di trattato commerciale tra Napoli e Venezia nel 1739. *Studi Economici ed Aziendali*, Anno III, pp. 1–16.

Romano, R. (1951). *Le commerce du Royaume de Naples avec la France et les pays de l'Adriatique an XVIII siécle*. Paris: Armand Colin.

Romano, R. (1968). *Prezzi, salari e servizi a Napoli nel secolo XVIII (1734–1806)*. Milan: Banca Commerciale Italiana.

Romano, R. (1970). Economia e finanza nella Napoli spagnola. In *Storia di Napoli*, volume VI, Naples: Società Editrice Storia di Napoli, pp. 537–606.

Romano, R. (1976). *Dal Viceregno al Regno. Storia Economica*. Turin: Einaudi.

Romeo, G. (1976). Per la Storia del Sant'Ufficio a Napoli tra '500 e '600. Documenti e problem. *Campania Sacra*, VII, pp. 5–109.

Roncaglia, A. (2005). *The Wealth of Ideas*. Cambridge: Cambridge University Press.

Rosselli, A. (2000). Early Views on Monetary Policy: The Neapolitan Debate on the Theory of Exchange. *History of Political Economy*, 32:1, pp. 61–82.

Rosselli, A. (2001). The Role of The Precious Metals in *Della Moneta* by Ferdinando Galiani. *History of Economic Ideas*, Vol. 9, No. 3, pp. 43–60.

Rossetti, G. (1942). Galiani e la teoria dei gradi finali di utilità. *Rivista di Storia Economica*, Anno VII, pp. 111–116

Rossi, R. (2010). Il mercato laniero nel Regno di Napoli durante il Viceregno austriaco. Persistenze e mutamenti. In S. Russo, N. Guasti (eds.), *Il Viceregno austriaco (1707–1734)*. Rome, Carocci, pp. 137–153.

Rotta, S. (ed.) (1973). *L'illuminismo a Genova. Lettere di P.P. Celesia e F. Galiani*, Florence: La Nuova Italia.

Rotta, S. (1978). Introduzione a Paolo Mattia Doria. In R. Ajello, M. Berengo (eds.) *Politici ed economisti del primo settecento, dal Muratori al Cesarotti, La letteratura Italiana, Storia e testi*, vol. 5, Naples-Milan: Ricciardi, pp. 837–870.

Rothschild, E. (2001). *Economic Sentiments: Adam Smith, Condorcet, and the Enlightenment*. Cambridge (MS): Harvard University Press.

Rothschild, E. (2005). Axiom, Theorem, Corollary, Etc.: Condorcet and Mathematical Economics. *Social Choice and Welfare*, 25, pp. 287–302.

Rovito, P. L. (1981). *La Respublica dei togati. Giuristi e società nella Napoli del Seicento*.Naples: Jovene.

Rovito, P. L. (1987). Funzioni pubbliche e capitalismo signorile nel feudo napoletano del Seicento. *Bollettino del Centro di Studi Vichiani*, Anno XVI, pp. 95–156.

Rovito, P. L. (2003). *Il viceregno spagnolo di Napoli*. Naples: Arte Tipografica.

Ruggiero, R. (2018). La nozione storica di diritto naturale nel pensiero di Vico tra *De ratione* e *De uno*. *Bollettino del Centro di Studi Vichiani*, Anno XLVIII, pp. 89–103.

Russo, F. (2007). Il desiderio della società. Sulla fortuna di Grozio tra Westfalia e Napoli. *Annali dell'Università Suor Orsola Benincasa*, anno 2006–2007.

Russo, S., Guasti, N. (eds.). (2010). *Il Viceregno austriaco (1707–1734)*. Rome: Carocci.

Salinari, G. (1972). Appiano Buonafede. In *Dizionario Biografico degli Italiani*, Volume 15, Rome: Treccani, *ad vocem*.

Salvati, C. (1962). L'azienda e le altre Segreterie di Stato durante il primo periodo borbonico (1734–1806). *Quaderni della Rassegna degli Archivi di Stato*, 14, pp. 1–62.

Sargent, T. J, Velde, F. R. (2002). *The Big Problem of Small Change*. Princeton: Princeton University Pres.

Sasso, R. (1978). Voltaire et le système de la nature de d'Holbach. *Revue Internationale de Philosophie* Vol. 32, No. 124/125 (2/3), *Rousseau et Voltaire 1778–1978*, pp. 279–296.

Scazzieri, R. 2011. Paolo Mattia Doria. In *Il Contributo Italiano alla Storia del Pensiero. Economia*. Rome: Treccani, pp. 326–331.

Schelle, G. (1897). *Vincent de Gournay*, Paris: Guillaumin.

Schelle, G. (1907). *Le Docteur Quesnay. Chirurgien, Médecin de M.me de Pompadour et de Louis XV, Physiocrate*. Paris: Félix Alcan.

Scherillo,M.(1886).IlSocrateimmaginario.Saggiocritico.InF.Galiani,G.B.Lorenzi, *Socrate Immaginario. Commedia per musica, preceduta da un saggio critico e con note del dottor M. Scherillo*. Milan: Sonzogno, pp. 5–20.

Schipa, M. (1897). *Un ministro napoletano nel secolo XVIII. Domenico Caracciolo*. Naples: Pierro.

Schipa, M. (1899). Il Regno di Napoli descritto nel 1713 da P. M. Doria. *Archivio Storico per le Province Napoletane*, 1899, Anno XXIV, fascicolo I, IV, pp. 25–84; 329–350.

Schipa, M. (1902). *Il Muratori e la cultura napoletana del suo tempo*. Naples: Pierro.

Schipa, M. (1904). *Il Regno di Napoli al tempo di Carlo di Borbone*. Naples: Pierro.

Schipa, M. (1924). L'Università di Napoli nel secolo XVIII. In *Storia dell'Università di Napoli*. Naples: Ricciardi, pp. 436–466.

Schipa, M. (1938). *Nel Regno di Ferdinando IV di Borbone*. Florence: Vallecchi.

Schuhl, P.-M. (1938). Malebranche et Quesnay. *Revue Philosophique de la France et de l'Étranger*, 125, 3/4, pp. 313–315.

Schumpeter, J. A. (1954) [2006]. *History of Economic Analysis*. London: Routledge.

Schumpeter, J. A. (1970). *Das Wesen des Geldes*, Mann, F.K. (ed.), Gottingen: Ruprecht & Vandenhoeck.

Scibilia, A. (1976). Domenico Caracciolo. In *Dizionario Biografico degli Italiani*, Volume 19, Rome: Treccani, *ad vocem*.

Scognamiglio, A. (2010). Introduzione. In F. Galiani, *Socrate immaginario. Commedia per musica*. Naples: Denaro libri.

Screpanti, E., Zamagni, S. (2005). *An Outline of the History of Economic Thought. Second Edition Revised and Expanded*. Oxford: Oxford University Press.

Senut, B. (2012). Fifty years of the Debate on the Origin of Human Bipedalism. *Journal of Biological Research - Bollettino della Società Italiana di Biologia Sperimentale*, 85 (1), pp. 37–46.

Setaro, P. (2021). Una città in fermento. Gli intellettuali napoletani e il ruolo del viceré Francisco de Benavides, IX conte di Santisteban (1688–1696), *Pedralbes*, 41, pp. 255–298.

Shank, J. B. (2008). *The Newton Wars and the Beginning of the French Enlightenment*. Chicago: University of Chicago Press.

Shaw, W. (1896). *The history of currency, 1252 to 1894*, Second Edition, New York: Burt Franklin.

Simiand, F. (1934). La monnaie, réalité sociale. *Les Annales Sociologiques*, série D, fascicule 1, pp. 1–54.

Simmel, G. (1907) [2004]. *Philosophie des Geldes*, Leipzig, Duncker & Humblot. English Translation, *The Philosophy of Money*, London: Routledge.

Sirago, M. (2018). Le rôle de Ferdinando Galiani à la signature du Traité de commerce entre la Russie et le Royaume des Deux-Siciles (1787). In A. Tiran, C. Carnino, (eds.), *Ferdinando Galiani, économie et politique*. Paris: Classiques Garnier, pp. 295–317.

Sirago, M. (2019). La politica marittima di Bernardo Tanucci nell'epistolario con Carlo III Re di Spagna. *Cuadernos de Ilustración y Romanticismo. Revista Digital del Grupo de Estudios del Siglo XVIII*, n° 25, pp. 507–538.

Skornicki, A. (2018). Le pour et le contre Galiani, la diplomatie et le commerce des blés. In A. Tiran, C. Carnino (eds.), *Economie et politique chez Ferdinando Galiani*. Paris: Classiques Garnier, pp. 319–340.

Soldovieri, U. (2019). L'Abate Galiani epigrafista. In L. Calvelli, G. Cresci Marrone, A. Buonopane, (eds.) *Altera pars laboris Studi sulla tradizione manoscritta delle iscrizioni antiche*, Venezia Edizioni Ca' Foscari pp. 304–322.

Souffrin, P., Segonds, A. P. (eds.). (1988). *Nicolas Oresme, Tradition et innovation chez un intellectuel du XIVe siècle*. Paris: Les Belles Lettres.

Soulange-Bodin, A. (1894). *La diplomatie de Louis XV et le Pacte de Famille*. Paris: Didier, Perrin & Cie.

Soliani, R., Clément, A. (2018). Les fondaments philosophiques de l'approche èconomique de Ferdinando Galiani. In A. Tiran, C. Carnino, (eds.), *Ferdinando Galiani, économie et politique*. Paris: Classiques Garnier, pp. 121–154.

Sonenscher, M. (2002). Physiocracy as a theodicy. *History of Political Thought*, 23, pp. 326–339.

Spagnoletti, A. (1997). *Storia del Regno delle Due Sicilie*, Bologna: il Mulino.

Spooner, F. C. (1956). The Principle of Utility: The Contribution of Ferdinando Galiani. *Cambridge Historical Journal*, 12 (1), pp. 81–82.

Stapelbroek, K. (2005). The Devaluation Controversy in Eighteenth-Century Italy. *History of Economic Ideas*, Vol. 13, No. 2, pp. 79–110.

Stapelbroek, K. (2006). Preserving the Neapolitan State: Antonio Genovesi and Ferdinando Galiani on commercial society and planning economic growth. *History of European Ideas*, Volume 32, Issue 4, pp. 406–429.

Stapelbroek, K. (2008a). *Love, Self-Deceit and Money. Commerce and Morality in the Early Neapolitan Enlightenment*. Toronto: University of Toronto Press.

Stapelbroek, K. (2008b). Universal Society, Commerce and the Rights of Neutral Trade: Martin Hübner, Emer de Vattel and Ferdinando Galiani. In P. Korkman, V. Mäkinen, (eds.) *Universalism in International Law and Political Philosophy*, COLLeGIUM: Studies Across Disciplines in the Arts and Humanities, vol. 4, Helsinki: Helsinki Collegium for Advanced Studies, pp. 63–89.

Stapelbroek, K. (2011). The progress of humankind in Galiani's *Dei Doveri dei Principi Neutrali*: Natural law, Neapolitan trade and Catherine the Great. In Stapelbroek, K. (ed.) *Trade and War: The Neutrality of Commerce in the Inter-State System*. COLLeGIUM: Studies Across Disciplines in the Arts and Humanities, vol. 10, Helsinki: Helsinki Collegium for Advanced Studies, pp. 161–183.

Stapelbroek, K. (2016), "To Console and Alleviate the Human Mind": Ferdinando Galiani's Attempted Republication of Serra in the 1750s, in Patalano, R., - Reinert, S. A. (eds.), Antonio Serra and the Economics of Good Government. New York: Palgrave Macmillan, pp. 234–262.

Stapelbroek, K. (2018). Les fondements de l'économie politique de Galiani: L'art du gouvernement, le luxe et l'histoire de l'humanité. In A. Tiran, C. Carnino, (eds.), *Ferdinando Galiani, économie et politique*. Paris: Classiques Garnier, pp. 457–483.

Stapelbroek, K. (2020). *Commercio, passioni e mercato. Napoli nell'Europa del Settecento*, Milan: Franco Angeli.

Steegmuller, F. (1983). *A Woman, a Man, and Two Kingdoms: The Story of Madame d'Épinay and Abbé Galiani*. Princeton: Princeton University Press.

Steegmuller, F. (1988). The Abbé Galiani: The Laughing Philosopher. *The American Scholar*, 57, 4 (Autumn), pp. 589–597.

Steiner, P. (1993). L'économie politique du royaume agricole: François Quesnay, In A. Béraud, G. Faccarello, (eds.), *Nouvelle histoire de la pensée économique*. Volume I, *Des Scolastiques au classiques*. Paris: La Découverte, pp. 225–253.

Steinke, H. (2022). Religion, Marriage, and Burial in Vico's Scienza nuova: A Reappraisal. *Laboratorio dell'ISPF* (Istituto per la storia del pensiero filosofico e scientifico moderno), XIX, n. 8, 2022.

Stephenson, M. A. (1972). The Paradox of Value: A Suggested Interpretation. *History of Political Economy*, 4 (1), pp. 127–139.

Stigler, S. (1996). The Bernoullis of Basel. *Journal of Econometrics*, vol. 75, n°1, pp. 7–13.

Stone, H. S. (1997). *Vico's Cultural History. The Production and Transmission of Ideas in Naples 1685–1750*. New York: Brill.

Strazzullo, F. (1982). Il "Ragguaglio di Parnaso" dell'abate Galiani e la reazione dei napoletani a Winckelmann. In *Scritti in onore di Ottavio Morisani*, Catania: Università degli studi, pp. 415–425.

Strazzullo, F. (1997). *Il marchese di Squillace. Leopoldo de Gregorio ministro di Carlo di Borbone*. Naples: Liguori.

Strenski, E.M. (1967). Diderot, for and against the physiocrats. *Studies on Voltaire and the 18th Century*, vol. LVII, pp. 1435–1455.

Swann, J. (1995). *Politics and Parlamento of Paris under Louis XV (1754–1774)*. Cambridge: Cambridge University Press.

Tagliacozzo, G. (1937). *Economisti napoletani dei secoli XVII e XVIII*. Bologna: Cappelli.

Tagliacozzo, G. (1968). Economic Vichism (Vico, Galiani, Croce - Economics, Economic Liberalism). *BNL Quarterly Review*, 21 (85), pp. 96–119.

Tiran, A. (2011). Pompeo Neri. In *Il Contributo Italiano alla Storia del Pensiero. Economia*. Rome: Treccani, pp. 380–383.

Tiran, A. (2014). La monnaie ct les prix dans la pensée italienne au dix-huitième siècle. In J Blanc, L. Desmedt (eds.) *Les Pensées monétaires dans l'histoire. L'Europe, 1517–1776*. Paris: Classiques Garnier, pp. 645–700.

Tiran, A. 2018. Galiani (1728–1787) et Della Moneta (1751). In A. Tiran, C. Carnino, (eds.), *Ferdinando Galiani, économie et politique*. Paris: Classiques Garnier, pp. 57–94.

Torrini, M. (1981). L'accademia degli Investiganti. Napoli 1663–1670. *Quaderni storici*, Vol. 16, No. 48 (3), *Accademie scientifiche del 600; Professioni borghesi*, pp. 845–883.

Toutain, J. C. (1961). *Le produit de l'agriculture francaise de 1700 à 1958. La Croissance. Histoire Quantitative De L'Économie Francaise. Cahiers De L'Institut De Science Économique Appliquée*, Paris: Isea.

Trampus, A. (2011a). Gian Rinaldo Carli. In *Il Contributo Italiano alla Storia del Pensiero. Economia*. Rome: Treccani, pp. 299–303.

Trampus, A. (2011b). *La massoneria nell'età moderna*: Bari: Laterza.

Trampus, A. (2020). *Emer de Vattel and the Politics of Good Government, Constitutionalism, Small States and the International System*. London: Palgrave Macmillan.

Troisi, M. (1941). Aspetti teorici e normativi del sistema di economia civile di Antonio Genovesi. Il valore e la dottrina monetario-creditizia (con appendice di documenti inediti). *Rassegna Monetaria*, anno XXXVIII, n. 5, maggio 1941, pp. 729–761.

Trombetta, V. (2002). *Storia e cultura delle biblioteche napoletane*. Naples: Vivarium.

Tubaro, P. (2002). A Case Study in Early Mathematical Economics: Pietro Verri and Paolo Frisi, 1772. *Journal of the History of Economic Thought*, 24 (2), pp. 193–214.

Tucci, U. (1981). Le emissioni monetarie di Venezia e i movimenti internazionali dell'oro. In *Mercanti, navi, monete nel Cinquecento veneziano*, Bologna: Il Mulino, pp. 275–316.

Tucci, U. (1986). Monete e riforme monetarie nell'Italia del Settecento. *Rivista Storica Italiana*, Anno XCVIII, I, pp. 78–119.

Tucci, U. (1996). Teoria e pratica delle idee monetarie di Gian Rinaldo Carli. *Acta Historiae*, V, pp. 11–24.

Tuccillo, A. (2013). *Il commercio infame. Antischiavismo e diritti dell'uomo nel Settecento italiano*, Naples: ClioPress.

Tuccillo, A. (2018). L'esprit de commerce à l'épreuve de la colonisation dans le traité *Della moneta*. In A. Tiran, C. Carnino, (eds.), *Ferdinando Galiani, économie et politique*. Paris: Classiques Garnier, pp. 485–505.

Tusset, G. (2020). Gian Rinaldo Carli (1720–1795): Diagnosis and treatment of a monetary plague. *History of Economic Thought and Policy*, 2–2020, pp. 39–65.

Ullmer, J. H. (2011). The scientific method of Sir William Petty. *Erasmus Journal for Philosophy and Economics*, Volume 4, Issue 2, pp. 1–19.

Vaggi, G. (1987). *The Economics of François Quesnay*. London: Macmillan.

Valentino, H. (1952). *Madame d'Épinay, une femme d'esprit sous Louis XV*, Paris: Librairie Académique Perrin.

Valerio, V. (2007). Cartography in the Kingdom of Naples during the Early Modern Period. In D. Woodward, (ed.), *The History of Cartography, Volume 3. Cartography in the European Renaissance*, Chicago: The University Chicago Press, pp. 940–974.

Valerio, V. (2013). Representation and Self-Perception: Plans and Views of Naples in the Early Modern Period. In T. Astarita (ed.), *A Companion to Early Modern Naples*. Leiden-Boston: Brill, pp. 63–88.

Van Bever, P. (1976). L'abbé Galiani et les signes sociaux. *Etudes sur le XVIIIe siècle*, 3, pp. 255–263.

Van Der Wee, H. (1977). Monetary, Credit and Banking Systems. In *The Cambridge Economic History*, volume V, Cambridge; Cambridge University Press, pp. 290–392.

Van Kley, D. K. (2018). *Reform Catholicism and the International Suppression of the Jesuits in Enlightenment Europe*. New Haven: Yale University Press.

Vardi, L. (2012). *The Physiocrats and the World of the Enlightenment*. Cambridge: Cambridge University Press.

Vaughan, F. (1972). *The Political Philosophy of Giambattista Vico an Introduction to La Scienza Nuova*. The Hague: Martinus Nijhoff.

Velde, F. (2012). The Life and Times of Nicolas Dutot. *Journal of the History of Economic Thought*, Vol. 34, 1, pp. 67–107.

Velde, F. (2020). The Money Doctors of Seventeenth-Century Naples. *Capitalism: A Journal of History and Economics*, Volume 1, Number 2, Spring m2020, pp. 405–455.

Velde, F. R., Weber, W. E. (2000). Fiat money in 17th century Castile. *Federal Reserve Bank of Minneapolis and University of Minnesota Minneapolis.*

Venturi F. (1959a). Alle origini dell'Illuminismo napoletano. Dal carteggio di Bartolomeo Intieri. *Rivista Storica Italiana*, a. LXXI, fascicolo III, pp. 416–456.

Venturi, F. (1959b). Was ist Aufklärung? Sapere aude. *Rivista Storica Italiana,* a. LXXI, fascicolo II, pp. 119–128.

Venturi, F. (1960a). Le lezioni di commercio di Antonio Genovesi. Manoscritti, edizioni e traduzioni. *Rivista Storica italiana*, anno LXXII, fascicolo III, pp. 511–530.

Venturi, F. (1960b). Galiani tra enciclopedisti e fisiocrati. *Rivista Storica Italiana*, anno LXXII, fascicolo I, pp. 45–64.

Venturi, F. (1971a). *Utopia and Reform in the Enlightenment*, Cambridge: Cambridge University Press.

Venturi, F. (1971b). Napoli capitale nel pensiero dei riformatori illuministi. In *Storia di Napoli*, Vol. VIII, Naples: Società Editrice Napoletana, pp. 3–73.

Venturi, F. (1973). 1764: Napoli nell'anno della fame. *Rivista storica italiana*, Anno LXXXV fasc. 2, pp. 394–472.

Venturi, F. (1997). Nota introduttiva. In F. Venturi (ed.) *Illuministi italiani. Riformatori napoletani*, vol. II, tomo I. Milano: Mondadori, pp. 3–46.

Venturi, F. (1998). *Settecento riformatore. Da Muratori a Beccaria*, Turin: Einaudi.

Verga, M. (2013). Pompeo Neri. In *Dizionario Biografico degli Italiani*, Vol. 78, *ad vocem.*

Vianello, A. (ed.) (1939). La riforma monetaria in Lombardia nella Seconda metà del '700. Milan: Bocconi.

Vidal, E. (1953). *Il pensiero civile di P.M. Doria negli scritti inediti: con il testo del manoscritto Del Commercio del Regno di Napoli.* Milan: Giuffrè.

Vidari, E. (1868). Ferdinando Galiani, Giovanni Maria Lampredi e Alberto Domenico Azuni. *Archivio Giuridico,* vol. I, pp. 210–241.

Vilar, Pierre. (1991). *A History of Gold and Money, 1450 to 1920.* London: Verso.

Villani, P. (1977). *Mezzogiorno tra riforme e rivoluzione.* Bari: Laterza.

Villari, L. (1958). *Il pensiero economico di Antonio Genovesi.* Florence: Le Monnier.

Villari, L. (1965). La fisiocrazia nel dibattito illuministico. *Studi Storici*, Anno 6, No. 1, pp. 25–39.

Villari, L. (1968). Note sulla fisiocrazia e sugli economisti napoletani del '700. In E. Sestan (ed.), *Saggi e ricerche sul Settecento*, Naples: Istituto Italiano per gli Studi Filosofici, pp. 224–251.

Villari, R. (1961). *Mezzogiorno e contadini nell'età moderna*, Bari: Laterza.

Villari, R. (1967). *La rivolta antispagnola a Napoli (1585–1647). Le origini.* Bari: Laterza.

Villari, R. (2012). *Un sogno di libertà. Napoli nel declino di un impero. 1585–1648.* Milan: Mondadori.

Viviani Della Robbia, E. (1942). *Bernardo Tanucci e il suo più importante carteggio*. Florence: Sansoni.

Walras, L. (1881). *Théorie mathématique du bimétallisme*, Paris: Guillamin.

Weinreb, R. (1992). *Eagle in a Gauze Cage: Louise d'Épinay, femme de lettres*, New York: AMS Press.

Weiss, R. W. (1970) The Issue of Paper Money in the American Colonies, 1720-1774, The Journal of Economic History, Vol. 30, No. 4, pp. 770–784.

Wennerlind, C. (2019). Money and its Ideas: Enlightenment debates about the Morality of Money. In C. Desan (ed.) *A Cultural History of Money*, Vol. IV, *A Cultural History of Money in the Age of Enlightenment*. London: Bloomsbury Academic, pp. 53–74.

Weulersse, G. (1910). *Le mouvement physiocratique en France (de 1750 à 1770)*. Paris: Alcan.

Williams, D. (2004). *Condorcet and Modernity*. Cambridge: Cambridge University Press.

Zambelli, P. (1972). *La formazione filosofica di Antonio Genovesi*, Naples: Morano.

Zambelli, P. (1973). Il rogo postumo di Paolo Mattia Doria. In *Ricerche sulla cultura dell'Italia moderna*, Bari: Laterza, pp. 149–198.

Zambelli, P. (1977). Prime iniziative di un Cappellano Maggiore. Una lettera inedita di Celestino Galiani. *Bollettino del Centro di Studi Vichiani*, Anno VII, pp. 113–121.

Zambelli, P. (1985). Letture vichiane e illuministiche del Segretario del Regno Niccolò Fraggianni. *Bollettino del Centro di Studi Vichiani*, Anno XIV–XV (1984–5), pp. 215–227.

Zaretsky, R. (2019). *Catherine & Diderot: The Empress, the Philosopher, and the Fate of the Enlightenment*. Cambridge (MS): Harvard University Press.

Zazo, A. (1929). Antonio Genovese e il suo contributo alle riforme scolastiche nel napoletano (1767–1769). *Samnium*, II, pp. 55–65

Zilli, I. (1990). *Carlo di Borbone e la rinascita del Regno di Napoli. Le finanze pubbliche (1734–1742)*. Naples: ESI.

Zoli, S. (1989). *Europa libertina tra Controriforma e Illuminismo: l'Oriente dei libertini e le origini dell'illuminismo: studi e ricerche*. Bologna: Capelli.

Index[1]

[1] Note: Page numbers followed by 'n' refer to notes.

R. Patalano, *Ferdinando Galiani*,
https://doi.org/10.1007/978-3-032-02793-1

B

G

Q

FSC
www.fsc.org
MIX
Papier | Fördert gute Waldnutzung
FSC® C083411

Kolibri 360 GmbH
Ferdinand-Jühlke-Straße 7
99095 Erfurt, Deutschland
produktsicherheit@kolibri360.de